WHERE THE LOCALS EAT

A Guide to the Best Restaurants in America

Compiled by the editors
and researchers of Magellan Press:

L. Lee Wilson, William B. King,
K. Joy Wood, Carole Cunningham,
Stephen Taylor, Gregory Leaming, Devona Matthews,
Clinton Blair Ryals, Caroline Barham, Joy Rice,
Scott Raulie, Geneva McSweeney, Monte Pennington,
and Steve Boyce

MAGELLAN PRESS, INC.
Nashville, Tennessee

647.95
ω

Where the Locals Eat: A Guide to the Best Restaurants in America

Second Edition

Compiled by the editors and researchers of Magellan Press:
L. Lee Wilson, William B. King, K. Joy Wood, Carole Cunningham,
Stephen Taylor, Gregory Leaming, Devona Matthews, Clinton Blair
Ryals, Caroline Barham, Joy Rice, Scott Raulie, Geneva McSweeney,
Monte Pennington, and Steve Boyce

© 1998 Magellan Press, Inc.
All rights reserved.

Published by Magellan Press, Inc., P.O. Box 121075,
Nashville, Tennessee 37212.
Printed in the United States of America.

To order additional copies of *Where the Locals Eat*, use the order
form in the back of the book or call the publisher at 800/624-5359.
Quantity discounts are available.

Cover design by John Robertson, Robertson Design,
Brentwood, Tennessee.
Text design by Bruce Gore, Gore Studio,
Brentwood, Tennessee.
Printed by Malloy Lithographing,
Ann Arbor, Michigan.

Library of Congress Catalog Card Number: 97-69885

ISBN: 0-9634403-4-9

Contents

Introduction

It's 6:30. You've had a hard day. Your hotel room is nothing fancy, but it's clean and quiet and the mattress is comfortable. You need to review your notes for your meeting tomorrow, but first you want to eat—after a day during which you had no time for breakfast and only an airline sandwich for lunch, you're famished. But how do you find a decent meal in a city you've never visited before?

Or maybe you're traveling with your children. They ate too much junk food at the theme park and they'd gladly eat pizza again for dinner, but you'd like to find a nice family restaurant where *you* can order something less fattening. There's a phone book in your motel room, but that doesn't tell you what you want to know, which is *Where in this city can I feed two adults and three ravenous kids for under $35*?

Or maybe you want to take your client to lunch. He's old enough to be your father and you think he thinks you're wet behind the ears. You've never been to Boston before, but you don't want *him* to realize that this is your first trip. Where can you take him that will impress him with your *savoir faire* and allow you to close your deal?

Where the Locals Eat is the first book that can answer these questions. There are other restaurant guides, but most of them don't take into account that people travel to cities smaller than New York and Los Angeles. Others are geared more toward the gourmet in search of the ultimate *escargot* experience than the average traveler caught in Detroit overnight. And, whatever they say, those "dining guides" you find in hotel rooms are sometimes no more useful than the Yellow Pages— what a coincidence that every restaurant listed in these slick publications is also the subject of a nice, big ad!

Our researchers have gathered information on the best and most popular restaurants in more than 1,000 American cities. We have included restaurants named as the best in town in local newspaper and magazine readers' polls, by local restaurant critics and editors, and by local business and professional people and field reviewers. None of the restaurants in our guide paid to be included—in fact, the only way a restaurant can make it into *Where the Locals Eat* is to be recommended by someone who lives in the area and knows which restaurants his or her neighbors like best. We believe that *Where the Locals Eat* is the most reliable restaurant guide on the market—after all, who knows better where to eat in San Jose or Seattle or Wichita than the people who live there?

A word about the information included in each restaurant listing. We have purposefully kept our listings brief. Each contains the name, telephone number, and street address of the recommended restaurant. We figure that knowing what sort of food a restaurant serves and that local people like it is all the information a traveler really needs to know about any restaurant except how to get there. For other information about a restaurant, such as its hours of operation or whether it requires reservations, we suggest that you simply call before leaving your hotel. After all, if you're in Austin, it's a local call to the best steak place in town.

Be sure to look not only at the listings for the town where you're staying, but also at those for nearby cities. Where the locals eat in Marietta, Georgia, may be, sometimes, in restaurants within the sprawl of Atlanta. The reverse situation also occurs. While many suburban communities are large enough to have earned their own listings, the best way to find good seafood near you may be to look at the recommended restaurants in the nearest city, especially if you are visiting a populous area where suburbs of the principal cities have grown to meet each other. If a town name is given as part of the address for a restaurant, that restaurant is in a neighboring town.

Knowing that readers have diverse tastes, we have gathered information on 75 different categories of restaurants—restaurants known for everything from their barbecue or burgers to their vegetarian menu or wine list. However, because we were dependent on the recommendations of our local sources and because you just can't find a coffeehouse or good Spanish food or sushi in every town and city, the restaurant listings for most of the cities in our guide include far fewer than 75 categories.

You'll notice that in most cities, there is more than one best restaurant listed for many categories. Again, this is reflective of our research. If our sources named several best Italian restaurants, so did we. This is because even though we consider all our sources to be reliable, the opinions of reliable people differ. We also knew that you'd want to know about *all* the best Indian restaurants in Orlando. So we included all the recommendations we gathered. You can decide for yourself if one of several great restaurants outshines the others.

Because our guide is designed to be useful to real people rather than to appeal only to traveling gourmets, we have sometimes included in our listings the names of chain restaurants when they were recommended to us as the best restaurants of their sort in a particular town or city. We did this for several reasons. We know that, in some smaller cities, the best burgers in town *are* at Sonic. And we know that sometimes travelers don't *want* to experiment with dinner—they just want a decent meal at a reasonable price. However, most of the restaurants listed in our guide are unique in the universe—the majority of those listed are not chain restaurants and most exist in only one location.

We think **Where the Locals Eat** is an invaluable tool for travelers who want to experience the flavor of the cities they visit. We hope you enjoy using it. Happy trails and *bon appetit!*

Lee Wilson
Editor-in-Chief

Alabama

Best Barbecue/Ribs
Betty's Barbecue
  401 S. Quintard Ave., 256/237-1411
Dad's Barbecue
  3101 McClellan Blvd., 256/238-4323
Old Smokehouse Bar-B-Q
  631 S. Quintard Ave., 256/237-5200

Best Burgers
Sonic Drive-In
  3109 Noble St., 256/236-6796

Best Chinese Food
China Luck
  503 Quintard Dr., Oxford, 256/831-5221

Best Dinner
The Victoria
  1604 Quintard Ave., 256/236-0503

Best Mexican Food
Los Tres Amigos
  320 S. Quintard Ave., 256/237-4404

Best Pizza
Pizza Inn
  2017 Quintard Ave., 256/236-5671

Best Seafood
Top of the River
  3220 McClellan Blvd., 256/238-0097

Best Steaks
Zack's Mesquite Grill
  1613 Snow St., Oxford, 256/831-9334

AUBURN, AL

Best All-You-Can-Eat Buffet
Mister J's Family Steak House
2027 Pepperell Pkwy., Opelika, 334/749-5741

Best Atmosphere
Legends Bar and Grill
1408 Opelika Rd., 334/826-0712

Best Barbecue/Ribs
Barbecue House
345 S. College St., 334/826-8277
Chuck's Bar-B-Que
622 Shug Jordan Pkwy., 334/826-2400

Best Burgers
Auburn Grille
104 N. College St., 334/821-6626
Cheeburger, Cheeburger
160 N. College St., 334/826-0845
Lil' Ireland's
122B W. Magnolia Ave., 334/821-5634

Best Chinese Food
Ruby's Chinese Restaurant
2360 Pepperell Pkwy., Opelika, 334/705-0108

Best Coffee/Coffeehouse
The Coffee Banque
101 N. College St., 334/887-1005

Best Desserts
The Coffee Banque
101 N. College St., 334/887-1005

Best Diner
Tiger Time Diner
1645 S. College St., 334/826-2000

Best Fine Dining
The Warehouse Bistro
105C Rocket Ave., Opelika, 334/745-6353

Best Inexpensive Meal
Auburn Grille
104 N. College St., 334/821-6626

Best Italian Food
Denaro's
103 N. College St., 334/821-0349

Best Mexican Food
La Fiesta Restaurant
820 Opelika Rd., 334/826-7259

Best Restaurant in Town
Breeze Way
213 S. Eighth St., Opelika, 334/749-5167
Venable's
913 S. Railroad Ave., Opelika, 334/745-0834

Best Romantic Dining
Provino's Italian Restaurant
3903A Pepperell Pkwy., Opelika, 334/742-0340

A

Best Steaks
Mister J's Family Steak House
   2027 Pepperell Pkwy., Opelika, 334/749-5741

Best Sunday Brunch
Horizons Restaurant
   Auburn University Hotel and Conference Center
      241 S. College St., 334/821-8200

BESSEMER, AL

Best Barbecue/Ribs
Bob Sykes Bar-B-Q
   1724 Ninth Ave. N., 205/426-1400

Best Chinese Food
China Doll
   505 Nineteenth St. N., 205/426-8077

Best Homestyle Food
Hobo Joe's Family Restaurant
   1030 Fourth Ave. N., 205/424-1622

Best Restaurant in Town
Bright Star Restaurant
   304 Nineteenth St. N., 205/424-9444

Best Seafood
Bright Star Restaurant
   304 Nineteenth St. N., 205/424-9444

BIRMINGHAM, AL

Best American Food
Fish Market Restaurant
   611 21st St. S., 205/322-3330

Best Atmosphere
Arman's
   2117 Cahaba Park Circle, 205/871-5551

Best Bar
Highlands Restaurant
   2011 Eleventh Ave. S., 205/939-1400
Lou's Pub
   726 29th St. S., 205/322-7005

Best Barbecue/Ribs
Dreamland Bar-B-Que
   1427 Fourteenth Ave. S., 205/933-2133

Best Breakfast
The Original Pancake House
   1931 Eleventh Ave. S., 205/933-8837

Best Burgers
Heights Cafe
   3135 Cahaba Heights Rd., 205/967-3132

Best Business Lunch
Bottega Cafe
   2242 Highland Ave. S., 205/933-2001

Best Casual Dining
Magic City Brewery
   420 21st St. S., 205/328-2739

Best Chinese Food
Chop Suey Inn
837 Green Springs Hwy., Homewood, 205/942-9782

Best Coffee/Coffeehouse
O'Henry's Coffee
2831 Eighteenth St. S., Homewood, 205/870-1198

Best Delicatessen
Vincent's Market
531 Brookwood Village Center, 205/871-2800

Best Diner
Maryanne's Diner
75 Church St., 205/871-7281

Best Fine Dining
Arman's at Park Lake
2117 Cahaba Rd., 205/871-5551

Best French Food
Cafe de France
2612 Lane Park Rd., 205/871-1000

Best Greek/Mediterranean Food
Connie Kanakis' Cafe
3423 Colonnade Pkwy., 205/967-5775

Best Homestyle Food
Irondale Cafe
1906 First Ave. N., Irondale, 205/956-5258

Best Indian Food
Bombay Cafe
2839 Seventh Ave. S., 205/322-1930

Best Inexpensive Meal
Purple Onion Deli and Grill
1931 Second Ave. N., 205/252-4899

Best Italian Food
Ciao Italian Restaurant
2031 Cahaba Rd., Mountain Brook, 205/871-2426

Best Japanese Food
Asahi Japanese Restaurant
444 Cahaba Park Circle, 205/991-5542

Best Late-Night Food
Moneer's
932 Oxmoor Rd., Homewood, 205/871-0306

Best Lunch
The Magic Bagel
3320 Clairmont Ave. S., 205/326-3354

Best Mexican Food
La Fiesta Restaurant
1941 Hoover Ct., 205/979-7314
La Paz Mexican Restaurant
99 Euclid Ave., 205/879-2225

Best Middle Eastern Food
Pita Stop Cafe
1106 Twelfth St. S., 205/328-2749

Best Other Ethnic Food
Ali Baba (Persian)
110 Centre at Riverchase, 205/823-2222

Best Pizza
Cosmo's Pizza
2012 Magnolia Ave. S., 205/930-9971

Best Place to Eat Alone
Pete's Famous Hot Dogs
1925 Second Ave. N., 205/252-2905

Best Place to Take the Kids
Chuck E. Cheese Pizza
500 Old Town Rd., 205/979-3420
9323 Parkway E., 205/833-8807

Best Restaurant in Town
Highlands Restaurant
2011 Eleventh Ave. S., 205/939-1400

Best Romantic Dining
Merritt House
2220 Highland Ave. S., 205/933-1200

Best Salad/Salad Bar
Fifth Quarter Steakhouse
195 Vulcan Rd., 205/942-0108

Best Sandwiches
Forest Park Deli and Catering
3811 Clairmont Ave. S., 205/595-5577

Best Seafood
Fish Market Restaurant
611 21st St. S., 205/322-3330

Best Soul Food
La'Vase Fine Food
328 Sixteenth St. N., 205/328-9327

Best Southwestern Food
Arizona Rib Company
217 Lakeshore Pkwy., 205/290-2190

Best Sports Bar
P.T.'s
350 Hollywood Blvd., 205/879-8519

Best Steaks
Michael's
431 Twentieth St. S., 205/322-0419

Best Sunday Brunch
The Tutwiler Restaurant
Wyndham Grand Heritage Hotel, 2021 Park Pl. N.,
205/322-2100

Best Tea Room
Cobb Lane Restaurant
1 Cobb Lane S., 205/933-0462

Best Undiscovered Restaurant
Bro' Chette's Que and Bayou
1709 Fourth Ave. N., 205/326-3663

A

Best Vegetarian Food
Golden Temple Natural Grocery
   1901 Eleventh Ave. S., 205/933-6333
   3309 Lorna Rd., 205/823-7002

Best Wine Selection
Highlands Restaurant
   2011 Eleventh Ave. S., 205/939-1400

DECATUR, AL

Best Barbecue/Ribs
B.B. Perrins BBQ
   608 Holly St. NE, 205/355-1045
Big Bob Gibson's Bar-B-Que
   2520 Danville Rd. SW, 205/350-0404
   1715 Sixth Ave. SE, 205/350-6969
Whitt's Barbecue
   2532 Spring Ave. SW, 205/350-2748
   918 Sixth Ave. SE, 205/351-6294

Best Chinese Food
Formosa Chinese Restaurant
   2136 Sixth Ave. SE, 205/350-3300

Best Coffee/Coffeehouse
Cafe 113
   113 Grant St. SE, 205/351-1400

Best Homestyle Food
City Cafe
   101 First Ave. SE, 205/353-9126
Shelley's Iron Gate Restaurant
   402 Johnston St. SE, 205/350-6795

Best Mexican Food
Camino Real Mexican Restaurant
   2504 Sixth Ave. SE, 205/353-6727

Best Pizza
Mando's Italian Food
   1416 Sixth Ave. SE, 205/355-4430

Best Place to Take the Kids
Camino Real Mexican Restaurant
   2504 Sixth Ave. SE, 205/353-6727

Best Salad/Salad Bar
Court Street Cafe
   103 Second St. SW, 205/350-5777
Shelley's Iron Gate Restaurant
   402 Johnston St. SE, 205/350-6795
Mando's Italian Food
   1416 Sixth Ave. SE, 205/355-4430

Best Sandwiches
Court Street Cafe
   103 Second St. SW, 205/350-5777

Best Seafood
McCollum's Catfish and Seafood
   2057 Gordon Terry Pkwy., 205/353-9321

Best Steaks
Brangus Feed Lot
   1807 Sixth Ave. SE, 205/355-9499

A

DEMOPOLIS, AL

Best Atmosphere
Foscue House Restaurant
21333 Hwy. 80W, 334/289-2221

Best Chinese Food
China Inn Chinese Restaurant
123 W. Washington St., 334/289-4528

Best Dinner
Foscue House Restaurant
21333 Hwy. 80W, 334/289-2221

Best Family Restaurant
Robert's Family Restaurant
880 Hwy. 80E, 334/289-1505

Best Italian Food
Mr. G's
602 N. Walnut Ave., 334/289-4149

Best Regional Food
The Cotton Patch
Union Rd., Eutaw, 205/372-4235

Best Seafood
Ellis V Restaurant
708 Hwy. 80E, 334/289-3446
Red Barn
901 Hwy. 80E, 334/289-0595

Best Steaks
Ellis V Restaurant
708 Hwy. 80E, 334/289-3446
Red Barn
901 Hwy. 80E, 334/289-0595

DOTHAN, AL

Best Burgers
Mrs. Boomer's
256 N. Foster St., 334/793-7810

Best Chinese Food
Ruby Palace
2240 Ross Clark Circle, 334/677-6677

Best Desserts
Garland House
200 N. Bell St., 334/793-2043
Old Mill Restaurant
2501 Murphy Mill Rd., 334/794-8530

Best Homestyle Food
Pat's Diner
1905 Montgomery Hwy., 334/671-8244

Best Italian Food
Tony's Italian Restaurant
3803 Ross Clark Circle, 334/794-4457

Best Mexican Food
Old Mexican
2920 Ross Clark Circle, 334/712-1434

A

Best Pizza
Mama Rosa's Pizza
3074H Ross Clark Circle, 334/794-2252
2111 Southview Shopping Ctr., 334/793-6868

Best Seafood
Old Mill Restaurant
2557 Murphy Mill Rd., 334/794-8530

Best Steaks
Conestoga Steak House
3549 Montgomery Hwy., 334/794-4445
Old Mill Restaurant
2501 Murphy Mill Rd., 334/794-8530

ENTERPRISE, AL

Best Bar
Top's Restaurant and Lounge
734 Glover Ave., 334/393-2297

Best Barbecue/Ribs
Carolina Bar-B-Que
608 E. Park Ave., 334/347-1096
Kelly's Bar-B-Q
853 Troy Hwy., Elba, 334/897-5212

Best Breakfast
Dottie's Country Kitchen
925 N. Main St., 334/393-1439

Best Business Lunch
Cutts Restaurant
417 E. Lee St., 334/347-1110

Best Chinese Food
China Gate Restaurant
654 Hwy. 84 Bypass, 334/347-2722
Hunan Chinese Restaurant
1034 Rucker Blvd., 334/393-1417

Best Homestyle Food
Cutts Restaurant
417 E. Lee St., 334/347-1110
Magnolia Room
107 N. Main St., 334/347-0697

Best Mexican Food
Effie's Cantina
913 Rucker Blvd., 334/347-0838
El Palacio
621 Boll Weevil Circle, Ste.1, 334/347-0313

Best Regional Food
Cutt's Restaurant
417 E. Lee St., 334/347-1110

Best Steaks
Indigo Head
1009 Rucker Blvd., 334/393-9566
Western Steer Steakhouse
650 Boll Weevil Circle, 334/347-6556

A

FLORENCE, AL

Best Barbecue/Ribs
Bunyan's Bar-B-Que
901 W. College St., 256/766-3522

Best Burgers
Princeton's Restaurant
251 Cox Creek Pkwy., 256/766-7163

Best Cajun/Creole Food
Louisiana the Restaurant
406 N. Montgomery Ave., Sheffield, 256/386-0801

Best Desserts
Court Street Cafe
116 E. Mobile St., 256/766-6196
201 N. Seminary St., 256/767-4300

Best Italian Food
Stephano's Italian Cafe and Catering
218 N. Court St., 256/764-7407

Best Salad/Salad Bar
Dale's Restaurant
1001 Mitchell Blvd., 256/766-4961

Best Seafood
J.C. Scott's
230 E. Tennessee St., 256/757-3819
Renaissance Grille
1 Hightower Pl., 256/718-0092

Best Steaks
Dale's Restaurant
1001 Mitchell Blvd., 256/766-4961
George's Steak Pit
1206 S. Jackson Hwy., Sheffield, 256/381-1531

Best View While Dining
Renaissance Grille
1 Hightower Pl., 256/718-0092

GADSDEN, AL

Best American Food
Thee Grill
135 N. Seventh St., 256/546-7788
Warehouse
315 S. Second St., Southside, 256/547-5548

Best Bar
Chestnut Station
410 Chestnut St., 256/546-4229

Best Barbecue/Ribs
Pruitt's
1617 Rainbow Dr., 256/547-4118

Best Burgers
Magic Burger Drive-in
915 Cleveland Ave., Attalla, 256/538-7350

Best Chinese Food
China Doll Restaurant
2723 Rainbow Dr., Rainbow City, 256/442-8528

A

Golden China
957 W. Meighan Blvd., 256/546-9443

Best Diner
Tony's Bar-B-Q
227 S. Third St., 256/547-0230

Best Homestyle Food
West Gadsden Cafe
906 Forrest Ave., 256/547-9183

Best Inexpensive Meal
Nelson's Variety Store
422 Broad St., Southside, 256/547-8871

Best Mexican Food
Mi Casita Mexican Restaurant
624 Walnut St., 256/547-9824
Villa Fiesta
825 Rainbow Dr., Southside, 256/546-5161

Best Pizza
Mater's Pizza
329 Locust St., Southside, 256/547-2556

Best Place to Be "Seen"
Fuzzy Duck
231 E. Broad St., 256/546-9149

Best Restaurant in Town
Chestnut Station
410 Chestnut St., Southside, 256/546-4229

Best Soul Food
Cunningham's BBQ
1901 E. Meighan Blvd., 256/494-0914

GULF SHORES, AL

[See also: Mobile.]

Best Barbecue/Ribs
Katy's Barbecue Smokehouse
603 S. McKenzie St., Foley, 334/943-7427

Best Breakfast
Gulf State Park Resort Hotel Dining Room
21250 E. Beach Blvd., 334/948-4853

Best Casual Dining
Papa Rocco's
6359 Hwy. 59S, 334/948-7262
Wolf Bay Lodge
9050 Pinewood Ave., Elberta, 334/986-7267

Best Chinese Food
Hunan Chinese Restaurant
306 E. Laurel Ave., Foley, 334/943-3909

Best Family Restaurant
De Soto's Restaurant
138 W. First Ave., 334/948-7294

A

Best Inexpensive Meal
Hunan Chinese Restaurant
306 E. Laurel Ave., Foley, 334/943-3909

Best Italian Food
Gambino's Restaurant
18 Laurel Ave., Fairhope, 334/928-5444

Best Mexican Food
Mexico Rock
27121 Canal Rd., Orange Beach, 334/981-6441

Best Pizza
Papa Rocco's
6359 Hwy. 59S, 334/948-7262

Best Regional Food
Gift Horse
309 W. Laurel Ave., Foley, 334/943-3663
Punta Clara Kitchen
17111 Scenic Hwy. 98, Point Clear, 334/928-8477

Best Salad/Salad Bar
Gift Horse
309 W. Laurel Ave., Foley, 334/943-3663

Best Seafood
Gambino's Restaurant
18 Laurel Ave., Fairhope, 334/928-5444
Wolf Bay Lodge
9050 Pinewood Ave., Elberta, 334/986-7267

HUNTSVILLE, AL

Best American Food
Green Hills Grille
5100 Sanderson St. NW, 256/837-8282

Best Bar
West End Grill
6610 Old Madison Pike NW, 256/722-8040

Best Barbecue/Ribs
Greenbrier Barbecue
15050 Hwy. 20, Madison, 256/353-9769

Best Business Lunch
Bubba's
109 Washington St. NE, 256/534-3133

Best Continental Food
Green Bottle Grill and Bakery
975 Airport Rd. SW, 256/882-0459

Best Dinner
West End Grill
6610 Old Madison Pike NW, 256/722-8040

Best French Food
Pho's Cafe and Lounge
2006 Country Club Ave. NW, 256/533-5001

Best German Food
Cafe Berlin
505 Airport Rd. SW, 256/880-9920
Ol Heidelberg Cafe
6125 University Dr. NW, 256/922-0556

A

Best Homestyle Food
Eunice's Country Kitchen
  1006A Andrew Jackson Way NE, 256/534-9550
Five Points Restaurant
  816 Wellman Ave. NE, 256/536-7356

Best Indian Food
Bombay Cuisine
  420 Jordan Ln. NW, 256/536-3360

Best Italian Food
Fratelli's Italian Restaurant
  4800 Whitesburg Dr. S., 256/650-5944
  501 Jordan Ln. NW, 256/830-1660

Best Japanese Food
Shogun Japanese Steak House
  3780 University Dr. NW, 256/534-3000

Best Lunch
Victoria's Cafe
  7500 Memorial Pkwy. SW, 256/881-0403

Best Mexican Food
Bandito Burrito
  3017 Governors Dr. SW, 256/534-0866

JACKSON, AL

Best Burgers
Ed's Drive-In
  3018 College Ave., 334/246-3054

Best Family Restaurant
Jackson Steak House and Seafood
  3701 College Ave., 334/246-4441

Best Mexican Food
Nolasco's Mexican and American Restaurant
  1204 College Ave., 334/246-6822

Best Sandwiches
Delightful Treats
  1916 College Ave., 334/246-3685

Best Seafood
Jackson Steak House and Seafood
  3701 College Ave., 334/246-4441

MOBILE, AL

Best Barbecue/Ribs
Johnny's Smokehouse Restaurant
  3758 Dauphin Island Pkwy., 334/478-8172
Rodger's B-B-Q
  2350 St. Stephens Rd., 334/330-0285
Saucy-Que Barbecue
  1301 Springhill Ave., 334/433-7427

Best Cajun/Creole Food
Oliver's Restaurant
  Radisson Hotel, 251 Government St., 334/432-8000

Best Eclectic Menu
Almost Six
  6 1/2 N. Jackson St., 334/438-3447

Best Inexpensive Meal
Dew Drop Inn Restaurant
   1808 Old Shell Rd., 334/473-7872

Best Homestyle Food
Cock of the Walk
   4815 Halls Mill Rd., 334/666-1875

Best Lunch
Queen G's Cafe
   2518 Old Shell Rd., 334/471-3361

Best Mexican Food
El Giro
   2518 Government Blvd., 334/478-9886

Best Restaurant in Town
Lighthouse Restaurant
   12495 Padgent Switch, Bayou La Batre,
      334/824-2500
Loretta's Restaurant
   19 S. Conception St., 334/432-2200
Michael's Midtown Cafe
   153 S. Florida St., 334/473-5908

Best Seafood
Bailey's Carry Out Seafood
   10805 Dauphin Island Pkwy., Theodore,
      334/973-1572
Lighthouse Restaurant
   12495 Padgent Switch, Bayou La Batre,
      334/824-2500
The Blue Gill Restaurant and Club
   3775 Battleship Pkwy., Spanish Fort, 334/626-9852

Best Thai Food
Bangkok Thai Cuisine
   5345 Hwy. 90W, 334/666-7788

MONTGOMERY, AL

Best American Food
Char House Restaurant
   92 Knollwood Blvd., 334/272-3995

Best Barbecue/Ribs
Sam's Bar-B-Q
   3510 Atlanta Hwy., 334/279-0008

Best Burgers
Hamburger King
   547 S. Decatur St., 334/262-1798
Sommer's Place
   7972 Vaughn Rd., 334/279-5401

Best Business Lunch
Chappy's Deli
   1611 Perry Hill Rd., 334/279-7477

Best Chinese Food
Choices Chinese Restaurant
   80 Commerce St., 334/262-0888
Ming's Garden Chinese Restaurant
   1741 Eastern Blvd., 334/277-8188

A

Best Fine Dining
Panache at Rosehill
   1741 Eastern Blvd., 334/215-7620

Best Greek/Mediterranean Food
Sahara Restaurant
   511 E. Edgemont Ave., 334/264-9178

Best Homestyle Food
Down the Street Cafe
   2739 Zelda Rd., 334/279-1009
Kountry Cafe
   3951 Norman Bridge Rd., 334/613-2822
Martin's Restaurant
   1796 Carter Hill Rd., 334/265-1767
Shashy's Bakery and Fine Food
   1700 Mulberry St., 334/263-7341

Best Italian Food
Corsino's Italian-American
   911 S Court St., 334/263-9752
Vittorio's Italian Restaurant
   5338 Atlanta Hwy., 334/270-8888

Best Mexican Food
La Fiesta Restaurant
   2131 Eastern Blvd., 334/272-4130
San Marcos
   61 N. Burbank Dr., 334/279-6680

Best Pizza
Tony's Pizza and Steak Restarant
   1985 Bell St., 334/264-7081

Best Restaurant in Town
Sahara Restaurant
   511 E. Edgemont Ave., 334/264-9178

Best Sandwiches
Chappy's Deli
   1611 Perry Hill Rd., 334/279-7477

Best Seafood
Igor's
   3619 Eastern Blvd., 334/271-3535
Sundown East Sandwich and Oyster
   3416 Atlanta Hwy., 334/271-0501

Best Soul Food
Moses Crawford Catering
   700 Columbus St., 334/265-3520

Best Steaks
Green Lantern
   5725 Troy Hwy., 334/288-9947

Best Thai Food
Lek's Taste of Thailand
   5421 Atlanta Hwy., 334/244-8994

PHENIX CITY, AL

Best Barbecue/Ribs
Mike and Ed's Bar-B-Q
   2001 Crawford Rd., 334/297-1012

Best Breakfast
Tyler's Restaurant
  800 Thirteenth St., 334/297-5778

Best Chinese Food
King House
  1821 Stadium Dr., 334/480-4009

Best Mexican Food
El Vaquero
  913 Hwy. 280 Bypass, 334/298-8009

SELMA, AL

Best Barbecue/Ribs
Lannie's Bar-B-Q Spot
  2115 Minter Ave., 334/874-4478

Best Breakfast
Glass House Restaurant
  108 Hwy. 80E, 334/874-9290

Best Chinese Food
China Cook
  128 Broad St., 334/872-2778

Best Homestyle Food
Downtowner Restaurant
  1114 Selma Ave., 334/875-5933

Best Steaks
Steak Pit
  Hwy. 80W, 334/872-3509

TUSCALOOSA, AL

Best American Food
Harvey's Restaurant
  2710 McFarland Blvd. E., 205/553-8466

Best Bar
Kozy's
  3510 Loop Rd., 205/556-0665

Best Barbecue/Ribs
Dreamland Drive-Inn Bar-B-Que
  5535 Fifteenth Ave. E., 205/758-8135
Woodrow's Pit BBQ
  9711 Hwy. 43N, Northport, 205/333-1033

Best Breakfast
The Waysider
  1512 Greensboro Ave., 205/345-8239

Best Brewpub
Barrett's Brewpub and Eatery
  2325 University Blvd., 205/366-0380

Best Business Lunch
Fifteenth Street Diner
  1036 Fifteenth St., 205/750-8750

Best Casual Dining
City Cafe
  408 Main Ave., Northport, 205/758-9171

A

Best Chinese Food
Pearl Garden
2719 Lurleen B. Wallace Blvd., Northport,
205/339-0880
Trey Yuen Chinese Restaurant
4200 McFarland Blvd. E., 205/752-0088

Best Coffee/Coffeehouse
Crimson Cafe
508 Thirteenth Ave., 205/750-0203
Liberty Cafe
1407 University Blvd., 205/758-1833

Best Delicatessen
International Deli
1225 University Blvd., 205/345-9878
Subs-N-You
2427 University Blvd., 205/758-0088

Best Desserts
Crimson Cafe
508 Thirteenth Ave., 205/750-0203

Best Diner
Fifteenth Street Diner
1036 Fifteenth St., 205/750-8750
North River Grill
19039 Hwy. 43N, Northport, 205/339-7951

Best Family Restaurant
Cypress Inn
501 Rice Mine Rd. N., 205/345-6963

Best Fine Dining
Kozy's
3510 Loop Rd., 205/556-0665

Best Homestyle Food
City Cafe
408 Main Ave., Northport, 205/758-9171
Mama Jewel's Country Cookin'
5600 McFarland Blvd. E., 205/752-7580

Best Italian Food
Depalma's Italian Cafe
2300 University Blvd., 205/759-1879
Mr. G's Restaurant
908 McFarland Blvd., Northport, 205/339-8505

Best Japanese Food
Benkei Japanese Steak House
1223 McFarland Blvd. NE, 205/759-5300

Best Lunch
City Cafe
408 Main Ave., Northport, 205/758-9171

Best Mexican Food
Patio Grill
1301 McFarland Blvd. E., 205/391-4861
La Fiesta Mexican Restaurant
1434 McFarland Blvd. E., Holt, 205/759-2371
3408 University Blvd. E., Holt, 205/554-7956

A

Best Pizza
Depalma's Italian Cafe
2300 University Blvd., 205/759-1879
Tut's Place
1400 University Blvd., 205/759-1004

Best Place to Take the Kids
Baumhover's Wings
500 Harper Lee Dr., 205/556-5658

Best Regional Food
Cypress Inn
501 Rice Mine Rd. N., 205/345-6963

Best Restaurant in Town
Globe Restaurant
430 Main Ave., Northport, 205/391-0949

Best Salad/Salad Bar
Subs-N-You
2427 University Blvd., 205/758-0088

Best Sandwiches
Liberty Cafe
1407 University Blvd., 205/758-1833

Best Seafood
Cypress Inn
501 Rice Mine Rd. N., 205/345-6963

Best Sports Bar
Champs
320 Paul W. Bryant Dr., 205/752-3200

Best Steaks
Nick's Filet House
4018 Eutaw Hwy., 205/758-9316

Best Thai Food
Siam House Thai Cuisine
1306D University Blvd., 205/758-4246

Best Vegetarian Food
Manna Grocery Natural Gourmet
2300 McFarland Blvd. E., Ste. 12, 205/752-9955

Best Wine Selection
Globe Restaurant
430 Main Ave., Northport, 205/391-0949

Alaska

ANCHORAGE, AK

Best Burgers
Arctic Roadrunner
  2477 Arctic Blvd., 907/279-7311
  5300 Old Seward Hwy., 907/561-4016
O'Brady's Burgers and Brew
  800 E. Dimond Blvd., Ste. 159, 907/344-8033
Phillip's International Inn
  2902 Minnesota Dr., 907/274-3637
  5121 Arctic Blvd., 907/562-6188
  3801 Debarr Rd., 907/258-3199
  335 Muldoon Rd., 907/338-7606
Red Robin
  3401 Penland Pkwy., 907/276-7788
  401 E. Dimond Blvd., 907/522-4321
Village Inn
  720 W. Dimond Blvd., 907/344-0010
  1130 E. Northern Lights Blvd., 907/279-6012

Best Lunch
Humpy's
  610 W. Sixth Ave., 907/276-2337

Best Pizza
L'Aroma
  3700 Old Seward Hwy., 907/562-9797
Pizza Olympia
  2809 Spenard Rd., 907/561-5264
Sorrento's
  1011 E. Dimond Blvd., 907/344-9986
  610 E. Fireweed Ln., 907/278-3439

A

Best Seafood
Elevation 92
   1007 W. Third Ave., 907/279-1578
Sea Galley
   4101 Credit Union Dr., 907/563-3520
Simon and Seafort's
   420 L St., 907/274-3502

Best Sushi
New Sagaya
   3700 Old Seward Hwy., 907/561-5173
Tempura Kitchen
   3826 Spenard Rd., 907/277-2741

BETHEL, AK

Best Desserts
Diane's Cafe
   1220 Hoffman Hwy., 907/543-4305

Best Greek/Mediterranean Food
Dimitri's Restaurant
   281 Fourth Ave., 907/543-3434

Best Pizza
Brother's Pizza
   1725 State Hwy., 907/543-3878

FAIRBANKS, AK

Best Atmosphere
Pike's Landing
   4438 Airport Way, 907/479-6500
Two Rivers Lodge Fine Dining
   Mile 16.9 Chena Hot Springs Rd., 907/488-6815

Best Breakfast
Sam's Sourdough Cafe
   3702 Cameron St., 907/479-0523

Best Burgers
Triggers
   900 Noble St., 907/457-8747

Best Chinese Food
Golden Shang Hai
   1900 Airport Way, 907/451-1100

Best Coffee/Coffeehouse
Cookie Jar's Garden Cafe
   1006 Cadillac Ct., 907/479-8319
Wolf Run Desserts and Coffeehouse
   3360 Wolf Run, 907/458-0636

Best Desserts
Wolf Run Desserts and Coffeehouse
   3360 Wolf Run, 907/458-0636

Best Health-Conscious Menu
Cookie Jar's Garden Cafe
   1006 Cadillac Ct., 907/479-8319
Whole Earth Grocery and Deli
   1157 Deborah Ave., 907/479-2052

A

Best Homestyle Food
Klondike Lounge and Dining Hall
  1347 Bedrock St., 907/479-2224

Best Ice Cream/Yogurt
Hot Licks Homemade Ice Cream
  3549 College Rd., 907/479-7813

Best Italian Food
Vallata
  2190 Goldstream Rd., 907/455-6600

Best Pizza
Pizza Bella
  1694 Airport Way, 907/456-5657

Best Sandwiches
Food Factory
  1707 S. Cushman St., 907/452-6348
  44 College Rd., 907/452-3313
Wolf Run Desserts and Coffeehouse
  3360 Wolf Run, 907/458-0636

Best Seafood
Ivory Jack's
  2581 Goldstream Rd., 907/455-6666
Two Rivers Lodge Fine Dining
  Mile 16.9 Chena Hot Springs Rd., 907/488-6815

Best Steaks
Ivory Jack's
  2581 Goldstream Rd., 907/455-6666
Two Rivers Lodge Fine Dining
  Mile 16.9 Chena Hot Springs Rd., 907/488-6815

Best Thai Food
Thai Taste Cuisine
  338 Old Steese Hwy., 907/452-7419

HOMER, AK

Best Breakfast
Cafe Cups
  162 W. Pioneer Ave., 907/235-8330

Best Burgers
Boatyard Cafe
  41955 Kachemak Dr., 907/235-5638
Glacier Drive In
  3789 Homer Spit Rd., 907/235-7148

Best Desserts
Smith Family Restaurant
  412 E. Pioneer Ave., 907/235-8600

Best Dinner
Homestead Restaurant
  55775 E. End Rd., Ste. 83, 907/235-8723
Lands End
  4786 Homer Spit Rd., 907/235-2500

Best Health-Conscious Menu
Cafe Cups
  162 W. Pioneer Ave., 907/235-8330

A

Best Mexican Food
Don Jose's Restaurant
127 Pioneer Ave., 907/235-7963

Best Seafood
Boardwalk Fish and Chips
4287 Homer Spit Rd., 907/235-7749

Best Sunday Brunch
Two Sisters Espresso-Bakery
106B W. Bunnell Ave., 907/235-2280

JUNEAU, AK

Best Mexican Food
Armadillo Tex-Mex Cafe
431 S. Franklin St., 907/586-1880

Best Pizza
Vito and Nick's
9342 Glacier Hwy., 907/789-7070

Best Restaurant in Town
Douglas Cafe
916 Third St., Douglas, 907/364-3307
Hot Bite
Auke Bay Boat Harbor, Auke Bay, 907/790-2483
Summit Restaurant
455 S. Franklin St., 907/586-2050
The Fiddlehead Restaurant and Bakery
429 W. Willoughby Ave., 907/586-3150

KETCHIKAN, AK

Best Desserts
5-Star Cafe
5 Creek St., Ste. 1, 907/247-7827

Best Fine Dining
Heen Ka Hidi
Westmark Hotel, 800 Venetia Way, 907/225-8001

Best Health-Conscious Menu
5-Star Cafe
5 Creek St., Ste.1, 907/247-7827

Best Italian Food
Ocean View Italian
3159 Tongass Ave., 907/225-7566

Best Pizza
Ocean View Italian
3159 Tongass Ave., 907/225-7566
Papa's Ketchikan Cafe
316 Front St., 907/247-7272

Best Vegetarian Food
5-Star Cafe
5 Creek St., Ste. 1, 907/247-7827

SEWARD, AK

Best Breakfast
Breeze Inn Restaurant and Lounge
Breeze Inn Motel, 1311 Fourth Ave.,
907/224-5237

A

Best Chinese Food
Peking Chinese Restaurant
  338 Fourth Ave., 907/224-5444

Best Coffee/Coffeehouse
Resurrect Art Coffee House
  320 Third Ave., 907/224-7161

Best Desserts
Ranting Raven Bakery
  228 Fourth Ave., 907/224-2228

Best Family Restaurant
Apollo Restaurant
  229 Fourth Ave., 907/224-3092

Best Homestyle Food
Mainstreet Cafe
  203 Fourth Ave., 907/224-3068

Best Pizza
Apollo Restaurant
  229 Fourth Ave., 907/224-3092

Best Seafood
Ray's Waterfront
  1316 Fourth Ave., 907/224-5606

Best Steaks
Harbor Dinner Club
  220 Fifth Ave., 907/224-3012

SITKA, AK

Best Atmosphere
Back Door
  104 Barracks St., 907/747-8856

Best Dinner
Channel Club
  2906 Halibut Point Rd., 907/747-9916
Van Winkle and Daigler
  228 Harbor Dr., 907/747-3396

Best Greek/Mediterranean Food
Marina Restaurant
  205 Harbor Dr., 907/747-8840

Best Lunch
Back Door
  104 Barracks St., 907/747-8856
Raven's Room
  Westmark Hotel, 330 Seward St., 907/747-6241

Best Seafood
Channel Club
  2906 Halibut Point Rd., 907/747-9916
Marina Restaurant
  205 Harbor Dr., 907/747-8840

Best Steaks
Channel Club
  2906 Halibut Point Rd., 907/747-9916

Best View While Dining
Marina Restaurant
  205 Harbor Dr., 907/747-8840

A

SOLDOTNA, AK

Best Casual Dining
Paradiso's Pizza
  Main St., Kenai, 907/283-2222

Best Dinner
Paradiso's Pizza
  Main St., Kenai, 907/283-2222

Best Fine Dining
Mykel's Restaurant and Lounge
  35041 Kenai Spur Hwy., 907/262-4305

Best Homestyle Food
King Salmon Restaurant
  35674 Kenai Spur Hwy., 907/262-1062

Best Lunch
Paradiso's Pizza
  Main St., Kenai, 907/283-2222

Best Mexican Food
Don Jose's Mexican Restaurant
  44109 Sterling Hwy., 907/262-5700

Best Pizza
Giovanni's Restaurant
  43977 Sterling Hwy., 907/262-2344
Pizza Pete's
  35433 Kenai Spur Hwy., 907/262-5306

WASILLA, AK

Best Barbecue/Ribs
JD's Bar-B-Que Pit
  1595 E. Parks Hwy., 907/376-1097

Best Breakfast
Windbreak Cafe
  2201 E. Parks Hwy., 907/376-4484

Best Chinese Food
Peking Garden
  500 E. Railroad Ave., 907/376-4919

Best Coffee/Coffeehouse
The Deli
  185 E. Parks Hwy., 907/376-2914

Best Desserts
The Deli
  185 E. Parks Hwy., 907/376-2914

Best Dinner
Shore Line Restaurant
  Best Western Lake Lucille Inn, 1300 Lake Lucille
    Dr., 907/373-1776

Best Health-Conscious Menu
Windbreak Cafe
  2201 E. Parks Hwy., 907/376-4484

Best Italian Food
Evangelo's Trattoria
  301 W. Parks Hwy., 907/376-1212

A

Best Mexican Food
Chepo's Fiesta Mexican Restaurant
731 W. Parks Hwy., 907/373-5656

Best Romantic Dining
Mat-Su Resort
1850 Bogard Rd., 907/376-3228

Best Seafood
Mat-Su Resort
1850 Bogard Rd., 907/376-3228

Best Steaks
Mat-Su Resort
1850 Bogard Rd., 907/376-3228

Best Sunday Brunch
Shore Line Restaurant
Best Western Lake Lucille Inn, 300 Lake Lucille
Dr., 907/373-1776

Best View While Dining
Mat-Su Resort
1850 Bogard Rd., 907/376-3228

Arizona

Best American Food
Rawhide Steak House
  1226 Riverview Dr., 520/758-8083

Best Chinese Food
China Panda Restaurant
  2164 Hwy. 95, 520/763-8899
China Szechuan Restaurant
  1890 Hwy. 95, 520/763-2610

Best Homestyle Food
Frontier Cafe
  16118 E. Hwy. 66, Peach Springs, 520/769-8255

Best Italian Food
Joey D's Pizza
  1081 Hwy. 95, 520/754-5300

Best Mexican Food
Casa Serrano Mexican Restaurant
  5230 Hwy. 95, Ft. Mohave, 520/768-1881
El Palacio
  1884 Hwy. 95, 520/763-2494

Best Atmosphere
Paloverde Dining Room
  Francisco Grande Resort, 26000 W. Gila Bend
    Hwy., 520/836-6444

Best Breakfast
Casa Grande Cafe
  301 N. Picacho St., 520/426-1424

A

Best Burgers
Casa Grande Cafe
  301 N. Picacho St., 520/426-1424

Best Homestyle Food
Mr. K's Food and Spirits
  777 N. Pinal Ave., 520/426-3500

Best Pizza
Dell's Pizza and Sports Bar
  1654 N. Pinal Ave., 520/836-2972

Best Southwestern Food
Be Dillon's Cactus Garden
  800 N. Park Ave., 520/836-2045

CHANDLER, AZ

[See also: Mesa and Phoenix.]

Best Barbecue/Ribs
Tom's BBQ Chicago-Style
  2050 N. Alma School Rd., Ste. 35, 602/899-5722

Best Breakfast
J.B.'s Restaurant
  600 N. Arizona Ave., 602/963-0512
Marie Callender's
  7455 W. Chandler Blvd., 602/961-9673

Best Chinese Food
C-Fu Gourmet
  2051 W. Warner Rd., 602/899-3888
House of Egg Roll
  961 W. Ray Rd., 602/899-9331
Shangri La Restaurant
  2992 N. Alma School Rd., 602/821-5388

Best Coffee/Coffeehouse
Bagel Nosh
  985 W. Elliot Rd., 602/814-7608

Best Desserts
Frontier Pie Restaurant
  2130 N. Arizona Ave., 602/963-1243

Best French Food
Citrus Cafe
  2330 N. Alma School Rd., 602/899-0502

Best Ice Cream/Yogurt
Cold Stone Creamery
  2095 N. Alma School Rd., 602/963-1292
  4939 W. Ray Rd., 602/940-0343
  1926 E. Ray Rd., 602/857-9268

Best Italian Food
Rigatony's Authentic Italian Restaurant
  1374 N. Arizona Ave., 602/899-1111

Best Lunch
Sierra Grill
  9645 E. E.V. Robson Blvd., Sun Lakes,
  602/802-4303

A

Best Mexican Food
Guedo's Taco Shop
71 E. Chandler Blvd., 602/899-7841
Serrano's Mexican Food Restaurant
141 S. Arizona Ave., 602/899-3318

Best Sandwiches
AJ's Cafe
1 S. San Marcos Pl., 602/899-1335
Cafe 181
181 N. Dakota St., 602/857-1181
Hogi Yogi
2040 W. Chandler Blvd., 602/963-0505
Pesto's Pizza, Pasta, and Calzones
1960 W. Ray Rd., Ste. 4, 602/821-2949
Surf City Squeeze
3029 N. Alma School Rd., 602/756-0014

Best Seafood
Chops Classic Steak and Seafood
1371 N. Alma School Rd., 602/899-6735

Best Steaks
Chops Classic Steak and Seafood
1371 N. Alma School Rd., 602/899-6735

FLAGSTAFF, AZ

Best Atmosphere
Pasto
19 E. Aspen Ave., 520/779-1937

Best Bar
Buster's Restaurant and Bar
1800 S. Milton Rd., Ste. 111, 520/774-5155

Best Breakfast
Kathy's Cafe
7 N. San Francisco St., 520/774-1951
Mike and Ronda's
21 S. Milton Rd., 520/774-7008

Best Casual Dining
Beaver Street Brewery
11 S. Beaver St., Ste. 1, 520/779-0079
Charly's
23 N. Leroux St., 520/779-1919
Granny's Closet
218 S. Milton Rd., 520/774-8331

Best Chinese Food
Szechuan Restaurant
1451 S. Milton Rd., 520/774-8039

Best Coffee/Coffeehouse
Cafe Express
16 N. San Francisco St., 520/774-0541
La Bellavia Restaurant
18 S. Beaver St., 520/774-8301
Macy's European Coffee House
14 S. Beaver St., 520/774-2243

A

Best Continental Food
Christmas Tree Restaurant
  5200 E. Cortland Blvd., 520/526-0776

Best Dinner
Horseman Lodge and Restaurant
  8500 N. Hwy. 89, 520/526-2655

Best Fine Dining
Chez Marc Bistro
  503 N. Humphreys St., 520/774-1343
Cottage Place
  126 W. Cottage Ave., 520/774-8431

Best French Food
Chez Marc Bistro
  503 N. Humphreys St., 520/774-1343

Best German Food
Gretel's Blackforesthouse
  605 Riordan Rd., 520/773-1551

Best Italian Food
Pasta Works
  2700 Woodlands Village, 520/774-6775
Pasto
  19 E. Aspen Ave., 520/779-1937
Strombolli's Restaurant
  1435 S. Milton Rd., 520/773-1960

Best Japanese Food
Sakura Restaurant
  1175 W. Rte. 66, 520/773-9118

Best Lunch
Kathy's Cafe
  7 N. San Francisco St., 520/774-1951

Best Mexican Food
Black Bean
  12 E. Rte. 66, 520/779-9905
El Charro
  409 S. San Francisco St., 520/779-0552
Kachina Restaurant
  522 E. Rte. 66, 520/779-1944
Ramona's Mexican Food
  2800 Woodland Ave., 520/774-3397
Salsa Brava
  1800 S. Milton Rd., 520/774-1083

Best Pizza
Alpine Spaghetti Station
  2400 E. Rte. 66, 520/779-4138
Ni Marco's Pizza
  101 S. Beaver St., 520/779-2691

Best Sandwiches
Coaches' Club Restaurant
  1481 S. Milton Rd., 520/774-2988

Best Seafood
Buster's Restaurant and Bar
  1800 S. Milton Rd., Ste. 111, 520/774-5155

A

Best Steaks
Black Bart's Steak House Saloon
2760 E. Butler Ave., 520/779-3142

Best Vegetarian Food
Cafe Espress
16 N. San Francisco St., 520/774-0541
Kathy's Cafe
7 N. San Francisco St., 520/774-1951

GLENDALE, AZ

[See also: Phoenix.]

Best American Food
Mercer's Restaurant
9720 W. Peoria Ave., Ste. 101, Peoria, 602/972-0933
Nancy's Country Cupboard Restaurant and Bakery
15400 N. 99th Ave., Sun City, 602/933-0663

Best Barbecue/Ribs
El Paso Barbeque Company
4303 W. Peoria Ave., 602/931-3218

Best Breakfast
Kiss The Cook Restaurant
4915 W. Glendale Ave., 602/939-4663

Best Burgers
Johnny Rockets
7700 W. Arrowhead Towne Ctr., 602/412-8605
Red Robin Restaurant
5830 W. Bell Rd., 602/978-3828

Best Chinese Food
Chang Lee Restaurant
13600 N. 99th Ave., Sun City, 602/974-3601

Best Coffee/Coffeehouse
Global Grind Coffeehouse
15224 N. 59th Ave., 602/938-2452
Italian Coffee Cafe
7700 W. Arrowhead Towne Ctr., 602/979-0083
Java The Hut
5800 W. Peoria Ave., Ste. 102, 602/412-7895

Best Fine Dining
Terrace Dining Room
Wigwam Resort, 300 E. Indian School Rd.,
Litchfield Park, 602/935-3805

Best German Food
Ritter's German Chalet
13232 N. 111th Ave., Youngtown, 602/933-6023

Best Ice Cream/Yogurt
Cold Stone Creamery
5800 W. Peoria Ave., 602/487-1707

Best Italian Food
Cucina Tagliani
17045 N. 59th Ave., 602/547-2782

Lo Perchio's
16901 N. Village Dr. W., Surprise, 602/954-0646
Portofino Ristorante
6020 W. Bell Rd., 602/938-1902
Rosario Ristorante
9250 N. 43rd Ave., 602/931-1810

Best Japanese Food
Ah-So
6033 W. Bell Rd., 602/978-1177

Best Lunch
Bitzee Mama's Restaurant
7023 N. 58th Ave., 602/931-0562

Best Mexican Food
Josie's Mexican Food
6633 N. 55th Ave., 602/937-8224
La Perla
5912 W. Glendale Ave., 602/939-7561
Minga's Fine Mexican Food
4323 W. Cactus Rd., 602/978-5167

Best Pizza
Bola's Pizza Buffet
6756 W. Camelback Rd., 602/848-7574

Best Seafood
Rosario Ristorante
Olive Crossing Shopping Center, 9250 N. 43rd
Ave., 602/931-1810

Best Southwestern Food
Arizona Kitchen
Wigwam Resort, 300 E. Indian School Rd.,
Litchfield Park, 602/935-3811

Best Steaks
Barn Steak House
6508 W. Bell Rd., 602/979-5811
Carver's
8172 W. Bell Rd., 602/412-0787

Best Thai Food
Siam Imports Restaurant
5008 W. Northern Ave., Ste. 1, 602/931-2102
Siamese Kitchen
4352 W. Olive St., 602/931-3229

Best Vietnamese Food
Spring Restaurant
5850 N. 43rd Ave., 602/937-2195

HOLBROOK, AZ

Best All-You-Can-Eat Buffet
Arizona Country Cafe
1851 I-40 Exit 292, 520/524-2686
R and R Pizza Express
1002 W. Hopi Dr., 520/524-2888

Best Burgers
Wayside Drive Inn
1150 W. Hopi Dr., 520/524-3167

A

Best Chinese Food
Sundown Restaurant
915 W. Hopi Dr., 520/524-3785

Best Family Restaurant
Romo's Cafe
121 W. Hopi Dr., 520/524-2153

Best Homestyle Food
Roadrunner Cafe
1501 Navajo Blvd., 520/524-2787

Best Italian Food
Mesa Italiana Restaurant
2318 Navajo Blvd., 520/524-6696

Best Mexican Food
Joe and Aggie's Cafe
120 W. Hopi Dr., 520/524-6540

Best Place to Take the Kids
R and R Pizza Express
1002 W. Hopi Dr., 520/524-2888

Best Seafood
Butterfield Stage Company Steakhouse
609 W. Hopi Dr., 520/524-3447
Plainsman Restaurant
1001 W. Hopi Dr., 520/524-3345

LAKE HAVASU CITY, AZ

Best American Food
London Arms Pub and Restaurant
422 English Village, 520/855-8782

Best Breakfast
Sir James Kafe
1425 N. McCulloch Blvd., 520/855-7669

Best Continental Food
Shugrue's Restaurant Bakery
1425 S. McCulloch Blvd., 520/453-1400

Best Mexican Food
Casa de Miguel Mexican Restaurant
1550 Palo Verde Blvd. S., 520/453-1550
El Rio Cantina and Grill
2131 N. McCulloch Blvd., 520/680-0088

Best Restaurant in Town
The Captain's Table
Nautical Inn Resort, 1000 N. McCulloch Blvd.,
520/855-2141
The Pepper Mill Cafe
2187 N. McCulloch Blvd., 520/855-4405

Best Seafood
Krystal's Fine Dining
460 El Camino Dr., 520/453-2999

Best Steaks
Homestead Saloon and Steakhouse
3465 Maricopa Ave., 520/855-1078

A

[See also: Chandler, Phoenix, Scottsdale, and Tempe.]

Best American Food
American Grill
  1233 S. Alma School Rd., 602/844-1918
The Landmark Restaurant
  809 W. Main St., 602/962-4652
Tortilla Flats
  1678 W. Superstition Blvd., Apache Junction,
    602/984-1776

Best Breakfast
The Farm House
  11421 S. Gilbert Rd., Gilbert, 602/926-0676

Best Burgers
Johnny Rockets
  1445 W. Southern Ave., 602/844-2408

Best Diner
Community Restaurant
  535 N. Country Club Dr., 602/833-3971
  5601 E. Hermosa Vista Dr., 602/832-0640

Best Fine Dining
Bavarian Point Restaurant
  4815 E. Main St., 602/830-0999

Best German Food
Zur-Kate
  4815 E. Main St., 602/830-4244

Best Greek/Mediterranean Food
Euro Cafe
  1111 S. Longmore, 602/962-4224

Best Inexpensive Meal
Golden Canyon Restaurant
  1133 S. Dobson Rd., 602/835-7343

Best Italian Food
Raffaele's
  2909 S. Dobson Rd., Ste. 21, 602/838-0090

Best Japanese Food
Golden Canyon Restaurant
  1133 S. Dobson Rd., 602/835-7343

Best Lunch
Red Hot Shack Deli
  2051 S. Dobson Rd., Ste.18, 602/838-4664
The Farm House
  11421 S. Gilbert Rd., Gilbert, 602/926-0676

Best Mexican Food
El Charro
  105 N. Country Club Rd., 602/964-1851
El Taquito
  9201 S. Avenida Del Yaqui, Ste. 6, Guadalupe,
    602/839-8170

Lulu's Taco Shop
610 N. Gilbert Rd., Gilbert, 602/545-8219
Serrano's Mexican Food Restaurant
1964 E. McKellips Rd., 602/649-3503
1955 W. Guadalupe Rd., 602/756-2992

Best Other Ethnic Food
Bavarian Point Restaurant (central European)
4815 E. Main St., 602/830-0999

Best Pizza
Nello's Pizza
2950 S. Alma School Rd., 602/820-5995

Best Seafood
San Diego Bay Seafood Restaurant
9201 S. Avenida Del Yaqui, Guadalupe,
602/839-2991

Best Thai Food
Mint Thai Cafe
1111 N. Gilbert Rd., Gilbert, 602/497-5366

Best Wine Selection
Brunello
1954 S. Dobson Rd., 602/897-0140

PAGE, AZ

Best Barbecue/Ribs
Ken's Old West
718 Vista Ave., 520/645-5160

Best Breakfast
M Bar H Cafe
819 N. Navajo Dr., 520/645-1420

Best Coffee/Coffeehouse
Beans Gourmet Coffee House
Page Factory Stores, 644 N. Navajo St.,
520/645-6858

Best Desserts
Sweet Memories
660 Elm St., 520/645-1678

Best Family Restaurant
Glen Canyon Steak House
201 N. Lake Powell Rd., 520/645-3363

Best Homestyle Food
Empire House
107 S. Lake Powell Blvd., 520/645-2406

Best Ice Cream/Yogurt
Big Dipper
819 N. Hwy. 89A, 520/645-1456

Best Italian Food
Bella Napoli
810 N. Navajo Dr., 520/645-2706

Best Mexican Food
Zapata's Mexican Food
614 N. Navajo Dr., 520/645-9006

A

Best Sandwiches
Sandwich Place
662 Elm St., 520/645-5267

Best Seafood
Rainbow Room
Wahweap Resort, 100 Lakeshore Dr., 520/645-2433

Best Steaks
Rainbow Room
Wahweap Resort, 100 Lakeshore Dr., 520/645-2433

PHOENIX, AZ

[See also: Glendale, Mesa, and Tempe.]

Best American Food
Latilla
The Boulders Resort and Club, 34631 N.
Tom Darlington Dr., Carefree, 602/488-9009
Stuart Anderson's Black Angus Restaurant
2125 E. Camelback Rd., 602/955-9741
10021 E. Metro Pkwy., 602/944-1517
The Eggery
5109 N. 44th St., 602/840-5734

Best Atmosphere
Los Dos Molinos
8646 S. Central Ave., 602/243-9113

Best Bar
Pomeroy's
5551 N. Seventh St., 602/264-5411
The Monastery
4114 N. 28th St., 602/840-7510

Best Barbecue/Ribs
A and J Chicago Style Barbecue
6102B N. Sixteenth St., 602/241-7519
Honey Bear's Barbecue
5012 E. Van Buren St., 602/273-9148

Best Breakfast
Four B's Cafe
Old Black Canyon Hwy., Black Canyon City,
602/374-5736

Best Burgers
Lenny's Burger Shop
1530 W. Camelback Rd., 602/274-4471

Best Business Lunch
Desert Jade
3215 E. Indian School Rd., 602/954-0048
Tucchetti
2135 E. Camelback Rd., 602/957-0222

Best Cafeteria
Palm Grove Food Court
1850 N. Central Ave., Viad Corporate Ctr.,
602/207-7107

A

Best Cajun/Creole Food
Baby Kay's Cajun Kitchen
  2119 E. Camelback Rd., 602/955-0011

Best Casual Dining
Eddie's Grill
  4747 N. Seventh St., 602/241-1188
Tucchetti
  2135 E. Camelback Rd., 602/957-0222

Best Chinese Food
China Best
  3275 E. McDowell Rd., 602/267-9520
Desert Jade
  3215 E. Indian School Rd., 602/954-0048
New Panda Restaurant
  4234 W. Indian School Rd., 602/278-4060
Sing High
  27 W. Madison St., 602/253-7848

Best Coffee/Coffeehouse
Rembrandt's
  2655 N. Alma School Rd., 602/812-1070
The Good Egg
  2957 W. Bell Rd., 602/993-2797

Best Continental Food
Chaparral Restaurant
  5402 E. Lincoln Dr., 602/948-6644

Best Delicatessen
Miracle Mile Deli
  Park Central Mall, 3110 N. Central Ave.,
    602/277-4783

Best Desserts
Christopher's
  2398 E. Camelback Rd., 602/957-3214

Best Diner
Five and Diner
  5220 N. Sixteenth St., 602/264-5220

Best Dinner
Central Cafe
  15820 N. 35th Ave., 602/938-3383
Harris' Restaurant
  3101 E. Camelback Rd., 602/508-8888
Houston's
  2425 E. Camelback Rd., Ste. 110, 602/957-9700
Richardson's Cuisine of New Mexico
  1582 E. Bethany Home Rd., 602/265-5886
Timothy's
  6335 N. Sixteenth St., 602/234-2205

Best Fine Dining
Vincent Guerithault on Camelback
  3930 E. Camelback Rd., 602/224-0225

Best French Food
Mimi's Cafe
  4901 E. Ray Rd., 602/705-4811

A

Best Greek/Mediterranean Food
Central Cafe
15820 N. 35th Ave., 602/938-3383
Greekfest
1940 E. Camelback Rd., 602/265-2990

Best Health-Conscious Menu
Blue Burrito Grille
3118 E. Camelback Rd., 602/955-2377

Best Homestyle Food
R.J. Osborn's Restaurant
2333 E. Osborn Rd., 602/956-4420

Best Ice Cream/Yogurt
Bavarian Alps Ice Cream Store
2452 E. Camelback Rd., 602/957-9716

Best Indian Food
India Palace
16842 N. Seventh St., 602/942-4224

Best Inexpensive Meal
Gabriel's
Viad Corporate Ctr., 1850 N. Central Ave.,
602/207-2070
Via Delosantos
9120 N. Central Ave., 602/997-6239

Best Italian Food
Che Bella Tuscan Grill and Bakery
2420 E. Camelback Rd., 602/956-5705
La Fontanella
4231 E. Indian School Rd., 602/955-1213

Best Japanese Food
Fish Market Restaurant
1720 E. Camelback Rd., 602/277-3474
Tokyo Express
4105 N. 51st Ave., 602/245-1166

Best Kosher Food
Segal's
4818 N. Seventh St., 602/263-9377

Best Late-Night Food
Five and Diner
5220 N. Sixteenth St., 602/264-5220

Best Lunch
Central Cafe
15820 N. 35th Ave., 602/938-3383
Souper Salad
2651 N. 44th St., 602/840-5686

Best Mexican Food
Ajo Al's Mexican Cafe
5101 N. Sixteenth St., 602/222-9902
Blue Burrito Grille
3118 E. Camelback Rd., 602/955-2377
Carlos O'Brien's Mexican Food
1133 E. Northern Ave., 602/997-2871
Carolina's Mexican Food Service
1202 E. Mohave St., 602/252-1503

Chevy's Mexican Restaurant
2650 E. Camelback Rd., 602/955-6677
El Bravo
8338 N. Seventh St., 602/943-9753
El Pollo Asado
1601 E. Bethany Home Rd., 602/265-6147
El Portal
117 W. Grant St., 602/257-4531
Garcia's
3301 W. Peoria Ave., 602/866-1850
4420 E. Camelback Rd., 602/952-8031
La Canasta
2501 W. Van Buren St., 602/278-7097
5508 N. Seventh Ave., 602/242-4252
3824 W. Indian School Rd., 602/269-2101
Marilyn's First Mexican Restaurant
12631 N. Tatum Blvd., 602/953-2121
Matador Restaurant
125 E. Adams St., 602/254-7563
The Original Garcia's
2212 N. 35th Ave., 602/272-5584

Best Other Ethnic Food
Eliana's Restaurant (Salvadoran)
1627 N. 24th St., 602/225-2925
Havana Cafe (Cuban)
4235 E. Camelback Rd., 602/952-1991
Havana Patio Cafe (Cuban)
6245 E. Bell Rd., 602/991-1496
Seamus McCaffrey's Pub (Irish)
18 W. Monroe St., 602/253-6081

Best Outdoor Dining
The Farm at South Mountain
6106 S. 32nd St., 602/276-6360

Best Pizza
Nello's Pizza
4710 E. Warner Rd., 602/893-8930
Streets of New York
multiple locations

Best Place to Take the Kids
Chuck E. Cheese Pizza
8039 N. 35th Ave., 602/973-1945
Ed Debevic's Short Orders Deluxe
2102 E. Highland Ave., 602/956-2760

Best Romantic Dining
The Compass Room
Hyatt Regency Hotel, 122 E. Second St.,
602/252-1234

Best Salad/Salad Bar
Sweet Tomatoes
52 E. Camelback Rd., 602/274-5414

Best Sandwiches
Pugzie's
4700 N. Sixteenth St., 602/279-3577

A

Best Seafood
Taylor's Chowder House
   3538 W. Calavar Rd., 602/978-1815
The Oyster Grill
   455 N. Third St., 602/252-6767

Best Soul Food
Mrs. White's Golden Rule Cafe
   808 E. Jefferson St., 602/262-9256

Best Southwestern Food
Coyote Grill
   3027 E. Greenway Rd., Ste. 1315, 602/404-8966
Sam's Cafe
   455 N. Third St., Ste.114, 602/252-3545
   2566 E. Camelback Rd., 602/954-7100
Terra Cotta Cafe
   6166 N. Scottsdale Rd., Paradise Valley,
      602/948-8100
Palo Verde
   The Boulders Resort and Club, 34631 N. Tom
      Darlington Dr., Carefree, 602/488-9009

Best Spanish Food
Altos
   5029 N. 44th St., 602/808-0890

Best Sports Bar
Field Goal Bar
   3430 W. Glendale Ave., 602/249-4123

Best Steaks
Morton's of Chicago
   2501 E. Camelback Rd., 602/955-9577
Ruth's Chris Steak
   2201A E. Camelback Rd., Ste. 106, 602/957-9600

Best Sunday Brunch
Terrace Restaurant
   Phoenician Resort, 6000 E. Camelback Rd.,
      602/941-8200

Best Sushi
Ayako of Tokyo
   2564 E. Camelback Rd., 602/955-7007

Best Vegetarian Food
Vegetarian House
   Suma Ching Hai International Association,
      4812 N. Seventh Ave., 602/264-3480

Best View While Dining
Different Pointe of View
   Pointe Hilton, 11111 N. Seventh St., 602/863-0912

Best Wine Selection
Timothy's
   6335 N. Sixteenth St., 602/234-2205

PRESCOTT, AZ

Best American Food
Zeke's Eatin' Place
   1781 E. State Road 69, Ste. 35, 520/776-4602

Best Italian Food
Panzullo's
1350 Iron Springs Rd., 520/776-7062

Best Mexican Food
El Chaparral
628 Miller Valley Rd., 520/445-8447
El Charro
120 N. Montezuma St., 520/445-7130
Pancho's Place
1459 W. Gurley St., 520/771-9505

Best Restaurant in Town
Murphy's
201 N. Cortez St., 520/445-4044

SCOTTSDALE, AZ

[See also: Mesa, Phoenix, and Tempe.]

Best American Food
Rawhide Steakhouse
23023 N. Scottsdale Rd., 602/502-5600

Best Atmosphere
Impeccable Pig
7042 E. Indian School Rd., 602/941-1141

Best Bar
AZ 88
7353 Scottsdale Mall, 602/994-5576

Best Beer Selection
The Crow's Nest
4321 N. Scottsdale Rd., 602/941-0602

Best Breakfast
Arcadia Farms
7014 E. First Ave., 602/941-5665
Pierre's Pastry Cafe
7119 E. Shea Blvd., Ste. 100, 602/443-2510
The Original Pancake House
6840 E. Camelback Rd., 602/946-4902

Best Burgers
Johnny Rockets
7014 E. Camelback Rd., Ste. 576, 602/423-1505

Best Cajun/Creole Food
Baby Kay's Cajun Kitchen
7216 E. Shoeman Ln., 602/990-9080

Best Chinese Food
P.F. Chang's Chinese Bistro
7014 E. Camelback Rd., 602/949-2610

Best French Food
Chez Georges
7000 E. Shea Blvd., 602/991-9484

Best German Food
Mueller's Black Forest Inn
4441 N. Buckboard Trail, 602/970-3504

Best Indian Food
Taste of India
1609 E. Bell Rd., 602/788-3190

Best Italian Food
Franco's Trattoria
8120 N. Hayden Rd., 602/948-6655

Best Japanese Food
Mikado
7111 E. Camelback Rd., 602/481-9777

Best Kosher Food
Boman's Restaurant Deli
3731 N. Scottsdale Rd., 602/947-2934

Best Mexican Food
Blue Burrito Grille
7318 E. Shea Blvd., Ste. 101, 602/951-3151
Carlsbad Tavern
3309 N. Scottsdale Rd., 602/970-8164
La Hacienda
7575 E. Princess Dr., 602/585-4848
Such is Life
7000 E. Shea Blvd., 602/948-1753

Best Pizza
Nello's Pizza
8658 E. Shea Blvd., 602/922-5335
Pizzeria Bianco
4709 N. Twentieth St., 602/381-1779
Sidney's Pizza Cafe
8260 N. Hayden Rd., 602/922-9009

Best Seafood
Salt Cellar Restaurant
550 N. Hayden Rd., 602/947-1963

Best Southwestern Food
Old Town Tortilla Factory
6910 E. Main St., 602/945-4567
Z Tejas Grill
7014 E. Camelback Rd., 602/946-4171

Best Spanish Food
Marquesa
Scottsdale Princess Hotel, 7575 E. Princess Dr.,
602/585-4848
Pepin
7363 E. Scottsdale Mall, 602/990-9026

Best Steaks
Ruth's Chris Steak House
7001 N. Scottsdale Rd., 602/991-5988

Best Sunday Brunch
Marquesa
Scottsdale Princess Hotel, 7575 E. Princess Dr.,
602/585-4848

Best Sushi
Yamaska Restaurant
9301 E. Shea Blvd., Ste.126, 602/860-5605

Best Thai Food
Malee's on Main
  7131 E. Main St., 602/947-6042

Best Vegetarian Food
Lalibela
  8946 N. Nineteenth Ave., 602/870-4555

SHOW LOW, AZ

Best Breakfast
Country Kitchen
  201 E. Deuce of Clubs, 520/537-4774

Best Chinese Food
Asia Gardens Restaurant
  59 W. Deuce of Clubs, 520/537-9333

Best Coffee/Coffeehouse
High in the Pines
  1201 E. Hall St., 520/537-1453

Best Desserts
J.B.'s Restaurant
  480 W. Deuce of Clubs, 520/537-1156

Best Family Restaurant
Pat's Place
  981 E. Deuce of Clubs, 520/537-2337

Best Homestyle Food
Country Kitchen
  201 E. Deuce of Clubs, 520/537-4774
J.B.'s Restaurant
  480 W. Deuce of Clubs, 520/537-1156

Best Mexican Food
Guayo's
  350 E. Deuce of Clubs, 520/537-9503

Best Pizza
Pat's Place
  981 E. Deuce of Clubs, 520/537-2337

Best Sandwiches
High in the Pines
  1201 E. Hall St., 520/537-1453

Best Seafood
Branding Iron Steak House
  1231 E. Deuce of Clubs, 520/537-5151

Best Steaks
Branding Iron Steak House
  1231 E. Deuce of Clubs, 520/537-5151

SIERRA VISTA, AZ

Best Continental Food
The Outside Inn
  4907 S. Hwy. 92, 520/378-4645

Best Mexican Food
Ricardo's Mexican Restaurant
  8177 S. Downey St., Hereford, 520/378-3220

Best Restaurant in Town
The Mesquite Tree Restaurant
   6398 S. Hwy. 92, 520/378-2758

Best Steaks
The Bright Spot
   10989 E. Hwy. 92, Hereford, 520/366-5203

TEMPE, AZ

[See also: Chandler, Mesa, Phoenix, and Scottsdale.]

Best American Food
Brown Derby Restaurant
   4400 S. Rural Rd., 602/345-8223
House of Tricks
   114 E. Seventh St., 602/968-1114
Red Robin Restaurant
   1375 W. Elliot Rd., 602/940-9900
Ted's Jumbo Red Hots
   1755 E. Broadway Rd., 602/968-6678

Best Atmosphere
Monti's La Casa Vieja
   3 W. First St., 602/967-7594

Best Breakfast
The Great Bagel and Coffee Company
   816 E. Camelback Rd., 602/230-7800

Best Brewpub
Bandersnatch Brew Pub
   125 E. Fifth St., 602/966-4438
Beeloc's
   501 S. Mill Ave., 602/894-1230

Best Burgers
Island's
   730 S. Mill Ave., 602/929-9769
The Chuck Box
   202 E. University Dr., 602/968-4712

Best Chinese Food
C-Fu Gourmet
   6438 S. McClintock Dr., 602/831-8899

Best Coffee/Coffeehouse
Cabana Cafe and Juice Bar
   9020 S. McClintock Dr., 602/838-2844
Java Road
   11 E. Seventh St., 602/829-3797
The Coffee Grounds
   5394 S. Lakeshore Dr., 602/820-0660
The Great Bagel and Coffee Company
   816 E. Camelback Rd., 602/230-7800

Best Continental Food
Top of the Rock Bar
   2000 W. Westcourt Way, 602/225-9000

Best Delicatessen
Dilly's Deli
   3330 S. Price Rd., 602/491-1196
In Season Deli
   414 S. Mill Ave., Ste. 111, 602/966-0334

Best Dinner
May West Restaurant
   1825 E. University Dr., 602/966-2761

Best Family Restaurant
Coco's Restaurant
   1717 S. Rural Rd., 602/966-9854

Best Fine Dining
Top of the Rock Bar
   2000 W. Westcourt Way, 602/225-9000

Best Health-Conscious Menu
Saigon Healthy Deli
   820 S. Mill Ave., 602/967-4199

Best Homestyle Food
Coco's Restaurant
   1717 S. Rural Rd., 602/966-9854

Best Ice Cream/Yogurt
Mill Avenue Creamery
   501 S. Mill Ave., 602/894-2202

Best Indian Food
Indian Cuisine
   933 E. University Dr., 602/921-2200

Best Italian Food
John Henry's
   909 E. Elliot Rd., 602/730-9009

Best Korean Food
Korean Garden
   1324 S. Rural Rd., 602/967-1133

Best Mexican Food
Casa Reynoso
   3138 S. Mill Ave., 602/966-0776
El Chilito
   914 E. Baseline Rd., 602/839-5899
Guerrero's Mexican Food
   2148 E. Apache Blvd., 602/966-4118
Monti's La Casa Vieja
   3 W. First St., 602/967-7594
Palapa
   640 S. Mill Ave., 602/921-8011
Restaurant Mexico
   16 E. Seventh St., 602/967-3280

Best Middle Eastern Food
Cafe Istanbul
   903 S. Rural Rd., Ste. 103, 602/731-9499
Haji Baba Middle Eastern
   1513 E. Apache Blvd., 602/966-4672
Tasty Kabob
   1250 E. Apache Blvd., 602/966-0260

A

Best Pizza
Pizzeria Uno Restaurant and Bar
  690 S. Mill Ave., 602/968-1300

Best Regional Food
Crocodile Cafe
  525 S. Mill Ave., 602/966-5883

Best Salad/Salad Bar
Brown Derby Restaurant
  4400 S. Rural Rd., 602/345-8223

Best Seafood
C-Fu Gourmet
  6438 S. McClintock Dr., 602/831-8899
Rusty Pelican
  1606 W. Baseline Rd., 602/345-0972

Best Southwestern Food
Top of the Rock Bar
  2000 W. Westcourt Way, 602/225-9000

Best Sports Bar
McDuffy's
  230 W. Fifth St., 602/966-5600

Best Steaks
Plum Tree Ranch Cookhouse
  3300 S. Price Rd., 602/756-2580

Best Sushi
Ichi Ban Japanese Restaurant
  1435 E. University Dr., 602/968-3234
  3333 S. Rural Rd., 602/345-9848

Best View While Dining
Top of the Rock Bar
  2000 W. Westcourt Way, 602/225-9000

TUCSON, AZ

Best American Food
Arizona Inn
  2200 E. Elm St., 520/325-1541
Tack Room
  2800 N. Sabino Canyon Rd., 520/722-2800

Best Barbecue/Ribs
Rod's KC Barbeque
  601 N. Fourth Ave., 520/623-0182

Best Bistro
Boccata Bistro Bar
  5605 E. River Rd., 520/577-9309
Le Bistro
  2574 N. Campbell Ave., 520/327-3086

Best Breakfast
Cottonwood Cafe
  60 N. Alvernon Way, 520/326-6000
Frank's Restaurant
  3843 E. Pima St., 520/881-2710
Garland Restaurant
  119 E. Speedway Blvd., 520/792-4221

A

Best Burgers
Big A Restaurant
  2033 E. Speedway Blvd., 520/326-1818
Carter's Drive In
  575 S. Haskell Ave., Willcox, 520/384-2277
Lucky Wishbone
  10 N. Swan Rd., 520/327-5679
  1104 S. Wilmot Rd., 520/747-7181
  2545 N. Campbell Ave., 520/323-9329
  4092 N. Oracle Rd., 520/887-9160
  5220 S. Nogales Hwy., 520/294-7607

Best Casual Dining
Austin's Ice Cream
  2920 E. Broadway Blvd., 520/327-3892

Best Chinese Food
Mei Hon Chinese Restaurant
  1030 E. Irvington Rd., 520/294-8739
Peking Palace
  6970 E. 22nd St., 520/750-9614

Best Coffee/Coffeehouse
Coffee Etc.
  2830 N. Campbell Ave., 520/881-8070
  6091 N. Oracle Rd., 520/544-8588
Not Just Java
  149 N. Stone Ave., 520/620-1504

Best Delicatessen
Feig's Kosher Foods
  5071 E. Fifth St., 520/325-2255

Best Diner
Little Anthony's Diner
  7010 E. Broadway Blvd., 520/296-0456

Best Dinner
City Grill
  6350 E. Tanque Verde Rd., 520/733-1111
Cottonwood Cafe
  60 N. Alvernon Way, 520/326-6000
Ventana Grill
  6866 E. Sunrise Dr., 520/299-3666

Best Eclectic Menu
Ventana Room
  Loew's Ventana Canyon Resort, 7000 N. Resort Dr.,
    520/299-2020

Best Fine Dining
Charles Restaurant
  6400 E. El Dorado Circle, 520/296-7173
Gold Room
  Westward Look Resort, 245 E. Ina Rd.,
    520/297-1151
Jano's Restaurant
  150 N. Main Ave., 520/884-9426
Kingfisher Bar and Grill
  2564 E. Grant Rd., 520/323-7739
Scordato's in the Foothills
  4405 W. Speedway Blvd., 520/624-8946

A

Best French Food
Le Rendez-Vous
    2844 E. Fort Lowell Rd., 520/323-7373
Vivace Restaurant
    4811 E. Grant Rd., 520/795-7221

Best Greek/Mediterranean Food
Athens on Fourth Avenue
    500 N. Fourth Ave., 520/624-6886

Best Health-Conscious Menu
Blue Willow Restaurant Bakery
    2616 N. Campbell Ave., 520/795-8736
La Salsa Restaurant
    4861 E. Grant Rd., 520/325-2200

Best Ice Cream/Yogurt
Austin's Ice Cream
    2920 E. Broadway Blvd., 520/327-3892

Best Indian Food
India Oven Cuisine of India
    2727 N. Campbell Ave., 520/326-8635

Best Inexpensive Meal
Maya Quetzal
    429 N. Fourth Ave., 520/622-8207
Reay's Foothill's Market
    4751 E. Sunrise Dr., 520/299-8858
Yoeme Tortillas
    1545 N. Stone Ave., 520/623-2046

Best Italian Food
Daniel's Restaurant and Trattoria
    4340 N. Campbell Ave., 602/742-3200
Fio Rito's
    2702 E. Grant Rd., 520/325-6913
Gavi Italian Restaurant
    7865 E. Broadway Blvd., 520/290-8380
Larocca's Classic Italian
    5689 N. Swan Rd., 520/299-4301
Old Chicago Deli
    175 S. La Canada Dr., Green Valley, 520/625-3354
Scordato's in the Foothill's
    4405 W. Speedway Blvd., 520/624-8946
Vivace
    4811 E. Grant Rd., 520/795-7221

Best Late-Night Food
Congress Grill
    100 E. Congress St., 520/623-7621

Best Lunch
Cafe Dolomitti
    5575 E. River Rd., Ste. 141, 520/529-1811
Cafe Magritte
    254 E. Congress St., 520/884-8004
Coffee Etc.
    6091 N. Oracle Rd., 520/544-8588
    2830 N. Campbell Ave., 520/881-8070
Cottonwood Cafe
    60 N. Alvernon Way, 520/326-6000

A

Delectables Restaurant
  533 N. Fourth Ave., 520/884-9289
Ric's Cafe
  5605 E. River Rd., 520/577-7272

Best Mexican Food
Cora's Cafe
  24 W. Irvington Rd., 520/294-2146
El Charro
  587 Morris Rd., Hayden, 520/356-7050
  601 W. Main St., Safford, 520/428-4134
El Charro Cafe
  311 N. Court Ave., 520/903-1922
  6310 E. Broadway Blvd., 520/745-1922
El Mariachi
  106 W. Drachman St., 520/791-7793
El Parador
  2744 E. Broadway Blvd., 520/881-2808
La Indita Restaurant
  622 N. Fourth Ave., 520/792-0523
La Salsa Restaurant
  4861 E. Grant Rd., 520/325-2200

Best Middle Eastern Food
Tork's Cafe
  1701 N. Country Club Rd., 520/325-3737

Best Other Ethnic Food
Seri Melaka (Thai/Malaysian)
  6133 E. Broadway Blvd., 520/747-7810

Best Outdoor Dining
Blue Willow Restaurant Bakery
  2616 N. Campbell Ave., 520/795-8736
Tohono Chul Tea Room
  7366 N. Paseo Del Norte, 520/797-1222

Best Pizza
Fio Rito's
  2702 E. Grant Rd., 520/325-6913
Mama's Pizza and Heros
  7965 N. Oracle Rd., 520/297-3993
  831 N. Park Ave., 520/882-3993
  6996 E. 22nd St., 520/750-1919
Old Chicago Deli
  175 S. La Canada Dr., Green Valley, 520/625-3354
Zachary's Classic Pan
  1019 E. Sixth St., 520/623-6323

Best Romantic Dining
Le Rendez-Vous
  3844 E. Fort Lowell Rd., 520/323-7373

Best Salad/Salad Bar
Souper Salad Restaurant
  6129 E. Broadway Blvd., 520/790-4181
  4490 N. First Ave., 520/690-1111

Best Sandwiches
Austin's Ice Cream
  2920 E. Broadway Blvd., 520/327-3892
Baggin's Gourmet Sandwiches
  multiple locations

A

Best Seafood
Chuy's Baja Broiler
  3312 S. Sixth Ave., 520/622-0964
  4185 W. Ina Rd., 520/579-3395
  6453 N. Oracle Rd., 520/797-1233
Kingfisher Bar and Grill
  2564 E. Grant Rd., 520/323-7739
Marisco's Chihuahua
  1009 N. Grande Ave., 520/623-3563
Solarium Restaurant
  6444 E. Tanque Verde Rd., 520/886-8186
Ye Olde Lantern Restaurant
  1800 N. Oracle Rd., 520/622-6761

Best Southwestern Food
Cafe Terra Cotta
  4310 N. Campbell Ave., 520/577-8100
Fuego Restaurant and Bar
  6958 N. Campbell Ave., 520/886-1745
Gold Room
  245 E. Ina Rd., 520/297-1151
Jano's Restaurant
  150 N. Main Ave., 520/884-9426

Best Steaks
Lil' Abner's Steak House
  8501 N. Silverbell Rd., 520/744-2800
OK Corral Catering and Restaurant
  7710 E. Wrightstown Rd., 520/885-2373
Pinnacle Peak
  6541 E. Tanque Verde Rd., 520/296-0911

Best Sunday Brunch
Canyon Cafe
  Loews Ventana Canyon Resort, 7000 N. Resort Dr.,
    520/299-2020
Rincon Market
  2513 E. Sixth St., 520/327-6653

Best Sushi
Sachiko Sushi
  1101 N. Wilmot Rd., 520/886-7000
Sushi-Cho Restaurant
  1830 E. Broadway Blvd., 520/628-8800

Best Tea Room
Tohono Chul Tea Room
  7366 N. Paseo Del Norte, 520/797-1711

Best Vegetarian Food
Garland Restaurant
  119 E. Speedway Blvd., 520/792-4221
Govinda's Natural Foods
  711 E. Blacklidge Dr., 520/792-0630

YUMA, AZ

Best Bar
Hungry Hunter
  2355 S. Fourth Ave., 520/782-3637
Johnny's Sports Bar and Grill
  244 E. Sixteenth St., 520/783-9367

Best Breakfast
Brownie's Restaurant
   1145 S. Fourth Ave., 520/783-7911
Ligurta Station
   19702 E. Hwy. 80, Wellton, 520/785-4361

Best Burgers
Lute's Casino
   221 S. Main St., 520/782-2192

Best Business Lunch
Crossing Restaurant
   2690 S. Fourth Ave., 520/726-5551
Famous Sam's Restaurant and Bar
   2052 S. Fourth Ave., 520/783-7267
Panda Restaurant and Lounge
   711 E. 32nd St., 520/341-0323

Best Chinese Food
Mandarin Palace
   350 E. 32nd St., 520/344-2805

Best Desserts
Mostly Muffins
   2451 W. Sixteenth St., 520/783-7484

Best Diner
Brownie's Restaurant
   1145 S. Fourth Ave., 520/783-7911

Best Family Restaurant
Chateau Basque Restaurant
   4340 E. Hwy. 80, 520/341-9776

Best Inexpensive Meal
La Casa Gutierrez
   520 S. Orange Ave., 520/782-1402

Best Italian Food
Bella Vita Restaurant
   2755 S. Fourth Ave., 520/344-3989

Best Late-Night Food
Copper Miner's Kitchen
   10800 N. Frontage Rd., 520/342-2110

Best Mexican Food
Chretin's Mexican Food
   485 S. Fifteenth Ave., 520/782-1291
El Charro
   601 W. Eighth St., 520/783-9790

Best Pizza
Bernardo's Pizza
   11242 S. Foothills Blvd., 520/342-2034

Best Place to Eat Alone
Copper Miner's Kitchen
   10800 N. Frontage Rd., 520/342-2110

Best Place to Take the Kids
Famous Sam's Restaurant and Bar
   2052 S. Fourth Ave., 520/783-7267

Best Romantic Dining
Shilo Inn
   1550 S. Castle Dome Ave., 520/782-9511

A

Best Salad/Salad Bar
Chateau Basque Restaurant
  4340 E. Hwy. 80, 520/341-9776

Best Steaks
Jack and Rosie's
  1551 W. Fifth St., 520/783-9172

Best Sunday Brunch
Hungry Hunter
  2355 S. Fourth Ave., 520/782-3637

Arkansas

BATESVILLE, AR

Best All-You-Can-Eat Buffet
Kelly Wyatt's Restaurant
  1220 S. Saint Louis St., 870/793-5756

Best Barbecue/Ribs
Batesville BBQ
  1351 Lyon St., 870/793-4668

Best Breakfast
Kelly Wyatt's Restaurant
  1220 S. Saint Louis St., 870/793-5756

Best Burgers
Kelly Wyatt's Restaurant
  1220 S. Saint Louis St., 870/793-5756

Best Desserts
Cafe Indigo
  231 E. Main St., 870/698-0200

Best Fine Dining
Teal's in the Ramada Inn
  1325 N. Saint Louis St., 870/698-1800

Best Lunch
Cafe Indigo
  231 E. Main St., 870/698-0200

Best Mexican Food
La Fiesta Cafe Mexican
  4530 Harrison St., 870/793-4999

Best Regional Food
Fred's Fish House
  3777 Harrison St., 870/793-2022

Best Restaurant in Town
Cafe Indigo
231 E. Main St., 870/698-0200

Best Seafood
Fred's Fish House
3777 Harrison St., 870/793-2022

BLYTHEVILLE, AR

Best Barbecue/Ribs
Dixie Pig
701 N. Sixth St., 870/763-4636

Best Breakfast
Sharecropper's
211 W. Ash St., 870/763-5818

Best Burgers
Burger Broil
698 N. Sixth St., 870/763-6202

Best Chinese Food
Hong Kong Chinese Steak and Seafood
829 E. Main St., 870/763-5664
Kowloon Chinese Restaurant
357 S. Division St., 870/762-2828

Best Family Restaurant
Grecian Steak House
165 E. State Hwy. 18, 870/763-7550

Best Homestyle Food
Sharecropper's
211 W. Ash St., 870/763-5818

Best Regional Food
Ed's Country Catfish House
2075 S. Division St., 870/762-2603

Best Steaks
Grecian Steak House
165 E. State Hwy. 18, 870/763-7550
Harry's
200 S. First St., 870/763-0443

CONWAY, AR

Best Atmosphere
Breakaway Cafe
505 Donaghey Ave., 501/327-6700

Best Barbecue/Ribs
Shorty's
1101 Harkrider St., 501/329-9213
Smitty's Bar-B-Q
740 S. Harkrider St., 501/327-8304

Best Burgers
Mean Bean Cafe
2501 Hwy. 286W, 501/336-9957

Best Homestyle Food
Dixie Cafe
1101 Fendley Dr., 501/327-4777

A

Best Ice Cream/Yogurt
Dixie Cafe
  1101 Fendley Dr., 501/327-4777

Best Italian Food
Fazoli's
  1100 Hwy. 65N, 501/336-0006

Best Mexican Food
El Chico Restaurant
  201 Hwy. 65N, 501/327-6553
Los Amigos Mexican Restaurant
  2850 Prince St., 501/329-7919

Best Sandwiches
Place to Eat
  808 Front St., 501/327-6858

Best Seafood
Fish House
  116 S. Harkrider St., 501/327-9901
Hart's Seafood Restaurant
  Hwy. 64 at Hwy. 65, 501/327-7041

Best Steaks
Chuck's Steak House
  3105 Hwy. 25B, Heber Springs, 501/362-7676

DUMAS, AR

Best American Food
Cow Pen
  5198 Hwy. 82E, Lake Village, 870/265-9992

Best Barbecue/Ribs
Sassy Jones Barbeque
  3738 Hwy. 65 and 82S, Lake Village, 870/265-5400

Best Burgers
Sonic Drive-In
  714 Hwy. 65S, 870/382-2520

Best Chinese Food
House of Lee Restaurant
  350 Twin River Ctr., 870/382-2388

Best Family Restaurant
Dude's Restaurant
  Hwy. 65S, 870/382-2879

Best Mexican Food
Cow Pen
  5198 Hwy. 82E, Lake Village, 870/265-9992

Best Other Ethnic Food
Tradewinds Restaurant (Asian)
  Hwy. 65N, McGehee, 870/222-4022

EL DORADO, AR

Best American Food
Barron's Restaurant
  1920 Junction City Rd., 870/862-5191

Best Barbecue/Ribs
J J's Smokehouse BBQ
  1000 E. Main St., 870/862-1777

A

Massey's Pit Bar-B-Q
321 W. Grove St., 870/863-0802

Best Breakfast
Andy's Restaurant
1305 N. West Ave., 870/864-0144
Union Station Cafe
208 E. Elm St., 870/863-9719

Best Burgers
Burger Blast
1409 E. Main St., Magnolia, 870/234-2034

Best Cajun/Creole Food
The French Quarter
825 Jackson St. SW, Camden, 870/837-1010

Best Chinese Food
Oriental Garden
3401 N. West Ave., 870/862-7771

Best Diner
Beef and Bisquits
417 E. Main St., Magnolia, 870/234-8659

Best Family Restaurant
Marlar's Cafeteria
2116 N. Vine St., Magnolia, 870/234-6900
Miller 's Cafeteria
2402 N. Vine St., Magnolia, 870/234-2181

Best Homestyle Food
Marlar's Cafeteria
2116 N. Vine St., Magnolia, 870/234-6900

Best Inexpensive Meal
Good Times Grill
2500 N. West Ave., 870/862-6922

Best Regional Food
Wood's Place
1173 W. Washington St., Camden, 870/836-0474

Best Restaurant in Town
Al's On the Square
200 E. Main St., 870/863-0404

Best Seafood
Catfish Cove
4414 W. Hillsboro St., 870/862-5814
Rails
902 E. McKissack St., Waldo, 870/693-2243

Best Steaks
Georgia's Restaurant
2630 Columbia Rd., Ste. 15, Magnolia,
870/696-3942
White House Cafe
323 Adams Ave. SE, Camden, 870/836-4663

FAYETTEVILLE, AR

Best All-You-Can-Eat Buffet
J.D. China Chinese Restaurant
1466 N. College Ave., 501/442-5875

A

Best American Food
Kirby's Grill and Bakery
3722 N. Front St., 501/443-3900

Best Bar
George's Majestic Lounge
519 W. Dickson St., 501/442-4226

Best Barbecue/Ribs
B and B Bar-B-Q
230 S. East Ave., 501/582-3663

Best Breakfast
Jerry's Homestyle Cooking
241 N. College Ave., 501/521-2480
Uncle Gaylord's
315 W. Mountain St., 501/444-0605

Best Burgers
Hoffbrau Steaks
31 E. Center St., 501/442-4444
Hugo's
25 1/2 N. Block Ave., 501/521-7585

Best Business Lunch
Hog City Diner
1 W. Center Sq., 501/443-5588

Best Casual Dining
Ozark Brewing Company
430 W. Dickson St., 501/521-2739

Best Chinese Food
Lin's Chinese Restaurant
704 N. College Ave., 501/521-2022

Best Coffee/Coffeehouse
Arsaga's Espresso Cafe
2418 N. Gregg Ave., 501/444-6557
Hog City Diner
1 W. Center Sq., 501/443-5588

Best Eclectic Menu
Restaurant on the Corner
248 W. Dickson St., 501/521-2674

Best French Food
Zachary's Restaurant
708 N. College Ave., 501/444-7774

Best Health-Conscious Menu
Kirby's Grill and Bakery
3722 N. Front St., 501/443-3900

Best Homestyle Food
Vida Drake's Restaurant
1023 S. Morningside Dr., 501/521-3244

Best Inexpensive Meal
J.D. China Chinese Restaurant
1466 N. College Ave., 501/442-5875

Best Italian Food
Belvedeer's
3061 N. College Ave., 501/443-7778

A

Best Late-Night Food
Tony C's Italiano Ristorante
2366 N. College Ave., 501/442-4433

Best Lunch
Muley's Restaurant and Club
1 Colt Square Dr., 501/443-3911

Best Mexican Food
Cafe Santa Fe and Bar
25 E. Center St., 501/442-5673
Jose's
324 W. Dickson St., 501/521-0194
La Huerta
2356 N. College Ave., 501/521-7990

Best Pizza
Tim's Pizza
21 W. Mountain St., 501/521-5551
2730 N. College Ave., 501/521-4151

Best Place to Eat Alone
Jim's Razorback Pizza
University of Arkansas Student Union, Sixth St.,
501/575-7345

Best Regional Food
The Hush Puppy Catfish Restaurant
3582 N. Hwy. 112, 501/521-5914

Best Restaurant in Town
Kirby's Grill and Bakery
3722 N. Front St., 501/443-3900

Best Seafood
Ozark Brewing Company
430 W. Dickson St., 501/521-2739
Powerhouse Seafood and Grill
112 N. University Ave., 501/442-8300

Best Southwestern Food
Jose's
324 W. Dickson St., 501/521-0194

Best Sports Bar
Cuckoo's Sports Grill
965 S. Razorback Rd., 501/521-5100

Best Steaks
Herman's Ribhouse
2901 N. College Ave., 501/442-9671
Ozark Brewing Company
430 W. Dickson St., 501/521-2739

Best Sunday Brunch
Belvedeer's
3061 N. College Ave., 501/443-7778
Uncle Gaylord's
315 W. Mountain St., 501/444-0605

A

FT. SMITH, AR

Best American Food
Goodson's
  5111 Rogers Ave., Ste. 62, 501/452-0929
Re-Pete's Place
  7830 Hwy. 71S, 501/646-4333

Best Barbecue/Ribs
Jerry Neel's B-B-Q
  1823 S. Phoenix Ave., 501/646-8085

Best Bistro
Folie A Deux
  2909 Old Greenwood Rd., Ste. 6, 501/648-0041
  3514 Country Club Ave., 501/649-9711

Best Burgers
Burgers and More
  2800 Albert Pike Rd., 501/767-4601

Best Casual Dining
Varsity Sports Grill
  318 Garrison Ave., 501/494-7173

Best Chinese Food
Peking Palace Chinese Restaurant
  5819 Rogers Ave., 501/452-6070

Best Delicatessen
Dora's Pie Shop and Deli
  4300 Rogers Ave., Ste. 18, 501/782-0170

Best Fine Dining
John Q's Fine Dining
  700 Rogers Ave., 501/783-1000

Best French Food
Folie A Deux
  2909 Old Greenwood Rd., Ste. 6, 501/648-0041

Best German Food
Emmy's German Restaurant
  602 N. Sixteenth St., 501/783-0012

Best Greek/Mediterranean Food
George's Restaurant
  2120 Grand Ave., 501/785-1199

Best Homestyle Food
Calico County Restaurant
  2401 S. 56th St., 501/452-3299
Creative Kitchen Cafe
  3702 Century Dr., 501/646-3221
Eunice's Country Cookin'
  3615 Jerry Lind Rd., 501/646-3638

Best Italian Food
Bella Italia
  407 N. Eighth St., 501/785-1550

Best Mexican Food
Puebla Restaurant
  4020A Midland Blvd., 501/783-3755

Best Pizza
Pizza Parlour
  8901 Rogers Ave., 501/452-2228

A

Best Regional Food
Catfish Cove Restaurant
  1615 S. Phoenix Ave., 501/646-8835

Best Romantic Dining
Light House Inn
  6000 Midland Blvd., 501/783-9420

Best Sandwiches
Corner House
  2711 Park Ave., 501/783-9015

Best Seafood
Light House Inn
  6000 Midland Blvd., 501/783-9420

Best Sports Bar
Varsity Sports Grill
  318 Garrison Ave., 501/494-7173

Best Steaks
John Q's Fine Dining
  700 Rogers Ave., 501/783-1000
Red Barn Steak House
  3716 Newlon Rd., 501/783-4075
Tommy's Seafood and Steaks
  2428 N. Midland Blvd., 501/783-9523

Best View While Dining
Light House Inn
  6000 Midland Blvd., 501/783-9420
Old Mill Inn Restaurant
  9417 Rogers Ave., 501/452-4777

HARRISON, AR

Best Barbecue/Ribs
Circle J BBQ and Steakhouse
  108 Lakeshore Dr., 870/743-2881

Best Casual Dining
Townhouse Cafe
  119 W. Rush Ave., 870/741-2130

Best Diner
D W's Diner
  103 W. Rush Ave., 870/741-8207

Best Fine Dining
Benton House
  811 S. Pine St., 870/365-7275

Best Italian Food
DeVito's Restaurant
  350 DeVito Loop, 870/741-8832

Best Mexican Food
Miguel's Mexican Villa
  416 S. Hwy. 62/65 Bypass, 870/743-2824

Best Regional Food
Catfish Wharf
  1318 N. Hwy. 62/65 Bypass, 870/741-9200

Best Sunday Brunch
Benton House
  811 S. Pine St., 870/365-7275

DeVito's Restaurant
350 DeVito Loop, 870/741-8832

Best All-You-Can-Eat Buffet
Buffy's Buffet
3815 Central Ave., 501/525-5793

Best American Food
Johnny's
3413 Central Ave., 501/623-9788
Miller's Chicken and Steak House
4723 Central Ave., 501/525-8861

Best Barbecue/Ribs
Stubby's BBQ
3024 Central Ave., 501/624-2484

Best Breakfast
Colonial Pancake and Waffle House
111 Central Ave., 501/624-9273
Pancake Shop
216 Central Ave., 501/624-9465

Best Burgers
Burgers and More
622 Carpenter Dam Rd., 501/262-2253

Best Chinese Food
The Panda
3520 Central Ave., 501/624-5403

Best German Food
Brau Haus
801 Central Ave., 501/624-7866

Best Homestyle Food
Mary's Cafe
1010 Central Ave., 501/624-2988
Mollie's Restaurant
538 W. Grand Ave., 501/623-6582

Best Italian Food
Agostino's Italian Restaurant
510 Central Ave., 501/624-5500
Facci's Italian Restaurant
2910 Central Ave., 501/623-9049
Rocky's Corner
2600 Central Ave., 501/624-0199

Best Mexican Food
Acapulco Restaurant
320 Ouachita Ave., 501/623-8030
Cafe Santa Clare
323 Whittington Ave., 501/624-0166
La Hacienda Restaurant
3836 Central Ave., 501/525-8203

Best Other Ethnic Food
Bohemia Restaurant (Czech/German)
417 Park Ave., 501/623-9661

Best Pizza
Rocky's Corner
2600 Central Ave., 501/624-0199

A

Rod's Pizza Cellar
   3350 Central Ave., 501/624-7637

Best Regional Food
Fish Net Family Restaurant
   Hwy. 7N, 501/321-1910
Miller's Chicken and Steak House
   4723 Central Ave., 501/525-8861

Best Restaurant in Town
Coy's Steakhouse
   300 Coy St., 501/321-1414
Miller's Chicken and Steak House
   4723 Central Ave., 501/525-8861
The Hamilton House
   130 Van Lyell Dr., 501/525-2727

Best Seafood
Pirate's Cove Restaurant and Bar
   200 River Heights Terrace, 501/767-8517

Best Steaks
Coy's Steakhouse
   300 Coy St., 501/321-1414
The Hamilton House
   130 Van Lyell Dr., 501/525-2727

Best Sunday Brunch
Arlington Fountain and Venetian Restaurant
   239 Central Ave., 501/623-7771

JONESBORO, AR

Best All-You-Can-Eat Buffet
Barnhill's Country Buffet
   111 Caraway Rd., 870/931-7322

Best Atmosphere
The Candlelite Steakhouse
   1116 Linwood Dr., Paragould, 870/239-8391

Best Barbecue/Ribs
Couch's Bar-B-Q
   5323 E. Nettleton Ave., 870/932-0710
Rib Shack
   112 Jones Rd., Paragould, 870/239-5773

Best Burgers
The Hamburger Station
   110 E. Main St., Paragould, 870/239-9956

Best Chinese Food
China Garden Restaurant
   906 S. Caraway Rd., 870/932-6083

Best Fine Dining
501 Club and Restaurant
   2628 Phillips Dr., 870/972-6501

Best Homestyle Food
Guy's Buffet
   403 W. Kings Hwy., Paragould, 870/236-2299

Best Italian Food
Piero and Company
   314 Union St., 870/933-0034

A

Best Lunch
Potlicker's Uptown Deli
  311B Main St., 870/931-4195

Best Mexican Food
El Acapulco
  1900 E. Highland Dr., 870/935-6692
Poncho's
  2240 S. Caraway Rd., 870/972-6640

Best Regional Food
Ed's Country Catfish House
  5071 Hwy. 1S, 870/972-1498
Fishboat Restaurant
  3905 E. Nettleton Ave., 870/935-0951
Ron's Catfish Buffet
  63 Dan Ave., 870/930-9639

Best Restaurant in Town
Dixie Cafe
  2406 S. Caraway Rd., 870/932-9400
Oaks Restaurant
  3006 S. Caraway Rd., 870/935-2030
The Candlelite Steakhouse
  1116 Linwood Dr., Paragould, 870/239-8391

Best Steaks
Grecian Steakhouse
  625 N. Fourteenth St., Paragould, 870/239-2822
The Candlelite Steakhouse
  1611 Linwood Dr., Paragould, 870/239-8391

LITTLE ROCK, AR

Best All-You-Can-Eat Buffet
Brown's Country Store and Restaurant
  18718 I-30, Benton, 501/778-5033

Best American Food
Faded Rose Restaurant
  1615 Rebsamen Park Rd., 501/663-9734
  400 N. Bowman Rd., Ste. 28, 501/224-3377

Best Atmosphere
Ashley's Restaurant
  111 W. Markham St., 501/374-7474
Josephine's
  3 Statehouse Plz., 501/375-5000

Best Barbecue/Ribs
Casey's Bar-B-Q
  600 Reservoir Rd., 501/224-9493
Corky's Ribs and Barbecue
  400 N. Bowman Rd., 501/954-7427
Hickory Joe's
  7300 W. Twelfth St., 501/663-3427
Sim's Bar-B-Que
  7601 Geyer Springs Rd., 501/562-8844
  1307 Barrow Rd., 501/224-2057
  716 W. 33rd St., 501/372-6868

A

Best Breakfast
Ozark Mountain Smokehouse and Family Restaurant
201 Keightly Dr., 501/663-7319

Best Burgers
Buffalo Grill
1611 Rebsamen Park Rd., 501/663-2158
Buffalo Grill West
400 N. Bowman Rd., 501/224-0012
Canon Grill
2811 Kavanaugh Blvd., 501/664-2068
Doe's Eat Place
1023 W. Markham St., 501/376-1195

Best Business Lunch
Cafe St. Moritz
225 E. Markham St., 501/372-0411

Best Casual Dining
Black Eyed Pea Restaurant
219 N. Shackleford Rd., 501/227-9967
Julie's
110 S. Shackleford Rd., 501/224-4501

Best Chinese Food
Chi's Chinese Cuisine
6 Shackleford Dr., 501/221-7737
China Garden
324 W. Main St., Jacksonville, 501/982-2712
Fantastic China
1900 N. Grant St., 501/663-8999
Forbidden City Chinese Restaurant
6000 W. Markham St., Ste. 1034, 501/663-9099
Fu Lin Chinese Restaurant
200 N. Bowman Rd., 501/225-8989

Best Coffee/Coffeehouse
Cafe D'Roma
2701 Kavanaugh Blvd., 501/663-7397
Community Bakery
1200 Main St., 501/375-7105
Wycoff Coffee
10700 N. Rodney Parham Rd., 501/228-4448

Best Continental Food
1620 Restaurant
1620 Market St., 501/221-1620
Andre's in Hillcrest
605 N. Beechwood Ave., 501/666-9191
Ashley's Restaurant
111 W. Markham St., 501/374-7474
Cafe St. Moritz
225 E. Markham St., 501/372-0411

Best Delicatessen
Cordell's
1500 Rebsamen Park Rd., 501/666-5405
Jason's Deli
301 N. Shackleford Rd., 501/954-8700

Best Diner
Homer's
2001 E. Roosevelt Rd., 501/374-1400

Lucky Seven Diner and Catering
  314 E. Sixth St., 501/375-2526
Starlite Diner
  250 E. Military Dr, North Little Rock, 501/753-1433
Your Mama's Good Food
  402 Louisiana St., 501/372-1811

Best Eclectic Menu
Brave New Restaurant
  3701 Old Cantrell Rd., 501/663-2677
Spaule'
  5713 Kavanaugh Blvd., 501/664-3663

Best French Food
Alouette's French Company
  11401 N. Rodney Parham Rd., 501/225-4152
Andre's in Hillcrest
  605 N. Beechwood Ave., 501/666-9191

Best Homestyle Food
Bard's Restaurant
  1902 N. Grant St., 501/666-9933
Cody's Cafe
  96 Industrial Dr., Jacksonville, 501/982-8386
Dixie Cafe
  1220 Rebsamen Park Rd., 501/663-9336
  10700 N. Rodney Parham Rd., 501/224-3728
  8523 Geyer Springs Rd., 501/568-6444
Lucky Seven Diner and Catering
  314 E. Sixth St., 501/375-2526
Your Mama's Good Food
  402 Louisiana St., 501/372-1811

Best Indian Food
Star of India Restaurant
  301 N. Shackleford Rd., 501/227-9900

Best Italian Food
Bruno's Little Italy
  315 N. Bowman Rd., Ste. 15, 501/224-4700
Cassinelli 1700 Swiss Italian
  1700 Main St., North Little Rock, 501/753-9399
Lascala Italian Restaurant
  2721 Kavanaugh Blvd., 501/663-1196
Villa Italian Restaurant
  201 S. Shackleford Rd., 501/219-2244

Best Japanese Food
Mount Fuji Japanese Restaurant
  10301 N. Rodney Parham Rd., 501/227-6498
Shogun Japanese Steakhouse
  2815 Cantrell Rd., 501/666-7070

Best Lunch
Doe's Eat Place
  1023 W. Markham St., 501/376-1195
The Vineyard in the Park
  Arkansas Art Center, Ninth St. at Commerce Ave.,
  501/372-4000

Best Mexican Food
Casa Manana Restaurant
  5820 Asher Ave., 501/565-7992

A

Juanita's Mexican Cafe and Bar
1300 Main St., 501/372-1228
Tia's Tex-Mex Grill
4305 Warden Rd., North Little Rock, 501/753-8675
225 N. Shackleford Rd., 501/224-9336

Best Pizza
Shotgun Dan's Pizza
10923 W. Markham St., 501/224-9519
U S Pizza Company
2814 Kavanaugh Blvd., 501/663-2198
9300 N. Rodney Parham Rd., 501/224-6300
U S Pizza Company
5524 Kavanaugh Blvd., 501/664-7071
3324 Pike Ave., North Little Rock, 501/758-5997
Vino's
923 W. Seventh St., 501/375-8466

Best Place to Take the Kids
Dixie Cafe
1220 Rebsamen Park Rd., 501/663-9336
10700 N. Rodney Parham Rd., 501/224-3728
8523 Geyer Springs Rd., 501/568-6444

Best Restaurant in Town
Alouette's French Company
11401 N. Rodney Parham Rd., 501/225-4152
Andre's in Hillcrest
605 Beechwood Ave., 501/666-9191
Brave New Restaurant
3701 Old Cantrell Rd., 501/663-2677
Cafe St. Moritz
225 E. Markham St., 501/372-0411
Lascala Italian Restaurant
2721 Kavanaugh Blvd., 501/663-1196
Spaule
5713 Kavanaugh Blvd., 501/664-3663

Best Romantic Dining
Alouette's French Company
11401 N. Rodney Parham Rd., 501/225-4152

Best Sandwiches
Grady's Pizza And Subs
6801 W. Twelfth St., 501/663-1918

Best Seafood
Atlantic Seafood Chowderhouse
11121 N. Rodney Parham Rd., 501/228-5622

Best Spanish Food
Tapas
10301 N. Rodney Parham Rd., 501/224-7707

Best Steaks
Faded Rose Restaurant
1615 Rebsamen Park Rd., 501/663-9734
400 N. Bowman Rd., Ste. 28, 501/224-3377

Best Sunday Brunch
Cafe Saint Moritz
225 E. Markham St., 501/372-0411

A

Best Tea Room
Victorian Garden
  4801C N. Hills Blvd., North Little Rock,
    501/758-4299

Best Thai Food
Siam Restaurant
  1415 W. Main St., Jacksonville, 501/982-3651

Best Vegetarian Food
Vegetable Garden
  3000 Kavanaugh Blvd., 501/663-8033

PINE BLUFF, AR

Best American Food
Arnold's Catfish Place
  2122 S. Blake St., 870/536-1834
Jones Cafe
  3910 Hwy. 65S, 870/534-6678

Best Barbecue/Ribs
Bar-B-Que Hut
  2203 W. 26th Ave., 870/536-3801

Best Bread
Sonny's
  128 S. Main St., 870/534-8887

Best Burgers
Sno-White Grill
  310 E. Fifth Ave., 870/534-9811

Best Casual Dining
Tommy's Restaurant
  812 S. Poplar St., 870/534-9622

Best Chinese Food
China Rose Restaurant
  4012 Old Warren Rd., 870/541-0311
East Winds Chinese Restaurant
  500 Fifth St., 870/535-0108

Best Desserts
Jones Cafe
  3910 Hwy. 65S, 870/534-6678
Lybrand's Bakery
  2900 S. Hazel St., 870/534-4607

Best Homestyle Food
Southern Cook's Kitchen
  3007 S. Olive St., 870/534-0625

Best Pizza
Big Banjo Pizza Parlor
  6000 Sheridan Rd., 870/247-3801

Best Sandwiches
Sonny's
  128 S. Main St., 870/534-8887

Best Steaks
Colonial Steak House
  111 W. Eighth Ave., 870/536-3488
Jones Cafe
  3910 Hwy. 65S, 870/534-6678

Tommy's Restaurant
812 S. Poplar St., 870/534-9622

ROGERS, AR

Best American Food
Cotton Patch Cafe
1949 W. Walnut St., 501/936-8088

Best Atmosphere
Crumpet Tea Room
107 W. Elm St., 501/636-7498

Best Bar
Cafe Santa Fe of Rogers
117 W. Walnut St., 501/636-4242

Best Barbecue/Ribs
Armadillo Grill
1100 48th Pl., Springdale, 501/756-0066
Bubba's Barbecue
60 Kings Hwy., Eureka Springs, 501/253-7706
Smokin' Joe's Ribhouse
803 W. Poplar St., 501/621-0021

Best Breakfast
Tiffany Grille
Holiday Inn, 1500 S. 48th St., Springdale,
501/751-8300

Best Casual Dining
Cotton Patch Cafe
1949 W. Walnut St., 501/936-8088

Best Chinese Food
Aloha Chinese Restaurant
208 S. Eighth St., 501/631-1781
China Town
1610 S.Eighth St., 501/636-2152
Far East Restaurant
812 N. Thompson St., Springdale, 501/756-2460

Best Continental Food
Blackboard Cafe
12 Cunningham Rd., Bella Vista, 501/855-0739
Plaza Restaurant
55 Main St., Eureka Springs, 501/253-8866

Best Delicatessen
Vicenza's
835 E. Henri de Tonti Blvd., Springdale,
501/361-9024

Best Desserts
Spring Street Grill and Catering
101 N. Spring St., Springdale, 501/751-0323

Best Diner
Wesner's Grill
117 W. Chestnut St., 501/636-9723

Best Family Restaurant
AQ Chicken House
Hwy. 71B, Springdale, 501/751-4633

A

Best Health-Conscious Menu
Aunt Clyde's Bakery
200 W. Poplar St., 501/621-8959

Best Homestyle Food
Monte Ne Chicken Restaurant
Hwy. 94E, 501/636-5511
Neal's Cafe
806 N. Thompson St., Springdale, 501/751-9996

Best Italian Food
Mary Maestri's
956 E. Henri de Tonti Blvd., Springdale,
501/361-2536
Vicenza's
835 E.Henri De Tonti Blvd., Springdale,
501/361-9024

Best Mexican Food
Cafe Santa Fe
179 N. Main St., Eureka Springs, 501/253-9617
Cafe Santa Fe of Rogers
117 W. Walnut St., 501/636-4242
Chimi's
2850 W.Walnut St., 501/636-2512

Best Pizza
Mazzio's Pizza
817 W. Walnut St., 501/636-0003

Best Place to Eat Alone
Hunan Chinese Restaurant
509 S. Eighth St., 501/621-5300

Best Place to Take the Kids
AQ Chicken House
Hwy. 71B, Springdale, 501/751-4633

Best Regional Food
Catfish John's
447 W. Hudson Rd., 501/631-6908

Best Romantic Dining
Fred's Hickory Inn
1502 N. Walton Blvd., Bentonville, 501/273-3303

Best Sandwiches
Fatiga's Sub Station
808 S. Mount Olive St., Siloam Springs,
501/524-6277

Best Seafood
Tale of the Trout
4611 W. New Hope Rd., 501/636-0508

Best Steaks
Butcher Block Steak House
4309 S. Thompson St., Springdale, 501/751-0006

Best Sunday Brunch
Tiffany Grill
Holiday Inn, 1500 S. 48th St., Springdale,
501/751-8300

Best Tea Room
Crumpet Tea Room
107 W. Elm St., 501/636-7498

A

Best Barbecue/Ribs
Old Post Bar-B-Que
   407 S. Arkansas Ave., 501/968-2421

Best Breakfast
Stoby's Depot and Dining Car
   405 W. Parkway, 501/968-3816

Best Burgers
Stoby's Depot and Dining Car
   405 W. Parkway, 501/968-3816

Best Chinese Food
New China
   2211 N. Arkansas Ave., 501/968-8881
Tran's Oriental Palace
   2621 W. Main St., 501/968-1933

Best Pizza
Cici's Pizza
   3063 E. Main St., Ste. C, 501/967-4432

Best Steaks
Brangus Feed Lot
   1509 E. Main St., 501/968-1999

Best Barbecue/Ribs
Slick Willie's
   1100 Ingram Blvd., 870/735-3656

Best Chinese Food
Dragon China
   500 W. Broadway St., 870/735-8888
Fu Gai
   526 E. Broadway St., 870/735-3133

Best Homestyle Food
Earl's Hot Biscuits
   2005 I-55, 870/735-5380
Granny's Front Porch
   109 S. Worthington Dr., 870/735-9468

Best Sandwiches
Munchy's
   108 E. Broadway St., 870/735-7358

Best Seafood
Kelly's Restaurant
   Hwy. 64W, Wynne, 870/238-2616

California

[See also: Garden Grove, Irvine, Long Beach, Los Angeles, Orange, and Santa Ana.]

Best Barbecue/Ribs
Chris and Pitt's of Anaheim
  601 N. Euclid St., 714/635-2601

Best Breakfast
Mimi's Cafe
  22651 Lake Forest Dr., Lake Forest, 714/457-9078
  1240 N. Euclid St., 714/535-1552
  17231 Seventeenth St., Tustin, 714/544-5522
  18342 Imperial Hwy., Yorba Linda, 714/996-3650
  18461 Brookhurst St., Fountain Valley,
    714/964-2533

Best Burgers
Angelo's Hamburger
  511 S. State College Blvd., 714/533-1401
Chris and Pitt's of Anaheim
  601 N. Euclid St., 714/635-2601

Best Chinese Food
Mandarin Pavillion
  1050 W. Valencia Dr., Fullerton, 714/870-7950

Best Continental Food
Mimi's Cafe
  22651 Lake Forest Dr., Lake Forest, 714/457-9078
  1240 N. Euclid St., 714/535-1552
  17231 Seventeenth St., Tustin, 714/544-5522
  18342 Imperial Hwy., Yorba Linda, 714/996-3650

C

18461 Brookhurst St., Fountain Valley,
714/964-2533

Best Dinner
Mimi's Cafe
22651 Lake Forest Dr., Lake Forest, 714/457-9078
1240 N. Euclid St., 714/535-1552
17231 Seventeenth St., Tustin, 714/544-5522
18342 Imperial Hwy., Yorba Linda, 714/996-3650
18461 Brookhurst St., Fountain Valley,
714/964-2533

Best Homestyle Food
Marie Callender's
5711 E. La Palma Ave., 714/779-0600
540 N. Euclid St., 714/774-1832

Best Ice Cream/Yogurt
Golden Spoon Frozen Yogurt
101 W. Imperial Hwy., Brea, 714/256-4727

Best Italian Food
Luigi's D'Italia
801 S. State College Blvd., 714/490-0990
1287 E. Lincoln Ave., 714/533-1300
Mama Cozza's
2170 W. Ball Rd., 714/635-0063

Best Japanese Food
Mikoshi Japanese Noodle House
955 E. Birch St. at F St., Brea, 714/255-9456

Best Mexican Food
El Torito Grill
2020 E. Ball Rd., 714/956-4880
555 Pointe Dr., Ste. 5, Brea, 714/990-2411
Fresca's Mexican Grill
22681 Lake Forest Dr., Lake Forest, 714/837-8397

Best Other Ethnic Food
Hatam Restaurant (Persian)
1112 N. Brookhurst St., 714/991-6262

Best Regional Food
Crocodile Cafe
975 E. Birch St., Brea, 714/529-2233

Best Southwestern Food
El Torito Grill
2020 E. Ball Rd., 714/956-4880
555 Pointe Dr., Ste. 5, Brea, 714/990-2411

Best Steaks
Stuart Anderson's Black Angus
2011 E. La Palma Ave., 714/776-5550

Best Wine Selection
Mr. Stox
1105 E. Katella Ave., 714/634-2994

ANTIOCH, CA

Best Mexican Food
La Plaza Mexican Restaurant
2370 Buchanan Rd., 925/754-6556

New Mecca
324 Railroad Ave., Pittsburg, 925/432-7433
Taqueria Salsa
3612 Delta Fair Blvd., 925/778-9281

Best Pizza
Skipolini's Pizza
901 Fitzuren Rd., 925/757-7770

Best Restaurant in Town
Humphrey's Restaurant
1 Marina Plaza, 925/778-5800

Best Seafood
Riverview Lodge
Foot of I St., 925/757-2272

Best Thai Food
Thai Derm Thai Cuisine
1884 A St., 925/757-8835

APPLE VALLEY, CA

Best Homestyle Food
Molly's
21851 U.S. Hwy. 18, 760/240-6130

Best Mexican Food
Las Brisas Restaurant
21919 U.S. Hwy. 18, 760/240-1051

Best Restaurant in Town
Jeff's Cafe
21660 Bear Valley Rd., 619/961-8687

Best Steaks
The Bum Steer
23323 U.S. Hwy. 18, 760/247-1336

APTOS, CA

Best Desserts
Kelly's French Pastry
7486 Soquel Dr., 408/662-2911

Best Fine Dining
Sanderling's Restaurant
Seascape Resort, 1 Seascape Resort Dr.,
408/662-7120

Best Pizza
Pizza Amore
783 Rio Del Mar Blvd., Ste. 45, 408/688-1477

Best Regional Food
Chez Renee
9051 Soquel Dr., 408/688-5566

Best Restaurant in Town
Pacific Rim Buffet
8035 Soquel Dr., 408/688-5208
Palapas Restaurant and Cantina
21 Seascape Village, 408/662-9000
Seacliff Inn
7500 Old Dominion Ct., 408/688-7300

C

Best Sandwiches
Erik's DeliCafe
  102 Rancho Del Mar, 408/688-5656

Best View While Dining
Cafe Rio
  131 Esplanade, 408/688-8917

ARCATA, CA

Best Burgers
Maggie's Burgers
  1884 Central Ave., McKinleyville, 707/839-2871

Best Coffee/Coffeehouse
Ramone's Bakery
  600 F St., 707/826-9000

Best Fine Dining
Folie Douce
  1551 G St., 707/822-1042

Best Health-Conscious Menu
Daybreak Cafe
  768 Eighteenth St., 707/826-7543
Wildberries Marketplace
  747 Thirteenth St., 707/822-0095
Wildflower Cafe and Bakery
  1604 G St., 707/822-0360

Best Italian Food
Abruzzi
  791 Eighth St., 707/826-2345
Tomaso's
  100 Erickson Ct., 707/822-6190

Best Lunch
Tomaso's
  100 Erickson Ct., 707/822-6190

Best Mexican Food
Luzmilla's Mexican Restaurant
  5000 Valley West Blvd., 707/822-5100

Best Pizza
Murphy's Take and Bake Pizza
  2015 Central Ave., McKinleyville, 707/839-8763
Round Table
  600 F St., 707/822-3761

Best Romantic Dining
Abruzzi
  791 Eighth St., 707/826-2345
Larrupin Cafe
  1658 Patricks Point Dr., Trinidad, 707/677-0230
Merryman's
  100 Moonstone Beach Rd., Trinidad, 707/677-3111

BAKERSFIELD, CA

Best Breakfast
24th Street Cafe
  1415 24th St., 805/323-8801

Best Burgers
Happy Jack's Hamburgers
  1800 Twentieth St., 805/323-1661

Best Casual Dining
Gatsby's
  1300 Coffee Rd., 805/588-3088

Best Chinese Food
Peking Palace
  5600 Auburn St., 805/872-9686

Best Fine Dining
City Lights by Patrick Beck
  1800 Chester Ave., 805/633-2283
J.C. Scott's
  4001 Auburn St., 805/872-3818
Mama Tosca's Ristorante
  6631 Ming Ave., 805/831-1242
Maxwell's
  5600 Auburn St., 805/872-5171
Tavern By the Green
  6218 Sundale Ave., 805/831-5225
The Bistro
  5105 California Ave., 805/323-3905

Best French Food
Wool Growers Restaurant
  620 E. Nineteenth St., 805/327-9584

Best German Food
Bit of Germany
  1901 Flower St., 805/325-8874

Best Greek/Mediterranean Food
Goose Loonie's Sports Bar
  1623 Nineteenth St., 805/631-1242

Best Ice Cream/Yogurt
Dewar's Candy Shop
  1120 Eye St., 805/322-0933
Rosemary's Family Creamery
  2733 F St., 805/395-0555
  6401 White Lane, 805/833-8166

Best Indian Food
Taj Mahal Cuisine of India
  5416 California Ave., 805/633-2222

Best Italian Food
Joseph's Italian Restaurant
  3013 F St., 805/322-7710
Luigi's
  725 E. Nineteenth St., 805/322-0929
Sorello Italian
  7800 McNair Ln., 805/396-8603

Best Japanese Food
Izumo Sushi
  4412 Ming Ave., 805/398-0608

Best Mexican Food
Cactus Valley Cafe
  9517 Rosedale Hwy., 805/588-8440

C

El Guanaco Restaurant
807 Baker St., 805/633-2892
El Pueblo
9705 Main St., Lamont, 805/845-4545
Garcia's Mexican Restaurant
6051 White Lane, 805/836-2747
Jake's Original Tex-Mex Cafe
1710 Oak St., 805/322-6380
La Costa Foods of Mexico
716 21st St., 805/322-2655
Taco Fresco
3701 California Ave., 805/328-0500
The Red Pepper Restaurant
2641 Oswell St., 805/871-5787

Best Other Ethnic Food
Noriega Hotel (Basque)
525 Sumner St., 805/322-8419
Pyrenees Cafe (Basque)
601 Sumner St., 805/323-0053

Best Pizza
Jerry's Pizza and Deli
1817 Chester Ave., 805/633-1000
Sbarro
2701 Ming Ave., 805/398-9842
3000 Mall View Rd., 805/871-9844

Best Salad/Salad Bar
The Garden Spot
3320 Truxtun Ave., 805/323-3236

Best Sunday Brunch
The California Grill
Doubletree Hotel Bakersfield,
3100 Camino Del Rio Court, 805/323-7111

Best Wine Selection
Frugatti's Restaurant
600 Coffee Rd., 805/836-2000

BANNING, CA

Best Burgers
Ramsey Burger
1901 W. Ramsey St., 909/849-1185

Best Chinese Food
Wing's Garden Cafe
116 W. Ramsey St., 909/849-2914

Best Family Restaurant
Billy T's Family Restaurant
3285 W. Ramsey St., 909/849-4115

Best Homestyle Food
Gramma's Country Kitchen
2579 W. Ramsey St., 909/849-8385
The Farmhouse
6261 W. Fifth St., 908/845-2027

Best Italian Food
Guy's Italian Restaurant
5970 W. Ramsey St., 909/845-9095

C

Best Pizza
Paradise Pizza
575 W. Ramsey St., 909/849-9131

Best Vietnamese Food
Daoreuang
1498 W. Ramsey St., 909/849-2587

BEAUMONT, CA

Best Restaurant in Town
Jimmy's Casa Figueroa
1310 E. Sixth St., 909/845-9047
The Rusty Lantern
1316 E. Sixth St., 909/845-9000

BARSTOW, CA

Best Barbecue/Ribs
Slash X Cafe
28040 Barstow Rd., 760/252-1197

Best Family Restaurant
Rosita's Restaurant
540 W. Main St., 760/256-1058

Best Homestyle Food
Coco's Restaurant
1311 E. Main St., 760/256-8992

Best Mexican Food
Plata's Mexican Food
36491 Irwin Rd., 760/256-5596
1521 W. Main St., 760/255-1750
25569 Main St., 760/253-2449
Rosita's Restaurant
540 W. Main St., 760/256-1058

Best Seafood
Idle Spurs Steak House
690 U.S. Hwy. 58, 760/256-8888

Best Steaks
Idle Spurs Steak House
690 U.S. Hwy. 58, 760/256-8888

BENICIA, CA

Best Atmosphere
Mabel's
2032 Columbus Pkwy., 707/746-7068

Best Breakfast
Washington House Deli Cafe
333A First St., 707/745-3364

Best Coffee/Coffeehouse
Benicia Cafe
714 First St., 707/745-8232

Best Greek/Mediterranean Food
Blandini's
907 First St., 707/747-5263

C

Best Mexican Food
Sandoval's
640 First St., 707/746-7830

Best Restaurant in Town
Mabel's
2032 Columbus Pkwy., 707/746-7068

Best Thai Food
Sala Thai Restaurant
807 First St., 707/745-4331

BERKELEY, CA

[See also: Oakland, Richmond, and San Francisco.]

Best Beer Selection
Jupiter
2181 Shattuck Ave., 510/843-8277

Best Breakfast
Bette's Ocean View Diner
1807A Fourth St., 510/644-3230
Cafe Fanny
1603 San Pablo Ave., 510/524-5451
Rick & Ann's
2922 Domingo Ave., 510/649-8538

Best Burgers
Barney's Gourmet Hamburger
1591 Solano Ave., 510/526-8185
Fatapple's Restaurant and Bakery
7525 Fairmount Ave., El Cerrito,
510/528-3433
1346 Martin Luther King Jr. Way,
510/526-2260

Best Chinese Food
King Yen Restaurant
2995 College Ave., 510/845-1286
Kirin Chinese Restaurant
1767 Solano Ave., 510/524-1677
Long Life Vegi House
2129 University Ave., 510/845-6072

Best Coffee/Coffeehouse
Caffe Strada
2300 College Ave., 510/843-5282
Peet's Coffee and Tea
2124 Vine St., 510/841-0564
1825 Solano Ave., 510/526-9607
2916 Domingo Ave., 510/843-1434
1776 Fourth St., 510/525-3207

Best Delicatessen
Saul's Restaurant and Delicatessen
1475 Shattuck Ave., 510/848-3354
Ultra Lucca Delicatessen
2905 College Ave., 510/849-2701

C

Best Desserts
Just Desserts
2925 College Ave., 510/841-1600
1823 Solano Ave., 510/527-7344

Best French Food
Chez Panisse
1517 Shattuck Ave., 510/548-5525

Best Greek/Mediterranean Food
Cafe Rouge
1782 Fourth St., 510/525-1440
Lalime's
1329 Gilman St., 510/527-9838

Best Health-Conscious Menu
O'Chame
1830 Fourth St., 510/841-8783
Rivoli Restaurant
1539 Solano Ave., 510/526-2542

Best Indian Food
New Delhi Junction
2556 Telegraph Ave., 510/486-0477
Pasand Madras Cuisine
2286 Shattuck Ave., 510/549-2559

Best Italian Food
Venezia Cafe
1799 University Ave., 510/849-4681

Best Japanese Food
Kirala Japanese Restaurant
2100 Ward St., 510/549-3486
O'Chame
1830 Fourth St., 510/841-8783
Sushi Sho
1645 Solano Ave., 510/525-4551

Best Lunch
Bette's-To-Go
1807A Fourth St., 510/548-9494
Chez Panisse
1517 Shattuck Ave., 510/548-5525

Best Mexican Food
Cactus Taqueria
1881 Solano Ave., 510/528-1881
Picante Cocina Mexicana
1328 Sixth St., 510/525-3121

Best Other Ethnic Food
Cafe de la Paz (Latin-American)
1600C Shattuck Ave., 510/843-0662
Cambodiana's (Cambodian)
2156 University Ave., 510/843-4630
The Blue Nile (Ethiopian)
2525 Telegraph Ave., 510/540-6777

Best Outdoor Dining
Chester's Cafe
1508B Walnut St., 510/849-9995

C

Best Pizza
Zachary's Chicago Pizza
  1835 Solano Ave., 510/525-5950

Best Place to Take the Kids
Fatapple's Restaurant and Bakery
  1346 Martin Luther King Jr. Way,
    510/526-2260
  7525 Fairmount Ave., El Cerrito,
    510/528-3433
Walker's Pie Shop
  1491 Solano Ave., Albany, 510/525-4647

Best Restaurant in Town
Chez Panisse
  1517 Shattuck Ave., 510/548-5525

Best Romantic Dining
Skates on the Bay
  100 Seawall Dr., 510/549-1900

Best Sunday Brunch
Chester's Cafe
  1508B Walnut St., 510/849-9995

Best Sushi
Kirala Japanese Restaurant
  2100 Ward St., 510/549-3486
Sushi Ko
  64 Shattuck Sq., 510/845-6601

Best Thai Food
Cha Am
  1543 Shattuck Ave., 510/848-9664
Plearn Thai Cuisine No. 2
  2050 University Ave., 510/841-2148

Best Vegetarian Food
Long Life Vegi House
  2129 University Ave., 510/845-6072

BEVERLY HILLS, CA

[See also: Burbank, Glendale, Los Angeles, Pasadena, and Santa Monica.]

Best Continental Food
The Dining Room
  Regent Beverly Wilshire Hotel,
    9500 Wilshire Blvd., 310/274-8179

Best Fine Dining
The Dining Room
  Regent Beverly Wilshire Hotel,
    9500 Wilshire Blvd., 310/274-8179

Best Health-Conscious Menu
Whole Foods Market and Cafe
  239 N. Crescent Dr., 310/274-3360

Best Italian Food
Il Pastilo
  400 N. Canon Dr., 310/205-5444

C

Best Japanese Food
Benihana of Tokyo
  38 N. La Cienega Blvd., 310/659-1511
Matsuhisa
  129 N. La Cienega Blvd., 310/659-9639

Best Salad/Salad Bar
R.J.'s Restaurant
  252 N. Beverly Dr., 310/274-3474

Best Seafood
McCormick and Schmick's, The Fish House
  206 N. Rodeo Dr., 310/859-0434

Best Steaks
The Prime Rib
  100 N. La Cienega Blvd., 310/652-2827

Best Sushi
Crazy Fish
  9105 W. Olympic Blvd., 310/550-8547

BLYTHE, CA

Best Breakfast
Steaks and Cakes
  9026 E. Hobson Way, 760/922-4241

Best Burgers
Jerry's Restaurant
  320 S. Lovekin Blvd., 760/922-9521

Best Coffee/Coffeehouse
Judy's Restaurant
  9266 E. Hobson Way, 760/922-6015

Best Ice Cream/Yogurt
Fosters Old Fashioned Freeze
  540 E. Hobson Way, 760/922-3912

Best Steaks
Steaks and Cakes
  9026 E. Hobson Way, 760/922-4241

BUELLTON, CA

Best Seafood
A.J. Spurs Restaurant and Saloon
  350 E. Hwy. 246, 805/686-1655
Buellton Hitching Post
  406 E. Hwy. 246, 805/688-0676
Zaca Creek Restaurant and Saloon
  1297 U.S. Hwy. 101, 805/688-2412

Best Steaks
A.J. Spurs Restaurant and Saloon
  350 E. Hwy. 246, 805/686-1655
Buellton Hitching Post
  406 E. Hwy. 246, 805/688-0676
Zaca Creek Restaurant and Saloon
  1297 U.S. Hwy. 101, 805/688-2412

BURBANK, CA

[See also: Beverly Hills, Glendale, Los Angeles, Pasadena, and Santa Monica.]

Best Burgers
Great Grill
1909 W. Burbank Blvd., 818/842-9226
126 N. San Fernando Blvd., 818/567-0060
916 W. Magnolia Blvd., 818/841-0066

Best Coffee/Coffeehouse
Starbucks Coffee
4702 W. Riverside Dr., 818/563-9830
300 N. San Fernando Blvd., 818/567-0630

Best Desserts
Crocodile Cafe
201 N. San Fernando Blvd., 818/843-7999

Best Homestyle Food
Don's Restaurant and Coffee Shop
509 S. Glenoaks Blvd., 818/846-9521

Best Mexican Food
Bahia Caporales Restaurant
3821 W. Magnolia Blvd., 818/842-7845

Best Pizza
Pizza Pie
1700 W. Magnolia Blvd., 818/846-5141

Best Seafood
Bahia Caporales Restaurant
3821 W. Magnolia Blvd., 818/842-7845

Best Steaks
Stewart Anderson's Black Angus
235 S. First St., 818/848-8880
Smokehouse
4420 W. Lakeside Dr., 818/845-3731

BURLINGAME, CA

Best Coffee/Coffeehouse
Pete's
1309 Burlingame Ave., 650/548-0494
Starbucks Coffee
1160 Burlingame Ave., 650/348-5138

Best Delicatessen
Brother's Deli Restsaurant
1351 Howard Ave., 650/343-2311

Best Desserts
Max's Opera Cafe
1250 Bayshore Hwy., 650/342-6297

CAMARILLO, CA

Best Breakfast
Eggs and Things
1101 E. Daily Dr., 805/527-0055

C

Best Coffee/Coffeehouse
Low Key Bagels
  4972 Verdugo Way, 805/383-0772
Starbucks Coffee
  540 Las Posas Rd., 805/383-7130

Best Italian Food
Presto Pasta
  1701 Daily Dr., 805/383-1583

Best Regional Food
California Grill
  67 E. Daily Dr., 805/987-1922

CAMPBELL, CA

Best Bar
The Black Watch
  141 1/2 N. Santa Cruz Ave., Los Gatos,
    408/354-2200

Best Barbecue/Ribs
Andy's Oakwood Bar-B-Que
  700 E. Campbell Ave., 408/378-2838
The Original Hick'ry Pit
  980 E. Campbell Ave., 408/371-2400

Best Burgers
Kirk's Steakburgers
  2388 S. Bascom Ave., 408/371-3565

Best Chinese Food
Blue Sky Chinese Restaurant
  2028 Winchester Blvd., 408/378-0424
Fung Lum Restaurant
  1815 S. Bascom Ave., 408/377-6955

Best Coffee/Coffeehouse
Barado's Coffee Company
  266 E. Campbell Ave., 408/364-2157
Starbucks Coffee
  1696 S. Bascom Ave., 408/371-6703

Best Delicatessen
Erik's Deli Cafe
  1777 S. Bascom Ave., 408/371-8282
Togo's Eatery
  866 E. Campbell Ave., 408/371-3696
  900 E. Campbell Ave., Ste. 1, 408/377-1754

Best French Food
Le Mouton Noir
  14560 Big Basin Way, Saratoga, 408/867-7017

Best Indian Food
Royal Taj
  1350 Camden Ave., 408/559-6801

Best Japanese Food
Komatsu Japanese Cuisine
  300 Orchard City Dr., 408/379-3000

Best Other Ethnic Food
Shebele Ethiopian Restaurant (Ethiopian)
  422 E. Campbell Ave., 408/378-3131

C

Best Romantic Dining
La Fondue
14510 Big Basin Way, Saratoga, 408/867-3332

Best Vegetarian Food
Good Earth Restaurant and Bakery
206 N. Santa Cruz Ave., Los Gatos, 408/395-6868

Best Vietnamese Food
Golden Chopsticks
1765 Winchester Blvd., 408/370-6610

Best Wine Selection
Plumed Horse
14555 Big Basin Way, Saratoga, 408/867-4711

CANYON COUNTRY, CA

Best Bar
Santa Clarita Brewing Company
20655 Soledad Canyon Rd., 805/298-5676

Best Breakfast
Coco's Restaurant
16526 Soledad Canyon Rd., 805/251-7725

Best Brewpub
Santa Clarita Brewing Company
20655 Soledad Canyon Rd., 805/298-5676

Best Burgers
Cuzzin's Burgers
19318 Soledad Canyon Rd., 805/298-4200

Best Casual Dining
Caruso's II
18340 Sierra Hwy., 805/251-8450

Best Fine Dining
Backwoods Inn
17846 Sierra Hwy., 805/252-5522

Best Sunday Brunch
El Chaparral Mexican Restaurant
19132 Soledad Canyon Rd., 805/252-5599

CAPITOLA, CA

Best Desserts
Gayle's Bakery and Rosticceria
504 Bay Ave., 408/462-1200

Best Fine Dining
Shadowbrook Restaurant
1750 Wharf Rd., 408/475-1222

Best Health-Conscious Menu
Dharma's Restaurant
4250 Capitola Rd., 408/462-1717
Fresh Choice Restaurant
3555 Clares St., 408/479-9873

Best Ice Cream/Yogurt
Yogurt Delite
1420 41st Ave., 408/462-9393

C

Best Pizza
Pizza My Heart
  209 Esplanade, 408/475-5714
Pleasure Pizza
  4000 Portola Ave., 408/475-4999
Tony and Alba's Pizza
  1501 41st Ave., 408/475-4450

Best Sandwiches
Erik's DeliCafe
  1601 41st Ave., 408/475-4646
Togo's Eatery
  1550 41st Ave., 408/476-7330

Best Seafood
Shadowbrook Restaurant
  1750 Wharf Rd., 408/475-1222

Best Vegetarian Food
Dharma's Restaurant
  4250 Capitola Rd., 408/462-1717

Best Wine Selection
Balzac Bistro
  112 Capitola Ave., 408/476-5035

CARLSBAD, CA

Best Breakfast
Kahala Cafe
  795 Carlsbad Village Dr., 760/729-5448

Best Chinese Food
Golden Garden
  2216 S. El Camino Real, Ste. 107, 760/722-8210

Best Coffee/Coffeehouse
Kafana
  3076 Carlsbad Blvd., 760/720-0074

Best Desserts
The Claim Jumper
  5958 Avenida Encinas, 760/431-0889

Best Italian Food
Amedeo's Italian Cafe
  2780 State St., 760/729-8799
Tuscany Ristorante-Bar-Cafe
  6981 El Camino Real, 760/929-8111

Best Mexican Food
Fidel's Norte, Inc.
  3003 Carlsbad Blvd., 760/729-0903

Best Other Ethnic Food
Armenian Cafe (Armenian)
  3126 Carlsbad Blvd., 760/720-2233

Best Restaurant in Town
Neiman's Seagrill American Bar
  2978 Carlsbad Blvd., 760/729-4131
The Claim Jumper
  5958 Avenida Encinas, 760/431-0889

C

Best Sandwiches
Grand Deli
595 Grand Ave., 760/729-4015

Best Seafood
Fish House Veracruz
417 Carlsbad Village Dr., 760/434-6777

Best Southwestern Food
Coyote Bar and Grill
300 Carlsbad Village Dr., 760/729-4695

Best Sports Bar
Hennessey's Tavern
2777 Roosevelt St., 760/729-6951

CARMEL, CA

Best Old Favorite Restaurant
Golden Buddha
3678 The Barnyard, 408/625-1668

Best Outdoor Dining
The General Store
Fifth at Junipero, 408/624-2233

Best Pizza
Allegro Gourmet Pizzeria
3770 The Barnyard, 408/648-4363

Best Regional Food
Pacific's Edge
Hwy. 1, 408/622-5445

Best Restaurant in Town
Rio Grill
159 The Crossroad, 408/625-5436

Best Salad/Salad Bar
Allegro Gourmet Pizzeria
3770 The Barnyard, 408/648-4363

Best Sushi
Robata Grill
3658 The Barnyard, 408/624-2643

Best Thai Food
Thai Bistro
55 W. Carmel Valley Rd., Carmel Valley,
408/659-5900

Best View While Dining
The Pacific Edge
Highlands Inn, Hwy. 1, 408/624-3801

CHICO, CA

Best Desserts
Cory's Sweet Treats and Gallery
230 W. Third St., 530/345-2955

Best Italian Food
Dancing Noodles Cafe
131 Broadway St., 530/891-1383
Gina Marie's
305 Main St., 530/342-2420

C

Best Mexican Food
La Fonda
   243 W. Second St., Ste. 4, 530/345-5289
La Hacienda Mexican Restaurant
   2635 Esplanade, 530/893-8270
Ricardo's Mexican Food
   2365 Esplanade, 530/895-9607

Best Restaurant In Town
Italian Cottage Restaurant
   2525 Dominic Dr., 530/342-7771
   2234 Esplanade, 530/343-7000

Best Salad/Salad Bar
Redwood Forest
   121 W. Third St., 530/343-4315

CHINO, CA

Best Barbecue/Ribs
Joey's Bar-B-Q
   3689 Riverside Dr., 909/628-1231

Best Business Lunch
Cask and Cleaver
   12206 Central Ave., 909/627-6011

Best Cajun/Creole Food
Cafe Orleans
   5460 Philadelphia St., 909/591-4537

Best Ice Cream/Yogurt
Penguins Place Frozen Yogurt
   5525 Philadelphia St., 909/591-2844

Best Inexpensive Meal
Carrows Family Restaurant
   12325 Mountain Ave., 909/627-0271

Best Other Ethnic Food
Centro Basquo (Basque)
   13432 Central Ave., 909/628-9014

Best Pizza
Papa Paul's
   12345 Mountain Ave., 909/590-0063

Best Salad/Salad Bar
Cask and Cleaver
   12206 Central Ave., 909/627-6011

Best Seafood
Cafe Orleans
   5460 Philadelphia St., 909/591-4537

CITRUS HEIGHTS, CA

Best Homestyle Food
Sam's Kosher-Style Restaurant and Deli
   8121 Greenback Ln., Fair Oaks, 916/726-7267

Best Japanese Food
Mikuni Japanese Restaurant
   4323 Hazel Ave., Fair Oaks, 916/961-2112

C

Best Mexican Food
Carmelita's Mexican Restaurant
  4071 Howard St., Fair Oaks, 916/961-3327

Best Outdoor Dining
Bernice's Cookery
  5132 Arden Way, Carmichael, 916/484-6632

Best Romantic Dining
Cliff House of Folsom
  9900 Greenback Ln., Folsom, 916/989-9243
Slocum House
  7992 California Ave., Fair Oaks, 916/961-7211

Best Steaks
Cattlemen's Restaurant
  2000 Taylor Rd., Roseville, 916/782-5587
  12409 Folsom Blvd., Rancho Cordova,
    916/985-3030

CLAREMONT, CA

Best Business Lunch
BC Cafe
  701 S. Indian Hill Blvd., 909/482-1414

Best Delicatessen
Greene's Delicatessen and Restaurant
  1025 W. Foothill Blvd., 909/626-8802

Best Desserts
Some Crust Bakery
  119 Yale Ave., 909/621-9772

Best Ice Cream/Yogurt
21 Choices
  328 S. Indian Hill Blvd., 909/621-7175

Best Italian Food
Aruffo's Italian Cuisine
  126 Yale Ave., 909/949-8426

Best Other Ethnic Food
Walter's Restaurant (Afghan)
  308 Yale Ave., 909/624-2779

Best Seafood
Shrimp House
  962 W. Foothill Blvd., 909/621-6805

CLOVIS, CA

Best Burgers
Fat Jack's
  625 W. Shaw Ave., 209/299-1104
Red Robin
  950 Shaw Ave., 209/299-4500

Best Chinese Food
China Buffet
  140 W. Shaw Ave., 209/297-9255

Best Family Restaurant
Lyon's
  1125 Shaw Ave., 209/297-1212

C

Best Italian Food
Luna Pizzeria
349 Pollasky Ave., 209/299-4141

Best Japanese Food
Daruma Tei
300 W. Shaw Ave., 209/298-1011
Japanese Kitchen
711 W. Shaw Ave., Ste. 107, 209/297-1100

Best Mexican Food
Bobby Salazar's Mexican Restaurant and Cantina
434 Clovis Ave., 209/298-7898
El Quetzal
180 Shaw Ave., 209/298-6271
La Posada
311 Pollasky Ave., 209/298-2211

Best Other Ethnic Food
Mediterranean Corner (Armenian)
135 Shaw Ave., 209/297-7801

Best Pizza
Aldo's Pizza
1414 Clovis Ave., 209/298-0801

Best Salad/Salad Bar
Fresh Choice
10 Shaw Ave., 209/297-4272
Grandy's
80 W. Shaw Ave., 209/299-1083

Best Sandwiches
Full O' Bull
632 Fifth St., 209/299-3076

Best Thai Food
Thai Garden
135 W. Shaw Ave., 209/299-0183
Thai House
3185 Willow Ave., 209/292-5774

CORONA, CA

*[See also: Ontario, Orange, Pomona, Rancho
Cucamonga, San Bernadino, and Upland.]*

Best Breakfast
Mimi's Cafe
2230 Griffin Way, 909/734-2073

Best Burgers
Red Robin
419 N. McKinley St., 909/737-1130

Best Coffee/Coffeehouse
Jitters Coffee
304 N. Main St., 909/737-3787

Best Fine Dining
Villa Amalfi Ristorante
1237 W. Sixth St., 909/278-3393

C

Best Homestyle Food
Mimi's Cafe
  2230 Griffin Way, 909/734-2073

Best Italian Food
Pasta Pasta
  1296 Border Ave., 909/371-7874
Petrelli's Restaurant
  113 E. Sixth St., 909/734-3003
Villa Amalfi Ristorante
  1237 W. Sixth St., 909/278-3393

Best Japanese Food
Misato Restaurant
  261 S. Lincoln Ave., 909/272-2900

Best Mexican Food
Hacienda Del Rey
  1353 W. Sixth St., 909/737-9440
Live Oak Inn
  21700 Temescal Canyon Rd., 909/277-0605
Miguel Sonora Style Mexican
  1703 W. Sixth St., 909/371-9299
Puerto Vallarte Mexican Restaurant
  511 N. Main St., 909/270-0152

Best Place to Take the Kids
Chuck E. Cheese Pizza
  191 N. McKinley St., 909/279-9903

Best Salad/Salad Bar
Mimi's Cafe
  2230 Griffin Way, 909/734-2073

Best Seafood
Claim Jumper Restaurant
  380 N. McKinley St., 909/735-6567
TB Scott's
  103 N. Lincoln Ave., 909/340-3474

Best Steaks
TB Scott's
  103 N. Lincoln Ave., 909/340-3474

CORTE MADERA, CA

[See also: Larkspur, Mill Valley, San Anselmo, San Francisco, and San Rafael.]

Best Delicatessen
Ultra Lucca Delicatessen
  107 Corte Madera Town Ctr., 415/927-4347

Best Health-Conscious Menu
Fresh Choice
  131 Corte Madera Town Ctr., 415/924-0540

Best Italian Food
Il Fornaio
  223 Corte Madera Town Ctr., 415/927-4400

C

Best Late-Night Food
Marin Joe's
  1585 Casa Buena Dr., 415/924-2081

Best Seafood
Baby Sal's Seafood Grill
  60 Corte Madera Ave., 415/927-0149

COSTA MESA, CA

*[See also: Anaheim, Garden Grove, Irvine, Long
Beach, Los Angeles, Orange, Santa Ana, and
San Rafael.]*

Best Barbecue/Ribs
Zubie's
  1712 Placentia Ave., 714/645-8091

Best Breakfast
Mimi's Cafe
  1835 Newport Blvd., 714/722-6722

Best Burgers
Ruby's Diner
  3333 Bear St., 714/662-7829

Best Health-Conscious Menu
Mother's Market and Kitchen
  225 E. Seventeenth St., 714/631-4741

Best Homestyle Food
Marie Callender's
  353 E. Seventeenth St., 714/642-0822

Best Ice Cream/Yogurt
Golden Spoon Frozen Yogurt
  488 E. Seventeenth St., 714/548-9147
  2801 Harbor Blvd., 714/641-7495

Best Mexican Food
Avila's El Ranchito
  2101 Placentia Ave., 714/645-0209
El Torito Grill
  633 Anton Blvd., 714/662-0798

Best Pizza
Me and Ed's Pizza Parlor
  410 E. Seventeenth St., 714/646-7136

Best Place to Take the Kids
Zubie's
  1712 Placentia Ave., 714/645-8091

Best Steaks
Barn Steak House
  2300 Harbor Blvd., Ste. 31, 714/641-9777

Best Thai Food
Bangkok Four Restaurant
  3333 Bear St., Ste. 320, 714/540-7661

Best Vegetarian Food
Mother's Market and Kitchen
  225 E. Seventeenth St., 714/631-4741

C

COVINA, CA

[See also: Los Angeles, Pasadena, Pomona, and Whittier.]

Best Chinese Food
Shanghai Chinese Restaurant
316 N. Azusa Ave., 626/966-1890

Best Delicatessen
Danny's Kosher Pickle Restaurant
402 N. Azusa Ave., 626/339-1373

Best Italian Food
Giovanni's Ristorante
143 N. Citrus Ave., 626/332-9539

Best Japanese Food
Restaurant Hayakawa
750 Terrado Plz., 626/332-8288
Sakura of Tokyo
533 S. Glendora Ave., West Covina, 626/960-7155

Best Restaurant in Town
Northwood's Inn of Covina
540 N. Azusa Ave., 626/331-7444

DANA POINT, CA

Best Mexican Food
Olamendi's Mexican Cuisine
34660 Pacific Coast Hwy., Capistrano Beach,
714/661-1005

Best Wine Selection
The Dining Room
Ritz-Carlton, 1 Ritz Carlton Dr., 714/240-2000

DANVILLE, CA

Best Breakfast
Country Waffles
130 Hartz Ave., 925/838-0651

Best Fine Dining
Bridges
44 Church St., 925/820-7200

Best Ice Cream/Yogurt
Yogurt Park
684 Hartz Ave., 925/838-2243

Best Inexpensive Meal
Economy Restaurant
202 Sycamore Valley Rd. W., 925/838-2333

Best Italian Food
Father Nature's Shed
172 E. Prospect Ave., 925/820-3160

DAVIS, CA

Best Breakfast
Baker's Square Restaurant
255 Second St., 530/756-4190

Best Burgers
Murder Burger
  978 Olive Dr., 530/756-2142

Best Chinese Food
Hing's Restaurant
  707 Second St., 530/756-0666

Best Coffee/Coffeehouse
Caffino Inc.
  980 Olive Dr., 530/758-0972
Delta of Venus
  122 B St., 530/753-8639

Best Desserts
Farmer's Wife
  330 G St., 530/756-1107

Best French Food
La Brioche Restaurant
  129 E St., 530/756-8676

Best German Food
Sudwerk
  2001 Second St., 530/758-8700

Best Italian Food
Caffe Italia
  1121 Richards Blvd., 530/758-7200

Best Mexican Food
La Esperanza
  200 G St., 530/753-4449
  825 Russell Blvd., 530/757-7579

Best Pizza
Graduate Restaurant
  805A Russell Blvd., 530/758-4723
Woodstock's Pizza
  219 G St., 530/757-2525

Best Sandwiches
Caffe Italia
  1121 Richards Blvd., 530/758-7200
Mustard Seed
  231 G St., 530/758-5750
Togo's Eatery
  715 Second St., 530/753-5330

Best Southwestern Food
Dos Coyotes Border Cafe
  1411 W. Covell Blvd., 530/753-0922

DIXON, CA

Best Mexican Food
Cueva's Restaurant
  143 N. First St., 707/678-9685

Best Steaks
Cattlemen's Restaurant
  I-80 at Curry Rd., 916/678-5518

C

EL CAJON, CA

Best Burgers
Boll Weevil
  335 N. Second St., 619/444-4438
Rally's Hamburgers
  1261 E. Main St., 619/444-3496

Best Business Lunch
Black Angus Restaurant
  1000 Graves Ave., 619/440-5055

Best Chinese Food
Lucky Chinese Fast Food
  201 N. Magnolia Ave., 619/448-3101

Best Mexican Food
Antonio's Hacienda
  700 N. Johnson, 619/442-9827
Marieta's Restaurant
  1746 E. Main St., 619/442-6671

Best Restaurant Meal Value
Lucky Chinese Fast Food
  201 N. Magnolia Ave., 619/448-3101

Best Sandwiches
Patty's Subs
  164 E. Main St., 619/588-0878

EL CENTRO, CA

Best Chinese Food
Airport
  1093 Airport Rd., Imperial, 760/355-2838
China Palace Restaurant
  1075 Adams Ave., 760/353-2798
Lucky Chinese Restaurant
  500 S. Fourth St., 760/352-7680
Ma's Kitchen
  290 N. Imperial Ave., 760/352-8713

Best Mexican Food
Adobe Hacienda
  538 E St., Brawley, 760/344-9750
Celia's Restaurant
  1530 Adams St., 760/352-4570
El Sombrero Cafe
  841 W. Main St., 760/353-8118
Mi Casita Restaurant
  729 W. Main St., 760/353-8690

Best Restaurant in Town
Barbara Worth Golf Resort and Convention Center
  2050 Country Club Dr., Holtville, 760/356-2806

ENCINITAS, CA

Best American Food
Red Robin
  294 N. El Camino Real, 760/436-4488

Best Cajun/Creole Food
Paradise Grill
  1476 Encinitas Blvd., 760/943-9997

C

Shrimply Delicious
559 First St., 760/944-9172

Best Chinese Food
Golden Bowl Restaurant
1337 Encinitas Blvd., 760/436-8669

Best Coffee/Coffeehouse
Pannikin Coffee and Tea
510 N. Hwy. 101, 760/436-0033

Best Family Restaurant
Oscar's
1505 Encinitas Blvd., 760/632-0222
Red Robin
294 N. El Camino Real, 760/436-4488

Best French Food
Chez Henri
1555 Camino Del Mar, Del Mar, 619/793-0067
La Bonne Bouffe
471 Encinitas Blvd., 760/436-3081
Mille Fleurs
6009 Paseo Delicias, Rancho Santa Fe,
619/756-3085

Best Health-Conscious Menu
Ki's Juice Bar
206 Birmingham Dr., Cardiff By The Sea,
760/436-5236

Best Japanese Food
Mr. Sushi
Ralph's Shopping Center, 111 N. El Camino Real,
760/944-2800
Nobu
315 S. Hwy. 101, Solana Beach, 619/755-7787
Sakura Bana Sushi Bar
1031 South Coast Hwy. 101, Ste. 101, 760/942-6414
Samurai
979 Lomas Santa Fe Dr., Solana Beach,
619/481-0032

Best Mexican Food
Tony's Jacal
621 Valley Ave., Solana Beach, 619/755-2274

Best Other Ethnic Food
Khayyam Cuisine (Jordanian/Lebanese)
437 S. Hwy. 101, Solana Beach, 619/755-6343

Best Outdoor Dining
Jake's Del Mar
1660 Coast Blvd., Del Mar, 619/755-2002

Best Pizza
Borrelli's Pizza
285 El Camino Real N., 760/436-1501

Best Romantic Dining
Jake's Del Mar
1660 Coast Blvd., Del Mar, 619/755-2002

C

Best Sandwiches
Giovanni's Sandwich Shop
  764 First St., 760/943-8620

Best Seafood
Pacifica del Mar
  1555 Camino del Mar, Del Mar, 619/792-0476

Best Southwestern Food
Cilantro's
  3702 Via De La Valle, Del Mar, 619/259-8777

Best Sports Bar
Yogi's
  2005 San Elijo Ave., Cardiff By The Sea, 760/943-
9644

Best Sunday Brunch
Marie Callender's Restaurant
  162 S. Rancho Santa Fe Rd., 760/632-0204
Rancho Valencia Dining Room
  Rancho Valencia Resort, 5921 Valencia Circle,
    Rancho Santa Fe, 619/756-1123

ESCONDIDO, CA

Best American Food
150 Grand Cafe
  150 W. Grand Ave., 760/738-6868

Best Atmosphere
Castle Creek Country Club
  8797 Circle R Dr., 760/749-2877

Best Breakfast
Champion's Family Restaurant
  117 W. Grand Ave., 760/747-0288

Best Chinese Food
China Panda
  330 W. Felicita Ave., 760/741-3982

Best Coffee/Coffeehouse
Metaphor Cafe
  258 E. Second Ave., 760/489-8890

Best Continental Food
Sirino's Restaurant
  113 W. Grand Ave., 760/745-3835

Best Diner
Chicken Pie Diner
  14727 Pomerado Rd., Poway, 619/748-2445

Best Dinner
Castle Creek Country Club
  8797 Circle R Dr., 760/749-2877

Best French Food
Sirino's Restaurant
  113 W. Grand Ave., 760/745-3835

Best Health-Conscious Menu
Metaphor Cafe
  258 E. Second Ave., 760/489-8890

C

Best Homestyle Food
Champion's Family Restaurant
117 W. Grand Ave., 760/747-0288

Best Italian Food
Joe's Italian Dinners
403 W. Grand Ave., 760/489-6835

Best Mexican Food
Cocina Del Charro
525 N. Quince St., 760/745-1382
La Tapatia Restaurant
340 W. Grand Ave., 760/747-8282

Best Pizza
Filippi's Pizza Grotto
114 W. Grand Ave., 760/747-2650

Best Regional Food
150 Grand Cafe
150 W. Grand Ave., 760/738-6868

Best Seafood
Sandcrab Cafe
2229 Micro Pl., 760/480-2722

Best Steaks
Brigantine Restaurant
421 W. Felicita Ave., 760/743-4718

EUREKA, CA

Best Breakfast
Chalet House of Omelettes
1935 Fifth St., 707/442-0333
Gill's by the Bay
77 Halibut Ave., 707/442-2554
Loring's Simply the Best
332 Harris St., 707/441-8555
The Cutten Inn Restaurant
3980 Walnut Dr., 707/445-9217

Best Burgers
Fresh Freeze
3023 F St., 707/442-6967
Mike's Drive-Up
637 Broadway St., 707/442-4755
No Brand Burger Stand
989 Milton Ave., Ferndale, 707/786-9474
Stars
2009 Harrison Ave., 707/445-2061

Best Chinese Food
Gonsea
2335 Fourth St., 707/444-8899
Hunan Restaurant
2912 E St., 707/444-9241

Best Coffee/Coffeehouse
Gold Rush Express
Bayshore Mall, 3300 Broadway St., 707/445-4617
Stanton's Coffee Shop
1111 Fifth St., 707/442-8141

C

Udder Place
  2228 Fourth St., 707/442-6487

Best Delicatessen
Deo's Sandwich Shop
  428 Grotto St., 707/445-1111
Enrico's
  1595 Myrtle Ave., 707/442-1771
Hole in the Wall
  1331 Broadway St., 707/443-5362

Best Family Restaurant
Adel's Restaurant
  1724 Broadway, 707/445-9777
Sweetriver Saloon
  3300 Broadway St., 707/444-9704

Best Fine Dining
Restaurant 301
  Hotel Carter, 301 L St., 707/444-8062

Best Health-Conscious Menu
Eureka Natural Foods Deli
  1626 Broadway, 707/442-6325
The Flour Garden
  712 Fifth St., 707/443-1890

Best Italian Food
Mazzotti's Italian Food
  305 F St., 707/445-1912
Parlato's
  320 Main St., Fortuna, 707/725-9961
Roy's
  218 D St., 707/442-4574

Best Japanese Food
Samurai
  621 Fifth St., 707/442-6802
Tomo Japanese Restaurant
  2120 Fourth St., 707/444-3318

Best Lunch
Adel's Restaurant
  1724 Broadway, 707/445-9777
Bay City Grill
  508 Henderson St., 707/444-9069
Cafe Marina
  601 Startare Dr., 707/443-2233
Ron's American Bistro
  521 Fourth St., 707/444-8018

Best Mexican Food
Cosina Michoacana
  427 V St., 707/443-7840
Jalisco Cafe'
  1718 Fourth St., 707/445-9324
Luna's Mexican Restaurant
  1134 Fifth St., 707/445-9162
Reyes Y Casas Viejas
  1436 Second St., 707/445-4960

C

Best Pizza
Celestino's Live from New York
  421 Third St., 707/444-8995
Murphy's Take and Bake Pizza
  906 West Ave., 707/442-1499
Pizzeria Pizza
  1604 Fourth St., 707/444-9681
  519 Everdint St., 707/444-0990
Round Table
  2810 E St., 707/445-3227
  1735 Fourth St., 707/443-3187
Tom's Sourdough Pizza Villa
  1611 Myrtle Ave., 707/443-2728

Best Romantic Dining
Restaurant 301
  Hotel Carter, 301 L St., 707/444-8062
The Rib Room
  Eureka Inn, 518 Seventh St., 707/442-6441

Best Seafood
Cafe Marina
  601 Startare Dr., 707/443-2233
Ernie's Briefing Room
  608 A St., 707/442-7146
Lazio's
  327 Second St., 707/443-9717
Seafood Grotto
  605 Broadway St., 707/443-2075
The Sea Grill
  316 E St., 707/443-7187

Best Steaks
Geri's Myrtletowne House
  1672 Myrtle Ave., 707/443-8209
O-H's Town House
  206 W. Sixth St., 707/443-4652
Parlato's
  320 Main St., Fortuna, 707/725-9961
The Embers
  4485 Broadway St., 707/443-1807
Whaler's Inn
  6690 Fields Landing Dr., Fields Landing, 707/443-6026

Best Thai Food
Smile of Siam
  210 Fourth St., 707/442-6999

FAIRFIELD, CA

Best All-You-Can-Eat Buffet
J.J. North
  1315 Gateway Blvd., 707/428-6000

Best Bar
Suite 21
  1721 N. Texas St., 707/425-8352

Best Burgers
Dave's Giant Hamburger
  1055 N. Texas St., 707/425-1818

Nations Foodservice
1955 W. Texas St., 707/425-1800

Best Business Lunch
Heart Key Cafe
1123 W. Texas St., 707/425-8800
Strings Italian Cafe
2401C Waterman Blvd., 707/428-3882

Best Chinese Food
Mandarin Restaurant
219 W. Texas St., 707/428-9736

Best Desserts
Marie Callender's
1750 Travis Blvd., 707/428-4745

Best Family Restaurant
J.J. North
1315 Gateway Blvd., 707/428-6000

Best Health-Conscious Menu
Fresh Choice
1501 The Courtyard, 707/429-2560

Best Italian Food
Fusilli Ristorante
620 Jackson St., 707/428-4211
Strings Italian Cafe
2401C Waterman Blvd., 707/428-3882

Best Mexican Food
El Azteca Mexican Food
1731 N. Texas St., 707/422-2108
Los Gallos Taqueria
936 Texas St., 707/429-2155

Best Pizza
Scenario's
1955 W. Texas St., Ste. 9, 707/425-1000

Best Place to Eat Alone
Lyon's Restaurant
2390 N. Texas St., 707/429-5330

Best Place to Take The Kids
Chuck E. Cheese Pizza
1027 Oliver Rd., 707/426-4500

Best Salad/Salad Bar
Carl Jr.'s Restaurant
Solano Mall, 1401A Travis Blvd., 707/422-9263
2380 N. Texas St., 707/425-6993

Best Vegetarian Food
Fresh Choice
1501 The Courtyard, 707/429-2560

FALLBROOK, CA

Best Breakfast
Wayside Cafe
507C S. Main Ave., 760/723-9633

Best French Food
Le Bistro
119 N. Main St., 760/723-3559

Best Italian Food
Vince's Italian Restaurant
  1331 S. Mission Rd., 760/723-1221

Best Pizza
Sourdough Pizza
  321 E. Alvarado St., 760/723-3106

Best Sandwiches
Dominick's Sandwiches
  1672 S. Mission Rd., 760/728-7911

FREMONT, CA

[See also: Hayward, Palo Alto, and Pleasanton.]

Best American Food
Dina's Family Restaurant
  40800 Fremont Blvd., 510/770-1930
Norman's Family Restaurant
  4949 Stevenson Blvd., 510/226-7777

Best Breakfast
Hobee's
  39222 Fremont Blvd., 510/797-1244

Best Chinese Food
Hong Kong Buffet
  41063 Fremont Blvd., 510/656-6908

Best Coffee/Coffeehouse
Java Bean
  2000 Driscoll Rd., 510/656-5517

Best Homestyle Food
Mission Pine Cafe
  129 Anza St., 510/770-8815

Best Italian Food
Camilio's Italian Restaurant
  40900 Fremont Blvd., 510/657-3027

Best Mexican Food
La Casita Restaurant
  41240 Fremont Blvd., 510/657-8602
Mi Pueblo Restaurant
  41025A Fremont Blvd., 510/656-8177
Pollo Ranchero
  39620 Mission Blvd., 510/792-8761
Taqueria Los Gallos
  39459 Fremont Blvd., 510/770-0526

Best Pizza
Mission Pizza
  43468 Ellsworth St., 510/651-6858

FRESNO, CA

Best Burgers
Chubby's
  4388 W. Shaw Ave., 209/276-7633
  6451 N. Blackstone Ave., 209/448-9999

C

Best Casual Dining
Wiliker's
  1713 E. Shaw Ave., 209/226-1985

Best Chinese Food
Helen's Gourmet Chinese Food
  7444 N. Fresno St., 209/432-4241

Best Delicatessen
Piemontes Italian Deli
  616 E. Olive Ave., 209/237-2038

Best Family Restaurant
Lyon's
  1746 W. Shaw Ave., 209/432-3806
  4965 N Fresno St., 209/224-3566
Marie Callender's
  1781 E. Shaw Ave., 209/224-8434
Spoons
  613 E. Shaw Ave., 209/221-6117

Best French Food
Ripe Tomato
  5064 N. Palm Ave., 209/225-1850

Best Indian Food
Bombay Cuisine
  4937 E. Kings Canyon Rd., 209/255-4496
Brahma Bull
  3050 W. Shaw Ave., 209/275-1100
India Sweet and Spice
  3209 W. Shaw Ave., 209/225-2824

Best Italian Food
Giulia's
  3050 W. Shaw Ave., 209/276-3573
Il Forno
  6755 N. Palm Ave., 209/438-0901
Mike's Pizzeria
  3228 N. West Ave., 209/229-2635
Nicola's
  3075 N. Maroa Ave., 209/224-1660

Best Japanese Food
Bando-Ya Japanese Cuisine
  3050 W. Shaw Ave., 209/275-7535
Dai Ichi
  7058 N. Cedar Ave., 209/297-1110
  2736 Divisadero St., Ste. 106, 209/266-7843
Kame Sushi House
  1089 E. Shaw Ave., 209/226-3701

Best Mexican Food
Plaza Mexican Restaurant
  3085 E. Shields Ave., 209/226-9780
  2074 E. Dayton Ave., 209/229-8465
Toledos Mexican Restaurant
  367 E. Shaw Ave., 209/224-0975

Best Other Ethnic Food
Andre's (Armenian)
  4743 N. Blackstone Ave., 209/229-6353

George's Shish Kebab (Armenian)
2405 Capitol St., 209/264-9433
The Mediterranean (Armenian)
4631 N Fresno St., 209/226-7856
Zlfred's (Armenian)
1803 E. Dakota Ave., 209/229-7853
4030 N. Blackstone St., 209/229-7852

Best Pizza
BC's Pizza
1056 W. Shaw Ave., 209/224-2224
DaVinci's
7795 N. First St., 209/435-8200
Popolo's Pizza
6775 N. Blackstone Ave., 209/276-7600
2760 W. Shaw Ave., 209/276-7600

Best Restaurant in Town
Harland's
722 W. Shaw Ave., 209/225-7100
Nicola's
3705 N. Maroa Ave., 209/224-1660
Primaveras Ristorante
2075 W. Bullard Ave., 209/435-2006
Veni Vidi Vici
1116 N. Fulton St., 209/266-5510

Best Salad/Salad Bar
Brooks Ranch
4131 S. Chestnut Ave., 209/485-6951
4278 W. Ashlan Ave., 209/275-8483
Grandy's
5180 N. Blackstone Ave., 209/221-8262
2340 N. Blackstone Ave., 209/225-9255
4898 E. Kings Canyon Rd., 209/251-4851
Happy Steak
2345 N. Blackstone Ave., 209/227-0016
5625 E. Kings Canyon Rd., 209/255-9026

Best Sandwiches
Geno's
1615 E. Ashlan Ave., 209/227-1812
Grape Tray
5091 N Fresno St., 209/226-6828
Packing Shed
5183 E. Kings Canyon Rd., 209/252-3518
Pat's Blue Ribbon
5042 N. West Ave., 209/431-3450
389 E. Shaw Ave., 209/227-1949

Best Seafood
Pacific Seafood Restaurant
1055 E. Herndon, 209/439-2778

Best Steaks
Black Angus
1737 E. Shaw Ave., 209/224-2205
Richard's
1609 E. Belmont Ave., 209/266-4077

C

Best Sunday Brunch
B.J.'s Kountry Kitchen
   1831 E. Ashlan Ave., 209/229-1036
   4109 E. Ashlan Ave., 209/222-5206
   6700 N. Cedar Ave., 209/298-5456

Best Thai Food
Bai Tong
   2021 W. Bullard Ave., 209/436-1516
Daruma Tei
   5096 N. West Ave., 209/431-2625
Lanna Thai Restaurant
   1069 E. Shaw Ave., 209/221-7245
Toom Thai Cuisine
   66 E. Herndon Ave., 209/446-0607

GARDEN GROVE, CA

[See also: Anaheim, Costa Mesa, Long Beach, Los Angeles, Orange, and Santa Ana.]

Best Breakfast
Mimi's Cafe
   7955 Garden Grove Rd., 714/898-5042

Best French Food
Mimi's Cafe
   7955 Garden Grove Rd., 714/898-5042

Best Greek/Mediterranean Food
Mad Greek Restaurant
   12120 Beach Blvd., Stanton, 714/898-5181

Best Mexican Food
Acapulco Mexican Restaurant
   12101 Valley View St., 714/893-7513

Best Salad/Salad Bar
Souplantation
   5939 Chapman Ave., 714/895-1314

Best Steaks
Stuart Anderson's Black Angus
   12900 Euclid St., 714/638-9981

Best Vietnamese Food
Ahn Hong Restaurant
   10195 Westminster Ave., 714/537-5230
Tu Hai
   14271 Brookhurst St., 714/531-8253

GILROY, CA

Best Continental Food
Harvest Time
   7397 Monterey Hwy., 408/842-7575

Best Greek/Mediterranean Food
Station 55 Bar and Grill
   55 Fifth St., 408/847-5555

Best Homestyle Food
Dunneville Store
5970 San Felipe Rd., Hollister, 408/636-9191

Best Restaurant in Town
O.D.'s Kitchen
28 Martin St., 408/847-3818

GLENDALE, CA

[See also: Beverly Hills, Los Angeles, Pasadena, and Santa Monica.]

Best American Food
Java City
134 N. Brand Blvd., 818/956-3925

Best Bar
Jax Bar and Grill
339 N. Brand Blvd., 818/500-1604

Best Breakfast
Porto's Bakery
315 N. Brand Blvd., 818/956-5996

Best Chinese Food
Gourmet 88
315 S. Brand Blvd., 818/547-9488

Best Coffee/Coffeehouse
Starbucks Coffee
114 N. Brand Blvd., 818/547-3694

Best Health-Conscious Menu
Whole Foods Market and Cafe
826 N. Glendale Ave., 818/240-9350

Best Steaks
Damon's Steak House
317 N. Brand Blvd., 818/507-1510

Best Thai Food
Indra Restaurant
517 S. Verdugo Rd., 818/247-3176

HAYWARD, CA

[See also: Fremont, Pleasanton, and San Leandro.]

Best American Food
Dino's Restaurant
3600 Castro Valley Blvd., Castro Valley,
510/537-1454

Best Chinese Food
Fong's Restaurant
3335 Castro Valley Blvd., Castro Valley,
510/581-9707

Best Continental Food
A Street Cafe
1213 A St., 510/582-2558

C

Best Diner
Val's Burgers
2115 Kelly St., 510/889-8257

Best Family Restaurant
Cafe Vasiliki
25202 Hesperian Blvd., 510/785-0184

Best Italian Food
Suzio Ristorante Italiano
20400 Lake Chabot Rd., Castro Valley,
510/733-0788

Best Japanese Food
Ichiban Restaurant
22560 Foothill Blvd., 510/537-4466

Best Lunch
Pablito's Authentic Mexican
22800 Mission Blvd., 510/886-6732

Best Mexican Food
La Imperial Restaurant
948 C St., 510/537-6227
Los Compadres Restaurant
944 C St., 510/582-1937
Pablito's Authentic Mexican
22800 Mission Blvd., 510/886-6732

Best Restaurant in Town
A Street Cafe
1213 A St., 510/582-2558

Best Seafood
Hayward Fishery and Restaurant
1065 C St. at Foothill Blvd., 510/537-6410

HEMET, CA

Best Breakfast
Millie's Country Kitchen
2020 E. Florida Ave., 909/658-9068

Best Burgers
Jimbo Burgers
1031 W. Florida Ave., 909/658-0203

Best Casual Dining
Hamby's Cafe
980 N. State St., 909/652-9772
Hamby's Cafe II
43430 Florida Ave., 909/927-8511

Best Chinese Food
Royal Mandarin Restaurant
525 N. San Jacinto St., 909/925-6624

Best Delicatessen
Rodolfo's Pizza and Deli
1947 E. Florida Ave., 909/658-6000

Best Italian Food
Arturo's Restaurant
117 N. Harvard St., 909/658-0165
Dattilo Ristorante
2288 E. Florida Ave., 909/658-4248

C

Best Mexican Food
Chagolla Taqueria
1287 E. Florida Ave., 909/925-7644
Esmeralda Restaurant
521 N. San Jacinto St., 909/652-1514
La Fogata Mexican Restaurant
2999 W. Florida Ave., 909/925-4147

Best Pizza
Milano Brothers Pizza
269 E. Stetson Ave., 909/929-2599

Best Steaks
Steer and Stein Restaurant
3104 W. Florida Ave., 909/658-6838

HUNTINGTON BEACH, CA

Best Italian Food
Shore House Cafe
520 Main St., 714/960-8091

Best Seafood
King Neptune Sea Foods
17115 Pacific Coast Hwy., Sunset Beach,
562/592-4878

Best Vegetarian Food
Mother's Market and Kitchen
19770 Beach Blvd., 714/963-6667

IRVINE, CA

*[See also: Anaheim, Costa Mesa, Garden Grove, Long
Beach, Los Angeles, Mission Viejo, Orange, and
Santa Ana.]*

Best American Food
Claim Jumper Restaurant
25332 McIntyre St., Laguna Hills, 714/768-0662

Best Coffee/Coffeehouse
Starbucks Coffee
2801 E. Coast Hwy., Corona Del Mar, 714/675-4416

Best Continental Food
Five Crowns
3801 E. Coast Hwy., Corona Del Mar, 714/760-0331

Best Desserts
Five Crowns
3801 E. Coast Hwy., Corona Del Mar, 714/760-0331

Best Eclectic Menu
Bistango
19100 Von Karman Ave., 714/752-5222

Best Ice Cream/Yogurt
Golden Spoon Frozen Yogurt
2445 E. Coast Hwy., Corona Del Mar, 714/673-2339

Best Indian Food
Natraj Cuisine of India Restaurant
24861 Alicia Pkwy., Laguna Hills, 714/581-4200

C

Niki's Tandoori Express
  24155 Laguna Hills Mall, Laguna Hills,
    714/586-0663
The Bombay Duck
  229 Ocean Ave., Laguna Beach, 714/497-7303

Best Italian Food
Rumari Ristorante
  1826 S. Coast Hwy., Laguna Beach, 714/494-0400

Best Mexican Food
Kachina
  222 Forest Ave., Laguna Beach, 714/497-5546

Best Other Ethnic Food
Five Feet (Pacific Rim cuisine)
  328 Glenneyre St., Laguna Beach, 714/497-4955

Best Pizza
California Pizza Kitchen
  24155 Laguna Hills Mall, Laguna Hills, 714/458-9600
  2957 Michelson Dr., 714/975-1585

Best Restaurant Meal Value
Bistango
  19100 Von Karman Ave., 714/752-5222

Best Seafood
McCormick and Schmick's
  2000 Main St., 714/756-0505

Best Southwestern Food
El Torito Grill
  1910 Main St., 714/975-1220

LA JOLLA, CA

Best American Food
Top O' The Cove
  1216 Prospect St., 619/454-7779

Best Bar
Piatta
  2182 Avenida de La Playa, 619/454-1589
The Whaling Bar and Grill
  La Valencia Hotel, 1132 Prospect St., 619/454-0771
Triangles
  4370 La Jolla Village Dr., 619/453-6650

Best Breakfast
Harry's
  7545 Girard Ave., 619/454-7381

Best Brewpub
La Jolla Brewing Company
  7536 Fay Ave., 619/456-2739

Best Business Lunch
Cindy Black's
  5721 La Jolla Blvd., 619/456-6299

Best Chinese Food
Panda Country Restaurant
  4150 Regents Park, Ste. 190, 619/552-1345

C

Best Coffee/Coffeehouse
Pannikin
 7467 Girard Ave., 619/454-5453
Wall Street Cafe
 1044 Wall St., 619/551-1044

Best Continental Food
The Mediterranean Room
 La Valencia Hotel, 1132 Prospect St., 619/454-0771

Best Fine Dining
Crab Catcher
 1298 Prospect St., 619/454-9587
George's at the Cove
 1250 Prospect St., 619/454-4244

Best Health-Conscious Menu
Whole Foods Market and Cafe
 8825 Villa La Jolla Dr., 619/642-6700

Best Indian Food
Ashoka Cuisine of India
 8008 Girard Ave., Second Fl., 619/454-6263

Best Inexpensive Meal
Come On In
 1030 Torrey Pines Rd., 619/551-1063

Best Mexican Food
Alfonso's of La Jolla
 1251 Prospect St., 619/454-2232

Best Middle Eastern Food
Marrakesh Restaurant
 634 Pearl St., 619/454-2500

Best Pizza
Sammy's California Wood-fired Pizza
 702 Pearl St., 619/456-5222

Best Place to Take the Kids
Hard Rock Cafe
 909 Prospect St., 619/454-5101

Best Restaurant in Town
Top O' The Cove
 1216 Prospect St., 619/233-5757

Best Romantic Dining
Elario's Restaurant
 7955 La Jolla Shores Dr., Eleventh Fl., 619/459-0541
Marine Room
 2000 Spindrift Dr., 619/459-7222
The Sky Room
 La Valencia Hotel, 1132 Prospect St., 619/454-0771

Best Seafood
Crab Catcher
 1298 Prospect St., 619/454-9587

Best View While Dining
George's at the Cove
 1250 Prospect St., 619/454-4244
Top O' The Cove
 1216 Prospect St., 619/454-7779

C

Best Wine Selection
Elario's Restaurant
  7955 La Jolla Shores Dr., Eleventh Fl., 619/459-0541

LAFAYETTE, CA

Best Breakfast
Millie's Kitchen
  1018 Oak Hill Rd., 925/283-2397

Best Chinese Food
Uncle Yu's Szechuan
  999 Oak Hill Rd., 925/283-1688

Best Coffee/Coffeehouse
Starbucks Coffee
  3547A Mt. Diablo Blvd., 925/284-5811

Best French Food
Le Marquis
  3524 Mt. Diablo Blvd., 925/284-4422

Best Sunday Brunch
Duck Club Restaurant
  The Lafayette Park Hotel, 3287 Mt. Diablo Blvd.,
    925/283-7108

LA MESA, CA

Best Family Restaurant
Claim Jumper
  Grossmont Center Mall,
    5500 Grossmont Center Dr., 619/469-3927

Best Southwestern Food
Marieta's Restaurant
  8949 La Mesa Blvd., 619/462-3500

Best Sports Bar
Trophy's
  Grossmont Center Mall,
    5500 Grossmont Center Dr., 619/469-3927

Best Steaks
Claim Jumper
  Grossmont Center Mall,
    5500 Grossmont Center Dr., 619/469-3927

LARKSPUR, CA

*[See also: Corte Madera, Mill Valley, San Anselmo,
San Francisco, and San Rafael.]*

Best Beer Selection
Marin Brewing Company
  1809 Larkspur Landing Circle, 415/461-4677

Best Chinese Food
CJ Chinese Cuisine
  435 Magnolia Ave., 415/924-0717

C

Best Coffee/Coffeehouse
Java
320 Magnolia Ave., 415/ 927-1501

Best Desserts
Pasticerria Rulli
464 Magnolia Ave., 415/924-7478

Best French Food
Left Bank
507 Magnolia Ave., 415/927-3331

Best Health-Conscious Menu
Good Earth
2231 Larkspur Landing Circle, 415/461-7322

Best Japanese Food
Sushi-Ko
1819 Larkspur Landing Circle, 415/461-8400

Best Mexican Food
Roadrunner Burrito
1813 Larkspur Landing Circle, 415/461-4646

Best Restaurant in Town
Lark Creek Inn
234 Magnolia Ave., 415/924-7766

LOMPOC, CA

Best Breakfast
Tom's Educated Burgers
115 E. College Ave., 805/736-9996

Best Italian Food
La Botte Italian Cuisine
812 N. H St., 805/736-2050

Best Restaurant in Town
Sissy's Uptown Cafe
112 S. I St., 805/735-4877

Best Salad/Salad Bar
Tom's Educated Burgers
115 E. College Ave., 805/736-9996

Best Seafood
The Jetty Restaurant
304 W. Ocean Ave., 805/735-2400
The Outpost Restaurant
1501 E. Ocean Ave., 805/735-1130

Best Steaks
The Jetty Restaurant
304 W. Ocean Ave., 805/735-2400
The Outpost Restaurant
1501 E. Ocean Ave., 805/735-1130

Best Thai Food
Good Choice Thai Cuisine
920 N. I St., 805/736-7450

LONG BEACH, CA

[See also: Anaheim, Costa Mesa, Garden Grove, Los Angeles, Montebello, Santa Ana, and Whittier.]

Best All-You-Can-Eat Buffet
Arnold's Family Restaurant
   3925 Atlantic Ave., 562/424-8573

Best Business Lunch
Simon and Seafort's Fish Chop
   340 Golden Shore St., 562/435-2333

Best Coffee/Coffeehouse
Portfolio Cafe and Gallery
   2300 E. Fourth St., 562/434-2486

Best Delicatessen
Katella Deli-Restaurant
   4470 Katella Ave., Los Alamitos, 562/594-8611

Best Desserts
Grandma's Sugarplums
   4908 E. Second St., 562/439-3363

Best Diner
Babe's Kitchen
   1106 E. Wardlow Rd., 562/427-4897
Cafe Bixby
   3900 Atlantic Ave., 562/427-2233

Best Family Restaurant
Coco's Restaurant
   4750 E. Los Coyotes Diagonal, 562/498-1140
   6405 E. Pacific Coast Hwy., 562/431-6306

Best Fine Dining
Mustard Seed
   5624 Atlantic Ave., 562/422-6090

Best Italian Food
Andiamo In Citta
   217 Pine Ave., 562/435-1225
Andiamo's Ristorante
   The Airport Hilltop Hilton,
      5711 W. Pacific Coast Hwy., 562/493-5529

Best Mexican Food
Avila's El Ranchito Mexican Restaurant
   5345 N. Long Beach Blvd., 562/428-7348
La Salsa Restaurant
   243 Pine Ave., 562/491-1104
Mi Lupita
   1202 E. Broadway, 562/432-0163

Best Pizza
Pizza Place
   1431 E. Broadway, 562/432-6000

Best Restaurant in Town
Mustard Seed
   5624 Atlantic Ave., 562/422-6090

C

Best Salad/Salad Bar
Colonial Buffet
355 E. First St., 562/590-0220

Best Seafood
Original Fish Company
11061 Los Alamitos Blvd., Los Alamitos,
562/594-4553
Simon at Catalina Landing
340 Golden Shore St., 562/435-2333

Best Steaks
Twin Wheels Steak House
1654 W. Anaheim St., 562/435-4744

Best Vegetarian Food
Papa Jon's
5006 E. Second St., 562/439-1059

LOS ANGELES, CA

*[See also: Beverly Hills, Burbank, Glendale, Long
Beach, Montebello, Pasadena, Santa Monica,
Whittier, and West Covina.]*

Best 24-Hour Restaurant
Canter's
419 N. Fairfax Ave., 213/651-2030
The Original Pantry Cafe
877 S. Figueroa St., 213/972-9279

Best American Food
Alice's Restaurant
23000 Pacific Coast Hwy., Malibu, 310/456-6646
Eclipse
8800 Melrose Ave., West Hollywood, 310/724-5959
Pacific Dining Car
1310 W. Sixth St., 213/483-6000
Stepps On the Court
330 S. Hope St., 213/626-0900
Vida
1930 Hillhurst Ave., 213/660-4446

Best Bar
Bar Deluxe
1710 N. Las Palmas Ave., Hollywood, 213/469-1991
Birds
5925 Franklin Ave., 213/465-0175
Jones
7205 Santa Monica Blvd., 213/850-1727
Lava Lounge
1533 N. La Brea Ave., Hollywood, 213/876-6612
The Smog Cutter
864 N. Virgil Ave., 213/660-4626

Best Barbecue/Ribs
Benny's Barbecue
4077 Lincoln Blvd., Marina Del Rey, 310/821-6939
Phillips Barbecue
4307 Leimart Blvd., 213/292-7613

C

Woody's Barbecue
3446 W. Slauson Ave., 213/294-9443

Best Bistro
Chaya Venice
110 Navy St., Venice, 310/396-1179

Best Breakfast
Du-par's Restaurants and Bakeries
16055 Ventura Blvd., Ste. 1109, Encino,
818/990-1919
Fred's Burger
6225 S. Broadway, 213/753-6310
Mimi's Cafe
19710 Nordhoff Pl., Chatsworth, 818/717-8334
Pacific Dining Car
1310 W. Sixth St., 213/483-6000

Best Brewpub
Westwood Brewing Company
1097 Glendon Ave., 310/209-2739

Best Burgers
Apple Pan
10801 W. Pico Blvd., 310/475-3585
Cassell's Hamburgers
3266 W. Sixth St., 213/480-8668
Fred's Burger
6225 S. Broadway, 213/753-6310
Johnny Rocket's
7507 Melrose Ave., 213/651-3361
10959 Weyburn Ave., 310/824-5656
1888 Century Park E., Ste. 224, 310/556-8811
100 N. La Cienega Blvd., 310/657-6073
10250 Santa Monica Blvd., 310/788-9020

Best Cajun/Creole Food
Jonake's French Quarters
621 W. Manchester Blvd., Inglewood, 310/412-1920

Best Casual Dining
Musso and Frank Grill
6667 Hollywood Blvd., 213/467-5123

Best Chinese Food
Chin Chin Restaurant
11740 San Vicente Blvd., 310/826-2525
8618 W. Sunset Blvd., 310/652-1818
Empress Pavillion
988 N. Hill St., Ste. 201, 213/617-9898
Mandarin Deli
356 E. Second St., 213/617-0231
Ocean Seafood
750 N. Hill St., 213/687-3088
Panda Inn Chinese Restaurant
10800 W. Pico Blvd., 310/470-7790
VIP Harbor Seafood Restaurant
11701 Wilshire Blvd., 310/979-3377
Won Kok Restaurant
210 Alpine St., 213/613-0700

C

Best Coffee/Coffeehouse
Coffee Brake
  1507 1/2 S. Robertson Blvd., 310/277-6741
Highland Grounds
  742 N. Highland Ave., Hollywood, 213/466-1507
Insomnia Cafe
  7286 Beverly Blvd., 213/931-4943
Piper's Coffee Shop
  222 N. Western Ave., 213/465-7701

Best Continental Food
La Brasserie
  Wyndham Plaza, 1020 N. San Vicente Blvd.,
    West Hollywood, 310/854-1111
Musso and Frank Grill
  6667 Hollywood Blvd., Hollywood, 213/467-7788

Best Delicatessen
Art's Delicatessen and Restaurant
  12224 Ventura Blvd., Studio City, 818/762-1221
Canter's Deli
  419 N. Fairfax Ave., 213/651-2030
Greenblatt's Delicatessen
  8017 W. Sunset Blvd., Hollywood, 213/656-0606
Jerry's Famous Deli
  16650 Ventura Blvd., Encino, 818/906-1800
  13181 Mindanao Way, Marina Del Rey,
    310/821-6626
Langers Delicatessen and Restaurant
  704 S. Alvarado St., 213/483-8050
Metro Deli
  624A S. Alvarado St., 213/353-4771

Best Desserts
Campanile Restaurant
  624 S. La Brea Ave., 213/938-1447
Cheesecake Factory
  11647 San Vicente Blvd., 310/826-7111
Water Grill
  544 S. Grand Ave., 213/891-0900

Best Diner
Engine Company 28 Restaurant
  644 S. Figueroa St., 213/624-6996
Ozzie's
  7780 E. Slauson Ave., 213/726-0300

Best Eclectic Menu
Out Take Cafe
  12159 Ventura Blvd., Studio City, 818/760-1111
Spago
  1114 Horn Ave., West Hollywood, 310/652-4025
West Beach Cafe
  60 N. Venice Blvd., Venice, 310/823-5396

Best Family Restaurant
Jerry's Famous Deli
  16650 Ventura Blvd., Encino, 818/906-1800
  13181 Mindanao Way, Marina Del Rey,
    310/821-6626

C

Best Fine Dining
Bernard's
  Biltmore Hotel, 506 S. Grand Ave., 213/612-1580
L'Orangerie Restaurant
  903 N. La Cienega Blvd., 310/652-9770
La Cachette Restaurant
  10506 Little Santa Monica Blvd., 310/470-4992
Rex Restaurant
  617 S. Olive St., 213/627-2300
Sisley Italian Kitchen
  24201 W. Valencia Blvd., 805/287-4444
The Ivy
  1100 Wall St., 213/746-6124
  113 N. Robertson Blvd., 310/274-8303

Best French Food
Cafe des Artistes
  1534 N. McCadden Pl., 213/461-6889
Citrus Restaurant
  6703 Melrose Ave., 213/857-0034
L'Orangerie Restaurant
  903 N. La Cienega Blvd., 310/652-9770
La Cachette Restaurant
  10506 Little Santa Monica Blvd., 310/470-4992
Patina Restaurant
  5955 Melrose Ave., 213/467-1108

Best Greek/Mediterranean Food
Byblos Restaurant
  1964 Westwood Blvd., 310/475-9558
Noura
  8479 Melrose Ave., West Hollywood, 310/651-4581

Best Health-Conscious Menu
Whole Foods Market and Cafe
  11737 San Vicente Blvd., 310/826-4433
  9350 Reseda Blvd., Northridge, 818/701-5122
  11666 National Blvd., 310/996-8840

Best Homestyle Food
Paty's Restaurant
  10001 Riverside Dr., North Hollywood,
   818/761-9126

Best Ice Cream/Yogurt
Humphrey Yogart
  11677 San Vicente Blvd., 310/207-2206

Best Indian Food
Bombay Cafe
  12113 Santa Monica Blvd., Ste. 205, 310/820-2070
Clay Pit
  3465 W. Sixth St., 213/382-6300
India's Oven
  11645 Wilshire Blvd., 310/655-4596
  7231 Beverly Blvd., 213/936-1000
Paru's Vegetarian Indian Restaurant
  5140 W. Sunset Blvd., 213/661-7600

Best Inexpensive Meal
La Parrilla Restaurant
  2126 E. Caesar E. Chavez Ave., 213/262-3434

Mandarin Deli
356 E. Second St., 213/617-0231
Rosalind's
1044 S. Fairfax Ave., 213/936-2486
Rosti
908 S. Barrington Ave., 310/447-8695
Versailles Restaurant
10319 Venice Blvd., 310/558-3168

Best Italian Food
Alejo's
8343 Lincoln Blvd., Westchester, 310/670-6677
4002 Lincoln Blvd., Marina del Rey, 310/822-0095
Alto Palato
755 N. La Cienega Blvd., West Hollywood, 310/657-9271
Farfalla
1978 Hillhurst Ave., 213/661-7365
La Loggia
11814 Ventura Blvd., Studio City, 818/985-9222
Louise's Trattoria
10645 W. Pico Blvd., 310/475-6084
232 N. Larchmont Blvd., 213/962-9510
7505 Melrose Ave., 213/651-3880
4500 Los Feliz Blvd., 213/667-0777
11645 San Vicente Blvd., 310/826-2000
Toscana
11633 San Vicente Blvd., 310/820-2448
Tra Di Noi
3835 Cross Creek Rd., Malibu, 310/456-0169
Valentino Cafe
698 Irolo St., 213/384-0394

Best Japanese Food
Ashai Ramen
2027 Sawtelle Blvd., 310/479-2231
Katsu Third
8636 W. Third St., 310/273-3605
Macos
1820 N. Vermont Ave., 213/660-1211
Yamashiro Restaurant
1999 N. Sycamore Ave., 213/466-5125

Best Late-Night Food
Caffe Luna
7463 Melrose Ave., 213/655-8647
Jerry's Famous Deli
16650 Ventura Blvd., Encino, 818/906-1800

Best Mexican Food
Acapulco Mexican Restaurant
3280 Glendale Blvd., 213/663-8275
1109 Glendon Ave., 310/208-3884
7038 W. Sunset Blvd., 213/469-5131
4444 W. Sunset Blvd., 213/665-5751
El Cholo Restaurant
1121 S. Western Ave., 213/734-2773
La Fonda de Los Camperos
2501 Wilshire Blvd., 213/380-5055

C

La Parrilla Restaurant
2126 E. Caesar E. Chavez Ave., 213/262-3434
La Serenata de Garibaldi
1842 E. First St., 213/265-2887
Senor Fish
4803 Eagle Rock Blvd., 213/257-7167
422 E. First St., 213/625-0566
Super Antojitos Mexicanos
4508 Whittier Blvd., East Los Angeles,
213/262-2116
Yuca's Hut
2056 Hillhurst Ave., 213/662-1214

Best Middle Eastern Food
Dar Maghreb Restaurant
7651 W. Sunset Blvd., 213/876-7651
Zankou Chicken
5065 W. Sunset Blvd., 213/665-7842

Best Other Ethnic Food
Cava Restaurant (Caribbean)
8384 W. Third St., 213/658-8898
El Floridita Restaurant (Cuban)
1253 N. Vine St., 213/871-8612
Gaucho Grill (Argentinian)
7980 Sunset Blvd., Hollywood, 213/656-4152
Koutoubia (Moroccan)
2116 Westwood Blvd., 310/475-0729
Messob Ethiopian Restaurant (Ethiopian)
1041 S. Fairfax Ave., 213/938-8827
Mobay Restaurant (Caribbean)
1031 Abbot Kinney Blvd., Venice, 310/452-7472
Perestroyka (Georgian)
5468 Wilshire Blvd., 213/934-2215
Rincon Criollo (Cuban)
4361 Sepulveda Blvd., Culver City, 310/391-4478
Rosalind's (African)
1044 Fairfax Ave., Hollywood, 213/936-2486
Uzbekistan (Uzbeki)
7077 W. Sunset Blvd., 213/464-3663
Versailles Restaurant (Cuban)
10319 Venice Blvd., 310/558-3168

Best Outdoor Dining
Bel Air Hotel
701 Stone Canyon Rd., 310/472-1211
Sidewalk Cafe
1401 Ocean Front Walk, Venice, 310/399-5547

Best Pizza
California Pizza Kitchen
121 N. La Cienega Blvd., 310/854-6555
330 S. Hope St., 213/626-2616
6053 W. Century Blvd., 310/342-5000
11677 San Vicente Blvd., 310/826-3573
1640 S. Sepulveda Blvd., Ste. 200, 310/575-3000
Damiano's Mr. Pizza
1511 1/2 S. Robertson Blvd., 310/475-6751
Palermo
1858 N. Vermont Ave., 213/663-1430

C

Vittorio!
  16646 Marquez Ave., Pacific Palisade,
    310/459-3755

Best Regional Food
Fenix
  Argyle Hotel, 8358 W. Sunset Blvd.,
    West Hollywood, 310/654-7100

Best Restaurant in Town
Citrus Restaurant
  6703 Melrose Ave., 213/857-0034
Fenix
  Argyle Hotel, 8358 W. Sunset Blvd.,
    West Hollywood, 310/654-7100
L'Orangerie Restaurant
  903 N. La Cienega Blvd., 310/652-9770
Patina Restaurant
  5955 Melrose Ave., 213/467-1108
Spago
  1114 Horn Ave., West Hollywood, 310/652-4025

Best Restaurant Meal Value
Ashai Ramen
  2027 Sawtelle Blvd., 310/479-2231
Bombay Cafe
  12113 Santa Monica Blvd., Ste. 205, 310/820-2070
Caffe Luna
  7463 Melrose Ave., 213/655-8647
Out Take Cafe
  12159 Ventura Blvd., Studio City, 818/760-1111

Best Romantic Dining
La Brasserie
  Wyndham Plaza Hotel, 1020 N. San Vicente Blvd.,
    West Hollywood, 310/854-1111
Giorgio Malibu
  21337 Pacific Coast Hwy., Malibu, 310/317-0207
Yamashiro
  1999 N. Sycamore Ave., 213/466-5125

Best Sandwiches
Saigon Sandwich
  828 N. Broadway, 213/625-8721

Best Seafood
Empress Pavillion
  988 N. Hill St., Ste. 201, 213/617-9898
Fish House
  3440 W. Slauson Ave., 213/293-1300
Full House Seafood Restaurant
  963 N. Hill St., 213/617-8382
Gladstone's
  1000 Universal Center Dr., Universal City,
    818/622-3474
Killer Shrimp
  523 Washington Blvd., Marina Del Rey,
    310/578-2293
Lobster Connection
  2201 Lincoln Blvd., Venice, 310/822-4062

C

Ocean Seafood
750 N. Hill St., 213/687-3088
VIP Harbor Seafood Restaurant
11701 Wilshire Blvd., 310/979-3377
Water Grill
544 S. Grand Ave., 213/891-0900

Best Soul Food
Roscoe's Chicken and Waffles
1514 N. Gower St., 213/466-7453
106 W. Manchester Blvd., 213/752-6211
5006 W. Pico Blvd., 213/934-4405

Best Southwestern Food
Authentic Cafe
7605 Beverly Blvd., 213/939-4626

Best Spanish Food
La Masia Restaurant
9077 Santa Monica Blvd., West Hollywood,
310/273-7066
La Paella
476 S. San Vicente Blvd., 213/951-0745

Best Steaks
Monty's Steak House
1100 Glendon Ave., 21st Fl., 310/208-8787

Best Sunday Brunch
The Restaurant
Bel Air Hotel, 701 Stone Canyon Rd., 310/472-1211
French Quarter Market
7985 Santa Monica Blvd., 213/654-0898
House of Blues
8430 W. Sunset Blvd., West Hollywood,
213/654-1457

Best Sushi
Cafe Sushi
8459 Beverly Blvd., 213/651-4020
Hama Sushi
335 E. Second St., 213/680-3454
Shibucho
3114 Beverly Blvd., 213/387-8498
Sushi Gen
422 E. Second St., 213/617-0552
Teru Sushi
11940 Ventura Blvd., Studio City, 818/763-6201

Best Thai Food
Chan Dara Restaurant
11940 W. Pico Blvd., 310/479-4461
1511 N. Cahuenga Blvd., 213/464-8585
Chuam Chin
5644 Hollywood Blvd., Hollywood, 213/462-6221
Jitlada
11622 Ventura Blvd., Studio City, 818/506-9355
Lumpinee Thai
11020 Vanowen St., North Hollywood,
818/505-0761
Toi on Sunset
7505 1/2 Sunset Blvd. W., Hollywood, 213/874-8062

C

Tommy Tang's
7313 Melrose Ave., 213/937-5733
Vim Thai-Chinese
5132 Hollywood Blvd., 213/662-1017

Best Vegetarian Food
A Votre Sante
345 N. La Brea Ave., 213/857-0412
1025 Abbot Kinney Blvd., Venice, 310/314-1187
13016 San Vicente Blvd., 310/451-1813
Follow Your Heart
21825 Sherman Way, Canoga Park, 818/348-3240
Vegetable Delight
17823 Chatsworth St., Granada Hills, 818/360-3997

Best Vietnamese Food
Mandalay
611 N. La Brea Ave., 213/933-0717

Best View While Dining
Fenix
Argyle Hotel, 8358 W. Sunset Blvd.,
West Hollywood, 213/654-7100
Gladstone's Four Fish
17300 Pacific Coast Hwy., Pacific Palisade,
310/454-3474
Inn of the Seventh Ray
128 Old Topanga Canyon Rd., Topanga, 310/455-1311
Saddle Peak Lodge
419 Cold Canyon Rd., Calabasas, 818/222-3888
Yamashiro Restaurant
1999 N. Sycamore Ave., 213/466-5125

Best Wine Selection
Philippe the Original Restaurant
1001 N. Alameda St., 213/628-3781

MADERA, CA

Best French Food
Pinchette
1816 Howard Rd., 209/675-0433

Best Regional Food
Erna's Elderberry House
48688 Victoria Ln., Oakhurst, 209/683-6800

Best Restaurant in Town
Eppie's Restaurant
1101 Country Club Dr., 209/674-0368
Farnesi's Restaurant
20885 W. Kennedy, 209/673-9164
Lucca's Restaurant
325 N. Gateway Dr., 209/674-6744
Perko's Cafe
1825 W. Cleveland Ave., 209/675-8020
The Vineyard
605 S. I St., 209/674-0923
Vintage House
30338 Avenue Twelve, 209/674-1560

C

MANHATTAN BEACH, CA

Best American Food
Chicken Factory and More
  901 N. Sepulveda Blvd., 310/372-7442

Best Bar
Pancho's
  3615 Highland Ave., 310/545-6670

Best Breakfast
Local Yolk
  3414 Highland Ave., 310/546-4407

Best Casual Dining
Grunions Sports Bar and Grill
  1501 N. Sepulveda Blvd., 310/545-9910

Best Chinese Food
Szechwan
  924 N. Sepulveda Blvd., 310/379-9712

Best Delicatessen
Bristol Farms
  1570 Rosecrans Ave., 310/643-5229

Best Lunch
Manhattan Coolers
  309 Manhattan Beach Blvd., 310/546-7344

Best Mexican Food
Pancho's
  3615 Highland Ave., 310/545-6670

Best Other Ethnic Food
Barnabey's Hotel and Restaurant (British)
  3501 N. Sepulveda Blvd., 310/545-5693

Best Sports Bar
Grunions Sports Bar and Grill
  1501 N. Sepulveda Blvd., 310/545-9910

Best Sunday Brunch
Pancho's
  3615 Highland Ave., 310/545-6670

MANTECA, CA

Best American Food
The Table
  1185 N. Main St., 209/823-7777

Best Chinese Food
Sun Kwong Buffet
  1460 W. Yosemite Ave., 209/239-3288

Best Italian Food
Pietro's Italian Restaurant
  1020 N. Main St., 209/239-4181

Best Mexican Food
La Estralia Taqueria
  1361 E. Yosemite Ave., 209/829-8481

Best Restaurant in Town
Isadore's
  680 N. Main St., 209/825-4300

String's Italian Cafe
   1125 S. Main St., 209/823-9777

MERCED, CA

Best Italian Food
D'Angelo's
   350 W. Main St., 209/383-3020

Best Japanese Food
Nagami
   2650 W. Sixteenth St., 209/384-1677

Best Seafood
D'Angelo's
   350 W. Main St., 209/383-3020

Best Steaks
Branding Iron
   640 W. Sixteenth St., 209/722-1822
Pine Cone Bar and Grill
   1500 W. Thirteenth St., 209/384-9223
The Ranch
   245 W. Sixteenth St., 209/722-7351

Best Thai Food
Star Garden
   235 W. Twelfth St., 209/383-5350

MILL VALLEY, CA

*[See also: Corte Madera, Larkspur, San Anselmo,
San Francisco, and San Rafael.]*

Best Burgers
Phyllis' Giant Burgers
   72 E. Blithedale Ave., 415/381-5116

Best Delicatessen
La Petite
   33 Reed Blvd., 415/381-2336
Perry's Delicatessen
   246 E. Blithedale Ave., 415/381-0407

Best Desserts
Sweet Things
   1 Blackfield Dr., Tiburon, 415/388-8583
True Confections
   17 Madrona St., 415/383-3832

Best French Food
Guernica
   2009 Bridgeway, Sausalito, 415/332-1512

Best Ice Cream/Yogurt
Ultimate Yogurt
   214 Strawberry Village, 415/383-4881

Best Indian Food
India Palace
   707 Redwood Hwy., 415/388-3350

Best Inexpensive Meal
High Tech Burrito
118 Strawberry Village, 415/388-7002

Best Italian Food
Piazza D'Angelo
22 Miller Ave., 415/388-2185

Best Mexican Food
Cactus Cafe and Taqueria
393 Miller Ave., 415/388-8226
Guaymas
5 Main St., Tiburon, 415/435-6300
The Cantina
651 E. Blithedale Ave., 415/381-1070

Best Middle Eastern Food
Cairo Cafe
411 Strawberry Village, 415/389-1101

Best Outdoor Dining
Guaymas
5 Main St., Tiburon, 415/435-6300

Best Pizza
Muzzarella di Bufla
711 E. Blithedale Ave., 415/381-3972
Round Table Pizza
50 Belvedere Dr., 415/383-5100

Best Restaurant in Town
Buckeye Roadhouse
15 Shoreline Hwy., 415/331-2600

Best Romantic Dining
Caprice
200 Paradise Dr., Tiburon, 415/435-3400
El Paseo
17 Throckmorton, 415/388-0741

Best Seafood
Scoma's
588 Bridgeway, Sausalito, 415/332-9551

Best Sunday Brunch
Dipsea Cafe
200 Shoreline Hwy., 415/381-0298
Horizons Restaurant
558 Bridgeway, Sausalito, 415/331-3232
Sam's Anchor Cafe
27 Main St., Tiburon, 415/435-4527

Best View While Dining
Horizons Restaurant
558 Bridgeway, Sausalito, 415/331-3232

MISSION VIEJO, CA

[See also: Irvine and San Clemente.]

Best Burgers
Knowl Wood Restaurant
27755 Santa Margarita Pkwy., 714/588-9113

Ruby's Diner
    27762 Vista Del Lago, 714/770-7829

Best Coffee/Coffeehouse
Diedrich Coffee
    26137 La Paz Rd., 714/699-0566
    27775 Santa Margarita Pkwy., 714/472-3733

Best Diner
Ruby's Diner
    27762 Vista Del Lago, 714/770-7829

Best Family Restaurant
Peppino's Pizzeria
    27782 Vista Del Lago, 714/859-9556

Best Ice Cream/Yogurt
Golden Spoon Frozen Yogurt
    27775 Santa Margarita Pkwy., 714/454-0402

Best Italian Food
Capriccio Italian Restaurant
    25380 Marguerite Pkwy., 714/855-6866
Peppino's Pizzeria
    27782 Vista Del Lago, 714/859-9556

Best Restaurant in Town
Capriccio Italian Restaurant
    25380 Marguerite Pkwy., 714/855-6866

Best Restaurant Meal Value
Taco Mesa
    22922 Los Alisos Blvd., 714/472-3144

Best Sandwiches
Knowl Wood Restaurant
    27755 Santa Margarita Pkwy., 714/588-9113

Best Seafood
Tony's Sea Landing
    26032 Marguerite Pkwy., 714/582-8844

MODESTO, CA

Best American Food
Farmer's Catfish House Restaurant
    4937 Beckwith Rd., 209/526-0969

Best Atmosphere
Hazel's Elegant Dining
    513 Twelfth St., 209/578-3463

Best Bar
Mallard's
    1700 McHenry Ave., 209/522-3825

Best Breakfast
Opus 13
    421 McHenry Ave., 209/576-7508
Sundial Lodge and Restaurant
    808 McHenry Ave., 209/524-4375

Best Brewpub
St. Stan's Brewery Restaurant
    821 L St., 209/524-4782

C

Best Burgers
Scenic Drive-In
1151 Scenic Dr., 209/522-3536
Smoky's Pub and Grill
2625 Coffee Rd., 209/524-3317

Best Business Lunch
Tresetti's World Caffe
927 Eleventh St., 209/572-2990

Best Casual Dining
Benni's
1105 Yosemite Blvd., 209/571-3657

Best Coffee/Coffeehouse
Deva
1202 J St., 209/572-3382
Espresso Caffe
3025D McHenry Ave., 209/571-3337

Best Continental Food
Hazel's Elegant Dining
513 Twelfth St., 209/578-3463

Best Delicatessen
Ferrarese's Deli Restaurant
1161 E. F St., Oakdale, 209/847-2079

Best Eclectic Menu
Deja Vu Cafe
825 W. Roseburg Ave., 209/571-3333

Best Fine Dining
Maxi's Restaurant and Lounge
1150 Ninth St., 209/526-6000

Best Health-Conscious Menu
The Brighter Side
1125 K St., 209/524-7531

Best Indian Food
India Oven Restaurant
1022 Eleventh St., 209/572-1805

Best Inexpensive Meal
Noah's Hof Brau
1311 J St., 209/527-1090

Best Italian Food
Benni's
1105 Yosemite Blvd., 209/571-3657

Best Mexican Food
La Morenita
1410 E. Hatch Rd., 209/537-7900

Best Place to Take the Kids
Strings Italian Cafe
2601 Oakdale Rd., 209/578-9777

Best Lunch
China Gate Restaurant
1601E Yosemite Blvd., 209/526-6666

Best Restaurant in Town
Hazel's Elegant Dining
513 Twelfth St., 209/578-3463

Best Salad/Salad Bar
Fresh Choice Restaurant
2225 Plaza Pkwy., 209/523-8875

Best Seafood
Fisherman's Galley
3008 McHenry Ave., 209/527-3450

Best Southwestern Food
R.J. Sweetwater's
1029 Ninth St., 209/526-4060

Best Sunday Brunch
Fruityard
7948 Yosemite Blvd., 209/577-3093
Mallard's
1700 McHenry Ave., 209/522-3825

Best Thai Food
Thailand Restaurant
950 Tenth St., 209/544-0505

Best Undiscovered Restaurant
Bon Appetit Cafe
500 Ninth St., Ste. K-1, 209/526-7000

Best Vegetarian Food
Village Health Food
1700 McHenry Ave., 209/523-3466

Best Wine Selection
Bon Appetit Cafe
500 Ninth St., Ste. K-1, 209/526-7000

MONTEBELLO, CA

[See also: Los Angeles, Pasadena, West Covina, and Whittier.]

Best Bar
Mister C's Lounge
612 W. Whittier Blvd., 213/727-0681

Best Breakfast
Jimmie's Family Restaurant
701 W. Whittier Blvd., 213/726-7783

Best Burgers
Golden Ox
902 W. Whittier Blvd., 213/722-2865

Best Business Lunch
Baker's Square Restaurant
1322 W. Beverly Blvd., 213/722-6324
Quiet Cannon
901 Via San Clemente, 213/724-9284

Best Casual Dining
Gotham Bar and Grill
5811 Firestone Blvd., South Gate, 562/806-2224

Best Chinese Food
Harbor Village
111 N. Atlantic Blvd., Monterey Park,

C

628/300-8833

Paul's Kitchen
  1950 S. Atlantic Blvd., Monterey Park,
    213/724-1855

Best Homestyle Food
Ordonez Mexican Restaurant And Cantina
  872 N. Garfield Ave., 213/724-6383

Best Inexpensive Meal
Argos Jr. Chicken and Beef Bowl
  1001 W. Whittier Blvd., 213/721-6426

Best Italian Food
Salvatore Pizza and Italian Restaurant
  125 N. Sixth St., 213/727-2803

Best Mexican Food
Ordonez Mexican Restaurant and Cantina
  872 N. Garfield Ave., 213/724-6383

Best Restaurant in Town
Quiet Cannon
  901 Via San Clemente, 213/724-9284

Best Steaks
Steven's Steak House
  5332 Stevens Pl., Commerce, 213/723-9856

MONTEREY, CA

Best Beer Selection
London Bridge Pub
  Fisherman's Wharf, Ste. 2, 408/655-2879
Mucky Duck
  479 Alvarado St., 408/655-3031

Best Breakfast
The Breakfast Club
  1130 Fremont Blvd., Ste. 201, Seaside,
    408/394-3238

Best Burgers
Del Monte Express
  2329 Fremont St., 408/394-5434
Duffy's Tavern
  282 High St., 408/372-2565

Best Chinese Food
Chef Lee's
  2031 Fremont St., 408/375-9551

Best Coffee/Coffeehouse
Morgan's Coffeehouse
  498 Washington St., 408/373-5601

Best Eclectic Menu
Roy's at Pebble Beach
  2700 Seventeen Mile Dr., Pebble Beach,
    408/647-7423

Best Inexpensive Meal
Papa Chano's
  462 Alvarado St., 408/646-9587

C

Best Italian Food
Tutto Buono
    469 Alvarado St., 408/372-1880

Best Restaurant in Town
Fresh Cream
    99 Pacific St., Ste. 100C, 408/375-9798
Sardine Factory
    701 Wave St., 408/373-3775

Best Restaurant Meal Value
London Bridge Pub
    Fisherman's Wharf, Ste. 2, 408/655-2879

Best Romantic Dining
Wente Brothers Vineyards
    37990 Elm Ave., Greenfield, 408/674-5642

Best Sandwiches
Bagel Bakery
    201 Lighthouse Ave., 408/649-1714

Best Seafood
Fishwife
    789 Trinity Ave., Seaside, 408/394-2027

Best Sports Bar
Characters
    350 Calle Principal, 408/647-4023

Best Steaks
Whaling Station
    763 Wave St., 408/373-3778

Best Vietnamese Food
Thuy Duong
    1104 Broadway Ave., Seaside, 408/393-9338

Best Wine Selection
Sardine Factory
    701 Wave St., 408/373-3775

MORENO VALLEY, CA

Best American Food
Mrs. Knott's Restaurant
    12625T Frederick St., 909/697-4480
New York Deli and Catering
    12190 Perris Blvd., 909/924-4910

Best Japanese Food
Matsuri Japanese Restaurant
    25100E Alessandro Blvd., 909/247-0767

Best Other Ethnic Food
Banig Restaurant (Filipino)
    23962F Alessandro Blvd., 909/653-5268
Nipa Hut (Filipino)
    14420 Elsworth St., 909/653-1729

Best Thai Food
Pattaya Palace
    24050 Alessandro Blvd, Ste. 8, 909/242-3189
River Kwai Thai Cuisine
    22920 Alessandro Blvd., 909/656-3355

C

MOUNTAIN VIEW, CA

Best Beer Selection
Tied House Cafe and Brewery
  954 Villa St., 650/965-2739

Best Breakfast
Hobee's
  2312 Central Expressway at Rengstorff,
    650/968-6050

Best Brewpub
Tied House Cafe and Brewery
  954 Villa St., 650/965-2739

Best Indian Food
Amber India
  2290 W. El Camino Real, 650/968-7511

Best Sunday Brunch
Hobee's
  2312 Central Expressway at Rengstorff,
    650/968-6050

Best Vietnamese Food
Pho Hoa Restaurant
  220 Castro St., 650/969-5805

NAPA, CA

Best Breakfast
Old Adobe Restaurant
  376 Soscol Ave., 707/255-4310

Best Burgers
Geezer's Grill and Bar
  829 Main St., 707/224-4322
Nation's Hamburgers
  1441 Third St., 707/252-8500

Best Chinese Food
Asia Cafe
  825 Main St., 707/224-0840

Best Coffee/Coffeehouse
Napa Valley Coffee Roasting Company
  948 Main St., 707/224-2233

Best Desserts
Marie Callender's
  1990 Trower Ave., 707/253-7754

Best Eclectic Menu
French Laundry Restaurant
  6640 Washington St., Yountville, 707/944-2380

Best French Food
Chanterelle Restaurant
  804 First St., 707/253-7300
Domaine Chandon
  1 California Dr., Yountville, 707/944-2892
La Boucane
  1778 Second St., 707/253-1177
Trilogy
  1234 Main St., St. Helena, 707/963-5507

Best Ice Cream/Yogurt
Swensen's Ice Cream
  3138 Jefferson St., 707/252-3212

Best Italian Food
Pietro's Pizza Restaurant
  999 Trancas St., 707/252-1033
Tra Vigne Restaurant
  1050 Charter Oak Ave., St. Helena, 707/963-4444

Best Mexican Food
Red Hen Cantina
  5091 Saint Helena Hwy., 707/255-8125

Best Regional Food
Mustards Grill
  7399 Saint Helena Hwy., 707/944-2424

Best Restaurant in Town
Mustard's Grill
  7399 Saint Helena Hwy., 707/944-2424

Best Seafood
Penguin's
  1533 Trancas St., 707/252-4343

NEWPORT BEACH, CA

Best Breakfast
Haute Cakes
  1807 Westcliff Dr., 714/642-4114

Best Chinese Food
China Palace
  2899 W. Coast Hwy., 714/631-8031

Best Coffee/Coffeehouse
Starbucks Coffee
  1128 Irvine Ave., 714/650-0369

Best Continental Food
The Ritz Restaurant and Garden
  880 Newport Center Dr., 714/720-1800

Best Desserts
The Cheesecake Factory
  Fashion Island, 1141 Newport Center Dr.,
    714/720-8333

Best French Food
Pascal
  1000 N. Bristol St., 714/752-0107

Best Mexican Food
El Torito Grill
  Fashion Island, 951 Newport Center Dr.,
    714/640-2875

Best Pizza
California Pizza Kitchen
  Fashion Island, 1151 Newport Center Dr.,
    714/759-5543

Best Place To Be "Seen"
Tutto Mare
  Fashion Island, 545 Newport Center Dr.,
    714/640-6333

C

Best Salad/Salad Bar
Farmer's Market
  Fashion Island, 401 Newport Center. Dr.,
    714/760-0403

Best Seafood
Crab Cooker
  2200 Newport Blvd., 714/673-0100

OAKLAND, CA

[See also: Berkeley, San Leandro, and San Francisco.]

Best American Food
Mama's Royal Cafe
  4012 Broadway, 510/547-7600

Best Barbecue/Ribs
Doug's Barbecue
  1048 36th St., Emeryville, 510/655-9048

Best Burgers
Barney's Gourmet Hamburger
  4162 Piedmont Ave., 510/655-7180
  5819 College Ave., 510/601-0444

Best Chinese Food
Hong Kong East Ocean
  3199 Powell St., Emeryville, 510/655-3388
King Yen
  4080 Piedmont Ave., 510/652-9678

Best Coffee/Coffeehouse
Peet's Coffee and Tea
  2066 Antioch Court, 510/339-6704
  4050 Piedmont Ave., 510/655-3228
  3258 Lakeshore Ave., 510/832-6761

Best Delicatessen
Genova Delicatessen and Ravioli Factory
  5095A Telegraph Ave., 510/652-7401
Ultra Lucca Delicatessen
  4001A Piedmont Ave., 510/547-7222
  6119 La Salle Ave., 510/339-9716

Best Desserts
Just Desserts
  4001B Piedmont Ave., 510/601-7780

Best Greek/Mediterranean Food
Bay Wolf Restaurant
  3853 Piedmont Ave., 510/655-6004

Best Inexpensive Meal
Economy Restaurant
  399 Eighth St., 510/832-9886

Best Italian Food
Oliveto
  5655 College Ave., 510/547-5356

Best Korean Food
Koryo Wooden Charcoal Restaurant
  4390 Telegraph Ave., 510/652-6007

Best Lunch
Cafe Cheneville
  499 Ninth St., 510/893-5439
Soizic Restaurant
  300 Broadway, 510/521-8100

Best Mexican Food
Cactus Taqueria
  5525 College Ave., 510/547-1305

Best Old Favorite Restaurant
Citron Restaurant
  5484 College Ave., 510/653-5484

Best Other Ethnic Food
Asmara (African)
  5020 Telegraph Ave., 510/547-5100
Red Sea Restaurant (African)
  5200 Claremont Ave., 510/655-3757

Best Pizza
Zachary's Chicago Pizza
  5801 College Ave., 510/655-6385

Best Restaurant in Town
Bay Wolf Restaurant
  3852 Piedmont Ave., 510/655-6004
Citron Restaurant
  5484 College Ave., 510/653-5484

Best Romantic Dining
Bay Wolf Restaurant
  3852 Piedmont Ave., 510/655-6004

Best Seafood
Scott's Seafood Grill and Bar
  2 Broadway, 510/444-3456

Best Sushi
Tachibana
  5812 College Ave., 510/654-3668

Best Vietnamese Food
Le Cheval
  1007 Clay St., 510/763-8495
  344 Twentieth St., 510/763-3610
Pho 84
  354 Seventeenth St., 510/832-1338
  416 Thirteenth St., 510/832-1499

OCEANSIDE, CA

Best Chinese Food
Chin's Szechwan Restaurant
  4140 Oceanside Blvd., 760/631-4808

Best Coffee/Coffeehouse
Hill Street Coffee House
  524 S. Coast Hwy., 760/966-0985

Best Desserts
Carrow's Restaurant
  936 N. Hill St., 760/722-9435

C

Best Family Restaurant
Spoons California Grill
  2725 Vista Way, 760/757-7070

Best Greek/Mediterranean Food
Mykonos Greek and Seafood Restaurant
  258 Harbor Dr. S., 760/757-8757

Best Health-Conscious Menu
Secret Garden
  Fire Mountain Shopping Ctr., 2530 W. Vista Way,
    760/722-3870

Best Japanese Food
Kurando Restaurant
  3815 Mission Ave., 760/754-9343

Best Mexican Food
Roberto's Taco Shop
  1209 S. Hill St., 760/757-2377
Rockin' Baja Lobster
  264 Harbor Dr. S., 760/754-2252

Best Southwestern Food
Spoons California Grill
  2725 Vista Way, 760/757-7070

Best View While Dining
Chart House
  314 Harbor Dr. S., 760/722-1345

ONTARIO, CA

*[See also: Corona, Pomona, Rancho Cucamonga,
Riverside, San Bernardino, and Upland.]*

Best Breakfast
Molly's Cafe
  230 N. Euclid Ave., 909/391-6907

Best Chinese Food
Panda Inn Chinese Restaurant
  3223 Centre Lake Dr., 909/983-2888
Yangtze Restaurant
  126 N. Euclid Ave., 909/986-8941

Best Continental Food
Calla Restaurant
  Ontario Hilton, 700 N. Haven Ave., 909/980-0400

Best Desserts
Coco's Restaurant
  2322 S. Mountain Ave., 909/984-3930

Best Fine Dining
Cask and Cleaver
  12206 Central Ave., Chino, 909/627-6011
Rosa's Restaurant
  425 N. Vineyard Ave., 909/391-1971

Best French Food
La Cheminee Restaurant
1133 W. Sixth St., 909/983-7900

Best Italian Food
Vince's Spaghetti
1206 W. Holt Blvd., 909/986-7074

Best Mexican Food
Juan Pollo
1702 S. Euclid Ave., 909/988-4888
Zendejas Mexican Restaurant
2411 S. Vineyard Ave., 909/947-1400

Best Restaurant in Town
La Cheminee Restaurant
1133 W. Sixth St., 909/983-7900

Best Seafood
Misty's Restaurant and Lounge
Red Lion Inn, 222 N. Vineyard Ave., 909/983-0909

Best Steaks
Black Angus Restaurant
3640 Porsche Way, 909/944-6882
Misty's Restaurant and Lounge
Red Lion Inn, 222 N. Vineyard Ave., 909/983-0909

Best Sunday Brunch
El Torito Restaurant
3680 Inland Empire Blvd., 909/944-9102
Marie Callender's
2149 E. Convention Center Way, 909/973-0214

Best Sushi
New Peking
816 N. Euclid Ave., 909/983-6939
Tokyo Kitchen
8851 Central Ave., Montclair, 909/625-5588

ORANGE, CA

[See also: Anaheim, Corona, Costa Mesa, Garden Grove, Irvine, Los Angeles, and Santa Ana.]

Best Italian Food
Raffaello Ristorante
1998 N. Tustin St., 714/283-8230

OXNARD, CA

Best American Food
Marie Callender's
1600 Ives Ave., 805/487-7437

Best Breakfast
Coco's Restaurant
150 W. Vineyard Ave., 805/485-4779
Mrs. Olsen's Coffee Hut
117 Los Altos St., 805/985-9151

C

Best Chinese Food
China Square Restaurant
141 W. Gonzales Rd., 805/988-1922
Lao's Garden
2655 N. Ventura Rd., Port Hueneme, 805/382-8106

Best Coffee/Coffeehouse
Starbucks Coffee
587 W. Channel Islands Blvd., Port Hueneme,
805/984-1172

Best Family Restaurant
Uncle Herb's Restaurant
5141 Saviers Rd., 805/488-5515

Best Fine Dining
Kona Ranch House
2800 Harbor Blvd., 805/985-5723

Best Greek/Mediterranean Food
Greek
2343 N. Oxnard Blvd., 805/981-1891

Best Health-Conscious Menu
Sano Cafe
301 E. Hueneme Rd., 805/488-4844

Best Indian Food
Yasmeen's
2311 N. Oxnard Blvd., 805/485-3804

Best Italian Food
Armando's Italian Restaurant
641 S. Ventura Rd., 805/984-4500
Mariann's Italian Villa
301 W. Channel Islands Blvd., Port Hueneme,
805/985-8663

Best Japanese Food
Hiro Sushi
804 Wagon Wheel Rd., 805/485-9898

Best Mexican Food
Montezuma Restaurant
112 E. Stroube St., 805/983-0033
Sal's Mexican Inn
1450 S. Oxnard Blvd., 805/483-9015

Best Romantic Dining
Cielito Lindo Cafe
637 S. Oxnard Blvd., 805/483-3131

Best Seafood
Whale's Tail
3950 Blue Fin Circle, 805/985-2511

PACIFIC GROVE, CA

Best Bistro
Taste Cafe and Bistro
1199 Forest Ave, 408/655-0324

Best Breakfast
First Awakenings
125 Ocean View Blvd., 408/372-1125

Best Coffee/Coffeehouse
Pacific Grove Coffee Roasting Company
510 Lighthouse Ave., 408/655-5633

Best Italian Food
Pasta Mia
481 Lighthouse Ave., 408/375-7709
Vito's
1180A Forest Ave., 408/375-3070

Best Mexican Food
Peppers Mexicali Cafe
170 Forest Ave., 408/373-6892

Best Pizza
Allegro Gourmet Pizzeria
1184 Forest Ave., 408/373-5656

Best Regional Food
Vivolo's Chowder House
127 Central Ave., 408/372-5414

Best Romantic Dining
The Old Bath House
620 Ocean View Blvd., 408/375-5195

Best Seafood
Fishwife Seafood Restaurant
1996 1/2 Sunset Dr., 408/375-7107

Best Thai Food
Thai Bistro
159 Central Ave., 408/372-8700

Best Vegetarian Food
Tillie Gort's Cafe
111 Central Ave., 408/373-0335

PACIFICA, CA

[See also: San Francisco and San Mateo.]

Best Chinese Food
Tam's
494 Manor Plaza, 650/359-7575

Best Japanese Food
Kani-Kosen
580 Crespi Dr., 650/355-1281

Best Restaurant in Town
Nick's Rockaway
100 Rockaway Beach Ave., 650/359-3900

Best Sunday Brunch
The Moonraker
105 Rockaway Beach Ave., 650/359-0303

PALM DESERT, CA

Best American Food
Biga, The California Grill
4394 Hwy. 111, Rancho Mirage, 760/324-4535

Kaiser Grill
8689 U.S. Hwy. 111, 760/779-1988

Best Bar
Gila Bar and Grill
74950 Country Club Dr., 760/346-4452

Best Beer Selection
Beer Hunter
8043 U.S. Hwy. 111, 760/340-4222

Best Bistro
Palomino Euro-Bistro
7565 U.S. Hwy. 111, 760/773-9091

Best Burgers
Hamburger Hamlet
7304 U.S. Hwy. 111, 760/341-4335

Best Chinese Food
Chen Ling
4604 Hwy. 111, Rancho Mirage, 760/770-0788
China Jo's
73091 Country Club Dr., 760/340-4172
Dragon Gate
44491 Town Center Way, 760/341-6588
Panda Express
36101 Bob Hope Dr., Rancho Mirage, 714/459-0978
Tsing Tao Chinese Cuisine
8504 U.S. Hwy. 111, 760/779-9593

Best Continental Food
Doug Arango's
7984 El Paseo, 760/341-4120
Players Fine Dining
84-245 Indio Springs Dr., Indio, 760/342-5000

Best Delicatessen
Backstreet Deli and Pub
7159 U.S. Hwy. 111, Ste. 7, 760/341-7966

Best Diner
Heavenly Diner
77682 Country Club Dr., 760/772-2047

Best French Food
Cuistot Restaurant
73111 El Paseo, 760/340-1000
Le Paon Restaurant
45640 Hwy. 74, a760/568-3651

Best Homestyle Food
Keedy's Fountain Grill
8097 U.S. Hwy. 111, 760/346-6492
Louise's Pantry
44491 Town Center Way, 760/346-1315

Best Ice Cream/Yogurt
Big Scoop Yogurt and Ice Cream
73131 Country Club Dr., 760/341-3104
Goldmine Yogurt
42414 Bob Hope Dr., Rancho Mirage, 760/568-5540

C

Best Italian Food
Andreino's King of Fettucine
  7562 U.S. Hwy. 111, 760/773-3365
Cafe Valentino
  73375 El Paseo, 760/776-7535
Mama Gina's Restaurant
  73705 El Paseo, 760/568-9898
Tuscany's Ristorante
  74855 Country Club Dr., 760/341-2211

Best Japanese Food
Midori Japanese Restaurant
  74880 Country Club Dr., 760/340-1466

Best Mexican Food
Casuela's Cafe
  8167 U.S. Hwy. 111, 760/568-0011

Best Outdoor Dining
Las Casuelas Nuevas
  4514 Hwy. 111, Rancho Mirage, 760/328-8844

Best Sandwiches
That Sandwich Place
  9332A Joni Dr., Ste. 1, 760/340-5882
Windy City Sandwich Company
  75110 Saint Charles Pl., 760/773-0400

Best Seafood
Captain Cook's Sea Grill
  6655 U.S. Hwy. 111, 760/341-8333

Best Steaks
LG's Steakhouse
  8689 U.S. Hwy. 111, 760/779-9799
Morton's of Chicago
  74880 Country Club Dr., 760/340-6885

PALM SPRINGS, CA

Best Chinese Food
Chen Ling Garden
  787 N. Palm Canyon Dr., 760/322-0039
Flower Drum Restaurant
  424 S. Indian Canyon Dr., 760/323-3020

Best Continental Food
Blue Coyote Grill
  445 N. Palm Canyon Dr., 760/327-1196

Best Delicatessen
The Gaiety
  448 S. Indian Canyon Dr., 760/323-5691

Best Greek/Mediterranean Food
Mykonos Greek Restaurant
  139 E. Andreas Rd., 760/322-0223

Best Homestyle Food
Louise's Pantry
  124 S. Palm Canyon Dr., 760/325-5124
Vern's Place
  590 S. Vella Rd., 760/325-3514

C

Best Ice Cream/Yogurt
Palm Springs Penguin's
333 N. Palm Canyon Dr., Ste. 102, 760/327-6455

Best Indian Food
Delhi Palace Cuisine of India
1422 N. Palm Canyon Dr., 760/325-3411

Best Italian Food
Trilussa
123 N. Palm Canyon Dr., 760/323-4255

Best Outdoor Dining
Cedar Creek Inn
1555 S. Palm Canyon Dr., 760/325-7300

Best Restaurant in Town
El Mirasol Regional Cuisines
140 E. Palm Canyon Dr., 760/323-0721
La Provence
254 N. Palm Canyon Dr., 760/416-4418

PALMDALE, CA

Best Breakfast
Karen's Kitchen
840 W. Palmdale Blvd., 805/947-0550
1003 E. Palmdale Blvd., 805/947-1920

Best Burgers
Pete's Burgers
2330 E. Palmdale Blvd., 805/266-0353

Best Chinese Food
Lucky Garden Chinese Restaurant
2542 E. Palmdale Blvd., 805/273-7892

Best Coffee/Coffeehouse
Westerfield's Coffee Shop
300 W. Palmdale Blvd., 805/273-1200

Best Inexpensive Meal
El Pollo Loco
2221 E. Palmdale Blvd., 805/265-1615

Best Italian Food
Eduardo's Italian Restaurant
819 W. Palmdale Blvd., 805/273-0955

Best Late-Night Food
Pete's Burgers
2330 E. Palmdale Blvd., 805/266-0353

Best Mexican Food
El Toreo East
3025 E. Avenue S, 805/266-8496

Best Pizza
Cafe Fresco
42010 N. 50th St. W., Lancaster, 805/722-5555
Round Table Pizza
1823K E. Palmdale Blvd., 805/947-8944

Best Romantic Dining
Forty-Niner Saloon
31908 Crown Valley Rd., Acton, 805/269-1360

C

Best Seafood
Forty-Niner Saloon
  31908 Crown Valley Rd., Acton, 805/269-1360

Best Steaks
Forty-Niner Saloon
  31908 Crown Valley Rd., Acton, 805/269-1360

PALO ALTO, CA

[See also: Redwood City, San Jose, and Sunnyvale.]

Best Bar
Blue Chalk Cafe
  630 Ramona St., 650/326-1020
Los Altos Bar and Grille
  169 Main St., Los Altos, 650/948-4332

Best Breakfast
Hobee's
  67 Town and Country Village, 650/327-4111
  4224 El Camino Real, 650/856-6124
Mike's
  2680 Middlefield Rd., 650/473-6453

Best Desserts
Max's Opera Cafe
  711 Stanford Shopping Ctr., 650/323-6297

Best French Food
L 'Amie Donia
  530 Bryant St., 650/323-7614

Best Health-Conscious Menu
Fresh Choice
  379 Stanford Shopping Ctr., 650/322-6995
Good Earth Restaurant and Bakery
  185 University Ave., 650/321-9449

Best Ice Cream/Yogurt
Double Rainbow Gourmet Ice Cream
  520 Ramona St., 650/321-7466

Best Italian Food
Piatti's
  2 Stanford Shopping Ctr., 650/324-9733

Best Japanese Food
Miyake Restaurant
  140 University Ave., 650/323-9449

Best Pizza
Murphy's Pizza Take and Bake
  2730 Middlefield Rd., 650/328-5200

Best Regional Food
Star's
  265 Lytton Ave., 650/321-4466

Best Salad/Salad Bar
Fresh Choice
  379 Stanford Shopping Ctr., 650/322-6995

Best Sandwiches
Simply Sandwiches
   2435 Ash St., 650/329-1266

Best Seafood
Fish Market Restaurant
   3150 El Camino Real, 650/493-9188
Scott's Seafood Grill and Bar
   2300 E. Bayshore Rd., 650/856-1046

Best Sunday Brunch
Mike's Cafe
   2680 Middlefield Rd., 650/473-6453

Best Thai Food
Bangkok Cuisine
   407 Lytton Ave., 650/322-6533

Best Vegetarian Food
Good Earth Restaurant and Bakery
   185 University Ave., 650/321-9449

PASADENA, CA

[See also: Beverly Hills, Burbank, Glendale, Los Angeles, and Montebello.]

Best Bar
Barney's Limited
   93 W. Colorado Blvd., 626/577-2739

Best Breakfast
Marston's Restaurant
   151 E. Walnut St., 626/796-2459

Best Brewpub
Crown City Brewery
   300 S. Raymond Ave., 626/577-5548
Gordon Biersch Brewery Restaurant
   1 Colorado Courtyard, 626/449-0052

Best Burgers
Burger Continental
   535 S. Lake Ave., 626/792-6634
Crocodile Cafe
   140 S. Lake Ave., 626/449-9900
Wolfe Burgers
   46 N. Lake Ave., 626/792-7292

Best Casual Dining
Dodsworth Bar and Grill
   2 W. Colorado Blvd., 626/578-1344

Best Chinese Food
Grandview Palace
   590 S. Fair Oaks Ave., 626/449-0348
Panda Inn Restaurant
   3488 E. Foothill Blvd., 626/793-7300

Best Coffee/Coffeehouse
Il Fornaio
   24 W. Union St., 626/683-8585

Best Continental Food
Raymond Restaurant
1250 S. Fair Oaks Ave., 626/441-3136

Best French Food
D'Lyon
713 E. Green St., 626/796-9501
Xiomara
69 N. Raymond Ave., 818/796-2520

Best Homestyle Food
Marston's Restaurant
151 E. Walnut St., 626/796-2459

Best Ice Cream/Yogurt
Fair Oaks Pharmacy and Soda Fountain
1526 Mission St., South Pasadena, 626/799-1414
Golden Spoon Frozen Yogurt
1103 Fair Oaks Ave., South Pasadena,
626/799-0643

Best Inexpensive Meal
Tarantino's Pizza
784 E. Green St., 626/796-7836

Best Italian Food
Mi Piace Italian Kitchen
25 E. Colorado Blvd., 626/795-3131

Best Mexican Food
Acapulco Mexican Restaurant
2936 E. Colorado Blvd., 626/795-4248
2060 E. Foothill Blvd., 626/449-7273
Margarita's Mexican Food
155 S. Rosemead Blvd., 626/449-4193
Super Antojitos Mexicanos
40 N. Mentor Ave., 626/449-4071

Best Other Ethnic Food
Barney's Limited (British Isles)
93 W. Colorado Blvd., 626/577-2739
El Emperador Maya (Yucatan)
1823 S. San Gabriel Blvd., San Gabriel,
626/288-7265
Kuala Lumpur (Malaysian)
69 W. Green St., 626/577-5175
Merida Restaurant (Yucatan)
20 E. Colorado Blvd., 626/792-7371
Rose Tree Cottage (British Isles)
828 E. California Blvd., 626/793-3337

Best Pizza
Tarantino's Pizza
784 E. Green St., 626/796-7836

Best Restaurant in Town
Parkway Grill
510 S. Arroyo Pkwy., 626/795-1001
Sesame Grill
308 E. Huntington Dr., Arcadia, 626/821-0880
Yujean Kang's Gourmet Chinese Cuisine
67 N. Raymond Ave., 626/585-0855

C

C

Best Restaurant Meal Value
Out Take Cafe
  1065 E. Green St., 626/449-4519

Best Salad/Salad Bar
Kathleen's Restaurant
  595 N. Lake Ave., 626/578-0722

Best Sandwiches
Crown City Brewery
  300 S. Raymond Ave., 626/577-5548

Best Seafood
Cameron's Seafood Market
  1978 E. Colorado Blvd., 626/793-3474
McCormick and Schmick's
  111 N. Los Robles Ave., 626/405-0064

Best Steaks
Beckham Place
  77 W. Walnut St., 626/796-3399
Dodsworth Bar and Grill
  2 W. Colorado Blvd., 626/578-1344

Best Thai Food
Tommy Tang's
  24 W. Colorado Blvd., 626/792-9700

Best Vegetarian Food
Good Earth Restaurant
  257 N. Rosemead Blvd., 626/351-5488

PETALUMA, CA

Best Barbecue/Ribs
Jerome's Mesquite Barbeque
  1390 N. McDowell Blvd., 707/795-2114

Best Breakfast
Marvin's Restaurant
  317 Petaluma Blvd. S., 707/765-2808

Best Brewpub
Dempsey's Ale House
  50 E. Washington St., 707/765-9694

Best Burgers
Mike's at The Yard
  84 Corona Rd., 707/769-1082

Best Chinese Food
Canton
  951 Lakeville St., 707/762-7201

Best Coffee/Coffeehouse
Copperfield's Books
  140 Kentucky St., 707/762-0563
Deaf Dog Coffee
  351 S. McDowell Blvd., 707/763-8111

Best Homestyle Food
Tivoli
  219 Lakeville St., 707/762-9927

Best Italian Food
Buona Sera
  148 Kentucky St., 707/763-3333

Giacomo's Ristorante
  2000 Lakeville Hwy., 707/765-1700
Graziano's
  170 Petaluma Blvd. N., 707/762-5997
Volpi's
  122 Washington St., 707/765-0695

Best Middle Eastern Food
Aram's Cafe
  122 Kentucky St., 707/765-9775

Best Pizza
Old Chicago Pizza
  41 Petaluma Blvd. N., 707/763-3897

Best Wine Selection
De Schmire Restaurant
  304 Bodega Ave., 707/762-1901
The Twisted Vine
  16 Kentucky St., 707/766-8162

PISMO BEACH, CA

Best 24-Hour Restaurant
Fat Cats
  480 Front St., Avila Beach, 805/595-2204

Best Burgers
Garland's Hamburgers
  1090 Price St., 805/773-3376

Best Ice Cream/Yogurt
Burnardo'z Candy and Ice Cream
  750 Grand Ave., Grover Beach, 805/481-7784

Best Italian Food
Giuseppe's Italian Restaurant
  891 Price St., 805/773-2873
Rosa's Italian Restaurant
  491 Price St., 805/773-0551

Best Outdoor Dining
The Old Custom House
  324 Front St., Avila Beach, 805/595-7555

Best Seafood
Olde Port Inn Restaurant
  Port San Luis, Pier 3, Avila Beach, 805/595-2515

Best Sunday Brunch
Sea Venture
  100 Ocean View Ave., 805/773-3463
The Old Custom House
  324 Front St., Avila Beach, 805/595-7555

Best Wine Selection
Rosa's Italian Restaurant
  491 Price St., 805/773-0551

C

PLEASANTON, CA

[See also: Fremont and Hayward.]

Best Seafood
Hayward Fishery Restaurant
  7400 San Ramon Rd., Dublin, 925/828-8882

POMONA, CA

[See also: Los Angeles, Ontario, Rancho Cucamonga, West Covina, and Whittier.]

Best Desserts
Coco's Restaurant
  309 E. Foothill Blvd., 909/596-5909

Best Italian Food
Rillo's Restaurant
  510 E. Foothill Blvd., 909/621-4954

Best Pizza
Warehouse Pizza
  2340 D St., La Verne, 909/593-2714

PORTERVILLE, CA

Best American Food
Palace Restaurant
  Palace Hotel, 22 E. Oak Ave., 209/784-7086

Best Barbecue/Ribs
Oak Pit
  615 N. Main St., 209/781-7427

Best Breakfast
Green Valley Cafe
  450 W. Olive Ave., 209/783-0747

Best Ice Cream/Yogurt
Ginger's Corner Store
  1170 W. Henderson Ave., 209/784-6386

Best Inexpensive Meal
Cellar
  244 1/2 N. Main St., 209/784-4235

Best Italian Food
Rosa's Italian Restaurant
  949 W. Henderson Ave., 209/781-6423

Best Mexican Food
El Nuevo Mexicali
  370 N. Main St., 209/781-1742
El Tapatillo Restaurant
  134 E. Orange Ave., 209/781-2115
Mission Restaurant
  247 N. Main St., 209/781-8814

Best Pizza
Poor Richard's Pizza
  205 N. Main St., 209/784-4410

Best Salad/Salad Bar
Palace Restaurant
  Palace Hotel, 22 E. Oak Ave., 209/784-7086

Best Seafood
Fish Net
  210 N. Main St., 209/784-2226

C

RANCHO CUCAMONGA, CA

[See also: Corona, Pomona, Riverside, San Bernardino, and Upland.]

Best American Food
Magic Lamp Inn
  8189 Foothill Blvd., 909/981-8659

Best Barbecue/Ribs
Chuck's Diner
  8890 Eighth St., 909/982-5119
The Pit
  8661 Baseline Rd., 909/948-5252

Best Burgers
Final Score
  8411 Foothill Blvd., 909/985-4515
The Deli
  9671 Foothill Blvd., 909/989-8122

Best Business Lunch
Cask and Cleaver
  8689 Ninth St., 909/982-7108

Best Coffee/Coffeehouse
Coffee Klatch
  8916 Foothill Blvd., 909/944-5282
Rose's Caffe Luna
  8038 Haven Ave., 909/941-9822

Best Continental Food
Magic Lamp Inn
  8189 Foothill Blvd., 909/981-8659
Sycamore Inn
  8318 Foothill Blvd., 909/982-1104

Best Delicatessen
Deli
  9671 Foothill Blvd., 909/981-8122
Togo's Eatery
  7900 Haven Ave., 909/944-7888

Best Desserts
Claim Jumper Restaurant
  12499 Foothill Blvd., 909/899-8022

Best Family Restaurant
Vince's Spaghetti
  8241 Foothill Blvd., 909/981-1003

Best Italian Food
Cafe Calato
  9640 Center Ave., Ste. 150, 909/948-3671

Vince's Spaghetti
8241 Foothill Blvd., 909/981-1003

Best Mexican Food
El Kiosco Restaurant
916 S. Riverside Ave., Rialto, 909/820-0198
Zendejas Mexican Restaurant
7945 Vineyard Ave., 909/466-0633

Best Pizza
Brooklyn Deli Pizza Restaurant
8403 Haven Ave., 909/945-3557
Cafe Calato
9640 Center Ave., Ste. 150, 909/948-3671
Final Score
8411 Foothill Blvd., 909/985-4515
Sal's Pizza
6622 Carnelian St., Alta Loma, 909/989-5547

Best Salad/Salad Bar
Cask and Cleaver
8689 Ninth St., 909/982-7108
Souplantation
8966 Foothill Blvd., 909/980-9690

Best Sandwiches
Deli
9671 Foothill Blvd., 909/981-8122

Best Steaks
Magic Lamp Inn
8189 Foothill Blvd., 909/981-8659
Steer and Stein of Cucamonga
8348 Archibald Ave., 909/987-4447

Best Sushi
Ken's Japanese Restaurant
10006 Foothill Blvd., 909/989-3019

REDDING, CA

Best American Food
Grady's Steak and Seafood House
1100 Center St., 530/241-3624
Jack's Grill
1743 California St., 530/241-9705

Best Chinese Food
Peter Chu's Skyroom
6751 Woodrum Circle, 530/222-1364

Best Coffee/Coffeehouse
Serendipity
236 Hartnell Ave., 530/223-4497
167 Lake Blvd., 530/244-3780

Best Fine Dining
Hatch Cover Restaurant
202 Hemsted Dr., 530/223-5606

Best Mexican Food
Chevys Mexican Restaurant
1691 Hilltop Dr., 530/223-5797
Taco Shop
775 E. Cypress Ave., 530/222-8443

Best Other Ethnic Food
C.R. Gibbs Alehouse and Restaurant (British)
2300 Hilltop Dr., 530/221-2335

C

REDLANDS, CA

Best American Food
Clara's
101 E. Redlands Blvd., 909/335-1466
Greensleeves
220 Orange St., 909/792-6969

Best Breakfast
Bagel Peddler
1150 Brookside Ave., 909/792-1399

Best Continental Food
The Wild Rabbit
1502 Barton Rd., 909/793-2038
Umberto's
101 E. Redlands Blvd., 909/335-1466

Best French Food
Gigi et Jean French Restaurant
499 New York St., 909/793-3714

Best Middle Eastern Food
Caprice Cafe
104 E. State St., 909/793-8787

Best Seafood
Dillon's
1045 Parkford Dr., 909/793-2221

Best Steaks
Dillon's
1045 Parkford Dr., 909/793-2221

Best Thai Food
Rama Garden Restaurant
309 W. State St., 909/798-7747

REDONDO BEACH, CA

Best Barbecue/Ribs
Chicago Ribs
1410 S. Pacific Coast Hwy., 310/316-7427

Best Breakfast
Backburner Cafe
87 Fourteenth St., Hermosa Beach, 310/372-6973

Best Burgers
Fat Face Fenner's Falloon
837 Hermosa Ave., Hermosa Beach, 310/376-0996

Best Business Lunch
The Cheesecake Factory
605 N. Harbor Dr., 310/376-0466

Best Coffee/Coffeehouse
Java Man
157 Pier Ave., Hermosa Beach, 310/379-7209

Best Continental Food
Chez Melange
1718 S. Pacific Coast Hwy., 310/540-9135

C

Best Desserts
The Cheesecake Factory
  605 N. Harbor Dr., 310/376-0466

Best Health-Conscious Menu
Whole Foods Market and Cafe
  405 N. Pacific Coast Hwy., 310/376-6931

Best Indian Food
Clay Pit
  1815 Hawthorne Blvd., Third Fl., 310/214-0888

Best Inexpensive Meal
Good Stuff
  1286 The Strand, Hermosa Beach, 310/374-2334

Best Italian Food
Brogino's
  2423 Artesia Blvd., 310/370-4828

Best Mexican Food
Riviera Bar and Grill
  1615 S. Pacific Coast Hwy., 310/540-2501

Best Middle Eastern Food
Jerusalem Restaurant
  120 International Boardwalk, 310/372-4344

Best Pizza
Mama's Original Pizza and Pasta
  2205 Pacific Coast Hwy., Hermosa Beach,
    310/376-8486

Best Restaurant in Town
Chez Melange
  1718 S. Pacific Coast Hwy., 310/540-9135

Best Romantic Dining
Casablanca
  53 Pier Ave., Hermosa Beach, 310/379-4177

Best Seafood
Captain Kidd's
  209 N. Harbor Dr., 310/372-7703

Best Steaks
The Bull Pen
  314 Ave. I, 310/375-7797

Best Thai Food
Thai Thani
  1109 S. Pacific Coast Hwy., 310/375-7797

Best Vegetarian Food
Spot the Natural Food Restaurant
  110 Second St., Hermosa Beach, 310/376-2355

REDWOOD CITY, CA

[See also: San Mateo and Palo Alto.]

Best Burgers
Donovan's
  1450 Veterans Blvd., 650/361-9702

C

Best Business Lunch
Dal Baffo European Cuisine
878 Santa Cruz Ave., Menlo Park, 650/325-1588

Best Chinese Food
Speedy's Broasted Chicken
756 Woodside Rd., 650/369-3767

Best Family Restaurant
Fifth Quarter Pizza
976 Woodside Rd., 650/369-2686

Best French Food
Dante's on Woodside
1515 Woodside Rd., 650/363-0949

Best Italian Food
Lucia's
1725 Woodside Rd., 650/365-3812
Messina's Italian Restaurant
542 El Camino Real, San Carlos, 650/593-9116
Piacere Restaurant
727 Laurel St., San Carlos, 650/592-3536

Best Mexican Food
La Azteca
1531 Main St., 650/368-3486

Best Other Ethnic Food
Estampas Peruanas (Peruvian)
715 El Camino Real, 650/368-9340

Best Pizza
Round Table Pizza
128 Woodside Plz., 650/365-2770
1483 Broadway St., 650/365-7226

Best Place to Eat Alone
Happi House Restaurant
30 Woodside Plz., 650/368-3306

Best Sandwiches
Erik's Deli Cafe
400C Walnut St., 650/364-1717

Best Sports Bar
Sneakers Pub and Grill
1163 San Carlos Ave., San Carlos, 650/802-0177

RICHMOND, CA

[See also: Berkely, Oakland and San Rafael.]

Best Barbecue/Ribs
Ernie Foods Bar-B-Q
2401 MacDonald Ave., 510/237-2346

Best Breakfast
Baker's Square Restaurant
12323 San Pablo Ave., 510/232-6350

Best Coffee/Coffeehouse
Bear Claw Bakery
2340 San Pablo Ave., Pinole, 510/724-3105

C

Rosemary Bakery
101 Park Pl., 510/234-2384

Best Italian Food
Angelo's Poultry and Deli
12025 San Pablo Ave., 510/234-2485
Salute
1900 Esplanade Dr., 510/215-0803

Best Regional Food
Hidden City Cafe
109 Park Pl., 510/232-9738

Best Sandwiches
Angelo's Poultry and Deli
12025 San Pablo Ave., 510/234-2485

Best Seafood
Hotel Mac Restaurant
50 Washington Ave., 510/233-0576
Salute
1900 Esplanade Dr., 510/215-0803

Best Steaks
Hotel Mac Restaurant
50 Washington Ave., 510/233-0576

RIDGECREST, CA

Best Chinese Food
China Garden
206 S. China Lake Blvd., 760/375-3533

Best Coffee/Coffeehouse
Casa Java
972 N. Norma St., 760/446-9161

Best Mexican Food
La Fiesta Sandwiches and Things
119 N. China Lake Blvd., 760/375-5901
Santa Fe Grill
901 N. Heritage Dr., 760/446-5404

Best Sandwiches
Blimpie's
1028 N. Norma St., 760/446-6969

RIVERSIDE, CA

[See also: Corona, Ontario, Pomona, Rancho Cucamonga, San Bernardino, and Upland.]

Best American Food
Casual Elegance
26848 Hwy. 189, Blue Jay, 909/337-8932
Coachman Dinner House
1805 University Ave., 909/788-0310
Mission Inn
3649 Mission Inn Ave., 909/784-0300
Riverside Brewing Company
3397 Mission Inn Ave., 909/784-2739

Sire Bar and Grill
   10909 Magnolia Ave., 909/358-0570
Steer Grill
   2395 Hamner Ave., Norco, 909/734-5441
Terry's Kitchen
   2382 Third St., 909/788-8512

Best Bar
Frank's Bar and Grill
   3221 Iowa Ave., 909/788-7630

Best Barbecue/Ribs
Gram's Mission Barbecue Palace
   3646 Seventh St., 909/782-8219

Best Breakfast
La Cascada Mexican Restaurant
   6154 Magnolia Ave., 909/684-8614

Best Brewpub
Riverside Brewing Company
   3397 Mission Inn Ave., 909/784-2739

Best Burgers
Frank's Bar and Grill
   3221 Iowa Ave., 909/788-7630

Best Cajun/Creole Food
A Taste of New Orleans
   5225 Canyon Crest Dr., 909/788-1829
Crescent City Creole
   5250 Arlington Ave., 909/351-6934

Best Chinese Food
Dragon House
   10466 Magnolia Ave., 909/354-2080
Little Emperor
   5225 Canyon Crest Dr., 909/683-1073

Best Continental Food
Creola's Restaurant
   1015 E. Alessandro Blvd., 909/653-8150
   3221 Iowa Ave., 909/788-7630
Mario's Place
   1725 Spruce St., 909/684-7755

Best French Food
Gerard's French Restaurant
   9814 Magnolia Ave., 909/687-4882

Best Greek/Mediterranean Food
Grapeleaves
   4085 Vine St., 909/784-3033

Best Homestyle Food
Terry's Kitchen
   2382 Third St., 909/788-8512

Best Ice Cream/Yogurt
Golden Spoon Frozen Yogurt
   Galleria at Tyler, Ste. 1310, 909/352-8895

Best Indian Food
Bengal Kitchen
   3375 Iowa Ave., 909/784-3811

Bombay Restaurant
1725 University Ave., 909/788-4994

Best Italian Food
Frank's Bar and Grill
3221 Iowa Ave., 909/788-7630
Magnone Cucina
1630 Spruce St., 909/781-8840
Mario's Place
1725 Spruce St., 909/684-7755
Pietro's Italian Cucina
3812 Pierce St., 909/687-9980

Best Japanese Food
Akina Sushi-Teppan Restaurant
195 E. Alessandro Blvd., 909/789-2621

Best Mexican Food
El Toro
6611 Arlington Ave., 909/359-0999
El Trigo Tortilleria Y Comida
4155 Park Ave., 909/787-6937
La Cascada Mexican Restaurant
6154 Magnolia Ave., 909/684-8614
Rubio's Cocina Mexicana
6749 Brockton Ave., 909/683-9537
Templo del Sol
1365 University Ave., 909/682-6562
Zacatecas Cafe
2472 University Ave., 909/683-3939

Best Middle Eastern Food
Grapeleaves
4085 Vine St., 909/784-3033
Kebob-It
365 Iowa Ave., 909/686-4904

Best Restaurant in Town
Akina Sushi-Teppan Restaurant
195 E. Alessandro Blvd., 909/789-2621

Best Seafood
La Cascada Mexican Restaurant
6154 Magnolia Ave., 909/684-8614
Market Broiler
6104B Riverside Ave., 909/682-9850
3525 Merrill Ave., 909/276-9007

Best Soul Food
Gram's Mission Barbecue Palace
3646 Seventh St., 909/782-8219

Best Sports Bar
Events Sports Grill
10560 Magnolia Ave., 909/352-2693

Best Steaks
Cask and Cleaver
1333 University Ave., 909/682-4580
Coachman Dinner House
1805 University Ave., 909/788-0310

C

Best Thai Food
Little Emperor
  5225 Canyon Crest Dr., 909-683-1073
Thai Ice Tea Restaurant
  7207 Arlington Ave., 909/687-2270

Best Vegetarian Food
Bengal Kitchen
  3375 Iowa Ave., 909/784-3811

Best Vietnamese Food
Pho Que Huong
  10051 Magnolia Ave., 909/352-9548

SACRAMENTO, CA

Best American Food
Morrison's Upstairs
  428 1/2 First St., Woodland, 530/666-6176

Best Barbecue/Ribs
Texas Bar-B-Que
  180 Otto Circle, 916/424-3520

Best Breakfast
Cafe Bernardo
  2726 Capitol Ave., 916/443-1180
Fox and Goose
  1001 R St., 916/443-8825
Lucky Cafe
  1111 21st St., 916/442-9620

Best Burgers
Ford's Real Hamburgers
  1948 Sutterville Rd., 916/452-6979
Willie's Burgers and Chiliburgers
  2415 Sixteenth St., 916/444-2006

Best Business Lunch
Delta King
  1000 Front St., 916/441-4440
Land Park Grill
  1517 Broadway, 916/552-2893
Paragary's Bar and Oven
  1401 28th St., 916/457-5737
  2384 Fair Oaks Blvd., 916/485-7100
  705 Goldlake Dr., Folsom, 916/457-5737

Best Chinese Food
Chinois City Cafe
  3535 Fair Oaks Blvd., 916/485-8690
Frank Fat's
  806 L St., 916/442-7092
Great Wall Mongolian Bar-B-Q
  1537 Howe Ave., 916/925-7813
  4314 Florin Rd., 916/427-8888
Hoi Sing Chinese Sea Food Restaurant
  7007 S. Land Park Dr., 916/392-9630
Luau Garden
  1890 Arden Way, 916/929-3690
Tea Cup Cafe
  1614 21st St., 916/448-6212

C

Best Coffee/Coffeehouse
Starbucks Coffee
508 Pavilions Ln., 916/485-6922
2100 Arden Way, Ste. 190, 916/485-6922
1 Adobe Ct., 916/485-6922
4301 Arden Way, 916/482-1205
1401 Alhambra Blvd., 916/452-1707

Best Delicatessen
Corti Brothers
5810 Folsom Blvd., 916/736-3800

Best Desserts
Caffe Ettore
2376 Fair Oaks Blvd., 916/482-0708
Leatherby's Family Creamery
2333A Arden Way, 916/920-8382
Rick's Dessert Diner
2322 K St., 916/444-0969

Best Diner
Artie's Star-Lite Fountain
3839 J St., 916/454-4555

Best Diners
Huey's Diner
2100 Arden Way, 916/929-1950

Best Fine Dining
Biba
2801 Capitol Ave., 916/455-2422
Firehouse
1112 Second St., 916/442-4772
Morton's of Chicago
521 L St., 916/442-5091

Best French Food
Aldo's Restaurant
2914 Pasatiempo Ln., 916/483-5031
La Boheme
1001 K St., 916/443-7336

Best Homestyle Food
Lucky Cafe
1111 21st St., 916/442-9620
Silva's Sheldon Inn
9000 Grant Line Rd., Elk Grove, 916/686-8330

Best Ice Cream/Yogurt
Leatherby's Family Creamery
2333A Arden Way, 916/920-8382

Best Inexpensive Meal
Pescado's
2801 P St., 916/452-7237
Squeeze Inn
7918 Fruitridge Rd., 916/386-8599
Taqueria Taco Loco
2326 J St., 916/447-0711

Best Italian Food
Amerigo
2000 Capitol Ave., 916/442-8119

Biba
2801 Capitol Ave., 916/455-2422
Old Spaghetti Factory
1910 J St., 916/443-2862
Pheasant Club
2525 Jefferson Blvd., West Sacramento,
916/371-9530
String's Italian Cafe
1620 W. El Camino Ave., 916/567-1111

Best Japanese Food
Fuji
2422 Thirteenth St., 916/446-4135
Hana Tsubaki
5006 J St., 916/456-2849

Best Mexican Food
El Charro
306 Sixth St., Woodland, 530/662-3804
El Novillero
4216 Franklin Blvd., 916/456-4287
El Torito Restaurant and Cantina
1212 Howe Ave., 916/924-1000
1598 Arden Way, 916/927-0071
Ernesto's Mexican Food
1901 Sixteenth St., 916/441-5850

Best Outdoor Dining
Jammin' Salmon
1801 Garden Hwy., 916/929-6232
The Pilothouse Restaurant
The Delta King, 1000 Front St., 916/441-4440
Tower International Cafe
1518 Broadway, 916/441-0222

Best Pizza
Paragary's Bar and Oven
1401 28th St., 916/457-5737
2384 Fair Oaks Blvd., 916/485-7100
705 Goldlake Dr., Folsom, 916/457-5737
Steve's Place Pizza
813 Howe Ave., 916/920-8600
4303 Arden Way, 916/487-5100
Zelda's Original Gourmet Pizza
1415 21st St., 916/447-1400

Best Restaurant in Town
Harlow's Bar and Restaurant
2708 J St., 916/441-4693
Lemon Grass Thai Cuisine
601 Munroe St., 916/486-4891
Paragary's Bar and Oven
2384 Fair Oaks Blvd., 916/485-7100
1401 28th St., 916/457-5737
Ristorante Piatti
569 Pavilions Ln., 916/649-8885

Best Romantic Dining
Aldo's Restaurant
2914 Pasatiempo Ln., 916/483-5031
2673 El Paseo Ln., 916/483-5031

Grand Island Mansion
  13415 Grand Island Rd., Wlnut Grove,
    916/775-1705
The Pilot House Restaurant
  The Delta King, 1000 Front St., 916/441-4440
John Q's
  300 J St., 916/446-0100
Mace's Restaurant
  501 Pavilions Ln., 916/922-0222

Best Salad
String's Italian Cafe
  1827 Broadway, 916/658-1950

Best Salad/Salad Bar
Eat Your Vegetables
  1841 Howe Ave., 916/922-8413
Fresh Choice
  535 Howe Ave., 916/649-8046
  1689 Arden Way, 916/649-3839

Best Seafood
The Pilothouse Restaurant
  The Delta King, 1000 Front St., 916/441-4440
Scott's Seafood Grill and Bar
  545 Munroe St., 916/489-1822
The Fish Restaurant
  2310 Fair Oaks Blvd., 916/927-3474

Best Steaks
Fulton's Prime Rib
  900 Second St., 916/444-9641
Morton's of Chicago
  521 L St., 916/442-5091
Stuart Anderson's Black Angus
  1625 Watt Ave., 916/973-1901
  6601 Florin Rd., 916/381-4900

Best Sunday Brunch
Ciao Yama
  Hyatt Regency Hotel, 1209 L St., 916/443-1234
The Coffee Garden
  Double Tree Hotel, 2001 Point West Way,
    916/929-8855
The Pilothouse Restaurant
  The Delta King, 1000 Front St., 916/441-4440

Best Sushi
Fuji
  2422 Thirteenth St., 916/446-4135
Shige Sushi
  1608 Howe Ave., 916/929-1184
Sushi-Sei Japanese Restaurant
  2372 Fair Oaks Blvd., 916/971-1222

Best Thai Food
Lemon Grass Thai Cuisine
  601 Munroe St., 916/486-4891
Siam
  5100 Franklin Blvd., 916/452-8382
Thai Palms
  943 Howe Ave., 916/929-5915

C

Best Vegetarian Food
Eat Your Vegetables
  1841 Howe Ave., 916/922-8413
Fresh Choice
  535 Howe Ave., 916/649-8046
  1689 Arden Way, 916/649-3839
Mum's Vegetarian
  2968 Freeport Blvd., 916/444-3015

Best View While Dining
Crawdad's River Cantina
  1375 Garden Hwy., 916/929-2268
Jammin' Salmon
  1801 Garden Hwy., 916/929-6232
The Pilothouse Restaurant
  The Delta King, 1000 Front St., 916/441-4440

Best Wine Selection
Aldo's Restaurant
  2914 Pasatiempo Ln., 916/483-5031
  2673 El Paseo Ln., 916/483-5031
Biba
  2801 Capitol Ave., 916/455-2422
Mace's Restaurant
  501 Pavilions Ln., 916/922-0222
Terrace Grill
  544 Pavilions Ln., 916/920-3800

SALINAS, CA

Best American Food
Giant Artichoke Restaurant
  11261 Merritt St., Castroville, 408/633-3204

Best Atmosphere
Steinbeck House
  132 Central Ave., 408/424-2735

Best Barbecue/Ribs
Big Joe's BBQ
  1104 S. Main St., 408/422-4213
Central Texan Barbecue
  10500 Merritt St., Castroville, 408/633-2285

Best Homestyle Food
Steinbeck House
  132 Central Ave., 408/424-2735

Best Italian Food
La Scuola
  10700 Merritt St., Castroville, 408/633-2111

Best Mexican Food
Chapala Restaurant
  438 Salinas St., 408/757-4959
Cozumel Mexican Restaurant
  1447 N. Main St., 408/442-2854
El Pollo Dorado
  701 E. Alisal St., 408/424-5444
Gutierrez and Rico Drive-In
  61 Sherwood Dr., 408/424-8382
Mi Tierra Restaurant
  18 E. Gabilan St., 408/422-4631

C

SAMOA, CA

Best Family Restaurant
Samoa Cookhouse
Samoa Rd., 707/442-1659

SAN ANSELMO, CA

[See also: Corte Madera, Larkspur, Mill Valley, San Francisco, and San Rafael.]

Best Chinese Food
Maylee's Chinese Restaurant
115 San Anselmo Ave., 415/455-9988

Best Health-Conscious Menu
Comforts
337 San Anselmo Ave., 415/454-6790

Best Mexican Food
Pancho Villa's
1625 Sir Francis Drake Blvd., Fairfax,
415/459-9606

Best Pizza
Filippo Lococo Italian Pizzeria
638 San Anselmo Ave., 415/883-0564

Best Place to Eat Alone
Bubba's Diner
566 San Anselmo Ave., 415/459-6862

Best Thai Food
Orchid
726 San Anselmo Ave., 415/457-9470

SAN BERNARDINO, CA

[See also: Corona, Ontario, Rancho Cucamonga, Riverside, and Upland.]

Best Bar
Celebrities
3993 N. Sierra Way, 909/882-9144
Pig's Ear Pub
1987 Diners Ct., 909/889-1442

Best Barbecue/Ribs
Bobby Ray's Barbecue
1657 W. Base Line St., 909/885-9177

Best Breakfast
D.J. Coffee Shop
265 E. 40th St., 909/882-3917

Best Burgers
Celebrities
3993 N. Sierra Way, 909/882-9144

Best Business Lunch
Bon Appetito Restaurant
246 E. Base Line St., 909/884-5054

Isabella's
201 N. E St., 909/884-2534

Best Chinese Food
South Sea Restaurant
204 E. Hospitality Ln., 909/885-2338

Best Continental Food
Gazzolo's European Restaurant
132 E. Highland Ave., 909/886-3213

Best Eclectic Menu
Castaways Restaurant
670 Kendall Dr., 909/881-1502

Best French Food
Le Rendezvous Restaurant
4775 N. Sierra Way, 909/883-1231

Best German Food
Gazzolo's European Restaurant
132 E. Highland Ave., 909/886-3213

Best Homestyle Food
Celebrities
3993 N. Sierra Way, 909/882-9144
Soup Asylum
1471 N. Waterman Ave., 909/885-5777

Best Ice Cream/Yogurt
Fosdick's Grinders and Ice Cream
3970 N. Sierra Way, 909/882-0523

Best Italian Food
Alfredo's Pizza and Restaurant
251 W. Base Line St., 909/885-0218
Isabella's
201 N. E St., 909/884-2534

Best Mexican Food
Mexico Restaurant
892 E. Highland Ave., 909/882-3000
Nena's Restaurant
642 N. D St., 909/885-4161
Rosa Maria's Drive-In
4202 N. Sierra Way, 909/881-1731
7275 Boulder Ave., Highland, 909/862-5762
Su Casa Mexican Restaurant
1566 E. Highland Ave., 909/883-4640

Best Other Ethnic Food
Bambino's (Argentinian)
27208 Base Line St., Highland, 909/864-6292

Best Pizza
Alfredo's Pizza and Restaurant
251 W. Base Line St., 909/885-0218

Best Sandwiches
Fosdick's Grinders and Ice Cream
3970 N. Sierra Way, 909/882-0523

Best Steaks
Black Angus Restaurant
290 E. Hospitality Ln., 909/885-7551

Best Sunday Brunch
South Sea Restaurant
  204 E. Hospitality Ln., 909/885-2338

C

SAN CLEMENTE, CA

[See also: Mission Viejo.]

Best Breakfast
Antoine's Cafe
  218 S. El Camino Real, 714/492-1763

Best Chinese Food
Eastern Winds
  201 N. El Camino Real, 714/492-3008
New Mandarin Garden
  111 W. Avenida Palizada, 714/492-7432

Best Diner
Harbor House Cafe
  34157 Pacific Coast Hwy., Dana Point,
    714/496-9270

Best Seafood
Fisherman's Restaurant
  611 Avenida Victoria, 714/498-6390

Best Thai Food
Mongkut Thai
  212 Avenida Del Mar, 714/492-3871

SAN DIEGO, CA

Best American Food
Bread Basket
  1347 Tavern Rd., Alpine, 619/445-0706
The Grill
  Wyndham Hotel, 400 W. Broadway, 619/239-4500
Trophy's
  7510 Hazard Center Dr., Ste. 215, 619/296-9600

Best Bar
Blue Point Coastal Cuisine
  565 Fifth Ave., 619/233-6623
Croce's Restaurant Jazz Bar
  802 Fifth Ave., 619/233-4355
Karl Strauss Brewery and Grill
  1157 Columbia St., 619/234-2739
Karl Strauss Brewery Gardens
  9675 Scranton Rd., 619/587-2739

Best Barbecue/Ribs
Buffalo Joe's
  600 Fifth Ave., 619/236-1616
Kansas City Barbecue
  610 W. Market St., 619/231-9860

Best Breakfast
Hob Nob Hill
  2271 First Ave., 619/239-8176
Original Pancake House
  3906 Convoy St., 619/565-1740

Best Brewpub
Baja Brewing Company
  203 Fifth Ave., 619/231-9279
Callahan's Pub and Brewery
  8280A Mira Mesa Blvd., 619/578-7892
Hops! Bistro and Brewery
  4353 La Jolla Village Dr., 619/587-6677
Karl Strauss Brewery and Grill
  1157 Columbia St., 619/234-2739
Karl Strauss Brewery Gardens
  9675 Scranton Rd., 619/587-2739
San Diego Brewing Company
  10450 Friars Rd., 619/284-2739
Terrific Pacific Brewery and Grill
  721 Grand Ave., 619/270-3596

Best Burgers
Bully's East
  2401 Camino Del Rio S., 619/291-2665
Grant Grill
  326 Broadway, 619/239-6806

Best Business Lunch
Dakota Grill and Spirits
  901 Fifth Ave., 619/234-5554
Rainwater's on Kettner
  1202 Kettner Blvd., 619/233-5757

Best Chinese Food
Emerald Chinese Seafood
  3709 Convoy St., 619/565-6888
Fortune Cookie Restaurant
  16425 Bernardo Center Dr., 619/451-8958
Mandarin House
  2604 Fifth Ave., 619/232-1101
  1820 Garnet Ave., 619/272-2288
Ming's Court
  12750 Carmel Country Rd., Ste. 107, 619/793-2933
Panda Inn
  506 Horton Plaza, 619/233-7800
PF Chang's China Bistro
  4540 La Jolla Village Dr., 619/458-9007

Best Delicatessen
Ingrid's German Delicatessen
  1520 Garnet Ave., 619/270-4250
Samson's 501
  501 W. Broadway, 619/232-2340
Submarina
  3225 Sports Arena Blvd., 619/523-1053

Best Desserts
Cafe Pacifica
  2414 San Diego Ave., 619/291-6666
Extraordinary Desserts
  2929 Fifth Ave., 619/294-7001

Best Diner
Corvette Diner Bar and Grill
  3946 Fifth Ave., 619/542-1001

C

Ruby's Diner
  1640 Camino Del Rio N., Ste. 360P, 619/294-7829

Best Fine Dining
Marius Restaurant
  The Marriott Hotel, 2000 Second St., Coronado,
    619/435-3000

Best German Food
House of Munich Restaurant
  230 Third Ave., Chula Vista, 619/426-5172
Ingrid's German Delicatessen
  1520 Garnet Ave., 619/270-4250
Kaiserhof Restaurant
  2253 Sunset Cliffs Blvd., 619/224-0606

Best Greek/Mediterranean Food
Aesop's Tables Greek Cafe
  Costa Verde Center, 8650 Genesee Ave.,
    619/455-1535
Athens Market Cafe
  11640 Carmel Mountain Rd., 619/675-2225
Cafe Athena
  1846 Garnet Ave., 619/274-1140

Best Health-Conscious Menu
Daily's Restaurant
  8915 Towne Centre Dr., 619/453-1112
Greek Corner Restaurant
  13185 Black Mountain Rd., 619/484-9197
  5841 El Cajon Blvd., 619/287-3303
The Vegetarian Zone
  2949 Fifth Ave., 619/298-7302
Whole Foods Market and Cafe
  711 University Ave., 619/294-2800

Best Homestyle Food
Bread Basket
  1347 Tavern Rd., Alpine, 619/445-0706

Best Indian Food
Passage to India
  13185 Black Mountain Rd., Ste. 1, 619/484-9688
Star of India
  423 F St., 619/544-9891

Best Inexpensive Meal
Bread Basket
  1347 Tavern Rd., Alpine, 619/445-0706
Lorna's
  3945 Governor Dr., 619/452-0661
Osteria Panevino
  722 Fifth Ave., 619/595-7959
Rubio's Baja Grill
  910 Grand Ave., 619/270-4800
  3555 Rosecrans St., Ste. 101B, 619/223-2631
  5157 College Ave., 619/286-3844
  12002 Carmel Mountain Rd., 619/675-9398
Rubio's Restaurant
  multiple locations

C

Best Italian Food
Bella Luna
  748 Fifth Ave., 619/239-3222
Fio's Cucina Italiana
  801 Fifth Ave., 619/234-3467
La Strada
  702 Fifth Ave., 619/239-3400
Mama Anna's
  644 Fifth Ave., 619/235-8144
Osteria Panevino
  722 Fifth Avel, 619/595-7959
Salvatore's
  750 Front St., 619/544-1865

Best Japanese Food
Ichiban
  1441 Garnet Ave., 619/270-5755
  1449 University Ave., 619/299-7203
Sushi Ota
  4529 Mission Bay Dr., 619/270-5670

Best Late-Night Food
Croce's
  802 Fifth Ave., 619/233-4355
Dobson's
  956 Broadway Circle, 619/231-6771
Saska's
  3768 Mission Blvd., 619/488-7311

Best Mexican Food
Casa Sanchez
  3332 Adams Ave., 619/283-0355
Chilangos Mexico City Grill
  142 University Ave., 619/294-8646
El Indio Mexican Restaurant
  3695 India St., 619/299-0333
Fins Mexican Seafood Palace
  15817 Bernardo Center Dr., 619/451-3055
La Salsa
  415 Horton Plaza, 619/234-6906
  9172 Mira Mesa Blvd., 619/530-0607
  8750 Genesee Ave., 619/455-7229
  1010 University Ave., 619/543-0777
Old Town Mexican Cafe
  2489 San Diego Ave., 619/297-4330

Best Other Ethnic Food
Aladdin (Lebanese)
  5420 Clairemont Mesa Blvd., 619/573-0000

Best Outdoor Dining
Casa de Pico
  2754 Calhoun St., 619/296-3267
Osteria Panevino
  722 Fifth Ave., 619/595-7959

Best Pizza
Filippi's Pizza Grotto
  10330 Friars Rd., 619/281-3511
  5353 Kearny Villa Rd., 619/279-7240
  1747 India St., 619/232-5094

C

9969 Mira Mesa Blvd., 619/586-0888
962 Garnet Ave., 619/483-6222
Oscar's
12045 Carmel Mountain Rd., 619/592-0222
Pizza Nova
3955 Fifth Ave., 619/296-6682
5120 N. Harbor Dr., 619/226-0268

Best Place to Take the Kids
Casa de Bandini
2754 Calhoun St., 619/297-8211
Chuck E. Cheese Pizza
3146 Sports Arena Blvd., 619/523-4385
9840 Hibert St., 619/578-5860

Best Restaurant in Town
Belgian Lion
2265 Bacon St., 619/223-2700
Lamont Street Grill
4445 Lamont St., 619/270-3060
Old Town Brigantine Restaurant
2725 Shelter Island Dr., 619/224-2871
Old Town Mexican Cafe
2489 San Diego Ave., 619/297-4330
Seaport Village
879 W. Harbor Dr., 619/230-1343
The Brigantine Restaurant
2444 San Diego Ave., 619/298-9840

Best Romantic Dining
Humphrey's
2241 Shelter Island Dr., 619/224-3577

Best Salad/Salad Bar
Souplantation
6171 Mission Gorge Rd., 619/280-7087
3960 W. Point Loma Blvd., 619/222-7404
8105 Mira Mesa Blvd., 619/566-1172
17210 Bernardo Center Dr., 619/675-3353

Best Sandwiches
Submarina
3225 Sports Arena Blvd., 619/523-1053

Best Seafood
Anthony's Fish Grotto
11666 Avena Pl., 619/451-2070
5232 Lovelock St., 619/457-5008
Athens Market Downtown
109 W. F St., 619/234-1955
Blue Point Coastal Cuisine
565 Fifth Ave., 619/233-6623
Cafe Pacifica
2414 San Diego Ave., 619/291-6666
Casa Sanchez
3332 Adams Ave., 619/283-0355
Fins Mexican Seafood Palace
9460H Mira Mesa Blvd., 619/549-3467
Fish Merchant
7005 Navajo Rd., 619/462-3811

C

Point Loma Seafoods
  2805 Emerson St., 619/223-1109
Red Sails Inn
  2614 Shelter Island Dr., 619/223-3030
Top of the Market
  750 N. Harbor Dr., 619/234-3474

Best Soul Food
Sister Pee Wee's Soul Food
  2971 1/2 Imperial Ave., 619/236-0470

Best Spanish Food
Cafe Sevilla
  555 Fourth Ave., 619/233-5979
La Gran Tapa
  611 B St., 619/234-8272
Tapas Picasso
  3923 Fourth Ave., 619/294-3061

Best Sports Bar
The Rancho Bernardo Sports Cafe
  15817 Bernardo Center Dr., 619/487-0224

Best Steaks
Bully's East
  2401 Camino Del Rio S., 619/291-2665
Chart House
  525 E. Harbor Dr., 619/233-7391
Kelly's
  Town and Country Hotel, 500 Hotel Circle N.,
    619/291-7131
Rainwater's On Kettner
  1202 Kettner Blvd., 619/233-5757

Best Sunday Brunch
The Cavapappi
  Hilton Hotel, 1775 E. Mission Bay Dr.,
    619/276-4010
Charlie Brown's
  880 E. Harbor Island Dr., 619/291-1870
The Crown Room
  Hotel Del Coronado, 1500 Orange Ave., Coronado,
    619/435-6611
Marius Restaurant
  The Marriott Hotel, 2000 Second St., Coronado,
    619/435-3000

Best Sushi
Cafe Japengo
  8960 University Center Ln., 619/450-3355
Sushi Ota
  4529 Mission Bay Dr., 619/270-5670

Best Thai Food
Saffron Thai Grill Chicken
  3731V India St., 619/574-0177
Spices Thai Cafe
  16441 Bernardo Center Dr., 619/674-4665
  3810 Valley Center Dr., Ste. 903, 619/259-0889
Taste of Thai
  527 University Ave., 619/291-7525

Thai Spices Cafe
  3810 Valley Center Dr., Ste. 903, 619/259-0889

Best Undiscovered Restaurant
Bread Basket
  1347 Tavern Rd., Alpine, 619/445-0706

Best Vegetarian Food
Monsoon
  3975 Fifth Ave., 619/298-3155
The Vegetarian Zone
  2949 Fifth Ave., 619/298-7302

Best Vietnamese Food
A Dong Restaurant
  8660 Miramar Rd., 619/298-4420
Chieu-Anh Vietnamese Cuisine
  16769 Bernardo Ctr. Dr., Ste. 10, 619/485-1231
Pho 54 Vietnamese Restaurant
  4016 54th St., 619/583--0611

Best View While Dining
Mr. A's
  2550 Fifth Ave., 619/239-1377

Best Wine Selection
The WineSellar and Brasserie
  9550 Waples St., Ste. 115, 619/450-9576

SAN FRANCISCO, CA

[See also: Berkeley, Corte Madera, Larkspur, Mill Valley, Oakland, and Pacifica.]

Best 24-Hour Restaurant
Sparky's Diner
  242 Church St., 415/626-8666

Best American Food
Bread Basket
  1471 E. Plaza Blvd., National City
    619/474-1821
Cafe For All Seasons
  150 W. Portal Ave., 415/665-0900
Doidge's Kitchen
  2217 Union St., 415/921-2149
Firefly
  4288 24th St., 415/821-7652
JoAnn's Cafe
  1131 El Camino Real
    South San Francisco, 650/872-2810
Sally's Cafe and Bakery
  300 De Haro St., 415/626-6006
Sam's Grill
  374 Bush St., 415/421-0594
Stars Cafe
  500 Van Ness Ave., 415/861-4344
  555 Golden Gate Ave., 415/861-7827
Trio Cafe
  1870 Fillmore St., 415/563-2248

C

Universal Cafe
  2814 Nineteenth St., 415/821-4608

Best Atmosphere
Kan Zaman
  1793 Haight St., 415/751-9656

Best Bar
One Market Restaurant
  1 Market Plaza, 415/777-5577

Best Barbecue/Ribs
The Bear Pit
  10825 Sepulveda Blvd., Mission Hills
    818/365-2509

Best Breakfast
Art's Cafe
  747 Irving St., 415/665-7440
Brother Juniper's Restaurant
  1065 Sutter St., 415/771-8929
Campton Place Restaurant
  340 Stockton St., 415/955-5555
Chava's Mexican Restaurant
  3248 Eighteenth St., 415/552-9387
Chloe's Cafe
  1399 Church St., 415/648-4116
Dottie's True Blue Cafe
  522 Jones St., 415/885-2767
Ella's Restaurant
  500 Presidio Ave., 415/441-5669
Home Plate
  2274 Lombard St., 415/922-4663
Just For You Bakery and Cafe
  1453 Eighteenth St., 415/647-3033
Kate's Kitchen
  471 Haight St., 415/626-3984
M's Cafe
  1376 Ninth Ave., 415/665-1821
Mama's Restaurant
  1701 Stockton St., 415/362-6421
Mel's Drive-In
  2165 Lombard St., 415/921-3039
  3355 Geary Blvd., 415/387-2255
The Park Grill
  The Park Hyatt Hotell, 333 Battery St.,
    415/392-1234
People's Cafe
  1419 Haight St., 415/553-8842
Pork Store Cafe
  1451 Haight St., 415/864-6981
Postrio Restaurant
  545 Post St., 415/776-7825
Silks at Mandarin Oriental
  222 Sansome St., 415/986-2020
Town's End Restaurant and Bakery
  2 Townsend St., 415/512-0749
U.S. Restaurant and Coffee Shop
  431 Columbus Ave., 415/362-6251

C

Best Burgers
Barney's Hamburgers
  4138 24th St., 415/282-7770
  3344 Steiner St., 415/563-0307
Bill's Place
  2315 Clement St., 415/221-5262
Hamburger Mary's
  1582 Folsom St., 415/626-1985
Mo's Restaurant
  1322 Grant Ave., 415/788-3779

Best Chinese Food
Fook Yuen Seafood Restaurant
  195 El Camino Del Mar, 415/692-8600
Hong Kong Flower Lounge Restaurant
  5322 Geary Blvd., 415/668-8998
House of Nanking
  919 Kearny St., 415/421-1429
Taiwan Restaurant
  289 Columbus Ave., 415/989-6789
  445 Clement St., 415/387-1789
Tommy Toy's Haute Cuisine Chinoise
  655 Montgomery St., 415/397-4888
Ton Kiang Restaurant
  5821 Geary Blvd., 415/386-8530
Wu Kong Restaurant
  101 Spear St., 415/957-9300
Yank Sing Restaurant
  427 Battery St., 415/781-1111
  49 Stevenson St., 415/541-4949

Best Coffee/Coffeehouse
The Horse Shoe
  566 Haight St., 415/626-8852
Peet's Coffee and Tea
  multiple locations

Best Desserts
Hawthorne Lane
  22 Hawthorne St., 415/777-9779
Just Desserts
  836 Irving St., 415/681-1277
  3 Embarcadero Center, 415/421-1609
  3735 Buchanan St., 415/922-8675
  248 Church St., 415/626-5774

Best Eclectic Menu
Boulevard
  1 Mission St., 415/543-6084
Campton Place
  340 Stockton St., 415/955-5555
Carta
  1772 Market St., 415/863-3516
Eos
  901 Cole St., 415/566-3063
Flying Saucer
  1000 Guerrero St., 415/641-9955
Infusion
  555 Second St., 415/543-2282

C

Oritalia
1915 Fillmore St., 415/346-1333
Postrio Restaurant
545 Post St., 415/776-7825
R & G Lounge
631 Kearny St., 415/982-7877
Woodward's Garden
1700 Mission St., 415/621-7122

Best Fine Dining
Plumpjack Cafe
3127 Fillmore St., 415/563-4755
Rubicon Restaurant
558 Sacramento St., 415/434-4100

Best French Food
Alain Rondelli Restaurant
126 Clement St., 415/387-0408
Baker Street Bistro
2953 Baker St., 415/931-1475
Cafe Jacqueline
1454 Grant Ave., 415/981-5565
Fleur de Lys
777 Sutter St., 415/673-7779
La Folie
2316 Polk St., 415/776-5577
Le Charm
315 Fifth St., 415/546-6128
Masa's Restaurant
648 Bush St., 415/989-7154
The Dining Room
Ritz-Carlton Hotel, 600 Stockton St.,
415/296-7465
Ti Couz Creperie
3108 Sixteenth St., 415/252-7373

Best German Food
Speckmann's
1550 Church St., 415/282-6850

Best Greek/Mediterranean Food
42 Degrees
235 Sixteenth St., 415/777-5558
Bruno's
2389 Mission St., 415/550-7455
La Mediterranee
288 Noe St., 415/431-7210
2210 Fillmore St., 415/921-2956
Mecca
2029 Market St., 415/621-7000
Plumpjack Cafe
3127 Fillmore St., 415/563-4755
Square One Restaurant
190 Pacific Ave., 415/788-1110
The Helmand
430 Broadway, 415/362-0641
Zak's
2330 Taylor St., 415/563-6266
Zuni Cafe
1658 Market St., 415/552-2522

C

Best Ice Cream/Yogurt

Mitchell's Ice Cream
  688 San Jose Ave., 415/648-2300
Pure T Ice Cream
  2238 Polk St., 415/441-7878
St. Francis Fountain and Candy
  2801 24th St., 415/826-4200

Best Indian Food

Gaylord India Restaurant
  1 Embarcadero Ctr., 415/397-7775
  900 N. Point St., 415/771-8822
Maharani Restaurant
  1122 Post St., 415/775-1988
North India Restaurant
  3131 Webster St., 415/931-1556
Zante Pizza and Indian Cuisine
  3489 Mission St., 415/821-3949

Best Inexpensive Meal

Caffe Delle Stelle
  395 Hayes St., 415/252-1110
Timo's
  842 Valencia St., 415/647-0558

Best Italian Food

Acquerello
  1722 Sacramento St., 415/567-5432
Albona
  545 Francisco St., 415/441-1040
Antica Trattoria
  2400 Polk St., 415/928-5797
Buca Giovanni
  800 Greenwich St., 415/776-7766
Caffe Macaroni
  59 Columbus Ave., 415/956-9737
Enrico's Sidewalk Cafe
  504 Broadway, 415/982-6223
Il Fornaio
  1265 Battery St., 415/986-0100
Kuleto's Italian Restaurant
  221 Powell St., 415/397-7720
L'Osteria Del Forno
  519 Columbus Ave., 415/982-1124
La Felce Italian Cuisine
  1570 Stockton St., 415/392-8321
Laghi
  1801 Clement St., 415/386-6266
Mario's Bohemian Cigar Store Cafe
  2209 Polk St., 415/776-8226
North Beach Restaurant
  1512 Stockton St., 415/392-1700
Pane e Vino Restaurant
  3011 Steiner St., 415/346-2111
Rose Pistola
  532 Columbus Ave., 415/399-0499
Scala's Bistro
  432 Powell St., 415/395-8555

C

Stinking Rose
253 Columbus Ave., 415/781-7673
Vivande Ristorante
670 Golden Gate Ave., 415/673-9245

Best Japanese Food
Ebisu Restaurant
1283 Ninth Ave., 415/566-1770
Kabuto Sushi
5116 Geary Blvd., 415/752-5652
Kyo-Ya Restaurant
Sheraton Palace Hotel
2 New Montgomery St.
415/392-8600
Maki
1825 Post St., 415/921-5215
Matsuya
3856 24th St., 415/282-7989
Mifune
1737 Post St., 415/922-0337
Murasaki
211 Clement St., 415/668-7317
Yoshida-Ya Japanese Restaurant
2909 Webster St., 415/346-3431

Best Korean Food
Korea House
1640 Post St., 415/563-1388

Best Lunch
Zuni Cafe
1658 Market St., 415/552-2522

Best Mexican Food
Cafe Marimba
2317 Chestnut St., 415/776-1506
Campo Santo
240 Columbus Ave., 415/433-9623
Chevy's Mexican Restaurant
2 Embarcadero Ctr., 415/391-2323
150 Fourth St., 415/543-8060
3251 Twentieth Ave., 415/665-8705
141 Hickey Blvd., South San Francisco,
650/755-1617
La Cumbre
515 Valencia St., 415/863-8205
La Taqueria
2889 Mission St., 415/285-7117
Roosevelt Tamale Parlor
2817 24th St., 415/550-9213

Best Other Ethnic Food
Angkor Wat Cambodian
Restaurant (Cambodian)
4217 Geary Blvd., 415/221-7887
Bahia Cabana (Brazilian)
1600 Market St., 415/626-3306
Betelnut (Asian)
2030 Union St., 415/929-8855
Cha Cha Cha (Central/South American)
1801 Haight St., 415/386-5758

C

El Zocalo (Salvadoran)
  3230 Mission St., 415/282-2572
Geva's Caribbean Cuisine (Caribbean)
  482 Hayes St., 415/863-1220
Helmand Restaurant (Afghani)
  430 Broadway, 415/362-0641
Irrawaddy (Burmese)
  1769 Lombard St., 415/931-2830
Lhasa Moon (Tibetan)
  2420 Lombard St., 415/674-9898
Massawa (African)
  1538 Haight St., 415/621-4129
Matterhorn (Swiss)
  2323 Van Ness Ave., 415/885-6116
Miss Pearl's Jam House (Central/South American)
  601 Eddy St., 415/775-5267
Phnom Penh Cambodian Restaurant (Cambodian)
  631 Larkin St., 415/775-5979
Rasselas Ethiopian Cuisine (Ethiopian)
  2801 California St., 415/567-5010

Best Pizza
North Beach Pizza
  1310 Grant Ave., 415/433-2444
  3054 Taraval St., 415/242-9100
  1499 Grant Ave., 415/433-2444
  4787 Mission St., 415/586-1400
  800 Stanyan St., 415/751-2300
Vicolo Pizzeria
  201 Ivy St., 415/863-2382

Best Regional Food
Cafe Flore
  2298 Market St., 415/621-8579
Cafe Kati
  1963 Sutter St., 415/775-7313
Fly Trap
  606 Folsom St., 415/243-0580
Fringale
  570 Fourth St., 415/543-0573
Hawthorne Lane
  22 Hawthorne St., 415/777-9779
Kelly's on Trinity
  333 Trinity Alley, 415/362-4454

Best Restaurant in Town
Brava Terrace
  3010 St. Helena Hwy. N., 707/963-9300

Best Sandwiches
Specialty's Cafe and Bakery
  1 Post St., 415/512-9550
  22 Battery St., 415/512-9550
  312 Kearney St., 415/512-9550
  150 Spear St., 415/512-9550

Best Seafood
Aqua
  252 California St., 415/956-9662
Hayes Street Grill
  320 Hayes St., 415/863-5545

C

PJ's Oyster Bed
737 Irving St., 415/566-7775
Plouf
40 Belden Pl., 415/986-6491
Rocco's Seafood Grill
2080 Van Ness Ave., 415/567-7600
Swan Oyster Depot
1517 Polk St., 415/673-1101

Best Spanish Food
Thirstybear Brewing Company
661 Howard St., 415/974-0905
Zarzuela
2000 Hyde St., 415/346-0800

Best Steaks
Harris' Restaurant
2100 Van Ness Ave., 415/673-1888
Izzy's Steak and Chop House
3345 Steiner St., 415/563-0487

Best Tea Room
The Garden Court
Sheraton Palace Hotel, 2 New Montgomery St.,
415/512-1111
The Dining Room
Ritz-Carlton Hotel, 600 Stockton St.
415/296-7465
The Compass Rose
Westin St. Francis Hotel, 335 Powell St.
415/774-0118

Best Thai Food
Cha Am
701 Folsom St., 415/546-9710
Khan Toke Thai House
5937 Geary Blvd., 415/668-6654
Manora's Thai Cuisine
3226 Mission St., 415/550-0856
Royal Thai Restaurant
951 Clement St., 415/386-1795
San Francisco BBQ
1328 Eighteenth St., 415/431-8956
Thep-Phanom
400 Waller St., 415/431-2526
Yukol Place Thai Cuisine
2380 Lombard St., 415/922-1599

Best Vegetarian Food
Greens
204 Bay St., 415/771-6222
Millennium Vegetarian Restaurant
246 McAllister St., 415/487-9800

Best Vietnamese Food
Golden Turtle
2211 Van Ness Ave., 415/441-4419
La Vie
5830 Geary Blvd., 415/668-8080
The Golden Turtle Vietnamese Restaurant
2211 Van Ness Ave., 415/441-4419

C

308 Fifth Ave., 415/221-5285
The Slanted Door Restaurant
584 Valencia St., 415/861-8032
Tu Lan
8 Sixth St., 415/626-0927

Best View While Dining
Buena Vista Cafe
2765 Hyde St., 415/474-5044
Cliff House
1090 Point Lobos Ave., 415/386-3330
Greens
204 Bay St., 415/771-6222

SAN JOSE, CA

[See also: Sunnyvale and Palo Alto.]

Best All-You-Can-Eat Buffet
Soong Soong Restaurant
3680C Stevens Creek Blvd., 408/249-2272

Best Bar
Britannia Arms
5027 Almaden Expwy., 408/266-0550
9511 DeAnza Blvd., 408/252-7262
Drying Shed
402 Toyon Ave., 408/272-1512

Best Breakfast
Hobee's
920 Town and Country Village, 408/244-5212
680 River Oaks Pkwy. at Montague
Expressway, North San Jose, 408/232-0190

Best Brewpub
Tied House Cafe and Brewery
65 N. San Pedro St., 408/295-2739

Best Burgers
Kirk's Steakburgers
1330 Saratoga Ave., 408/446-2988

Best Delicatessen
Erik's Deli Cafe
5705 Cottle Rd., 408/365-1515
4611 Almaden Expwy., 408/265-1818
1120 Branham Ln., 408/265-1818

Best French Food
Rue de Paris
19 N. Market St., 408/298-0704

Best Indian Food
Pasand Madras Cuisine
3701 El Camino Real, Santa Clara, 408/241-5150

Best Inexpensive Meal
Old Spaghetti Factory
51 N. San Pedro St., 408/288-7488

C

Best Italian Food
Florentine Italian Foods
   1070 Commercial St., Ste. 107, 408/452-0170
   745 S. Winchester Blvd., 408/243-4040
   1057 Blossom Hill Rd., 408/723-3211

Best Japanese Food
Kikusushi
   1187B S. De Anza Blvd., 408/725-1749

Best Mexican Food
Aqui Mex-Grill
   1145 Lincoln Ave., 408/995-0381

Best Other Ethnic Food
Emile's (Swiss)
   545 S. Second St., 408/289-1960

Best Steaks
Stuart Anderson's Black Angus
   380 Kiely Blvd. S., 408/261-6900
   1011 Blossom Hill Rd., 408/266-6602

Best Thai Food
Thepthai
   23 N. Market St., 408/292-7515

Best Vegetarian Food
Good Earth Restaurant and Bakery
   2705 The Alameda, Santa Clara, 408/984-0960
White Lotus
   80 N. Market St., 408/977-0540

Best Vietnamese Food
Pho Hoa
   1834 Tully Rd., 408/238-1481
   1089 S. De Anza Blvd., 408/366-0544
   3484 El Camino Real, Santa Clara, 408/249-8598

SAN LEANDRO, CA

[See also: Oakland and Hayward.]

Best American Food
Cornerstone Cafe
   600 Dutton Ave., 510/562-2535

Best Breakfast
Sabino's Coffee
   1273 MacArthur Blvd., 510/357-5282

Best Chinese Food
Lucky's Chinese Restaurant
   1456 E. Fourteenth St., 510/351-8131

Best Family Restaurant
Harry's Hofbrau
   14900 E. Fourteenth St., 510/357-1707

Best French Food
Le Gourmet French Restaurant
   635 E. Fourteenth St., 510/635-8260

C

Best Italian Food
Strizzi's Restaurant
1376 E. Fourteenth St., 510/483-4883

SAN LUIS OBISPO, CA

Best All-You-Can-Eat Buffet
China Bowl and Kyoto
685 Higuera St., 805/546-9700
Fresh Choice
Downtown Centre, 876 Marsh St., 805/543-0943

Best Breakfast
Big Sky Cafe
1121 Broad St., 805/545-5401
Hobee's
1443 Calle Joapuin, 805/549-9186
Margie's Diner
1575 Calle Joaquin, 805/541-2940

Best Burgers
Hudson's Grill
1005 Monterey St., 805/541-5999
Scrubby and Lloyd's Cafe
1136 Carmel St., 805/543-5885

Best Chinese Food
Golden China
1085 Higuera St., 805/543-7354
675 Higuera St., 805/543-7576

Best Coffee/Coffeehouse
Coffee Merchant
1065 Higuera St., 805/543-6701
Linnaea's Cafe
1110 Garden St., 805/541-5888
Starbucks Coffee
Downtown Centre, 876 Marsh St., 805/547-0465

Best Delicatessen
Ben Franklin's Sandwich Company
313 Higuera St., 805/544-4948
Cisco's
594 California Blvd., 805/543-3334
778G Higuera St., 805/543-5555
Gus' Grocery
1683 Osos St., 805/543-8684

Best Desserts
Madonna Inn
100 Madonna Rd., 805/543-3000

Best Ice Cream/Yogurt
Country Culture Yogurt Bar
746 Higuera St., 805/544-9007
Froggie's Frozen Yogurt
578 California Blvd., 805/546-8181

Best Italian Food
Buona Tavola
1037 Monterey St., 805/545-8000
Cafe Roma
1819 Osos St., 805/541-6800

C

Best Mexican Food
Izzy Ortega's Mexican Restaurant
  1850 Monterey St., 805/543-3333
Pepe Delgado's Mexican Restaurant
  1601 Monterey St., 805/544-6660
Pete's Southside Cafe
  1815 Osos St., 805/549-8133

Best Pizza
Upper Crust
  785 Foothill Blvd., 805/542-0400
Woodstock's Pizza Parlor
  1000 Higuera St., 805/541-4420

Best Place to Take the Kids
Apple Farm Restaurant
  2015 Monterey St., 805/544-6100
F. McClintock's Saloon and Dining
  686 Higuera St., 805/541-0686

Best Restaurant in Town
1865
  1865 Monterey St., 805/544-1865
Benvenuti
  450 Marsh St., 805/541-5393

Best Steaks
F. McClintock's Saloon and Dining
  686 Higuera St., 805/541-0686
This Old House
  740 W. Foothill Rd., 805/543-2690

Best Sunday Brunch
Sea Cliffs Restaurant
  2757 Shell Beach Rd., Shell Beach, 805/773-3555

SAN MARCOS, CA

Best American Food
Quails Inn Dinnerhouse
  1035 La Bonita Dr., 760/744-2445

Best Bar
Camelot Inn
  887 W. San Marcos Blvd., 760/744-1332

Best Brewpub
San Marcos Brewery
  1080 W. San Marcos Blvd., 760/471-0050

Best Burgers
George's Burgers
  122 N. Las Poisas Rd., 760/744-0164

Best Cajun/Creole Food
Cajun Connection
  740 Nordahl Rd., Ste. 114, 760/741-5680

Best Greek/Mediterranean Food
Grecian Gardens
  1020 W. San Marcos Blvd., 760/744-3790

Best Health-Conscious Menu
Panda Garden
  748 S. Rancho Santa Fe Rd., 760/727-2322

Best Italian Food
Bruno's Italian Restaurant
1020 W. San Marcos Blvd., 760/744-7700

Best Japanese Food
Katsu Seafood and Steak House
1020 W. San Marcos Blvd., 760/744-7156

Best Mexican Food
Marietta's Restaurant
1020 W. San Marcos Blvd., 760/752-1765
Rockin' Baja Lobster
1020 W. San Marcos Blvd., 760/744-7550

Best Sandwiches
Sub Marina
997 W. San Marcos Blvd., 760/471-7707

Best Seafood
Fish House Veracruz
360 Via Vera Cruz, 760/744-8000

SAN MATEO, CA

[See also: Pacifica, Redwood City and San Francisco.]

Best Breakfast
First Watch
201 Second Ave., 650/342-2356
Stacks
361 California Dr., Burlingame, 650/579-1384

Best Chinese Food
Toa Yuen Restaurant
3170 Campus Dr., 650/349-0414

Best Coffee/Coffeehouse
Noah's Bagels
50 E. Fourth Ave., 650/347-2364

Best Desserts
Capellini Ristorante
310 Baldwin Ave., 650/348-2296

Best Health-Conscious Menu
Fresh Choice
1952 S. El Camino Real S., 650/341-8498

Best Italian Food
Bella Mangiata Caffe
233 Baldwin Ave., 650/343-2404
Capellini Ristorante
310 Baldwin Ave., 650/348-2296
Luceti's on 25th Avenue
109 W. 25th Ave., 650/574-1256

Best Pizza
Amici's East Coast Pizzeria
69 E. Third Ave., 650/342-9392
Jack's Pizza
770 Polhemus Rd., 650/574-2233
212 Second Ave., 650/343-9229

Best Regional Food
Buffalo Grill
   66 31st Ave., 650/358-8777

Best Seafood
Clamhouse San Mateo
   33 W. 25th Ave., 650/571-1846

Best Steaks
Barley and Hopps
   201 S. B St., 650/348-7808

Best Thai Food
Bow Thai Cafe
   43 S. B St., 650/340-8424
Chao Praya Thai Cuisine
   4300 S. El Camino Real, 650/571-9123
Nipa-Pon
   121 W. 25th Ave., 650/578-9211

Best Vegetarian Food
World Wrapps
   1318 Burlingame Ave., Burlingame, 650/342-9777

SAN RAFAEL, CA

[See also: Corte Madera, Larkspur, Mill Valley, and San Anselmo.]

Best Beer Selection
Pacific Tap and Grill
   812 Fourth St., 415/457-9711

Best Burgers
Phyllis' Giant Burgers
   2202 Fourth St., 415/456-0866

Best Chinese Food
Pier 6
   1559 Fourth St., 415/457-1733

Best Delicatessen
Belli-Deli
   1304 Second St., 415/456-2626

Best French Food
La Petite Auberge
   704 Fourth St., 415/456-5808

Best Ice Cream/Yogurt
Double Rainbow Gourmet Ice Cream
   860 Fourth St., 415/457-0803
   112 Vintage Way, Novato, 415/898-8500

Best Indian Food
India Village
   555 Francisco Blvd., 415/456-2411
Pasand Madras Cuisine
   802 B St., 415/456-6099

Best Inexpensive Meal
High Tech Burrito
   942 Diablo Ave., Novato, 415/897-8083
   2042 Fourth St., 415/485-0214

C

Best Italian Food
Ristorante Dalecio
340 Ignacio Blvd., Novato, 415/883-0960
Salute
706 Third St., 415/453-7596

Best Japanese Food
Kamikaze Sushi Bar
223 Third St., 415/457-6776
Sushi to Dai For
869 Fourth St., 415/721-0392

Best Mexican Food
Las Camelias
912 Lincoln Ave., 415/453-5850

Best Other Ethnic Food
Kasbah (Moroccan)
200 Merrydale Rd., 415/472-6666

Best Pizza
Lococo's Pizzeria
631 Del Ganado Rd., 415/472-3323
Mulberry Street Pizza
101 Smith Ranch Rd., 415/472-7272
Redboy Pizzeria
1115 Fourth St., 415/454-3131
Round Table Pizza
186 Northgate One, 415/472-3232
Stefano's Pizzeria
3815 Redwood Hwy., 415/491-1900

Best Thai Food
Anita's Kitchen
534 Fourth St., 415/454-2626
My Thai
1230 Fourth St., 415/456-4455

SAN RAMON, CA

Best Chinese Food
Uncle Yu's Szechuan
2005 Crow Canyon Pl., 925/275-1818

Best Delicatessen
Max's Diner, Bakery, and Bar
2015 Crow Canyon Pl., 925/277-9300

Best Sports Bar
Tommy T's
2410 San Ramon Valley Blvd., 925/743-1500

Best Vegetarian Food
Mudd's Restaurant
10 Boardwalk Pl., 925/837-9387

SANTA ANA, CA

[See also: Anaheim, Costa Mesa, Garden Grove, Irvine, and Orange.]

C

Best All-You-Can-Eat Buffet
Country Harvest Buffet
1008 E. Seventeenth St., 714/541-3020

Best Breakfast
Pop's Cafe
112 E. Ninth St., 714/543-2772

Best Burgers
Knowl Wood Restaurant
2107 E. Seventeenth St., 714/541-0555
Mo's Food Service
1504 W. Edinger Ave., 714/540-9673

Best Continental Food
Gustaf Anders Restaurant
Bear St. at MacArthur St., 714/668-1737

Best Health-Conscious Menu
Whole Foods Market
14945 Holt Ave., Tustin, 714/731-3400

Best Indian Food
Niki's Tandoori Express
2031 E. First St., 714/542-2969
3705 S. Bristol St., 714/850-0595

Best Italian Food
Antonello Ristorante
1611 W. Sunflower Ave., 714/751-7153
Caffe Piemonte
498 E. First St., Tustin, 714/532-3296

Best Pizza
California Pizza Kitchen
2800 N. Main St., 714/479-0604
Pizza Cucina
1106 Irvine Blvd., Tustin, 714/669-1599

Best Sandwiches
Zov's Bistro and Bakery
17440A Enderle Center, Tustin, 714/838-8855

Best Steaks
Crazy Horse Steak House
1580 Brookhollow Dr., 714/549-1512
Morton's of Chicago
1661 W. Sunflower Ave., 714/444-4834

SANTA BARBARA, CA

Best Bar
Mel's
6 E. De La Guerra St., 805/963-2211

Best Barbecue/Ribs
Woody's Bodacious Barbecue
5112 Hollister Ave., 805/967-3775

Best Beer Selection
Trader Joe's
  29 South Milpas St., 805/564-7878

Best Breakfast
Esau's
  403 State St., 805/965-4416

Best Burgers
Chubbie's
  1027 State St., 805/965-6004

Best Cajun/Creole Food
The Palace Grill
  8 E. Cota St., 805/966-3133

Best Chinese Food
China Castle
  1202 Chapala St., 805/965-9219

Best Coffee/Coffeehouse
Coffee Cat
  3615 State St., 805/569-8868
  1201 Anacapa St., 805/962-7164
S.B. Roasting Company
  321 Motor Way, 805/962-0320

Best Delicatessen
Italian-Greek Deli
  636 State St., 805/962-6815

Best Fine Dining
Downey's
  1305 State St., 805/966-5006
El Encanto Dining Room
  1900 Lasuen Rd., 805/687-5000
La Marina
  Four Seasons Biltmore Hotel, 1260 Channel Dr.,
    Montecito, 805/969-2261
The Stonehouse
  900 San Ysidro Ln., 805/969-5046
The Wine Cask
  813 Anacapa St., 805/966-9463

Best French Food
Mousse Odile Restauarnt
  18 E. Cota St., 805/962-5393

Best Health-Conscious Menu
Natural Cafe
  508 State St., 805/962-9494

Best Ice Cream/Yogurt
McConnell's
  201 W. Mission St., 805/569-2323
  835 E. Canon Perdido St., 805/965-3764
Penguin's
  935 State St., 805/965-0255

Best Inexpensive Meal
Fresh Choice
  740 State St., 805/965-6599

Best Italian Food
Palazzio Trattoria Italiana
 1151 Coast Village Rd., 805/969-8565

Best Japanese Food
Azuma
 24 W. Figueroa St., 805/966-2139

Best Mexican Food
La Super Rica Taqueria
 622 N. Milpas St., 805/963-4940

Best Outdoor Dining
Earthling Bookstore Cafe
 1137 State St., 805/564-6096
Paradise Cafe
 702 Anacapa St., 805/962-4416

Best Pizza
Giovanni's
 5003 Carpinteria Ave., Carpinteria, 805/684-8288
 3020 State St., 805/682-3621
 1187 Coast Village Rd., Montecito, 805/969-1277

Best Place to Eat Alone
Sojourner Cafe
 134 E. Canon Perdido St., 805/965-7922

Best Romantic Dining
El Encanto Dining Room
 1900 Lasuen Rd., 805/687-5000

Best Seafood
Brophy Brothers
 119 Harbor Way, 805/966-4418
Palms
 701 Linden Ave., Carpinteria, 805/684-3811

Best Steaks
Chuck's of Hawaii
 3888 State St., 805/687-4414
Palms
 701 Linden Ave., Carpinteria, 805/684-3811

Best Sunday Brunch
La Marina
 Four Seasons Biltmore Hotel, 1260 Channel Dr.,
  Montecito, 805/969-2261

Best Sushi
Arigato Sushi
 11 W. Victoria St., 805/965-6074

Best Thai Food
Your Place
 22 N. Milpas St., 805/966-5151

SANTA CLARITA, CA

Best German Food
German Place Deli
 23115 Lyons Ave., Newhall, 805/255-9790

Best Sandwiches
Final Score Food and Beverage
 23942 Lyons Ave., Newhall, 805/254-6557

C

Best Spanish Food
El Mas Cafe
  24367 San Fernando Rd., Newhall, 805/253-0609

Best Undiscovered Restaurant
La Cocina Bar and Grill
  28022 Seco Canyon Rd., 805/297-4546

Best Vegetarian Food
Nature's Harvest
  25067 Peachland Ave., Newhall, 805/259-0807

SANTA CRUZ, CA

Best Barbecue/Ribs
Hindquarter Bar and Grille
  303 Soquel Ave., 408/426-7770

Best Beer Selection
99 Bottles of Beer on the Wall Beer Pub
  104 Walnut Ave., 408/459-9999
Seabright Brewery
  519 Seabright Ave., 408/426-2739
The Catalyst
  1011 Pacific Ave., 408/423-1336

Best Breakfast
Hobee's
  Galleria de Santa Cruz, 740 Front St.,
    408/458-1212
Linda's Seabreeze Cafe
  542 Seabright Ave., 408/427-9713
Walnut Avenue Cafe
  106 Walnut Ave., 408/457-2307
Zachary's Restaurant
  819 Pacific Ave., 408/427-0646

Best Brewpub
Santa Cruz Brewing Company
  516 Front St., 408/429-8838

Best Burgers
Carpo's
  2400 Porter St., Soquel, 408/476-6260
Hindquarter Bar and Grille
  303 Soquel Ave., 408/426-7770
Jack's Hamburgers
  202 Lincoln St., 408/423-4421
Pontiac Grill
  429 Front St., 408/427-2290

Best Chinese Food
O'Mei Sichuan Chinese Restaurant
  2316 Mission St., 408/425-8458

Best Coffee/Coffeehouse
Cafe Pergolesi
  418 Cedar St., 408/426-1775
Coffee Roasting Company
  1330 Pacific Ave., 408/459-0100
Espresso Royale Caffe
  1545 Pacific Ave., 408/429-9804

Jahva House
120 Union St., 408/459-9876

Best Desserts
Cafe Bittersweet
2332 Mission St., 408/423-9999
Kelly's French Pastry
1547 Pacific Ave., 408/423-9059

Best Fine Dining
Casablanca Restaurant
101 Main St., 408/426-9063
Chaminade
1 Chaminade Ln., 408/475-5600
Compass Grille and Bar
175 W. Cliff Dr., 408/426-4330

Best Health-Conscious Menu
Aragona's
2591 S. Main St., Soquel, 408/462-5100

Best Ice Cream/Yogurt
Polar Bear Ice Cream
1224 Soquel Ave., 408/425-5188
Yogurt Delite
1306 Mission St., 408/429-6400

Best Inexpensive Meal
Marcelo's the Restaurant
1520 Mission St., 408/423-2845

Best Late-Night Food
Saturn Cafe
1230 Mission St., 408/429-8505
The Crepe Place
1134 Soquel Ave., 408/429-6994

Best Mexican Food
Costa Brava
505 Seabright Ave., 408/423-8190
Crow's Nest Restaurant
2218 E. Cliff Dr., 408/476-4560
Rosa's Rosticeria
439 Lake Ave., 408/479-3536
Taqueria Vallarta
608 Soquel Ave., 408/457-8226
Tucson Taqueria
218 Mount Hermon Rd., Scotts Valley,
408/439-8470

Best Pizza
Pizza Amore
103 Cliff St., 408/423-2336
Pizza My Heart
1116 Pacific Ave., 408/426-2511
Tony and Alba's Pizza
817 Soquel Ave., 408/425-8669

Best Restaurant in Town
Oswald's
1547 Pacific Ave., 408/423-7427

C

Best Sandwiches
Erik's Delicafe
  222 Mount Hermon Rd., Scotts Valley,
    408/438-4646
  1664 Soquel Ave., 408/458-1414
  712 Front St., 408/425-5353
Togo's Eatery
  1315 Pacific Ave., 408/426-8441
  266 Mount Hermon Rd., Scotts Valley,
    408/438-0742
  1917 Mission St., 408/457-9294
Zoccoli's Delicatessen
  1534 Pacific Ave., 408/423-1711

Best Seafood
Riva Fish House
  31 Municipal Wharf, 408/429-1223
Sea Cloud Restaurant
  49B Municipal Wharf, 408/458-9393

Best Vegetarian Food
Asian Rose Cafe
  1547 Pacific Ave., 408/458-3023
Malabar Cafe
  1116 Soquel Ave., 408/423-7906

Best View While Dining
Casablanca Restaurant
  101 Main St., 408/426-9063
Chaminade
  1 Chaminade Ln., 408/475-5600
Compass Grille and Bar
  175 W. Cliff Dr., 408/426-4330
Crow's Nest Restaurant
  2218 E. Cliff Dr., 408/476-4560

Best Wine Selection
Pearl Alley Bistro
  110 Pearl Alley, 408/429-8070
Theo's French Restaurant
  3101 N. Main St., Soquel, 408/462-3657

SANTA MARIA, CA

Best American Food
Far Western Tavern
  899 Guadalupe St., Guadalupe, 805/343-2211

Best Homestyle Food
Jack's
  156C S. Broadway St., 805/937-1871

Best Italian Food
Marianne's
  800 S. Broadway, 805/347-2737

Best Restaurant in Town
Central City Broiler
  1520 N. Broadway, 805/922-3700
Santa Maria Inn
  801 S. Broadway, 805/928-7777

Best Seafood
Jetty Restaurant
135 E. Foster Rd., 805/937-5144

Best Steaks
Shaw's
714 S. Broadway, 805/925-5862

SANTA MONICA, CA

[See also: Beverly Hills and Los Angeles.]

Best American Food
17th Street Cafe
1610 Montana Ave., 310/453-2771
Bob Burns Restaurant
202 Wilshire Blvd., 310/393-6777
Tavern on Main
2907 Main St., 310/392-2772
Wolfgang Puck Cafe
1323 Montana Ave., 310/393-0290

Best Breakfast
Omelette Parlor
2732 Main St., 310/399-7892
Pacific Dining Car
2700 Wilshire Blvd., 310/453-4000

Best Brewpub
Brewhouse
1246 Third St. Promenade, 310/393-2629

Best Chinese Food
Chinois on Main
2709 Main St., 310/392-3037

Best Delicatessen
Broadway Deli
1457 Third St. Promenade, 310/451-0616

Best Diner
Patrick's Roadhouse
106 Entrada Dr., 310/459-4544

Best Eclectic Menu
Abiqui
1413 Fifth St., 310/395-8611
DC3 Restaurant
2800 Donald Douglas Loop N., 310/399-2323

Best Fine Dining
Schatzi on Main
3110 Main St., 310/399-4800

Best French Food
Rockenwagner
2435 Main St., 310/399-6504

Best German Food
Knoll's Black Forest Inn
2454 Wilshire Blvd., 310/395-2212

C

Best Ice Cream/Yogurt
Golden Spoon Frozen Yogurt
155 Santa Monica Pl., 310/576-7781

Best Inexpensive Meal
Tavern on Main
2907 Main St., 310/392-2772

Best Italian Food
Drago Restaurant
2628 Wilshire Blvd., 310/828-1585
Il Ristorante di Giorgio Baldi
114 W. Channel Rd., 310/573-1660
Valentino Italian Restaurant
3115 Pico Blvd., 310/829-4313

Best Mexican Food
Border Grill 2
1445 Fourth St., 310/451-1655

Best Other Ethnic Food
Babalu (Caribbean)
1002 Montana Ave., 310/395-2500

Best Seafood
Back on the Beach
445 Palisades Beach Rd., 310/393-8282
Ocean Avenue Seafood
1401 Ocean Ave., 310/394-5669

Best Southwestern Food
Border Grill 2
1445 Fourth St., 310/451-1655

Best Vegetarian Food
Real Food Daily
514 Santa Monica Blvd., 310/451-7544

Best View While Dining
DC3 Restaurant
2800 Donald Douglas Loop N., 310/399-2323
Michael's
1147 Third St., 310/451-0843

SANTA ROSA, CA

Best American Food
Bistro Ralph
109 Plaza St., Healdsburg, 707/433-1380
Willowside Cafe
3535 Guerneville Rd., 707/523-4814

Best Beer Selection
The English Rose
2024 Armory Dr., 707/544-7673

Best Breakfast
Omelette Express
112 Fourth St., 707/525-1690

Best Brewpub
Santa Rosa Brewing Company
458 B St., 707/544-4677

C

Best Chinese Food
Gary Chu's
611 Fifth St., 707/526-5840

Best Coffee/Coffeehouse
A' Roma Roasters
95 Fifth St., 707/576-7765

Best Delicatessen
Traverso's Gourmet Foods
106 B St., 707/542-2530

Best Desserts
Michelle Marie's Patisserie
2404 Magowan Dr., 707/575-1214

Best Fine Dining
John Ash and Company
4330 Barnes Rd., 707/527-7687

Best French Food
Babette's
464 First St. E., Sonoma, 707/939-8921
La Gare
208 Wilson St., 707/528-4355

Best German Food
Cafe Europe
65 Brookwood Ave., 707/526-2200

Best Indian Food
Sizzling Tandoor
409 Mendocino Ave., 707/579-5999

Best Italian Food
Checkers
523 Fourth St., 707/578-4000
Italian Affair
1612 Terrace Way, 707/528-4336

Best Pizza
La Vera
629 Fourth St., 707/575-1113

Best Thai Food
Thai House
525 Fourth St., 707/526-3939

Best Wine Selection
Gaffney's Wine Bar
404 Mendocino Ave., 707/542-8463

SANTEE, CA

Best Breakfast
Omelette Factory
7941 Mission Gorge Rd., 619/596-9686

Best Burgers
Boll Weevil
9535 Mission Gorge Rd., 619/448-1744

Best Mexican Food
Marieta's Restaurant
8915 Carlton Hills Blvd., 619/449-2365

Best Pizza
Tanino's Pizza House
  9730 Cuyamaca St., 619/562-4383

C

SAUGUS, CA

Best Barbecue/Ribs
Pit BBQ Restaurant
  26057 Bouquet Canyon Rd., 805/253-0115

Best Homestyle Food
Saugus Cafe
  25861 San Fernando Rd., 805/259-7886

Best Italian Food
L'Italiano
  28200 Bouquet Canyon Rd., 805/296-1200

Best Japanese Food
Kotobuki Restaurant
  27665 Bouquet Canyon Rd., 805/296-1353

Best Pizza
Round Table Pizza
  26524 Bouquet Canyon Rd., 805/297-3556

SEBASTOPOL, CA

Best Burgers
Rocco's
  12750 Bodega Hwy., Freestone, 707/823-7765

Best Japanese Food
Sushi Hana
  6930 Burnett St., 707/823-3778

Best Outdoor Dining
Topolos at Russian River Vineyards
  5700 Gravenstein Hwy. N., Forestville,
    707/887-1575

Best Seafood
Lucas Wharf
  595 S. Hwy. 1, Bodega Bay, 707/875-3522

Best Vegetarian Food
East West Cafe
  128 N. Main St., 707/829-2822

SHERMAN OAKS, CA

Best Health-Conscious Menu
Whole Foods Market and Cafe
  4520 Sepulveda Blvd., 818/382-3700
  12905 Riverside Dr., 818/762-5548

Best Italian Food
Posto Restaurant
  14928 Ventura Blvd., 818/784-4400

SIMI VALLEY, CA

Best Barbecue/Ribs
Red's BBQ and Grillery
  2892 Cochran St., 805/581-9076

C

Best Burgers
Del Taco
  2990 Cochran St., 805/583-3717
Hudson's Grill
  2900 Cochran St., 805/581-1740

Best Fine Dining
Ciao Restaurant
  1627 E. Los Angeles Ave., 805/522-1049

Best Greek/Mediterranean Food
It's Greek To Me
  2375 Sycamore Dr., 805/527-5316

Best Italian Food
Giovanni's Italian Kitchen
  4210 E. Los Angeles Ave., 805/582-2375
Paul's Italian Villa
  1951 Erringer Rd., 805/526-5360

Best Japanese Food
Ken of Japan
  4340 Cochran St., 805/527-6490

Best Mexican Food
Carrillo's Mexican Deli
  2836 Cochran St., 805/522-8939
Familia Diaz
  245 S. Tenth St., 805/525-2813
Tico's Taco
  2090 First St., 805/527-6456

Best Steaks
Maverick's
  5225 Cochran St., 805/527-8730

Best Thai Restaurant
Siam Cuisine
  1960 Sequoia Ave., 805/581-5526

SOUTH LAKE TAHOE, CA

Best American Food
Angie's Cafe
  Best Western, Timber Cave Lodge,
    3411 Lake Tahoe Blvd., 530/541-6722
Forest Inn
  3855 Montreal Rd., 530/541-6655
Izzy's Burger Spa
  2591 Lake Tahoe Blvd., 530/544-5030

Best Continental Food
Zackary's
  Embassy Suites, 4130 Lake Tahoe Blvd.,
    530/544-5400

Best Fine Dining
Evan's
  536 Emerald Bay Rd., 530/542-1990

Best Italian Food
Cafe Fiore
  1169 Ski Run Blvd., 530/541-2908
Lake Tahoe Pizza Company
  1168 Hwy. 50, 530/544-1919

Best Other Ethnic Food
McP's Irish Pub and Grill (Irish)
    4090 Lake Tahoe Blvd., 530/542-4435

Best Restaurant In Town
Sunnyside Restaurant and Lodge
    1850 W. Lake Blvd., Tahoe City, 530/583-7200
Wolfdale's Cuisine Unique
    640 N. Lake Blvd., Tahoe City, 530/583-5700

Best Sandwiches
Yellow Submarine
    983 Tallac Ave., 530/541-8808

STOCKTON, CA

Best Breakfast
Hoosier Inn
    1537 N. Wilson Way, 209/463-0271

Best Chinese Food
Dave Wong's Chinese Cuisine
    5620 N. Pershing Ave., 209/951-4150
Yen Ching Restaurant
    6511 Pacific Ave., 209/473-9813

Best Continental Food
Albert's Restaurant
    8103 Hwy. 99N, 209/476-1763

Best French Food
Le Bistro
    3121 W. Benjamin Holt Dr., 209/951-0885

Best Greek/Mediterranean Food
Papapavlo's Gourmet Greek Cafe
    7555 Pacific Ave., 209/477-6855

Best Homestyle Food
Hoosier Inn
    1537 N. Wilson Way, 209/463-0271

Best Italian Food
Ernie's Pasta Barn
    10880 Hwy. 99N, 209/931-5330
Ristorante Primavera
    856 W. Benjamin Holt Dr., 209/477-6128

Best Lunch
Yasoo Yani Restaurant
    326 E. Main St., 209/464-3108

Best Mexican Food
Santiago's Cocina Mexicana
    222 Lincoln Ctr., 209/478-6444

Best Seafood
Bud's Seafood Grill
    314 Lincoln Ctr., 209/956-0270

SUNNYVALE, CA

[See also: Palo Alto and San Jose.]

C

Best Bar
Britannia Arms Pub
  1087 Peanza Blvd., 408/252-7262
Paul and Eddie's
  10014 Peninsula Ave., Cupertino,
    408/252-2226

Best Breakfast
Hobee's
  800 Ahwanee Ave., 408/524-3580
  21267 Stevens Creek Blvd., Cupertino,
    408/255-6010

Best Brewpub
Stoddard's Brewhouse and Eatery
  111 S. Murphy Ave., 408/733-7824

Best Chinese Food
Tao Tao Cafe
  175 S. Murphy Ave., 408/736-3731

Best Delicatessen
Erik's Deli Cafe
  717 E. El Camino Real, 408/737-0202
Togo's Eatery
  1253 W. El Camino Real, 650/969-8646
  528 N. Lawrence Expwy., 408/738-8761
  561 E. El Camino Real, 408/732-3680
  1200 Crossman Ave., 408/745-1557

Best German Food
Hardy's Bavaria
  111 W. Evelyn Ave., Ste. 108,
    408/720-1531

Best Italian Food
Il Postale
  127 W. Washington Ave., 408/733-9600

Best Japanese Food
Miyake
  10650 S. De Anza Blvd., Cupertino,
    408/253-2668
Tsumami Grill
  220 Town and Country, 408/773-8776

Best Mexican Food
Chevy's Mexican Restaurant
  204 S. Mathilda Ave., 408/737-7395

Best Other Ethnic Food
Kabul Afghan Cuisine (Afghanian)
  833 W. El Camino Real, 408/245-4350

Best Salad/Salad Bar
Fresh Choice
  1105 W. Camino Blvd., 408/732-7788
  333 Moffett Park Dr., 408/734-0661

Best Thai Food
Thai Basil
　101 S. Murphy Ave., 408/773-1098

C

Best Vegetarian Food
Good Earth Restaurant and Bakery
　20807 Stevens Creek Blvd., Cupertino,
　　408/252-3555
Hobee's Restaurant
　800 Ahwanee Ave., 408/524-3580

TEMECULA, CA

Best American Food
Temet Grill
　44501 Rainbow Canyon Rd., 909/694-1000

Best Chinese Food
Little Chung King
　27371 Jefferson Ave., 909/699-1234

Best Coffee/Coffeehouse
Rio De Java
　26459 Ynez Rd., 909/699-8082

Best Desserts
Katie McGuire's Pie Shoppe
　27495 Ynez Rd., 909/676-9194

Best Ice Cream/Yogurt
Sweet Bean
　30590 Rancho California Rd., 909/699-8443

Best Italian Food
Marino's Pasta House
　31361 Riverside Dr., Lake Elsinore, 909/674-5657
Pasquale's
　27315 Jefferson Ave., 909/699-4428
Scarcella's
　27485 Ynez Rd., 909/676-5450
Vera's Italian Restaurant
　27326 Jefferson Ave., Ste. 17, 909/676-6474

Best Mexican Food
Rosa's Cantina
　28636 Front St., 909/677-1453

Best Pizza
Filippi's Pizza Grado
　27309 Jefferson Ave., 909/699-8900

Best Sandwiches
European Deli
　28860 Front St., Ste. A1, 909/695-0201

Best Seafood
Cafe Champagne
　32575 Rancho California Rd., 909/699-0088
Fish Exchange
　24910 Washington Ave., Murrieta, 909/677-9449
Pirates of the Caribbean
　41925 Third St., 909/695-1405

Best Steaks
Black Angus
　27735 Ynez Rd., 909/699-8000

Hungry Hunter
27600 Jefferson Ave., 909/694-1475

TEMPLETON, CA

Best Chinese Food
Golden China
7425 El Camino Real, Atascadero, 805/466-1828

Best Desserts
Linn's Fruit Bin
2485 Village Ln., Cambria, 805/927-1499

Best Restaurant in Town
McPhee's Grille
416 Main St., 805/434-3204
Robin's on Burton
4095 Burton Dr., Cambria, 805/927-5007

Best Seafood
Great American Fish Company
1185 Embarcadero, Morro Bay, 805/772-4407

Best Steaks
A.J. Spur's Saloon and Dining Hall
508 N. Main St., 805/434-2700

THOUSAND OAKS, CA

Best Chinese Food
Hunan Chinese Restaurant
1352 N. Moorpark Rd., 805/371-0075

Best Coffee/Coffeehouse
Starbucks Coffee
33 N. Moorpark Rd., 818/381-1848

Best Desserts
Coco's Bakery Restaurant
55 Rolling Oaks Dr., 805/379-3939

Best French Food
The Rendezvous
1282 Newbury Rd., Newbury Park, 818/498-1019

Best Health-Conscious Menu
Whole Foods Market and Cafe
451 E. Avenida De Los Arboles, 805/492-5340

Best Italian Food
Allegro Italian Restaurant
579A N. Ventu Park Rd., Newbury Park,
805/499-6767

Best Restaurant Meal Value
Los Robos Inn
299 S. Moorpark Rd., 818/889-0722

Best Sandwiches
Roxy's Famous Deli
1345 E. Thousand Oaks Blvd., 805/379-6767

Best Steaks
Black Angus Restaurant
139 W. Thousand Oaks Blvd., 805/497-0757
Hungry Hunter
487 N. Moorpark Rd., 805/497-3925

C

TORRANCE, CA

Best American Food
The Depot
1250 Cabrillo Ave., 310/787-7501

Best Burgers
Snax Home-Original Superburger
4535 Sepulveda Blvd., 310/316-6631

Best Business Lunch
Misto Caffe and Bakery
24558 Hawthorne Blvd., 310/375-3608

Best Chinese Food
Szechwan Restaurant
22529 Hawthorne Blvd., 310/378-4235

Best Family Restaurant
Carrow's
20535 Hawthorne Blvd., 310/371-6444
Vince's Spaghetti Restaurant
23609 Hawthorne Blvd., 310/375-1455

Best Greek/Mediterranean Food
Papadakis Taverna
301 W. Sixth St., San Pedro, 310/548-1186

Best Japanese Food
Kanda Japanese Sushi Buffet
23305 Hawthorne Blvd., 310/378-6699

Best Mexican Food
El Torito Restaurant
23225 Hawthorne Blvd., 310/378-0331
La Salsa II
24223 Crenshaw Blvd., 310/326-1444

Best Other Ethnic Food
El Pollo Inka (Peruvian)
23705 Hawthorne Blvd., 310/373-0062

Best Salad/Salad Bar
Misto Caffe and Bakery
24558 Hawthorne Blvd., 310/375-3608

TRACY, CA

Best Chinese Food
Mandarin Villa Restaurant
2501 Tracy Blvd., 209/836-1818

Best Italian Food
Fabio's
88 W. Tenth St., 209/836-2012

Best Lunch
Gerard's Deli
939 Central Ave., 209/835-6655

Best Mexican Food
Casa Nachos Family Mexican
2321 Tracy Blvd., 209/835-9402

Best Thai Food
Thai Cafe
614 Central Ave., 209/835-6001

TULARE, CA

Best Bar
Papa Joe's Place
424 N. N St., 209/686-5472

Best Burgers
Monty's Walk-Up Drive-In
700 W. Inyo Ave., 209/686-3491

Best Chinese Food
Jean Jean Chinese Restaurant
72 N. Tower Sq., 209/688-1818
Rice Bowl
300 W. Inyo Ave., 209/686-5634

Best Homestyle Food
Apple Annie's
1165 N. Blackstone St., 209/686-3411

Best Italian Food
Rosa's Italian Restaurant
1351 E. Tulare Ave., 209/686-3938

Best Mexican Food
Papa Joe's Place
424 N. N St., 209/686-5472
Ricardo's Mexican
262 E. Cross Ave., 209/688-6782
Vejar's Mexican Restaurant
533 E. Cross Ave., 209/688-0279
1293 S. K St., 209/688-0355

Best Sandwiches
Hazel's Kitchen
237 N. L St., 209/685-0455
Nielson's Restaurant
137 S. M St., 209/688-8563

TURLOCK, CA

Best Chinese Food
Golden Hour Restaurant
415 E. Main St., 209/634-8677

Best Homestyle Food
Latif's Restaurant
111 N. Golden State Blvd., 209/634-5351

Best Italian Food
Angelini's Italian Restaurant
2251 Geer Rd., 209/667-6644

Best Mexican Food
El Jardin
409 E. Olive Ave., 209/632-0932

Best Outdoor Dining
La Creme Restaurant
310 E. Main St., 209/667-2293

Best Regional Food
La Creme Restaurant
310 E. Main St., 209/667-2293

C

Best Steaks
Marty's Inn
29030 U.S. Hwy. 33, Newman, 209/862-1323
Trax Bar and Grill
10 E. Main St., 209/668-8729

UPLAND, CA

[See also: Corona, Ontario, Pomona, Rancho Cucamonga, Riverside, and San Bernardino.]

Best Barbecue/Ribs
Joey's Barbecue
1964 W. Foothill Blvd., 909/982-2128

Best Business Lunch
Mimi's Cafe
370 N. Mountain Ave., 909/982-3038

Best Chinese Food
China Gate
365 S. Mountain Ave., 909/982-2449

Best Coffee/Coffeehouse
Espresso Yourself
350 W. Foothill Blvd., 909/946-0927

Best Delicatessen
Dr. Don's Deli
250 C St., 909/982-2011
Togo's Eatery
110B S. Mountain Ave., 909/982-5445

Best Desserts
Coco's Restaurant
60 W. Foothill Blvd., 909/985-9604
150 E. Seventh St., 909/946-2324

Best French Food
Cafe Provencal
967 W. Foothill Blvd., 909/608-7100

Best Ice Cream/Yogurt
Goldmine Yogurt
110A S. Mountain Ave., 909/946-0623

Best Mexican Food
El Gato Gordo
1241 W. Foothill Blvd., 909/981-8380

Best Pizza
Corina's
670 N. Mountain Ave., 909/985-0218

Best Seafood
Charley's Grill and Pub
2035 W. Foothill Blvd., 909/982-4513

Best Sushi
Kishi Japanese Restaurant
320 W. Foothill Blvd., 909/981-1770

C

VACAVILLE, CA

Best Bar
T.J.'s Tavern
554 Main St., 707/448-9993

Best Breakfast
Coffee Tree
100 Nut Tree Pkwy., 707/448-8435

Best Chinese Food
China House Restaurant
513 Main St., 707/446-8068

Best Coffee/Coffeehouse
Starbucks
1031 Helen Power Dr., Ste. D100, 707/447-9668

Best Diner
Chubby's Diner
1989 Peabody Rd., 707/446-9640
2091 Harbison Dr., 707/451-2954

Best Fine Dining
Buckhorn Cafe
210 Railroad Ave., Winters, 530/795-4503

Best Health-Conscious Menu
Fresh Choice
1001 Helen Power Dr., 707/446-1056

Best Inexpensive Meal
Favela's Taqueria
2040 Harbison Dr., 707/447-1120

Best Late-Night Food
Lyon's Restaurant
909 Merchant St., 707/447-4600

Best Mexican Food
Pelayo's Mexican Dining
1160 E. Monte Vista Ave., 707/449-9365

Best Pizza
Pepperoni's Pizza
700 Merchant St., 707/451-0370

Best Sandwiches
Tortellini Original Deli
5139 Quinn Rd., 707/453-1514

Best Vegetarian Food
Favela's Taqueria
2040 Harbison Dr., 707/447-1120

VALENCIA, CA

Best Bar
Hamburger Hamlet
27430 The Old Rd., 805/253-0888

Best Continental Food
Gerard's Fine Dining
23329 Lyons Ave., 805/253-0995

Best Indian Food
Tandoori Grill
23360 W. Valencia Blvd., 805/288-1200

C

Best Southwestern Food
El Torito
27510 The Old Rd., 805/254-2994

Best Tea Room
A Touch of Class
25914 McBean Pkwy., 805/259-1625

Best Thai Food
Thai Dishes
23328 Valencia Blvd., 805/253-3663

VALLEJO, CA

Best Breakfast
Joy of Eating
1828 Springs Rd., 707/644-5315

Best Chinese Food
Szechuan Chinese Cuisine
2079 Solano Ave., 707/554-4657
Yet Wah
20050 San Pablo Ave., Crockett, 510/787-3011

Best Eclectic Menu
Breakfast Break
301 Georgia St., 707/644-6421

Best Italian Food
Napoli Pizzeria and Italian Food
124 Tennessee St., 707/644-9270

Best Seafood
Harbor House Restaurant
23 Harbor Way, 707/642-8984
Sardine Can
0 Harbor Way, 707/553-9492

Best Steaks
Black Angus Restaurant
124 Plaza Dr., 707/647-0595
Harbor House Restaurant
23 Harbor Way, 707/642-8984

VENTURA, CA

Best Bar
Bombay Bar and Grill
143 S. California St., 805/643-4404

Best Barbecue/Ribs
RD's Famous Barbecue
11012 Violeta St., 805/647-7427

Best Breakfast
Cottage Cafe
1907 E. Thompson Blvd., 805/643-1231
Vagabond Coffee Shop
760 E. Thompson Blvd., 805/643-1390

Best Chinese Food
Golden China Restaurant
1105 S. Seaward Ave., 805/652-0688

C

Best Diner
Busy Bee Cafe
478 E. Main St., 805/643-4864

Best Fine Dining
Mattie's
Pierport Inn, 550 San Jon Rd., 805/643-6144

Best German Food
Old Vienna Restaurant
3845 Telegraph Rd., 805/654-1214

Best Greek/Mediterranean Food
Greek at the Harbor
1583 Spinnaker Dr., Ste. 101, 805/650-5350

Best Italian Food
Ferraro's Italian Restaurant
2788 E. Main St., 805/648-7270

Best Lunch
Casa de Soria
1961 E. Thompson Blvd., 805/648-2083
Greek at the Harbor
1583 Spinnaker Dr., Ste. 101, 805/650-5350

Best Mexican Food
Casa de Soria
1961 E. Thompson Blvd., 805/648-2083
Yolanda's Mexican Restaurant
2753 E. Main St., 805/643-2700

Best Pizza
Beachside Pizzeria
1141 S. Seaward Ave., 805/648-7858

Best Sandwiches
66 California
66 S. California St., 805/648-2266

Best Seafood
Alexander's
1050 Schooner Dr., 805/658-2000
Eric Ericsson's Fish Company
668 Harbor Blvd., 805/643-4783
Sportsman Restaurant and Lounge
53 S. California St., 805/643-2851

Best Southwestern Food
Rosarito Beach Cafe
629 E. Main St., 805/653-7343

Best Steaks
Tony's Steak and Sea Food
2009 E. Thompson Blvd., 805/643-3322

Best View While Dining
Eric Ericsson's Fish Company
668 Harbor Blvd., 805/643-4783
Mattie's
Pierport Inn, 550 San Jon Rd., 805/643-6144

C

VICTORVILLE, CA

Best Burgers
Jason's Hamburgers
14876 Bear Valley Rd., 760/241-8858

Best Chinese Food
Chateau Chang Restaurant
15425 Anacapa Rd., 760/241-3040

Best Fine Dining
Pagano's Restaurant
14747 Bear Valley Rd., Hesperia, 619/948-4880

Best Homestyle Food
Mollie's Kountry Kitchen
15775 Mojave Dr., 760/241-4900

Best Mexican Food
John's Pizza Pasta Parlor
15010 Circle Dr., 760/243-3801

Best Place to Take the Kids
Cask and Cleaver
13885 Park Ave., 760/241-7318
Steer and Stein
12224 Mariposa Rd., 760/241-0775

VISALIA, CA

Best All-You-Can-Eat Buffet
Gumbo Chinese Buffet Restaurant
101 W. Main St., 209/732-4263

Best Bar
Michael's on Main
123 W. Main St., 209/635-2686
Vintage Press Restaurant
216 N. Willis St., 209/733-3033

Best Barbecue/Ribs
Breenie's
314 W. Main St., 209/741-1466
Tour's Mesquite Grill
3730 S. Mooney Blvd., 209/635-8687

Best Breakfast
Dala Horse
1531 Draper St., Kingsburg, 209/897-7762
Valhalla Restaurant
314 W. Center Ave., 209/627-2113

Best Burgers
Checkers
401 W. Acequia Ave., 209/733-4227

Best Business Lunch
Cafe 225
225 W. Main St., 209/733-2967
Michael's on Main
123 W. Main St., 209/635-2686

Best Chinese Food
Lum-Lum's
417 E. Center Ave., 209/733-5292

C

Best Coffee/Coffeehouse
Java Jungle Espresso Bar
208 W. Main St., 209/732-5282
The Fox Den
214 W. Main St., 209/635-4265
Visalia Coffee Company
2933 S. Mooney Blvd., 209/732-6333

Best Desserts
Michael's on Main
123 W. Main St., 209/635-2686
Vintage Press Restaurant
216 N. Willis St., 209/733-3033

Best Diner
Main Street Diner
127 W. Main St., 209/739-1822

Best Family Restaurant
Alpine Station
610 W. Main St., 209/627-2643
Shagnasty's Big Play Cafe
210 W. Center Ave., 209/625-8910

Best Fine Dining
Vintage Press Restaurant
216 N. Willis St., 209/733-3033

Best Health-Conscious Menu
Watson's Veggie Garden
615 W. Main St., 209/635-7355

Best Homestyle Food
Valhalla Restaurant
314 W. Center Ave., 209/627-2113

Best Ice Cream/Yogurt
Alpine Station
610 W. Main St., 209/627-2643

Best Inexpensive Meal
A&W Family Restaurant
2611 S. Mooney Blvd., 209/733-4445
301 N. Willis St., 209/625-1513

Best Italian Food
Little Italy Italian Restaurant
303 W. Main St., 209/734-2906

Best Mexican Food
Las Palmas Restaurant
309 E. Main St., 209/734-5405

Best Pizza
Coastal Pizza
106 S. Locust St., 209/733-4210
VIP Pizza
449 E. Pine St., Exeter, 209/592-5170

Best Place to Be "Seen"
Vintage Press Restaurant
216 N. Willis St., 209/733-3033

Best Place to Eat Alone
Bulene's Restaurant
208 W. Main St., 209/739-8136

Best Place to Take the Kids
Alpine Station
  610 W. Main St., 209/627-2643

Best Romantic Dining
Bulene's Restaurant
  208 W. Main St., 209/739-8136
Michael's on Main
  123 W. Main St., 209/635-2686
Vintage Press Restaurant
  216 N. Willis St., 209/733-3033

Best Sandwiches
Picnic Sandwich Shop
  114 W. Main St., 209/734-1847

Best Seafood
Bulene's Restaurant
  208 W. Main St., 209/739-8136

Best Steaks
The Double L Steakhouse
  401E E. Center Ave., 209/627-1126

Best Tea Room
The Fox Den
  214 W. Main St., 209/635-4265

WALNUT CREEK, CA

Best Bar
Crogan's Bar and Grill
  1387 Locust St., 925/933-7800

Best Coffee/Coffeehouse
Buttercup Kitchen
  2387 N. Main St., 925/938-2270
Peet's Coffee and Tea
  1343 Locust St., 925/933-9580
Starbucks Coffee
  1146 Broadway Plz., 925/937-1377

Best Delicatessen
Genova Delicatessen
  1105 S. California Blvd., 925/939-3838

Best French Food
La Cigale Restaurant Francais
  2195 N. Broadway, 925/937-8800

Best Ice Cream/Yogurt
Yogurt Park
  1499 N. California Blvd., 925/246-0456
  80 Broadway Ln., 925/944-4748

Best Italian Food
Spiedini Northern Italian Ristorante
  101 Ygnacio Valley Rd., 925/939-2100

Best Regional Food
California Cafe
  1540 N. California Blvd., 925/938-9977
High Tech Burrito
  1815 Ygnacio Valley Rd., 925/938-3888

C

Best Sandwiches
A Sweet Affair
  5345 Clayton Rd., Clayton, 925/672-0936
  1815 Ygnacio Valley Rd., 925/944-1910

Best Seafood
Scott's Seafood Grill and Bar
  1333 N. California Blvd., 925/934-1300

Best Vegetarian Food
Fresh Choice Restaurant
  1275 S. Main St., 925/938-1529
  486 Sun Valley Mall, Concord, 925/671-7222

Best Wine Selection
Prima Trattoria e Negozio di Vini
  1522 N. Main St., 925/935-7780

WATSONVILLE, CA

Best Chinese Food
Bamboo Garden
  1012 E. Lake Ave., 408/724-1486

Best Mexican Food
Jalisco Restaurant
  618 Main St., 408/728-9080
Zuniga's Mexican Food
  100 Aviation Way, 408/724-5788

Best Restaurant in Town
Green Valley Grill
  40 Penny Ln., 408/728-0644
The Villager
  1032 E. Lake Ave., 408/722-5200

WESTLAKE VILLAGE, CA

Best Continental Food
Boccaccio's Restaurant
  32123 Lindero Canyon Rd., 818/889-8300

Best Desserts
Baker's Square Restaurant
  3887 E. Thousand Oaks Blvd., 805/496-7437

Best Italian Food
Tuscany Il Ristorante
  968 S. Westlake Blvd., Ste. 4, 818/880-5642

Best Sandwiches
Oak Tree Restaurant
  3955 E. Thousand Oaks Blvd., 818/991-8454
Plug Nickel Restaurant
  717 Lakefield Rd., Ste. 1, 805/495-3469

Best Seafood
Fins Seafood Grill
  982 S. Westlake Blvd., Ste. 8, 805/494-6494

WESTMINSTER, CA

Best Mexican Food
El Torito Mexican Restaurant
  15042 Goldenwest St., 714/898-6621

Best Seafood
Seafood Paradise Number Two
  8602 Westminster Blvd., 714/893-6066

Best Vietnamese Food
Grand Garden
  8894 Bolsa Ave., 714/893-1200
Pagolac Restaurant
  14580 Brookhurst St., 714/531-4740
Vien Huong Restaurant
  14092 Magnolia St., 714/373-1876

WHITTIER, CA

[See also: Anaheim, Long Beach, Los Angeles, and West Covina.]

Best Breakfast
Mimi's Cafe
  15436 Whittier Blvd., 562/947-0339
Spire's Restaurant
  10140 Carmenita Rd., 562/941-5673

Best Chinese Food
Mandarin Inn
  10120 Carmenita Rd., 562/946-4539

Best Family Restaurant
Baker's Square Restaurant
  16255 Whittier Blvd., 562/943-6756

Best Health-Conscious Menu
Mimi's Cafe
  15436 Whittier Blvd., 562/947-0339

Best Homestyle Food
Marie Callender's
  9829 La Serna Dr., 562/945-3471
  12402 Washington Blvd., 562/693-2724

Best Mexican Food
Green Burrito
  8536 Norwalk Blvd., 562/699-9143

Best Pizza
Pizza Mania
  13547 Telegraph Rd., 562/944-8803

Best Place to Be "Seen"
Acapulco Mexican Restaurant
  13473 Telegraph Rd., 562/946-7577

Best Steaks
Stuart Anderson's Black Angus Steakhouse
  15500 Whittier Blvd., 562/947-2200

YUBA CITY, CA

Best Cajun/Creole Food
Al's Cafe American
  1538 Poole Blvd., 530/674-3213

C

Best Fine Dining
The Refuge Restaurant and Lounge
  1501 Butte House Rd., 530/673-7620

Best Italian Food
Pasquini's Fine Food and Spirits
  6241 Live Oak Blvd., Live Oak, 530/695-3384

Best Mexican Food
Casa Lupe
  655 W. Onstott Rd., 530/673-2190
La Palma Restaurant
  440 Garden Hwy., 916/755-4749
Lucio's
  890 W. Onstott Rd., 916/671-2050

Colorado

C

ALAMOSA, CO

Best Chinese Food
Hunan Chinese Restaurant
419 Main St., 719/589-9002

Best Eclectic Menu
Cafe Maya
529 Main St., 719/589-6175

Best Health-Conscious Menu
Lara's Soft Spoken Restaurant
801 State Ave., 719/589-6769

Best Pizza
Pizza Den
1419 Main St., 719/589-3039

Best Sandwiches
St. Ives A Pub and Eatery
719 Main St., 719/589-0711

ASPEN, CO

Best Barbecue/Ribs
Rusty's Hickory House
730 W. Main St., 970/925-2313

Best Breakfast
Wienerstube Restaurant
633 E. Hyman Ave., 970/925-3357

Best Brewpub
Flying Dog Brew Pub
425 E. Cooper St., 970/925-7464

Best Burgers
Little Annie's Eating House
617 E. Hyman Ave., 970/925-1098

C

Best Casual Dining
Cache Cache Restaurant
  205 S. Mill St., 970/925-3835
O' Leary's Pizza Pub
  521 E. Hyman Ave., 970/925-2233
Woody Creek Tavern
  2858 Woody Creek Rd., Ste. 2, Woody Creek,
    970/923-4585

Best Coffee/Coffeehouse
Explore Coffeehouse
  221 E. Main St., 970/925-5338
Zele Gourmet Coffee
  121 S. Galena St., 970/925-5745

Best Dinner
Charthouse
  219 E. Durant St., 970/925-3525
Crystal Palace Theatre Restaurant
  300 E. Hyman Ave., 970/925-1455
Howling Wolf
  316 E. Hopkins Ave., 970/920-7771

Best Fine Dining
Century Room
  Hotel Jerome, 330 E. Main St., 970/920-1000
Krabloonik
  4250 Divide Rd., Snowmass Village, 970/923-3953
Pinion's
  105 S. Mill St., 970/920-2021

Best French Food
Ute City Bar and Grill
  501 E. Hyman Ave., 970/920-4699

Best Italian Food
Il Poggio
  57 Elbert Ln., Snowmass Village, 970/923-4292

Best Lunch
Aspen Grove Cafe
  525 E. Cooper St., 970/925-6162
Charcuterie and Cheese Market
  520 E. Durant Ave., 970/925-8010
Johnny McGuire's Deli
  730 E. Cooper St., 970/920-9255
The Ajax Tavern
  685 E. Durant Ave., 970/920-9333
Wienerstube Restaurant
  633 E. Hyman Ave., 970/925-3357

Best Mexican Food
Cantina
  411 E. Main St., 970/925-3663
La Cocina
  308 E. Hopkins Ave., 970/925-9714
Su Casa Mexican Restaurant
  315 E. Hyman Ave., 970/920-1488

Best Outdoor Dining
Little Nell Restaurant
  675 E. Durant Ave., 970/920-4600

C

Best Seafood
Butch's Lobster Bar
  264 Snowmelt Rd., Snowmass Village,
    970/923-4004

Best Steaks
Steak Pit
  305 E. Hopkins Ave., 970/925-8624

Best Sushi
Kenichi
  533 E. Hopkins Ave., 970/920-2212
Takah Sushi
  420 E. Hyman Ave., 970/925-8588

Best Vegetarian Food
Explore Coffeehouse
  221 E. Main St., 970/925-5338

BOULDER, CO

Best All-You-Can-Eat Buffet
Boulder Salad Company
  2595 Canyon Blvd., 303/447-8272

Best Brewpub
Mountain Sun Pub and Brewery
  1535 Pearl St., 303/546-0886
Oasis Brewery and Restaurant
  1095 Canyon Blvd., 303/449-0363
Walnut Brewery
  1123 Walnut St., 303/447-1345

Best Burgers
Dark Horse
  2922 Baseline Rd., 303/442-8162
Red Robin
  2580 Arapahoe Ave., 303/442-0320
Tom's Tavern
  1047 Pearl St., 303/442-9363

Best Chinese Food
First Wok Express
  2835 28th St., 303/444-8886
Hunan Garden
  949 Walnut St., 303/442-2772
Orchid Pavilion
  1050 Walnut St., 303/449-4353
Young's Place on the Hill
  1083 Fourteenth St., 303/447-9837

Best Coffee/Coffeehouse
Bookend Cafe
  1115 Pearl St., 303/440-6699
Downtown Brewing Market
  1918 Thirteenth St., 303/443-2098
Caffe Mars
  1425 Pearl St., 303/938-1750
Peaberry Coffee
  2721 Arapahoe Ave., 303/449-4111
  947 Pearl St., 303/449-9646
Starbucks Coffee
  1402 Broadway St., 303/442-9199

C

3033 Arapahoe Ave., 303/440-5090
Trident Booksellers and Cafe
940 Pearl St., 303/443-3133

Best Delicatessen
Deli Zone
2900 Valmont Rd., 303/447-9349
New York Deli
1117 Pearl St., 303/449-5161
On the Hill
1091 Thirteenth St., 303/449-6952
Salvaggio's Italian Deli
2655 Pearl St., 303/938-1981

Best French Food
Fawnbrook Inn
Hwy. 7 Business District, Ste. 357, Allenspark,
303/747-2556

Best German Food
Marie's Inn
400 Mountain Ave., Berthoud, 970/532-2648

Best Greek/Mediterranean Food
The Mediterranean Restaurant
1002 Walnut St., 303/444-5335

Best Ice Cream/Yogurt
Boulder Ice Cream
2660A Canyon Blvd., Ste. 2, 303/444-6624

Best Indian Food
MijBani Indian Restaurant
2005 Eighteenth St., 303/442-7000

Best Japanese Food
Sushi Tora
2014 Tenth St., 303/444-2280

Best Korean Food
Korea House
2750 Glenwood Dr., 303/449-1657

Best Mexican Food
Juanita's
1043 Pearl St., 303/449-5273
Zolo Grill
2525 Arapahoe Ave., 303/449-0444

Best Other Ethnic Food
Narayan's Nepal Restaurant (Nepalese)
921 Pearl St., 303/447-2816

Best Outdoor Dining
Chautauqua Dining Hall
900 Baseline Rd., 303/440-3776
West End Tavern
926 Pearl St., 303/444-3535

Best Pizza
Abo's
2761 Iris Ave., 303/443-1921
Beau Jo's
1600 28th St., 303/444-5135

C

14th Street Bar and Grill
1400 Pearl St., 303/444-5854
Jalino's
1647 Arapahoe Ave., 303/443-6300
Nick-n-Willy's
801 Pearl St., 303/444-9898
4800 Baseline Rd., 303/499-9898
Old Chicago
1102 Pearl St., 303/443-5031

Best Romantic Dining
European Cafe
2460 Arapahoe Ave., 303/938-8250
Flagstaff House
1138 Flagstaff Dr., 303/442-4640
Greenbriar
8735 N. Foothills Hwy., 303/440-7979
John's Restaurant
2328 Pearl St., 303/444-5232
Q's
2115 Thirteenth St., 303/442-4880
The Boulder Cork Restaurant
3295 30th St., 303/443-9505

Best Sandwiches
Alfalfa's
1651 Broadway St., 303/442-0909
New York Deli
1117 Pearl St., 303/449-5161
Pressto
3960 Broadway St., 303/444-0780
Quizno's
2875 Pearl St., 303/444-6744
601E S. Broadway St, 303/494-5360
6525 Gunpark Dr., 303/530-4920
1136 Pearl St., 303/449-3366

Best Sunday Brunch
The Boulder Broker Restaurant
Boulder Broker Inn, 555 30th St., 303/444-3330
The Greenbriar Inn
8735 N. Foothills Hwy., 303/440-7979
Lucile's
2124 Fourteenth St., 303/442-4743

Best Thai Food
Sawaddee
1401 Pearl St., 303/447-3321
Siamese Plate
1575 Folsom St., 303/447-9718

Best Vegetarian Food
Creative Vegetarian Cafe
1837 Pearl St., 303/449-1952
Harvest Restaurant
1738 Pearl St., 303/449-6223
Rudi's
4720 Table Mesa Dr., 303/494-5858
Turley's
2350 Arapahoe Ave., 303/442-2800

C

Best Vietnamese Food
Chez Thuy
2655 28th St., 303/442-1700

Best Wine Selection
Flagstaff House
1138 Flagstaff Dr., 303/442-4640

COLORADO SPRINGS, CO

Best Breakfast
Olive Branch Restaurant
2140 Vickers Dr., 719/593-9522
333 N. Tejon St., 719/475-1199

Best Brewpub
Beckett's Brewhouse and Restaurant
128 S. Tejon St., 719/633-3230
Judge Baldwin's Brewing Company
4 S. Cascade Ave., 719/955-5600
Phantom Canyon Brewing Company
2 E. Pikes Peak Ave., 719/635-2800

Best Burgers
Conway's Red Top Restaurant
3589 N. Carefree Circle, 719/596-6444

Best Casual Dining
Juniper Valley Ranch
16350 State Hwy. 115, 719/576-0741
Luigi's Restaurant
947 S. Tejon St., 719/632-0700

Best Continental Food
Briarhurst Manor
404 Manitou Ave., Manitou Springs, 719/685-1864

Best Diner
King's Chef Diner
110 E. Costilla St., 719/634-9135

Best French Food
La Petit Maison
1015 W. Colorado Ave., 719/632-4887

Best German Food
Edelweiss Restaurant
34 E. Ramona Ave., 719/633-2220

Best Health-Conscious Menu
Adams Mountain Cafe
110 Canyon Ave., Manitou Springs, 719/685-1430

Best Inexpensive Meal
Keg Lounge
730 Manitou Ave., Manitou Springs, 719/685-9531

Best Italian Food
Giuseppe's Depot Restaurant
10 S. Sierra Madre St., 719/635-3111
Panino's
1732 S. Eighth St., 719/635-1188
604 N. Tejon St., 719/635-7452

C

Best Lunch
Beckett's Brewhouse and Restaurant
128 S. Tejon St., 719/633-3230

Best Mexican Food
El Taco Rey
330 E. Colorado Ave., 719/475-9722
Jose Muldoon's
222 N. Tejon St., 719/636-2311
Pepe's Restaurante and Cantina
2427 N. Academy Blvd., 719/574-5801

Best Other Ethnic Food
Mataam Fez Moroccan Restaurant (Moroccan)
101 N. Tejon St., 719/634-2101

Best Pizza
Old Chicago Pasta Pizza and Beer
7115 Commerce Center Dr., 719/593-7678
118 N. Tejon St., 719/634-8812

Best Sandwiches
Bell's Deli
154 E. Cheyenne Mountain Blvd., 719/576-8633
Ritz Grille
15 S. Tejon St., 719/635-8484

Best Seafood
Hatch Cover Restaurant
252 E. Cheyenne Mountain Blvd., 719/576-5223

DENVER, CO

Best All-You-Can-Eat Buffet
Mr. Panda
6206 W. Alameda Ave., Lakewood, 303/922-7562

Best American Food
Keys on the Green
29614 Upper Bear Creek Rd., Evergreen,
303/674-4095

Best Barbecue/Ribs
Bennett's
3700 Peoria St., 303/375-0339
1201 Sixteenth St., 303/893-3399
County Line
8351 Southpark Ln., Littleton, 303/797-3727
M and D's Bar-B-Que and Fish Place
2004 E. 28th Ave., 303/296-1760

Best Beer Selection
Old Chicago
multiple locations

Best Breakfast
Annie's Cafe
4012 E. Eighth Ave., 303/355-8197
Breakfast Inn
6135 E. Evans Ave., 303/757-7491
Chef Zorba's Cuisine
2630 E. Twelfth Ave., 303/321-0091
Crown Burger
2192 S. Colorado Blvd., 303/753-9696

C

Fratelli's Italian Restaurant
 1200 E. Hampden Ave., Englewood, 303/761-4771
Hot Cakes
 1400 E. Eighteenth Ave., 303/830-1909
Racine's Restaurant
 850 Bannock St., 303/595-0418
Simm's Landing
 11911 W. Sixth Ave., Golden, 303/237-0465
Wynkoop Brewery Company
 1634 Eighteenth St., 303/297-2700

Best Brewpub
Broadway Brewery Pub
 2441 Broadway, 303/292-2555

Best Burgers
Brooklyn's
 2644 W. Colfax Ave., 303/572-3999
Good Times
 multiple locations
Mutdear's
 4900 E. 35th Ave., 303/321-2050
My Brother's Bar
 2376 Fifteenth St., 303/455-9991
Red Robin
 3333 S. Wadsworth Blvd., 303/989-8448
Spanky's
 1800 E. Evans Ave., 303/733-6886
The Cherry Cricket
 2641 E. Second Ave., 303/322-7666
Trinity Grille
 1801 Broadway, 303/293-2288

Best Business Lunch
Ellyngton's
 Brown Palace Hotel, 321 Seventeenth St.,
  303/297-3111
Ship Tavern
 Brown Palace Hotel, 321 Seventeenth St.,
  303/297-3111
Strings
 1700 Humboldt St., 303/831-7310

Best Casual Dining
Jackson's Hole All-American Sports Grill
 990 S. Oneida St., 303/388-2883
 1520 Twentieth St., 303/298-7625
Peppers
 3500 Morrison Rd., 303/975-0285

Best Chinese Food
China Jade
 375 S. Federal Blvd., 303/935-0033
China Terrace
 1512 Larimer St., 303/592-1032
Empress Seafood Restaurant
 2825 W. Alameda Ave., 303/922-2822
Golden Plate Chinese
 7180 E. Hampden Ave., 303/639-9898
 9880 W. Girton Dr., 303/763-9028

C

Imperial Chinese Restaurant
  431 S. Broadway, 303/698-2800
Jade Garden
  5120 E. Arapahoe Rd., Littleton, 303/770-5188
Little Shanghai Cafe
  456 S. Broadway, 303/777-9838
Pavilion Chinese Cuisine
  3333 S. Tamarac Dr., 303/743-9777

Best Coffee/Coffeehouse
Common Grounds
  3484 W. 32nd Ave., 303/458-5248
Daily Grind Coffee House and Bakery
  1999 Broadway, 303/292-5282
  900 Auraria Pkwy., Ste. 240, 303/573-5282
Gallery Coffeehouse
  6035 W. Alameda Ave., Lakewood, 303/202-2024
Peaberry Coffee
  multiple locations
Pizza Colore Cafe
  1512 Larimer St., Ste. 12R, 303/534-6844
Starbucks Coffee
  multiple locations
The Market at Larimer Square
  1445 Larimer St., 303/534-5140

Best Delicatessen
New York Deli News
  7105 E. Hampden Ave., 303/759-4741
Zaidy's
  121 Adams St., 303/333-5336

Best Diner
Southside Cafe
  560 S. Broadway, 303/777-2391

Best Eclectic Menu
Firehouse Bar and Grill
  1525 Blake St., 303/820-3308
Melting Pot
  2707 W. Main St., Littleton, 303/794-5666
Michael's of Cherry Creek
  2710 E. Third Ave., 303/321-2324
Rock Bottom Brewery
  1001 Sixteenth St., 303/534-7616

Best Family Restaurant
Marie Callender's
  3535 S. Yosemite St., 303/779-0216
White Fence Farm
  6263 W. Jewell Ave., Lakewood, 303/935-5945

Best Fine Dining
Brasserie Z
  815 Seventeenth St., 303/293-2322
Fourth Story
  2955 E. First Ave., 303/322-1824

Best French Food
Le Central
  112 E. Eighth Ave., 303/863-8094

C

Tante Louise
  4900 E. Colfax Ave., 303/355-4488
The Normandy
  1515 Madison St., 303/321-3312

Best Greek/Mediterranean Food
Central 1
  300 S. Pearl St., 303/778-6675
Thai's Cafe
  6495 E. Evans Ave., 303/757-5828
Yanni's: A Greek Taverna
  2223 S. Monaco Pkwy., 303/692-0404

Best Health-Conscious Menu
Bocaza Mexican Grill
  1740 E. Seventeenth Ave., 303/393-7545
Mediterranean Health Cafe
  2817 E. Third Ave., 303/399-2940
Noodles and Company
  2360 E. Third Ave., 303/331-6600

Best Ice Cream/Yogurt
Cucina Leone
  763 S. University Blvd., 303/722-5466

Best Indian Food
Gandhi India's Cuisine
  5071B S. Syracuse St., 303/694-7388
India's
  3333 S. Tamarac Dr., 303/755-4284
Taj Mahal
  8665 Sheridan Blvd., Arvada, 303/427-4340

Best Inexpensive Meal
Bocaza Mexican Grill
  1740 E. Seventeenth Ave., 303/393-7545
Chef Noodle House
  10400 E. Sixth Ave., Aurora, 303/363-6888
Las Delicias
  439 E. Nineteenth Ave., 303/839-5675
Las Delicias II
  50 E. Del Norte, 303/430-0422
Las Delicias III
  1530 Blake St., 303/629-5051
Lim's Mongolian BBQ and Lim's Chinese Kitchen
  1530 Blake St., 303/893-1158
Lucero's
  3657 Fillmore St., 303/322-1662
Taqueria Mexico
  3800 W. Colfax Ave., 303/595-0085

Best Italian Food
Barolo Grill
  3030 E. Sixth Ave., 303/393-1040
Cafe Jordano
  11068 W. Jewell Ave., Lakewood, 303/988-6863
Carmine's on Penn
  92 S. Pennsylvania St., 303/777-6443
Fratelli's Restaurant
  1200 E. Hampden Ave., Englewood, 303/761-4771

C

Gaetano's Restaurant
  3760 Tejon St., 303/455-9852
Grisanti's
  4100 E. Mexico Ave., 303/782-5170
Josephina's
  1433 Larimer St., 303/623-0166
Marsala's Ristorante
  12041 Pecos St., 303/450-5444
Mauro's Restaurant
  25797 Conifer Rd., Conifer, 303/838-5707
Pasquini's Pizzeria
  1310 S. Broadway, 303/744-0917
The Old Spaghetti Factory
  1215 Eighteenth St., 303/295-1864

Best Japanese Food
Benihana
  3295 S. Tamarac Dr., 303/750-0200
Gasho of Japan
  5071B S. Syracuse St., 303/773-3277
Mori Japanese Restaurant
  2019 Market St., 303/298-1864
Sonoda's
  1620 Market St., 303/595-9500
Sushi Den
  1487 S. Pearl St., 303/777-0826
Sushi Tazu
  300 Fillmore St., 303/320-1672

Best Korean Food
Silla
  3005 S. Peoria St., Aurora, 303/338-5070

Best Lunch
Aubergine Cafe
  225 E. Seventh Ave., 303/832-4778
Cafe Galileo
  535 Sixteenth St., 303/573-7600
Ellyngton's
  Brown Palace Hotel, 321 Seventeenth St.,
    303/297-3111
Gandhi India's Cuisine
  5071B S. Syracuse St., 303/694-7388
Lucero's
  3657 Fillmore St., 303/322-1662
Pony Expresso and Dessert Bar
  501 W. Twelfth Ave., 303/573-7669
Pressto
  555 Seventeenth St., 303/294-0449
The Palm Restaurant at Westin Hotel Tabor Center
  1672 Lawrence St., 303/825-7256
Tommy's Oriental Food
  3410 E. Colfax Ave., 303/377-4244
Trinity Grille
  1801 Broadway, 303/293-2288
Twentieth Street Cafe
  1123 Twentieth St., 303/295-9041

C

Best Mexican Food
Blue Bonnet Cafe
  457 S. Broadway, 303/778-0147
Chez Jose
  3027 E. Second Ave., 303/322-9160
  5910 S. University Blvd., Littleton, 303/798-8753
El Azteca
  3960 Federal Blvd., 303/761-3639
El Bronquito Cafe
  3023 W. 44th Ave., 303/458-9203
El Taco de Mexico
  714 Santa Fe Dr., 303/623-3926
La Casita
  4390 W. 44th Ave., 303/455-2190
  3561 Tejon St., 303/477-2899
La Cueva
  9742 E. Colfax Ave., Aurora, 303/367-1422
Lucero's
  3657 Fillmore St., 303/322-1662
Mama Josefina's
  2336 E. 46th Ave., 303/292-9907
RosaLinda's Mexican Cafe
  2005 W. 33rd Ave., 303/455-0608
Taqueria Mexico
  3800 W. Colfax Ave., 303/595-0085
Taqueria Paztcuaro
  2616 W. 32nd Ave., 303/455-4389
Tortilla Flat Restaurant
  2850 W. Church Ave., Littleton, 303/794-7300

Best Middle Eastern Food
Damascus
  2276 S. Colorado Blvd., 303/757-3515
House of Kabob
  2246 S. Colorado Blvd., 303/756-0744
Jerusalem Restaurant
  1890 E. Evans Ave., 303/777-8828

Best Other Ethnic Food
Cafe Brazil (South American)
  3611 Navajo St., 303/480-1877
Los Cabos II (South American, Peruvian)
  1512 Curtis St., 303/571-0007
Mataam Fez Moroccan Food (Moroccan)
  4609 E. Colfax Ave., 303/399-9282
Queen of Sheba (Ethiopian)
  7225 E. Colfax Ave., 303/399-9442
Rodizio Grill and Steakhouse (South American)
  7900 W. Quincy Ave., Littleton, 303/972-0806
Sabor Latino Restaurant (South American)
  3464 W. 32nd Ave., 303/455-8664
Sadie's Caribbean (Caribbean)
  2033 Colfax, 303/780-9982
The Ethiopian Restaurant (Ethiopian)
  2816 E. Colfax Ave., 303/322-5939
Tommy Tsunami's Pacific Diner (Pacific Rim)
  1432 Market St., 303/534-5050

C

Best Outdoor Dining
Chopper's Sports Grill
   80 S. Madison St., 303/399-4448
Cucina Colore
   3041 E. Third Ave., 303/393-6917
Emerald Isle
   4385 S. Parker Rd., Aurora, 303/690-3722
La Coupole Cafe
   2191 Arapahoe St., 303/297-2288
Maria's Bakery and Deli
   3705 Shoshone St., 303/477-3372
P.F. Chang's China Bistro
   8315 S. Park Meadows Center Dr., Littleton,
   303/790-7744
Rock Bottom Brewery
   1001 Sixteenth St., 303/534-7616

Best Pizza
Anthony's Pizza and Pasta
   1628 E. Evans Ave., 303/744-3137
   1550 California St., 303/573-6236
   10890 E. Dartmouth Ave., Aurora, 303/306-9755
Beau Jo's
   2710 S. Colorado Blvd., 303/758-1519
Carl's Pizzeria
   3800 W. 38th Ave., 303/477-1694
Frontroom Pizza
   13795 W. Jewell Ave., Lakewood, 303/969-8880
Pantaleone's New York Pizza
   2120 S. Holly St., 303/757-3456
Pasquini's Pizzeria
   1310 S. Broadway, 303/744-0917
Pizza Colore Cafe
   1512 Larimer St., Ste. 12R, 303/534-6844
Wazee Supper Club
   1600 Fifteenth St., 303/623-9518

Best Place to Take the Kids
Grand Slam Sports Cafe
   9660 E. Arapahoe Rd., Englewood, 303/799-1300
Paul's Place Restaurant
   3000 E. First Ave., Ste. 115, 303/321-5801
   6818 S. Yosemite, 303/321-5801

Best Regional Food
Pepper Pod Restaurant
   530 Fir St., Hudson, 303/536-4736

Best Restaurant in Town
Briarwood Inn
   1630 Eighth St., Golden, 303/279-3121
Buckhorn Exchange
   1000 Osage St., 303/534-9505
Racine's Restaurant
   850 Bannock St., 303/595-0418
Strings
   1700 Humboldt St., 303/831-7310
Today's Gourmet Highland Gardens Cafe
   3927 W. 32nd Ave., 303/458-5920

C

Best Restaurant Meal Value
The Old Spaghetti Factory
  1215 Eighteenth St., 303/295-1864

Best Romantic Dining
Anastasia Vieux Carre
  5946 S. Holly St., Englewood, 303/770-2073
Baby Doe's Matchless Mine
  2023 W. 23rd Ave., 303/433-3386
Cliff Young's Restaurant
  700 E. Seventeenth Ave., 303/831-8900
Tuscany Restaurant
  4150 E. Mississippi Ave., 303/782-9300

Best Salad/Salad Bar
Coos Bay Bistro
  2076 S. University Blvd., 303/744-3591
Denver Salad Company
  102 Inverness Terrace E., Englewood,
    303/790-7706
  14201 E. Public Market Dr., Aurora, 303/750-1339
  2010 E. County Line Rd., Littleton, 303/798-3453
  8936 W. Bowles Ave., Littleton, 303/932-2080
Gussie's Restaurant and Lounge
  2345 W. 112th Ave., 303/469-5281
Healthy Habits
  14195 W. Colfax Ave., Golden, 303/277-9293
  7418 S. University Blvd., Littleton, 303/740-7044
Laughing Dog Market and Deli
  1925 Blake St., 303/293-2364

Best Sandwiches
Old-Fashioned Italian Deli
  395 W. Littleton Blvd., Littleton, 303/794-1402
Taqueria Patzcuaro
  2616 W. 32nd Ave., 303/455-4389
Wild Oats Community Market
  1111 S. Washington St., 303/733-6201

Best Seafood
Fresh Fish Company
  7800 E. Hampden Ave., 303/740-9556
Jax Fish House
  1539 Seventeenth St., 303/292-5767
McCormick's Fish House and Bar
  1659 Wazee St., 303/825-1107
Star Fish Restaurant
  300 Fillmore St., 303/333-1133

Best Soul Food
Ethel's House of Soul
  2622 Welton St., 303/295-2125
Kapre Lounge and Fried Chicken
  2729 Welton St., 303/295-9207
M and D's Bar-B-Que and Fish Place
  2004 E. 28th Ave., 303/296-1760
Pierre's Supper Club
  2157 Downing St., 303/861-8236

C

Best Steaks
Aurora Summit
  2700 S. Havana St., Aurora, 303/751-2112
Beacon Grill
  303 Sixteenth St., 303/592-4745
Luke's
  4990 Kipling St., Wheat Ridge, 303/422-3300
Morton's of Chicago
  1710 Wynkoop St., 303/825-3353
Stuart Anderson's Black Angus
  1295 Cortez St., 303/426-6010
  6875 S. Broadway, Littleton, 303/795-0686
  3000 S. Havana St., Aurora, 303/751-5985
  375 Union Blvd., Lakewood, 303/988-5753

Best Sunday Brunch
Ellyngton's
  Brown Palace Hotel, 321 Seventeenth St.,
    303/297-3111
Grand Slam Sports Cafe
  810 S. Wadsworth Blvd., Lakewood, 303/922-3400
Kate's at 35th Avenue
  3435 Albion St., 303/333-4816
Today's Gourmet Highland Gardens Cafe
  3927 W. 32nd Ave., 303/458-5920
Tuscany Restaurant
  Loews Giorgio Hotel, 4150 E. Mississippi Ave.,
    303/782-9300

Best Sushi
Kobe An
  85 S. Union Blvd., Lakewood, 303/989-5907
Restaurant Japon
  1028 S. Gaylord St., 303/744-0330

Best Tea Room
Brown Palace Hotel
  321 Seventeenth St., 303/297-3111

Best Thai Food
J's Noodles
  945 S. Federal Blvd., 303/922-5495
Taste of Thailand
  504 E. Hampden Ave., Englewood, 303/762-9112
Tommy's Oriental Food
  3410 E. Colfax Ave., 303/377-4244

Best Vegetarian Food
Creative Vegetarian Cafe
  330 E. Sixth Ave., 303/777-7373
Harvest
  430 S. Colorado Blvd., 303/399-6652
Healthy Habits Restaurant
  865 S. Colorado Blvd., 303/733-2105
Hugh's
  1469 S. Pearl St., 303/744-1940
Porter Memorial Hospital Cafeteria
  2525 Downing St., 303/778-1955
St. Mark's Coffeehouse
  2019 E. 17th Ave., 303/322-8384
  1416 Market St., 303/446-2925

C

Best Vietnamese Food
Little Saigon
  201 Steele St., Ste. 3C, 303/333-4569
New Orient Restaurant
  10203 E. Iliff Ave., 303/751-1288
New Saigon Restaurant
  630 S. Federal Blvd., 303/936-4954
Oodles
  1529 S. Pearl St., 303/765-2880
Rose's Cafe
  731 Quebec St., 303/377-7649
T-Wa Inn
  555 S. Federal Blvd., 303/922-4584
Vietnam Inn Restaurant
  6510 S. Broadway, Littleton, 303/797-7990

Best View While Dining
Baby Doe's Matchless Mine
  2023 W. 23rd Ave., 303/433-3386

Best Wine Selection
Fourth Story
  2955 E. First Ave., 303/322-1824

DURANGO, CO

Best Chinese Food
Golden Dragon Restaurant
  992 Main Ave., 970/259-0956
May Palace
  909 Main Ave., 970/259-4836

Best Coffee/Coffeehouse
Durango Coffee Company
  730 Main Ave., 970/259-2059
Steaming Bean Coffee Company
  915 Main Ave., 970/385-7901

Best Desserts
Carver's Bakery Cafe
  1022 Main Ave., 970/259-2545
Le Rendezvous Swiss Bakery
  750 Main Ave., 970/385-5685

Best Diner
Durango Diner
  957 Main Ave., 970/247-9889

Best Fine Dining
Ariano's Italian Restaurant
  150 E. Sixth St., 970/247-8146
Randy's Restaurant and Bar
  152 E. Sixth St., 970/247-9083
Seasons Grill
  764 Main Ave., 970/382-9790
Sow's Ear
  49617 550N, 970/247-3527

Best Ice Cream/Yogurt
Durango Country Creamery
  600 Main Ave., 970/247-8111

Best Lunch
K-Bob's Steakhouse
    381 S. Camino Del Rio, 970/247-1940
Lori's Family Dining
    800 S. Camino Del Rio, 970/247-1224
Old Tymer's Cafe
    1000 Main Ave., 970/259-2990

Best Mexican Food
Francisco's
    619 Main Ave., 970/247-4098
Gazpacho New Mexican Restaurant
    431 E. Second Ave., 970/259-9494

Best Pizza
a'Roma Restaurant and Tavern
    2659 Main Ave., 970/259-0188
Pronto Pizza and Pasta
    160 E. Sixth St., 970/247-1510

Best Seafood
Ore House
    147 E. College Dr.., 970/247-5707

Best Steaks
Henry's at the Strater
    669 Main Ave., 970/247-4431
Ore House
    147 E. College Dr.., 970/247-5707
Palace Grill
    501B Main Ave., 970/247-2018
Sow's Ear
    49617 550N, 970/247-3527

Best Vegetarian Food
Durango's Meeting Place
    666 E. Sixth Ave., 970/247-5322

FT. COLLINS, CO

Best Bar
Bruce's Bar
    345 First St., Severence, 970/686-2320

Best Beer Selection
Old Chicago
    147 S. College Ave., 970/482-8599

Best Bistro
Jay's
    151 S. College Ave., 970/482-1876

Best Breakfast
Cafe Bluebird
    524 W. Laurel St., 970/484-7755
Heartland Cafe
    301 E. Fourth St., Loveland, 970/669-7774
Silver Grill Cafe
    218 Walnut St., 970/484-4656
The Egg and I
    2525 N. Lincoln Ave., Loveland, 970/635-0050

C

2809 S. College Ave., 970/223-5271

Best Brewpub
Coopersmith's Pub and Brewing
5 Old Town Sq., 970/498-0483

Best Burgers
Red Robin Spirits Emporium
701 E. Harmony Rd., 970/223-0111
Round the Corner Restaurant
101 W. Swallow Rd., 970/226-2705

Best Chinese Food
China Dragon
1525 W. Eisenhower Blvd., Loveland, 970/663-3734
China Palace
117 S. College Ave., 970/221-0448

Best Coffee/Coffeehouse
Black Cup
4527 W. Eisenhower Blvd., Loveland, 970/663-0795
Boyer's Coffee Emporium
257D E. 29th St., Loveland, 970/593-0635
Deja Vu Coffeehouse
646 1/2 S. College Ave., 970/221-3243
Starbucks Coffee
2601 S. Lemay Ave., 970/223-6308
3600 S. College Ave., 970/204-9948
Starry Night Coffee Company
112 S. College Ave., 970/493-3039

Best Continental Food
Parsonage Restaurant
405 E. Fifth St., Loveland, 970/962-9700

Best Desserts
Pour La France Bakery and Cafe
100 W. Mountain Ave., 970/482-9868
Schmidt's Bakery and Deli
2248 W. First St., Loveland, 970/667-9811

Best Fine Dining
Bisetti's Italian Restaurant
120 S. College Ave., 970/493-0086
Cuisine Cuisine
130 S. Mason St., 970/221-0399
Nico's Catacombs
115 S. College Ave., 970/482-6426

Best Health-Conscious Menu
Cabin Country Natural Foods
248 E. Fourth St., Loveland, 970/669-9280
Peaks Cafe
425 E. Fourth St., Loveland, 970/669-6158
Rainbow Limited
212 W. Laurel St., 970/221-2664
The Egg and I
2809 S. College Ave., 970/223-5271
2525 N. Lincoln Ave., Loveland, 970/635-0050

Best Ice Cream/Yogurt
Walrus Ice Cream
125 W. Mountain Ave., 970/482-5919

C

Best Italian Food
Bisetti's Italian Restaurant
   120 S. College Ave., 970/493-0086
Canino's Italian Restaurant
   613 S. College Ave., 970/493-7205
Johnny Carino's Italian Kitchen
   4235 S. College Ave., 970/223-9455
Pasta Jay's Old Town
   11 Old Town Sq., 970/224-5800

Best Lunch
Deli-Works
   6001 S. College Ave., 970/226-4308
Joe's Fireside Cafe
   238 S. College Ave., 970/482-2233

Best Mexican Food
Adelita's Fine Mexican Food
   414 E. Sixth St., Loveland, 970/669-9577
Armadillo's
   354 Walnut St., 970/493-4440
El Burrito Tortillas
   402 Linden St., 970/493-6606
Gonzalo's Restaurant
   172 N. College Ave., 970/493-2002
Juan's Cantina
   128 E. Fourth St., Loveland, 970/593-9197
Tortilla Marissa
   2635 S. College Ave., 970/225-9222

Best Pizza
Beau Jo's
   100 N. College Ave., 970/498-8898
Cozzola's Pizza
   241 Linden St., 970/482-3557
Justine's Pizza
   1906 W. Eisenhower Blvd., Loveland, 970/667-8808
Woody's Woodfired Pizza and Watering Hole
   518 W. Laurel St., 970/482-7100

Best Salad/Salad Bar
Fort Collins Salad Company
   116 E. Foothills Pkwy., 970/223-6363
Red Robin Spirits Emporium
   701 E. Harmony Rd., 970/223-0111

Best Sandwiches
Avogadro's Number
   605 S. Mason St., 970/493-5555
Colorado Grill
   106 E. 29th St., Loveland, 970/663-5698
   2225 W. Eisenhower Blvd., Loveland, 970/669-7377
Coopersmith's Pub and Brewing
   5 Old Town Sq., 970/498-0483
Maggie McCullough's Bread Shop
   116 E. Foothills Pkwy., 970/282-8460
Pickle Barrel
   122 W. Laurel St., 970/484-0235

C

Best Seafood
Black Steer
  436 N. Lincoln Ave., Loveland, 970/667-6679
Nate's Steak and Seafood Place
  3620 S. Mason St., 970/223-9200
Pelican Fish
  3512 S. Mason St., 970/226-1522
Summit Restaurant
  3208 W. Eisenhower Blvd., Loveland, 970/669-6648

Best Southwestern Food
Cactus Grille
  125 E. Fourth St., Loveland, 970/663-4500

Best Steaks
Black Steer
  436 N. Lincoln Ave., Loveland, 970/667-6679
Charco Broiler
  1716 E. Mulberry St., 970/482-1472

Best Vegetarian Food
Rainbow Limited
  212 W. Laurel St., 970/221-2664

Best Vietnamese Food
Saigon 17
  146 N. College Ave., 970/484-7255

GLENWOOD SPRINGS, CO

Best American Food
Jack's 82 Grill
  6824 Hwy. 82, 970/945-8803

Best Barbecue/Ribs
Buffalo Valley Inn
  3637 Hwy. 82, 970/945-5297
Smokin' Willie's
  101 W. Sixth St., 970/945-2479

Best Burgers
Charcoalburger Drive In
  5965 Hwy. 6 at 24, 970/945-6652

Best Chinese Food
China Town
  2830 S. Glen Ave., 970/945-0307
May Palace
  820 Grand Ave., 970/945-0472

Best Continental Food
Sopris Restaurant
  7215 Hwy. 82, 970/945-7771

Best Desserts
Rosi's Little Bavarian
  141 W. Sixth St., 970/928-9186

Best Family Restaurant
Fireside Restaurant
  51701 Hwy. 6, 970/945-6613

Best Italian Food
Florindo's Italian Cuisine
  721 Grand Ave., 970/945-1245

C

Best Mexican Food
Dos Hombres Restaurant
  51683 Hwy. 6, 970/928-0490
Los Desperados
  55 Mel Rey Rd., 970/945-6878

Best Pizza
Italian Underground
  715 Grand Ave., 970/945-6422

Best Seafood
Rivers
  2525 Grand Ave., 970/928-8813

GRAND JUNCTION, CO

Best American Food
Furr's Cafeteria
  2817 North Ave., 970/243-4415

Best Barbecue/Ribs
Bennett's
  2440 Hwy. 6 at 50, 970/256-7427

Best Breakfast
Crystal Cafe and Bake Shop
  314 Main St., 970/242-8843
Starvin' Arvin's
  752 Horizon Dr., 970/241-0430
  2516 Broadway, 970/245-8028

Best Casual Dining
WW Peppers
  735 Horizon Dr., 970/245-9251

Best Chinese Food
China Garden
  2931 North Ave., 970/256-9758
Far East Restaurant
  1530 North Ave., 970/242-8131

Best Family Restaurant
Raintree Restaurant
  492 Morning Glory Ln., Ste. 1, 970/241-3530

Best Fine Dining
Winery Restaurant
  642 Main St., 970/242-4100

Best Greek/Mediterranean Food
Blue Moon Bar and Grille
  120 N. Seventh St., 970/242-4506

Best Health-Conscious Menu
Goodpasture's Restaurant
  733 Horizon Dr., 970/243-3058

Best Italian Food
Dolce Vita
  336 Main St., Ste. 101, 970/242-8482
Mama Longo's
  2830 North Ave., Ste. 6C, 970/245-6600
Pantuso's Ristorante and Lounge
  2782 Crossroads Blvd., 970/243-0000

C

Best Lunch
Crystal Cafe and Bake Shop
314 Main St., 970/242-8843

Best Mexican Food
Dos Hombres Restaurant
421 Branch Dr., 970/242-8861
Los Reyes Restaurant
811 S. Seventh St., 970/245-8392

Best Pizza
Big Cheese Pizza
810 North Ave., 970/245-9263
Old Chicago
120 North Ave., 970/244-8383

Best Sandwiches
Papa Kelsey's and Fred's Pizza and Subs
1234 N. Twelfth St., 970/241-4033

GREELEY, CO

Best Bar
Fat Albert's
1717 23rd Ave., 970/356-1999
Lucky Star Lounge
33131 U.S. Hwy. 85, Lucerne, 970/351-8000
The Smiling Moose
2501 Eleventh Ave., 970/356-7010
The Gambler
618 25th Ave., 970/351-7575

Best Breakfast
The Egg and I
3830 Tenth St., 970/353-7737
The Kitchen
905 Sixteenth St., 970/351-7396

Best Burgers
Jackson's Hole
2118 35th Ave., 970/330-3400
JB's
2501 Eighth Ave., 970/352-3202
Neighborhood Grill
3000 23rd Ave., 970/356-4449

Best Chinese Food
Canton Garden
1330 Eighth Ave., 970/353-7314
Hunan
2028 35th Ave., 970/330-0755
Jade Palace
3605 Tenth St., 970/356-3388

Best Coffee/Coffeehouse
Margie's Java Joint
931 Sixteenth St., 970/356-6364
Village Inn and Pancake House and Restaurant
2729 Eighth Ave., 970/353-5187
921 30th Ave., 970/356-5449

C

Best Italian Food
Cable's End
  3780 W. Tenth St., 970/356-4847
Roma
  728 Sixteenth St., 970/352-9511

Best Mexican Food
Alberto's
  2525 Tenth St., 970/356-1417
Armadillo
  111 S. First St., La Salle, 970/284-5565
Farmer's Inn
  109 S. Third Ave., La Salle, 970/284-6100

Best Pizza
Old Chicago
  2349 29th St., 970/330-1116
Roma
  728 Sixteenth St., 970/352-9511

Best Sandwiches
Fat Albert's
  1717 23rd Ave., 970/356-1999
Neighborhood Grill
  3000 23rd Ave., 970/356-4449
The Egg and I
  3830 W. Tenth St., 970/353-7737

Best Seafood
New Plantation
  3520 S. Eleventh Ave., Evans, 970/330-7903
Potato Brumbaugh's
  2400 Seventeenth St., 970/356-6340

Best Sports Bar
Jackson's Hole
  2118 35th Ave., 970/330-3400
Old Chicago
  2349 29th St., 970/330-1116
The Dugout
  2509 Eleventh Ave., 970/356-8739

Best Steaks
The Ebony Room
  3313 Eleventh Ave., Evans, 970/339-5241
Potato Brumbaugh's
  2400 Seventeenth St., 970/356-6340
Rafferty's
  5990 W. Tenth St., 970/352-1664

GUNNISON, CO

Best Dinner
Palisades Saloon and Restaurant
  820 N. Main St., 970/641-9223

Best Fine Dining
The Trough Restaurant
  Hwy. 50, 970/641-3724

Best Inexpensive Meal
W Cafe
  114 N. Main St., 970/641-1744

C

Best Pizza
Pie-Zans Pizza
730 N. Main St., 970/641-4319

Best Sandwiches
Chatterbox Sandwich Shop
206 N. Main St., 970/641-0330

Best Steaks
Cattleman's Inn
301 W. Tomichi Ave., 970/641-1061

LAMAR, CO

Best Barbecue/Ribs
Hickory House
1115 N. Main St., 719/336-5018

Best Breakfast
Ranchers Restaurant
Lamar Truck Plaza, 33110 County Rd. 7,
719/336-3445

Best Burgers
BJ's Burger and Beverage
1510 S. Main St., 719/336-5386

Best Chinese Food
Green Garden
601 E. Olive St., 719/336-3264

Best Mexican Food
The Main Cafe
114 S. Main St., 719/336-5736

Best Steaks
Blackwell Station
1301 S. Main St., 719/336-7575

MONTROSE, CO

Best Bar
JJ's Restaurant
613 E. Main St., 970/249-5349

Best Breakfast
Starvin' Arvin's
1320 S. Townsend Ave., 970/249-7787

Best Coffee/Coffeehouse
Mocha Joe's
833 S. Townsend Ave., 970/240-1808

Best Family Restaurant
Backwoods Inn
103 Rose Ln., 970/249-1961
Red Barn Restaurant
1413 E. Main St., 970/249-8100

Best Mexican Food
El Sombrero
82 Rose Ln., 970/249-0217

Best Pizza
Sicily's Italian Restaurant
1135 E. Main St., 970/240-9199

Best Sandwiches
Backstreet Bagel Shop
192 S. Townsend Ave., 970/240-3675

C

Best All-You-Can-Eat Buffet
Country Buffet
3020 Hart Rd., 719/545-3502
Mi Ranchito Mexican Restaurant
24500 Hwy. 50E, Blende, 719/583-1098

Best Bar
Gold Dust Saloon
130 S. Union Ave., 719/545-0741
Gus's Place
1201 Elm St., 719/542-0756
Irish Brewpub and Grille
108 W. Third St., 719/542-9974

Best Business Lunch
Cactus Flower
2149 Jerry Murphy Rd., 719/545-8218
The Deli
612 N. Main St., 719/543-8165
Magpie's
229 S. Union Ave., 719/542-5522

Best Casual Dining
Southern Classic Cuisine
1123 W. Thirteenth St., 719/545-9338

Best Chinese Food
China Lantern Restaurant
315 W. Fourth St., 719/546-0640
Mandarin Chinese Restaurant
240 W. 29th St., 719/542-5151
Saigon Garden Cuisine
1301 N. Main St., 719/542-0280
Tian Jin Restaurant
3400 W. Northern Ave., 719/560-0903

Best Diner
Pantry Restaurant
107A E. Abriendo Ave., 719/543-8072
Pass Key 50 West
1901 Pass Key 50W, 719/542-9144
Pass Key Restaurant
518 E. Abriendo Ave., 719/542-0827

Best Family Restaurant
Black-Eyed Pea
801 W. U.S. Hwy. 50, 719/583-9544
Country Kitchen
4137 N. Elizabeth St., 719/545-3179

Best Fine Dining
Rendezvous Restaurant
218 W. Second St., 719/542-2247

Best French Food
Le Petit Chablis
512 Royal Gorge Blvd., Canon City, 719/269-3333

C

Best Inexpensive Meal
Don's Cafe
  2921 N. Elizabeth St., 719/543-5814
Pinon Restaurant Stop
  4803 N. I-25, 719/545-3990

Best Italian Food
Gaetano's Restaurant
  910 W. U.S. Hwy. 50, 719/546-0949
Giadone's Bar and Grill
  23344 U.S. Hwy. 50E, 719/542-9751
Ianne's Whiskey Ridge
  4333 Thatcher Ave., 719/564-8551
La Tronica's
  1143 E. Abriendo Ave., 719/542-1113

Best Lunch
Carriage House Restaurant
  Fifteenth at Grand St., 719/595-0098
DeJoy's Italian Cafe
  115 W. B St., 719/584-3410

Best Mexican Food
Don Carlos
  1234 S. Prairie Ave., 719/566-1447
Grand Prix Restaurant and Lounge
  615 E. Mesa Ave., 719/542-9825
Mill Stop Cafe
  317 Bay State Ave., 719/564-0407

Best Pizza
Ianne's Pizzeria Number 1
  515 W. Northern Ave., 719/542-5942
Ianne's Whiskey Ridge
  4333 Thatcher Ave., 719/564-8551

Best Restaurant in Town
Ivywood Inn
  3915 Ivywood Ln., 719/564-1476
La Renaissance
  217 E. Routt Ave., 719/543-6367
La Tronica's
  1143 E. Abriendo Ave., 719/542-1113

Best Sandwiches
All Seasons Gourmet Deli Cafe
  2800 N. Elizabeth St., 719/543-5060
Mostly Bagels
  218 S. Victoria Ave., 719/546-0858
Pagano's
  3416 W. Northern Ave., 719/566-0067
Quizno's Classic Subs
  405 N. Union Ave., 719/546-9339

Best Steaks
D J's Steak House
  4289 N. Elizabeth St., 719/545-9354
Mozart's Lounge
  1120 N. Main St., 719/542-9662
Park East Restaurant
  720 Goodnight Ave., 719/561-8707

Best Sunday Brunch
Pueblo West Inn
  Best Western, 201 S. McCulloch Blvd.,
    719/547-2111

Best Tea Room
Tivoli's
  325 S. Union Ave., 719/545-1448

STEAMBOAT SPRINGS, CO

Best Barbecue/Ribs
Double Z Bar and Bar BQ
  1124 Yampa St., 970/879-0890

Best Breakfast
The Shack Cafe
  740 Lincoln Ave., 970/879-9975

Best Brewpub
Steamboat Brewery and Tavern
  436 Lincoln Ave., 970/879-2233

Best Chinese Food
Canton Chinese Restaurant
  720 Lincoln Ave., 970/879-4480

Best Coffee/Coffeehouse
Mocha Molly's
  635 S. Lincoln Ave., 970/879-0587
Off The Beaten Path
  56 Seventh St., 970/879-6830

Best Mexican Food
La Montana Mexican Restaurant
  2500 Village Dr., 970/879-5800

Best Place to Take the Kids
Old Town Pub and Restaurant
  600 S. Lincoln Ave., 970/879-2101

Best Restaurant in Town
El Rancho Restaurant and Lounge
  425 Lincoln Ave., 970/879-0658
River Bend Inn
  26795 Hwy. 40W, 970/879-1615

Best Seafood
Coral Grill
  Sundance Plaza, Anglers Dr., Ste. 1, 970/879-6858
Ore House at the Pine Grove
  1465 Pine Grove Rd., 970/879-1190

Best Steaks
Old West Steak House
  1104 Lincoln Ave., 970/879-1441
Ore House at the Pine Grove
  1465 Pine Grove Rd., 970/879-1190

Best View While Dining
Hazie's
  2305 Mount Werner Circle, 970/879-6111

C

Best Breakfast
City Cafe
  207 Main St., Ft. Morgan, 970/867-2287
Village Inn
  203 N. Fourth Ave., 970/522-4882

Best Chinese Food
China Garden Restaurant
  126 W. Main St., 970/522-1137

Best Coffee/Coffeehouse
Hot Java Cafe
  202 N. Third Ave., 970/522-1120

Best Diner
J & L Cafe
  423 N. Third Ave., 970/522-3625

Best Dinner
Country Steak Out
  19592 E. Eighth Ave., Ft. Morgan, 970/867-7887
Steak House
  I-76 at Hwy. 63, Atwood, 970/522-7088

Best Eclectic Menu
Fort Restaurant and Lounge
  1409 Barlow Rd., Ft. Morgan, 970/867-9481

Best Family Restaurant
Memories Restaurant
  725 Main St., Ft. Morgan, 970/867-8205
Prairie Cafe
  73501 Hwy. 14, Stoneham, 970/735-2736

Best Italian Food
Cabel's Italian Grill
  431 Main St., Ft. Morgan, 970/867-6144

Best Lunch
Quilted Tea Pot
  109 Lincoln Ave., 970/522-3665

Best Mexican Food
Cocina Alvarado
  715 W. Main St., 970/522-8884
Momma Conde's
  100 Broadway St., 970/522-0802

Best Seafood
TJ Bummer's
  203 Broadway St., 970/522-8397

Best Steaks
TJ Bummer's
  203 Broadway St., 970/522-8397

Best Tea Room
Quilted Tea Pot
  109 Lincoln Ave., 970/522-3665

Best Barbecue/Ribs
Fat Alley BBQ
  122 S. Oak St., 970/728-3985

Best Breakfast
Maggie's Bakery
  217 E. Colorado Ave., 970/728-3334

Best Italian Food
Baked in Telluride
  127 S. Fir St., 970/728-4775

Best Lunch
Maggie's Bakery
  217 E. Colorado Ave., 970/728-3334

Best Mexican Food
Sofio's Restaurant
  110 E. Colorado Ave., 970/728-4882

VAIL, CO

Best American Food
Hong Kong Cafe
  227 Wall St., 970/476-1818

Best Breakfast
The Daily Grind
  288 Bridge St., 970/476-5856

Best Desserts
Villager Restaurant and Bar
  100 E. Meadow Dr., 970/476-8683

Best Pizza
Pazzo's Pizzeria
  122 E. Meadow Dr., 970/476-9026

Best Place to Take the Kids
The Bully Ranch
  Sommen Alp Resort, 20 Vail Rd., 970/476-5656

Best Seafood
Montauk Seafood Grill
  549 E. Lionshead Circle, 970/476-2601

Best Steaks
Red Lion
  304 Bridge St., 970/476-7676

Best Thai Food
Siamese Orchid
  12 S. Frontage Rd. W., 970/476-9417

Connecticut

Best American Food
Nineteenth Hole Restaurant
  650 Brooklawn Ave., 203/333-5752

Best Bar
Black Rock Castle
  2895 Fairfield Ave., 203/336-3990

Best Breakfast
Frankie's Diner
  1660 Barnum Ave., 203/334-8971

Best Business Lunch
Ralph and Rich's
  121 Wall St., 203/366-3597

Best Continental Food
Ralph and Rich's
  121 Wall St., 203/366-3597

Best Diner
New Colony Diner Bridgeport
  2321 Main St., 203/367-1217

Best Family Restaurant
Jennie's Family Restaurant
  380 Monroe Turnpike, Rte. 111, 203/452-2435

Best Health-Conscious Menu
Marisa's Ristorante
  6540 Main St., Trumbull, 203/459-4225

Best Homestyle Food
Rhythms
  1328 Main St., 203/576-7427

C

Best Italian Food
La Scogliera Restaurant
   697 Madison Ave., 203/333-0673
Marisa's Ristorante
   6540 Main St., Trumbull, 203/459-4225
Tartaglia's Restaurant
   1439 Madison Ave., 203/576-1281
Testo's Restaurant
   920 Madison Ave., 203/367-4298

Best Lunch
Ritz Lunchette
   2816 Fairfield Ave., 203/335-6977
Roberto's Pizza and Restaurant
   899 Main St., 203/368-6599

Best Mexican Food
Taco Loco
   3170 Fairfield Ave., 203/335-8228

Best Other Ethnic Food
Black Rock Castle (Irish)
   2895 Fairfield Ave., 203/336-3990
Kossuth Club (Hungarian)
   2931 Fairfield Ave., 203/335-7877
Minabela Restaurant (Portuguese/Italian)
   1282 North Ave., 203/384-1159
Omanel Restaurant (Portuguese)
   1909 Main St., 203/335-1676

Best Pizza
Emmylio's Restaurant and Pizza
   960 Main St., 203/333-1761
Famous Pizza House
   430 Park Ave., 203/333-8173

Best Restaurant in Town
Wellington's Market Restaurant
   2521 Main St., 203/335-9431

Best Sandwiches
Corporate Deli
   130 John St., 203/576-1116

Best Seafood
Seascape Restaurant
   14 Beach Dr., Stratford, 203/375-1332

Best Southwestern Food
Arizona Flats
   3001 Fairfield Ave., 203/334-8300

Best Thai Food
King and I
   545 Broadbridge Rd., 203/374-2081

DANBURY, CT

Best Breakfast
JK's
   126 South St., 860/743-4004
Station Break
   13 Durant Ave., Bethel, 860/790-1577

Best Casual Dining
Tuxedo Junction and the Living Room
2 Ives St., 860/748-2561

Best Chinese Food
Panda West
93 Mill Plain Rd., 860/730-8888

Best Coffee/Coffeehouse
Seattle Espresso
262 Main St., 860/748-6618

Best French Food
Ondine Restaurant
69 Pembroke Rd., Rte. 37, 860/746-4900
Stonehenge Inn and Restaurant
1 Stonehenge Rd., Ridgefield, 860/438-6511

Best Italian Food
Bentley's Restaurant
1 Division St., 860/778-3637
Ciao! Cafe and Wine Bar
2B Ives St., 860/791-0404

Best Middle Eastern Food
Hanna's
72 Lake Ave., 860/748-5713

Best Other Ethnic Food
Goulesh Place (Hungarian)
42 Highland Ave., 860/744-1971
O'Faia Restaurant (Portuguese)
58 Main St., 860/791-2208

Best Seafood
Down the Hatch Restaurant
292 Candlewood Lake Rd., Brookfield, 860/775-6635

Best Southwestern Food
Two Steps
5 Ives St., 860/794-0032

Best Steaks
Chuck's Steak House
20 Segar St., 860/748-6688
Kabuki Japanese Steak House
39 Lake Extension, 860/744-6885

Best Tea Room
Elizabeth's Tea Room
187 S. Main St., Newtown, 860/426-1655

FAIRFIELD, CT

Best American Food
Gregory's Cafe and Bar
1599 Post Rd., 203/259-7417
Rawley's Drive In
1886 Post Rd., 203/259-9023

Best Barbecue/Ribs
Ash Creek Saloon
93 Post Rd., 203/255-5131

C

Best Breakfast
Firehouse Deli
22 Reef Rd., 203/255-5527

Best Burgers
Archie Moore's Bar and Restaurant
48 Sanford St., 203/256-9295
Breakaway Restaurant and Bar
2316 Post Rd., 203/255-0026
Duchess Drive-In
625 Post Rd., 203/259-4874
Stuart Anderson's Black Angus Restaurant
2133 Black Rock Turnpike, 203/366-5902
Tommy's
1418 Post Rd., 203/254-1478

Best Chinese Food
Hunan Pavillion
80 Post Rd., 203/254-3444

Best Coffee/Coffeehouse
P. Gordon Coffee Roaster
1740 Post Rd., 203/254-2034

Best Diner
Athena Diner
3350 Post Rd., Southport, 203/259-0603

Best Health-Conscious Menu
Sprouts Natural Foods Market and Cafe
2057 Black Rock Turnpike, 203/333-3455

Best Italian Food
Avellino's
1813 Post Rd., 203/254-2339
Baci
52 Sanford St., 203/254-3781
Centro
1435 Post Rd., 203/255-1210
Cinzano's
1920 Black Rock Turnpike, 203/367-1199
Luigi's Restaurant
170 Post Rd., 203/259-7816

Best Japanese Food
Mako of Japan
941 Black Rock Turnpike, 203/367-5319

Best Other Ethnic Food
Pearl of Budapest (Hungarian)
57 Unquowa Rd., 203/259-4777

Best Pizza
Spazzi
1229 Post Rd., 203/256-1629
Uno Chicago Bar and Grill
2320 Black Rock Turnpike, 203/372-2909

Best Sandwiches
Gold's Delicatessen
873 Post Rd., 203/259-2233
Maggie's Pantry
1891 Post Rd., 203/255-1579

Best Sunday Brunch
Sidetracks Restaurant
2070 Post Rd., 203/254-3606

GREENWICH, CT

Best American Food
Thataway Cafe
409 Greenwich Ave., 203/622-0947

Best Burgers
Manero's
559 Steamboat Rd., 203/869-0049

Best French Food
Thomas Henkelmann
Homestead Inn, 420 Field Point Rd., 203/869-7500
Jean Louis Restaurant
61 Lewis St., 203/622-8450
Le Figaro Bistro De Paris
372 Greenwich Ave., 203/622-0018

Best Health-Conscious Menu
Greenwich Health Mart
30 Greenwich Ave., 203/869-9658

Best Italian Food
Terra Ristorante Italiano
156 Greenwich Ave., 203/629-5222

Best Japanese Food
Abis Japanese Tradition
381 Greenwich Ave., 203/862-9100

Best Pizza
DaVinci's Ristorante
235 Greenwich Ave., 203/661-5831

Best Salad/Salad Bar
Thataway Cafe
409 Greenwich Ave., 203/622-0947

Best Sandwiches
Gourmet Galley
100 Greenwich Ave., 203/869-9617

Best Seafood
DaVinci's Ristorante
235 Greenwich Ave., 203/661-5831

Best Southwestern Food
Boxcar Cantina
44 Old Field Point Rd., 203/661-4774

Best Steaks
Manero's
559 Steamboat Rd., 203/869-0049

Best Vietnamese Food
La Maison Indochine
107 Greenwich Ave., 203/869-2689

HARTFORD, CT

Best American Food
Avon Old Farms Inn
1 Nod Rd., Avon, 860/677-2818

C

Best Breakfast
Freddie's Restaurant
  2756 Main St., 860/522-6313
Municipal Cafeteria
  485 Main St., 860/278-4844

Best Business Lunch
Civic Cafe
  150 Trumbull St., 860/493-7412

Best Chinese Food
Butterfly
  831 Farmington Ave., West Hartford, 860/236-2816

Best Continental Food
Ann Howard's Apricots
  1593 Farmington Ave., Farmington, 860/673-5405

Best Diner
Freddie's Restaurant
  2756 Main St., 860/522-6313
Hal's Aquarius Restaurant
  2790 Main St., 860/247-0435

Best Dinner
Civic Cafe on Trumbull
  150 Trumbull St., 860/493-7412
Peppercorn's Grill
  357 Main St., 860/547-1714

Best Family Restaurant
Spaghetti Warehouse
  45 Bartholomew Ave., 860/951-1680

Best Fine Dining
Carbone's Ristorante
  588 Franklin Ave., 860/296-9646
Skywalk Restaurant
  242 Trumbull St., 860/522-7623

Best German Food
Edelweiss Restaurant
  980 Farmington Ave., West Hartford, 860/236-3096

Best Greek/Mediterranean Food
Tapa's Restaurant
  1150 New Britain Ave., West Hartford, 860/521-4609

Best Italian Food
Carbone's Ristorante
  588 Franklin Ave., 860/296-9646
Gaetano's Restaurant
  1 Civic Center Plz., 860/249-1629
Hot Tomato's
  1 Union Pl., 860/249-5100
Max Downtown
  185 Asylum St., 860/522-2530
Sorrento Ristorante
  371 Franklin Ave., 860/296-2490

Best Japanese Food
Fuji Japanese Restaurant
  1144 New Britain Ave., West Hartford,
    860/232-1732

C

Best Mexican Food
Margarita's
144 Albany Turnpike, Canton, 860/693-8237

Best Other Ethnic Food
Casa Lisboa (Portuguese)
1911 Park St., 860/233-3184
Shish-Kebab House (Afghan)
360 Franklin Ave., 860/296-0301

Best Pizza
First and Last Tavern
939 Maple Ave., 860/956-6000
North Main Pizza
3347 Main St., 860/527-6497

Best Sandwiches
Chicken by George
1 Civic Center Plz., 860/724-5501
Congress Rotisserie
208 Trumbull St., 860/525-5141
274 Farmington Ave., 860/278-7711

Best Seafood
USS Chowder Pot IV
165 Brainard Rd., 860/244-3311

Best Soul Food
Hal's Aquarius Restaurant
2790 Main St., 860/247-0453

Best Spanish Food
Costa Del Sol Restaurante
901 Wethersfield Ave., 860/296-1714

Best Sports Bar
Coach's Sports Bar and Grille
187 Allyn St., 860/522-6224

Best Steaks
Chuck's Steakhouse
1 Civic Center Plz., 860/241-9100

Best Thai Food
Lemon Grass Restaurant
7 S. Main St., West Hartford, 860/233-4405

Best Vietnamese Food
Truc Orient Express
735 Wethersfield Ave., 860/296-2818

MANCHESTER, CT

Best Breakfast
Chez Den Diner
927 Center St., 860/649-4011
Fani's Kitchen
1015 Main St., 860/643-2603

Best Burgers
Shady Glen Dairy Store
840 Middle Turnpike, 860/649-4245
360 Middle Turnpike W., 860/643-0511

C

Best Chinese Food
Golden Dragon Restaurant
1131U Tolland Turnpike, 860/645-0300
House of Chung
363 Broad St., 860/649-4958

Best French Food
Cavey's Restaurant
45 E. Center St., 860/643-2751

Best Ice Cream/Yogurt
Shady Glen Dairy Store
840 Middle Turnpike, 860/649-4245
360 Middle Turnpike W., 860/643-0511

Best Indian Food
Bombay Rajnahal
836 Main St., 860/646-5330

Best Italian Food
Acadia Restaurant
103 Tolland Turnpike, 860/643-1179
Nullis' Italia Ristorante
706 Hartford Rd., 860/647-1500
Pagani's Brick Oven Restaurant
55 E. Center St., 860/645-7777

Best Mexican Food
Loco Perro
191 High St., 860/267-2945

Best Pizza
Pizzeria Uno
180 Deming St., 860/648-2238
Sarantino's
238 N. Main St., 860/646-0836

Best Romantic Dining
Cavey's Restaurant
43 E. Center St., 860/643-2751

Best Sandwiches
Shady Glen Dairy Store
840 Middle Turnpike, 860/649-4245
360 Middle Turnpike W., 860/643-0511

Best Steaks
Willie's Steak House
444 Center St., 860/649-5271

Best Vegetarian Food
Bombay Rajnahal
836 Main St., 860/646-5330

MERIDEN, CT

Best American Food
Eli Cannon's
695 Main St., Middleton, 860/347-3547
Fareways Restaurant
688 Westfield Rd., 203/237-3030
Yankee Silversmith Inn
1033 N. Colony Rd., Wallingford, 203/269-5444

Best Breakfast
Fischer's Fine Food
  21 Colony Pl., 203/235-1221
Justin Time Diner
  82 W. Main St., 203/238-3301
Mike and Dee's Dinette
  85 W. Main St., 203/630-1331
Neptune House Restaurant
  1086 N. Colony Rd., Wallingford, 203/269-9317
O'Rourke's Diner
  728 Main St., Middletown, 860/346-6101

Best Burgers
O'Rourke's Diner
  728 Main St., Middletown, 860/346-6101

Best Chinese Food
King's Garden
  1231 E. Main St., 203/630-2188
Wa Wah Kitchen
  98 State St., 203/238-2100

Best Continental Food
Sans- Souci
  2003 N. Broad St., 203/639-1777

Best Diner
Justin Time Diner
  82 W. Main St., 203/238-3301
Mike and Dee's Dinette
  85 W. Main St., 203/630-1331
Olympus Diner
  1130 E. Main St., 203/235-5636

Best Dinner
Cabin Restaurant
  103 Colony St., 203/237-7471

Best Health-Conscious Menu
Fiasco
  98 Washington St., Middletown, 860/344-0222

Best Indian Food
Taj of India
  170 Main St., Middletown, 860/346-2050

Best Italian Food
Lido's Italian Foods
  361 Liberty St., 203/634-3959
Mister D's Restaurant
  34 River Rd., 203/235-1967

Best Mexican Food
Coyote Blue Tex Mex Cafe
  1960 Saybrook Rd., Middletown, 860/354-2403

Best Pizza
Lido's Italian Foods
  361 Liberty St., 203/634-3959
Little Rendezvous
  256 Pratt St., 203/235-0110
Zorba's Pizza
  1257 E. Main St., 203/238-2077

C

Best Sandwiches
Goldilocks
   612 E. Main St., 203/237-4087
Huxley's Cafe
   1231 E. Main St., 203/237-4087

Best Seafood
Hawthorne Inn
   2387 Wilbur Cross Hwy., Berlin, 203/828-4181

Best Steaks
Hawthorne Inn
   2387 Wilbur Cross Hwy., Berlin, 203/828-4181
Jacoby's Restaurant
   1388 E. Main St., 203/634-3222

MYSTIC, CT

Best Breakfast
Kitchen Little
   81A Greenmanville Ave., 860/536-2122
Noah's Restaurant
   113 Water St., Stonington, 860/535-3925
Restaurant Bravo Bravo
   The Whaler's Inn, 20 E. Main St., 860/536-3228

Best Fine Dining
Seamen's Inn Restaurant and Pub
   105 Greenmanville Ave., 860/536-9649

Best French Food
Harbor View Restaurant
   60 Water St., Stonington, 860/535-2720

Best Italian Food
Restaurant Bravo Bravo
   The Whaler's Inn, 20 E. Main St., 860/536-3228

Best Mexican Food
Margaritas
   12 Water St., 860/536-4589

Best Pizza
Mystic Pizza
   56 W. Main St., 860/536-3700

Best Sandwiches
Two Sisters Deli
   4 Pearl St., 860/536-2068

Best Seafood
Abbott's Lobster in the Rough
   117 Pearl St., 860/536-7719
Floodtide Restaurant
   Rte. 1 at Hwy. 27, 860/536-8140

Best Steaks
Steak Loft
   I-95, Exit 90, 860/536-2661

NAUGATUCK, CT

Best Breakfast
Coddington's on Meadow
   262 Meadow St., 203/729-6551

C

Best Casual Dining
Old Corner Cafe
178 N. Main St., 203/729-8087

Best Chinese Food
Hunan Pearl Restaurant
727 Rubber Ave., 203/729-8281

Best Homestyle Food
Coddington's on Meadow
262 Meadow St., 203/729-6551

Best Italian Food
Casa Nuova
1 S. Main St., 203/723-4212

Best Pizza
American Pie Pizza and Restaurant
500 S. Main St., 203/723-8661

Best Restaurant in Town
Milestone Inn
18 Neumann St., 203/723-6693

NEW BRITAIN, CT

Best American Food
Angelico's Cafe
542 E. Main St., 860/224-3811

Best Breakfast
Guy's Place
224 S. Main St., 860/224-7883

Best Chinese Food
Great Taste
597 W. Main St., 860/827-8988

Best German Food
East Side Restaurant
131 Dwight St., 860/223-1188

Best Health-Conscious Menu
Good Times Deli
298 Main St., 860/225-2233

Best Ice Cream/Yogurt
Guida's Dairy Bar
975 Farmington Ave., 860/229-0063

Best Other Ethnic Food
Fatherland Restaurant (Polish)
450 S. Main St., 860/224-3345
Guy's Place (French Canadian)
224 S. Main St., 860/224-7883

Best Pizza
Paradise Pizza
10 East St., 860/827-8123

Best Sandwiches
Good Times Deli
298 Main St., 860/225-2233

Best Steaks
Angelico's Cafe
542 E. Main St., 860/224-3811

NEW HAVEN, CT

Best American Food
Eli's Restaurant
2392 Whitney Ave., Hamden, 203/287-1101

Best Bar
Five Hundred Blake Street
500 Blake St., 203/387-0500
Eli's Restaurant
2392 Whitney Ave., Hamden, 203/287-1101

Best Barbecue/Ribs
Amber Restaurant
132 Middletown Ave., North Haven, 203/239-4072
Bar-B-Q Restaurant
591 Boston Post Rd., Milford, 203/874-5653
The Rib House
16 Main St., East Haven, 203/468-6695

Best Breakfast
Parthenon Diner Restaurant
374 E. Main St., Branford, 203/481-0333

Best Burgers
Bennigan's
290 Old Gate Ln., Milford, 203/877-1903
Louis' Lunch
263 Crown St., 203/562-5507

Best Chinese Food
China Pavilion
185 Boston Post Rd., Orange, 203/795-3555
Dynasty Chinese Restaurant
419 Universal Dr. N., North Haven, 203/239-2449
Shong Fa Jaing
670 Foxon Rd., East Haven, 203/468-2066

Best Coffee/Coffeehouse
Elfie's
58 River St., Milford, 203/878-8393
Willoughby's Coffee and Tea
550 E. Main St., Branford, 203/481-1700

Best Diner
Twin Pines Diner Restaurant
34 Main St., East Haven, 203/468-6887
Yankee Doodle Coffee Shop
258 Elm St., 203/865-1074
258 Elm St., 203/865-1074

Best Fine Dining
Five Hundred Blake Street
500 Blake St., 203/387-0500
Colonial Tymes
2389 Dixwell Ave., Hamden, 203/230-2301
Delmonaco's
232 Wooster St., 203/865-1109
Sachem Country House
111 Goose Ln., Guilford, 203/453-5261
Tre Scalini
100 Wooster St., 203/777-3373

C

Best French Food
Union League Cafe
1032 Chapel St., 203/562-4299

Best Ice Cream/Yogurt
Carvel
1081 Bridgeport Ave., Milford, 203/874-1427
866 Boston Post Rd., Milford, 203/874-5498

Best Indian Food
India Palace
65 Howe St., 203/776-9010

Best Inexpensive Meal
Seafood Peddler
1950 Dixwell Ave., Hamden, 203/248-9907

Best Italian Food
Adriana Restaurant
771 Grand Ave., 203/865-6474
Gabriele Restaurant and Pizza
326 Boston Post Rd., Orange, 203/799-2633
Gennaro's Ristorante D'Amalfi
937 State St., 203/777-5490
Pasta Fair Restaurant
262 Boston Post Rd., Orange, 203/799-9601

Best Japanese Food
Akasaka
1450 Whalley Ave., 203/387-4898
Hama Japanese Restaurant
1206 Dixwell Ave., Hamden, 203/281-4542

Best Mexican Food
El Torero Mexican Restaurant
1698 Boston Post Rd., Milford, 203/878-7734
Su Casa
400 E. Main St., Branford, 203/481-5001

Best Pizza
Bella Napoli Pizza
864 Boston Post Rd., Milford, 203/877-1102
Bertucci's
550 Boston Post Rd., Milford, 203/799-6828
Frank Pepe Pizzeria
157 Wooster St., 203/865-5762
Sally's Pizza
237 Wooster St., 203/624-5271
237 Wooster St., 203/624-5271

Best Restaurant Meal Value
Captain's Galley
19 Beach St., West Haven, 203/932-1811

Best Romantic Dining
Adriana Restaurant
771 Grand Ave., 203/865-6474

Best Salad/Salad Bar
Vito's News
45 Center St., 203/624-1533

Best Sandwiches
Humphrey's East
175 Humphrey St., 203/782-1506

Vito's News
45 Center St., 203/624-1533

Best Seafood
Chowder Pot Family Restaurant
560 E. Main St., Branford, 203/481-2356
Scribner's
31 Village Rd., Milford, 203/878-7019
The Gathering
989 Boston Post Rd., Milford, 203/878-6537

Best Soul Food
Sandra's Place
636 Congress Ave., 203/562-4535

Best Sports Bar
Bobby Valentine's Sports Gallery Cafe
304 Old Gate Ln., 203/878-5262

Best Steaks
Charlie B's Steakhouse
1157 Chapel St., 203/776-7689
Chart House
100 S. Water St., 203/787-3466
Delmonaco's
232 Wooster St., 203/865-1109
Indian River Steak and Seafood
471 New Haven Ave., Milford, 203/874-4624
The Gathering
989 Boston Post Rd., Milford, 203/878-6537

Best Sushi
Miya Japanese Restaurant
68 Howe St., 203/777-9760

Best Vegetarian Food
Claire's Corner Copia
1000 Chapel St., 203/562-3888

NEW LONDON, CT

Best Bar
Cherrystones
218 Shore Rd., Old Lyme, 860/434-1721

Best Barbecue/Ribs
Russell's Ribs
214 Rte. 12, Groton, 860/445-8849

Best Breakfast
Bee and Thistle Inn
100 Lyme St., Old Lyme, 860/434-1667

Best Family Restaurant
Yantic River Inn
270 W. Town St., Yantic, 860/887-2440

Best Pizza
Recovery Room Cafe
445 Ocean Ave., 860/443-2619

Best Romantic Dining
Bee and Thistle Inn
100 Lyme St., Old Lyme, 860/434-1667

C

Best Steaks
Chuck's Steakhouse
  250 Pequot Ave., 860/443-1323
Ye Olde Tavern
  345 Bank St., 860/442-0353

Best Thai Food
Bangkok City
  123 Captains Walk, 860/442-6970

NORWALK, CT

Best American Food
Three Bears
  333 Wilton Rd., Westport, 203/227-7219

Best Barbecue/Ribs
Cogburn's, The Place For Ribs
  16 River St., 203/866-2112

Best Breakfast
Penny's Diner and Restaurant
  212 East Ave., 203/852-0326
Whistle Stop Muffin Company
  7 Station Rd., Wilton, 203/762-9778

Best Brewpub
Brewhouse Restaurant
  13 Marshall St., 203/853-9110

Best Burgers
Bobby Valentine's Sports Gallery
  280 Connecticut Ave., 203/854-9300

Best Chinese Food
Panda Pavilion
  1300 Post Rd. E., Westport, 203/255-3988

Best Continental Food
Restaurant Zanghi
  2 Post Rd. W., Westport, 203/221-7572

Best Diner
Orem's Diner
  209 Danbury Rd., Wilton, 203/762-7370
Silvermine Tavern
  194 Perry Ave., 203/847-4558

Best Family Restaurant
Brock's Restaurant
  606 Main Ave., 203/853-3663

Best Italian Food
Arturo's
  426 Main Ave., 203/845-0808
Maria's Trattoria
  172 Main Ave., 203/847-5166
Via Sforza Trattoria Pizzeria
  250 Westport Ave., 203/846-1116

Best Japanese Food
Plum Tree Japanese Restaurant
  70 Main St., New Canaan, 203/966-8050
Sakura
  680 Post Rd. E., Westport, 203/222-0802

C

Best Pizza
Bertucci's Brick Oven Pizzeria
    833 Post Rd. E., Westport, 203/454-1559
Sunrise Pizza Cafe
    211 Liberty Sq., 203/838-0166

Best Restaurant Meal Value
Mario's
    36 Railroad Pl., Westport, 203/226-0308

Best Romantic Dining
Cobb's Mill Inn
    12 Weston Rd., Weston, 203/227-7221

Best Salad/Salad Bar
Brock's Restaurant
    606 Main Ave., 203/853-3663

Best Seafood
Allen's Clam and Lobster House
    191 Hillspoint Rd., Westport, 203/226-4411
Skipper's Restaurant
    Beach Rd., 203/838-2211

Best Spanish Food
Meson Galicia
    10 Wall St., 203/866-8800

Best Steaks
Eric and Michael's Steak House
    205 Wilton Town Green, Wilton, 203/834-2000

NORWICH, CT

Best American Food
Modesto's Restaurant
    10 Rte. 32, North Franklin, 860/887-7755

Best Breakfast
Olde Tymes Restaurant
    360 W. Main St., 860/887-6865

Best Chinese Food
Pagoda Chinese Restaurant
    47 Town St., 860/887-7500
Phoenix Chinese Restaurant
    595 W. Main St., 860/889-8868

Best Coffee/Coffeehouse
Liberty Tree Coffee House
    2 Market St., 860/886-4465

Best Outdoor Dining
Americus on the Wharf
    1 American Wharf, 860/887-8555

Best Pizza
Olympic Pizza Restaurant
    372 W. Main St., 860/887-0196

Best Seafood
Americus on the Wharf
    1 American Wharf, 860/887-8555

C

PUTNAM, CT

Best All-You-Can-Eat Buffet
The White Horse Inn at Vernon Stiles
Rte. 193, Thompson, 860/923-9571

Best American Food
Golden Lamb Buttery
469 Bush Hill Rd., Brooklyn, 860/774-4423

Best Bistro
Vine Bistro
85 Main St., 860/928-1660

Best Breakfast
Marketplace
319 Kennedy Dr., 860/928-3346

Best Chinese Food
Jade Garden II
243 Kennedy Dr., 860/928-5351

Best Coffee/Coffeehouse
The Vanilla Bean Cafe
450 Deerfield Rd., Pomfret, 860/928-1562

Best Family Restaurant
Golden Greek Restaurant
474 Putnam Pike, Dayville, 860/774-0167
Jason's Restaurant
274 Riverside Dr., Thompson, 860/923-2908

Best Pizza
Someplace Special
58 Main St., 860/928-2884

Best Romantic Dining
Golden Lamb Buttery
469 Bush Hill Rd., Brooklyn, 860/774-4423

Best Seafood
Inn at Woodstock Hill
94 Plaine Hill Rd., Woodstock, 860/928-0528

Best Steaks
J.D. Cooper's
146 Park Rd., 860/928-0501

Best Sunday Brunch
The White Horse Inn at Vernon Stiles
Rte. 193, Thompson, 860/923-9571

STAMFORD, CT

Best American Food
Boxing Cat Grill
1392 E. Putnam Ave., Old Greenwich,
203/698-1995

Best Bar
Hacienda Don Emilio
222 Summer St., 203/324-0577

Best Chinese Food
Hunan Spring Restaurant
323 Hope St., 203/359-2086

C

Best Coffee/Coffeehouse
Starbucks Coffee
1079 High Ridge Rd., 203/461-9049

Best Dinner
Kathleen's
25 Bank St., 203/323-7785

Best Family Restaurant
Pellicci's Restaurant
96 Stillwater Ave., 203/323-2542

Best German Food
The European Chef
83 Bedford St., 203/325-0789

Best Indian Food
Bonani Indian Cuisine
490 Summer St., 203/348-8138
Meera
227 Summer St., 203/496-9916

Best Italian Food
Columbus Park Trattoria
205 Main St., 203/967-9191
Mario the Baker
864 High Ridge Rd., 203/329-0440
Papa Joe's Restaurant
1973 Post Rd., Darien, 203/655-1330
Pellicci's Restaurant
96 Stillwater Ave., 203/323-2542
Valbella
1309 E. Putnam Ave., Old Greenwich,
203/637-1155

Best Lunch
Kathleen's
25 Bank St., 203/323-7785

Best Mexican Food
Hacienda Don Emilio
222 Summer St., 203/324-0577
Ole Mole
1030 High Ridge Rd., 203/461-9962

Best Pizza
Arcuri's Pizza and Salads
226 E. Putnam Ave., Cos Cob, 203/869-6999
Hope Pizza Restaurant
230 Hope St., 203/325-0660
Pappa's Pizza Inc.
201 Main St., 203/324-7800
Stamford Restaurant and Pizzeria
1122 E. Main St., 203/325-1856

Best Restaurant in Town
Amadeus
201 Summer St., 203/348-7775
Kathleen's
25 Bank St., 203/323-7785
La Bretagne French Restaurant
2010 W. Main St., 203/324-9539

Best Restaurant Meal Value
Ole Mole
  1030 High Ridge Rd., 203/461-9962

Best Romantic Dining
Mona Lisa Ristorante
  133 Atlantic St., 203/349-1070

Best Salad/Salad Bar
Winfield's Restaurant
  1800 E. Putnam Ave., Old Greenwich,
    203/637-1234

Best Sandwiches
Dairy Inn
  1092 Hope St., 203/322-5138

Best Seafood
Crab Shell
  46 Southfield Ave., 203/967-7229
Fjord Fisheries
  49 Brownhouse Rd., 203/325-0255

Best Spanish Food
Fonda La Paloma
  531 Boston Post Rd., Cos Cob, 203/661-9395

Best Sports Bar
Bobby Valentine's Sports Gallery
  280 Connecticut Ave., 203/854-9300

TORRINGTON, CT

Best American Food
Hilltop Inn
  1057 Torringford St., 860/482-3326
West Street Grill
  43 West St., Litchfield, 860/567-3885

Best Coffee/Coffeehouse
Talk of the Town
  77 Main St., 860/489-9627

Best Diner
Central Lunch
  31 Hungerford St., 860/496-0297

Best Italian Food
Venetian Restaurant
  52 E. Main St., 860/489-8592

Best Late-Night Food
Twin Colony Diner
  417 E. Elm St., 860/482-5346

Best Mexican Food
La Tienda Cafe
  Rte. 202, Litchfield, 860/567-8778

Best Pizza
Berkshire Cafe
  71 Albert St., 860/489-0600

Best Restaurant Meal Value
Aspen Garden
  51 West St., Litchfield, 860/379-1094

C

Best Seafood
The Tributary
19 Rowley St., Winsted, 860/379-7679

VERNON, CT

Best Barbecue/Ribs
Little Mark's Big BBQ
226 Talcottville Rd., 860/872-1410

Best Breakfast
Bickford's Family Fare
415 Hartford Turnpike, 860/871-0621

Best Chinese Food
Panda Palace Chinese Restaurant
519 Talcottville Rd., 860/872-1977
Wong's Too
75 East St., 860/871-9311

Best Delicatessen
Rein's New York Style Deli
435 Hartford Turnpike, 860/875-1344

Best Inexpensive Meal
Bickford's Family Fare
415 Hartford Turnpike, 860/871-0621
Wong's Too
75 East St., 860/871-9311

Best Italian Food
New England Pizza and Restaurant
911 Hartford Turnpike, 860/871-9300

Best Pizza
Anthony's Pizza and Giant Grinders
216 Hartford Turnpike, 860/643-7570

Best Sandwiches
Rein's New York Style Deli
435 Hartford Turnpike, 860/875-1344

Best Seafood
Valley Fish Market and Restaurant
80 West Rd., Ellington, 860/872-9659

Best Vietnamese Food
Lotus Restaurant
409 Hartford Turnpike, 860/871-8962

WATERBURY, CT

Best American Food
Hill's
Park Rd., 203/755-1331

Best Barbecue/Ribs
Big Daddy's Rib Shack
55 Moran St., 203/753-0505

Best Breakfast
Leo's Restaurant
900 Straits Turnpike, Middlebury, 203/598-0166

Best Burgers
Morcey's
572 Watertown Ave., 203/574-9175

Best Delicatessen
Ann's Deli
  1622 Baldwin St., 203/575-9051

Best Desserts
Pie Plate
  835 Wolcott St., 203/757-8555

Best Ice Cream/Yogurt
Big Dipper Ice Cream Parlour
  91 Waterbury Rd., Prospect, 203/758-3200

Best Italian Food
Diorio
  231 Bank St., 203/754-5111
San Marino Restaurant
  111 Thomaston Ave., 203/755-1148

Best Other Ethnic Food
Lisboa Restaurante (Portuguese)
  19 Lafayette St., 203/754-0789

Best Pizza
Bacco's
  1230 Thomaston Ave., 203/755-1173

Best Romantic Dining
Cafe 457
  457 W. Main St., 203/574-4507

Best Seafood
Seafood Peddler
  689 Wolcott St., 203/597-9466

Best Steaks
The Olive Tree Restaurant
  20 Sherman Hill Rd., Woodbury, 203/263-4555

WILLIMANTIC, CT

Best All-You-Can-Eat Buffet
Homestead Restaurant
  50 Higgins Hwy., Mansfield Center, 860/456-2240

Best Breakfast
Bud's Coffee Nook
  69 Church St., 860/423-4373
Gil's Restaurant
  725 Main St., 860/423-0062

Best Burgers
Main Street Cafe
  967 Main St., 860/423-6777

Best Family Restaurant
Angellino's Restaurant
  135 Storrs Rd., Mansfield Center, 860/450-7071

Best Homestyle Food
Homestead Restaurant
  50 Higgins Hwy., Mansfield Center, 860/456-2240

Best Mexican Food
Chuck's and Margarita's
  Rte. 32, Mansfield Center, 860/429-1900

C

Best Pizza
Alexandra's Family Restaurant
  1310 Main St., 860/423-5407
Tony's Pizza and Restaurant
  117 Main St., 860/423-7717

Best Place to Take the Kids
Main Street Cafe
  967 Main St., 860/423-6777

Best Seafood
Husky Blues
  1254 Storrs Rd., Storrs, 860/429-2587

Best Steaks
Chuck's and Margarita's
  Rte. 32, Mansfield Center, 860/429-1900
Husky Blues
  1254 Storrs Rd., Storrs, 860/429-2587

Delaware

DEWEY BEACH, DE

Best Breakfast
Crystal Restaurant
  620 Rehoboth Ave., 302/227-1088
Starboard Restaurant
  2009 Hwy. 1, 302/227-4600

Best Burgers
Irish Eyes Pub and Restaurant
  15 Wilmington Ave., 302/227-2888

Best Lunch
Arena's Deli
  149 Rehoboth Ave., 302/227-1271

Best Mexican Food
Tijuana Taxi
  207 Rehoboth Ave., 302/227-1986

Best Outdoor Dining
Rusty Rudder Restaurant
  113 Dickinson St., 302/227-3888

Best Pizza
Nicola Pizza
  8 N. First St., 302/226-2654

Best Seafood
Coconut's Seafood House
  Dagsworthy St., 302/227-3317
Crabbers Cove
  113 Dickinson St., 302/227-4888
Jake's Seafood House
  29 Baltimore Ave., 302/227-6237

D

DOVER, DE

Best Barbecue/Ribs
Bull on the Beach
    3072 Dover Mall, 302/736-0337
Where Pigs Fly
    Edgehill Shopping Center,
        617 E. Lockerman St. at Hwy. 13,
        302/678-0586

Best Chinese Food
Sing House Chinese Restaurant
    45 Greentree Dr., 302/678-4844

Best Delicatessen
Bradford Street Cafe
    150 S. Bradford St., 302/736-6200

Best Desserts
Kirby and Holloway Restaurant
    656 N. DuPont Hwy., 302/734-7133
Paradiso Restaurant
    115B Lebanon Rd., 302/697-3055

Best Italian Food
Attilio's
    1628 S. Governors Ave., 302/674-8700

Best Japanese Food
Hibachi Japanese Steak House
    691 N. DuPont Hwy., 302/734-5900

Best Mexican Food
El Sombrero Mexican Restaurant
    655 N. DuPont Hwy., 302/678-9445
La Tolteca Restaurant
    245 S. DuPont Hwy., 302/734-3444

Best Salad/Salad Bar
Kathy's Kitchen
    1819 S. DuPont Hwy., 302/734-4111

Best Seafood
Shucker's Pier 13
    889 N. DuPont Hwy., 302/674-1190

MILFORD, DE

Best Breakfast
J and F Bagels
    917 N. DuPont Blvd., 302/424-0708
Second Cup
    1 N. Walnut St., 302/424-2287

Best Burgers
Library Square Cafe
    227 N. Rehoboth Blvd., 302/424-0515

Best Chinese Food
Shang Hai
    113 N. Walnut St., 302/422-2270

Best Coffee/Coffeehouse
Second Cup
    1 N. Walnut St., 302/424-2287

Best Desserts
Geyer's Restaurant
  556 S. DuPont Blvd., 302/422-5327

Best Diner
Milford Diner
  1042 N. Walnut St., 302/422-6111

Best Italian Food
Attilio's
  664 N. DuPont Hwy., 302/422-2730

Best Pizza
Milford's Pizza
  923 N. DuPont Hwy., 302/422-8499

Best Steaks
Geyer's Restaurant
  556 S. DuPont Blvd., 302/422-5327
Sail Loft Restaurant
  Rte. 113, 302/422-5858

Best Vegetarian Food
Library Square Cafe
  227 N. Rehoboth Blvd., 302/424-0515

NEW CASTLE, DE

Best American Food
Air Transport Command
  143 N. DuPont Hwy., 302/328-3527

Best Breakfast
Cellar Gourmet
  208 Delaware St., 302/323-0999

Best Chinese Food
Wok's
  132 Sunset Blvd., 302/328-6833

Best Delicatessen
Arner's Family Restaurant
  215 N. DuPont Hwy., 302/322-3279

Best Diner
Golden Dove Diner
  1101 N. DuPont Hwy., 302/322-1180

Best Indian Food
Casablanca Restaurant
  4010 N. DuPont Hwy., 302/652-5344

Best Pizza
Portofino Pizza and Restaurant
  730 Ferry Cut-Off St., 302/322-3330

Best Romantic Dining
Air Transport Command
  143 N. DuPont Hwy., 302/328-3527

Best Seafood
Alex's Seafood Restaurant
  110 N. DuPont Hwy., 302/328-5666
Arsenal on the Green
  30 Market St., 302/328-1290

Best Steaks
Arsenal on the Green
30 Market St., 302/328-1290
Lone Star Steakhouse and Saloon
113 S. DuPont Hwy., 302/322-3854

D

NEWARK, DE

Best Burgers
Jake's Hamburgers
1100 Ogletown Rd., 302/737-1118

Best Casual Dining
Italian Bistro
425 Christiana Mall, 302/366-8566

Best Chinese Food
Authentic Chinese Restaurant
200 University Plz., 302/368-0660
Wing Wah
Chestnut Hill Plz., State Rd. 4, 302/738-7681

Best Coffee/Coffeehouse
Borders Books and Music
101 Geoffrey Dr., 302/366-8144
Brew-HaHa
Galleria Mall, 45 E. Main St., 302/369-2600

Best Diner
Bob's Big Boy Restaurant
530 JFK Memorial Hwy., 302/737-5956

Best Eclectic Menu
Mirage
100 Elkton Rd., 302/453-1711

Best Family Restaurant
Beeches
748 E. Chestnut Hill Rd., 302/292-2700
Michael's Family Restaurant
1000 Churchmans Rd., 302/368-4230
Oliver's Restaurant
Holiday Inn, 1283 Christiana Rd., 302/737-2899

Best Health-Conscious Menu
Sinclair's Cafe Ltd.
177 E. Main St., 302/368-7755

Best Indian Food
Taste of India Restaurant
2628 Capitol Trail, 302/737-9483

Best Korean Food
Korean Barbecue and Sushi Bar
Liberty Plz., 3602 Kirkwood Hwy., Ste. 3,
302/455-9100

Best Mexican Food
El Sombrero
160 Elkton Rd., 302/738-0808
Santa Fe Bar and Grill
9 University Plz., Delaware Rte. 73, 302/738-0758

Best Outdoor Dining
Klondike Kate's
158 E. Main St., 302/737-6100

D

Best Restaurant Meal Value
Alyson's Restaurant
16 Marrows Rd., 302/368-4545

Best Romantic Dining
Mirage
100 Elkton Rd., 302/453-1711

Best Sandwiches
Daffy Deli
111 Elkton Rd., 302/737-8848
Jake's Hamburgers
1100 Ogletown Rd., 302/737-1118

Best Sunday Brunch
Alyson's Restaurant
16 Marrows Rd., 302/368-4545
Deer Park Tavern
108 W. Main St., 302/731-5315

Best Vegetarian Food
90 East Main Street
90 E. Main St., 302/368-9040

Best Vietnamese Food
Saigon Vietnam Restaurant
207 Newark Shopping Center, 302/737-1590

REHOBOTH BEACH, DE

Best Barbecue/Ribs
JR's, The Place for Ribs
Rte. 1, 302/227-1777

Best Cajun/Creole Food
Sydney's, the Blues and Jazz Place
25 Christian St., 302/227-1339

Best Desserts
Back Porch Cafe
59 Rehoboth Ave., 302/227-3674
Blue Moon Restaurant
35 Baltimore Ave., 302/227-6515

Best Family Restaurant
The Roadhouse Steak Joint
4572 Hwy. 1N, 302/645-8273

Best Fine Dining
Blue Moon Restaurant
35 Baltimore Ave., 302/227-6515
Garden Gourmet
4121 Hwy. 1, 302/227-4747

Best Middle Eastern Food
The Camel's Hump Restaurant
21 Baltimore Ave., 302/227-0947

Best Pizza
Nicola Pizza
8 N. First St., 302/227-6211

Best Salad/Salad Bar
Fran O'Brien's Beach House
59 Lake Avenue, 302/227-6121

D

Best Seafood
Taylor's Seashore Restaurant
  51 Wilmington Ave., 302/227-5685

Best Sunday Brunch
DiNardo's By The Sea
  330 Rehoboth Ave., 302/227-7451
Victoria's
  2 Olive Ave., 302/227-0615

SEAFORD, DE

Best Breakfast
Dillard's Restaurant
  501 N. Dual Hwy., 302/629-4814

Best Homestyle Food
Dillard's Restaurant
  501 N. Dual Hwy., 302/629-4814

Best Pizza
Pizza King
  300 W. Stein Hwy., 302/629-6003

Best Sandwiches
Bon Appetit
  312 High St., 302/629-3700
Dairy Bar and Restaurant
  511 King St., 302/629-9403

Best Steaks
Flagship Restaurant
  920 Concord Rd., 302/629-9767

WILMINGTON, DE

Best American Food
Columbus Inn
  2216 Pennsylvania Ave., 302/571-1492
Harry's Savoy Grill
  2020 Naamans Rd., 302/475-3000

Best Bar
O'Friel's Irish Pub
  600 Delaware Ave., 302/654-9952

Best Beer Selection
Bottlecaps Bar and Restaurant
  216 W. Ninth St., 302/427-9119
Stanley's Restaurant and Tavern
  2038 Foulk Rd., 302/475-1887

Best Bistro
European Bistro
  1710 Naamans Rd., 302/529-7773

Best Breakfast
Alyson's Restaurant
  714 Greenbank Rd., 302/998-8853
Big Sky Bread Company
  1812 Marsh Rd., 302/475-9494
Post House Restaurant
  4303 N. Market St., 302/764-1248
  105 N. Union St., 302/654-4414

D

Best Brewpub
Brandywine Brewing Company Restaurant
  3801 Kennett Pike, Greenville, 302/655-8000

Best Burgers
Charcoal Pit
  5200 Pike Creek Blvd., 302/999-7483
  2600 Concord Pike, 302/478-2165
Deerhead
  905 N. Orange St., 302/656-1400

Best Business Lunch
Brandywine Room
  Hotel DuPont, 100 W. Eleventh St., 302/594-3156

Best Casual Dining
Italian Bistro
  4301 Kirkwood Hwy., 302/996-0700

Best Chinese Food
China Palace
  837 N. Market St., 302/654-0200
China Royal
  1845 Marsh Rd., 302/475-3686
Tung Yan
  3007 Concord Pike, 302/478-0660

Best Coffee/Coffeehouse
Brew-HaHa
  Branmar Plz., 1612 Marsh Rd., 302/529-1125
Il Fornaio Bakery Cafe
  1602 Delaware Ave., 302/888-0148

Best Delicatessen
Capriotti's Sandwich Shop
  510 N. Union St., 302/571-8929
  2124 Silverside Rd., 302/479-9818
Casapulla's Elsmere Steak Shop
  514 Philip St., 302/994-5934

Best Desserts
Brandywine Room
  Hotel DuPont, 100 W. Eleventh St., 302/594-3156

Best Diner
Hop Diner Restaurant
  4542 Kirkwood Hwy., 302/633-1955

Best Eclectic Menu
Queen Bean Cafe
  8 Commonwealth Ave., Claymont, 302/792-5995

Best Family Restaurant
Alyson's Restaurant
  714 Greenbank Rd., 302/998-8853
Charcoal Pit
  2600 Concord Pike, 302/478-2165
  5200 Pike Creek Blvd., 302/999-7483
Lotsa Pasta Restaurant and Lounge
  2314 Carpenter Rd., 302/475-0840
Robino's Restaurant
  520 N. Union St., 302/652-9223
Wing Wah Chinese Restaurant
  3901 Concord Pike, 302/478-9500

D

Best Fine Dining
Terrace at Greenhill
   800 N. DuPont Rd., 302/575-1990

Best German Food
Edda's Delicatessen
   12A Trolley Sq., 302/658-3361

Best Greek/Mediterranean Food
Tarabicos Restaurant
   803 N. Union St., 302/654-9780

Best Ice Cream/Yogurt
Temptations
   11A Trolley Sq., 302/429-9162

Best Indian Food
India Palace
   101 N. Maryland Ave., 302/655-8772

Best Inexpensive Meal
Charcoal Pit
   2600 Concord Pike, 302/478-2165
   5200 Pike Creek Blvd., 302/999-7483

Best Italian Food
Attilo's Ristorante
   1900 Lancaster Ave., 302/428-0909
Buckley's Tavern
   5812 Kennett Pike, 302/656-9776
Cafe Napoli Restaurant and Pizza
   4391 Kirkwood Hwy., 302/999-7553
Griglia Toscana
   1412 N. DuPont St., 302/654-8001
Piccolo Mondo
   Talleyville Towne Shoppes, 3604 Silverside Rd.,
302/478-9028
Ristorante Trevi
   3100 Naamans Rd., 302/478-7434
Robino's Restaurant
   520 N. Union St., 302/652-9223
Rosauri's Pizza and Pasta Restaurant
   1323 McKennans Church Rd., 302/996-0301
Toscana
   1402 N. DuPont St., 302/655-8600
Vincente's Restaurant
   1601 Concord Pike, 302/625-5142

Best Japanese Food
Hibachi Japanese Steak House
   5607 Concord Pike, 302/477-0194
Mikasa
   3602 Kirkwood Hwy., 302/995-8905
Utage Japanese Restaurant
   1601 Concord Pike, 302/652-1230
Yama Restaurant
   1726 Marsh Rd., 302/478-4863

Best Mexican Food
La Tolteca Mexican Restaurant
   4701 Concord Pike, 302/477-0433

D

Best Other Ethnic Food
Genelle's Bakery Cafe (Caribbean)
730 Market St., 302/654-5322

Best Outdoor Dining
Kid Shelleens
1801 W. Fourteenth St., 302/658-4600

Best Pizza
Cafe Riviera
4737 Concord Pike, 302/478-8288
Gerardo's
111 W. Eighth St., 302/658-1225
114 N. Union St., 302/658-0569
Grotto Pizza
2311 Concord Pike, 302/888-2222
303 Rocky Run Pkwy., 302/479-8300
Pala's Cafe
701 N. Union St., 302/658-2346
Pappy's Family Restaurant
4753 Kirkwood Hwy., 302/998-0123
Pizza by Elizabeth
4019A Kennett Pike, 302/654-4478

Best Restaurant in Town
Columbus Inn
2216 Pennsylvania Ave., 302/571-1492
Green Room
Hotel DuPont, 100 W. Eleventh St., 302/594-3154
Griglia Toscana
1412 N. DuPont St., 302/654-8001
Hunter's Den
3517 Old Capitol Trail, 302/998-4790

Best Restaurant Meal Value
Alyson's Restaurant
714 Greenbank Rd., 302/998-8853
Caffe Bellisimo Seafood
3421 Kirkwood Hwy., 302/994-9200

Best Romantic Dining
Bourbon Street Cafe
105 Kirkwood Sq., 302/633-1944
Carucci
504 Greenhill Ave., 302/654-2333
Columbus Inn
2216 Pennsylvania Ave., 302/571-1492
Green Room
Hotel DuPont, 100 W. Eleventh St., 302/594-3154

Best Sandwiches
Borgia's Subs and Steaks
414 N. Union St., 302/654-5061
Glasgow Deli
5916 Kirkwood Hwy., 302/994-2700
Talkin' Turkey
907 N. Shipley St., 302/428-0665

Best Seafood
DiNardo's Restaurant
405 N. Lincoln St., 302/656-3685

Feby's Fishery
   3701 Lancaster Pike, 302/998-9501

Best Steaks
Constantinou's House of Beef
   1616 Delaware Ave., 302/652-0653
Kid Shelleens
   1801 W. Fourteenth St., 302/658-4600
Walter's Steakhouse and Saloon
   802 N. Union St., 302/652-6780

Best Thai Food
Bangkok House Restaurant
   104 N. Union St., 302/654-8555

Best Vegetarian Food
Indian Paradise Restaurant
   1710A Newport Gap Pike, 302/999-0855

Best Wine Selection
Green Room
   Hotel DuPont, 100 W. Eleventh St., 302/594-3154

District of Columbia

D

[See also: Bethesda, Gaithersburg, and Rockville, MD; and Alexandria, Arlington, Fairfax, McLean, and Reston, VA.]

Best American Food
1789 Restaurant
    1226 36th St. NW, 202/965-1789
Cashion's Eat Place
    1819 Columbia Rd. NW, Washington, 202/797-1819
Mick's
    2401 Pennsylvania Ave. NW, 202/331-9613
Morrison Clark Inn
    1015 L St. NW, 202/289-8580
New Heights Restaurant
    2317 Calvert St. NW, 202/234-4110
Sam and Harry's Restaurant
    1200 Nineteenth St. NW, 202/296-4333
Vidalia Restaurant
    1990 M St. NW, 202/659-1990

Best Atmosphere
Old Ebbitt Grill
    675 Fifteenth St. NW, 202/347-4800

Best Bistro
The Bistro Restaurant
    2401 M St. NW, 202/457-5020

Best Brewpub
John Harvard's Brew House
    1299 Pennsylvania Ave. NW, 202/333-2313

D

Best Casual Dining
Centre Cafe
  50 Massachusetts Ave. NW, 202/682-0143
Clyde's of Georgetown
  3236 M St. NW, 202/333-9180

Best Chinese Food
City Lights of China
  1731 Connecticut Ave. NW, 202/265-6688

Best Delicatessen
Krupin's Restaurant
  4620 Wisconsin Ave. NW, 202/686-1989

Best Desserts
Cheesecake Factory
  5345 Wisconsin Ave. NW, 202/364-0500

Best Dinner
Red Sage Restaurant
  605 Fourteenth St. NW, 202/638-4444
Trumpets Restaurant
  1633 Q St. NW, 202/232-4141

Best Eclectic Menu
Afterwords Cafe
  1517 Connecticut Ave. NW, 202/387-1462
Restaurant Nora
  2132 Florida Ave. NW, 202/462-5143

Best French Food
Bistrot Lepic
  1736 Wisconsin Ave. NW, 202/333-0111
Gerard's Place Restaurant
  915 Fifteenth St. NW, 202/737-4445
Jean-Louis at the Watergate
  2650 Virginia Ave. NW, 202/298-4488
La Chaumiere
  2813 M St. NW, 202/338-1784
Les Halles de Paris
  1201 Pennsylvania Ave. NW, 202/347-6848

Best Greek/Mediterranean Food
Eye Street Cafe
  1915 I St. NW, 202/457-0773
Skewers Restaurant
  1633 P St. NW, 202/387-7400

Best Indian Food
Aditi Indian Cuisine
  3299 M St. NW, 202/625-6825
Bombay Place Restaurant
  2020 K St. NW, 202/331-4200

Best Italian Food
Donatello Restaurant
  2514 L St. NW, 202/333-1485
Galileo Restaurant
  1110 21st St. NW, 202/293-7191
Goldoni Restaurant
  1113 23rd St. NW, 202/293-1511
i Ricchi Tuscan Italian Food
  1220 Nineteenth St. NW, 202/835-0459

Il Radicchio
1509 Seventeenth St. NW, 202/986-2627
Luigino
1100 New York Ave. NW, 202/371-0595
Obelisk
2029 P St. NW, 202/872-1180

Best Japanese Food
Makoto Restaurant
4822 MacArthur Blvd. NW, 202/298-6866
Samurai Japanese Restaurant
3222 M St. NW, Ste. 120, 202/333-1001

Best Late-Night Food
Au Pied de Cochon
1335 Wisconsin Ave. NW, 202/333-5440

Best Lunch
Mendocino Grille and Wine Bar
2917 M St. NW, 202/333-2912

Best Mexican Food
Austin Grill
2404 Wisconsin Ave. NW, 202/337-8080
Cactus Cantina
3300 Wisconsin Ave. NW, 202/686-7222
Coco Loco
810 Seventh St. NW, 202/289-2626
El Tamarindo Restaurant
1785 Florida Ave. NW, 202/328-3660
Gabriel
2121 P St. NW, 202/956-6690

Best Other Ethnic Food
Afghan Kabob (Afghan)
3320 M St. NW, 202/337-0300
Ascot Restaurant (Basque)
1708 L St. NW, 202/296-7640
Marrakesh Restaurant (Moroccan)
617 New York Ave. NW, 202/393-9393
Meskerem Ethiopian Restaurant (Ethiopian)
2434 Eighteenth St. NW, 202/462-4100
Red Sea Ethiopian Restaurant (Ethiopian)
2463 Eighteenth St. NW, 202/483-5000
Zed's Ethiopian Cuisine (Ethiopian)
3318 M St. NW, 202/333-4710

Best Pizza
Coppi's Restaurant
1414 U St. NW, 202/319-7773
Paolo's
1305 Wisconsin Ave. NW, 202/333-7353
Pizzaria Paradiso
2029 P St. NW, 202/223-1245

Best Restaurant in Town
Felix Restaurant and Lounge
2406 Eighteenth St. NW, 202/483-3549

Best Restaurant Meal Value
Music City Roadhouse
1050 30th St. NW, 202/337-4444

D

Best Seafood
Kinkead's Restaurant
  2000 Pennsylvania Ave. NW, 202/296-7700
La Rivage Restaurant
  1000 Water St. SW, 202/488-8111
Market Inn
  200 E St. SW, 202/554-2100
Pesce Trattoria
  2016 P St. NW, 202/466-3474
Phillip's Flagship Restaurant
  900 Water St. SW, 202/488-8515

Best Soul Food
B Smith's DC
  50 Massachusetts Ave. NE, 202/289-6188
Georgia Brown's Restaurant
  950 Fifteenth St. NW, 202/393-4499

Best Southwestern Food
Red Sage Restaurant
  605 Fourteenth St. NW, 202/638-4444

Best Spanish Food
Jaleo
  480 Seventh St. NW, 202/628-7949
Taberna De Alabardero
  1776 I St. NW, 202/429-2200

Best Sports Bar
Champions
  1206 Wisconsin Ave., 202/965-4005

Best Steaks
Capitol Grille
  601 Pennsylvania Ave. NW, 202/737-6200
Morton's of Chicago
  3251 Prospect St. NW, 202/342-6258
Paramont Steak House
  1609 Seventeenth St. NW, 202/232-0395
Prime Rib
  2020 K St. NW, 202/466-8811
Ruppert's Restaurant
  1017 Seventh St. NW, 202/783-0699

Best Thai Food
Sala Thai Restaurant
  2016 P St. NW, 202/872-1144
Star of Siam
  2446 Eighteenth St. NW, 202/986-4133

Best Vegetarian Food
Bombay Club Restaurant
  815 Connecticut Ave. NW, Ste. 302, 202/659-3727
Food for Thought
  1738 Connecticut Ave. NW, 202/797-1095
Restaurant Nora
  2132 Florida Ave. NW, 202/462-5143

Florida

F

Best Barbecue/Ribs
Barney's Bar-B-Q
  1049 E. Altamonte Dr., 407/831-0813

Best Diner
Angel's Diner
  254 W. Hwy. 436, 407/774-1957

Best French Food
Maison et Jardin
  430 S. Wymore Rd., 407/862-4410

Best Health-Concious Menu
Chamberlin's Natural Foods
  1086 Montgomery Rd., 407/894-8866

Best Mexican Food
Amigos Original Tex-Mex
  120 N. Westmonte Dr., 407/774-4334

Best Other Ethnic Food
Don Pepe's (Cuban)
  941 W. State Rd. 436, 407/682-6834

Best Seafood
Straub's Fine Seafood
  512 E. Altamonte Dr., 407/831-2250

Best Brewpub
The Tap Room Brewery
  207 Atlantic Blvd., 904/241-7877

Best Burgers
The Loop
  211 Third St., 904/241-8476

Best Fine Dining
Sergio's
1021 Atlantic Blvd., 904/249-0101

Best Italian Food
Sergio's
1021 Atlantic Blvd., 904/249-0101

Best Seafood
Ragtime Tavern and Seafood Grill
207 Atlantic Blvd., 904/241-7877
The Tap Room Brewery
207 Atlantic Blvd., 904/241-7877

BELLE GLADE, FL

Best Barbecue/Ribs
Fat Boy's Bar-B-Q
255 U.S. Hwy. 27N, South Bay, 561/996-5554

Best Chinese Food
Bob Yee Chinese Food
531 S. Main St., 561/996-1903

Best Homestyle Food
Kountry Kitchen
1525 NW Avenue L, 561/996-0284

Best Pizza
Dino's Pizza Restaurant
1100 N. Main St., 561/996-1901

Best Seafood
Drawbridge
3300 E. Lake Rd., 561/992-9370

Best Steaks
Drawbridge
3300 E. Lake Rd., 561/992-9370

BOCA RATON, FL

[See also: Coral Springs, Deerfield Beach, Ft. Lauderdale, Pompano Beach, and West Palm Beach.]

Best American Food
Carson's
5798 N. Federal Hwy., 561/995-2500
Max's Grille
404 Plaza Real, 561/368-0080
Maxwell's Chophouse
501 E. Palmetto Park Rd., 561/347-7077
Pete's
7940 Glades Rd., 561/487-1600
Sweetwater
2200 Glades Rd., 561/368-7427
Wilt Chamberlain's
8903 Glades Rd., 561/488-8881

F

Best Barbecue/Ribs
Mississippi Sweet's Barbecue Company
2399 N. Federal Hwy., 561/394-6779
Park Avenue BBQ and Grill
2401 N. Dixie Hwy., Lake Worth, 561/586-7427

Best Chinese Restaurant
Pine Garden
1668 N. Federal Hwy., 561/395-7534

Best Continental Food
Cafe Gloria
855 S. Federal Hwy., 561/338-9692
Gazebo Cafe
4199 N. Federal Hwy., 561/395-6033
La Finestra
171 E. Palmetto Park Rd., 561/392-1838
Rabelais
461 E. Palmetto Park Rd., 561/347-7444

Best Fine Dining
Hoot, Toot and Whistle
290 E. Atlantic Ave., Delray Beach, 561/243-0140

Best French Food
Auberge Le Grillon
6900 N. Federal Hwy., 561/997-6888
La Veille Maison
770 E. Palmetto Park Rd., 561/391-6701
Marcel's
1 S. Ocean Blvd., 561/362-9911

Best Italian Food
Addison's Flavors of Italy
2 E. Camino Real, 561/391-9800
Arturo's Trattoria Romano
499 E. Palmetto Park Rd., 561/393-6715
6750 N. Federal Hwy., 561/997-7373
Baci
344 Plaza Real, 561/362-8500
Basil Garden
5837 N. Federal Hwy., 561/994-2554
Bennardo's
116 NE Sixth Ave., Delray Beach, 561/274-0051
Buona Sera
499 S. Federal Hwy., 561/338-8780
Cafe Bellino
180 S. Federal Hwy., 561/393-2844
Calogero's Restaurant
5155 W. Atlantic Ave., Delray Beach, 561/495-0991
Carlucci's
23001 U.S. Hwy. 441, 561/479-2960
Four Brothers Italian Restaurant
2495 Tenth Ave. N., Lake Worth, 561/969-6046
La Trattoria
6060 SW Eighteenth St., 561/750-1296
La Villetta
4351 N. Federal Hwy., 561/362-8403
Marcello's Place
306 W. Mango St., Lantana, 561/585-2110

F

Marianne's
169 NE Fourth Ave., Delray Beach, 561/278-3349
Maxaluna Tuscan Grill
5050 Town Center Circle, 561/391-7177
Prezzo
7820 Glades Rd., 561/451-2800
Renzo's of Boca Italian Restaurant
5999 N. Federal Hwy., 561/994-3495
Roboli Restaurante Italiano
2901 Clint Moore Rd., 561/995-9940
Vito's
3013 Yamato Rd., 561/995-0800

Best Japanese Food
Fuji Japanese Restaurant
21191 Powerline Rd., 561/392-8778

Best Mexican Food
Baja Cafe/Cantina
2399 N. Federal Hwy., 561/391-5300

Best Other Ethnic Food
Caribbean Grill (Cuban)
1332 NW Second Ave., 561/362-0161
Cuban Cafe (Cuban)
3350 NW Boca Raton Blvd., 561/750-8860

Best Pizza
California Pizza Kitchen
2006 Executive Center Ctr. NW, 561/241-2664

Best Place to Take the Kids
Boomer's Cafe
2001 Tenth Ave. N., Lake Worth, 561/582-5422

Best Romantic Dining
Riggins Crab House
607 N. Ridge Rd., Lantana, 561/586-3000

Best Seafood
Nick's Italian Fishery
2255 Glades Rd., Ste. 128, 561/994-2201
Seafood Connection Restaurant
6998 N. Federal Hwy., 561/997-5562

Best Steaks
New York Prime
2350 Executive Center Dr. NW, 561/998-3881

Best Thai Food
Siam Garden
680 Glades Rd., 561/368-9013
Uncle Tai's
5250 Town Center Circle, Ste. 143, 561/368-8806

Best Vietnamese Food
La Truc Vietnamese Restaurant
249 E. Palmetto Park Rd., 561/392-4568

BRADENTON, FL

Best Barbecue/Ribs
J and J Bar-B-Que
2620 Ninth St. W., 941/746-6683

Sonny's Real Pit Bar-B-Q
 6515 Fourteenth St. W., 941/753-3993

Best Breakfast
Gulf Drive Cafe
 900 Gulf Dr. N., 941/778-1919

Best Burgers
Council's Bradenton Recreation
 536 Twelfth St. W., 941/746-8350
Rotten Ralph's Restaurant
 902 Bay Blvd. S., Anna Maria, 941/778-3953

Best Casual Dining
Cafe on the Beach
 4000 Gulf Dr. N., 941/778-0784

Best Chinese Food
Asia
 6844 Fourteenth St. W., 941/758-7133
China Blossom Restaurant and Lounge
 15 Avenue of the Flowers, Longboat Key,
  941/383-9533
Panda Garden Restaurant
 3240 Fourteenth St. W., 941/747-0201

Best Desserts
Euphemia Haye Restaurant
 5540 Gulf of Mexico Dr., Longboat Key,
  941/383-3633

Best Homestyle Food
Al-Jan's
 6650 Cortez Rd. W., 941/794-5150
Peach's Restaurant
 5702 44th Ave. W., 941/794-5140
 3201 Manatee Ave. W., 941/747-2894

Best Italian Food
Demetrio's Pizza House
 1720 Cortez Rd. W., 941/758-6478
Piccirilli's Italian Restaurant
 6713 Fourteenth St. W., 941/758-4491

Best Other Ethnic Food
Miller's Dutch Kitchen (Amish)
 3401 Fourteenth St. W., 941/746-8253

Best Seafood
Euphemia Haye Restaurant
 5540 Gulf of Mexico Dr., Longboat Key,
  941/383-3633
Leverock's Seafood House
 12320 Manatee Ave. W., 941/794-8900
Pier Restaurant
 1200 First Ave. W., 941/748-8087
Seafood Shack
 4110 127th St. W., Cortez, 941/794-1235

Best View While Dining
Sandbar Restaurant
 100 Spring Ave., Anna Maria, 941/778-0444

F

BROOKSVILLE, FL

Best Barbecue/Ribs
Florida Boy's Barbeque
915 W. Jefferson St., 352/796-6333

Best Homestyle Food
Country Kitchen
20020 Cortez Blvd., 352/796-2041

Best Pizza
Five Star Pizza
31156 Cortez Blvd., 352/799-3787

Best Seafood
Zip's Restaurant
11738 Broad St., 352/799-8985

Best Steaks
Pier 688 Restaurant
1177 S. Broad St., 352/799-5200

CLEARWATER, FL

[See also: Dunedin, St. Petersburg, Tampa.]

Best All-You-Can-Eat Buffet
Stacey's Family Buffet
1451 Missouri Ave. N., Largo, 813/585-3543
21838 Hwy. 19N, 813/726-0040

Best American Food
O'Keefe's Tavern and Restaurant
1219 S. Fort Harrison Ave., 813/442-9034

Best Bar
Shephard's Restaurant and Lounge
601 S. Gulfview Blvd., 813/441-6875

Best Bistro
Michael's Bistro
2410 Commercial Way, Spring Hill, 352/683-8420

Best Breakfast
Robby's Pancake House
5399 Commercial Way, Spring Hill, 352/596-6699

Best Brewpub
Hops Grill and Bar
18825 Hwy. 19N, 813/531-5300

Best Chinese Food
Hao Wah
10704 U.S. Hwy. 19N, Port Richey, 813/869-2400

Best Diner
Rody's Country Cookin'
914 S. Pinellas Ave., Tarpon Springs, 813/937-9279

Best Dinner
Bobby's Bistro and Wine Bar
447 Mandalay Ave., 813/446-9463
Heilman's Beachcomber
447 Mandalay Ave., 813/442-4144

Best Eclectic Menu
Blue Heron Cafe
  5770 Roosevelt Blvd., 813/532-9970

Best Family Restaurant
Corner House Family Restaurant
  2836 Alternate 19, Palm Harbor, 813/786-3736

Best French Food
Cafe Largo
  12551 Indian Rocks Rd., Largo, 813/596-6282
Ile de France
  13911 Old Dixie Hwy., Hudson, 813/863-7994

Best Greek/Mediterranean Food
Hellas
  784 Dodecanese Blvd., Tarpon Springs,
    813/934-8400

Best Health-Conscious Menu
Smoothie's
  1590 N. McMullen Booth Rd., 813/797-0955

Best Italian Food
Sorrento's Restaurant
  5526 Commercial Way, Spring Hill, 352/596-5383

Best Mexican Food
Carambas
  1842 Drew St., 813/446-7469
Carmelita's
  5042 E. Bay Dr., 813/524-8226

Best Outdoor Dining
Palm Court Restaurant
  1825 N. Highland Ave., 813/446-8168
The Blue Dolphin
  8825 State Rd. 52, Hudson, 813/862-9300

Best Seafood
Adams Mark Caribbean Grill
  430 S. Gulfview Blvd., 813/443-5714
Frenchy's Saltwater Cafe
  419 Poinsettia Ave., 813/461-6295
Frenchy's Shrimp and Oyster Cafe
  41 Baymont St., 813/446-3607
Guppy's
  1701 Gulf Blvd., Indian Rocks Beach,
    813/595-8647
Heilman's Beachcomber
  447 Mandalay Ave., 813/442-4144
Hungry Fisherman
  19915 Gulf Blvd., Indian Rocks Beach,
    813/595-4218

Best Spanish Food
Tio Pepe Restaurant
  2930 Gulf to Bay Blvd., 813/799-3082

Best Steaks
Black Angus Stockyard
  13707 58th St. N., 813/531-0019

F

Best Sunday Brunch
Shephard's Restaurant and Lounge
  601 S. Gulfview Blvd., 813/441-6875

Best Sushi
Kiku Japanese Restaurant
  13505 Icot Blvd., 813/532-9559

Best View While Dining
Rockaway Grill
  7 Rockaway St., 813/446-4844
Sweetwater's
  2400 Gulf to Bay Blvd., 813/799-0818

CORAL SPRINGS, FL

Best American Food
Dan Marino's Town Tavern
  901 N. University Dr., 954/341-4658

Best Brewpub
Hops Grill and Bar
  2600 N. University Dr., 954/340-3868

Best Lunch
Borders Bookstore
  700 N. University Dr., 954/340-3307

Best Steaks
Dan Marino's Town Tavern
  901 N. University Dr., 954/341-4658

DAYTONA BEACH, FL

Best Bar
MC K's Pub
  218 S. Beach St., 904/238-3321

Best Barbecue/Ribs
Sonny's Real Pit Bar-B-Q
  1840 S. Ridgewood Ave., 904/761-0371

Best Beer Selection
Mr. Dunderbak's
  1700 International Speedway Blvd., 904/258-1600

Best Breakfast
Aunt Catfish's on the River
  4009 Halifax Dr., 904/767-4768

Best Burgers
Earl Street Grill
  715 Earl St., 904/239-8781

Best Coffee/Coffeehouse
Cafe Bravo
  176 N. Beach St., 904/252-7747
Java Lava
  550 Seabreeze Blvd., 904/257-0599

Best Delicatessen
Sorrento's Restaurant
  1344 W. International Speedway Blvd.,
    904/255-1817

F

Best Eclectic Menu
Cafe Frappes
174 N. Beach St., 904/254-7999

Best Family Restaurant
Booth's Bowery
957 Herbert St., 904/761-9464

Best German Food
Mr. Dunderbak's
1700 International Speedway Blvd., 904/258-1600

Best Greek/Mediterranean
Stavros'
709 S. Nova Rd., 904/672-6111

Best Homestyle Food
Aunt Catfish's on the River
4009 Halifax Dr., 904/767-4768

Best Ice Cream/Yogurt
Flamingo Homemade Ice Cream
559 N. Beach St., 904/255-8090

Best Japanese Food
Sapporo
501 Seabreeze Blvd., 904/257-4477
3340 S. Atlantic Ave., 904/756-0480

Best Mexican Food
Rio Bravo Cantina
1735 W. International Speedway Blvd.,
904/255-6500

Best Other Ethnic Food
Hungarian Village (Hungarian)
424 S. Ridgewood Ave., 904/253-5712
Tropical Gourmet (Caribbean)
1420 Mason Ave., 904/274-4450

Best Outdoor Dining
Cafe Frappes
174 N. Beach St., 904/254-7999
JC'S Oyster Deck
79 Dunlawton Ave., 904/767-1881

Best Pizza
New York Pizza
725 Broadway Ave., 904/257-2050
Pantheon Pizza
505 White St., 904/258-7180

Best Salad/Salad Bar
Chart House
1100 Marina Point Dr., 904/255-9022

Best Sandwiches
Booth's Bowery
957 Herbert St., 904/761-9464
Bopper's Sandwich Emporium
137 W. International Speedway Blvd.,
904/253-3778

Best Seafood
Park's Seafood Restaurant
951 N. Beach St., 904/258-7272

Shells Restaurant
200 S. Atlantic Ave., 904/258-0007
Top Of Daytona Restaurant
2625 S. Atlantic Ave., 904/767-5791

Best Steaks
Top Of Daytona Restaurant
2625 S. Atlantic Ave., 904/767-5791
Webber's Penn Jersey Bar
2017 S. Ridgewood Ave., 904/761-5982

Best Sushi
Sapporo
501 Seabreeze Blvd., 904/257-4477

Best Wine Selection
Norwood's
400 E. Second Ave., New Smyrna Beach,
904/252-9296

DEERFIELD BEACH, FL

[See also: Boca Raton, Coral Springs, and Ft. Lauderdale.]

Best American Food
Cove Restaurant and Marina
1645 SE Third Ct., 954/421-9272
Pal's Charley's Crab
1755 SE Third Ct., 954/427-4000

Best Barbecue/Ribs
Roadhouse Grill
401 N. Federal Hwy., 954/428-9080

Best Delicatessen
New York Deli Restaurant
1310 S. Federal Hwy., 954/725-7100

Best Desserts
Olympia Flame Diner
80 S. Federal Hwy., 954/480-8402

Best French Food
Cafe Claude
1544 SE Third Ct., 954/421-7337
Le Val de Loire
1576 SE Third Ct., 954/427-5354

Best Greek/Mediteranean Food
Olympia Flame Diner
80 S. Federal Hwy., 954/480-8402

Best Italian Food
Brusco Italian Restaurant
1380 S. Federal Hwy., 954/428-2676
Carafiello's Restaurant
949 S. Federal Hwy., 954/421-2481
Pasta Cafe
490 W. Hillsboro Blvd., 954/698-6445

F

Best Mexican Food
Rattlesnake Jake's
2060 NE Second St., 954/421-4481

Best Salad/Salad Bar
Pete's Garden Cafe
700 W. Hillsboro Blvd., Ste. 106, 954/429-3989

Best Sandwiches
Dry Dock Cafe
250 S. Federal Hwy., 954/480-9084

Best Seafood
Cove Restaurant and Marina
1645 SE Third Ct., 954/421-9272
Whales Rib
2031 NE Second St., 954/421-8880

Best View While Dining
Cove Restaurant and Marina
1645 SE Third Ct., 954/421-9272

DESTIN, FL

Best Breakfast
Silver Sands Restaurant
285 Hwy. 98E, 850/837-9493

Best Brewpub
Harbour Docks
538 Hwy. 98E, 850/837-2506

Best Continental Food
Marina Cafe
404 Hwy. 98E, 850/837-7960

Best Delicatessen
Village Cheese Shop
209 Main St., 850/837-8032

Best Fine Dining
Flamingo Cafe
414 Hwy. 98E, 850/837-0961
Marina Cafe
404 Hwy. 98E, 850/837-7960
Ocean Club
8955 Emerald Coast Pkwy. W., 850/267-3666

Best Italian Food
Guglielmo's Ristorante and Lounge
529 Hwy. 98E, 850/654-9880

Best Restaurant in Town
Flamingo Cafe
414 Hwy. 98E, 850/837-0961
Marina Cafe
404 Hwy. 98E, 850/837-7960

Best Seafood
Captain Dave's on the Gulf
3796 Hwy. 98E, 850/837-2627
Captain Jewel Melvin's Seafood
602 Hwy. 98E, 850/837-2020
Harbour Docks
538 Hwy. 98E, 850/837-2506

Marina Cafe
  404 Hwy. 98E, 850/837-7960

Best View While Dining
Harbour Docks
  538 Hwy. 98E, 850/837-2506
Harry T's Boathouse
  320 Hwy. 98E, 850/654-4800
Lucky Snapper Grill and Bar
  76 Hwy. 98E, 850/654-0900

F

DUNEDIN, FL

[See also: Clearwater and Tampa.]

Best All-You-Can-Eat Buffet
The Crystal Room at K-Lynn's Banquet Hall
  1106 Overcash Dr., 813/734-3767

Best Breakfast
Kelly's For Just About Anything
  319 Main St., 813/736-5274

Best Casual Dining
Sea Sea Rider's
  221 Main St., 813/734-1445

Best Homestyle Food
Iris Family Restaurant
  234 Douglas Ave., 813/734-0779

Best Other Ethnic Food
Flanagan's Hunt Irish Pub (Irish)
  465 Main St., 813/736-4994

Best Seafood
Bon Appetit
  148 Marina Plz., 813/733-2151
Jesse's Dockside
  345 Causeway Blvd., 813/736-2611

ENGLEWOOD, FL

Best Chinese Food
China Fair
  1720 S. McCall Rd., 941/475-6887

Best Mexican Food
Prime Time Steak and Spirits
  5800 Placida Rd., Ste. 100, 941/697-7799

Best Regional Food
Lock and Key Restaurant and Pub
  2045 N. Beach Rd., 941/474-1517

Best View While Dining
Mad Sam's
  1375 Beach Rd., 941/475-9505

F

FT. LAUDERDALE, FL

[See also: Boca Raton, Coral Springs, Deerfield Beach, Hollywood, Hallandale, Miami, and Pompano Beach.]

Best American Food
Michael's Cafe
    2304 NE 62nd St., 954/776-6191
Riverwalk Eatery
    215 SW Second St., 954/760-4373

Best Barbecue/Ribs
Bobby Rubino's Place for Ribs
    6001 Kimberly Blvd., North Lauderdale,
    954/971-4740
Shorty's Bar-B-Q
    5989 S. University Dr., Davie, 954/944-0348

Best Breakfast
Rainbow Restaurant and Diner
    2726 David Blvd., 954/792-5860

Best Business Lunch
Cave's Restaurant
    2205 N. Federal Hwy., 954/561/4622

Best Casual Dining
Ship's Galley Restaurant
    2830 NE 29th Ave., Lighthouse Point,
    954/781-6144

Best Chinese Food
Dynasty Chinese Restaurant
    3232 David Blvd., 954/584-7828
Mai Kai Restaurant and Catering
    3599 N. Federal Hwy., 954/563-3272

Best Eclectic Menu
Max's Beach Place
    17 S. Atlantic Blvd., 954/525-5022

Best Fine Dining
East City Grill
    505 N. Atlantic Blvd., 954/565-5569
Mark's Las Olas
    1032 E. Las Olas Blvd., 954/463-1000

Best French Food
Christina Crepe Restaurant
    2736 N. Federal Hwy., 954/566-2880
Jean-Claude Patisserie
    3320 NE 33rd St., 954/563-5406
Left Bank
    214 SE Sixth Ave., 954/462-5376

Best Indian Food
Punjab Indian Restaurant
    5975 N. Federal Hwy., Ste. 103, 954/491-6710

Best Inexpensive Meal
Shells Restaurant
    2019 N. University Dr., Sunrise, 954/749-0557

Best Italian Food
Mario's East
  1313 E. Las Olas Blvd., 954/523-4990
Randazzo's Restaurant
  6029 Kimberly Blvd., North Lauderdale,
  954/972-4330
Regalo
  4215 N. Federal Hwy., 954/566-6661
Tina's Spaghetti House
  2110 S. Federal Hwy., 954/522-9943

Best Kosher Food
Tel-Aviv Min- Market and Restaurant
  4305 NW 88th Ave., Sunrise, 954/746-3996

Best Lunch
Michael's Cafe
  2304 NE 62nd St., 954/776-6191
Rainbow Restaurant and Diner
  2726 David Blvd., 954/792-5860

Best Mexican Food
Carlos and Pepe's
  1302 SE Seventeenth St., 954/467-7192
Mark's Las Olas
  1032 E. Las Olas Blvd., 954/463-1000

Best Other Ethnic Food
Aruba Beach Cafe (Caribbean)
  1 E. Commercial Blvd., 954/776-0001
Don Arturo Restaurant (Cuban)
  1198 SW 27th Ave., 954/584-7966
La Bamba (Cuban)
  5552 W. Oakland Park Blvd., 954/735-1891

Best Pizza
California Pizza Kitchen
  2301 N. Federal Hwy., 954/565-1196

Best Romantic Dining
Le Dome
  333 Sunset Dr., 954/463-3303

Best Seafood
Fifteenth Street Fisheries
  1900 SE Fifteenth St., 954/763-2777
Rustic Inn Crabhouse
  4331 Ravenswood Rd., 954/584-1637
Sea Watch Restaurant and Lounge
  6002 N. Ocean Blvd., 954/781-2200

Best Soul Food
Betty's Restaurant and Barbecue
  601 NW 22nd Rd., 954/583-9121

Best Sports Bar
Wings Plus
  87 W. Prospect Rd., Oakland Park, 954/771-9877
  1354 SW 160th St., Sunrise, 954/389-1933

Best Steaks
Kansas City Steak House
  5645 S. University Dr., Davie, 954/680-0322

Roadhouse Grill
  3300 E. Commercial Blvd., 954/772-3777
  1900 S. University Dr., Davie, 954/370-3044

Best Thai Food
Siam Cuisine
  Wilton Manors, 2010 Wilton Dr., 954/564-3411
Thai Spice Restaurant
  1514 E. Commercial Blvd., Oakland Park,
  954/771-4335

Best View While Dining
Aruba Beach Cafe
  1 E. Commercial Blvd., 954/776-0001
East City Grill
  505 N. Atlantic Blvd., 954/565-5569
Sea Watch Restaurant and Lounge
  6002 N. Ocean Blvd., 954/781-2200

FT. MYERS/CAPE CORAL, FL

Best Barbecue/Ribs
Hickory Barbecue
  15400 McGregor Blvd., Ft. Myers, 941/481-2626
Rib City Grill
  12575 S. Cleveland Ave., Ft. Myers, 941/278-1300
Santa Fe Barbecue and Steakhouse
  4400 Hancock Bridge Pkwy., Ft. Myers,
  941/656-5002
Sonny's Real Pit Barbecue
  5980 Winkler Rd., Ft. Myers, 941/481-0090
  3701 Fowler St., Ft. Myers, 941/936-5747

Best Breakfast
Jimbo's Restaurant
  1604 SE 46th St., Cape Coral, 941/549-1818

Best Casual Dining
Shells of Fort Myers
  4606 S. Cleveland Ave., Ft. Myers, 941/278-9011

Best Chinese Food
Brass Phoenix
  16520 Tamiami Trail, Ft. Myers, 941/489-4242
Magic Wok
  6900 Daniels Pkwy., Ft. Myers, 941/561/2066

Best Dinner
Prawnbroker
  13451 McGregor Blvd., Ste. 16, Ft. Myers,
  941/489-2226
Sasse Il Pizzauolo
  3651 Evans Ave., Ft. Myers, 941/278-5544
Sunshine Cafe
  14900 Captiva Dr., Captiva, 941/472-6200
The Veranda
  2122 Second St., Ft. Myers, 941/332-2065

Best Eclectic Menu
The Bubble Room
  15001 Captiva Dr., Captiva, 941/472-5558

F

Best Fine Dining
Chez Le Bear
  17260 Harbour Point Dr., Ft. Myers, 941/466-4000

Best French Food
Michel and Michelle's Restaurant
  1400 Colonial Blvd., Ft. Myers, 941/275-6212
Peter's LA Cuisine
  2224 Bay St., Ft. Myers, 941/332-2228

Best German Food
Little Oak
  1708 Cape Coral Pkwy. W., Cape Coral,
    941/542-7889
Tannengarten Restaurant
  3724 Del Prado Blvd. S., Cape Coral, 941/549-1300

Best Homestyle Food
Farmer's Market Restaurant
  2736 Edison Ave., Ft. Myers, 941/334-1687
Mel's Diner
  19050 S. Tamiami Trail, Ft. Myers, 941/267-2468
Mel's Diner Commissary
  12350 Palm Beach Blvd., Tice, 941/693-5833
Mel's Diner Too
  4820 S. Cleveland Ave., Ft. Myers, 941/275-7850

Best Italian Food
Carrabba's Italian Grill
  12990 S. Cleveland Ave., Ft. Myers, 941/433-0877
Dario's Restaurant and Lounge
  1805 Del Prado Blvd. S., Cape Coral, 941/574-7798
Gabriello's Italian Ristorante
  12791 Kenwood Ln., Ft. Myers, 941/275-0076

Best Japanese Food
Osaka Japanese Steakhouse
  12951 McGregor Blvd., Ft. Myers, 941/489-2414
Yokahama
  4650 S. Cleveland Ave., Ft. Myers, 941/936-4007

Best Mexican Food
Garibaldi's
  11605 S. Cleveland Ave., Ft. Myers, 941/939-2323
Iguana Mia Mexican Restaurant
  4329 Cleveland Ave., Ft. Myers, 941/939-5247
  1027 Cape Coral Pkwy. E., Cape Coral,
    941/542-1351

Best Other Ethnic
Delilah's Garden (Polish)
  12375-25 Cleveland Ave., Ft. Myers, 941/278-9987

Best Outdoor Dining
Anthony's on the Gulf
  3040 Estero Blvd., Ft. Myers Beach, 941/463-2600

Best Restaurant in Town
Melanie's Restaurant
  2158 McGregor Blvd., Ft. Myers, 941/334-3139
Mucky Duck
  2500 Estero Blvd., Ft. Myers Beach, 941/463-5519

The Veranda
  2122 Second St., Ft. Myers, 941/332-2065

Best Sandwiches
Englund's Deli II
  1109 Del Prado Blvd. S., Cape Coral, 941/458-0183
Palate Pleasers Cafe and Pub
  3512 Del Prado Blvd. S., Cape Coral, 941/945-6333

Best Seafood
Cape Crab House
  2301 Del Prado Blvd. S., Cape Coral, 941/574-2722
New England Moorings
  1326 SE Sixteenth Pl., Cape Coral, 941/772-9900
Prawnbroker
  13451 McGregor Blvd., Ste. 16, Ft. Myers,
  941/489-2226
Shells of Fort Myers
  4606 S. Cleveland Ave., Ft. Myers, 941/278-9011
Smitty's on MacGregor
  3583 McGregor Blvd., Ft. Myers, 941/939-7300

Best Steaks
Bubba's Road House and Saloon
  1719 Cape Coral Pkwy. E., Cape Coral,
  941/540-0400
Cape Crab House
  2301 Del Prado Blvd. S., Cape Coral, 941/574-2722
Santa Fe Barbecue and Steakhouse
  4400 Hancock Bridge Pkwy., Ft. Myers,
  941/656-5002

Best Thai Food
Siam Hut Thai Food
  1873 Del Prado Blvd. S., Cape Coral, 941/772-3131
Thai Gardens
  7091 College Pkwy., Ft. Myers, 941/275-0999

Best View While Dining
Anthony's on the Gulf
  3040 Estero Blvd., Ft. Myers Beach, 941/463-2600
Mucky Duck
  11546 Andy Rosse Ln. SW, Captiva, 941/472-3434
Mariners Inn Grog and Galley
  3448 Marinatown Ln., Ft. Myers, 941/997-8300

Best Wine Selection
Peter's LA Cuisine
  2224 Bay St., Ft. Myers, 941/332-2228

FT. PIERCE, FL

Best Bar
Tiki Bar and Restaurant
  1 Avenue A, 561/467-1188

Best Barbecue/Ribs
Dale's Barbecue
  3362 S. U.S. Hwy. 1, 561/567-6640
  3900 Okeechobee Rd., 561/464-6766
Norris's Famous Place For Ribs
  3080 N. U.S. Hwy. 1, 561/464-4000

Sonny's Real Pit Bar-B-Q
  3120 S. U.S. Hwy. 1, 561/468-9086

Best Beer Selection
Pig and Whistle Pub
  217 Orange Ave., 561/489-3969

Best Breakfast
Captain's Galley
  825 N. Indian River Rd., 561/466-8495
JJ Plum's II
  4131 S. U.S. Hwy. 1, 561/468-8622

Best Burgers
Billy's Bar and Grill
  4810 S. U.S. Hwy. 1, 561/460-1411
Norris's Famous Place For Ribs
  3080 N. U.S. Hwy. 1, 561/464-4000
Pineapple Joe's Grill and Bar
  6297 N. U.S. Hwy. 1, 561/465-6930
Theo Thudpucker's Raw Bar
  2025 Seaway Dr., 561/465-1078

Best Chinese Food
Chang-Chun Chinese Restaurant
  4903 S. U.S. Hwy. 1, 561/465-8622
Peking Chinese Restaurant
  1012 S. U.S. Hwy. 1, 561/464-5960

Best Diners
Crystal's Restaurant
  127 S. Second St., 561/461-9550

Best Family Restaurant
Dino's Family Restaurant
  2001 N. U.S. Hwy. 1, 561/465-5217
JJ Plum's II
  4131 S. U.S. Hwy. 1, 561/468-8622

Best Health-Conscious Menu
Lee's Sub and Salad Shop
  850 S. 21st St., 561/466-4243

Best Ice Cream/Yogurt
Bresler's Ice Cream and Yogurt
  4420 Okeechobee Rd., 561/466-9490

Best Italian Food
Italian Grill
  2180 58th Ave., Vero Beach, 561/567-6640

Best Mexican Food
Enriqo's Mexican Kitchen
  3215 S. U.S. Hwy. 1, 561/465-1608
Guadalajara Mexican Food
  1702 Delaware Ave., 561/489-2403

Best Restaurant In Town
Ocean Grill
  1050 Sexton Plz., Vero Beach, 561/231-5409

Best Romantic Dining
Toucan's Top Of The Dock
  201 Fisherman's Wharf, 561/465-1334

F

Best Sandwiches
Sharky's
  1012 Shorewinds Dr., 561/466-2757

Best Seafood
Captain's Galley
  825 N. Indian River Dr., 561/466-8495
Chuck's Seafood Restaurant
  822 Seaway Dr., 561/461-9484
Galley Grille
  927 N. U.S. Hwy. 1, 561/468-2081
Oceans Village Restaurant
  2400 S. Ocean Dr., 561/465-4200
Ramp Raw Bar and Diner
  20 Seaway Dr., 561/468-0760
Theo Thudpucker's Raw Bar
  2025 Seaway Dr., 561/465-1078

Best Steaks
Galley Grille
  927 N. U.S. Hwy. 1, 561/468-2081
Gator Trace
  4302 Gator Trace, 561/464-7442
Mangrove Mattie's
  1640 Seaway Dr., 561/466-1044
Norris's Famous Place For Ribs
  3080 N. U.S. Hwy. 1, 561/464-4000
Oceans Village Restaurant
  2400 S. Ocean Dr., 561/465-4200
Out of Bounds Cafe
  2838 S. U.S. Hwy. 1, 561/468-4363

Best View While Dining
Tiki Bar and Restaurant
  1 Avenue A, 561/467-1188

FT. WALTON BEACH, FL

Best Barbecue/Ribs
Daddy's, The Place for Ribs
  I-40, W. Miracle Strip Pkwy., 850/244-3445

Best Fine Dining
Pandora's Restaurant and Lounge
  1120B Santa Rosa Blvd., 850/244-8669
Summerhouse Restaurant
  2 Miracle Strip Pkwy. SW, 850/244-1553

Best French Food
Bay Cafe French Restaurant
  233 Alconese Ave. SE, 850/244-3550

Best Homestyle Food
Brooks Bridge Barbecue and Cafe
  240 Miracle Strip Pkwy. SE, 850/244-3003

Best Italian Food
Caffe Italia
  189 Brooks St. SE, 850/664-0035

Best Late-Night Food
Joe and Eddie's Restaurant
  206 Florida Pl. SE, 850/243-0733

Best Outdoor Dining
Bay Cafe French Restaurant
  233 Alconese Ave. SE, 850/244-3550

Best Pizza
Caffe Italia
  189 Brooks St. SE, 850/664-0035

Best Seafood
Staff's Seafood Restaurant
  24 Miracle Strip Pkwy. SE, 850/243-3482

GAINESVILLE, FL

Best Barbecue/Ribs
David's Real Pit Bar-B-Que
  5121A NW 39th Ave., 352/373-2002

Best Chinese Food
China Palace
  2445 SW Thirteenth St., 352/375-8021
Jade Gardens
  3510 SW Thirteenth St., 352-376-7800
Mr. Han's Restaurant
  6944 NW Tenth Pl., Ste. 1, 352/331-6400

Best Italian Food
Amelia's Italian Cuisine
  235 S. Main St., 352/373-1919
Ruscito's Restaurant
  521 NE 23rd Ave., 352/373-2575

Best Mexican Food
Ashley's Mexican and American Restaurant
  3236 SW 35th Blvd., 352/375-4064
El Indio
  407 NW Thirteenth St., 352/377-5828
  5011 NW 34th St., 352/374-8647
El Toro Mexican Food
  1203 SW Sixteenth Ave., 352/374-8100

Best Pizza
Leonardo's Pizza In a Pan
  4131 NW Sixteenth Blvd., 352/376-2001
Pizza Palace
  608 NW Thirteenth St., 352/372-1546

Best Sandwiches
43 Street Deli and Breakfast House
  4401 NW 25th Pl., 352/373-2927
Copper Monkey Restaurant
  5109 NW 39th Ave., 352/377-1365
  1702 W. University Ave., 352/374-4984

Best Seafood
Harry's Seafood Bar and Grille
  110 SE First St., 352/372-1555

Best Steaks
Steak and Pasta Works
  3620 NW Thirteenth St., 352/377-2782

Best Thai Food
Tim's Thai Restaurant
  501 NW 23rd Ave., 352/372-5424

HALLANDALE, FL

[See also: Ft. Lauderdale, Hollywood, and Miami.]

Best Bar
Flanagan's Seafood Bar and Grill
  4 N. Federal Hwy., 954/458-2566

Best Breakfast
Tom's Coffee and Sandwich Shop
  826 W. Hallandale Beach Blvd., 954/454-6819

Best Chinese Food
Mott Street Chinese Restaurant
  1295 E. Hallandale Beach Blvd., 954/456-7555

Best Italian Food
Manero's Steak House
  2600 E. Hallandale Beach Blvd., 954/456-1000

Best Japanese Food
Koto Japanese Restaurant
  1111 E. Hallandale Beach Blvd., 954/457-0078

Best Lunch
Miami Subs
  116 W. Hallandale Beach Blvd., 954/454-4488

HOLLYWOOD, FL

[See also: Ft. Lauderdale, Miami, and Pompano Beach.]

Best Casual Dining
Sara's
  3944 N. 46th Ave., 954/986-1770

Best Continental Food
Impromptu Fine Dining
  2039 Hollywood Blvd., 954/923-7099

Best Diner
Jimmy's Place North
  2209 S. State Rd. 7, 954/961-3547

Best Family Restaurant
Dave and Buster's
  3000 Oakwood Blvd., 954/923-5505

Best Fine Dining
Martha's Supper Club
  6024 N. Ocean Dr., 954/923-5444

Best German Food
Bavarian Village Restaurant
  1401 N. Federal Hwy., 954/922-7321

Best Kosher Food
Pita Plus Hollywood
  5650 Stirling Rd., 954/985-8028

F

Best Middle Eastern Food
Lucy's Glatt Kosher Restaurant
  2832 Stirling Rd., 954/927-9277

Best Other Ethnic Food
Martha's Supper Club (Caribean)
  6024 N. Ocean Dr., 954/923-5444

Best Restaurant In Town
Revolution 2029
  2029 Harrison St., 954/920-4748

Best Seafood
Martha's Supper Club
  6024 N. Ocean Dr., 954/923-5444
Sugar Reef
  600 N. Surf Rd., 954/922-1119

Best Steaks
The Palm Cafe
  1855 Griffin Rd., Dania, 954/929-4243

Best View While Dining
Martha's Supper Club
  6024 N. Ocean Dr., 954/923-5444
Tugboat Annie's
  815 NE Third St., Dania, 954/925-3399

HOLMES BEACH, FL

Best Bar
Duffy's Tavern
  3901 Gulf Dr. N., 941/778-2501

Best Breakfast
Cafe on the Beach
  4000 Gulf Dr. N., 941/778-0784

Best Burgers
Duffy's Tavern
  3901 Gulf Dr. N., 941/778-2501

Best Eclectic Menu
Beach Bistro
  6600 Gulf Dr. N., 941/778-6444

HOMESTEAD, FL

Best Barbecue/Ribs
Shiver's Bar-B-Q
  28001 S. Dixie Hwy., 305/248-2272

Best Chinese Food
Canton Chinese Restaurant
  1657 NE Eighth St., 305/248-9956

Best Homestyle Food
Potlikker's Restaurant
  591 Washington Ave., 305/248-0835

Best Italian Food
Capri Restaurant
  935 N. Krome Ave., Florida City, 305/247-1542

Best Lunch
Shiver's Bar-B-Q
  28001 S. Dixie Hwy., 305/248-2272

JACKSONVILLE, FL

Best American Food
Beech Street Grill
   801 Beech St., Fernandina Beach, 904/277-3662

Best Barbecue/Ribs
Bono's Pit Barbecue
   9250 Baymeadows Rd., 904/636-5500
Homestead Restaurant
   1712 Beach Blvd., Jacksonville Beach,
      904/249-5240

Best Breakfast
Beach Hut Cafe
   1281 Third St. S., 904/249-3516
Metro Diner
   3302 Hendricks Ave., 904/398-3701

Best Brewpub
River City Brewing Company
   9810-3 Baymeadows Rd., 904/642-6310
   835 Museum Circle, 904/398-2299

Best Burgers
The Loop
   9965 San Jose Blvd., 904/262-2210
   4000 St. Johns Ave., 904/384-7301
   8221 Southside Blvd., 904/645-7788
   2014 San Marco Blvd., 904/399-5667
   6426 Bowden Rd., 904/448-0322
   9331 Arlington Expwy., 904/725-0850

Best Chinese Food
Mandarin Dragon Chinese Restaurant
   11362 San Jose Blvd., Ste. 8, 904/260-4681

Best Coffee/Coffeehouse
Biscotti's
   3556 St. John's Ave., 904/387-2060
The Coffee Grinder
   9834 Baymeadows Rd., 904/642-7600

Best Continental Food
Horizons Restaurant
   802 Ash St., Fernandina Beach, 904/321-2430
The Cafe and Grill
   Ritz-Carlton Hotel, 4740 Amelia Island
      Pkwy., Amelia Island, 904/277-1100

Best Delicatessen
Worman's Bakery and Delicatessen
   204 Broad St., 904/354-5702

Best Desserts
Cafe Carmon
   1986 San Marco Blvd., 904/399-4488

Best Diner
Metro Diner
   3302 Hendricks Ave., 904/398-3701

Best Dinner
Dolphin Depot
   704 E. First St., 904/270-1424

F

F

Marker 32
  14549 Beach Blvd., Jacksonville Beach,
    904/223-1534

Best Fine Dining
24 Miramar
  4446 Hendricks Ave., 904/448-2424
Amore Cafe
  1406 Beach Blvd., 904/246-5373
Beech Street Grill
  801 Beech St., Fernandina Beach, 904/227-3662
Gio's Cafe
  900 Sawgrass Village Dr., Ponte Verde Beach,
904/273-0101
Island Grill
  981 First St. N., Jacksonville Beach, 904/241-1881
Marker 32
  14549 Beach Blvd., 904/223-1534
Max's Place
  1316 Beach Blvd., 904/247-4422
Raspberry's On The Water
  2321 Beach Blvd., 904/247-8720
Sarnelli's
  2023 Park Ave., Orange Park, 904/269-1331
Sterling's Cafe
  3551 St. Johns Ave., 904/387-0700
The Augustine Grille
  1000 TPC Blvd., Ponte Verde Beach, 904/285-7777
West River
  1711 Edgewood Ave. S., 904/389-4171

Best Greek/Mediterranean Food
First Street Grille
  807 E. First St., 904/246-6555

Best Indian Food
Bombay Tandoor
  7404 Atlantic Blvd., 904/725-5711

Best Inexpensive Meal
Blue Diner
  410 N. Julia St., 904/632-1270
Slider's Cafe
  218 First St., 904/246-0881

Best Italian Food
La Cena Ristorante
  6271 St. Augustine Rd., 904/737-5350
Nino's Pasta House
  4456 Hendricks Ave., 904/733-1011
  7457 103rd St., 904/779-7568
Sarnelli's
  2023 Park Ave., Orange Park, 904/269-1331
Tonino's Ristorante Italiano
  1266 Third St. S., Jacksonville Beach,
    904/241-5425

Best Japanese Food
Chizu Japanese Steak House
  1227 Third St. S., Jacksonville Beach,
    904/241-8455

Mikado
10460 Philips Hwy., 904/886-0900

Best Lunch
A Tasteful Cafe
717 Post St., 904/358-1813
European Street Restaurant
2753 Park St., 904/384-9999
9501 Arlington Expwy., 904/725-8992
Schmagel's Bagels
9825 San Jose Blvd., Ste. 1, 904/268-5273
Tidbits
1076 Hendricks Ave., 904/396-0528

Best Mexican Food
Sierra Grille
331 Marsh Landing Pkwy., Jacksonville Beach,
904/273-2090

Best Other Ethnic Food
Lynch's Irish Pub (Irish)
514 First St. N., Jacksonville Beach, 904/249-5181

Best Outdoor Dining
First Street Grille
807 E. First St., 904/246-6555

Best Pizza
Al's Pizza
14286 Beach Blvd., Jacksonville Beach,
904/223-0991
Pizza Palace
1526 King St., 904/399-8815

Best Regional Food
Clark's Fish Camp and Seafood
12903 Hood Landing Rd., 904/268-3474

Best Romantic Dining
24 Miramar
4446 Hendricks Ave., 904/448-2424
The Augustine Grille
1000 TPC Blvd., Ponte Vedra Beach, 904/285-7777
The Hilltop
2030 Wells Rd., Orange Park, 904/279-5959
West River
1711 Edgewood Ave. S., 904/389-4171

Best Salad/Salad Bar
Jacksonville Kennel Club
1440 N. McDuff Ave., 904/646-0001
Silver Spoon Bar and Grill
2 Independent Dr., Ste. 2, 904/353-4503

Best Sandwiches
Larry's Giant Subs
11701 San Jose Blvd., 904/292-2666
12777 Atlantic Blvd., 904/221-7827

Best Seafood
Aw Shucks
950 Sawgrass Village Dr., Ponte Vedra Beach,
904/285-3017

F

Crab Pot
    12 First St. N., Jacksonville Beach, 904/241-4188
Dolphin Depot
    704 First St. N., Jacksonville Beach, 904/270-1424
Harry's Oyster Bar
    2 Independent Dr., 904/353-4927

Best Sunday Brunch
Crawdaddy's
    1643 Prudential Dr., 904/396-3546
Juliette's
    245 Water St., 904/355-6664

Best Thai Food
Old Siam
    1616 W. Third St., 904/247-7763
Pattaya Thai
    10916 Atlantic Blvd., 904/646-9506

Best Vegetarian Food
Heartworks Gallery
    820 Lomax St., 904/355-6210

Best Wine Selection
Wine Cellar
    1314 Prudential Dr., 904/398-8989

KEY LARGO, FL

Best Barbecue/Ribs
B.J.'s Barbecue
    102570 Overseas Hwy., 305/451-0900

Best Japanese Food
Makoto Japanese Restaurant
    1691 Overseas Hwy., 305/451-7083

Best Seafood
Islamorada Fish Company Restaurant
    81620 Overseas Hwy., Islamorada, 305/664-8363

Best View While Dining
Islamorada Fish Company Restaurant
    81620 Overseas Hwy., Islamorada, 305/664-8363

KEY WEST, FL

Best Chinese Food
Dynasty Chinese Restaurant
    918 Duval St., 305/294-2943

Best Continental Food
Bagatelle
    115 Duval St., 305/296-6609

Best Diner
Harpoon Harry's
    832 Caroline St., 305/294-8744

Best Fine Dining
The Palm Grill
    1029 Southard St., 305/296-1744

Best French Food
Cafe Des Artistes
    1007 Simonton St., 305/294-7100

F

Best Homestyle Food
Camille's Restaurant
703 1/2 Duval St., 305/296-4811

Best Italian Food
La Trattoria Venezia
524 Duval St., 305/296-1075

Best Restaurant in Town
Louie's Back Yard
700 Waddell Ave., 305/294-1061

Best Seafood
Martha's
3591 S. Roosevelt Blvd., 305/294-3466
Quay Restaurant
12 Duval St., 305/294-4446

Best Sports Bar
P.T.'s Late Night Bar and Grill
920 Caroline St., 305/296-4245

Best Steaks
Pepe's Cafe
806 Caroline St., 305/294-7192

Best View While Dining
Pier House Restaurant
1 Duval St., 305/296-4600

LAKELAND, FL

Best Barbecue/Ribs
Brothers Bar-B-Q
1046 Martin Luther King Jr. Ave., 941/688-5303
Jaybird's Bar-B-Q
6120 U.S. Hwy. 98N, 941/858-1970
Jimbo's Pit Bar-B-Q
1215 E. Memorial Blvd., 941/683-3777

Best Breakfast
Dale's Kitchen
223 N. Wabash Ave., 941/683-3702
Reececliff Restaurant
940 S. Florida Ave., 941/686-6661

Best Burgers
Fat Jack's Deli and Pub
2940 S. Florida Ave., 941/687-0262

Best Chinese Food
Pan Ye's Restaurant
743 E. Memorial Blvd., 941/686-2052

Best Desserts
Palm Court
819 S. Florida Ave., 941/682-4140
Strollo's Cucina
1295 E. Main St., 941/686-1295

Best Italian Food
CDB Pizza and Italian Restaurant
804 E. Memorial Blvd., 941/688-6444
Palm Court
819 S. Florida Ave., 941/682-4140

F

Strollo's Cucina
1295 E. Main St., 941/686-1295

Best Japanese Food
Shogun Japanese Steak House
3234 S. Florida Ave., 941/647-2114
4949 U.S. Hwy. 98N, 941/853-6800
2306 E. Edgewood Dr., 941/665-1165

Best Other Ethnic Food
El Coqui Restaurant (Puerto Rican)
4417 S. Florida Ave., 941/648-4374

Best Place to Take the Kids
Chuck E. Cheese Pizza
3558 U.S. Hwy. 98N, 941/853-8668

Best Sandwiches
Deli Delicacies
4110E S. Florida Ave., 941/644-3363
Fat Jack's Deli and Pub
2940 S. Florida Ave., 941/687-0262

Best Seafood
Catfish Country Restaurant
2400 E.F. Griffin Rd., Bartow, 941/646-6767

Best Steaks
Farmer Jones Red Barn House
6150 New Tampa Hwy., 941/686-2754
Texas Cattle Company
735 E. Main St., 941/686-1434

MELBOURNE, FL

Best Barbecue/Ribs
Woody's Bar-B-Que
2227 W. New Haven Ave., 407/951-9163

Best Breakfast
Sue's Wrangler
914 W. New Haven Ave., 407/984-0770

Best Homestyle Food
Ethel and Fred's Restaurant
3016 W. New Haven Ave., 407/725-6855
Sue's Wrangler
914 W. New Haven Ave., 407/984-0770

Best Italian Food
Dove Restaurant
1790 A1A Hwy., Satellite Beach, 407/777-5817
Paolo's Italian Kitchen
476 Ballard Dr., 407/259-2089

Best Pizza
Leaning Tower of Pizza
681 N. Wickham Rd., 407/259-6100

Best Sandwiches
Don's Famous Hoagies
784 S. Apollo Blvd., 407/676-7030
Doubles Hoagies
1897 S. Patrick Dr., Satellite Beach, 407/773-5341
575 S. Wickham Rd., 407/676-6945

Best Seafood
Bone Fish Willy's
  2459B Pineapple Ave., 407/255-0735
Jack Baker's Lobster Shanty
  2200 S. Orlando Ave., Cocoa Beach, 407/783-1350
Rooney's
  2641 Palm Bay Rd. NE, Palm Bay, 407/724-8520
Shells Restaurant
  1490 W. New Haven Ave., 407/722-1122

Best Steaks
Durango Steak House
  6765 N. Wickham Rd., 407/259-2955

F

MIAMI, FL

[See also: Ft. Lauderdale, Hallandale, and Hollywood.]

Best Barbecue/Ribs
79th Street Barbecue
  1772 NW 79th St., 305/836-4142
Peoples Bar-B-Q
  360 NW Eighth St., 305/373-8080
Shorty's Bar-B-Q
  9200 S. Dixie Hwy., Kendall, 305/670-7732
  11575 SW 40th St., 305/227-3196
The Pit Bar-B-Q
  16400 SW Eighth St., 305/226-2272

Best Casual Dining
Bayside Seafood
  3501 Rickenbacker Causeway, 305/361-0808
The Booking Table
  728 Ocean Dr., Miami Beach, 305/672-3476

Best Chinese Food
Canton Chinese Restaurant
  14487 S. Dixie Hwy., 305/255-5115
  9796 SW Eighth St., 305/226-8032
  2614 Ponce De Leon Blvd., Coral Gables,
    305/448-3736
China Grill
  404 Washington Ave., Miami Beach, 305/534-2211
Christine Lee's Gaslight
  17082 Collins Ave., 305/931-7700
Chrysanthemum
  1256 Washington Ave., Miami Beach, 305/531-5656
South Garden
  10855 Sunset Dr., 305/274-8788
Tropical Chinese Restaurant
  7991 SW 40th St., 305/262-7576
Wok and Roll
  1451 Collins Ave., S. Miami Beach, 305/672-0911

Best Coffee/Coffeehouse
The Grind
  12573 Biscayne Blvd., North Miami, 305/899-9979

Best Continental Food
Crystal Cafe
726 NW 41st St., 305/673-8266

Best Delicatessen
Arnie and Richie's
525 41st St., 305/531-7691

Best Desserts
Cheesecake Factory
3015 Grand Ave., 305/447-9898
Mark's Place
2286 NE 123rd St., North Miami, 305/893-6888

Best Diner
11th Street Diner
1065 Washington Ave., Miami Beach, 305/534-6373
Il Piccolo Diner
2112 NE 123rd St., North Miami, 305/893-6538

Best Eclectic Menu
Astor Place Bar and Grill
956 Washington Ave., 305/672-7217
Gourmet Diner
13951 Biscayne Blvd., North Miami Beach,
305/947-2255
Pacific Time
915 Lincoln Rd., Miami Beach, 305/534-5979

Best Family Restaurant
Shells Seafood Restaurant
7390 SW 117th Ave., 305/274-5552

Best Fine Dining
Chef Allen
19008 NE 29th Ave., 305/935-2900
China Grill
404 Washington Ave., Miami Beach, 305/534-2211
Kaleidoscope Restaurant
3112 Commodore Plz., 305/446-5010
Osteria Del Teatro
1443 Washington Ave., Miami Beach, 305/538-7850
Raleigh Tiger Oak Room
1775 Collins Ave., Miami Beach, 305/534-6300
The Grand Cafe
2669 S. Bayshore Dr., 305/858-9600
Veranda at Turnberry Isle Resort Club
19999 Country Club Dr., 305/932-6200

Best French Food
Le Festival
2120 Salzedo St., Coral Gables, 305/442-8545
The Bistro
2611 Ponce de Leon Blvd., Coral Gables,
305/442-9671

Best German Food
Edelweiss Restaurant
2655 Biscayne Blvd., 305/573-4421
Treffpunkt Biergarten
18090 Collins Ave., 305/933-3942

Best Greek/Mediterranean Food
Maria's Greek Restaurant
    1363 Coral Way, 305/856-0938
Two Sisters
    50 Alhambra Plz., Coral Gables, 305/441-1234

Best Health-Conscious Menu
Unicorn Village Market and Restaurant
    3599 NE 207th St., 305/933-8829

Best Ice Cream/Yogurt
Das GUTT Yogurt
    10793 Biscayne Blvd., 305/893-9550
The Frieze
    1626 Michigan Ave., Miami Beach, 305/538-0207

Best Indian Food
Darbar
    276 Alhambra Circle, Coral Gables, 305/448-9691
House of India Restaurant
    22 Merrick Way, Coral Gables, 305/444-2348
Kebab Indian Restaurant
    514 NE 167th St., 305/940-6309

Best Inexpensive Meal
Danny's Restaurant
    9516 Harding Ave., Surfside, 305/865-2331
Monty's on the Beach
    300 Alton Rd., Miami Beach, 305/673-3444
Paulo Luigi's
    3324 Virginia St., 305/445-9000

Best Italian Food
Bocca di Rosa
    2833 Bird Ave., 305/444-4222
Cafe Prima Pasta
    414 71st St., 305/867-0106
Caffe Abbracci
    318 Aragon Ave., Coral Gables, 305/441-0700
Giacosa
    394 Giralda Ave., Coral Gables, 305/445-5858
Il Tulipano
    11052 Biscayne Blvd., North Miami Beach,
        305/893-4811
La Bussola
    264 Giralda Ave., Coral Gables, 305/445-8783
Oggi Caffe
    1740 79th St. Causeway, 305/866-1238
Osteria Del Teatro
    1443 Washington Ave., Miami Beach, 305/538-7850
Prezzo
    18831 Biscayne Blvd., Aventura, 305/933-9004
    8888 SW 136th St., 305/234-1010
Sport Cafe
    538 Washington Ave., Miami Beach, 305/674-9700

Best Japanese Food
Akashi Japanese Restaurant
    5830 S. Dixie Hwy., 305/665-6261
Benihana
    8727 S. Dixie Hwy., 305/665-0044

Tani Guchi's Place
San Souci Plaza East, 2224 NE 123rd St.,
North Miami Beach, 305/892-6744
Toni's Sushi Bar
1208 Washington Ave., Miami Beach, 305/673-9368

Best Kosher Food
Rascal House Restaurant
17190 Collins Ave., 305/947-4581
Sara's
2214 NE 123rd St., 305/891-3312

Best Late-Night Food
Big Pink
157 Collins Ave., Miami Beach, 305/532-4700
David's Coffee Shop
1058 Collins Ave., Miami Beach, 305/534-8736
La Sandwicherie
229 Fourteenth St., 305/532-8934
News Cafe
800 Ocean Dr., Miami Beach, 305/538-6397
San Loco
235 Fourteenth St., Miami Beach, 305/538-3009
Versailles Restaurant
3555 SW Eighth St., 305/444-0240

Best Lunch
Restaurant Le Pavillon
100 Chopin Plz., 305/372-4494

Best Mexican Food
Chilango's Mexican Grill
5839 SW 73rd Ave., 305/663-9333
El Rancho Grande Restaurant
1626 Pennsylvania Ave., Miami Beach,
305/673-0480
Paquito's Mexican Restaurant
16265 Biscayne Blvd., Miami Beach, 305/947-5027
Senor Frog's
3480 Main Hwy., 305/448-0999

Best Middle Eastern Food
El Manara
5811 Sunset Dr., 305/665-3374
Khoury's Mediterranean Restaurant
5887 SW 73rd Ave., 305/662-7707

Best Other Ethnic Food
Antigua Guatemala Cafeteria (Guatemalan)
2170 NW Seventh St., 305/643-4960
El Meson Castellano (Cuban)
2395 NW Seventh St., 305/642-4087
Exquisito Restaurant (Cuban)
1510 SW Eighth St., 305/643-0227
Fleming A Taste Of Denmark (Danish)
8511 SW 136th St., 305/232-6444
Granny B's Kitchen (Caribbean)
1700 NW 183rd St., Opa Locka, 305/624-8878
Islas Canarias (Cuban)
13695 Coral Way, 305/559-6666
285 NW 27th Ave., 305/649-0440

La Casita (Cuban)
112 Giralda Ave., Coral Gables, 305/461-2729
3805 SW Eighth St., Coral Gables, 305/448-8224
La Casona (Cuban)
6355 SW Eighth St., West Miami, 305/262-2828
Lario's On The Beach (Cuban)
820 Ocean Dr., Miami Beach, 305/532-9577
Latin-American Cafeteria (Cuban)
2940 Coral Way, Coral Gables, 305/448-6809
Mango's Tropical Cafe (Caribbean)
900 Ocean Dr., Miami Beach, 305/673-4422
Norma's on the Beach (Caribbean)
646 Lincoln Rd., Miami Beach, 305/532-2809
Porcao (Brazilian)
801 Brickell Dr., 305/373-2777
Atlakat Restaurant (Salvadoran)
2273 NW Seventh St., 305/643-2545
Rincon Argentino (Argentinian)
2345 SW 37th Ave., 305/444-2494
Shabeen Restaurant (Caribbean)
1200 Collins Ave., Miami Beach, 305/931-7700
Tap Tap Haitian Restaurant (Haitian)
819 SW Fifth St., Miami Beach, 305/672-2898
Versailles Restaurant (Cuban)
3555 SW Eighth St., 305/445-7614
World Resources (multicultural cuisine)
719 Lincoln Rd., Miami Beach, 305/534-9095
Yambo (Nicaraguan)
1643 SW First St., 305/642-6616
Yuca Restaurant (Venezuelan)
501 Lincoln Rd., Miami Beach, 305/532-9822

Best Outdoor Dining
La Sandwicherie
229 Fourteenth St., 305/532-8934
Monty's Raw Bar
300 Alton Rd., Miami Beach, 305/674-0580
Nemo
100 Collins Ave., Miami Beach, 305/532-4550
News Cafe
800 Ocean Dr., Miami Beach, 305/538-6397
Van Dyke Cafe
846 Lincoln Rd., Miami Beach, 305/534-3600

Best Pizza
Au Natural Gourmet Pizza
1427 Alton Rd., Miami Beach, 305/531-0666
Casola's Pizza
2437 SW Seventeenth Ave., 305/858-0090
Mark's Place
2286 NE 123rd St., North Miami, 305/893-6888
Steve's Pizza
12101 Biscayne Blvd., North Miami, 305/891-0202

Best Restaurant in Town
China Grill
404 Washington Ave., Miami Beach, 305/534-2211
Marco's In The Grove
3339 Virginia St., 305/444-5333

Pacific Time
915 Lincoln Rd., Miami Beach, 305/534-5979
Paparazzi Ristorante and Nightclub
940 Ocean Dr., Miami Beach, 305/531-3500
Rusty Pelican
3201 Rickenbacker Causeway, Key Biscayne,
305/361-3818
The Grand Cafe
2669 S. Bayshore Dr., 305/858-9600
Wolfie's Restaurant
2038 Collins Ave., Miami Beach, 305/538-6626

Best Restaurant Meal Value
Flamingo Restaurant
16701 S. Dixie Hwy., 305/235-3051
Oggi Caffe
1740 79th St. Causeway, 305/866-1238

Best Romantic Dining
Cafe Baci
2522 Ponce De Leon Blvd., Coral Gables,
305/442-0600
Caffe Abbracci
318 Aragon Ave., Coral Gables, 305/441-0700
Caffe Da Vinci
1009 Kane Concourse, Miami Beach, 305/861-8166
Grand Cafe
Grand Bay Hotel, 2669 S. Bayshore Dr.,
305/858-9600
The Forge
432 W. 41st St., Miami Beach, 305/538-8533
Tuna's Waterfront Grille
17201 Biscayne Blvd., North Miami Beach,
305/945-2567

Best Salad/Salad Bar
Hooligan's Pub and Oyster Bar
13135 SW 89th Pl., 305/252-9155

Best Sandwiches
Chili's Grill and Bar
11900 SW 88th St., 305/596-5025
Football Sandwich Shop
8484 NE Second Ave., 305/759-3602

Best Seafood
Bayside Seafood
3501 Rickenbacker Causeway, 305/361-0808
Fishbone Grille
650 S. Miami Ave., 305/530-1915
Joe's Stone Crab Restaurant
227 S. Biscayne St., Miami Beach, 305/673-0365

Best Southwestern Food
The Heights
2530 Ponce De Leon Blvd., Coral Gables,
305/461-1774

Best Spanish Food
Casa Juancho
2436 SW Eighth St., 305/642-2452

Malaga Restaurant
740 SW Eighth St., 305/858-4224
Mango's Tropical Cafe and Hotel
900 Ocean Dr., Miami Beach, 305/673-4422

Best Steaks
Christy's Restaurant
3101 Ponce de Leon Blvd., Coral Gables,
305/446-1400
Linda B. Steak House
320 Crandon Blvd., Key Biscayne, 305/361-1111
Los Ranchos of Bayside
401 Biscayne Blvd., 305/375-0666
Miami Palm Restaurant
9650 E. Bay Harbor Dr., 305/868-7256
Shula's Steak House
7601 Miami Lakes Dr., 305/820-8102
The Capital Grille
444 Brickell Ave., 305/374-4500

Best Sunday Brunch
K.C. Cagney Eatery
11230 SW 137th Ave., 305/386-1555
Courtyard Cafe
Biltmore Hotel, 1200 Anastasia Ave., Coral Gables,
305/445-1926

Best Sushi
Sushi Hana
1131 Washington Ave., Miami Beach, 305/604-0300

Best Thai Food
Cafe Thai Bistro
1533 Washington Ave., Miami Beach, 305/531-4181
Siam River
3455 NE 163rd St., North Miami Beach,
305/945-8079
Thai House
1137 Washington Ave., Miami Beach, 305/531-4841
Thai Toni
890 Washington Ave., Miami Beach, 305/538-8424

Best Vegetarian Food
Here Comes the Sun
2188 NE 123rd St., North Miami, 305/893-5711
Neal's
2570 NE Miami Gardens Dr., North Miami Beach,
305/936-8333
The Last Carrot
3133 Grand Ave., 305/445-0805

Best Vietnamese Food
Hy-Vong
3458 SW Eighth St., 305/446-3674

Best View While Dining
Chart House
51 Charthouse Dr., 305/856-9741
Rusty Pelican
3201 Rickenbacker Causeway, Key Biscayne,
305/361-3818

Best Wine Selection
The Forge
432 W. 41st St., Miami Beach, 305/538-8533
The Grand Cafe
2669 S. Bayshore Dr., 305/858-9600

NAPLES, FL

F

Best All-You-Can-Eat Buffet
Grouper House
396 Goodlette Rd., 941/263-4900

Best Barbecue/Ribs
Michelbob's
869 103rd Ave. N., 941/594-7675
371 Airport Pulling Rd. N., 941/643-2877

Best Breakfast
First Watch Restaurant
1400 Gulf Shore Blvd. N., 941/434-0005

Best Burgers
Lindburgers
330 Ninth St. S., 941/262-1127

Best Eclectic Menu
Savannah
5200 Tamiami Trail N., 941/261-2555

Best Fine Dining
Edgewater
1901 Gulf Shore Blvd., 941/262-6511
The Dining Room
The Ritz-Carlton Naples, 936 Fifth Ave. S.,
941/598-3300
Trios
1170 Third St. S., 941/649-8333

Best French Food
Chardonnay Restaurant
2331 Tamiami Trail N., 941/261-1744
Sign Of The Vine Restaurant
980 Solano Rd., 941/261-6745

Best Italian Food
Antonia's
2327 County Rd. 951, 941/455-2000
Frascatti's Italian Restaurant
1258 Airport Pulling Rd. N., 941/643-5709
Il Posto Cafe
1170 Third St. S., 941/261-8650
Vincenzo's on the Bay
5370 Bonita Beach Rd., Bonita Springs,
941/992-1159

Best Salad/Salad Bar
Pewter Mug
12300 Tamiami Trail N., 941/597-3017

Best Seafood
Grouper House
396 Goodlette Rd. S., 941/263-4900
Riverwalk Fish and Ale House
1200 Fifth Ave. S., 941/263-2734

St. George and The Dragon
  936 Fifth Ave. S.,The Ritz-Carlton Naples,
    941/262-6546

Best Steaks
Andre's Steakhouse
  2800 Tamiami Trail N., 941/263-5851
Riverwalk Fish and Ale House
  1200 Fifth Ave. S., 941/263-2734
St. George and The Dragon
  The Ritz-Carlton Naples, 936 Fifth Ave. S.,
    941/262-6546

Best Thai Food
Bangkok Cuisine
  572 Ninth St. N., 941/261-5900

Best View While Dining
The Rooftop
  25999 Hickory Blvd., Bonita Springs, 941/992-0033

OCALA, FL

Best American Food
Carmichael's Restaurant
  3105 NE Silver Springs Blvd., 352/622-3636

Best Bar
Dooley's Eating and Drinking
  3305 NE Silver Springs Blvd., 352/629-2740

Best Barbecue/Ribs
Sonny's Real Pit Bar-B-Q
  4102 NE Silver Springs Blvd., 352/236-1012
  1845 SW College Rd., 352/629-2663

Best Casual Dining
Mom and Dad's Italian Restaurant
  Hwy. 27S, Lady Lake, 352/753-2722

Best Continental Food
Carmichael's Restaurant
  3105 NE Silver Springs Blvd., 352/622-3636

Best Diner
Wayne's Brick City Cafe
  10 NE First St., 352/629-4700

Best French Food
Petite Jardin
  2209 E. Silver Springs Blvd., 352/351-4140

Best Greek/Mediterranean Food
Laki's Greek Restaurant
  1605 SE Magnolia Ext., 352/351-2550

Best Japanese Food
The Wokery I
  2701 SW College Rd., Ste. 309, 352/873-3222

Best Mexican Food
El Toreo
  3790 NE Silver Springs Blvd., 352/694-1401

Best Pizza
Abio's Italian Restaurant
  2377 SW College Rd., Ste. 200, 352/629-4886

F

Best Place to Be "Seen"
Fiddlestix Edibles and Libations, Inc.
  1016 SE Third Ave., 352/629-8000

Best Romantic Dining
Petite Jardin
  2209 E. Silver Springs Blvd., 352/351-4140

Best Salad/Salad Bar
Holiday House
  4011 NE Silver Springs Blvd., 352/236-3014

Best Sandwiches
Charley Horse Restaurant
  2426 E. Silver Springs Blvd., 352/622-4050

Best Seafood
Sam's St. John's Seafood
  7119 N. U.S. Hwy. 441, 352/622-2927

Best Southwestern Food
Lone Star Saloon
  3410 SW College Rd., 352/873-1133

Best Spanish Food
Latinos Y Mas
  2030 S. Pine Ave., 352/622-4777

Best Sports Bar
Ocala Ale House
  305 SE Seventeenth St., 352/620-8989

Best Sunday Brunch
Ocala Hilton
  3600 SW 36th Ave., 352/854-1400

Best Sushi
Kotobuki Japanese Steak House
  2463 SW 27th Ave., 352/629-6649

ORLANDO, FL

Best American Food
College Park Cafe
  2304 Edgewater Dr., 407/420-9892
Pebbles Restaurant
  2110 State Rd. 434W, Longwood, 407/774-7111

Best Barbecue/Ribs
B's Bar-B-Q
  617 N. Primrose Ave., 407/894-9981
  1210 N. Nebraska St., 407/896-6746
Barney's Bar-B-Q
  7323 S. Orange Ave., 407/851-7480
Cecil's Bar-B-Q
  2800 S. Orange Ave., 407/423-9871

Best Casual Dining
Pebbles Restaurant
  12551 State Rd. 535, 407/827-1111

Best Chinese Food
China Jade
  220 N. Orlando Ave., Maitland, 407/539-1999

Best Continental Food
The Black Swan
  1 N. Jacaranda Dr., 407/239-1999
Victoria and Albert
  Grand Floridian Resort and Spa, Lake Buena
    Vista, 407/939-7707

Best Diner
Angel's Diner
  502 E. Main St., Apopka, 407/886-2230
  7220 S. Orange Blossom Trail, 407/856-1968
  4580 S. Semoran Blvd., 407/249-1955
  7300 W. Irlo Bronson Memorial Hwy., Kissimmee,
    407/397-1960
  1345 Lee Rd., 407/291-4832
  304 W. Colonial Dr., 407/426-2029
Brian's
  1409 N. Orange Ave., 407/896-9912
Patsio's
  1419 E. Semoran Blvd., Casselberry, 407/657-8404

Best Dinner
Townsend's Fish House and Tavern
  35 W. Michigan St., 407/422-5560

Best Eclectic Menu
Harvey's Bistro
  390 N. Orange Ave., 407/246-6560

Best Family Restaurant
Pete's Bubble Room
  1351 S. Orlando Ave., Maitland, 407/628-3331

Best Fine Dining
Arthur's 27
  1900 Buena Vista Dr., 407/827-3450

Best French Food
Le Coq Au Vin
  4800 S. Orange Ave., 407/851-6980
Le Provence
  50 E. Pine St., 407/843-1320

Best Greek/Mediterranean Food
Athena Roasted Chicken
  487 S. Orlando Ave., Maitland, 407/539-0669
  2401 State Rd. 434W, Longwood, 407/869-0669
Olympia Restaurant
  8505 E. Colonial Dr., 407/381-3637
Victoria Restaurant
  6524 Carrier Dr., 407/345-0095

Best Health-Conscious Menu
Chamberlin's Natural Foods
  7600 Dr. Phillips Blvd., 407/352/2130

Best Italian Food
Amalfi Italian Restaurant
  523 S. Chickasaw Trail, 407/282-6283
Bacco Ristorante Italiano
  10065 University Blvd., 407/678-8833
Enzo's Restaurant on the Lake
  1130 S. U.S. Hwy. 17-92, Longwood, 407/834-9872

Gargi's Italian Restaurant
  1421 N. Orange Ave., 407/894-7907
Lido's Italian Restaurant
  2509 S. Orange Ave., 407/423-8933
Numero Uno Restaurant
  2499 S. Orange Ave., 407/841-3840

Best Japanese Food
Kobe Japanese Steakhouse
  8460 Palm Pkwy., 407/239-1119
  2110 E. Colonial Dr., 407/895-6868

Best Lunch
Tanqueray's Bar and Grille
  100 S. Orange Ave., 407/649-8540

Best Mexican Food
Amigos Original Tex-Mex
  6036 S. Orange Blossom Trail, 407/857-3144
L.A. Tacos
  2117 E. Colonial Dr., 407/894-5590
PR's Mexican Restaurant
  4768 S. Kirkman Rd., 407/293-8226

Best Pizza
Antonio's Restaurant and Pizza
  3916 S. Semoran Blvd., 407/273-6799

Best Romantic Dining
Manuel's on the 28th
  390 N. Orange Ave., 407/246-6580

Best Sandwiches
Dan's Sandwich Shoppes
  28 S. Orange Ave., 407/425-8881

Best Seafood
Shells Restaurant
  852 Lee Rd., 407/628-3968
Straub's Fine Seafood
  5101 E. Colonial Dr., 407/273-9330
The Catfish Place of Apopka
  311 S. Forest Ave., Apopka, 407/889-7980

Best Steaks
Del Frisco's Steak House
  729 Lee Rd., 407/645-4443
Roadhouse Grill
  1870 N. Semoran Blvd., 407/679-1222
Yachtsman Steakhouse
  1700 Epcot Resorts Blvd., 407/934-7000

Best Sunday Brunch
La Coquina
  1 Grand Cypress Blvd., 407/239-1234

Best Thai Food
Siam Orchid
  7575 Republic Dr., 407/351-0821
Viet Garden
  1237 E. Colonial Dr., 407/896-4154

Best Vegetarian Food
Pebbles Restaurant
   12551 State Rd. 535, 407/827-1111
   17 W. Church St., 407/839-0892

ORMOND BEACH, FL

Best Chinese Food
Royal Dynasty
   1482 W. Granada Blvd., 904/676-2266

Best French Food
Le Crepe en Haut
   142 E. Granada Blvd., 904/673-1999

Best Italian Food
Mario's
   521 S. Yonge St., 904/677-2711

Best Sandwiches
Mr. Wich
   21 N. Nova Rd., 904/677-1106

Best Sports Bar
Houligan's
   1110 W. Granada Blvd., 904/673-7878

Best Vegetarian Food
Rosemary's Garden Restaurant
   670 S. Yonge St., 904/677-5363

Best Vietnamese Food
Bamboo Garden
   749 S. Nova Rd., 904/677-9517

PANAMA CITY, FL

Best Breakfast
Bayou Joe's
   112A E. Third Ct., 850/763-6442
Dock at Jr.'s, Eat at Joe's
   112A E. Third Ct., 850/763-6442
Panama Cafe
   4607 W. Hwy. 98, 850/763-8753

Best Continental Food
Terrace Restaurant
   13741 E. Emerald Coast Pkwy., 850/231-5202

Best Desserts
Canopies
   4423 W. Hwy. 98, 850/872-8444
Cheese Barn
   440 Grace Ave., 850/769-3892

Best Japanese Food
Mikato Japanese Seafood
   7724 Front Beach Rd., Panama City Beach,
   850/235-1338

Best Pizza
Red Rose Pizzeria
   8730 Thomas Dr., 850/233-0955

F

Best Sandwiches
Sweet Magnolia's Deli
   2117 E. Third St., 850/769-3218

Best Seafood
Captain Anderson's Restaurant
   5551 N. Lagoon Dr., 850/234-2225
Harbour House Restaurant
   3001 W. Tenth St., 850/785-9053
Saltwater Grill
   4305 W. Hwy. 98, 850/784-1441

Best Steaks
Angelo's Steak Pit
   9527 Front Beach Rd., Panama City Beach,
      850/234-2531

Best Sunday Brunch
Hawk's Nest Restaurant
   123 E. Beach Dr., 850/872-1333

PENSACOLA, FL

Best Barbecue/Ribs
Billy Bob's Barbeque
   911 Gulf Breeze Pkwy., Gulf Breeze, 850/934-2999
   6403 N. Ninth Ave., 850/484-5480
King's Bar-B-Q
   2120 N. Palafox St., 850/433-4479
Rodger's Barbecue
   4708 N. Davis Hwy., 850/478-7864

Best Breakfast
Coffee Cup Restaurant
   520 E. Cervantes St., 850/432-7060

Best Coffee/Coffeehouse
Bean and Leaf Coffeehouse
   4350 Bayou Blvd., 850/477-7469

Best Desserts
Jubilee Restaurant and Cafe
   400 Quietwater Beach Rd., Gulf Breeze,
      850/934-3108

Best Family Restaurant
Montana's Bar-B-Q and Seafood
   7813 N. Davis Hwy., 850/477-1313

Best French Food
Jamie's French Restaurant
   424 E. Zarragossa St., 850/434-2911

Best Greek/Mediterranean Food
Georgio's Pizza
   3000 E. Cervantes St., 850/432-5996

Best Homestyle Food
H and O Cafe
   301 E. Gonzalez St., 850/432-1991
Hopkins Boarding House
   900 N. Spring St., 850/438-3979

Best Italian Food
Marchelo's Italian Restaurant
   620 S. Navy Blvd., 850/456-5200

F

Best Japanese Food
Yamato
   131 N. New Warrington Rd., 850/453-3461

Best Pizza
Fournaris Brothers Restaurant
   1015 N. Ninth Ave., 850/432-0629
Godfather's Pizza
   6847B N. Ninth Ave., 850/484-9900
   4479 Mobile Hwy., 850/455-5438

Best Sandwiches
McGuire's Irish Pub and Brewery
   600 E. Gregory St., 850/433-6789
Napoleon Bakery
   101 S. Jefferson St., 850/434-9701
New Yorker Deli
   3001 E. Cervantes St., 850/469-0029

Best Seafood
Boy On A Dolphin Restaurant
   400 Pensacola Beach Blvd., Gulf Breeze,
   850/932-7954
Chet's Food Restaurant
   3708 W. Navy Blvd., 850/456-0165
Cock of the Walk
   550 Scenic Hwy., 850/432-6766
Flounder's Chowder and Ale House
   800 Quietwater Beach Rd., Pensacola Beach,
   850/932-2003
Jubilee Restaurant and Cafe
   400 Quietwater Beach Rd., Gulf Breeze,
   850/934-3108
Oscar's Restaurant
   2805 W. Cervantes St., 850/432-8388
Skopelos Seafood and Steak
   670 Scenic Hwy., 850/432-6565

Best Steaks
McGuire's Irish Pub and Brewery
   600 E. Gregory St., 850/433-6789
Mesquite Charlie's
   5901 N. W St., 850/434-0498

POMPANO BEACH, FL

*[See also: Boca Raton, Coral Springs, Deerfield
Beach, Ft. Lauderdale, Hallandale, and Hollywood.]*

Best American Food
Flaming Pit Restaurant
   1150 N. Federal Hwy., 954/943-3484
Wings and Things Restaurant
   150 SW Sixth St., 954/781-9464

Best Barbecue/Ribs
Bobby Rubino's Place for Ribs
   2501 N. Federal Hwy., 954/781-7550
   6001 N. Kimberly Blvd., 954/971-9740

Best Breakfast
Galaxy Diner
  560 S. Dixie Hwy. W., 954/941/3331

Best Casual Dining
McDivitt's
  3011 N. Rock Island Rd., Margate, 954/753-3500

Best Chinese Food
Peking Duck House
  1200 E. Atlantic Blvd., 954/946-0436
Wong's China Town Restaurant
  10 SW Sixth St., 954/785-1320

Best Eclectic Menu
Cafe Arugula
  3110 N. Federal Hwy., 954/785-7732

Best French Food
Chez Max of Tamarac
  8096 W. McNab Rd., Tamarac, 954/721-1126

Best Italian Food
Alceo Italian Restaurant
  1340 N. Federal Hwy., 954/786-0004
Gianni's Italian Restaurant
  1601 E. Atlantic Blvd., 954/942-1733
Vesuvio Italian Restaurant
  2715 E. Atlantic Blvd., 954/941/1594

Best Kosher Food
Pita Nosh
  2900 W. Sample Rd., 954/968-5747

Best Lunch
Chez Porky's Barbecue Restaurant
  105 SW Sixth St., 954/946-5590

Best Mexican Food
Cielito Lindos Restaurant
  600 S. Dixie Hwy., 954/782-1600

Best Pizza
Frank's Ristorante
  3428 E. Atlantic Blvd., 954/785-4140
Pompano Pizza and Italian Eatery
  1606 S. Cypress Rd., 954/782-5800

Best Restaurant in Town
Cafe Arugula
  3150 N. Federal Hwy., 954/785-7732

Best Romantic Dining
Cafe Arugula
  3150 N. Federal Hwy., 954/785-7732

Best Seafood
Calypso Restaurant
  460 Cypress Rd., 954/942-1633
Cap's Place Island Restaurant
  4081 N. Federal Hwy., Ste. 110C, 954/941-0418

Best Spanish Food
Cielito Lindos Restaurant
  600 S. Dixie Hwy., 954/782-1600

Best Thai Food
Jasmine Thai and Chinese Restaurant
  5103 Coconut Creek Pkwy., Margate, 954/979-5530

PORT CHARLOTTE, FL

Best Barbecue/Ribs
Bibb's
  2020 Tamiami Trail, 941/764-7427
Sonny's Real Pit Bar-B-Q
  SE State Rd. 70, Arcadia, 941/494-1990

Best Chinese Food
China Fair
  3092 Tamiami Trail, 941/625-2225

Best Fine Dining
Chantalle's
  3822 Tamiami Trail, 941/766-1251
Pepin's on the Water
  5098 Melbourne St ., 941/629-0007

Best French Food
Chantalle's
  3822 Tamiami Trail, 941/766-1251

Best Health-Conscious Menu
Chef's Garden Restaurant
  3575 Tamiami Trail, 941/627-5322

Best Italian Food
Buddy's Pizza
  625 Tamiami Trail N., Nokomis, 941/484-6614
Mama Nunzia Ristorante
  1975 Tamiami Trail, 941/575-7575

Best Outdoor Dining
Almonds Cafe
  3591 Tamiami Trail, 941/627-0500

Best Seafood
Captain Eddie's Seafood Restaurant and Oyster Bay
  107 Colonial Ln. E., Nokomis, 941/484-4372
Fishery Restaurant
  13000 Fishery Rd., Placida, 941/697-2451

Best Sushi
Asuka Japanese Steakhouse
  1900 Tamiami Trail, 941/255-1119
Ichiban Japanese Steak House
  4200 Tamiami Trail, 941/629-1766

Best Thai Food
Thai Cafe
  4200 Tamiami Trail, Ste. 14, 941/629-0727

Best Vegetarian Food
Nature's Way
  3821 Tamiami Trail, 941/629-0047

PORT ST. LUCIE, FL

Best Chinese Food
China Delight
  1756 SE Port St. Lucie Blvd., 561/335-0733

Best Family Restaurant
Johnny's Corner Family Restaurant
7180 S. U.S. Hwy. 1, 561/878-2686

Best French Food
Le Brittany
899A E. Prima Vista Blvd., 561/871-2231

Best Italian Food
Da Vinci's Restaurant
6692 S. U.S. Hwy. 1, 561/466-9331

Best Sunday Brunch
Christopher's
1420 SE Westmoreland Blvd., 561/335-0800

PUNTA GORDA, FL

Best Casual Dining
Harpoon Harry's
1200 W. Retta Esplanade, 941/637-7917

Best Fine Dining
The Captain's Table
1200 W. Retta Esplanade, 941/637-1177

Best Pizza
Monty's Restaurant and Pizzeria
2515 Tamiami Trail, 941/637-0008

Best Sandwiches
Waldo's Bistro
139 W. Marion Ave., 941/639-0908

Best Seafood
Riviera Oyster Bar Restaurant
5500 Deltona Dr., 941/639-2633
Salty's Harborside Restaurant
5000 Burnt Store Rd. N., 941/639-3650

Best View While Dining
Harpoon Harry's
1200 W. Retta Esplanade, 941/637-7917

SANFORD, FL

Best Breakfast
Colonial Room Restaurant
115 E. First St., 407/323-2999

Best Chinese Food
China King
2508 S. French Ave., 407/323-6166

Best Desserts
Holiday House
704 N. Woodland Blvd., De Land, 904/734-6319

Best Homestyle Food
M and M Sandwich Shop and Deli
205 S. Spring Garden Ave., De Land, 904/734-9663

Best Mexican Food
Don Pablo's
100 Towne Center Blvd., 407/328-1885

Best Seafood
The Marina Hotel
530 N. Palmetto Ave., 407/323-1910

SANIBEL ISLAND, FL

Best Eclectic Menu
Mad Hatter Restaurant
6467 Sanibel Captiva Rd., 941/472-0033

Best Fine Dining
The Greenhouse Grill
2407 Periwinkle Way, 941/472-6882

Best Restaurant in Town
The Jacaranda
1223 Periwinkle Way, 941/472-1771

Best Seafood
Windows on the Water
1451 Middle Gulf Dr., 941/395-6014

SANTA ROSA BEACH, FL

Best Casual Dining
Grayton Corner Cafe
1 Hotz Ave., 850/231-1211
Shades
Seaside Ave., 850/231-1950

Best Continental Food
Bud and Alley's Restaurant
Hwy. 30A, Seaside, 850/231-5900

Best Fine Dining
Criolla's
170 E. County Hwy. 30A, 850/267-1267
Elephant Walk
9801 U.S. Hwy. 98W, 850/267-4800

SARASOTA, FL

Best American Food
Michael's on East
1212 S. East Ave., 941/366-0007
Ophelia's Restaurant
9105 Midnight Pass Rd., 941/349-2212
Patrick's Restaurant
1400 Main St., 941/952-1170

Best Atmosphere
The Summerhouse
6101 Midnight Pass Rd., 941/349-1100

Best Barbecue/Ribs
Oaks Open Pit BBQ
6112 S. Tamiami Trail, 941/922-7778
Sonny's Real Pit Bar-B-Q
3926 S. Tamiami Trail, 941/364-5833

Best Breakfast
Chef Paul's
Days Inn, 4900 N. Tamiami Trail, 941/365-5976
First Watch Restaurant
8383 S. Tamiami Trail, 941/923-6754

1395 Main St., 941/954/1395

Best Burgers
Stock Yard Steakhouse
4041 Cattlemen Rd., 941/378-9699

Best Business Lunch
Michael's on East
1212 S. East Ave., 941/366-0007

Best Chinese Food
Mr. Wong's Restaurant and Lounge
830 Tamiami Trail, 941/966-3689

Best Continental Food
Alley Cat Cafe
1558 Fourth St., 941/954/1228
Bijou Cafe
1287 First St., 941/366-8111
Cafe L'Europe Restaurant
431 St. Armands Circle, 941/388-4415

Best Diner
Fifty's Diner
3737 Bahia Vista St., 941/953-4637
Mel's Diner
3730 Bee Ridge Rd., 941/923-6070
Mel-O-Dee Restaurant
4685 N. Tamiami Trail, 941/355-5768

Best Family Restaurant
Yoder's Restaurant
3434 Bahia Vista St., 941/955-7771

Best French Food
Cafe of the Arts
5230 N. Tamiami Trail, 941/351-4304
Chez Sylvie's Restaurant
1526 Main St., 941/953-3232

Best Italian Food
Gastronomia
7119 S. Tamiami Trail, 941/927-8331
Nick's Italian Restaurant
230 Sarasota Quay, 941/954/3839

Best Lunch
Hillview Grill
1920 Hillview St., 941/952-0045

Best Mexican Food
El Adobe
4023 S. Tamiami Trail, 941/921-7476
Two Senoritas
1355 Main St., 941/366-1618

Best Other Ethnic Food
Colombia Restaurant (Colombian)
411 St. Armands Circle, 941/388-3987
Yoder's Restaurant (Amish)
3434 Bahia Vista St., 941/955-7771

Best Restaurant in Town
Burns Lane Cafe
516 Burns Lane, 941/955-1653

Best Sandwiches
Nellie's Deli
  3688 Webber St., 941/921-4571

Best Seafood
Captain Brian's Seafood Market and Restaurant
  8441 N. Tamiami Trail, 941/351-4492
Coasters of Sarasota
  1500 Stickney Point Rd., 941/923-4848

Best Steaks
Joto Japanese Steak House
  7971 N. Tamiami Trail, 941/351-4677

Best Thai Food
Bangkok Restaurant
  4791 Swift Rd., 941/922-0703
Siam Orchid
  4141 S. Tamiami Trail, 941/923-7447

Best View While Dining
Coasters of Sarasota
  1500 Stickney Point Rd., 941/923-4848
Marina Jack
  2 Marina Plz., 941/365-4232

ST. AUGUSTINE, FL

Best American Food
Creekside
  160 Nix Boat Yard Rd., 904/829-6113
Old City House
  115 Cordova St., 904/826-0781

Best Brewpub
A1A Ale Works
  1 King St., 904/829-2977

Best Burgers
OC White's
  118 Avenida Menendez, 904/824-0808

Best Chinese Food
Ocean Palace Chinese Restaurant
  9 Anastasia Blvd., 941/829-5151

Best Continental Food
Le Pavillon
  45 San Marco Ave., 904/824-6202

Best Eclectic Menu
Gypsy Cab Company
  828 Anastasia Blvd., 904/824-8244

Best Family Restaurant
Salt Water Cowboy's
  299 Dondanville Rd., 904/471-2332

Best Fine Dining
Fiddler's Green Oceanside Bar and Grille
  2750 Anahama Dr., 904/824-8897
Raintree Restaurant
  102 San Marco Ave., 904/824-7211

F

Best French Food
La Parisienne
60 Hypolita St., 904/829-0055

Best Greek/Mediterranean Food
Athena Restaurant
14 Cathedral Pl., 904/823-9076

Best Health-Conscious Menu
Gypsy Cab Company
828 Anastasia Blvd., 904/824-8244

Best Homestyle Food
Mom and Pop's Buffet and Bakery
2005 U.S. Hwy. 1S, 904/829-3642

Best Other Ethnic Food
A1A Ale Works (Caribbean)
1 King St., 904/829-2977

Best Pizza
Dino's Pizza Restaurant
4660 U.S. Hwy. 1N, 904/823-9193

Best Seafood
A1A Ale Works
1 King St., 904/829-2977
Conch House Restaurant
57 Comares Ave., 904/824-2046
Marty's Seafood and Steak House
2703 N. Ponce de Leon Blvd., 904/829-8679
O'Steen's Restaurant
205 Anastasia Blvd., 904/829-6974
Salt Water Cowboy's
299 Dondanville Rd., 904/471-2332
Sea Fair Restaurant and Cocktails
1 Anastasia Blvd., 904/824-2316

Best Spanish Food
Colombia Restaurant
98 Saint George St., 904/824-3341

Best Steaks
Arruano's Italian Restaurant
105 D St., 904/471-9373

Best View While Dining
Compton's Seafood Restaurant
4100 Coastal Hwy., 904/824-8051
Fiddler's Green Oceanside Bar
2750 Anahma Dr., 904/824-8897

ST. PETERSBURG, FL

[See also: Clearwater and Tampa.]

Best American Food
Harvey's Fourth Street Grill
3121 Fourth St. N., 813/821-6316

Best Barbecue/Ribs
Big Tim's Bar-B-Q
530 34th St. S., 813/327-7388

Hickory Smoke House Bar-B-Que
  6769 U.S. Hwy. 19N, Pinellas Park, 813/525-0948

Best Breakfast
Frog Pond
  16909 Gulf Blvd., North Redington Beach,
    813/384-4803
Skyway Jack's Restaurant
  2795 34th St. S., 813/866-3217

Best Burgers
El Cap
  3500 Fourth St. N., 813/521-1314

Best Chinese Food
Hao Wah
  700 34th St. N., 813/321-4904
  10454 66th St., Pinellas Park, 813/544-4656

Best Coffee/Coffeehouse
Espresso Yourself
  111 Second Ave. NE, 813/822-6646

Best Family Restaurant
Family Kitchen Restaurant
  2339 Ninth St. N., 813/822-8500

Best Fast Food
Coney Island Sandwich Shop
  250 Ninth St. N., 813/822-4493

Best Fine Dining
Don Cesar Beach Resort
  3400 Gulf Blvd., 813/360-1881
Fetishes Restaurant
  6690 Gulf Blvd., 813/363-3700
Keystone Club
  320 Fourth St. N., 813/822-6600
Wine Cellar Restaurant
  17307 Gulf Blvd., 813/393-3491

Best French Food
La Cote Basque Winehouse
  3104 Beach Blvd. S., 813/321-6888

Best German Food
Der Eisenhut Bistro
  357 Corey Ave., St. Petersburg Beach,
    813/367-6495

Best Inexpensive Meal
Family Kitchen Restaurant
  2339 Ninth St. N., 813/822-8500

Best Italian Food
Brunello
  3861 Gulf Blvd., St. Petersburg Beach,
    813/367-1851
C.D. Roma's
  1280 66th St. N., 813/344-3837
Gigi's Italian Restaurant
  6852 Gulfport Blvd. S., South Pasadena,
    813/345-0191
  105 Treasure Island Causeway, 813/360-6905

F

Best Japanese Food
Arigato Japanese Steak House
  3600 66th St. N., 813/343-5200

Best Lunch
Mama Leone's
  1952 49th St. S., Gulfport, 813/328-9122

Best Mexican Food
Carmelita's
  5211 Park St. N., 813/545-2956

Best Other Ethnic Food
La Teresita Restaurant (Cuban)
  7101 66th St. N., Pinellas Park, 813/546-5785

Best Restaurant Meal Value
Durango Steak House
  3901 Fourth St. N., 813/251-2421

Best Romantic Dining
Black Angus Stockyard
  333 Pasadena Ave. S., 813/360-7878
Leverock's Waterfront Restaurant
  8800 Bay Pines Blvd., 813/345-5335
Marchand's Bar and Grill
  501 Fifth Ave. NE, 813/894-1000

Best Sandwiches
Williams Submarine Sandwich
  3801 Tyrone Blvd. N., 813/347-9497

Best Seafood
Leverock's Seafood House
  4801 37th St. S., 813/864-3883
Lobster Pot Restaurant
  17814 Gulf Blvd., Redington Shores, 813/391-8592
Shells Seafood Restaurant
  17855 Gulf Blvd., Redington Shores, 813/393-8990
  7005 Fourth St. N., 813/522-9229

Best Soul Food
Atwater's Cafeteria
  895 22nd Ave. S., 813/823-7018

Best Spanish Food
Pepin Restaurant
  4125 Fourth St. N., 813/345-5335

Best Sports Bar
Bleachers
  10478 Roosevelt Blvd. N., 813/576-2216

Best Steaks
Cody's Original Roadhouse
  7022 22nd Ave. N., 813/345-1022
The Steak Joint
  4871 Park St. N., 813/545-9481

Best Thai Food
Thai-Am
  14363 Gulf Blvd., 813/398-9700

Best Vietnamese Food
East Wind
  6139 Park Blvd., Pinellas Park, 813/541-6377

STUART, FL

Best Chinese Food
China Star
1501 S. Federal Hwy., 561/283-8378

Best Continental Food
11 Maple Street
3177 NE Maple Ave., Jensen Beach, 561/334-7714
Country Place
1205 NE Dixie Hwy., Jensen Beach, 561/334-4563

Best Family Restaurant
Flamingo Family Restaurant
2583 SE Federal Hwy., 561/286-4475

Best Health-Conscious Menu
Nature's Way Cafe
25 SW Osceola St., 561/220-7306

Best Italian Food
Mario's
1924 SE Federal Hwy., 561/283-6660
Scoozi's Italian Restaurant
2075 NE Indian River Dr., Jensen Beach,
561/225-0700

Best Lunch
Gentleman Jim's
1651 SE Federal Hwy., 561/287-1250
Harbour Bay Gourmet
3716 SE Ocean Blvd., 561/286-9463

Best Mexican Food
Cantina Dos Amigos
300 SE Federal Hwy., 561/286-2546
Don Ramon's
100 SW Monterey Rd., 561/221-7711

Best Other Ethnic Food
Jolly Sailor Pub (English)
1 SW Osceola St., 561/221-1111

Best Pizza
Doe's Italian Deli
2413 SE Dixie Hwy., 561/223-8077
Luna Italian Restaurant
49 SW Flagler Ave., 561/288-0550

Best Restaurant in Town
Ashley Restaurant
61 SW Osceola St., 561/221-9476
Prawnbroker Restaurant and Fish
3754 SE Ocean Blvd., 561/288-1222

Best Seafood
Guytano's Grille
2220 SE Ocean Blvd., 561/286-7550
Shells Restaurant
2107 SE Ocean Blvd., 561/283-1099

Best Sunday Brunch
Walter's
Holiday Inn Oceanside, 1209 S. Federal Hwy.,
561/287-6200

F

TALLAHASSEE, FL

Best All-You-Can-Eat Buffet
Kitcho Japanese Restaurant
  1415 Timberlane Rd., 850/893-7686

Best Atmosphere
Chez Pierre Restaurant
  1215 Thomasville Rd., 850/222-0936

Best Barbecue/Ribs
Jim and Milt's Bar-B-Q
  1923 W. Pensacola St., 850/576-3998

Best Breakfast
Bagel Peddler's New York Deli
  1400 Village Square Blvd., 850/668-2345
Cross Creek Restaurant
  6725 Mahan Dr., 850/877-4130

Best Chinese Food
Lucy Ho's Oriental Court
  1700 Halstead Blvd., Ste. 5, 850/893-4112

Best Continental Food
Anthony's Italian Restaurant
  1950 Thomasville Rd., 850/224-1447

Best Dinner
Chez Pierre Restaurant
  1215 Thomasville Rd., 850/222-0936
Mustard Tree
  1415 Timberlane Rd., Ste. 215, 850/893-8733

Best Health-Conscious Menu
Hopkins Eatery
  1840 N. Monroe St., 850/386-4258
  1415 Market St., 850/668-0311

Best Italian Food
Anthony's Italian Restaurant
  1950 Thomasville Rd., 850/224-1447

Best Lunch
Chez Pierre Restaurant
  1215 Thomasville Rd., 850/222-0936
Food Glorious Food
  1950C Thomasville Rd., 850/224-9974

Best Mexican Food
La Fiesta Mexican Restaurant
  911 Apalachee Pkwy., 850/656-3392

Best Romantic Dining
Melting Pot Restaurant
  1832 N. Monroe St., 850/386-7440

Best Seafood
Wharf Seafood Restaurant
  4141 Apalachee Pkwy., 850/656-2332

Best Steaks
Texas Steak Restaurant and Saloon
  3212 Apalachee Pkwy., 850/877-2986

TAMPA, FL

[See also: Clearwater, Dunedin, and St. Petersburg.]

Best American Food
First Watch Restaurant
  11610 N. Dale Mabry Hwy., 813/961-4947
Mise En Place
  442 W. Kennedy Blvd., 813/254-5373
Next City Grill
  2902 W. Kennedy Blvd., 813/879-1990

Best Bar
Four Green Fields
  205 W. Platt St., 813/254-4444

Best Barbecue/Ribs
Jimbo's Pit Barbecue
  4103 W. Kennedy Blvd., 813/289-9724

Best Barbecue/Ribs/Ribs
Kojak's House of Ribs
  2808 W. Gandy Blvd., 813/837-3774

Best Beer Selection
The Oak Barrel
  1901 N. Thirteenth St., 813/247-1164

Best Breakfast
Village Inn
  7011 W. Hillsborough Ave., 813/884-5292

Best Brewpub
Hops Grill and Bar
  1241 E. Fowler Ave., 813/632-0717
  14303 N. Dale Mabry Hwy., 813/264-0522

Best Burgers
Jimmy Mac's Restaurant
  113 S. Armenia Ave., 813/879-0591
Old Meeting House
  901 S. Howard Ave., 813/251-1754

Best Cajun/Creole Food
Cafe Creole and New Orleans Bar
  1330 E. Ninth Ave., 813/247-6283

Best Chinese Food
Hao Wah Chinese Restaurant
  1713 S. Dale Mabry, 813/253-2095

Best Coffee/Coffeehouse
Barnie's Coffee and Tea Company
  2136 University Square Mall, 813/971-2192
Bean There
  3203 W. Bay to Bay Blvd., 813/837-7022
Joffrey's Coffee and Tea Company
  1628 W. Snow Circle, 813/251-3315

Best Delicatessen
Wright's Gourmet House
  1200 S. Dale Mabry Hwy., 813/253-3838

Best Desserts
Jeff's Desserts
 1704 E. Seventh Ave., 813/896-9866
Le Cheesecake
 1515 S. Dale Mabry Hwy., 813/835-4999
Village Inn
 7011 W. Hillsborough Ave., 813/884-5292
 215 N. Dale Mabry Hwy., 813/877-2617
 8602 N. Dale Mabry Hwy., 813/935-6342
 11302 N. 30th St., 813/977-7925

Best Eclectic Menu
Ovo Cafe
 1901 E. Seventh Ave., 813/248-6979

Best Fine Dining
Malio's Cafe
 301 S. Dale Mabry Hwy., 813/879-3233

Best French Food
Le Bordeaux Jazz Bistro
 1502 S. Howard Ave., 813/254-4387

Best Greek/Mediterranean Food
Papo's Cafe
 5135 W. Cypress St., 813/282-1060

Best Ice Cream/Yogurt
Old Meeting House
 901 S. Howard Ave., 813/251-1754

Best Indian Food
Bombay Masala
 4023 W. Waters Ave., 813/880-7511

Best Inexpensive Meal
Lauro Ristorante Italiano
 3915 Henderson Blvd., 813/281-2100

Best Italian Food
Armani's
 6200 W. Courtney Campbell Causeway,
  813/281-9165
Cafe Italia
 3114 W. Bay to Bay Blvd., 813/831-0600
Caffe Paradiso
 4205 S. MacDill Ave., 813/835-6622
Carrabba's Italian Grill
 405 N. Reo St., Ste. 210, 813/288-8286
Lauro Ristorante Italiano
 3915 Henderson Blvd., 813/281-2100
Primadonna Trattoria Restaurant
 915 S. Howard Ave., 813/258-3358

Best Japanese Food
Arigato Japanese Steak House
 13755 N. Dale Mabry Hwy., 813/960-5050
Jo-To Japanese Restaurant
 310 S. Dale Mabry Hwy., 813/875-4842

Best Korean Food
Sam Oh Jung
 602 N. Dale Mabry Hwy., 813/871-3233

Best Middle Eastern Food
Antranik's Bakery and Food Store
  5710 E. Fowler Ave., 813/988-3737

Best Other Ethnic Food
Capdevila at La Teresita Restaurant (Cuban)
  3248 W. Columbus Dr., 813/879-9704
Colombia Restaurant (Cuban)
  2025 E. Seventh Ave., 813/248-4961
El Sol De Cuba (Cuban)
  3101 N. Armenia Ave., 813/872-9880
La Teresita Restaurant (Cuban)
  3248 W. Columbus Dr., 813/879-4909
Silver Ring Cafe (Cuban)
  1831 E. Seventh Ave., 813/248-2549
Valencia Garden Restaurant (Cuban)
  811 W. Kennedy Blvd., 813/253-3773

Best Pizza
CDB Italian Restaurant
  5305 Ehrlich Rd., 813/962-1221
Lenny and Vinny's Pizzeria
  11111 N. Dale Mabry Hwy., 813/960-4032
Windy City Pizza
  12908 N. Dale Mabry Hwy., 813/960-1400

Best Restaurant Meal Value
Colonnade
  3401 Bayshore Blvd., 813/839-7558

Best Romantic Dining
Cafe Italia
  3114 W. Bay to Bay Blvd., 813/831-0600

Best Salad/Salad Bar
Sweet Tomatoes
  14703 N. Dale Mabry Hwy., 813/960-5220

Best Sandwiches
Miami Subs
  1915 E. Fowler Ave., 813/971-0995

Best Seafood
Armani's
  6200 W. Courtney Campbell Causeway,
    813/281-9165
Bern's Steak House
  1208 S. Howard Ave., 813/251-2421
Colonnade
  3401 Bayshore Blvd., 813/839-7558
Oystercatcher's
  6200 W. Courtney Campbell Causeway,
    813/281-9116

Best Southwestern Food
Cactus Club
  1601 W. Snow Ave., 813/251-4089

Best Spanish Food
Colombia Restaurant
  2025 E. Seventh Ave., 813/248-4961
La Teresita Restaurant
  8218 Hanley Rd., 813/888-8988

F

Valencia Garden Restaurant
811 W. Kennedy Blvd., 813/253-3773

Best Steaks
Arigato Japanese Steak House
13755 N. Dale Mabry Hwy., 813/960-5050
Bern's Steak House
1208 S. Howard Ave., 813/251-2421

Best Thai Food
Jasmine Thai Restaurant
13248 N. Dale Mabry Hwy., 813/968-1501
Sukhothai Restaurant
8201 N. Dale Mabry Hwy., 813/933-7990
Sunee's Thai Restaurant
5224 S. Dale Mabry Hwy., 813/837-6484

Best Vegetarian Food
NK Cafe
4100 W. Kennedy Blvd., 813/287-1385

TITUSVILLE, FL

Best Barbecue/Ribs
Paul's Smokehouse
3665 S. Washington Ave., 407/267-3663

Best Breakfast
New York-New York
3434 S. Washington Ave., 407/264-2585
Village Inn
2925 S. Washington Ave., 407/267-6611

Best Burgers
Moonlight Drive-In
1515 S. Washington Ave., 407/267-8222

Best Italian Food
Lorenzo's Italian Cuisine
3350 S. U.S. Hwy. 1, 407/269-0202

Best Seafood
Dixie Crossroads
1475 Garden St., 407/268-5000
Steamer's
801 Marina Rd., 407/269-1012

VENICE, FL

Best Barbecue/Ribs
Sonny's Real Pit Bar-B-Q
406 E. Venice Ave., 941/485-1575

Best Business Lunch
Crow's Nest Marina Restaurant and Tavern
1968 Tarpon Center Dr., 941/484-9551

Best Diner
Uncle B's Coney Dog
602 Tamiami Trail S., 941/484-7243

Best Italian Food
Buddy's Pizza
822 Pinebrook Rd., 941/484-6551

Best Sandwiches
Johnny's One Stop
  101 Shamrock Blvd., 941/492-9807

Best Seafood
Frenchy's Saltwater Cafe
  1071 Tamiami Trail S., 941/488-3775

Best View While Dining
Oyster Crackers
  147 Tampa Ave. E., 941/486-0909

F

WEST PALM BEACH, FL

[See also: Boca Raton.]

Best Breakfast
Tiesta's Restaurant
  221 Royal Poinciana Way, Palm Beach,
  561/832-0992

Best Business Lunch
Casablanca Cafe Americain
  101 N. County Rd., Palm Beach, 561/655-1115
Dontee's 1
  620 Belvedere Rd., 561/655-6001
Pollo Tropical
  2611 Okeechobee Blvd., 561/688-0578

Best French Food
Chez Jean Pierre
  7504 S. Dixie Hwy., 561/586-9579
  132 N. County Rd., Palm Beach, 561/833-1171

Best Italian Food
Amici Restaurant
  288 S. County Rd., Palm Beach, 561/832-0201
Malsori's Pizza and Restaurant
  523 Clematis St., 561/835-8522

Best Japanese Food
Sagami Japanese Restaurant
  871 Village Blvd., 561/683-4600

Best Mexican Food
La Taqueria
  419 Clematis St., 561/655-5450
Margarita Y Amigas
  2030 Palm Beach Lakes Blvd., 561/684-7788

Best Other Ethnic Food
Havana Restaurant (Cuban)
  6803 S. Dixie Hwy., 561/547-9799
Olympia Cafe (Greek)
  2514 PGA Blvd., 561/622-4845

Best Pizza
California Pizza Kitchen
  3101 PGA Blvd., 561/625-4682
Zuccarelli
  1937 N. Military Trail, 561/686-7739

Best Seafood
Bimini Bay Cafe
  104 Clematis St., 561/833-9554
The Breakers Hotel
  1 S. County Rd., Palm Beach, 561/655-6611

Best Steaks
Morton's of Chicago
  777 S. Flagler Dr., 561/835-9664
Raindancer Steak House
  2300 Palm Beach Lakes Blvd., 561/684-2810

Best Thai Food
Bangkok House
  1847 N. Military Trail, 561/697-4704
  2062 Palm Beach Lakes Blvd., 561/471-7711

WINTER HAVEN, FL

Best Barbecue/Ribs
Fat Boy's Bar-B-Q
  3000 Cypress Gardens Rd., 941/324-1537
Sonny's Real Pit Bar-B-Q
  4600 Recker Hwy., 941/293-4744

Best Burgers
Andy's Drive-In Restaurant and Igloo
  703 Third St. SW, 941/293-0019

Best Seafood
Harborside
  2435 Seventh St. SW, 941/293-7070
Harry's Old Place
  3751 Cypress Gardens Rd., 941/324-0301

Best Steaks
Christy's Sundown Restaurant
  1100 Third St. SW, 941/293-0069

WINTER PARK, FL

Best American Food
Briar Patch
  252 N. Park Ave., 407/645-4566
Grady's American Grill
  227 S. Semoran Blvd., 407/671-9905
Pebbles Restaurant
  2516 Aloma Ave., 407/678-7001

Best Barbecue/Ribs
Bubbalou's Bodacious BBQ
  1471 Lee Rd., 407/629-4309

Best Health Concious Menu
Chamberlin's Natural Foods
  1271 S. Semoran Blvd., Ste. 105, 407/678-3100

Best Health-Concious Menu
Chamberlin's Natural Foods
  430 N. Orlando Ave., 407/647-6661

Best Mexican Food
Amigos Original Tex-Mex
  494 N. Semoran Blvd., 407/657-8111

Pico's Mex-Cafe
  1915 Aloma Ave., 407/671-6123

Best Seafood
Boston's Fish House
  6860 Aloma Ave., 407/678-2107

Best Sunday Brunch
Park Plaza Gardens
  319 Park Ave. S., 407/645-2475

F

Georgia

ALBANY, GA

Best Barbecue/Ribs
Black Beard's and B & B Bar-B-Que
  2709 N. Slappey Blvd., 912/878-6369
Gus' Barbecue
  2347 Dawson Rd., 912/883-2404

Best Cafeteria
Pearly's
  814 N. Slappey Blvd., 912/432-0141

Best Chinese Food
China Palace
  301 E. Oglethorpe Blvd., 912/883-2084
House of China Restaurant
  1514 N. Slappey Blvd., 912/432-1001
  2526 Dawson Rd., 912/883-7156
China Buffet
  2413 Dawson Rd., 912/436-9261

Best Coffee/Coffeehouse
Pat's French Press
  2610 Dawson Rd., 912/889-9045

Best Homestyle Food
Aunt Fannie's Checkered Apron
  826 Byron Rd., 912/888-8416

Best Italian Food
Gargano's East
  1710 E. Oglethorpe Blvd., 912/432-0241

Best Mexican Food
El Maya Mexican Restaurant
  106 N. Slappey Blvd., 912/889-9712
  2800 Old Dawson Rd., 912/434-1566

Best Salad/Salad Bar
Yesterday's Ole Time Saloon and Restaurant
2601 Dawson Rd., 912/883-7543

Best Sandwiches
Cookie Shoppe
115 N. Jackson St., 912/883-3327
Ye Olde World Sandwich Shoppe
1116A W. Broad Ave., Ste. 1, 912/436-6496

Best Seafood
Black Beard's and B & B Bar-B-Que
2709 N. Slappey Blvd., 912/878-6369

Best Steaks
Austin's Cattle Company Steak House
101 S. Slappey Blvd., 912/889-0699
Texas Star Steak House
1111 Dawson Rd., 912/888-7797

ATHENS, GA

Best All-You-Can-Eat Buffet
Pinecrest Lodge
1 Pinecrest Lodge Rd., 706/353-2606

Best Barbecue/Ribs
Barbecue Shack
4320 Lexington Rd., 706/613-6752

Best Burgers
Locos Deli
3190 Atlanta Hwy., 706/549-7700
1985 Barnett Shoals Rd., 706/208-0911
581 S. Harris St., 706/548-7803

Best Cajun/Creole Food
Gautreau's Cajun Cafe
24 Greensboro Hwy., Watkinsville, 706/769-9330
Harry Bissett's Restaurant
279 E. Broad St., 706/353-7065

Best Eclectic Menu
The Last Resort Grill
184 W. Clayton St., 706/549-0810

Best Italian Food
DePalma's Italian Cafe
1965 Barnett Shoals Rd., 706/369-0085
401 E. Broad St., 706/354-6966

Best Mexican Food
Compadre's
320 E. Clayton St., 706/546-0190

Best Pizza
DaVinci's Pizza-in-a-Pan
1065 Baxter St., 706/353-1065
Rocky's Pizzeria
233 E. Clayton St., 706/353-0000

Best Restaurant in Town
Dogwood Cafe
311 E. Broad St., 706/548-5187
East West Bistro
351 E. Broad St., 706/546-9378

The Grill
233 E. Clayton St., 706/543-4770

Best Steaks
T-Bones Steak House and Saloon
1061 Baxter St., 706/548-8702

Best Vegetarian Food
Guaranteed
167 E. Broad St., 706/208-0962
The Bluebird Cafe
493 E. Clayton St., 706/549-3663
The Grill
233 E. Clayton St., 706/543-4770

G

ATLANTA, GA

Best American Food
Agnes and Muriel's
1514 Monroe Dr. NE, 404/885-1000
American Roadhouse
842 N. Highland Ave. NE, 404/872-2822
Blue Ridge Grill
1261 W. Paces Ferry Rd. NW, 404/233-5030
Grady's American Grill
4764 Ashford Dunwoody Rd., Dunwoody,
770/393-3316
Indigo Coastal Grill
1397 N. Highland Ave. NE, 404/876-0676
Mick's
4505 Ashford Dunwoody Rd. NE, 770/394-6425
229 Peachtree St. NE, 404/688-6425
1320 Cumberland Mall, 770/431-7190
557 Peachtree St. NE, 404/875-6425
75 Upper Alabama St. SW, 404/525-2825
489 Peachtree St. NE, 404/872-1400
2110 Peachtree St.. NW, 404/351-6425
3393 Peachtree Rd. NE, 404/262-6425
Paschal's Center
830 Martin Luther King Jr. Dr. SW, 404/577-3150
South City Kitchen
1144 Crescent Ave. NE, 404/873-7358
Terra Cotta
1044 Greenwood Ave. NE, 404/853-7888

Best Barbecue/Ribs
Abdullah The Butcher House of Ribs and Chinese Food
2387 Fairburn Rd. SW, 404/629-2332
Aleck's Barbecue Heaven
783 Martin Luther King Jr. Dr. NW, 404/525-2062
Dusty's Barbecue Restaurant
1815 Briarcliff Rd. NE, 404/320-6264
Fat Matt's Rib Shack
1811 Piedmont Rd. NE, 404/607-1622
Jilly's, The Place For Ribs
2655 Cobb Pkwy., 770/952-7437
Rib Ranch
25 Irby Ave. NW, 404/233-7644
Thomas Marketplace Restaurant
16 Forest Pkwy., Forest Park, 404/361-1367

Best Beer Selection
Alon's
   659 Peachtree St. NE, 404/724-0444
Three Dollar Cafe
   3002 Peachtree Rd. NW, 404/266-8667
   8595 Roswell Rd., 770/992-5011

Best Bistro
Tom Tom
   3393 Peachtree Rd. NE, 404/264-1163
Toulouse
   2293B Peachtree Rd. NE, 404/351-9533

Best Breakfast
Beautiful Restaurant
   397 Auburn Ave. , 404/223-0080
   2200 Cascade Rd., SW, 404/752-5931
Java Jive
   790 Ponce De Leon Ave. NE, 404/876-6161

Best Brewpub
The Phoenix Brewing Company
   5600 Roswell Rd. NE, Ste. 21, 404/843-2739

Best Burgers
Johnny Rocket's
   5 W. Paces Ferry Rd. NW, 404/231-5555
The Varsity
   61 North Ave. NW, 404/881-1706
The Vortex
   878 Peachtree St. NE, 404/875-1667
   438 Moreland Ave. NE, 404/688-1828
Zesto Drive-In
   377 Moreland Ave. NE, 404/523-1973
   2469 Piedmont Rd. NE, 404/237-8689
   544 Ponce De Leon Ave. NE, 404/607-1118
   1181 E. Confederate Ave. SE, 404/622-4254

Best Business Lunch
Delectables
   Atlanta Fulton Public Library, 1 Margaret Mitchell
      Sq. NW, 404/681-2909
Kudzu Cafe
   3215 Peachtree Rd. NE, 404/262-0661

Best Cajun/Creole Food
French Quarter Food Shop
   923 Peachtree St. NE, 404/875-2489
McKinnon's Louisiane Restaurant and Seafood Grill
   3209 Maple Dr. NE, 404/237-1313
New Orleans Cafe
   7887 Roswell Rd., 404/396-9665

Best Chinese Food
Chopstix
   4279 Roswell Rd. NE, 404/255-4868
First China Restaurant
   5295 Buford Hwy. NE, 404/457-6788
Golden Buddha
   1905 Clairmont Rd., Decatur, 404/633-5252
Hong Kong Harbor
   2184 Cheshire Bridge Rd. NE, 404/325-7630

Honto Restaurant
3295 Chamblee Dunwoody Rd., Chamblee,
404/458-8088
Little Szechuan
5091C Buford Hwy. NE, 770/451-0192
Panda Inn
5389 New Peachtree Rd., 770/451-4568
Pung Mei
5145 Buford Hwy. NE, 770/455-0435
Yen Jing
5302 Buford Hwy. NE, Doraville, 770/454-6688

Best Coffee/Coffeehouse
Aurora Coffee
992 N. Highland Ave. NE, 404/607-1300
Cafe Intermezzo
4505 Ashford Dunwoody Rd. NE, 770/396-1344
1845 Peachtree St. NE, 404/355-0411
Cyberstache
772 N. Highland Ave.NE, 404/892-0266

Best Continental Food
103 West
103 W. Paces Ferry Rd. NW, 404/233-5993
Hedgerose
490 E. Paces Ferry Rd. NE, 404/233-7673
Palisades
1829 Peachtree Rd. NE, 404/350-6755

Best Delicatessen
St. Charles Deli
2470 Briarcliff Rd. NE, 404/636-5201

Best Desserts
Corner Cafe and Buckhead Bread Company
3070 Piedmont Rd. NE, 404/240-1978
The Dessert Place
1000 Virginia Ave. NE, 404/892-8921
279 E. Paces Ferry Rd. NE, 404/233-2331

Best Diner
Buckhead Diner
3073 Piedmont Rd., 404/262-3336
Silver Grill
900 Monroe Dr. NE, 404/876-8145

Best Eclectic Menu
Cafe Tu Tu Tango
220 Pharr Rd. NE, 404/841-6222
City Grill
50 Hurt Plaza SE, Ste. 200, 404/524-2489
Dante's Down the Hatch
60 Upper Alabama St. SW, Ste. 1, 404/577-1800
3380 Peachtree Rd. NE, 404/266-1600
Nickiemoto's
247 Buckhead Ave. NE, 404/842-0334
Tiburon Grille
1190B N. Highland Ave. NE, 404/892-2393

Best Fine Dining
Country Place
1197 Peachtree St. NE, 404/881-0144

G

Dining Room at the Ritz-Carlton
  3434 Peachtree Rd. NE, 404/237-2700
Luna Si
  1931 Peachtree Rd. NE, 404/355-5993
Pano's and Paul's
  1232 W. Paces Ferry Rd. NW, 404/261-3662
Pricci
  500 Pharr Rd. NE, 404/237-2941

Best French Food
Anis
  2974 Grandview Ave. NE, 404/233-9889
Brasserie Le Coze
  3393 Peachtree Rd. NE, 404/266-1440
Ciboulette Restaurant
  1529 Piedmont Rd. NE, 404/874-7600
Petite Auberge Restaurant
  2935 N. Druid Hills Rd. NE, 404/634-6268
Riviera
  519 E. Paces Ferry Rd. NE, 404/262-7112
Violette Restaurant
  2948 Clairmont Rd. NE, 404/633-3323

Best Greek/Mediterranean Food
Athens Pizza
  1341 Clairmont Rd., Decatur, 404/636-1100
Caribbean Cafe
  1213 Columbia Dr., Decatur, 404/284-8400

Best Health-Conscious Menu
Rainbow Restaurant
  2118 N. Decatur Rd., Decatur, 404/633-3538

Best Homestyle Food
Satterwhite Restaurant and Catering
  590 Cascade Ave. SW, 404/758-9825
Sooky's Kitchen
  3693 Main St., College Park, 404/762-8105

Best Ice Cream/Yogurt
Gorin's Homemade Ice Cream
  1043 Ponce De Leon Ave. NE, 404/875-3795
  2903 N. Druid Hills Rd. NE, 404/634-7042

Best Indian Food
Indian Delights
  1707 Church St., Decatur, 404/296-2965
Touch of India Tandoori
  1037 Peachtree St. NE, 404/876-7777

Best Inexpensive Meal
Cafe Diem
  640 N. Highland Ave. NE, 404/607-7008
Eats
  600 Ponce De Leon Ave. NE, 404/888-9149
El Taco Veloz
  5084 Buford Hwy. NE, 770/936-9094
Grecian Gyro Restaurant
  855 Virginia Ave., 404/762-1627
Madras Cafe
  3092 Briarcliff Rd. NE, 404/320-7120

Best Italian Food
Abruzzi
  2355 Peachtree Rd. NE, 404/261-8186
Fratelli Di Napoli Restaurant
  2101 Tula St. NW, 404/351-1533
La Grotta Ristorante Italiano
  2637 Peachtree Rd. NE, 404/231-1368
  4355 Ashford Dunwoody Rd. NE, 770/395-9925
Lindy's Neighborhood Italian Cafe
  10 Kings Circle NE, 404/231-4112
Pasta da Pulcinella
  1027 Peachtree St. NE, 404/892-6195
Provino's
  4387 Roswell Rd. NE, 404/256-4300
Veni, Vidi, Vici
  41 Fourteenth St. NE, 404/875-8424

G

Best Japanese Food
Benihana of Tokyo
  2143 Peachtree Rd. NE, 404/355-8565
  229 Peachtree St. NE, 404/522-9627
Kamogawa
  3300 Peachtree Rd. NE, 404/841-0314
Kobe Steaks
  5600 Roswell Rd. NE, 404/256-0810
Yakitori Den Chan
  3099 Peachtree Rd. NE, 404/842-0270

Best Korean Food
Chosun Ok
  5865 Buford Hwy. NE, 770/452-1821

Best Late-Night Food
Beautiful Restaurant
  2260 Cascade Rd. SW, 404/752-5931
Majestic Food Shops
  1031 Ponce De Leon Ave. NE, 404/875-0276
R. Thomas Deluxe Grill
  1812 Peachtree St. NW, 404/872-2942

Best Lunch
Atlanta Bread Company
  595 Piedmont Ave. NE, 404/881-9555
Bella Cucina Artful Food
  489 Peachtree St. NE, 404/872-4553
OK Cafe
  1284 W. Paces Ferry Rd. NW, 404/233-2888

Best Mexican Food
Cinco de Mayo
  1332 Blvd. SE, 404/624-0210
El Azteca
  939 Ponce De Leon Ave. NE, 404/881-6040
El Charro
  2581 Piedmont Rd. NE, 404/264-0613
La Paz Restaurant y Cantina
  6410 Roswell Rd. NE, 404/256-3555
  2950 New Paces Ferry Rd. SE, 770/801-0020
Las Americas Mexican Taqueria
  3652 Shallowford Rd. NE, Doraville, 404/458-7062

Nuevo Laredo Cantina
  1495 Chattahoochee Ave. NW, 404/352-9009
Rio Bravo Cantina
  3172 Roswell Rd. NW, 404/262-7431
  2250 Pleasant Hill Rd., 404/623-1096
  4749 Ashford Dunwoody Rd., 770/395-6603
Zocalo
  990 Piedmont Ave. NE, 404/249-7576

Best Middle Eastern Food
Lawrence's Cafe
  2888 Buford Hwy. NE, 404/320-7756
Nicola's
  1602 La Vista Rd. NE, 404/325-2524

Best Other Ethnic Food
Abday (Ethiopian)
  3375 Buford Hwy. NE, Ste. 1050, 404/321-5808
Bridgetown Grill (Caribbean)
  7285 Roswell Rd. NE, 770/394-1575
  1156 Euclid Ave. NE, 404/653-0110
  689 Peachtree St. NE, 404/873-5361
Coco Loco (Cuban)
  2625G Piedmont Rd. NE, Ste. 40, 404/364-0212
Imperial Fez Moroccan Restaurant (Moroccan)
  2285 Peachtree Rd. NE, 404/351-0850
La Fonda Latina (Cuban)
  2813 Peachtree Rd. NE, 404/816-8311
  1150B Euclid Ave. NE, 404/577-8317
Machu Picchu (Peruvian)
  3375 Buford Hwy. NE, 404/320-3226
Mambo Restaurante Cubano (Cuban)
  1402 N. Highland Ave. NE, 404/876-2626
Taste of Africa Restaurant (African)
  4813 Old National Hwy., College Park,
    404/684-0333

Best Outdoor Dining
Einstein's
  1077 Juniper St. NE, 404/876-7925
St. Agnes Tea Garden
  222 E. Howard Ave., Decatur, 404/370-1995

Best Pizza
Cameli's Pizza Joint
  699 Ponce De Leon Ave. NE, Ste. 12, 404/249-9020
Everybody's Pizza
  1040 N. Highland Ave. NE, 404/873-4545
Fellini's Pizza
  1634 McLendon Ave. NE, 404/687-9190
  422 Seminole Ave. NE, 404/525-2530
Rocky's Brick Oven Pizzeria
  1770 Peachtree Rd. NW, 404/876-1111
  1394 N. Highland Ave., 404/872-9331

Best Regional Food
Colonnade Restaurant
  1879 Cheshire Bridge Rd. NE, 404/874-5642
Mary Mac's Tea Room
  224 Ponce De Leon Ave. NE, 404/876-1800

Pittypat's Porch
  25 International Blvd. NW, 404/525-8228
Silver Grill
  900 Monroe Dr. NE, 404/876-8145
The Horseradish Grill
  4320 Powers Ferry Rd. NW, 404/255-7277

Best Salad/Salad Bar
Lettuce Souprise You
  5975 Roswell Rd. NE, 404/250-0304
  1009 Cumberland Mall SE, 770/438-2288
  595 Piedmont Ave. NE, 404/874-4998
  2470 Briarcliff Rd. NE, 404/636-8549
Virginia's Koffie House
  1243 Virginia Ave., 404/875-4453

Best Sandwiches
J.R. Crickets
  631 Spring St. NW, 404/881-1950
Monterey Jack's Sandwich Company
  3330 Piedmont Rd. NE, 404/233-8020
Sensational Subs
  782 Ponce De Leon Ave. NE, 404/872-4424
  33 Edgewood Ave. SE, 404/523-1420
  1690 Howell Mill Rd. NW, 404/350-0720

Best Seafood
Atlanta Fish Market
  265 Pharr Rd. NE, 404/262-3165
Thomas Marketplace Restaurant
  16 Forest Pkwy., Forest Park, 404/361-1367
Yasin's Fish Supreme
  3541 Martin Luther King Jr. Dr. SW, 404/696-3277
  5340 Old National Hwy., 404/765-9823
  387 Cleveland Ave. SW, 404/559-0336
  300 Simpson Terrace NW, 404/873-9971

Best Soul Food
Heath's Cascade Grocery and Ms. Bea's Kitchen
  787 Cascade Ave. SW, 404/755-0543
Son's Place
  100 Hurt St. NE, 404/581-0530
Southfork
  737 Ralph McGill Blvd. NE, 404/522-4809

Best Southwestern Food
Azuni Grill
  4279 Roswell Rd. NE, 404/255-5501
Nava
  3060 Peachtree Rd. NW, 404/240-1984
Sundown Cafe
  2165 Cheshire Bridge Rd. NE, 404/321-1118

Best Sports Bar
Frankie's
  The Prado, 5600 Roswell Rd. NE, 404/843-9444

Best Steaks
Bone's Steak and Seafood
  3130 Piedmont Rd. NE, 404/237-2663
Chops
  70 W. Paces Ferry Rd. NW, 404/262-2675

G

Houston's
　3539 Northside Pkwy. NW, 404/262-7130
　2946 Hillwood Dr., 404/351-2442
　3321 Lenox Rd. NE, 404/237-7534
McKendrick's Steak House
　4505 Ashford Dunwoody Rd. NE, 770/512-8888
Morton's of Chicago
　303 Peachtree St. NE, 404/577-4366
　3379 Peachtree Rd. NE, 404/816-6535
The Palm
　3391 Peachtree Rd. NE, 404/814-1955
Thomas Marketplace Restaurant
　16 Forest Pkwy., Forest Park, 404/361-1367

Best Sunday Brunch
Canoe
　4199 Paces Ferry Rd. SE, 770-432-2663
Le Peep Restaurant
　233 Peachtree St. NE, 404/688-3782
　2484 Briarcliff Rd. NE, 404/325-7069
Murphy's
　997 Virginia Ave. NE, 404/872-0904

Best Sushi
Harry and Son's
　820 N. Highland Ave., 404/873-2009

Best Thai Food
Annie's Thai Castle
　3195 Roswell Rd. NE, 404/264-9546
Bai Tong
　2329C Cheshire Bridge Rd. NE, 404/728-9040
My Thai Restaurant
　1248 Clairmont Rd., Decatur, 404/636-4280
Pad Thai Restaurant
　1021 Virginia Ave. NE, 404/892-2070
Surin of Thailand
　810 N. Highland Ave. NE, 404/892-7789
Thai Chili
　2169 Briarcliff Rd. NE, 404/315-6750

Best Vegetarian Food
Atlantis Natural Foods and Cafe
　2488 Mount Vernon Rd., Dunwoody, 770/393-1297
Cafe Sunflower
　5975 Roswell Rd. NE, 404/256-1675
Flying Biscuit Cafe
　1655 McLendon Ave. NE, 404/687-8888
Mellow Mushroom Pizza Bakers
　6218 Roswell Rd. NE, 404/252-5560
　931 Monroe Dr. NE, 404/874-2291
　1679 La Vista Rd. NE, 404/325-0330
　1715 Howell Mill Rd. NW, 404/350-0501
　30 Pharr Rd. NW, 404/233-3443

Best Vietnamese Food
Bien Thuy
　5095 Buford Hwy. NE, Doraville, 404/454-9046
Cha Gio
　132 Tenth St. NE, 404/885-9387

Vietnamese Cuisine
3375 Buford Hwy. NE, 404/321-1840

Best View While Dining
Ray's on the River
6700 Powers Ferry Rd. NW, 770/955-1187

Best Wine Selection
Aldo's Italian Restaurant
6690 Roswell Rd. NE, 404/252-4832
Bacchanalia
3125 Piedmont Rd. NE, 404/365-0410

G

AUGUSTA, GA

Best American Food
Michael's Fine Food
2860 Washington Rd., 706/733-0913

Best Barbecue/Ribs
Sconyer's Barbecue
2250 Sconyers Way, 706/790-5411

Best Breakfast
Duke Restaurant
1920 Walton Way, 706/736-6879
Whistle Stop Cafe
573 Greene St., 706/724-8224

Best Brewpub
King George
2 Eighth St., 706/724-4755

Best Cajun/Creole Food
Cafe Du Teau
1855 Central Ave., 706/733-3505

Best Casual Dining
Boll Weevil
10 Ninth St., 706/722-7772
Cotton Patch
816 Cotton Ln., 706/724-4511
Snug Tavern and Grill
240 Davis Rd., 706/863-1118

Best Desserts
Boll Weevil
10 Ninth St., 706/722-7772
Caffe Allegro
3830 Washington Rd., 706/650-5959

Best Diner
Duke Restaurant
1920 Walton Way, 706/736-6879

Best Eclectic Menu
Word of Mouth Cafe
724 Broad St., 706/722-3477

Best Fine Dining
Andrews Restaurant
2651 Perimeter Pkwy., 706/855-8100
Cadwallader's
106 Davis Rd., 706/860-7444

G

Best French Food
Cafe Du Teau
  1855 Central Ave., 706/733-3505
La Maison on Telfair
  404 Telfair St., 706/722-4805

Best German Food
Villa Europa Restaurant and Lounge
  3044 Deans Bridge Rd., 706/798-6211

Best Homestyle Food
Cotton Row Cafe and Meeting Place
  2 Eighth St., River Walk, 706/722-6901

Best Indian Food
Moghul Restaurant
  2501 Washington Rd., 706/738-4500

Best Italian Food
Augustino's an Italian Eatery
  2 Tenth St., 706/823-6521
Luigi's Restaurant
  590 Broad St., 706/722-4056
Villa Europa Restaurant and Lounge
  3044 Deans Bridge Rd., 706/798-6211

Best Japanese Food
Kyoto Japanese Restaurant
  2834 Washington Rd., 706/737-4015
Mikoto Japanese Restaurant
  3102 Washington Rd., 706/855-0009
Sho Gun
  3043 Washington Rd., 706/863-9690

Best Lunch
Partridge Inn
  2110 Walton Way, 706/737-8888
Sixth at Watkins
  559 Watkins St., 706/722-8877

Best Mexican Food
Nacho Mama's Burritos
  976 Broad St., 706/724-0501
Vallarta Restaurante Mexicano
  3144 Wrightsboro Rd., 706/731-0321
  2808 Washington Rd., 706/733-5584

Best Sandwiches
Sunshine Bakery
  1209 Broad St., 706/724-2302

Best Seafood
Beamie's at the River
  865 Reynolds St., 706/724-6593
Calvert's Restaurant
  475 Highland Ave., 706/738-4514
The Snug Tavern and Grill and Cub House Banquets
  240 Davis Rd., 706/863-1118
French Market Grille
  424 Highland Ave., 706/737-4865
Rinehart's Oyster Bar
  3051 Washington Rd., 706/860-2337

T's Seafood Restaurant
2856 Washington Rd., 706/737-8325
Williams Seafood Restaurant
3160 Wrightsboro Rd., 706/737-9415

Best Steaks
T-Bone's Steakhouse of Augusta
2856 Washington Rd., 706/737-8325
1654 Gordon Hwy., 706/796-1875

BRUNSWICK, GA

G

Best Barbecue/Ribs
Mack's Barbecue Place
2809 Glynn Ave., 912/264-0605
Twin Oaks
2618 Norwich St., 912/265-3131

Best Breakfast
Mama's and Papa's Home Cooking
120 Old Jesup Rd., 912/264-8080

Best Chinese Food
New China Restaurant
3202 Glynn Ave., 912/265-3312

Best Delicatessen
P & C Deli
3015 Norwich St., 912/265-7582
Salvador's Delicatessen
205 Gloucester St., 912/264-1543

Best Italian Food
Matteo's Italian Restaurant
5448 New Jesup Hwy., 912/267-0248
Scarpinato's Italian Deli
3421 Cypress Mill Rd., 912/264-5878

Best Mexican Food
El Potro Mexican Restaurant
2806 Cypress Mill Rd., 912/264-1619

Best Restaurant In Town
Royal Cafe
1618 Newcastle St., 912/262-1402

Best Sandwiches
Grapevine Cafe
1519 Newcastle St., 912/265-0115

Best Seafood
Captain Joe's Seafood
3303 Glynn Ave., 912/262-9878
5296 New Jesup Hwy., 912/264-8771
Jinright's Seafood House
2815 Glynn Ave., 912/267-1590
Spanky's
1200 Glynn Ave., 912/267-6100

COLUMBUS, GA

Best Casual Dining
Tavern on the Square
14 Eleventh St., 706/324-2238

Best Continental Food
Bludau's Goetchius House
  405 Broadway, 706/324-4863

Best Desserts
Minni's Uptown Restaurant
  104 Eighth St., 706/322-2766

Best Diner
Gabby's 24-Hour Diner
  5753 Milgen Rd., 706/568-4435
  5915 Veterans Pkwy., 706/323-2226

G

Best Dinner
Olive Branch Cafe
  1024 Broadway, 706/322-7410

Best Family Restaurant
Country's Barbecue
  1329 Broadway, 706/596-8910
  3137 Mercury Dr., 706/563-7604
  6298 Veterans Pkwy., 706/660-1415
Speakeasy Pub
  3123 Mercury Dr., 706/561-0411

Best German Food
Amadeus
  3747 Macon Rd., 706/563-7427

Best Italian Food
Olive Branch Cafe
  1024 Broadway, 706/322-7410

Best Japanese Food
Mikata Japanese Steakhouse
  5300 Sidney Simons Blvd., 706/327-5100

Best Mexican Food
El Vaquero Mexican Restaurante
  3135 Cross Country, 706/569-1420

Best Sandwiches
W.D. Crowley's Restaurant
  3111 Manchester Expwy., 706/324-3463

DALTON, GA

Best Italian Food
Flammini's Cafe Italia
  1205 W. Walnut Ave., 706/226-0667

Best Restaurant in Town
Dalton Depot
  110 Depot St., 706/226-3160
Oakwood Cafe
  201 W. Cuyler St., 706/278-4421
Powell's Country Kitchen
  116 W. King St., 706/278-1545

DULUTH, GA

Best American Food
Buffalo's Cafe
  911 Duluth Hwy., Ste. 120, Lawrenceville,
  770/338-0505

Best Chinese Food
Golden Buddha
  2055 Beaver Ruin Rd., Norcross, 770/448-3377
  3200 Buford Hwy., 770/497-1954
  2283 Thompson Bridge Rd., Gainesville,
    770/534-0767

Best Delicatessen
Harry's Farmers Market
  2025 Satellite Blvd., 770/416-6900

Best Eclectic Menu
Mick's
  3525 Mall Blvd., 770/623-1855

Best Family Restaurant
Dominick's
  95 S. Peachtree St., Norcross, 770/449-1611

Best Fine Dining
Little Gardens Restaurant
  3571 Lawrenceville Hwy., Lawrenceville,
    770/923-3434

Best Greek/Mediterranean Food
Evelyn's Cafe
  3853F Lawrenceville Hwy., Tucker, 770/496-0561

Best Homestyle Food
County Seat Cafe
  450 Hurricane Shoals Rd. NE, Lawrenceville,
    770/963-0666

Best Japanese Food
Kabuki Japanese Restaurant
  455 Grayson Hwy., Lawrenceville, 770/995-7796
Shiki
  1492 Pleasant Hill Rd., 770/279-0097

Best Mexican Food
El Toro
  1210 Rockbridge Rd., Norcross, 770/381-0849

Best Pizza
Mellow Mushroom Pizza Bakers
  6135 Peachtree Pkwy., Norcross, 770/729-1555
Stone Mountain Pizza Cafe
  5370 Hwy. 78, Ste. 600, Stone Mountain,
    770/413-6717

Best Place to Take the Kids
La Cazuela Mexican Restaurant
  3585 Peachtree Industrial Blvd., 770/497-1730

Best Sandwiches
Manhattan Bagel Company
  2180 Pleasant Hill Rd., 770/495-9959

Best Sports Bar
Time Out Sports Bar and Grill
  9775-R Medlock Bridge, 770/495-9113

Best Steaks
Skeeter's Grille
  3505 Satellite Blvd., 770/476-3131

G

Best Thai Food
Taste of Thai
  5775 Jimmy Carter Blvd., Ste. B2, Norcross,
  770/662-8575

GRIFFIN, GA

Best Barbecue/Ribs
Southern Pit Bar-B-Que
  2964 N. Expressway, 770/229-5887

G

Best Breakfast
Anderson's Cafeteria
  814 W. Taylor St., 770/227-2962

Best Sandwiches
Jasmine's
  315 W. Solomon St., 770/227-1155

Best Steaks
Manhattan's Restaurant
  1707 N. Expressway, 770/228-5442

LA GRANGE, GA

Best Bar
Knickers Restaurant
  1510 Lafayette Pkwy., 706/882-3873

Best Breakfast
Tyler's Restaurant
  401 Vernon St., 706/884-4158

Best Diner
Landmark Cafe
  22 Main St., Grantville, 770/583-2599

Best Dinner
Cleve's Place
  Roanoke Road., 706/884-2222

Best Homestyle Food
Jimmy's
  120 Main St., 706/845-0406

Best Lunch
The Lemon Tree
  200 S. Morgan St., 706/882-5382

Best Mexican Food
Los Nopales Mexican Restaurant
  1014 Hogansville Rd., 706/883-8547

Best Sandwiches
Hogan's Hero's Too
  306 Cherry St., 706/882-3354

Best Steaks
Spring House Inn
  1 Youngs Mill Rd., 706/812-1546

MACON, GA

Best All-You-Can-Eat Buffet
S & S Cafeteria
  2626 Riverside Dr., 912/746-9406

Best Barbecue/Ribs
Fincher's Barbecue
  891 Gray Hwy., 912/743-5866
  3057 Columbus Rd., 912/742-2220
  3947 Houston Ave., 912/788-1900
Satterfield's
  120 New St., 912/742-0352

Best Burgers
Grey Goose Players Club
  4524 Forsyth Rd., 912/471-0987
Polly's Corner Cafe
  6351 Zebulon Rd., 912/757-9926

Best Casual Dining
Hotlanta Wings
  3485 Mercer University Dr., 912/742-8090

Best Chinese Food
China King
  2444 Pio Nono Ave., 912/781-7616
Golden Palace
  172 Tom Hill Sr. Blvd., 912/471-0732
Hong Kong Express
  610 North Ave., 912/745-7975

Best Fine Dining
Green Jacket Restaurant
  325 Fifth St., 912/746-4680

Best Italian Food
Napoli's on Forsyth
  4524 Forsyth Rd., Ste. 304, 912/952-7307
Natalia's
  2720 Riverside Dr., 912/741-1380

Best Lunch
Between the Bread Cafe
  588 Mulberry St., 912/743-3999
H & H Restaurant
  807 Forsyth St., 912/742-9810
Len Berg's Carryout Meal
  240 Post Office Alley, 912/742-9255
Sid's Sandwich Shop
  336 Second St., 912/746-1772

Best Mexican Food
El Sombrero
  610 North Ave., 912/750-8159

Best Pizza
Ingleside Village Pizza
  2396 Ingleside Ave., 912/750-8488

Best Seafood
Harbor Pointe Restaurant
  6420 Moseley Dixon Rd., 912/471-0393
Jim Shaw's Restaurant
  3040 Vineville Ave., 912/746-3697
Polly's Corner Cafe
  6351 Zebulon Rd., 912/757-9926
Mikata Japanese Steakhouse
  2972 Riverside Dr., 912/471-7573

G

Best Thai Food
Bangkok Express
   3311 Pio Nono Ave., 912/788-6848

MARIETTA, GA

Best All-You-Can-Eat Buffet
Cici's
   2731 Sandy Plains Rd., 770/579-2424
   1455 Terell Mill Rd. SE, 770/952-4400

Best Beer Selection
Taco Mac
   2359 Windy Hill Rd. SE, 770/953-6382

Best Chinese Food
Lee's Golden Buddha
   2524 Cobb Pkwy. SE, Smyrna, 770/980-1800

Best Delicatessen
Harry's Farmers Market
   70 Powers Ferry Rd. SE, 770/578-4400

Best Indian Food
Haveli Indian Cuisine
   2650 Cobb Pkwy. SE, Smyrna, 770/955-4525

Best Pizza
Cici's
   1455 Terrell Mill Rd. SE, 770/952-4400
   2731 Sandy Plains Rd., 770/579-2424
Pizza by Tomaselli
   365 Pat Mell Rd. E, 770/438-1819

Best Regional Food
1848 House Restaurant
   780 S. Cobb Dr. SE, 770/428-1848

Best Restaurant in Town
Jimmy's on the Square
   164 Roswell St. NE, 770/428-5627
Shilling's on the Square
   19 N. Park Sq. NE, 770/428-9520

Best Seafood
Squid Roe
   2995 Johnson Ferry Rd., 770/587-3474

ROME, GA

Best Barbecue/Ribs
Bubba's Barbecue
   1 Broad St., 706/291-0618
Sonny's Real Pit Barbecue
   2103 Shorter Ave., 706/234-1441

Best Breakfast
Jo Jo's City Diner
   313 Broad St., 706/234-5520

Best Chinese Food
China City Restaurant
   1803 Martha Berry Blvd., 706/291-2499
Happy Family Chinese Restaurant
   2004 Shorter Ave., 706/234-6888

Best Delicatessen
Schroeder's New Deli
   406 Broad St., 706/234-4613

Best Diner
Patridge Cafe
   330 Broad St., 706/291-4048
Rick's Diner
   900 Martha Berry Blvd., 706/235-7851

Best Homestyle Food
Country Gentleman Restaurant
   26 Chateau Dr. SE, 706/295-0205
Homestead
   1401 Kingston Rd. NE, 706/291-4290

Best Italian Food
Pasquale's Pizza
   4011 Martha Berry Hwy. NW, 706/235-6063
Ragazzi's Italian Restaurant
   226 Shorter Ave., 706/234-0333
The Gondolier Pizza Italian Restaurant
   152 Shorter Ave., 706/291-8080

Best Lunch
Duffy's Deli
   500 E. Second Ave., 706/291-0531
Tootsie's Deli
   2017 Maple Ave., 706/291-0396

Best Mexican Food
El Zarape Mexican Restaurant
   429 Broad St., 706/295-5330

ROSWELL, GA

Best Barbecue/Ribs
Slopes' BBQ of Roswell
   10360 Alpharetta St., 770/518-7000

Best Delicatessen
Harry's Farmers Market
   1180 Upper Hembree Rd., 770/664-6300

Best Desserts
Martha's
   555 S. Atlanta St., 770/955-2900

Best Homestyle Food
Lickskillet Farm Restaurant
   1380 Old Roswell Rd., 770/475-6484

Best Kosher Food
Bagelicious
   2500 Old Alabama Rd., 770/998-3401

Best Other Ethnic Food
Janousek's Restaurant (Czech)
   1475 Holcomb Bridge Rd., 770/587-2075

Best Pizza
Mellow Mushroom Pizza Bakers
   1570 Holcomb Bridge Rd., 770/998-8260

G

Best Regional Food
The Smith House
   84 S. Chestatee St., Dahlonega, 706/867-7000

Best Vegetarian Food
Cafe Sunflower
   5975 Roswell Rd. NE, Sandy Springs, 912/256-1675

SAVANNAH, GA

Best Barbecue/Ribs
Johnny Harris Restaurant
   1651 E. Victory Dr., 912/354-7810

Best Brewpub
Oglethorpe Brewing Company
   21 W. Bay St., 912/232-0933

Best Burgers
Crystal Beer Parlor
   301 W. Jones St., 912/691-1033

Best Diner
Clary's Cafe
   404 Abercorn St., 912/233-0402

Best Italian Food
Il Pasticcio
   2 E. Broughton St., 912/231-8888

Best Mexican Food
Pepe's
   325 E. Bay St., 912/236-0530

Best Pizza
Vinnie Van Go-Go's
   317 W. Bryan St., 912/233-6394

Best Regional Food
Barnes Restaurant
   5320 Waters Ave., 912/354-8745
   4685 U.S. Hwy. 80E, 912/898-0220
The Lady and Sons
   311 W. Congress St., 912/233-6200
Wilkes' Dining Room
   107 W. Jones St., 912/232-5997
Nita's Place
   140 Abercorn St., 912/238-8233
Wall's Bar B Que Restaurant
   515 E. York St., 912/232-9754

Best Sandwiches
Sam Fink's Deli
   11 W. Liberty St., 912/236-3354

Best Seafood
Shrimp Factory
   313 E. River St., 912/236-4229
Williams Seafood Restaurant
   8010 U.S. Hwy. 80E, 912/897-2219

ST. SIMONS ISLAND, GA

Best Bar
Brogen's
   200 Pier Alley, 912/638-1660

3600 Frederica Rd., 912/638-2060

Best Breakfast
Dressner's Village Cafe
223 Mallory St., 912/634-1217

Best Burgers
Brogen's
200 Pier Alley, 912/638-1660
3600 Frederica Rd., 912/638-2060

Best Desserts
Sweet Mama's
1201 Ocean Blvd., 912/638-9011
Sweet Mama's Too
1627 Frederica Rd., 912/634-6022

G

Best Italian Food
Allegro
2465 Demere Rd., 912/638-7097
CJ's Italian Restaurant
520 Ocean Blvd., Ste. 210, 912/638-3857

Best Japanese Food
Kyoto Japanese Restaurant
202 Retreat Plz., 912/638-0885

Best Lunch
Frannie's Place
318 Mallory St., 912/638-1001

Best Regional Food
Fourth of May
444 Mallory St., 912/638-5444

Best Seafood
Blanche's Courtyard Restaurant
440 Ocean Blvd., 912/638-3030
Crab Trap
1209 Ocean Blvd., 912/638-3552
Crabdaddy's Seafood Bar
1219 Ocean Blvd., 912/634-1120

Best Steaks
Bennie's Red Barn
5514 Frederica Rd., 912/638-2844

Best Sunday Brunch
King and Prince Beach Resort
201 Arnold Rd., 912/638-3631

STATESBORO, GA

Best Family Restaurant
Beaver House
121 S. Main St., 912/764-2821

Best Health-Conscious Menu
Health Attack Cafe and Yogurt
609 Brannen St., 912/764-7858

Best Mexican Food
El-Sombrero Restaurant
406 Fair Rd., 912/764-9828

Best Pizza
Holiday Pizza
  406 Fair Rd., 912/764-7669
Mellow Mushroom Pizza Bakers
  6 University Plz., 912/681-8788

VALDOSTA, GA

Best All-You-Can-Eat Buffet
Country Buffet
  2801 N. Ashley St., 912/242-0863

Best Atmosphere
Fiddlers Green
  4479 N. Valdosta Rd., 912/247-0366

Best Barbecue/Ribs
Bono's Barbeque
  1531 Baytree Rd., 912/244-5006
Old South Barbecue House
  1706 W. Hill Ave., 912/247-0505
Sonny's Real Pit Barbecue
  2037 Bemiss Rd., 912/242-8257

Best Breakfast
King's Grill
  200 N. Patterson St., 912/242-5897

Best Desserts
Lulu's
  132 N. Patterson St., 912/242-4000

Best Diner
King's Grill
  200 N. Patterson St., 912/242-5897

Best Dinner
Giulio's Greek and Italian
  105 E. Ann St., 912/333-0929

Best German Food
Willy Hofbrau
  2325 N. Ashley St., 912/247-0611

Best Greek/Mediterranean Food
Giulio's Greek and Italian
  105 E. Ann St., 912/333-0929
Mom and Dad's Italian Restaurant
  4143 N. Valdosta Rd., 912/333-0848

Best Mexican Food
El Potro Mexican Restaurant
  3022 N. Ashley St., 912/241-7249

Best Pizza
Buffalo Brady's Wooden Nickel
  3104 N. Oak St., 912/242-5842

Best Restaurant in Town
Big O's Country Buffet
  2801 N. Ashley St., 912/242-0863

Best Sandwiches
Buffalo Brady's Wooden Nickel
  3104 N. Oak St., 912/242-5842

Covington's Dining and Catering
310 N. Patterson St., 912/242-2261

Best Seafood
J.P. Mulldoon's Restaurant
1405 Gornto Rd., 912/247-6677

Best Steaks
J.P. Mulldoon's Restaurant
1405 Gornto Rd., 912/247-6677

Best Sunday Brunch
Captain T's
2905 N. Ashley St., 912/247-7590

G

WARNER ROBINS, GA

Best Chinese Food
China Palace
306 Russell Pkwy., 912/923-8263
Top Wok
1244 Watson Blvd., 912/929-4655

Best Mexican Food
Casa Maria Mexican Restaurant
1855 Watson Blvd., 912/328-1906

Best Restaurant in Town
Richard's Restaurant
604 Russell Pkwy., 912/922-1547

Best Steaks
Montana Steak House
2212 Watson Blvd., 912/929-9555

WAYCROSS, GA

Best All-You-Can-Eat Buffet
Adolph's
410 Plant Ave., 912/283-1766
Holiday Inn Restaurant
Holiday Inn, 1725 Memorial Dr., 912/283-4170

Best Barbecue/Ribs
B & E Bar-B-Q
2403 Plant Ave., 912/283-3516
The Pig
768 State St., 912/283-4875

Best Burgers
Jerry J's
1404 Plant Ave., 912/287-1303
1809 Reynolds St., 912/285-3657

Best Chinese Food
Wong's Palace Restaurant
903 Knight Ave., 912/285-8747

Best Coffee/Coffeehouse
Huddle House
1010 Memorial Dr., 912/283-0915

Best Mexican Food
El Potro Mexican Restaurant
1506 Memorial Dr., 912/285-2855

Best Sandwiches
Downtown Sandwich Shoppe
  417 Tebeau St., 912/285-8476
Michael's Deli
  910 Memorial Dr., 912/283-3724

Best Steaks
Whitfield's
  514 Mary St., 912/285-9027

G

Hawaii

HILO, HI

Best American Food
Scruffle's Restaurant
1438 Kilauea Ave., 808/935-6664

Best Chinese Food
Kow's Restaurant
87 W. Kawailani St., 808/959-3766

Best Dinner
Seaside Restaurant
1790 Kalanianaole Ave., 808/935-8825

Best Family Restaurant
Don's Grill
485 Hinano St., 808/935-9099
Scruffle's Restaurant
1438 Kilauea Ave., 808/935-6664

Best Inexpensive Meal
Cafe 100
969 Kilauea Ave., 808/935-8683

Best Italian Food
Cafe Pesto
308 Kamehameha Ave., 808/969-6640

Best Japanese Food
Nihon Restaurant and Cultural Center
123 Lihiwai St., 808/969-1133
Scruffle's Restaurant
1438 Kilauea Ave., 808/935-6664

Best View While Dining
Seaside Restaurant
1790 Kalanianaole Ave., 808/935-8825

HONOLULU, HI

Best American Food
Orchids
   Halekulani Hotel, 2199 Kalia Rd., 808/923-2311

Best Bar
Row Bar
   500 Ala Moana Blvd., 808/528-2345

Best Burgers
W & M Bar-B-Q Burger
   3104 Waialae Ave., 808/734-3350

Best Business Lunch
Byron II Steak House
   1450 Ala Moana Blvd., 808/949-8855
Sunset Grill
   500 Ala Moana Blvd., Ste. 1A, 808/521-4409

Best Chinese Food
Dew Drop Inn
   1088 S. Beretania St., 808/526-9522
Golden Dragon
   2005 Kalia Rd., 808/946-5336
Hee Hing Restaurant
   449 Kapahulu Ave., 808/735-5544
Maple Garden
   909 Isenberg St., 808/941-6641
Mini Garden Restaurant
   50 N. Hotel St., 808/538-1273

Best Coffee/Coffeehouse
Coffee Manoa
   Manoa Marketplace, 2752 Woodlawn Dr.,
      808/988-5113
Coffee Talk
   3601 Waialae Ave., 808/737-7444
Like Like Drive Inn Restaurant
   745 Keeaumoku St., 808/941-2515
Lion Coffee
   831 Queen St., 808/591-2479

Best Diner
Kelly's Diner
   2908 Kamehameha Hwy., 808/836-3444

Best Dinner
Eggs and Things
   1911B Kalakaua Ave., 808/949-0820

Best Fine Dining
Maile Restaurant
   5000 Kahala Ave., 808/734-2211
The Bali
   2005 Kalia Rd., 808/941-2254

Best French Food
Alfred's Restaurant
   1750 Kalakaua Ave., 808/955-5353
La Mer
   2199 Kalia Rd., 808/923-2311

Best Italian Food
Auntie Pasto's, Inc.
  1099 S. Beretania St., 808/523-8855
Matteo's Italian Restaurant
  364 Seaside Ave., 808/922-5551
Salerno Italian Restaurant
  1960 Kapiolani Blvd., Ste. 204, 808/946-3299
Verbano Italiano Ristorante
  3571 Waialae Ave., Ste. 101, 808/735-1777

Best Japanese Food
Kyo-Ya Japanese Restaurant
  2057 Kalakaua Ave., 808/947-3911
Tanaka of Tokyo
  131 Kaiulani Ave., Third Fl., 808/922-4233
  1777 Ala Moana Blvd., 808/945-3443
  2250 Kalakaua Ave., Fourth Fl., 808/922-4702
Yanagi Sushi
  762 Kapiolani Blvd., 808/597-1525

Best Korean Food
Kim Chee
  1040 S. King St., 808/536-1426
Kim Chee II Restaurant
  3569 Waialae Ave., 808/737-0006
Sorabol
  805 Keeaumoku St., 808/947-3113
Yummy Korean Bar-B-Q
  7192 Kalanianaole Hwy., 808/395-4888
  801 Kaheka St., 808/942-0288

Best Mexican Restaurant
Compadres Mexican Bar and Grill
  Ward Centre Mall, 1200 Ala Moana Blvd., Ste. 3,
    808/523-1307
La Bamba
  847 Kapahulu Ave., 808/737-1956
Quintero's
  1102 Piikoi St., 808/593-1561

Best Other Ethnic Food
Elena's (Filipino)
  2153 N. King St., 808/845-0340
Mabuhay (Filipino)
  1049 River St., 808/545-1956

Best Pizza
California Pizza Kitchen
  4211 Waialae Ave., 808/737-9446

Best Regional Food
3660 on the Rise
  3660 Waialae Ave., 808/737-1177
Alan Wong's Restaurant
  1857 S. King St., 808/949-2526
Cascada Restaurant
  440 Olohana St., 808/945-0270
Helena's Hawaiian Food
  1364 N. King St., 808/845-8044
Roy's Restaurant
  6600 Kalanianaole Hwy., 808/396-7697

Best Restaurant Meal Value
Swiss Inn
  5730 Kalanianaole Hwy., 808/377-5447

Best Seafood
Horatio's
  1050 Ala Moana Blvd., 808/591-2005
John Dominis
  43 Ahui St., 808/523-0955
Legend Seafood Restaurant
  100 N. Beretania St., 808/532-1868
Nick's Fishmarket
  Waikiki Gateway Hotel, 2070 Kalakaua Ave.,
808/955-6333
Orson's
  1050 Ala Moana Blvd., Ste. 2, 808/591-8681

Best Steaks
Hy's Steak House
  2440 Kuhio Ave., 808/922-5555
Ruth's Chris Steak House
  500C Ala Moana Blvd., Ste. 6, 800/544-0808

Best Sunday Brunch
The Plumeria Beach Cafe
  5000 Kahala Ave., 808/734-2211

Best Thai Food
Keo's Thai Cuisine
  Ward Centre Mall, 1200 Ala Moana Blvd.,
    808/596-0020
  625 Kapahulu Ave., 808/737-8240
Mekong Thai
  1295 S. Beretania St., 808/591-8841
Siam Orchid Thai Restaurant
  1614 Kona St., 808/955-6161
Singha Thai Cuisine
  1910 Ala Moana Blvd., 808/941-2898

Best Vietnamese Food
A Little Bit of Saigon
  1160 Maunakea St., 808/528-3663
Diem Vietnamese
  2633 S. King St., 808/941-8657
Duc's Bistro
  1188 Maunakea St., 808/531-6325
Hale Vietnam
  1140 Twelfth Ave., 808/735-7581

KAHULUI, HI

Best Barbecue/Ribs
S.W. Bar-B-Q
  Maui Mall Shopping Center, 808/877-0706

Best Burgers
Cupie's Drive-In
  134 W. Kaahumanu Ave., 808/877-3055

Best Chinese Food
Ming Yuen Chinese Restaurant
  162 Alamaha St., 808/871-7787

H

Best Coffee/Coffeehouse
Coffee Store
275 W. Kaahumanu Ave., 808/871-6860
Sir Wilfred's
Lahaina Cannery Mall, 1221 Honoapiilani Hwy.,
808/667-1941

Best Family Restaurant
Koho Grill and Bar
275 W. Kaahumanu Ave., 808/877-5588

Best Italian Food
Luigi's Pasta Pizzeria
PCB 426 Maui Mall, 808/877-3761

Best Japanese Food
Maui Palms Hotel
170 W. Kaahumanu Ave., 808/877-0071

Best Sandwiches
Marco's Grill and Deli
444 Hana Hwy., 808/877-4446

Best Seafood
Chart House
500 N. Puunene Ave., 808/877-2476

Best View While Dining
Mama's Fish House
799 Poho Pl., Paia, 808/579-8488

KAILUA KONA, HI

Best Dinner
Chart House Restaurant
75-5770 Alii Dr., 808/329-2451

Best French Food
La Bourgogne French Restaurant
77-6400 Nalani St., Ste. 101, 808/329-6711

Best Regional Food
Ocean View Inn
75-5683 Alii Dr., 808/329-9998
Sam Choy's
73-5576 Kauhola St., Ste. 1, 808/326-1545

Best Restaurant in Town
Edward's at the Terrace
Kanaloa at Kona Condominiums, 78-261 Manukai
St., 808/322-1434
Merriman's
Opelo Plz., Hwy. 19, Kamuela, 808/885-6822
Palm Cafe
75-5819 Alii Dr., 808/329-7765

LAHAINA, HI

Best Atmosphere
Roy's Kahana Bar and Grill
4405 Honoapiilani Hwy., 808/669-6999

Best Restaurant in Town
Gerard's Restaurant
174 Lahainaluna Rd., Ste. 1, 808/661-8939

Best Seafood
Erik's Seafood Grotto
4242 Lower Honoapiilani Rd., 808/669-4806

LIHUE, HI

Best Coffee/Coffeehouse
Cafe Espresso
Coconut Marketplace, 4-484 Kuhio Hwy., Kapaa,
808/822-9421

Best Dinner
A Pacific Cafe
4-831 Kuhio Hwy., Ste. 220, Kapaa, 808/822-0013

Best Japanese Food
Restaurant Kintaro Japanese
4-370 Kuhio Hwy., Kapaa, 808/822-3341

Best Lunch
Gaylord's Restaurant
3-2087 Kaumualii Hwy., 808/245-9593

Best Restaurant in Town
Hanamaulu Restaurant
3-4291 Kuhio Way, 808/245-2511
The Bull Shed
796 Kuhio Hwy., Kapaa, 808/822-3791

Best Seafood
Hanalei Dolphin Restaurant
55020 Kuhio Hwy., Ste. 5-5016, Hanalei,
808/826-6113

WAILUKU, HI

Best Barbecue/Ribs
Lone Star Cookout
1234 Lower Main St., 808/242-6616

Best Breakfast
Chums Family Restaurant
1900 Main St., 808/244-1000

Best Desserts
Maui Bake Shop and Deli
2092 W. Vineyard St., 808/242-0064

Best Health-Conscious Menu
Saigon Cafe A
1792 Main St., 808/243-9560

Best Japanese Food
Ichiban Okazuya Hawaii
2133 Kaohu St., 808/244-7276

Best Lunch
Bentos and Banquets by Bernard
85 N. Church St., 808/244-1124

Best Mexican Food
Ramon's
2102 W. Vineyard St., 808/244-7243

Best Thai Food
Saeng's Thai Cuisine
2119 W. Vineyard St., 808/244-1567

Saim Thai Cuisine
123 N. Market St., 808/244-3817

Idaho

BOISE, ID

Best Chinese Food
Panda Chinese Restaurant
  415 E. Parkcenter Blvd., 208/336-3113

Best Coffee/Coffeehouse
Cafe Soho
  6932 W. State St., 208/853-4641

Best Family Restaurant
Noodles Pizza Pasta Pizzazz
  800 Idaho St., 208/342-9300
Red Robin
  211 W. Parkcenter Blvd., 208/344-7471
  267 N. Milwaukee St., 208/323-0023

Best Lunch
Angell's Bar and Grill
  999 Main St., 208/342-4900

Best Pizza
Chicago Connection Pizza
  3931 Overland Rd., 208/344-6838
  10668 Overland Rd., 208/323-0216
  7766 Lemhi St., 208/323-1231
  7070 Fairview Ave., 208/377-5551
  3504 W. State St., 208/345-3278
Flying Pie Pizzeria
  6508 Fairview Ave., 208/376-3454
  1016 Broadway Ave., 208/384-0000
  4320 W. State St., 208/345-8585
Lucky 13
  1602 N. Thirteenth St., 208/344-6967

Best Sunday Brunch
Cristina's Bakery and Coffee Bar
504 Main St., 208/385-0133
Murphy's Seafood Bar and Grill
1555 Broadway Ave., 208/344-3691
The Pacific Grill
Doubletree Riverside, 2900 Chinden Blvd.,
208/343-1871

COEUR D'ALENE, ID

Best Restaurant in Town
Beverly's Restaurant
250 Northwest Blvd., Ste. 7, 208/765-4000
Cedars Floating Restaurant
Blackwell Island, 208/664-2922
Chef In The Forest
7900 E. Hauser Lake Rd., Post Falls, 208/773-3654
Jimmy D's
320 E. Sherman Ave., 208/664-9774
Tomato Street
221 W. Appleway Ave., 208/667-5000

IDAHO FALLS, ID

Best American Food
The Sandpiper
750 Lindsay Blvd., 208/524-3344

Best Barbecue/Ribs
Bubba's BBQ Restaurant
888 E. Seventeenth St., 208/523-2822
Snake River Smokehouse Restaurant
680 Lindsay Blvd., 208/523-1865

Best Burgers
Blue Room
500 W. 21st St., 208/525-9659

Best Casual Dining
Sugar Factory Smokehouse
422 N. 4000 E, Rigby, 208/745-7070

Best Coffee/Coffeehouse
D.D. Mudd Espresso Cafe
439 A St., 208/535-9088

Best Eclectic Menu
Rutabaga's Espresso Bar
415 River Pkwy., 208/529-3990

Best Family Restaurant
Smitty's Pancake and Steakhouse
645 W. Broadway St., 208/523-6450

Best Fine Dining
Downtowner
365 River Pkwy., 208/524-2524
O'Callahan's
The Shiloh Hotel, 740 Lindsay Blvd., 208/523-1818

Best Lunch
Bagelby's Bagel Bakery
1902 Jennie Lee Dr., 208/523-6867

Half Moon Coffee and Tea
401 Park Ave., 208/529-2650
Louie's Pizza and Italian Restaurant
340 E. Anderson St., 208/524-1010

Best Mexican Food
Mama Inez
344 Park Ave., 208/525-8968
Mi Casa
235 Cliff St., 208/523-9381

Best Restaurant in Town
Hawg Smoke Cafe
4330 N. Yellowstone Hwy., 208/523-4804

Best Sandwiches
Big Al's Sandwich Joint
545 Shoup Ave., 208/529-4615
Pap Kelsey's Pizza and Subs
2285 E. Seventeenth St., 208/523-3136

Best Seafood
Jake's
851 Lindsay Blvd., 208/524-5240

Best Southwestern Food
Snake Bite
425 River Pkwy., 208/525-2522

Best Steaks
Jake's
851 Lindsay Blvd., 208/524-5240

KETCHUM, ID

Best American Food
Baldy's Bistro
241 N. Main St., 208/726-2267

Best Coffee/Coffeehouse
Galleria Wine and Espresso Bar
351 Leadville Ave. N., 208/726-1707

Best Italian Food
Ketchum Grill
520 East Ave. N., 208/726-4660

Best Mexican Food
Chapala
502 N. Main St., Hailey, 208/788-5065

Best Pizza
Da Vinci's
17 W. Bullion St., 208/788-6699

Best Restaurant In Town
Soupcon Restaurant
231 1/2 Leadville Ave. N., 208/726-5034

Best Sushi
Sushi On Second
260 Second St., 208/726-5181

LEWISTON, ID

Best American Food
Helm Restaurant
  1824 Main St., 208/746-9661
The Nobby Inn
  501 S. Main St., Moscow, 208/882-2932
Zany's
  2004 Nineteenth Ave., 208/746-8131

Best Atmosphere
The Wayback Cafe
  2138 Thirteenth Ave., 208/743-2396

Best Breakfast
Anytime Tavern and Grill
  1350 Main St., 208/746-6230
Panhandler Pies
  1407 Main St., 208/746-0010
Waffles and More
  1421 Main St., 208/743-5189

Best Burgers
Effie's Tavern
  1120 Main St., 208/746-1889

Best Casual Dining
Dutch Goose
  226 W. Sixth St., Moscow, 208/883-4847
Rusty's Ranch Cafe
  2418 North And South Hwy., 208/746-5054
Zany's
  2004 Nineteenth Ave., 208/746-8131

Best Chinese Food
Mandarin Pine Restaurant
  833 21st St., 208/746-4919

Best Desserts
Panhandler Pies
  1407 Main St., 208/746-0010
The Nobby Inn
  501 S. Main St., Moscow, 208/882-2932

Best Dinner
Helm Restaurant
  1824 Main St., 208/746-9661

Best Eclectic Menu
Mikey's Gyros
  527 S. Main St., Moscow, 208/882-0780

Best Health-Conscious Menu
Carter's Cafe
  1303 Main St., 208/743-2463

Best Homestyle Food
Granny's
  232 Thain Rd., 208/746-7328

Best Inexpensive Meal
Strike and Spare Bar and Grill
  Orchards Lane, 244 Thain Rd., 208/743-8883

Best Italian Food
Gambino's Italian Restaurant
308 W. Sixth St., Moscow, 208/882-4545

Best Mexican Food
El Sombrero Mexican Restaurant
629 Bryden Ave., 208/746-0658

Best Restaurant in Town
The Broiler
Best Western University Inn, 1516 Pullman Rd.,
Moscow, 208/882-0550

Best Seafood
Helm Restaurant
1824 Main St., 208/746-9661
Jonathan's
301 D St., 208/746-3438

Best Steaks
Bojack's Broiler Pit
311 Main St., 208/746-9532
Jonathan's
301 D St., 208/746-3438

Best Sunday Brunch
Meriwether's
621 21st Ave., 208/746-9390

NAMPA, ID

Best American Food
Generations
112 Third St. S., 208/467-4941
Little Kitchen Restaurant
1224 First St. S., 208/467-9677

Best Breakfast
The Koffee Pot
1730 Garrity Blvd., 208/466-2979

Best Chinese Food
Hong Kong Restaurant
117 Twelfth Ave. S., 208/466-1244

Best Lunch
Noodle's Pizza Pasta Pizzazz
1802 Franklin Blvd., 208/888-2821

Best Seafood
O'Callahan's
1401 Shilo Dr., 208/465-5908

POCATELLO, ID

Best Restaurant in Town
Blue Ribbon Restaurant
2036 Thunderbolt St., 208/233-8002
Continental Bistro
140 S. Main St., 208/233-4433
Sandpiper
1400 Bench Rd., 208/233-1000
Wagon Wheel Inn
2720 Bannock Hwy., 208/232-9850

Whistle Stop
  200 S. Main St., 208/233-1037

Best Seafood
Remo's
  160 W. Cedar St., 208/233-1710

SALMON, ID

Best Barbecue/Ribs
Lewis and Clark Cafe
  HC 10, Hwy. 93N, North Fork, 208/865-2244
North Fork Cafe
  Hwy. 93N, North Fork, 208/865-2412

Best Burgers
A & W
  609 Hwy. 93N, 208/756-3630
BG's Burnt Buns
  516 S. Challis St., Ste.1, 208/756-2062

Best Family Restaurant
Savage Circle
  1111 Main St., 208/756-3458

Best Pizza
Garbonzo's Pizza
  Hwy. 28, 208/756-4565

Best Restaurant in Town
The Shady Nook and-Brandin' Iron Saloon
  Hwy. 93N, 208/756-4182

TWIN FALLS, ID

Best Breakfast
Buffalo Cafe
  218 Fourth Ave. W., 208/734-0271
Java Blue Coffee Bar
  653 Blue Lakes Blvd., 208/734-7973
Kelly's
  110 Main Ave. N., 208/733-0466

Best Brewpub
Mugger's Brewpub
  516 Second St. S., 208/733-2322

Best Casual Dining
JB's Restaurant
  835 Blue Lakes Blvd., 208/734-0642
Sharis
  1601 Blue Lakes Blvd. N., 208/734-2110

Best French Food
Uptown Bistro
  117 Main Ave. S., 208/733-0900

Best Italian Food
A'Roma Italian Cuisine
  147 Shoshone St. N., 208/733-0167

Best Lunch
Dunken's Draught House
  102 Main Ave. N., 208/733-8114
Kelly's
  110 Main Ave. N., 208/733-0466

Metropolis Bakery Cafe
  125 Main Ave. E., 208/734-4457

Best Mexican Food
Eduardo's Mexican Restaurant
  2096 Kimberly Rd., 208/734-5345
Garivalbi's
  1118 Blue Lakes Blvd., 208/736-7408
La Casita Mexican Restaurant
  111 S. Park Ave., 208/734-7974
Mama Inez
  164 Main Ave. N., 208/734-0733

Best Other Ethnic Food
Basque Kitchen (Basque)
  360 Main Ave. N., 208/733-9231

Best Pizza
Bernardi's Pizza
  222 Blue Lakes Blvd., 208/733-5678
Maxie's Pizza and Pasta
  170 Blue Lakes Blvd., 208/733-3963

Best Restaurant in Town
Cafe Ole Restaurant and Cantina
  1288 Blue Lakes Blvd. N., 208/734-0685
Jaker's
  1598 Blue Lakes Blvd. N., 208/733-8400
Rock Creek
  200 Addison Ave. W., 208/734-4154
The Sandpiper Restaurant
  1309 Blue Lakes Blvd. N., 208/734-7000

Best Steaks
Creekside Steakhouse
  360 Main Ave. N., 208/733-9231

Illinois

ALTON, IL

Best American Food
Joshua's Restaurant
  1900 E. Homer M. Adams Pkwy., 618/465-0886

Best Coffee/Coffeehouse
A Taste of Class
  210 Market St., 618/465-7507

Best Desserts
My Just Desserts
  31 E. Broadway, 618/462-5881
Old Post Office Mall
  300 Alby St., 618/462-8204

Best Health-Conscious Menu
Midtown Restaurant
  1026 E. Seventh St., 618/465-1321

Best Ice Cream/Yogurt
Kerr's Drug Store
  2512 College Ave., 618/465-5631

Best Italian Food
Moonlight Restaurant
  3400 Fosterburg Rd., 618/462-4620
Tony's Restaurant and Third Street Cafe
  312 Piasa St., 618/462-8384

Best Sandwiches
Old Post Office Mall
  300 Alby St., 618/462-8204

Best Tea Room
Franklin House
  202 State St., 618/463-1078

ARLINGTON HEIGHTS, IL

[See also: Des Plaines, Glenview, Lake Zurich, Northbrook, and Wheeling.]

Best All-You-Can-Eat Buffet
Old Country Buffet
  445 E. Palatine Rd., 847/255-0066

Best American Food
Arlington Gardens
  710 E. Kensington Rd., 847/255-4675
Arlington Place
  902 E. Northwest Hwy., 847/253-2190
Bailey's Restaurant
  208 S. Arlington Heights Rd., 847-394-3950
Bovis Restaurant
  900 W. Northwest Hwy., 847/577-6888
Brown's Chicken and Pasta
  1000 E. Northwest Hwy., 847/255-5500
Eddie's Restaurant and Lounge
  10 E. Northwest Hwy., 847/253-1320
Eros Restaurant
  18 S. Dryden Pl., 847/255-3171
Higgley's Restaurant
  2240 S. Arlington Heights Rd., 847/593-8199
Jameson's Char House
  1331 W. Dundee Rd., 847/392-7100
Jimmy's Place
  640 W. Northwest Hwy., 847/398-9783
Max and Erma's
  306 E. Rand Rd., 847/590-9400
Prime Time Inn Restaurant
  150 E. Rand Rd., 847/398-6571
Riviera Restaurant
  5 W. Campbell St., 847/394-1930
Seigelman's Restaurant
  912 W. Algonquin Rd., 847/398-0222
Wellington
  2121 S. Arlington Heights Rd., 847/439-6610
Zippy's
  1720 W. Algonquin Rd., 847/342-9797

Best Bar
Harry's of Arlington
  1 N. Vail Ave., 847/577-2525

Best Barbecue/Ribs
Yogie's Ribs
  5 E. Golf Rd., 847/290-9100

Best Breakfast
Egg Harbor Cafe
  140 Wing St., 847/253-4363
Vail Street Cafe
  19 N. Vail Ave., 847/392-1164
Village Grill
  2 E. Northwest Hwy., 847/577-9292

Walker Brothers Original Pancake House
  825 W. Dundee Rd., 847/392-6600

Best Brewpub
O'Grady's Brewery and Pub
  372 E. Golf Rd., 847/640-0060

Best Burgers
Brandt's - The Little Cafe
  807 W. Baldwin Rd., Palatine, 847/359-6373

Best Chinese Food
Chin's Restaurant
  10 E. Miner St., 847/255-9080
China Wok
  1451 E. Palatine Rd., 847/255-1001
Chinese Munch In
  1091 E. Golf Rd., 847/593-2227
Ding Ho
  915 W. Rand Rd., 847/394-1240
Heng Wing
  121 W. Palatine Rd., Palatine, 847/358-3061
Mandarin Garden Restaurant
  915 W. Rand Rd., 847/394-1240
  155 W. Rand Rd., 847/255-3434
Moy Fong's Restaurant
  932 W. Algonquin Rd., 847/259-9422
New Hong Kong
  100 W. Campbell St., 847/392-6699
Wing Wah Restaurant
  337 E. Rand Rd., 847/259-8882
Yen Yen Restaurant
  4226 N. Arlington Heights Rd., 847/259-3400

Best Coffee/Coffeehouse
Barjen's Coffee, Beans, and Brews
  140 E. Golf Rd., 847/437-9932

Best Delicatessen
Ada's Deli
  902 W. Dundee Rd., 847/577-7444
Aunt Betty's Bagels and Deli
  136 E. Golf Rd., 847/364-1616
Continental Deli
  10 S. Evergreen Ave., 847/259-9544
Out to Lunch
  1039 S. Arlington Heights Rd., 847/290-8618

Best Desserts
Le Titi de Paris
  1015 W. Dundee Rd., 847/506-0222

Best Family Restaurant
Dunton House
  11 W. Davis St., 847/394-5885

Best Fine Dining
Sage's Sages Restaurant
  75 W. Algonquin Rd., 847/593-6200
Wellington of Arlington
  2121 S. Arlington Heights Rd., 847/439-6629

Best French Food
Le Titi de Paris
   1015 W. Dundee Rd., 847/506-0222

Best Health-Conscious Menu
Chowpatti Vegetarian Restaurant
   1035 S. Arlington Heights Rd., 847/640-9554

Best Homestyle Food
Granny's Restaurant
   24 E. Miner St., 847/398-1720

Best Inexpensive Meal
Billy's
   1729 E. Central Rd., 847/439-2031
Mr. Allison's Snack Shop
   1711 E. Central Rd., 847/228-5870

Best Japanese Food
Bowl House
   1918 S. Arlington Heights Rd., 847/437-7878
Edoya
   282 E. Algonquin Rd., 847/593-2470
Rokbonki Japanese Steak House
   876 W. Dundee Rd., 847/506-1212

Best Korean Food
Jin Mee
   940 W. Algonquin Rd., 847/577-8949

Best Mexican Food
La Chicanita Mexican Restaurant
   202 N. Dunton Ave., 847/255-7075
Los Jardines
   712 E. Kensington Rd., 847/255-4744

Best Pizza
Home Run Inn Pizza
   222 E. Algonquin Rd., 847/427-9696
Paulogruto's Restaurant
   820 E. Rand Rd., 847/392-9090
Regina's Restaurant
   27 W. Campbell St., 847/394-2728
Toma Rosa Pizza
   210 E. Grove St., 847/506-9400
Tortorice's Pizzeria
   1735 E. Central Rd., 847/437-7668

Best Place to Take the Kids
Barnaby's
   933 W. Rand Rd., 847/394-5270
Higgley's Restaurant
   2240 S. Arlington Heights Rd., 847/593-8199

Best Sandwiches
Portillo's Hot Dogs
   806 W. Dundee Rd., 847/870-0870

Best Seafood
Chin's Restaurant
   10 E. Miner St., 847/255-9080
Dover Straits
   1149 W. Golf Rd., Hoffman Estates, 847/884-3900

Rusty Pelican
   10 E. Algonquin Rd., 847/228-0040

Best Sports Bar
Sports Page Restaurant and Bar
   1330 E. Rand Rd., 847/392-5332

Best Steaks
Jameson's Char House
   1331 W. Dundee Rd., 847/392-7100
Lone Star Steak House
   115 W. Rand Rd., 847/392-9789
Palm Court
   1912 N. Arlington Heights Rd., 847/870-7770
Wellington of Arlington
   2121 S. Arlington Heights Rd., 847/439-6610

Best Thai Food
Bangkok Cafe
   30 E. Golf Terrace, 847/437-3870

Best Vegetarian Food
Chowpatti Vegetarian Restaurant
   1035 S. Arlington Heights Rd., 847/640-9554

Best Vietnamese Food
Bowl House
   1918 S. Arlington Heights Rd., 847/437-7878

Best Wine Selection
Sage's Sages Restaurant
   75 W. Algonquin Rd., 847/593-6200

AURORA, IL

[See also: Elmhurst, Lombard, and Naperville.]

Best All-You-Can-Eat Buffet
Epic Buffet
   1 New York St., Hollywood Casino Aurora,
   630/801-7000

Best American Food
Fairbanks Steakhouse
   1 New York St., Hollywood Casino Aurora,
   630/801-7000

Best Breakfast
Aurora Pancake House
   321 N. Lake St., 630/859-1122
Epic Buffet
   1 New York St., Hollywood Casino Aurora,
   630/801-7000
Harner's Bakery Restaurant
   10 W. State St., North Aurora, 630/892-4400

Best Burgers
The Office
   746 S. Lincoln Ave., 630/896-5510

Best Business Lunch
Tavern on the Fox
   24 N. Broadway, 630/896-6667

Best Family Restaurant
Nikarry's Restaurant
  1055 N. Lake St., 630/264-1500

Best Mexican Food
La Cabana Restaurant
  835 S. River St., 630/859-8885

Best Pizza
Nancy's Pizza
  2616 Ogden Ave., 630/585-9600

Best Seafood
Fisherman's Inn
  43W 901 Main Street Rd., Elburn, 630/365-6265

Best Steaks
Hi-Way Lounge and Steakhouse
  1518 E. New York St., 630/820-8222

BARRINGTON, IL

Best American Food
Greenery Restaurant
  117 North Ave., 847/381-9000

Best Breakfast
Egg Harbor
  210 S. Cook St., 847/304-4033

Best Brewpub
Millrose Brewing Company
  45 S. Barrington Rd., South Barrington,
    847/382-7673

Best Continental Food
Barn of Barrington
  1415 S. Barrington Rd., 847/381-8585

BELLEVILLE, IL

Best American Food
Fischer's Restaurant
  2100 W. Main St., 618/233-1131

Best Barbecue/Ribs
Hickory Hut
  1030 Freeburg Ave., 618/277-7138

Best Breakfast
The Shrine Restaurant
  422 S. De Mazenod Dr., 618/397-6700

Best Burgers
Shenanigan's
  15 N. 64th St., 618/398-6979
Sports Page Inn
  2635 Old State Rte. 3, East Carondelet,
    618/286-5628

Best Coffee/Coffeehouse
Rebo's
  7410 Westchester Dr., 618/398-3255

Best Desserts
Pie Pantry
  301 E. Main St., 618/277-4140

Best Ice Cream/Yogurt
White Cottage
  102 Lebanon Ave., 618/234-1120

Best Italian Food
Viviano's Italian Restaurant
  6A Wade Sq., 618/235-1558

Best Mexican Food
Casa Gallardo Mexican Restaurant
  6600 N. Illinois St., Fairview Heights,
    618/632-4404

Best Pizza
Wolf's Den
  211 N. Main St., Freeburg, 618/539-5829

Best Southwestern Food
The Mansion
  1680 Mansion Way, O' Fallon, 618/628-0800

Best Steaks
Andria's
  6805 Old Collinsville Rd., O' Fallon, 618/632-4866
Valentine's Restaurant
  605 S. State St., Freeburg, 618/539-9169

BLOOMINGTON, IL

Best Chinese Food
Dragon Palace Chinese Restaurant
  1407 N. Veterans Pkwy., 309/663-1388
Tien Tsin Mandarin Chinese
  1500 E. Empire St., 309/663-9361

Best Coffee/Coffeehouse
The Coffeehouse
  114 E. Beaufort St., Normal, 309/452-6774

Best Family Restaurant
Ozark House
  704 McGregor St., 309/827-3900

Best German Food
The Bayern Stube
  209 N. Sangamon Ave., Gibson City, 217/784-8304

Best Mexican Food
Delgado's Mexican Food and Drink
  201 N. Landmark Dr., Normal, 309/454-4747

Best Pizza
Sonoma Cucina
  1603 Morrissey Dr., 309/664-0044

Best Romantic Dining
Le Radishe Rouge
  Jumer's Chateau, 1601 Jumer Dr., 309/662-2020

Best Sandwiches
Bennigan's
  115 Veterans Pkwy., Normal, 309/454-5577

BRIDGEVIEW, IL

Best American Food
Daniel's Restaurant
  8930 S. Harlem Ave., 708/598-5225
JC George's
  7200 W. 87th St., 708/430-2920

Best Chinese Food
See Through Chinese Kitchen
  7665 S. Harlem Ave., 708/430-8098

Best Italian Food
Brown's Chicken and Pasta
  8719 S. Harlem Ave., 708/430-8677

Best Mexican Food
Mr. Burrito
  9014 S. Harlem Ave., 708/430-8555

CARBONDALE, IL

Best Bar
Hangar 9
  511 S. Illinois Ave., 618/549-0511

Best Burgers
Rally's Hamburgers
  709 S. Illinois Ave., 618/549-7882

Best Chinese Food
Hunan Village
  710 E. Main St., 618/529-1108

Best Coffee/Coffeehouse
Melange
  607 S. Illinois Ave., 618/549-9161

Best Family Restaurant
Italian Village
  405 S. Washington St., 618/457-0212
Mugsy McGuire's
  1620 W. Main St., 618/457-6847

Best Homestyle Food
Murphy's Bar and Grill
  501 E. Walnut St., 618/457-5544

Best Italian Food
Pasta House Company
  1245 E. Main St., 618/457-5545

Best Late-Night Food
Sam's Cafe
  521 S. Illinois Ave., 618/549-2234

Best Mexican Food
El Bajio
  1010 E. Main St., 618/529-1648

Best Pizza
La Roma's Pizza
  515 1/2 S. Illinois Ave., 618/529-1344
Pagliai's Pizza and Pasta
  515 S. Illinois Ave., 618/457-0321
Quatro's Deep Pan Pizza
  222 W. Freeman St., 618/549-5326

Best Sandwiches
Jimmy John's Gourmet Sub Shop
519 S. Illinois Ave., 618/549-3334

Best Steaks
Murphy's Bar and Grill
501 E. Walnut St., 618/457-5544

CHAMPAIGN, IL

Best Breakfast
Original Pancake House
1909 W. Springfield Ave., 217/352-8866

Best Burgers
Vriner's Restaurant
55 E. Main St., 217/359-5408

Best Cajun/Creole Food
City of New Orleans
116 N. Chestnut St., 217/359-2489

Best Chinese Food
First Wok
1805 Philo Rd., Urbana, 217/344-4500

Best Coffee/Coffeehouse
Cafe Kopi
109 N. Walnut St., 217/359-4266

Best Diner
Silver Creek Restaurant
402 N. Race St., Urbana, 217/328-3402

Best Italian Food
Great Impasta
132 W. Church St., 217/359-7377

Best Korean Food
Miko Steak House
407 W. University Ave., Urbana, 217/367-0822

Best Other Ethnic Food
Asiana (Asian)
408 E. Green St., 217/398-3344

Best Pizza
Papa Del's Pizza
206 E. Green St., 217/359-7700

Best Steaks
Prime Room
The Chancellor Hotel, 1501 S. Neil St.,
217/352-8178

CHICAGO, IL

[See also: Des Plaines, Elmhurst, Evanston, Glenview, Oak Lawn, Skokie, and Wilmette.]

Best American Food
The Blackhawk Lodge
41 E. Superior St., 312/280-4080

Charlie Trotter's
816 W. Armitage Ave., 773/248-6228
Colonial Restaurant
5459 S. Kedzie Ave., 773/737-6942
Daniel J's
3811 N. Ashland Ave., 773/404-7772
Gold Coast Dogs
418 N. State St., 312/527-1222
Gordon Restaurant
500 N. Clark St., 312/467-9780
Nookies
1746 N. Wells St., 312/337-2454
Park Avenue Cafe
199 E. Walton St., 312/944-4414
Prairie
500 S. Dearborn St., 312/663-1143

Best Bar
Cullen's Bar and Grill
3741 N. Southport Ave., 773/975-0600
Jimmy's Woodlawn Tap and Liquor Store
1172 E. 55th St., 773/643-5516

Best Barbecue/Ribs
Bones
7110 N. Lincoln Ave., 847/677-3350
Carson's Place for Ribs
5970 N. Ridge Ave., 773/271-4000
612 N. Wells St., 312/280-9200
Gale Street Inn
4914 N. Milwaukee Ave., 773/725-1300

Best Beer Selection
Fireside Restaurant and Lounge
5739 N. Ravenswood Ave., 773/878-5942
Goose Island Brewery
1800 N. Clybourn Ave., 312/915-0071
Quencher's Saloon
2401 N. Western Ave., 773/276-9730
Village Tap
2055 W. Roscoe St., 773/883-0817

Best Bistro
Brasserie Jo
59 W. Hubbard St., 312/595-0800

Best Breakfast
Breakfast Club
1381 W. Hubbard St., 312/666-2372
Gladys' Luncheonette
4527 S. Indiana Ave., 773/548-6848

Best Burgers
Ed Debevic's
640 N. Wells St., 312/664-1707

Best Chinese Food
Emperor's Choice
2238 S. Wentworth Ave., 312/225-8800
Furama Restaurant
4936 N. Broadway St., 773/271-1161

Mars Restaurant
  3124 N. Broadway St., 773/404-1600
Triple Crown Chinese Seafood Restaurant
  211 W. 22nd Pl., 312/791-0788

Best Coffee/Coffeehouse
La Piazza Cafe
  3845 N. Broadway St., 773/868-0998
Starbucks Coffee
  227 W. Monroe St., 312/346-4360
  209 W. Jackson Blvd., 312/341-9850
  617 W. Diversey Pkwy., 773/880-5172
  430 N. Clark St., 312/670-3920
  105 W. Adams St., 312/855-0099

Best Delicatessen
Bagel Restaurant and Deli
  3107 N. Broadway St., 773/477-0300
Frances' Restaurant and Deli
  2552 N. Clark St., 773/248-4580
Manny's Coffee Shop and Deli
  1141 S. Jefferson St., 312/939-2855
Max's New York Deli
  2301 N. Clark St., 773/281-9100

Best Desserts
Gateway Bar and Grill
  7545 N. Clark St., 773/262-5767
Lutz Continental Cafe
  2458 W. Montrose Ave., 773/478-7785

Best Diner
Ed Debevic's
  640 N. Wells St., 312/664-1707
Lou Mitchell's Restaurant
  565 W. Jackson Blvd., 312/939-3111

Best Dinner
Pump Room
  1301 N. State Pkwy., 312/266-0360

Best Eclectic Menu
Cafe Absinthe
  1954 W. North Ave., 773/278-4488
Cafe Selmarie
  2327 W. Giddings St., 773/989-5595
Emilio's Tapas Bar
  4100 W. Roosevelt Rd., Hillside, 708/547-7177
Emilio's Tapas Chicago Restaurant
  444 W. Fullerton Pkwy., 773/327-5100
Printers Row Restaurant
  550 S. Dearborn St., 312/461-0780

Best Fine Dining
Gordon Restaurant
  500 N. Clark St., 312/467-9780
Whitehall Place
  105 E. Delaware Pl., 312/573-6300

Best French Food
Ambria
  2300 N. Lincoln Park W., 773/472-5959

Everest
440 S. La Salle St., 312/663-8920
Kiki's Bistro
900 N. Franklin St., 312/335-5454
Le Bouchon
1958 N. Damen Ave., 773/862-6600
Les Nomades
222 E. Ontario St., 312/649-9010
Marche
833 W. Randolph St., 312/226-8399
Ritz-Carlton Dining Room
Ritz-Carlton Hotel, 160 E. Pearson St.,
312/266-1000
Un Grand Cafe
2300 N. Lincoln Park W., 773/348-8886

Best German Food
Berghoff Restaurant Company
17 W. Adams St., 312/427-3170
The Berghoff Restaurant
17 W. Adams St., 312/427-3170
Zum Deutschen Eck
2924 N. Southport Ave., 773/525-8389

Best Greek/Mediterranean Food
Athenian Room
807 W. Webster Ave., 773/348-5155
Greek Islands Restaurant
200 S. Halsted St., 312/782-9855
Papagus Greek Taverna
620 N. State St., 312/642-8450
Parthenon Restaurant
314 S. Halsted St., 312/726-2418
Rodity's Restaurant
222 S. Halsted St., 312/454-0800
Santorini's Restaurant
138 S. Halsted St., 312/829-8820

Best Homestyle Food
Granny's Country Kitchen
8401 S. Roberts Rd., Justice, 708/233-1510

Best Indian Food
Bukara
2 E. Ontario St., 312/943-0188
Klay Oven
414 N. Orleans St., 312/527-3999
Moti Mahal
1035 W. Belmont Ave., 773/348-4392
2525 W. Devon Ave., 773/262-2080
Udupi Palace
2543 W. Devon Ave., 773/338-2152

Best Italian Food
Avanzare
161 E. Huron St., 312/337-8056
Bruna's Ristorante
2424 S. Oakley Ave., 773/254-5550
Cafe Spiaggia
980 N. Michigan Ave., 312/280-2764

Coco Pazzo
  300 W. Hubbard St., 312/836-0900
Da Nicola Ristorante
  3114 N. Lincoln Ave., 773/935-8000
Maggiano's
  516 N. Clark St., 312/644-7700
Rico's Restaurant
  626 S. Racine Ave., 312/421-7262
Rosebud Cafe
  1500 W. Taylor St., 312/942-1117
  751 N. Rush St., 312/266-6444
Scoozi!
  410 W. Huron St., 312/943-5900
Stefani's
  1418 W. Fullerton Ave., 773/348-0111
Topo Gigio
  1516 N. Wells St., 312/266-9355
Vivere
  The Italian Village Restaurant, 71 W. Monroe St.,
    312/332-4040

Best Japanese Food
Ron of Japan
  230 E. Ontario St., 312/644-6500

Best Late-Night Food
Bar Louie
  226 W. Chicago Ave., 312/337-3313

Best Lunch
Big Bowl
  159 W. Erie St., 312/787-8297
Caffe Baci
  231 S. La Salle St., 312/629-1818
Food Life
  Water Tower Pl., 835 N. Michigan Ave.,
    312/335-3663
Mity Nice Grill
  Water Tower Pl., 835 N. Michigan Ave.,
    312/335-4745
Nick and Tony's
  1 E. Wacker Dr., 312/467-9449
Wishbone Restaurant and Cafeteria
  1001 W. Washington Blvd., 312/850-2663

Best Mexican Food
Don Juan's
  6730 N. Northwest Hwy., 773/775-6438
El Presidente Restaurant
  2558 N. Ashland Ave., 773/525-7938
Frida's
  2143 N. Damen Ave., 312/337-4327
Frontera Grill and Topolobampo
  445 N. Clark St., 312/661-1434
Hat Dance
  325 W. Huron St., 312/649-0066
Las Mananitas
  3523 N. Halsted St., 773/528-2109
Nuevo Leon Restaurant
  3659 W. 26th St., 773/522-1515

1515 W. Eighteenth St., 312/421-1517
Tecalitlan Restaurant
  820 N. Ashland Ave., 312/243-1166
  1814 W. Chicago Ave., 773/384-4285
Twisted Lizard
  1964 N. Sheffield Ave., 773/929-1414
  600 E. Grand Ave., 312/494-9400

Best Middle Eastern Food
Reza Restaurant
  5255 N. Clark St., 773/561-1898
  432 W. Ontario St., 312/664-4500
The Casbah
  3151 N. Broadway St., 773/935-3339

Best Other Ethnic Food
Ann Sather's Restaurant (Swedish)
  5207 N. Clark St., 773/271-6677
  929 W. Belmont Ave., 773/348-2378
Busy Bee Restaurant (Polish)
  1546 N. Damen Ave., 773/772-4433
Cafe Ba-Ba-Reeba (Spanish)
  2024 N. Halsted St., 773/935-5000
Cafe Iberico (Spanish)
  739 N. La Salle Dr., 312/573-1510
Churrascos (South American)
  1960 N. Clybourn Ave., 773/248-4800
Healthy Food Restaurant (Lithuanian)
  3236 S. Halsted St., 312/326-2724
Hirickey's Asia Noodle Shop and Satay Bar (Pan-Asian)
  1852 W. North Ave., 773/276-8300
L'Olive Mediterranean Bistro (Moroccan)
  3915 N. Sheridan Rd., 773/472-2400
Little Bucharest (Eastern European)
  3001 N. Ashland Ave., 773/929-8640

Best Outdoor Dining
Black Cat Chicago
  2856 N. Southport Ave., 773/404-8400
Southport City Saloon
  2548 N. Southport Ave., 773/975-6110

Best Pizza
Bacino's
  3146 N. Sheffield Ave., 773/404-1658
  2204 N. Lincoln Ave., 773/472-7400
  75 E. Wacker Dr., 312/263-0070
Edwardo's Natural Pizza
  2662 N. Halsted St., 773/871-3400
  1937 W. Howard St., 773/761-7040
  521 S. Dearborn St., 312/939-3366
  1321 E. 57th St., 773/241-7960
  1212 N. Dearborn St., 312/337-4490
Gino's Pizzeria
  160 E. Superior St., 312/943-1124
Lou Malnati's Pizzeria
  439 N. Wells St., 312/828-9800
  3859 W. Ogden Ave., 773/762-0800
Pizzeria Due
  619 N. Wabash Ave., 312/943-2400

Pizzeria Uno
  29 E. Ohio St., 312/321-1000

Best Place to Take the Kids
Barnaby's
  2832 W. Touhy Ave., 773/973-4550
Ed Debevic's
  640 N. Wells St., 312/664-1707

Best Romantic Dining
Da Nicola Ristorante
  3114 N. Lincoln Ave., 773/935-8000
Geja's Cafe
  340 W. Armitage Ave., 773/281-9101
O' Brien's
  1528 N. Wells St., 312/787-3131
Spiaggia Cafe
  980 N. Michigan Ave., 312/280-2764
Trattoria Dinotto
  163 W. North Ave., 312/787-3345

Best Salad/Salad Bar
Claim Company
  900 N. Michigan Ave., 312/787-5757
Corosh
  1072 N. Milwaukee Ave., 773/235-0600
R.J. Grunt's
  2056 N. Lincoln Park W., 773/929-5363

Best Sandwiches
L'Appetito
  875 N. Michigan Ave., 312/337-0691
Moran's Bar and Grill
  1983 N. Clybourn Ave., 773/549-2337

Best Seafood
65 Seafood Restaurant
  336 N. Michigan Ave., 312/372-0065
Bones
  7110 N. Lincoln Ave., 847/677-3350
Carmine's Clamhouse
  1043 N. Rush St., 312/988-7676
Catch 35
  35 W. Wacker Dr., 312/346-3500
Gale Street Inn
  4914 N. Milwaukee Ave., 773/725-1300
Gateway Bar and Grill
  7545 N. Clark St., 773/262-5767

Best Soul Food
Army and Lou's
  422 E. 75th St., 773/483-3100
Edna's Restaurant
  3175 W. Madison St., 773/638-7079
Soul Kitchen
  1576 N. Milwaukee Ave., 773/342-9742

Best Sports Bar
Sluggers World Class Sports Bar
  3540 N. Clark St., 773/248-0058

Best Steaks

Chicago Chop House
  60 W. Ontario St., 312/787-7100
Eli's The Place For Steak
  215 E. Chicago Ave., 312/642-1393
Gene and Georgetti
  500 N. Franklin St., 312/527-3718
Gibson's Steakhouse
  1028 N. Rush St., 312/266-8999
Morton's of Chicago
  1050 N. State St., 312/266-4820
Myron and Phil's
  3900 W. Devon Ave., 847/677-6663

Best Sunday Brunch

Celebrity Cafe
  Westin River North Chicago, 320 N. Dearborn St.,
    312/744-1900
Erwin's
  2925 N. Halsted St., 773/528-7200
Southport City Saloon
  2548 N. Southport Ave., 773/975-6110

Best Tea Room

The Palm Court
  Drake Hotel, 140 E. Walton St., 312/787-2200
The Walnut Room
  111 N. State St., 312/781-3125

Best Thai Food

Arun's Restaurant
  4156 N. Kedzie Ave., 773/539-1909
P.S. Bangkok
  3345 N. Clark St., 773/871-7777
Penny's Noodle Shop
  3400 N. Sheffield Ave., 773/281-8222
  950 W. Diversey Pkwy., 773/281-8448
Roongpetch Restaurant
  1828 W. Montrose Ave., 773/989-0818
Star of Siam
  11 E. Illinois St., 312/670-0100
Thai Borrahn
  16 E. Huron St., 312/440-6003
The Bangkok
  3542 N. Halsted St., 773/327-2870

Best Vegetarian Food

Chicago Diner
  3411 N. Halsted St., 773/935-6696
Ethio Cafe
  3462 N. Clark St., 773/929-8300
Feast
  1835 W. North Ave., 773/235-6361
Hatsuhana
  160 E. Ontario St., 312/280-8287
Heartland Cafe
  7000 N. Glenwood Ave., 773/465-8005
Jane's
  1655 W. Cortland St., 773/862-5263

John's Place
1202 W. Webster Ave., 773/525-6670
Kanval Palace
2501 W. Devon Ave., 773/465-3928

Best Vietnamese Food
Thai Binh
1113 W. Argyle St., 773/728-0283

Best View While Dining
Seasons Restaurant
Four Seasons Hotel, 120 E. Delaware Pl.,
312/280-8800
The Signature Room
John Hancock Bldg., 875 N. Michigan Ave.,
Ste. 95, 312/787-9596
Spiaggia Cafe
980 N. Michigan Ave., 312/280-2764

Best Wine Selection
Entre Nous
Fairmont Hotel at Grant Park, 200 N. Columbus
Dr., 312/565-7997
Four Farthings Tavern
2060 N. Cleveland Ave., 773/935-2060
Vivere
Italian Village Restaurant, 71 W. Monroe St.,
312/332-4040

CHICAGO HEIGHTS, IL

[See also: Chicago and Oak Lawn.]

Best American Food
Enzo's
1710 Chicago Rd., 708/754-7040

Best Barbecue/Ribs
Princess Cafe
502 S. Dixie Hwy., Beecher, 708/946-3141

Best Breakfast
Egg and I
222 Dixie Hwy., 708/754-0909
Looking Glass Restaurant
1425 Western Ave., 708/747-7970

Best Burgers
Big Boy's
405 W. Fourteenth St., 708/481-3369

Best Chinese Food
Liang's Garden Restaurant
480 W. Lincoln Hwy., 708/481-5438

Best Homestyle Food
Mama Mary's
96 E. 24th St., 708/754-1147

Best Italian Food
Carlo Lorenzetti
560 W. Fourteenth St., 708/747-9480

La Pergola Restaurant
  525 Dixie Hwy., 708/756-2327

Best Mexican Food
Coco's Tacos
  2617 Chicago Rd., South Chicago Heights,
    708/754-5940
L.A. Cafe
  22835 Govenors Hwy., Richton Park, 708/747-4440

Best Pizza
Nino's Pizza
  203 156th Pl., Calumet City, 708/862-5555

Best Sandwiches
Enrico's
  427 N. La Grange Rd., Frankfort, 815/469-4187
  7717 W. Saint Francis Rd., Frankfort,
    815/469-1000
Gabe's Place
  9 E. Main St., Glenwood, 708/757-7171

Best Steaks
Glenwood Oaks Restaurant
  106 N. Main St., Glenwood, 708/758-4400

DANVILLE, IL

Best Barbecue/Ribs
Bud's
  504 N. Bowman Ave., 217/442-0614
Kag's Bar-B-Q
  612 1/2 E. Seminary St., 217/442-9679

Best Breakfast
Cahill's Family Restaurant
  334 N. Gilbert St., 217/442-3992
Danville Family Restaurant
  515 N. Vermilion St., 217/431-6044

Best Burgers
Gross's Burgers
  25 Henderson St., 217/442-8848
Moonglow
  324 Perrysville Rd., 217/442-9519

Best Chinese Food
Great Wall
  2 E. Main St., 217/443-2888

Best Coffee/Coffeehouse
Java Hut
  1419 N. Bowman Ave., 217/477-1033

Best Greek/Mediterranean Food
Deluxe Restaurant
  21 W. North St., 217/442-0685

Best Ice Cream/Yogurt
Custard Cup
  2507 N. Vermilion St., 217/443-0221

Best Lunch
Regina's Kitchen
  34 N. Vermilion St., 217/446-3354

Best Mexican Food
Buen Apetito
  3 E. Woodbury St., 217/442-6086
Mi Casa
  129 N. Vermilion St., 217/446-9856

Best Seafood
O'Leary's Pub
  510 N. Gilbert St., 217/442-1485

Best Steaks
O'Leary's Pub
  510 N. Gilbert St., 217/442-1485

DECATUR, IL

Best Business Lunch
Robbie's
  122 N. Merchant St, 217/ 423-0448

Best Bar
Lock Stock and Barrel
  129 S. Oakland Ave., 217/ 429-7411

Best Burgers
Krekel's Custard
  1355 N. State Rte. 48, 217/ 362-0121
  3727 N. Woodford St., 217/ 875-4044
  801 E. Wood St., 217/ 429-1122
Krekel's Dairy Maid
  2320 E. Main St., 217/423-1719

Best Chinese Food
First Wok
  702 Keokuk St., Lincoln, 217/732-7862

Best Fine Dining
Central Park West
  170 N. Merchant St., 217/ 429-0669

Best Health-Conscious Menu
Felice's Italian Restaurant
  2880 N. Oakland Ave., 217/ 872-0303

Best Late-Night Food
Blue Mill
  1099 W. Wood St, 217/ 423-7717

Best Seafood
Marcia's Waterfront Restaurant
  2301 E. Lake Shore Dr., 217/422-7202

Best View While Dining
Marcia's Waterfront Restaurant
  2301 E. Lake Shore Dr., 217/422-7202

DES PLAINES, IL

[See also: Arlington Heights, Chicago, Glenview, Skokie, Northbrook, and Wheeling.]

Best Breakfast
Grandma Sally's Waffle House
  1145 Elmhurst Rd., 847/364-0883

Best Coffee/Coffeehouse
Java Junction
  605 Lee St., 847/298-2828

Best Continental Food
Cafe La Cave
  2777 Mannheim Rd., 847/827-7818

Best Ice Cream/Yogurt
Sugar Bowl Sweet Shop and Restaurant
  1949 Miner St., 847/824-7380

Best Italian Food
Giuseppe's La Cantina
  1062 Lee St., 847/824-4230
Little Villa Restaurant
  660 N. Wolf Rd., 847/296-7763

Best Japanese Food
The Kampai
  2330 S. Elmhurst Rd., Mt. Prospect,
    847/640-6700

Best Pizza
Gino's East
  9751 W. Higgins Rd., Rosemont, 847/698-4949
  1321 Golf Rd., Rolling Meadows, 847/364-6644

Best Place to Take the Kids
Barnaby's
  636 E. Touhy Ave., 847/297-8866
Choo-Choo Restaurant
  600 Lee St., 847/298-5949

Best Seafood
Black Ram
  1414 E. Oakton St., 847/824-1227
Crab and Things
  1249 Elmhurst Rd., 847/437-1595
Don's Dock
  1220 E. Northwest Hwy., 847/827-1817
Knickers
  1050 E. Oakton St., 847/299-0011

Best Steaks
Black Ram
  1414 E. Oakton St., 847/824-1227
Knickers
  1050 E. Oakton St., 847/299-0011
Morton's of Chicago
  9525 Bryn Mawr Ave., Rosemont, 847/678-5155

EFFINGHAM, IL

Best Barbecue/Ribs
Stix
  1310 N. Keller Dr., 217/347-2222

Best Burgers
Cruiser's
  806 E. Fayette Ave., 217/342-3760

Best Chinese Food
Golden China
  1603 W. Fayette Ave., 217/342-2412

Best Coffee/Coffeehouse
Niemerg's Steak House
 1410 W. Fayette Ave., 217/342-3921

Best Desserts
Thelma's
 Ramada Inn, N. Rte. 32 at Rte. 33, 217/342-2131

Best Family Restaurant
Niemerg's Steak House
 1410 W. Fayette Ave., 217/342-3921
Trailways Restaurant
 2402 N. Third St., 217/342-2680

Best Inexpensive Meal
China Buffet
 1500 W. Fayette Ave., 217/342-3188

Best Mexican Food
El Rancherito
 1313 N. Keller Dr., 217/342-4753

Best Pizza
Pizza Man
 604 W. Jefferson Ave., 217/347-7766

Best Sandwiches
Deb's Wings and Subs
 3002 Four Seasons Dr., 217/536-9464
Old Grey Dog Bar and Grill
 303 E. Fayette Ave., 217/342-2035

Best Seafood
Rexroat's Distinctive Dining
 221 W. Jefferson Ave., 217/347-5831

Best Steaks
Rexroat's Distinctive Dining
 221 W. Jefferson Ave., 217/347-5831

ELGIN, IL

*[See also: Arlington Heights, Des Plaines, and
Schaumburg.]*

Best All-You-Can-Eat Buffet
Mack's Silver Pheasant
 6N543 Illinois Rt. 25, St. Charles, 847/888-8400

Best Breakfast
Paul's Family Restaurant
 1300 Lawrence Ave., 847/695-8687

Best Brewpub
Prairie Rock Brewing Company
 127 S. Grove Ave., 847/622-8888

Best Burgers
Leitner's Hamburgers
 992 Saint Charles St., 847/742-8380

Best Chinese Food
Green Jade Chinese Restaurant
 10 Tyler Creek Plz., 847/888-8010

Best Desserts
Hob Nob Restaurant
  4419 Northwest Hwy., Crystal Lake, 815/459-7234

Best Ice Cream/Yogurt
Al's Cafe and Creamery
  43 DuPage Ct., 847/742-1180
Colonial Ice Cream Restaurant
  600 S. McLean Blvd., 847/888-3939

Best Italian Food
Facaccia's Restaurant
  50 N. Spring St., 847/695-4495

Best Pizza
Geno Nottolini's
  1061 N. Liberty St., 847/888-4884
Gino's East
  1590 E. Main St., St. Charles, 630/513-1311

ELMHURST, IL

[See also: Chicago, Des Plaines, and Lombard.]

Best American Food
Dave and Buster's
  1155 N. Swift Rd., Addison, 630/543-5151
Zealous
  174 N. York St., 630/834-9300

Best Breakfast
Our Kitchen
  363 W. Lake St., 630/279-3738
Rainbow Restaurant
  233 N. York St., 630/833-0556

Best Burgers
Elmhurst Public House
  683 W. Saint Charles Rd., 630/834-8989
Silverado Grill
  447 Spring Rd., 630/833-1602

Best Chinese Food
Great China Restaurant
  737 North Ave., Glendale Heights, 630/858-1188
Red Dragon
  117 W. First St., 630/832-8326

Best Ice Cream/Yogurt
Fresco's Ice Cream Cafe
  143 N. York Rd., 630/834-3333
Yummy Armadillo Ice Cream Shop
  489A Spring Rd., 630/530-9866

Best Italian Food
Angelo's Pizza and Restaurant
  247 N. York St., 630/833-2400

Best Mexican Food
Cafe Las Bellas Artes
  112 W. Park Ave., 630/530-7725

Best Pizza
Two Brothers From Italy
 128 W. Park Ave., 630/833-0414

Best Steaks
Morton's of Chicago
 1 Westbrook Corporate Ctr., Westchester,
  708/562-7000
Steven's Steak House
 476 N. York St., 630/834-6611

EVANSTON, IL

*[See also: Chicago, Glenview, Des Plaines, Highland
Park, Northbrook, Skokie, and Wilmette.]*

Best American Food
Stir Fire Grill
 1729 Benson Ave., 847/328-2920

Best Barbecue/Ribs
Hecky's Barbecue
 1902 Green Bay Rd., 847/492-1182
Merle's Number 1 Barbecue
 1727 Benson Ave., 847/475-7766

Best Breakfast
Clarke's
 720 Clark St., 847/864-1610
La Peep
 827 Church St., 847/328-4880
Sarkis' Cafe
 2632 Gross Point Rd., 847/328-9703

Best Chinese Food
Central Restaurant
 1714 Central St., 847/475-8820
Lulu's
 626 Davis St., 847/869-4343
Mandarin House
 819 Noyes St., 847/869-4344
Pine Yard
 924 Church St., 847/475-4940
Szechuan Palace
 1627 Chicago Ave., 847/475-2500

Best Coffee/Coffeehouse
Bean Counter Cafe
 1932 Central St., 847/332-1116
Kafein Inc.
 1621 Chicago Ave., 847/491-1621
Unicorn Cafe
 1723 Sherman Ave., 847/332-2312

Best Delicatessen
Cafe Express
 615 Dempster St., 847/864-1868
Cafe Express South
 500 Main St., 847/328-7940

Jimmy John's
824 Clark St., 847/328-8858

Best Diner
Prairie Joe's
1921 Central St., 847/491-0391

Best Eclectic Menu
Trio Restaurant
1625 Hinman Ave., 847/733-8746

Best Family Restaurant
Gold Mine Restaurant
1901 Howard St., 847/332-2200

Best Greek/Mediterranean Food
Cross-Rhodes Restaurant
913A Chicago Ave., 847/475-4475

Best Italian Food
Dave's Italian Kitchen
906 Church St., 847/864-6000
Giordano's
500 Davis St., 847/475-5000
Symphony's
1945 Central St., 847/869-0818
Trattoria Diem
1571 Sherman Ave., 847/332-2330
Va Pensiero
1566 Oak Ave., 847/475-7779

Best Japanese Food
Daruma Japanese Restaurant
2901 Central St., 847/864-6633
Kuni's Japanese Restaurant
511 Main St., 847/328-2004

Best Mexican Food
Coyote Joe's Cafe
817 University Pl., 847/332-1700
Las Palmas
1642 Maple Ave., 847/328-2555
Salsa Borracha
750 Chicago Ave., 847/733-0308

Best Middle Eastern Food
Olive Mountain
814 Church St., 847/475-0380

Best Other Ethnic Food
Lucky Platter (Jamaican)
514 Main St., 847/869-4064

Best Pizza
Carmen's Pizzeria of Evanston
1012 Church St., 847/328-0031
Da Vinci's Pizza
724 Clark St., 847/328-9999
Trattoria Diem
1571 Sherman Ave., 847/332-2330

Best Seafood
Davis Street Fish Market
501 Davis St., 847/869-3474

Oceanique
505 Main St., 847/864-3435

Best Spanish Food
Barcelona Tapas
1615 Chicago Ave., 847/866-9900

Best Steaks
Pete Miller's Steak House
1557 Sherman Ave., 847/328-0399

Best Thai Food
Noodle Garden
1241 Chicago Ave., 847/332-2775
Thai Sookdee Restaurant
810 Church St., 847/866-8012

Best Vegetarian Food
Blind Faith Cafe
525 Dempster st., 847/328-6875

Best Wine Selection
Trio Restaurant
1625 Hinman Ave., 847/733-8746

FREEPORT, IL

Best Atmosphere
Cannova's Pizza
1101 W. Empire St., 815/233-0032

Best Chinese Food
Imperial Palace Chinese Restaurant
1735 S. Ihm Blvd., 815/233-5944

Best Delicatessen
Garden Deli
1264 W. Galena Ave., 815/235-3913

Best Family Restaurant
Spring Grove Family Restaurant
1521 S. West Ave., 815/233-3181

Best Italian Food
Cannova's Pizza
1101 W. Empire St., 815/233-0032
Mama Cimino's Pizzeria
1713 S. West Ave., 815/235-3545

Best Seafood
Club Esquire
1121 W. Empire St., 815/235-7404

Best Steaks
Club Esquire
1121 W. Empire St., 815/235-7404

GALESBURG, IL

Best Mexican Food
John's Taco Hide Out
1256 W. Berrien St., 309/343-5610

Best Restaurant in Town
Cerar's Barnstormer Restaurant
1201 W. Broadway, Monmouth, 309/734-9494

Grady's 2100 Club
   2100 Grand Ave., 309/342-6414
Jumer's Dining Room
   Jumer's Continental Inn, Soangataha Rd.,
      309/343-7151
Landmark Cafe and Creperie
   62 S. Seminary St., 309/343-5376

Best Steaks
The Steak House
   951 N. Henderson St., 309/343-9994

GLENVIEW, IL

[See also: Arlington Heights, Chicago, Des Plaines, Evanston, Highland Park, Northbrook, Skokie, Wilmette, and Wheeling.]

Best Beer Selection
Glenview House
   1843 Glenview Rd., 847/724-7999

Best Breakfast
Egg Harbor
   2853 Pfingsten Rd., 847/559-9905
Walker Brothers Pancake House
   1615 Waukegan Rd., 847/724-0220

Best Burgers
Hackney's
   1241 Harms Rd., 847/724-5577
   1514 E. Lake Ave., 847/724-7171

Best Italian Food
Lucci's Pasta Facce
   609 N. Milwaukee Ave., 847/729-2268

HIGHLAND PARK, IL

[See also: Arlington Heights, Des Plaines, Evanston, Glenview, Mundelein, Skokie, Waukegan, Wilmette, and Wheeling.]

Best American Food
South Gate Cafe
   655 Forest Ave., Lake Forest, 847/234-8800

Best Barbecue/Ribs
Nite and Gale
   346 Waukegan Ave., Highwood, 847/432-9744

Best Breakfast
Egg Harbor
   512 N. Western Ave., Lake Forest, 847/295-3449

Best Coffee/Coffeehouse
Carlos'
   429 Temple Ave., 847/432-0770

Best Delicatessen
Ada's Famous Restaurant and Deli
405 Lake Cook Rd., Deerfield, 847/564-4446
Harrie's Delicatessen and Restaurant
317 Park Ave., Glencoe, 847/835-1000

Best Family Restaurant
Ed Debevic's
660 Lake Cook Rd., Deerfield, 847/945-3242

Best French Food
Carlos'
429 Temple Ave., 847/432-0770
Froggy's French Cafe
306 Green Bay Rd., Highwood, 847/433-7080
Ravinia Bistro
581 Roger Williams Ave., 847/432-1033

Best Italian Food
Gabriel's
310 Green Bay Rd., Highwood, 847/433-0031

Best Mexican Food
Las Tres Hermanas
329 Waukegan Ave., Highwood, 847/432-0774

Best Seafood
Shaw's Seafood Grill
660 Lake Cook Rd., Deerfield, 847/948-1020

Best Steaks
Morton's of Chicago
1876 First St., 847/432-3484

Best Sunday Brunch
The English Room
Deerpath Inn, 255 E. Illinois Rd., Lake Forest,
847/234-2280

HINSDALE, IL

Best American Food
Zarrosta Grill
118 Oakbrook Ctr., 630/990-0177

Best Breakfast
Egg Harbor Cafe
777 N. York Rd., 630/920-1344

Best Business Lunch
Tuscany
1425 W. 22nd St., 630/990-1993

Best Family Restaurant
Maggiano's Little Italy
240 Oakbrook Ctr., 630/368-0300

Best Italian Food
Maggiano's Little Italy
240 Oakbrook Ctr., 630/368-0300

Best Pizza
California Pizza Kitchen
551 Oakbrook Ctr., 630/571-7800

Best Sandwiches
Corner Bakery
240 Oakbrook Ctr., 630/368-0505

JOLIET, IL

Best Burgers
Heroes and Legends Original Bar
2400 W. Jefferson St., 815/725-1113

Best Chinese Food
Dragon Light Restaurant
1809 N. Larkin Ave., 815/725-1006

Best Coffee/Coffeehouse
Bakers Square Restaurant
2211 W. Jefferson St., 815/729-1531

Best Diner
Steak and Shake Restaurant
2675 Plainfield Rd., 815/439-9145

Best Family Restaurant
Diamond's Family Restaurant
3000 Plainfield Rd., 815/436-1070

Best Fine Dining
Al's Steak House
1990 W. Jefferson St., 815/725-2388

Best Ice Cream/Yogurt
Creamy Delight
920 N. Broadway St., 815/723-5298

Best Italian Food
Earl's Cafe
1987 W. Jefferson St., 815/729-1971

Best Mexican Food
Los Primos
2219 W. Jefferson St., 815/744-5144

Best Pizza
Maurie's Table
2360 Glenwood Ave., 815/744-2619

Best Sandwiches
Merichka's
604 Theodore St., 815/723-9371

Best Seafood
Syl's Restaurant and Lounge
829 Moen Ave., 815/725-1977

Best Steaks
Syl's Restaurant and Lounge
829 Moen Ave., 815/725-1977

Best Vegetarian Food
Bakers Square Restaurant
2211 W. Jefferson St., 815/729-1531

LAKE ZURICH, IL

[See also: Arlington Heights, Mundelein, and Wheeling.]

Best Family Restaurant
Hackney's
  880 N. Old Rand Rd., 847/ 537-4141

Best French Food
D and J Bistro
  466 S. Rand Rd., 847/ 438-8001

Best German Food
Fritzl's
  900 Ravinia Terrace, 847/ 540-8844

Best Japanese Food
The Great Kahn
  139 S. Rand Rd., 847/ 550-9622

Best Mexican Food
Mexico Lindo
  35 N. Old Rand Rd., 847/438-3770

Best Other Ethnic Food
Julio's Latin Cafe (Latin American)
  95 S. Rand Rd., 847/ 438-3484

LIBERTYVILLE, IL

Best American Food
Buffalo Bar and Grill
  1760 N. Milwaukee Ave., 847/362-8202
Centre Lights Restaurant
  200 W. Golf Rd., 847/816-6100

Best Beer Selection
Mickey Finn's Brewery
  412 N. Milwaukee Ave., 847/362-6688

Best Casual Dining
Princess
  1290 S. Milwaukee Ave., 847/362-1290

Best Chinese Food
Hunan Palace Restaurant
  1318 S. Milwaukee Ave., 847/367-0338
Yan's Hunan Inn
  100 N. Milwaukee Ave., 847/816-6988

Best Delicatessen
Picnic Basket
  501 N. Milwaukee Ave., 847/367-8336

Best Desserts
Bakers Square Restaurant
  1195 S. Milwaukee Ave., 847/362-8550

Best Family Restaurant
Fodrak's
  327 S. Milwaukee Ave., 847/816-8111
Liberty Restaurant
  419 S. Milwaukee Ave., 847/362-9494

Towne Square Restaurant
508 N. Milwaukee Ave., 847/367-9144

Best Fine Dining
Tavern in the Town
519 N. Milwaukee Ave., 847/367-5755

Best Mexican Food
Rancho Grande
513 E. Park Ave., 847/816-1040

Best Southwestern Food
Austin's
481 Peterson Rd., 847/549-1972

Best Sunday Brunch
Hidden Cove
926 S. Milwaukee Ave., 847/367-0021

LOMBARD, IL

[See also: Chicago, Des Plaines, and Elmhurst.]

Best Barbecue/Ribs
Carson's Place for Ribs
400 E. Roosevelt Rd., 630/627-4300

Best Bistro
Bistro Banlieue
44 Yorktown Conveniece Ctr., 630/629-6560

Best Greek/Mediterranean Food
Greek Islands Restaurant West
300 E. 22nd St., 630/932-4545

Best Ice Cream/Yogurt
Bresler's
154 Yorktown Shopping Center, 630/495-4227

Best Italian Food
Lorica Ristorante
229 W. Saint Charles Rd., 630/495-0470

Best Japanese Food
Benihana of Tokyo
747 E. Butterfield Rd., 630/ 571-4440

Best Seafood
Casey's Restaurant
415 E. North Ave., 630/932-4777
Terrace Restaurant
315 E. North Ave., 630/ 629-9500

MOLINE, IL

Best Barbecue/Ribs
Jim's Rib Haven
1600 Tenth St., East Moline, 309/ 752-1240

Best Breakfast
Village Inn
560 Seventeenth Ave., 309/ 764-9222
2122 53rd St., 309/ 797-5556

Best Coffee/Coffeehouse
Peabody's Espresso
  1603 Fifth Ave., 309/764-5282

Best French Food
C'est Michele
  1514 Fifth Ave., 309/762-0585

Best Ice Cream/Yogurt
Whitey's Ice Cream
  2525 41st St., 309/ 762-4548

Best Mexican Food
Rudy's Tacos
  2414 16th St., 309/ 762-3293

Best Pizza
Happy Joe's Pizza and Ice Cream
  2041 Sixteenth St., 309/764-3388

Best Sandwiches
Lagomarcino's Confectionary
  1422 Fifth Ave., 309/764-9548

Best Seafood
Captain's Table
  4801 River Dr., 309/797-9222
Harold's on the Rock
  2600 N. Shore Dr., 309/764-4813
Sky Line Inn
  2621 Airport Rd., 309/764-9128

Best Steaks
Captain's Table
  4801 River Dr., 309/797-9222
Harold's on the Rock
  2600 N. Shore Dr., 309/764-4813
Sky Line Inn
  2621 Airport Rd., 309/764-9128

Best Vietnamese Food
Le Mekong Vietnamese Cuisine
  1606 Fifth Ave., 309/797-3709

MUNDELEIN, IL

[See also: Lake Zurich and Waukegan.]

Best American Food
Frank's for the Memories
  645 E. Hawley St., 847/949-9464
Gilmer Road House
  25792 N. Midlothian Rd., 847/566-5009

Best Bar
Annex Lounge
  U.S. Hwy. 45 at U.S. Hwy. 83, 847/566-0230

Best Barbecue/Ribs
Brothers Ribs
  1565 S. Lake St., 847/949-7427
Gale Street Inn-Diamond Lake
  906 Diamond Lake Rd., 847/566-1090

Best Chinese Food
Hong Kong Chop Suey
  428 N. Lake St., 847/949-9019
House of Joy
  310 Townline Rd., 847/949-6181
Mundelein Garden Restaurant
  510 E. Hawley St., 847/566-5020
Royal Cantonese Restaurant
  Rt. 45 at Rt. 83, 847/680-8888

Best Delicatessen
Brown Bag Deli
  22 E. Park St., 847/949-9123

Best Dinner
Crossroads of Ivanhoe
  20915 Park Ave., 847/949-9009
Tops Restaurant
  10 E. Maple Ave., 847/949-6666

Best Eclectic Menu
Katz and Dogs
  1452 S. Butterfield Rd., 847/816-8913

Best Lunch
Villiage Square
  115 N. Seymour Ave., 847/949-5350

Best Mexican Food
El Barrio Restaurant and Lounge
  1122 Diamond Lake Rd., 847/566-0475
El Norte Tacos
  822 S. Lake St., 847/949-9345
El Salvador Restaurant
  141A N. Seymour Ave., 847/949-9421
Terry's Mexican Restaurant
  325 N. Seymour Ave., 847/566-9530

Best Pizza
Bill's Pizza and Pub
  624 S. Lake St., 847/566-6508
Emil's Pizza
  604 N. Lake St., 847/566-8879
Journey's End
  2077 Rte. 45, 847/566-4400
Papa Pia's Pizzaria
  1408 S. Butterfield Rd., 847/566-2345
Sonny's
  46 Oak Creek Plaza, 847/566-3333
The Silo
  625 Rockland Rd., Lake Bluff, 847/234-6660

Best Seafood
Dover Straits
  890 E. U.S. Hwy. 45, 847/949-1550
Family Fishery
  412 N. Lake St., 847/566-2580

Best Southwestern Food
Little Big Horn
  2045 W. Maple Ave., 847/566-1134

Best Vegetarian Food
Rainbow Restaurant
  900 S. Lake St., 847/566-1450

NAPERVILLE, IL

[See also: Aurora and Lombard.]

Best Breakfast
Egg Harbor
  221 Town Sq., Wheaton, 630/510-1344
Grandma Sally's Waffle House
  450 E. Ogden Ave., 630/355-7771
Omega Restaurant
  1300 Ogden Ave., Downers Grove, 630/963-0300

Best Burgers
The Lantern
  8 W. Chicago Ave., 630/355-7099

Best Chinese Food
Jin Mandarin Restaurant
  790 Royal St. George Dr., 630/416-1188
New China Chef Restaurant
  614 E. Ogden Ave., 630/717-1199

Best Coffee/Coffeehouse
Green Mountain Coffee Roasters
  131 W. Jefferson Ave., 630/355-6444
Starbucks Coffee
  42 W. Jefferson Ave., 630/778-8614
  1163 E. Ogden Ave., 630/355-5884

Best Family Restaurant
Steven's Restaurant
  2001 63rd St., Downers Grove, 630/810-9812

Best Fine Dining
Washington Square Restaurant
  218 S. Washington St., 630/357-3462

Best French Food
Montparnasse Restaurant
  200 E. Fifth Ave., 630/961-8203

Best Ice Cream/Yogurt
Colonial Ice Cream
  8 W. Gartner Rd., 630/420-7722

Best Italian Food
Cafe Buonaro's
  300 E. Fifth Ave., 630/717-0006
Sorella Di Francesca
  18 W. Jefferson Ave., 630/961-2706

Best Late-Night Food
Omega Restaurant
  1300 W. Ogden Ave., Downers Grove, 630/963-0300

Best Mexican Food
Potter's Place
  29 W. Jefferson Ave., 630/355-9165

Best Other Ethnic Food
Tahiti Terrace Restaurant (Polynesian)
  1224 W. Ogden Ave., 630/355-7420

Best Pizza
Aurelio's Pizza
  1002 Warren Ave., Downers Grove, 630/810-0097
Bacino's
  1504 N. Naper Blvd., 630/505-0600
Lou Malnati's Pizzeria
  131 W. Jefferson Ave., 630/717-0700
Papa Passero's
  6326 S. Cass Ave., Westmont, 630/963-7660

Best Sandwiches
Rocco's Pizza
  192 W. Gartner Ave., 630/369-8899
Teddy's Red Hots
  6310 Main St., Downers Grove, 630/968-8444

Best Seafood
Chinn's 34th Street Restaurant
  3011 W. Ogden Ave., Lisle, 630/637-1777

Best Spanish Food
Emilio's Meson Sabika
  1025 Aurora Ave., 630/983-3000

Best Sunday Brunch
Allgauer's
  Hilton Hotel, 3003 Corporate West Dr., Lisle,
  630/505-0900

NORTHBROOK, IL

[See also: Arlington Heights, Des Plaines, Evanston, Glenview, Highland Park, Skokie, Wilmette, and Wheeling.]

Best American Food
Ceiling Zero
  500 Anthony Trail, 847/272-8111
Garden Grill Restaurant
  933 Skokie Blvd., 847.498-6500
Woody's Roadhouse
  1775 Lake Cook Rd., 847/564-8877

Best Delicatessen
Max and Benny's Restaurant
  461 Waukegan Rd., 847/272-9490

Best Eclectic Menu
Next Door Restaurant
  250 Skokie Blvd., 847/272-1491

Best Italian Food
Francesco's Hole in the Wall
  254 Skokie Blvd., 847/272-0155
Stefani's
  601 Skokie Blvd., 847/564-3950
Trattoria Oliverii
  1358 Shermer Rd., 847/559-8785

Best Japanese Food
Ron of Japan
 633 Skokie Blvd., 847/564-9450

Best Pizza
Edwardo's Natural Pizza
 240 Skokie Blvd., 847/272-5222

Best Place to Take the Kids
Barnaby's
 960 Skokie Blvd., 847/498-3900

Best Steaks
The Prime Minister
 3355 Milwaukee Ave., 847/296-4423

Best Sunday Brunch
Allgauer's Fireside Restaurant
 2855 N. Milwaukee Ave., 847/480-7500

Best Thai Food
Jasmine
 242 Skokie Blvd., 847/205-1414

I

OAK LAWN, IL

[See also: Chicago and Chicago Heights.]

Best American Food
Michael A's
 10033 Ridgeland Ave., 708/422-3665
Oak Lawn Restaurant
 5769 W. 95th St., 708/425-4949

Best Bar
Petey's Bungalow Lounge
 4401 W. 95th St., 708/424-8210

Best Barbecue/Ribs
Pit Boss Rib House
 9430 S. Roberts Rd., 708/599-7576

Best Breakfast
Omelette House
 4002 W. 111th St., 708/229-1235

Best Burgers
Grill Time
 9634 S. Pulaski Rd., 708/422-6732
Hackney's
 123rd at Rte. 45, Palos Park, 708/448-8300
Schoop's Hamburgers
 7847 W. 95th St., Hickory Hills, 708/598-9993
Top-Notch Beefburgers West
 4720 W. 95th St., 708/422-5544

Best Chinese Food
Chef's Chop Suey
 10427 S. Cicero Ave., 708/229-2889
China Wok Restaurant
 8821 Ridgeland Ave., 708/598-3080
Great Wall Chinese Restaurant
 9304 S. Roberts Rd., Hickory Hills, 708/599-6260

Ho Sai Gai Chinese Chop Suey
  10832 S. Cicero Ave., 708/425-1262
Imperial Palace
  6246 W. 95th St., 708/430-0090
Jade Palace Chop Suey
  8625 W. 95th St., Hickory Hills, 708/430-5075
Jedi's Garden Restaurant
  9266 S. Cicero Ave., 708/499-4545
Wing Wan Express
  9231 S. Cicero Ave., 708/499-2208
MG Chop Suey
  8014 S. Cicero Ave., Burbank, 708/229-1192

Best Continental Food
Jalisco Restaurant
  6547 W. 79th St., Burbank, 708/430-7903
Whitney's Bar and Grille
  9333 S. Cicero Ave., 708/229-8888

Best Diner
Suzy's Grill and Ice Cream
  10315 Central Ave., 708/636-4466

Best Dinner
Alexander's
  9940 Southwest Hwy., 708/422-4070
Paragon Restaurant
  4510 W. 95th St., 708/423-9050

Best French Food
Les Brother's Restaurant
  7730 W. 95th St., Hickory Hills, 708/233-0333

Best Greek/Mediterranean Food
Mr. Gyro's
  9229 S. Cicero Ave., 708/499-3883

Best Homestyle Food
Oak Ridge Restaurant
  6616 W. 95th St., 708/430-4544

Best Italian Food
Brown's Chicken and Pasta
  4740 W. 111th St., 708/424-9280
Giordano's
  9630 Southwest Hwy., 708/499-3232
Rickette's Italian Ristorante
  5172 W. 95th St., 708/499-9900
Vincenzo's Restaurante Italiano
  5819 W. 87th St., 708/425-1200
Volante Restaurant
  4750 W. 103rd St., 708/425-8772

Best Mexican Food
Al-Gallo De'Oro
  10846 S. Cicero Ave., 708/422-4040
Jalepeno's
  9600 S. Pulaski Rd., 708/423-2255
Senor Pancho
  10812 S. Cicero Ave., 708/422-5290

Best Pizza
Bacino's
15256 S. La Grange Rd., Orland Park,
708/403-3535
Beggars Pizza
10240 Central Ave., 708/499-0505
Fox's Oak Lawn Restaurant
9240 S. Cicero Ave., 708/499-2233
Palmero's Italian Cuisine
4849 W. 95th St., 708/425-6262
Papa Joe's Restaurant
10745 S. Cicero Ave., 708/636-5030
Pudgy's Pizza
5651 W. 87th St., 708/425-1060

Best Romantic Dining
The Pump Room
6908 W. 111th St., Worth, 708/448-8542

Best Sandwiches
All Star Submarines
10806 S. Cicero Ave., 708/346-0046

Best Seafood
Wagner Seafood
9626 S. Pulaski Rd., 708/636-2646

Best Sports Bar
11th Frame
4730 W. 103rd St., 708/857-7343

Best Steaks
Frankie's Beef House
5707 W. 95th St., 708/423-4444
Ken's Guest House
9848 Southwest Hwy., 708/422-4014
Louie's Chop House
4642 W. 103rd St., 708/425-6530

Best Wine Selection
Senese's Winery Restaurant
10345 S. Central Ave., 708/499-2969

PEKIN, IL

Best American Food
Chateau on the Lake
901 Chateau Dr., 309/382-3414

Best Bar
Yesterday's Bar and Grill
363 Court St., 309/346-3255

Best Burgers
Ernie's Family Restaurant
613 Derby St., 309/353-8109
Steak N Shake
3205 Court St., 309/347-5191

Best Mexican Food
Margarita's
121 S. Second St., 309/353-8226

Best Sandwiches
Larkin's Home Bakery
 1526 N. Eighth St., 309/353-2414

Best Steaks
Normandy Club
 1703 S. Second St., 309/346-3803
The Summit
 1620 Summit Dr., 309/347-4154

PEORIA, IL

Best American Food
Carnegie's
 Hotel Pere Marquette, 501 Main St., 309/637-6500
River Station
 212 SW Constitution Ave., 309/676-7100
Stephanie's Restaurant
 1825 N. Knoxville Ave., 309/682-7300

Best Atmosphere
Jumer's Castle Lodge
 117 N. Western Ave., 309/673-8181

Best Bar
King's Restaurant
 7327 N. Galena Rd., 309/691-3046

Best Barbecue/Ribs
Big John's North
 7805 N. University St., 309/693-7800

Best Beer Selection
Hofbrau Restaurant
 2210 NE Jefferson Ave., 309/686-9739

Best Breakfast
Doc's Mt. Hawley Inn
 8412 N. Knoxville Ave., 309/691-3122
Joe's International Deli
 425 Hamilton Blvd., 309/637-3354

Best Cajun/Creole Food
Alligator Bar and Grill
 308 Walnut St., 309/673-5244

Best Chinese Food
China Gate Express
 4100 W. Willow Knolls Dr., 309/692-6503

Best Coffee/Coffeehouse
Mocha Joe's Beanery
 4700 N. University St., 309/689-9800

Best Diner
Grill on Fulton
 456 Fulton St., 309/674-6870

Best German Food
Hofbrau Restaurant
 2210 NE Jefferson Ave., 309/686-9739

Best Italian Food
Agatucci's Restaurant
 2607 N. University St., 309/688-8200

Avanti's Italian Restaurant
  4711 N. Rockwood Dr., 309/688-6565
  1301 W. Main St., 309/674-4923
Capponi's Restaurant
  302 N. Main St., Toluca, 815/452-2343
Mona's Italian Foods
  202 N. Main St., Toluca, 815/452-2303
Paparazzi
  4315 N. Voss St., Peoria Heights, 309/682-5205
Rizzi's Ristorante
  4613 N. Sheridan Rd., Peoria Heights,
    309/689-0025

Best Other Ethnic Food
Haddad's (Lebanese)
  1024 W. Main St., 309/672-5339

Best Steaks
Alexander's Steakhouse
  100 Alexander Ave., 309/688-0404
Jim's Downtown Steak House
  110 SW Jefferson Ave., 309/673-5300
Lariat Club
  2232 W. Glen Ave., 309/691-4731
Sky Harbor Steak House
  2017 Airport Rd., 309/697-9598

Best Sunday Brunch
O'Leary's
  3300 W. Willow Knolls Dr., 309/692-9030

QUINCY, IL

Best Bar
Abbey
  1736 Spring St., 217/228-8868
Kelly's Tavern
  2902 Broadway, 217/222-5579

Best Barbecue/Ribs
Bill's Bar-B-Q
  207 N 36th St., 217/223-2233
Patio
  133 S. Fourth St., 217/222-1281

Best Breakfast
Sprout's Inn
  2814 N. Twelfth St., 217/223-6294
Village Inn
  200 N. 36th St., 217/228-1817

Best Burgers
Artie's Scoreboard
  234 S. Eighth St., 217/222-3793
Lakeview Restaurant and Patio
  4300 Broadway, 217/222-9661

Best Coffee/Coffeehouse
CJ's Coffee Shoppee
  234 N. Twelfth St., 217/223-3333

Best Delicatessen
Deli 1
  129 S. Fourth St., 217/224-3282

Best Desserts
Mike's Place
  Hwy. 104N, Liberty, 217/645-3399

Best Homestyle Food
Stipp's Restaurant
  1130 S. Sixth St., 217/223-1212

Best Ice Cream/Yogurt
Deter's Dairy Farms
  4801 State St., 217/223-5484

Best Mexican Food
Gem City Pizzeria
  1801 State St., 217/228-0550
Santino's Mexican Restaurant
  512 Hampshire St., 217/228-8777

Best Pizza
Tower of Pizza
  1221 Broadway, 217/224-6030

Best Sandwiches
Maid Rite
  507 N. Twelfth St., 217/222-9767
  3120 Broadway, 217/224-5622
Plaza
  900 N. Twelfth St., 217/222-0690
River House
  238 N. Front St., 217/224-6888

Best Seafood
Tony's Old Place
  810 Hampshire St., 217/224-4800

Best Steaks
Lakeview Restaurant and Patio
  4300 Broadway, 217/222-9661
Patio
  133 S. Fourth St., 217/222-1281

ROBINSON, IL

Best Barbecue/Ribs
Poor Little Mikey's
  508 S. Cross St., 618/546-5212

Best Breakfast
Judy's Cafe
  108 E. Main St., 618/544-8864

Best Chinese Food
Yen Ching Mandarin Restaurant
  507 N. Jackson St., 618/546-1307

Best Desserts
Studio Cafe
  206 N. Cross St., 618/544-3732

Best Italian Food
Joe's Italian Food and Pizza
  1111 E. Main St., 618/544-8212

ROCK ISLAND, IL

Best Barbecue/Ribs
Jim's Rib Haven
531 24th Ave., 309/786-8084
RJ Boar's
4110 Blackhawk Rd., 309/ 786-0667

Best Breakfast
14th Avenue Waffle Shop
4128 Fourteenth Ave., 309/788-4181
Bixby's Bagels
140 Eighteenth St., 309/788-6610

Best Brewpub
Blue Cat Brew Pub
113 Eighteenth Ave., 309/788-8247

Best Ice Cream/Yogurt
Whitey's Ice Cream
2516 Eighteenth Ave., 309/788-5948

Best Pizza
Charlie's Pizza
1407 30th St., 309/786-0911
Original Huckleberry's Pizza
223 Eighteenth Ave., 309/786-1122

Best Sandwiches
Hunter's Club
2107 Fourth Ave., 309/786-9880

Best Soul Food
Aunt Bea's Cafe
2429 Ninth St., 309/793-0905

Best Steaks
O'Melia's Supper Club
2900 Blackhawk Rd., 309/788-5635

Best View While Dining
Skarfi's
4619 34th St., 309/793-7700

ROCKFORD, IL

Best American Food
Track Inn
301 E. Pacific Ave., Davis Junction, 815/645-2381

Best Atmosphere
Beef-A-Roo
6116 N. Second St., Loves Park, 815/633-6585
6380 E. Riverside Blvd., Loves Park, 815/877-5610

Best Bar
The Olympic Tavern
2327 N. Main St., 815/962-8758

Best Barbecue/Ribs
Box's Bar-B-Q
815 Marchesano Dr., 815/962-9629

Best Breakfast
Stockholm Inn
2420 Charles St., 815/397-3534

Best Burgers
Mary's Kitchen
 2515 S. Main St., 815/987-4509

Best Coffee/Coffeehouse
Mary's Market
 4431 E. State St., 815/397-7291
 1659 N. Alpine Rd., 815/394-0765

Best Diner
The Huddle
 1100 N. State St., Belvidere, 815/544-9214

Best Family Restaurant
Rummel's Barn
 4058 S. Spielman Rd., Seward, 815/247-8755

Best Fine Dining
Lucerne's Fondue and Spirits
 845 N. Church St., 815/968-2665

Best French Food
Cafe Patou
 3929 Broadway, 815/227-4100

Best Italian Food
Lino's
 5611 E. State St., 815/397-2077

Best Pizza
Capri Restaurant and Pizza
 313 E. State St., 815/965-6341
Franchesco's
 2404 S. Perryville Rd., 815/332-4992
Giordano's Restaurant and Pizzeria
 333 N. Mulford Rd., 815/398-5700
Sam's Pizza
 2134 Charles St., 815/398-5952

Best Seafood
Cliffbreaker's
 700 W. Riverside Blvd., 815/282-3033
Michael's
 601 N. Perryville Rd., 815/226-8286

Best Steaks
Michael's
 601 N. Perryville Rd., 815/226-8286
Tumbleweed Southwest Mesquite Grill and Bar
 5494 E. State St., 815/227-0192

Best Sunday Brunch
Cliffbreaker's
 700 W. Riverside Blvd., 815/282-3033

SCHAUMBURG, IL

[See also: Arlington Heights and Des Plaines.]

Best Burgers
Assembly
 2570 Hassell Rd., 847/843-3993

Best Family Restaurant
Rainforest Cafe
 Woodfield Mall, Ste. D121, 847/619-1900

Best Japanese Food
Daruma Japanese Restaurant
 1823 W. Golf Rd., 847/310-8877

Best Place to Take the Kids
Barnaby's
 134 W. Golf Rd., 847/882-3220

SKOKIE, IL

[See also: Chicago, Des Plaines, Evanston, Glenview, Highland Park, Northbrook, and Wilmettte.]

Best Barbecue/Ribs
Carson's Place for Ribs
 8617 Niles Center Rd., 847/275-3499

Best Breakfast
Omega Restaurant
 9100 W. Golf Rd., Niles, 847/296-7777

Best Delicatessen
Bagel Restaurant and Deli
 50 Old Orchard Shopping Ctr., 847/677-0100
Barnum and Bagel
 4700 Dempster St., 847/676-4466

Best German Food
Black Forest Chalet
 8840 Waukegan Rd., Morton Grove, 847/965-6830

Best Greek/Mediterranean Food
Mykonos
 8660 W. Golf Rd., Niles, 847/296-6777

Best Mexican Food
Mexico Lindo
 8990 N. Milwaukee Ave., Niles, 847/296-2540

Best Place to Take the Kids
Barnaby's
 7950 N. Caldwell Ave., Niles, 847/967-8600

Best Salad/Salad Bar
Sasha's Cafe
 9599 Skokie Blvd., 847/675-3300

Best Seafood
Don's Fishmarket
 9335 Skokie Blvd., 847/677-3424

Best Vegetarian Food
Slice of Life
 4120 Dempster St., 847/674-2021

SPRINGFIELD, IL

Best Barbecue/Ribs
Popeye's
 1100 S. Martin Luther King Jr., 217/522-0386

Best Desserts
George Warburton's Food and Drink
  Rte. 3, Petersburg, 217/632-7878

Best Italian Food
Saputo's
  801 E. Monroe St., 217/544-2523

Best Late-Night Food
Mr. Ted's Grill
  926 W. Jefferson St., 217/525-8368

Best Pizza
Joe's Italian Pizza
  1552 W. Jefferson St., 217/787-6005

Best Thai Food
Magic Kitchen Thai Restaurant
  4112 N. Peoria Rd., 217/525-2230

VERNON HILLS, IL

Best Bistro
Cafe Pyrenees
  701 Milwaukee Ave., Ste. 316, 847/918-8850

Best Chinese Food
The Silk Mandarin
  4 E. Phillip Rd., 847/680-1760

Best Italian Food
Gilardi's Restaurant
  23397 U.S. Hwy. 45N, 847/634-1811

Best Japanese Food
Tsukasa of Tokyo
  700 Milwaukee Ave., 847/816-8770

WATERLOO, IL

Best Bar
Wartburg Inn
  5831 Maeystown Rd., 618/939-8981

Best Breakfast
Hoefft's Village Inn
  1026 Main St., Maeystown, 618/458-6425

Best Coffee/Coffeehouse
Courthouse Espresso Cafe
  219 S. Main St., 618/939-5995

Best Family Restaurant
Dreamland Palace
  3043 State Rte. 156, 618/939-9922
Lincoln Trail Restaurant
  108 N. Market St., 618/939-7310

Best Lunch
JV's
  117 N. Main St., 618/939-7127

WAUKEGAN, IL

[See also: Mundelein and Highland Park.]

Best Family Restaurant
Rainforest Cafe
  6170 Grand Ave., Gurnee, 847/855-7800

Best Mexican Food
Pepe's Mexican Restaurant
  760 N. Green Bay Rd., 847/244-7887

Best Romantic Dining
Parkway Restaurant
  3035 Belvidere Rd., 847/336-0222

WHEELING, IL

[See also: Arlington Heights, Des Plaines, Glenview, Highland Park, and Northbrook.]

Best Burgers
Hackney's
  241 Milwaukee Ave., 847/537-2100

Best Business Lunch
Harry Caray's
  933 N. Milwaukee Ave., 847/537-2827

Best French Food
Le Francais
  269 S. Milwaukee Ave., 847/541-7470

Best German Food
Hans' Bavarian Lodge
  931 N. Milwaukee Ave., 847/537-4141

Best Salad/Salad Bar
Don Roth's
  612 N. Milwaukee Ave., 847/537-5800

Best Seafood
Bob Chinn's Crab House
  393 S. Milwaukee Ave., 847/520-3633

Best Steaks
The Weber Grill Restaurant
  920 N. Milwaukee Ave., 847/215-0996

WILMETTE, IL

[See also: Chicago, Des Plaines, Evanston, Glenview, Highland Park, Northbrook, and Skokie.]

Best Breakfast
Walker Brothers
  153 Green Bay Rd., 847/251-6000

Best Burgers
Old Ouilmette Depot
  1139 Wilmette Ave., 847/256-0771

Best Chinese Food
Tsing Tao Mandarin Chinese Restaurant
  537 Green Bay Rd., 847/251-7760

Best Coffee/Coffeehouse
Marie's Restaurant
  415 Fourth St., 847/251-1636
Ridgeview Restaurant
  827 Ridge Rd., 847/251-2770

Best French Food
Betise
  1515 Sheridan Rd., 847/853-1711

Best Ice Cream/Yogurt
Homer's Ice Cream
  1237 Green Bay Rd., 847/251-0477

Best Italian Food
Convito Italiano
  1515 Sheridan Rd., 847/251-3654

Best Japanese Food
Akai Hana
  3223 Lake Ave., 847/251-0384

Best Sandwiches
A La Carte
  111 Green Bay Rd., 847/256-4102
Butt'ry
  1137 Greenleaf Ave., 847/256-1133
C.J. Arthur's
  1168 Wilmette Ave., 847/256-8870

Indiana

ANDERSON, IN

Best Bar
Elliott's Downtown
709 Main St., 765/640-0150

Best Barbecue/Ribs
Damon's the Place for Ribs
840 S. State Rd. 9, 765/649-8742

Best Burgers
Madewell Food and Ice Cream
2326 Columbus Ave., 765/649-8918

Best Chinese Food
Magic Wok
817 S. State Rd. 9, 765/643-7000

Best Italian Food
Fazoli's
4410 S. Scatterfield Rd., 765/622-9163

Best Late-Night Food
Steak and Shake Restaurant
5825 S. Scatterfield Rd., 765/622-9367

Best Mexican Food
Tio's Restaurant
2902 Broadway St., 765/649-5655

Best Middle Eastern Food
Nile Restaurant
723 E. Eighth St., 765/640-9028

BLOOMINGTON, IN

Best Bar
Nick's English Hut
423 E. Kirkwood Ave., 812/332-4040

Second Story Nightclub
201 S. College Ave., 812/336-2582
The Irish Lion
212 W. Kirkwood Ave., 812/336-9076

Best Barbecue/Ribs
Damon's Clubhouse
216 S. College Ave., 812/339-4347

Best Burgers
Hinkle's Hamburgers
206 S. Adams St., 812/339-3335
Mustard's
300 College Mall Rd., Ste. 511, 812/334-3344
Opie Taylor's Burger Works
212 N. Walnut St., 812/333-7287
The Trojan Horse
100 E. Kirkwood Ave., 812/332-1101

Best Business Lunch
Malibu Grill
106 N. Walnut St., 812/332-4334

Best Casual Dining
White River Cafe and Coffee
910 N. College Ave., 812/330-1212

Best Chinese Food
Dragon Chinese Restaurant
3261 W. Third St., 812/332-6610
214 W. Kirkwood Ave., 812/336-8877
Leofoo Chinese Cuisine
110 N. Walnut St., 813/333-4474
Marc Pie's China Gate
3020 E. Third St., 812/323-1688
Phoenix Dumpling
307 E. Third St., 812/333-5262
The Wok
430 E. Kirkwood Ave., Ste. 2, 812/339-4296
Yen Cheng Chinese Restaurant
1143 S. College Mall Rd., 812/334-1334

Best Coffee/Coffeehouse
Runcible Spoon Cafe and Restaurant
412 E. Sixth St., 812/334-3997
The Daily Grind and Daily Bread
430 E. Kirkwood Ave., Ste. 4, 812/339-6038
919 S. College Mall Rd., 812/339-2253

Best Desserts
Encore Cafe
316 W. Sixth St., 812/333-7312
Tina's Carryout and Cuisine
309 E. Third St., 812/332-0464

Best Family Restaurant
Encore Cafe
316 W. Sixth St., 812/333-7312

Best Fine Dining
Michael's Uptown Cafe and Bakery
102 E. Kirkwood Ave., 812/339-0900

Best French Food
Le Petit Cafe
308 W. Sixth St., 812/334-9747

Best Homestyle Food
Cloverleaf Family Restaurant`
2500 W. Third St., 812/334-1077
Gib and Denzil's Restaurant
2130 S. Walnut St., 812/332-7810
Ladyman's Cafe
122 E. Kirkwood Ave., 812/336-5557

Best Ice Cream/Yogurt
White Mountain Ice Creamery
107 N. Dunn St., 812/333-8975

Best Inexpensive Meal
Cloverleaf Family Restaurant
2500 W. Third St., 812/334-1077
Laughing Planet
322 E. Kirkwood Ave., 812/323-2233

Best Italian Food
Grisanti's Casual Italian
850 E. Auto Mall Rd., 813/339-9391
Puccini's International Restaurant
420 E. Fourth St., 812/333-5522

Best Mexican Food
La Charreada
1720 N. Walnut St., 812/332-2343

Best Other Ethnic Food
Snow Lion (Tibetan)
113 S. Grant St., 812/336-0835

Best Outdoor Dining
Bakehouse
125 N. College Ave., 812/331-6029

Best Pizza
Lennie's Restaurant
1795 E. Tenth St., 812/323-2112
Monroe County Pizza Department
3890 W. Third St., 812/331-2345
Mother Bear's Pizza
1402 N. Walnut St., 812/332-6812
1428 E. Third St., 812/332-4495
Rockit's Famous Pizza
222 N. Walnut St., 812/336-7625

Best Romantic Dining
Chapman's Restaurant and Lounge
300 S. State Rd. 446, 812/337-9999

Best Sandwiches
Dagwood's Deli-Sub Shop
116A S. Indiana Ave., 812/333-3000
Loaf and Ladle
104 W. Sixth St., 812/334-3500
Macri's Deli
1221 S. College Mall Rd., 812/333-0606
The Village Deli
409 E. Kirkwood Ave., 812/336-2303

Best Seafood
Fisherman's Dock
    4501 E. Third St., 812/336-3474
Mikado Japanese Restaurant
    895 S. College Mall Rd., 812/333-1950

Best Steaks
Colorado Steakhouse
    1800 College Ave., 812/339-9979
Crazy Horse Food and Beverage
    214 W. Kirkwood Ave., 812/336-8877
Little Zagreb
    223 W. Sixth St., 812/332-0694

Best Tea Room
Casablanca
    402 E. Fourth St., 812/335-9094

Best Thai Food
Siam House
    430 E. Fourth St., 812/331-1233

Best Vegetarian Food
Ekimae Japanese Restaurant
    825 N. Walnut St., 812/334-1661
Siam House
    430 E. Fourth St., 812/331-1233
Wild Beet
    123A S. Walnut St., 812/323-3000

COLUMBUS, IN

Best Burgers
Lucas Brothers Sandwich Shop
    1842 Indiana Ave., 812/376-7010

Best Casual Dining
Grindstone Charley's
    2607 Central Ave., 812/372-2532

Best Eclectic Menu
Zaharako's Confectionery
    329 Washington St., 812/379-9329

Best Fine Dining
Weinantz Food and Spirits
    3450 W. Jonathan Moore Pike, 812/379-2323

Best Pizza
Noble Roman's
    2995 N. National Rd., 812/376-9438
    4140 W. Jonathan Moore Pike, 812/342-4477

Best Seafood
Peter's Bay Restaurant
    310 Commons Mall, 812/372-2270

Best Southwestern Food
La Bomba's Tex-Mexican Restaurant
    2326 25th St., 812/379-1234

Best Steaks
Ribeye Steak and Ribs
    2506 25th St., 812/376-6410
Sirloin Stockade
    3114 N. National Rd., 812/378-3867

CROWN POINT, IN

Best Breakfast
Schoop's Hamburgers
1124 N. Main St., 219/663-2288
Twelve Islands
114 S. Main St., Ste. 1, 219/663-5070

Best Chinese Food
Twin Happiness Chinese Restaurant
1188 N. Main St., 219/663-4433

Best Delicatessen
Pap's Deli
119 W. Joliet St., 219/663-9745

Best Family Restaurant
Bronko's
1244 N. Main St., 219/662-0145
Twelve Islands
114 S. Main St., Ste. 1, 219/663-5070

Best Homestyle Food
Crown Kitchen
111 N. Main St., 219/663-7466

Best Mexican Food
Fiesta Mexico
1 N. Court St., 219/663-5890

Best Pizza
Chicago's Restaurant and Lounge
109 W. Joliet St., 219/663-6040

Best Restaurant Meal Value
Truffles
400 N. Main St., 219/662-7764

Best Seafood
Chicago's Restaurant and Lounge
109 W. Joliet St., 219/663-6040

Best Steaks
Chicago's Restaurant and Lounge
109 W. Joliet St., 219/663-6040

Best Sunday Brunch
Bon Appetit
302 S. Main St., 219/663-6363

EVANSVILLE, IN

Best American Food
Greeley's
100 NW Second St., 812/425-5553
Jungle Mornings Coffee Company
416 Main St., 812/425-5282

Best Bar
Bockelman's Restaurant
4001 Big Cynthiana Rd., 812/963-9017
Jacob's Pub and Restaurant
4428 N. First Ave., 812/423-0050

Best Barbecue/Ribs
Shyler's Bar-B-Q
405 S. Green River Rd., 812/476-4599

Best Breakfast
Merry-Go-Round Restaurant
  5115 Monroe Ave., 812/479-6388
  2101 Hwy. 41N, 812/423-6388
Pie Pan
  905 N. Park Dr., 812/425-2261

Best Business Lunch
TK Pepper's Restaurant
  217 Main St., 812/422-2555

Best Chinese Food
Canton Inn Restaurant
  915 N. Park Dr., 812/428-6611
Shing-Lee Chinese Restaurant
  215 Main St., 812/464-2769

Best Delicatessen
Bits and Bytes
  216 NW Fourth St., 812/423-5113

Best Family Restaurant
Bockelman's Restaurant
  4001 Big Cynthiana Rd., 812/963-9017
Wolf's Bar-B-Q Restaurant
  6600 N. First Ave., 812/424-8891
  1414 E. Columbia St., 812/423-3599

Best Homestyle Food
Jojo's Family Restaurant
  3901 Hwy. 41N, 812/425-1486

Best Italian Food
Crazy Tomato Italian
  500 S. Green River Rd., 812/474-9977

Best Lunch
Emge's Deli in the Alley
  206 Main St., 812/422-3026

Best Mexican Food
Los Bravos Mexican Restaurant
  900 W. Buena Vista Rd., 812/424-4101
  640 S. Green River Rd., 812/474-9078

Best Steaks
Haub Steak House
  Main St., Haubstadt, 812/768-6462
The Sunset Dining Room
  Bernie Little's Riverhouse Hotel,
    20 Walnut St., 812/425-6500

FT. WAYNE, IN

Best All-You-Can-Eat Buffet
Back 40 Junction
  1011 N. Thirteenth St., Decatur, 219/724-3355

Best Bar
Damon's Restaurant
  4820 N. Clinton St., 219/471-2296
Park Place Grill
  200 E. Main St., 219/420-7275
Triangle Park
  3010 Trier Rd., 219/482-4342

Best Breakfast
Ice Cream Shoppe
    3235 N. Anthony Blvd., 219/483-3213
    211 E. Tillman Rd., 219/447-2121
Willie's Family Restaurant
    6342 Saint Joe Rd., 219/485-3144

Best Burgers
Flanagan's Restaurant and Pub
    6525 Covington Rd., 219/432-6666
Powers Hamburger Shop
    1904 Maumee Ave., 219/422-3227
    1402 S. Harrison St., 219/422-6620

Best Casual Dining
Canterbury House
    3232 Saint Joe Circle, 219/485-7640
Don Hall's Factory Restaurant
    5811 Coldwater Rd., 219/484-8693
Munchie Emporium
    1109 Taylor St., 219/424-6883

Best Chinese Food
House of Hunan
    5626 Coldwater Rd., 219/482-9402
Mandarin
    1026 E. Dupont Rd., 219/497-0353
    5978 Stellhorn Rd., 219/485-9175

Best Delicatessen
Bagel Station
    3009 E. State Blvd., 219/471-2272

Best Desserts
Epicurean Delights
    5958 W. Jefferson Blvd., 219/436-7640

Best Diner
Cindy's Diner
    830 S. Harrison St., 219/422-1957

Best Eclectic Menu
Dash-In Cafe
    817 S. Calhoun St., 219/423-3595

Best Family Restaurant
Don Hall's Old Gas House
    305 E. Superior St., 219/426-3411
Richard's Restaurant
    629 E. Paulding Rd., 219/745-7432
    717 W. Washington Center Rd., 219/489-4279
    2912 Getz Rd., 219/432-0913

Best Fine Dining
Oyster Bar
    1830 S. Calhoun St., 217/744-9490
Park Place Grill
    200 E. Main St., 219/420-7275
Paula's Seafood and Mangy Moose
    1732 W. Main St., 219/422-4322

Best French Food
Cafe Johnell
    2529 S. Calhoun St., 219/456-1939

Chappell's French Quarter
   3311 N. Anthony Blvd., 219/482-2628

Best Indian Food
Taj Mahal Indian Restaurant
   6410 W. Jefferson Blvd., Ste. 9B, 219/432-8993
Taste of India
   4614 Coldwater Rd., 219/482-1612

Best Japanese Food
Takaoka of Japan
   305 E. Superior St., 219/424-3183
Yokohama Japanese Restaurant
   5320 Coldwater Rd., 219/482-4040

Best Mexican Food
Bandido's Mexican Restaurant
   933 Northcrest Shopping Ctr., 219/482-9497
   7510 Winchester Rd., 219/478-1587
   6060 E. State Blvd., 219/493-0607
Casa
   7545 W. Jefferson Blvd., 219/436-2272
Casa D'Angelo
   4111 Parnell Ave., 219/483-0202
   3402 Fairfield Ave., 219/745-7200
El Azteca
   535 E. State Blvd., 219/482-2172
La Hacienda Mexican Restaurant
   3938 W. Jefferson Blvd., 219/432-9721
La Margarita
   2713 S. Calhoun St., 219/456-5857

Best Other Ethnic Food
Zoli's Family Restaurant (Hungarian)
   2426 Broadway, 219/745-2740

Best Pizza
Munchie Emporium
   1109 Taylor St., 219/424-6883
Oley's Pizza
   10910 U.S. Hwy. 24W, 219/432-6996
   1427 N. Coliseum Blvd., 219/424-8900
Redwood Inn Pizza
   1432 W. Main St., 219/426-7543

Best Regional Food
Hilger's Farm Restaurant
   5215 Butt Rd., 219/625-4181

Best Romantic Dining
Peppercorn Restaurant and Lounge
   6135 Plantation Ln., 219/486-5661

Best Sandwiches
Bagel Station
   3009 E. State Blvd., 219/471-2272
Cheddar's
   305 W. Coliseum Blvd., 219/484-4631
Munchie Emporium
   1109 Taylor St., 219/424-6883

Best Seafood
Chappell's Coral Grill
  2723 Broadway, 219/456-9652
Fish of Stroh
  3929 E. State Blvd., 219/483-0561
  1571 Goshen Ave., 219/484-8602
Oyster Bar
  1830 S. Calhoun St., 219/744-9490

Best Soul Food
Mama's Place
  1714 E. Pontiac St., 219/745-0418

Best Sports Bar
Alumni Sports Club
  6200 W. Jefferson Blvd., 219/436-2651

Best Steaks
Chappell's Coral Grill
  2723 Broadway, 219/456-9652
Ernie's Steakhouse
  602 E. Dupont Rd., 219/489-5389
  2787 Maplecrest Rd., 219/486-7244
Red River Steaks and Barbecue
  305 E. Washington Center Rd., 219/484-1921

Best View While Dining
Window Garden Restaurant
  1300 One Summit Sq., 219/426-4086

GARY, IN

Best American Food
L.L. Coney Island
  1744 Broadway, 219/882-2287
Purple Steer
  1402 Indianapolis Blvd., Whiting, 219/659-3950

Best Breakfast
Big Wheel Restaurant
  6140 Melton Rd., 219/938-3516

Best Chinese Food
Great Wall Restaurant
  5920 U.S. Hwy. 6, Portage, 219/763-7776
Ming Ling
  566 S. Lake St., 219/938-6617

Best French Food
Chez Criton
  1700 Grant St., 219/944-0775

Best Mexican Food
Pepe's Mexican Restaurant
  6400 Melton Rd., 219/938-0777

Best Seafood
Phil Smidt and Son Restaurant
  1205 Calumet Ave., Hammond, 219/659-0025
Ray's Shrimp House
  4499 W. Fifth Ave., 219/944-8545
  3770 Grant St., 219/884-5707

Best Steaks
Freddy's Steakhouse
6442 Kennedy Ave., Hammond, 219/844-1500

INDIANAPOLIS, IN

Best All-You-Can Eat Buffet
Heritage House Smorgasbord
4990 Hwy. 31S, 317/783-9388

Best Bar
Ale Emporium
8617 Allisonville Rd., 317/842-1333
2650 Lake Circle Dr., 317/879-1212
Broad Ripple Brew Pub
840 E. 65th St., 317/253-2739
C T Pepper's Ltd.
6283 N. College Ave., 317/257-6277
Charlie and Barney's Bar
1130 W. 86th St., Nora, 317/844-2399
225 E. Ohio St., Ste. 1, 317/637-5851
1 Merchants Plz., Ste. 101, 317/636-3101
723 Broad Ripple Ave., 317/253-5263
Daddy Jack's Restaurant and Bar
9419 N. Meridian St., 317/843-1609
Loughmiller's Pub and Eatery
301 W. Washington St., 317/638-7380
Red Key Tavern
5170 N. College Ave., 317/283-4601

Best Barbecue/Ribs
G T South's Rib House
5711 E. 71st St., 317/849-6997
King Ribs Bar-B-Q
5610 Georgetown Rd., 317/291-2695
4130 N. Keystone Ave., 317/543-0841
2660 Lafayette Rd., 317/488-0223
Mountain Jack's
6901 W. 38th St., 317/329-6929
3650 W. 86th St., 317/872-4500
Odie's Pit Bar-B-Que
6825 Graham Rd., 317/849-6901

Best Beer Selection
Shallow's Antique Restaurant
8811 Hardegan St., Ste. 1B, 317/882-7997
Union Jack Pub
6225 W. 25th St., 317/243-3300

Best Breakfast
Cafe Patachou
4911 N. Pennsylvania St., 317/925-2823
Le Peep
8255 Craig St., Ste. 102, 317/576-0433
301 N. Illinois St., 317/237-3447
Original Pancake House
1518 W. 86th St., 317/872-0022

Best Brewpub
Alcatraz Brewing Company
49 W. Maryland St., 317/488-1230

Rock Bottom Brewery
   10 W. Washington St., 317/681-8180

Best Burgers
Flakey Jake's
   6530 E. 82nd St., 317/841-0274
   7975 E. Washington St., 317/359-1456

Best Cafeteria
Jonathan Byrd's Cafeteria
   100 Byrd Way, Greenwood, 317/881-8888
Laughner's Cafeteria
   4030 S. East St., 317/787-3745
   1616 E. 86th St., 317/846-1112
   20 N. Franklin Rd., 317/356-3388

Best Cajun/Creole Food
Jazz Cooker
   925 Westfield Blvd., 317/253-2883
New Orleans House
   8845 Township Line Rd., 317/872-9670

Best Chinese Food
China Garden Restaurant
   7015 Madison Ave., 317/781-0943
Chinese Ruby Restaurant
   7280 N. Keystone Ave., Nora, 317/253-6451
Forbidden City
   2606 E. 65th St., 317/257-7388
   3517 W. 86th St., 317/872-2888
   3837 N. High School Rd., 317/298-3588
Oriental Inn
   1421 N. Arlington Ave., 317/352-0348
Yen Ching
   1300 E. 86th St., 317/844-1910
   8512 E. Washington St., 317/889-3270

Best Coffee/Coffeehouse
Abbey Coffee House II
   5909 E. 86th St., 317/598-9864
Coffee Zon's Courtyard
   137 E. Ohio St., 317/684-0432
Cornerstone Coffee and Espresso
   651 E. 54th St., 317/726-1360
Houlihan's Old Place
   Glendale Mall, 6101 N. Keystone Ave., 317/257-3285
The Abbey Coffeehouse
   771 Massachusetts Ave., 317/269-8426

Best Delicatessen
D'Amico's Deli and Bagel
   9546 Allisonville Rd., Ste. 138, 317/845-5460
   6311 Guilford Ave., 317/475-1209
IKA's Gourmet Delicatessen
   8255 Craig St., Ste. 128, 317/595-9400
Shapiro's Deli Cafeteria
   2370 W. 86th St., 317/872-7255
   808 S. Meridian St., 312/631-4041

Best Desserts
Dutch Oven
4004 Hwy. 31S, 317/784-0305
Finale
3953 E. 82nd St., Nora, 317/841-3953

Best Diner
Post Restaurant
State Rd. 967 at Hwy. 9, Pendleton, 317/778-4651

Best Dinner
Palomino
49 W. Maryland St., Ste. 189, 317/974-0400

Best Family Restaurant
Daddy O's
3744 N. Keystone Ave., 317/921-1922
Moe's Place
646 E. 38th St., 317/923-5674

Best Fine Dining
Keystone Grill
8650 Keystone Crossing, 317/848-5202
Pendleton House
118 N. Pendleton Ave., Pendleton, 317/778-8061
Something Different
2411 E. 65th St., 317/257-7973

Best French Food
Renee's French Restaurant
839 E. Westfield Blvd., 317/251-4142

Best German Food
Heidelberg Haus Cafe
7625 Pendleton Pike, 317/547-1230
Rathskeller
401 E. Michigan St., 317/636-0396

Best Greek/Mediterranean Food
Acropolis
1625 E. Southport Rd., 317/787-8883
Aesop's Tables
600 Massachusetts Ave., 317/631-0055
Hellas Cafe
8501 Westfield Blvd., 317/257-6211
Kory's Restaurant
1850 E. 62nd St., 317/251-2252

Best Homestyle Food
Dodd's Townhouse
5694 N. Meridian St., 317/257-1872
Hollyhock Hill
8110 N. College Ave., 317/251-2294

Best Ice Cream/Yogurt
Nick's Sweet Retreat
920 Broad Ripple Ave., 317/251-8379

Best Indian Food
India Garden
830 Broad Ripple Ave., 317/253-6060
Star of India
1043 Broad Ripple Ave., 317/465-1100

Best Inexpensive Meal
Kory's Restaurant
   1850 E. 62nd St., 317/251-2252
Old Spagetti Factory
   210 S. Meridian St., 317/635-6325
Shapiro's Deli Cafeteria
   808 S. Meridian St., 317/631-4041
   2370 W. 86th St., 317\872-7255

Best Italian Food
Arturo's Ristorante Italiano
   2727 E. 86th St., Ste. 232, 317/257-4806
Bravo!
   8651 Castle Creek Pkwy., 317/577-2211
Iaria's
   317 S. College Ave., 317/638-7706
Italian Gardens Restaurant
   8336 E. Washington St., 317/898-7333
Milano Inn
   231 S. College Ave., 317/638-7706
Some Guys Pizza and Pasta
   6235 Allisonville Rd., 317/257-1364

Best Japanese Food
Benihana of Tokyo
   8830 Keystone Crossing, 317/846-2495
Ginza Japanese Steakhouse
   5380 W. 38th St., 317/298-3838

Best Late-Night Food
Rock Lobster
   820 Broad Ripple Ave., 317/257-9001

Best Mexican Food
Don Pablo's Restaurant
   8150 Hwy. 31S, 317/888-0363
   6929 W. 38th St., 317/293-2178
   3824 E. 82nd St., 317/576-0819
   7600 Old Trails Rd., 317/353-6754
El Sol de Tala Mexican Restaurante Y Cantina
   2444 E. Washington St., 317/635-8252
Zorro's
   1300 E. 86th St., Nora, 317/571-1001

Best Outdoor Dining
Blue Heron
   11699 Fall Creek Rd., 317/845-8899
Rick's Cafe Boatyard
   4100 Dandy Trail, 317/290-9300
   6201 La Pas Trail, Ste. 130, 317/290-9300

Best Pizza
Bazbeaux Pizza
   334 Massachusetts Ave., 317/636-7662
   832 E. Westfield Blvd., 317/255-5711
Enzo
   29 E. McCarty St., 317/638-0337
   222 E. Market St., 317/266-0498
   8701 Keystone Crossing, 317/846-9332
   25 W. Market St., 317/635-1144

Jack's Pizza
  5172 N. College Ave., 317/283-8124
Marco's Pizza
  2380 E. 54th St., 317/251-7000
Puccini's Smiling Teeth
  3944 E. 82nd St., 317/570-0160
  1508 W. 86th St., 317/875-9223

Best Place to Take the Kids
Arni's
  3443 W. 86th St., 317/875-7034
Hollyhock Hill
  8110 N. College Ave., 317/251-2294
Max and Erma's
  8817 U.S. Hwy. 31S, 317/882-4477
  8930 Wesleyan Rd., 317/872-2300
  5899 E. 86th St., 317/841-1411

Best Restaurant in Town
Johnson County Line
  1265 N. Madison Ave., Greenwood, 317/887-0404
Majestic
  47 S. Pennsylvania St., 317/636-5418
Malibu Grill
  4503 E. 82nd St., 317/845-4334
Peter's Restaurant and Bar
  8505 Keystone Crossing, 317/465-1155

Best Romantic Dining
Restaurant at the Canterbury
  123 S. Illinois St., 317/634-3000

Best Seafood
Kona Jack's Fish Market and Oyster Bar
  9413 N. Meridian St., 317/843-2600
Mary's Seafood
  5523 E. 38th St., 317/546-1667

Best Soul Food
Big Mama's
  2356 N. Sherman Dr., 317/547-6262
Lauren's Southern Soul
  2172 E. 54th St., 317/255-3554
Pa and Ma's
  974 W. 27th St., 317/924-3698

Best Sports Bar
Dave's Finish Line
  115 E. Ohio St., 317/637-6253
Bench Warmers
  Holiday Inn, 3850 De Pauw Blvd., 317/871-5655
  Holiday Inn, 2501 S. High School Rd., 317/244-6861

Best Steaks
Broad Ripple Steakhouse
  929 E. Westfield Blvd., 317/253-8101
Charleston's
  6815 E. 82nd St., 317/841-0442
Del Frisco's
  5 E. Market St., 317/687-8888

Fifth Quarter Steakhouse
   8225 Allison Pointe Trail, 317/577-9840
Kang's Express
   2989 W. 71st St., Ste. 3, New Augusta, 317/297-3451
Murphy's Steak House
   4189 N. Keystone Ave., 317/545-3707
St. Elmo Steak House
   127 S. Illinois St., 317/365-0636
Stuart Anderson's Cattle Company
   7853 Hwy. 31S, 317/887-1833
   8621 Keystone Crossing, Nora, 317/844-9512

Best Sunday Brunch
Porch Restaurant
   Hyatt Hotel, 1 S. Capitol Ave., 317/632-1234

Best Sushi
Sakura
   7201 N. Keystone Ave., 317/259-4171

Best Thai Food
Bangkok
   7269 N. Keystone Ave., 317/255-7799

Best Vegetarian Food
Brother Juniper's
   150 E. Sixteenth St., Ste. 1, 317/924-9529
Brother Juniper's
   339 Massachusetts Ave., 317/636-3115
Essential Edibles
   115 E. 49th St., 317/931-1080
   429 E. Vermont St., 317/266-8797
Nature's Pantry
   3000 N. Meridian St., 317/926-8439

Best Wine Selection
Corner Wine Bar
   6331 Guilford Ave., 317/255-5159
Schaffer's
   6125 Hillside Ave., 317/253-1404

JEFFERSONVILLE, IN

Best Breakfast
Wall Street Cafe
   401 Wall St., 812/288-6466

Best Chinese Food
China Palace Restaurant
   839 Spring St., 812/284-2888

Best Family Restaurant
Ann's on the River
   149 Spring St., 812/284-2667

Best Fine Dining
Inn on Spring
   348 Spring St., 812/284-5545

Best Italian Food
Parrella's Italian Restaurant
   214 W. Court Ave., 812/283-7933

Best Pizza
Pizza King
1066 Kehoe Ln., 812/282-8286
Rocky's Sub Pub
1207 E. Market St., 812/282-3844

Best Sandwiches
Jenny Lind Tea Room
249 Spring St., 812/283-4832
Rocky's Sub Pub
1207 E. Market St., 812/282-3844
Soup Line
320 E. Court Ave., 812/282-7765

Best Seafood
Moby Dick Seafood Restaurant
1700 E. Tenth Street, 812/282-6168
Towboat Annie's
707 W. Riverside Dr., 812/282-2368

Best Steaks
Frank's Steak House
520 W. Seventh St., 812/283-3383

KOKOMO, IN

Best Burgers
Sycamore Grill
113 W. Sycamore St., 765/457-2220

Best German Food
Pumpernickel
1906 S. Elizabeth St., 765/868-7453

Best Ice Cream/Yogurt
Del's Ice Cream and Yogurt
1233 1/2 S. Reed Rd., 765/452-3440
Freshens Premium Yogurt
Kokomo Mall, 1826 E. Boulevard, 765/452-9478
Kokomo Frozen Custard
3107 S. Webster St., 765/453-2482

Best Italian Food
Fazoli's
622 S. Reed Rd., 765/868-2538
Martino's Italian Villa
1929 N. Washington St., 765/457-6621

Best Mexican Food
Hacienda Mexican Restaurant
2006 S. Plate St., 765/452-8231

Best View While Dining
Country Cook-Inn
1050 E. 180S, Greentown, 765/628-7676

LA PORTE, IN

Best Breakfast
Christo's Family Restaurant
1462 W. State Rd. 2, 219/326-1644
Louie's Cafe
920 Lincoln Way, 219/326-9686

Round the Clock Restaurant
219 Pine Lake Ave., 219/326-5817

Best Burgers
Dick's Bar
912 Lincoln Way, 219/326-9702

Best Coffee/Coffeehouse
Temple News Agency
816 Jefferson Ave., 219/362-2676

Best Family Restaurant
Christo's Family Restaurant
1462 W. State Rd. 2, 219/326-1644
Louie's Cafe
920 Lincoln Way, 219/326-9686
Roskoe's
1004 Lakeside St., 219/325-3880

Best Pizza
Albano's Pizza
325 J St., 219/325-3331
Mancino's
41 Pine Lake Ave., 219/362-9032

Best Sandwiches
Indiana Deli and Catering Company
805 Indiana Ave., 219/324-3383

Best Seafood
Kelsey's Steak House
304 Detroit St., 219/325-0000
Ole's Meat, Fish, and Liquor
502 State St., 219/362-8270
Tangerine
601 Michigan Ave., 219/326-8000

Best Steaks
Kelsey's Steak House
304 Detroit St., 219/325-0000
Roskoe's
1004 Lakeside St., 219/325-3880
Tangerine
601 Michigan Ave., 219/326-8000

LAFAYETTE, IN

Best Bar
The Other Pub
3000 S. Ninth St., 765/474-9527

Best Breakfast
Four Boys Manor
1201 Teal Rd., 765/474-6675

Best Burgers
Steak 'N Shake Restaurant
2 Sagamore Pkwy. N., 765/447-6091

Best Desserts
Jane's Gourmet Deli and Catering
524 N. Fourth St., 765/742-5000

Best Family Restaurant
Arni's
2200 Elmwood Ave., 765/447-1108

2323 Wallace Ave., 765/447-9436

Best Fine Dining
Sarge Oak on the Alley
721 Main St., 765/742-5230

Best Inexpensive Meal
Hacienda Mexican Restaurant
112 N. Third St., 765/423-2347

Best Italian Food
Spaghetti Shop
1947 Elmwood Ave., 765/447-4177

Best Mexican Food
Don Pablo's Mexican Restaurant
50 N. Creasy Ln., 765/449-0511

Best Pizza
Noble Roman's
2919 Sagamore Pkwy. S., 765/447-6905

Best Salad/Salad Bar
Sergeant Preston's of the North
6 N. Second St., 765/742-7378

Best Seafood
Patout's
3614 State Rd. 38E, 765/447-5400

Best Steaks
Sarge Oak on the Alley
721 Main St., 765/742-5230

MARION, IN

Best Barbecue/Ribs
King Gyros
215 S. Miller Ave., 765/668-1944

Best Breakfast
Jim Dandy Restaurant
1229 N. Baldwin Ave., 765/664-6702

Best Burgers
Myers Drive-In
938 S. Washington St., 765/664-9736

Best Chinese Food
Main Moon
3316 S. Western Ave., 765/662-0503

Best Health-Conscious Menu
Marion Cafeteria
201 W. Third St., 765/664-2443

Best Pizza
Noble Roman's
1414 W. Kem Rd., 765/662-9941
Pizza King
1212 N. Baldwin Ave., 765/664-0523
3404 S. Adams St., 765/674-6966

Best Place to Take the Kids
Ivanhoe's Drive-In
914 S. Main St., Upland, 765/998-7261

Best Sandwiches
Downtown Deli
201 W. Third St., 765/664-2443

Best Seafood
Brassery Restaurant
501 E. Fourth St., 765/668-8801
Erma's Restaurant
1197 N. Washington St., 765/668-7680

Best Steaks
Icehouse
1412 W. Kem Rd., 765/664-6646

MERRILLVILLE, IN

Best Burgers
Miner-Dunn Hamburger Shoppe
510 W. 81st Ave., 219/769-5611

Best Chinese Food
New Hong Kong Restaurant
7856 E. 37th Ave., Hobart, 219/962-3992

Best Family Restaurant
Odyssey
7876 Broadway, 219/738-2242

Best Fine Dining
Teibel's Restaurant
1775 Hwy. 3 at Hwy. 41, Schererville, 219/865-2000

Best Italian Food
Cafe Venezia
405 W. 81st Ave., 219/736-2203

Best Lunch
Jolly Ginger's
800 E. 81st Ave., 219/769-6311
Patio
7706 Broadway, 219/769-7990

Best Pizza
Giordano's
31 W. 81st Ave., 219/769-6114
Old Mill Pizzeria and Lounge
35 W. 73rd Ave., 219/769-4511
Uno's Pizzeria
2385 Southlake Mall, 219/736-4885

Best Place to Take the Kids
Celebration Station
8121 Georgia St., 219/769-7672

MICHIGAN CITY, IN

Best American Food
Matey's Restaurant
110 Franklin St., 219/872-9471
Top Dog Restaurant
701 Washington St., 219/874-3647

Best Breakfast
Howard's Restaurant
1708 Franklin St., 219/879-3426

Lindo's Restaurant
  3940 Franklin St., 219/872-0056

Best Burgers
Schoop's Hamburgers
  4105 Franklin St., 219/872-0170
Swing Belly's
  103 S. Lake Ave., 219/874-5718

Best Chinese Food
Fortune House
  312 Hwy. 20W, 219/872-6664

Best Fine Dining
Rodini's
  4125 Franklin St., 219/879-7388
Scottie's
  2134 Hwy. 20E, 219/879-2626

Best Mexican Food
Hacienda Mexican Restaurant
  1099 N. Karwick Rd., 219/879-4404

Best Pizza
Albano's Villa
  1612 Franklin St., 219/872-0571

Best Sandwiches
5th Street Deli
  431 Washington St., 219/872-5204
Blue Ribbon Cafe
  1407 Franklin St., 219/879-5702

Best Seafood
Matey's Restaurant
  110 Franklin St., 219/872-9471

Best Steaks
Rodini's
  4125 Franklin St., 219/879-7388

MUNCIE, IN

Best All-You-Can-Eat Buffet
Tasty Chinese Food
  1001 W. Jackson St., 765/287-8888

Best Breakfast
Bruner's Family Restaurant
  2200 W. Kilgore Ave., 765/288-2711
Richard's Restaurant
  1501 N. Broadway Ave., 765/288-5888
Sue's Kitchen
  600 S. Walnut St., 765/288-4786
Sunshine Cafe
  3113 N. Oakwood Ave., 765/288-5221

Best Burgers
Burkie's Drive In
  1515 W. Jackson St., 765/282-4355
Rally's
  220 E. McGalliard Rd., 765/286-0350
  400 S. Madison St., 765/282-4732
Richard's Restaurant
  1501 N. Broadway Ave., 765/288-5888

Best Business Lunch
Thornburg's
    Radisson Hotel Roberts, 420 S. High St., 765/741-7777

Best Chinese Food
House of Yu
    3511 W. Fox Ridge Ln., 765/289-2790
Szechuan Garden
    1312 W. McGalliard Rd., 765/289-8007
Tasty Chinese Food
    1001 W. Jackson St., 765/287-8888

Best Coffee/Coffeehouse
Dill Street Bar and Grill
    421 N. Dill St., 765/288-3630

Best Family Restaurant
Country Kitchen
    208 S. Main St., Winchester, 765/584-1688
Foxfires Restaurant
    3300 N. Chadam Ln., 765/284-5235
J.R. Brook's
    1101 W. McGalliard Rd., 765/282-1321
MCL Cafeteria
    3501 N. Granville Ave., 765/289-2955

Best Fine Dining
Vince's Restaurant
    5201 N. Walnut St., 765/284-6364

Best Italian Food
Aljeano's
    3212 E. Jackson St., 765/288-0787

Best Lunch
Judge's Chamber
    125 E. Charles St., 765/284-2202
Spot Lunch
    118 N. Walnut St., 765/282-8895

Best Mexican Food
La Hacienda
    2620 S. Madison St., 765/289-0909
Puerto Vallarta Mexican Restaurant
    4000 N. Broadway Ave., 765/287-8897

Best Pizza
Noble Roman's
    3001 N. Oakwood Ave., 765/284-0999

Best Southwestern Food
Culpepper's Southwestern Grill
    4008 W. Bethel Ave., 765/741-8522

Best Sports Bar
Tony's Locker Room
    2915 W. Bethel Ave., 765/288-9938

Best Steaks
Sirloin Stockade
    4949 W Hessler Rd., 765/287-9051

NEW ALBANY, IN

Best Bar
Sam's Food and Spirits
  3800 Payne Koehler Rd., 812/945-9757

Best Burgers
Ranch House
  2612B Charlestown Rd., 812/944-9199

Best Family Restaurant
Tommy Lancaster Restaurant
  1629 E. Market St., 812/945-2389

Best Homestyle Food
South Side Inn
  114 E. Main St., 812/945-9645

Best Mexican Food
Tumbleweed
  1638 Slate Run Rd., 812/945-9333
  2005 State St., 812/945-0177

Best Pizza
Hoosier Pizza
  2152 State St., 812/948-2229

Best Sandwiches
Mancino
  330 Grant Line Center, 812/949-7777
Stella's Sandwich Cafe
  128 W. Main St., 812/948-2541

Best Seafood
Hungry Pelican
  2604 Charlestown Rd., 812/948-1692

Best Steaks
Tommy Lancaster Restaurant
  1629 E. Market St., 812/945-2389

RICHMOND, IN

Best Barbecue/Ribs
Damon's Clubhouse
  Ramada Inn, 4700 National Rd. E., 765/962-5555

Best Breakfast
Olde Richmond Inn
  138 S. Fifth St., 765/962-2247

Best Burgers
Circus Shoppe
  820 Promenade, 765/962-4441

Best Chinese Food
Jade Palace Chinese Restaurant
  4340 National Rd. E., 765/935-4575

Best Coffee/Coffeehouse
Anything Goes
  704 Promenade, 765/966-4637

Best Health-Conscious Menu
MCL Cafeteria
  3801 E. Main St., 765/966-2939

Best Italian Food
Fazoli's
4711 National Rd. E., 765/935-6219

Best Mexican Food
Pedro's Mexican Restaurant
540 W. Eaton Pike, 765/966-1330

Best Pizza
Clara's Pizza King
203 W. Main St., 765/966-1541

Best Sandwiches
Court Cafe
211 S. Fifth St., 765/962-0359

Best Steaks
Country Rib Eye Steakhouse
725 Progress Dr., 765/966-4902

SOUTH BEND, IN

Best All-You-Can-Eat Buffet
Miller's Home Cafe
110 E. Michigan St., New Carlisle, 219/654-3431

Best American Food
La Salle Grill
115 W. Colfax Ave., 219/288-1155
Tippecanoe Place Restaurant
620 W. Washington St., 219/234-9077

Best Barbecue/Ribs
Heartland Texas Barbecue
222 S. Michigan St., 219/234-5200

Best Breakfast
Morse Inn
Notre Dame University, Notre Dame Ave., 219/631-2000

Best Burgers
Bonnie Doon Ice Cream
52446 N. Dixie Way, 219/272-2500

Best German Food
Hans Haus
2803 S. Michigan St., 219/291-5522

Best Homestyle Food
Miller's Home Cafe
110 E. Michigan St., New Carlisle, 219/654-3431

Best Mexican Food
Hacienda Mexican Restaurant
1224 Scottsdale Mall, 219/291-2566
1501 N. Ironwood Dr., 219/272-5922

Best Pizza
Edwardo's Natural Pizza
235 S. Michigan St., 219/233-1000
Macri's Milano Inn Pizza
61021 U.S. Hwy. 31, 219/291-4308

Best Soul Food
Franny's Restaurant
416 S. Main St., 219/232-2165

Best Steaks
East Bank Emporium
121 S. Niles Ave., 219/234-9000
Morse Inn
Notre Dame University, Notre Dame Ave., 219/631-2000

TERRE HAUTE, IN

Best Bar
Ballyhoo Pizza King
2405 Poplar St., 812/232-3423
900 Chestnut St., 812/232-3939
Larry Bird's Boston Connection
555 S. Third St., 812/235-3333
The Terminal
820 Wabash Ave., 812/232-8480

Best Burgers
Bohannon's
2961 S. Seventh St., 812/232-9305
1728 Wabash Ave., 812/234-2638

Best Chinese Food
Peking Chinese Restaurant
2828 S. Third St., 812/232-0665

Best Italian Food
Louise's Restaurant
1849 S. Third St., 812/232-4989

Best Mexican Food
Cancun Mexican Restaurant
3495 S. Fourth St., 812/232-4347

Best Place to Be "Seen"
Garfield's Restaurant
3401 Hwy. 41S at I-70, 812/238-1755

Best Romantic Dining
Pino's Il Sonetto
4234 S. Seventh St., 812/299-9255

Best Salad/Salad Bar
Western Rib-Eye Restaurant
100 S. Fruitridge Ave., 812/232-5591

Best Sandwiches
Candy's Deli Corner
3030 S. Seventh St., 812/234-0222

Best Steaks
Runyon's Black Angus
502 S. Third St., 812/235-5549

VALPARAISO, IN

Best Barbecue/Ribs
Wagner's Too
597 W. Hwy. 30, 219/759-6334

Best Breakfast
Big Wheel Restaurant
902 Lincolnway, 219/462-4169
Round the Clock Restaurant
217 Lincolnway, 219/462-6339

Schoop's Hamburgers
 2816 Calumet Ave., 219/464-2996

Best Chinese Food
China House
 120 Lincoln Way, 219/462-5788

Best Coffee/Coffeehouse
Coffee and Tea Market
 157 Lincolnway, 219/462-7265

Best Homestyle Food
Birky's Cafe
 205 N. Main St., Kouts, 219/766-3851
Strongbow Inn
 2405 U.S. Hwy. 30, 219/462-5121

Best Italian Food
Billy Jack's Cafe and Grill
 2904 Calumet Ave., 219/477-3797
Fazoli's
 2809 Calumet Ave., 219/531-0001

Best Sandwiches
D'Ouevres by Dottie
 21 E. Lincolnway, 219/462-1416

Best Seafood
Clayton's
 66 Lincolnway, 219/531-0612

Best Steaks
Kelsey's Steak House
 1905 Morthland Dr., 219/465-4022

VINCENNES, IN

Best Barbecue/Ribs
Oink's Gourmet BBQ
 1003 Main St., 812/882-3311

Best Burgers
Market Restaurant and Pub
 106 St. Honore Pl., 812/886-5201

Best Chinese Food
Hong Kong Restaurant
 2447 N. Sixth St., 812/882-0508
Marone's Formosa Gardens
 101 N. Second St., 812/882-0460

Best Ice Cream/Yogurt
Lic's Ice Cream and Sandwich Shop
 2815 N. Sixth St., 812/882-3526

Best Pizza
Bill Bobe's Pizzeria
 1651 N. Sixth St., 812/882-2992

Best Sandwiches
Market Restaurant and Pub
 106 St. Honore Pl., 812/886-5201

WARSAW, IN

Best Breakfast
American Table Restaurant
  3575 Lake City Hwy., 219/267-8171
Richard's Restaurant
  975 Anchorage Rd., 219/267-3244

Best Cajun/Creole Food
Orion's Restaurant
  937 N. Detroit St., 219/269-9100

Best Pizza
Gordy's Sub Pub
  321 S. Buffalo St., 219/269-6963

Best Sandwiches
Barbee Hotel Bar and Grill
  3620 N. Barbee Rd., 219/834-2984
Gordy's Sub Pub
  321 S. Buffalo St., 219/269-6963

Best Seafood
Barbee Hotel Bar and Grill
  3620 N. Barbee Rd., 219/834-2984
Mosaique
  115 S. Buffalo St., 219/269-5080
Wolfgang's Restaurant
  617 S. Buffalo St., 219/269-6678

Best Steaks
Barbee Hotel Bar and Grill
  3620 N. Barbee Rd., 219/834-2984
Wolfgang's Restaurant
  617 S. Buffalo St., 219/269-6678

WOODBRIDGE, IN

Best Bar
Nick's English Hut
  423 E. Kirkwood Ave., 812/332-4040
Yogi's Bar and Grill
  519 E. Tenth St., 812/323-9644

Best Breakfast
Runcible Spoon Cafe and Restaurant
  412 E. Sixth St., 812/334-3997

Best French Food
Chez Nous
  416 E. Fourth St., 812/323-8962

Best Other Ethnic Food
Norbu Cafe (Tibetan)
  415 E. Fourth St., 812/335-1297
Siam House (Asian)
  430 E. Fourth St., 812/331-1233

Best Pizza
Cafe Pizzeria
  405 Kirkwood Ave., 812/332-2111

Best Vegetarian Food
Bloomington Foods
  419 E. Kirkwood Ave., 812/336-5300

Laughing Planet Cafe
  322 E. Kirkwood Ave., 912/323-2233

Best Wine Selection
Lennie's Restaurant
  1795 E. Tenth St., 812/323-2112

Iowa

AMANA, IA

Best German Food
Brick Haus Restaurant
  728 47th Ave., 319/622-3278
Colony Inn
  741 47th Ave., 319/622-6270
Ox Yoke Inn
  4420 220th Trail, 319/622-3441

Best Regional Food
Ronneburg Restaurant
  4408 220th Trail, 319/622-3641

AMES, IA

Best American Food
Aunt Maude's
  547 Main St., 515/233-4136
Grove Cafe
  124 Main St., 515/232-9784
Wallaby's
  3720 Lincoln Way, 515/292-1167

Best Barbecue/Ribs
Battle's Bar-B-Q
  112 Hayward Ave., 515/292-1670
Hickory Park
  121 S. Sixteenth St., 515/232-8940

Best Chinese Food
House of Chen
  2508 Ferndale Ave., 515/233-3144

Best Homestyle Food
Grove Cafe
  124 Main St., 515/232-9784

Ivy's Garden Cafe
517 Grand Ave., 515/232-0275

Best Italian Food
Lucullan's Restaurant
400 Main St., 515/232-8484
Valentino's
2500 Ferndale Ave., 515/233-2111

Best Mexican Food
O'Malley and McGee's Cafe
716 S. Duff Ave., 515/232-0007

Best Other Ethnic Food
Cafe Baudelaire (Brazilian)
2504 E. Lincoln Way, 515/292-7429

Best Pizza
Great Plains Sauce and Dough Company
129 Main St., 515/232-4263

Best Steaks
Broiler Steakhouse
6008 Lincoln Way, 515/292-2516
Cafe Northwest
114 S. Duff Ave., 515/232-5328

Best Vietnamese Food
Le's Restaurant
113 Colorado Ave., 515/292-0002

BETTENDORF, IA

Best American Food
Ross' Restaurant
430 Fourteenth St., 319/355-7573

Best Barbecue/Ribs
R.J. Boar's
1804 State St., 319/359-8949

Best Pizza
Sports Fans Pizza
1723 Grant St., 319/359-5555

Best Restaurant in Town
Jumers Restaurant
900 Spruce Hills Dr., 319/359-1607

BURLINGTON, IA

Best Barbecue/Ribs
Dillon's Real Pit Barbeque
2107 N. Roosevelt Ave., 319/752-4263

Best Chinese Food
Great Wall
3103 Kirkwood St., 319/753-6788

Best Ice Cream/Yogurt
Bridgeman's Restaurant
1414 N. Roosevelt Ave., 319/752-8541

Best Sandwiches
Big Muddy's
710 N. Front St., 319/753-1699

Pantry Restaurant
  325 Angular St., 319/753-1593

Best Steaks
Big Muddy's
  710 N. Front St., 319/753-1699
J.J. Maguire's Restaurant
  3001 Winegard Dr., 319/753-2291

CEDAR FALLS, IA

Best American Food
Tally's
  4214 University Ave., 319/268-1655

Best Breakfast
Joe's Country Grill
  4117 University Ave., 319/277-8785

Best Burgers
Danny's Diner
  1525 W. First St., 319/266-1462

Best Business Lunch
Tally's
  4214 University Ave., 319/268-1655

Best Seafood
Olde Broom Factory Restaurant
  110 N. Main St., 319/268-0877

Best Steaks
Olde Broom Factory Restaurant
  110 N. Main St., 319/268-0877

Best Sunday Brunch
Green Streets
  Holiday Inn, 5826 University Ave., 319/277-2230

CEDAR RAPIDS, IA

Best All-You-Can-Eat Buffet
Bishop Buffet
  4444 First Ave. NE, 319/393-9794
LongBranch Motor Inn
  90 Twixt Town Rd. NE, 319/377-6386

Best American Food
Tic-Toc
  600 Seventeenth St. NE, 319/364-9685

Best Atmosphere
Ced-Rel Supper Club
  11909 Sixteenth Ave. SW, 319/446-7300
Windows
  350 First Ave. NE, 319/363-8161

Best Barbecue/Ribs
Al and Irene's Barbeque House
  2020 N. Towne Ln. NE, 319/393-6242
Winifred's
  3847 First Ave. SE, 319/364-6125

Best Brewpub
Cedar Brewing Company
  500 Blairs Ferry Rd. NE, 319/378-9090

Best Burgers
Starlite Room
  3300 First Ave. NE, 319/362-4759

Best Casual Dining
David's Restaurant and Lounge
  1107 Seventh Ave., Marion, 319/373-0414

Best Chinese Food
Pei's Mandarin Restaurant
  3287 Sixth St. SW, 319/362-6165
  5131 Council St. NE, 319/395-9741

Best Coffee/Coffeehouse
Coffee Emporium
  220 Third Ave. SE, 319/362-3384

Best Continental Food
Cafe de Klos
  821 Third Ave. SE, 319/362-9340

Best Delicatessen
Ashley's Restaurant
  201 Third Ave. SE, Ste. 50, 319/364-2509
Emil's Delicatessen
  100 Fifth St. NE, 319/364-3123

Best Diner
Ragtop Diner
  240 Classic Car Ct. SW, 319/366-6070
  5010 Council St. NE, 319/393-5959

Best Family Restaurant
Maid-Rite
  621 First Ave. SW, 319/364-4415
  2600 Edgewood Rd., Ste. 550, 319/396-9049
  4444 First Ave. NE, 319/395-0886
Sports Page Family Restaurant
  3707 First Ave. SE, 319/362-3350
Spring House
  3980 Center Point Rd. NE, 319/393-4995

Best Greek/Mediterranean Food
Greek Place Vernon Inn
  Vernon Inn, 2663 Mount Vernon Rd., 319/366-7817

Best Homestyle Food
Spring House
  3980 Center Point Rd. NE, 319/393-4995

Best Indian Food
Taj Mahal Cuisine of India
  5454 Blairs Forest Way NE, 319/393-4500

Best Italian Food
Zio Johno's Spaghetti House
  355 Edgewood Rd. NW, 319/396-1700
  1125 First Ave. SE, 319/362-9667

Best Mexican Food
Cancun
  433 Seventh Ave., Marion, 319/377-2032
Hacienda Las Glorias
  715 First Ave. SW, 319/363-7344

Papa Juan's Mexican Restaurant
    5505 Center Point Rd. NE, 319/393-0258

Best Other Ethnic Food
Cafe de Klos (Dutch)
    821 Third Ave. SE, 319/362-9340
Konecny's Restaurant (Czechoslovakian)
    72 Sixteenth Ave. SW, 319/364-9492
Zindrick's Czech Restaurant (Czechoslovakian)
    86 Sixteenth Ave. SW, 319/365-5257

Best Outdoor Dining
Ellis Landing
    1895 Ellis Blvd. NW, 319/365-7049

Best Pizza
Happy Joe's Pizza and Ice Cream
    3419 Sixteenth Ave. SW, 319/396-0626
    4444 NE First Ave., Ste. 454, 319/393-0017
Pizza Village and Brewery
    350 Edgewood Rd. NW, 319/396-1010
Riverside and Company
    1550 A St. SW, 319/362-2631
Zoey's Pizzeria
    690 Tenth St., Marion, 319/377-2840

Best Romantic Dining
Ced-Rel Supper Club
    11909 Sixteenth Ave. SW, 319/446-7300

Best Salad/Salad Bar
Drake's Salad Bar
    219 Second St. SE, 319/363-8880

Best Sandwiches
Al's Red Frog
    88 Sixteenth Ave. SW, 319/369-3940
Deb's Ice Cream and Deli
    315 Third St. SE, 319/365-1010
Doc and Eddy's
    3325 Sixteenth Ave. SW, 319/365-8478
Flamingo Pizza Palace
    1211 Ellis Blvd. NW, 319/364-9926
Irish Democrat Pub and Grille
    3207 First Ave. SE, 319/364-9896
Little Bohemia
    1317 Third St. SE, 319/364-9396
Sykora Bakery
    73 Sixteenth Ave. SW, 319/364-5271

Best Seafood
Boston Fish
    804 Fifth St. SE, 319/363-9627

Best Southwestern Food
Lone Star Steakhouse and Saloon
    4545 First Ave. SE, 319/393-9648

Best Sports Bar
Cedar Brewing Company
    500 Blairs Ferry Rd. NE, 319/378-9090
CJ's Sports Bar and Grill
    62 Seventeenth Ave. SW, 319/365-9001

Best Steaks
The LongBranch Restaurant
  The Best Western Longbranch Hotel, 90 Twixt
    Town Rd. NE, 319/377-6386

Best Vietnamese Food
Nha Trang Restaurant
  3635 First Ave. SE, 319/364-8090

CLINTON, IA

Best American Food
Kernan's Riverview Restaurant
  333 River Dr., Princeton, 319/289-5137

Best Chinese Food
Yen Ching Restaurant
  1105 N. Second St., 319/242-6422

Best Restaurant in Town
Holiday Harry's
  226 Fifth Ave. S., 319/243-5736
McKinley Street Taverne
  2301 McKinley St., 319/242-3134
Rastelli's
  238 Main Ave., 319/242-7441
The Frontier
  The Best Western, 2300 Lincolnway St.,
    319/242-7112
The Unicorn
  1004 N. Second St., 319/242-7355

CORALVILLE, IA

Best Bar
Wig and Pen
  1220 Hwy. 6W, 319/354-2767

Best Burgers
Flannigan's Bar and Grill
  501 First Ave., 319/351-1904
Sluggers Sports Bar and Grill
  303 Second St., 319/354-4459

Best Chinese Food
China Garden Restaurant
  93 Second St., 319/338-8686
Hunan Chinese Restaurant
  118 Second St., 319/338-8885

Best Inexpensive Meal
Hawk I Feed and Relay
  903 First Ave., 319/354-3335
Randall's Pantry
  Hwy. 6W, 319/354-4990

Best Italian Food
Mondo's Tomato Pie
  516 Second St., 319/337-3000

Best Restaurant in Town
House of Lords
  The Best Western Canterbury Inn, 704 First Ave.,
    319/351-0400

Best Romantic Dining
Iowa River Power Company
501 First Ave., 319/351-1904

Best Sunday Brunch
Plum Tree Cafe
1895 27th Ave., 319/354-7770

Best Vietnamese Food
Mekong Vietnamese and Chinese
222 First Ave., 319/337-9910

COUNCIL BLUFFS, IA

Best Breakfast
Hy Vee's Kitchen
1706 N. Sixteenth St., 712/328-9792
1745 Madison Ave., 712/322-9260

Best Business Lunch
Bleu Ox West
3549 W. Broadway, 712/323-6848

Best Casual Dining
Christy Creme
2733 N. Broadway, 712/322-2778

Best Desserts
Village Inn
2935 W. Broadway, 712/328-7377

Best Fine Dining
Royal Fork Buffet
1751 Madison Ave., 712/323-3398

Best Homestyle Food
Iowa Feed and Grain
14759 Rosewood Rd., Crescent, 712/545-3190

Best Mexican Food
Romeo's
1821 W. Broadway, 712/323-0042

Best Restaurant in Town
Pizza King
1101 N. Broadway, 712/323-4911

Best Seafood
Gurney's Restaurant
229 S. Sixth St., Missouri Valley, 712/642-2580

Best Tea Room
Garden Cafe
1707 Madison Ave., 712/322-2233

DAVENPORT, IA

Best American Food
Riefe's Restaurant
1417 W. Locust St., 319/324-4732

Best Business Lunch
Duck City Delicatessen
115 E. Third St., 319/322-3825
Pat McGuire's Irish American Grille
3333 N. Harrison St., 319/386-0090

Best Homestyle Food
Dempsey's Bar
  501 N. Marquette St., 319/322-9109
Iowa Machine Shed Restaurant
  7256 N. Blvd., 319/391-2427

Best Italian Food
Lunardi's Italian Restaurant
  102 E. Kimberly Rd., 319/388-0001

Best Mexican Food
Rudy's Tacos
  4334 N. Brady St., 319/386-2475
  2214 E. Eleventh St., 319/322-0668
  326 Cedar St., 319/322-0662

Best Pizza
Dudley's Davenport Pizza
  1720 E. Kimberly Rd., 319/359-4411
Happy Joe's Pizza and Ice Cream
  2630 Rockingham Rd., 319/324-0477
  1414 W. Locust St., 319/324-5656
  201 E. 50th St., 319/386-1766
  320 W. Kimberly Rd., 319/386-5415

Best Restaurant in Town
Thunderbay Grille
  6511 N. Brady St., 319/386-2722
Windows On The River
  200 E. Third St., 319/323-5226

Best Seafood
The Dock Steak, Seafood, & Spirits
  125 S. Perry St., 319/322-5331

Best Steaks
Captain's Table
  4801 River Dr., Moline, 309/797-9222

Best View While Dining
Dock Steak Seafood Spirits
  125 S. Perry St., 319/322-5331

DES MOINES, IA

Best American Food
Greenbrier Restaurant and Bar
  5810 Merle Hay Rd., Johnston, 515/253-0124

Best Breakfast
Drake Diner
  1111 25th St., 515/277-1111

Best Burgers
Stella's Blue Sky Diner
  400 Locust St., 515/246-1953

Best Business Lunch
Jimmy's American Cafe
  1238 Eighth St., West Des Moines, 515/224-1212

Best Diner
Drake Diner
  1111 25th St., 515/277-1111

Best Family Restaurant
Iowa Machine Shed Restaurant
  11151 Hickman Rd., Clive, 515/270-6818

Best Italian Food
Christopher's Restaurant
  2816 Beaver Ave., 515/274-3694
Cosi Cucina Italian Grill
  1975 NW 86th St., Clive, 515/278-8148
8th Street Seafood Bar and Grill
  1261 Eighth St., West Des Moines, 515/223-8808
Noah's Ark Restaurant and Lounge
  2400 Ingersoll Ave., 515/288-2246
Riccelli's Restaurant
  3803 Indianola Ave., 515/288-7755

Best Mexican Food
Nacho Mamma's
  216 Court Ave., 515/280-6262

Best Pizza
Orlondo's Italian Restaurant
  3835 University Ave., 515/277-3600
Tavern
  205 Fifth St., West Des Moines, 515/255-9827

Best Salad/Salad Bar
Chicago Speakeasy
  1520 Euclid Ave., 515/243-3141
Stella's Blue Sky Diner
  400 Locust St., 515/246-1953

Best Steaks
Iowa Beef Steak House
  1201 E. Euclid Ave., 515/262-1138

DUBUQUE, IA

Best All-You-Can-Eat Buffet
Bishop Buffet
  The Kennedy Mall, 555 John F. Kennedy Rd.,
    319/588-2031

Best Bar
Circle Saloon
  806 Pleasant St., La Motte, 319/773-2352

Best Breakfast
Timmerman's
  7777 Timmerman Dr., East Dubuque,
    815/747-3181

Best Burgers
Dubuque Mining Company
  The Kennedy Mall, 555 John F. Kennedy Rd.,
    319/557-1729
West Dubuque Tap
  1701 Asbury Rd., 319/556-9647

Best Chinese Food
Yen Ching Restaurant
  926 Main St., 319/556-2574

Best Coffee/Coffeehouse
Take Five
  371 Bluff St., 319/557-2506
The Last Drop Java Joint
  1120 University Ave., 319/583-1577

Best Diner
Beanie's Cafe
  1400 Central Ave., 319/557-9533
Dottie's Cafe
  504 Central Ave., 319/556-9617

Best Family Restaurant
Papa Sarducci's
  1895 John F. Kennedy Rd., 319/583-1371
The Shot Tower Inn
  390 Locust St., 319/556-1061

Best Fine Dining
Timmermans
  7777 Timmerman Dr., East Dubuque,
    815/747-3316

Best Homestyle Food
Busy Bee Cafe
  1958 Central Ave., 319/583-1567

Best Ice Cream/Yogurt
Happy Joe's Pizza and Ice Cream Parlor
  1099 University Ave., 319/556-0823
  855 Century Dr., 319/556-0820
Yogurt D'Lite Coffee Shop
  469 Bluff St., 319/557-8825

Best Inexpensive Meal
Papa Sarducci's
  1895 John F. Kennedy Rd., 319/583-1371

Best Italian Food
Twisted Taco
  301 N Main St., Galena, 815/777-0033
Mario's Pizza and Restaurant
  1298 Main St., 319/582-0904
Papa Sarducci's
  1895 John F. Kennedy Rd., 319/583-1371
Pusateri's Restaurant
  2400 Central Ave., 319/583-9104

Best Mexican Food
The Silver Dollar Cantina
  342 Main St., 319/556-9327

Best Pizza
Happy Joe's Pizza and Ice Cream
  1099 University Ave., 319/556-0823
  855 Century Dr., 319/556-0820
Marco's
  2022 Central Ave., 319/588-0007

Best Romantic Dining
Mario's Pizza and Restaurant
  1298 Main St., 319/556-9424
Tollbridge Inn
  2800 Rhomberg Ave., 319/556-5566

Best Salad/Salad Bar
Hoffman House Restaurant
  3100 Dodge St., 319/557-8900

Best Steaks
Cedars Restaurant
  2155 S. Park Ct., 319/588-7189
Tollbridge Inn
  2800 Rhomberg Ave., 319/556-5566

Best Sunday Brunch
Timmermans
  7777 Timmerman Dr., East Dubuque,
    815/747-3316

FT. DODGE, IA

Best American Food
Colonial Inn
  1306 A St., 515/576-5757
Hickory House
  3022 Fifth Ave. S., 515/955-2722

Best Desserts
Bloomer's on Central
  900 Central Ave., 515/955-2221

Best Restaurant In Town
Marvin's Garden
  809 Central Ave., 515/955-5333
The Sports Page Bar and Grill
  2707 N. Fifteenth St., 515/955-1890

Best Sandwiches
Bloomer's on Central
  900 Central Ave., 515/955-2221

Best Sunday Brunch
Colonial Inn
  1306 A St., 515/576-5757

Best Thai Food
Won Ton Inn
  425 Second Ave. S., 515/573-5929

IOWA CITY, IA

Best American Food
Ground Round
  830 S. Riverside Dr., 319/351-2370

Best Atmosphere
Mondo's Sports Cafe
  212 S. Clinton St., 319/337-6787

Best Beer Selection
Sanctuary Restaurant and Pub
  405 S. Gilbert St., 319/351-5692

Best Breakfast
Hamburg Inn No. 2
  214 N. Linn St., 319/337-5512

Best Chinese Food
Yen Ching Restaurant
  1803 Boyrum St., 319/951-3001

Yen Ching Cafe
  Lenock Cilek Shopping Center, 130 S. Dubuque
    St., 319/338-6395

Best Continental Food
Vito's
  118 E. College St., 319/338-1393

Best Desserts
Season's Best Restaurant and Bar
  325 E. Washington St., Ste. 15, 319/337-2378

Best Family Restaurant
Country Kitchen
  1402 S. Gilbert St., 319/337-7696

Best Fine Dining
Highlander Inn Restaurant
  2525 N. Dodge St., 319/354-2000
The State Room
  IMU Bldg., 2nd Fl., Madison St. at Jefferson St.,
    319/335-1507

Best Ice Cream/Yogurt
Great Midwestern Ice Cream Company
  126 E. Washington St., 319/337-7243

Best Indian Food
India Cafe
  227 E. Washington St., 319/354-2775
Masala Indian Vegetarian Cuisine
  9 S. Dubuque St., 319/338-6199

Best Italian Food
Brown Bottle
  115 E. Washington St., 319/351-6704
Givanni's
  109 E. College St., 319/338-5967

Best Late-Night Food
Panchero's Mexican Grill
  32 S. Clinton St., 319/338-6311
Village Inn
  9 Sturgis Corner Dr., 319/351-1094

Best Lunch
Bread Garden Bakery and Cafe
  224 S. Clinton St., 319/354-4246

Best Mexican Food
Gringos
  115 E. College St., 319/338-3000
La Perlita Mexican Cafe
  327 E. Market St., 319/354-9046

Best Pizza
A and A Patliai's Pizza
  302 E. Bloomington St., 319/351-5073
Sanctuary Restaurant and Pub
  405 S. Gilbert St., 319/351-5692
The Mill Restaurant
  120 E. Burlington St., 319/351-9529

Best Romantic Dining
Linn Street Cafe
  121 N. Linn St., 319/337-7370

Best Steaks
House of Lords Restaurant
  704 First Ave., 319/351-0400
Iowa River Power Company
  501 First Ave., 319/351-1904
Lark Supper Club
  Hwy. 6W, Tiffin, 319/645-2461

Best Sunday Brunch
Swan's Restaurant
  Holiday Inn, 210 S. Dubuque St., 319/337-4058

Best Vegetarian Food
Masala Indian Vegetarian Cuisine
  9 S. Dubuque St., 319/338-6199

I

LE MARS, IA

Best All-You-Can-Eat Buffet
King Sea Chinese Restaurant
  630 Eighth Ave. SW, 712/546-1666

Best Family Restaurant
Bob's Drive-In
  Hwy. 75S, 712/546-5445
Country Kitchen
  511 Hawkeye Ave. SW, 712/546-4016
East Side Restaurant
  125 Plymouth St. NE, 712/546-4406
Pantry Cafe
  15 First St. NE, 712/546-6800

Best Pizza
Godfather's Pizza
  Hwy. 75S, 712/546-4159

Best Steaks
Archie's Waeside
  224 Fourth Ave. NE, 712/546-7011
The Depot Steak House and Lounge
  45 Third Ave. NE, 712/546-5918

MARSHALLTOWN, IA

Best Burgers
Maid-Rite
  106 S. Third Ave., 515/753-9684

Best Coffee/Coffeehouse
Muddy Waters
  14 W. Main, 515/754-9082

Best Homestyle Food
Country Kitchen
  2003 S. Center St., 515/752-7363

Best Mexican Food
Taco John's
  907 S. Center St., 515/753-6211

Best Pizza
Zeno's Pizza
109 E. Main St., 515/752-1245

Best Steaks
Rube's Lounge and Supper Club
118 Elm St., Montour, 515/492-6222

MASON CITY, IA

Best Barbecue/Ribs
Bill's Bar-B-Q
215 S. Madison Ave., 515/424-4944

Best Breakfast
Country Kitchen
1519 Fourth St. SW, 515/423-4000

Best Ice Cream/Yogurt
Birdsall Ice Cream
518 N. Federal Ave., 515/423-5365
100 S. Federal Ave., 515/424-5445

Best Mexican Food
Pastime Gardens
404 S. Madison Ave., 515/423-8896

Best Sandwiches
Bagel Depot
124 Fourth St. SW, 515/424-0100
The Hungry Mind
16 S. Commercial Alley, 515/423-0121

Best Seafood
Max Sea's
1828 S. Taft Ave., 515/424-0438
Prime and Wine
3000 Fourth St. SW, 515/424-8153

Best Steaks
Prime and Wine
3000 Fourth St. SW, 515/424-8153

MUSCATINE, IA

Best Barbecue/Ribs
Dillon's
1109 Grandview Ave., 319/262-8838

Best Chinese Food
Imperial Restaurant
1519 Park Ave., 319/264-8978
New Peking Restaurant
1700 Park Ave., 319/263-6321

Best Dinner
The Elms
2108 Grandview Ave., 319/263-8123

Best Fine Dining
Riverbend Bistro
Hotel Muscatine, 101 W. Mississippi Dr.,
319/262-4030

Best Lunch
Dutch Treat Restaurant
   203 E. Second St., 319/263-5181

Best Mexican Food
Imelda's Mexican Restaurant
   114 E. Second St., 319/263-3188

Best Sports Bar
Bootleggers
   214 Iowa Ave., 319/264-2686

OTTUMWA, IA

Best All-You-Can-Eat Buffet
Sirloin Stockade
   2645 Northgate Dr., 515/682-8731

Best Barbecue/Ribs
Carl's Barbeque Pit
   708 E. Main St., 515/682-3828

Best Breakfast
Country Kitchen
   1107 N. Quincy Ave., 515/682-0776

Best Chinese Food
Ching Dow Restaurant
   704 Richmond Ave., 515/683-3133
Wang's Chinese Kitchen
   121 N. Market St., Oskaloosa, 515/673-7777

Best Family Restaurant
Stanley's Restaurant
   345 Richmond Ave., 515/682-1213

Best Homestyle Food
Canteen Lunch in the Alley
   112 E. Second St., 515/682-5320
Ellis Tenderloins and Ice Cream
   233 N. Sheridan Ave., 515/683-1105
Maid-Rite
   1110 N. Quincy Ave., 515/684-8823
   107 N. Market St., 515/682-7385

Best Mexican Food
Fiesta Cantina
   2517 Northgate St., 515/682-8541

Best Pizza
Breadeaux Pizza
   401 E. Main St., 515/684-4617
Happy Joe's Pizza and Ice Cream
   315 Church St., 515/682-0125

Best Seafood
Fisherman's Bay
   221 N. Wapello St., 515/682-6325

Best Steaks
Greenbriar
   1207 N. Jefferson St., 515/682-8147

RED OAK, IA

Best All-You-Can-Eat Buffet
Burning Red Coach Inn
  Red Coach Inn Hotel, N. Hwy. 34, 712/623-4864

Best Breakfast
JD's Cafe
  709 N. Broadway St., 712/623-9600
Reed Street Cafe
  311 Reed St., 712/623-4322

Best Mexican Food
Taco Tico
  900 Senate Ave., 712/623-2012

Best Pizza
Breadeaux Pizza
  308 Coolbaugh St., 712/623-5488

Best Salad/Salad Bar
Red Coach Inn
  N. Hwy. 34, 712/623-4864

Best Steaks
Johnny's Steak House
  101 Broadway, 712/623-3136
Red Lion Steakhouse
  203 Coolbaugh St., 712/623-9545

SIOUX CITY , IA

Best Business Lunch
First Edition
  416 Jackson St., 712/277-4566

Best Chinese Food
Hunan Palace
  4280 Sergeant Rd., 712/274-2336
King Sea
  512 Fifth St., 712/255-0222

Best Family Restaurant
Green Gables
  1800 Pierce St., 712/258-4246
Harvey's
  5307 Military Rd., 712/233-1337

Best Salad/Salad Bar
John's Steak House
  1100 Steuben St., 712/277-4403
Theo's Steak House
  1911 Hwy. 20, Lawton, 712/944-5731

Best Vegetarian Food
Minerva's
  2901 Hamilton Blvd., 712/252-1012

STORM LAKE, IA

Best All-You-Can-Eat Buffet
Ken-A-Bob Buffet
  606 Flindt Dr., 712/732-2091

Best Breakfast
Lakeshore Family Restaurant
  1520 Lake Ave., 712/732-9800

Best Burgers
Boz-Wellz
  507 Erie St., 712/732-3616
Embers
  723 Lake Ave., 712/732-9887
Malarky's Pub
  147 Flindt Dr., 712/732-2055

Best Chinese Food
China House
  624 W. Milwaukee Ave., 712/732-1676

Best Coffee/Coffeehouse
Flying Pig Cafe
  617 Lake Ave., 712/732-5636

Best Homestyle Food
Pantry
  505 Lake Ave., 712/732-3240
Villager Restaurant
  421 Flindt Dr., 712/732-2372

Best Pizza
Godfather's Pizza
  811 Lake Ave., 712/732-2965

Best Steaks
Baker's Court
  1605 W. Milwaukee Ave., 712/732-6298
Boat House
  502 Lake Ave., 712/732-1462

WATERLOO, IA

Best Breakfast
Village Inn
  212 W. Ridgeway Ave., 319/291-2010

Best Chinese Food
Golden China Restaurant
  2046 E. Ridgeway Ave., 319/232-3928
Yen Ching
  107 Commercial St., 319/236-5005

Best Diner
Garfield's Cafe and Catering
  2820 Falls Ave., 319/291-6742

Best Family Restaurant
Lone Star Steakhouse and Saloon
  4045 Hammond Ave., 319/232-3233

Best Italian Food
The Brown Bottle
  209 W. Fifth St., 319/232-3014

Kansas

COLBY, KS

Best All-You-Can-Eat Buffet
Deep Rock Cafe
  1170 S. Range Ave., 785/462-8806
Prairie Rose Restaurant
  Ramada Inn , 1950 S. Range Ave., 785/462-3933
Sirloin Stockade
  1855 S. Range Ave., 785/462-7178

Best Breakfast
Prairie Rose Restaurant
  Ramada Inn , 1950 S. Range Ave., 785/462-3933

Best Burgers
A and W
  965 E. Fourth St., 785/462-3033
Victory Lane
  735 W. College Dr., 785/462-7888

Best Chinese Food
Big Wong Restaurant
  1715 W. Fourth St., 785/462-7722

Best Homestyle Food
Bourquin's Old Depot Restaurant
  155 E. Willow Rd., 785/462-3300
Deep Rock Cafe
  1170 S. Range Ave., 785/462-8806

Best Mexican Food
Alejandro's
  320 N. Franklin Ave., 785/462-7855

Best Steaks
Victory Lane
  735 W. College Dr., 785/462-7888

DODGE CITY, KS

Best American Food
Peppercorn's Bar and Grill
   1301 W. Wyatt Earp Blvd., 316/225-2335

Best Barbecue/Ribs
Fat and Happy's
   412 E. Wyatt Earp Blvd., 316/225-2476

Best Mexican Food
Casa Alvarez
   1701 W. Wyatt Earp Blvd., 316/225-7164
El Charro Restaurant
   1209 W. Wyatt Earp Blvd., 316/225-0371

Best Restaurant in Town
Cafe Potpourri
   100 Military Ave., Ste. 207, 316/225-0477

Best Steaks
Silver Spur Club
   1510 W. Wyatt Earp Blvd., 316/225-9362

Best Vietnamese Food
Saigon Market
   1202 E. Wyatt Earp Blvd., 316/225-9099

EMPORIA, KS

Best American Food
Chicken House Cafe
   8 Hwy. 99E, Olpe, 316/475-3386
Coach's Restaurant and Bar
   1408 Industrial Rd., 316/343-6362

Best Chinese Food
House of Ma
   1404 Industrial Rd., 316/342-3433

Best Family Restaurant
Love's
   205 Commercial St., Hartford, 316/392-5548

Best Mexican Food
El Palenque Cafe
   315 Commercial St., 316/342-0200

Best Steaks
Lujan's Waterworks
   402 Merchant St., 316/343-9980

GARDEN CITY, KS

Best 24-Hour Restaurant
Red Baron Restaurant and Lounge
   Hwy. 50C, 316/275-1797

Best Atmosphere
China Restaurant
   1518 Taylor Plaza E., 316/275-0304

Best Bar
Grain Bin Supper Club
   1301 E. Fulton St., 316/275-5954

Best Barbecue/Ribs
Adam's Rib Barbecue
1135 College Dr., 316/275-7427

Best Burgers
Herb's Carry Out
110 W. Kansas Ave., 316/276-8021

Best Chinese Food
China Restaurant
1518 Taylor Plaza E., 316/275-0304
Golden Dragon Restaurant
519 W. Mary St., Ste. 111, 316/275-8661

Best Desserts
Herb's Carry Out
110 W. Kansas Ave., 316/276-8021

Best Mexican Food
Casa Alvarez
1109 College Dr., 316/275-5494
El Conquistador Restaurant
1601 Jones Ave., 316/276-3836
El Zarape
606 W. Fulton St., 316/275-5401
El Zarape West
2212 Jones Ave., 316/275-2420
Irma's Cafe
1203 E. Fulton St., 316/275-6462

Best Steaks
Grain Bin Supper Club
1301 E. Fulton St., 316/275-5954
Wheat Lands Motor Inn and Restaurant
1408 E. Fulton St., 316/276-2768
Widow McGee's Restaurant
Plaza Inn, 1911 E. Kansas Ave., 316/275-7471

Best Sunday Brunch
Widow McGee's Restaurant
Plaza Inn, 1911 E. Kansas Ave., 316/275-7471

Best Vietnamese Food
Pho Hoa One Restaurant
713 E. Fulton St., 316/276-3993

HAYS, KS

Best All-You-Can-Eat Buffet
Alloway's Restaurant
105 W. Second St., Ellis, 785/726-3188

Best Desserts
Corner Garden
700 Main St., 785/625-8680

HUTCHINSON, KS

Best Barbecue/Ribs
Roy's BBQ
1018 Nickerson Blvd., 316/663-7421

Best Homestyle Food
Mom's Cafe
501 N. Main St., 316/662-1543

The Dutch Kitchen
6803 State Hwy. 61W, 316/662-2554

Best Italian Food
Tommassi Italian Restaurant
17 E. Second Ave., 316/663-9633

Best Mexican Food
The Anchor Inn
128 S. Main St., 316/669-0311

Best Other Ethnic Food
The Carriage Crossing (Amish)
10002 S. Yoder Rd., Yoder, 316/465-3612

Best Steaks
The Airport Steakhouse
1100 Airport Rd., 316/662-4281

INDEPENDENCE, KS

[See also: Kansas City, MO.]

Best All-You-Can-Eat Buffet
Applewood's
120 W. Laurel St., 316/331-7960

Best Breakfast
Eggbert's International
1724 W. Main St., 316/331-0520

Best Chinese Food
Great China Restaurant
2001 W. Main St., 316/331-0060

Best Diner
Eggbert's International
1724 W. Main St., 316/331-0520

Best Ice Cream/Yogurt
Braum's Ice Cream and Dairy
1415 N. Pennsylvania Ave., 316/331-1973

Best Mexican Food
Ortega's
1100 E. Main St., 316/331-3027

Best Pizza
Big Cheese Pizza
103 E. Main St., 316/331-2330

Best Steaks
Applewood's
120 W. Laurel St., 316/331-7960

JUNCTION CITY, KS

Best All-You-Can-Eat Buffet
Sirloin Stockade
426 Goldenbelt Dr., 785/238-1817

Best Barbecue/Ribs
Chubby's
203 S. Washington St., 785/762-2773

Best Breakfast
Stacy's Restaurant
  118 Flint Hills Blvd., 785/238-3039

Best Chinese Food
Peking Chinese Restaurant
  836 S. Washington St., 785/238-2336

Best German Food
Gasthaus Erika's
  610 N. Washington St., 785/762-6414

Best Mexican Food
Pinata Mexican Restaurant
  322 W. Sixth St., 785/238-7346

Best Steaks
Sirloin Stockade
  426 Goldenbelt Dr., 785/238-1817

KANSAS CITY, KS

[See also: Overland Park and Shawnee; and Kansas City, MO.]

Best Breakfast
Fritz's Union Station
  250 N. Eighteenth St., 913/281-2777

Best Delicatessen
Gino Deli
  901 N. Seventh St., 913/342-8225
Sophie's Deli and Catering
  553 Central Ave., 913/321-9454

Best Dinner
Mrs. Peter's Chicken Dinners
  4960 State Ave., 913/287-7711

Best Homestyle Food
Loretta's Cafe
  838 Minnesota Ave., 913/371-9175
Mrs. Peter's Chicken Dinners
  4960 State Ave., 913/287-7711

Best Lunch
Jennie's Restaurant
  402 N. Fifth St., 913/621-4222
Loretta's Cafe
  838 Minnesota Ave., 913/371-9175

Best Mexican Food
Casa De Tacos
  1817 Park Dr., 913/342-6226

Best Steaks
Frontier Restaurant
  9338 State Ave., 913/788-9159

LAWRENCE, KS

Best Breakfast
Paradise Cafe
  728 Massachusetts St., 785/842-5199

Village Inn Pancake House
821 Iowa St., 785/842-3251

Best Brewpub
Free State Brewing Company
636 Massachusetts St., 785/843-4555

Best Burgers
Johnny's Tavern
401 N. Second St., 785/842-0377

Best Chinese Food
Panda Garden
1500 W. Sixth St., 785/843-4312
Royal Peking
711 W. 23rd St., 785/841-4599

Best Fine Dining
Fifi's Restaurant
925 Iowa St., 785/841-7226

Best Mexican Food
Pancho's Mexican Restaurant
711 W. 23rd St., 785/843-4044

Best Pizza
Old Chicago
2320 S. Iowa St., 785/841-4124
Teller's
746 Massachusetts St., 785/843-4111

Best Sandwiches
Paradise Cafe
728 Massachusetts St., 785/842-5199

Best Steaks
Mr. Steak
920 W. 23rd St., 785/841-3454
Sirloin Stockade
1015 Iowa St., 785/749-3005

LEAVENWORTH, KS

Best American Food
Bootleggers' Steak and Barbecue
1709 Metropolitan St., 913/758-0775
Mama Mia's Pizza
402 S. 20th St., 913/682-2131

Best Atmosphere
Skyview
504 Grand Ave., 913/682-2653
The Tea Room
505 Delaware St., 913/682-0777

Best Barbecue/Ribs
High Noon Saloon
206 Choctaw St., 913/682-4876

Best Brewpub
High Noon Saloon
206 Choctaw St., 913/682-4876

Best Chinese Food
New China Inn
3519 S. Fourth St., 913/651-8088

Best Diner
Pullman Place
232 Cherokee St., 913/682-8658

Best Fine Dining
Skyview
504 Grand Ave., 913/682-2653

Best Italian Food
Mama Mia's Pizza
402 S. Twentieth St., 913/682-2131

Best Lunch
The Tea Room
505 Delaware St., 913/682-0777

Best Mexican Food
El Sambre Restaurant
781 Shawnee St., 913/682-3200

LIBERAL, KS

K

Best Barbecue/Ribs
King's Pit Bar BQ
355 E. Oancake Blvd., 316/624-2451

Be4st Chinese Food
Hong kong Restaurant
802 Hwy. 54E, 316/624-7012

Best Homestyle Food
Dean's Family Restaurant
339 E. Pancake Blvd., 316/624-1875

Best Mexican Food
Casa Alvarez
1010 S. Kansas Ave., 316/624-5205

MANHATTAN, KS

Best Barbecue/Ribs
Calico Inn Restaurant
105 S. Broadway, Riley, 785/485-2622

Best Cajun/Creole Food
Hibachi Hut
608 N. Twelfth St., 785/539-9393

Best Chinese Food
Hunan Chinese Restaurant
1304 Westloop Pl., 785/539-8888
Yen Ching Chinese Restaurant
1005 N. Seth Child Rd., 785/776-2020

Best Coffee/Coffeehouse
Espresso Royale
616 N. Manhattan Ave., 785/537-2345

Best Desserts
Harry's Uptown Supper Club
418 Poyntz Ave., 785/537-1300

Best Family Restaurant
Village Inn
204 Tuttle Creek Blvd., 785/537-3776

Best Mexican Food
Texas Star Cafe
  608 N. Twelfth St., 785/537-9077

Best Pizza
Pyramid Pizza
  1130 Moro St., 785/539-4888

Best Steaks
Harry's Uptown Supper Club
  418 Poyntz Ave., 785/537-1300
Little Apple Brewing Company
  1110 Westloop Pl., 785/539-5500

Best Sunday Brunch
Scampi's
  Holiday Inn, 530 Richards Dr., 785/539-5311

OLATHE, KS

K

[See also: Kansas City, Overland Park, and Shawnee; and Kansas City, MO.]

Best Burgers
Austin's
  2103 E. 151st St., 913/829-2106
Back Yard Burgers
  124 N. Claiborne Rd., 913/780-4114

Best Business Lunch
Ambrosia's
  Holiday Inn, 101 W. 151st St., 913/829-4000

Best Chinese Food
Golden Bowl Restaurant
  1808 E. Santa Fe St., 913/829-3435

Best Coffee/Coffeehouse
Christian Book and Gift Shoppe
  1229 E. Santa Fe St., 913/764-1752
Cinnamon's Deli
  2097 E. Santa Fe St., 913/782-7887

Best Diner
West Side Diner
  117 S. Kansas Ave., 913/780-6611

Best Family Restaurant
Kansas Machine Shed Restaurant
  12080 S. Strangline Rd., 913/780-2697

Best Italian Food
Pizzetti's Pizza
  2018 E. Santa Fe St., 913/764-9300

Best Sandwiches
Cinnamon's Deli
  2097 E. Santa Fe St., 913/782-7887

OVERLAND PARK, KS

*[See also: Kansas City, Olathe, and Shawnee; and
Kansas City, MO.]*

Best Barbecue/Ribs
Boardroom Bar B-Q
9600 Antioch Rd., 913/642-6273

Best Ice Cream/Yogurt
Maggie Moo's
9218 Metcalf Ave., 913/642-7888

SALINA, KS

Best American Food
Red Coach Inn Restaurant
2110 W. Crawford St., 913/825-2166
Tom's Appletree Restaurant
2404 S. Ninth St., 785/823-7339

Best Beer Selection
Shooter's Bar and Grill
107 N. Santa Fe Ave., 785/827-0922

Best Breakfast
Russell's Restaurant
649 Westport Blvd., 785/825-5733

Best Chinese Food
Beijing Restaurant
1601 W. Crawford St., 785/823-1685

Best Coffee/Coffeehouse
Coffee Gallery
104 S. Fifth St., 785/823-5093

Best Delicatessen
Mr. Goodcents Subs and Pasta
2344 Planet Ave., 785/826-9500

Best Greek/Mediterranean Food
The Captain's Quarters
Ramada Inn, 1949 N. Ninth St., 785/825-8211

Best Homestyle Food
Grandma Max's Restaurant
1944 N. Ninth St., 785/825-5023

Best Ice Cream/Yogurt
Bogey's
1417 S. Ninth St., 785/823-8066

Best Outdoor Dining
JC's Bar and Grill
2030 S. Ohio St., 785/823-8549

Best Pizza
Scheme Restaurant
123 N. Seventh St., 785/823-5125

Best Romantic Dining
Ranger's Steak and Seafood House
150A S. Broadway Blvd., 785/823-3491

K

Best Salad/Salad Bar
Sirloin Stockade
  2351 S. Ninth St., 785/823-2787

Best Sports Bar
JC's Bar and Grill
  2030 S. Ohio St., 785/823-8549

Best Vegetarian Food
The Captain's Quarters
  Ramada Inn, 1949 N. Ninth St., 785/825-8211

SHAWNEE, KS

*[See also: Kansas City, Olathe, and Overland Park;
and Kansas City, MO.]*

K

Best Barbecue/Ribs
K.C. Masterpiece Barbecue
  10985 Metcalf Ave., 913/345-1199

Best Breakfast
First Watch
  9916 College Blvd., 913/339-6686
  4117 W. 83rd St., 913/649-8875
  7305 W. 95th St., 913/383-2904
Le Peep Restaurant
  7218 College Blvd., 913/661-9441

Best Brewpub
Rock Bottom Brewery
  11721 Metcalf Ave., 913/663-2422

Best Burgers
Dick Clark's American Bandstand Grill
  10975 Metcalf Ave., 913/451-1600
Fred P. Ott's Bar and Grill
  6700 College Blvd., 913/451-2999
Talk of the Town Grill and Bar
  11922 W. 119th St., 913/661-9922

Best Coffee/Coffeehouse
101 Bean Company
  9220 Metcalf Ave., 913/642-3267
Mildred's Coffeehouse
  7921 Santa Fe Dr., 913/341-0301

Best Homestyle Food
The Black-Eyed Pea
  11836 W. 95th St., 913/599-3222
  11900 Shawnee Mission Pkwy., 913/962-0900

Best Ice Cream/Yogurt
Maggie Moo's Creamery
  6471 Quivira Rd., 913/268-8500
  7628 State Line Rd., 913/649-0979
  12014 College Blvd., 913/339-9009
  4308 W. 119th St., 913/338-1428

Best Mexican Food
Jalapeno's Mexican Restaurant
  7729 W. 151st St., 913/681-3555

Jose Pepper's
   10316 Metcalf Ave., 913/341-5673
La Cocina Del Puerco
   9097 Metcalf Ave., 913/341-2800
Margarita's West
   12200 Johnson Dr., 913/631-5553

Best Sandwiches
Bagel and Bagel
   7940 Lee Blvd., 913/341-2080
   4949 W. 119th St., 913/338-2080

Best Seafood
J. Alexander's
   11471 Metcalf Ave., 913/469-1995

Best Southwestern Food
Coyote Grill
   4843 Johnson Dr., 913/362-3333

Best Steaks
Houston's Restaurant
   7111 W. 95th St., 913/642-0630
J. Alexander's
   11471 Metcalf Ave., 913/469-1995
Martini's Restaurant
   11723 Roe Ave., 913/451-4515

Best Thai Food
Bangkok Pavilion
   7249 W. 97th St., 913/341-3005
Thai Orchid
   6504 Mission W. St., 913/384-2800

TOPEKA, KS

Best Atmosphere
Heritage House
   3635 SW Sixth Ave., 785/233-3808

Best Barbecue/Ribs
Grover's Smokehouse
   100 SW 29th St., 785/272-0033
   1217 SW Gage Blvd., 785/273-7331

Best Bistro
JJ's Bistro
   2121 SW Belle Ave., 785/272-3100

Best Breakfast
Courtney's Family Restaurant
   2833 SW Fairlawn Rd., 785/273-7155
Kozy Kitchen
   315 SE 29th St., 785/267-6128

Best Brewpub
Barley's Brewhaus
   801 S. Kansas Ave., 785/357-5300
Blind Tiger Brewery and Restaurant
   417 SW 37th St., 785/267-2739

Best Burgers
Heidelberger Cafe
   1409 NW Topeka Blvd., 785/233-9065

K

Prize Package Store
1420 SE Sixth Ave., 785/232-5764

Best Business Lunch
Charley Porubsky's
508 NE Sardou Ave., 785/234-5788
China Pavilion
5348 SW Seventeenth St., 785/271-5656
Po'e Richard's
705 S Kansas Ave., 785/233-4276

Best Chinese Food
Evergreen Chinese Restaurant
2038 SW Gage Blvd., 785/271-2038
Great Wall Chinese Restaurant
1336 SW Seventeenth St., 785/234-1060

Best Coffee/Coffeehouse
PT's Cafe Expresso
Fleming Place Shopping Center, 4025 SW Tenth
Ave., 785/271-8188
The Classic Bean
628 S. Kansas Ave., 785/232-1001

Best Delicatessen
Mr. Goodcents Subs and Pastas
1001 S. Kansas Ave., 785/233-2368

Best Desserts
Paisano's Italian Ristorante
4043 SW Tenth Ave., 785/273-0100
The Heritage House
3535 SW Sixth Ave., 785/233-3800

Best Eclectic Menu
New City Cafe
4005 Gage Center Dr., 785/271-8646

Best Italian Food
Paisano's Italian Ristorante
4043 SW Tenth Ave., 785/273-0100
Pappas' Eatery and Pub
926 S. Kansas Ave., 785/232-6161

Best Japanese Food
Kobe Steak House of Japan
5331 SW 22nd Pl., 785/272-6633

Best Mexican Food
Pepe and Chela's
1001 SW Tyler St., 785/357-8332
Rosa's Mexican Restaurant
2025 SE California Ave., 785/233-9842

Best Pizza
Grazie's the Italian Bistro
435 S. Kansas Ave., 785/357-6545

Best Restaurant in Town
The Heritage House
3535 SW Sixth Ave., 785/233-3800

Best Sandwiches
Corner Pocket Carryout
623 Poke Ave., 785/232-5522

Willie C's Cafe and Bar
2047 SW Topeka Blvd., 785/232-8080

Best Sports Bar
Remington's
1155 SW Wanamaker Rd., 785/271-8700

Best Steaks
Topeka Steak House
526 SE Dupont Rd., Tecumseh, 785/379-9994

Best Sunday Brunch
Aboud's at Western Hills Country Club
8533 SW 21st St., 785/478-9290

WICHITA, KS

Best Barbecue/Ribs
Miller's Bar B Que
4788 E. Thirteenth St. N., 316/684-8080

Best Breakfast
Willie C's Cafe and Bar
1320 E. Kellogg Dr., 316/262-3424
7525 E. Douglas Ave., 316/686-0753
656 S. West St., 316/942-4077

Best Chinese Food
Kwan Wah
795 N. West St., 316/945-5484
4600 W. Kellogg Dr., 316/945-8099
7700 E. Kellogg Dr., 316/686-8396
945 S. Oliver St., 316/682-1081

Best Delicatessen
Piccadilly Market
7728 E. Central Ave., 316/681-1100

Best Diner
Old Mill Tasty Shop
604 E. Douglas Ave., 316/264-6500
Rock Island Cafe
725 E. Douglas Ave., 316/263-1616

Best Greek/Mediterranean Food
Piccadilly Market
7728 E. Central Ave., 316/681-1100

Best Italian Food
Angelo's Italian Foods
3105 E. Harry St., 316/682-1473
Savute's Italian Ristorante
3303 N. Broadway St., 316/838-0455

Best Pizza
Piccadilly Market
7728 E. Central Ave., 316/681-1100

Best Sandwiches
Artichoke Sandwich Bar
811 N. Broadway St., 316/263-9164
Old Mill Tasty Shop
604 E. Douglas Ave., 316/264-6500

K

Best Steaks
Doc's Steak House
   1515 N. Broadway St., 316/264-4735

K

Kentucky

ASHLAND, KY

Best Barbecue/Ribs
Damon's
500 Winchester Ave., 606/325-8929

Best Italian Food
Italian Oven
1069 U.S. Hwy. 60, 606/928-4222

Best Steaks
Columbia Steak House
1290 Montgomery Ave., 606/329-1012

BEREA, KY

Best Breakfast
Dinner Bell Restaurant
I-75 Plaza, 606/986-2777

Best Coffee/Coffeehouse
Berea Coffee and Tea Company
124 Main St., 606/986-7656

Best Dinner
Boone Tavern Hotel
100 Main St. N., 606/986-9358

Best Family Restaurant
Columbia Mountain Grill
107 Peggy Flats, I-75, Exit 77, 606/986-3639

Best Pizza
Papaleno's Restaurant
108 Center St., 606/986-4497

Best Sandwiches
Papaleno's Restaurant
108 Center St., 606/986-4497

BOWLING GREEN, KY

Best Barbecue/Ribs
Split Tree Barbecue
  8872 Scottsville Rd., Alvaton, 502/842-2268

Best Breakfast
Murray's Restaurant
  1313 31W Bypass, 502/842-7504

Best Business Lunch
440 Main Restaurant and Bar
  440 E. Main St., 502/793-0450

Best Chinese Food
Beijing Restaurant
  1951 Scottsville Rd., 502/842-2288

Best Fine Dining
Andrew's Restaurant and Bar
  2019 Scottsville Rd., 502/781-7680

Best Homestyle Food
Judy's Castle
  3102 31W Bypass, 502/842-8736

Best Ice Cream/Yogurt
Clark's Drive In
  129 31W Bypass, 502/842-5101

Best Mexican Food
Pepe's Mexican Restaurant
  2001 Russellville Rd., 502/782-3902
  600 31W Bypass, Ste. 21, 502/781-6292

Best Pizza
Mancino's Grinders and Pizza
  1620A Scottsville Rd., 502/783-8000

Best Restaurant in Town
Parakeet Cafe and Bar
  522 Morris Alley, 502/781-1538

Best Sandwiches
Cambridge Market and Cafe
  830 Fairview Ave., 502/782-9367

Best Seafood
Mariah's
  801 State St., 502/842-6878

Best Thai Food
Taste of Thai
  410 E. Main St., 502/781-6961

CORBIN, KY

Best Burgers
Crabtree Restaurant
  129 Eighteenth St., 606/528-4163

Best Pizza
Pizza and Company
  1500 S. Main St., 606/523-1400

Best Regional Food
Dixie Cafe
  208 S. Main St., 606/523-1999

COVINGTON, KY

Best American Food
Anchor Grill
   438 Pike St., 606/431-9498
Barleycorn's Yacht Club
   201 Riverboat Row, Newport, 606/292-2978
Coach and Four Restaurant
   214 Scott St., 606/431-6700
Remington's Roadhouse
   301 Riverboat Row, Newport, 606/491-7500

Best Breakfast
Old Towne Tavern
   32 W. Seventh St., 606/581-3509

Best Casual Dining
Di John Restaurant and Bar
   724 Madison Ave., 606/581-5646
Old Towne Tavern
   32 W. Seventh St., 606/581-3509

Best Coffee/Coffeehouse
Awakenings Coffee and Tea Company
   2343 Buttermilk Crossing, Crescent Springs,
      606/578-0033
Behle Street Cafe
   50 E. Rivercenter Blvd., 606/291-4100

Best Fine Dining
E Room Restaurant
   Embassy Suites Hotel, 10 E. Rivercenter Blvd.,
      606/261-8400

Best German Food
Wertheim's Restaurant
   514 W. Sixth St., 606/261-1233

Best Italian Food
Pompilio's
   600 Washington Ave., Newport, 606/581-3065

Best Lunch
Calico Kitchen
   106 E. Fourth St., 606/261-6700
Gold Star Chili
   635 Madison Ave., 606/491-0029
The Point
   45 W. Pike St., 606/491-0602
Skyline Chili
   617 W. Third St., 606/261-8474

Best Sports Bar
Willie's Sports Cafe & Bar and Grill
   401 Crescent Ave., 513/581-1500

Best Restaurant in Town
Dee Felice Cafe
   529 Main St., 606/261-2365
Mike Fink Restaurant
   Greenup St., 606/261-4212

DANVILLE, KY

Best Breakfast
Beaumont Inn
  638 Beaumont Dr., Harrodsburg, 606/734-3381
Shakertown Inn
  3501 Lexington Rd., Harrodsburg, 606/734-5411

Best Desserts
Sweet Difference
  132 Church St., 606/236-9847

Best Family Restaurant
Western Steer Steakhouse
  U.S. Hwy. 150W Bypass, 606/236-2944

Best Mexican Food
Guadalajara Mexican Restaurant
  917 Hustonville Rd., 606/238-7551

Best Regional Food
Pioneer Playhouse
  840 Stanford Rd., 606/236-2747

Best Tea Room
Tea Leaf
  230 W. Broadway St., 606/236-7456

ELIZABETHTOWN, KY

Best Dinner
Depot Restaurant
  201 E. Main St., Glendale, 502/369-6000

Best Fine Dining
Stone Hearth
  1001 N. Mulberry St., 502/765-4898

Best Lunch
Old Vault Deli
  45 Public Square, 502/737-7550

Best Sandwiches
Back Home
  251 W. Dixie Ave., 502/769-2800
Back Home Again
  2004 N. Mulberry St., 502/769-2822

FRANKFORT, KY

Best American Food
Bullfrog's Restaurant
  243 W. Broadway St., 502/875-0090
Market Cafe
  238 W. Main St., 502/223-5548

Best Burgers
Cliffside Restaurant
  Lawrenceburg Rd., 502/223-3173

Best Lunch
Kelley's Garden
  334 St. Clair St., 502/227-7287
Pot Belly Deli
  120 Brighton Park Blvd., 502/695-8494

Best Mexican Food
Aranda's
    193 Versailles Rd., 502/695-4002
La Fiesta Grande
    314 Versailles Rd., 502/695-8378

Best Seafood
Jim's Seafood
    950 Wilkinson Blvd., 502/223-7448

Best Thai Food
Smile of Siam
    19 Century Plz. S., 502/227-9934

FT. MITCHELL, KY

Best American Food
Burbanks Real Barbecue
    400 Buttermilk Pike, 606/341-2806

Best Barbecue/Ribs
Walt's Hitching Post
    3300 Madison Pike, 606/331-0494

Best Continental Food
Josh's
    The Drawbridge Estate, I-75 at Buttermilk Pike,
       606/341-2800

Best Regional Food
Skyline Chili
    2196 Dixie Hwy., 606/331-8352

Best Restaurant In Town
Greyhound Tavern
    2500 Dixie Hwy., 606/331-3767

HENDERSON, KY

Best American Food
The Mill
    526 S. Main St., 502/826-8012

Best Barbecue/Ribs
Ralph's Hickory Pit
    739 N. Green St., 502/826-5656

Best Breakfast
Downtown Diner
    122 First St., 502/827-9671

Best Chinese Food
Hunan Chinese Restaurant
    1765 S. Green St., 502/827-2229

Best Coffee/Coffeehouse
Planters Coffeehouse
    130 N. Main St., 502/830-0927

Best Mexican Food
Los Toribo
    1739 S. Green St., 502/831-2367

Best Salad/Salad Bar
Mezzaluna
    104 N. Water St., 502/826-9401

K

Planters Coffeehouse
130 N. Main St., 502/830-0927

HOPKINSVILLE, KY

Best American Food
Bartholomew's
914 S. Main St., 502/886-5768
J's on Main
1004 S. Main St., 502/885-2896

Best Barbecue/Ribs
Bar B Q Shack
468 Pembroke Rd., Pembroke, 502/475-4844

Best Breakfast
Roundie's Restaurant
115 E. First St., 502/886-4240

Best Burgers
Ferrell's Snappy Service
1001 S. Main St., 502/886-1445

Best Homestyle Food
Owen's Delicatessen
206 North Dr., 502/886-2022

Best Seafood
Bartholomew's
914 S. Main St., 502/886-5768

Best Steaks
Charlie's Steakhouse
Hwy. 41A, Oak Grove, 502/439-4592

LEXINGTON, KY

Best American Food
Ed and Fred's Desert Moon
148 Grand Blvd., 606/231-1161
Roy and Nadine's
3735 Harrodsburg Rd., 606/223-0797

Best Bar
Buffalo and Dad's
805 N. Broadway, 606/252-7602
Cheapside Bar and Grill
131 Cheapside, 606/254-0046
Rosebud Restaurant and Bar
121 N. Mill St., 606/254-1907

Best Barbecue/Ribs
Billy's Bar-B-Q
101 Cochran Rd., 606/269-9593
Spuds Grill and Tavern
3130 Pimlico Pkwy., 606/273-8885

Best Brewpub
Lexington City Brewery
1050 S. Broadway, 606/259-2739

Best Burgers
Buffalo and Dad's
805 N. Broadway, 606/252-7602
Linus Irish Pub and Grill
388 Woodland Ave., 606/255-6614

K

Max and Erma's
153 Patchen Dr., 606/269-5692

Best Business Lunch
De Sha's Grille and Bar
101 N. Broadway, 606/259-3771

Best Coffee/Coffeehouse
Common Grounds Coffee House
343 E. High St., 606/233-9761

Best Continental Food
A La Lucie
159 N. Limestone, 606/252-5277

Best Dinner
Coach House
855 S. Broadway, 606/252-7777

Best Eclectic Menu
Cheapside Bar and Grill
131 Cheapside, 606/254-0046

Best Fine Dining
Coach House
855 S. Broadway, 606/252-7777
Merrick Inn
3380 Tates Creek Rd., 606/269-5417

Best Homestyle Food
Ramsey's Diner
4053 Tates Creek Centre Dr., 606/271-2638
496 E. High St., 606/259-2708

Best Inexpensive Meal
Tolly-Ho
395 S. Limestone, 606/253-2007

Best Italian Food
Bravo Pitino Restaurant
401 W. Main St., 606/255-2222
Lexitalia Ristorante
1765 Alexandria Dr., 606/277-1116

Best Lunch
Phil Dunn's Cook Shop
431 Old Vine St., 606/231-0099

Best Mexican Food
Don Pablo's Mexican Restaurant
3737 Nicholasville Rd., 606/271-7094
Mesa Bar and Grill
401 W. Main St., 606/231-6372
Mi Mexico
818 New Circle Rd. NE, 606/253-0690
Ricon Mexicano
818 E. Euclid Ave., 606/268-8160

Best Pizza
Joe Bologna's Restaurant
380 S. Mill St., 606/259-0495
120 W. Maxwell St., 606/252-4933

Best Regional Food
Hall's on the River Restaurant
1225 Boonesboro Rd., Winchester, 606/255-8105

Best Seafood
New Orleans House
  1510 Newtown Pike, 606/254-3474

Best Sports Bar
Two Keys Tavern
  333 S. Limestone, 606/254-5000

Best Steaks
Cliff Hagan's Ribeye
  941 Winchester Rd., 606/253-0750
Columbia Steak House
  261 Midland Ave., 606/231-0008

Best Vegetarian Food
Alfalfa Restaurant
  557 S. Limestone, 606/253-0014
Everybody's Natural Foods Deli
  503 E. Euclid Ave., 606/255-4162

K

LONDON, KY

Best Burgers
Dairy Dart
  1255 S. Main St., 606/864-5051
Weaver's Hot Dogs
  131 N. Main St., 606/864-9937

Best Desserts
Frisch's Big Boy Restaurant
  Hwy. 192 at Hwy. 75, 606/878-2620

Best Family Restaurant
Charcoal House
  2035 W. Hwy. 192, 606/864-7383

LOUISVILLE, KY

Best Barbecue/Ribs
Bibby's
  3812 Bardstown Rd., 502/451-2122
Gib's
  2224 Dundee Rd., 502/451-5154
Mark's Feed Store
  11422 Shelbyville Rd., Middletown, 502/244-0140
Rib Tavern
  4157 Bardstown Rd., 502/499-1515
Vince Staten's Old Time Barbecue
  9219 U.S. Hwy. 42, 502/228-7427

Best Bistro
Baxter Station Bar and Grill
  1201 Payne St., 502/584-1635
Bobby J's
  1314 Bardstown Rd., 502/452-2665
Deitrich's
  2862 Frankfort Ave., 502/897-6076
Uptown Cafe
  1624 Bardstown Rd., 502/458-4212

Best Breakfast
Lynn's Paradise Cafe
  984 Barrett Ave., 502/583-3447

Best Burgers
W.W. Cousins
  900 Dupont Rd., 502/897-9684
  2101 S. Hurstbourne Pkwy., 502/896-8881

Best Cafeteria
Blue Boar
  3008 Bardstown Rd., 502/458-7262
  802 Eastern Pkwy., 502/634-1052
  106 Bauer Ave., 502/899-3030
  7900 Shelbyville Rd., 502/426-3310
Colonnade
  455 S. Fourth Ave., Ste.120, 502/584-6846
Jay's Cafeteria
  1812 W. Muhammad Ali Blvd., 502/538-2534
Miller's
  429 S. Second St., 502/582-9135
Morrison's
  4801 Outer Loop, 502/964-5756
  133 S. Hurstbourne Pkwy., 502/423-1733

Best Chinese Food
Asian Pearl
  2060 S. Hurstbourne Pkwy., 502/495-6800
August Moon
  2296 Lexington Rd., 502/456-6569
Empress of China
  210 Holiday Manor, 502/426-1717
  2249 Hikes Ln., 502/451-2500
Sichuan Garden
  9850 Linn Station Rd., 502/426-6767

Best Coffee/Coffeehouse
John Conti
  4023 Bardstown Rd., 502/499-8602
Twice Told
  1604 Bardstown Rd., 502/456-0507

Best Continental Food
211 Clover Lane Restaurant
  The Colony Center, 211 Clover Ln., 502/896-9570

Best Delicatessen
Karem Deeb Liquors and Deli
  2228 Taylorsville Rd., 502/458-1668
Cafe LaPeche
  4941 Holiday Manor Shopping Plaza, 502/339-7593
Stevens and Stevens
  1114 Bardstown Rd., 502/584-3354
Wall Street Deli
  400 W. Market St., 502/585-4202

Best Desserts
La Crepe Ermin
  1538 Bardstown Rd., 502/485-9755
Cafe LaPeche
  4941 Holiday Manor Shopping Plaza, 502/339-7593
Queen of Tarts
  1649 Cowling Ave., 502/473-0735
Sweet Surrender
  2311 Frankfort Ave., 502/896-0519

K

Best Eclectic Menu
Ramsi's Cafe
   1293 Bardstown Rd., 502/451-0700
Uptown Cafe
   1624 Bardstown Rd., 502/458-4212

Best Family Restaurant
Austin's
   4950 U.S. Hwy. 42, 502/423-1990
KT's
   2300 Lexington Rd., 502/458-8888
W.W. Cousins
   2101 S. Hurstbourne Pkwy., 502/896-8881
   900 Dupont Rd., 502/897-9684

Best Fine Dining
Jack Fry's
   1007 Bardstown Rd., 502/452-9244
Le Relais
   2817 Taylorsville Rd. at Bowman Field, 502/451-9020
The English Grill
   The Brown Hotel, 335 W. Broadway, 502/583-1234
Timothy's
   826 E. Broadway, 502/561-0880

Best German Food
Gasthaus
   4818 Brownsboro Rd., 502/899-7177

Best Greek/Mediterranean Food
Grape Leaf
   2217 Frankfort Ave., 502/897-1774
Pita Delights
   1015 Barrett Ave., 502/583-2926

Best Italian Food
Bravo's
   600 W. Main St., 502/568-2222
Ferd Grisanti
   10212 Taylorsville Rd., Jeffersontown,
      502/267-0050
Mama Grisanti
   3938 Dupont Circle, 502/893-0141
Porcini
   2730 Frankfort Ave., 502/894-8686
Romano's Macaroni Grill
   401 S. Hurstbourne Pkwy., 502/423-9220
Vincenzo's
   150 S. Fifth St., 502/580-1350

Best Japanese Food
Sesame
   9409 Shelbyville Rd., 502/339-7000
Shogun
   9026 Taylorsville Rd., 502/499-5700

Best Korean Food
A Little Bit of Seoul
   2206 Frankfort Ave., 502/894-9807
Koreana
   5009 Preston Hwy., 502/966-2115

Best Lunch
Bravo's
  600 W. Main St., 502/568-2222
Jack Fry's
  1007 Bardstown Rd., 502/452-9244
Timothy's
  826 E. Broadway, 502/561-0880

Best Mexican Food
El Caporal
  2209 Meadow Dr., 502/473-7840
El Mundo
  2345 Frankfort Ave., 502/899-9930
Frontero
  10602 Shelbyville Rd., 502/244-8889
La Cazuela
  7707 Preston Hwy., 502/966-2828
Tumbleweed Mexican Cafe
  7900 Shelbyville Rd., 502/339-8411
  12975 Shelbyville Rd., 502/245-2113

Best Middle Eastern Food
Mo Flav
  3334 Frankfort Ave., 502/896-1773

Best Other Ethnic Food
Cafe Kilimanjaro (Caribbean/South American)
  649 S. Fourth St., 502/583-4332
De La Torre's (Spanish/Mediterranean)
  1606 Bardstown Rd., 502/456-4955

Best Restaurant in Town
Allo Spiedo
  2309 Frankfort Ave., 502/895-4878
Cafe Metro
  700 Bardstown Rd., 502/458-4830
De La Torre's
  1606 Bardstown Rd., 502/456-4955
Equus
  122 Sears Ave., 502/897-9721
Shariats
  2901 Brownsboro Rd., 502/899-7878

Best Romantic Dining
Le Relais
  2817 Taylorsville Rd. at Bowman Field,
    502/451-9020
Lilly's
  1147 Bardstown Rd., 502/451-0447
Vincenzo's
  150 S. Fifth St., 502/580-1350

Best Salad/Salad Bar
Bluegrass Brewing Company
  3929 Shelbyville Rd., 502/899-7070
Lilly's
  1147 Bardstown Rd., 502/451-0447
Melrose Inn
  13306 W. Hwy. 42, Prospect, 502/228-1461

K

Best Sandwiches
Another Place
  1514 Bardstown Rd., 502/458-8141
Bluegrass Brewing Company
  3929 Shelbyville Rd., 502/899-7070
J.P. Kayrouz
  130 St. Matthews Ave., St. Matthews, 502/897-9300

Best Seafood
Carolina Shrimp and Seafood
  3922 Westport Rd., 502/894-8947
New Orleans House
  9424 Shelbyville Rd., 502/426-1577

Best Southwestern Food
Alameda
  1381 Bardstown Rd., 502/459-6300
Baja Bay
  1801 Bardstown Rd., 502/459-6398
Chico's
  3003 Breckenridge Ln., 502/452-2479
Judge Roy Bean's
  1801 Bardstown Rd., 502/451-4982
Mexico Tipico
  6517 Dixie Hwy., 502/933-9523

Best Steaks
Del Frisco's
  4107 Oechsli Ave., 502/897-7077
Dillon's
  2101 S. Hurstbourne Pkwy., 502/499-7106
John E's
  3708 Bardstown Rd., 502/456-1111
Pat's Steak House
  2437 Brownsboro Rd., 502/893-2062

Best Sunday Brunch
Bristol Bar and Grille
  1308 Bardstown Rd., 502/456-1702
Oak Room
  Seelbach Hotel, 500 S. Fourth Ave., 502/585-3200

Best Thai Food
Cafe Mimosa
  1216 Bardstown Rd., 502/458-2233
Thai Siam
  3002 1/2 Bardstown Rd., 502/458-6871

Best Vegetarian Food
Lynn's Paradise Cafe
  984 Barrett Ave., 502/583-3447
Rainbow Blossom
  12401 Shelbyville Rd., 502/244-2022
Twice Told
  1604 Bardstown Rd., 502/456-0507

Best Vietnamese Food
Vietnam Kitchen
  5339 Mitscher Ave., 502/363-5154·

MAYSVILLE, KY

Best Breakfast
Victoria's
  Ramada Inn, 484 Moody Dr., 606/564-6793

Best Burgers
De Sha's Restaurant
  1166 U.S. Hwy. 68, 606/564-9275

Best Chinese Food
Asian Garden
  1152 U.S. Hwy. 68, 606/564-8889
China Pearl Restaurant
  1569 U.S. Hwy. 68, Ste. 4, 606/759-5959

Best Homestyle Food
Ole Country Inn
  Main St., Germantown, 606/728-2912

Best Italian Food
Pasquale's Pizza
  186 U.S. Hwy. 68, 606/564-4039

Best Seafood
De Sha's Restaurant
  1166 U.S. Hwy. 68, 606/564-9275

Best Steaks
Cutter's Roadhouse
  140 Trademore Shopping Ctr., 606/783-1153
De Sha's Restaurant
  1166 U.S. Hwy. 68, 606/564-9275

MURRAY, KY

Best Chinese Food
August Moon Chinese Restaurant
  506 N. Twelfth St., 502/759-4653
New Hong Kong Restaurant
  1205 Stadium View, Hwy. 641N at Twelfth St.,
    502/753-4488

Best Family Restaurant
Martha's Restaurant
  1407 N. Twelfth St., 502/759-1648
Rudy's Restaurant
  104 S. Fifth St., 502/753-1632
T.J.'s Barbecue
  806 Chestnut St., 502/753-0045

Best Italian Food
Pagliai's Pizza and Italian
  970 Chestnut St., 502/753-2975

Best Mexican Food
Los Portales Mexican Restaurant
  12 Olympic Plaza, 502/767-0315

Best Steaks
Sirloin Stockade Family Steak House
  926 S. Twelfth St., 502/753-0440
  1502 Spring Hill Court, 502/753-0963

K

OWENSBORO, KY

Best Bar
Martin's
622 1/2 E. Second St., 502/684-3306

Best Barbecue/Ribs
George's Barbecue
1346 E. Fourth St., 502/926-9276
Kettle Barbecue
2530 W. Third St., 502/684-3800
Moonlight Bar-B-Que Inn
2840 W. Parrish Ave., 502/684-8143
Old Hickory Pit Barbecue
338 Washington Ave., 502/926-9000
Shady Rest Barbecue
3955 E. Fourth St., 502/926-8234

Best Breakfast
The Patio Dining Room
Executive Inn, 1 Executive Blvd., 502/926-8000

Best Burgers
Eight-Ball Restaurant
1846 Triplett St., 502/683-3693

Best Chinese Food
House of Hunan
2845 W. Parrish Ave., 502/683-6267

Best Diner
Jack and Jenny's Diner
201 E. Ninth St., 502/685-0226

Best Fine Dining
Briar Patch
2760 Veach Rd., 502/685-3329
Campbell Club
521 Frederica St., 502/684-4249

Best Inexpensive Meal
Jay Dee's Restaurant
1420 Breckenridge St., 502/683-9419

Best Italian Food
Mancino's Pizza and Grinders
2686 Frederica St., 502/688-8900

Best Mexican Food
Los Toribios
3034 E. Fourth St., 502/683-8361

Best Place to be "Seen"
Colby's
204 W. Third St., 502/685-4239
Red's Place
7046 State Rte. 56, 502/771-4007

Best Salad/Salad Bar
Trotters Restaurant
1100 Walnut St., 502/685-2771

Best Sandwiches
Colby's Deli and Cafe
401 Frederica St., 502/684-2495

Famous Deli
  102 W. Second St., 502/686-8202

Best Steaks
Briar Patch
  2760 Veach Rd., 502/685-3329

PADUCAH, KY

Best Barbecue/Ribs
Starnes Bar-B-Q
  1008 Joe Clifton Dr., 502/444-9555

Best Breakfast
Skin Head's Restaurant
  1020 S. 21st St., 502/442-6471

Best Burgers
Downtown Diner
  308 Broadway St., 502/443-1288

Best Chinese Food
Double Happiness
  3794 Hinkleville Rd., 502/443-5010

Best Homestyle Food
Little Castle Restaurant
  1008 Jefferson St., 502/442-1979

Best Italian Food
Cynthia's Ristorante
  127 S. Second St., 502/443-3319

Best Lunch
Hillbilly Cooker
  2530 Jackson St., 502/443-8748

Best Pizza
The Parlor
  3033 Lone Oak Rd., 502/554-3707

Best Seafood
Whaler's Catch Restaurant
  123 N. Second St., 502/444-7701

Best Steaks
Jeremiah's
  225 Broadway St., 502/443-3991

PIKEVILLE, KY

Best Chinese Food
Peking Chinese Restaurant
  293 Weddington Hollow, 606/437-6788

Best Casual Dining
Log Cabin Restaurant
  308 Town Mountain Rd., 606/437-9918

Best Mexican Food
Sam An Tonio's Ribs Nachos and More
  518 S. Mayo Trail, 606/432-3600
  U.S. Hwy. 23, Betsy Layne, 606/452-4000

Best Restaurant in Town
Landmark Inn
  146 S. Mayo Trail, 606/432-2545

K

Log Cabin Restaurant
 308 Town Mountain Rd., 606/437-9918
Windmill Family Restaurant
 90 Weddington Branch Rd., 606/432-2222

Best Steaks
Western Steer Steakhouse
 270 S. Mayo Trail, 606/437-9613

RICHMOND, KY

Best Bar
Madison Garden
 152 N. Madison Ave., 606/623-9720

Best Breakfast
Country Kettle
 1424 E. Main St., 606/625-5587
Early Bird Restaurant
 1417 E. Main St., 606/624-1649

Best Burgers
Jet Drive-In
 613 Big Hill Ave., 606/624-2018

Best Chinese Food
Tsing Tao Restaurant
 300 W. Main St., 606/624-0133
Wok and Go
 410 Eastern Bypass, 606/623-0660

Best Dinner
Woody's
 246 W. Main St., 606/623-5130

Best Family Restaurant
Country Kettle
 1424 E. Main St., 606/625-5587

Best Lunch
Gibson Bay Cafe
 2000 Gibson Bay Dr., 606/625-0704

Best Mexican Food
Casa Cafe
 459 Eastern Bypass, 606/623-8582
Paco's Mexican Restaurant
 124 S. First St., 606/623-0021

Best Pizza
Apollo Pizza
 228 S. Second St., 606/623-0330

Best Regional Food
Country Kettle
 1424 E. Main St., 606/625-5587

Louisiana

ALEXANDRIA, LA

Best Bar
Mirror Room
  Bentley Hotel, 200 DeSoto St., 318/448-9600

Best Breakfast
Pitt Grill Restaurant
  2360 S. MacArthur Dr., 318/442-9675

Best Burgers
Speedy Bee's
  2705 Shreveport Hwy., Pineville, 318/640-9755

Best Business Lunch
Tobe's
  Ramada Inn, 2211 N. MacArthur Dr., 318/443-2561

Best Casual Dining
Lea's Lunch Room
  1810 Hwy. 71S, Lecompte, 318/776-5178
Tunk's Cypress Inn Restaurant
  9507 Hwy. 28, Boyce, 318/487-4014

Best Chinese Food
Oriental Wok
  6 N. Bolton Ave., 318/448-8247

Best Coffee/Coffeehouse
Coffee Unlimited
  5820 Jackson St. Ext., 318/445-7451

Best Desserts
Lee J's Restaurant
  208 Main St., Pineville, 318/443-8789

Best Fine Dining
Bentley Room
  Bentley Hotel, 200 DeSoto St., 318/448-9600

Gray Fox Inn
  5521 Jackson St. Ext., 318/487-8333

Best Inexpensive Meal
Red Kettle Grill
  3746 S. MacArthur Dr., 318/445-6642

Best Italian Food
Suburban Garden
  3322 Jackson St., 318/442-6974

Best Late-Night Food
Ann's Coffee Shoppe
  2314 N. MacArthur Dr., 318/448-9073

Best Mexican Food
Julia's Mexican Restaurant
  2204 Worley Dr., 318/445-2405

Best Pizza
B.J. Pizza
  902 Versailles Blvd., 318/448-4104

Best Place to Eat Alone
Piccadilly Cafeteria
  1400 MacArthur Dr., 318/445-0209
  3451 Masonic Dr., 318/445-9574

Best Place to Take the Kids
Chuck E. Cheese Pizza
  1725 Metro Dr., 318/445-9843

Best Restaurant in Town
Mariner's Seafood and Steak House
  Hwy. 1 Bypass, 318/357-1220

Best Sandwiches
Critics' Choice
  5208 Rue Verdun, 318/445-1680
  415 Murray St., 318/442-3333

Best Seafood
Cajun Landing
  2728 N. MacArthur Dr., 318/487-4912

BATON ROUGE, LA

Best American Food
Cafe America Restaurant
  7521 Jefferson Hwy., 504/927-1626
Frank's Restaurant
  8353 Airline Hwy., 504/926-5977
Piccadilly Cafeteria
  3164 Government St., 504/293-9440
  3232 S. Sherwood Forest Blvd., 504/293-9440

Best Barbecue/Ribs
Jay's Bar-B-Q
  4215 Government St., 504/343-5082
Podnuh's Bar-B-Q
  7026 Florida Blvd., 504/926-3341
  5565 Essen Ln., 504/769-6617
  2648 S. Sherwood Forest Blvd., 504/295-7056
Sonny's Real Pit Bar-B-Q
  12475 Florida Blvd., 504/272-5028

T J Ribs
  2324 S. Acadian Thruway, 504/383-7427

Best Cajun/Creole Food
Drusilla Seafood Restaurant
  3482 Drusilla Ln., 504/923-0896
French Market Bistro
  16645 Highland Rd., 504/753-3500
Juban's Restaurant
  3739 Perkins Rd., 504/346-8422
Mansur's Restaurant
  3044 College Dr., 504/923-3366
The Factory
  3130 College Dr., 504/924-6735

Best Casual Dining
Superior Grill
  5435 Government St., 504/927-2022

Best Chinese Food
Bamboo Garden
  5207 Essen Ln., 504/769-2877
Hunan Chinese Restaurant
  4215 S. Sherwood Forest Blvd., 504/291-6868
Taste of China
  9716 Airline Hwy., 504/928-9911

Best Continental Food
Chalet Brandt
  7655 Old Hammond Hwy., 504/927-6040
DaJoNel's
  7327 Jefferson Hwy., 504/924-7537
Maison Lacour
  11025 N. Harrells Ferry Rd., 504/275-3755

Best Family Restaurant
Copeland's of New Orleans
  4957 Essen Ln., 504/769-1800
Giamanco's
  4624 Government St., 504/928-5045

Best Fine Dining
Chalet Brandt Restaurant
  7655 Old Hammond Hwy., 504/927-6040
Juban's Restaurant
  3739 Perkins Rd., 504/346-8422
Mansur's Restaurant
  3044 College Dr., 504/923-3366

Best French Food
Maison Lacour
  11025 N. Harrells Ferry Rd., 504/275-3755

Best Greek/Mediterranean Food
Zorba's Greek Place
  9990 Perkins Rd., 504/769-8833

Best Italian Food
Cippriani's
  4550 Concord Ave., 504/924-3930
Digiulio Brothers
  2903 Perkins Rd., 504/383-4203

L

Gino's
4542 Bennington Ave., 504/927-7156
Sarmando's
10763 Old Hammond Hwy., 504/273-9900

Best Lunch
The Daily Grind
2834 S. Sherwood Forest Blvd., Ste. C4,
504/291-3970

Best Mexican Food
Carlos Mexican Food
8740 Florida Blvd., 504/924-4712
Mamacita's Restaurant and Cantina
7524 Bluebonnet Blvd., 504/769-3850
Ninfa's Mexican Restaurant
4738 Constitution Ave., 504/924-0377
Superior Grill
5435 Government St., 504/927-2022

Best Other Ethnic Food
Arzi's Ethnic Cafe (Lebanese)
4625 S. Sherwood Forest Blvd., 504/293-2999
Serop's (Lebanese)
4065 Government St., 504/383-3658

Best Restaurant in Town
Chalet Brandt Restaurant
7655 Old Hammond Hwy., 504/927-6040
DaJoNel's Restaurant
7327 Jefferson Hwy., 504/924-7537
Joe's Dreyfus Store Restaurant
2731 Maringouin Rd. W., Hwy. 77S, Livonia,
504/637-2625
The Place Restaurant
5255 Florida Blvd., 504/924-5069

Best Romantic Dining
Drusilla Seafood Restaurant
3482 Drusilla Ln., 504/923-0896

Best Sandwiches
Brew Bacher's Grill
5580 Government St., 504/927-8131
5251 Nicholson Dr., 504/766-8491
3410 S. Sherwood Forest Blvd., 504/291-7669
3554 Drusilla Ln., 504/927-3344
George's
2943 Perkins Rd., 504/343-2363

Best Seafood
Don's Seafood and Steaks
6823 Airline Hwy., 504/357-0601
Mike Anderson's Seafood
1031 W. Lee Dr., 504/766-7823
Ralph and Kacoo's Seafood Restaurant
6110 Bluebonnet Blvd., 504/766-2113
7110 Airline Hwy., 504/356-2361

Best Sports Bar
Chelsea's Cafe
148 W. State St., 504/387-3679

Best Steaks
Ruth's Chris Steak House
  4836 Constitution, 504/925-0163
The Place Restaurant
  5255 Florida Blvd., 504/924-5069

Best Wine Selection
Don's Seafood and Steaks
  6823 Airline Hwy., 504/357-0601

CHALMETTE, LA

Best Barbecue/Ribs
Luther's Barbeque
  8740 W. Judge Perez Dr., 504/277-8167

Best Breakfast
Breakfast Club
  2200 Paris Rd., 504/279-7364

Best Italian Food
Rocky and Carlo Restaurant and Bar
  613 E. Saint Bernard Hwy., 504/279-8323

Best Seafood
Bubba John's Seafood Restaurant
  9212 W. Judge Perez Dr., 504/279-1589
Marina Wharf Seafood Restaurant
  5353 Paris Rd., 504/277-8215
Par 3 Restaurant
  1530 E. Judge Perez Dr., 504/279-9114
Rocky and Carlo Restaurant and Bar
  613 E. Saint Bernard Hwy., 504/279-8323

HAMMOND, LA

Best Casual Dining
Taste of Bavaria
  14476 Hwy. 22, Ponchatoula, 504/386-3634

Best Chinese Food
Trey Yuen Cuisine of China
  2100 N. Morrison Blvd., 504/345-6789

Best Seafood
Middendorf's Seafood Restaurant
  30160 U.S. Hwy. 51, Ponchatoula, 504/386-6666

HOUMA, LA

Best Breakfast
Abear's Restaurant
  209 Bayou Black Dr., 504/872-6306

Best Desserts
Your Just Desserts
  2731 W. Main St., 504/851-3336

Best Ice Cream/Yogurt
Scarlett Scoop Ice Cream
  300 Barrow St., 504/872-5114

Best Inexpensive Meal
Lunch Basket
  649 W. Main St., 504/876-7420

Best Mexican Food
Cuco's Border Cafe
   3038 E. Park Ave., 504/868-0800
La Casa Del Sol Fine Mexican Restaurant
   101 Monarch Dr., 504/872-3474

Best Seafood
Dave's Cajun Kitchen
   6240 W. Main St., 504/868-3870

KENNER, LA

Best Barbecue/Ribs
Texas Bar-B-Que Company
   2001 Williams Blvd., 504/464-4404

Best Casual Dining
Harbor Seafood and Oyster Bar
   3201 Williams Blvd., 504/443-6454

Best Chinese Food
Fortune Garden Chinese
   3804 Williams Blvd., 504/443-4114

Best Coffee/Coffeehouse
Chateau Coffee Cafe
   3501 Chateau Blvd., 504/465-9444

Best Dinner
Harbor Seafood and Oyster Bar
   3201 Williams Blvd., 504/443-6454

Best Eclectic Menu
Semolina
   3501 Chateau Blvd., 504/468-1047

Best Homestyle Food
Chateau Pub
   3535 Chateau Blvd., 504/466-7272

Best Italian Food
Andy Messina's Restaurant
   2717 Williams Blvd., 504/469-7373
Brick Oven Cafe
   2805 Williams Blvd., 504/466-2097

Best Mexican Food
Casa Tequila
   3229 Williams Blvd., 504/443-5423
El Patio Mexican Restaurant
   3244 Georgia Ave., 504/443-1188

Best Regional Food
Come Back Inn
   3826 Williams Blvd., 504/443-1623
Mosca's Restaurant
   4137 Hwy. 90W, Westwego, 504/436-9942

Best Sandwiches
Short Stop Po Boys
   4041 Williams Blvd., 504/443-3211

Best Seafood
Harbor Seafood and Oyster Bar
   3203 Williams Blvd., 504/443-6454

Jazz Seafood and Steaks
2722 Williams Blvd., 504/468-3237

LAFAYETTE, LA

Best Bar
Charley G's Seafood Grill
3809 Ambassador Caffery Pkwy., 318/981-0108

Best Breakfast
A La Carte Restaurant
301 Heymann Blvd., 318/235-8493
Bayou Bistro
Best Western Hotel, 1801 W. Pinhook Rd.,
318/233-8120
Cafe Des Amis
140 E. Bridge St., Breaux Bridge, 318/332-5273

Best Burgers
Bun's
105 St. Landry St., 318/232-3287
1406 Surrey St., 318/232-0979
Judice Inn
3134 Johnston St., 318/984-5614

Best Business Lunch
City Club of Lafayette
600 Jefferson St., Ste. 1600, 318/266-2250

Best Cajun/Creole Food
Prudhomme's Cajun Cafe
4676 NE Evangeline Thruway, Carencro,
318/896-1026

Best Casual Dining
Poor Boy's Riverside Inn
240 Tubing Rd., Broussard, 318/235-8559

Best Chinese Food
Kim's Chinese and Seafood Restaurant
1523 N. Bertrand Dr., 318/235-7874

Best Coffee/Coffeehouse
Anjo's Bakery
1507A Kaliste Saloom Rd., 318/989-1977

Best Desserts
A La Carte Restaurant
301 Heymann Blvd., 318/235-8493

Best Diner
Hub City Diner
1412 S. College Rd., 318/235-5683
Mel's Diner
112 Oil Center Dr., 318/234-7112
2946 Johnston St., 318/235-6129

Best Family Restaurant
Don's Seafood Hut
4309 Johnston Rd., 318/981-1141

Best Homestyle Food
T-Coon's
740 Jefferson St., 318/232-3803

L

Best Inexpensive Meal
La Fonda
    3809 Johnston St., 318/984-5630
Laura's Drive Inn
    918A Voorhies St., 318/234-3915

Best Italian Food
Baracca's Italian Grill
    3502 Ambassador Caffery Pkwy., 318/988-6119
Monelli Italian Restaurant
    4017 Johnston St., 318/989-9291

Best Late-Night Food
Hub City Diner
    1412 S. College Rd., 318/235-5683

Best Mexican Food
Ninfa's Mexican Restaurant
    3551 Ambassador Caffery Pkwy., 318/988-2333

Best Pizza
Louisiana Pizza Kitchen
    1926 W. Pinhook Rd., 318/237-5800

Best Place to Be "Seen"
Charley G's Seafood Grill
    3809 Ambassador Caffery Pkwy., 318/981-0108

Best Place to Eat Alone
Dwyer's Cafe
    323 Jefferson Blvd., 318/235-9364

Best Restaurant in Town
Blair House Restaurant
    1316 Surrey St., 318/234-0357
Cafe Vermilionville
    1304 W. Pinhook Rd., 318/237-0100
Randall's
    2320 Kaliste Saloom Rd., 318/981-7080

Best Sandwiches
Cedar Grocery
    1115 Jefferson St., 318/233-5460
Chris' Po-Boys
    3304 Johnston St., 318/981-5073
    1900 W. Pinhook Rd., 318/234-6333
    631 Jefferson St., 318/234-1696
    1941 Moss St., 318/237-1095
Old Tyme Grocery
    218 W. Saint Mary Blvd., 318/235-8165

Best Seafood
Charley G's Seafood Grill
    3809 Ambassador Caffery Pkwy., 318/981-0108
Prejean's Restaurant
    3480 Hwy. 167N, 318/896-3247

Best Steaks
Ruth's Chris Steak House
    507 W. Pinhook, 318/237-6123

Best Sunday Brunch
Cafe Jardin
    Hilton Hotel, 1521 W. Pinhook Rd., 318/235-6111

Best Vegetarian Food
Baracca's Italian Grill
3502 Ambassador Caffery Pkwy., 318/988-6119

LAKE CHARLES, LA

Best Bar
Toucan on the Bayou
1103 W. Prien Lake Rd., 318/477-3337

Best Breakfast
Pitt Grill
928 Shady Ln., 318/478-4166

Best Business Lunch
Jean Lafitte Inn
501 W. College St., 318/474-2730

Best Casual Dining
Piccadilly Classic American
316 W. Prien Lake Rd., 318/477-7010

Best Chinese Food
China Garden Restaurant
419 W. Prien Lake Rd., 318/477-4447

Best Family Restaurant
Mr. Gatti's Pizza
3522 Ryan St., 318/474-6625

Best Fine Dining
Hunter's Harlequin Steaks and Seafood
1717 Hwy. 14, 318/439-2780

Best French Food
Pat's of Henderson
1500 Siebarth Dr., 318/439-6618

Best Italian Food
Italian Villa
3716 Ryan St., 318/477-8376
Tony's Pizza and Restaurant
335 W. Prien Lake Rd., 318/477-1611

Best Late-Night Food
Pitt Grill
715 W. Prien Lake Rd., 318/478-4166

Best Lunch
Pujo Street Cafe
508 Pujo St., 318/439-2054

Best Mexican Food
Casa Manana Mexican Restaurant
2510 Ryan St., 318/433-4112
Pepper's
545 W. Prien Lake Rd., 318/474-9869

Best Place to Take the Kids
Mr. Gatti's Pizza
3522 Ryan St., 318/474-6625

Best Sandwiches
Darrell's
119 W. College St., 318/474-3651

Best Seafood
Mr. D's on the Bayou
  3205 Common St., 318/433-9652
Steamboat Bill's
  1004 Lake Shore Dr., 318/494-1070

Best Steaks
Hunter's Harlequin Steaks and Seafood
  1717 Hwy. 14, 318/439-2780

METAIRIE, LA

Best American Food
Charley G's
  111 Veterans Memorial Blvd., Ste. 2, 504/837-6408
Mickey's Express Restaurant
  400 E. William David Pkwy., 504/833-7351

Best Barbecue/Ribs
Corky's Bar-B-Q
  4141 Veterans Memorial Blvd., Ste. 335,
    504/456-1732
Luther's Bar-B-Q
  2750 Severn Ave., 504/888-6370

Best Bistro
La Madaleine French Bistro
  3300 Severn Ave., Ste. 201, 504/456-1624
Tailgators Cafe
  933 Metairie Rd., 504/832-0122

Best Burgers
Lee's Hamburgers
  904 Veterans Memorial Blvd., 504/836-6804
O'Henry's Food and Spirits
  8859 Veterans Memorial Blvd., 504/461-9840
  3020 Severn Ave., 504/888-9383

Best Cajun/Creole Food
King Creole
  1517 Metairie Rd., 504/831-7009

Best Casual Dining
Houston's Restaurant
  4241 Veterans Memorial Blvd., 504/889-2301

Best Chinese Food
Royal China Restaurant
  600 Veterans Memorial Blvd., 504/831-9633

Best Coffee/Coffeehouse
Coffee Cottage
  2559 Metairie Rd., 504/833-3513
Morning Call Coffee Stand
  3325 Severn Ave., 504/885-4068

Best Delicatessen
Bayou Cowboy Deli and Seafood
  123 N. Lester Ave., 504/737-0862

Best Eclectic Menu
Straya California Creole Cafe
  4517 Veterans Memorial Blvd., 504/887-8873

Best French Food
Chez Daniel
  2037 Metairie Rd., 504/837-6900
Crozier's Restaurant Francias
  3216 W. Esplanade Ave. N., 504/833-8108

Best Greek/Mediterranean Food
Byblos Restaurant
  1501 Metairie Rd., 504/834-9773
Zissis Greek Restaurant
  2051 Metairie Rd., 504/837-7890

Best Indian Food
India Palace
  3322 N. Turnbull Dr., 504/889-2436
Taj Mahal Indian Cuisine
  923 Metairie Rd., 504/836-6859

Best Italian Food
Andrea's Restaurant
  3100 Nineteenth St., 504/834-8583
Barreca's Restaurant
  3100 Metairie Rd., 504/831-4546
Pomodorro Restaurant
  4634 Veterans Memorial Blvd., 504/888-3008

Best Japanese Food
Shogun Japanese Restaurant
  2325 Veterans Memorial Blvd., 504/833-7477

Best Mexican Food
Casa Garcia Mexican Restaurant
  8814 Veterans Memorial Blvd., 504/464-0354
Lucio's Mexican Restaurant
  3540 Eighteenth St., 504/456-1295

Best Middle Eastern Food
Casablanca Restaurant
  3030 Severn Ave., 504/888-2209

Best Pizza
Mark Twain's Pizza Landing
  2035 Metairie Rd., 504/832-8032
R & O Pizza Place
  216 Hammond Hwy., 504/831-1248

Best Seafood
Bozo's Restaurant
  3117 21st St., 504/831-8666
Charley G's
  111 Veterans Memorial Blvd., Ste. 2, 504/837-6408
Deanie's
  1713 Lake Ave., 504/831-4141
Drago's Seafood Restaurant
  3232 N. Arnoult Rd., 504/888-9254
Ralph and Kacoo's Seafood Restaurant
  601 Veterans Memorial Blvd., 504/831-3177
Sid-Mars Restaurant and Lounge
  1824 Orpheum Ave., 504/831-9541

Best Steaks
Ruth's Chris Steak House
  3633 Veterans Blvd., 504/888-3600

L

Saia's Beef Room
  2645 N. Causeway Blvd., 504/835-8555

Best Sunday Brunch
Peppermill Restaurant
  3524 Severn Ave., 504/455-2266

MINDEN, LA

Best Barbecue/Ribs
Neta's Drive-In
  1433 Shreveport Rd., 318/377-5675

Best Burgers
Hamburger Happiness
  11927 Hwy. 80, 318/371-0609
Trucker's Paradise
  1745 Hwy. 531, 318/371-1310

Best Chinese Food
China Town Restaurant
  712 Homer Rd., 318/377-7121

Best Seafood
Earl's Bayou Inn
  1 Dorcheat St., 318/371-0287

MONROE, LA

Best Barbecue/Ribs
Podnuh's Bar-B-Q
  1510 MLK Jr. Dr., 318/325-8747
  1810 Louisville Ave., 318/325-4261
  2021 Hudson Ln., 318/387-7684

Best Beer Selection
Trenton Street Bar
  207 Trenton St., West Monroe, 318/387-2157

Best Burgers
Melvyn's Restaurant
  2000 N. Eighteenth St., 318/325-2055

Best Cafeteria
Piccadilly Cafeteria
  2203 Louisville Ave., 318/325-5414

Best Cajun/Creole Food
Captain Avery Louisiana Restaurant
  1500 Hwy. 165N, 318/345-0100
Cormier's Cajun Restaurant
  1205 Forsythe Ave., 318/322-0414

Best Chinese Food
Peking Chinese Restaurant
  903 N. Fourth St., 318/361-0231

Best Coffee/Coffeehouse
The Coffee Bean
  1420 N. Eighteenth St., 318/324-9114

Best Desserts
Not Just Pie
  2117 Forsythe Ave., 318/322-9928

Best Homestyle Food
Kitchen Restaurant
202 S. Sixth St., 318/322-4224

Best Italian Food
Cascio's Italian and Cajun
305 Finks Hideaway Rd., 318/345-4536
Genusa's Italian Restaurant
815 Park Ave., 318/387-3083

Best Mexican Food
Rio Cafe
3211 Sterlington Rd., 318/324-0500

Best Pizza
Johnny's Pizza House
3812 Desiard St., 318/343-1835
1126 Hwy. 139, 318/345-0540
1707 McKeen Pl., 318/387-8668
801 S. Second St., 318/323-4458
3001 Sterlington Rd., 318/343-2992

Best Restaurant in Town
Chateau
2007 Louisville Ave., 318/325-0384
The Atrium Grille
Holiday Inn Atrium Hotel, 2001 Louisville Ave.,
318/325-0641
Warehouse No. 1 Restaurant
1 Olive St., 318/322-1340

Best Sandwiches
Ray's Pe Ge
8209 Desiard St., 318/343-0710

Best Seafood
Captain Avery Louisiana Restaurant
1500 Hwy. 165N, 318/345-0100
Mohawk Tavern Seafood Restaurant
704 Louisville Ave., 318/322-5481

Best Steaks
Monroe's Steak House
1301 N. Nineteenth St., 318/387-0908

MORGAN CITY, LA

Best Breakfast
Brannigan's
Holiday Inn, 520 Roderick St., 504/385-2200
Manny's Restaurant and Grill
7027 Hwy. 90E, 504/384-2359

Best Chinese Food
Formosa Gardens
7545 Hwy. 90E, 504/384-9436

Best Ice Cream/Yogurt
Tastee Freez
7708 Hwy. 90E, 504/384-1284

Best Mexican Food
Tampico Restaurant
1025 Victor II Blvd., 504/385-2784
1425 Hwy. 90W, 504/395-2859

Best Seafood
Landry's Seafood Inn
  6509 Hwy. 90E, 504/385-2285
Pat and Carolyn's Seafood Inn
  6701 Hwy. 90E, 504/384-8550
Rita Mae's Kitchen
  711 Federal Ave., 504/384-3550

NATCHITOCHES, LA

Best Cajun/Creole Food
Landing Restaurant
  530 Front St., 318/352-1579
Lasyone's Meat Pie Kitchen
  622 Second St., 318/352-3353

Best French Food
Merci Beaucoup
  127 Church St., 318/352-6634

Best Homestyle Food
Almost Home
  729 Third St., 318/352-2431

Best Mexican Food
Nicky's Mexican Restaurant
  4108 Hwy. 6, 318/352-1538

Best Steaks
Mariners Seafood and Steak House
  Hwy. 1 Bypass, 318/357-1220

NEW IBERIA, LA

Best Burgers
Duffy's Diner
  1120 Center St., 318/365-2326
Freez-O
  1215 Center St., 318/369-9391
Lil's Kitchen
  521 Main St., Jeanerette, 318/276-9600

Best Mexican Food
Tampico Restaurant
  602 W. Admiral Doyle Dr., 318/365-9547

Best Seafood
Landry's Seafood Restaurant
  20371 Hwy. 90, Jeanerette, 318/276-4857
Patio Restaurant
  105 N. Main St., Loreauville, 318/229-8281
Yellow Bowl Restaurant
  19466 Hwy. 182W, Jeanerette, 318/276-5512

NEW ORLEANS, LA

Best 24-Hour Restaurant
Clover Grill
  900 Bourbon St., 504/523-0904

Best All-You-Can-Eat Buffet
Court of the Two Sisters
  613 Royal St., 504/522-7261

Best American Food
Clancy's Restaurant
  6100 Annunciation St., 504/895-1111

Best Bistro
Di Piazza's Restaurant
  337 Dauphine St., 504/525-3335
Mr. B's Bistro
  201 Royal St., 504/523-2078

Best Breakfast
Bluebird Cafe
  7801 Panola St., 504/866-7577
  3625 Prytania St., 504/895-7166
New City Diner
  828 Gravier St., 504/522-8198
  1340 Poydras Dr., 504/561-0061

Best Brewpub
Crescent City Brewhouse
  527 Decatur St., 504/522-0571

Best Burgers
Port of Call
  838 Esplanade Ave., 504/523-0120

Best Cajun/Creole Food
Bon Ton Cafe
  401 Magazine St., 504/524-3386
Brennan's Restaurant
  417 Royal St., 504/525-9711
Cafe Rue Bourbon Restaurant
  241 Bourbon St., 504/524-0114
Christian's Restaurant
  3835 Iberville Rd., 504/482-4924
Copeland's of New Orleans
  4338 Saint Charles Ave., 504/897-2325
Dooky Chase Restaurant
  2301 Orleans Ave., 504/821-0600
Mandich Restaurant and Bar
  3200 Saint Claude Ave., 504/947-9553
Mike Anderson's Seafood Restaurant
  215 Bourbon St., 504/524-3884
  1400 Poydras St., 504/525-6334
  1 Poydras St., Ste. 163, 504/522-7727
Sazerac
  Fairmont Hotel, 123 Baronne St., 504/529-4733
The Alpine Restaurant
  620 Chartres St., 504/523-3005
Zachary's Restaurant
  8400 Oak St., 504/865-1559

Best Chinese Food
Five Happiness
  3605 S. Carrollton Ave., 504/482-3935

Best Coffee/Coffeehouse
Cafe Du Monde
  1 Poydras St., Ste. 27, 504/587-0841
  1400 Poydras St., 504/587-0842
  800 Decatur St., 504/525-4544
  1401 W. Esplanade, 504/468-3588
  197 Westbank Expressway 504/587-0849

P. J.'s
   24 McAlister Dr., 504/865-5705

Best Desserts
Camellia Grill
   626 S. Carrollton Ave., 504/866-9573
Caribbean Room
   Ponchartrain Hotel, 2031 Saint Charles Ave.,
   504/524-0581

Best Eclectic Menu
G and E Courtyard Grill
   1113 Decatur St., 504/528-9376

Best Fine Dining
Antoine's Restaurant
   713 Saint Louis St., 504/581-4422
Commander's Palace Restaurant
   1403 Washington Ave., 504/899-8221
The Pelican Club Restaurant and Bar
   312 Exchange Pl., 504/523-1504
Sazerac
   Fairmont Hotel, 123 Baronne St., 504/529-4733
Tujague's Restaurant
   823 Decatur St., 504/525-8676

Best French Food
Bizou Restaurant
   701 Saint Charles Ave., 504/524-4114
Louis XVI
   730 Bienville St., 504/581-7000

Best Greek/Mediterranean Food
Mystic Cafe
   3226 Magazine St., 504/891-1992

Best Health-Conscious Menu
Back to the Garden
   920 Saint Charles Ave., 504/522-8792
Red Bike
   746 Tchoupitoulas St., 504/529-2453
Whole Foods Market
   3135 Esplanade Ave., 504/943-1626

Best Homestyle Food
Mother's Restaurant
   401 Poydras St., 504/523-9656

Best Italian Food
Bacco Restaurant
   310 Chartres St., 504/522-2426
Semolina
   3242 Magazine St., 504/895-4260
   5080 Pontchartrain Blvd., 504/486-5581

Best Late-Night Food
Camellia Grill
   626 S. Carrollton Ave., 504/866-9573

Best Mexican Food
Vaquero's
   4938 Prytania St., 504/891-6441

Best Pizza
Cafe Roma
 1901 Sophie Wright Pl., 504/524-2419
 615 S. Carrolton Ave., 504/866-5900
Louisiana Pizza Kitchen
 95 French Market Pl., 504/522-9500
 2800 Esplanade Ave., 504/488-2800
New York Pizza
 5201 Magazine St., 504/891-2376
 208 N. Carrollton Ave., 504/482-2376
Pizza Roma
 4840 Bienville St., 504/483-9949

Best Place To Be "Seen"
Emeril's Restaurant
 800 Tchoupitoulas St., 504/528-9393

Best Regional Food
Emeril's Restaurant
 800 Tchoupitoulas St., 504/528-9393
Galatoire's Restaurant
 209 Bourbon St., 504/525-2021
Remoulade
 309 Bourbon St., 504/523-0377

Best Restaurant in Town
Bayona
 430 Dauphine St., 504/525-4455
Brigtsen's Restaurant
 723 Dante St., 504/861-7610
Casamento's Restaurant
 4330 Magazine St., 504/895-9761
Commander's Palace Restaurant
 1403 Washington Ave., 504/899-8221
Emeril's Restaurant
 800 Tchoupitoulas St., 504/528-9393
Gautreau's Restaurant
 1728 Soniat St., 504/899-7397
The Grill Room
 Windsor Court Hotel, 300 Gravier St.,
  504/522-1992
Mike's on the Avenue
 628 Saint Charles Ave., 504/523-1709
Peristyle
 1041 Dumaine St., 504/593-9535
Sapphire
 228 Camp St., 504/524-0081

Best Sandwiches
Louisiana Seafood Exchange
 433 Jefferson Hwy., Jefferson, 504/834-9393
Maspero's
 440 Chartres St., 504/524-8990
Parasol's Restaurant and Bar
 2533 Constance St., 504/899-2054
Trolly Car Sandwiches
 1434 S. Carrollton Ave., 504/866-4321
Uglesich Restaurant and Bar
 1238 Baronne St., 504/523-8571

L

Best Seafood
Acme Oyster and Seafood House
  724 Iberville St., 504/522-5973
Bruning's Seafood Restaurant
  1924 Westend Park, 504/282-9395
Deanie's
  1016 Annunciation St., 504/561-9251
Fitzgerald's Seafood Restaurant
  1932 Westend Park, 504/282-9254
Franky and Johnny's Restaurant
  321 Arabella St., 504/899-9146
Gumbo Shop
  630 Saint Peter St., 504/525-1486
Jaeger's Seafood Beer Garden
  1928 Westbend Pkwy., 504/283-7585
Mandina's
  3800 Canal St., 504/482-9179
Palace Cafe
  605 Canal St., 504/523-1661
Pascal's Manale
  1838 Napoleon Ave., 504/895-4877
State Street Cafe
  5961 Magazine St., 504/895-1441

Best Soul Food
Praline Connection
  542 Frenchmen St., 504/943-3934
  901 S. Peters St., 504/523-3973

Best Southwestern Food
Kokopelli's
  3150 Calhoun St., 504/861-3922

Best Sports Bar
Hyttop's Sports Bar and Grill
  Hyatt Regency New Orleans, Poydras at Loyola
    Ave., 504/561-1234

Best Steaks
Ruth's Chris Steak House
  711 N. Broad St., 504/486-0810

Best Thai Food
Bangkok Cuisine
  4137 S. Carrollton Ave., 504/482-3606

Best Vietnamese Food
Lemon Grass Cafe
  216 N. Carrollton Ave., 504/488-8335

Best View While Dining
Bella Luna
  914 N. Peters St., 504/529-1583
Fitzgerald's Seafood Restaurant
  1932 Westend Park, 504/282-9254
Jaeger's Seafood Beer Garden
  1928 Westbend Pkwy., 504/283-7585

RUSTON, LA

Best Burgers
Trenton Street Cafe
  201 N. Trenton St., 318/251-2103

Best Delicatessen
Sundown
111 E. Park Ave., 318/255-8028

Best Italian Food
Anthony's Pasta and Seafood
109 N. Trenton St., 318/255-9000

Best Soul Food
Sarah's Kitchen
607 Lee Ave., 318/255-1726

SHREVEPORT, LA

Best Barbecue/Ribs
Podnuh's Bar-B-Q
1146 Shreveport Barksdale Hwy., 318/869-3371
1915 N. Market St., 318/222-7480
8995 Mansfield Rd., 318/688-0818

Best Breakfast
Grandy's Restaurant
6811 Pines Rd., 318/687-0718
6605 Youree Dr., 318/797-0316

Best Chinese Food
Ming Garden Restaurant
1250 Shreveport Barksdale Hwy., 318/861-2741

Best Fine Dining
Monsieur Patou French Restaurant
855 Pierremont Rd., 318/868-9822
Village Grille
1313 Louisiana Ave., 318/424-2874

Best Homestyle Food
M & P Superior Kitchen
3530 Jewella Ave., 318/636-0633

Best Italian Food
Monjuni's Italian Cafe and Grocery
1315 Louisiana Ave., 318/227-0847

Best Mexican Food
Superior Bar and Grill
6123 Line Ave., 318/869-3243

Best Seafood
Ralph and Kacoo's Seafood Restaurant
1700 Old Minden Rd., Bossier City, 318/747-6660

Best Soul Food
Pete Harris Cafe
1351 Milam St., 318/425-4277

L

Maine

AUBURN, ME

Best Breakfast
Bagels and Things
213 Center St., 207/782-4426

Best Burgers
Gipper's Sports Grill
120 Center St., 207/786-0715

Best Coffee/Coffeehouse
Austin's Fine Wines and Foods
78 Main St., 207/783-6312

Best Pizza
George's Pizza
563 Center St., 207/782-7141

Best Seafood
Fishery Seafood Market
250 Center St., 207/786-2299
Village Inn
165 High St., 207/782-7796

Best Steaks
Mac's Grill
1052 Minot Ave., 207/783-6885

AUGUSTA, ME

Best American Food
Senator Restaurant
284 Upper Western Ave., 207/622-0320
The A-1 Diner
3 Bridge St., Gardiner, 207/582-4804

Best Chinese Food
Hong Kong Isle Restaurant
  208 Western Ave., 207/623-8878

Best Coffee/Coffeehouse
Java Joe's
  287 Water St., 207/622-1110

Best Eclectic Menu
Slate's Restaurant
  167 Water St., Hallowell, 207/622-9575

Best Mexican Food
Margarita's Mexican Restaurant
  390 Western Ave., 207/622-7874

Best Other Ethnic Food
River Cafe (Lebanese)
  119 Water St., Hallowell, 207/622-2190

Best Pizza
Pat's Pizza
  292 State St., 207/623-1748

M **Best Steaks**
Mike's Restaurant
  15 Bangor St., 207/622-3221

BANGOR, ME

Best Breakfast
Brown Bag of Brewer
  272 State St., 207/989-9980
Harborside Restaurant
  9 Main St., 207/989-2040

Best Brewpub
Sea Dog Brewing Company
  26 Front St., 207/947-8004

Best Burgers
Dana's Grill
  72 Summer St., 207/945-3899

Best Chinese Food
Oriental Jade Restaurant
  555 Stillwater Ave., 207/947-6969
Panda Garden
  123 Franklin St., 207/942-2704
Sing's Polynesian Restaurant
  41 Washington St., 207/947-8308

Best Coffee/Coffeehouse
Bagel Shop
  1 Main St., 207/947-1654

Best Fine Dining
Pilots Grill
  1528 Outer Hammond St., 207/942-6325

Best Health-Conscious Menu
Lemon Tree
  167 Center St., 207/945-3666

Best Inexpensive Meal
Governor's Restaurant
  643 Broadway, 207/947-3113

Best Italian Food
Momma Baldacci's Restaurant
12 Alden St., 207/945-5813

Best Lunch
Whig and Courier Pub
18 Broad St., 207/947-4095

Best Mexican Food
Margarita's Mexican Restaurant
15 Mill St., Orono, 207/866-4863

Best Pizza
Pat's Pizza
11 Mill St., Orono, 207/866-2111

Best Romantic Dining
Lucerne Inn
Bar Harbor Rd., Holden, 207/843-5123

Best Sandwiches
Brown Bag of Brewer
272 State St., 207/989-9980
Paul's Restaurant
605 Hogan Rd., 207/942-6726

M

Best Seafood
Captain Nick's
1165 Union St., 207/942-6444
Sea Dog Brewing Company
26 Front St., 207/947-8004

Best Sunday Brunch
Harborside Restaurant
9 S. Main St., 207/989-2040
Miller's Restaurant
427 Main St., 207/942-6361

Best Vegetarian Food
Old World Gourmet Shop
38 Main St., 207/942-1500

BIDDEFORD, ME

Best Breakfast
Jonesy's Restaurant
273 Main St., 207/282-6406
Wonderbar Restaurant
12 Washington St., 207/282-9926

Best Chinese Food
Happy Dragon Chinese
115 Main St., 207/282-0440

Best Dinner
Dan's Restaurant
106 Elm St., 207/284-5970

Best French Food
Joseph's By The Sea
55 W. Grand Ave., Old Orchard Beach,
207/934-5044

Best Italian Food
George's Sandwich Shop
43 Franklin St., 207/282-9713

Best Lunch
Cole Road Cafe
    1 Cole Rd., 207/283-4103
Dry Dock
    631A Elm St., 207/282-3775
Wonderbar Restaurant
    12 Washington St., 207/282-9926

Best Pizza
Alex's Pizza
    91 Alfred St., 207/283-0002

Best Restaurant in Town
Cascade Inn Restaurant
    941 Portland Rd., Saco, 207/283-3271

Best Restaurant Meal Value
Wonderbar Restaurant
    12 Washington St., 207/282-9926

Best Sandwiches
D' Angelo's Sandwich Shop
    352 Alfred St., 207/282-6870
George's Sandwich Shop
    43 Franklin St., 207/282-9713

Best Seafood
Captain's Galley Restaurant
    168 Saco Ave., Old Orchard Beach, 207/934-1336
Clambake Restaurant
    358 Pine Point Rd., Scarborough, 207/883-4871

Best Sports Bar
Mulligan's at Millside
    12 Lincoln St., 207/284-9283

Best Steaks
Hurricane Restaurant
    50 Oarweed Cove Rd., Ogunquit, 207/646-6348
Village Inn
    213 Saco Ave., Old Orchard Beach, 207/934-7370

LEWISTON, ME

Best All-You-Can-Eat Buffet
Jim's Jungle Restaurant
    729 Main St., 207/783-4900

Best Atmosphere
Eli's
    Rte. 117, Turner, 207/224-7090
Sedgley Place
    Sedgley Rd., Greene, 207/946-5990

Best Chinese Food
Chopsticks Restaurant
    37 Park St., 207/783-6300

Best Coffee/Coffeehouse
Nothing But the Blues Cafe
    81 College St., 207/784-6493

Best Desserts
Marois Restaurant
    249 Lisbon St., 207/782-9055

Best Homestyle Food
Fran's Place
  1485 Lisbon St., 207/786-0667

Best Ice Cream/Yogurt
Cote's Old Fashioned Ice Cream
  902 Lisbon St., 207/753-0853
  688 Main St., 207/783-1105

Best Italian Food
Ristorante Bella Italia
  700 Lisbon St., 207/783-1202

Best Mexican Food
Margarita's
  838 Lisbon St., 207/782-6036

PORTLAND, ME

Best Atmosphere
Bella Bella
  606 Congress St., 207/780-1260

Best Breakfast
Becky's
  390 Commercial St., 207/773-7070

Best Brewpub
Gritty McDuff's
  396 Fore St., 207/772-2739

Best Burgers
Rosie's
  330 Fore St., 207/772-5656
Ruby's Choice
  127 Commercial St., 207/773-9099
Stone Coast Brewery
  14 York St., 207/773-2337

Best Casual Dining
Anthony's Italian Kitchen
  151 Middle St., 207/774-8668

Best Coffee/Coffeehouse
Green Mountain Coffee Roasters
  15 Temple St., 207/773-4475
Java Joe's
  13 Exchange St., 207/761-5637

Best Family Restaurant
Village Cafe
  112 Newbury St., 207/772-5320

Best Fine Dining
Back Bay Grill
  65 Portland St., 207/772-8833
Cafe Always
  47 Middle St., 207/774-9399
David's Restaurant
  164 Middle St., 207/773-4340
Walter's
  15 Exchange St., 207/871-9258

Best Health-Conscious Menu
Mesa Verde
  618 Congress St., 207/774-6089

M

Pepperclub
78 Middle St., 207/772-0531

Best Homestyle Food
Katahdin Restaurant
106 High St., 207/774-1740

Best Italian Food
G'vanni's
37 Wharf St., 207/775-9061
Perfetto
28 Exchange St., 207/828-0001
Roma Cafe
769 Congress St., 207/773-9873

Best Pizza
Ricetta's Brick Oven Pizzeria
29 Western Ave., South Portland, 207/775-7400
Turino's Stone Oven Pizzeria
164 Middle St., 207/780-6600

Best Regional Food
Gilbert's Chowder House
92 Commercial St., 207/871-5636
Lobster Shack
225 Two Lights Rd., Cape Elizabeth, 207/799-1677

Best Restaurant Meal Value
Anthony's Italian Kitchen
151 Middle St., 207/774-8668

Best Salad/Salad Bar
Raff's
285 Forest Ave., 207/773-7763

Best Sandwiches
Amato's Sandwich Shop
160 Main St., Sanford, 207/324-7407

Best Seafood
Di Millo's Floating Restaurant
25 Long Wharf, 207/772-2216
Newark's Seafood Restaurant
740 Broadway, South Portland, 207/799-3090
Street and Company
33 Wharf St., 207/775-0887

Best Steaks
F. Parker Reidy's
83 Exchange St., 207/773-4731

Best Tea Room
Sweet Annie's Tea Shop
642 Congress St., 207/773-3353

Best Thai Food
Sala Thai Restaurant
1363 Washington Ave., 207/797-0871

SANFORD, ME

Best Breakfast
Jerry's Diner
Main St., 207/324-0909

Best Chinese Food
Golden Palace Restaurant
520 Main St., 207/490-3800

Best Diner
Jerry's Diner
Main St., 207/324-0909

Best Family Restaurant
Le Beau's Pub and Grille
277 Main St., 207/324-5664
The Falls Restaurant
Riverside Ave., 207/324-5430
Weathervane Seafood Restaurant
Rural Route 109, 207/324-0084

Best Ice Cream/Yogurt
Shain's
Wells Rd. S., 207/324-1449

Best Pizza
House of Pizza
270 Main St., 207/324-3161

Best Sandwiches
Moe's Italian Sandwiches
4 School St., 207/490-0088

Best Seafood
Le Beau's Pub and Grille
277 Main St., 207/324-5664

Best Steaks
The Falls Restaurant
Riverside Ave., 207/324-5430

M

WATERVILLE, ME

Best Atmosphere
Last Unicorn
8 Silver St., 207/873-6378
Silver Street Tavern
2 Silver St., 207/873-2277

Best Coffee/Coffeehouse
Jorgensen's
103 Main St., 207/872-8711
Main Street Cafe
45 Main St., 207/872-8748

Best Family Restaurant
Governor's Restaurant
356 Main St., 207/872-0677
Villager's Restaurant
40 W. Concourse, 207/872-6231
Weathervane Seafood Restaurant
470 Kennedy Memorial Dr., 207/873-4522

Best Ice Cream/Yogurt
Gifford's Ice Cream
170 Silver St., 207/872-6631

Best Italian Food
Steve's Restaurant
14 Silver St., 207/872-9887

Best Japanese Restaurant
Jade Island Restaurant
  99 W. River Rd., 207/873-7181

Best Steaks
Steve's Restaurant
  14 Silver St., 207/872-9887

Best Thai Restaurant
Mei Lam Lau Restaurant
  8 Silver St., 207/873-6378

M

Maryland

ABERDEEN, MD

Best Homestyle Food
New Ideal Diner
  104 S. Philadelphia Blvd., 410/272-1880

Best Italian Food
The Olive Tree
  1005 Beards Hill Rd., 410/272-6217

Best Sandwiches
Frank's Pizza
  37 W. Bel Air Ave., 410/272-2878

Best Seafood
Tidewater Grille
  300 Franklin St., Havre De Grace, 410/939-3313

Best Steaks
Colonel's Choice Ballroom
  Carol Avenue at Rte. 40, 410/272-6500
Towne House Restaurant
  705 S. Philadelphia Blvd., 410/272-4404

ANNAPOLIS, MD

Best American Food
Acme Bar and Grill
  163 Main St., 410/280-6486
Northwood's
  609 Melvin Ave., 410/268-2609

Best Atmosphere
Middleton Tavern
  2 Market St., 410/263-3323
Reynold's Tavern
  7 Church Circle, 410/626-0380

Best Bar
McGarvey's Saloon
8 Market Space, 410/263-5700
11 Pinkney St., 410/263-5772
Middleton Tavern
2 Market Space, 410/263-3323

Best Barbecue/Ribs
Adam's the Place for Ribs
921 Chesapeake Ave., 410/267-0064
Burkes Barn Yard
801 Compass Way, 410/266-0816

Best Breakfast
Main Ingredient
914 Bay Ridge Rd., 410/626-0388
Mum's Waterfront
136 Dock St., 410/263-3353

Best Casual Dining
Riordan's Saloon
26 Market Space, 410/263-5449

Best Chinese Food
China House
228 Main St., 410/263-0002

Best Delicatessen
Jo's Deli
117 Hillsmere Dr., 410/263-1818

Best Eclectic Menu
New Moon Cafe
137 Prince George St., 410/280-1956
Paul's Homewood Cafe
919 West St., 410/267-7891

Best Family Restaurant
Broadneck Grill
1364 Cape Saint Claire Rd., 410/757-0002

Best Fine Dining
Northwoods
609 Melvin Ave., 410/268-2609
O'Brien's Oyster Bar and Restaurant
113 Main St., 410/268-6288
Treaty of Paris Restaurant
16 Church Circle, 410/263-2641

Best French Food
Cafe Normandie Restaurant
185 Main St., 410/263-3382

Best Health-Conscious Menu
Canton Restaurant
11 Ridgley Ave., 410/280-8658

Best Indian Food
Indian Palace
186 Main St., 410/263-7900

Best Italian Food
Scirrocco Mediterranean Grill
2552 Riva Rd., 410/573-0970

M

Best Mexican Food
Caliente Restaurant
  50 West St., 410/268-8548

Best Other Ethnic Food
Maria's Sicilian Ristorante (Sicilian)
  12 Market St., 410/268-2112

Best Pizza
Rocco's Pizzeria
  125 Hillsmere Dr., 410/263-9444

Best Regional Food
Sam's Waterfront Cafe
  2020 Chesapeake Harbour Dr. E., 410/263-3600

Best Seafood
Chart House Restaurant
  300 Second St., 410/268-7166
O'Leary's Seafood Restaurant
  310 Third St., 410/263-0884

Best Southwestern Food
Armadillo's Bar and Gill
  132 Dock St., 410/268-6680

Best Steaks
Lewne's Steakhouse
  401 Fourth St., 410/263-1617
McGarvey's Saloon
  8 Market Space, 410/263-5700
  11 Pinkney St., 410/263-5772

Best Sunday Brunch
Griffin's Restaurant
  2049 West St., 410/266-7662
  22 Market Space, 410/268-2576

Best Sushi
Joss Cafe and Sushi Bar
  195 Main St., 410/263-4688

Best View While Dining
Buddy's Crabs and Ribs
  100 Main St., 410/626-1100
Carrol's Creek Cafe
  410 Severn Ave., 410/263-8102
Chart House Restaurant
  300 Second St., 410/268-7166

Best Wine Selection
Cafe Du Vin
  1410 Forest Dr., 410/268-6677
Chart House Restaurant
  300 Second St., 410/268-7166

M

BALTIMORE, MD

Best American Food
Birds of a Feather
  1712 Aliceanna St., 410/675-8466
Central Station Restaurant and Pub
  1001 N. Charles St., 410/752-7133
Louie's The Bookstore Cafe
  518 N. Charles St., 410/962-1224

McCabe's
3845 Falls Rd., 410/467-1000
Tamber's Nifty Fifties Diner
3327 Saint Paul St., 410/243-0383
The Chart House Restaurant
601 E. Pratt St., 410/539-6616
Tyson Place
227 W. Chase St., 410/539-4850
Women's Industrial Exchange
333 E. Charles St., 410/685-4388

Best Bar
Henninger's Tavern
1812 Bank St., 410/342-2172
Jerry's Belvedere Tavern
5928 York Rd., 410/435-8600
Peter's Inn
504 S. Ann St., 410/675-7313
The Rendezvous Lounge
136 W. 25th St., 410/467-3860

Best Breakfast
Jimmy's Restaurant
801 S. Broadway, 410/327-3273
Morning Edition Cafe
153 N. Patterson Park Ave., 410/732-5133
Rallo's Restaurant
838 E. Fort Ave., 410/727-7067
The Bridge Restaurant
353 N. Calvert St., 410/727-8858

Best Brewpub
Baltimore Brewing Company
104 Albemarle St., 410/837-5000
Bertha's Dining Room
734 S. Broadway, 410/327-5795
Sisson's South Baltimore Brew
36 E. Cross St., 410/539-2093
Wharf Rat Brew Pub
206 W. Pratt St., 410/244-8900

Best Casual Dining
Buddies Pub and Jazz Club
313 N. Charles St., 410/332-4200
Cafe Tattoo
4825 Belair Rd., 410/325-7427
Frazier's Restaurant and Tap Room
857 W. 33rd St., 410/889-1143
Mick O'Shea's Irish Pub
328 N. Charles St., 410/539-7504

Best Chinese Food
Golden Crown Restaurant
3341 Belair Rd., 410/276-4242
3320 Greenmount Ave., 410/467-3213
Szechuan Restaurant
1125 S. Charles St., 410/752-8409
Tony Cheng's Szechuan
801 N. Charles St., 410/539-6666
Uncle Lee's Szechuan
3313 Greenmount Ave., 410/366-3333

44 South St., 410/727-6666

Best Coffee/Coffeehouse
City Cafe
  1001 N. Cathedral St., 410/539-4252
The Coffee and Tea Cafe
  6303 York Rd., 410/435-3040
Funk's Democratic Coffee Spot
  1818 Eastern Ave., 410/276-3865
The Daily Grind
  1726 Thames St., 410/558-0399
Ze Mean Bean Cafe
  1739 Fleet St., 410/675-5999

Best Continental Food
The Brass Elephant
  924 N. Charles St., 410/547-8480

Best Delicatessen
Attman's Delicatessen
  1019 E. Lombard St., 410/563-2666
Henry and Jeff's Restaurant
  1218 N. Charles St., 410/727-3322

Best Desserts
Spike and Charlie's
  1225 Cathedral St., 410/752-8144
Vaccaro's Italian Pastry
  222 Albemarle St., 410/685-4905

Best Diner
Double T Diner
  6300 Baltimore National Pike, 410/744-4151
Hollywood Diner
  400 E. Saratoga St., 410/962-5379
Overlea Diner
  6652 Belair Rd., 410/254-8356
Paper Moon Diner
  227 W. 29th St., 410/889-4444
Pete's Grille
  3130 Greenmount Ave., 410/467-7698
Roland Restaurant
  850 W. 36th St., 410/235-2915
State Diner
  2821 Wilkens Ave., 410/947-2288
Wyman Park Restaurant
  138 W. 25th St., 410/235-5100

Best Dinner
Zorba's Bar and Grill
  4710 Eastern Ave., 410/276-4484

Best Eclectic Menu
Corky's Grill
  225 W. 23rd St., 410/243-4377
Margaret's Cafe
  909 Fell St., 410/276-5605
Wild Mushroom
  641 S. Montford Ave., 410/675-4225

Best Fine Dining
Polo Grill
  Inn at the Colonnade, 4 W. University Pkwy.,
    410/235-8200

M

Tio Pepe Restaurant
  10 E. Franklin St., 410/539-4675

Best French Food
Jeannier's Restaurant
  105 W. 39th St., 410/889-3303

Best German Food
Haussner's Restaurant
  3242 Eastern Ave., 410/327-8365

Best Indian Food
Akbar Restaurant
  823 N. Charles St., 410/539-0944
Banjara
  1017 S. Charles St., 410/962-1554
Bombay Grill Restaurant
  2 E. Madison St., 410/837-2973
Mughal Garden
  920 N. Charles St., 410/547-0001

Best Inexpensive Meal
Cafe Hon
  1002 W. 36th St., 410/243-1230
Nice and Easy Restaurant
  700 S. Broadway, 410/732-8821
Saigon Restaurant
  3345 Belair Rd., 410/276-0055

Best Italian Food
Amicci's
  2903 O' Donnell St., 410/675-3207
  231 S. High St., 410/528-1096
Cafe Troia
  28 W. Allegheny Ave., 410/337-0133
La Tavoll
  248 Albemarle St., 410/685-1859
Palmer House Restaurant
  108 N. Eutaw St., 410/752-8969
Sabatino's Italian Restaurant
  901 Fawn St., 410/727-9414
Velleggia's
  829 E. Pratt St., 410/685-2620

Best Japanese Food
Kawasaki Japanese Food
  413 N. Charles St., 410/659-7600
Matsuri Japanese Restaurant
  1105 S. Charles St., 410/752-8561
Sushi Cafe
  1640 Thames St., 410/732-3570

Best Korean Food
Nam Kang
  2126 Maryland Ave., 410/685-6237
New No Da Ji Restaurant
  2501 N. Charles St., 410/235-4846

Best Kosher Food
Kosher Bite
  6309 Reisterstown Rd., 410/358-6349
Miller's Cafe
  2849 Smith Ave., 410/602-2233

M

Best Late-Night Food
Paper Moon Diner
227 W. 29th St., 410/889-4444
Sip and Bite
2200 Boston St., 410/675-7077

Best Lunch
Cosmos
5427 Harford Rd., 410/426-2775
Three Squares Restaurant
3300 Odonnell St., 410/563-0014

Best Mexican Food
Lista's
1637 Thames St., 410/327-0040
Loco Hombre
413 W. Cold Spring Ln., 410/889-2233
Mencken's Cultured Pearl
1114 Hollins St., 410/837-1947
Nacho Mama's
2911 O' Donnell St., 410/675-0898
Rotisseria
219 S. Broadway, 410/563-3712

Best Other Ethnic Food
Braznell's Caribbean Kitchen (Caribbean)
1623 E. Baltimore St., 410/327-2445
The Helmand (Afghan)
806 N. Charles St., 410/752-0311

Best Outdoor Dining
Gypsy's Cafe
1103 Hollins St., 410/625-9310

Best Pizza
Ledo Pizza
1020 W. 41st St., 410/243-4222
Uno Pizzeria
201 E. Pratt St., 410/625-5900

Best Regional Food
Angelina's Restaurant
7135 Harford Rd., 410/444-5545
Koco's Pub
4301 Harford Rd., 410/426-3519
Ransome's Harbor Hill Cafe
1030-32 Riverside Ave., 410/576-9720

Best Seafood
Bo Brook's Crab House
5415 Belair Rd., 410/488-8144
Fisherman's Wharf
826 Dulaney Valley Rd., 410/337-2909
Obrycki's Crab House and Seafood Restaurant
1727 W. Pratt St., 410/732-6399

Best Soul Food
Kimmy's Restaurant and Carryout
5016 Sinclair Ln., 410/483-0085

Best Steaks
McCafferty's
1501 Sulgrave Ave., 410/664-2200

M

Prime Rib
  1101 N. Calvert St., 410/539-1804
Ruth's Chris Steak House
  600 Water St., 410/783-0033

Best Sunday Brunch
Louie's The Bookstore Cafe
  518 N. Charles St., 410/962-1224
Morning Edition Cafe
  153 N. Patterson Park Ave., 410/732-5133
Bistro 300
  The Hyatt, 300 Light St., 410/528-1234

Best Sushi
Sushi Cafe
  1640 Thames St., 410/732-3570

Best Thai Food
Thai Landing
  1207 N. Charles St., 410/727-1234
Thai Restaurant
  3316 Greenmount Ave., 410/889-7303
The Bangkok Place
  5230 York Rd., 410/433-0040

Best Vegetarian Food
One World Cafe
  904 S. Charles St., 410/234-0235

Best Vietnamese Food
Saigon Restaurant
  3345 Belair Rd., 410/276-0055

Best View While Dining
Piccolo's at Fells Point
  1629 Thames St., 410/522-6600

BETHESDA, MD

[See also: Washington, DC; Rockville, MD; and Arlington and McLean, VA.]

Best American Food
Houston's Restaurant
  7715 Woodmont Ave., 301/656-9755

Best Bar
Gulf Coast Kitchen
  7750 Woodmont Ave., 301/652-6278
Montgomery Grill
  7200 Wisconsin Ave., 301/654-3595

Best Chinese Food
Foong Lin Restaurant
  7710 Norfolk Ave., 301/656-3427

Best French Food
La Madeleine French Bistro
  7607 Old Georgetown Rd., 301/215-9139

Best Indian Food
Bombay Dining
  4931 Cordell Ave., 301/656-3373

Best Italian Food
Pines of Rome
4709 Hampden Ln., 301/657-8775
Red Tomatoe Cafe
4910 Saint Elmo Ave., 301/652-4499

Best Japanese Food
Matuba Japanese Restaurant
4918 Cordell Ave., 301/652-7449
Tako Grill
7756 Wisconsin Ave., 301/652-7030

Best Late-Night Food
Tastee Diner of Bethesda
7731 Woodmont Ave., 301/652-3970

Best Mexican Food
Cottonwood Cafe
4844 Cordell Ave., 301/656-4844
Rio Grande Cafe
4919 Fairmont Ave., 301/656-2981

Best Sandwiches
Philadelphia Mike's
7732 Wisconsin Ave., 301/656-0103

Best Seafood
O'Donnell's Restaurant
8301 Wisconsin Ave., 301/654-5753

Best Steaks
Ruth's Chris Steak House
7315 Wisconsin Ave., 301/652-7877

Best Thai Food
Bangkok Garden
4906 Saint Elmo Ave., 301/951-0670
Taro Thai Restaurant
4828 Bethesda Ave., 301/657-0488

BOWIE, MD

Best American Food
Rip's Country Inn
3809 Crain Hwy., 301/805-5901

Best Italian Food
Ristorante Mare E Monti
15554B Annapolis Rd., 301/262-9179

Best Lunch
Jasper's Restaurant
1651 State Rte. 3N, Crofton, 410/261-3505

Best Seafood
Sly Horse Tavern
1678 Village Green, Crofton, 410/721-4550

Best Steaks
Rip's Country Inn
3809 Crain Hwy., 301/805-5901

CAMBRIDGE, MD

Best Breakfast
English's Family Restaurant
710 Sunburst Hwy., 410/228-4344

Best Family Restaurant
Old Salty's Restaurant
  2560 Hooper's Island Rd., Fishing Creek,
    410/397-3752

Best Health-Conscious Menu
McGuigan's Pub
  411 Muir St., 410/228-7110

Best Italian Food
Rusticana Pizza
  Shoal Creek Mall, 410/228-1515

Best Outdoor Dining
Snapper's
  112 Commerce St., 410/228-0112

Best Pizza
Hyser's Old Time Soda Fountain
  824 Locust St., 410/228-3465
Rusticana Pizza
  Shoal Creek Mall, 410/228-1515

Best Place to Take the Kids
High Spot
  303 High St., 410/228-3410
Spicer's Seafood Restaurant
  802 Wood St., 410/221-0222

Best Sandwiches
Creek Deli
  106 Market Sq., 410/228-1161

Best Steaks
High Spot
  303 High St., 410/228-3410

COLUMBIA, MD

Best American Food
Black Eyed Pea
  8335 Benson Dr., 410/290-1522
Clyde's of Columbia
  10221 Wincopin Circle, 410/730-2828
Morgan's Food and Spirits
  5485 Twin Knolls Rd., 410/964-3750

Best Casual Dining
Coho Grill
  11130 Willow Bottom Dr., 410/740-2096

Best Chinese Food
China Chefs
  10801 Hickory Ridge Rd., 410/730-1200
China Moon Restaurant
  8775 Centre Park Dr., 410/715-1298
Peking Chef Restaurant
  6420 Freetown Rd., 410/531-2828

Best Continental Food
King's Contrivance
  10150 Shaker Dr., 410/995-0500

Best Health-Conscious Menu
Waterside Restaurant
  10207 Wincopin Circle, 410/730-3900

Best Indian Food
Bombay Peacock Grill
  10005 Old Columbia Rd., 410/381-7111

Best Italian Food
Piccolo's Restaurant
  7090 Deepage Dr., 410/381-8866
Tomato Palace
  10221 Wincopin Circle, 410/715-0211

Best Japanese Food
Nichi Bei Kai
  9400 Snowden River Pky., Ste. 120, 410/381-5800

Best Restaurant in Town
Bangkok Delight
  8825 Central Park Dr., 410/730-0032

Best Sandwiches
American Cafe
  10400 Little Patuxent Pkwy., 410/740-7200

Best Thai Food
Bangkok Delight
  8825 Central Park Dr., 410/730-0032

M

Best View While Dining
Clyde's of Columbia
  10221 Wincopin Circle, 410/730-2828
Waterside Restaurant
  10207 Wincopin Circle, 410/730-3900

CUMBERLAND, MD

Best American Food
Harrigan's
  Holiday Inn, 100 S. George St., 301/724-8800

Best Breakfast
D'Atri's Restaurant
  1118 National Hwy., 301/729-2774

Best Seafood
When Pigs Fly
  18 Valley St., 301/722-7447

Best Steaks
Carmichael's
  209 N. Mechanic St., 301/777-2523

ELLICOTT CITY, MD

Best American Food
Kelsey's Restaurant
  8480 Baltimore National Pike, 410/418-9076

Best Brewpub
Bare Bones Restaurant and Brewery
  Saint John's Plz., 9150 Baltimore National Pike,
    410/461-0770

Best Burgers
Phoenix Emporium
  8049 Main St., 410/465-5665

Best Chinese Food
Uncle YY's Szechuan
   8601 Baltimore National Pike, 410/418-8888

Best Coffee/Coffeehouse
Cappuccino Books and Cafe
   8480 Baltimore National Pike, 410/461-0775

Best French Food
Tersiguel's
   8293 Main St., 410/465-4004

Best Romantic Dining
Tersiguel's
   8293 Main St., 410/465-4004

Best Seafood
Captains Choice Restaurant
   8450 Baltimore National Pike, 410/465-6171
Crab Shanty Restaurant
   3410 Plumtree Dr., 410/465-9660

M

FREDERICK, MD

Best All-You-Can-Eat Buffet
Dan-Dee Motel and Country Inn
   7817 Baltimore National Pike, 301/473-8282

Best Bar
Red Horse Restaurant
   996 W. Patrick St., 301/663-3030

Best Breakfast
Beans and Bagels
   49 E. Patrick St., 301/620-2165

Best Business Lunch
Deli Restaurant
   57 E. Patrick St., 301/663-8122
Jennifer's Restaurant
   207 W. Patrick St., 301/662-0373

Best Coffee/Coffeehouse
Beans and Bagels
   49 E. Patrick St., 301/620-2165

Best Italian Food
Nido Italiano
   111 E. Patrick St., 301/694-5939
Tauraso's Ristorante
   4 East St., 301/663-6600

Best Mexican Food
La Paz Mexican Restaurant
   18 Market Space, 301/694-8980

Best Sandwiches
Griff's Landing
   43 S. Market St., 301/694-8696
Jennifer's Restaurant
   207 W. Patrick St., 301/662-0373

Best Seafood
Dutch's Daughters
   5901 Old National Pike, 301/663-0297

Best Vegetarian Food
Orchard Restaurant
45 N. Market St., 301/663-4912

GAITHERSBURG, MD

[See also: Rockville.]

Best Barbecue/Ribs
Bare Bones
617 S. Frederick Ave., 301/948-4344

Best Brewpub
Olde Towne Tavern and Brewery
227 E. Diamond Ave., 301/948-4200

Best Burgers
Hamburger Hamlet
9811 Washingtonian Blvd., 301/417-0773

Best Chinese Food
Wok Express Chinese Restaurant
9615 Lost Knife Rd., 301/948-8788

Best Dinner
Gentleman Jim's Restaurant
18917 Earhart Ct., 301/963-7778
Golden Bull Grand Cafe
7 Dalamar St., 301/948-3666

Best French Food
Le Paradis Restaurant
347 Muddy Branch Rd., 301/208-9493

Best Lunch
Muldoon's and JJ
16143 Shady Grove Rd., 301/258-8866

Best Sandwiches
Roy's Place
2 E. Diamond Ave., 301/948-5548

Best Sports Bar
Chris' Restaurant
201 E. Diamond Ave., 301/869-6116

Best Steaks
Bugaboo Creek Steakhouse
15710 Shady Grove Rd., 301/548-9200

Best Thai Food
Thai Sa Mai Restaurant
8369 Snouffers School Rd., 301/963-1800

GLEN BURNIE, MD

Best Breakfast
Breakfast Shoppe
360 Ritchie Hwy., Severna Park, 410/544-8599
Honey Bee Drive-In
7346 Ritchie Hwy., 410/761-0477

M

Best Dinner
Sunset Restaurant
  625 Greenway Rd. SE, 410/768-1417

Best Fine Dining
Trattoria Alberto
  1660 Crain Hwy. S., 410/761-0922

Best Seafood
Seaside Seafood and Crab Shack
  224 Crain Hwy. N., 410/760-2200

HAGERSTOWN, MD

Best German Food
Schmankerl Stube Bavarian Restaurant
  58 S. Potomac St., 301/797-3354

Best Health-Conscious Menu
Grille at Park Circle
  325 Virginia Ave., 301/797-9100

Best Japanese Food
House of Kobe
  757 Dual Hwy., 301/797-6979

Best Seafood
Nick's Airport Inn
  18615 Terminal Dr., 301/733-8560

LUTHERVILLE-TIMONIUM, MD

Best Bar
Michael's Cafe
  2119 York Rd., 410/252-2022

Best Barbecue/Ribs
Charred Rib Restaurant
  2010 York Rd., 410/561-0735

Best Casual Dining
Vito's Cafe
  10249 York Rd., Cockeysville, 410/666-3100

Best Chinese Food
Hunt Valley Szechuan
  9 Schilling Rd., Hunt Valley, 410/527-1818

Best Diner
Ralphie's Diner
  9690 Deereco Rd., 410/252-3990

Best Eclectic Menu
Pacific Rim Restaurant
  9726 York Rd., Cockeysville, 410/666-2336

Best Health-Conscious Menu
Harvey's Restaurant
  2350 W. Joppa Rd., 410/296-9526

Best Italian Food
Liberatore's Ristorante
  9515 Deereco Rd., 410/561-3300

Best Romantic Dining
The Milton Inn
  14833 York Rd., Sparks Glencoe, 410/771-4366

Best Seafood
Gibby's Seafood Restaurant
22 W. Padonia Rd., 410/560-0703
Ocean Pride Restaurant
1534 York Rd., 410/321-7744

OCEAN CITY, MD

Best All-You-Can-Eat Buffet
Phillip's Crab House
2004 N. Philadelphia Ave., 410/289-6821

Best Chinese Food
Charlie Chiang's Restaurant
5401 Coastal Hwy., 410/723-4600

Best Fine Dining
The Atlantic Hotel Restaurant
2 N. Main St., Berlin, 410/641-0189

Best Inexpensive Meal
Happy Chinese Restaurant
9936 Stephen Decatur Hwy., 410/213-2663

Best Italian Food
Adolfo's Italian Family Restaurant
806 S. Baltimore Ave., 410/289-4001

Best Mexican Food
Tio Gringo's
5309 Coastal Hwy., 410/524-6244

Best Seafood
Phillip's by the Sea
1301 Atlantic Ave., 410/289-9121
Phillip's Crab House
2004 N. Philadelphia Ave., 410/289-6821

PIKESVILLE, MD

Best American Food
Jasper's Pimlico
1777 Reisterstown Rd., 410/486-1400
Jilly's
1012 Reisterstown Rd., 410/653-0610

Best Chinese Food
Mr. Chan Szechuan Restaurant
1010 Reisterstown Rd., 410/484-1100

Best Delicatessen
Suburban House Restaurant
911 Reisterstown Rd., 410/484-7775

Best Italian Food
San Marco Restaurant
1726 Reisterstown Rd., 410/653-9090

M

ROCKVILLE, MD

[See also: Washington, DC; and Bethesda and Gaithersburg, MD.]

Best Casual Dining
Silver Diner
  11806 Rockville Pike, 301/770-2828

Best Chinese Food
House of Chinese Chicken
  12710 Twinbrook Pkwy., 301/881-4500

Best Diner
Tastee Diner
  8516 Georgia Ave., Silver Spring, 301/589-8171

Best Dinner
Houston's Restaurant
  12256 Rockville Pike, 301/468-3535

Best Italian Food
Il Pizzico
  15209 Frederick Rd., 301/309-0610

Best Late-Night Food
Silver Diner
  11806 Rockville Pike, 301/770-0333

Best Seafood
Crisfield Seafood Restaurant
  8606 Colesville Rd., Silver Spring, 301/588-1572

Best Vietnamese Food
Taste of Saigon
  410 Hungerford Dr., 301/424-7222

SALISBURY, MD

Best Chinese Food
Imperial Gallery Restaurant
  321 Civic Ave., 410/546-3103

Best Family Restaurant
English's Family Restaurant
  735 S. Salisbury Blvd., 410/742-5812
  302 N. Salisbury Blvd., 410/742-8183

Best Inexpensive Meal
Nacho Pete's
  1322 S. Salisbury Blvd., 410/546-0779

Best Italian Food
Zia's Pastaria
  2408 N. Salisbury Blvd., 410/543-9118

TOWSON, MD

Best Family Restaurant
Mick's
  425 York Rd., 410/825-0071

Best Homestyle Food
Silver Diner
  825 Dulaney Valley Rd., 410/823-5566

Best Late-Night Food
Casa Mia's
40 York Rd., 410/321-8707

Best Mexican Food
Saguaro's Restaurant
2 W. Pennsylvania Ave., 410/339-7774

Best Other Ethnic Food
Orchard Market and Cafe (Persian)
8815 Orchard Tree Ln., 410/339-7700

Best Pizza
Uno Pizzeria
435 York Rd., 410/825-8667

Best Place to Be "Seen"
Gettier's Orchard Inn
1528 E. Joppa Rd., 410/823-0384

Best Place to Eat Alone
Borders Bookstore
415 York Rd., 410/296-0791

Best Place to Take the Kids
Chuck E. Cheese Pizza
809 Goucher Blvd., 410/823-1756

Best Restaurant in Town
Orchard Market and Cafe
8815 Orchard Tree Ln., 410/339-7700

Best Salad/Salad Bar
Paolo's Italian Restaurant
1 W. Pennsylvania Ave., 410/321-7000

Best Southwestern Food
Saguaro's Restaurant
2 W. Pennsylvania Ave., 410/339-7774

WALDORF, MD

Best Barbecue/Ribs
Lefty's Bar-B-Que Unlimited
2064 Crain Hwy., 301/870-8998

Best Burgers
Flamers Charburgers
5000 U.S. Hwy. 301, 301/870-7995

Best Chinese Food
Aloha
175 Smallwood Village Ctr., 301/645-8907

Best Italian Food
Topolin, An Italian Bistro
2940 Festival Way, 301/645-9647

Best Pizza
Uno Chicago Bar and Grill
11215 Mall Circle, 301/705-8420

Best Place to Take the Kids
Chuck E. Cheese Pizza
2928 Festival Way, 301/932-4640

Best Seafood
Chesapeake Bay Seafood House
  3205 Plz. Way, 301/645-5622
Rip's
  2111 Crain Hwy., 301/870-6800

Best Steaks
Lone Star Steak House
  11075 Mall Circle, 301/870-0949

M

Massachusetts

AMHERST, MA

Best Bar
Rafters
  422 Amity St., 413/549-4040

Best Breakfast
Daisy's
  1185 N. Pleasant St., 413/549-6643

Best Brewpub
The Pub
  15 E. Pleasant St., 413/549-1200

Best Casual Dining
Season's Restaurant
  248 Belchertown Rd., 413/253-9909

Best Chinese Food
Amherst Chinese Food
  62 Main St., 413/253-7835
Panda East Chinese Restaurant
  103 N. Pleasant St., 413/256-8923

Best Fine Dining
Seasons Restaurant
  248 Belchertown Rd., 413/253-9909

Best Health-Conscious Menu
Judie's
  51 N. Pleasant St., 413/253-3491

Best Indian Food
New India Restaurant
  17 Kellogg Ave., 413/253-4200
Paradise of India Restaurant
  87 Main St., 413/256-1067

Best Italian Food
La Cucina Di Pinocchio
  30 Boltwood Walk, 413/256-4110

Best Lunch
Antonio's Pizza
  31 N. Pleasant St., 413/253-0808

Best Restaurant in Town
Amber Waves
  63 Main St., 413/253-9200
Judie's
  51 N. Pleasant St., 413/253-3491

Best Thai Food
Amber Waves
  63 Main St., 413/253-9200

ANDOVER, MA

[See also: Lawrence and Methuen.]

M

Best Breakfast
Shawsheen Luncheonette
  3 Lowell St., 978/475-9750

Best Chinese Food
Beijing Restaurant
  1250 Osgood St., 978/689-9500

Best Continental Food
Backstreet Restaurant
  19 Essex St., 978/475-4411

Best Dinner
Palmer's Restauarnt and Tavern
  18 Elm St., 978/470-1606

Best Italian Food
Vincenzo's
  12 Main St., 978/475-7711

Best Lunch
99 Restaurant
  464 Lowell St., 978/475-8033

Best Pizza
Bertucci's Brick Oven
  90 Main St., 978/470-3939

ATHOL, MA

Best Breakfast
Cinnamon's Restaurant
  491 Main St., 978/249-6033

Best Chinese Food
King Sing Restaurant
  46 W. Main St., Orange, 978/544-8853

Best Pizza
Athol House of Pizza Restaurant
  522 Main St., 978/249-3762

Best Sandwiches
Deli Patch
   131 S. Main St., 978/249-9956

Best Steaks
King Phillip Restaurant
   35 State Rd., 978/249-6300

ATTLEBORO, MA

Best Delicatessen
Bagels and Cream
   5 Bank St., 508/222-1318

Best Dinner
Union Station
   88 Union St., 508/222-3760
Williams Restaurant
   16 S. Main St., 508/222-8834

Best Family Restaurant
Morin's Diner
   16 S. Main St., 508/222-9875

Best Fine Dining
Ann's Place
   48 Bay Rd., Norton, 508/285-9766

Best Pizza
Eli's Pizza
   99 County St., 508/222-1824

Best Steaks
Bugaboo Creek Steak House
   1125 Fall River Ave., Seekonk, 508/336-2200

Best Sunday Brunch
Audrey's
   Johnson & Wales Inn, 213 Taunton Ave.,
      Seekonk, 508/336-4636

BEVERLY, MA

[See also: Boston.]

Best Breakfast
Brothers Restaurant and Deli
   446 Rantoul St., 978/927-8535
Omelette Headquarters
   218 Cabot St., 978/922-8126

Best Eclectic Menu
Tapas Corner
   284 Cabot St., 978/927-9983

Best Greek/Mediterranean Food
Brothers Restaurant and Deli
   446 Rantoul St., 978/927-8535

Best Italian Food
Bella Venezia
   218 Cabot St., 978/927-2365

M

MA3

Best Mexican Food
Casa De Lucca
  146 Rantoul St., 978/922-7660

Best Romantic Dining
Chianti Cafe and Grill
  285 Cabot St., 978/921-9343

Best Salad/Salad Bar
Beverly Depot Restaurant
  10 Park St., 978/927-5402

Best Seafood
Cabot Place Restaurant
  256 Cabot St., 978/927-3920

Best Steaks
Roscoe's Restaurant
  208 Rantoul St., 978/927-2028

BOSTON, MA

M

[See also: Brookline, Cambridge, Needham, Somerville, and Woburn.]

Best American Food
Icarus
  3 Appleton St., 617/426-1790
Joe's American Bar and Grill
  279 Dartmouth St., 617/536-4200
Milk Street Cafe
  50 Milk St., 617/542-3663
Olive's
  10 City Sq., Charlestown, 617/242-1999
Seasons Restaurant
  Regal Bostonian Hotel, 24 North St., 617/523-3600

Best Bar
Mercury Bar
  116 Boylston St., 617/482-7799

Best Beer Selection
Boston Beer Works
  61 Brookline Ave., 617/536-2337
Commonwealth Brewing Company
  138 Portland St., 617/523-8383
Sunset Grill and Tap
  130 Brighton Ave., Allston, 617/254-1331

Best Bistro
Hamersley's Bistro
  553 Tremont St., 617/423-2700

Best Breakfast
Blue Diner
  150 Kneeland St., 617/695-0087
Geoffrey's Cafe Bar South End
  578 Tremont St., Roxbury, 617/266-1122
Sonsie Restaurant
  327 Newbury St., 617/351-2500

Best Brewpub
Back Bay Brewing Company
   755 Boylston St., 617/424-8300
Brew Moon Restaurant
   115 Stuart St., 617/523-6467
Commonwealth Brewing Company
   138 Portland St., 617/523-8383

Best Burgers
Charley's Eating and Drinking Saloon
   284 Newbury St., 617/266-3000
Division Sixteen
   955 Boylston St., 617/353-0870

Best Casual Dining
M. Cooke
   80 Atlantic Ave., 617/723-6722
Sage
   69 Prince St., 617/248-8814
Upstairs Grille
   Lenox Hotel, 710 Boylston St., 617/421-4960

Best Chinese Food
China Pearl Restaurant
   9 Tyler St., 617/426-4338
Chinatown Cafe
   262 Harrison Ave., 617/451-2395
Grand Chau Chow
   45 Beach St., 617/292-5166
New Shanghai Restaurant
   21 Hudson St., 617/338-6688

Best Coffee/Coffeehouse
Caffe Vittoria
   296 Hanover St., 617/227-7606

Best Desserts
Other Side Cosmic Cafe
   407 Newbury St., 617/536-9477

Best Diner
Metropolis Cafe
   584 Tremont St., Roxbury, 617/247-2931

Best Dinner
Bread and Circus
   15 Westland Ave., 617/375-1010

Best Eclectic Menu
Ambrosia on Huntington
   116 Huntington Ave., 617/247-2400
Cafe Eurosia
   Park Plaza Hotel, 54 Park Plz., 617/542-1616

Best Family Restaurant
J.J. Grimsby and Company
   1 Lynn Fells Pkwy., Melrose, 781/665-1123

Best Fine Dining
Biba
   272 Boylston St., 617/426-7878
Morton's of Chicago
   1 Exeter Plz., 617/266-5858

M

Rowe's Wharf Restaurant and Cafe
  Boston Harbor Hotel, 70 Rowes Wharf,
    617/439-3995

Best French Food
Aujourd'Hui
  200 Boylston St., 617/338-4400
Elephant Walk
  900 Beacon St., 617/247-1500
Julien
  Hotel Meridien, 250 Franklin St., 617/451-1900
L'Espalier
  30 Gloucester St., 617/262-3023
Maison Robert
  45 School St., 617/227-3370

Best Greek/Mediterranean Food
Mediterraneo Bistro
  323 Turnpike St., Canton, 781/821-8881
Omonia Greek Restaurant
  75 Charles St., 617/426-4310
Steve's Restaurant
  316 Newbury St., 617/267-1817

Best Indian Food
Bombay Cafe
  175 Massachusetts Ave., 617/247-0555
Kashmir Indian Restaurant
  279 Newbury St., 617/536-1695

Best Italian Food
Artu
  6 Prince St., 617/742-4336
Artu on Charles Street
  89 Charles St., 617/227-9023
Bertucci's
  43 Stanhope St., 617/247-6161
Caffe Bella
  19 Warren Ave., Randolph, 781/961-7729
Ciao Bella
  240A Newbury St., 617/536-2626
Club at Il Panino
  11 Parmenter St., 617/720-1336
  295 Franklin St., 617/338-1000
Davio's Restaurant
  269 Newbury St., 617/262-4810
L'Osteria
  104 Salem St., 617/723-7847
Mama Maria
  3 North Sq., 617/523-0077
Mother Anna's
  211 Hanover St., 617/523-8496
Papa Gino's
  417 Main St., Melrose, 781/662-4227
Pleasant Cafe and Restaurant
  4515 Washington St., Roslindale, 617/323-2111
Ristorante Toscano
  47 Charles St., 617/723-4090
Terramia Ristorante
  98 Salem St., 617/523-3112

Best Japanese Food
Ginza Japanese Restaurant
  16 Hudson St., 617/338-2261
Gyuhama
  827 Boylston St., 617/437-0188
Lotus Cafe
  105 Beach St., 617/542-9526
Miyako Japanese Restaurant
  279A Newbury St., 617/236-0222

Best Korean Food
Jae's Cafe and Grill
  520 Columbus Ave., Roxbury, 617/421-9405

Best Lunch
Rebecca's
  21 Charles St., 617/742-9747

Best Mexican Food
Casa Romero
  30 Gloucester St., 617/536-4341
Sol Azteca
  914A Beacon St., 617/262-0909

Best Middle Eastern Food
Cafe Jaffa
  48 Gloucester St., 617/536-0230
Phoenicia
  240 Cambridge St., 617/523-4606
Sami's
  350 Longwood Ave., 617/730-8105
Sultan's Kitchen
  72 Broad St., 617/338-7819

Best Other Ethnic Food
Addis Red Sea Ethiopian Restaurant (Ethiopian)
  544 Tremont St., 617/426-8727

Best Pizza
California Pizza Kitchen
  800 Boylston St., 617/247-0888
Figs
  67 Main St., Charlestown, 617/242-2229
Mona Lisa Pizza
  57 Fairmount Ave., Hyde Park, 617/361-6258
Pizzeria Regina
  11 1/2 Thacher St., 617/227-0765
Pizzeria Uno
  1 Brookline Ave., 617/262-4911
  1230 Commonwealth Ave., Allston, 617/739-0034
  280 Huntington Ave., 617/424-1697
  22 Clinton St., 617/523-5722
  731 Boylston St., Copley Square, 617/267-8554
Umberto Galleria
  289 Hanover St., 617/227-5709

Best Regional Food
Boston Sail Loft Restaurant
  80 Atlantic Ave., 617/227-7280
Durgin Park
  340 Faneuil Hall Market Pl., 617/227-2038

M

Union Oyster House
    41 Union St., 617/227-2750

Best Restaurant in Town
Durgin park
    5 Fanewil Hall Market Place, 617/227-2038

Best Romantic Dining
Bay Tower Room
    Sheraton World Headquarters, 60 State St.,
        33rd Fl., 617/723-1666
Cafe Budapest
    90 Exeter St., 617/266-1979
Hungry I
    71 Charles St., 617/227-3524
L'Espalier
    30 Gloucester St., 617/ 262-3023

Best Sandwiches
Charlie's Sandwich Shoppe
    429 Columbus Ave., 617/536-7669

Best Seafood
Barking Crab
    88 Sleeper St., 617/426-2722
Daily Catch Restaurant
    259 Northern Ave., 617/426-8220
    323 Hanover St., 617/523-8567
East Ocean City Restaurant
    27 Beach St., 617/542-2504
Jimmy's Harborside Restaurant
    242 Northern Ave., 617/423-1000
Legal Sea Foods
    multiple locations
No Name Restaurant
    15A Fish Pier St. W., 617/423-2705
Skipjack's Seafood Emporium
    199 Clarendon St., 617/536-3500
    500 Boylston St., 617/536-3500
Turner Fisheries
    Westin Hotel, 10 Huntington Ave., 617/424-7425

Best Southwestern Food
Cottonwood Cafe
    222 Berkeley St., 617/247-2225
Zuma's Tex Mex Cafe
    7 Faneuil Hall Market Pl., 617/367-9114

Best Steaks
Capital Grille
    359 Newbury St., 617/262-8900
Faneuil Charcoal Grill
    200 Faneuil Hall Market Pl., 617/248-3960
Grill 23 and Bar
    161 Berkeley St., 617/542-2255
Morton's of Chicago
    1 Exeter Plz., 617/266-5858

Best Sunday Brunch
Cafe Fleuri
    Hotel Meridien, 250 Franklin St., 617/451-1900

Ritz-Carlton Dining Room
  Ritz-Carlton Hotel, 15 Arlington St., 617/536-5700
Rowe's Wharf Restaurant and Cafe
  Boston Harbor Hotel, 70 Rowes Wharf,
    617/439-3995

Best Thai Food
Bangkok Blue
  651 Boylston St., 617/266-1010
Bangkok City Restaurant
  167 Massachusetts Ave., 617/266-8884
King and I
  259 Newbury St., 617/437-9611
  145 Charles St., 617/227-3320
Thai Village
  592 Tremont St., Roxbury, 617/536-6548

Best Undiscovered Restaurant
Anchovies
  433 Columbus Ave., 617/266-5088
On the Park
  315 Shawmut Ave., Roxbury, 617/426-0862
Uva
  1418 Commonwealth Ave., Brighton, 617/566-5670

Best Vegetarian Food
Buddha's Delight Vegetarian
  5 Beach St., 617/451-2395
Country Life Vegetarian Buffet
  200 High St., 617/951-2462
Five Seasons
  669A Centre St., Jamaica Plain, 617/524-9016
Sepal's
  555 Mt. Auburn St., East Watertown, 617/924-5753
Small Planet Bar and Grill
  565 Boylston St., 617/536-4477

Best Vietnamese Food
Ba Dat
  28 Harrison Ave., 617/426-8838
Elephant Walk
  900 Beacon St., 617/247-1500
King and I
  259 Newbury St., 617/437-9611
  145 Charles St., 617/227-3320
Pho Pasteur Restaurant
  682 Washington St., 617/967-2452
  137 Brighton Ave., Allston, 617/783-2340
  8 Kneeland St., 617/451-0247

Best Wine Selection
Capital Grille
  359 Newbury St., 617/262-8900
Michael's Waterfront
  85 Atlantic Ave., 617/367-6425
Ritz-Carlton Dining Room
  Ritz-Carlton Hotel, 15 Arlington St., 617/536-5700

M

BROCKTON, MA

Best American Food
Cape Cod Cafe
   979 Main St., 508/583-9420
George's Cafe
   228 Belmont St., 508/588-4231

Best Bar
Sidelines Sports Bar and Pub
   232 E. Ashland St., 508/587-5511

Best Breakfast
Dew Drop Inn
   610 N. Main St., 508/588-4147
Dorothy Lou Pastry Shop
   605 Belmont St., 508/583-7035

Best Casual Dining
Sidelines Sports Bar and Pub
   232 E. Ashland St., 508/587-5511

Best Chinese Food
Chang Feng Restaurant
   379 Belmont St., 508/587-5993

Best Dinner
Cape Cod Cafe
   979 Main St., 508/583-9420

Best Greek/Mediterranean Food
Christo's
   782 Crescent St., 508/588-4200

Best Homestyle Food
Dew Drop Inn
   610 N. Main St., 508/588-4147

Best Italian Food
George's Cafe
   228 Belmont St., 508/588-4231
Italian Kitchen
   1071 Main St., 508/586-2100

Best Thai Food
Chaophraya
   165 Westgate Dr., 508/586-8530

BROOKLINE, MA

Best Barbecue/Ribs
Village Smokehouse
   6 Harvard Sq., 617/566-3782

Best Chinese Food
Chef Chang's House
   1006 Beacon St., 617/277-4226
Chef Chow's House
   230 Harvard St., 617/739-2469
Golden Temple
   1651 Beacon St., 617/277-9722

Best Delicatessen
B and D Deli
   1653 Beacon St., 617/232-3727

KJ's Deli and Restaurant
335 Harvard St., 617/738-3354

Best Indian Food
Bombay Bistro
1353B Beacon St., 617/734-2879

Best Seafood
Skipjack's Fish House
2 Brookline Pl., 617/739-6428

Best Thai Food
Bangkok Basil
1374 Beacon St., 617/739-1236

CAMBRIDGE, MA

[See also: Boston, Brookline, Somerville, and Woburn.]

Best Beer Selection
John Harvard's Brew House
33 Dunster St., 617/868-3585

Best Burgers
Mr. Bartley's Burger Cottage
1246 Massachusetts Ave., 617/354-6559

Best Chinese Food
Joyce Chen
390 Rindge Ave., 617/825-3688
Shilla Restaurant
57 J.F.K. St., 617/547-7971

Best Delicatessen
S & S Restaurant and Deli
1334 Cambridge St., 617/354-0777

Best Indian Food
Bombay Club
57 John F. Kennedy St., 617/661-8100

Best Italian Food
Rialto
The Charles Hotel, 1 Bennett St., 617/864-1200

Best Japanese Food
Jae's Cafe and Grill
1281 Cambridge St., 617/497-8380

Best Mexican Food
Border Cafe
32 Church St., 617/864-6100

Best Middle Eastern Food
Middle East
472 Massachusetts Ave., 617/354-8238

Best Pizza
Pizzeria Uno
820 Somerville Ave., 617/864-1916
22 JFK St., 617/497-1530

M

Best Regional Food
Boston Sail Loft Cafe and Bar
1 Memorial Dr., 617/225-2222

Best Southwestern Food
Cottonwood Cafe
1815 Massachusetts Ave., 617/661-7440

Best Thai Food
Jae's Cafe and Grill
1281 Cambridge St., 617/497-8380

Best Undiscovered Restaurant
Grendel's Den
89 Winthrop St., 617/491-1160

CENTERVILLE, MA

Best Ice Cream/Yogurt
Four Seas Ice Cream
360 S. Main St., 508/775-9253

CHATHAM, MA

Best American Food
Christian's
443 Main St., 508/945-3362

Best Lunch
Impudent Oyster
15 Chatham Bars Ave., 508/945-3545

Best Regional Food
The Squire Restaurant
487 Main St., 508/945-0945

CHELMSFORD, MA

[See also: Lowell.]

Best American Food
Bainbridge's
75 Princeton St., North Chelmsford, 978/251-8670

Best Breakfast
Town Meeting Restaurant
88 Chelmsford St., 978/250-1550

Best Burgers
Ground Round
185 Chelmsford St., 978/256-0051

Best Chinese Food
Szechuan Chef
6 Vinal Sq., North Chelmsford, 978/251-9888

Best Family Restaurant
Skip's Restaurant
116 Chelmsford St., 978/256-2631

Best Italian Food
Vincenzo's Restaurant
170 Concord Rd., 978/256-1250

Best Pizza
Bertucci's
14E Littleton Rd., 978/250-8800
Ciro's Pizzeria
170 Concord Rd., 978/256-6008

DENNIS PORT, MA

Best Bar
Michael Patrick's Publick House
435 Main St., 508/398-1620

Best Breakfast
Bonatt's Bakery
537 Rte. 28, Harwich Port, 508/432-7199

Best Family Restaurant
Oliver's
6 Bray Farm Rd., Yarmouth Port, 508/362-6062

Best Ice Cream/Yogurt
Sundae School
387 Lower County Rd., 508/394-9122

Best Lunch
Red Cottage
36 Old Bass River Rd., South Dennis, 508/394-2923

Best Regional Food
Scargo Cafe
799 Rt. 6A, Dennis, 508/385-8200

Best Seafood
Gina's by the Sea
134 Taunton Ave., Dennis, 508/385-3213
Kream and Kone
527 Main St., 508/394-0808
Thompson's Clam Bar
23 Snow Inn Rd., Harwich Port, 508/432-3595

Best Sunday Brunch
Christine's Restaurant
581 Main St., West Dennis, 508/394-7333

Best View While Dining
Brax Landing
705 Rte. 28, Harwich Port, 508/432-5515

EDGARTOWN, MA

Best Breakfast
Daggett House
59 N. Water St., 508/627-4600

Best Delicatessen
Edgartown Deli
52 Main St., 508/627-4789

Best Diner
Main Street Diner
65 Main St., 508/627-9337

Best Fine Dining
Savoir Faire
14 Church St., 508/627-9864

M

Best Regional Food
The Navigator Restaurant
  2 Main St., 508/627-4320

Best Sunday Brunch
L'Etoile
  27 S. Summer St., 508/627-5187

FALL RIVER, MA

Best American Food
Eagle Restaurant
  35 N. Main St., 508/677-3788

Best Chinese Food
China Royal
  542 Pleasant St., 508/674-2310
China Star
  390 Rhode Island Ave., 508/677-1218

Best Other Ethnic Food
Lusitano Restaurant (Portuguese)
  822 King Philip St., 508/672-9104

FALMOUTH, MA

Best Bar
Bobby Byrne's Pub
  Mashpee Commons, Mashpee, 508/477-0600

Best Breakfast
Food for Thought Restaurant
  37 N. Main St., 508/548-4498
Marshland
  109 Rte. 6A, Sandwich, 508/888-9824

Best Diner
Betsy's Diner
  457 Main St., 508/540-0060

Best Dinner
Chapoquoit
  410 W. Falmouth Hwy., 508/540-7794

Best Family Restaurant
Beehive Restaurant
  406 Rte. 6A, East Sandwich, 508/833-1184
Hearth and Kettle
  874 Main St., 508/548-6111

Best Fine Dining
Dan'l Webster Inn
  149 Main St., Sandwich, 508/888-3622
The Regatta of Cotuit
  4631 Falmouth Rd., Cotuit, 508/428-5715

Best Lunch
Chikadee Room
  881 Palmer Ave., 508/548-4006
Quarterdeck
  164 Main St., 508/548-9900

Best Outdoor Dining
Flying Bridge
  220 Scranton Ave., 508/548-2700

Best Pizza
Paul's Pizza and Seafood
  14 Benham Rd., 508/548-5838

Best Regional Food
The Flume
  Lake Ave., Mashpee, 508/477-1456

Best Romantic Dining
Coonamessett Inn
  311 Gifford St., 508/548-2300

Best Seafood
Clam Shack
  227 Clinton Ave., 508/540-7758

Best View While Dining
The Chart Room
  1 Shore Rd., Buzzards Bay, 508/563-5350
Regatta of Falmouth By-The-Sea
  357 Scranton Ave., 508/548-5400

FITCHBURG, MA

Best Chinese Food
Fitchburg Jade Chinese Restaurant
  447 Main St., 978/343-0287

Best Fine Dining
Rendezvous Restaurant
  100 Franklin Rd., 978/343-9624

Best Sandwiches
Dagwood's Deli
  490 Main St., 978/345-2141

Best Seafood
S.S. Lobster Ltd.
  691 River St., 978/342-6135

Best Sports Bar
Slatterly's Back Room
  106 Lunenburg St., 978/342-8880

FRAMINGHAM, MA

Best American Food
Finally Michael's
  1280 Worcester Rd., 508/879-7345

Best Chinese Food
Lotus Flower Chinese Restaurant
  341 Cochituate Rd., 508/872-6005
Uncle Chung's
  266 Worcester Rd., 508/872-9200

Best Greek/Mediterranean Food
Aegean Restaurant
  47 Beacon St., 508/879-8424

Best Italian Food
La Cantina Restaurant
  911 Waverley St., 508/879-7874

Best Japanese Food
Chef Orient
  1538 Worcester Rd., 508/628-9227

M

Best Pizza
Bertucci's Brick Oven Pizzeria
150 Worcester Rd., 508/879-9161
Pizzeria Uno
71 Worcester Rd., 508/620-1816

Best Sandwiches
D'Angelo's Sandwich Shop
290 Worcester Rd., 508/626-0028

Best Seafood
Legal Sea Foods
1400 Worcester St., Natick, 508/820-1115
The Dolphin
12 Washington St., Natick, 508/650-3474
7 South Ave., Natick, 508/655-0669

Best Thai Food
Bangkok Oriental Thai Restaurant
50 Worcester Rd., 508/879-6001

M

GLOUCESTER, MA

Best Dinner
Patio Restaurant of Magnolia
12 Lexington Ave., 978/525-3230

Best Family Restaurant
Cameron's Restaurant
206 Main St., 978/281-1331

Best Inexpensive Meal
Magnolia Breakfast Nook
16 Lexington Ave., 978/525-3895

Best Italian Food
Il Porto
40 Railroad Ave., 978/282-4606

Best Restaurant in Town
Gull Restaurant
75 Essex Ave., 978/283-6565
Patio Restaurant of Magnolia
12 Lexington Ave., 978/525-3230
White Rainbow
65 Main St., 617/281-0017

GREENFIELD, MA

Best Casual Dining
Taylor's Tavern
238 Main St., 413/773-8313

Best Chinese Food
New Fortune China Restaurant
249 Mohawk Trail, 413/772-0838
Royal Panda
10 Fiske Ave., 413/772-2531

Best Coffee/Coffeehouse
Timberhill Coffee House
233 Main St., 413/772-0201

Best Eclectic Menu
Sienna
6B Elm St., South Deerfield, 413/665-0215

Best Family Restaurant
Bill's Restaurant
  30 Federal St., 413/773-9230
Turnbull's Restaurant
  242 Mohawk Trail, 413/773-8203

Best Italian Food
Andiamo Restaurant
  Huckle Hill Rd., Bernardston, 413/648-9107

Best Sandwiches
Bricker's
  184 Shelburne Rd., 413/774-2857

Best Seafood
Deerfield Inn
  81 Old Main St., Deerfield, 413/774-5587
Herm's
  91 Main St., 413/772-6300
Pete's Fish Market and Seafood
  54 School St., 413/772-2153

Best Steaks
Herm's
  91 Main St., 413/772-6300

M

HAVERHILL, MA

[See also: Lawrence, and Methuen.]

Best Chinese Food
Oriental Garden
  400 Lowell Ave., 978/373-5626

Best Delicatessen
A-1 Deli
  92 Merrimack St., 978/372-7951

Best Dinner
The Cobblestone
  130 Washington St., 978/373-2410

Best Family Restaurant
Al's Place
  251 Primrose St., Ste. 13, 978/374-9846

Best Lunch
Jimmy's Restaurant III
  2 Essex St., 978/372-8822

Best Pizza
Sal's Pizza
  95 Winter St., 978/521-7575

Best Sandwiches
Bagel Express
  35 Railroad Sq., 978/521-4333

HYANNIS, MA

Best Barbecue/Ribs
Mitchell's Steak and Rib House
  451 Iyanough Rd., 978/775-6700

Best Breakfast
Hearth and Kettle
  23 Richardson Rd., Centerville, 508/775-8878

Best Chinese Food
Dragon Lite Restaurant
  620 Main St., 508/775-9494
Golden Fountain Restaurant
  203 W. Main St., 508/771-3332

Best Desserts
D'Olimpio's New York Deli
  55 Iyanough Rd., 508/771-3220

Best Fine Dining
Paddock Restaurant
  20 Scudder Ave., 508/775-7677

Best Italian Food
Alberto's Ristorante
  360 Main St., 508/778-1770
Roadhouse Cafe
  488 South St., 508/775-2386

Best Mexican Food
Sam Diego's
  950 Iyanough Rd., 508/771-8816

Best Outdoor Dining
Tugboats
  21 Arlington St., 508/775-6433

Best Regional Food
Mildred's Chowder House
  290 Iyanough Rd., 508/775-1045

Best Restaurant in Town
Paddock Restaurant
  20 Scudder Ave., 508/775-7677

Best Romantic Dining
Alberto's Ristorante
  360 Main St., 508/778-1770

Best Seafood
Cooke's Seafood
  1120 Iyanough Rd., 508/775-0450
Main Street Restaurant and Grill
  426 Main St., 508/771-8585

Best Southwestern Food
Sweetwaters Grille
  644 Main St., 508/775-3323

Best View While Dining
Baxter's Boathouse Club and Fish-N-Chips
  177 Pleasant St., 508/775-4490
Mattakeese Wharf
  271 Mill Way, Barnstable, 508/362-4511

LAWRENCE, MA

[See also: Andover and Methuen.]

Best American Food
Cedar Crest Restaurant
187 Broadway, 978/685-5722

Best Burgers
Lawton's Famous Frankfurters
606 Canal St., 978/686-9603

Best Lunch
Brother's Pizza
145 Lawrence St., 978/688-7039

Best Middle Eastern Food
Bishop's Restaurant
99 Hampshire St., 978/683-7143

Best Spanish Food
Capricornio Restaurant
216 Hampshire St., 978/688-2444

M

LOWELL, MA

[See also: Chelmsford.]

Best American Food
Bel Gusto's D'Italia
Sheraton Hotel, 50 Warren St., 978/937-9447

Best Bar
The Office Pub
660 Rogers St., 978/441-9040

Best Brewpub
Brewhouse Cafe and Grill
201 Cabot St., 978/937-2690

Best Business Lunch
Old Worthen
147 Worthen St., 978/441-3189

Best Delicatessen
Deli King
885 Main St., Tewksbury, 978/858-3855

Best Dinner
Cobblestones
91 Dutton St., 978/970-2282

Best French Food
La Boniche Restaurant
143 Merrick St., 978/458-9473

Best Greek/Mediterranean Food
Olympia Restaurant
453 Market St., 978/452-8092

Best Indian Food
Bombay Mahal Restaurant
45 Middle St., 978/441-2222

Best Italian Food
Bel Gusto's D'Italia
    Sheraton Hotel, 50 Warren St., 978/937-9447

Best Pizza
Queen's Pizza
    287 Chelmsford St., 978/452-8606

MANSFIELD, MA

Best American Food
Jimmy's Pub
    141 N. Main St., 508/339-7167

Best Breakfast
Old Colony Diner
    16 Old Colony Rd., 508/339-4983

Best Italian Food
Ladonna
    131 Copeland Dr., 508/261-7000

Best Pizza
House of Pizza
    175 N. Main St., 508/339-6400

Best Sandwiches
Bagel Train
    350 N. Main St., 508/339-1800

MARLBOROUGH, MA

Best Bar
Kennedy's Pub
    247A Maple St., 508/485-5800
Pastimes Bar and Grill
    277 Main St., 508/485-0098

Best Burgers
Boston Market
    185 Boston Post Rd., 508/229-2525

Best Chinese Food
Royal Mandarin
    350 E. Main St., 508/485-8366

Best Coffee/Coffeehouse
Starbucks Coffee
    189 Boston Post Rd. E, 508/485-8223

Best Ice Cream/Yogurt
Trombetta's Tee-Rarium
    655 Farm Rd., 508/485-6429

Best Italian Food
Rocco's Restaurant and Pub
    127 Lakeside Ave., 508/485-7717
The Oxford
    109 Lakeside Ave., 508/485-0077

Best Pizza
Bertucci's Brick Oven Pizzeria
    388 Boston Post Rd., 508/460-0911
Papa Gino's
    205 E. Main St., 508/481-5245

Best Sandwiches
D'Angelo's Sandwich Shop
28 Boston Post Rd. E., 508/485-2363
JD Craig's Fine Food To Go
241 Boston Post Rd. W., 508/485-1588

Best Seafood
American Lobster
19 Northboro Rd., 508/481-9898

Best Steaks
Wildwood
189 Boston Post Rd. E., 508/481-2021

Best Thai Food
Chez Siam Restaurant
280 E. Main St., 508/485-3880

MARSHFIELD, MA

Best Breakfast
Arthur and Pat's Restaurant
239 Ocean St., 781/834-9755

Best Dinner
Fairview
133 Ocean St., 781/834-9144

Best Family Restaurant
Bridgeway Inn
1289 Ferry St., 781/834-6505

Best Lunch
Hung's Chinese Cuisine
43 Careswell St., 781/837-4440

Best Pizza
American Pie
25 Webster Sq., 781/837-5211

Best Restaurant in Town
Fairview
133 Ocean St., 781/834-9144

MARTHA'S VINEYARD, MA

Best Pizza
Papa's Pizza
158 Circuit Ave., Oak Bluffs, 508/693-1400

Best View While Dining
Black Dog Tavern
Beach Street Extension, 2219 Vineyard Haven,
508/693-9223

METHUEN, MA

[See also: Lawrence.]

Best Breakfast
Country Kitchen
18 Hampshire Ct., 978/687-9632

Best Burgers
1859 House
  16 Hampshire St., 978/682-1859
Fireside Restaurant
  171 Pelham St., 978/683-2945

Best Coffee/Coffeehouse
Green Mountain Coffee
  Flicks Video Center, 234 Pleasant St.,
    978/794-0068

Best Desserts
Hampstead Manor
  251 Hampstead St., 978/687-9876

Best Family Restaurant
Methuen Family Restuarant
  246 Broadway, 978/683-7050

Best Health-Conscious Menu
Cosmos Restaurant
  940 Riverside Dr., 978/682-2330
Jackson's Restaurant
  478 Lowell St., 978/688-5021

Best Ice Cream/Yogurt
Jay Gee's Ice Cream
  602 Lowell St., 978/689-0456

Best Italian Food
Mamma Mary's
  322 Merrimack St., 978/682-6299

Best Other Ethnic Food
Shadi's Restaurant (Lebanese)
  58 Osgood St., 978/687-9698

Best Pizza
Espresso Pizza
  246 Broadway, 978/686-1606
Theo's Pizza
  26 Hampshire Cir., 978/686-8288

Best Place to Take the Kids
Stagger Lee's
  114 Cross St., 978/688-9600

Best Seafood
Jackson's Restaurant
  478 Lowell St., 978/688-5021

Best Steaks
Jimmy's Restaurant II
  106 Lowell Blvd., 978/682-5542

MILFORD, MA

Best Barbecue/Ribs
Coachmen's Lodge
  273 Wrentham Rd., Bellingham, 508/883-9888

Best Chinese Food
The Milford Mandarin
  Quarry Square, 196 E. Main St., 508/478-8893

Best Restaurant in Town
Pete's Bluebird
  85 Mendon St., Bellingham, 508/966-9717

NANTUCKET, MA

Best Breakfast
Jared Coffin House
  29 Broad St., 508/228-2400
Le Languedoc Inn and Restaurant
  24 Broad St., 508/228-2552

Best Burgers
Atlantic Cafe
  15 S. Water St., 508/228-0570

Best Delicatessen
Provisions
  3 Harbour Sq., 508/228-3258

Best Family Restaurant
The Hearth
  The White Elephant Resort, S. Beach St.,
    508/228-1500

Best Fine Dining
21 Federal
  21 Federal St., 508/228-2121
Boarding House
  12 Federal St., 508/228-9622

Best Greek/Mediterranean Food
West Creek Cafe
  11 W. Creek Rd., 508/228-4943

Best Ice Cream/Yogurt
The Juice Bar
  12 Broad St., 508/228-5799

Best Mexican Food
Tacos Tacos
  10 Broad St., 508/228-5418

Best Pizza
Vincent's Italian Restaurant
  21 S. Water St., 508/228-0189

Best Romantic Dining
The Woodbox Inn
  29 Fair St., 561/842-0201

Best Seafood
Galley on Cliffside Beach
  32 Jefferson Ave., 508/228-9641
Topper's at the Wauwinet
  120 Wauwinet Rd., 508/228-8768

Best Sunday Brunch
Harbor House
  The White Elephant Resort, S. Beach St.,
    508/228-1500

Best View While Dining
Ropewalk
  1 Straight Wharf, 508/228-8886

M

NEEDHAM, MA

[See also: Boston, Brookline, and Cambridge.]

Best Breakfast
What's Cookin'
  942 Great Plain Ave., 781/444-9600

Best Burgers
Ground Round
  1 First Ave., 781/444-6360

Best Chinese Food
The Joy Luck Club
  1037 Great Plain Ave., 781/455-8908

Best Coffee/Coffeehouse
Bergson's Ice Cream Shop
  1077 Great Plain Ave., 781/444-6997

Best Greek/Mediterranean Food
Four Stars Restaurant
  1430 Highland Ave., 781/444-1011

Best Inexpensive Meal
What's Cookin'
  942 Great Plain Ave., 781/444-9600

Best Middle Eastern Food
Karoun
  839 Washington St., Newton, 617/964-3400

Best Pizza
Mom and Pop's Pizza
  315 Chestnut St., 781/449-2255
Pizzeria Uno
  287 Washington Ave., Newton, 617/964-2296

Best Thai Food
Amarin of Thailand
  287 Centre St., Newton, 617/527-5255
Bai Thong
  1257 Highland Ave., 781/433-0272

NEW BEDFORD, MA

Best American Food
Miguel's Restaurant
  253 Union St., 508/990-8781

Best Barbecue/Ribs
Skewers
  142 Huttleston Ave., Fairhaven, 508/996-3303

Best Breakfast
Newport Creamery Restaurant
  1071 Kempton St., 508/997-8383
  950 Kings Hwy., 508/998-5323

Best Business Lunch
Manny's Cafe Restaurant
  175 Sawyer St., 508/999-9804

Best Chinese Food
China Lantern
116 Nauset St., 508/997-4474

Best Diner
Shawmut Diner
943 Shawmut Ave., 508/993-3073

Best Family Restaurant
Spearfield's
1 Johnny Cake Hill, 508/993-4848

Best Homestyle Food
Shawmut Diner
943 Shawmut Ave., 508/993-3073

Best Italian Food
Pa Raffa's Italian Restaurant
2857 Acushnet Ave., 508/995-7711
Pasta House
100 Alden Rd., Fairhaven, 508/993-9913

Best Other Ethnic Food
Miguel's Restaurant (Portuguese)
253 Union St., 508/990-8781
Portuguese Shanty (Portuguese)
2980 Acushnet Ave., 508/998-2645

Best Pizza
Fay's Knotty Pine Kitchen
2164 Acushnet Ave., 508/995-9838
Riccardi's Italian Restaurant
901 Hathaway Rd., 508/996-3921

Best Sandwiches
Manny's Cafe Restaurant
175 Sawyer St., 508/999-9804
Three Flags
894 Purchase St., 508/997-6212

Best Seafood
Davy's Locker
1480 E. Rodney French Blvd., 508/992-7359
Three Flags
894 Purchase St., 508/997-6212

NORTHAMPTON, MA

Best Breakfast
Gwen and Deb's
14 Pleasant St., 413/586-7953

Best Cajun/Creole Food
Eastside Grill
19 Strong Ave., 413/586-3347

Best Casual Dining
Fitzwilly's
23 Main St., 413/584-8666
Packard's
14 Masonic St., 413/584-5957

Best Chinese Food
Hunan Gourmet Chinese Restaurant
261 King St., 413/585-0202

M

Best Desserts
Bananarama
  186 Main St., 413/586-9659

Best French Food
Martini's
  5 Bridge St., 413/584-1197

Best Indian Food
India House
  45 State St., 413/586-6344

Best Inexpensive Meal
Blue Bonnet Diner
  324 King St., 413/584-3333
Miss Florence Diner
  99 Main St., 413/584-3137

Best Italian Food
Fresh Pasta Company
  249 Main St., 413/586-5875
Melina's Trattoria
  21 Center St., 413/586-8900
Spoleto Restaurant
  50 Main St., 413/586-6313

Best Lunch
Cha Cha Cha
  134 Main St., 413/586-7311

Best Mexican Food
La Cazuela Mexican Restaurant
  7 Old South St., 413/586-0400
La Veracruzana
  31 Main St., 413/586-7181

Best Pizza
Geraldine's
  86 Green St., 413/586-5443
Pizzeria Paradiso
  12 Crafts Ave., 413/586-1468

Best Sandwiches
D'Angelo's Sandwich Shop
  388 King St., 413/584-9776
Jake's
  17 King St., 413/584-9613

Best Seafood
Eastside Grill
  19 Strong Ave., 413/586-3347
Penguin Fish Market
  29 Union St., Easthampton, 413/527-7480

Best Steaks
Aqua Vitae
  37 Russell St., Hadley, 413/584-9892
Eastside Grill
  19 Strong Ave., 413/586-3347

Best Sunday Brunch
Sylvester's Restaurant
  111 Pleasant St., 413/586-5343

Best Vegetarian Food
Bela Vegetarian Restaurant
   68 Masonic St., 413/586-8011
Paul and Elizabeth's
   150 Main St., 413/584-4832
Raw Carrot
   9 Pleasant St., 413/549-4240

ORLEANS, MA

Best Family Restaurant
Lobster Claw
   Rte. 6A, 508/255-1800

Best Fine Dining
Chillingsworth
   3449 Main St., Brewster, 508/896-3640

Best Italian Food
Nauset Beach Club
   222 Main St., East Orleans, 508/255-8547
Rosina's Cafe
   54 Main St., 508/240-5513

Best Outdoor Dining
Kadee's Lobster and Clam Bar
   212 Main St., East Orleans, 508/255-6184

Best Pizza
Binnacle Tavern
   20 S. Orleans Rd., 508/255-7901

Best Restaurant in Town
Land Ho Restaurant
   Rte. 6A at Main St., 508/255-5165
Off the Bay Cafe
   28 Main St., 508/255-5505

Best Romantic Dining
Captain Linnell House
   137 Skaket Beach Rd., 508/255-3400

Best Seafood
Cooke's Seafood
   Rte. 28, 508/255-5518

PITTSFIELD, MA

Best Breakfast
Court Square Breakfast and Deli
   95 East St., 413/442-9896

Best Coffee/Coffeehouse
Sip of Seattle
   216 Elm St., 413/445-5143

Best Continental Food
Wendell House
   17 Wendell Ave., 413/448-6072

Best Fine Dining
Truffles and Such
   Allendale Shopping Center, Allendale Rd.,
      413/442-0151

M

Best Italian Food
Sweet Basil Grille
306 Pittsfield Rd., 413/637-1270

Best Pizza
East Side Cafe
378 Newell St., 413/447-9405
Elizabeth's Restaurant
1264 East St., 413/448-8244

Best Seafood
Sweet Basil Grille
306 Pittsfield Rd., 413/637-1270

Best Steaks
Dakota's Restaurant
1035 South St., 413/499-7900

PLYMOUTH, MA

Best American Food
The Colonial Restaurant
39 Main St., 508/746-0838

Best Restaurant in Town
Handlebar Harry's
Bldg. 3, 3 Cordage Park, 508/747-1922
Run of the Mill Tavern
6 Spring Ln., 508/830-1262

Best Seafood
Souza's Seafood Restaurant
Town Wharf Rd., 508/746-5354
Wood's Seafood
Town Wharf Rd., 508/746-0261

PROVINCETOWN, MA

Best Bar
Fat Jack's Cafe
335 Commercial St., 508/487-4822

Best Casual Dining
Gallerani's
133 Commercial St., 508/487-4433

Best Family Restaurant
Lobster Pot
321 Commercial St., 508/487-0842

Best Fine Dining
Whitman House
Rte. 6, North Truro, 508/487-1740

Best Lunch
Box Lunch
4205 Rte. 6, Eastham, 508/255-0799

Best Other Ethnic Food
Moors Restaurant (Portuguese)
5 Bradford St., 508/487-0840

Best Outdoor Dining
Cafe Blase
328 Commercial St., 508/487-9465

Best Pizza
Upper Crust Pizza
90 Commercial St., Wellfleet, 508/349-9562

Best Regional Food
Friendly Fisherman
4500 Rte. 6, North Eastham, 508/255-6770
PJ's Family Restaurant
261 Rte. 6, Wellfleet, 508/349-2126

Best Romantic Dining
Aesop's Tables
Main St., Wellfleet, 508/349-6450

Best Seafood
Lobster Pool
4380 Rte. 6, North Eastham, 508/255-9706
Mayflower Cafe
300 Commercial St., 508/487-0212
Napi's
7 Freeman St., 508/487-1145
Tips for Tops
31 Bradford St., 508/487-1811

Best View While Dining
Sal's Place
99 Commercial St., 508/487-1279
The Mews
359 Commercial St., 508/487-1500

M

QUINCY, MA

Best American Food
Alfredo's Restaurant
75 Franklin St., 617/472-1115

Best Delicatessen
Common Market
97 Willard St., 617/773-9532

Best Italian Food
Bertucci's
90 Derby St., Hingham, 617/740-4405
Gennaro's Eatery
12 Blanchard Rd., 617/773-1500

Best Mexican Food
La Paloma
195 Newport Ave., 617/773-0512

SALEM, MA

[See also: Beverly.]

Best American Food
Blue Point Roast Beef and Seafood
100 Boston St., 978/741-3479

Best Breakfast
Red's Sandwich Shop
15 Central St., 978/745-3527

Best Italian Food
Bertini's
284 Canal St., 978/744-1436

Best Japanese Food
Asahi Restaurant
21 Congress St., 978/744-5376

Best Pizza
Mandee's Pizza
408 Essex St., 978/745-6400

Best Restaurant in Town
Chase House
Bldg. K, Pickering Wharf, 978/744-0000
Victoria Station
86 Wharf St., 978/745-3400

SOMERVILLE, MA

[See also: Boston, Brookline, Cambridge, and Woburn.]

Best Barbecue/Ribs
Redbones
55 Chester St., 617/628-2200

Best Burgers
Casey's
171 Broadway, 617/625-5195

Best Chinese Food
Chang Feng Restaurant
289 Beacon St., 617/864-6265
Fortune Palace
146 Broadway, 617/625-9194

Best Family Restaurant
Paddock Lounge and Pizza
249 Pearl St., 617/628-6525

Best Greek/Mediterranean Food
Dali
415 Washington St., 617/661-3254

Best Mexican Food
Rudy's Cafe
248 Holland St., 617/623-9201

Best Salad/Salad Bar
Victor's Meat and Deli
710 Broadway, 617/625-3076

Best Seafood
Mount Vernon Restaurant
14 Broadway, 617/666-3830

Best Steaks
Mount Vernon Restaurant
14 Broadway, 617/666-3830

Best Undiscovered Restaurant
Union Square Bistro
16 Bow St., 617/628-3344

Best Vietnamese Food
Elephant Walk
  70 Union Sq., 617/623-9939

SOUTHBRIDGE, MA

Best Atmosphere
Publick House
  295 Main St., Sturbridge, 508/347-3313
Salem Cross Inn
  260 W. Main St., West Brookfield, 508/867-2345

Best Breakfast
Annie's Country Kitchen
  140 Main St., Sturbridge, 508/347-2320
Elm Centre Coffee Shop
  39 Elm St., 508/764-7288

Best Family Restaurant
Hook and Ladder Restaurant
  177 Elm St., 508/764-8405

Best French Food
Le Bearn Restaurant
  12 Cedar St., 508/347-5800

Best Greek/Mediterranean Food
Golden Greek Restaurant
  6 Sandersdale Rd., 508/765-0211

Best Health-Conscious Menu
Margaux's Deli and Catering
  33 Crystal St., 508/765-0954

Best Ice Cream/Yogurt
Coop's Scoops
  204 Worcester St., 508/764-3043

Best Italian Food
Mario's Restaurant
  274 Main St., 508/765-5338

Best Pizza
Central Pizza
  57 Central St., 508/764-2541
Great Oak Pizza
  922 Main St., 508/765-2929

SPRINGFIELD, MA

Best 24-Hour Restaurant
Bickford's Family Restaurant
  1296 Riverdale Rd., West Springfield, 413/733-6055

Best Breakfast
Route 66 Diner
  950 Bay St., 413/737-4921

Best Business Lunch
Mexitalia Cafe
  1441 Main St., 413/781-6101

Best Chinese Food
Golden Dragon
  2223 Northampton St., Holyoke, 413/536-4299

M

Best German Food
Student Prince and The Fort
8 Fort St., 413/734-7475

Best Greek/Mediterranean Food
Mykonos European Restaurant
1060 Wilbraham Rd., 413/783-6333

Best Indian Food
Sitar Restaurant
1688 Main St., 413/732-8011

Best Italian Food
Lido Restaurant
555 Worthington St., 413/736-9433
Silvano's Restaurant
680 Worthington St., 413/734-9774

Best Lunch
Cafe Manhattan
301 Bridge St., 413/737-7913

Best Pizza
Buona Pizza
1441 Main St., 413/731-0881
Liquori's Pizza
659 Westfield St., West Springfield, 413/737-9690
Mamma Mia's Pizzeria
60 Park Avenue Ct., West Springfield,
413/732-0400

Best Seafood
Delaney House
1 Country Club Rd., Holyoke, 413/532-1800
Tilly's Restaurant
1390 Main St., 413/732-3613

Best Steaks
Take Five
944 Springfield St., Feeding Hills, 413/786-0962

WESTFIELD, MA

Best American Food
Point East Lounge
The Sheraton, 385 E. Main St., 413/568-1315

Best Chinese Food
China Star
36 Southwick Rd., 413/568-9698

Best Delicatessen
Farmer's Daughter
36 Elm St., 413/568-5888

Best Dinner
Sheraton Inn
880 Russell Rd., 413/562-6505

Best Greek/Mediterranean Food
Cafe Santorini
930 Southhampton Rd., 413/572-1022
Davio's Restaurant
198 Elm St., 413/562-5033

Best Pizza
Daniele's Pizza
 1029 North Rd., 413/533-7400

WOBURN, MA

Best Chinese Food
Kowloon
 948 Broadway, Saugus, 617/233-0077

Best Family Restaurant
99 Restaurant
 291 Mishawum Rd., 781/935-7210
 194 Cambridge Rd., 781/938-8999

Best Fine Dining
Cafe Escadrille
 26 Cambridge St., Burlington, 781/273-1916

Best Restaurant in Town
Joe's Bar & Grill
 311 Mishawum Rd., 781/935-7200

Best Steaks
Hilltop Steak House
 855 Broadway, Saugus, 781/324-9200

WORCESTER, MA

Best American Food
Union House Pub
 18 Bridge St., Blackstone, 508/883-5353

Best Barbecue/Ribs
Cactus Pete's
 400 Park Ave., 508/752-3038

Best Chinese Food
Ping's Garden
 60 Madison St., 508/791-9577

Best Coffee/Coffeehouse
Cafe Dolce
 154 Shrewsbury St., 508/754-3761
Coffee Kingdom
 2 Richmond Ave., 508/755-8936

Best Diner
The Parkway Diner
 148 Shrewsbury St., 508/753-9968

Best Indian Food
House of India
 439 Park Ave., 508/752-1330
Sweetheart Restaurant
 270 Shrewsbury St., 508/752-3700

Best Italian Food
Dino's Ristorante
 13 Lord St., 508/753-9978

Best Japanese Restaurant
Sakura Tokyo
 640 Park Ave., 508/792-1078

M

Best Late-Night Food
Kenmore Diner
  250 Franklin St., 508/753-9541

Best Mexican Food
Acapulco Mexican Restaurant
  107 Highland St., 508/791-1746

Best Other Ethnic Food
Caribbean Cuisine (Caribbean)
  5 E. Mountain St., 508/856-9199
El Morocco (Lebanese)
  100 Wall St., 508/756-7117
O'Connor's Restaurant and Bar (Irish/European)
  1160 W. Boylston St., 508/853-0789

Best Pizza
Wonder Bar
  121 Shrewsbury St., 508/752-9909

Best Place to Take the Kids
Chuck E. Cheese Pizza
  Redmont Sq. Mall, 5612 Albemarle St.,
    508/754-5151

Best Restaurant Meal Value
Webster House
  1 Webster St., 508/757-7208

Best Romantic Dining
Castle Restaurant
  1230 Main St., Leicester, 508/892-9090
Tiano's
  108 Grove St., 508/752-8901

Best Salad/Salad Bar
Abdow's Big Boy
  442 Southbridge St., Auburn, 508/832-3229

Best Sandwiches
Elsa's Bushel and Peck
  17 E. Mountain St., 508/856-0516
  358 Main St., 508/752-9001
Regatta Deli
  28 Lake Ave., 508/756-6916

Best Seafood
Sole Proprietor
  118 Highland St., 508/798-3474

Best Steaks
Cactus Pete's
  400 Park Ave., 508/752-3038
Chuck's Steak House
  10 Prospect St., Auburn, 508/832-2553

Best Vegetarian Food
The Living Earth
  232 Chandler St., 508/753-1896

Best Vietnamese Food
Da-Lat Restaurant
  425 Park Ave., 508/753-6036

Michigan

ADRIAN, MI

Best American Food
The Hathaway House
424 W. Adrian St., Blissfield, 517/486-2141

Best Breakfast
Kate and Emily's
104 Toledo St., 517/263-0890
Main Stop Restaurant
1003 N. Main St., 517/263-9873

Best Chinese Food
China Chef
124 S. Main St., 517/264-6868

Best Dinner
Brass Lantern
1853 W. Maumee St., 517/263-0411

Best Family Restaurant
Miller's Family Restaurant
1545 W. Maumee St., 517/265-7170

Best Mexican Food
CC Margarita and Company
521 S. Meridian Rd., Hudson, 517/448-7111
El Chapulin Restaurant
118 S. Winter St., 517/265-6670
Espo's Mexican Grill
1416 S. Main St., 517/265-9099

ANN ARBOR, MI

Best American Food
Dominick's
812 Monroe St., 734/662-5414

Red Hawk Bar and Grill
316 S. State St., 734/994-4004

Best Chinese Food
China Gate
1201 S. University Ave., 734/668-2445

Best Coffee/Coffeehouse
Sweet Water Cafe
123 W. Washington St., 734/769-2331

Best Delicatessen
Amer's Mediterranean Deli
312 S. State St., 734/761-6000
611 Church St., 734/769-1210
Zingermann's Delicatessen
422 Detroit St., 734/663-3354

Best Diner
Fleetwood Diner
300 S. Ashley St., 734/995-5502

Best Fine Dining
Escoffier
300 S. Thayer St., 734/995-3800
Moveable Feast
326 W. Liberty St., 734/663-3278

Best German Food
Heidelberg Restaurant
215 N. Main St., 734/663-7758

Best Health-Conscious Menu
Seva Restaurant and Market
314 E. Liberty St., 734/662-1111

Best Homestyle Food
Fleetwood Diner
300 S. Ashley St., 734/995-5502

Best Indian Food
Raja Rani
400 S. Division St., 734/995-1545

Best Inexpensive Meal
Afternoon Delight
251 E. Liberty St., 734/665-7513
Grizzly Peak Brewing Company
120 W. Washington St., 734/741-7325

Best Italian Food
Argiero's Italian Restaurant
300 Detroit St., 734/665-0444
The Earle
121 W. Washington St., 734/994-0211

Best Lunch
Seva Restaurant and Market
314 E. Liberty St., 734/662-1111

Best Mexican Food
Prickly Pear Southwest Cafe
328 S. Main St., 734/930-0047

Best Pizza
Brown Jug Restaurant
1204 S. University Ave., 734/761-3355

Best Restaurant in Town
Bella Ciao Trattoria
  118 W. Liberty St., 734/995-2107
The Earle
  121 W. Washington St., 734/994-0211

Best Seafood
Lord Fox
  5400 Plymouth Rd., 734/662-1647

Best Vegetarian Food
Maude's Restaurant
  314 S. Fourth Ave., 734/662-8485
Seva Restaurant and Market
  314 E. Liberty St., 734/662-1111

BATTLE CREEK, MI

Best American Food
Moonraker Lounge and Restaurant
  14490 Beadle Lake Rd., 616/962-7779

Best Barbecue/Ribs
Sam's Joint
  1600 State Rte. 66, Athens, 616/729-5010

Best Chinese Food
Golden Dragon Restaurant
  906 Capital Ave. NE, 616/968-7159
Hong Kong Restaurant
  174 Columbia Ave. E., 616/965-4848
Tony's Chop Suey
  215 Michigan Ave. W., 616/964-8138

Best Ice Cream/Yogurt
Pastamazoo
  55 S. Twentieth St., 616/963-1177

Best Italian Food
Roma Cafe and Spaghetti Factory
  217 Michigan Ave. W., 616/968-6377

Best Mexican Food
Bit O'Mexico
  605 North Ave., 616/964-6100

Best Pizza
Mancino's Pizza
  5285 Beckley Rd., 616/979-3100
Pennfield Pizza
  1432 Capital Ave. NE, 616/964-9465

Best Steaks
Finley's American Restaurant
  140 Columbia Ave. E., 616/968-3938

Best Sunday Brunch
Clara's on the River
  44 N. McCamly St., 616/963-0966

BAY CITY, MI

Best Breakfast
Krzysiak's House
  1605 Michigan Ave., 517/894-5531

M

Best Burgers
Mulligan's Pub
  109 Center Ave., 517/893-4555
O'Hare's
  608 E. Midland St., 517/893-5181
Steamer's Pub
  108 N. Linn St., 517/895-8559

Best Chinese Food
Mandarin House Chinese Restaurant
  1415 W. Center Rd., Essexville, 517/893-9499

Best Coffee/Coffeehouse
Espresso Express
  916 N. Water St., 517/893-8898

Best Ice Cream/Yogurt
Jamie's Dairies
  1023 Broadway St., 517/893-7862
  110 N. Madison Ave., 517/893-7871
  1309 S. Farragut St., 517/893-7804
  603 Columbus Ave., 517/893-7849

M

Best Italian Food
Grampa Tony's Restaurant
  1108 Columbus Ave., 517/893-4795
O Sole Mio Restaurant
  1005 Saginaw St., 517/893-3496

BIRMINGHAM, MI

Best Coffee/Coffeehouse
Lonestar Coffeehouse
  207 S. Woodward Ave., 248/642-2233

Best Continental Food
Beverly Hills Grill
  31471 Southfield Rd., Beverly Hills, 248/642-2355

Best Delicatessen
Albans Restaurant and Deli
  190 N. Hunter Blvd., 248/258-5788

Best Middle Eastern Food
Pita Cafe
  239 N. Woodward Ave., 248/645-6999

Best Restaurant in Town
Rugby Grille
  Townsend Hotel, 100 Townsend St., 248/642-5999

Best Seafood
Streetside Seafood
  273 Pierce St., 248/645-9122

COLDWATER, MI

Best Atmosphere
Clairmont House
  32 Railroad St., 517/278-5257

Best Chinese Food
Charlie's II Restaurant
  599 E. Chicago St., 517/278-2982

Best Coffee/Coffeehouse
Dutch Uncle Donuts
58 E. Chicago St., 517/278-8965

Best Greek/Mediterranean Food
Coldwater Gardens
432 E. Chicago St., 517/278-3172

Best Pizza
Mancino's Pizza
510 Chicago Rd., 517/278-2127

Best Sandwiches
Allen's Root Beer Drive-In
378 W. Chicago Rd., 517/279-9048
Irma's Restaurant
14 W. Chicago St., 517/279-9965

Best Steaks
Monroe Street Station
19 S. Monroe St., 517/278-3149
Narrows
191 Narrows Rd., 517/278-5088

M

DEARBORN, MI

[See also: Detroit and Southgate.]

Best Breakfast
Andoni's Family Dining
1620 N. Telegraph Rd., 313/278-9100
Dimitri's Fine Food
2424 S. Telegraph Rd., 313/565-7066

Best Business Lunch
La Shish
12918 Michigan Ave., 313/584-4477

Best Chinese Food
Lim's Village Cafe
24418 Michigan Ave., 313/565-5788
New Peking Restaurant
29105 Ford Rd., Garden City, 734/425-2230

Best Delicatessen
Matti's on Monroe
1842 Monroe St., 313/277-3253

Best Family Restaurant
Andoni's Family Dining
1620 N. Telegraph Rd., 313/278-9100

Best Indian Food
Peacock Restaurant
4045 Maple St., 313/582-2344

Best Italian Food
Antonio's Cucina Italiana
26356 Ford Rd., Dearborn Heights, 313/278-6000
La Trattoria Italian Restaurant
13736 Michigan Ave., 313/581-6055
Roman Village
9924 Dix, 313/842-2100

Best Middle Eastern Food
Al-Berdouni Restaurant
  5821 Chase Rd., 313/582-6116
Cedarland Restaurant
  13007 W. Warren Ave., 313/582-4849
La Shish
  12918 Michigan Ave., 313/584-4477
La Shish East
  22039 Michigan Ave., 313/562-7200
M and M Cafe
  13355 Michigan Ave., 313/581-5775
Talal's Restaurant
  22041 Michigan Ave., 313/565-5500

Best Salad/Salad Bar
Salad Bar
  22023 Michigan Ave., 313/274-7520

Best Sandwiches
Lile's Sandwich Shop
  13800 Michigan Ave., 313/581-2821
Noah's Sandwich Factory
  14500 Michigan Ave., 313/582-8361

Best Seafood
Big Fish
  700 Town Center Dr., 313/336-6350

Best Soul Food
Southern Connections Family Restaurant
  18900 Michigan Ave., 313/240-8403

M

DETROIT, MI

[See also: Dearborn, Livonia, Royal Oak, Southgate, and Warren.]

Best American Food
Rattlesnake Club
  300 River Place Dr., 313/567-4400
The Whitney
  4421 Woodward Ave., 313/832-5700

Best Breakfast
Mesquite Creek
  222 E. Jefferson Ave., 313/964-5500

Best Brewpub
Franklin Street Brewing Company
  1560 Franklin St., 313/568-0390

Best Cajun/Creole Food
Fishbones Rhythm Kitchen Cafe
  400 Monroe St., 313/965-4600

Best Delicatessen
Bread Basket Deli
  26052 Greenfield Rd., Oak Park, 248/968-0022
Lou's Deli
  19440 W. Seven Mile Rd., 313/538-0274
  8220 W. McNichols Rd., 313/861-1321

Maxie's Deli and More
1501 Michigan Ave., 313/961-7968

Best Desserts
Traffic Jam and Snug
511 W. Canfield St., 313/831-9470

Best Dinner
Edmund Place
69 Edmund Pl., 313/831-5757

Best Fine Dining
Opus One
565 E. Larned St., 313/961-7766
Rattlesnake Club
300 River Place Dr., 313/567-4400

Best French Food
Twingo's Cafe
4710 Cass Ave., 313/832-3832

Best Greek/Mediterranean Food
Zefs Coney Island Restaurant
2469 Russell St., 313/259-4705

Best Inexpensive Meal
National Coney Island
19019 Mack Ave., Grosse Pointe, 313/881-5509

Best Italian Food
Giovanni's Ristorante
330 S. Oakwood, 313/841-0122
Intermezzo Italian Ristorante
1435 Randolph St., 313/961-0707
Lelli's Inn
7618 Woodward Ave., 313/871-1590

Best Mexican Food
Armando's Mexican Cuisine
4242 W. Vernor Hwy., 313/554-0666
El Zocalo Mesican Restaurant
3400 Bagley St., 313/841-3700
Xochimilco Restaurant
3409 Bagley St., 313/843-0179

Best Middle Eastern Food
Pita Cafe
25282 Greenfield Rd., Oak Park, 248/968-2225
Steve's Back Room
19872 Kelly Rd., Harper Woods, 313/527-5047

Best Other Ethnic Food
Cadieux Cafe (Belgian)
4300 Cadieux Rd., 313/882-8560
Ivanhoe Cafe (Polish)
5249 Joseph Campau St., 313/925-5335
Polish Villiage Cafe (Polish)
2990 Yemans St., Hamtramck, 313/874-5726
Trapper's Bar and Grill (Lebanese)
508 Monroe St., 313/965-1574
Under the Eagle (Polish)
9000 Joseph Campau St., Hamtramck,
313/875-5905

M

Best Pizza
Buddy's Rendezvous Pizza
  17125 Conant St., Hamtramck, 313/892-9001
Gregg's Pizza and Bar-B-Que
  7630 E. Seven Mile Rd., 313/892-2400
  17160 Livernois Ave., 313/341-2400

Best Sandwiches
Ham Heaven Sandwich Shop
  70 Cadillac Sq., 313/961-8818

Best Seafood
Joe Muer's
  2000 Gratiot Ave., 313/567-1088

Best Soul Food
Steve's Soul Food
  8443 Grand River Ave., 313/894-7978

EAST LANSING, MI

Best Burgers
USA Cafe
  4750 S. Hagadorn Rd. S., 517/332-3660

Best Chinese Food
Gourmet Village Chinese Restaurant
  The Hannah Plaza, 4790 S. Hagadorn Rd.,
  517/333-6666

Best Diner
USA Cafe
  4750 S. Hagadorn Rd. S., 517/332-3660

Best Italian Food
Michelangelo's Restaurant
  213 E. Grand River Ave., 517/332-4825

Best Middle Eastern Food
Sultan's
  The Hannah Plaza, 4790 S. Hagadorn Rd.,
  517/333-6666

Best Restaurant in Town
Beggars Banquet
  218 Abbott Rd., 517/351-4573
Dustys English Inn
  728 S. Michigan Rd., Eaton Rapids, 517/663-2500
Pistachios Restaurant
  2827 E. Grand River Ave., 517/351-1551

Best Salad/Salad Bar
Pretzel Bell
  1020 Trowbridge Rd., 517/351-0300

FENTON, MI

Best Atmosphere
Fenton Hotel
  302 N. Leroy St., 810/750-9463

Best Barbecue/Ribs
Fenton House Restaurant
  413 S. Leroy St., 810/629-0661

Best Burgers
Halo Burger
1464 N. Leroy St., 810/750-1952

Best Seafood
Frank's Tavern
14331 Eastview Dr., 810/629-9133

FLINT, MI

Best American Food
Danny's Restaurant
G-1405 W. Pierson Rd., 810/733-6720
Greenery Restaurant
6468 W. Vienna Rd., Clio, 810/686-9318
White Horse
621 W. Court St., 810/234-3811

Best Breakfast
Balkan Bakery
1325 W. Dayton St., 810/235-3431
White Horse
621 W. Court St., 810/234-3811

Best Burgers
Bill Thomas' Halo Burger
800 S. Saginaw St., 810/238-4015

Best Business Lunch
Red Rooster Makuch's Restaurant
1302 Davison Rd., 810/742-9310

Best Casual Dining
Bailiwick Pub and Grill
836 S. Saginaw St., 810/235-1230

Best Chinese Food
Empress of China Restaurant
2320 S. Dort Hwy., 810/234-8971

Best Continental Food
Broadstreet
103 W. Broad St., Linden, 810/735-5844

Best Diner
The Diner
522 W. Broad St., Linden, 810/735-9741

Best Dinner
White Horse
621 W. Court St., 810/234-3811

Best Fast Food
Bill Thomas' Halo Burger
800 S. Saginaw St., 810/238-4015

Best Italian Food
Danny's Restaurant
G4070 S. Saginaw St., 810/743-8970
Italia Gardens
401 W. Court St., 810/233-4112
Russo's Casual Italian Dining
11225 S. Saginaw St., Grand Blanc, 810/695-1671
Salvatore Scallopini
G3227 Miller Rd., 810/732-1070

M

Best Mexican Food
Don Pablo's
  3145 Miller Rd., 810/235-2262

Best Middle Eastern Food
Aidas Mid East Food
  1 Water St., 810/233-5347

Best Pizza
Pesto's
  5275 Miller Rd., 810/732-4390
Ruggero's
  G-2995 S. Linden Rd., 810/733-7633
Ruggero's at Water Street
  303 S. Saginaw St., 810/232-1411

Best Seafood
Whitey's Restaurant
  109 S. State Rd., Davison, 810/653-6666

Best Steaks
Big John Steak and Onion
  multiple locations

Best Thai Food
Bangkok 1 Thai Cuisine
  3096 S. Dort Hwy., 810/715-1115

Best View While Dining
City Lights Restaurant
  432 N. Saginaw St., Ste. 12, 810/232-8888

M

GAYLORD, MI

Best American Food
Sugar Bowl Bakery
  216 W. Main St., 517/732-5524

Best French Food
Blue Goose
  900 Charles Brink Rd., 517/732-8254

Best German Food
Sclang's Bavarian Inn
  3917 Old Hwy. 27S, 517/732-9288

Best Homestyle Food
Gobblers Restaurant
  900 S. Otsego Ave., 517/732-9002

GRAND RAPIDS, MI

Best American Food
Gidson's Restaurant
  1033 Lake Dr. SE, 616/774-8535

Best Barbecue/Ribs
Sam's Joint
  7449 68th St. SE, Dutton, 616/698-1833
  107 E. Main St. SE, Caledonia, 616/891-1128
  4312 S. Division Ave., 616/538-9601

Best Beer Selection
Flanagan's
  139 Pearl St. NW, 616/454-7852

Best Breakfast
Red Geranium Cafe
  352 Michigan Ave. NE, 616/235-4680
Wolfgang's Just Breakfast
  1530 Wealthy St. SE, 616/454-5776

Best Burgers
Cottage Bar and Restaurant
  18 La Grave Ave. SE, 616/454-9088

Best Business Lunch
Hong Kong Inn
  121 Monroe Center St. NW, 616/451-3835
Teazer's
  819 Ottawa Ave. NW, 616/459-2481

Best Casual Dining
Arnie's Bakery Restaurant
  710 Leonard St. NW, 616/454-3098
  East Brook Mall, 3561 28th St. SE, 616/956-7901
  1960 Breton Rd. SE, 616/949-3801
Grand River Saloon
  151 Ottawa Ave. NW, 616/458-2229
Honey Creek Inn
  8025 Cannonsburg Rd. NE, Cannonsburg,
    616/874-7849
Rose's
  550 Lakeside Dr. SE, 616/458-1122

Best Chinese Food
First Wok
  2301 44th St. SE, 616/281-0681
  3509 Alpine Ave. NW, 616/784-1616
Hong Kong Inn
  121 Monroe Center St. NW, 616/451-3835
Yen Ching
  57 Monroe Center St. NW, 616/235-6969

Best Coffee/Coffeehouse
Gaia Coffee House
  209 Diamond Ave. SE, 616/454-6233
Kava House
  1445 Lake Dr. SE, 616/451-8600

Best Continental Food
Pagano's
  9948 Cherry Valley Ave. SE, Caledonia,
    616/891-0160

Best Delicatessen
Eastown Deli
  3730 28th St. SE, 616/458-5439
Schnitzelbank Delicatessen
  342 Jefferson Ave. SE, 616/459-9527
  1315 E. Fulton St., 616/451-4444
Solomon's Deli
  221 Michigan St. NE, 616/774-0272

Best Desserts
Arnie's Bakery Restaurant
  710 Leonard St. NW, 616/454-3098
  East Brook Mall, 3561 28th St. SE, 616/956-7901
  1960 Breton Rd. SE, 616/949-3801

M

East Brook Mall
  3561 28th St. SE, 616/959-7901
  710 Leonard St. NW, 616/454-3098
The Gathering Place
  6886 Cascade Rd. SE, 616/949-3188

Best Diner
Brandywine
  1345 Lake Dr. SE, 616/774-8641

Best Family Restaurant
Bono's Italian Restaurant
  1418 Plainfield Ave.NE, 616/451-0010
Finley's American Restaurants
  1420 28th St. SW, 616/538-8600
  1950 44th St. SE, 616/455-9640
  4095 Plainfield Ave. NE, 616/364-0058

Best Fine Dining
Cygnus
  Amway Grand Plaza Hotel, 187 Monroe Ave. NW,
    616/776-6425
Sayfees
  3555 Lake Eastbrook Blvd. SE, 616/949-5750

Best Homestyle Food
Fingers Restaurant
  4981 Plainfield Ave.NE, 616/363-3836
Teazer's
  819 Ottawa Ave. NW, 616/459-2481

Best Italian Food
Florentine Pizzeria Restaurant
  4301 Kalamazoo Ave. SE, 616/455-2230
Johnny Noto's Italian Ristorante
  4259 Lake Michigan Dr. NW, 616/791-0092
Pietro's Ristorante
  5301 Northland Dr. NE, 616/365-3550
  2780 Birchcrest Dr. SE, 616/452-3228
Tuscan Express
  6450 28th St. SE, 616/956-5522
Vitale's Italian Restaurant
  834 Leonard St. NE, 616/458-3766

Best Korean Food
Seoul Garden
  2409 E. Beltline Ave. SE, 616/956-1522

Best Lunch
Forest Hills Inn
  4609 Cascade Rd. SE, 616/949-4771

Best Mexican Food
Alma Latina
  45 S. Division Ave., 616/454-6790
Jose Babushka's
  1820 44th St. SW, 616/534-0704
Texas Cafe
  956 E. Fulton St., 616/451-0976

Best Other Ethnic Food
Osta's (Lebanese)
  2228 Wealthy St. SE, 616/456-8999

Wisla Shop (Polish)
644 Stocking Ave. NW, 616/458-2903

Best Pizza
Pallino's
Gaslight Village, 2224 Wealthy St. SE,
616/458-4646

Best Romantic Dining
Rembrandt's
333 Bridge St. NW, 616/459-8900

Best Sandwiches
Buddie's Delicatessen and Bagelry
2150 Wealthy St. SE, 616/235-3354
Eastown Deli
3730 28th St. SE, 616/458-5439
Ski's Sub Shop
96 Monroe Center St. NW, 616/451-9504

Best Seafood
Charley's Crab
63 Market Ave. SW, 616/459-2500

Best Southwestern Food
Beltline Bar
16 28th St. SE, 616/245-0494

Best Spanish Food
San Chez Bistro
38 W. Fulton St., 616/774-8272

Best Steaks
Brann's Steak and Seafood
401 Leonard St. NW, 616/454-9368
5080 Alpine Ave. NW, Comstock Park,
616/784-2100
4157 S. Division Ave., 616/534-5421
Duck's Restaurant and Lounge
740 Michigan St. NE, 616/451-2767
Pietro's Ristorante
2780 Birchcrest Dr. SE, 616/452-3228
5301 Northland Dr. NE, 616/365-3550

Best Thai Food
Thai House Restaurant
6447 28th St. SE, 616/285-9944

GROSSE POINTE WOODS, MI

Best Breakfast
Jumps
63 Kercheval, Grosse Pointe Farms, 313/882-9555

Best Coffee/Coffeehouse
Daily Grind Coffee House
20962 Mack Ave., 313/417-0020

Best Pizza
Buddy's Rendezvous Pizza
19163 Mack Ave., 313/884-7400

HOLLAND, MI

Best American Food
Pereddie's Bakery Deli
447 Washington Ave., 616/394-3061

Best Breakfast
Russ' Restaurant
361 E. Eighth St., 616/396-2348
210 N. River Ave., 616/392-6300
1060 Lincoln Ave., 616/396-4036

Best Casual Dining
Calypso's
Holland Holiday Inn, 650 E. 24th St., 616/394-0111
The Auburn
478 E. Sixteenth St., 616/392-3017

Best Chinese Food
China Inn
457 E. 32nd St., 616/395-8383
2863 W. Shore Dr., Ste. 105, 616/786-9230

Best Continental Food
Alpen Rose
4 E. Eighth St., 616/393-2111

Best Delicatessen
Pumpernickels
202 Butler St., Saugatuck, 616/857-1196

Best Health-Conscious Menu
Till Midnight
208 College Ave., 616/392-6883

Best Ice Cream/Yogurt
Captain Sundae
365 Douglas Ave., 616/396-5938

Best Italian Food
84 East
84 E. Eighth St., 616/396-8484
Mancino's
12465 James St., 616/786-0600
Pereddie's Bakery Deli
447 Washington Ave., 616/394-3061

Best Mexican Food
Cantu's Mexican Restaurant
380 W. Sixteenth St., 616/396-6622
Jose Babushka's
12420 Felch St., 616/392-9900

Best Other Ethnic Food
Queen's Inn Restaurant (Dutch)
12350 James St., 616/393-0310

Best Regional Food
Sandpiper Restaurant
2225 S. Shore Rd., Macatawa, 616/335-5866

Best Sandwiches
Eighth Street Grill
20 W. Eighth St., 616/392-5888

Best Steaks
Prime Tyme Restaurant
1080 Lincoln Ave., 616/396-1071

JACKSON, MI

Best Barbecue/Ribs
West Texas Barbeque Company
2190 Brooklyn Rd., 517/784-0510

Best Burgers
Kelly's Lunch
640 E. Michigan Ave., 517/787-9010
Schlenker's Sandwich Shop
1104 E. Ganson St., 517/783-1667

Best Ice Cream/Yogurt
Jackson All Star Dairy
1401 Daniel Rd., 517/782-7141

Best Pizza
Jaxon Pizza Factory
800 N. Waterloo St., 517/788-8366

Best Seafood
Brandywine Pub and Food
2125 Horton Rd., 517/783-2777
Eagle's Nest
1200 Eagle Point Rd., Clarklake, 517/529-9121

Best Steaks
Brandywine Pub and Food
2125 Horton Rd., 517/783-2777
Gilbert's Steak House
2323 Shirley Dr., 517/782-7135
Ye Old Steakhouse
1319 E. Michigan Ave., 517/784-6744

KALAMAZOO, MI

Best All-You-Can-Eat Buffet
Dane's Buffet
4217 Portage St., 616/343-4264

Best American Food
Burdick's
100 W. Michigan Ave., 616/343-3333

Best Bar
Main Street Pub
4574 W. Main St., 616/342-9710

Best Breakfast
Food Dance Cafe
161 E. Michigan Ave., 616/382-1888
Maggie's Bakery and Cafe
2715 W. Michigan Ave., 616/381-1312

Best Burgers
McGinnis Landing Restaurant
5031 W. Main St., 616/388-9911

Best Chinese Food
Great Wall of China
3025 S. Westnedge Ave., 616/343-9888

M

Best Coffee/Coffeehouse
Water Street Coffee Joint
315 E. Water St., 616/373-2840

Best Desserts
Aries Cafe
127 E. Bridge St., Plainwell, 616/685-9495

Best Eclectic Menu
Aries Cafe
127 E. Bridge St., Plainwell, 616/685-9495
Aries London Grill
200 E. Bridge St., Plainwell, 616/685-1877

Best Family Restaurant
Finley's American Restaurant
5160 W. Main St., 616/342-4360

Best Fine Dining
The Great Lakes Shipping Company Restaurant
4525 W. KL Ave., 616/375-3650
Webster's
100 W. Michigan Ave., 616/343-4444

Best Greek/Mediterranean Food
Blue Dolphin
502 S. Burdick St., 616/343-4993
Nikos Landing
5852 King Hwy., 616/342-8626

Best Health-Conscious Menu
Food Dance Cafe
161 E. Michigan Ave., 616/382-1888

Best Homestyle Food
Bill Knapp's
4315 W. Main St., 616/342-0227
Blake Diner
402 S. Burdick St., 616/381-4333

Best Ice Cream/Yogurt
Carousel Ice Cream
819 S. Westnedge Ave., 616/343-8493

Best Inexpensive Meal
Mancino's Pizza
3911 Gull Rd., 616/383-0066
5363 N. Westnedge Ave., 616/382-2527

Best Italian Food
Fricano's
7454 N. Sixth St., 616/342-0808
Josephine's
601 S. Burdick St., 616/349-6749

Best Late-Night Food
McGinnis Landing Restaurant
5031 W. Main St., 616/388-9911

Best Mexican Food
Carlos Murphy's
5650 W. Main St., 616/343-0330
Juanita's Store
1801 S. Burdick St., 616/383-0750

Mi Ranchito
   3806 S. Westnedge Ave., 616/343-7262
   3112 S. Ninth St., 616/375-5861

Best Place to Eat Alone
Damon's
   3124 S. Westnedge Ave., 616/342-4753

Best Place to Take the Kids
The Pizza Parlor
   3301 W. Michigan Ave., 616/962-8061

Best Sandwiches
Burdick's
   100 W. Michigan Ave., 616/343-3333

Best Steaks
Great Lakes Shipping Company
   4525 W. KL Ave., 616/375-3650

Best Vegetarian Food
Burdick's
   100 W. Michigan Ave., 616/343-3333

M

KENTWOOD, MI

Best Bar
Beltline Bar
   16 28th St. N., 616/245-0494

Best Barbecue/Ribs
Damon's
   4515 28th St. SE, 616/956-1211

Best Casual Dining
Brann's
   4157 S. Division Ave., 616/534-5421

Best Dinner
Kentwood Station Restaurant
   1665 Viewpond Dr. SE, 616/455-4150

Best Italian Food
Russo's Italian Restaurant
   6209 S. Division Ave., 616/534-7877

Best Japanese Food
Tokyo Grill and Sushi
   4478 Breton Rd. SE, 616/455-3433

Best Sports Bar
Cheddar's Restaurant
   4284 28th St. SE, 616/940-1837

Best Steaks
Mountain Jack's
   3600 28th St. SE, 616/949-9033

LANSING, MI

Best American Food
Falsetta's Restaurant and Lounge
   138 S. Waverly Rd., 517/323-9181

Best Bar
Buddies Pub and Grill
   1937 W. Grand River Ave., Okemos, 517/347-0443

Best Brewpub
Blue Coyote Brewing Company
    113 Pere Marquette Dr., 517/485-2583

Best Chinese Food
House of Ing
    4113 S. Cedar St., 517/393-4848

Best Eclectic Menu
Clara's Restaurant
    637 E. Michigan Ave., 517/372-7120

Best Italian Food
Coscarelli's Restaurant and Lounge
    2420 S. Cedar St., 517/482-4919

Best Mexican Food
El Azteco
    1016 W. Saginaw St., 517/485-4589
Famous Taco
    2012 W. Saginaw St., 517/371-5171
Jalapenos Mexican Restaurant
    307 S. Washington Sq., 517/482-2326
Ramon's Restaurant and Lounge
    718 E. Grand River Ave., 517/482-6690
    3020 E. Kalamazoo St., 517/372-3010

Best Pizza
Deluca's Restaurant
    2006 W. Willow St., 517/487-6087

Best Regional Food
Restaurant Villegas
    1735 W. Grand River Ave., Okemos, 517/347-2080

Best Restaurant in Town
Mountain Jack's
    5800 W. Saginaw Hwy., 517/321-2770

Best Steaks
Best Steak House
    3020 E. Kalamazoo St., 517/337-2210

LIVONIA, MI

[See also: Dearborn, and Detroit.]

Best Breakfast
Golden Lantern
    33251 Five Mile Rd., 734/421-1012

Best Burgers
Bill Knapp's
    32955 Plymouth Rd., 734/427-0511
    16995 S. Laurel Park Dr. S., 734/464-6363
Max and Erma's
    37714 Six Mile Rd., 734/462-9870

Best Chinese Food
Szechuan Empire
    37097 Six Mile Rd., 734/591-1901

29215 Five Mile Rd., 734/458-7160

Best Continental Food
Cafe Bon Homme
844 Penniman Ave., Plymouth, 734/453-6260

Best Eclectic Menu
Misty Duck Bistro
45250 Ford Rd., Canton, 734/459-7100

Best Italian Food
DePalma's Dining
31735 Plymouth Rd., 734/261-2430
Fonte D'Amore Ristorante
32030 Plymouth Rd., 734/422-0770

Best Mexican Food
El Nibble Nook Restaurant
27725 W. Eight Mile Rd., 248/474-0755

Best Pizza
Buddy's Rendezvous Pizza
33605 Plymouth Rd., 734/261-3550

Best Salad/Salad Bar
Buddy's Rendezvous Pizza
33605 Plymouth Rd., 734/261-3550
D. Dennison's
37716 Six Mile Rd., 734/464-9030

Best Sandwiches
Max and Erma's
37714 Six Mile Rd., 734/462-9870

Best Seafood
D. Dennison's
37716 Six Mile Rd., 734/464-9030

Best Steaks
Mountain Jack's
31501 Schoolcraft Rd., 734/458-7333

Best Thai Food
Thai Bostro
45620 Ford Rd., Canton, 734/416-2122

MARQUETTE, MI

Best Coffee/Coffeehouse
Sweetwater Cafe
517 N. Third St., 906/226-7009

Best Health-Conscious Menu
Sweetwater Cafe
517 N. Third St., 906/226-7009

Best Italian Food
Pasta Shop
824 N. Third St., 906/228-6620
Villa Capri Italian Cuisine
155 Bayou St., 906/225-1153

Best Mexican Food
Entre Amigos
142 W. Washington St., 906/228-4531

Best Restaurant in Town
Northwoods Supper Club
   260 Northwoods Rd., 906/228-4343
The Vierling Saloon and Samplery
   119 S. Front St., 906/228-3533

Best Sports Bar
Whiskers Sports Bar and Eatery
   1700 Presque Isle Ave., 906/228-9038

MIDLAND, MI

Best Bar
101 Main Street Food and Spirits
   101 E. Main St., 517/839-2896

Best Breakfast
Omeletes and More
   112 E. Main St., 517/839-0930
Shirlene's Cuisine
   1716 W. Wackerly St., 517/631-8750
Texan Family Restaurant
   2008 N. Saginaw Rd., 517/631-4600

Best Chinese Food
Bamboo Garden
   2600 N. Saginaw Rd., 517/832-7967

Best Desserts
Sweet Onion
   1415 S. Saginaw Rd., 517/631-2062

Best Fine Dining
The Crossings Restaurant and Lounge
   Ashman Court Hotel, 111 W. Main St.,
   517/839-0500

Best Regional Food
Cafe Edward
   5010 Bay City Rd., 517/496-3012

Best Sandwiches
101 Main Street Food and Spirits
   101 E. Main St., 517/839-2896

Best Seafood
Cafe Edward
   5010 Bay City Rd., 517/496-3012

Best Steaks
Corky's Steakhouse
   5100 Bay City Rd., 517/839-0541

MONROE, MI

Best Breakfast
Ernie's Gathering Place
   15425 S. Dixie Hwy., 734/242-2330
Monroe Diner
   546 S. Telegraph Rd., 734/242-4077

Best Burgers
McGeady's Town Pub
   39 S. Monroe St., 734/243-1220

Best Ice Cream/Yogurt
Independent Dairy
126 N. Telegraph Rd., 734/241-6016
7373 Bluebush Rd., 734/587-2112

Best Italian Food
Dominic's Italian Restaurant
15215 S. Dixie Hwy., 734/242-6300
Restaurant Italia and Lounge
1110 N. Telegraph Rd., 734/241-7151

Best Mexican Food
Carl's Hide-A-Way
2838 Lewis Ave., Ida, 734/269-6288

Best Pizza
Detroit Beach Restaurant
2630 N. Dixie Hwy., 734/289-3122
Ron's Pizzeria and Restaurant
1119 Monroe St., Carleton, 734/654-6233

Best Regional Food
Ernie's Gathering Place
15425 S. Dixie Hwy., 734/242-2330

M

Best Seafood
Francesco's Pier House
6975 Laplaisance Rd., 734/242-6470
Quatro's
1295 Stewart Rd., 734/242-6788

Best Steaks
Quatro's
1295 Stewart Rd., 734/242-6788

MT. PLEASANT, MI

Best Burgers
Brass Saloon
128 S. Main St., 517/772-0864

Best Coffee/Coffeehouse
Max and Emily's Bakery Cafe
125 E. Broadway St., 517/772-7460

Best Desserts
Sweet Onion
102 N. Mission St., 517/772-0801

Best Homestyle Food
J.W. Filmore's
903 N. Mission St., 517/772-5950
Stanley's Famous Restaurant
220 E. Broadway St., 517/773-3259

Best Ice Cream/Yogurt
Doozie's Ice Cream
1310 E. Pickard Rd., 517/772-2332

Best Italian Food
Italian Oven
2336 S. Mission St., 517/773-6836

Best Mexican Food
La Senorita Mexican Restaurant
1516 S. Mission St., 517/772-1331

Best Seafood
Embers
    1217 S. Mission St., 517/773-5007
Pickard Street Bar and Grill
    Holiday Inn, 5665 E. Pickard St., 517/772-2905

MUSKEGON, MI

Best Barbecue/Ribs
Sam's Joint
    15520 48th Ave., Coopersville, 616/837-8558

Best Breakfast
Goober's Bakery
    4165 Grand Haven Rd., 616/798-1213
Hearthstone
    3350 Glade St., 616/733-1056
Papa Bear's
    2280 E. Apple Ave., 616/773-2067

Best Casual Dining
Kirby Grill
    2 Washington Ave., Grand Haven, 616/846-3299

Best Chinese Food
House of Chan
    375 Gin Chan Ave., 616/733-9624

Best Coffee/Coffeehouse
Anton's Bakery
    927 W. Laketon Ave., 616/759-7676

Best Dinner
Carmen's Cafe
    315 W. Clay Ave., 616/726-6317
USA Cafe
    2020 Lakeshore Dr., 616/755-7454

Best Family Restaurant
Cherokee Restaurant
    1971 W. Sherman Blvd., 616/759-7006

Best Italian Food
Tony's Club
    785 W. Broadway Ave., 616/739-7196

Best Lunch
G and L Chili Dogs
    885 Jefferson St., 616/722-9119
    771 W. Sherman Blvd., 616/733-1505

Best Mexican Food
Flamingo II
    1163 E. Laketon Ave., 616/722-1679

Best Pizza
Fricano's Pizza
    1400 Fulton St., Grand Haven, 616/842-8640

Best Romantic Dining
Rafferty's
    601 Terrace Point Rd., 616/722-4461

Best Sandwiches
Hearthstone
    3350 Glade St., 616/733-1056

Best Seafood
Chesapeake Crab House
    939 Third St., 616/728-2204

Best Breakfast
Americana The Pancake House
    U.S. Hwy. 31, 616/347-5530

Best Burgers
Elias Brothers
    751 Spring St., 616/347-2931
Mitchell Street Pub
    426 E. Mitchell St., 616/347-1801

Best Chinese Food
Chee Peng Chinese Restaurant
    1129 N. U.S. Hwy. 31, 616/347-2542

Best Coffee/Coffeehouse
Roast and Toast
    309 E. Lake St., 616/347-7767

Best Desserts
H.O. Rose Room
    Perry Hotel, Bay St. at Lewis St., 616/347-4000

Best Ice Cream/Yogurt
Kilwin Chocolates
    355 N. Division Rd., 616/347-4831

Best Italian Food
Villa Ristorante Italiano
    U.S. Hwy. 131S, 616/347-1440

Best Mexican Food
La Senorita
    1285 N. U.S. Hwy. 31, 616/347-7750

Best Pizza
Mighty Fine Pizza
    222 E. Mitchell St., 616/347-3255

Best Restaurant in Town
Andante
    321 Bay St., 616/348-3321

Best Steaks
Schelde's
    1315 N. U.S. Hwy. 31, 616/347-7747

[See also: Rochester, Rochester Hills, and Troy.]

Best Bar
Industry Night Club
    15 S. Saginaw St., 248/334-1999

Best Barbecue/Ribs
Beale Street Blues
    8 N. Saginaw St., 248/334-7900

Best Breakfast
Coney Jack's
  101 N. Saginaw St., 248/338-2797

Best Burgers
Coyote Club
  1 N. Saginaw St., 248/332-4695
Griff's Grill
  49 N. Saginaw St., 248/334-9292

Best Coffee/Coffeehouse
Gargoyle's Coffeehouse
  7 N. Saginaw St., 248/745-9790

Best Ice Cream/Yogurt
Leeon Restaurant
  1252 N. Perry St., 248/334-1929

Best Italian Food
Allegro's
  1 N. Saginaw St., 248/338-7337

Best Mexican Food
El Taco Loco
  143 S. Telegraph Rd., 248/334-9933
Tenuta's Villa Rio
  454 W. Huron St., 248/338-9639

Best Sandwiches
Maya's Delicatessen
  22 N. Saginaw St., 248/332-8787
Pete's Coney Island
  839 W. Huron St., 248/334-5050

Best Seafood
Pike Street Restaurant
  18 W. Pike St., 248/334-7878

Best Soul Food
Chuck's Coney and Soul Food
  370 Martin Luther King Jr. Blvd. N., 248/334-7624

Best Steaks
Wide Track Diner
  1551 Wide Track Dr., 248/332-4097

PORT HURON, MI

Best Breakfast
Thomas Edison Inn
  500 Thomas Edison Pkwy., 810/984-8000

Best Burgers
Huron Athletic Club
  321 Huron Ave., 810/984-2299

Best Fine Dining
Victorian Inn
  1229 Seventh St., 810/984-1437

Best Homestyle Food
Loxton's Family Restaurant
  3535 Lapeer Rd., 810/982-7771

Best Ice Cream/Yogurt
London Dairy
  2136 Pine Grove Ave., 810/984-5111

Best Sandwiches
Main Street Deli
  902 Military St., 810/984-2940

Best Seafood
Fogcutter Restaurant
  511 Fort St., 810/897-3300

Best Steaks
Fogcutter Restaurant
  511 Fort St., 810/897-3300

PORTAGE, MI

Best Casual Dining
Finley's American Restaurant
  6301 S. Westnedge Ave., 616/323-1104

Best Chinese Food
Peking Palace
  5640 S. Westnedge Ave., 616/388-5100

Best Desserts
Hawthorne Restaurant and Cafe
  9110 Portage Rd., 616/323-1327

Best Family Restaurant
Finley's American Restaurant
  6301 S. Westnedge Ave., 616/323-1104

Best Fine Dining
Hawthorne Restaurant and Cafe
  9110 Portage Rd., 616/323-1327

Best Health-Conscious Menu
Hawthorne Restaurant and Cafe
  9110 Portage Rd., 616/323-1327

Best Homestyle Food
Bill Knapp's
  5135 Portage Rd., 616/345-8655

Best Inexpensive Meal
Mancino's Pizza
  10100 Shaver Rd., 616/327-5121

Best Pizza
Mancino's Pizza
  10100 Shaver Rd., 616/327-5121

Best Place to Be "Seen"
Hawthorne Restaurant and Cafe
  9110 Portage Rd., 616/323-1327

Best Romantic Dining
Hawthorne Restaurant and Cafe
  9110 Portage Rd., 616/323-1327

Best Steaks
Mountain Jack's Restaurant
  6701 S. Westnedge Ave., 616/327-6797

M

[See also: Pontiac, Rochester Hills, Sterling Heights, and Troy.]

Best Bar
Mr. B's Food and Spirits
423 S. Main St., 248/651-6534

Best Business Lunch
Kruse and Muer on Main
327 S. Main St., 248/652-9400

Best Casual Dining
Kruse and Muer on Main
327 S. Main St., 248/652-9400

Best Fine Dining
Scallops
1002 N. Main St., 248/656-2525

Best Health-Conscious Menu
Elias Brothers
3756 Rochester Rd., 248/852-5540

Best Homestyle Food
Rochester Cafe and Family Dining
630 N. Main St., 248/652-0820

Best Late-Night Food
Rochester Chop House and Bar
306 S. Main St., 248/651-2266

Best Middle Eastern Food
Angie's Place
134 W. University Dr., 248/650-4715

Best Pizza
Hungry Howie's Pizza and Subs
606 N. Main St., 248/652-2010

Best Place to Eat Alone
Paint Creek Tavern
4480 Orion Rd., 248/651-8361

Best Restaurant in Town
Kruse and Muer on Main
327 S. Main St., 248/652-9400
Rochester Chop House
306 S. Main St., 248/651-2266

Best Seafood
Rochester Chop House and Bar
306 S. Main St., 248/651-2266

ROCHESTER HILLS, MI

[See also: Pontiac, Rochester, Sterling Heights, and Troy.]

Best Burgers
Bill Knapp's
  3010 Walton Blvd., 248/375-1515

Best Business Lunch
Murdock's
  2086 Crooks Rd., 248/852-0550

Best Casual Dining
Max and Erma's Restaurant
  70 N. Adams Rd., 248/375-1535

Best Chinese Food
Pearl City North Restaurant
  2601 S. Rochester Rd., 248/852-0170

Best Diner
Bill Knapp's
  3010 Walton Blvd., 248/375-1515

Best Family Restaurant
Max and Erma's Restaurant
  70 N. Adams Rd., 248/375-1535

Best Italian Food
Alfoccino of Rochester
  2091 S. Rochester Rd., 248/853-6633
Eastside Mario's
  2273 Crooks Rd., 248/853-9622
Lino's
  50 W. Tienken Rd., 248/652-9002

Best Place to Take the Kids
Family Buggy Restaurant
  870 S. Rochester Rd., 248/656-0850

Best Salad/Salad Bar
Max and Erma's Restaurant
  70 N. Adams Rd., 248/375-1535

Best Sandwiches
Pic-A-Deli
  3134 Walton Blvd., 248/375-1330

ROYAL OAK, MI

[See also: Detroit, Sterling Heights, Troy, and Warren.]

Best All-You-Can-Eat Buffet
BD's Mongolian Barbecue
  310 S. Main St., 248/398-7755

Best Barbecue/Ribs
Mitchell's Barbecue and Grill
  1824 W. Fourteen Mile Rd., 248/280-0050

Oxford Inn
1214 S. Main St., 248/543-5619

Best Casual Dining
Beau Jacks Restaurant
4108 W. Maple Rd., Bloomfield Hills, 248/626-2630
Gallery Restaurant
6638 Telegraph Rd., Bloomfield Hills,
248/851-0313

Best Ice Cream/Yogurt
Ray's Ice Cream
4233 Coolidge Hwy., 248/549-5256

Best Italian Food
Sila Italian Dining and Pizza
4033 W. Twelve Mile Rd., Berkley, 248/548-3650

Best Seafood
Big Fish Too
1111 W. Fourteen Mile Rd., Madison Heights,
810/585-9533

Best Steaks
Clawson Steak House
56 S. Rochester Rd., Clawson, 248/588-5788
Masters Restaurant
1775 E. Thirteen Mile Rd., Madison Heights,
248/588-0915
Mountain Jack's Restaurant
2262 S. Telegraph Rd., Bloomfield Hills,
810/334-4694

Best Thai Food
Thai House
4254 N. Woodward Ave., 248/776-3660

Best Vegetarian Food
Inn Season Natural Food Cafe
500 E. Fourth St., 248/547-7916
O M Cafe
23136 Woodward Ave., Ferndale, 248/548-1941

SAGINAW, MI

Best 24-Hour Restaurant
Ram's Horn
2575 Tittabawassee Rd., 517/249-4223

Best Bar
Hamilton Street Pub
308 S. Hamilton St., 517/790-2670

Best Breakfast
Bringer Inn
516 W. Genesee Ave., 517/753-1462

Best Business Lunch
Holly's Landing
1134 N. Niagara St., 517/754-4461

Best Chinese Food
East Wind
3747 East St., 517/754-3031
Hunan Chinese Restaurant
3109 Bay Plaza Dr., 517/792-0303

Panda House
1010 N. Niagara St., 517/755-5394

Best Family Restaurant
Tony's Original Restaurant
2612 State St., 517/793-1801
1205 Lapeer Ave., 517/754-6001
2525 E. Genesee Ave., 517/753-4321
1029 Gratiot Ave., 517/792-1113
Zehnders of Frankenmuth
730 S. Main St., Frankenmuth, 517/652-9925

Best Fine Dining
The Montague Inn
1581 S. Washington Ave., 517/752-3939

Best Greek/Mediterranean Food
Blue Dolphin
175 E. Jefferson St., Frankenmuth, 517/652-3900

Best Health-Conscious Menu
Heart House Inn
419 N. Michigan Ave., 517/753-3145

Best Homestyle Food
Bill Knapp's
4600 State St., 517/793-2150
Sullivan's
5235 Gratiot Rd., 517/799-1940

Best Ice Cream/Yogurt
Mooney Ice Cream Store
812 Williams St., 517/754-6641

Best Lunch
Cafe Suz
6099 Gratiot Rd., 517/791-2343
Treasure Island
924 N. Niagara St., 517/755-6577

Best Mexican Food
El Farolito Restaurant
1346 N. Washington Ave., 517/771-9460
115 N. Hamilton St., 517/799-8959
La Senorita
3823 Bay Rd., 519/793-6312

Best Pizza
Guido's
116 N. Michigan Ave., 517/790-1000

Best Place to Be "Seen"
Levi's Saloon
6407 State St., 517/790-3538
5212 Bay Rd., 517/793-6670

Best Place to Take the Kids
Chuck E. Cheese Pizza
5105 Bay Rd., 517/791-1116

Best Romantic Dining
Delphine's
4960 Towne Center Rd., 517/790-5050
Montague Inn
1400 Weiss St., 517/752-3939

M

Treasure Island
    924 N. Niagara St., 517/755-6577

Best Sandwiches
Intermission Deli
    2128 Bay Rd., 517/790-6777
Wally's Old Fashioned Sandwich Shop
    216 S. Washington Ave., 517/752-8877

Best Steaks
Big John Steak and Onion
    3300 E. Holland Rd., 517/754-5012

SOUTHGATE, MI

[See also: Dearborn and Detroit.]

Best 24-Hour Restaurant
Louie's Family Dining
    12119 Fort St., 734/283-3055

Best Mexican Food
Mexican Gardens Restaurant
    15950 Eureka Rd., 734/282-5633
Mi Casa
    12950 Northline Rd., 734/282-0527

Best Other Ethnic Food
The Hungarian Rhapsody Restaurant (Hungarian)
    14315 Northline Rd., 734/283-9622

Best Pizza
Roma Pizzeria
    13020 Eureka Rd., 734/282-4900

Best Restaurant in Town
Charlie's Chop House
    Holiday Inn, 17201 Northline Rd., 734/283-4400

STERLING HEIGHTS, MI

[See also: Rochester, Rochester Heights, Royal Oak, Troy, and Warren.]

Best Italian Food
Antonio's Italian Cuisine
    2505 E. Fourteen Mile Rd., 810/264-5252

Best Late-Night Menu
Ram's Horn
    35264 Dodge Park Rd., 810/983-4121

Best Middle Eastern Food
Ike's Family Dining
    39064 Van Dyke Ave., 810/979-4460

Best Steaks
Loon River Cafe
    34911 Van Dyke Ave., 810/979-1420

TRAVERSE CITY, MI

Best Breakfast
Omelette Shoppe and Bakery
 1209 E. Front St., 616/946-0590
 124 S. Cass St., 616/946-0912

Best Burgers
Dill's Olde Towne Saloon
 423 S. Union St., 616/947-7534
Don's Drive In
 2030 N. U.S. Hwy. 31N, 616/938-1860

Best Casual Dining
Bowers Harbor Inn
 13512 Peninsula Dr., 616/223-4222
Torch Riviera
 12899 Cherry Ave., Rapid City, 616/322-4100

Best Chinese Food
Hunan Chinese Restaurant
 1425 S. Airport Rd. W., 616/947-1388

Best Desserts
Windows
 7677 E. Shore Rd., 616/941-0100

Best Family Restaurant
Bowery
 13512 Peninsula Dr., 616/223-4333
Sweitzer's by the Bay
 13890 SW Bay Shore Dr., 616/947-0493

Best Health-Conscious Menu
Cousin Jenny's Gourmet Cornish
 129 S. Union St., 616/941-7821
Exquisite Edibles
 223 W. Grandview Pky., 616/941-4529
Mabel's Restaurant
 472 Munson Ave., 616/947-0252

Best Ice Cream/Yogurt
Kilwin Chocolates
 129 E. Front St., 616/946-2403

Best Italian Food
Auntie Pasta's
 2030 S. Airport Rd. W., 616/941-8147
Papa Romano's
 703 S. Garfield Ave., 616/941-7272

Best Mexican Food
La Senorita
 1245 S. Garfield Ave., 616/947-8820

Best Other Ethnic Food
Reflections Restaurant (Caribbean)
 2061 N. U.S. Hwy. 31N, 616/938-2321

Best Outdoor Dining
La Cuisine Amical
 229 E. Front St., 616/941-8888

Best Pizza
Upper Crust
 720 W. Front St., 616/946-5252

M

Best Seafood
Hattie's Restaurant
    111 N. Saint Josephs, Suttons Bay, 616/271-6222

Best Steaks
Boone's Long Lake Inn
    7208 Secor Rd., 616/946-3991
Mode's Bum Steer
    125 E. State St., 616/947-9832

Best View While Dining
Grand Traverse Dinner Train
    642 Railroad Pl., 616/933-3768

TROY, MI

*[See also: Pontiac, Rochester, Rochester Hills,
Sterling Heights, and Warren.]*

M

Best American Food
Alibi
    6700 Rochester Rd., 248/879-0014

Best Barbecue/Ribs
T-Birds Chicken and Ribs
    4970 Livernois Rd., 248/689-4690

Best Chinese Food
Mon Jin Lau
    1515 E. Maple Rd., 248/689-2332

Best Delicatessen
Hershel's Deli and Hot Bakery
    585 W. Big Beaver Rd., 248/524-4770
Metro Deli
    2495 Livernois Rd., 248/362-3101

Best Italian Food
Picano's Restaurant and Lounge
    3775 Rochester Rd., 248/689-8050

Best Japanese Food
Kyoto Japanese Steak House
    1985 W. Big Beaver Rd., 248/649-6340

Best Other Ethnic Food
American Polish Cultural Center (Polish)
    2975 E. Maple Rd., 248/689-3636

Best Salad/Salad Bar
Leo's Souvlaki Coney Island
    841 E. Big Beaver Rd., 248/680-0094

Best Sandwiches
Bruschetta Cafe
    586 W. Fourteen Mile Rd., 248/589-2900

Best Thai Food
Orchid Cafe
    3303 Rochester Rd., 248/524-5047

WARREN, MI

[See also: Detroit, Royal Oak, Sterling Heights, and Troy.]

Best Breakfast
Bi-Centennial Family Restaurant
  11747 E. Thirteen Mile Rd., 810/939-6580

Best Brewpub
The Brewery
  39950 Hayes Rd., Clinton Township, 810/286-3020

Best Burgers
Teddy's Tavern
  7231 Chicago Rd., 810/268-7070

Best Chinese Food
Empire Szechuan Gourmet
  4203 E. Eight Mile Rd., 810/757-4040
Pearl City Restaurant
  20753 E. Thirteen Mile Rd., Roseville,
    810/293-4640

Best Coffee/Coffeehouse
Chocolate Gallery Cafe
  3672 Chicago Rd., 810/979-1140
Deebe's Coffee Bar
  29200 Hoover Rd., 810/558-3290
Lilli's in the Park
  31800 Van Dyke Ave., 810/939-2991

Best Desserts
Michelle's Restaurant
  31920 Van Dyke Ave., 810/795-1665

Best Greek/Mediterranean Food
Louie's Ham and Corn Beef Shop
  11450 E. Nine Mile Rd., 810/757-1330

Best Homestyle Food
Bi-Centennial Family Restaurant
  11747 E. Thirteen Mile Rd., 810/939-6580

Best Ice Cream/Yogurt
Leason's Dairy Bar and Grille
  11475 E. Thirteen Mile Rd., 810/977-2680

Best Italian Food
Andiamo Italia
  7096 E. Fourteen Mile Rd., 810/268-3200
Arriva Italia Ristorante
  6880 E. Twelve Mile Rd., 810/573-8100
Juliano's Restaurant
  27380 Van Dyke Ave., 810/754-8383

Best Other Ethnic Food
La Shish (Lebanese)
  32401 Van Dyke Ave., 810/977-2177

Best Pizza
Buddy's Rendezvous Pizzeria
  14156 E. Twelve Mile Rd., 810/777-3400
  8100 E. Thirteen Mile Rd., 810/574-9200

M

Juliano's Restaurant
27380 Van Dyke Ave., 810/754-8383

Best Salad/Salad Bar
National Coney Island
30140 Van Dyke Ave., 810/751-7700
28628 Dequindre Rd., 810/558-9180

Best Steaks
L-Bow Room
28655 Schoenherr Rd., 810/558-9393
Mountain Jack's Restaurant
5702 E. Twelve Mile Rd., 810/574-1040

YPSILANTI, MI

Best Burgers
Boomba's Beer and Burgers
23 N. Washington St., 734/481-0101
The Sidetrack
56 E. Cross St., 734/483-1035

Best Chinese Food
Old China Restaurant
505 W. Cross St., 734/482-8333

Best Delicatessen
Max's Delicatessen
6 W. Michigan Ave., 734/485-4610

Best Italian Food
Cady's Grill
36 E. Cross St., 734/483-2800
Cottage Inn Cafe
1531 Washtenaw Rd., 734/487-1515
Louis Cafe
205 W. Michigan Ave., 734/486-5544

Best Mexican Food
Aubree's Saloon
39 E. Cross St., 734/483-1870

Best Steaks
Haab's Restaurant
18 W. Michigan Ave., 734/483-8200

M

Minnesota

ALBERT LEA, MN

Best Breakfast
Cafe Don'l
   1701 W. Main St., 507/373-3420
   2510 Bridge Ave., 507/377-8831

Best Burgers
Elbow Room
   310 E. Eighth St., 507/373-1836
Office II
   1119 S. Broadway Ave., 507/373-1536

Best Chinese Food
China Restaurant
   805 E. Main St., 507/377-8888
Chinese Tea House
   126 W. William St., 507/377-1899
Hong Kong Restaurant
   212 E. Clark St., 507/373-1044

Best Coffee/Coffeehouse
Kaffe Hus
   522 S. Broadway Ave., 507/377-2951

Best Desserts
Trumble's Restaurant
   1811 E. Main St., 507/373-2638
Turtle Dove Tea House and Garden
   510 W. Main St., 507/377-9381

Best Mexican Food
Casa Zamora Restaurant
   2006 E. Main St., 507/373-6475

Best Pizza
A Taste of the Big Apple
   105 N. Broadway Ave., 507/373-2666
Jake's Pizza
   126 W. Clark St., 507/373-7350

Best Sandwiches
Trumble's Restaurant
   1811 E. Main St., 507/373-2638

Best Steaks
Philly's Bar and Grill
   804 E. Main St., 507/373-2450

AUSTIN, MN

Best Barbecue/Ribs
Old Mill Restaurant
   Rural Rte. 1, 507/437-2076

Best Breakfast
Watts Cooking
   1509 Tenth Pl. NE, 507/433-2633

Best Burgers
Oak Grill
   307 W. Oakland Ave., 507/437-4135

Best Chinese Food
China Wok
   323 N. Main St., 507/433-8360

Best Delicatessen
Grinder's Deli
   604 Third Ave. NW, 507/433-6808

Best Desserts
Jerry's Other Place
   1207 N. Main St., 507/433-2331
Oak Leaf
   208 S. Main St., 507/437-8555
Plaza Dining
   123 Third Ave. NE, 507/433-7271

Best Pizza
Steve's Pizza
   215 Second Ave. NE, 507/437-3249

Best Salad/Salad Bar
Tolly's Time Out Restaurant
   100 Fourteenth St. SW, 507/437-6078

Best Steaks
Old Mill Restaurant
   Rural Route 1, 507/437-2076

BEMIDJI, MN

Best Bar
Back Yard
   2450 Paul Bunyan Dr., 218/751-7853
Stats Sports Bar
   101 First St. W., 218/751-0441

M

Best Burgers
Classic Burgers
701 Paul Bunyan Dr. NW, 218/751-1212

Best Coffee/Coffeehouse
Clementine's
205 Second St. NW, 218/751-9063
Griffy's Eating Establishment
319 Minnesota Ave. NW, 218/751-3609

Best Desserts
Union Station
128 First St. NW, 218/751-9261

Best Mexican Food
T. Juan's Restaurante and Cantina
305 Park Ave. SW, 218/751-6879

Best Other Ethnic Food
Che-Wa-Ka-E-Gon Restaurant (Native American)
Hwy. 2E, Cass Lake, 218/335-8378

Best Seafood
Northern Inn
3600 Moberg Dr. NW, 218/751-9500
Stats Sports Bar
101 First St. W., 218/751-0441

Best Steaks
Union Station
128 First St. NW, 218/751-9261

BLOOMINGTON, MN

Best Burgers
Lion's Tap Family Restaurant
16180 Flying Cloud Dr., Eden Prairie,
612/934-5299

Best Chinese Food
Szechuan Express
9818 Aldrich Ave. S., 612/881-8068

Best Indian Food
Tandoor Restaurant India House
8062 Morgan Circle S., 612/885-9060

Best Italian Food
Buca Little Italy
7711 Mitchell Rd., Eden Prairie, 612/724-7266

Best Middle Eastern Food
Da-Afghan
929 W. 80th St., 612/888-5824

Best Pizza
Edwardo's Natural Pizza
2633 Southtown Dr., 612/884-8400

Best Seafood
Kincaid's Steak, Chop and Fish
8400 Normandale Lake Blvd., 612/921-2255

Best Thai Food
Sawatdee
8501 Lyndale Ave. S., 612/888-7177

M

Best Wine Selection
Napa Valley Grille
  Mall of America, 220 W. Market, 612/858-9934

DULUTH, MN

Best Burgers
Scenic Cafe
  5461 N. Shore Dr., 218/525-6274

Best Casual Dining
Afterburner Restaurant
  4701 Airport Rd., 218/727-1152

Best Chinese Food
Taste of Saigon
  394 S. Lake Ave., 218/727-1598

Best Coffee/Coffeehouse
Barnes and Noble
  625 W. Central Entrance, 218/727-0191

Best Delicatessen
Erbert and Gerbert's Subs
  234 W. First St., 218/723-2330

Best Desserts
Amazing Grace
  394 S. Lake Ave., 218/723-0075

Best Family Restaurant
Grandma's Saloon and Grill
  2202 Maple Grove Rd., 218/722-9313
Grandma's Sports Garden
  425 S. Lake Ave., 218/722-4724

Best Fine Dining
Bellows
  2230 London Rd., 218/724-8531
Pickwick
  508 E. Superior St., 218/727-8901

Best Ice Cream/Yogurt
Bridgeman's Restaurant
  2202 Mountain Shadow Dr., 218/727-0196

Best Italian Food
Bella Vita Ristorante
  21 N. Fourth Ave. W., 218/722-2211

Best Mexican Food
Hacienda Del Sol
  319 E. Superior St., 218/722-7296

Best Regional Food
Angry Trout Cafe
  408 Hwy. 61W, Grand Marais, 218/387-1265

Best Romantic Dining
Porter's
  200 E. Superior St., 218/727-6746

Best Sandwiches
Sir Benedict's by the Lake
  805 E. Superior St., 218/728-1192

Best Seafood
Pickwick
508 E. Superior St., 218/727-8901

Best Vietnamese Food
Taste of Saigon
394 S. Lake Ave., 218/727-1598

GRAND RAPIDS, MN

Best Breakfast
Forest Lake Restaurant
1201 NW Fourth St., 218/326-3423

Best Burgers
Jack Pine Junction
11851 Hwy. 38, 218/326-9854

Best Chinese Food
Hong Kong Garden Restaurant
220 NE Second St., 218/327-1131

Best Coffee/Coffeehouse
Brewed Awakenings
204 NW First Ave., 218/327-1088

Best Desserts
First Grade
10 NW Fifth St., 218/326-9361

Best Homestyle Food
Whalen's Cafe
18 NW Fourth St., 218/326-8646

Best Pizza
Beno's Pizza and Video
324 NE Fourth St., 218/327-1400

Best Seafood
Captain Hook's Supper Club
29 Crystal Springs Rd., 218/326-0235

Best Steaks
Cedars Dining Room
Sawmill Inn, 2301 S. Pokegama Ave., 218/326-8501
Forest Lake Restaurant
1201 NW Fourth St., 218/326-3423

HIBBING, MN

Best Bar
Atrium Restaurant
531 E. Howard St., 218/262-6145
Mr. Nick's Corner Bar
2001 First Ave., 218/262-1639

Best Breakfast
Country Kitchen
Hwy. 169 at 25th St., 218/263-3689

Best Coffee/Coffeehouse
Androy Coffee Shop
502 E. Howard St., 218/263-5917

Best Desserts
Sunrise Bakery
1813 Third Ave. E., 218/263-4985

M

Best Ice Cream/Yogurt
Cookies and Cream
  Irongate Mall, Hwy. 169 at Neuberg Rd.,
    218/262-5060

Best Italian Food
Valentini's Supper Club
  31 W. Lake St., Chisholm, 218/254-2607

Best Pizza
Sammy's Pizza and Restaurant
  106 E. Howard St., 218/263-7574

Best Sandwiches
Sunrise Deli-Lybba
  2135 First Ave., 218/263-5713

Best Seafood
Main Street Supper Club
  408 E. Howard St., 218/262-4815
Riverside Inn
  7477 Hwy. 5, Side Lake, 218/254-2322

Best Steaks
Bil-Mars Supper Club
  2114 Hwy. 73, 218/262-6201
Main Street Supper Club
  408 E. Howard St., 218/262-4815
Old Howard Saloon and Eatery
  413 E. Howard St., 218/262-1031

MANKATO, MN

Best Breakfast
Embers Restaurant
  209 N. Riverfront Dr., 507/387-6539

Best Burgers
Eagle's Nest
  100 N. Second St., Eagle Lake, 507/257-9996
Ruttle's '50s Grill
  River Hills Mall, 1850 Adams St., 507/625-1955
  1270 E. Madison Ave., 507/345-1950

Best Chinese Food
Hunan Garden Restaurant
  1400 E. Madison Ave., Ste. 104, 507/345-8812
Tonni's Restaurant
  625 E. Madison Ave., 507/388-7475

Best Coffee/Coffeehouse
Barnes and Noble
  1857 Adams St., 507/386-0110
Coffee Hag
  329 N. Riverfront Dr., 507/387-5533

Best Desserts
Baker's Square Restaurant
  1861 E. Madison Ave., 507/345-4240

Best Eclectic Menu
Stoney's Restaurant
  900 N. Riverfront Dr., 507/387-4813

Best French Food
Meray's
113 E. Hickory St., 507/625-9217

Best Greek/Mediterranean Food
Massad's
River Hills Mall, 1850 Adams St., Ste. 618,
507/387-7111

Best Homestyle Food
Adrian's Eatery and Saloon
1812 S. Riverfront Dr., 507/625-6776
Charley's Restaurant
920 E. Madison Ave., 507/388-6845
Embers Restaurant
209 N. Riverfront Dr., 507/387-6539

Best Ice Cream/Yogurt
Adele's Frozen Custard
950 E. Madison Ave., 507/625-7071

Best Mexican Food
Mexican Village Restaurant
1630 E. Madison Ave., 507/387-4455

Best Pizza
Jake's Stadium Pizza
1614 Monks Ave., 507/345-5420
Pagliai's Pizza
524 S. Front St., 507/345-6080

Best Sandwiches
Embers Restaurant
209 N. Riverfront Dr., 507/387-6539

Best Seafood
Country Pub
Rte. 1, Kasota, 507/931-5888

Best Steaks
Applewood
Rural Route 6, Box 52, 507/625-4105

Best Sunday Brunch
Applewood
Rural Route 6, Box 52, 507/625-4105

MINNEAPOLIS, MN

[See also: St. Paul.]

Best All-You-Can-Eat Buffet
Odaa Ethiopian Restaurant
408 Cedar Ave. S., 612/338-4459

Best American Food
Curran's Family Restaurant
4201 Nicollet Ave., 612/822-5327
Grandma's Saloon and Deli
1810 Washington Ave. S., 612/340-0516
4301 W. 80th St., Bloomington, 612/897-0533
J.D. Hoyt's
301 Washington Ave. N, 612/338-1560

Kincaid's Steak, Chop and Fish
  8400 Normandale Lake Blvd., 612/921-2255
Shelly's Woodroast
  6501 Wayzata Blvd., 612/593-5050

Best Barbecue/Ribs
Famous Dave's Barbecue Shack
  4264 Upton Ave. S., 612/929-1200
  3001 Hennepin Ave. S., 612/822-9900
  14601 Hwy. 7, Minnetonka, 612/933-9600
Market Barbecue
  1414 Nicollet Ave., 612/372-1111
  15320 Wayzata Blvd., Minnetonka, 612/475-1770
Rudolph's Barbecue
  1933 Lyndale Ave. S., 612/871-8969
Scott Ja-Mama's Barbecue
  3 W. Diamond Lake Rd., 612/823-4450
Ted Cook's Nineteenth Hole Barbecue
  2814 E. 38th St., 612/721-2023

Best Beer Selection
Williams Pub and Peanut Bar
  2911 Hennepin Ave., 612/823-6271

Best Bistro
Cafe Un Deux Trois
  114 S. Ninth St., 612/673-0686
Caffe Solo
  123 N. Third St., 612/332-7108
Palomino Euro-Bistro
  Fall Plaza, 825 E. Hennepin Ave., 612/339-3800

Best Breakfast
Al's Breakfast
  413 Fourteenth Ave. SE, 612/331-9991
Keys Restaurant
  8299 University Ave. NE, 612/785-6004
  1007 Nicollet Mall, 612/339-6399
  7532 Brooklyn Blvd., 612/561-5233

Best Brewpub
Rock Bottom Brewery
  Fall Plaza, 825 E. Hennepin Ave., 612/332-2739
Sherlock's Home
  11000 Red Circle Dr., Hopkins, 612/931-0203

Best Burgers
Annie's Parlour
  1827 Riverside Ave., 612/339-6207
  313 Fourteenth Ave. SE, 612/379-0744
Big 10 Restaurant and Bar
  606 Washington Ave. SE, 612/378-0467

Best Chinese Food
Dragon House
  3970 Central Ave. NE, 612/781-8884
Hunan Chinese Restaurant
  8066 Morgan Circle S., 612/881-2280
Leeann Chin
  1571 Plymouth Rd., Minnetonka, 612/545-3600

Best Delicatessen
Kramarczuk East European Deli
   215 E. Hennepin Ave., 612/379-3018

Best Desserts
Cafe Royale
   Hotel Sofitel, 5601 W. 78th St., 612/835-1900
Pannekoeken Griddle and Grille
   3020 W. 66th St., Richfield, 612/866-7731

Best Eclectic Menu
California Cafe, Bar and Grill
   368 South Ave., 612/854-2233
Napa Valley Grill
   220 W. Market, 612/858-9934
Palomino Euro-Bistro
   825 E. Hennepin Ave., 612/339-3800
Pickled Parrott
   26 N. Fifth St., 612/332-0673

Best Fine Dining
Goodfellow's
   40 S. Seventh St., 612/332-4800
La Terrasse
   5601 W. 78th St., 612/835-1900
Murray's
   26 S. Sixth St., 612/339-0909
Sophia
   65 Main St. SE, 612/379-1111

Best French Food
La Terrasse
   5601 W. 78th St., 612/835-1900
New French Cafe
   128 N. Fourth St., 612/338-3790

Best German Food
Black Forest Inn
   1 E. 26th St., 612/872-0812
Gasthof Zur Gemutlichkeit
   2300 University Ave. NE, 612/781-3860

Best Ice Cream/Yogurt
Crema Cafe
   3403 Lyndale Ave. S., 612/824-3868
Sebastian Joe's
   4321 Upton Ave. S., 612/926-7916
   1007 W. Franklin Ave., 612/870-0065

Best Indian Food
Sri-Lanka Curry House
   2821 Hennepin Ave. S., 612/871-2400

Best Inexpensive Meal
Gallery 8
   725 Vineland Place, 612/374-3701

Best Italian Food
A Figlio Restaurant and Bar
   3001 Hennepin Ave. S., 612/822-1688
Broder's Cucina Italiana
   2308 W. 50th St., 612/925-3113

M

Buca
  11 S. Twelfth St., 612/638-2225
Campiello
  1320 W. Lake St., 612/825-2222
D'Amico Cucina
  100 N. Sixth St., Ste. 160, 612/338-2401
Lucia's
  1432 W. 31st St., 612/823-7125

Best Japanese Food
Ichiban Japanese Steak House
  1333 Nicollet Mall, 612/339-0540
Origami
  30 N. First St., 612/333-8430
Samurai Japanese Steak and Seafood
  850 Louisiana Ave. S., 612/542-9922

Best Late-Night Food
Pizza Luce
  119 N. Fourth St., 612/333-7359
Village Wok
  610 Washington Ave. SE, 612/331-9041

Best Mexican Food
Don Pablo's Mexican Kitchen
  980 W. 78th St., 612/861-9686
La Cucaracha
  533 N. Hennepin Ave., 612/339-1161
Pepito's
  4820 Chicago Ave., 612/822-2104

Best Middle Eastern Food
Jerusalem's
  1518 Nicollet Ave., 612/871-8883

Best Other Ethnic Food
Chez Bananas (Caribbean)
  129 N. Fourth St., 612/340-0032
Da-Afghan Restaurant (Afghan)
  929 W. 80th St., 612/888-5824
Jacob's 101 Restaurant (Lebanese)
  101 Broadway St. NE, 612/379-2508
Machu Picchu (Peruvian)
  2940 Lyndale Ave. S., 612/822-2125
Pannekoeken Griddle and Grille (Dutch)
  3020 W. 66th St., Richfield, 612/866-7731

Best Outdoor Dining
Annie's Parlour
  313 Fourteenth Ave. SE, 612/379-0744
Black Forest Inn
  1 E. 26th St., 612/872-0812
La Terrasse
  5601 W. 78th St., 612/835-1900
Loring Cafe
  1624 Harmon Pl., 612/332-1617

Best Pizza
Broadway Pizza
  5607 W. Broadway, 612/535-5010
D'Amico and Sons
  7804 Olson Memorial Hwy., 612/546-1166

555 Nicollet Mall, 612/342-2700
2210 Hennepin Ave. S., 612/374-1858
2724 W. 43rd St., 612/920-2646
Edwardo's Natural Pizza
1125 Marquette Ave., 612/339-9700
Leaning Tower
2324 Lyndale Ave. S., 612/377-3532
Pizza Luce
119 N. Fourth St., 612/333-7359
Sidney's Pizza Cafe
2120 Hennepin Ave., 612/870-7000
3520 Galleria, 612/925-2002
15600 Hwy. 7, Minnetonka, 612/933-1000
Uptown Express
5 N. Seventh St., 612/338-4814
1409 W. Lake St., 612/822-7400

Best Place to Eat Alone
Moose and Sadie's
212 Third Ave. N., 612/371-0464

Best Restaurant in Town
Jax Cafe
1928 University Ave. NE, 612/789-7297
Lucia's
1432 W. 31st St., 612/823-7125

Best Romantic Dining
Nicollet Island Inn
95 Merriam St., 612/331-3035

Best Salad/Salad Bar
Linguini and Bob
100 N. Sixth St., 612/332-1600
Nikki's Cafe
107 Third Ave. N., 612/340-9098
Q Cumbers
7465 France Ave. S., 612/831-0235

Best Sandwiches
The Monte Carlo
219 Third Ave. N., 612/335-5900

Best Seafood
Anthony's Wharf Seafood Restaurant
201 Main St. SE, 612/378-7058

Best Southwestern Food
Tejas
3910 W. 50th St., 612/926-0800

Best Spanish Food
El Meson
1115 Vicksburg Ln. N., 612/475-0233
3450 Lyndale Ave. S., 612/822-8062

Best Steaks
Mancini's Char House
531 Seventh St. W., 612/224-7345
Manny's Steakhouse
Hyatt Hotel, 1300 Nicollet Mall, 612/339-9900
Murray's
26 S. Sixth St., 612/339-0909

M

Best Sunday Brunch
Jax Cafe
  1928 University Ave. NE, 612/789-7297
Soba's Restaurant
  2558 Lyndale Ave. S., 612/871-6631
Whitney Grille
  150 Portland Ave., 612/372-6405

Best Thai Food
Bangkok Thai Restaurant
  425 Thirteenth Ave. SE, 612/331-6830
King and I
  1034 Nicollet Ave., 612/332-6928
Pattaya Thai Restaurant
  2627 E. Franklin Ave., 612/375-9942
Royal Orchid Restaurant
  1835 Nicollet Ave., 612/872-1938
Sawatdee
  607 Washington Ave. S., 612/338-6451

Best Vegetarian Food
Cafe Brenda
  300 First Ave. N., 612/342-9230
Good Earth
  3460 W. 70th St., 612/925-1001
Mud Pie
  2549 Lyndale Ave. S., 612/872-9435

Best Vietnamese Food
Chinn Fua Restaurant
  2219 Central Ave. NE, 612/781-5931
Lotus Restaurant
  113 W. Grant St., 612/870-1213
  Stadium Village, 313 SE Oak St., 612/331-1781
  3037 Hennepin Ave., 612/825-2263
Que Viet Village House
  2211 Johnson St. NE, 612/781-4744
  6100 Brooklyn Blvd., 612/560-0215
Vina Vietnamese Restaurant
  6401 Nicollet Ave., 612/866-5034

Best View While Dining
Lord Fletcher's Of The Lake
  3746 Sunset Dr., Spring Park, 612/471-8513

Best Wine Selection
Goodfellow's
  40 S. Seventh St., 612/332-4800
Lucia's
  1432 W. 31st St., 612/823-7125

MOORHEAD, MN

Best Atmosphere
Speak Easy Restaurant and Lounge
  1001 30th Ave. S., 218/233-1326

Best Burgers
Hi Ho Tavern
  10 Center Ave. E., Dilworth, 218/287-2975

Best Chinese Food
Golden Phoenix
  816 30th Ave. S., 218/236-7089

Best Coffee/Coffeehouse
Atomic Coffee
  15 Fourth St. S., 218/299-6161

Best Desserts
Treetop Restaurant
  403 Center Ave., Ste. 7, 218/233-1393

Best Family Restaurant
Speak Easy Restaurant and Lounge
  1001 30th Ave. S., 218/233-1326

Best Fine Dining
Treetop Restaurant and Lounge
  403 Center Ave., 218/233-1393
Victoria's Restaurant
  101 First St., Wolverton, 218/995-2000

Best Homestyle Food
Peggy's Pantry
  28 Fourth St. N., 218/233-8795

Best Italian Food
Speak Easy Restaurant and Lounge
  1001 30th Ave. S., 218/233-1326

Best Pizza
Duane's House of Pizza
  1024 Center Ave., 218/236-0550

Best Romantic Dining
Treetop Restaurant and Lounge
  403 Center Ave., 218/233-1393

Best Sandwiches
Atomic Coffee
  15 Fourth St. S., 218/299-6161
Hi-Ho Tavern
  10 Center Ave. E., Dilworth, 218/287-2975
Moorhead Host
  Moorhead Center Mall, 218/236-8805

ROCHESTER, MN

Best Bar
Smiling Moose Bar and Grill
  1829 Hwy. 52N, 507/289-1689

Best Barbecue/Ribs
Roscoe's Great Barbecue
  603 Fourth St. SE, 507/285-0501
  2810 N. Broadway, 507/288-8684

Best Breakfast
Bakers Square
  3539 22nd Ave. NW, 507/289-2468
Cheap Charlie's
  11 Fifth St. NW, 507/289-9591
Grandma's Kitchen
  1514 N. Broadway, 507/289-0331

M

Best Burgers
Smiling Moose Bar and Grill
  1829 Hwy. 52N, 507/289-1689

Best Business Lunch
Michael's Restaurant
  15 S. Broadway, 507/288-2020

Best Chinese Food
China Dynasty
  701 S. Broadway, 507/289-2333
Hunan Garden
  1120 Seventh St. NW, 507/285-1438

Best Coffee/Coffeehouse
Barnes and Noble
  15 First St. SW, 507/288-3848

Best Diner
Cheap Charlie's
  11 Fifth St. NW, 507/289-9591

Best Family Restaurant
Shakey's Pizza Parlor
  1816 Hwy. 52N, 507/288-6565
Smiling Moose Bar and Grill
  1829 Hwy. 52N, 507/289-1689

Best Fine Dining
Chardonnay
  732 Second St. SW, 507/252-1310
The Meadows
  Radisson Hotel, 150 S. Broadway, 507/281-8000

Best French Food
Victoria House French Restaurant
  709 Parkway Ave. S., Lanesboro, 507/467-3457

Best Health-Conscious Menu
Zorba's Greek Restaurant
  924 Seventh St. NW, 507/281-1540

Best Homestyle Food
Cheap Charlie's
  11 Fifth St. NW, 507/289-9591

Best Ice Cream/Yogurt
Nelson Cheese Factory
  210 N. Broadway, 507/288-1888

Best Late-Night Food
The Greenhouse
  Kahler Hotel, 20 Second Ave. SW, 507/282-2581

Best Mexican Food
Fiesta Mexicana
  301 Seventeenth Ave. SW, 507/288-1116

Best Pizza
Redwood Room and the Broadstreet Cafe
  300 First Ave. NW, 507/281-2451

Best Place to Eat Alone
Daube's Konditorei
  14 Third St. SW, 507/280-6446

Best Romantic Dining
Elizabethan Room
  Kahler Hotel, 20 Second Ave. SW, 507/282-2581

Best Salad/Salad Bar
John Barleycorn
  2804 S. Broadway, 507/285-0178

Best Sandwiches
Nelson Cheese Factory
  210 N. Broadway, 507/288-1888

Best Seafood
Fishermen's Inn
  8 Fisherman Dr. NW, Oronoco, 507/367-4567

Best Steaks
Michael's Restaurant and Lounge
  15 S. Broadway, 507/288-2020

Best Sunday Brunch
Legends Restaurant
  Rochester Athletic Club, 3100 Nineteenth St. NW,
  507/287-9333

Best Vegetarian Food
The Open Table
  16 S. Broadway, 507/287-8939

M

ST. CLOUD, MN

Best Breakfast
Copper Lantern
  15 Hwy. 10S, 320/252-0672
McMillan's Restaurant
  3219 W. Division St., 320/252-7115

Best Brewpub
O'Hara Brothers Pub and Restaurant
  3308 Third St. N., 320/251-9877

Best Burgers
O'Hara Brothers Pub and Restaurant
  3308 Third St. N., 320/251-9877

Best Chinese Food
Dong Khanh Chinese Restaurant
  810 W. Saint Germain St., 320/251-0656
Dong Khanh Express
  3616 W. Division St., 320/253-2633
Hong Kong Restaurant
  37 33rd Ave. N., 320/251-5907
Phoenix Too Chinese Cuisine
  Crossroads Center, 4101 Division St., 320/251-3588

Best Coffee/Coffeehouse
Sano's Coffee and Tea House
  419 W. Saint Germain St., 320/253-6811

Best Delicatessen
Bo Diddley's Deli
  216 Sixth Ave. S., 320/255-9811
  1501 Northway Dr., 320/255-1500
  129 25th Ave. S., 320/252-9475

Best Desserts
D.B. Searle's
  18 Fifth Ave. S., 320/253-0655

Best Health-Conscious Menu
Good Earth Food Co-Op
  2010 Eighth St. N., 320/253-9290

Best Homestyle Food
Alvie's Family Restaurant
  42 32nd Ave. S., 320/252-0955
  451 E. Saint Germain St., 320/251-7575

Best Italian Food
Ciatti's Italian Restaurant
  660 Germain Mall, 320/251-5255

Best Mexican Food
Bravo Burritos Mexicatessen
  26 Fifth Ave. S., 320/252-5441
  68 33rd Ave. S., 320/654-1269
Mexican Village Restaurant
  Germain Mall, Ste. 509, 320/252-7134

Best Pizza
House of Pizza
  19 Fifth Ave. S., 320/252-9300

Best Sandwiches
Bo Diddley's Deli
  1501 Northway Dr., 320/255-1500
  129 25th Ave. S., 320/252-9475
  216 Sixth Ave. S., 320/255-9811
Carmel Crisp Shop
  201 E. Saint Germain St., 320/253-5310
Erbert and Gerbert's Subs
  8 Fifth Ave. N., 320/253-9963
O'Hara Brothers Pub
  3308 Third St. N., 320/251-9877

Best Seafood
Angus McGee's
  139 S. Second Ave., 320/255-1207
Anton's
  2001 W. Division St., 320/253-3611

Best Steaks
Angus McGee's
  139 S. Second Ave., 320/255-1207
Anton's
  2001 W. Division St., 320/253-3611
O'Hara Brothers Pub
  3308 Third St. N., 320/251-9877

ST. PAUL, MN

[See also: Minneapolis.]

Best American Food
Green Mill Restaurant
  1000 Gramsie Rd., 612/482-1600
  6025 Hudson Rd., 612/735-1000

1342 Grand Ave., 612/690-0539
St. Paul Grill
350 Market St., 612/224-7455

Best Barbecue/Ribs
Famous Dave's Barbecue Shack
2131 Snelling Ave. N., 612/633-4800

Best Breakfast
Keys Restaurant
1192 Fifth Ave. NW, 612/636-0662
2208 Fourth St., 612/426-2885
1682 Lexington Ave. N., 612/487-5397
767 Raymond Ave., 612/646-5756
500 Robert St. N., 612/222-4083
The Egg and I
2550 University Ave., 612/647-1292
Uptown Bar and Grill
2399 University, 612/646-7827

Best Cajun/Creole Food
Dixie's Smokehouse Bar and Grill
695 Grand Ave., 612/222-7345

Best Casual Dining
Lexington Restaurant
1096 Grand Ave., 612/222-5878

Best Chinese Food
Leeann Chin
214 E. Fourth St., 612/224-8814

Best Coffee/Coffeehouse
Cafe Latte
850 Grand Ave., 612/224-5687
Caribou Coffee
multiple locations
The Prairie Star Coffeehouse
2399 University Ave. W., 612/646-7827

Best Delicatessen
Cecil's Deli
651 Cleveland Ave. S., 612/698-6276

Best Desserts
Cafe Latte
850 Grand Ave., 612/224-5687
Dixie's Smokehouse Bar and Grill
695 Grand Ave., 612/222-7345
W.A. Frost and Company
374 Selby Ave., 612/224-5715

Best Fine Dining
St. Paul Grill
350 Market St., 612/224-7455
Vintage
579 Selby Ave., 612/222-7000

Best French Food
Tulips Restaurant
452 Selby Ave., 612/221-1061

Best German Food
Gasthaus Bavarian Hunter
8390 Lofton Ave. N., Stillwater, 612/439-7128

Best Greek/Mediterranean Food
Christo's Greek Restaurant
214 Fourth St. E., 612/224-6000
Khyber Pass Cafe
1399 St. Clair Ave., 612/698-5403

Best Indian Food
Taste of India
1745 Cope Ave. E., Maplewood, 612/773-5477

Best Italian Food
Buca Little Italy
2728 Gannon Rd., 612/772-4388
Ristorante Luci
470 Cleveland Ave. S., 612/699-8258

Best Japanese Food
Sakura Restaurant
350 Saint Peter St., 612/224-0185

Best Lunch
Cafe Latte
850 Grand Ave., 612/224-5687

Best Mexican Food
Don Pablo's Mexican Kitchen
2700 Lincoln Dr., 612/639-3916
La Corvina
1570 Selby Ave., 612/645-5288
La Cucaracha
36 S. Dale St., 612/221-9682

Best Middle Eastern Food
Caravan Serai
2175 Ford Pkwy., 612/690-1935
Old City Cafe
1571 Grand Ave., 612/699-5347

Best Outdoor Dining
W.A. Frost and Company
374 Selby Ave., 612/224-5715

Best Pizza
Grampa Tony's
631 Snelling Ave. S., 612/690-3297
Green Mill Restaurant
1000 Gramsie Rd., 612/482-1600
6025 Hudson Rd., 612/735-1000
1342 Grand Ave., 612/690-0539

Best Regional Food
Dakota Bar and Grill
1021 Energy Park Dr., 612/642-1442

Best Restaurant Meal Value
Sidney's Pizza Cafe
917 Grand Ave., 612/227-5000

Best Romantic Dining
Forepaugh's
276 Exchange St. S., 612/224-5606
Ristorante Luci
470 Cleveland Ave. S., 612/699-8258

Best Sandwiches
Cossetta's Italian Market and Pizzeria
211 W. Seventh St., 612/222-3476

Best Soul Food
Arnellia's
1183 University Ave. W., 612/642-5975

Best Sports Bar
Champp's Sports Bar
2401 Seventh St. W., 612/698-5050

Best Steaks
Freight House
305 Water St. S., Stillwater, 612/439-5718
Lindey's Prime Steak House
3600 Snelling Ave. N., 612/633-9813

Best Sushi
Saji-Ya
695 Grand Ave., 612/292-0444

Best Thai Food
Ruam Mit Thai Cafe
475 Saint Peter St., 612/290-0067
Sawatdee
289 Fifth St. E., 612/222-5859

Best Vegetarian Food
Old City Cafe
1571 Grand Ave., 612/699-5347

Best Vietnamese Food
Lotus
867 Grand Ave., 612/228-9156
Que Viet Village House
1272 Town Centre Dr., 612/452-5018

Best View While Dining
Clyde's On The St. Croix
101 Fifth Ave. S., Bayport, 612/439-6555

Best Wine Selection
St. Paul Grill
350 Market St., 612/224-7455

M

WINONA, MN

Best Burgers
Jefferson Pub and Grill
58 Center St., 507/452-2718

Best Chinese Food
Great Hunan Restaurant
111 W. Third St., 507/452-1556

Best Coffee/Coffeehouse
Natural Habitat Coffeehouse
451 Huff St., 507/452-7020

Best Health-Conscious Menu
Natural Habitat Coffeehouse
451 Huff St., 507/452-7020

Best Homestyle Food
Hot Fish Shop
965 Mankato Ave., 507/452-5002

Best Sandwiches
Beno's Cheese and Deli
72 Center St., 507/452-2761
Jefferson Pub and Grill
58 Center St., 507/452-2718

Best Steaks
Winona Steakhouse
3480 Service Dr., 507/452-3968

WORTHINGTON, MN

Best Breakfast
Gobbler by the Mall
1861 Oxford St., 507/372-2200

Best Chinese Food
Panda House Chinese Restaurant
913 Fourth Ave., 507/372-5155

Best Desserts
Ruttle's '50s Grill
1709 N. Humiston Ave., 507/376-1955

Best Family Restaurant
Michael's
1305 Spring Ave., 507/376-3187

Best Homestyle Food
Windmill Cafe
609 Kragness Ave. N., 507/376-5223

Best Ice Cream/Yogurt
W.T. Berrie Ice Cream
1635 Oxford St., 507/376-9220

Best Sandwiches
W.T. Berrie Ice Cream
1635 Oxford St., 507/376-9220

Best Seafood
Brandywine
Holiday Inn, 2015 N. Humiston Ave., 507/372-2991

Best Steaks
Michael's
1305 Spring Ave., 507/376-3187

Best Sunday Brunch
Brandywine
Holiday Inn, 2015 N. Humiston Ave., 507/372-2991

Best Thai Food
Bangkok Cuisine
1719 East Ave., 507/376-9009

M

Mississippi

BILOXI, MS

Best Casual Dining
Port-O-Call Seafood Restaurant
15200 Lemoyne Blvd., 228/392-0335

Best Fine Dining
Germaine's Restaurant
1203 Bienville Blvd., Ocean Springs, 228/875-4426

Best Late-Night Food
Anthony's Under the Oaks
1217 Washington Ave., Ocean Springs,
228/872-4564

Best Seafood
Aunt Jenny's Catfish Restaurant
1217 Washington Ave., Ocean Springs,
228/875-9201
McElroy's Harbor House
695 Beach Blvd., 228/435-5001

CLARKSDALE, MS

Best Barbecue/Ribs
Abe's Barbecue Drive In
616 State St., 601/624-9947
Boss Hog's Barbecue
1101 Fourth St., 601/627-5264
Ranchero
1907 N. State St., 601/624-9768

Best Homestyle Food
Sarah's Kitchen
224 Sunflower Ave., 601/627-3239

Best Seafood
Ramon's
535 Oakhurst Ave., 601/624-9230

COLUMBUS, MS

Best American Food
Harvey's
200 Main St., 601/327-1639

Best Barbecue/Ribs
Miz Lou's
903 Waterworks Rd., 601/327-2281

Best Breakfast
Pete's Restaurant
2123 Main St., 601/328-9861

Best Chinese Food
Gold Star Chinese Restaurant
1205 Hwy. 45N, 601/329-5247

Best Steaks
Old Hickory Steakhouse
1301 Hwy. 45N, 601/328-9793

GREENVILLE, MS

Best Homestyle Food
Jim's Cafe
314 Washington Ave., 601/332-5951

Best Italian Food
Fermo's
700 Hwy. 1S, 601/334-9934

Best Seafood
Seafood Place and Oyster Bar
1801 Hwy. 1S, 601/335-3393
Sherman's Restaurant
1400 S. Main St., 601/332-6924

Best Steaks
Doe's
502 Nelson St., 601/334-3315

GULFPORT, MS

Best Breakfast
Helen's Coffee Shop
2313 Fourteenth St., 228/863-8788

Best Casual Dining
Li'l Ray's Po-Boys
500A Courthouse Rd., 228/896-9601

Best Dinner
Vrazel's Fine Food Restaurant
3206 W. Beach Blvd., 228/863-2229

Best Homestyle Food
Cafe Reef
439 Hwy. 90, Waveland, 228/467-7333

Best Seafood
Chappy's Seafood Restaurant
624 E. Beach Blvd., 228/865-9755

Best Steaks
Blow-Fly Inn
  1201 Washington Ave., 228/896-9812

HATTIESBURG, MS

Best Barbecue/Ribs
Gold Post Sandwich House
  2210 Hardy St., 601/583-9454
Strick's Barbecue
  2830 Edwards St., 601/582-1228

Best Breakfast
Rocket City Diner
  4700 Hardy St., 601/264-7893

Best Chinese Food
Mandarin House
  4400 Hardy St., Ste. A7, 601/264-5511

Best Fine Dining
Purple Parrot Cafe
  3810 Hardy St., 601/264-0656

Best Mexican Food
Mexican Kitchen
  5693 U.S. Hwy. 49, 601/544-4811

Best Sandwiches
California Sandwich Shoppe
  217 E. Front St., 601/582-0726
Gus's Cafe
  144 E. Front St., 601/544-4939
McAlister's Deli
  2300 Hardy St., 601/545-1876

Best Seafood
Bea's Broiler
  3616 Hwy. 42W, 601/261-0133
Crescent City Grill
  3810 Hardy St., 601/264-0657
Mack's Fish Camp
  820 River Rd., 601/582-5101

Best Steaks
Conestoga Steak House
  6713 U.S. Hwy. 49N, 601/264-8816

Best Sunday Brunch
Purple Parrot Cafe
  3810 Hardy St., 601/264-0656

HOLLY SPRINGS, MS

Best Barbecue/Ribs
Pete's Bar-B-Q
  540 Hwy. 7N, 601/252-9879

Best Breakfast
City Cafe
  135A W. Van Dorn Ave., 601/252-9895

Best Chinese Food
Canton Chinese Restaurant
  152 E. College Ave., 601/252-1589

M

Best Family Restaurant
Holly Inn Restaurant
350 Hwy. 78W, 601/252-1870

Best Homestyle Food
Country Kitchen
133A E. Van Dorn Ave., 601/252-4298

Best Place to Take the Kids
Phillips Grocery
541 E. Van Dorn Ave., 601/252-4671

JACKSON, MS

Best Barbecue/Ribs
Chimneyville Smoke House
970 High St., 601/354-4665

Best Chinese Food
Peking Chinese Restaurant
5315 I-55N, 601/362-7000

Best Coffee/Coffeehouse
Beagle Bagel Cafe
898 Avery Blvd., Ridgeland, 601/956-1773

Best Dinner
Edison Walthall Hotel
225 E. Capitol St., 601/948-6161

Best Greek/Mediterranean Food
Bill's Greek Tavern
4762 McWillie Dr., 601/982-9295

Best Health-Conscious Menu
Beagle Bagel Cafe
898 Avery Blvd., Ridgeland, 601/956-1773

Best Homestyle Food
Cherokee Inn
5020 N. State St., 601/362-6388
Elite Restaurant
141 E. Capitol St., 601/352-5606

Best Seafood
Dennery's Restaurant
330 Greymont Ave., 601/354-2527
Iron Horse Grill
320 W. Pearl St., 601/355-8419

Best Steaks
Dennery's Restaurant
330 Greymont Ave., 601/354-2527
Iron Horse Grill
320 W. Pearl St., 601/355-8419

MERIDIAN, MS

Best All-You-Can-Eat Buffet
Plaza Restaurant
2409 Fifth St., 601/482-7659

Best American Food
D.T. Grinder's Restaurant and Pub
1600 24th Ave., 601/693-1988

The Landing
  5005 Hwy. 493, 601/693-5623

Best Barbecue/Ribs
Coleman's Barbecue
  2111 Hwy. 45N, 601/485-3006

Best Breakfast
Weidmann's
  210 22nd Ave., 601/693-1751

Best Chinese Food
China Palace Restaurant
  806 Hwy. 19N, Ste. 320, 601/483-5082

Best Desserts
Weidmann's
  210 22nd Ave., 601/693-1751

Best Fine Dining
Hollybrook Fine Dining
  1200 22nd Ave., 601/693-7584

Best Homestyle Food
Jean's Restaurant
  2114 Front St., 601/482-2348

M

Best Mexican Food
Lapinata Mexican Restaurant
  814 Eighteenth Ave. S., 601/693-7187
San Marcos Mexican Restaurant
  802 Hwy. 19N, 601/693-6683

Best Regional Food
Weidmann's
  210 22nd Ave., 601/693-1751

Best Restaurant in Town
Hollybrook Fine Dining
  1200 22nd Ave., 601/693-7584

Best Steaks
Rustler Steakhouse and Lounge
  5915 Hwy. 80W, 601/693-6499

NATCHEZ, MS

Best Burgers
Scrooge's Old English Pub
  315 Main St., 601/446-9922

Best Homestyle Food
Cock of the Walk Restaurant
  200 N. Broadway St., 601/446-8920

Best Restaurant in Town
West Bank Eatery
  710 Levee Rd., Vidalia, LA, 318/336-9669

Best Salad/Salad Bar
Clara Nell's Downtown Deli
  412 Main St., 601/445-7799

Best View While Dining
West Bank Eatery
  710 Levee Rd., Vidalia, LA, 318/336-9669

OXFORD, MS

Best All-You-Can-Eat Buffet
Abbeville Catfish Restaurant
Hwy. 7N, 601/234-8898
Cobb's Seafood and Steaks
Hwy. 6W, 601/236-6380

Best Atmosphere
Gin Restaurant
1302 Harrison St., 601/234-0024
Proud Larry's
211 S. Lamar Blvd., 601/236-0050

Best Barbecue/Ribs
Dixie Creek Meat Market
2304 Jackson Ave. W., 601/236-4100
Handy Andy Grocery
800 N. Lamar Blvd., 601/234-4621

Best Breakfast
Bottletree Bakery
923 Van Buren Ave., 601/236-5000

Best Casual Dining
Downtown Grill Restaurant
110 Courthouse Sq., 601/234-2659

Best Chinese Food
Far East Oriental Restaurant
1536 University Ave., 601/236-3600
Ruby Chinese Restaurant
2301 Jackson Ave. W., 601/234-8811

Best Coffee/Coffeehouse
Smitty's
208 S. Lamar Blvd., 601/234-9111
Square Books
160 Courthouse Sq., 601/236-2262

Best Delicatessen
McAlister's Deli
1515 University Ave., 601/234-1363

Best Desserts
Downtown Grill Restaurant
110 Courthouse Sq., 601/234-2659

Best Family Restaurant
Beacon Restaurant
1200 N. Lamar Blvd., 601/234-5041
Cedars
1007 College Hill Rd., 601/234-3855

Best Fine Dining
City Grocery
1118 Van Buren Ave., 601/232-8080
Yocona River Inn
842 Hwy. 334, 601/234-2464

Best Greek/Mediterranean Food
Kalo's Restaurant
1414 Jackson Ave. W., 601/236-0026

Best Homestyle Food
Blind Jim's
  1112 Van Buren Ave., 601/234-6147

Best Italian Food
Dino's Pizza Restaurant
  1420 Jackson Ave. W., 601/234-6777

Best Mexican Food
El Charro Mexican Restaurant
  1908 Jackson Ave. E., 601/236-0058

Best Seafood
Cobb's Seafood and Steaks
  Hwy. 6W, 601/236-6380
Oxford Seafood
  1520 Jackson Ave. W., 601/238-2847

Best Spanish Food
Don Pancho's Spanish Restaurant
  512 Jackson Ave. E., 601/238-2736

Best Steaks
Oxford Steak Company
  302 S. Eleventh St., 601/236-6460
Yocona River Inn
  842 Hwy. 334, 601/234-2464

M

PASCAGOULA, MS

Best Chinese Food
China Garden Restaurant
  3141 Denny Ave., 228/762-6186

Best Italian Food
Marguerite's Italian Village
  2318 Ingalls Ave., 228/762-7464

Best Lunch
Fillets Family Restaurant
  1911 Denny Ave., 228/769-0280

Best Seafood
River Docks Seafood Pier
  525 Denny Ave., 228/762-0570

Best Steaks
La Font Inn
  2703 Denny Ave., 228/762-7111

STARKVILLE, MS

Best Barbecue/Ribs
Little Dooey
  100 Fellowship St., 601/323-6094

Best Burgers
Christy's Hamburger
  446 Hwy. 12W, 601/323-6497

Best Chinese Food
Peking Chinese Restaurant
  840 Hwy. 12W, 601/324-0555

Best Desserts
Harvey's
  406 Hwy. 12E, 601/323-1639

Best Mexican Food
Mexico Tipico
123 Hwy. 12W, 601/323-2117

Best Pizza
CJ's Pizza
806 Hwy. 12E, 601/323-8897

Best Sandwiches
Starkville Cafe
211 University Dr., 601/323-1665

TUPELO, MS

Best Barbecue/Ribs
Johnnie's Drive-In
908 E. Main St., 601/842-6748
Omar's Ranch House
712 S. Gloster St., 601/840-1009
Rib Cage
206 Troy St., 601/840-5400

Best Breakfast
Shockley's
927 S. Gloster St., 601/842-6036

Best Burgers
Harvey's
424 S. Gloster St., 601/842-6763
Jefferson Place Dining Room
823 W. Jefferson St., 601/844-8696

Best Chinese Food
China Capital
530 N. Gloster St., 601/841-0484
Sun-Kai Chinese Restaurant
775 E. Main St., 601/844-7047
726 S. Gloster St., 601/680-8888

Best Ice Cream/Yogurt
Dairy Kream
796 E. Main St., 601/842-7838
Yummy Yogurt
105D Rankin Blvd., 601/841-1133

Best Mexican Food
Casa Monterrey
700 W. Main St., 601/844-0440

Best Pizza
Pizza Doctor
621 Joyner St., 601/844-2600
Vanelli's Restaurant
1302 N. Gloster St., 601/844-4410

Best Sandwiches
Finney's Sandwich and Soda Shop
1009 W. Main St., 601/842-1746

Best Seafood
Woody's Restaurant
619 N. Gloster St., 601/840-0460

Best Steaks
Gloster 205
205 N. Gloster St., 601/842-7205

VICKSBURG, MS

Best American Food
Beechwood Restaurant and Lounge
  4451 E. Clay St., 601/636-3761

Best Barbecue/Ribs
Goldie's Trail Bar-B-Q
  4127 Washington St., 601/636-9839

Best Chinese Food
Sun Koon Restaurant
  3535 S. Frontage Rd., 601/638-4941

Best Homestyle Food
Walnut Hills
  1214 Adams St., 601/638-4910

Best Steaks
Maxwell's Restaurant
  4207 Clay St., 601/636-1344

WAYNESBORO, MS

Best All-You-Can-Eat Buffet
Carol's Roundtable
  103 Mississippi Dr., 601/735-2819
Magnolia Restaurant
  109 Turner St., 601/735-5231

Best Burgers
Steve's Place
  912 Robinson St., 601/735-3435

Best Chinese Food
Golden China
  503 Azalea Dr., 601/735-9966

Best Family Restaurant
Carol's Roundtable
  103 Mississippi Dr., 601/735-2819
Magnolia Restaurant
  109 Turner St., 601/735-5231

M

Missouri

BLUE SPRINGS, MO

Best Barbecue/Ribs
Zarda Bar-B-Q
  214 State Rte. 7N, 816/229-9999

Best Homestyle Food
Betty's Family Dining
  1428 SW Hwy. 40, 816/229-2260

Best Mexican Food
Jose Miguel's
  1130 NW South Outer Rd., 816/228-6606

Best Seafood
Nader's Steak House and Lounge
  1605 State Rte. 7S, 816/229-9040

Best Steaks
Marina Grog and Galley
  22A Northshore Dr., Lake Lotawana,
    816/578-4400
Nader's Steak House and Lounge
  1605 State Rte. 7S, 816/229-9040

BRANSON, MO

Best All-You-Can-Eat-Buffet
Gator's Steak House
  3404 W. State Hwy. 76, 417/339-3451

Best Barbecue/Ribs
Lodge Of The Ozarks
  3431 W. State Hwy. 76, 417/334-7535

Best Breakfast
Kenny's Country Kitchen
  State Hwy. 165, 417/337-5025

Raftors Restaurant
3431 W. State Hwy. 76, 417/334-7535

Best Cajun/Creole Food
Champagne's Seafood
3400 W. State Hwy. 76, 417/334-6370

Best Casual Dining
Rocky's Italian Restaurant
120 N. Sycamore St., 417/335-4765

Best Fine Dining
Candlestick Inn
127 Taney St., 417/334-3633

Best Greek/Mediterranean Food
Dimitri's Restaurant
500 E. Main St., 417/334-0888

Best Homestyle
The Shack
108 S. Commercial St., 417/334-3490

Best Lunch
Branson Cafe
120 W. Main St., 417/334-3021
Uptown Cafe
285 State Hwy. 165, 417/336-3535

Best Mexican Food
Garcia's Mexican Food
207 S. Francis St., 417/334-5801

Best Regional Food
Farmhouse Restaurant
119 W. Main St., 417/334-9701

Best Restaurant Meal Value
Pzazz
Hwy. 165 at Pointe Royale Dr., 417/335-2798

Best Southwestern Food
Gilley's Texas Cafe
3457 W. State Hwy. 76, 417/335-2755

Best Sunday Brunch
Stage Door Canteen
1984 State Hwy. 165, 417/336-3575

Best Vegetarian Food
Club Celebrity Lounge
3425 W. State Hwy. 76, 417/334-7535

CAPE GIRARDEAU, MO

Best Barbecue/Ribs
Mac's Smoke House
6611 County Rd. 532, Pocahontas, 573/833-6552
Pilot House
3532 Perryville Rd., 573/335-9953

Best Breakfast
Sand's Pancake House
1448 N. Kingshighway St., 573/335-0420

Best Cajun/Creole Cuisine
Broussard's Cajun Cuisine
120 N. Main St., 573/334-7235

Best Chinese Food
Pagoda Gardens Chinese Restaurant
329 S. Kingshighway St., 573/334-8931

Best Diner
Wimpy's
506 S. Kingshighway St., 573/335-9679

Best French Food
Mollie's Cafe and Bar
11 S. Spanish St., 573/339-1661

Best Italian Food
Pasta House Company
W. Park Mall, Ste. 155, 573/335-4450

Best Mexican Food
El Torero
2120 William St., 573/339-2040

CHILLICOTHE, MO

Best Burgers
Hick's Hometown Drive-In
1311 Washington St., 660/646-1008

Best Chinese Food
Beijing Chinese Restaurant
327 Washington St., 660/646-4112

Best Homestyle Food
Country Kitchen
1029 S. Washington St., 660/646-6500

Best Ice Cream/Yogurt
Francine's Ice Cream and Bakery
1007 Bryan St., 660/646-3333

Best Pizza
Royal Inn Pizza
411 Park Ln., 660/646-5990

Best Seafood
Washington Street Food and Drink
1100 Washington St., 660/646-4058

Best Steaks
Harlow's Dining and Lounging
609 Jackson St., 660/646-6812

Best Sunday Brunch
Willows Restaurant
Grand River Inn, 606 W. Old Hwy. 36,
660/646-6590

CLINTON, MO

Best Barbecue/Ribs
Win-Mill Restaurant
219 NW State Rte. 7, 660/885-8434

Best Chinese Food
Egg Roll King Chinese Restaurant
701 N. Third St., 660/885-6547

Best Homestyle Food
Uchie's Fine Foods
127 W. Franklin St., 660/885-3262

M

Best Korean Food
Happy Garden
  1407 E. Ohio St., 660/885-8940

Best Mexican Food
Cancun
  1502 N. Second St., 660/885-4550
El Sambre Restaurant
  1107 S. Second St., 660/885-4333

Best Pizza
Pizza Glen
  205 E. Rives Rd., 660/885-8021

COLUMBIA, MO

Best Breakfast
Heidelberg Restaurant
  410 S. Ninth St., 573/449-6927

Best Brewpub
Flat Branch Pub and Brewing
  115 S. Fifth St., 573/499-0400

Best Burgers
Booches Billiard Hall
  110 S. Ninth St., 573/874-9519
Harpo's Bar and Grill
  29 S. Tenth St., 573/443-5418

Best Chinese Food
House of Chow
  2101 W. Broadway, 573/445-8800
Peking Chinese Restaurant
  122 S. Ninth St., 573/449-3716

Best Coffee/Coffeehouse
Lakota Coffee Company
  24 S. Ninth St., 573/874-2852

Best Italian Food
Bambino's
  203 Hitt St., 573/443-4473
Trattoria Strada Nova
  21 N. Ninth St., 573/442-8992

Best Mexican Food
Los Bandidos Mexican Restaurant
  220 S. Eighth St., 573/443-2419

Best Pizza
Rome Pizzeria
  1101 E. Broadway, 573/449-3104
Shakespeare's Pizza
  225 S. Ninth St., 573/449-2454

Best Sandwiches
Ninth Street Deli
  28 N. Ninth St., 573/875-8890
St. Louis Bread Company
  102 S. Ninth St., 573/442-4455
  Columbia Mall, 2300 Bernadette Dr., 573/446-7374

Best Seafood
Glenn's Cafe
  29 S. Ninth St., 573/443-3094

Best Steaks
Jack's Gourmet Restaurant
 1903 Business Loop 70E, 573/449-3927

Best Sunday Brunch
Boone Tavern and Restaurant
 811 E. Walnut St., 573/442-5123

Best Thai Food
Bangkok Gardens
 26 N. Ninth St., 573/874-3284

HANNIBAL, MO

Best Casual Dining
TJ's Supper Club
 211 Munger Ln., 573/221-5551

Best Chinese Food
Hunan Chinese Restaurant
 2905 Palmyra Rd., 573/221-1817

Best Sandwiches
Mark Twain Dinette and Drive In
 400 N. Third St., 573/221-5300
Twainland Cheesecake Company and Cafe
 116 North St., 573/221-3355

Best View While Dining
Riverview Cafe
 Hwy. 79N, 573/221-8292

INDEPENDENCE, MO

Best American Food
Montana Steak Company
 12712 Hwy. 40E, 816/373-8777

Best Business Lunch
Courthouse Exchange Restaurant
 113 W. Lexington Ave., 816/252-0344

Best Chinese Food
Magic Wok Restaurant
 3681 S. Noland Rd., 816/461-0218

Best Family Restaurant
Furr's Cafeteria
 16202 Hwy. 24E, 816/257-1258

Best German Food
Rheinland
 208 N. Main St., 816/461-5383

Best Homestyle Food
Stephenson's Old Apple Farm
 16401 Hwy. 40E, 816/373-5405

Best Italian Food
V's Italiano Ristorante
 10819 Hwy. 40E, 816/353-1241

Best Sandwiches
Clinton's Drugstore Giftshop
 100 W. Maple Ave., 816/833-2625
Courthouse Exchange Restaurant
 113 W. Lexington Ave., 816/252-0344

M

M

JEFFERSON CITY, MO

Best Breakfast
Park Place Restaurant
  Capitol Plaza Hotel, 415 W. McCarty St.,
    573/635-1234
Country Kitchen
  1650 Jefferson St., 573/634-5353
Mel's Country Cafe
  2421 Industrial Dr., 573/893-9115

Best Burgers
Ecco Lounge
  703 Jefferson St., 573/636-8751

Best Chinese Food
Yen Ching Restaurant
  2208 Missouri Blvd., 573/635-5225

Best Fine Dining
Alexandro's
  2125 Missouri Blvd., 573/634-7740
Cafe Deville
  319 W. Miller St., 573/636-5231

Best Homestyle Food
Veit's Diamond Restaurant
  2001 Missouri Blvd., 573/635-1213

Best Italian Food
Domenico's Italian Restaurant
  3702 W. Truman Blvd., 573/893-5454
Madison's Cafe
  216 Madison St., 573/893-6020

Best Mexican Food
La Casa Mexican Restaurant
  1102 Missouri Blvd., 573/636-7868

Best Pizza
Arris' Pizza Palace
  117 W. High St., 573/635-9225
Breadeaux Pisa
  510 Ellis Blvd., 573/635-7472
Mo and Waldo's
  126 E. Dunklin St., 573/893-6020

Best Sandwiches
Silverado Cafe
  103 E. High St., 573/635-9194

JOPLIN, MO

Best Barbecue/Ribs
Butcher's Block
  2412 S. Main St., 417/624-1000
Jim Bob's Steaks and Ribs
  2040 S. Range Line Rd., 417/781-3300

Best Burgers
Kitchen Pass Restaurant
  1212 S. Main St., 417/624-9095

Best Italian Food
Travetti's Restaurante and Bar
  3010 E. Twentieth St., 417/781-4344

Best Mexican Food
Casa Montez Restaurant
  2324 S. Range Line Rd., 417/781-3610

Best Seafood
Crabby's Seafood Bar and Grill
  815 W. Seventh St., 417/782-7372

Best Steaks
Wilder's Fine Foods
  1216 S. Main St., 417/623-2058

KANSAS CITY, MO

Best Bar
Zola
  4113 Pennsylvania Ave., 816/561-9191

Best Barbecue/Ribs
Arthur Bryant Barbecue
  1727 Brooklyn Ave., 816/231-1123
Gates and Sons Bar-B-Q
  1411 Swope Pkwy., 816/921-0409
Gates Bar-B-Q
  4707 Paseo Blvd., 816/923-0900
  1221 Brooklyn Ave., 816/483-3880

Best Beer Selection
Charlie Hooper's
  12 W. 63rd St., 816/361-8841

Best Breakfast
Corner Restaurant
  4059 Broadway St., 816/931-6630
First Watch
  1022 Westport Rd., 816/931-4401

Best Brewpub
75th Street Brewery
  520 W. 75th St., 816/523-4677
River Market Brewing Company
  500 Walnut St., 816/471-6300

Best Burgers
Town Topic Sandwich Shop
  1900 Baltimore Ave., 816/471-6038
  2021 Broadway St., 816/842-2298
Westport Flea Market and Bar
  817 Westport Rd., 816/931-1986
Winstead's
  101 Brush Creek Blvd., 816/753-2244
  1628 Burlington St., 816/842-5952

Best Business Lunch
Grand Street Cafe
  4740 Grand Ave., 816/561-8000
Plaza III: The Steakhouse
  4749 Pennsylvania Ave., 816/753-0000

Best Cafeteria
Furr's Cafeteria
  5407 NE Antioch Rd., 816/452-6400

M

Best Cajun/Creole Food
Jazz: A Louisiana Kitchen
  1823 W. 39th St., 816/531-5556
Kiki's Bon Ton Maison
  1515 Westport Rd., 816/931-9417

Best Casual Dining
Romanelli Grill
  7122 Wornall Rd., 816/333-1321

Best Chinese Food
Bo Ling's Chinese Restaurant
  4800 Main St., 816/753-1718
Double Dragon
  5031 Main St., 816/531-5778

Best Coffee/Coffeehouse
Broadway Cafe
  4106 Broadway St., 816/531-2432
East 51st Street Coffee House
  318 E. 51st St., 816/756-3121
Latte Land
  318 W. 47th St., 816/931-7477

Best Delicatessen
D'Bronx
  3904 Bell St., 816/531-0550
Margerita's
  7013 N. Oak, 816/468-0337
  13401 Holmes Ave., 816/941-9411
  2829 Southwest Blvd., 816/931-4849

Best Desserts
Tippin's Restaurant and Pie
  9145 Hillcrest Rd., 816/761-3966
  5080 N. Oak Trafficway, 816/459-7550

Best Diner
Chubby's
  1835 Independence Ave., 816/842-2482

Best Dinner
The American Restaurant
  2450 Grand Blvd., 816/426-1133

Best Eclectic Menu
Classic Cup Cafe
  301 W. 47th St., 816/753-1840
  4130 Pennsylvania Ave., 816/756-0771
Zola
  4113 Pennsylvania Ave., 816/561-9191

Best Family Restaurant
Stroud's
  1015 E. 85th St., 816/333-2132
  5410 NE Oak Ridge Rd., 816/454-9600

Best German Food
Berliner Bear
  7815 Wornall Rd., 816/444-2828
Emil's European Deli and Restaurant
  302 Nichols Rd., 816/753-2771

Best Italian Food
Garozzo's Ristorante
526 Harrison St., 816/221-2455

Best Japanese Food
Gojo Japanese Steak House
4163 Broadway St., 816/561-2501

Best Late-Night Food
Antonio's Pizza
3834 Main St., 816/561-1988
1100 Main St., 816/421-4888
Nichol's Lunch
3906 Waddell Ave., 816/561-5200
Velvet Dog
400 E. 31st St., 816/753-9990

Best Lunch
Boulevard Cafe
703 Southwest Blvd., 816/842-6984

Best Mexican Food
California Taqueria
700 Southwest Blvd., 816/474-5571
Guadalajara Restaurant
822 Southwest Blvd., 816/471-3235
Ponak's Mexican Restaurant
2856 Southwest Blvd., 816/756-3850

Best Middle Eastern Food
Jerusalem Cafe
431 Westport Rd., 816/756-2770

Best Outdoor Dining
The Classic Cup Cafe
301 W. 47th St., 816/753-1840
4130 Pennsylvania Ave., 816/756-0771

Best Pizza
D'Bronx
3904 Bell St., 816/531-0550
Minsky's Pizza
5105 Main St., 816/561-5100
Waldo Pizza and Bar
7433 Broadway St., 816/363-5242

Best Restaurant in Town
Cafe Allegro
1815 W. 39th St., 816/561-3663
The American Restaurant
2450 Grand Blvd., 816/426-1133

Best Romantic Dining
Peppercorn Duck Club
Hyatt Regency Center, 2345 McGee St.,
816/435-4199
Skies
Hyatt Regency Center, 2345 McGee St.,
816/435-4199

Best Seafood
Savoy
219 W. Ninth St., 816/842-3890

M

Best Soul Food
Ruby's
   1506 Brooklyn Ave., 816/221-2370

Best Steaks
Hereford House Restaurant
   2 E. Twentieth St., 816/842-1080

Best Sunday Brunch
Micheal Forbes Grill
   7539 Wornall Rd., 816/444-5445
Tomfooleries Restaurant and Bar
   612 W. 47th St., 816/753-0555

Best Vegetarian Food
Daily Bread
   645 E. 59th St., 816/531-1452
Eden Alley
   707 W. 47th St., 816/561-5415

Best Vietnamese Food
Hien Vuong Restaurant
   417 Main St., 816/842-1020
Saigon 39
   1806 1/2 W. 39th St., 816/531-4447

Best Wine Selection
Harry Starker's
   200 Nichols Rd., 816/756-2770
Joe D's Wine Bar-Cafe
   6227 Brookside Plz., 816/333-6116

KIRKSVILLE, MO

Best Breakfast
Pancake City
   2101 N. Baltimore St., 660/665-6002

Best Chinese Food
China Palace Restaurant
   124 N. Franklin St., 660/627-8888
Minn's Tea House
   102 S. Elson St., 660/665-9610

Best Fine Dining
Minn's Cuisine
   216 N. Franklin St., 660/665-2842

Best Homestyle Food
Country Kitchen
   2700 S. Baltimore St., 660/627-4555

Best Italian Food
Wooden Nickel
   114 S. Elson St., 660/665-2760

Best Pizza
Pagliai's Pizza
   101 W. Washington St., 660/665-6678

Best View While Dining
Thousand Hills Dining Lodge
   Rural Route 3, 660/665-7119

M

MOBERLY, MO

Best Chinese Food
Chinese Chef
  721 N. Morley St., 660/269-8221
Hunan Chinese Restaurant
  537 W. Reed St., 660/263-6803

Best Family Restaurant
Country Kitchen
  530 E. Hwy. 24, 660/263-3191

Best Pizza
Pizza Works
  319 N. Morley St., 660/263-8102

Best Seafood
Jeffrey's
  107 N. Williams St., 660/263-3005

Best Steaks
CC Sawyer's Restaurant Lounge
  104 W. Wrightman St., 660/263-7744
Richard's Steak House
  1633 S. Morley St., 660/263-2221

POPLAR BLUFF, MO

Best All-You-Can-Eat Buffet
Johnson's Cafe
  919 E. Rte. 53, 573/785-9949

Best Barbecue/Ribs
Hayden Drive-In
  807 W. Maud St., 573/785-4705

Best Homestyle Food
Myrtle's Place
  109 N. Broadway St., 573/785-9203

Best Restaurant in Town
Dumplin's of Poplar Bluff
  2201 N. Westwood Blvd., 573/686-6777

ROLLA, MO

Best Barbecue/Ribs
Johnny's Smoke Stak
  201 W. State Rt. 72, 573/364-4838

Best Chinese Food
Great Wall Chinese Restaurant
  1505 N. Bishop Ave., 573/341-9922

Best Pizza
Alex's Pizzeria
  122 W. Eighth St., 573/364-2669

Best Steaks
Sirloin Stockade
  1401 Martin Springs Dr., 573/364-7168

SIKESTON, MO

Best Barbecue/Ribs
Bo's Pit Bar BQ
  1609 E. Malone Ave., 573/471-9927

M

Best Burgers
Kirby's Sandwich Shop
  109 N. Kingshighway St., 573/471-1318

Best Business Lunch
Prime and Wine Restaurant
  2608 E. Malone Ave., 573/471-4700

Best Chinese Food
China Pearl
  2301 E. Malone Ave., 573/472-1552

Best Homestyle Food
Lambert's Cafe
  2515 E. Malone Ave., 573/471-4261

Best Pizza
Mazzio's Pizza
  1511 E. Malone Ave., 573/471-7120

Best Sandwiches
Rodchester's Deli
  400 N. Main St., 573/471-2139

M

Best Seafood
Fisherman's Net
  915 River Birch Mall, 573/471-8102

SPRINGFIELD, MO

Best All-You-Can-Eat Buffet
Silk Road Restaurant
  400 S. Glenstone Ave., 417/869-4403
  310 W. Battlefield St., 417/886-0999

Best American Food
Diamond Head Restaurant
  2734 S. Campbell Ave., 417/883-9581
Ziggie's Family Restaurant
  2222 S. Campbell Ave., 417/883-0900

Best Breakfast
Anton's Coffee Shop
  937 S. Glenstone Ave., 417/869-7681
Village Inn
  4222 S. Campbell Ave., 417/887-4774

Best Burgers
Taylor's Drive In
  139 Memorial Plz., 417/862-3278

Best Chinese Food
Diamond Head Restaurant
  2734 S. Campbell Ave., 417/883-9581
Gee's East Wind
  2951 E. Sunshine St., 417/883-4567
Leong's Tea House
  1036 W. Sunshine St., 417/869-4444

Best Delicatessen
Nearly Famous Deli and Pasta
  1828 S. Kentwood Ave., 417/883-3403

Best Dinner
Hamby's Steak House
  901 N. Boonville Ave., 417/869-7615

Best Family Restaurant
McGuffey's Restaurant
 2101 W. Chesterfield Blvd., 417/882-2484

Best Greek/Mediterranean Food
Sophia's Cafe
 3522 S. National Ave., 417/883-3367

Best Homestyle Food
Heritage Cafeteria
 1364 E. Battlefield St., 417/883-3033
 1310 S. Glenstone Ave., 417/881-7770

Best Italian Food
J. Parrino's Pasta House and Bar
 1550 E. Battlefield St., 417/882-1808
Soup-N-Sandwich
 2259 S. Campbell Ave., 417/882-5166

Best Japanese Food
Nakato Japanese Steak House
 2615 S. Glenstone Ave., 417/881-7171

Best Mexican Food
Cielito Lindo Mexicano
 2953 S. National Ave., 417/886-3320
 3530 S. Campbell Ave., 417/886-7676
 2626 N. Glenstone Ave., 417/863-1879
La Mexican Kitchen
 3322D S. Campbell Ave., 417/886-0073
Mexican Villa
 multiple locations
Tres Hombres
 3371 E. Montclair St., 417/887-6767

Best Pizza
McSalty's Pizza Cafe
 1550 E. Battlefield St., 417/883/4324
 2627 E. Sunshine St., 417/887-2589
 1141 E. Delmar St., 417/869-0982

Best Seafood
Hemingway's
 1935 S. Campbell Ave., 417/887-3388

Best Steaks
Shady Inn
 524 W. Sunshine St., 417/862-0369

ST. JOSEPH, MO

Best Chinese Food
Chu's Garden
 1521 Saint Joseph Ave., 816/232-9968
 2243 N. Belt Hwy., 816/364-3368

Best Homestyle Food
Jerre Anne Cafeteria and Bakery
 2640 Mitchell Ave., 816/232-6585

Best Italian Food
Fazoli's
 504 N. Belt Hwy., 816/387-9539

Best Mexican Food
Barbosa's
  906 Sylvanie St., 816/233-4970
  4804 Frederick Ave., 816/232-0221
Palma's Authentic Mexican Restaurant
  2715 N. Belt Hwy., 816/279-9445

Best Sandwiches
Common Ground Cafe
  614 Francis St., 816/279-4577
Maid-Rite
  522 Felix St., 816/279-8382
  2701 Frederick Ave., 816/387-8867

Best Steaks
Black Angus Restaurant
  102 S. Third St., 816/279-8000
D & G Restaurant
  1918 Frederick Ave., 816/232-7170
Frederick Inn Steakhouse
  1627 Frederick Ave., 816/364-5151
Hoof and Horn Steak House
  429 Illinois Ave., 816/238-0742

M

ST. LOUIS, MO

Best American Food
Jordan's Restaurant
  12908 New Halls Ferry Rd., Florissant,
    314/838-1155

Best Bar
McGurk's
  1200 Russell Blvd., 314/776-8309

Best Barbecue/Ribs
K.C. Masterpiece
  611 N. Lindbergh Blvd., 314/991-5811

Best Beer Selection
Blueberry Hill Restaurant
  6504 Delmar Blvd., 314/727-0880

Best Breakfast
Uncle Bill's Pancake and Dinner
  4000 Lemay Ferry Rd., 314/845-0660
  3427 S. Kingshighway Blvd., 314/832-1973

Best Burgers
Blueberry Hill Restaurant
  6504 Delmar Blvd., 314/727-0880

Best Business Lunch
Cardwell's Restaurant and Bar
  94 Plaza Frontenac, 314/997-8885
  8100 Maryland Ave., 314/726-5055

Best Cafeteria
Miss Sheri's
  5406 Southfield Center Dr., 314/849-1141
  6607 Chippewa St., 314/644-6063

Best Casual Dining
Flaco's Tacos
  515 Chestnut St., 314/241-0277

116 N. Sixth St., 314/231-8226
3852 Lindell Blvd., 314/534-8226

Best Chinese Food
Yen Ching
1012 Brentwood Blvd., 314/721-7507
Yen Wah Cafeteria and Restaurant
108 S. Main St., St. Charles, 314/723-0320

Best Coffee/Coffeehouse
Aesop's
6611 Clayton Rd., 314/727-0809
Brandt's Market and Cafe
6525 Delmar Blvd., 314/727-3663
Grind Coffee House
56 Maryland Plz., 314/454-0202
Meshuggah
565 Melville Ave., 314/726-5662
Oasis
8130 Big Bend Blvd., 314/968-3038

Best Delicatessen
Kopperman's
386 N. Euclid Ave., 314/361-0100

Best Desserts
Tippin's Restaurant and Pie Pantry
7331 Watson Rd., 314/352-0759
11440 Olive Blvd., 314/567-5694
10 Saint Louis Galleria, 314/721-3880
9807 Watson Rd., 314/822-0112

Best Diner
South City Diner
3141 S. Grand Blvd., 314/772-6100

Best Eclectic Menu
Big Sky Cafe
47 S. Old Orchard Ave., 314/962-5757
Piccolo's Mediterranean Cafe
Metropolitan Square Building, 211 N. Broadway,
314/421-2887

Best Fine Dining
Yacovelli's Restaurant
407 Dunn Rd., Florissant, 314/839-1000

Best French Food
Cafe de France
408 Olive St., 314/231-2204

Best German Food
Bevo Mill
4749 Gravois Ave., 314/481-2626

Best Greek/Mediterranean Food
Spiro's Restaurant
8406 Natural Bridge Rd., 314/382-8074
3122 Watson Rd., 314/645-8383

Best Health-Conscious Menu
Bonzai Express of St. Louis
7353 Forsyth Blvd., 314/725-5030

M

Best Ice Cream/Yogurt
Crown Candy Kitchen
  1401 St. Louis Ave., 314/621-9650
Fritz's Frozen Custard
  1055 Saint Catherine St., Florissant, 314/839-4100
Iggy's Frozen Yogurt
  10118 W. Florissant Ave., 314/867-5737
  1669 Pattern Dr., 314/653-1580
Lix Frozen Custard
  16043 Manchester Rd., Ballwin, 314/230-8202
Maggie Moo's Creamery
  8853 Ladue Rd., 314/862-6651
Ted Drewe's Frozen Custard
  6726 Chippewa St., 314/481-2652
  4224 S. Grand Blvd., 314/352-7376

Best Indian Food
India Palace
  4534 N. Lindbergh Blvd., Bridgeton, 314/731-3333
Star of India
  4569 Laclede Ave., 314/361-6911

Best Italian Food
Canolli's Restaurant
  462 Hwy. 67N, Florissant, 314/839-5988
Kemoll's
  Metropolitan Square Building, 211 W. Broadway,
    314/421-0555
Pasta House Company
  multiple locations

Best Japanese Food
Robata of Japan
  111 Westport Plz., Ste. 12, 314/434-1007

Best Late-Night Food
Eat-Rite Diner
  622 Chouteau Ave., 314/621-9621

Best Lunch
Fatted Calf
  12 S. Bemiston Ave., 314/726-1141

Best Mexican Food
Casa Gallardo Mexican Restaurant
  1491 Saint Louis Galleria, 314/727-2223
  1821 N. Market St., 314/421-6766

Best Middle Eastern Food
Saleem's Lebanese Cuisine
  6501 Delmar Blvd., 314/721-7947

Best Outdoor Dining
Busch's Grove Restaurant
  9160 Clayton Rd., 314/993-0011

Best Pizza
California Pizza Kitchen
  1493 Saint Louis Galleria, 314/863-4500
Talayna's Italian Restaurant
  276 N. Skinker Blvd., 314/863-2120
  510 Westport Plz., 314/434-6700

Best Place to Take the Kids
Chuck E. Cheese Pizza
2805 Target Dr., 314/741-8001
7499 S. Lindbergh Blvd., 314/487-6707
Fortel's Pizza Den
7922 Mackenzie Rd., 314/353-2360

Best Restaurant Meal Value
Hodak's Restaurant
2100 Gravois Ave., 314/776-7292

Best Romantic Dining
Tony's Restaurant
410 Market St., 314/231-7007

Best Sandwiches
St. Louis Bread Company
multiple locations

Best Seafood
Blue Water Grill
2607 Hampton Ave., 314/645-0707
Nantucket Cove
101 S. Hanley Rd., 314/726-4900
S & P Oyster Company
1644 Country Club Plaza Dr., St. Charles,
314/947-3300
14501 Manchester Rd., Ballwin, 314/256-3300

Best Soul Food
London and Sons Wing House
4739 Goodfellow Blvd., 314/389-8328
6731 Page Ave., 314/725-4710
3740 Dr. Martin Luther King Dr., 314/371-4925

Best Southwestern Food
Casa Grill
1491 Saint Louis Galleria, 314/727-2223

Best Sports Bar
Ozzie's Restaurant and Sports Bar
645 Westport Plz., 314/434-1000

Best Steaks
Tucker's Place
2117 S. Twelfth St., 314/772-5977

Best Sunday Brunch
Faust's
Adam's Mark Hotel, 315 Chestnut St.,
314/241-7400

Best Thai Food
King and I
3157 S. Grand Blvd., 314/771-1777

Best Vegetarian Food
Sunshine Inn
8 S. Euclid Ave., 314/367-1413

Best Vietnamese Food
Mai Lee
8440 Delmar Blvd., 314/993-3754
Pho Grand
3191 S. Grand Blvd., 314/664-7435

M

WEST PLAINS, MO

Best American Food
The Depot
  1717 N. Terra St., 417/257-2880

Best Breakfast
Kenny's Walleye and Catfish House
  612 Porter Wagoner Blvd., 417/256-1538

Best Chinese Food
Diamond Head Restaurant
  1214 Porter Wagoner Blvd., 417/256-4888

Best Coffee/Coffeehouse
Cornucopia Fine Foods
  Court Square, 3 Evans Arc, 417/256-0689
Yellow House Coffeehouse
  209 W. Cleveland St., 417/256-3554

Best Homestyle Food
Ozark Cafe
  104 Washington Ave., 417/256-3340

Best Pizza
Simple Simon's Pizza
  1836 Porter Wagoner Blvd., 417/257-7700

Best Steaks
TJ's Hickory House
  Hwy. 160W, 417/257-7614

Best Vegetarian Food
Bluebird Cafe
  480 First St., Ste. 2, Summersville, 417/932-5272

Montana

BILLINGS, MT

Best American Food
The Granary Restaurant
  1500 Poly Dr., 406/259-3488

Best Burgers
Casey's Golden Pheasant
  109 N. Broadway, 406/256-5200
King's Hat
  105 S. 37th St., 406/259-4746

Best Chinese Food
Golden Phoenix Chinese Restaurant
  79 Swords Ln., 406/256-0319

Best Coffee/Coffeehouse
Todd's Plantation Gourmet Coffee
  115 N. 29th St., 406/245-2720

Best Italian Food
Bruno's Italian Specialties
  1002 First Ave. N., 406/248-4146
  1523 Broadwater Ave., 406/252-1616

Best Lunch
Stella's Kitchen and Bakery
  110 N. 29th St., 406/248-3060

Best Pizza
Village Inn Pizza Parlor
  2048 Grand Ave., 406/656-6706

Best Romantic Dining
Rex Hotel
  2401 Montana Ave., 406/245-7477

Best Sandwiches
Pug Mahon's
  3011 First Ave. N., 406/259-4190

Best Seafood
Windmill Club
  3921 First Ave. S., 406/252-8100

Best Steaks
Kit Kat Cafe
  633 Main St., 406/259-9154
Walker's Grill
  301 N. 27th St., 406/245-9291
Windmill Club
  3921 First Ave. S., 406/252-8100

Best Thai Food
Thai Orchid Restaurant
  2926 Second Ave. N., 406/256-2206

BOZEMAN, MT

M

Best Barbecue/Ribs
Fred's Mesquite Diner
  451 E. Main St., 406/585-8558
Monkey Don's Rib Joint
  103 S. Fourth St., Manhattan, 406/585-7490

Best Brewpub
Spanish Peaks Brewing Company
  120 N. Nineteenth Ave., 406/585-2296

Best Chinese Food
Wong's Restaurant
  125 W. Main St., 406/587-1686

Best Delicatessen
Bacchus Pub
  105 W. Main St., 406/586-1314

Best Eclectic Menu
John Bozeman's Bistro
  242 E. Main St., 406/587-4100

Best Fine Dining
O'Brien's Restaurant
  312 E. Main St., 406/587-3973
The Gallatin Gateway Inn
  76405 Gallatin Rd., 406/763-4672

Best Italian Food
John Bozeman's Bistro
  242 E. Main St., 406/587-4100
Spanish Peaks Brewing Company
  120 N. Nineteenth Ave., 406/585-2296

Best Sandwiches
Pickle Barrel
  209 E. Main St., 406/582-0020
  809 W. College St., 406/587-2411
Spanish Peaks Brewing Company
  120 N. Nineteenth Ave., 406/585-2296

Best Thai Food
John Bozeman's Bistro
  242 E. Main St., 406/587-4100

BUTTE, MT

Best 24-Hour Restaurant
Gold Rush Casino
   22 W. Galena St., 406/723-3211

Best American Food
Lydia's
   4915 Harrison Ave., 406/494-2000

Best Burgers
The M & M Bar and Cafe
   9 N. Main St., 406/723-7612

Best Chinese Food
Chinatown Buffet
   3030 Elm St., 406/723-3888
Ming's Chinese Restaurant
   116 W. Park St., 406/782-7058
Peking Noodle Parlor
   117 S. Main St., 406/782-2217

Best Family Restaurant
Hanging Five Family Restaurant
   2110 Harvard Ave., 406/494-4309

Best French Food
Uptown Cafe
   47 E. Broadway St., 406/723-4735

Best Greek/Mediterranean Food
It's Greek To Me
   1640 Grand Ave., 406/782-3122

Best Italian Food
Spaghettini's
   101 Broadway St., 406/782-8855

Best Lunch
Columbia Garden Espresso
   27 N. Main St., 406/782-8808
Four B's Restaurant
   1935 Dewey Blvd., 406/494-1199
   23000 Nissler Rd., Ste. 48, 406/782-0080
Gamer's Cafe
   15 W. Park St., 406/723-5453
Joe's Pastry Shop
   1641 Grand Ave., 406/723-9071
Uptown Cafe
   47 E. Broadway St., 406/723-4735

Best Mexican Food
La Cosina Mexican Restaurant
   625 E. Front St., 406/723-9008
Ranchos Los Arcos Mexican
   815 E. Front St., 406/782-8421

Best Steaks
Chaparral Steak House Casino
   1300 S. Main St., 406/782-7656
Derby
   2016 Harrison Ave., 406/723-9086

M

CUT BANK, MT

Best Coffee/Coffeehouse
C & L Country Cafe
112 N. Central Ave., 406/873-5335

Best Homestyle Food
C & L Country Cafe
112 N. Central Ave., 406/873-5335

Best Pizza
Maxie's
1159 E. Railroad St., 406/873-4220

Best Place to Take the Kids
Point Drive Inn
1119 E. Main St., 406/873-2431
R Place
Northern Village Shopping Ctr., 615 Main St.,
406/873-4786

Best Sandwiches
Golden Harvest Cafe
13 W. Main St., 406/873-4010

Best Seafood
Glacier Motor Inn
15 First Ave. SW, 406/873-5555
JR's
918 E. Main St., 406/873-4401

Best Steaks
Glacier Motor Inn
15 First Ave. SW, 406/873-5555
JR's
918 E. Main St., 406/873-4401

DILLON, MT

Best Atmosphere
Centennial Inn
122 S. Washington St., 406/683-4454

Best Chinese Food
Western Wok
17 E. Bannack St., 406/683-2356

Best Coffee/Coffeehouse
Sweetwater Coffee
23 N. Idaho St., 406/683-4141

Best Desserts
Anna's Oven
120 S. Montana St., 406/683-5766
Centennial Inn
122 S. Washington St., 406/683-4454

Best Homestyle Food
Anna's Oven
120 S. Montana St., 406/683-5766
Longhorn Saloon
8 N. Montana St., 406/683-6839

Best Ice Cream/Yogurt
Arctic Circle
135 S. Atlantic St., 406/683-4146

Peppermint Stick
39 N. Idaho St., 406/683-6662

Best Pizza
Papa T's
10 N. Montana St., 406/683-6432

Best Sandwiches
Anna's Oven
120 S. Montana St., 406/683-5766
Sweetwater Coffee
23 N. Idaho St., 406/683-4141

Best Seafood
Lion's Den
725 N. Montana St., 406/683-2051

Best Steaks
Lion's Den
725 N. Montana St., 406/683-2051

GLENDIVE, MT

Best Burgers
Doc and Eddie's
1515 W. Bell St., 406/365-6782

Best Coffee/Coffeehouse
Hill-A-Beans
102 S. Merrill Ave., 406/365-2415

Best Italian Food
Bacio's
302 W. Towne St., 406/365-9664

Best Pizza
Greg's Silver Dollar Casino
1101 W. Towne St., 406/365-2074

Best Sandwiches
Beer Jug
313 N. Merrill Ave., 406/359-9986
Gust-Hauf
300 W. Bell St., 406/365-4451

Best Steaks
The Jordan
Best Western Inn, 222 N. Kendrick Ave.,
406/365-5655

GREAT FALLS, MT

Best Coffee/Coffeehouse
Big Sky Bagel Bakery
1229 Tenth Ave. S., 406/453-5747
Daily Grind
320 First Ave. N., 406/452-4529
Morning Light Coffee Roasters
900 Second Ave. N., 406/453-8443

Best Diner
Tracy's 24-Hour Family Restaurant
127 Central Ave., 406/453-6108

M

Best Dinner
Borries Family Restaurant
  1800 Smelter Ave., Black Eagle, 406/761-0300
Eddie's Supper Club and Coffee
  3725 Second Ave. N., 406/453-1616
Jaker's Steak, Ribs and Fish House
  1500 Tenth Ave. S., 406/727-1033

Best Homestyle Food
Dearborn Country Inn
  4 Cooper Dr., Cascade, 406/468-2838

Best Italian Food
Mama Cassie's Italian Restaurant
  319 First Ave. N., 406/454-3354

Best Lunch
Candie's of Times Square
  705 Central Ave. W., 406/727-1313
Dobie's
  122 Central Ave., 406/453-1686

Best Pizza
Howard's Pizza
  900 Eighth Ave. NW, 406/761-1321
  4300 Third Ave. S., 406/454-1325
  713 First Ave. N., 406/453-1212
MacKenzie River Pizza Company
  1220 Ninth St. S., 406/761-0085

HAMILTON, MT

Best Barbecue/Ribs
Bad Bubba's BBQ
  105 N. Second St., 406/375-0624

Best Breakfast
BJ's Family Restaurant
  900 N. First St., 406/363-4650

Best Burgers
Nap's Grill
  220 N. Second St., 406/363-0136

Best Chinese Food
Far East Village
  610 N. First St., 406/363-6976

Best Coffee/Coffeehouse
Coffee Cup Cafe
  500 S. First St., 406/363-3822

Best Family Restaurant
Four B's Restaurant
  1105 N. First St., 406/363-4620

Best Italian Food
La Trattoria
  315 S. Third St., 406/363-5030

Best Mexican Food
Sundance Cafe in Hamilton
  900 S. First St., 406/363-2810

Best Pizza
BJ's Family Restaurant
  900 N. First St., 406/363-4650

Best Sandwiches
Back Door Deli
  105 S. Third St., 406/363-4480

HAVRE, MT

Best American Food
Mediterranean Room
  1300 First St., 406/265-6111

Best Bar
15 West
  109 First St. W., 406/265-4747

Best Breakfast
Four B's Restaurant
  604 First St. W., 406/265-9721

Best Burgers
Rod's Drive Inn
  1827 Fifth Ave., 406/265-9781

M

Best Casual Dining
Four B's Restaurant
  604 First St. W., 406/265-9721
Vineyard Patio Restaurant
  1300 First St., 406/265-5355

Best Dinner
Andy's
  658 First St. W., 406/265-9963

Best Family Restaurant
Gallery Restaurant
  Hwy. 2W, 406/265-8851
Uncle Joe's
  1400 First St., 406/265-1013

Best Lunch
Lunch Box
  213 Third Ave., 406/265-6588
Quench and Bench
  220 Third Ave., 406/265-8911

Best Steaks
Andy's
  658 First St. W., 406/265-9963

HELENA, MT

Best Atmosphere
On Broadway
  106 E. Broadway St., 406/443-1929
Stonehouse Restaurant
  120 Reeders Alley, 406/449-2552
Windbag Saloon
  19 S. Last Chance Gulch St., 406/443-9669

Best Breakfast
No Sweat Cafe
  427 N. Last Chance Gulch St., 406/442-6954

Victor's
   Park Plaza Hotel, 22 N. Last Chance Gulch St.,
      406/443-2200
Uncle Ron's High Country Cafe
   3122 U.S. Hwy. 12E, 406/442-2332

Best Burgers
Overland Express
   2250 Eleventh Ave., 406/449-2635
York Bar
   7500 York Rd., 406/475-9949

Best Business Lunch
Bert and Ernie's Saloon
   361 N. Last Chance Gulch St., 406/443-5680

Best Chinese Food
Jade Gardens
   3128 N. Montana Ave., 406/443-8899

Best Family Restaurant
Uncle Ron's High Country Cafe
   3122 U.S. Hwy. 12E, 406/442-2332

Best Ice Cream/Yogurt
Ice Cream Parlor
   718 Logan St., 406/442-0117

Best Italian Food
On Broadway
   106 E. Broadway St., 406/443-1929
Pasta Pantry
   1218 Eleventh Ave., 406/442-1074

Best Lunch
Brewhouse Brew Pub and Grill
   939 Getchell St., 406/457-9390

Best Pizza
Godfather's Pizza
   2216 N. Montana Ave., 406/443-7050
Hugo's Pizza
   20 Hwy. 518, 406/449-4846
Miller's Crossing
   52 S. Park Ave., 406/442-3290

Best Sandwiches
Pasta Pantry
   1218 Eleventh Ave., 406/442-1074
Steffano's U-Bake Pizza
   2100 N. Main St., 406/442-2070

Best Seafood
The River Grille
   Northgate Plaza, 1225 Custer Ave., 406/442-1075

Best Steaks
Gilly's Casino
   920 E. Lyndale Ave., 406/442-6449

M

KALISPELL, MT

Best Breakfast
Finnegan's
660 E. Idaho St., 406/755-0322

Best Family Restaurant
Four Seasons Restaurant
350 N. Main St., 406/755-1374
Fred's Family Restaurant
1600 U.S. Hwy. 93S, 406/257-8666

Best Ice Cream/Yogurt
Alpine Frozen Yogurt
20 N. Main St., 406/752-4610

Best Italian Food
Rocco's
3796 U.S. Hwy. 2E, 406/756-5834

Best Mexican Food
Dos Amigos Mexican Restaurant
25 Second Ave. W., 406/752-2711

Best Pizza
Stageline Pizza
211 Second St. W., 406/755-4444

Best Sandwiches
Lighterside Restaurant
221 Main St., 406/752-3668
Stageline Pizza
211 Second St. W., 406/755-4444

Best Seafood
Montana Grill
5480 U.S. Hwy. 93S, Somers, 406/857-3889
Rocco's
3796 U.S. Hwy. 2E, 406/756-5834

Best Steaks
First Avenue West
139 First Ave. W., 406/755-4441
Hennessy's Restaurant
1701 U.S. Hwy. 93S, 406/755-6100
Montana Grill
5480 U.S. Hwy. 93S, Somers, 406/857-3889

Best Vietnamese Food
Alley Connection Restaurant
22 First St. W., 406/752-7077

LEWISTOWN, MT

Best Burgers
Four Aces Casino and Restaurant
508 First Ave. N., 406/538-9744

Best Casual Dining
Dash Inn
207 NE Main St., 406/538-3892

Best Dinner
Hackamore Casino and Lounge
U.S. Hwy. 87W, 406/538-5685

M

Best Homestyle Food
Empire Cafe
  214 W. Main St., 406/538-9912

Best Italian Food
Main Street Bistro
  122 W. Main St., 406/538-3666

Best Mexican Food
Taco Time
  501 E. Main St., 406/538-3435

Best Pizza
Howard's Pizza
  116 Sixth Ave. N., 406/538-2164
Little Big Men Pizza
  630 NE Main St., 406/538-2433

Best Salad/Salad Bar
Little Big Men Pizza
  630 NE Main St., 406/538-2433
Yogo Garden Restaurant
  211 E. Main St., 406/538-8721

Best Sandwiches
Simply Divine
  301 W. Broadway St., 406/538-7069
Whole Famdamily Restaurant
  206 W. Main St., 406/538-5161

Best Seafood
Sportsman Restaurant
  1660 W. Main St., 406/538-9053

Best Southwestern Food
Poor Man's Southwestern Cafe
  413 W. Main St., 406/538-4277

MILES CITY, MT

Best All-You-Can-Eat Buffet
New Hunan Chinese and American Restaurant
  716 N. Earling Ave., 406/232-3338

Best Breakfast
Cellar Casino
  5 N. Eighth St., 406/232-5611
Four B's Restaurant
  1406 S. Haynes Ave., 406/232-5772

Best Chinese Food
New Hunan Chinese and American Restaurant
  716 N. Earling Ave., 406/232-3338

Best Family Restaurant
Four B's Restaurant
  1406 S. Haynes Ave., 406/232-5772
Gallagher's Family Restaurant
  1215 S. Haynes Ave., 406/232-0099
Munchies
  1219 S. Haynes Ave., 406/232-1334

Best Sandwiches
Big Al's Sandwich Joint
  14 N. Eighth St., 406/232-1919

M

Best Seafood
Club 519
519 Main St., 406/232-5133

Best Steaks
Cellar Casino
5 N. Eighth St., 406/232-5611
Club 519
519 Main St., 406/232-5133

MISSOULA, MT

Best All-You-Can-Eat Buffet
Country Harvest Buffet
Southgate Mall, 2901 Brooks St., 406/728-6040

Best American Food
Del's Place
400 E. Broadway St., 406/728-0090

Best Atmosphere
Shadow's Keep
102 Ben Hogan Dr., 406/728-5132

Best Bar
Depot Restaurant and Bar
201 Railroad St. W., 406/728-9742

Best Brewpub
Iron Horse Brew Pub
100 Railroad St. W., 406/728-8866

Best Burgers
Missoula Club
139 W. Main St., 406/728-3740

Best Casual Dining
Nine Mile House
I-90, Exit 82, Nine Mile Rd., Nine Mile,
406/626-5668

Best Chinese Food
Mings
1049 W. Central Ave., 406/728-9000

Best Coffee/Coffeehouse
Break Espresso
432 N. Higgins Ave., 406/728-7300
Food for Thought
540 Daly Ave., 406/721-6033

Best Desserts
Alleycat Grill
125A W. Main St., 406/728-3535

Best Diner
Uptown Diner
120 N. Higgins Ave., 406/542-2449

Best French Food
The Bridge
515 S. Higgins Ave., 406/542-0002

Best Italian Food
Red Pies Over Montana
424 N. Higgins Ave., 406/549-7434

M

Best Lunch
Doc's Gourmet Sandwich Shop
   214 N. Higgins Ave., 406/542-7414

Best Mexican Food
Casa Pablo's
   147 W. Broadway St., 406/721-3854

Best Pizza
Red Pies Over Montana
   424 N. Higgins Ave., 406/549-7434

Best Romantic Dining
Alleycat Grill
   125A W. Main St., 406/728-3535

Best Southwestern Food
Old Post Pub and Pasta Parlor
   103 W. Spruce St., 406/721-7399

Best Sports Bar
Press Box Casino
   835 E. Broadway St., 406/721-1212

Best Steaks
Guy's Cold Creek Steak House
   6600 U.S. Hwy. 12W, Lolo, 406/273-2622

Best Sunday Brunch
Edgewater Dining Room
   Doubletree Hotel, 100 Madison St., 406/728-3100

Best Thai Food
Thai Spicy
   206 W. Main St., 406/543-0260
The Mustard Seed
   419 W. Front St., 406/728-7825

Nebraska

BEATRICE, NE

Best Breakfast
Beatrice Inn Motel Restaurant
   3500 N. Sixth St., 402/223-4074

Best Burgers
Michael J's Bar and Grill
   831 W. Court St., 402/228-9892

Best Chinese Food
Mar's Fine Foods
   2205 N. Sixth St., 402/223-2965

Best Coffee/Coffeehouse
Brickery Coffeehouse
   503 Court St., 402/228-3474

Best Continental Food
Black Crow
   405 Court St., 402/228-7200

Best Ice Cream/Yogurt
Goodrich Dairy
   817 Court St., 402/228-3677

Best Italian Food
Valentino's
   701 Court St., 402/223-3573

Best Restaurant in Town
Black Crow
   405 Court St., 402/228-7200

BROKEN BOW, NE

Best All-You-Can-Eat Buffet
Tumbleweed Cafe
   850 E. E St., 308/872-5454

Best Barbecue/Ribs
Lobby Restaurant and Lounge
  509 E. E St., 308/872-3363

Best Family Restaurant
Tumbleweed Cafe
  850 E St., 308/872-5454

Best Ice Cream/Yogurt
Dairy Corner Restaurant
  551 S. E St., 308/872-5950

Best Pizza
Casey's General Store
  125 S. E St., 308/872-9308

Best Seafood
Lobby Restaurant and Lounge
  509 S. Ninth Ave., 308/872-3363

Best Steaks
Lobby Restaurant and Lounge
  509 S. Ninth Ave., 308/872-3363

FREMONT, NE

Best American Food
Nick's Main Street Grill
  439 N. Main St., 402/727-9600

Best Chinese Food
Happy Inn Restaurant
  1035 E. 23rd St., 402/721-4711

Best Restaurant in Town
KC's Cafe and Bar
  631 N. Park Ave., 402/721-3353

Best Sandwiches
Irv's Deli and More
  35 W. Sixth St., 402/721-2015

GRAND ISLAND, NE

Best All-You-Can-Eat Buffet
Valentino's
  2245 N. Webb Rd., 308/382-7711

Best Breakfast
Country Kitchen
  3404 W. Thirteenth St., 308/382-7022
Tommy's Restaurant
  1325 S. Locust St., 308/381-0440

Best Chinese Food
Hunan Chinese Restaurant
  2249 N. Webb Rd., 308/384-6964
Yen Ching Chinese Restaurant
  610 W. Second St., 308/384-3020
  2623 S. Locust St., 308/384-8298

Best Homestyle Food
Conoco Motel Cafe
  2109 W. Second St., 308/382-9621

Best Italian Food
Nonna's Palazzo Restaurant
  820 W. Second St., 308/384-3029

Best Mexican Food
Dos Hermanos
  3311 W. Stolley Park Rd., 308/382-1080
El Tapatio
  2610 S. Locust St., 308/381-4511

Best Pizza
Valentino's
  2245 N. Webb Rd., 308/382-7711

Best Salad/Salad Bar
Western Charloin Steak
  1201 S. Locust St., 308/382-9011

Best Seafood
Dreisbach's
  1137 S. Locust St., 308/382-5450

Best Steaks
Dreisbach's
  1137 S. Locust St., 308/382-5450
Library Restaurant
  2530 Saint Patrick Ave., 308/381-1115

N

HASTINGS, NE

Best All-You-Can-Eat Buffet
Lo Rayne's Restaurant and Lounge
  1216 W. J St., 402/463-2784

Best American Food
Bernardo's Steakhouse and Lounge
  1109 S. Baltimore Ave., 402/463-4666

Best Breakfast
Garden Cafe
  2201 Osborne Dr. E., 402/463-8387

Best Chinese Food
Hunan Chinese Restaurant
  2727 W. Second St., Ste. 302, 402/463-4040

Best Dinner
Bernardo's Steakhouse and Lounge
  1109 S. Baltimore Ave., 402/463-4666
Taylor's Steak House
  1609 N. Kansas Ave., 402/462-8000

Best Homestyle Food
OK Cafe
  806 W. Sixteenth St., 402/461-4663

Best Lunch
Garden Cafe
  2201 Osborne Dr. E., 402/463-8387

Best Mexican Food
La Mejicana
  627 W. First St., 402/463-0606

Best Restaurant in Town
Back Rib Lounge
  2727 W. Second St., Ste. 440, 402/463-0546

Barrel Bar Lounge
  1200 E. South St., 402/463-9158
Big Dally's Deli
  801 W. Second St., 402/463-7666
Garden Cafe
  2201 Osborne Dr. E., 402/463-8387
Murphy's Wagon Wheel
  107 N. Lincoln Ave., 402/463-3011
OK Cafe
  806 W. Sixteenth St., 402/461-4663
Old Fashioned Garden Cafe
  2201 Osborne Dr., 402/463-8387
Taylor's Steak House
  1609 N. Kansas Ave., 402/462-8000

KEARNEY, NE

Best American Food
Lodge Restaurant
  1401 Second Ave., 308/234-2729

Best Breakfast
Country Kitchen
  407 Second Ave., 308/234-4531

Best Casual Dining
Cellar Bar and Grill
  3901 Second Ave., 308/236-6541
Habitat Restaurant
  121 W. 46th St., 308/237-2405

Best Continental Food
Alley Rose
  2013 Central Ave., 308/234-1261

Best Desserts
Simply Desserts
  2318 First Ave., 308/236-8288
The French Cafe
  2202 Central Ave., Kaufman Centre, 308/234-6808

Best Family Restaurant
Apple Annie's
  1010 Third Ave., 308/236-6550

Best Lunch
The French Cafe
  2202 Central Ave., Kaufman Centre, 308/234-6808

Best Steaks
Grandpa's Steakhouse
  Hwy. 44S, 308/237-2882

Best Sunday Brunch
Captain's Table Restaurant
  110 Second Ave., 308/237-5971

LINCOLN, NE

Best Chinese Food
House of Hunan Restaurant
  5601 S. 56th St., 402/423-8079
  4900 O St., 402/467-2393

Imperial Palace
 701 N. 27th St., 402/474-2688
Mr. Panda
 2900 N. 70th St., 402/464-8818

Best Coffee/Coffeehouse
Bagels and Joe
 1339 O St., 402/477-6266
 4701E Old Cheney Rd., 402/423-7797
The Mill
 800 P St., 402/475-5522

Best Dinner
Lazlo's Brewery and Grill
 710 P St., 402/434-5636

Best Greek/Mediterranean Food
George's Gyros
 1400 O St., 402/476-7147
Kuhl's Restaurant
 1038 O St., 402/476-1311
Pappa John's Family Restaurant
 114 S. Fourteenth St., 402/477-7657

Best Ice Cream/Yogurt
Colby Ridge Popcorn and Yogurt
 233 N. 48th St., 402/467-5811
 1126 S St., 402/477-6864
 3201 Pioneers Blvd., 402/489-9141
Goodrich Dairy
 1126 South St., 402/477-6864
 5501 Holdrege St., 402/466-1755
 5820 Fremont St., 402/464-8442
 4240 S. 48th St., 402/489-0149
I Can't Believe It's Yogurt
 101 N. Fourteenth St., 402/475-9117
 6940 Van Dorn St., Ste. 107, 402/489-9116

Best Italian Food
Grisanti's Restaurant
 6820 O St., 402/464-8444
Valentino's
 3920 W. Kearney St., 402/470-3800
 3457 Holdrege St., 402/467-3611

Best Lunch
Bum Steer Steaks
 6440 O St., 402/467-5110
Garden Cafe
 6891 A St., 402/434-3750
Lazlo's Brewery and Grill
 710 P St., 402/474-2337

Best Mexican Food
La Paz Mexican Restaurant
 321 N. Cotner Blvd., 402/466-9111
Tico's
 317 S. Seventeenth St., 402/475-1048

Best Seafood
Inn Harm's Way
 201 N. Seventh St., 402/438-3033

N

Best Sports Bar
Bleachers
  5601 S. 56th St., Ste. 21, 402/423-5381
Brewsky's Food and Spirits
  1602 S St., 402/438-2739
Sportscasters Bar and Grill
  3048 N. 70th St., 402/466-6679

Best Steaks
Misty's Restaurant and Lounge
  5508 S. 56th St., Ste. 5, 402/423-2288
  6235 Havelock Ave., 402/466-8424
The Steak House
  3441 Adams St., 402/466-2472

Best Sunday Brunch
Grandmother's Restaurant and Lounge
  6940 A St., 402/483-7855
Valentino's
  multiple locations

NORFOLK, NE

Best American Food
Sports Den
  715 Country Club Rd., 402/379-1111

Best Breakfast
Country Kitchen
  1221 Omaha Ave., 402/371-0477
Village Inn
  1915 Krenzien Dr., 402/371-8486

Best Chinese Food
China Gate
  1399 Michigan Ave., 402/379-3177
Panda Garden
  720 Benjamin Ave., 402/379-2013

Best Dinner
Brass Lantern
  1018 S. Ninth St., 402/371-2500
Prenger's Restaurant
  115 E. Norfolk Ave., 402/379-1900
Uptown Ballroom
  326 Norfolk Ave., 402/371-7171

Best Family Restaurant
Country Kitchen
  1221 Omaha Ave., 402/371-0477
Granary
  922 S. Thirteenth Pl., 402/371-5334
Mary's Restaurant
  801 E. Norfolk Ave., 402/371-5525

Best Fine Dining
Brass Lantern
  1018 S. Ninth St., 402/371-2500
Prenger's Restaurant
  115 E. Norfolk Ave., 402/379-1900
Uptown Ballroom
  326 Norfolk Ave., 402/371-7171

Best Restaurant Meal Value
Granary
   922 S. Thirteenth Pl., 402/371-5334

Best Sports Bar
Sports Den
   715 Country Club Rd., 402/379-1111

Best Sunday Brunch
Valentino's
   1025 S. Thirteenth St., 402/379-2500

NORTH PLATTE, NE

Best American Food
Hobb'E's
   217 E. Sixth St., 308/534-9998
Skelly Inn
   109 Rodeo Rd., 308/532-8720

Best Breakfast
Brick Wall
   507 N. Dewey St., 308/532-7545
Country Kitchen Restaurant
   202 W. Eugene Ave., 308/534-4710

Best Chinese Food
Golden Dragon
   120 W. Leota St., 308/532-8200
House of Oriental Food
   508 N. Jeffers St., 308/534-0422

Best Homestyle Food
Merrick's Ranch House
   1220 E. Fourth St., 308/532-8200
Roger's Fine Foods
   1401 S. Jeffers St., 308/534-3595

Best Mexican Food
La Casita Cafe
   1911 E. Fourth St., 308/534-4710
Little Mexico
   104 N. Jeffers St., 308/534-3052

Best Pizza
Valentino's
   802 S. Dewey St., 308/534-5367

Best Restaurant in Town
Airport Inn
   Lee Bird Field, 308/534-4340
Camino Inn
   2102 S. Jeffers St., 308/532-9090
Merrick's Ranch House
   1220 E. Fourth St., 308/532-8200
Stockman Inn
   1402 S. Jeffers St., 308/534-3630
The Brick Wall
   507 N. Dewey St., 308/532-7545
Depot Grill and Pub
   520 N. Jeffers St., 308/534-7844

Best Sandwiches
Philadelphia Bar and Grill
  1001 S. Dewey St., 308/534-6677

OMAHA, NE

Best American Food
Bohemian Cafe
  1406 S. Thirteenth St., 402/342-9838
Gallagher's Restaurant
  10730 Pacific St., 402/393-1421
Jams Bar and Grill
  7814 Dodge St., 402/399-8300
M's Pub
  422 S. Eleventh St., 402/342-2550
Old Chicago
  13110 Birch Dr., 402/445-9393
Upstream Brewing Company
  514 S. Eleventh St., 402/344-0200

Best Breakfast
Garden Cafe
  14330 U St., 402/895-5938
  1224 S. 103rd St., 402/397-1991
  3321 S. 72nd St., 402/397-3384
  11040 Oak St., 402/393-0252
  1212 Harney St., 402/422-1574
Market Basket
  911 S. 87th Ave., 402/397-1100

Best Burgers
Coyote's
  1217 Howard St., 402/345-2047
Goldberg's
  5008 Dodge St., 402/556-2006
  2936 S. 132nd St., 402/333-1086

Best Chinese Food
Chez Chong
  1015 S. Tenth St., 402/346-3635
House of Hunan
  2405 S. 132nd St., 402/334-5382
Imperial Palace
  11200 Davenport St., 402/330-3888
  7300 Dodge St., 402/393-1689
Imperial Palace Express
  10000 California St., 402/391-3885
Royal China Restaurant
  9006 Maple St., 402/571-6910

Best Continental Food
French Cafe
  1017 Howard St., 402/341-3547
La Strada 72
  3125 S. 72nd St., 402/397-8389
V. Mertz
  1022 Howard St., 402/345-8980

Best Dinner
Gorat's Steak House
  4917 Center St., 402/551-3733

Jams Bar and Grill
   7814 Dodge St., 402/399-8300
The Drover
   2121 S. 72nd St., 402/391-7440

Best Homestyle Food
Bohemian Cafe
   1406 S. Thirteenth St., 402/342-9838
Garden Cafe
   1212 Harney St., 402/422-1574
   14330 U St., 402/895-5938
   1224 S. 103rd St., 402/397-1991
   3321 S. 72nd St., 402/397-3384
   11040 Oak St., 402/393-0252

Best Italian Food
Cafe Di Coppia
   120 Regency Pkwy., 402/392-2806
Lo Sole Mio Ristorante Italiano
   3001 S. 32nd Ave., 402/345-5656
Mister C's Steakhouse
   5319 N. 30th St., 402/451-1998
Pasta Amore
   11027 Prairie Brook Rd., 402/391-2585
Vincenzo's Ristorante
   1818 N. 144th St., 402/498-3889
Vivace
   1110 Howard St., 402/342-2050

Best Mexican Food
Buena Vida
   7635 Cass St., 402/392-1021
El Alamo
   4917 S. 24th St., 402/731-8969
Fernando's
   380 N. 114th St., 402/330-5707
Julio's
   510 S. Thirteenth St., 402/345-6921
   7555 Pacific St., 402/399-8059
   13043 Arbor St., 402/330-2110
   5402 N. 90th St., 402/572-5223
O.J.'s Cafe
   9201 N. 30th St., 402/451-3266
Trini's
   1020 Howard St., 402/346-8400

Best Pizza
Big Fred's
   1301 S. 119th St., 402/333-4414
La Casa Pizzeria
   8216 Grover St., 402/556-6464
   4432 Leavenworth St., 402/556-6464
Zio's Pizzeria
   1213 Howard St., 402/344-2222
   7924 W. Dodge Rd., 402/391-1881
   13463 W. Center Rd., 402/330-1444

Best Romantic Dining
Amadeus
   Hotel Aquila, 1615 Howard St., 402/231-6019

N

Bistro At The Market
406 S. Twelfth St., 402/346-4060
French Cafe
1017 Howard St., 402/341-3547
Maxine's Restaurant
1616 Dodge St., 402/346-7600

Best Steaks
Austin's Steakhouse
1101 Harney St., 402/344-3585
1414 S. 72nd St., 402/397-0751
11224 W. Dodge Rd., 402/498-8502
12020 Anne St., 402/896-5373
Brother Sebastian's
1350 S. 119th St., 402/330-0300
Johnny's Cafe
4702 S. 27th St., 402/731-4774
Lone Star
3040 S. 143 Plz., 402/333-1563
655 N. 114th St., 402/493-1331
Omaha Prime Restaurant
415 S. Eleventh St., 402/341-7040

Best Sunday Brunch
Chardonnay
Marriott Regency, 10220 Regency Circle,
402/399-9000
Maxine's Restaurant
1616 Dodge St., 402/346-7600

Best View While Dining
Charlie's on the Lake
4150 S. 144th St., 402/894-9411
Maxine's Restaurant
1616 Dodge St., 402/346-7600

SCOTTSBLUFF, NE

Best All-You-Can-Eat Buffet
Buffalo Steakhouse
Scottsbluff Inn, 1901 21st Ave., 308/635-3111

Best Bar
O'Hara's Restaurant
2302 Frontage Rd., 308/635-0050

Best Breakfast
Country Kitchen
3485 Tenth St., Gering, 308/635-3800
Grampy's Pancake House
1802 E. Twentieth Pl., 308/632-6906

Best Chinese Food
Oriental House
1502 E. Twentieth St., 308/632-3922

Best Coffee/Coffeehouse
Java Hut
1813 Avenue A, 308/632-1522

Best Family Restaurant
Woodshed
18 E. Sixteenth St., 308/635-3684

Best Homestyle Food
Country Kitchen
  3485 Tenth St., Gering, 308/635-3800

Best Steaks
Gaslight Restaurant
  3315 Tenth St., Gering, 308/632-7315

VALENTINE, NE

Best Breakfast
Home Cafe
  103 W. Hwy. 20, 402/376-3222

Best Coffee/Coffeehouse
Ambrosia Garden
  105 N. Main St., 402/376-1927
Town Square
  269 N. Main St., 402/376-1424

Best Homestyle Food
Home Cafe
  103 W. Hwy. 20, 402/376-3222

Best Ice Cream/Yogurt
Ambrosia Garden
  105 N. Main St., 402/376-1927
Frosty Drive-In
  223 S. Main St., 402/376-2786

Best Sandwiches
Ambrosia Garden
  105 N. Main St., 402/376-1927
Celebrity Steak House
  103 W. Hwy. 20, 402/376-3222

Best Seafood
Jordan's Fine Dining
  E. Hwy. 20, 402/376-1255

Best Steaks
Jordan's Fine Dining
  E. Hwy. 20, 402/376-1255
Peppermill Restaurant
  112 N. Main St., 402/376-1440

N

Nevada

CARSON CITY, NV

Best American Food
Bodine's
5650 S. Carson St., 702/885-0303

Best Barbecue/Ribs
Pop's Bar-B-Que
224 S. Carson St., 702/884-4411

Best Breakfast
City Cafe and Bakery
701 S. Carson St., 702/882-2253
Heidi's Family Restaurant
1020 N. Carson St., 702/882-0486

Best Burgers
Juicy's Giant Burgers
2000 N. Carson St., 702/883-5600

Best Chinese Food
East Ocean Restaurant
1214 N. Carson St., 702/883-6668
Panda Kitchen
2416 Hwy. 50E, 702/882-8128

Best Coffee/Coffeehouse
Java Joe's
319 N. Carson St., 702/883-4004

Best Continental Food
Adele's
1112 N. Carson St., 702/882-3353

Best Family Restaurant
Thurman's Ranch House
2943 Hwy. 50E, 702/883-1773

Best Fine Dining
Bonanza Ranch
  3700 N. Carson St., 702/883-9696

Best Homestyle Food
Buffalo Club Grille and Bar
  2729 N. Carson St., 702/883-8488
Lone Eagle Grill
  111 Country Club Dr., Incline Village,
    702/832-3250
T's Rotisserie
  901 Tahoe Blvd., Incline Village, 702/831-2832

Best Italian Food
Garibaldi's
  301 N. Carson St., 702/884-4574

Best Lunch
Nick's Pizza
  303 N. Carson St., 702/885-8008
Tito's Restaurant Mexican
  444 E. William St., 702/885-0309

Best Mexican Food
El Charro Avitia
  4389 S. Carson St., 702/883-6261
Mi Casa Too
  3809 N. Carson St., 702/882-4080
Tequila Dan's Tex-Mex
  3449 S. Carson St., 702/885-7475

Best Outdoor Dining
Joe Garlic's Restaurant
  302 S. Carson St., 702/883-5775
Pop's Bar-B-Que
  224 S. Carson St., 702/884-4411

Best Restaurant in Town
Station Grill and Rotisserie
  1105 S. Carson St., 702/883-8400

Best Southwestern Food
Cafe Del Rio
  400 S. Carson St., 702/885-9088

Best Steaks
Heiss' Steak and Seafood House
  107 E. Telegraph St., 702/882-9012

ELKO, NV

Best Bar
Mattie's
  2525 Mountain City Hwy., 702/753-3877

Best Breakfast
Commercial Hotel and Casino
  345 Fourth St., 702/738-3181
Stockmen's Motor Hotel
  340 Commercial St., 702/738-5141

Best Burgers
Cimarron West Family Restaurant
  673 Cimarron Way, 702/753-8328

Best Coffee/Coffeehouse
Coffee Mug
 1309 Idaho St., 702/738-5999
Cowboy Joe
 376 Fifth St., 702/753-5612

Best Desserts
Commercial Hotel and Casino
 345 Fourth St., 702/738-3181
D'Orazio Italian Gardens
 217 Idaho St., 702/738-7088

Best Homestyle Food
Mattie's
 2525 Mountain City Hwy., 702/753-3877

Best Inexpensive Meal
Elko Dinner Station
 1430 Idaho St., 702/738-8528

Best Italian Food
D'Orazio Italian Gardens
 217 Idaho St., 702/738-7088

Best Salad/Salad Bar
Cimarron West Family Restaurant
 673 Cimarron Way, 702/753-8328

Best Sandwiches
Cowboy Joe
 376 Fifth St., 702/753-5612
Machi's
 778 Commercial St., 702/738-9772

Best Seafood
Pine Lodge
 Main St., Lamoille, 702/753-6363

Best Steaks
Pine Lodge
 Main St., Lamoille, 702/753-6363

ELY, NV

Best Breakfast
Cell Block Dining Room
 211 Fifth St., 702/289-3033
Kountry Kitchen Restaurant
 940 Avenue F, 702/289-8854

Best Burgers
Hotel Nevada and Gambling Hall
 501 Aultman St., 702/289-6665
Jerry's Restaurant
 2160 Aultman St., 702/289-3905

Best Chinese Food
Good Friends Chinese Restaurant
 1455 Aultman St., 702/289-4888
Orient Express
 562 Aultman St., 702/289-3431

Best Coffee/Coffeehouse
Flower Basket
 566 Aultman St., 702/289-2828

N

Best Family Restaurant
Cell Block Dining Room
   211 Fifth St., 702/289-3033
Hotel Nevada and Gambling Hall
   501 Aultman St., 702/289-6665

Best Homestyle Food
Kountry Kitchen Restaurant
   940 Avenue F, 702/289-8854
Silver State Restaurant
   1204 Aultman St., 702/289-2712

Best Ice Cream/Yogurt
Frosty Stand
   49A N. Fourth St., McGill, 702/235-7575
Ice Cream Fantasy
   301 Aultman St., 702/289-2585

Best Pizza
Shy Simon's Pizza
   905 Avenue F, 702/289-4162

Best Salad/Salad Bar
Evah's Copper Queen Restaurant
   Ramada Inn, 701 Avenue I, 702/289-4271

Best Seafood
Hotel Nevada and Gambling Hall
   501 Aultman St., 702/289-6665

Best Steaks
Evah's Copper Queen Restaurant
   Ramada Inn, 701 Avenue I, 702/289-4271
Hotel Nevada and Gambling Hall
   501 Aultman St., 702/289-6665

N

HENDERSON, NV

Best Late-Night Food
Renata's
   4451 E. Sunset Rd., Ste. 1, 702/435-4000

Best Restaurant in Town
Renata's
   4451 E. Sunset Rd., Ste. 1, 702/435-4000

LAS VEGAS, NV

Best All-You-Can-Eat Buffet
Carnival World Buffet
   Rio Suites Hotel and Casino, 3700 W. Flamingo
      Rd., 702/252-7698
Market Street Buffet
   Texas Gambling Hall and Casino, 2101 Texas Star
      Ln., North Las Vegas, 702/631-1000
Treasure Island
   3300 Las Vegas Blvd. S., 702/894-7111

Best American Food
Country Inn
   1401 S. Rainbow Blvd., 702/254-0520
   2425 E. Desert Inn Rd., 702/731-5035
Fog City Diner
   325 Hughes Center Dr., 702/737-0200

Molly's Country Kitchen
301 Fremont St., 702/388-2400
Poppa Gar's
1624 W. Oakey Blvd., 702/384-4513
The Tillerman
2245 E. Flamingo Rd., 702/731-4036

Best Barbecue/Ribs
Memphis Championship Barbecue
4379 Las Vegas Blvd. N., 702/644-0000

Best Breakfast
Hash House
6000 Spring Mountain Rd., 702/873-9479
Jamms Restaurant
2227 N. Rampart Blvd., 702/228-4151
Original Pancake House
4833 W. Charleston Blvd., 702/259-7755

Best Burgers
Fatburger
3765 Las Vegas Blvd. S., 702/736-4733
4851 W. Charleston Blvd., 702/870-4933
Red Robin Grill and Spirits
151 N. Nellis Blvd., 702/453-8611
Still
9495 Las Vegas Blvd. S., 702/361-7012

Best Chinese Food
Emperor's Table
4670 S. Decatur Blvd., 702/876-9588
Full Ho Chinese Cuisine
240 N. Jones Blvd., 702/878-2378
PF Chang's China Bistro
4165 Paradise Rd., 602/949-2610

Best Coffee/Coffeehouse
Cathay House
5300 Spring Mountain Rd., 702/876-3838
Enigma Cafe
918A S. Fourth St., 702/386-0999
Jitters
2457 E. Tropicana Ave., 702/898-0056
Peppermill Inn
2985 Las Vegas Blvd. S., 702/735-4177

Best Delicatessen
Celebrity Deli
4055 S. Maryland Pkwy., 702/733-7827
Max C's Place
603 Las Vegas Blvd. S., 702/382-6292

Best Desserts
Cadillac Grille
2801 N. Tenaya Way, 702/255-5555
Kenya's Gourmet Bakery
6400 S. Eastern Ave., Ste. 5, 702/261-0900
Marie Callender's
4875 W. Flamingo Rd., 702/365-6226

Best Eclectic Menu
Nicky Blair's Restaurant
3800 Howard Hughes Pkwy., 702/735-8622

N

Best Family Restaurant
Country Inn
 1401 S. Rainbow Blvd., 702/254-0520
 2425 E. Desert Inn Rd., 702/731-5035
Hush Puppy
 7185 W. Charleston Blvd., 702/363-5988
 1820 N. Ellis Blvd., 702/438-0005

Best French Food
Andre's
 401 S. Sixth St., 702/385-5016
Crepes Pierrette
 4794 S. Eastern Ave., 702/434-1234

Best Homestyle Food
Big Mama's Cooking
 3765 Las Vegas Blvd. S., 702/597-1616

Best Ice Cream/Yogurt
Danielle's Chocolates and Ice Cream
 West Sahara Town Plz., 638 W. Sahara Ave.,
  702/871-6871
Leatherby's Family Creamery
 577 E. Sahara Ave., 702/641-6088
Luv-It Frozen Custard
 505 E. Oakley Blvd., 702/384-6452

Best Indian Food
Gandhi India's Cuisine
 4080 Paradise Rd., 702/734-0094

Best Italian Food
North Beach Cafe
 2605 S. Decatur Blvd., 702/247-9530

Best Japanese Food
Hamada of Japan
 598 E. Flamingo Rd., 702/733-3005
Kabuki Japanese Restaurant
 1150 E. Twain Ave., 702/733-0066
Osaka Japanese Restaurant
 4205 W. Sahara Ave., 702/876-4988

Best Late-Night Food
Play It Again Sam
 4120 Spring Mountain Rd., 702/876-1550
Port Tack
 3190 W. Sahara Ave., 702/873-3345
Tap House
 5589 W. Charleston Blvd., 702/870-2111

Best Mexican Food
La Fiesta-A Mexican Restaurant
 2550 S. Rainbow Blvd., 702/871-5172
Macayo Vegas
 1375 E. Tropicana Ave., 702/736-1898
 1741 E. Charleston Blvd., 702/382-5605
 4457 W. Charleston Blvd., 702/878-7347
Pancho's Mexican Food
 3720 E. Sunset Rd., Ste. 110, 702/898-8488
Ricardo's
 2380 E. Tropicana Ave., 702/798-4515
 4300 Meadows Ln., 702/870-1088

4930 W. Flamingo Rd., 702/871-7119
Viva Mercado
6182 W. Flamingo Rd., 702/871-8826
Z Tejas Grill
3824 Paradise Rd., 702/732-1660

Best Other Ethnic Food
Marrakech Restaurant (Moroccan)
3900 Paradise Rd., 702/737-5611
Red Sea (African)
2226 Paradise Rd., 702/893-1740

Best Outdoor Dining
Bertolini's Authentic Italian
3500 Las Vegas Blvd. S., 702/735-4663
Cafe Michelle
1350 E. Flamingo Rd., 702/735-8686
Cafe Nicolle
4760 W. Sahara Ave., 702/870-7675
Kiefer's Atop The Carriage House
105 E. Harmon Ave., 702/739-8000

Best Pizza
Fasolini's Pizza Cafe
222 S. Decatur Blvd., 702/877-0071
The Cook's Shop Pizzeria
3375 E. Russell Rd., 702/451-5888

Best Place to Take the Kids
Blueberry Hill
1723 E. Charleston Blvd., 702/382-3330
1280 S. Decatur Blvd., 702/877-8867
5000 E. Bonanza Rd., 702/435-5555
3790 E. Flamingo Rd., 702/433-9999

Best Romantic Dining
Andre's
401 S. Sixth St., 702/385-5016
Kiefer's Atop The Carriage House
105 E. Harmon Ave., 702/739-8000
The Tillerman
2245 E. Flamingo Rd., 702/731-4036

Best Salad/Salad Bar
Wild Oats Community Market
6720 W. Sahara Ave., 702/253-7050

Best Sandwiches
Capriotti's Sandwich Shop
324 W. Sahara Ave., 702/474-0229
3981 E. Sunset Rd., 702/474-0229
Hush Puppy
1820 N. Nellis Blvd., 702/438-0005
7185 W. Charleston Blvd., 702/363-5988

Best Seafood
Landry's Seafood House
2160 E. Sahara Ave., 702/251-0101
The Tillerman
2245 E. Flamingo Rd., 702/731-4036

N

Best Steaks
Hilton Steakhouse
    The Hilton Inn, 3000 Paradise Rd., 702/732-5111
Hungry Hunter
    2380 S. Rainbow Blvd., 702/873-0433

Best Thai Food
Lotus of Siam
    953 E. Sahara Ave., 702/735-4463
Tanya Restaurant
    210 W. Sahara Ave., 702/338-9923
Thai Spice Restaurant
    4433 W. Flamingo Rd., 702/362-5308

Best Vegetarian Food
Kathy's Ranch Market
    3455 E. Flamingo Rd., 702/434-8115
    6720 W. Sahara Ave., 702/253-7050
Wild Oats Community Market
    3455 E. Flamingo Rd., 702/434-8115

RENO, NV

Best All-You-Can-Eat Buffet
Chefs' Pavilion Buffet
    Eldorado Hotel, 345 N. Virginia St., 702/786-5700
Toucan Charlie's Buffet and Grill
    Clarion Hotel and Casino, 3800 S. Virginia St.,
        702/825-4700

Best American Food
Branding Iron Cafe
    4720 N. Virginia St., 702/323-2724
Heidi's Family Restaurant
    8195 S. Virginia St., 702/852-0113
    2450 S. Virginia St., 702/826-3336
Landrum's Hamburger System
    6770 S. Virginia St., 702/852-5464
Truckee River Bar and Grill
    3466 Lakeside Dr., 702/825-5585
    1113 California Ave., 702/786-7971

Best Bar
Fireside Lounge
    2707 S. Virginia St., 702/826-2121

Best Breakfast
Peppermill Hotel Casino
    2707 S. Virginia St., 702/826-2121

Best Brewpub
Brew Brothers Microbrewery
    Eldorado Hotel, 345 N. Virginia St., 702/786-5700
Copper Summit Brewing Company
    7671 S. Virginia St., 702/851-2739

Best Burgers
Juicy's Giant Hamburgers
    301 S. Wells Ave., 702/322-2600

Best Casual Dining
Brew Brothers Microbrewery
    Eldorado Hotel, 345 N. Virginia St., 702/786-5700

Best Chinese Food
Asian Garden Restaurant
    1945 S. Virginia St., 702/825-5510

Best Coffee/Coffeehouse
Java Centrale
    5000 Smithridge Dr., 702/828-9194
    7695 S. Virginia St., 702/851-3730

Best Eclectic Menu
Cafe Soleil
    4796 Caughlin Pkwy., 702/828-6444

Best Health-Conscious Menu
Blue Heron Restaurant and Bakery
    1901 S. Virginia St., 702/786-4110

Best Italian Food
Cafe Andreotti
    219 N. Center St., 702/786-3232
Coco Pazzo
    3446 Lakeside Dr., 702/829-9449
Davo's Italian Restaurant
    3671 Kings Row, 702/746-4411
La Strada
    345 N. Virginia St., 702/786-5700
Lavecchia Varese Restaurant
    130 West St., 702/322-7486
Two Guys From Italy
    3501 S. Virginia St., 702/826-3700

Best Lunch
Cafe Alfresco
    3800 S. Virginia St., 702/825-4700
Cafe Soleil
    4796 Caughlin Pkwy., 702/828-6444
Skyline Cafe Delivery and Catering
    3005 Skyline Blvd., 702/825-5707
Wings and Things
    3080 Mill St., 702/329-3377

Best Mexican Food
Bertha Miranda's Mexican Restaurant
    336 Mill St., 702/786-9697
Cantina Los Tres Hombres
    7111 S. Virginia St., 702/852-0202
La Pinata Mexican Restaurant
    1575 Vassar St., 702/323-3210
Mi Casa Too
    2205 W. Fourth St., 702/323-6466

Best Other Ethnic Food
Palais De Jade (Asian)
    960 W. Moana Ln., 702/827-5233

Best Pizza
Blue Moon Gourmet Pizza
    6135 Lakeside Dr., 702/825-1120
Giorgio's Pizza
    6925 S. Virginia St., 702/853-1177
Round Table Pizza Restaurant
    1075 N. Hills Blvd., 702/677-2100

N

Best Seafood
Rapscallion Seafood House and Bar
  1555 S. Wells Ave., 702/323-1211

Best Steaks
Christmas Tree
  20007 Mount Rose Hwy., 702/849-0127
John Ascuaga's Nugget
  250 Edison Way, 702/856-0644

Best Sunday Brunch
Top of the Hilton
  Flamingo Hilton, 255 N. Sierra St., 702/322-1111

Best View While Dining
Christmas Tree
  20007 Mount Rose Hwy., 702/849-0127

SPARKS, NV

Best Breakfast
Craig's Restaurant and Bar
  430 N. McCarran Blvd., 702/331-2224
Sierra Sid's 76 Auto Truck Plaza
  200 N. McCarran Blvd., 702/359-0550

Best Brewpub
Great Basin Brewing Company
  846 Victorian Ave., 702/355-7711

Best Burgers
Scooper's Drive-In
  1356 Prater Way, 702/331-6221
Western Village Inn and Casino
  815 Nichols Blvd, 702/331-1069

Best Homestyle Food
Craig's Restaurant and Bar
  430 N. McCarran Blvd., 702/331-2224
Scooper's Drive-In
  1356 Prater Way, 702/331-6221

Best Inexpensive Meal
Plantation Station Casino
  2121 Victorian Ave., 702/359-9440

Best Mexican Food
Bertha Miranda's Mexican Restaurant
  2144 Greenbrae Dr., 702/356-1310
Las Trojes Restaurant
  1279 Baring Blvd., 702/359-3300

Best Romantic Dining
Trader Dick's
  1100 Nugget Ave., 702/356-3300

Best Steaks
John Ascuaga's Nugget
  1100 Nugget Ave., 702/356-3300
Victoria's Steakhouse
  Silver Club Hotel and Casino
    1040 Victorian Ave., 702/358-4771

WINNEMUCCA, NV

Best American Food
Red Lion Restaurant
Red Lion Inn, 741 W. Winnemucca Blvd.,
702/623-2565

Best Barbecue/Ribs
Flyin' Pig Barbecue
1100 W. Winnemucca Blvd., 702/623-4104

Best Breakfast
The Griddle
460 W. Winnemucca Blvd., 702/623-2977

Best Burgers
Dave's Dugout
329 E. Winnemucca Blvd., 702/623-2763

Best Chinese Food
Chinese Garden
1061 W. Fourth St., 702/623-6777

Best Mexican Food
Los Sanchez
Raley's Shopping Plaza, 1105 W. Fourth St.,
702/625-2000

Best Other Ethnic Food
Martin Hotel (Basque)
Railroad at Melarkey St., 702/623-3197
Restaurante San Fermin (Basque)
704 W. Winnemucca Blvd., 702/625-2555
Winnemucca Hotel (Basque)
95 N. Bridge St., 702/623-2908

Best Seafood
Ormachea's Dinner House
180 Melarkey St., 702/623-3455

N

New Hampshire

BERLIN, NH

Best All-You-Can-Eat Buffet
Balsam's Grand Resort Hotel
  Rte. 26, 603/255-3400

Best Atmosphere
Balsam's Grand Resort Hotel
  Rte. 26, 603/255-3400

Best Burgers
Mill Yard by Sinibaldi's
  207 E. Mason St., 603/752-6430

Best Desserts
Balsam's Grand Resort Hotel
  Rte. 26, 603/255-3400

Best Ice Cream/Yogurt
Northland Dairy Bar and Restaurant
  1808 Riverside Dr., 603/752-6210

Best Place to Take the Kids
Northland Dairy Bar and Restaurant
  1808 Riverside Dr., 603/752-6210

Best Seafood
Balsam's Grand Resort Hotel
  Rte. 26, 603/255-3400

CONCORD, NH

Best American Food
Cheers
  17 Depot St., 603/228-0180

Best Casual Dining
Harry's Steak House
  61 S. Main St., 603/229-0004

Best Chinese Food
Tea Garden Restaurant
  184 N. Main St., 603/228-4420

Best Diner
Capital City Diner
  25 Water St., 603/228-3463

Best Dinner
Angelina's
  11 Depot St., 603/228-3313
The Cat 'N Fiddle
  118 Manchester St., 603/228-8911

Best Family Restaurant
Scuffy's Family Restaurant
  25 Manchester St., 603/224-7164

Best Inexpensive Meal
Capital City Diner
  25 Water St., 603/228-3463
Veano's Italian Kitchen
  142 Loudon Rd., 603/224-2400

Best Italian Food
Angelina's
  11 Depot St., 603/228-3313
Pasta House
  11 Depot St., 603/226-4723
Veano's Italian Kitchen
  142 Loudon Rd., 603/224-2400

Best Lunch
The Cat 'N Fiddle
  118 Manchester St., 603/228-8911

Best Mexican Food
Hermanos Cocina Mexicana
  11 Hills Ave., 603/224-5669
Tio Juan's
  1 Bicentennial Sq., 603/224-2821

Best Pizza
Vinnie's Pizzaria
  200 S. Main St., 603/224-7727

Best Restaurant Meal Value
Pasta House
  11 Depot St., 603/226-4723

Best Salad/Salad Bar
Cheers
  17 Depot St., 603/228-0180

DOVER, NH

Best Breakfast
Charlotte's Copper Kettle
  499 Central Ave., 603/749-9383

Best Family Restaurant
Woodsky's
  887 Central Ave., 603/743-1811
Peppercorn's
  8 High St., Somersworth, 603/749-1470

Best Fine Dining
Ron's Place
2 Locust St., 603/749-4673

Best Lunch
Ron's Place
2 Locust St., 603/749-4673

Best Restaurant in Town
Weathervane Restaurant
2 Dover Point Rd., 603/749-2341

Best Seafood
16 Third Street Restaurant
16 Third St., 603/743-3767

Best Sports Bar
Kick-Off Sports Bar
20 Chesnut St., 603/749-2890

Best Steaks
Woodsky's
887 Central Ave., 603/743-1811

GORHAM, NH

Best Atmosphere
Birches
128 Main St., 603/466-5424

Best Breakfast
Loaf Around Bakery
19 Exchange St., 603/466-2706

Best Homestyle Food
Wilford's
117 Main St., 603/466-2380

Best Italian Food
La Bottega Saladino
152 Main St., 603/466-2520

Best Japanese Food
Yokohama Restaurant
288 Main St., 603/466-2501

Best Pizza
Mary's Pizza House
9 Cascade Flat, 603/752-6150

Best Steaks
Town and Country Motor Inn
Rural Route 2, 603/466-3315

KEENE, NH

Best Breakfast
Keene Bagel Works
120 Main St., 603/357-7751

Best Chinese Food
Imperial China
149 Emerald St., 603/357-0619

Best Coffee/Coffeehouse
Keene Bagel Works
120 Main St., 603/357-7751

N

Best Ice Cream/Yogurt
Piazza
  149 Main St., 603/352-5133

Best Italian Food
Martino's Spaghetti House
  276 West St., 603/357-0859

LACONIA, NH

Best Bar
Mame's
  8 Plymouth St., Meredith, 603/279-4631

Best Barbecue/Ribs
JT's Bar-B-Q
  Rural Route 3, 603/366-7322

Best Breakfast
Between the Bagel
  653 Main St., 603/524-0193
Soda Shoppe
  Laconia Mall, 603/524-2366

Best Burgers
JT's Bar-B-Q
  Rural Route 3, 603/366-7322

Best Family Restaurant
Mulligan's Restaurant
  Rural Route 3, Tilton, 603/528-4588

Best German Food
William Tell Inn
  Rural Route 11, 603/293-8803

Best Homestyle Food
Mulligan's Restaurant
  Rural Route 3, Tilton, 603/528-4588
Sawyer's Dairy Bar
  Rural Route 11, 603/293-4422
Soda Shoppe
  Laconia Mall, 603/524-2366
Weeks Restaurant
  331 S. Main St., 603/524-4100

Best Italian Food
Fratello's Ristorante Italiano
  799 Union Ave., 603/528-2022

Best Pizza
Giuseppe's Show Time Pizzeria
  312D Hwy. 13W, Meredith, 603/279-3313
Pizza Express
  4 Country Club Rd., 603/528-4200

Best Romantic Dining
Oliver's Bakery and Restaurant
  4 Sanborn Rd., Tilton, 603/286-7379

Best Salad/Salad Bar
Between the Bagel
  653 Main St., 603/524-0193

N

Best Sandwiches
Water Street Cafe
  141 Water St., 603/524-4144

Best Seafood
Rigione's Galley
  405 Union Ave., 603/524-0001

Best Steaks
Blackstone's
  76 Lake St., 603/524-7060
Hector's Fine Food and Spirits
  53 Beacon St., 603/524-1009
Mame's
  8 Plymouth St., Meredith, 603/279-4631

LEBANON, NH

Best Breakfast
Lou's Restaurant and Bakery
  30 S. Main St., Hanover, 603/643-3321

Best Chinese Food
Good Fortune Chinese Restaurant
  45 Hanover St., 603/448-3888

Best Coffee/Coffeehouse
Bean Gallery
  West Park on the Mall, 603/448-7302
Rosey Jeke's
  15 Lebanon St., Hanover, 603/643-3693

Best Family Restaurant
Friendly Family Restaurant
  Route 12A, West Lebanon, 603/298-7855
Riverside Grill Restaurant
  65 Riverside Dr., 603/448-2571

Best Italian Food
Sweet Tomatoes Trattoria
  1 Court St., 603/448-1711

Best Mexican Food
Shorty's Mexican Roadhouse
  10 Benning St., Ste. 1, West Lebanon,
    603/298-7200

Best Pizza
Lebanon Village Pizza
  24 Hanover St., 603/448-2772
Lui Lui's
  8 Glen Rd. W., Ste. 11, West Lebanon,
    603/298-7070

Best Sandwiches
Lebanon Village Pizza
  24 Hanover St., 603/448-2772

Best Seafood
Weathervane Seafoods
  7 Weathervane Dr., West Lebanon, 603/298-7805

Best Steaks
Jesse's Restaurant
  Lebanon Rd., Hanover, 603/643-4111

N

LITTLETON, NH

Best Atmosphere
Grand Depot Cafe
62 Cottage St., 603/444-5303
Tim-Bir Alley
Bethlehem Rd., Bethlehem, 603/444-6142

Best Coffee/Coffeehouse
Sunshine Bagel
19 Main St., 603/444-4090

Best Diner
Coffee Pot
35 Main St., 603/444-5722
Littleton Diner
170 Main St., 603/444-3994

Best Health-Conscious Menu
Cafe Munchies
363 Meadow St., 603/444-1222

Best Homestyle Food
Littleton Diner
170 Main St., 603/444-3994

N

Best Ice Cream/Yogurt
Bishop's Ice Cream Shoppe
78 Cottage St., 603/444-6039

Best Pizza
Gold House of Pizza and Greek Restaurant
77 Main St., 603/444-6190

Best Restaurant In Town
Eastgate Motor Inn
335 Cottage St., 603/444-3971
Grand Depot Cafe
62 Cottage St., 603/444-5303
Tim-Bir Alley
Bethlehem Rd., Bethlehem, 603/444-6142

Best Seafood
Clam Shell Restaurant
274 Dells Rd., 603/444-6445

Best Steaks
Clam Shell Restaurant
274 Dells Rd., 603/444-6445

MANCHESTER, NH

Best American Food
Back Room Restaurant
245 Hooksett Rd., 603/669-6890

Best Breakfast
Albee's on Amherst
36 Amherst St., 603/623-6907
Albee's on Pearl
15 Pearl St., 603/622-9015

Best Business Lunch
Aloha Restaurant
901 Hanover St., 603/647-2100

Best Chinese Food
Chen Yang Li
124 S. River Rd., 603/641-6922

Best Dinner
Back Room Restaurant
245 Hooksett Rd., 603/669-6890

Best Health-Conscious Menu
Sassafras
90 Dow St., 603/641-1862

Best Italian Food
Cafe Pavone
75 Arms Park Dr., 603/622-5488

Best Pizza
Luisa's Italian Kitchen
788 S. Willow St., 603/627-0006
Luisa's Italian Pizzeria
673 Hooksett Rd., 603/625-1331

Best Restaurant in Town
Yard Restaurant
1199 S. Mammoth Rd. Willow St., 603/623-3545

Best Salad/Salad Bar
Sassafras
90 Dow St., 603/641-1862

Best Seafood
Homestead Restaurant
176 Mammoth Rd., Londonderry, 603/437-2022

Best Steaks
99 Restaurant and Pub
1685 S. Willow St., 603/641-5999
1308 Hooksett Rd., Hooksett, 603/641-2999
Back Room Restaurant
245 Hooksett Rd., 603/669-6890
Homestead
176 Mammoth Rd., Londonderry, 603/437-2022

Best Sunday Brunch
Yard Restaurant
1199 S. Mammoth Rd., 603/623-3545

NASHUA, NH

Best American Food
Anthony's North End
28 Railroad Sq., 603/889-5797
Martha's Exchange Restaurant
185 Main St., 603/883-8781
Modern Restaurant and Lounge
116 W. Pearl St., 603/883-8422

Best Chinese Food
Golden Dragon Restaurant
300 Main St., 603/889-6122
Pearl City
6 Elm St., 603/883-8988

Best Italian Food
Ya Mama's
42 Canal St., 603/883-2264

Best Mexican Food
Shorty's Mexican Road House
 328 Nashua Mall, 603/882-4070

Best Pizza
Nashua House of Pizza
 40 E. Hollis St., 603/883-6177

Best Seafood
The Grainery
 36 Otterson Ct., 603/889-9524

NORTH CONWAY, NH

Best Fine Dining
Stonehurst Manor
 Route 16, 603/356-3113

Best Indian Food
Shalimar of India
 27 Seavey St., 603/356-0123

Best Italian Food
Bellini's Restaurant
 33 Seavey St., 603/356-7000

N

PORTSMOUTH, NH

Best Breakfast
Golden Egg
 967 Sagamore Ave., 603/436-0519

Best Burgers
Blue Mermaid World Grill
 409 The Hill, 603/427-2583

Best Indian Food
Shalimar Indian Restaurant
 80 Hanover St., 603/427-2959

Best Italian Food
Rosa's Restaurant
 80 State St., 603/436-9715

Best Other Ethnic Food
Blue Mermaid World Grill (Caribbean)
 409 The Hill, 603/427-2583

Best Pizza
Foodee's Pizza
 165 Deer St., 603/431-2100
Portsmouth Gas Light Company
 64 Market St., 603/430-9122
Rosa's Restaurant
 80 State St., 603/436-9715

Best Salad/Salad Bar
Belle Peppers
 41 Congress St., 603/427-2504

Best Sandwiches
Celebrity Sandwich
 171 Islington St., 603/433-7009

Best Seafood
Old Ferry Landing
 10 Ceres St., 603/431-5510

Ron's Beach House
965 Ocean Blvd., Hampton, 603/926-0583

Best Steaks
Ron's Beach House
965 Ocean Blvd., Hampton, 603/926-0583

Best Sunday Brunch
Molly Malone's Restaurant
177 State St., 603/433-7233

Best Vegetarian Food
Stockpot
53 Bow St., 603/431-1851

Best View While Dining
Dunfey's Aboard the John Wannamaker
1 Harbour Pl., 603/433-3111

SALEM, NH

Best Coffee/Coffeehouse
Antiquiteas
88 N. Broadway, 603/893-7337
Barnes and Noble
125 S. Broadway, 603/898-1930

N

Best Continental Food
Promises To Keep
199 Rockingham Rd., 603/432-1559

Best Desserts
Antiquiteas
88 N. Broadway, 603/893-7337
Millstone Manor
43 Pelham Rd., 603/898-1918

Best Fine Dining
Millstone Manor
43 Pelham Rd., 603/898-1918
Promises To Keep
199 Rockingham Rd., 603/432-1559

Best Health-Conscious Menu
Willow Tree
327 S. Broadway, 603/898-5206

Best Middle Eastern Food
Samantha & Sid's Restaurant
122 Main St., 603/898-2283

Best Pizza
Salem House of Pizza
115A Main St., 603/893-5250

Best Seafood
Weathervane Seafoods
41 S. Broadway, 603/893-6269

Best Steaks
T-Bones Great American Eatery
311 S. Broadway, 603/893-3444

Best Sunday Brunch
Samantha & Sid's Restaurant
122 Main St., 603/898-2283

New Jersey

ATLANTIC CITY, NJ

Best Bar
Dead Dog Saloon
  39th St. at Landis Ave., Sea Isle City, 609/263-7600
Deauville Inn
  201 Willard Rd., Strathmere, 609/263-2080
The Irish Pub
  164 Saint James Pl., 609/344-9063
The Oceanfront
  1400 Ocean Ave., Brigantine, 609/266-7731

Best Diner
Dino's Seaville Diner
  31 Rte. 50, Ocean View, 609/624-3100

Best Eclectic Menu
Gary's Little Rock Cafe
  5212 Atlantic Ave., Ventnor City, 609/823-2233

Best French Food
Le Palais
  1133 Boardwalk, 609/340-6400

Best German Food
The Dutchman's Brauhaus
  2500 E. Bay Ave., Cedar Bonnet Island,
    609/494-6910

Best Ice Cream/Yogurt
Tory's Ice Cream, Food, and Fun
  3308 Asbury Ave., Ocean City, 609/391-7933

Best Italian Food
Portofino
  Trump Castle, 1 Castle Blvd., 609/441-8342

Best Late-Night Food
Tony's Baltimore Grille
  2800 Atlantic Ave., 609/345-5766

Best Pizza
Angelo's Pizzeria and Restaurant
  4101 Landis Ave., Sea Isle City, 609/263-2845
Mack and Manco
  758 Boardwalk, Ocean City, 609/399-2738

Best Romantic Dining
The Green Gables Inn and Restaurant
  212 Centre St., Beach Haven, 609/492-3553

Best Sandwiches
Atlantic City Sub Shop
  307 N. Dorset Ave., Ventnor City, 609/823-9393
  4 Heather Croft, Pleasantville, 609/646-7799
The Cheese Board
  23 Central Sq., Linwood, 609/653-8088
White House Sub Shop
  2301 Arctic Ave., 609/345-1564

Best Seafood
Carmen's Seafood Restaurant
  343 43rd Pl., Sea Isle City, 609/263-3471
The Old Waterway Inn
  1700 W. Riverside Dr., 609/347-1793

Best Sushi
Tokyo Palace
  135 Somers Point Blvd., Longport, 609/927-8650

Best Wine Selection
Angeloni's II
  2400 Arctic Ave., 609/344-7875

N

BERGENFIELD, NJ

Best Burgers
Midway Tavern
  250 N. Washington Ave., 201/385-8556

Best Diner
Matthews Colonial Diner
  430 S. Washington Ave., 201/385-9496

Best Dinner
Cellar Bar and Grill
  47 Legion Dr., 201/385-5781

Best French Food
Chez Madeleine Restaurant
  4 Bedford Ave., 201/384-7637

Best Italian Food
Wagon Wheel Restaurant
  16 S. Front St., 201/384-9464

Best Pizza
Nick's Pizza
  44 W. Main St., 201/385-9240

Best Sports Bar
A's Rock and Sport Club
  260 S. Washington Ave., 201/384-3040

BRIDGETON, NJ

Best Bar
The Coach Room
59 W. Broad St., 609/451-0041

Best Breakfast
Westwood Restaurant
4 Townsend Ave., 609/451-6904

Best Greek/Mediterranean Food
Golden Pigeon
36 Landis Ave., 609/451-0940

Best Italian Food
Vito's Restaurant
2 West Ave., 609/451-2007

Best Lunch
Country Rose Restaurant
97 Trench Rd., 609/455-9294

Best Restaurant in Town
Benjamin's Restaurant
101 Commerce St. E., 609/451-6449

Best Seafood
Tinker's Seafood
17 Landis Ave., 609/455-1700

CAMDEN, NJ

Best Japanese Food
Sagami Japanese Restaurant
37 W. Crescent Blvd., Collingswood, 609/854-9773

Best Pizza
Danny's Pizzeria
714 Haddon Ave., 609/963-8484
Johnny's Pizza
513 Market St., 609/338-0444
Torelli's Pizzeria
3334 Federal St., 609/966-7979

CAPE MAY, NJ

Best American Food
Blackbeard's
1045 Beach Dr., 609/884-5611
The Merion Inn
106 Decatur St., 609/884-8363

Best Bar
Carney's
401 Beach Dr., 609/884-4424
Katie O'Brien's Pub and Restaurant
429 Beach Dr., 609/898-0900

Best Barbecue/Ribs
J and B's Barbecue
801 Lafayette St., 609/884-5444

Best Chinese Food
Number 1 Chinese Kitchen
1500 Rio Grande Ave., 609/898-1800

N

Best Coffee/Coffeehouse
Fish Tales
  9836 Third Ave., Stone Harbor, 609/967-3100

Best Family Restaurant
Hamann's Family Fare
  Cape May Court House, 16 S. Main St., 609/465-2288

Best Fine Dining
The Waters Edge
  Beach Dr. at Pittsburgh Ave., 609/884-1717

Best Italian

Best Italian Food
Mama Ferrari's
  3704 Bayshore Rd., 609/889-0330
Mangia Mangia Restaurant
  110 Broadway, 609/884-2429
Touch of Pasta
  6 Victorian Village Plz., 609/884-4886

Best Mexican Food
Tortilla Flat
  2540 Dune Dr., Avalon, 609/967-5658

Best Pizza
Louie's Pizza
  711 Beach Dr., 609/884-0305

Best Romantic Dining
Mad Batter
  19 Jackson St., 609/884-5970

Best Seafood
Lobster House Restaurant and Bar
  Fishermen's Wharf, 609/884-8296
Lund's Fisheries
  997 Ocean Dr., 609/884-7600
Oyster Bay Steak and Seafood
  615 Lafayette St., 609/884-2111

Best Steaks
Sea Grill Steak and Seafood
  225 21st St., Avalon, 609/967-5511

Best Vegetarian Food
Green Cuisine
  302 96th St., Stone Harbor, 609/368-1616

CHERRY HILL, NJ

Best American Food
Bennigan's
  1102 Rte. 73, Mount Laurel, 609/235-4190
Katie O'Brien's Pub and Restaurant
  427 Crystal Lake Ave., Haddonfield, 609/858-2253
The Forum Restaurant
  1300 Blackwood-Clementon Rd., Clementon, 609/627-9333
Viennese Cafe and Pastry Shop
  1442 Marlton Pike E., 609/795-0172

Best Bar
Braddock's Tavern
39 S. Main St., Medford, 609/654-1604

Best Barbecue/Ribs
Fat Jack's Barbecue and Blues
595 Rte. 73N, West Berlin, 609/767-0011

Best Burgers
Champs Americana
25 Rte. 73S, Marlton, 609/985-9333

Best Chinese Food
China Jade
450 Rte. 70E, 609/795-6668
Empress of China
1871 Rte. 70E, 609/424-4223

Best Continental Food
Viennese Cafe and Pastry Shop
1442 Marlton Pike E., 609/795-0172

Best Diner
Ponzio's Kingsway Diner
7 Marlton Pike W., 609/428-4808

Best Eclectic Menu
The Forum Restaurant
1300 Blackwood-Clementon Rd., Clementon,
609/627-9333

Best Greek/Mediterranean Food
Athens Cafe Restaurant
1030 Marlton Pike W., 609/429-1061

Best Indian Food
Tandoor Palace
328 White Horse Pike, Clementon, 609/435-1234

Best Italian Food
Italian Bistro
1509 Rt. 38 at Chapel Ave., 609/665-6900
Lamberti Restaurant
1491 Brace Rd., 609/354-1157
Pastavino
124 E. Kings Hwy., Maple Shade, 609/727-1001

Best Japanese Food
Kamakura
270 N. Elmwood Rd., Marlton, 609/983-2990

Best Middle Eastern Food
Al Khimah
1426 Marlton Pike E., 609/427-0888

Best Pizza
King of Pizza
2300 Rte. 70W, 609/665-9688
Pizzeria Uno
1854 Marlton Pike E., 609/424-8844

Best Sandwiches
Chick's Deli
906 Township Ln., 609/429-2022
Lou and Ann's Delicatessen
259 Rte. 70E, 609/795-2307

N

Best Seafood
Hardshell Cafe
  150 N. Rte. 73S, Marlton, 609/983-3180
Hideaway
  63 Kresson Rd., 609/428-7379
Pirate's Inn
  Moorestown Centerton Rd., Mt. Laurel, 609/235-5737
Ponzio's Kingsway Diner
  7 Marlton Pike W., 609/428-4808
Steak 38 Cafe and Raw Bar
  515 Rte. 38, 609/665-4090

Best Steaks
Gaetano's Steaks and Subs
  3131 Rte. 38, Mt. Laurel, 609/234-2255
Ponzio's Kingsway Diner
  7 Marlton Pike W., 609/428-4808
Steak 38 Cafe and Raw Bar
  515 Rte. 38, 609/665-4090

Best Thai Food
Bangkok City
  114 Berlin Rd., 609/795-6288
Siri's Thai-French Cuisine
  2117 Rte. 70W, 609/663-6781

CLIFTON, NJ

Best American Food
Alexus Steakhouse and Tavern
  955 Valley Rd., 973/746-6600

Best Bar
Harp and Bard
  363 Lakeview Ave., 973/772-7282

Best Breakfast
Tick-Tock Diner
  281 Allwood Rd., 973/777-0511

Best Chinese Food
China Garden Restaurant
  306 Main Ave., 973/773-7633

Best Italian Food
La Riviera Trattoria
  421 Piaget Ave., 973/478-4181
Mario's Restaurant and Pizzeria
  710 Van Houten Ave., 973/777-1559
Villa Romangna
  1014 Main Ave., 973/472-4422

Best Lunch
Tick-Tock Diner
  281 Allwood Rd., 973/777-0511

Best Other Ethnic Food
Lee's Hawaiian Islander (Pacific Rim)
  635 Lexington Ave., 973/578-1977
Villa Romangna (Romanian)
  1014 Main Ave., 973/472-4422

Best Pizza
Bruno's Pizza and Restaurant
1006 U.S. Hwy. 46, 973/473-3339

Best Place to Eat Alone
La Riviera Trattoria
421 Piaget Ave., 973/478-4181

Best Sports Bar
Rick's
550 Allword Rd., 973/778-7100

CRANFORD, NJ

Best American Food
The Coach and Four
24 North Ave. E., 908/276-3664

Best Breakfast
Cranford Restaurant
7 North Ave. E., 908/272-2800

Best Delicatessen
Mr. J's Deli
15 Walnut Ave., 908/272-0370

Best Diner
Summit Diner
1 Union Pl., Summit, 908/277-3256

Best French Food
Le Rendez-Vous
520 Boulevard, Kenilworth, 908/931-0888

Best Homestyle Food
Margie's Place
29 N. Union Ave., 908/272-6336

Best Italian Food
Cortina Restaurant
28 North Ave. W., 908/276-5749

Best Lunch
The Porca
Cranford Hotel, 1 S. Union Ave., 908/276-2121

Best Mexican Food
Mexico Lindo
221 Main St., Chatham, 973/635-2022

Best Pizza
Italy Express Restaurant
300 South Ave., Garwood, 908/789-9110

Best Seafood
Dennis Foy's Townsquare
6 Roosevelt Ave., Chatham, 973/701-0303

Best Steaks
The Office
3 South Ave. W., 908/272-3888

EAST BRUNSWICK, NJ

Best Breakfast
Colonial Diner
560 State Rte. 18, 732/254-4858

Best Casual Dining
Colonial Diner
  560 State Rte. 18, 732/254-4858

Best Diner
Colonial Diner
  560 State Rte. 18, 732/254-4858

Best Italian Food
Trattoria Moderna
  593 State Rte. 18, 732/651-7737

Best Salad/Salad Bar
Stuff Yer Face
  1050 State Rte. 18, 732/257-2666

EDISON, NJ

Best Continental Food
Culinary Renaissance
  12 Center St., Metuchen, 732/548-9202

Best Eclectic Menu
LouCa's
  Colonial Village, 9 State Route 27, 732/549-8580

Best Homestyle Food
Christopher's
  475 Old Post Rd., 732/248-8180

Best Indian Food
Akbar
  21 Cortlandt St., 732/632-8822

Best Italian Food
Christopher's
  475 Old Post Rd., 732/248-8180

ENGLEWOOD, NJ

Best Eclectic Menu
Jamie's
  574 Sylvan Ave., Englewood Cliffs, 201/568-4244

Best Italian Food
Baci
  47 N. Dean St., 201/568-3173
Michel's Ristorante
  126 Engle St., 201/871-1133

Best Mexican Food
Blue Moon Mexican Cafe
  21 E. Palisade Ave., 201/541-0600

FAIR LAWN, NJ

Best Diner
Empress Restaurant of Fair Lawn
  13-48 River Rd., 201/791-2895
Land and Sea Restaurant
  20-12 Fair Lawn Ave., 201/794-7240
  39-10 Broadway, 201/791-1936

Best Dinner
River Palm Terrace
  41-11 State Rte. 4, 201/703-3500

Best Family Restaurant
Rivara's Grill House
6-18 Maple Ave., 201/797-4878

Best Greek/Mediterranean Food
A Taste of Greece and More
6-11 Saddle River Rd., 201/475-0300

Best Italian Food
Branda's Restaurant
6-09 Fair Lawn Ave., 201/797-6767
The Picola Italia
14-13 Plaza Rd., 201/797-2510

FORT LEE, NJ

Best Business Lunch
Franco's Restaurant and Pizzeria
Plaza West Shopping Center, 1475 Bergen Blvd.,
201/461-6651

Best Chinese Food
Sally Ling's
1636 Palisade Ave., 201/346-1282

Best Italian Food
Archer's Ristorante
1310 Palisade Ave., 201/224-5652

Best Place to Take the Kids
Franco's Restaurant and Pizzeria
Plaza West Shopping Center, 1475 Bergen Blvd.,
201/461-6651

GARFIELD, NJ

Best Beer Selection
Sidewinder's Grille and Ale House
279 Passaic St., 973/778-7500

Best Casual Dining
Barcelona's Restaurant and Bar
38 Harrison Ave., 973/778-4930
Sidewinder's Grille and Ale House
279 Passaic St., 973/778-7500

Best Family Restaurant
Firehouse Family Restaurant
42 Plauderville Ave., 973/478-8900

Best Fine Dining
Good Fellas Ristorante and Bar
661 Midland Ave., 973/478-4000

Best Italian Food
Barcelona's Restaurant and Bar
38 Harrison Ave., 973/772-6960
Michele's Italian Restaurant
32 Passaic St., 973/365-9660
Pip's
226 MacArthur Ave., 973/478-0414

Best Other Ethnic Food
Pescador Restaurant (Portuguese)
1 Passaic St., 973/472-0503

Best Pizza
Barcelona's Restaurant and Bar
  38 Harrison Ave., 973/778-4930

Best Restaurant in Town
Good Fellas Ristorante and Bar
  661 Midland Ave., 973/478-4000

Best Southwestern Food
Sidewinder's Grille and Ale House
  279 Passaic St., 973/478-0414

HAWTHORNE, NJ

Best Diner
New Triangle Diner
  112 Goffle Rd., 973/427-8408

Best Eclectic Menu
Vernissage
  111 Wagaraw Rd., 973/423-5808

Best Italian Food
Benedetto's
  4 Garfield Ave., 973/423-0044
Cosenza's Ristorante
  184 Diamond Bridge Ave., 973/423-4044

HILLSIDE, NJ

Best American Food
New Blue Ribbon Restaurant
  256 Hollywood Ave., 973/965-0300

Best Breakfast
Bagel Masters
  1147 Liberty Ave., 973/527-8433

Best Italian Food
Alfonso's Seafood and Steak
  310 Hillside Ave., 973/688-8919

Best Pizza
M & M II Pizzeria
  1271 Liberty Ave., 973/923-0800

HOBOKEN, NJ

Best American Food
Amanda's
  908 Washington St., 201/798-0101
Lady Jane's Restaurant
  51 Fourteenth St., 201/659-9390
Park Cafe
  6013 Park Ave., 201/861-1077

Best Bar
Moran's
  501 Garden St., 201/795-2025

Best Chinese Food
Front Page Chinese Cuisine
  1120 Washington St., 201/653-5676

Best Continental Food
Baja Mexican Cuisine
104 Fourteenth St., 201/653-0610
Lady Jane's Restaurant
51 Fourteenth St., 201/659-9390

Best Family Restaurant
Leo's Grandevous
200 Grand St., 201/659-9467

Best Italian Food
Leo's Grandevous
200 Grand St., 201/659-9467
M and P Bianca Mano
1116 Washington St., 201/795-0274
Ricco's Ristorante
1024 Washington St., 201/792-5956

Best Mexican Food
Baja Mexican Cuisine
104 Fourteenth St., 201/653-0610

Best Pizza
Benny Tudino's Pizzeria
622 Washington St., 201/792-4132

Best Seafood
Onieal's Restaurant and Bar
341 Park Ave., 201/653-9388

N

JERSEY CITY, NJ

Best American Food
Casino-in-the-Park
Lincoln Park, 201/333-1045
VIP Diner Restaurant
175 Sip Ave., 201/792-1400

Best Business Lunch
Rosie Radigan's
10 Exchange Pl., 201/451-5566
VIP Diner Restaurant
175 Sip Ave., 201/792-1400

Best Chinese Food
Canton Tea Garden
920 Bergen Ave., 201/653-4728

Best Diner
Colonette Restaurant
405 State Rte. 440, 201/432-8222

Best Dinner
Lisbon Restaurant
256 Warren St., 201/432-9222

Best Italian Food
Casa Dante Restaurant
737 Newark Ave., 201/795-2750
Laico's Restaurant
67 Terhune Ave., 201/434-4115
Puccini's Restaurant
1064 Westside Ave., 201/432-4111

Best Restaurant in Town
Casino-in-the-Park
Lincoln Park, 201/333-1045

Best Seafood
Lincoln Inn
13 Lincoln St., 201/659-8686

Best Spanish Food
Lisbon Restaurant
256 Warren St., 201/432-9222

Best Steaks
Lincoln Inn
13 Lincoln St., 201/659-8686

KEARNEY, NJ

Best Chinese Food
Jade Fountain Restaurant
602 Ridge Rd., North Arlington, 201/991-5377

Best Diner
Arlington Diner
1 River Rd., North Arlington, 201/998-6262
Top's Diner
500 Passaic Ave., Harrison, 973/481-0490

Best Family Restaurant
Eagan's Restaurant
440 Belleville Turnpike, North Arlington, 201/991-8167

Best Other Ethnic Food
Argyle Fish and Chip Restaurant (English)
212 Kearny Ave., 201/991-3900
Torremolino's Restaurant (Portuguese)
188 Midland Ave., 201/991-1849

Best Pizza
Pete's Place
934 Passaic Ave., 201/998-0488

LIVINGSTON, NJ

Best American Food
Don's Restaurant
650 S. Orange Ave., 973/992-4010

Best Chinese Food
North Sea Village Cuisine
28 N. Livingston Ave., 973/992-7056

Best Diner
Ritz Diner
72 E. Mount Pleasant Ave., 973/533-1213

Best Italian Food
Nero's Restaurant and Lounge
618 S. Livingston Ave., 973/994-1410
Porto Bella
62 W. Mount Pleasant Ave., 973/992-1185

Best Pizza
Panevino Ristorante
637 W. Mount Pleasant Ave., 973/535-6160

LONG BRANCH, NJ

Best Barbecue/Ribs
Memphis Pig Out
67 First Ave., Atlantic Highlans, 732/291-5533

Best Burgers
Pour House
640 Shrewsbury Ave., Red Bank, 732/842-4337
Sitting Duck
104 Myrtle Ave., 732/229-5566

Best Coffee/Coffeehouse
Inkwell
665 Second Ave., 732/222-6886
No Ordinary Joe
51 Broad St., Red Bank, 732/530-4040

Best Desserts
Pleasure Bay
Ocean Place Hilton, 1 Ocean Blvd., 732/571-4000

Best Fine Dining
Mumford's Restaurant
45 Atlantic Ave., 732/222-2657

Best Ice Cream/Yogurt
Scoops Old Fashioned Ice Cream
50 Monmouth Rd., Oakhurst, 732/229-6266

Best Italian Food
Tuzzio's Italian Cuisine
224 Westwood Ave., 732/222-9614

Best Mexican Food
Casa Comida Mexican Restaurant
336 Branchport Ave., 732/229-7774

Best Pizza
Freddie's Pizzeria
563 Broadway, 732/222-0931
Guidetti's Pizzeria and Subs
15 Memorial Pkwy., 732/222-0504
Tony's
228 Morris Ave., 732/222-3535

Best Sandwiches
Primavera's Italian Specialty
140 Brighton Ave., 732/229-1518

Best Seafood
Doris and Ed's Seafood Restaurant
348 Shore Dr., Highlands, 732/872-1565
Pleasure Bay
Ocean Place Hilton, 1 Ocean Blvd., 732/571-4000

Best Steaks
What's Your Beef
21 W. River Rd., Rumson, 732/842-6205

LYNDHURST, NJ

Best Italian Food
Angelo's
263 Ridge Rd., 201/939-1922

N

La Dolce Vita
316 Valley Brook Ave., 201/935-4260

Best Other Ethnic Food
Lee's Hawaiian Islander (Pacific Rim)
768 Stuyvesant Ave., 201/939-3777

Best Spanish Food
La Cibeles
123 Ridge Rd., 201/438-9491

MARGATE CITY, NJ

Best Bar
Maynard's
9306 Amherst Ave., 609/822-8423

Best Casual Dining
Dino's Subs and Pizza
8016 Ventnor Ave., 609/822-6602

Best Chinese Food
Billy Ho's Imperial East
7800 Ventnor Ave., 609/487-1040

Best Delicatessen
Downbeach Deli
8 S. Essex, 609/823-7310

Best Eclectic Menu
Melissa's Bistro Fare
9307 Ventnor Ave., 609/823-1414

MAYS LANDING, NJ

Best Barbecue/Ribs
H.I. Rib and Company
6613 Black Horse Pike, Egg Harbor Township,
609/569-0050

Best Diner
Shore Diner
6710 Tilton Rd., Egg Harbor Township, 609/641-3669

Best Italian Food
Maplewood II
6126 Black Horse Pike, 609/625-1181

Best Romantic Dining
Cousin's Country House
3373 Bargaintown Rd., Egg Harbor Township,
609/927-5777
Inn at Sugar Hill
5704 Somers Point Rd., 609/625-2226

MILLBURN, NJ

Best Chinese Food
Ling Ling
59 Main St., 973/912-8838

Best Continental Food
Cafe Main
40 Main St., 973/376-4444

Best French Food
Chez Andre
1844 Springfield Ave., Maplewood, 973/762-9191

Best Italian Food
Giovanna
5 Highland Pl., Maplewood, 973/763-3083
Sergio's
343 Millburn Ave., 973/379-7020

Best Japanese Food
Sono
323 Millburn Ave., 973/467-2444

Best Pizza
The Brick Oven of Milford
343 Millburn Ave., 973/379-6700

MONTCLAIR, NJ

Best Casual Dining
Frankie's il Bacio
720 Bloomfield Ave., 973/746-4600

Best Eclectic Menu
Hudson Place
98 Walnut St., 973/746-0789

Best Italian Food
Frankie's il Bacio
720 Bloomfield Ave., 973/746-4600
Rispoli Restaurante Italiano
5 N. Fullerton Ave., 973/509-8544

Best Mexican Food
Mexicali Rose
10 Park St., 973/746-9005

NEW BRUNSWICK, NJ

Best American Food
Stage Left, An American Cafe
5 Livingston Ave., 732/828-4444

Best Bar
Old Man Rafferty's
106 Albany St., 732/846-6153

Best Business Lunch
The Old Bay Restaurant
61 Church St., 732/246-3114
Two Albany Restaurant
2 Albany St., 732/873-6600
Zia Grill
19 Dennis St., 732/249-1551

Best Cajun/Creole Food
The Old Bay Restaurant
61 Church St., 732/246-3114

Best Casual Dining
Church Street Trattoria
94 Church St., 732/828-4355

N

Best Eclectic Menu
The Frog and the Peach
  29 Dennis St., 732/846-3216
Stage Left, An American Cafe
  5 Livingston Ave., 732/828-4444

Best Fine Dining
La Fontana Restaurant
  120 Albany St., 732/249-7500
Stage Left, An American Cafe
  5 Livingston Ave., 732/828-4444

Best Italian Food
Church Street Trattoria
  94 Church St., 732/828-4355
La Fontana Restaurant
  120 Albany St., 732/249-7500
Leone's Italian Restaurant
  Lions Plaza, U.S. Hwy. 130N, North Brunswick,
    732/422-1230
Panico's
  103 Church St., 732/545-6100

Best Japanese Food
Sapporo Sushi and Steak House
  375 George St., 732/828-3888

Best Other Ethnic Food
The Round Grill (Mongolian)
  1 Penn Plz., 732/828-3337
Makeda Ethiopian Restaurant (Ethiopian)
  335 George St., 732/545-5115

Best Pizza
Stuff Yer Face
  49 Easton Ave., 732/247-1727

Best Southwestern Food
Zia Grill
  19 Dennis St., 732/249-1551

Best Thai Food
Pad Thai
  217 Raritan Ave., Highland Park, 732/247-9636

NEWARK, NJ

Best Italian Food
Casa Nostra Ristorante Italiano
  537 Bloomfield Ave., 973/484-0894
Il Tulipano Restaurant
  1131 Pompton Ave., Cedar Grove, 973/256-9300
La Fontanella Ristorante
  1640 Broad St., Bloomfield, 973/893-0188
Mangia Questa
  548 Bloomfield Ave., 973/239-7444
Michaelangelo's Restaurant
  544 Bloomfield Ave., 973/485-9057
Vesuvius Restaurant
  501 Bloomfield Ave., 973/485-2878

Best Spanish Food
Forno's of Spain
  47 Ferry St., 973/589-4767
Iberia Peninsula Restaurant
  63-69 Ferry St., 973/344-5611
Spanish Tavern Restaurant
  103 McWhorter St., 973/589-4959

NORTH BERGEN, NJ

Best Chinese Food
Phoenix Garden Too
  88 U.S. Hwy. 46W, Ridgefield, 201/313-0088

Best Continental Food
Arthur's Landing
  1 Pershing Circle, Weehawken, 201/867-0777
Stephen's Cafe
  7722 Bergenline Ave., 201/854-9666

Best French Food
Stephen's Cafe
  7722 Bergenline Ave., 201/854-9666

Best Greek/Mediterranean Food
Saray Mediterranean Restaurant
  520 Anderson Ave., Cliffside Park, 201/313-9118

Best Italian Food
Lantana Restaurant
  1148 Paterson Plank Rd., Secaucus, 201/867-1065

Best Other Ethnic Food
Mundo Latino Restaurant (Spanish-Cuban)
  8619 Bergenline Ave., 201/861-6902

Best Seafood
Arthur's Landing
  1 Pershing Circle, Weehawken, 201/867-0777
Fulton Crab House
  697 Anderson Ave., Cliffside Park, 201/945-2347
River Palm Terrace
  1416 River Rd., Edgewater, 201/224-2013
Salinger's
  1005 Edgewater Ave., Ridgefield, 201/945-9712

Best Steaks
River Palm Terrace
  1416 River Rd., Edgewater, 201/224-2013
Salinger's
  1005 Edgewater Ave., Ridgefield, 201/945-9712

PARAMUS, NJ

Best American Food
Saddle River Inn
  2 Barnstable Ct., Saddle River, 201/825-4016

Best French Food
Claude's Ho-Ho-Kus Inn
  E. Franklin Turnpike at Sheridan Ave.,
    Ho Ho Kus, 201/445-4115
Porquois Pas?
  6 Sycamore Ave., Ho Ho Kus, 201/251-8008

Saddle River Inn
  2 Barnstable Ct., Saddle River, 201/825-4016

Best Korean Food
Koreana
  257 State Rte. 4W, 201/487-8558

Best Seafood
Pier 17
  464 State Rte. 17N, 201/967-1079

PASSAIC, NJ

Best American Food
Manny's
  110 Moonachie Rd., Moonachie, 201/939-1244
Railroad Cafe
  240 Hackensack St., East Rutherford,
    973/939-9292

Best Bar
Railroad Cafe
  240 Hackensack St., East Rutherford,
    973/939-9292

Best Breakfast
Oasis Restaurant
  683 Main Ave., 973/773-7474

Best Chinese Food
Chin See Gardens
  603 Main Ave., 973/773-8627

Best Continental Food
Segovia
  150 Moonachie Rd., Moonachie, 973/641-4266

Best Delicatessen
Lenny Cohen's Deli
  210 Washington Pl., 973/779-1403

Best Diner
Bendix Diner
  Hwy. 17, Hasbrouck Heights, 203/288-0143
Candlewood Diner
  179 Paterson Ave., East Rutherford, 203/933-4446
Oasis Restaurant
  683 Main Ave., 973/773-7474

Best Italian Food
Bazzarelli Ristorante and Pizza
  117 Moonachie Rd., Moonachie, 201/641-4010
Il Villagio
  651 Rte. 17, Carlstadt, 203/935-7733

Best Seafood
North American Lobster Company
  430 Rte. 17, Carlstadt, 203/933-3300

Best Spanish Food
Segovia
  150 Moonachie Rd., Moonachie, 201/641-4266
Sevilla Restaurant
  505 Main Ave., 973/777-5827
Tatiana Restaurant
  235 Monroe St., 973/472-1091

Best Sports Bar
Jersey's Sports Cafe
  125 Park Ave., East Rutherford, 201/933-3308
Manny's Sports Bar Restaurant
  110 Moonachie Ave., Moonachie, 201/939-1244

PATERSON, NJ

Best American Food
Rosemary and Sage
  26 Hamburg Turnpike, Riverdale, 973/616-0606

Best Chinese Food
Soochow
  165 Rte. 46W, Saddle Brook, 201/368-2899

Best Italian Food
Cortina Ristorante
  118 Berkshire Ave., 973/942-1750
E and V Ristorante
  320 Chamberlain Ave., 973/942-4664
Lo Spuntino
  400 Minisink Rd., Totowa Plaza, Totowa, 973/812-0077
Nanni's Ristorante
  53 W. Passaic St., Rochelle Park, 201/843-1250
Valentino's
  103 Spring Valley Rd., Park Ridge, 201/391-2230

Best Mexican Food
La Hacienda
  102 McLean Blvd., 973/345-1255

Best Place to Take the Kids
Patsy's Tavern and Pizzeria
  72 Seventh Ave., 973/742-9596

Best Seafood
Sea Shack
  293 Polifly Rd., Hackensack, 201/489-7232

PRINCETON, NJ

Best Bar
Annex Restaurant
  128 1/2 Nassau St., 609/921-7555
Triumph's Brewing Company
  138 Nassau St., 609/924-7855

Best Breakfast
Carousel Luncheonette
  260 Nassau St., 609/924-2677
P.J.'s Pancake House Restaurant
  154 Nassau St., 609/924-1353

Best Burgers
J.B. Winberie Restaurant and Bar
  1 Palmer Sq. E., 609/921-0700

Best Chinese Food
Sunny Garden
  15 Farber Rd., 609/520-1881
The Tiger
  260 Nassau St., 609/252-0663

N

Best Coffee/Coffeehouse
Small World Coffee
  14 Witherspoon Ln., 609/924-4377

Best Diner
Harry's Luncheonette
  16 1/2 Witherspoon St., 609/921-9769

Best French Food
Lahiere's Restaurant
  5 Witherspoon St., 609/921-2798
Le Plumet Royal
  Peacock Inn, 20 Bayard Ln., 609/921-0050

Best Homestyle Food
Downtown Deluxe
  48 Leigh Ave., 609/921-3052

Best Ice Cream/Yogurt
Thomas Sweet Ice Cream
  181 Nassau St., 609/683-8720
  33 Palmer Sq. W., 609/683-1655

Best Indian Food
Palace of Asia
  400 Mercer Mall, Rte. 1, Lawrenceville,
  609/987-0606

Best Italian Food
Casabona
  47B State Rd., 609/252-0940
Teresa's Pizzetta Caffe
  21 Palmer Sq. E., 609/921-1974

Best Pizza
Pizza Colari
  124 Nassau St., 609/924-0777
Pizza Star
  301 N. Harrison St., 609/921-7422

Best Sandwiches
Hoagie Haven
  242 Nassau St., 609/921-7723

RIDGEWOOD, NJ

Best American Food
Smith Brothers Dining Saloon
  51 N. Broad St., 201/444-8111

Best Family Restaurant
Daily Treat Restaurant
  177 E. Ridgewood Ave., 201/652-9113

Best Indian Food
Kailash Indo-Thai Cuisine
  22 Oak St., 201/251-9693

Best Italian Food
Fratelli's
  119 E. Ridgewood Ave., 201/447-9377
Natalie's
  20 E. Ridgewood Ave., 201/444-7887

Best Restaurant in Town
The Office
32 Chestnut St., 201/652-1070

Best Thai Food
Kailash Indo-Thai Cuisine
22 Oak St., 201/251-9693

SOMERS POINT, NJ

Best Bar
Gregory's
900 Shore Rd., 609/927-6665

Best Romantic Dining
Hatteras Coastal Cuisine
801 Bay Ave., 609/926-3326

Best Sandwiches
Atlantic City Sub Shop
Acme Shopping Center, 226 New Rd.,
609/653-8181

SOMERVILLE, NJ

Best Bar
Green Knoll Grill
645 U.S. Hwy. 202/206N, Bridgewater,
908/526-7090

Best Breakfast
Country Fresh Pancake and Grill
145 W. Main St., 908/231-8090

Best Delicatessen
Steck's
325 U.S. Hwy. 202/206N, Bridgewater,
908/685-9587

Best Homestyle Food
Buffalo Bill's
24 W. Main St., 908/725-9558

Best Italian Food
Ferraro's Restaurant and Pizza
18 W. Main St., 908/707-0029
La Cuchina
125 W. Main St., 908/526-4907

Best Pizza
Central Pizzeria
122 W. Main St., 908/722-8272

Best Seafood
Scampi's Fish Market and Restaurant
198 W. Main St., 908/685-1323

TEANECK, NJ

Best Italian Food
Marcello and Dino Roman Cafe
12 Tappan Rd., Harrington Park, 201/767-4245
Villa Cortina
18 Piermont Rd., Tenafly, 201/567-6477

N

Best Japanese Food
East
  1405 Teaneck Rd., 201/837-1260
Kiku Alpine
  59 Rte. 9W, Alpine, 201/767-6322

Best Kosher Food
Noah's Ark
  493 Cedar Ln., 201/692-1200

Best Mexican Food
Mexicali Blues
  665 Cedar Ln., 201/836-9404

Best Seafood
La Posada
  368 Cedar Ln., 201/287-0412

Best Spanish Food
La Posada
  368 Cedar Ln., 201/287-0412
Meson Madrid
  343 Bergen Blvd., Palisades Park, 201/947-1038

TOMS RIVER, NJ

Best Burgers
Office Restaurant and Lounge
  820 Main St., 732/349-0800

Best Coffee/Coffeehouse
Java Joint
  73 Main St., 732/240-2123

Best Ice Cream/Yogurt
Rich's Ice Cream
  Rte. 37 at King Rd., 732/349-3459

Best Italian Food
Bella Di Notte
  247 Mantoloking Rd., Brick, 732/920-9158
Pier One Restaurant
  3430 Rte. 37E, 732/270-0914

Best Japanese Food
Hana Japanese Restaurant
  927 Rte. 166, 732/286-4465

Best Pizza
Vergona's Pizzeria and Restaurant
  K-Mart Shopping Plz., 213 Rte. 37E, 732/244-6616

Best Sandwiches
Jersey Mike's Submarines
  1501 Rte. 37E, 732/929-0222

Best Seafood
Jack Baker's Lobster Shanty
  4 Robbins Pkwy., 732/240-4800
The Old Time Tavern
  Rte. 166 at N. Main St., 732/349-8778
Pier One Restaurant
  3430 Rte. 37E, 732/270-0914

Best Steaks
Office Restaurant and Lounge
820 Main St., 732/349-0800
The Old Time Tavern
Rte. 166 at N. Main St., 908/349-8778
Pier One Restaurant
3430 Rte. 37E, 908/270-0914

TRENTON, NJ

Best Atmosphere
Diamond's
132 Kent St., 609/393-1000

Best Bar
Office Cafe
2 Elmwood Ave., 609/586-8600

Best Burgers
Rossi's Bar and Grill
501 Morris Ave., 609/394-9089

Best Desserts
Roebling Pub
801 S. Clinton Ave., 609/396-9411

Best Diner
Mastoris Diner-Restaurant
144 Hwy. 130, Bordentown, 609/298-4650

Best Fine Dining
Chianti's
701 Whittaker Ave., 609/695-0011

Best Italian Food
Amici's Restaurant
600 Chestnut Ave., 609/396-6300
Chianti's
701 Whittaker Ave., 609/695-0011

Best Pizza
De Lorenzo Pizza
1007 Hamilton, 609/393-2952

Best Romantic Dining
Sal Deforte's Ristorante
200 Fulton St., 609/396-6856

Best Sandwiches
Good Times Tavern
160 Ashmore Ave., 609/695-5067

Best Seafood
John Henry Seafood Restaurant
2 Mifflin St., 609/396-3083

Best Spanish Food
Malaga Spanish Restaurant
511 Lalor St., 609/396-8878

Best Steaks
Lorenzo's Cafe
66 S. Clinton Ave., 609/695-6868

N

VINELAND, NJ

Best Breakfast
Larry's II Restaurant
  907 N. Main Rd., 609/692-9001

Best Coffee/Coffeehouse
Coffee Time
  636 Landis Ave., 609/794-8900

Best Greek/Mediterranean Food
Greek Island Restaurant
  3513 S. Delsea Dr., 609/327-9462

Best Ice Cream/Yogurt
Ice Cream Palace
  205 S. Delsea Dr., 609/692-9416

Best Italian Food
Di Donato's Villa Restaurant
  376 E. Wheat Rd., 609/697-2900

Best Other Ethnic Food
Norma's Kitchen (Jamaican)
  7 S. Sixth St., 609/691-5411

Best Pizza
Pizza Pizzazz
  484 S. Brewster Rd., 609/692-7007

Best Sandwiches
Hello Deli
  2 LaSalle Dr., 609/691-3354

Best Seafood
Midway Inn
  Rte. 40 at Rte. 54, Buena, 609/697-0001
Pegasus II Restaurant
  251 S. Lincoln Ave., 609/692-6333

Best Steaks
Pegasus II Restaurant
  251 S. Lincoln Ave., 609/692-6333

WASHINGTON, NJ

Best Bar
Sports Scene Restaurant
  234 State Hwy. 31, 908/689-0310

Best Breakfast
Kelly's Corner Restaurant
  150 State Rte. 13N, 908/689-7486
Washington Diner Restaurant
  State Hwy. 31 at State Hwy. 57, 908/689-3059

Best Italian Food
Villa Scotto Pizza
  314 State Rte. 31N, 908/689-8900

Best Pizza
Sal's Pizza
  1 W. Washington Ave., 908/689-6336

Best Seafood
Backstage
  301 W. Washington Ave., 908/689-4071

Best Steaks
Backstage
  301 W. Washington Ave., 908/689-4071

WAYNE, NJ

Best Breakfast
King George Diner
  721 Paterson-Hamburg Turnpike, 973/696-3010

Best Family Restaurant
Bachagaloop's
  1467 State Rte. 23, 973/694-1116

Best Italian Food
La Gardenia
  2410 Hamburg Turnpike, 973/835-3585

WEST ORANGE, NJ

Best All-You-Can-Eat Buffet
The Manor
  111 Prospect Ave., 973/325-1400

Best Continental Food
Highlawn Pavilion
  Eaglerock Reservation, Eaglerock Ave.,
  973/731-3463
The Manor
  111 Prospect Ave., 973/325-1400

Best Dinner
Mayfair Farms
  481 Eagle Rock Ave., 973/731-4300

Best Italian Food
Cafe Arugula
  59 S. Orange Ave., South Orange, 973/378-9099
Due Amici
  450 Main St., 973/669-0027
Primavera Restaurant
  500 Pleasant Valley Way, 973/731-4779

Best Lunch
Pal's Cabin Restaurant
  265 Prospect Ave., 973/731-4000

Best Seafood
Sinclaire's Sea Grille
  74 First St., South Orange, 973/762-4776

WESTFIELD, NJ

Best American Food
B.G. Fields Restaurant
  560 Springfield Ave., 908/233-2260
Casual Times
  1085 Central Ave., Clark, 908/388-6511
Floridian Grill
  375 Terrill Rd., Scotch Plains, 908/322-2666
Jolly Trolley Saloon
  411 North Ave. W., 908/232-1207
Towne House Restaurant
  114 Central Ave., 908/232-4517

N

Westfield Diner
309 North Ave. E., 908/233-5200

Best Breakfast
Vicki's Diner
110 E. Broad St., 908/233-6887

Best Chinese Food
China Light
102 E. Broad St., 908/654-7797

Best Delicatessen
Duke's Sub and Deli
229 South Ave. W., 908/232-1160

Best Diner
Westfield Diner
309 North Ave. E., 908/233-5200

Best French Food
La Petite Rose
431 North Ave. W., 908/232-1680

Best Indian Food
Raagini Indian Restaurant
1085 U.S. Hwy. 22, Mountainside, 908/789-9777

Best Italian Food
Aliperti's Restaurant
1189 Raritan Rd., Clark, 732/381-2300
Ferraro's Italian Restaurant
14 Elm St., 908/232-1105
La Stalla
579 Raritan Rd., Roselle, 908/620-9520
Northside Trattoria
16 Prospect St., 908/232-7320
Theresa's Restaurant
47 Elm St., 908/233-9133

Best Japanese Food
Daimatsu
860 Mountain Ave., Mountainside, 908/233-7888
Kotobuki Japanese Restaurant
110 Central Ave., 908/233-6547

Best Lunch
Vicki's Diner
110 E. Broad St., 908/233-6887

Best Pizza
Buona Pizza
243 South Ave. E., 908/232-2066
Cosimo's Pizza
118 E. Broad St., 908/654-8787
La Fiorentina Pizzeria
338 South Ave. E., 908/654-7220
Sorrento's Restaurant and Pizzeria
631 Central Ave., 908/232-2642

Best Sandwiches
Duke's Sub and Deli
229 South Ave. W., 908/232-1160

Best Seafood
Wyckoff's Steak House
109 North Ave. W., 908/654-9700

Best Southwestern Food
Mojave Grill
235 North Ave. W., 908/233-7772

Best Steaks
Charlie Brown's Steakhouse
2376 North Ave., 908/232-3443
Wyckoff's Steak House
109 North Ave. W., 908/654-9700

WILDWOOD, NJ

Best Bar
Ye Olde Anglesea Pub
116 W. First Ave., 609/729-1133

Best Chinese Food
Dragon House
3616 Pacific Ave., 609/522-2320

Best Ice Cream/Yogurt
Island Ice Cream Company
118 E. Chestnut Ave., 609/522-0438

Best Italian Food
Little Italy Restaurant
5401 Atlantic Ave., 609/523-0999

Best Pizza
Al The Steak King and Pizza Shop
2501 New Jersey Ave., 609/729-1637

Best Seafood
Russo's Restaurant
4415 Park Blvd., 609/522-7038
Urie's Waterfront Restaurant
588 Old Rio Grande Ave., 609/522-4947

WILLINGBORO, NJ

Best Breakfast
Golden Dawn Diner
4387 Rte. 130S, Burlington, 609/877-2236
Prince Diner
805 Rte. 130S, Burlington, 609/386-5522

Best Diner
Edgewater Queen
2614 U.S. Hwy. 130S, Beverly, 609/871-5228

Best Steaks
Arthur's House of Fine Foods
630 E. Rte. 130, Burlington, 609/387-2334
Charlie Brown's Steakhouse
949 Rte. 541, Mount Holly, 609/265-1100

N

New Mexico

ALAMOGORDO, NM

Best Bar
Keg's Brewery
817 Scenic Dr., 505/437-9564

Best Breakfast
Our Lady of Mt. Carmel Restaurant
915 Texas Ave., 505/434-0722

Best Chinese Food
Taiwan Kitchen
110 N. White Sands Blvd., 505/434-4337

Best Coffee/Coffeehouse
Mastroddi's Espresso Cafe
804 New York Ave., 505/437-2323

Best Fine Dining
Rebecca's at the Lodge in Cloudcroft
1 Corona Pl., Cloudcroft, 505/682-3131

Best Health-Conscious Menu
Our Lady of Mt. Carmel Restaurant
915 Texas Ave., 505/434-0722

Best Mexican Food
Alfredo's Mexican Kitchen
801 Delaware Ave., 505/437-1745

Best Pizza
Peter Piper Pizza
101 S. White Sands Blvd., 505/434-1828

Best Steaks
Cattleman's Steak House
2904 N. White Sands Blvd., 505/434-5252
Eagle's Nest Restaurant
905 S. White Sands Blvd., 505/437-8644

Paul's Family Steakhouse
  3200 N. White Sands Blvd., 505/443-0145

Best Sunday Brunch
Danlika Restaurant
  Inn of the Mountain Gods, Hwy. 70, Rte. 4, Carrizo
    Canyon Rd., Mescalero, 505/257-5141

ALBUQUERQUE, NM

Best All-You-Can-Eat Buffet
Tomato Cafe
  5901 Wyoming Blvd. NE, 505/821-9300
  1930 Juan Tabo Blvd. NE, 505/293-5100

Best American Food
Monte Vista Fire Station Restaurant
  3201 Central Ave. NE, 505/255-2424
Stephen's
  1311 Tijeras Ave. NW, 505/842-1773

Best Bar
Gecko's Gallery and Grill
  3500 Central Ave. SE, 505/262-1848

Best Barbecue/Ribs
Rudy's Country Store and Barbecue
  2321 Carlisle Blvd. NE, 505/884-4000

Best Breakfast
Frontier Restaurant
  2400 Central Ave. SE, 505/266-0550

Best Burgers
Owl Cafe
  800 Eubank Blvd. NE, 505/291-4900

Best Business Lunch
Weck's For Breakfast and Lunch
  7200 Montgomery Blvd. NE, Ste. 3, 505/881-0019

Best Casual Dining
Garduno's of Mexico
  10551 Montgomery Blvd. NE, 505/298-5000
  8806 Fourth St. NW, 505/898-2772
  5400 Academy Rd. NE, 505/821-3030
  2100 Louisiana Blvd. NE, 505/880-0055

Best Chinese Food
Bamboo House Chinese Restaurant
  1745 Juan Tabo Blvd. NE, 505/293-0183

Best Coffee/Coffeehouse
Double Rainbow Bakery and Cafe
  3416 Central Ave. SE, 505/255-6633

Best French Food
Le Marmiton
  5415B Academy Rd. NE, 505/821-6279

Best Health-Conscious Menu
Souper Salad
  4411 San Mateo Blvd. NE, 505/255-8781
  2225 Wyoming Blvd. NE, 505/294-7585
  1606 Central Ave. SE, 505/243-9751

Best Homestyle Food
Black-Eyed Pea
 4701 San Mateo Blvd. NE, 505/880-8733

Best Inexpensive Meal
Frontier Restaurant
 2400 Central Ave. SE, 505/266-0550

Best Italian Food
Capo's Hide Away
 8938 Fourth St. NW, 505/898-2002
Scalo Northern Italian Grill
 3500 Central Ave. SE, 505/255-8781

Best Mexican Food
El Patio de Albuquerque
 142 Harvard Dr. SE, 505/268-4245
Maria Teresa
 618 Rio Grande Blvd. NW, 505/242-3900
Sadie's
 6230 Fourth St. NW, 505/345-5339
Viva Vira's Mexican Kitchen
 2202 State Rd. 17S, 505/756-2557

Best Pizza
Il Vicino Pizzeria
 3403 Central Ave. NE, 505/266-7855

Best Place to Eat Alone
Double Rainbow Bakery and Cafe
 3416 Central Ave. SE, 505/255-6633

Best Regional Food
La Placita Dining Room
 208 San Felipe St. NW, 505/247-2204

Best Restaurant in Town
Romano's Macaroni Grill
 2100 Louisiana Blvd. NE, 505/881-3400

Best Romantic Dining
Musashino Japanese Restaurant
 6205B Montgomery Blvd. NE, 505/880-0008

Best Salad/Salad Bar
Souper Salad
 4411 San Mateo Blvd. NE, 505/255-8781
 1606 Central Ave. SE, 505/243-9751
 2225 Wyoming Blvd. NE, 505/294-7585

Best Sandwiches
Woody's Cafe and Coffee Bar
 11200 Montgomery Blvd. NE, 505/292-6800

Best Seafood
Cafe Oceana
 1414 Central Ave. SE, 505/247-2233

Best Steaks
Paul's Monterey Inn
 1000 Juan Tabo Blvd. NE, 505/294-1461

Best Sunday Brunch
McGrath's/Hyatt Regency
 330 Tijeras Ave. NW, 505/766-6700

N

Best Thai Food
Bangkok Cafe
  5901 Central Ave. NE, 505/255-5036

Best Vegetarian Food
Wild Oats
  6300A San Mateo Blvd. NE, 505/823-1933

CARLSBAD, NM

Best Barbecue/Ribs
The Red Chimney Pit Bar-B-Q
  817 N. Canal St., 505/885-8744

Best Burgers
Queen Cafe
  3670 Queens Hwy., 505/981-2439
Sno To Go
  801 N. Pate St., 505/885-8864

Best Chinese Food
Golden China Restaurant
  509 S. Canal St., 505/885-2953
Kwan's Kitchen
  1511 S. Canal St., 505/887-5145

Best Mexican Food
Cortez Cafe
  508 S. Canal St., 505/885-4747
Lucy's Mexicali Restaurant
  701 S. Canal St., 505/887-7714
Spanish Inn
  805 W. Mermod St., 505/885-3489
Tina's Cafe
  3122 San Jose Blvd., 505/885-4239

Best Pizza
Pizza Mill and Sub Factory
  312 W. Church St., 505/887-5098

Best Seafood
Beaver's Restaurant
  1600 S. Canal St., 505/885-4515

Best Steaks
Sirloin Stockade
  710 S. Canal St., 505/887-7211

CLOVIS, NM

Best Barbecue/Ribs
Ben's BBQ
  1421 N. Prince St., 505/763-4241

Best Chinese Food
The Orient
  116 E. 21st St., 505/762-6238
China Star
  1221 N. Main St., 505/762-8489

Best Burgers
Bill's Jumbo Burgers
  501 N. Main St., 505/762-6300

N

Best Japanese Food
Shogun Steak House
  600 Pile St., 505/762-8577

Best Mexican Food
Guadalajara Restaurant
  916L Casillas Blvd., 505/769-9965
Juanito's Mexican Restaurant
  1608 Mabry Dr., 505/762-7822
Leal's Mexican Food Restaurant
  3100 Mabry Dr., 505/763-4075

Best Steaks
Cattleman's Cafe
  504 S. Hull St., 505/763-1897
K-Bob's Steak House
  1600 Mabry Dr., 505/763-4443
Poor Boy's Steak House
  2115 N. Prince St., 505/763-5222

FARMINGTON, NM

Best American Food
Clancy's Pub
  2703 E. Twentieth St., 505/325-8176

Best Barbecue/Ribs
Sparerib Barbecue Company
  1700 E. Main St., 505/325-4800

Best Breakfast
Kettle Restaurant
  685 Scott Ave., 505/326-0824
Village Inn
  514 Scott Ave., 505/325-3498

Best Brewpub
Chelsea's London Pub
  4601 E. Main St., Ste. 100, 505/327-9644
Clancy's Pub
  2703 E. Twentieth St., 505/325-8176

Best Chinese Food
Golden Dragon Restaurant
  2324 E. Main St., 505/325-5100

Best Family Restaurant
Furr's Family Dining
  3030 E. Main St., 505/327-6011

Best Lunch
Something Special Bakery and Tea Room
  116 N. Auburn Ave., 505/325-8183

Best Mexican Food
Coyote's
  Anasazi Inn, 903 W. Main St., 505/325-4564
El Charro Restaurant
  737 W. Main St., 505/327-2464
La Fiesta Grande Restaurant
  1916 E. Main St., 505/326-6476
Los Hermanitos
  3501 E. Main St., 505/326-5664

N

Los Rios Cafe
915 Farmington Ave., 505/325-5699
Senor Pepper's
1400 W. Navajo St., 505/327-0436

Best Regional Food
La Fiesta Grande Restaurant
1916 E. Main St., 505/326-6476

Best Restaurant Meal Value
K-Bob's Steakhouse
2210 E. Twentieth St., 505/327-5979

Best Seafood
Five Seasons Restaurant
1100 W. Broadway Ave., Bloomfield, 505/632-1196
K.B. Dillon's
101 W. Broadway, 505/325-0222

Best Steaks
Five Seasons Restaurant
1100 W. Broadway Ave., Bloomfield, 505/632-1196
K-Bob's Steakhouse
2210 E. Twentieth St., 505/327-5979
K.B. Dillon's
101 W. Broadway Ave., 505/325-0222

Best Sunday Brunch
Brass Apple Restaurant
Holiday Inn, 600 E. Broadway, 505/327-9811
Riverwalk Patio and Grille
Best Western Inn and Suites, 700 Scott Ave.,
505/327-5221

GALLUP, NM

Best Breakfast
Earl's Restaurant
1400 Hwy. 66E, 505/863-4201
Rocket Cafe
1719 S. Second St., 505/722-8972

Best Casual Dining
Pal Joey's Restaurant and Lounge
1648 S. Second St., 505/722-6383
Panz Alegra
1201 Hwy. 66E, 505/722-7229

Best Chinese Food
King Dragon
828 Hwy. 66N, 505/863-6300

Best Coffee/Coffeehouse
Kristy's Coffee Shop
1310 Hwy. 66E, 505/863-4742

Best Diner
El Sombrero Restaurant
1201 W. 66th Ave., 505/863-4554
Maria's
110 W. Coal Ave., 505/722-6135

Best Family Restaurant
Earl's Restaurant
1400 Hwy. 66E, 505/863-4201

Best Fine Dining
Nicole's
  Holiday Inn, 2915 Hwy. 66W, 505/722-2201

Best Italian Food
Dominic's Downtown Cafe
  303 W. Coal Ave., 505/722-0117

Best Mexican Food
El Sombrero Restaurant
  1201 W. 66th Ave., 505/863-4554
Panz Alegra
  1201 Hwy. 66E, 505/722-7229
Pedro's Restaurant and Lounge
  107 Burke Dr., 505/863-9755

Best Pizza
Big Cheese Pizza
  1316 Metro Ave., 505/722-4454

Best Restaurant Meal Value
Rocket Cafe
  1719 S. Second St., 505/722-8972

HOBBS, NM

N

Best American Food
Wallace's
  1403 E. Broadway St., 505/393-9025

Best Breakfast
Casey's
  209 W. Broadway St., 505/393-0308

Best Burgers
Saturday's
  312 W. Bender Blvd., 505/392-3651

Best Business Lunch
Furr's Cafeteria
  Broadmoore Mall, 726 E. Michigan Ave.,
    505/397-3211

Best Chinese Food
Mi Won
  1518 E. Marland St., 505/393-7644
Peking Restaurant
  2404 N. Grimes St., 505/392-2411

Best Family Restaurant
Kettle Restaurant
  505 N. Marland Blvd., 505/397-0663

Best Homestyle Food
Grandy's Restaurant
  1917 N. Turner St., 505/397-2219
Prairie Rose
  2004 N. Turner St., 505/393-9373

Best Mexican Food
Dan's Mexican Foods
  921 S. Dal Paso St., 505/397-0097
Goncho's Restaurant
  801 W. Bender Blvd., 505/397-3551
La Fiesta Restaurant
  604 E. Broadway St., 505/397-1235

La Fondita
  509 W. Broadway St., 505/397-0909

Best Restaurant in Town
Cattle Baron Steak and Seafood
  1930 N. Grimes St., 505/393-2800

LAS CRUCES, NM

Best Bistro
Brass Cactus Bistro
  1800 Avenida de'Mesilla, 505/527-4656

Best Eclectic Menu
Brass Cactus Bistro
  1800 Avenida de'Mesilla, 505/527-4656

Best Japanese Food
Tatsu
  930 El Paseo St., 505/526-7144

Best Mexican Food
Little Nellie's Chili Factory
  600 E. Amador Ave., 505/523-6407
Nellie's Cafe
  1226 W. Hadley Ave., 505/524-9982
Roberto's Mexican Food
  908 E. Amador Ave., 505/523-1851
The Hacienda
  2605 S. Espina St., 505/522-6380

Best Middle Eastern Food
Casbah Restaurant
  2404 S. Locust St., Ste. 3, 505/522-8530

LAS VEGAS, NM

Best American Food
El Alto Supper Club
  600 Sapello St., 505/454-0808

Best Burgers
Hillcrest Restaurant
  1106 Grand Ave., 505/425-7211

Best Chinese Food
Golden Dragon Restaurant
  1136 Grand Ave., 505/425-8522

Best Lunch
Spic and Span Bakery and Cafe
  713 Douglas Ave., 505/425-6481

Best Mexican Food
El Alto Supper Club
  600 Sapello St., 505/454-0808
El Rialto Restaurant
  141 Bridge St., 505/454-0037
Hillcrest Restaurant
  1106 Grand Ave., 505/425-7211
Johnny's Mexican Kitchen
  717 Grand Ave., 505/454-1769

Best Regional Food
Pancho's Cafe
  1154 N. Grand Ave., 505/454-8169

Best Steaks
El Alto Supper Club
600 Sapello St., 505/454-0808
K-Bob's of Las Vegas
1803 Seventh St., 505/425-6322

ROSWELL, NM

Best American Food
Nuthin' Fancy Cafe
2103 N. Main St., 505/623-4098
Peppers Grill
500 N. Main St., 505/623-1700

Best Fine Dining
Cattle Baron Steak and Seafood
1113 N. Main St., 505/622-2465

Best Italian Food
Giovanni's Italian Restaurant
3106 N. Main St., 505/623-0063
Mario's
200 E. Second St., 505/623-1740
Pasta Cafe
4501 N. Main St., 505/624-1111

Best Mexican Food
Cecilio's North
107 Twin Diamond Rd., 505/622-6180
Mario's
200 E. Second St., 505/623-1740
Martin's Capitol Cafe
110 W. Fourth St., 505/624-2111
Peppers Grill
500 N. Main St., 505/623-1700

Best Place to Take the Kids
Peter Piper Pizza
2601 N. Main St., 505/622-3474

Best Restaurant in Town
Peppers Grill
500 N. Main St., 505/623-1700

Best Romantic Dining
The Claim Restaurant
1310 N. Main St., 505/623-6042

Best Seafood
Cattle Baron Steak and Seafood
1113 N. Main St., 505/622-2465

Best Steaks
Cattle Baron Steak and Seafood
1113 N. Main St., 505/622-2465

Best Sunday Brunch
Roswell Inn
1815 N. Main St., 505/623-4920

Best Tea Room
Pecos Rose Tea Room
709 N. Main St., 505/625-9256
Creatively Yours Tea Cup
1501 W. Second St., 505/623-2586

N

SANTA FE, NM

Best All-You-Can-Eat Buffet
Furr's Cafeteria
   522 W. Cordova Rd., 505/982-3816
   De Vargas Shopping Mall, 187 Paseo de Peralta,
    505/988-4431

Best Bar
El Farol Restaurant and Lounge
   808 Canyon Rd., 505/983-9912

Best Breakfast
Cafe Pasqual's
   121 Don Gaspar Ave., 505/983-9340
Tia Sophia's
   210 W. San Francisco St., 505/983-9880

Best Burgers
San Francisco Bar and Grill
   114 W. San Francisco St., 505/982-2044

Best Business Lunch
Pranzo Italian Grill
   540 Montezuma Ave., 505/984-2645

Best Casual Dining
Tomasita's Cafe
   200 S. Guadalupe St., 505/983-5721

Best Chinese Food
Imperial Wok Oriental Gourmet
   731 Canyon Rd., 505/988-7100

Best Coffee/Coffeehouse
Downtown Subscriptions
   376 Garcia St., 505/983-3085

Best Continental Food
Pink Adobe
   406 Old Santa Fe Trail, 505/983-7712

Best Diner
Zia Diner
   326 S. Guadalupe St., 505/988-7008

Best Eclectic Menu
Atalaya Restaurant and Bakery
   320 S. Guadalupe St., 505/982-2709
Cafe Escalera
   130 Lincoln Ave., 505/989-8188
Santacafe
   231 Washington Ave., 505/984-1788

Best Family Restaurant
Garduno's of Santa Fe
   130 Lincoln Ave., 505/983-9797

Best French Food
Bistro 315
   315 Old Santa Fe Trail, 505/986-9190

Best Health-Conscious Menu
Natural Cafe
   1494 Cerrillos Rd., 505/983-1411

Best Homestyle Food
Bobcat Bite Restaurant
   Old Las Vegas Hwy., Rte. 3, 505/983-5319

Best Inexpensive Meal
Burrito Company
   111 Washington Ave., 505/982-4453

Best Italian Food
Andiamo
   322 Garfield St., 505/995-9595
Pranzo Italian Grill
   540 Montezuma Ave., 505/984-2645

Best Mexican Food
Old Mexico Grill
   2434 Cerrillos Rd., 505/473-0338
The Shed
   113 1/2 E. Palace Ave., 505/982-9030

Best Pizza
El Vicino
   321 W. San Francisco St., 505/986-8700

Best Place to Take the Kids
Furr's Cafeteria
   522 W. Cordova Rd., 505/982-3816
   De Vargas Shopping Mall, 187 Paseo de Peralta,
   505/988-4431

Best Regional Food
Guadalupe Cafe
   422 Old Santa Fe Trail, 505/982-9762
La Choza
   905 Alarid St., 505/982-0909
Rancho De Chimayo
   Hwy. 76, Chimayo, 505/351-4444
The Shed
   113 1/2 E. Palace Ave., 505/982-9030

Best Restaurant in Town
Coyote Cafe
   132 W. Water St., 505/982-2454
Michael's Kitchen
   100 E. San Francisco St., 505/758-4178
Pink Adobe
   406 Old Santa Fe Trail, 505/983-7712
Santacafe
   231 Washington Ave., 505/984-1788
The Bull Ring
   150 Washington Ave., 505/983-3328
Tiny's Restaurant and Lounge
   1015 Pen Rd., 505/983-9817

Best Romantic Dining
La Casa Sena Restaurant
   125 E. Palace Ave., 505/988-9232

Best Salad/Salad Bar
Souper Salad
   2428 Cerrillos Rd., 505/473-1211

N

Best Sandwiches
Carlos' Gosp'l Cafe
  Wells Fargo Bank Plz., 125 Lincoln Ave.,
    505/983-1841
Noon Whistle
  451 W. Alameda St., 505/988-2636

Best Seafood
Anthony's at the Delta
  228 E. Paseo de Onate Dr., Espanola, 505/753-4511

Best Southwestern Food
Cafe Pasqual's
  121 Don Gaspar Ave., 505/983-9340
Coyote Cafe
  132 W. Water St., 505/982-2454
Geronimo
  724 Canyon Rd., 505/982-1500
Inn of the Anasazi
  113 Washington Ave., 505/988-3236
La Casa Sena
  125 E. Palace Ave., 505/988-9232
The Old House Restaurant
  309 W. San Francisco St., 505/988-4455

Best Spanish Food
El Farol Restaurant and Lounge
  808 Canyon Rd., 505/983-9912

Best Steaks
Steaksmith at El Gancho
  Old Las Vegas Hwy., 505/988-3333

Best Sunday Brunch
The Eldorado Court
  Eldorado Hotel, 309 W. San Francisco St.,
    505/988-4455

Best Tea Room
Hotel St. Francis
  210 Don Gaspar Ave., 505/983-5700

Best Vegetarian Food
Healthy David's Cafe
  418 Cerrillos Rd., 505/982-4147

SILVER CITY, NM

Best Breakfast
Drifter Motel
  711 Silver Heights Blvd., 505/538-2916

Best Burgers
The Red Barn
  708 Silver Heights Blvd., 505/538-5666

Best Chinese Food
Chinese Palace Restaurant
  1608 N. Durango St., 505/538-9300

Best Pizza
R & R Pizza Express
  1602 Silver Heights Blvd., 505/388-3600

Best Sandwiches
Grinder Mill
  403 W. College Ave., 505/538-3366

Best Steaks
The Red Barn
  708 Silver Heights Blvd., 505/538-5666

TAOS, NM

Best Breakfast
Brother's Two Cafe and Deli
  115 E. Plaza, 505/758-4205
Ricky's Restaurant
  Santa Fe Rd. S., 505/758-3589

Best Burgers
Apple Tree Restaurant
  123 Bent St., 505/758-1900
Ogelvie's Bar and Grille
  103 E. Plaza, Ste. 1, 505/758-8866

Best Business Lunch
Trading Post Cafe
  101 Stakeout Dr., Ranchos de Taos, 505/758-2042

Best Coffee/Coffeehouse
Taos Coffee Company
  1807 S. Santa Fe Rd., Ranchos De Taos,
  505/758-3331

Best Family Restaurant
Michael's Kitchen
  304 Paseo Del Pueblo Norte, 505/758-4178

Best French Food
La Folie
  122 Dona Luz, 505/758-8800

Best Health-Conscious Menu
Amigo's Natural Grocery
  326 S. Santa Fe Rd., 505/758-8493

Best Ice Cream/Yogurt
Taos Cow Ice Cream
  591 Arroyo Hondo Seco Rd., Arroyo Seco,
  505/776-5640

Best Pizza
Outback Pizza
  712 Paseo Del Pueblo Norte, 505/758-3112

Best Place to Take the Kids
Michael's Kitchen
  304 Paseo Del Pueblo Norte, 505/758-4178

Best Spanish Food
Jacquelina's
  1541 Paseo Del Pueblo S., 505/751-0399

N

New York

ALBANY, NY

Best American Food
Barnsider
  480 Sand Creek Rd., 518/869-2448

Best Brewpub
Big House Brewing Company
  90 N. Pearl St., 518/445-2739

Best Burgers
Beff's
  15 Watervliet Ave., 518/482-2333
Kelty's Iron Horse Pub
  15 Colvin Ave., 518/458-2400
Sutter's Mill and Mining Company
  1200 Western Ave., 518/489-4910

Best Cajun/Creole Food
Justin's
  301 Lark St., 518/436-7008

Best Casual Dining
Big House Brewing Company
  90 N. Pearl St., 518/445-2739
Ginger Man Wine Bar and Restaurant
  234 Western Ave., 518/427-5963

Best Chinese Food
Amazing Wok Chinese
  267 Lark St., 518/434-3946
Dumpling House Chinese Restaurant
  120 Everett Rd., 518/458-7044
Emperor Palace
  423 Madison Ave., 518/465-3124
Pearl of the Orient
  471 Albany Shaker Rd., 518/459-0903

Peking Restaurant
 1100 Madison Ave., 518/489-0606

Best Coffee/Coffeehouse
Barnes and Noble Cafe
 20 Wolf Rd., 518/459-8183
Borders Books and Music Espresso Bar
 59 Wolf Rd., 518/482-5800
Professor Java's Coffee
 217 Wolf Rd., 518/435-0843
The Daily Grind
 204 Lark St., 518/427-0464

Best Diner
Miss Albany Diner
 893 Broadway, 518/465-9148
Quintessence
 11 New Scotland Ave., 518/434-8186

Best Eclectic Menu
Justin's
 301 Lark St., 518/436-7008

Best Fine Dining
La Serre Restaurant
 14 Green St., 518/463-6056
Ogden's Restaurant
 42 Howard St., 518/463-6605

Best French Food
L'Ecole Encore
 44 Fuller Rd., 518/437-1234
La Serre Restaurant
 14 Green St., 518/463-6056
Nicole's Bistro
 25 Albany St., 518/465-1111

Best Ice Cream/Yogurt
Kurver Kreme
 1349 Central Ave., 518/459-4120

Best Indian Food
Big House Brewing Company
 90 N. Pearl St., 518/445-2739
Shalimar Restaurant
 31 Central Ave., 518/434-0890
Sitar Indian Restaurant
 1929 Central Ave., 518/456-6670

Best Italian Food
Cafe Capriccio
 49 Grand St., 518/465-0439
Cavaleri Restaurant
 334 Second Ave., 518/463-4320
Draymond's Restaurant and Lounge
 269 Osborne Rd., 518/459-6364
Lombardo's Restaurant
 121 Madison Ave., 518/462-9180
Nicole's Restaurant
 556 Delaware Ave., 518/436-4952
Ristorante Paradiso
 198 Central Ave., 518/462-5812

Best Japanese Food
Arita Japanese Restaurant
  192 N. Allen St., 518/482-1080
Hiro's Japanese Restaurant
  1933 Central Ave., 518/456-1180

Best Mexican Food
Cactus Jack's
  455 Sand Creek Rd., 518/482-5297
El Loco Mexican Cafe
  465 Madison Ave., 518/436-1855
Garcia's Mexican Restaurant
  1673 Central Ave., 518/456-4116

Best Middle Eastern Food
BFS Catering and Imports
  1736 Western Ave., 518/452-6342
Mamoun's Falafel
  206 Washington Ave., 518/434-3901

Best Other Ethnic Food
Yono's (Indonesian)
  289 Hamilton St., 518/436-7747

Best Outdoor Dining
Cafe Hollywood
  275 Lark St., 518/472-9043
Cranberry Bog Restaurant
  56 Wolf Rd., 518/459-5110

Best Pizza
Fountain Restaurant
  283 New Scotland Ave., 518/482-9898
Inferno Pizzeria
  496 Albany Shaker Rd., 518/459-2121
Jeff's Pizzeria
  1038 Madison Ave., 518/489-2000
Sovrana Grocery Bakery and Deli
  63 N. Lake Ave., 518/465-0961

Best Place to See Celebrities
Jack's Oyster House
  42 State St., 518/465-8854

Best Restaurant in Town
La Serre Restaurant
  14 Green St., 518/463-6056
Yono's
  289 Hamilton St., 518/436-7747

Best Sandwiches
Debbie's Kitchen
  456 Madison Ave., 518/463-3829

Best Seafood
Jack's Oyster House
  42 State St., 518/465-8854
Real Seafood Company
  195 Wolf Rd., 518/458-2068
Scrimshaw Restaurant
  660 Albany Shaker Rd., 518/452-5801

N

Best Soul Food
Big John's Restaurant
   51 Elizabeth St., 518/463-5972

Best Steaks
Barnsider
   480 Sand Creek Rd., 518/869-2448
Butcher Block Steakhouse
   1632A Central Ave., 518/456-1653

Best Sunday Brunch
Madison's End Cafe
   1108 Madison Ave., 518/489-8859

Best Thai Food
Bangkok Thai Restaurant
   8 Wolf Rd., 518/435-1027

Best Vegetarian Food
Mother Earth's Cafe
   217 Western Ave., 518/434-0944
Shades Of Green
   187 Lark St., 518/434-1830

Best Vietnamese Food
My Linh's Restaurant
   137 Madison Ave., 518/434-6884

Best Wine Selection
Justin's
   301 Lark St., 518/436-7008
The Ginger Man Wine Bar and Restaurant
   234 Western Ave., 518/427-5963

AMSTERDAM, NY

Best Diner
Windmill Diner Restaurant
   4790 State Hwy. 30, 518/842-0087

Best Family Restaurant
Amsterdam Diner
   Rte. 30S, 518/842-9975

Best Italian Food
Lorenzo's Restaurant
   25 Union St., 518/842-9854

Best Pizza
Crystal Bar and Restaurant
   72 Lyon St., 518/842-9050

Best Steaks
Raindancer Steak Parlour
   4582 State Hwy. 30, 518/842-2606

AUBURN, NY

Best Coffee/Coffeehouse
Phoenix Cafe
   2 South St., 315/258-8681
Vermont Green Mountain Specialty Company
   50 E. Genesee St., Skaneateles, 315/685-1500

Best Desserts
Spirits Tavern and Cafe
  State Street Mall, 20 State St., 315/252-9702

Best Homestyle Food
Auburn Family Restaurant
  161 Genesee St., 315/253-2274
Hunter's Diner
  18 Genesee St., 315/255-3578

Best Italian Food
Curley's Restaurant
  96 State St., 315/252-5224
Hollywood Restaurant
  200A Clark St., 315/252-9775
Rosalie's Cucina
  841 W. Genesee St. Rd., Skaneateles, 315/685-2200

Best Restaurant in Town
Cassidy's Restaurant
  135 Grant Ave., 315/252-6162
Michael's Restaurant
  196 Clark St., 315/252-6194

Best Sandwiches
Downtown Deli
  119 Genesee St., 315/255-1919
Rick's Grocery and Deli
  449 N. Seward Ave., 315/253-0051

Best Seafood
Doug's Fish Fry
  8 Jordan St., Skaneateles, 315/685-3288

Best Steaks
Lasca's
  252 Grant Ave., 315/253-4885
Sunset Restaurant
  87 N. Division St., 315/252-9765

Best Sunday Brunch
Ripples Restaurant
  Holiday Inn, 75 North St., 315/253-4531
Springside Inn
  41 W. Lake Ave., 315/252-7247

Best Vegetarian Food
Phoenix Cafe
  2 South St., 315/258-8681
Spirits Tavern and Cafe
  State Street Mall, 20 State St., 315/252-9702

BINGHAMTON, NY

Best Barbecue/Ribs
Niko's Char Pit
  526 Court St., 607/724-2427
Theo's Restaurant
  11 Main St., Johnson City, 607/797-0088

Best Burgers
Uncle Tony's
  79 State St., 607/723-4488

Best Coffee/Coffeehouse
Java Joe's
  81 State St., 607/774-0966

Best Fine Dining
Number Five Restaurant
  33 S. Washington St., 607/723-0555

Best Ice Cream/Yogurt
Pat Mitchell's Ice Cream
  225 Harrison Ave., Endicott, 607/785-3080

Best Italian Food
Cortese Restaurant
  117 Robinson St., 607/723-6477
Orlando's
  107 W. Main St., Endicott, 607/757-9276

Best Japanese Food
Kampai Japanese Steak House
  108 Jensen Rd. at Vestal Pkwy. E., Vestal,
    607/798-7521

Best Pizza
Consol Family Kitchen
  101 Oak Hill Ave., Endicott, 607/754-7437
Cortese Restaurant
  117 Robinson St., 607/723-6477

Best Sandwiches
Old World Deli
  27 Court St., 607/722-5265

Best Seafood
Copper Cricket Cafe
  266 Main St., 607/729-5620

Best Sunday Brunch
Silo Restaurant
  Rte. 206E, Greene, 607/656-4377

Best Vietnamese Food
Mekong Vietnamese Restaurant
  29 Willow St., Johnson City, 607/770-9628

BRONX, NY

*[See also: Brooklyn, Manhattan, Queens, White
Plains, and Yonkers; and Englewood and Teaneck,
NJ.]*

Best American Food
Jack's Restaurant
  76 Westchester Sq., 718/892-3154
Piper's Kilt Restaurant
  170 W. 231st St., 718/548-9539

Best Chinese Food
Hawaii Sea Restaurant
  1477 Williamsbridge Rd., 718/863-7900
Lee Xing Chinese Restaurant
  3207 Westchester Ave., 718/829-7945

Meiya Kitchen
  858 Gerard Ave., 718/993-7710
Pyung Chang Restaurant
  6025 Broadway, 718/884-2134

Best Coffee/Coffeehouse
Unity Coffee Shop
  58 E. 161st St., 718/665-6180

Best Delicatessen
Court Deli
  96 E. 161st St., 718/993-1380
Gianluca's Salumeria
  1044 Morris Park Ave., 718/892-3080
Skyview Deli Kosher Restaurant
  5665 Riverdale Ave., 718/796-8596

Best Diner
Pelham Bay Diner
  1920 E. Gun Hill Rd., 718/379-4130
Riverdale Diner
  238 W. Kingsbridge Rd., 718/884-6050
Unity Coffee Shop
  58 E. 161st St., 718/665-6180

Best German Food
Castle Harbour Casino
  1118 Havemeyer Ave., 718/829-9459

Best Homestyle Food
Dominick's Restaurant
  2335 Arthur Ave., 718/733-2807

Best Italian Food
Ann and Tony's Restaurant
  2407 Arthur Ave., 718/364-8250
Artie's Manor Inn
  394 City Island Ave., 718/885-9885
Bella Vista Pizzeria
  904A Hunts Point Ave., 718/617-3939
Boschetto Italian Restaurant
  1660 E. Gun Hill Rd., 718/379-9335
Casa Mia Restaurant
  2143 Williamsbridge Rd., 718/792-8590
Fratelli's Restaurant
  2507 Eastchester Rd., 718/547-2489
Giovanni's Pizza and Restaurant
  3209 Westchester Ave., 718/892-4340
Mario's Restaurant
  2342 Arthur Ave., 718/584-1188
  842 Hunts Point Ave., 718/842-3636
Pasquale Rigoletto Restaurant
  2311 Arthur Ave., 718/365-6644
Venice Restaurant and Pizzeria
  772 E. 149th St., 718/585-5164

Best Japanese Food
Sakura Delight Japanese Restaurant
  1 Riverdale Ave., 718/549-2606

Best Kosher Food
Four Star Zion Kosher Deli
  750 Lydig Ave., 718/597-6360

Best Lunch
Mary's Luncheonette
 1339 Oakpoint Ave., 718/542-5656
Riverdale Diner
 238 Kingsbridge Rd., 718/884-6050

Best Other Ethnic Food
Hawaii Sea Restaurant (Polynesian)
 1477 Williamsbridge Rd., 718/863-7900
Jimmy's Bronx Cafe (Latin American)
 281 W. Fordham Rd., 718/329-2000

Best Pizza
Emilio's Pizza
 3843 E. Tremont Ave., 718/409-0929
Mario's Restaurant
 2342 Arthur Ave., 718/584-1188
Peppino's Pizza
 934 Morris Ave., 718/681-3879

Best Sandwiches
Gianluca's Salumeria
 1044 Morris Park Ave., 718/892-3080
Mary's Luncheonette
 1339 Oakpoint Ave., 718/542-5656

Best Seafood
Artie's Manor Inn
 394 City Island Ave., 718/885-9885
Crab Shanty One
 361 City Island Ave., 718/885-1810
Land and Sea Restaurant
 5535 Broadway, 718/543-3423

Best Spanish Food
Lebanon Restaurant
 555 E. 169th St., 718/293-5681

Best Sports Bar
Jimmy's Bronx Cafe
 281 W. Fordham Rd., 718/329-2000

Best Steaks
Frank's Soup Bowl
 3580 Bronxwood Ave., 718/519-9277
Land and Sea Restaurant
 5535 Broadway, 718/543-3423

BROOKLYN, NY

*[See also: Bronx, Manhattan, Staten Island, and
Queens; and Hoboken, Jersey City, and North
Bergen, NJ.]*

Best American Food
Chadwick's Restaurant
 8822 Third Ave., 718/833-9855
Gage and Tollner Restaurant
 372 Fulton St., 718/875-5181
Heights Cafe
 84 Montague St., 718/625-5555

River Cafe
1 Water St., 718/522-5200

Best Bistro
Seasons
556 Driggs Ave., 718/384-9695

Best Breakfast
Junior's Restaurant
386 Flatbush Ave., 718/852-5257

Best Chinese Food
Mr. Tang's Kitchen
7523 Third Ave., 718/748-0400
Ocean Restaurant
4911 Avenue D, 718/629-2255

Best Delicatessen
Lassen and Hennigs
114 Montague St., 718/522-5464
Monte's Deli and Catering
156 Avenue O, 718/259-1500

Best Eclectic Menu
Oznot's Dish
79 Berry St., 718/599-6596

Best Italian Food
Areo Restaurant
8424 Third Ave., 718/238-0079
Cucina
256 Fifth Ave., 718/230-0711
Milano Restaurant
7514 Eighteenth Ave., 718/259-4300
Salvi Restaurant
4220 Quentin Rd., 718/252-3030
Two Toms Restaurant
255 Third Ave., 718/875-8689

Best Lunch
Once Upon A Sundae
7702 Third Ave., 718/748-3412
Vegas Diner
1619 86th St., 718/331-2221

Best Mexican Food
Vera Cruz Restaurant
195 Bedford Ave., 718/599-7914

Best Pizza
Lento's Restaurant
7003 Third Ave. at Ovington St., 718/745-9197
Patsy's Pizzeria
19 Old Fulton St., New York, 718/858-4300

Best Restaurant in Town
La Bouillabaisse
145 Atlantic Ave., 718/522-8275
Moustache Mid Eastern Pitza
405 Atlantic Ave., 718/852-5555

Best Restaurant Meal Value
Aunt Suzie's Restaurant
247 Fifth Ave., 718/788-2868

Best Steaks
Peter Luger Steak House
178 Broadway, 718/387-7400

Best Thai Food
Planet Thailand
184 Bedford Ave., 718/599-5758
Thai Cafe
925 Manhattan Ave., 718/383-3562

BUFFALO, NY

Best American Food
Alice's Kitchen
3122 Sheridan Dr., 716/836-8954
Classics V
2443 Niagara Falls Blvd., 716/691-4585
Crean's
1245 Abbott Rd., 716/823-1255

Best Breakfast
Alice's Kitchen
3122 Sheridan Dr., 716/836-8954
Ambrosia Restaurant
467 Elmwood Ave., 716/881-2196
Country Kitchen
2043 Kensington Ave., 716/839-0290
First Ward Steel City Diner
93 Ridge Rd., 716/824-4607
Original Pancake House
5479 Main St., 716/634-5515

Best Brewpub
Buffalo Brew Pub
6861 Main St., 716/632-0552

Best Burgers
Zebb's Deluxe Grill and Bar
2875 Niagara Falls Blvd., 716/564-0610

Best Business Lunch
Hourglass Restaurant
981 Kenmore Ave., 716/877-8788

Best Casual Dining
Curly's Bar and Grill
647 Ridge Rd., 716/824-9716
Jimmy Mac's
555 Elmwood Ave., 716/886-9112

Best Chinese Food
Chang's Garden
938 Maple Rd., 716/689-3355

Best Diner
First Ward Steel City Diner
93 Ridge Rd., 716/824-4607

Best Family Restaurant
Dandelions Restaurant
1340 N. Forest Rd., 716/688-9714
Park Lane Restaurant
1360 Delaware Ave., 716/883-3344
33 Gates Circle, 716/883-3344

Best Fine Dining
E.B. Green's Steakhouse
  Hyatt Regency, 2 Fountain Plz., 716/856-1234
Oliver's Restaurant
  2095 Delaware Ave., 716/877-9662

Best French Food
Rue Franklin West
  341 Franklin St., 716/852-4416

Best Greek/Mediterranean Food
Spilio's
  5175 Transit Rd., 407/727-0239

Best Homestyle Food
Asa Ransom House Country Inn
  10529 Main St., Clarence, 716/759-2315

Best Ice Cream/Yogurt
Carvel Ice Cream Bakery
  3410 Delaware Ave., 716/876-6141
Sweet Jenny's
  5590 Main St., 716/631-2424

Best Italian Food
Chef's Restaurant
  291 Seneca St., 716/856-9187
Ilio Di Paolo's Restaurant
  3785 S. Park Ave., 716/825-3675
Little Talia Trattoria
  1458 Hertel Ave., 716/833-8667
Siena Restaurant
  4516 Main St., 716/839-3108

Best Mexican Food
Garcia's Mexican Restaurant
  3755 Union Rd., 716/681-9595
Mexican Joe's
  1300 N. Forest Rd., 716/632-4530

Best Pizza
Broadway Bobby's Pizzeria
  635 Ridge Rd., 716/827-8750
Jacobi's Restaurant
  1404 Abbott Rd., 716/825-5544
La Nova Pizzeria
  371 W. Ferry St., 716/881-3303

Best Place to Eat Alone
Red Carpet Restaurant
  5507 Main St., 716/634-1968

Best Restaurant in Town
Victoria Square Family Restaurant
  717 Ridge Rd., 716/825-6627

Best Sandwiches
Steve's Pig and Ox Roast
  951 Ridge Rd., 716/824-8601
Vito Fish and Chicken
  900 William St., 716/854-2442

N

Best Sunday Brunch
Christino's
Marriott Hotel, 1340 Millersport Hwy.,
716/689-6900

Best Vegetarian Food
Rutabaga's Vegetarian Cuisine
177 Hodge Ave., 716/882-2909

CENTEREACH, NY

Best Brewpub
Brick House Brewery and Restaurant
675 W. Main St., East Patchogue, 516/447-2337

Best Diner
Suffolk Diner
2101 Middle Country Rd., 516/981-9855

Best Mexican Food
Meson Ole Restaurant
2055 Middle Country Rd., 516/737-3346

Best Restaurant in Town
Bellport Chowder House
19 Bellport Ln., Bellport, 516/286-2343

Best Seafood
Bellport Chowder House
19 Bellport Ln., Bellport, 516/286-2343
Broadway Grill
115 W. Broadway, Port Jefferson, 516/473-1220

ELMIRA, NY

Best Italian Food
Moretti's Restaurant
800 Hatch St., 607/734-1535

Best Restaurant in Town
Pierce's 1894 Restaurant
228 Oakwood Ave., 607/734-2022
The Hill Top Inn
171 Jerusalem Hill Rd., 607/732-6728

ELMONT, NY

Best American Food
Murph's 935 Corp
935 Hempstead Turnpike, Franklin Square,
516/358-0548

Best Chinese Food
Szechuan Delight
24011 Linden Blvd., 516/285-6088

Best Continental Food
Luna Restaurant
127 Hempstead Turnpike, 516/488-3602

Best Diner
Stop 20 Diner
1336 Hempstead Turnpike, 516/358-7142

Best Italian Food
Cafe La Gondola
  1540 Hempstead Turnpike, 516/437-8381
King Umberto
  1339 Hempstead Turnpike, 516/352-8391
La Cantina Ristorante
  31 Rockaway Ave., Valley Stream, 516/825-2117

Best Lunch
Trotter's Tavern
  197 Mineola Blvd., Mineola, 516/746-9393

Best Other Ethnic Food
Little Portugal (Portuguese)
  241 Mineola Blvd., Mineola, 516/742-9797

Best Restaurant in Town
Piping Rock Restaurant
  130 Post Ave., Westbury, 516/333-5555

Best Restaurant Meal Value
Alpine Garden Restaurant
  11 Franklin Ave., Franklin Square, 516/354-5770

Best Seafood
Riverbay Seafood Bar and Grill
  700 Willis Ave., Williston Park, 516/742-9191

N

FREEPORT, NY

Best Breakfast
Imperial Diner
  63 W. Merrick Rd., 516/868-0303
Merrick Townhouse Diner
  2160 Sunrise Hwy. E., Merrick, 516/546-2664

Best Chinese Food
Hunan Palace
  129 W. Sunrise Hwy., 516/868-8899

Best Family Restaurant
Marybill Diner
  14 Merrick Ave. N., Merrick, 516/378-9715

Best Italian Food
Dockside Restaurant
  507 Guy Lombardo Ave., 516/378-5544

Best Seafood
Margo and Frank
  379 Woodcleft Ave., 516/546-3393
Moorings Restaurant
  392 Guy Lombardo Ave., 516/378-3244
Otto's Sea Grill
  271 Woodcleft Ave., 516/378-9480
Pier 95
  95 Hudson Ave., 516/867-9632
Tide's Inn
  340 Woodcleft Ave., 516/868-2231

Best Southwestern Food
Route 66
  33 Sunrise Hwy. W., Merrick, 516/623-7866

Best Spanish Food
House of Spain
 2008 Merrick Rd., Merrick, 516/378-8777

Best Steaks
Nautilus Cafe
 46 Woodcleft Ave., 516/379-2566

GARDEN CITY, NY

Best Burgers
Leo's Midway
 190 Seventh St., 516/742-0574

Best Casual Dining
Newport Grill
 176 Seventh St., 516/746-2592

Best Steaks
BK Sweeney's Steak House
 636 Franklin Ave., 516/746-3075

Best Sunday Brunch
The Polo Grill
 The Garden City Hotel, 45 Seventh St.,
 516/747-3000

HAUPPAUGE, NY

Best Diner
Paradise Diner
 579 Veterans Hwy., 516/724-1778

Best Italian Food
Forestier
 760 Townline Rd., 516/265-7475
San Marco Ristorante
 658 Vanderbilt Motor Pkwy., 516/273-0088

Best Japanese Food
Gasho of Japan
 356 Vanderbilt Motor Pkwy., 516/231-3400

HICKSVILLE, NY

Best American Food
Peppercorn's
 25 E. Marie St., 516/931-4002
Wickers Restaurant
 206 E. Old Country Rd., 516/433-6466

Best Chinese Food
Imperial Wok
 16 W. Marie St., 516/933-8688

Best Indian Food
Indian Oven
 67 E. Old Country Rd., 516/681-7070

Best Japanese Food
Century Noodle
 260 N. Broadway, 516/433-0622

Best Pizza
Gourmet Pizza and Things
 201 Broadway Mall, 516/681-8710

HUNTINGTON, NY

Best Coffee/Coffeehouse
Incredible Ices
362 New York Ave., 516/427-3737

Best French Food
Petite Gourmet
328 Main St., 516/271-3311

Best Greek/Mediterranean Food
Spartacus Restaurant
400 New York Ave., 516/549-9218

Best Italian Food
Cafe Trilussa
402 New York Ave., 516/271-8282
Piccolo Restaurant
215 Wall St., 516/424-5592

Best Japanese Food
Bonbori Japanese Restaurant
14 Elm St., 516/351-9163
Kurabarn Japanese Restaurant
479 New York Ave., 516/673-0060

Best Restaurant in Town
Calamari Kitchen
4 N. Cove Plz., Oyster Bay, 516/922-2999

Best Restaurant Meal Value
P.G. Steakhouse
1745 E. Jericho Turnpike, 516/499-1005

Best Romantic Dining
Mill River Inn
160 Mill River Rd., Oyster Bay, 516/922-7768

ITHACA, NY

Best 24-Hour Restaurant
State Diner of Ithaca
438 W. State St., 607/272-6189

Best Bar
The Rongovian Embassy
1 W. Main St., Trumansburg, 607/387-3334

Best Chinese Food
Main Moon Chinese Buffet
401 Elmira Rd., 607/277-3399

Best Continental Food
Renee's American Bistro
202 E. Falls St., 607/272-0656

Best Italian Food
Centini's Coddington Restaurant
124 Coddington Rd., 607/273-0802
Joe's Restaurant
602 W. Buffalo St., 607/273-2729
Lucatelli's Ristorante
205 Elmira Rd., 607/273-0777

Best Other Ethnic Food
Dano's on Cayuga (East European)
113 S. Cayuga St., 607/277-8942

N

Best Pizza
Little Joe's Restaurant
  410 Eddy St., 607/273-2771
Nines
  311 College Ave., 607/272-1888

Best Restaurant in Town
Taughannock Farms Inn
  2030 Gorge Rd., Trumansburg, 607/387-7711

Best Steaks
Antlers
  1159 Dryden Rd., 607/273-9725
Station Restaurant
  806 W. Buffalo St., 607/272-2609

Best Thai Food
Thai Cuisine
  501 S. Meadow St., 607/273-2031

Best Vegetarian Food
Moosewood Restaurant
  215 N. Cayuga St., 607/273-9610

JAMESTOWN, NY

N

Best Breakfast
Good Morning Farm
  2 Hadley Bay Rd., Stow, 716/763-1772

Best Dinner
Hultman's Four Coins Lounge
  232 W. Main St., Falconer, 716/665-6837
Ironstone Restaurant
  516 W. Fourth St., 716/487-1516
Vullo's Restaurant Veal House
  Rte. 430, Greenhurst, 716/487-9568

Best Homestyle Food
Grainery Restaurant
  1494 Thornton Rd., Cherry Creek, 716/287-3500
Ramsey's
  Rte. 430, Greenhurst, 716/488-3503

Best Italian Food
La Scala
  3202 Fluvanna Ave., 716/664-7534
The House of Petillo
  382 Hunt Rd., 716/664-7457

Best Lunch
Colonnade
  150 W. Fourth St., 716/664-3400
Joanne's Deli
  20 W. Third St., 716/664-7272
Kaldi's
  106 E. Third St., 716/484-8904

Best Restaurant in Town
Hare and Hounds Inn
  64 Lakeside Dr., Bemus Point, 716/386-2181

Best Seafood
Davidson's Restaurant
  398 E. Fairmount Ave., Lakewood, 716/763-9135

Vullo's Restaurant Veal House
Rte. 430, Greenhurst, 716/487-9568

Best Wine Selection
MacDuff's Restaurant
317 Pine St., 716/664-9414

KINGSTON, NY

Best Breakfast
Deising's Bakery and Coffee Shop
111 N. Front St., 914/338-7503
584 Broadway, 914/338-1580

Best Chinese Food
Rondout Golden Duck
11 Broadway, 914/331-3221

Best Japanese Food
Golden Ginza
24 Broadway, 914/339-8132

Best Mexican Food
Armadillo Bar and Grill
97 Abeel St., 914/339-1550

Best Outdoor Dining
Hoffman House Tavern
94 N. Front St., 914/338-2626

Best Seafood
Ship to Shore
15 W. Strand St., 914/331-7034

LACKAWANNA, NY

Best Restaurant in Town
Mansford Inn
3290 Abbott Rd., Orchard Park, 716/828-1115

LAKE PLACID, NY

Best Coffee/Coffeehouse
A New Leaf
8 Main St., 518/523-1847

Best Desserts
Three Guys and I
89 Saranac Ave., 518/523-4897

Best Italian Food
Jimmy's 21
21 Main St., 518/523-2353

Best Lunch
Three Guys and I
89 Saranac Ave., 518/523-4897

Best Pizza
Mr. Mike's Pizza
332 Main St., 518/523-9770

Best Steaks
Jimmy's 21
21 Main St., 518/523-2353

LOCKPORT, NY

Best American Food
Garlock's Restaurant
35 S. Transit St., 716/433-5595

Best Breakfast
Chet's Dog House
14 W. Main St., 716/433-1003

Best Family Dining
La Port's Pine Restaurant
48 Pine St., 716/433-9756

Best Homestyle Food
Boston Market
5849 S. Transit Rd., 716/439-5486
Finnan's
1191 Lincoln Ave., 716/438-2363

Best Italian Food
De Flippo's Restaurant
326 West Ave., 716/433-2913
Lorenzo's Restaurant
3919 Lockport Olcott Rd., 716/434-8446

Best Pizza
Pizza Oven
54 Vine St., 716/433-4390

Best Steaks
Danny Sheehan's Steak House
491 West Ave., 716/433-4666

MANHATTAN, NY

[See also: Bronx, Brooklyn, Staten Island, Queens, and Yonkers; and Englewood, Hoboken, Jersey City, and North Bergen, NJ.]

Best 24-Hour Restaurant
Wo Hop Kitchen
17 Mott St., 212/267-2536

Best American Food
America Restaurant
9 E. Eighteenth St., 212/505-2110
Corner Bistro
331 W. Fourth St., 212/242-9502
Fraunce's Tavern Restaurant
54 Pearl St., 212/269-0144
Marion's Continental Restaurant
354 Bowery, 212/475-7621
Mustang Grill
1633 Second Ave., 212/744-9194
Saloon
1920 Broadway, 212/874-1500
Tea and Sympathy
108 Greenwich Ave., 212/807-8329
Union Square Cafe
21 E. Sixteenth St., 212/243-4020

Best Atmosphere
Halcyon Restaurant
  151 W. 54th St., 212/247-0670
Kin Khao Restaurant
  171 Spring St., 212/966-3939
Rainbow Room
  30 Rockefeller Plz., Ste. 65, 212/632-5000
The Oak Room
  Algonquin Hotel, 59 W. 44th St., 212/840-6800

Best Bar
Bar Six
  502 Sixth Ave., 212/691-1363
DBA 41st Avenue
  41 First Ave., 212/475-5097
Donahue's Bar and Restaurant
  770 Second Ave., 212/883-1193
Fanelli's Cafe
  94 Prince St., 212/226-9412
King Cole Room
  St. Regis Hotel, 2 E. 55th St., 212/753-4500
McSorley's Old Ale House
  15 E. Seventh St., 212/473-9148
Monkey Bar
  60 E. 54th St., 212/838-2600
Riverrun Cafe
  176 Franklin St., 212/966-3894
The Round Bar
  Royalton Hotel, 44 W. 44th St., 212/869-4400
White Horse Tavern
  567 Hudson St., 212/989-3956

Best Barbecue/Ribs
Brother's Barbecue
  225 W. Varick St., 212/727-2775
Dallas BBQ
  1265 Third Ave., 212/772-9393
  27 W. 72nd St., 212/873-2004
Dallas Jones Barbecue
  315 Sixth Ave., 212/741-7390
Virgil's Real Barbeque
  152 W. 44th St., 212/921-9494
Wylie's Ribs and Company
  891 First Ave., 212/751-0700

Best Breakfast
Brasserie
  100 E. 53rd St., 212/751-4840
Chock Full O'Nuts
  422 Madison Ave., 212/754-9600
Kiev Restaurant, Ltd.
  117 Second Ave., 212/674-4040
Mom's Bagels and Tables
  15 W. 45th St., 212/764-1566
The 540 Park Restaurant
  Regency Hotel, 540 Park Ave., 212/759-4100
Royal Canadian Pancake House
  2286 Broadway, 212/873-6052
  1004 Second Ave., 212/980-4131

N

180 Third Ave., 212/777-9288

Best Burgers
Broome Street Bar
363 W. Broadway, 212/925-2086
Cafe Centro
200 Park Ave., 212/818-1333
Chelsea Grill
135 Eighth Ave., 212/929-9766
Churchill's Restaurant
1277 Third Ave., 212/650-1618
Corner Bistro
331 W. Fourth St., 212/242-9502
Jackson Hole Wyoming Burgers
521 Third Ave., 212/679-3264
232 E. 64th St., 212/371-7187
JG Melon Restaurant
1291 Third Ave., 212/650-1310

Best Business Lunch
An American Place
2 Park Ave., 212/684-2122
Four Seasons
99 E. 52nd St., 212/754-9494
Michael's Restaurant
24 W. 55th St., 212/767-0555
Nobu
105 Hudson St. at Franklin St., 212/219-0500

Best Cajun/Creole Food
Baby Jake's
14 First Ave., 212/254-2229
Louisiana Community Bar and Grill
622 Broadway, 212/460-9633
Two Boots
37 Avenue A, 212/777-2668

Best Casual Dining
Bryant Park Grill
25 W. 40th St., 212/840-6500
Carmine's
200 W. 44th St., 212/221-3800
Giorgio's Deli Market
27 E. 21st St., 212/477-0006
La Spaghetteria
178 Second Ave., 212/995-0900
Miracle Grill
112 First Ave., 212/254-2353
Patrick Conway's
40 E. 43rd St., 212/286-1873
Three of Cups
83 First Ave., 212/388-0059
Tivoli Restaurant
515 Third Ave., 212/532-3300

Best Chinese Food
Canton Restaurant
45 Division St., 212/226-4441
China Grill
52 W. 53rd St., 212/333-7788

N

Cottage East
713 Second Ave., 212/286-8811
Hong Fat
1461 Amsterdam Ave., 212/862-9322
Hunan Balcony Gourmet
1417 Second Ave., 212/517-2088
Joe's Shanghai Restaurant
9 Pell St., 212/233-8888
Lucky Cheng's
24 First Ave., 212/473-0516
Mr. Chow Restaurant
324 E. 57th St., 212/751-9030
Ollie's Noodle Shop and Grill
190B W. 44th St., 212/921-5988
2315 Broadway, 212/362-3712
Shanghai Manor Restaurant
141 E. 55th St., 212/753-3900
Shun Lee Palace East
155 E. 55th St., 212/371-8844
Sweet and Tart Cafe
76 Mott St., 212/334-8088
Wo On Restaurant
16 Mott St., 212/962-6475

Best Coffee/Coffeehouse
Alt Coffee
139 Avenue A, 212/529-2233
Cafe Tina
184 Prince St., 212/925-9387
Caffe Dante
79 MacDougal St., 212/982-5275
Figaro Cafe
184 Bleecker St., 212/677-1100
Philip's Coffee Company
155 W. 56th St., 212/582-7347

Best Continental Food
Campagna Restaurant
24 E. 21st St., 212/460-0903
Delegates Dining Room
46 First Ave., 212/963-7626
Knickerbocker Bar and Grill
33 University Pl., 212/228-8490
Le Madri
168 W. Eighteenth St. at Seventh Ave.,
212/727-8022
Tribeca Grill
375 Greenwich St., 212/941-3900

Best Delicatessen
Barney Greengrass
541 Amsterdam Ave., 212/724-4707
Carnegie Delicatessen and Restaurant
854 Seventh Ave., 212/757-2245
Katz's Delicatessan
205 E. Houston St., 212/254-2246
Lee and Elle
336 Madison Ave., 212/867-5322

Second Avenue Kosher Deli
156 Second Ave., 212/677-0606
Stage Deli and Restaurant
834 Seventh Ave., 212/245-7850

Best Desserts

Cascabel
218 Lafayette St. near Spring St., 212/431-7300
Home Restaurant
20 Cornelia St.., 212/243-9578
My Most Favorite Dessert Company
120 W. 45th St., 212/997-5032
Serendipity 3
225 E. 60th St., 212/838-3531
Veniero's Pasticceria and Cafe
342 E. Eleventh St., 212/674-7264

Best Diner

B and H Dairy and Vegetarian Cuisine
127 Second Ave., 212/505-8065
Buffa's Deli
54 Prince St., 212/226-0211
Cheyenne Diner
411 Ninth Ave. at 33rd St., 212/465-8750
Comfort Diner
214 E. 45th St., 212/867-4555
Eisenberg Sandwich Shop
174 Fifth Ave., 212/675-5096
Ellen's Stardust Diner
1650 Broadway, 212/307-7575
Joe Jr.'s Restaurant
482 Sixth Ave., 212/924-5220
167 Third Ave., 212/473-5150
Lucky Dog Diner
167 First Ave., 212/260-4220
Market Diner
572 Eleventh Ave. at 43rd St., 212/695-0415
Munson Diner
600 W. 49th St., 212/246-0964
Odessa's Restaurant
117 Avenue A, 212/473-8916
Ratner's Dairy Restaurant
138 Delancey St., 212/677-5588

Best Eclectic Menu

Alva
36 E. 22nd St., 212/228-4399
Aqua Grill
210 Spring St., 212/274-0505
Aureole Restaurant
34 E. 61st St., 212/319-1660
Blue Ribbon Brasserie
97 Sullivan St., 212/274-0404
Blue Water Grill
31 Union Sq. W., 212/675-9500
Bowery Bar
358 Bowery, 212/475-2220
Cafe C III
Washington Sq. Hotel, 103 Waverly Pl.,
212/254-1200

Cafe Des Artistes
1 W. 67th St., 212/877-3500
Cafe New Territories
179 W. Broadway, 212/219-2010
Candela Restaurant
116 E. Sixteenth St., 212/614-8666
Caprice Cafe
199 Columbus Ave., 212/580-6948
Cibo
767 Second Ave., 212/681-1616
Circa
103 Second Ave., 212/777-4120
City Crab and Seafood Company
235 Park Ave. S., 212/529-3800
First
87 First Ave., 212/674-3823
Flamingo East
219 Second Ave., 212/533-2860
Gramercy Tavern
42 E. Twentieth St., 212/477-0777
Hudson River Club
250 Vesey St., 212/786-1500
Indigo Restaurant
142 W. Tenth St., 212/691-7757
Jerry's Restaurant
101 Prince St., 212/966-9464
Judson Grill
152 W. 52nd St., 212/582-5252
Lola Restaurant
30 W. 22nd St., 212/675-6700
Luma Restaurant
200 Ninth Ave., 212/633-8033
M and R Bar-Dining Room
264 Elizabeth St., 212/226-0559
Mad Fish
2182 Broadway, 212/787-0202
Man Ray Restaurant
169 Eighth Ave., 212/627-4220
New World Grill
329 W. 49th St., 212/957-4745
Pisces Restaurant
95 Avenue A, 212/260-6660
Revolution
611 Ninth Ave., 212/489-8451
Sammy's Restaurant
157 Chrystie St., 212/475-9131
Scully on Spring
203 Spring St., 212/965-0057
Spartina
355 Greenwich St., 212/274-9310
Zarela
953 Second Ave., 212/644-6740
Zucca
227 Tenth Ave., 212/741-1970

Best Family Restaurant
Carmine's
2450 Broadway, 212/362-2200

200 W. 44th St., 212/221-3800
Knickerbocker Bar and Grill
  33 University Pl., 212/228-8490
Tivoli Restaurant
  515 Third Ave., 212/532-3300

Best Fine Dining
Alison on Dominick
  38 Dominick St., 212/727-1188
Aquavit Restaurant
  13 W. 54th St., 212/307-7311
Bolo
  23 E. 22nd St., 212/228-2200
Box Tree
  250 E. 49th St., 212/593-9810
Cafe Des Artistes
  1 W. 67th St., 212/877-3500
Chanterelle
  2 Harrison St., 212/966-6960
Four Seasons
  99 E. 52nd St., 212/754-9494
Gotham Bar and Grill
  12 E. Twelfth St., 212/620-4020
Jo Jo Restaurant
  160 E. 64th St., 212/223-5656
Le Colonial Restaurant
  149 E. 57th St., 212/752-0808
Lespinasse
  St. Regis Hotel, 2 E. 55th St., 212/339-6719
Lutece Restaurant
  249 E. 50th St., 212/752-2225
Maxim's New York Restaurant
  680 Madison Ave., 212/751-5111
Palm Restaurant
  837 Second Ave., 212/687-2953
Petrossian Restaurant
  182 W. 58th St., 212/245-2214
Restaurant Daniel
  20 E. 76th St., 212/288-0033
Sardi's
  234 W. 44th St., 212/221-8440
Smith and Wollensky Steak House
  797 Third Ave., 212/753-1530
Tavern on the Green
  Central Park West at 67th St., 212/873-3200
Union Square Cafe
  21 E. Sixteenth St., 212/243-4020
Vong
  200 E. 54th St., 212/486-9592
Water Club
  500 E. 30th St., 212/683-3333
Windows On The World
  1 World Trade Ctr., Ste. 106, 212/938-1100

Best French Food
Bruxelles
  118 Greenwich Ave., 212/206-1830

Cafe Lure
  169 Sullivan St., 212/473-2642
Cafe Luxembourg
  200 W. 70th St., 212/873-7411
Capsouto Freres Bistro
  451 Washington St., 212/966-4900
Chelsea Bistro and Bar
  358 W. 23rd St., 212/727-2026
Chez Jacqueline Restaurant
  72 MacDougal St., 212/505-0727
CT Restaurant
  111 E. 22nd St., 212/995-8500
Demarchelier Restaurant
  50 E. 86th St., 212/249-6300
Dix Et Sept
  181 W. Tenth St., 212/645-8023
Frontiere Restaurant
  199 Prince St., 212/387-0898
Gascogne
  158 Eighth Ave., 212/675-6564
Jean Claude Restaurant
  137 Sullivan St., 212/475-9232
Jubilee
  347 E. 54th St., 212/888-3569
Jules Restaurant
  65 St. Mark's Pl., 212/477-5560
Key Largo Bistro
  470 Sixth Ave., 212/243-2222
La Cote Basque
  60 W. 55th St., 212/688-6525
La Folie
  1422 Third Ave., 212/744-6327
La Jumelle
  55 Grand St., 212/941-9651
La Lunchontte, Jean Francois
  130 Tenth Ave., 212/675-0342
La Reserve
  4 W. 49th St., 212/247-2993
Lacajou Bar and Restaurant
  53 W. Nineteenth St., 212/645-1706
Le Bilboquet
  25 E. 63rd St., 212/751-3036
Le Jardin Bistro
  25 Cleveland Pl., 212/343-9599
Le Perigord
  405 E. 52nd St., 212/755-6244
Le Zoo
  314 W. Eleventh St., 212/620-0393
Les Deux Gamins
  170 Waverly Pl., 212/807-7357
Lespinasse
  St. Regis Hotel, 2 E. 55th St., 212/339-6719
Montrachet Restaurant
  239 W. Broadway, 212/219-2777
Park Bistro
  414 Park Ave. S., 212/689-1360

N

Pitachoune Restaurant
   226 Third Ave., 212/614-8641
Provence Restaurant
   38 MacDougal St., 212/475-7500
Raoul's Restaurant
   180 Prince St., 212/966-3518
Restaurant Daniel
   20 E. 76th St., 212/288-0033
Soho Steak
   90 Thompson St., 212/226-0602
Trois Canards
   184 Eighth Ave., 212/929-4320
Trois Jean Restaurant
   154 E. 79th St., 212/988-4858

Best German Food
Silver Swan
   41 E. Twentieth St., 212/254-3611

Best Greek/Mediterranean Food
Aegean Restaurant
   221 Columbus Ave., 212/873-5057
Eros
   1076 First Ave., 212/223-2322
Ithaka Restaurant
   48 Barrow St., 212/727-8886
Layla
   211 W. Broadway at Franklin St., 212/431-0700
Meltemi Restaurant
   905 First Ave., 212/355-4040
Mogador Restaurant
   101 Saint Mark's Pl., 212/677-2226
Moustache Pizza
   90 Bedford St., 212/229-2220
New Acropolis
   767 Eighth Ave., at 47th St., 212/246-8650
Salam Restaurant
   104 W. Thirteenth St., 212/673-0330
Sido First Restaurant
   203 First Ave., 212/995-1748
Turkish Kitchen
   386 Third Ave., 212/679-1810
Uncle Nick's Greek Cuisine
   747 Ninth Ave., 212/245-7992

Best Homestyle Food
Bubby's
   120 Hudson St., 212/219-0666
Community Bar and Grill
   216 Seventh Ave., 212/242-7900
Danal
   90 E. Tenth St., 212/982-6390
Eighteenth and Eighth Restaurant
   159 Eighth Ave., 212/242-5000
Home Restaurant
   20 Cornelia St., 212/243-9579
Jezebel
   630 Ninth Ave., 212/582-1045

Kitchenette
  73 W. Broadway, 212/267-6740
La Bodega
  136 W. Broadway, 212/285-1155
Pantry Cafe
  314 Bleecker St., 212/675-9463
Sylvia's Restaurant
  328 Lenox Ave., 212/996-0660
Tartine
  253 W. Eleventh St., 212/229-2611

Best Ice Cream/Yogurt
Peppermint Park Ice Cream Company
  1225 First Ave., 212/288-5054
Rumpelmayer's Restaurant
  50 Central Park S., 212/755-5800

Best Indian Food
Akbar Restaurant
  475 Park Ave., 212/838-1717
Baluchi's
  193 Spring St., 212/226-2828
  1565 Second Ave., 212/288-4810
Calcutta Cuisine of India
  175 E. 83rd St., 212/996-8037
Darbar Indian Restaurant
  44 W. 56th St., 212/432-7227
Dawat Haute Indian Cuisine
  210 E. 58th St., 212/355-7555
Haveli Restaurant
  100 Second Ave., 212/982-0533
India Grill
  240 E. 81st St., 212/988-4646
Mitali Restaurant
  334 E. Sixth St., 212/533-2508
Muriya Indian Restaurant
  129 E. 27th St. at Lexington Ave., 212/689-7925
Rose of India
  308 E. Sixth St., 212/533-5011
Salaam Bombay Indian Cuisine
  319 Greenwich St., 212/226-9400
Windows on India Restaurant
  344 E. Sixth St., 212/477-5956

Best Inexpensive Meal
Chelsea Commons
  Chelsea Commons, 242 Tenth Ave., 212/929-9424
Cucina Della Fontana Restaurant
  368 Bleecker St., 212/242-0636
Gray's Papaya
  2090 Broadway, 212/799-0243
Ruppert's Restaurant
  269 Columbus Ave., 212/873-9400
Trattoria Spaghetto
  232 Bleecker St., Ste. 232, 212/255-6752

Best Italian Food
Acappella
  1 Hudson St., 212/240-0163

Barolo Restaurant
398 W. Broadway, 212/226-1102
Bello Restaurant
863 Ninth Ave., 212/246-6773
Cafe Trevi
1570 First Ave., 212/249-0040
Cucina Della Fontana Restaurant
368 Bleecker St., 212/242-0630
Da Umberto's Restaurant
107 W. Seventeenth St., 212/989-0303
Doge Restaurant
142 W. 44th St., 212/944-3643
Felidia Ristorante
243 E. 58th St., 212/758-1479
Ferrara Pastries
195 Grand St., 212/226-6150
Forlini's Restaurant
93 Baxter St., 212/349-6779
Il Mulino
86 W. Third St., 212/673-3783
John's Restaurant
302 E. Twelfth St., 212/475-9531
823 Second Ave., 212/867-4955
Le Tre Venezie Restaurant
142 W. 46th St., 212/730-2135
Lombardi's
32 Spring St. at Mulberry, 212/941-7994
Lupa Bar and Restaurant
277 Church St., 212/343-1035
Osso Buco Restaurant
88 University Pl., 212/645-4525
Trattoria Spaghetto
228 Bleecker St., Ste. 232, 212/255-6752

Best Japanese Food
Avenue A Japanese Restaurant
105 Avenue A, 212/982-8109
Benihana
47 W. 56th St., 212/581-0930
Blue Ribbon Sushi
119 Sullivan St., 212/343-0404
Esashi Japanese Restaurant
32 Ave. A, 212/505-8726
Hasaki Restaurant
210 E. Ninth St., 212/473-3327
Honmura An
170 Mercer St. at Houston St., 212/334-5253
Japonica Restaurant
100 University Pl., 212/243-7752
Katana
179 Prince St., 212/677-1943
Kitchen Club
30 Prince St., 212/274-0025
La Maison Japonaise Restaurant
125 E. 39th St., 212/682-7375
NJ Sushi, Inc.
135 First Ave., 212/673-2547

Nobu
  105 Hudson St., 212/219-0500
Oikawa Restaurant
  805 Third Ave., 212/980-1400
Omen Restaurant
  113 Thompson St., 212/925-8923
Shabutatsu
  216 E. Tenth St., 212/477-2972
Sushisay Restaurant
  38 E. 51st St., 212/755-1780
Taka Japanese Restaurant
  61 Grove St., 212/242-3699
Takahashi Restaurant
  85 Avenue A, 212/505-6524
Tokubei 86
  314 E. 86th St., 212/628-5334
Totoya Restaurant
  1144 First Ave., 212/751-6123
Yama Japanese Restaurant
  49 Irving Pl. at Seventeenth St., 212/475-0969

Best Late-Night Food
Around The Clock Restaurant
  8 Stuyvesant St., 212/598-0402
Bar Six
  502 Sixth Ave., 212/691-1363
Bereket Turkish Kabob House
  187 E. Houston St., 212/475-7700
Blue Ribbon Brasserie
  97 Sullivan St., 212/274-0404
Coffee Shop
  29 Union Sqare W., 212/243-7969
Cub Room Cafe
  131 Sullivan St., 212/777-0030
Elaine's Restaurant
  1703 Second Ave., 212/534-8103
Florent Restaurant
  69 Gansevoort St., 212/989-5779
French Roast
  456 Sixth Ave., 212/533-2233
Kiev Restaurant, Ltd.
  117 Second Ave., 212/674-4040
Le Express
  249A Park Avenue, 212/254-5858
Lucky Strike
  59 Grand St., 212/941-0479
Odeon
  145 W. Broadway, 212/233-0507
Stingy Lulu's
  129 Saint Mark's Pl., 212/674-3545
The Galaxy
  15 Irving Pl., 212/777-3631
Tivoli Restaurant
  515 Third Ave., 212/532-3300
Veselka Restaurant
  144 Second Ave., 212/228-9682
Vynl Diner
  824 Ninth Ave., 212/974-2003

N

Yaffa Cafe
97 St. Mark's Pl., 212/674-9302

Best Lunch
Cottage East
713 Second Ave., 212/286-8811
Mary Ann's Chelsea Mexican Restaurant
116 Eighth Ave., 212/633-0877
Mezze
10 E. 44th St., 212/697-6644

Best Mexican Food
Alamo Restaurant
304 E. 48th St., 212/759-0590
Lupe's East L.A. Kitchen
110 Avenue of the Americas, 212/966-1326
Mary Ann's Chelsea Mexican Restaurant
116 Eighth Ave., 212/633-0877
Mi Cocina Restaurant
57 Jane St. at Hudson St., 212/627-8273
Rosa Mexicano Restaurant
1063 First Ave., 212/753-7407

Best Middle Eastern Food
Aja Restaurant
937 Broadway, 212/473-8388
Casa La Femme
150 Wooster St., 212/505-0005
Magic Carpet Restaurant
54 Carmine St., 212/627-9019
Moustache Pizza
90 Bedford St., 212/229-2220

Best Other Ethnic Food
Anyway Cafe (Russian)
32 E. Second St., 212/533-3412
Ariana Afghan Kabab Restaurant (Afghan)
787 Ninth Ave., 212/262-2323
Axum Cafe (African, Caribbean)
324 W. 49th St., 212/518-8265
Blue Nile (Ethiopian)
103 W. 77th St. at Columbus Ave., 212/580-3232
Boca Chica Restaurant (South American)
13 First Ave., 212/473-0108
Branigan's Pub and Restaurant (Irish)
104 Greenwich St., 212/267-4646
Caribe (Caribbean)
117 Perry St., 212/255-9191
Cendrillon (Filipino)
45 Mercer St., 212/343-9012
Gene's Restaurant (Caribbean)
73 W. Eleventh St., 212/242-9185
La Caridad Restaurant (Cuban)
2184 Amsterdam Ave., 212/568-4294
Negril (Caribbean)
362 W. 23rd St., 212/807-6411
Pamir Restaurant (Afghan)
1437 Second Ave., 212/734-3791
1065 First Ave., 212/644-9258

Pao (Portuguese)
    322 Spring St., 212/334-5464
Riodizio (Brazilian)
    417 Lafayette St., 212/529-1313
St. Dymphna's (Irish)
    118 Saint Mark's Pl., 212/254-6636
Tibetan Kitchen (Tibetan)
    444 Third Ave., 212/679-6286
Tibetan Restaurant (Tibetan)
    96 Second Ave., 212/979-9202

Best Outdoor Dining
Bar Pitti
    268 Sixth Ave., 212/982-3300
Barolo Restaurant
    398 W. Broadway, 212/226-1102
Miracle Grill
    112 First Ave., 212/254-2353

Best Pizza
2671 S and C Pizza Corp.
    2671 Broadway, 212/663-7651
Arturo's Pizza
    1610 York Ave., 212/288-2430
Ere's
    206 Dyckman St., 212/942-7736
Famous Ray's Pizza Greenwich
    465 Sixth Ave., Greenwich, 212/243-2253
John's Pizzeria
    278 Bleecker St., 212/243-1680
Le Madri
    168 W. Eighteenth St. at Seventh Ave.,
        212/727-8022
Sal's Pizzeria
    766 Second Ave., 212/986-1234
Stromboli Pizzeria
    112 University Pl., 212/255-0812
Two Boots
    37 Avenue A, 212/777-2668
World Room
    30 E. Sixteenth St., 212/243-1920

Best Restaurant in Town
33 Crosby Bar and Tapas
    33 Crosby St., 212/219-8856
American Festival Cafe
    20 W. 50th St., Rockefeller Plz., 212/332-7620
Anglers and Writers
    420 Hudson St., 212/675-0810
Bell Cafe
    310 Spring St., 212/334-2355
Bouley Restaurant
    165 Duane St., 212/608-3852
Bridge Cafe
    279 Water St., 212/227-3344
Caffe Rosso
    284 W. Twelfth St., 212/633-9277
Centanni Restaurant
    50 Carmine St., 212/989-9494

N

Chiam Restaurant
160 E. 48th St., 212/371-2323
Chin Chin Restaurant
216 E. 49th St., 212/888-4555
Coldwater's Restaurant
988 Second Ave., 212/888-2122
Cottage East
713 Second Ave., 212/286-8811
Cuisine De Saigon
154 W. Thirteenth St., 212/255-6003
Da Silvano Restaurant
260 Sixth Ave., 212/982-2343
Doge Restaurant
142 W. 44th St., 212/944-3643
Dojo West Restaurant
14 W. Fourth St., 212/505-8934
Duk Suni Doll Restaurant
119 First Ave., 212/477-9506
Ecco Restaurant
124 Chambers St., 212/227-7074
El Parador Cafe
325 E. 34th St., 212/679-6812
Elio's Restaurant
1621 Second Ave., 212/772-2242
Est Est Est
64 Carmine St., 212/255-6294
Fannie's Restaurant
765 Washington St., 212/255-5101
Fiorello's Roman Cafe
1900 Broadway, 212/595-5330
Follonico
6 W. 24th St., 212/691-6359
Four Seasons
99 E. 52nd St., 212/754-9494
Hakata Japanese Restaurant
224 W. 47th St., 212/730-6863
Havana New York
27 W. 38th St., 212/840-3035
Hudson River Club
250 Vesey St., 212/786-1500
Il Cantinori Restaurant
32 E. Tenth St., 212/673-6044
Il Monello Restaurant
1460 Second Ave., 212/535-9310
Jaiya Thai Restaurant
396 Third Ave. near 28th St., 212/889-1330
Kin Khao Restaurant
171 Spring St., 212/966-3939
Kom Tang Soot Bul House New York
32 W. 32nd St., 212/947-8482
Le Bernardin
155 W. 51st St., 212/489-1515
Le Cirque Restaurant
58 E. 65th St., 212/794-9292
Le Madri
168 W. Eighteenth St. at Seventh Ave.,
212/727-8022

Les Halles
411 Park Ave. S., 212/679-4111
Manhattan Cafe
1161 First Ave., 212/888-6556
Mappamondo Restaurant
11 Abingdon Sq., 212/675-3100
Mezzogiorno
195 Spring St., 212/334-2112
Mi Cocina Restaurant
57 Jane St., 212/627-8273
Nine Jones Street Restaurant
9 Jones St., 212/989-1220
Noho Star
330 Lafayette St., 212/925-0070
Old Town Bar and Restaurant
45 E. Eighteenth St., 212/529-6732
Panevino Restaurant
132 W. 65th St. at Lincoln Ctr., 212/874-7000
Patrissy's Restaurant
98 Kenmare St., 212/226-8509
Pedro Paramo
430 E. Fourteenth St., 212/475-4581
Periyali
35 W. Twentieth St., 212/463-7890
Post House Restaurant
28 E. 63rd St., 212/935-2888
Primavera Ristorante
1578 First Ave., 212/861-8608
Rectangel's Cafe and Bar
159 Second Ave., 212/677-8410
Regional Thai Taste Restaurant
208 Seventh Ave., 212/807-9872
Roettele A.G.
126 E. Seventh St., 212/674-4140
Rose Cafe
24 Fifth Ave., 212/260-4118
Savories Cafe
30 Rockefeller Plaza Concourse, 212/332-7630
Seven A Cafe
109 Avenue A, 212/475-9001
Shanghai Manor Restaurant
141 E. 55th St., 212/753-3900
Telephone Restaurant
149 Second Ave., 212/529-5000
Triple Eight Palace Restaurant
88 E. Broadway, 212/941-8886
Tropica Restaurant
200 Park Ave., 212/867-6767
Walker's
16 N. Moore St., 212/941-0142
Woo Lae Oak
77 W. 46th St., 212/869-9958

Best Restaurant Meal Value
Aunt Suzie's Italian Kitchen
126 E. 28th St., 212/689-1992
Cafe Gigi
417 E. Ninth St., 212/505-3341

Chez Brigitte
  77 Greenwich Ave., 212/929-6736
La Caridad
  2199 Broadway, 212/874-2780
Papaya King
  179 E. 86th St., 212/369-0648
Rice and Beans Restaurant
  744 Ninth Ave., 212/265-4444
Silver Palace Restaurant
  52 Bowery, 212/964-1204

Best Romantic Dining
Cafe Des Artistes
  1 W. 67th St., 212/877-3500
Cucina Della Fontana Restaurant
  368 Bleecker St., 212/242-0636
Erminia Italian Restaurant
  250 E. 83rd St., 212/879-4284
La Cote Basque
  60 W. 55th St., 212/688-6525
One If By Land, Two If By Sea
  17 Barrow St., 212/228-0822
Rainbow Room
  30 Rockefeller Plz., Ste. 65, 212/632-5000
Roettele A.G.
  126 E. Seventh St., 212/674-4140
Savoy Restaurant
  70 Prince St., 212/219-8570
Tavern on the Green
  Central Park West at 67th St., 212/873-3200
Terrace Restaurant
  400 W. 119th St., 212/666-9490
Water Club
  500 E. 30th St., 212/683-3333

Best Sandwiches
Barocco Restaurant
  301 Church St., 212/431-1445
Mangia Restaurant
  16 E. 48th St., 212/754-7600
Melampo Imported Foods
  105 Sullivan St., 212/334-9530
Paradise Muffin Company
  141 Eighth Ave., 212/647-0066

Best Seafood
City Crab and Seafood Company
  235 Park Ave. S., 212/529-3800
Dock's Restaurant
  633 Third Ave., 212/986-8080
  2427 Broadway, 212/724-5588
Manhattan Ocean Club
  57 W. 58th St., 212/371-7777
Oyster Bar and Restaurant
  89 E. 42nd St. at Vanderbilt Ave., 212/490-6650
Pisces Restaurant
  95 Avenue A, 212/260-6660

Best Soul Food
Pink Teacup, Inc.
  42 Grove St., 212/807-6755
Sylvia's Restaurant
  328 Lenox Ave., 212/996-0660
The Shark Bar
  307 Amsterdam Ave., 212/874-8500

Best Southwestern Food
Arizona 206 Restaurant
  206 E. 60th St., 212/838-0440
El Quijote Bar and Restaurant
  226 W. 23rd St., 212/929-1855
El Rio Grande Restaurant
  160 E. 38th St., 212/867-0922
Mesa Grill
  102 Fifth Ave., 212/807-7400

Best Spanish Food
Bolo
  23 E. 22nd St., 212/228-2200
El Castillo De Jagua Restauarnt
  113 Rivington St., 212/982-6412
El Quijote Bar and Restaurant
  226 W. 23rd St., 212/929-1855
Plaza Espana
  130 W. 58th St., 212/757-6434

Best Sports Bar
All State Cafe
  250 W. 72nd St., 212/874-1883
Mickey Mantle's Restaurant
  42 Central Park S., 212/688-7777
Polo Grounds Bar and Grill
  1472 Third Ave., 212/570-5590
Scores
  333 E. Sixtieth St., 212/421-3600
The Sporting Club
  99 Hudson St., 212/219-0900

Best Sunday Brunch
Anglers and Writers
  420 Hudson St., 212/675-0810
Cafe Botanica
  160 Central Park S., 212/484-5120
Cafe Noir
  32 Grand St., 212/431-7910
Cornelia Street Cafe
  29 Cornelia St., 212/989-9318
Museum Cafe
  366 Columbus Ave., 212/799-0150
Nadine's Restaurant
  99 Bank St., 212/924-3165
Oak Room and Bar at the Plaza
  Plaza Hotel, 768 Fifth Ave., 212/759-3000
Sign of the Dove
  1110 Third Ave., 212/861-8080
The Grange Hall
  50 Commerce St., 212/924-5246

West Fifty Seven Cafe
  312 W. 57th St., 212/489-9767
Zoe Restaurant
  90 Prince St., 212/966-6722

Best Sushi
Hasaki Restaurant
  210 E. Ninth St., 212/473-3327
Iso Restaurant
  175 Second Ave., 212/777-0361

Best Thai Food
Gingertoon
  417 Bleecker St., 212/924-6420
Jaiya Thai Restaurant
  396 Third Ave. near 28th St., 212/889-1330
Kin Khao Restaurant
  171 Spring St., 212/966-3939
Malaysia and Indonesia
  18 Doyers St., 212/267-0088
Penang Restaurant
  109 Spring St., 212/274-8883
Rain
  100 W. 82nd St., 212/501-0776
Regional Thai Taste Restaurant
  208 Seventh Ave., 212/807-9872
Thai House Cafe
  151 Hudson St., 212/334-1085

Best Vegetarian Food
Bachue Cafe
  36 W. 21st St., 212/229-0870
Buddha Green
  145 W. 58th St., 212/581-2288
Candle Cafe
  1307 Third Ave., 212/472-0970
Caravan of Dreams
  405 E. Sixth St., 212/254-1613
Dojo Restaurant
  26 St. Marks Pl., 212/674-9821
Hangawi
  12 E. 32nd St., 212/213-0077
Josie's
  300 Amsterdam Ave., 212/769-1212
Kate's Joint
  58 Avenue B, 212/777-7059
Luma Restaurant
  200 Ninth Ave., 212/633-8033
Nosmo King
  54 Varick St., 212/966-1239
Sacred Chow
  522 Hudson St., 212/337-0863
Souen Restaurant
  210 Sixth Ave. at Prince St., 212/807-7421
  28 E. Thirteenth St., 212/627-7150
Spring Street Natural Restaurant
  62 Spring St., 212/966-0290
Thali
  28 Greenwich Ave., 212/367-7411

Zen Palate Restaurant
  2170 Broadway, 212/614-9291
  663 Ninth Ave., 212/582-1669

Best Vietnamese Food
Indochine Restaurant
  430 Lafayette St., 212/505-5111
Mekong Restaurant
  44 Prince St., 212/343-8169
Miss Saigon Restaurant
  1425 Third Ave., 212/988-8828
  473 Columbus Ave., 212/595-8919
Monsoon Vietnamese Cooking
  435 Amsterdam Ave., 212/580-8686
Nha Trang Restaurant
  87 Baxter St., 212/233-5948
Pasteur Restaurant
  85 Baxter St., 212/608-3656
Vietnam Restaurant
  11 Doyers St., 212/693-0725

MIDDLETOWN, NY

Best Breakfast
Colonial Diner
  8 Dolson Ave., 914/342-3500

Best Italian Food
Orrio's Restaurant
  42 Ingrassia Rd., 914/343-9447

Best Japanese Food
Hana Restaurant and Sushi Bar
  339 Rte. 211E, 914/342-6634

Best Lunch
Middletown Forum Diner
  226 Wickham Ave., 914/342-5155

Best Pizza
Caffe Allegro
  21 W. Main St., 914/343-4567

NIAGARA FALLS, NY

[See also: Buffalo and North Tonawanda.]

Best American Food
Burgundy's On The River
  Best Western Inn, 7001 Buffalo Ave., 716/283-7612
Jon's Flaming Hearth
  1965 Military Rd., 716/694-5988

Best Chinese Food
Chu's Dining Lounge
  1019 Main St., 716/285-7278

Best Coffee/Coffeehouse
Mom's Coffee Shop and Restaurant
  8420 Niagara Falls Blvd., 716/297-6031

N

Best Family Restaurant
Club Joey Lounge
 1532 Pine Ave., 716/282-1108
Goose's Roost
 10158 Niagara Falls Blvd., 716/297-7497
 343 Fourth St., 716/282-6255

Best Greek/Mediterranean Food
Christos Restaurant
 2117 Military Rd., 716/297-9742

Best Homestyle Food
Basket Factory Restaurant
 2 Watson Ave., Middleport, 716/735-7001

Best Italian Food
Como Restaurant
 2220 Pine Ave., 716/285-9341
Dante's Ristorante
 2901 Pine Ave., 716/285-6711
Fortuna's Restaurant
 827 Nineteenth St., 716/282-2252
Goose's Roost
 343 Fourth St., 716/282-6255
 10158 Niagara Falls Blvd., 712/282-6255
La Hacienda
 3019 Pine Ave., 716/285-2536

Best Mexican Food
La Casa Cardenas
 921 Main St., 716/282-0231

Best Seafood
Riverside Inn
 115 S. Water St., Lewiston, 716/754-8206

Best Steaks
Burgundy's On The River
 Best Western Inn, 7001 Buffalo Ave., 716/283-7612
Pete's Market House Restaurant
 1701 Pine Ave., 716/282-7225

Best View While Dining
Burgundy's On The River
 Best Western Inn, 7001 Buffalo Ave., 716/283-7612

NORTH TONAWANDA, NY

[See also: Buffalo and Niagara Falls.]

Best Fine Dining
Daffodil's Restaurant
 930 Maple Rd., Williamsville, 716/688-5413

Best Homestyle Food
Nestor's Texas Red Hots
 102 Webster St., 716/695-3596

Best Italian Food
Pane's Pizzeria and Restaurant
 984 Payne Ave., 716/692-7076

Best Pizza
Frank's Pizza Shack
　452 Oliver St., 716/692-7984
J.V.'s Pizza and Pasta House
　354 Oliver St., 716/692-2796

PATCHOGUE, NY

Best Casual Dining
Harborside Restaurant
　503 E. Main St., 516/654-9290

Best German Food
Pine Grove Inn
　First St. at Chapel Ave., 516/475-9843

Best Italian Food
Umberto's Pizza and Restaurant
　33 E. Sunrise Hwy., 516/654-0070

Best Pizza
Delfiore's
　51 N. Ocean Ave., 516/475-6080
Gino's Pizzeria
　22 W. Main St., 516/289-2028
Guy's Pizza
　20 E. Main St., 516/654-5692

Best Steaks
The Good Steer
　2810 Middle Country Rd., Lake Grove,
　　516/585-8212

PLATTSBURGH, NY

Best Italian Food
Anthony's Restaurant
　538 State Rte. 3, 518/561-6420
Arnie's Restaurant
　20 Margaret St., 518/563-3003

Best Pizza
Zachary's Lounge
　86 Margaret St., 518/561-8876

Best Seafood
Butcher Block
　15 Booth Dr., 518/563-0920

PORT WASHINGTON, NY

Best American Food
Millie's Place
　2014 Northern Blvd., Manhasset, 516/365-4344

Best Bar
Finn MacCool's
　205 Main St., 516/944-3439

Best Barbecue/Ribs
Rib Roost
　110 Shore Rd., 516/944-3272

Best Breakfast
Friend of a Farmer East
　1382 Old Northern Blvd., Roslyn, 516/625-3808

Landmark Diner
  1023 Northern Blvd., Roslyn, 516/627-9635

Best Casual Dining
Millie's Place
  2014 Northern Blvd., Manhasset, 516/365-4344

Best Chinese Food
Chef Tai's Chinese Restaurant
  84 Old Shore Rd., 516/767-5111

Best Desserts
La Piccola Liguria
  47 Shore Rd., 516/767-6490

Best Diner
Landmark Diner
  1023 Northern Blvd., Roslyn, 516/627-9635

Best Dinner
Ken's Place
  64 Roslyn Ave., Sea Cliff, 516/674-3752
Tupelo Honey
  39 Roslyn Ave., Sea Cliff, 516/671-8300

Best Fine Dining
Bryant and Cooper Steak House
  2 Middleneck Rd., Roslyn, 516/627-7270

Best Greek/Mediterranean Food
Shish-Kebab Restaurant
  283 Main St., 516/883-9309

Best Homestyle Food
Publicans Restaurant
  550 Plandome Rd., Manhasset, 516/627-7722

Best Indian Food
Diwan Restaurant
  37 Shore Rd., 516/767-7878

Best Inexpensive Meal
Pazzo, Inc.
  181 Main St., 516/767-7117

Best Japanese Food
Yamaguchi Restaurant
  63 Main St., 516/883-3500

Best Mexican Food
Amigo's Mexican Restaurant
  52 Main St., 516/883-1315

Best Salad/Salad Bar
Club House
  987 Port Washington Blvd., 516/767-1112

Best Seafood
Louie's Shore Restaurant
  395 Main St., 516/883-4242

Best Sunday Brunch
Library Restaurant
  The Inn of Port Washington, 541 Port Washington
    Blvd., 516/883-3122

Best Wine Selection
Cottabella Ristorante
45A Shore Rd., 516/883-4920

POUGHKEEPSIE, NY

Best Cajun/Creole Food
Spanky's Restaurant
85 Main St., 914/485-2294

Best Chinese Food
Mill House Panda
289 Mill St., 914/454-2530

Best Coffee/Coffeehouse
Cappuccino by Coppola's
568 South Rd., 914/462-4545

Best Diner
Palace Diner
194 Washington St., 914/473-1576

Best Greek/Mediterranean Food
My Place Restaurant
322 Main Mall, 914/473-2815

Best Italian Food
Coppola's of Poughkeepsie
825 Main St., 914/452-3040
Milanese Restaurant
115 Main St., 914/471-9533

Best Japanese Food
Osho Fine Japanese Restaurant
763 South Rd., 914/297-0540

Best Lunch
Dickens Restaurant
796 Main St., 914/454-7322

Best Restaurant in Town
Christos Restaurant
155 Wilbur Blvd., 914/471-3400

Best Restaurant Meal Value
My Place Restaurant
322 Main Mall, 914/473-2815

Best Seafood
River Station Restaurant
25 Main St., 914/452-9207

QUEENS, NY

[See also: Bronx, Brooklyn, Manhattan, and New York.]

Best American Food
Sidetracks Restaurant and Bar
4508 Queens Blvd., Long Island City, 718/786-3570

Best Burgers
P.J. Horgan's
4217 Queens Blvd., Long Island City, 718/361-9680

Best Chinese Food
Joe's Shanghai Restaurant
  136-21 37th Ave., Flushing, 718/539-3838

Best Continental Food
First Edition
  4108 Bell Blvd., Flushing, 718/428-8522
Sidetracks Restaurant and Bar
  4508 Queens Blvd., Long Island City, 718/786-3570

Best Delicatessen
Pastrami King
  12424 Queens Blvd., Jamaica, 718/263-1717

Best Diner
Georgia Diner
  86-55 Queens Blvd., Flushing, 718/651-4687

Best Greek/Mediterranean Food
Telly's Taverna
  2813 23rd Ave., Long Island City, 718/728-9056

Best Ice Cream/Yogurt
Jahn's Since 1897
  81-04 37th Ave., Jackson Heights, 718/651-0700

Best Inexpensive Meal
Goody's Chinese Restaurant
  94-03B 63rd Dr., Flushing, 718/896-7159

Best Italian Food
Parkside Restaurant
  10701 Corona Ave., Flushing, 718/271-9871
Piccola Venezia Restaurant
  4201 28th Ave., Long Island City, 718/721-8470

Best Pizza
Milano Pizzeria
  1927 Ditmars Blvd., Long Island City,
    718/721-9722

Best Sandwiches
Ben's Best Kosher Deli
  96-40 Queens Blvd., Flushing, 718/897-1700

Best Soul Food
Carmichael's Diner
  117-08 Guy Brewer Blvd., Jamaica, 718/723-6908
Richard's Place
  200-05 Linden Blvd., Jamaica, 718/723-0041

Best Steaks
Kate Cassidy's Restaurant
  6398 Woodhaven Blvd., Flushing, 718/894-6200

Best Vegetarian Food
Bamboo Garden Restaurant
  4128 Main St., Flushing, 718/463-9240

RHINEBECK, NY

Best Bar
Foster's Coach House
  22 Montgomery St., 914/876-8052

Best Bistro
Le Petit Bistro
  8 E. Market St., 914/876-7400

Best Inexpensive Meal
Rolling Rock Cafe
  46 U.S. Hwy. 9N, 914/876-7655

Best Late-Night Food
Rolling Rock Cafe
  46 U.S. Hwy. 9N, 914/876-7655

Best Pizza
C.J.'s Restaurant and Pizzeria
  164 Old Post Rd., 914/876-7711

Best Sunday Brunch
Beekman Arms Restaurant
  4 Mill St., 914/871-1766

RIVERHEAD, NY

Best American Food
J.P. Michael's
  307 Griffing Ave., 516/727-9010

Best Breakfast
The Riverhead Grill
  85 E. Main St., 516/727-8495

Best Chinese Food
Hyting Restaurant
  54 W. Main St., 516/727-1557

Best Italian Food
Carlo's Pizza Oven
  435 Osborne Ave., 516/369-2010
Doc's Tavern
  424 Pulaski St., 516/727-3410

Best Lunch
Digger O'Dell's
  58 W. Main St., 516/369-3200

Best Other Ethnic Food
Birchwood (Polish)
  512 Pulaski St., 516/727-4449

Best Pizza
Primo's
  1091 Rte. 58, 516/727-8763

Best Sandwiches
Bagel Lover's
  136 E. Main St., 516/727-5080
Cooperage Inn
  Sound Ave., Calverton, 516/727-8994

Best Steaks
Cliff's Rendezvous Restaurant
  313 E. Main St., 516/727-6880

ROCHESTER, NY

Best 24-Hour Restaurant
Gitsis Texas Hots
  600 Monroe Ave., 716/271-8260

Best Beer Selection
Beers of the World
  3000 Winton Rd. S., 716/427-2852

Best Burgers
Highland Park Diner
  960 Clinton Ave. S., 716/461-5040
Zebb's Deluxe Grill and Bar
  1890 S. Clinton Ave., 716/271-1440

Best Chinese Food
House of Poon
  2185 Monroe Ave., 716/271-7371

Best Coffee/Coffeehouse
Java Joe's
  16 Gibbs St., 716/232-5282
Nancy's Coffee Collection
  213 Irondequoit Mall Dr., 716/338-7260
  3400 W. Henrietta Rd., 716/424-1630
Two Roses Cafe
  1308 Buffalo Rd., 716/235-4440

Best Indian Food
India House
  998 Clinton Ave. S., 716/244-9210

Best Inexpensive Meal
Aladdin's Natural Eatery
  141 State St., 716/546-5000
  646 Monroe Ave., 716/442-5000

Best Italian Food
Two Roses Cafe
  1308 Buffalo Rd., 716/235-4440

Best Japanese Food
Plumhouse Japanese
  686 Monroe Ave., 716/442-0778

Best Pizza
Chester Cab Pizza
  707 Park Ave., 716/244-8211
  1481 Dewey Ave., 716/458-0070

Best Romantic Dining
Edward's Restaurant
  13 S. Fitzhugh St., 716/423-0140

Best Sports Bar
Bathtub Billy's Sports Bar
  630 Ridge Rd. W., 716/865-6510
Distillery
  1142 Mount Hope Ave., 716/271-4105

Best Steaks
Rick's Prime Rib House
  788 Howard Rd., 716/235-2900
Scotch n' Sirloin
  3450 Winton Pl., Winton Place Plaza, 716/427-0808

Best Sunday Brunch
Charlie's Frog Pond
  652 Park Ave., 716/271-1970

Best Vietnamese Food
Mamasan's Restaurant
 309 University Ave., 716/546-3910

ROCKVILLE CENTRE, NY

Best American Food
MacArthur Park Bar
 1 Maple Ave., 516/766-8375

Best Bar
Alias Smith and Jones Restaurant
 2863 Woods Ave., Oceanside, 516/678-5888

Best Barbecue/Ribs
Raay-Nor's Cabin
 550 Sunrise Hwy., Baldwin, 516/223-4886

Best Business Lunch
George Martin Restaurant
 65 N. Park Ave., 516/678-7272

Best Coffee/Coffeehouse
International Delight Cafe
 241 Sunrise Hwy., 516/766-7557

Best Greek/Mediterranean Food
Metro Restaurant and Pizza
 245 Merrick Rd., Lynbrook, 516/887-4932

Best Pizza
Dodici
 12 N. Park Ave., 516/764-3000

ROME, NY

Best Bar
Aquino's Restaurant
 910 Floyd Ave., 315/337-7440

Best Breakfast
The Iron Kettle Coffee Shoppe
 215 E. Dominick St., 315/336-9543

Best Family Restaurant
Teddy's Restaurant
 851 Black River Blvd. N., 315/336-7839

Best Italian Food
Savoy
 255 E. Dominick St., 315/339-3166

Best Pizza
La Roma Pizzeria
 600 Floyd Ave., 315/336-1113

Best Seafood
Coalyard Charlie's
 100 Depeyster St., 315/336-9940

SCHENECTADY, NY

Best American Food
Union Hall Inn
 2 Union Place, Johnstown, 518/762-3210

Best Coffee/Coffeehouse
Caffe Dolce
142 Jay St., 518/347-2334

Best Delicatessen
Gershon's Deli
1600 Union St., 518/393-0617

Best Diner
Blue Ribbon Diner
1801 State St., 518/393-2600
Ruby's Silver Diner
167 Erie Blvd., 518/382-9741

Best Restaurant in Town
Brandywine Diner
970 Emmett St., 518/372-6030

Best Sandwiches
Maurice's Readi-Foods
268 State St., 518/377-7200

SCOTIA, NY

Best Burgers
Jumpin' Jack's Drive-In
5 Schonowee Ave., 518/393-6101

Best Continental Food
Glen Sanders Mansion
1 Glen Ave., 518/374-7262

Best Fine Dining
Glen Sanders Mansion
1 Glen Ave., 518/374-7262

STATEN ISLAND, NY

[See also: Brooklyn and Manhattan; and Hillside, Jersey City, and Newark, NJ.]

Best Bar
Choir Loft Bar
12 Cross St., 718/442-9615

Best Breakfast
Golden Dove
3281 Richmond Ave., 718/967-1900

Best Chinese Food
Loon Chuan Restaurant
85 Page Ave., 718/967-9819

Best Coffee/Coffeehouse
Colonnade Diner
2001 Hylan Blvd., 718/351-2900

Best Desserts
Alfonso's Pastry Shoppe
1899 Victory Blvd., 718/273-8802

Best Diner
Front Page Restaurant
75 Page Ave., 718/966-7882

Golden Dove
3281 Richmond Ave., 718/967-1900
New Dakota Diner
921 Richmond Ave., 718/983-9286

Best Dinner
MJ Supper Club
4864 Arthur Kill Rd., 718/948-9503

Best Family Restaurant
Elm Park Inn
238 Morningstar Rd., 718/720-1983
RH Tugs
1115 Richmond Terrace, 718/447-6369

Best Italian Food
La Strada Restaurant
139 New Dorp Ln., 718/667-4040

Best Lunch
Courthouse Cafe
1 Hyatt St., 718/816-6358

Best Pizza
Cosmo's on the Boulevard
4115 Hylan Blvd., 718/356-6565

N

Best Seafood
Marina Cafe
154 Mansion Ave., 718/967-3077

Best Steaks
Sammy's Steak House
1250 Hylan Blvd., 718/442-9595

Best Sunday Brunch
The Old Bermuda Inn
2512 Arthur Kill Rd., 718/948-7600

SYRACUSE, NY

Best Barbecue/Ribs
Dinosaur Bar-B-Q Express
246 W. Willow St., 315/476-4937

Best Brewpub
Empire Brewing Company
120 Walton St., 315/475-2337

Best Burgers
Zebb's Deluxe Grill and Bar
2803 Brewerton Rd., Mattydale, 315/455-5131

Best Chinese Food
China Pavilion Chinese Restaurant
2102 W. Genesee St., 315/488-2828
Ling Ling on the Square
218 W. Genesee St., 315/422-2800

Best Coffee/Coffeehouse
Nancy's Coffee Cafe
1 Carousel Center Dr., 315/466-0185
290 W. Jefferson St., 315/476-6550

Best Delicatessen
Brooklyn Pickle Catering
2222 Burnet Ave., 315/463-6220

1600 W. Genesee St., 315/487-8000

Best Desserts
Friendly's Family Restaurant
    3701 James St., 315/463-6781
    2720 Brewerton Rd., Mattydale, 315/455-2161
    3275 Erie Blvd. E., 315/446-8332
Happy Endings
    317 S. Clinton St., 315/475-1853

Best Diner
Anna Marie's Restaurant
    3900 New Court Ave., 315/463-9371

Best Family Restaurant
Rosie O'Grady's Tavern
    101 Hamilton St., 315/488-0881
Saratoga Steaks and Seafood
    200 Waring Rd., 315/445-1976

Best Fine Dining
Pascale Wine Bar and Restaurant
    204 W. Fayette St., 315/471-3040

Best Inexpensive Meal
Dominick's Restaurant
    1370 Burnet Ave., 315/471-4262

Best Italian Food
Carmella's Cafe
    705 N. Main St., North Syracuse, 315/458-4292

Best Mexican Food
Fresno's Southwest Restaurant and Bar
    4002 W. Genesee St., 315/468-5000
Juanita's Mexican Kitchen
    600 Court St., 315/478-2185
La Bamba Mexican and American Deli
    1305 Milton Ave., 315/488-0576

Best Pizza
Manhattan Onion
    4627 S. Salina St., 315/469-4907
Twin Trees
    1029 Milton Ave., 315/487-9638

Best Place to Take the Kids
Spaghetti Warehouse
    689 N. Clinton St., 315/475-1807

Best Salad/Salad Bar
Provisions Bakery
    216 Walton St., 315/472-3475

Best Seafood
Captain Ahab's Seafood and Steak
    3449 Erie Blvd. E., 315/446-3272

Best Steaks
Scotch and Sirloin
    3687 Erie Blvd. E., 315/446-1771

Best Wine Selection
Pascale Wine Bar and Restaurant
    204 W. Fayette St., 315/471-3040

TROY, NY

Best Bar
Smith's Restaurant of Cohoes
171 Remsen St., Cohoes, 518/237-9809

Best Beer Selection
Holmes and Watson, Ltd.
450 Broadway, 518/273-8526

Best Brewpub
Troy Pub and Brewery
417 River St., 518/273-2337

Best Chinese Food
China Inn
4 Northern Dr., 518/237-0031

Best Continental Food
The Van essler Room
New York Hwy. 7N, 518/663-5800

Best Diner
Colonial Restaurant and Coffee
880 Second Ave., 518/237-9384

Best Fine Dining
Allegro Cafe
33 Second St., 518/271-1942

Best Italian Food
Geno's Italian Sausage
601 23rd St., Watervliet, 518/273-1787
Italia Restaurant
24 Fourth St., 518/273-8773
Notty Pine Tavern
2301 Fifteenth St., 518/272-4557
Testo's Restaurant and Pizza Parlor
853 Fourth Ave. at 124th St., 518/235-0444
Verdile's Restaurant
572 Second Ave., 518/235-8879

Best Pizza
Dante's Pizzeria
70 Jefferson St., 518/272-4533
De Fazio's Pizzeria
266 Fourth St., 518/271-1111
Purple Pub
2 Cohoes Rd., Watervliet, 518/273-9646
Verdile's Restaurant
572 Second Ave., 518/235-8879

Best Seafood
Capehouse Seafood Restaurant
254 Broadway, 518/274-0167
Old Daley Inn
499 Second Ave., 518/235-2656

Best View While Dining
Mamma Maria Cuchina Italian
19 Clifton Country Rd., Clifton Park, 518/371-2106

Best Wine Selection
River Street Cafe
429 River St., 518/273-2740

UTICA, NY

Best Breakfast
Breakfast at Tiffany's
  40 Seneca Turnpike, Clinton, 315/853-8093

Best Burgers
Babe's Macaroni Grill and Bar
  80 N. Genesee St., 315/735-0777
Zebb's Deluxe Grill and Bar
  8428 Seneca Turnpike, New Hartford,
    315/735-8547

Best Coffee/Coffeehouse
Bagel Grove
  7 Burrstone Rd., 315/724-8015
Lu Lu's Cafe
  311 Turner St., 315/735-6587

Best Desserts
Desserts Beyond The Ordinary
  24 Bank Pl., 315/733-8799
Joey's Restaurant
  815 Mohawk St., 315/724-9769

Best Greek/Mediterranean Food
Symeon's Greek Restaurant
  4941 Commercial Dr., Yorkville, 315/736-4074

Best Homestyle Food
Hartford Queen Diner
  4784 Commercial Dr., New Hartford, 315/736-0312

Best Italian Food
Chesterfield Restaurant
  1713 Bleecker St., 315/732-9356
Joey's Restaurant
  815 Mohawk St., 315/724-9769
Tom Cavallo's Restaurant
  40 Genesee St., New Hartford, 315/735-1578

Best Pizza
Franco's Pizza Pasta Cafe
  2002 Genesee St., 315/724-4526
Sunset Pizza and Sub
  1428 Sunset Ave., 315/732-9000

Best Sandwiches
Bob's On Bank
  8 Bank Pl., 315/724-3998
Columbia
  500 Columbia St., 315/732-1596
Creative Cafe
  386 Main St., 717/726-7145
Tiny's Grill
  1014 State St., 315/732-9497

Best Seafood
Hook Line and Sinker Pub
  90 Seneca Turnpike, New Hartford, 315/732-3636
Jack Appleseed's Tavern
  151 N. Genesee St., 315/797-7979

Best Steaks
Kirby's American Restaurant
    4982 Commercial Dr., Yorkville, 315/736-4141
Raleigh Room
    Ramada Inn, 141 New Hartford St., New Hartford,
    315/735-3392

Best Wine Selection
Lu Lu's Cafe
    311 Turner St., 315/735-6587

WATERTOWN, NY

Best All-You-Can-Eat Buffet
Carriage House Restaurant
    300 Washington St., 315/782-8000
Partridge Berry Inn
    Black River Rd., 315/788-4610

Best Chinese Food
Fung Hing Chinese Restaurant
    225 State St., 315/785-9688

Best Diner
Longway's Diner
    23802 State Rte. 342, 315/782-1131

Best Italian Food
Art's Jug
    820 Huntington St., 315/782-9764
Giovanni's Ristorante
    616 Leray St., 315/788-6830
Sboro's Restaurant
    836 Coffeen St., 315/788-1728

Best Sandwiches
Clubhouse
    19271 U.S. Rte. 11, 315/788-5234

Best Steaks
Pete's Restaurant
    111 Breen Ave., 315/782-6640

N

WHITE PLAINS, NY

[See also: Bronx, Manhattan, and Yonkers.]

Best American Food
Ashley's
    51 Mamaroneck Ave., 914/683-5999

Best Burgers
Mr. Greenjeans Restaurant
    100 Main St., 914/997-8122

Best Chinese Food
White Plains Imperial Wok
    736 N. Broadway, 914/686-2700

Best Coffee/Coffeehouse
Dolce Vita Cafe
    100 Main St., 914/682-9378

Best Desserts
My Favorite Muffin
   100 Main St., 914/948-2136
Sweet Dreams Bake Shop
   333 Mamaroneck Ave., 914/448-9535

Best French Food
Bertrand
   1D Franklin Ave., Ste. 5, 203/661-4459

Best Health-Conscious Menu
Sweetwaters Restaurant
   577 N. Broadway, 914/328-8918

Best Italian Food
Mulino's of Westchester
   99 Court St., 914/761-1818

Best Japanese Food
Noda's Japanese Steakhouse
   200 Hamilton Ave., 914/949-0990

Best Mexican Food
Cactus Jack's
   210 Saw Mill River Rd., Elmsford, 914/345-3334

Best Pizza
Ernesto Restaurant
   130 W. Post Rd., 914/421-1414
Gianfranco Pizzeria
   88 Virginia Rd., 914/682-5655

Best Sandwiches
P and P Delicatessen
   670 N. Broadway, 914/683-8606

Best Seafood
Crystal Bay Dining and Catering
   5 John Walsh Blvd., Peekskill, 914/737-7234
Sam's of Gedney Way
   52 Gedney Way, 914/949-0978

Best Steaks
Oliver's Restaurant
   15 S. Broadway, 914/761-6111
Willet House
   20 Willett Ave., Port Chester, 914/939-7500

YONKERS, NY

[See also: Bronx, Manhattan, and White Plains.]

Best American Food
Freelance Cafe and Wine Bar
   506 Piermont Ave., Piermont, 914/365-3250

Best Barbecue/Ribs
Texas Grill
   1 Western Ave., 914/963-7427

Best Chinese Food
Golden Wok
   2250 Central Park Ave., 914/779-8438

Best Fine Dining
Daniel's Restaurant
    292 Columbus Ave., Tuckahoe, 914/337-1883

Best French Food
La Panetiere
    530 Milton Rd., Rye, 914/967-8140

Best Mexican Food
Corridos Mexicanos
    1771 Central Park Ave., 914/779-0990

Best Pizza
Bene Bene Italian Restaurant
    2500 Central Park Ave., 914/961-3795
Luciano's Italian Restaurant
    2192 Central Park Ave., 914/961-5550

Best Sandwiches
Epstein's Kosher Delicatessen
    2369 Central Park Ave., 914/793-3131

Best Seafood
East Harbor Seafood Restaurant
    1560 Central Park Ave., 914/961-0100

Best Steaks
Charlie Brown's Steakhouse
    1820 Central Park Ave., 914/779-7227

N

North Carolina

ASHEVILLE, NC

Best All-You-Can-Eat Buffet
Gerald's Fireplace Restaurant
   287 Old Weaverville Rd., 704/658-2992
Horizons
   Grove Park Inn, 290 Macon Ave., 704/252-2711

Best American Food
Southside Cafe
   1800 Hendersonville Rd., 704/274-4413

Best Bar
Barley's Taproom
   42 Biltmore Ave., 704/255-0504

Best Barbecue/Ribs
Barbecue Inn
   1341 Patton Ave., 704/253-9615
Little Pigs
   384 McDowell St., 704/254-4253
   1916 Hendersonville Rd., 704/684-0500
Mountain Smokehouse Restaurant
   20 S. Spruce St., 704/253-4871
Woody's Barbecue
   901 Smokey Park Hwy., Candler, 704/665-0000

Best Breakfast
Bruegger's Bagel Bakery
   670 Merrien Ave., 704/254-1560
Hot Shot Cafe
   7 Lodge St., 704/274-2170

Best Burgers
Westside Grill
   1190 Patton Ave., 704/252-9605

Best Cafeteria
J and S Cafeteria
  800 Fairview Rd., 704/298-0507

Best Chinese Food
China Inn
  777 Biltmore Ave., 704/252-6129
China Palace
  4 S. Tunnel Rd., 704/298-7098
Hong Kong Chinese Restaurant
  579 Tunnel Rd., 704/298-0505

Best Coffee/Coffeehouse
Beanstreet Coffee
  3 Broadway St., 704/255-8180

Best Continental Food
The Market Place
  20 Wall St., 704/252-4162

Best Desserts
Blue Moon Bakery
  60 Biltmore Ave., 704/252-6063
Grovewood Cafe
  111 Grovewood Rd., 704/258-8956
The Hop Ice Cream Shop
  507 Merrimon Ave., 704/252-8362

Best Diner
Battery Park Cafe
  1 Battle Sq., 704/255-7613
Hot Shot Cafe
  7 Lodge St., 704/274-2170

Best Dinner
La Caterina Trattoria
  5 Pack Sq., 704/254-1148

Best Fine Dining
Gabrielle's
  Richmond Hill Inn, 87 Richmond Hill Dr.,
    704/252-7313
La Caterina Trattoria
  5 Pack Sq., 704/254-1148
Windmill European Grill
  85 Tunnel Rd., 704/253-5285

Best Greek/Mediterranean Food
Apollo Flame Pizza
  485 Hendersonville Rd., 704/274-3582
Jerusalem Garden Cafe
  78 Patton Ave., 704/254-0255

Best Health-Conscious Menu
McGuffey's Restaurant
  13 Kenilworth Knoll, 704/252-0956

Best Ice Cream/Yogurt
Biltmore Dairy Bar
  800 Brevard Rd., 704/667-0213
  115 Hendersonville Rd., 704/274-2370

Best Italian Food
La Caterina Trattoria
  5 Pack Sq., 704/254-1148

Vincenzo's Ristorante
  10 N. Market St., 704/254-4698
Savoy Restaurant
  641 Merrimon Ave., 704/253-1077

Best Japanese Food
Heiwa Shokudo
  87 N. Lexington Ave., 704/254-7761
Tomo Japanese Cuisine
  2 Regent Park Blvd., 704/252-7177

Best Lunch
Cafe on the Square
  1 Biltmore Ave., 704/251-5565

Best Mexican Food
El Chapala
  1455 Patton Ave., 704/258-3730
  868 Merrimon Ave., 704/258-0899
La Paz Restaurant and Cantina
  10 Biltmore Plz., 704/277-8779
Rio Burrito
  11 Broadway St., 704/253-2422
Salsa Mexican Caribbean Food
  6 Patton Ave., 704/252-9805

Best Outdoor Dining
Max's Celebrity Deli, Grill, and Bar
  130 College St., 704/258-1162

Best Pizza
Apollo Flame Pizza
  485 Hendersonville Rd., 704/274-3582
Barley's Taproom
  42 Biltmore Ave., 704/255-0504
Blue Moon Bakery
  60 Biltmore Ave., 704/252-6063
Boston Pizza
  501 Merrimon Ave., 704/252-9474

Best Place to Eat Alone
Malaprop's Bookstore Cafe
  61 Haywood St., 704/254-6734

Best Sandwiches
Max and Rosie's
  25 N. Lexington Ave., 704/254-5342
New French Bar
  1 Battery Park Ave., 704/252-3685
Two Guys Original Olde Style Hoagies
  132 Charlotte St., 704/254-9955

Best Seafood
The Greenery Restaurant
  148 Tunnel Rd., 704/253-2809

Best Sunday Brunch
Grove Park Inn
  290 Macon Ave., 704/252-2711
Uptown Cafe
  22 Battery Park Ave., 704/253-2158

N

Best Vegetarian Food
Laughing Seed
    40 Wall St., 704/252-3445

Best View While Dining
Horizons
    Grove Park Inn, 290 Macon Ave., 704/252-2711

BLOWING ROCK, NC

Best Barbecue/Ribs
Woodlands Barbeque
    8332 Valley Blvd., Hwy. 321, 704/295-3395

Best Dinner
Original Emporium Restaurant
    8960 Valley Blvd., Hwy. 321, 704/295-7661
The Riverwood
    7179 Valley Blvd., Hwy. 321, 704/295-4162

Best Lunch
Woodlands Barbeque
    8332 Valley Blvd., Hwy. 321, 704/295-3395

Best Regional Food
Ham's Restaurant
    8960 Valley Blvd., Hwy. 321, 704/295-7661

Best Restaurant in Town
Best Cellar
    275 Little Springs Rd., Hwy. 321, 704/295-3466

Best Seafood
Dockside Ira's
    3148 Wonderland Trl., 704/295-4008

BOONE, NC

Best Breakfast
Mountain House Pancakes
    2174 Blowing Rock Rd., 704/264-4680

Best Casual Dining
Murphy's Patio Pub
    747 W. King St., 704/264-5117

Best Chinese Food
Hunan Chinese Restaurant
    214 Southgate Dr., 704/262-0555

Best Desserts
Macado's
    539 W. King St., 704/264-1375

Best Dinner
Peppers Restaurant
    240 Shadowline Dr., 704/262-1250

Best Fine Dining
Hound Ears Club
    Rural Route 3, Hwy. 105S, 704/963-4321

Best Inexpensive Meal
Caribbean Cafe
    489 W. King St., 704/265-2233

Best Italian Food
Casa Rustica Restaurant
1348 N.C. Hwy. 105S, 704/262-0551

Best Lunch
Murphy's Patio Pub
747 W. King St., 704/264-5117
Peppers Restaurant
240 Shadowline Dr., 704/262-1250
Red Onion Cafe
227 Hardin St., 704/264-5470

Best Pizza
Sollecito's Pizza Pasta
957 Rivers St., 704/264-2378

Best Regional Food
Daniel Boone Inn Restaurant
130 Hardin St., 704/264-8657

Best Restaurant in Town
Grandview Restaurant
10575-1 Hwy. 105S, Banner Elk, 704/963-4573
Louisiana Purchase
397 Shawneehaw Ave., Banner Elk, 704/898-5656
Stone Walls
N.C. Hwy. 184, Banner Elk, 704/963-6161

Best Steaks
Peddler Steak House
1972 Blowing Rock Rd., 704/264-4433
Sagebrush Steakhouse and Saloon
1111 N.C. Hwy. 105, 704/265-4488

N

BURLINGTON, NC

Best Coffee/Coffeehouse
Ham's Restaurant
1610 S. Church St., 910/570-3099

Best Diner
Blue Ribbon Diner
2465 S. Church St., 910/570-1120

Best Sandwiches
Ham's Restaurant
1610 S. Church St., 910/570-3099

Best Steaks
The Cutting Board
2619 Alamance Rd., 910/226-0291

CARY, NC

Best Breakfast
Bruegger's Bagel Bakery
122 SW Maynard Rd., 919/467-4566
Courtney's Restaurant
685 Cary Towne Blvd., 919/469-8410

Best Coffee/Coffeehouse
Gaulart and Maliclet French Cafe
957 N. Harrison Ave., 919/469-2288

Best Delicatessen
Horwitz's Delicatessen
   MacGregor Shopping Center, 107 Edenburgh St.,
      919/467-2007

Best Desserts
Rebecca's Gourmet Bakery
   115G W. Chatham St., 919/469-2516

Best Family Dining
Jasper's
   4300 NW Cary Pkwy., 919/319-3400

Best Ice Cream/Yogurt
Goodberry Creamery
   1146 Kildaire Farm Rd., 919/467-2386

Best Italian Food
Fiore's
   MacGregor Shopping Center, 107 Edinburgh Dr.,
      Ste. 135, 919/467-6028

Best Lunch
Wivi and Me Pub and Grill
   928 W. Chatham St., 919/467-1816

Best Mexican Food
Coyote Cafe
   1014 Ryan Rd., 919/469-5253

Best Other Ethnic Food
Ben's Jamaican Cuisine (Jamaican)
   8306 Chapel Hill Rd., 919/380-1818

Best Outdoor Dining
Ragazzi's Restaurant
   802 Cary Towne Blvd., 919/467-4075

Best Pizza
Brother's Pizza
   132 Kilmayne Dr., 919/481-0883

Best Restaurant in Town
Fox and Hound Restaurant and Pub
   107 Edinburgh Dr., Ste. 119, 919/380-0080

Best Sandwiches
D'Nardy's
   1259 Kildaire Farm Rd., 919/481-3381

Best Steaks
Vinnie's Steakhouse and Tavern
   107 Edinburgh Dr., 919/380-8210

CHAPEL HILL, NC

Best American Food
Ruben's Restaurant
   The Europa Hotel, 1 Europa Dr., 919/968-4900

Best Atmosphere
Spanky's Restaurant and Bar
   101 E. Franklin St., 919/967-2678

Best Beer Selection
Rathskeller
   157A E. Franklin St., 919/942-5158

Best Breakfast
Breadmen's Restaurant
 324 W. Rosemary St., 919/967-7110
Courtney's Restaurant
 1506 E. Franklin St., 919/967-2855
Elmo's Diner
 200 N. Greensboro St., Carrboro, 919/929-2909

Best Brewpub
Carolina Brewery
 460 W. Franklin St., 919/942-1800

Best Cajun/Creole Food
New Orleans Cookery
 401 W. Franklin St., 919/929-3192

Best Chinese Food
Oriental Garden Gourmet Restaurant
 503 W. Rosemary St., 919/967-8818

Best Coffee/Coffeehouse
Carolina Coffee Shop
 138 E. Franklin St., 919/942-6875

Best Desserts
La Residence
 202 W. Rosemary St., 919/967-2506

Best Diner
Owens 501 Diner
 1500 N. Fordham Blvd., 919/933-3505

Best Eclectic Menu
Saladelia Cafe
 105 N. Columbia St., 919/932-1020

Best Greek/Mediterranean Food
Mariakakis Restaurant and Bakery
 1 Mariakakis Plz., 1322 N. Fordham Blvd.,
  919/942-1453

Best Homestyle Food
Crook's Corner
 610 W. Franklin St., 919/929-7643
Dip's Country Kitchen
 405 W. Rosemary St., 919/942-5837

Best Indian Food
Star of India
 1301 E. Franklin St., 919/967-6622

Best Italian Food
411 West Italian Cafe
 411 W. Franklin St., 919/967-2782

Best Mexican Food
Flying Burrito Mexican Restaurant
 746A Airport Rd., 919/967-7744

Best Other Ethnic Food
Seeds of Sheba (Caribbean)
 110 N. Merritt Mill Rd., 919/967-9949

Best Regional Food
Pyewacket Restaurant
 431 W. Franklin St., 919/929-0297

N

Best Romantic Dining
La Residence
  202 W. Rosemary St., 919/967-2506

Best Seafood
Squids Restaurant
  1201 N. Fordham Blvd., 919/942-8757

Best Wine Selection
A Southern Season
  East Gate Shopping Center, 1800 E. Franklin St.,
    919/929-7133
Weathervane
  East Gate Shopping Center, 1800 E. Franklin St.,
    919/929-9466

CHARLOTTE, NC

Best American Food
Fifth Street Cafe
  118 W. Fifth St., 704/358-8334
Harper's Restaurant
  6518 Fairview Rd., 704/366-6688
  301 E. Woodlawn Rd., 704/522-8376
  320 S. Tryon St., Ste. 202, 704/375-9715
Jack Straw's, A Tavern of Taste
  1936 E. Seventh St., 704/347-8960
Palatable Pleasures
  2000 South Blvd., 704/377-9717

Best Barbecue/Ribs
Art's Barbecue and Deli
  900 E. Morehead St., 704/334-9424
Carolina Country Barbeque
  2501 Crownpoint Executive Dr., 704/847-4520
  838 Tyvola Rd., 704/525-0337
Old Hickory House Restaurant
  6538 N. Tryon St., 704/596-8014
Rogers Barbecue
  901 N. Wendover Rd., 704/364-2939

Best Bistro
Bistro 100
  100 N. Tryon St., 704/344-0515

Best Breakfast
Landmark Restaurant Diner
  4429 Central Ave., 704/532-1153
Original Pancake House
  4736 Sharon Rd., 704/332-3224

Best Brewpub
Dilworth Brewing Company
  1301 East Blvd., 704/377-2739
Southend Brewery and Smokehouse
  2100 South Blvd., 704/358-4677

Best Burgers
Lupie's Cafe
  2718 Monroe Rd., 704/374-1232

Best Cajun/Creole Food
Bayou Kitchen Restaurant
 1958 E. Seventh St., 704/332-2256
Cajun Queen
 1800 E. Seventh St., 704/377-9017
Hotel Charlotte
 705 S. Sharon Amity Rd., 704/364-8755

Best Casual Dining
300 East
 300 East Blvd., 704/332-6507

Best Chinese Food
Baoding
 4722F Sharon Rd., 704/552-8899
Fortune Garden
 809 E. Arrowood Rd., 704/523-2828
Great Wall of China
 6666 Carmel Rd., 704/542-5409
 5501 Central Ave., 704/536-3211
Tsing Tao
 1600 Montford Dr., 704/525-5803
Wan Fu
 10719 Kettering Dr., 704/541-1688

Best Coffee/Coffeehouse
Coffee Cup Grill
 914 S. Clarkson St., 704/375-8855
Coffeeworks
 7816 Fairview Rd., 704/367-1800
 8300 Providence Rd., 704/542-9975
Dillworth Coffee House
 320 S. Tryon St., 704/377-4788
Jackson's Java
 8544 University City Blvd., 704/548-1133
Jeremiah's Coffee and Tea Company
 1480BB East Blvd., 704/377-1680
La-Dee-Da's
 1942 E. Seventh St., 704/372-9599
Peabody's Coffee Shop
 4732 Sharon Rd., 704/556-1700
Queen City Coffee Roasters
 8502 Park Rd., 704/556-9771

Best Continental Food
Valentino's
 3014 E. Independence Blvd., 704/375-9200

Best Delicatessen
Chris's Deli Restaurant
 3619 E. Independence Blvd., 704/536-2670
Dikadees Deli
 1419A East Blvd., 704/333-3354
Rusty's Deli
 10612A Providence Rd., 704/845-8505
 5445 77 Center Dr., Ste. 80, 704/527-2650

Best Desserts
Dikadees Deli
 1419A East Blvd., 704/333-3354

N

Red Rocks
4223 Providence Rd., Ste. 8, 704/364-0402

Best Fine Dining
Hotel Charlotte
705 S. Sharon Amity Rd., 704/364-8755
Mimosa Grill
327 S. Tryon St., 704/343-0700
The Townhouse
1011 Providence Rd., 704/335-1546

Best French Food
La Bibliotheque
1901 Roxborough Rd., 704/365-5000

Best German Food
Rheinland Haus
2418 Park Rd., 704/376-3836

Best Greek/Mediterranean Food
Akropolis
8200 Providence Rd., Ste. 800, 704/541-5099
Town Center Plaza, 8500 University City Blvd.,
704/548-8584

Best Homestyle Food
Carver's Creek
131 E. Woodlawn Rd., 704/525-0333
6720 E. Independence Blvd., 704/535-3361
Diamond
1901 Commonwealth Ave., 704/375-8959
Fenwick's
511 Providence Rd., 704/333-2750
Liberty East
5112 E. Independence Blvd., 704/568-8640
Soul Shack
3418 Tuckaseegee Rd., 704/391-9636
The Country Inn of Matthews
341 N. Ames St., Matthews, 704/847-1447

Best Inexpensive Meal
Lupie's Cafe
2718 Monroe Rd., 704/374-1232
New Big Village
1537 Camden Rd., 704/332-3366
Tryon House Restaurant
130 Eastway Dr., 704/598-2611

Best Italian Food
Cafe 521
521 N. College St., 704/377-9100
Conte's Ristorante Italiano
2839D Selwyn Ave., 704/344-1110
Frankie's Italian Grille
800 E. Morehead St., 704/358-8004
Italian Isles Restaurant
5542 N. Tryon St., 704/596-4681
Mama Ricotta's
901 S. Kings Dr., 704/343-0148
Si! Italian Restaurant and Bar
8418 Park Rd., 704/556-0914

Best Japanese Food
Kabuto Japanese Steak House
   1001 E. White Harris, 704/548-1219
   446 Tyvola Rd., 704/529-0659
Tokyo Restaurant
   4603 South Blvd., 704/527-8787

Best Lunch
Providence Cafe
   110 Perrin Pl., 704/376-2008

Best Mexican Food
Azteca Mexican Restaurant
   116 E. Woodland Rd., 704/525-5110
La Paz Cantina and Restaurante
   523 Fenton Pl., 704/372-4168
Ole Ole
   709 S. Kings Dr., 704/358-1102

Best Middle Eastern Food
Ali Baba
   4113A Monroe Rd., 704/376-0750
Middle East Deli
   4508 E. Independence Blvd., 704/536-9847

Best Outdoor Dining
Village Tavern
   4201 Congress St., Ste. 190, 704/552-9983

Best Pizza
Luisa's Brick Oven
   1730 Abbey Pl., 704/522-8782
Mama Lena's Pizza and Pasta
   5135 Albemarle Rd., 704/568-0000
Southend Brewery and Smokehouse
   2100 South Blvd., 704/358-4077
Wolfman Pizza
   106 S. Sharon Amity Rd., 704/366-3666
   2839A Selwyn Ave., 704/377-4695
   8318-702 Pineville Matthews Rd., 704/543-9653
   10620A Providence Rd., 704/845-9888
   1819 Matthews Township Rd., 704/844-8272
Zepeddie's Pizzeria
   200D W. Woodlawn Rd., 704/522-7772

Best Romantic Dining
Lamplighter
   1328 Greenwood Cliffs, 704/372-5343
Tokyo Restaurant
   4603 South Blvd., 704/527-8787

Best Seafood
Blue Marlin
   2518 Sardis Rd. N., 704/847-1212
Caravel Seafood Restaurant
   201 Archdale Dr., 704/522-0911
Fishmarket Restaurant
   6631 Morrison Blvd., 704/365-0883

Best Soul Food
Simmons 4th Ward Restaurant
   516 N. Graham St., 704/334-6640

N

Best Spanish Food
Tio Montero
  207 Johnston St., Pineville, 704/889-2258

Best Steaks
Hereford Barn Steak House
  4320 I-85N Service Rd., 704/596-0854

Best Sunday Brunch
Providence Cafe
  110 Perrin Pl., 704/376-2008
Village Tavern
  4201 Congress St., Ste. 190, 704/552-9983

Best Thai Food
Thai Cuisine Restaurant
  4800 Central Ave., 704/532-7511
Thai House
  3210 N. Sharon Amity Rd., 704/532-6868
Thai Orchid
  4223 Providence Rd., 704/364-1134
Thai Taste
  324 East Blvd., 704/332-0001
  6701 N. Tryon St., 704/597-8880

Best Vegetarian Food
Ali Baba
  4113A Monroe Rd., 704/376-0750
Talley's Green Grocery
  1408C East Blvd., 704/334-9200

Best Vietnamese Food
Cafe Saigon
  8418 Park Rd., 704/556-9911
Huong Viet Vietnamese Restaurant
  4808 Central Ave., 704/537-8475
Lang Van
  3019 Shamrock Dr., 704/531-9525

Best Wine Selection
Sonoma
  201 S. College St., Ste. 280, 704/375-2004
Thirtieth Edition
  301 S. Tryon St., Ste. 3000, 704/372-7778

DURHAM, NC

Best 24-Hour Restaurant
Honey's Restaurant
  2700 Guess Rd., 919/477-2181

Best American Food
Colonial Inn
  153 W. King St., Hillsborough, 919/732-2461

Best Barbecue/Ribs
Bullock's Barbecue
  3330 Wortham Dr., 919/383-3211
Damon's The Place for Ribs
  3019 Auto Dr., 919/492-2574
Dillard's Barbecue
  3921 Fayetteville St., 919/544-1587

Best Burgers
Grady's American Grill
    4010 Chapel Hill Blvd., 919/419-7022

Best Casual Dining
Nana's Restaurant
    2514 University Dr., 919/493-8545
Sassy's Restaurant
    1821 Hillandale Rd., 919/383-0244

Best Chinese Food
China Inn
    2701 Hillsborough Rd., 919/286-2444
China Town Chinese Restaurant
    3500 N. Roxboro Rd., 919/220-1488

Best Delicatessen
Foster's Market
    2694 Chapel Hill Blvd., 919/489-3944

Best Desserts
Francesca's Dessert Caffe
    706B Ninth St., 919/286-4177

Best Eclectic Menu
Neo Renaissance
    5408 New Hope Commons Dr., 919/489-3838

N

Best Family Restaurant
Bullock's Barbecue
    3330 Wortham Dr., 919/383-3211

Best Fine Dining
Anotherthyme
    109 N. Gregson St., 919/682-5225
Magnolia Grill
    1002 Ninth St., 919/286-3609

Best Greek/Mediterranean Food
International Delights
    740 Ninth St., 919/286-2884
Parizade
    2200 W. Main St., 919/286-9712
Spartacus Restaurant
    4139 Durham Chapel Hill Blvd., 919/489-2848

Best Homestyle Food
Chicken Hut
    3019 Fayetteville St., 919/682-5697
Colonial Inn
    153 W. King St., Hillsborough, 919/732-2461

Best Italian Food
Pop's
    810 W. Peabody St., 919/956-7677
Romano's Macaroni Grill
    4020 Durham Chapel Hill Blvd., 919/489-0313

Best Lunch
Saladelia Cafe and Bakery
    4201 University Dr., 919/489-5776

Best Pizza
Mia Pizzeria
    748 Ninth St., 919/286-0404

Best Restaurant in Town
Anotherthyme
109 N. Gregson St., 919/682-5225
Magnolia Grill
1002 Ninth St., 919/286-3609
Nikos Taverna
905 W. Main St., Ste. 49, 919/682-0043
Papagayo Restaurant
501 Douglas St., 919/286-1910

Best Soul Food
Green Candle Restaurant
901 Fayetteville St., 919/682-6781

Best Southwestern Food
Cosmic Cantina
1920A Perry St., 919/286-1875
Papagayo Restaurant
501 Douglas St., 919/286-1910

Best Steaks
Grady's American Grill
4010 Durham Chapel Hill Blvd., 919/419-7022

N

FAYETTEVILLE, NC

Best Chinese Food
Great Wall Chinese Restaurant
3411 Murchison Rd., 910/630-1500

Best Fine Dining
La Terrace
270 SW Broad St., Southern Pines, 910/692-5622

Best Inexpensive Meal
Suds and Spuds
102 S. Eastern Blvd., 910/485-7770
The Haymount Grill and Steakhouse
1304 Morganton Rd., 910/484-0261
Vick's
506 Rowan St., 910/483-8652

Best Italian Food
Trio Cafe
201 S. McPherson Church Rd., Ste. 108,
910/868-2443

Best Pizza
Garo's Pizza
2805A Raeford Rd., 910/484-6336

Best Romantic Dining
De Lafayette
6112 Cliffdale Rd., 910/868-4600

Best Salad/Salad Bar
Boston Market
1909 Skibo Rd., 910/864-1666

Best Sandwiches
Dogwood Deli
315 N. Eastern Blvd., 910/484-9047

Best Seafood
Lobster House
448 Person St., 910/485-8866

Best Tea Rooms
The Coffee Scene
  411 Westwood Shopping Center, 910/864-7948

Best Thai Food
Bangkok Restaurant
  5034 Yadkin Rd., 910/868-6901
Tai Sho Restaurant
  4565 Yadkin Rd., 910/864-5550

GASTONIA, NC

Best American Food
Billie Jean's Grasshopper Farm
  911 Union Rd., 704/853-8661

Best Barbecue/Ribs
Black's Barbecue
  2902 York Hwy., 704/867-0941
Carolina Country Barbecue
  246 N. New Hope Rd., 704/865-2416
  1101 Union Rd., 704/867-2481

Best Burgers
Jigger's Drive-Inn
  1002 Gastonia Hwy., Bessemer City, 704/629-5050

Best Cafeteria
Jackson's Cafeteria
  401 Cox Rd., 704/868-4181

Best Chinese Food
Peking Chinese Restaurant
  1007 Union Rd., 704/864-6113
  3078 E. Franklin Blvd., 704/867-6600

Best Coffee/Coffeehouse
Coffee, Tea and Thee
  3044 E. Franklin Blvd., 704/867-2026

Best Homestyle Food
Firestone Grill
  908 W. Franklin Blvd., 704/868-3117

Best Ice Cream/Yogurt
Tony's Ice Cream Company
  604 E. Franklin Blvd., 704/867-7085

Best Italian Food
Angie's Spaghetti House
  1404 S. Marietta St., 704/864-0302
Benn-Benn's Italian Kitchen
  617 E. Garrison Blvd., 704/867-1446

Best Mexican Food
La Fuenete Bar and Grill
  3070 E. Franklin Blvd., 704/866-7744

Best Pizza
Milano's Italian Restaurant
  904 S. New Hope Rd., 704/854-3946

Best Salad/Salad Bar
Chantilly's Tea Room
  1003 Union Rd., 704/868-9500

N

Best Seafood
Lineberger Fish Fry
4253 S. New Hope Rd., 704/824-1587

GOLDSBORO, NC

Best Barbecue/Ribs
McCall's Barbecue and Seafood
139 Millers Chapel Rd., 919/751-0072
Wilber's Barbecue
4172 U.S. Hwy. 70E, 919/778-5218

Best German Food
Cafe Edelweiss
1809 N. Berkeley Blvd., 919/778-4446

Best Italian Food
Katlyn's Restaurant
335 N. Spence Ave., 919/778-9113
Mimmo's Italian Restaurant
2215 E. Ash St., 919/734-2228

Best Lunch
Michelle's Restaurant
1709 E. Ash St., 919/735-4128

Best Mexican Food
Mazatlan Mexican Restaurant
101 N. Berkeley Blvd., 919/751-9722

Best Restaurant in Town
Billie's Backstreet Restaurant
620 N. Madison Ave., 919/736-4406
The Lantern Inn
2201 E. Ash St., 919/734-5915

Best Seafood
Captain Bob's Seafood
430 N. Berkeley Blvd., 919/778-8332
Madison's Prime Rib and Steak
413 E. New Hope Rd., 919/751-2009

GREENSBORO, NC

Best American Food
Grady's American Grill
3011 High Point Rd., 910/292-1525

Best Atmosphere
Wild Magnolia Cafe
2200 Walker Ave., 910/378-0800

Best Barbecue/Ribs
Jed's Barbecue
2416 Randleman Rd., 910/274-2145
Stamey's Barbecue Inn
2812 Battleground Ave., 910/288-9275
2206 High Point Rd., 910/299-9888

Best Breakfast
Lox, Stock, and Bagel
2439 Battleground Ave., 910/288-2894

Best Brewpub
Spring Garden Brewing Company
714 Francis King St., 910/299-3649

Best Burgers
Fisher's Grille
  608 N. Elm St., 910/275-8300
Spring Garden Brewing Company
  714 Francis King St., 910/299-3653
Steak-Out
  1609B W. Friendly Ave., 910/271-0855

Best Casual Dining
Miami Subs
  2206 S. Holden Rd., 910/292-3661
Tripp's Restaurant
  4402 W. Wendover Ave., 910/299-9315
Village Tavern
  1219 Spring Garden St., 910/282-3063

Best Chinese Food
China Bowl
  2919 Battleground Ave., 910/282-3896
Lin's Garden
  1115 E. Bessemer Ave., 910/275-6057
Mr. Wonton
  5710H High Point Rd., 910/632-8700
  3220 Randleman Rd., 910/230-2222
  3709E Battleground Ave., 910/282-0044

Best Coffee/Coffeehouse
Cup A Joe
  411 Tate St., 910/275-2386
Stocks and Buns
  220 N. Elm St., 910/273-3941
Tate Street Coffeehouse
  334 Tate St., 910/275-2754

Best Delicatessen
Jay's Delicatessen
  627 Friendly Center Rd., 910/292-0741
T J's Deli
  3724 Battleground Ave., 910/545-1162

Best Desserts
Ganache Baking Company
  403 N. Elm St., 910/230-2253

Best Family Restaurant
Gate City Chop House
  106 S. Holden Rd., 910/294-9977
Robinson's Restaurant
  438 Battleground Ave., 910/272-6854
Tex and Shirley's Family Restaurant
  708 Pembroke Rd., 910/299-9315

Best Fine Dining
Lo Spiedo di Noble
  1720 Battleground Ave., 910/333-9833

Best Greek/Mediterranean Food
Acropolis Restaurant
  416 N. Eugene St., 910/273-3306

Best Ice Cream/Yogurt
Swensen's Ice Cream
  3124 Kathleen Ave., 910/299-2707

N

Best Indian Food
Nikita Indian Restaurant
  413 Tate St., 910/379-0744

Best Italian Food
Amalfi Harbour
  4514 W. Market St., 910/294-0020
Anton's Italian Cafe
  1628 Battleground Ave., 910/273-1386
Antonio's Restaurant
  4612 W. Market St., 910/852-3769
Ragazzi's Restaurant
  2629 Battleground Ave., 910/288-4065

Best Japanese Food
Asahi Japanese Steak House
  4520 W. Market St., 910/855-8883
Emperor's Garden
  2939 Battleground Ave., 910/282-5345

Best Lunch
Jack's Corner
  1601 Spring Garden St., 910/370-4400
Just One More
  3722G Battleground Ave., 910/282-2900

Best Mexican Food
Tijuana Fats
  360 Federal Pl., 910/272-1262

Best Outdoor Dining
Paisley's
  200 N. Davie St., 910/272-3222

Best Pizza
Pieworks
  3700 Lawndale Dr., 910/282-9003
  4508 W. Market St., 910/854-3555

Best Place to Take the Kids
Chuck E. Cheese Pizza
  702 Pembroke Rd., 910/855-0234
Elizabeth's Pizza
  918 Summit Ave., 910/274-3638
  5605E W. Friendly Ave., 910/299-1772
  2116 Lawndale Dr., 910/370-0800
  4516 High Point Rd., 910/852-7377

Best Restaurant in Town
Paisley's
  200 N. Davie St., 910/272-3222
Southern Lights Bistro and Bar
  105 Smyres Pl., 910/379-9414

Best Salad/Salad Bar
Harper's Restaurant
  601 Friendly Center Rd., 910/299-8850

Best Sandwiches
Ham's Restaurant
  201 Smyres Pl., 910/272-6721
  3709 Battleground Ave., 910/288-3334

Best Seafood
Bert's Seafood Grille
  2419 Spring Garden St., 910/854-2314
Mahi's Seafood Grill and Bar
  4721 Lawndale Dr., 910/282-8112
The Blue Marlin
  3017 High Point Rd., 910/854-5696

Best Thai Food
Rearn Thai Restaurant
  5412 W. Market St., 910/292-5901

Best Vegetarian Food
Sunset Cafe
  4608 W. Market St., 910/855-0349

HICKORY, NC

Best American Food
Vintage House Restaurant
  271 Third Ave. NW, 704/324-1210

Best Breakfast
Chesapeake Bagel Bakery
  1131 Second St. NE, 704/328-6116
Joel's Kitchen
  2145 N. Center St., 704/327-4816
Snack Bar Inc.
  1346 First Ave. SW, 704/322-5432

Best Burgers
Circus Hall of Cream
  1710 N. Center St., 704/322-2630
  211 22nd St. SW, 704/328-4214

Best Dinner
Hickory Station Restaurant
  232 Government Ave. SW, 704/322-1904

Best Place to Take the Kids
Village Inn Pizza Parlor
  326 Hwy. 70SW, 704/328-3010

Best Seafood
Jones Fish Camp
  2410 Springs Rd. NE, 704/256-8441

HIGH POINT, NC

Best Barbecue/Ribs
Henry James Barbecue
  2201 S. Main St., 336/882-8057
  621 Greensboro Rd., 336/884-8038
Smokey Joe's Barbecue
  1101 S. Main St., Lexington, 336/249-0315

Best Chinese Food
Hunan Chinese Restaurant
  1539 N. Main St., 336/885-6577

Best French Food
J. Basul Noble's Restaurant
  114 S. Main St., 336/889-3354

Best Homestyle Food
Rainbow Family Restaurant
  2116 Westchester Dr., 336/889-3133

Best Ice Cream/Yogurt
Yogurt Shoppe
  215 E. Lexington Ave., 336/885-6602

Best Pizza
Elizabeth's Pizza
  2505 Westchester Dr., 336/889-4030

Best Restaurant in Town
Atrium Cafe
  430 S. Main St., 336/889-9934

JACKSONVILLE, NC

Best Cafeteria
Piccadilly Cafeteria
  361 Jacksonville Mall, 910/577-2195

Best Chinese Food
Mai Tai Restaurant
  109 Henderson Dr., 910/346-5382

Best Homestyle Food
Helen's Kitchen
  2405B N. Marine Blvd., 910/455-9882

Best Mexican Food
El Cerro Grande
  505 N. Marine Blvd., 910/347-1307

Best Pizza
Tony's Pizza and Restaurant
  363 Western Blvd., 910/353-8666

KANNAPOLIS, NC

Best American Food
Oak's Restaurant
  1776 S. Cannon Blvd., 704/932-3900

Best Breakfast
Bojangles' Restaurant
  1301 S. Cannon Blvd., 704/932-5415
Troutman's Barbecue
  1875 Hwy. 601 Bypass S., Concord, 704/786-9714
  362 Church St. N., Concord, 704/786-5213

Best Italian Food
Villa Maria Italian Restaurant
  1445 Hwy. 29N, Concord, 704/788-1903

KILL DEVIL HILLS, NC

Best Casual Dining
RV's
  Nags Head Causeway, 740 S. Virginia Dare Trail,
    Nags Head, 919/441-4963
Sam and Omie's Restaurant
  7228 S. Virginia Dare Trail, Nags Head,
    919/441-7366
Tortugus Lie Shellfish Bar and Grill
  3018 N. Virginia Dare Trail, 919/441-7299

Best Chinese Food
North China Restaurant
  Outer Banks Mall, Mile Post 14 Bypass,
    Nags Head, 919/441-3454

Best Family Restaurant
Darrell's Restaurant
  Hwy. 64-264S, Manteo, 919/473-5366

Best Fine Dining
Colington Cafe
  1029 Colington Dr., 919/480-1123
Owens Restaurant
  7114 S. Virginia Dare Trail, Nags Head,
    919/441-7309

Best Italian Food
Chardo's Italian Ristorante
  1106 S. Croatan Hwy., 919/441-0276
Daredevil Inn Restaurant
  1112 S. Virginia Dare Trail, 919/441-6330

Best Mexican Food
Chilli Peppers Restaurant
  3001 N. Croatan Hwy., 919/441-8081

Best Seafood
Awful Arthur's Oyster Bar
  2104 N. Virginia Dare Trail, 919/441-5955

N

KINSTON, NC

Best All-You-Can-Eat Buffet
Abbott's Country Buffet
  3700 W. Vernon Ave., 919/527-5613

Best Barbecue/Ribs
Barbecue Lodge
  3647 W. Vernon Ave., 919/522-3021
King's Restaurant
  409 E. New Bern Rd., 919/527-2101
  602 N. McLewean St., 919/527-1661
  2404 N. Queen St., 919/523-3303

Best Breakfast
Lovick's Cafe
  320 N. Heritage St., 919/523-6854

Best Cafeteria
Christopher's
  217 N. Queen St., 919/527-3716

Best Chinese Food
China King
  2000 W. Vernon Ave., 919/527-7750

Best Pizza
Pizza Villa
  1400 W. Vernon Ave., 919/527-2260

Best Sandwiches
Supreme Deli and Subs
  106 E. Vernon Ave., 919/523-2230

Best Steaks
Baron and The Beef
  Hwy. 70E, 919/527-6787

KITTY HAWK, NC

Best Chinese Food
North China Express
  5416 N. Croatan Hwy., 919/261-5511

Best Mexican Food
La Fogata Mexican Restaurant
  3924 N. Croatan Hwy., 919/255-0934

Best Seafood
Black Pelican Seafood Company
  3848 Virginia Dare Trail, 919/261-5504

Best Sunday Brunch
Blue Point Bar and Grill
  The Waterfront Shop, 1240 Duck Rd.,
    919/261-8090

MAGGIE VALLEY, NC

Best Breakfast
Joey's Pancake House
  1315 Soco Rd., 704/926-0212

Best Fine Dining
J. Arthur's Restaurant
  2843 Soco Rd., 704/926-1817

Best Pizza
Two Brothers Pizza
  607 Soco Rd., 704/926-3244

Best Seafood
Key West Seafood Restaurant
  12 Soco Rd., Hwy. 19, 704/926-3112

MORGANTON, NC

Best Regional Food
Chesterfield Grill
  2000 Johns River LoopRd., 704/433-1581

Best Restaurant in Town
Judges Riverside Restaurant
  128 Greenlee Ford Rd., 704/433-5798
Original Emporium Restaurant
  1101 N. Green St., 704/433-9275

Best Steaks
Sagebrush Steakhouse Saloon
  101 Steakhouse Rd., 704/437-2242
Western Steer Steakhouse
  101 Bost Rd., 704/433-0800

NEW BERN, NC

Best All-You-Can-Eat Buffet
Latitude 35
  Sheraton Hotel, 1 Bicentennial Park,
    919/638-3585

Best Barbecue/Ribs
Moore's Barbecue
 3711 U.S. Hwy. 17S, 919/638-3937
Poppa Bear's Kitchen
 1020 Broad St., 919/635-1200

Best Burgers
Charburger
 1906 Clarendon Blvd., 919/633-4067

Best Chinese Food
Great Wall of China
 2500 Clarendon Blvd., 919/638-1188

Best Coffee/Coffeehouse
Trent River Coffee Company
 208 Craven St., 919/514-2030

Best Fine Dining
Harvey Mansion Historic Inn
 221 Tryon Palace Dr., 919/638-3205
Henderson House
 216 Pollock St., 919/637-4784

Best Homestyle Food
Billy's Ham and Eggs
 1300 S. Glenburnie Rd., 919/633-5498

Best Italian Food
Scalzo Italian Restaurant
 415 Broad St., 919/633-9898

Best Pizza
Franco's Pizza
 1226 S. Glenburnie Rd., 919/633-9711

Best Sandwiches
Carolina Bagel Company and Deli
 3601 Trent Rd., 919/636-0133
Fred and Claire's Restaurant
 247 Craven St., 919/638-5426
Pollock Street Delicatessen
 208 Pollock St., 919/637-2480

RALEIGH, NC

Best American Food
Charlie Goodnight's Restaurant
 861 W. Morgan St., 919/828-5233
Lucky 32 Restaurant
 832 Spring Forest Rd., 919/876-9932
Tripp's Restaurant
 3516 Wade Ave., 919/821-3990
Vertigo Diner
 426 S. McDowell St., 919/832-4477

Best Atmosphere
Charter Room
 1505 Hillsborough St., 919/828-0333
Seaboard Cafe
 707 Semart Dr., 919/821-7553

Best Barbecue/Ribs
Barbecue Lodge
 4600 Capital Blvd., 919/872-4755

N

Cooper's Barbecue
109 E. Davie St., 919/832-7614
Don Murray's Barbecue
2751 Capital Blvd., 919/872-6270
Oh Brian's Rack Shack
4638 Capital Blvd., 919/872-7422
5925 Glenwood Ave., 919/781-7427

Best Beer Selection
Greenshield's Brewery and Pub
214 E. Martin St., 919/829-0214
Mr. Dunderbak's Old World Deli
4325 Glenwood Ave., 919/781-7075

Best Breakfast
Big Ed's City Market Restaurant
220 Wolfe St., 919/836-9909
Farmers Market Restaurant
1240 Farmers Market Dr., 919/833-7973
Finch's Restaurant
401 W. Peace St., 919/834-7396

Best Brewpub
Greenshield's Brewery and Pub
214 E. Martin St., 919/829-0214

Best Burgers
Char-Grill
3211 Edwards Mill Rd., 919/781-2945
618 Hillsborough St., 919/821-7636
4617 Atlantic Ave., 919/954-9556
Fat Daddy's
6201 Glenwood Ave., 919/787-3773

Best Cafeteria
Hudson Belk Capital Room
4325 Glenwood Ave., 919/782-7010

Best Cajun/Creole Food
Cajun Charlie's Bayou Cuisine
607 Glenwood Ave., 919/836-1919

Best Casual Dining
Crowley's Old Favorites Restaurant
7330 Creedmoor Rd., 919/676-3431
3071 Medlin Dr., 919/787-3431
Simple Pleasures Market and Cafe
2923 Essex Cir., 919/782-9227

Best Coffee/Coffeehouse
3rd Place Coffeehouse
1811 Glenwood Ave., 919/834-6566
Cup A Joe
2109 Avent Ferry Rd., 919/828-9886
3100 Hillsborough St., 919/828-9665

Best Delicatessen
Deli Case
8323 Creedmoor Rd., 919/846-1222
New York Deli
109 S. Wilmington St., 919/832-3354

Best Desserts
Winston's Grille
  6401 Falls of Neuse Rd., 919/790-0700

Best Diner
Oak City Diner
  2305 Wake Forest Rd., 919/821-8020

Best Fine Dining
Cappers Restaurant and Tavern
  North Hills Plaza, 4421 Six Forks Rd., Ste. 319,
    919/787-8963
Maximillians Pasta Grille
  1284 Buck Jones Rd., 919/460-6299
The Angus Barn
  9401 Glenwood Ave., 919/787-3505

Best French Food
Jean Claude's French Cafe
  6112 Falls of Neuse Rd., 919/872-6224

Best Greek/Mediterranean Food
Alexander's Restaurant
  7909 Falls of Neuse Rd., 919/846-1994
Cafe Giorgios
  230 Newton Rd., Ste. 214, 919/846-9449

Best Health-Conscious Menu
The Museum Cafe
  2110 Blue Ridge Rd., 919/833-3548

Best Homestyle Food
Big Ed's City Market Restaurant
  220 Wolfe St., 919/836-9909
Capital Room Restaurant
  4325 Glenwood Ave., 919/782-7010
Griffin's Restaurant
  1604 N. Market Dr., 919/876-0125

Best Ice Cream/Yogurt
Goodberry's Creamery
  2421 Spring Forest Rd., 919/878-8159

Best Indian Food
India Mahal
  3212 Hillsborough St., 919/836-9742
Royal India Cuisine
  3901 Capital Blvd., 919/981-0849

Best Italian Food
Cafe Luna
  136 E. Hargett St., 919/832-6090
Casa Carbone Restaurant
  6019 Glenwood Ave., 919/781-8750
Casalinga Restaurant
  4538 Capital Blvd., 919/873-1334
Claudio's Ristorante
  6300 Creedmoor Rd., 919/847-0083
Maximillian's Pasta Grille
  1284 Buck Jones Rd., 919/460-6299
Piccola Italia
  6325 Falls of Neuse Rd., Ste. 17, 919/872-1131
  423 Woodburn Rd., 919/833-6888

N

Ragazzi's Restaurant
  5800 Glenwood Ave., 919/787-0434
  6305 Falls of Neuse Rd., 919/981-0160
Two Guy's Amer-Italian
  2504 Hillsborough St., 919/832-2324
Vinnie's Tap and Grille Room
  4015 University Dr., 919/493-0004

Best Japanese Food
Kanki Japanese House of Steaks
  4325 Glenwood Ave., 919/782-9708

Best Late Night Food
Raleighwood Cinema Grille
  6609 Falls of Neuse Rd., 919/847-0326

Best Lunch
Cloo's Coney Island
  2233 Avent Ferry Rd., Ste.102, 919/834-3354
Rock Ola Cafe
  2267 Avent Ferry Rd., 919/828-5533
  7371 Six Forks Rd., 919/848-4052

Best Mexican Food
Dos Taquitos Mexican Restaurant
  5629 Creedmoor Rd., 919/787-3373

Best Outdoor Dining
Zest
  8831 Six Forks Rd., 919/848-4792

Best Pizza
Andy's Pizza
  1302 E. Millbrook Rd., Ste. 1, 919/872-0797
  4217 Six Forks Rd., 919/781-9043
Brother's Pizza
  2508A Hillsborough St., 919/832-3664
Cafe Giorgio's
  230 Newton Rd., Ste. 214, 919/846-9449
Frank's Pizza and Italian Restaurant
  2030 New Bern Ave., 919/231-8990
Lilly's Pizza
  1813 Glenwood Ave., 919/833-0226
Milano's Pizza
  3001 Hillsborough St., 919/899-3500

Best Restaurant in Town
42nd Street Oyster Bar and Seafood
  508 W. Jones St., 919/831-2811
Capper's Restaurant and Tavern
  4421 Six Forks Rd., Ste. 319, 919/787-8963
Irregardless Cafe
  901 W. Morgan St., 919/833-8898

Best Romantic Dining
Margaux's Restaurant
  8111 Creedmoor Rd., 919/846-9846
Swain's Charcoal Steakhouse
  3201 New Bern Ave., 919/231-6873
Tartine's Bistro Provencal
  1110 Navaho Dr., 919/790-0091

Best Salad/Salad Bar
Sam's Restaurant and Wine Bar
  3050 Wake Forest Rd., 919/876-4056

Best Sandwiches
Manhattan Bakery
  3501 Capital Blvd., 919/954-0948

Best Seafood
42nd Street Oyster Bar and Seafood
  508 W. Jones St., 919/831-2811
Black Marlin Seafood Grille
  428 Daniels St., 919/832-7950

Best Sunday Brunch
Courtney's Restaurant
  407 E. Six Forks Rd., 919/834-3613
  2300 Gorman St., 919/859-3830
Gregory's Restaurant
  7420 Six Forks Rd., 919/847-6230

Best Thai Food
Thai Garden
  1408 Hardimont Rd., 919/872-6811

Best Vegetarian Food
Black Dog Cafe
  208 E. Martin St., 919/828-1994
Irregardless Cafe
  901 W. Morgan St., 919/833-9920
Rathskeller
  2412 Hillsborough St., 919/821-5342

N

ROCKY MOUNT, NC

Best American Food
Walnut Restaurant
  705 Walnut St., 919/446-0877

Best Barbecue/Ribs
Bob Melton's Barbecue
  631 E. Ridge St., 919/446-8513
Gardner's Barbecue
  835 N. Fairview Rd., 919/442-5522
  1331 N. Wesleyan Blvd., 919/442-0531
  Westridge Shopping Center, 3607 Sunset Ave.,
    919/443-3996

Best Dinner
Texas Steakhouse
  711 Sutters Creek Blvd., 919/443-3888

Best Family Restaurant
Carleton House
  213 N. Church St., 919/977-6576

SALISBURY, NC

Best Barbecue/Ribs
Wink's Barbecue
  1532 E. Innes St., 704/637-2410

Best Breakfast
Jim's Barbecue
  1624 W. Innes St., 704/633-1094

Best Dinner
Jasmine's
   Holiday Inn, 520 Jake Alexander Blvd. S.,
      704/637-3100

Best Family Restaurant
The Farmhouse Restaurant
   1602 Jake Alexander Blvd. S., 704/633-3276

Best Lunch
Bogart's
   2128 Statesville Blvd., 704/637-2227

Best Seafood
Blue Bay Seafood Restaurant
   8850 Statesville Blvd., 704/278-2226
   2050 Statesville Blvd., 704/639-9500

WAYNESVILLE, NC

Best Bar
Bogart's Restaurant and Lounge
   222 S. Main St., 704/452-1313
O'Malley's on Main Pub and Grill
   295 N. Main St., 704/452-4228

Best Burgers
Amon's Drive Inn and Dairy Bar
   2220 W. Dellwood Rd., 704/926-0734
Clyde's Restaurant
   1231 Balsam Rd., 704/456-9135
Duvall's Restaurant
   783 N. Main St., 704/452-9464

Best Italian Food
Angelo's Family Pizza
   550 N. Wall St., 704/452-1886
Antipasto's
   234 Waynesville Shopping Plaza, 704/452-0218

Best Lunch
Bogart's Restaurant and Lounge
   222 S. Main St., 704/452-1313
O'Malley's on Main Pub and Grill
   295 N. Main St., 704/452-4228

Best Mexican Food
Maria's Mexican Pueblo
   411 Branner Ave., 704/456-6413

Best Other Ethnic Food
Lomo Grill (Argentinian)
   121 Church St., 704/452-1704

Best Pizza
Angelo's Family Pizza
   550 N. Wall St., 704/452-1886

Best Seafood
Maggie's Galley Oyster Bar
   49 Howell Mill Rd., 704/456-8945

WILMINGTON, NC

Best Bar
Barbary Coast
  116 S. Front St., 910/762-8996
Caffe Phoenix
  9 S. Front St., 910/343-1395
Wave Hog Saloon
  12 Dock St., 910/762-2827

Best Barbecue/Ribs
Jackson's Big Oak Barbecue
  920 S. Kerr Ave., 910/799-1581

Best Breakfast
White Front Breakfast House
  1518 Market St., 910/762-5672

Best Burgers
Dockside Restaurant
  1308 Airlie Sound Rd., 910/256-2752
Katy's Great Eats
  1054 S. College Rd., 910/395-5289
P.T.'s Olde Fashioned Grille
  4544 Fountain Dr., 910/392-2293

Best Casual Dining
Annabelle's
  4106 Oleander Dr., 910/791-4955
Rucker Johns a Restaurant
  5511 Carolina Beach Rd., 910/452-1212

Best Chinese Food
Dragon Garden
  341 S. College Rd., 910/452-0708
Golden Dragon
  894 S. Kerr Ave., 910/791-0280
New China Restaurant
  3913 Oleander Dr., 910/799-3750
Szechuan Chinese Restaurant
  419 S. College Rd., 910/799-1426
Szechuan 130 Chinese Restaurant
  130 N. Front St., 910/762-5782
Wing Chinese Restaurant
  4002 Oleander Dr., 910/799-8178

Best Coffee/Coffeehouse
Fontana Caffe
  4555 Fountain Dr., 910/313-0227
Port City Java
  7 N. Front St., 910/762-5282

Best Delicatessen
Ken's Bagels and Deli
  5906 Oleander Dr., 910/313-0970

Best Desserts
Annabelle's
  4106 Oleander Dr., 910/791-4955

Best Fine Dining
Gardenias Restaurant
  7105 Wrightsville Ave., 910/256-2421

N

Pilot House Restaurant
  2 Ann St., 910/343-0200
Trail's End Steak House
  Trails End Rd., 910/791-2034

Best Ice Cream/Yogurt
Swensen's Ice Cream
  620 S. College Rd., 910/395-6740

Best Italian Food
Eddie Romanelli's Restaurant
  5400 Oleander Dr., 910/799-7000

Best Lunch
Candlelight Cafe
  417 S. College Rd., 910/392-5541
Rock Ola Cafe
  418 S. College Rd., 910/791-4288
Salt Works II
  6301 Oleander Dr., 910/350-0018
  4001 Wrightsville Ave., 910/392-1241
Temptations Gourmet Foods
  Hanover Center, 3501 Oleander Dr., 910/763-6662

Best Mexican Food
Burrito Bob's Mexican Restaurant
  5901 Wrightsville Ave., 910/392-6520
K-38 Baja Grill
  5410 Oleander Dr., 910/395-6040

Best Pizza
Gumby's Pizza
  1414D South College Rd., 910/313-0072
Incredible Gourmet Pizza
  1952 Eastwood Rd., 910/256-0339
  3600A S. College Rd., 910/791-7080

Best Romantic Dining
Harvest Moon Food and Spirits
  5704 Oleander Dr., 910/792-0172
Roy's Riverboat Landing Restaurant
  2 Market St., 910/763-7227

Best Sandwiches
Deli Downtown
  110 S. Front St., 910/762-6995
Sandwich Factory
  123 Princess St., 910/762-0100
Schlotzksy's
  3810 Oleander Dr., 910/395-0077

Best Seafood
Elijah's Restaurant
  2 Ann St., 910/343-1448
Pier 20 Seafood Restaurant
  614 S. College Rd., 910/791-1165
Pirate's Table Seafood
  3536 Carolina Beach Rd., 910/392-1470
Something Fishy Seafood
  3436 S. College Rd., 910/395-0909

Best Steaks
Beaches Restaurant
  2025 Eastwood Rd., 910/256-4622
Trail's End Steak House
  Trails End Rd., 910/791-2034

Best Sunday Brunch
Crook's by the River
  138 S. Front St., 910/762-8898
Deluxe
  114 Market St., 910/251-0333

Best Sushi
Kagetsu, Inc.
  4403 Wrightsville Ave., 910/452-5800

Best Vegetarian Food
Sahara Subs and Pitas
  6706 Market St., 910/392-4070

WILSON, NC

Best Barbecue/Ribs
Bill Ellis Barbecue
  3007 Downing St. SW, 919/237-4372
Parker's Barbecue
  2514 U.S. Hwy. 301S, 919/237-0972
R B's Restaurant
  300 Moyton Ave., Stantonsburg, 919/238-3014

Best Breakfast
Country Restaurant
  4600 Nash St. W., 919/237-8723

Best Desserts
Priscilla's
  2101 Tarboro St. S., 919/243-4944

Best Dinner
The Legacy
  301 E. Main St., Elm City, 919/236-3432

Best Seafood
Silver Lake Seafood Restaurant
  5335A Hwy. 58N, 919/243-2034

Best Steaks
Griff's Steak Barn
  2837 U.S. Hwy. 301S, 919/237-5935

WINSTON-SALEM, NC

Best Bar
Salem Tavern
  736 S. Main St., 336/748-8585
Ziggy's Tavern
  433 Baity St., 336/748-1064

Best Barbecue/Ribs
Little Richard's Barbecue
  4885 Country Club Rd., 336/760-3457
Mr. Barbecue
  1381 Peters Creek Pkwy., 336/725-7827

N

Best Bistro
Bistro 900
  900 S. Marshall St., 336/721-1336

Best Burgers
Corbin's Bar and Grill
  520 Hanes Mall Blvd., 336/768-3301
Rock Ola Cafe
  630 S. Stratford Rd., 336/765-7627

Best Casual Dining
Cumberland Cafe
  4665 Brownsboro Rd., 336/759-3113
Leon's Cafe
  924 S. Marshall St., 336/725-9593
Lucky 32 Restaurant
  109 S. Stratford Rd., 336/724-3232
Noble's Grille
  380 Knollwood St., 336/777-8477
Village Tavern
  221 Reynolda Village, 336/748-0221

Best Chinese Food
Sampan Chinese Restaurant
  985 Peters Creek Pkwy., 336/777-8266
Szechuan Palace
  3040 Healy Dr., 336/768-7123

Best Delicatessen
Buena Vista Delicatessen
  150 S. Stratford Rd., 336/723-9545

Best Family Restaurant
Ronni's Restaurant
  3656 Reynolda Rd., 336/924-1666
Village Tavern
  221 Reynolda Village, 336/748-0221

Best Fine Dining
Michael's on Fifth
  848 W. Fifth St., 336/777-0000

Best Italian Food
Franco's Italian Restaurant
  420 Jonestown Rd., 336/659-7778
Paul's Fine Italian Dining
  3443B Robinhood Rd., 336/768-2645

Best Japanese Food
Kyoto Japanese Restaurant
  585 Bethesda Rd., 336/765-7798

Best Lunch
Ham's Restaurant
  826 S. Stratford Rd., 336/760-1090

Best Mexican Food
La Carreta
  1796 Silas Creek Pky., 336/724-1114
  725 Coliseum Dr., 336/722-3709
Monterrey Mexican Restaurant
  1227 Corporation Pkwy., 336/773-0300

N

Best Pizza
Elizabeth's Italian Restaurant
2824 University Pky., 336/724-4650
Franco's Italian Restaurant
420 Jonestown Rd., 336/659-7778

Best Romantic Dining
South by Southwest
241 S. Marshall St., 336/727-0800

Best Sandwiches
Village Tavern
221 Reynolda Village, 336/748-0221

Best Seafood
Mayflower Seafood Restaurant
850 Peters Creek Pkwy., 336/725-3261
Oyster Bay
576 Hanes Mall Blvd., 336/659-0388
Shuckers Pelican Pointe
980 Peters Creek Pkwy., 336/724-2223
Yacht House Seafood Restaurant
4881 Country Club Rd., 336/768-3370

Best Steaks
Lone Star Steakhouse and Saloon
504 Hanes Mall Blvd., 336/760-9720
Staley's Charcoal Steakhouse
2000 Reynolda Rd., 336/723-8631
Western Steer Steakhouse
5920 University Pkwy., 336/377-2448
1750 S. Stratford Rd., 336/765-3526

N

WRIGHTSVILLE BEACH, NC

Best Bar
Clarence Foster's
22 N. Lumina Ave., 910/256-0224

Best Italian Food
Etrusca Restaurant
530 Causeway Dr., 910/256-5077

Best Seafood
Bridge Tender
1414 Airlie Rd., 910/256-4519
Oceanic Restaurant and Grill
703 S. Lumina Ave., 910/256-5551

North Dakota

N

BISMARCK, ND

Best All-You-Can-Eat Buffet
Royal Fork Buffet Restaurant
  1065 E. Interstate Ave., 701/222-0501

Best American Food
Captain Meriwether's Landing
  1700 River Rd., 701/224-0455
Peacock Alley Bar and Grill
  422 E. Main Ave., 701/255-7917

Best Atmosphere
Peacock Alley Bar and Grill
  422 E. Main Ave., 701/255-7917

Best Breakfast
Drumstick
  307 N. Third St., 701/223-8449
Kroll's Kitchen
  1915 E. Main St., 701/255-3850

Best Burgers
Ground Round
  526 S. Third St., 701/223-0000
It's Burger Time
  1320 E. Main Ave., 701/222-2458
Wood House
  1825 N. Thirteenth St., 701/255-3654

Best Business Lunch
Caspar's East Forty
  1401 Interchange Ave., 701/258-7222

Best Casual Dining
Green Earth Cafe and One World
  208 E. Broadway Ave., 701/223-8646

Best Chinese Food
Hong Kong Restaurant
1055 E. Interstate Ave., 701/223-2130
Jade Garden Restaurant
431 S. Third St., 701/222-8615

Best Coffee/Coffeehouse
Green Earth Cafe and One World
208 E. Broadway Ave., 701/223-8646
The Prairie Peddler
622 Kirkwood Mall, 701/223-1066

Best Continental Food
Bistro
1103 E. Front Ave., 701/224-8800

Best Diner
Drumstick
307 N. Third St., 701/223-8449
Little Cottage Cafe
2513 E. Main St., 701/223-4949

Best Dinner
Bistro
1103 E. Front Ave., 701/224-8800
Peacock Alley Bar and Grill
422 E. Main Ave., 701/255-7917

Best German Food
Drumstick
307 N. Third St., 701/223-8449
Kroll's Kitchen
1915 E. Main St., 701/255-3850

Best Health-Conscious Menu
Green Earth Cafe and One World
208 E. Broadway Ave., 701/223-8646
The International Restaurant
2240 N. Twelfth St., 701/258-6442

Best Homestyle Food
Cary's Kitchen
1307 Interchange Ave., 701/258-3470
Doublewood Inn
1400 Interchange Ave., 701/258-7000

Best Italian Food
Captain Meriwether's Landing
1700 River Rd., 701/224-0455

Best Mexican Food
Fiesta Villa
411 E. Main Ave., 701/222-8075
Los Amigos Mexican Restaurant
1010 Boundary Rd. NW, 701/663-1958
Paradiso Mexican Restaurant
2620 State St., 701/224-1111
Sergio's Mexican Bar and Grill
401 E. Bismarck Expwy., 701/223-3422

Best Pizza
A and B Pizza
1017 E. Interstate Ave., 701/258-6002
311 S. Seventh St., 701/222-3108

Best Place to Take the Kids
Ground Round
  526 S. Third St., 701/223-0000

Best Restaurant in Town
Bistro
  1103 E. Front Ave., 701/224-8800
Captain Meriwether's Landing
  1700 River Rd., 701/224-0455
Caspar's East Forty
  1401 Interchange Ave., 701/258-7222
Peacock Alley Bar and Grill
  422 E. Main Ave., 701/255-7917

Best Salad/Salad Bar
Royal Fork Buffet Restaurant
  1065 E. Interstate Ave., 701/222-0501

Best Steaks
Caspar's East Forty
  1401 Interchange Ave., 701/258-7222

Best Sunday Brunch
Peacock Alley Bar and Grill
  422 E. Main Ave., 701/255-7917
Seasons Cafe
  Radisson Inn, 800 S. Third St., 701/258-7700

Best View While Dining
Captain Meriwether's Landing
  1700 River Rd., 701/224-0455

N

DICKINSON, ND

Best Barbecue/Ribs
Jack's Family Restaurant
  1406 W. Villard St., 701/225-5905

Best Breakfast
Country Kitchen
  528 Twelfth St. E., 701/225-9376
Dakota Rose Restaurant
  Hospitality Inn, 532 Fifteenth St. W., 701/227-1853

Best Chinese Food
China Wok
  1173 Third Ave. W., 701/227-8889

Best Family Restaurant
Jack's Family Restaurant
  1406 W. Villard St., 701/225-5905

Best Homestyle Food
Georgia and the Owl
  Hwy. 85 at Main St., Amidon, 701/879-6289

Best Steaks
German Hungarian Lodge
  20 E. Broadway St., 701/225-3311

FARGO, ND

Best All-You-Can-Eat Buffet
Royal Fork Buffet Restaurant
  4325 Thirteenth Ave. SW, 701/282-9539

Best Breakfast
Fryin' Pan Family Restaurant
  302 Main Ave., 701/293-9952

Best Brewpub
Old Broadway Restaurant
  22 Broadway, 701/237-6161

Best Burgers
Fifties Cafe
  13 Eighth St. S., 701/298-0347

Best Business Lunch
Passages Cafe
  201 Fifth St. N., 701/293-6717

Best Casual Dining
Grandma's Saloon and Grill
  4201 Thirteenth Ave. S., 701/282-5439
Ground Round
  2902 Thirteenth Ave. SW, 701/280-2288
Jim Lauerman's Chili Sandwiches
  64 Broadway, 701/237-4747
Jim Lauerman's No. 2 Saloon
  2410 Great Northern Dr., 701/232-7671

Best Chinese Food
Chinese Dragon
  122 Broadway, 701/271-8682
Pearl Restaurant
  921 Fourth Ave. N., 701/232-1777
Phil Wong's Restaurant
  625 NP Ave., 701/235-6431

Best Desserts
Cynthia's Custom Cakes
  524 Broadway, 701/234-0664

Best Family Restaurant
Embers Restaurant
  3838 Main Ave., 701/282-6330

Best Fine Dining
Fargo Cork
  3301 S. University Dr., 701/237-6790
Grainery Restaurant and Bar
  3902 Thirteenth Ave. S., 701/282-6262
Seasons at Rose Creek
  1500 Rose Creek Pkwy. E., 701/235-5000

Best Greek/Mediterranean Food
Santa Lucia Family Restaurant
  505 40th St. SW, 701/281-8656

Best Italian Food
Luigi's
  613 First Ave. N., 701/241-4126

Best Mexican Food
Mexican Village
  814 Main Ave., 701/293-0120
Paradiso Mexican Restaurant
  801 38th St. SW, 701/282-5747

Best Pizza
Duane's House of Pizza
    1629 S. University Dr., 701/232-8908
Godfather's Pizza of Fargo
    1439 S. University Dr., 701/293-3701
    4340 Thirteenth Ave. SW, 701/277-1666
Sammy's Pizza and Restaurant
    301 Broadway, 701/235-5331

Best Steaks
Fargo Cork
    3301 S. University Dr., 701/237-6790

GRAND FORKS, ND

Best All-You-Can-Eat Buffet
Royal Fork Buffet
    2800 S. Columbia Rd, 701/746-0869

Best Bar
John Barleycorn
    2100 S. Columbia Rd., 701/775-0501
Players Sports Grill and Bar
    2120 S. Washington St., 701/780-9201

Best Burgers
Bronze Boot Steak House
    1804 N. Washington St., 701/746-5433

Best Casual Dining
Blue Moose Bar and Grill
    108 Demers Ave., East Grand Forks, MN,
        218/773-6516
Toppers
    3205 S. Washington St., 701/775-5911

Best Chinese Food
Hunan Chinese Restaurant
    Columbia Sq., 2100 S. Columbia Rd., 701/772-0556

Best Coffee/Coffeehouse
The Coffee Company
    Columbia Sq., 2100 S. Columbia Rd., 701/772-1995

Best Fine Dining
Grand Forks Good Ribs Steakhouse
    4223 Twelfth Ave. N., 701/746-7115

Best Health-Conscious Menu
Peartree Restaurant
    1210 N. 43rd St., 701/772-7131

Best Homestyle Food
Del's Coffee Shop
    1828 S. Washington St., 701/772-3311

Best Inexpensive Meal
Highway Host
    3615 Gateway Dr., 701/775-3141

Best Italian Food
Big Al's Pasta Parlor
    3500 Gateway Dr., 701/772-2222

N

Best Late-Night Food
Red Pepper
  1011 University Ave., 701/775-9671

Best Lunch
Toppers
  3205 S. Washington St., 701/775-5911

Best Pizza
Italian Moon
  810 S. Washington St., 701/772-7277

Best Place to Eat Alone
Ramada Inn
  1205 N. 43rd St., 701/775-3951

Best Place to Take the Kids
Happy Joe's Pizza and Ice Cream
  2909 S. Washington St., 701/772-6655

Best Steaks
Grand Forks Good Ribs Steakhouse
  4223 Twelfth Ave. N., 701/746-7115

Best Tea Room
The Coffee Company
  Columbia Sq., 2100 S. Columbia Rd., 701/772-1995

N

MANDAN, ND

Best All-You-Can-Eat Buffet
Midtowner
  111 Collins Ave., 701/663-4459

Best Homestyle Food
Dakota Farms Family Restaurant
  1120 E. Main St., 701/663-7322

Best Ice Cream/Yogurt
Lindy Sue's Third Street Emporium
  316 W. Main St., 701/663-5311

Best Restaurant in Town
Seven Seas
  2611 Old Red Trail, 701/663-7401

Best Steaks
Seven Seas
  2611 Old Red Trail, 701/663-7401

MINOT, ND

Best American Food
Econostop Cafe
  1712 Twentieth Ave. SE, 701/852-5044
Field and Stream Restaurant
  1711 Seventh St. NW, 701/852-3663
Ground Round
  2110 Burdick Expwy. E., 701/838-3500

Best Breakfast
Glady's Place
  1900 Fourth Ave. NW, 701/852-8221
Ryans Family Dining
  1418 S. Broadway, 701/852-3674

Schatz Crossroads Cafe
1305 Twentieth Ave. SE, 701/838-5588

Best Casual Dining
Embassy Food and Drink
112 Second Ave. SW, 701/852-4343
Green Mill Restaurant
2315 N. Broadway, 701/839-2110
Speedway Restaurant
Rural Route 2, 701/838-0649

Best Chinese Food
Fortune Cookie
1631 S. Broadway, 701/852-1471

Best Mexican Food
Sergio's Mexican Restaurant
1030 24th Ave. SW, 701/852-0181

Best Pizza
Green Mill Restaurant
2315 N. Broadway, 701/839-2110

Best Restaurant in Town
Embassy Food and Drink
112 Second Ave. SW, 701/852-4343
Homesteaders Restaurant
Hwy. 2W at 52S Bypass, 701/838-2274
Jake's Spice and Spirit
1910 S. Broadway, 701/852-8355
Roll-N-Pin
2145 N. Broadway, 701/839-8774
Sammy's Pizza Palace
400 N. Broadway, 701/852-4486

Best Seafood
Field and Stream Restaurant
1711 Seventh St. NW, 701/852-3663

Best Steaks
Field and Stream Restaurant
1711 Seventh St. NW, 701/852-3663
Speedway Restaurant
Rural Route 2, 701/838-0649

Best Sunday Brunch
The Green Mill
Ramada Inn, 2315 N. Broadway, 701/839-2110

WILLISTON, ND

Best All-You-Can-Eat Buffet
El Rancho Motor Hotel
1623 Second Ave. W., 701/572-6321

Best Burgers
Burger Queen and Pizza
2516 Second Ave. W., 701/572-1840

Best Chinese Food
Hunan Restaurant
1804 Second Ave. W., 701/572-3388
Ming Garden Restaurant
302 Fourteenth St. W., 701/774-1940

Best Coffee/Coffeehouse
Gramma Sharon's Cafe
  4201 Second Ave. W., 701/572-1412

Best Diner
Main Street Diner
  216 Main St., 701/774-0383

Best Family Restaurant
Dakota Farms Family Restaurant
  1906 Second Ave. W., 701/572-4480
The Brickyard
  6 W. 25th St., 701/572-3848

Best Pizza
Burger Queen and Pizza
  2516 Second Ave. W., 701/572-1840

Best Sandwiches
Trapper's Kettle
  3201 Second Ave. W., 701/774-2831

Best Steaks
Fourth Street Eatery
  408 First Ave. E., 701/774-1830
Jerry's Fireside Dining
  1002 Second Ave. W., 701/572-0677

N

Ohio

O

Best All-You-Can-Eat Buffet
Cathedral Buffet
2690 State Rd., Cuyahoga Falls, 330/922-0467

Best Barbecue/Ribs
Damon's, The Place for Ribs
150 Montrose West Ave., Copley, 330/665-5552

Best Breakfast
Country Kitchen
1245 E. Waterloo Rd., 330/724-9357
610 E. Cuyahoga Falls Ave., 330/928-1026
Primo's Deli
1707 Wooster Rd., 330/745-9056

Best Burgers
Coach's Cafe
1537 S. Main St., 330/773-1724

Best Business Lunch
Diamond Grill
77 W. Market St., 330/253-0041

Best Casual Dining
Nick Anthe's
1008 N. Main St., 330/929-6425
North Side Grill
111 N. Main St., 330/434-7625

Best Chinese Food
House of Hunan
376 E. Waterloo Rd., 330/773-1888
2717 W. Market St., 330/864-8215

Best Fine Dining
Ken Stewart's Grill
  1970 W. Market St., 330/867-2555
Tangier Restaurant and Cabaret
  532 W. Market St., 330/376-7171
Triple Crown Restaurant and Lounge
  335 S. Main St., Munroe Falls,
  330/633-5325

Best Greek/Mediterranean Food
Gus' Chalet
  938 E. Tallmadge Ave., 330/633-2322
Tangier Restaurant and Cabaret
  532 W. Market St., 330/376-7171

Best Ice Cream/Yogurt
Friendly's
  1040 Graham Rd., Cuyahoga Falls,
  330/928-4391
Strickland's Frozen Custard II
  2420 Wedgewood Dr., 330/733-0133

Best Inexpensive Meal
Bialy's at the Lake
  493 Portage Lakes Dr., 330/644-7177
Parasson's Italian Restaurant
  501 N. Main St., 330/376-2117
  959 E. Waterloo Rd., 330/724-9375

Best Italian Food
Luigi's Restaurant
  105 N. Main St., 330/253-2999

Best Mexican Food
Don Pablo's Mexican Kitchen
  145 Montrose West Ave., Copley,
  330/666-0239

Best Other Ethnic Food
Playwright's (Irish)
  1603 Home Ave., 330/630-1677

Best Outdoor Dining
Pelican Cove
  3720 S. Main St., 330/645-0635

Best Pizza
Emidio and Sons Italian Restaurant
  636 N. Main St., 330/253-4777
Mama Rosa's
  184 E. Tallmadge Ave., 330/253-8400
  1115 Brown St., 330/773-8235

Best Place to Take the Kids
East Side Mario's
  581 Howe Ave., Cuyahoga Falls,
  330/928-7288

Best Sandwiches
Louie's Bar and Grille
  739 E. Glenwood Ave., 330/535-5030

Best Steaks
Diamond Grille
  77 W. Market St., 216/253-0041

Young's Restaurant
2744 Manchester Rd., 330/745-6116

Best View While Dining
Old Harbour Inn
562 Portage Lakes Dr., 330/644-1664

ALLIANCE, OH

Best Bar
Roadhouse Charlie
2239 W. State St., 330/823-0578

Best Chinese Food
China House
251 Hester Ave., 330/823-7669

Best Health-Conscious Menu
Taster's Choice Cafe
1908 S. Union Ave., 330/821-6666

Best Homestyle Food
Shaffer's Diner
40 N. Park Ave., 330/823-0006

Best Italian Food
Polinori's Palm Garden Inn
1441 S. Liberty Ave., 330/821-2680

Best Mexican Food
Don Pancho's Fiesta Villa
9 S. Union Ave., 330/823-4390

Best Pizza
Pisanello's Pizza
344 W. State St., 330/823-7271

ASHLAND, OH

Best Breakfast
Lyn-Way Restaurant
1320 Cleveland Ave., 419/281-8911

Best Casual Dining
BW-3 Grill and Pub
630 Claremont Ave., 419/281-9464

Best Chinese Food
Great Dragon
1983 Baney Rd. S., 419/289-1688

Best Pizza
East of Chicago Pizza
614 Claremont Ave., 419/289-0605

Best Sandwiches
Kelly's Deli and Restaurant
622 Claremont Ave., 419/281-1313

Best Seafood
The Cabin
2106 State Rte. 603, 419/368-4457

ASHTABULA, OH

Best Family Restaurant
Hil-Mak Seafoods
449 Lake Ave., 216/964-3222

O

Best Italian Food
Caruso's Pizza and Spaghetti
  2313 West Ave., 216/964-2646

Best Restaurant in Town
Hulbert's Restaurant
  1033 Bridge St., 216/964-2594

Best Steaks
Lou's Stagecoach
  5205 Lake Rd. W., 216/964-7930

ATHENS, OH

Best Atmosphere
Seven Sauces
  66 N. Court St., 740/592-5555

Best Burgers
The Pub
  39 N. Court St., 740/592-9967

Best Chinese Food
Lam's Garden
  934 E. State St., 740/594-4424
  120 W. Union St., 740/592-1955

Best Delicatessen
Bagel Street Deli
  27 S. Court St., 740/593-3838
Zachary's
  30 N. Court St., 740/592-2000

Best Greek/Mediterranean Food
Souvlaki Sandwich Shop
  9 W. State St., 740/592-4131

Best Mexican Food
Casa Nueva
  4 W. State St., 740/592-2016

Best Pizza
Late Night Pizza
  122 W. Union St., 740/592-2008

Best Vegetarian Food
Casa Nueva
  4 W. State St., 740/592-2016
Purple Chopstix
  371 1/2 Richland Ave., 740/592-4798
Zachary's
  30 N. Court St., 740/592-2000

BARBERTON, OH

Best Breakfast
Nancy's Homestyle Cooking
  562 W. Tuscarawas Ave., 330/753-7750
Wink's Drive-In
  75 Fifth St. SE, 330/745-4141

Best Homestyle Food
Fa-Ray's Family Restaurant
  1115 Wooster Rd. N., 330/745-6091

Best Pizza
Parasson's Italian Restaurant
 234 Wooster Rd. N., 330/753-2264

Best Regional Food
Belgrade Gardens
 401 E. State St., 330/745-0113
Hopocan Gardens
 4396 Hopocan Ave., 330/825-9923
Whitehouse Chicken Dinners
 180 Wooster Rd. N., 330/745-0449

BEAVERCREEK, OH

Best American Food
Field's Restaurant
 3347 E. Patterson Rd., 937/426-6625

Best Breakfast
Debra Lee's
 3321 Dayton Xenia Rd., 937/429-3033

Best Burgers
Bellefair Restaurant
 1490 N. Fairfield Rd., 937/426-0788

Best Mexican Food
Don Pablo's
 2745 Fairfield Commons, 937/320-1777

Best Steaks
Grub Steak II
 2220 Rte. 35, 937/426-4117
Max and Erma's
 2739 Fairfield Commons, 937/320-2255

BOWLING GREEN, OH

Best All-You-Can-Eat Buffet
Kaufman's
 1628 E. Wooster St., 419/354-2535

Best Business Lunch
Junction Bar and Grill
 110 N. Main St., 419/352-9222

Best Coffee/Coffeehouse
Cosmo's Cafe
 126 E. Wooster St., 419/354-5282
Grounds For Thought
 174 S. Main St., 419/354-3266

Best Homestyle
McIntyre's Family Restaurant
 110 W. Poe Rd., 419/353-1890
Ranch Steak and Seafood
 1544 E. Wooster St., 419/352-0461

Best Lunch
Kaufman's
 163 S. Main St., 419/352-2595

Best Pizza
Di Benedetto's Pasta and Subs
 1432 E. Wooster St., 419/352-4663

O

Myles Pizza Pub and Sub Shop
516 E. Wooster St., 419/352-1504
Campus Pollyeyes
440 E. Court St., 419/352-9638

Best Restaurant in Town
Kaufman's
163 S. Main St., 419/352-2595

Best Sandwiches
Easy Street Cafe
104 S. Main St., 419/353-0988
Sam B's Restaurant
146 N. Main St., 419/353-2277

Best Steaks
Trotters Tavern
119 N. Main St., 419/352-5895

CANTON, OH

Best Atmosphere
356 Fighter Group Restaurant
4919 Mount Pleasant St. NW, 330-494-3500
Bender's Tavern
137 Court Ave. SW, 330/453-8424
Stables Hall of Fame Grille
2317 Thirteenth St. NW, 330/452-1230

Best Barbecue/Ribs
Damon's International
4220 Belden Village St. NW, 330/492-2413
Flaming Pit
3504 Tuscarawas St. W., 330/454-5248
Mulligan's Pub
4118 Belden Village St. NW, 330/493-8239

Best Breakfast
Ashley's Restaurant
320 Market Ave. S., 330/454-5000

Best Burgers
Rumours Cafe
725 30th St. NE, 330/452-0442

Best Chinese Food
Panda Garden Restaurant
3619 Cleveland Ave. NW, 330/492-2108
Ricky Ly's Chinese Gourmet
4725 Dressler Rd. NW, 330/492-5909

Best Coffee/Coffeehouse
Susan's Coffee and Tea
123 S. Main St., North Canton, 330/305-9284

Best Family Restaurant
Grinders and Such
3114 Whipple Ave. NW, 330/477-5411
John's Bar and Grille
2749 Cleveland Ave. NW, 330/454-1259

Best Fine Dining
Lolli's Restaurant
4801 Dressler Rd. NW, 330/492-6846

Best Greek/Mediterranean Food
Desert Inn
300 Twelfth St. NW, 330/456-1766

Best Ice Cream/Yogurt
Taggart's Ice Cream Parlor
1401 Fulton Rd. NW, 330/452-6844

Best Mexican Food
El Campesino
4048 Lincoln St. E., 330/477-8731

Best Pizza
Kraus Pizza Company
5440 Fulton Dr. NW, 330/494-7722
Pizza Oven
multiple locations
Pizza Plus
1909 Whipple Ave. NW, 330/478-5700

Best Romantic Dining
Mozart Restaurant
3520 Cleveland Ave. NW, 330/493-8664

Best Steaks
Baker's Cafe
1927 Stark Ave. SW, 330/454-0528

CHILLICOTHE, OH

Best Barbecue/Ribs
Damon's International
10 N. Plaza Blvd., 740/775-8383

Best Breakfast
J.R. Valentine's Restaurant
87 N. Bridge St., 740/774-2471

Best Chinese Food
Diamond Head Restaurant
33 N. Paint St., 740/773-8585

Best Homestyle Food
Carl's Town House
95 S. Paint St., 740/773-1660
Renick's Family Restaurant
47 S. Paint St., 740/773-5908

Best Pizza
Poppa Dino's Pizzeria
45 E. Water St., 740/773-1114

Best Steaks
Richard's House of Beef and Seafood
1641 N. Bridge St., 740/775-7099

Best Thai Food
Bangkok Palace
870 N. Bridge St., 740/773-8424

O

CINCINNATI, OH

[See also: Covington, KY.]

Best Barbecue/Ribs
Burbank's Real Bar-B-Q
   11167 Dowlin Dr., Sharonville,
      513/771-1440
The Montgomery Inn
   9440 Montgomery Rd., 513/791-3482
   The Boathouse, 925 Eastern Ave.,
      513/721-7427

Best Beer Selection
Allyn's Cafe
   3538 Columbia Pkwy., 513/871-5779

Best Breakfast
Big Sky Bread Company
   3012 Madison Rd., 513/631-8383
   265 Hosea Ave., 513/751-5050
First Watch
   8118 Montgomery Rd., 513/891-0088
   2692 Madison Rd., 513/531-7430
   700 Walnut St., Ste. 104, 513/721-4744
Inn the Wood
   277 Calhoun St., 513/221-3044
Lee's Family Diner
   1500 Queen City Ave., 513/921-7877

Best Burgers
Ollie's Trolley
   1607 Central Ave., 513/381-6100
Rookwood Pottery
   1077 Celestial St., 513/721-5456

Best Casual Dining
Remington's Roadhouse
   12185 Springfield Pike, 513/671-1110

Best Chinese Food
Blue Gibbon Chinese Restaurant
   1231 Tennessee Ave., 513/641-4100
Cheng 1 Cuisine
   203 W. McMillan St., 513/723-1999
China Gourmet
   3340 Erie Ave., 513/871-6612
Wong's East Restaurant
   7205 Beechmont Ave., 513/232-8899

Best Coffee/Coffeehouse
Awakenings Coffee and Tea Company
   2734 Erie Ave., 513/321-2525
   110 W. Fifth St., 513/621-2525
   121 E. Court St., 513/241-0033

Best Desserts
Petersen's Restaurant
   1111 Saint Gregory St., 513/651-4777
Take the Cake
   1437 Main St., 513/241-2772

Best Diner
Diner at 11700
  11700 Princeton Pike, 513/671-8225
Diner On Sycamore
  1203 Sycamore St., 513/721-1212

Best Eclectic Menu
Arboreta
  1133 Sycamore St., 513/721-1133
Boca
  4034 Hamilton Ave., 513/542-2022
Ciao Baby Cucina
  700 Walnut St., 513/929-0700
Petersen's Restaurant
  1111 Saint Gregory St., 513/651-4777
Plaza 600
  600 Walnut St., 513/721-8600

Best Family Restaurant
Proud Rooster Restaurant
  5709 Glenway Ave., 513/451-1142
Stone's Restaurant
  3605 Harrison Ave., 513/661-6849

Best Fine Dining
Orchids
  The Omni, 35 W. Fifth St., 513/421-9100
The Palace
  601 Vine St., 513/381-6006
The Phoenix Restaurant
  812 Race St., 513/721-8901

Best French Food
Maisonette
  114 E. Sixth St., 513/721-2260
Pigall's Cafe
  127 W. Fourth St., 513/651-2233

Best Homestyle
Lee's Family Diner
  1500 Queen City Ave., 513/921-7877

Best Indian Food
Ambar India
  350 Ludlow Ave., 513/281-7000

Best Inexpensive Meal
Big Sky Bread Company
  3012 Madison Rd., 513/631-8383
  265 Hosea Ave., 513/751-5050
  Kenwood Towne Center, 7875 Montgomery Rd.,
    513/984-6464
City View Tavern
  403 Oregon St., 513/241-8439
Courtyard Cafe
  1211 Main St., 513/723-1119
Stone Mill Bread Company
  8 West Fourth St., 513/651-0030

Best Japanese Food
Osaka
  11481 Chester Rd., 513/771-4488

O

Best Kosher Food
Izzy's
  800 Elm St., 513/721-4241

Best Lunch
Rookwood Pottery
  1077 Celestial St., 513/721-5456

Best Mexican Food
Allyn's Cafe
  3538 Columbia Pkwy., 513/871-5779

Best Outdoor Dining
Longworth's
  1108 St. Gregory St., 513/579-0900

Best Pizza
La Rosa's
  multiple locations
Pizzeria Uno
  342 Ludlow Ave., 513/281-8667
  7500 Beechmont Ave., 513/231-8667
  627 Walnut St., 513/621-8667
Pomodori's
  121 W. McMillan St., 513/861-0080

Best Salad/Salad Bar
Celestial
  1071 Celestial St., 513/241-4455

Best Sandwiches
Rookwood Pottery
  1077 Celestial St., 513/721-5456

Best Seafood
J's Fresh Seafood
  2444 Madison Rd., 513/871-2888

Best Spanish Food
Mallorca
  124 E. Sixth St., 513/723-9506

Best Sports Bar
Sorrento's Pizza and Sports Bar
  5141 Montgomery Rd., Norwood,
    513/531-5070
Blue Moon Saloon
  2686 Madison Rd., 513/871-2232

Best Steaks
Morton's of Chicago
  28 W. Fourth St., Tower Pl., 513/241-4104
The Precinct
  311 Delta Ave., 513/321-5454

Best Thai Food
Bangkok Thai Cuisine
  1055 Main St., Milford, 513/248-4853

Best Vegetarian Food
Carol's Corner Cafe
  825 Main St., 513/651-2667
Mullane's Parkside Cafe
  723 Race St., 513/381-1331

Ulysses
209 W. McMillan St., 513/241-3663

Best View While Dining
Primavista
810 Matson Pl., 513/251-6467
The Celestial
1071 Celestial St., 513/241-4455

CLEVELAND, OH

Best American Food
Wards' Inn
34105 Chagrin Blvd., Moreland Hills,
216/595-1954

Best Barbecue/Ribs
Winking Lizard Tavern
25380 Miles Rd., Bedford, 216/831-3488

Best Beer Selection
Harbor Inn
1219 Main St., 216/241-3232

Best Breakfast
Yours Truly
25300 Chagrin Blvd., Beachwood, 216/464-4848
13228 Shaker Sq., 216/751-8646

Best Brewpub
Rock Bottom Restaurant and Brewery
2000 Sycamore St., 216/623-1555

Best Burgers
Heck's Cafe
2927 Bridge Ave., 216/861-5464

Best Chinese Food
Bo Loong
3922 Saint Clair Ave. NE, 216/391-3113

Best Continental Food
Classics
Omni Hotel, 2065 E. 96th St., 216/791-1300

Best Diner
Ruthie and Moe's Diner
4002 Prospect Ave., 216/431-8063

Best French Food
Parker's
2801 Bridge Ave., 216/771-7130

Best German Food
Hofbrau Haus
1400 E. 55th St., 216/881-7773

Best Greek/Mediterranean Food
Sans Souci
Renaissance Cleveland Hotel, 24 Public Sq.,
216/696-5600
The Mad Greek Restaurant
2460 Fairmount Blvd., 216/421-3333

Best Health-Conscious Menu
Johnny Mango
3120 Bridge Ave., 216/575-1919

O

Best Indian Food
Saffron Patch
  20600 Chagrin Blvd., Beachwood, 216/295-0400

Best Italian Food
Baricelli Inn
  2203 Cornell Rd., 216/791-6500
Fratello's
  32085 Electric Blvd., Avon Lake, 216/871-3054
Guarino's Restaurant
  12309 Mayfield Rd., 216/231-3100
Johnny's Bar on Fulton
  3164 Fulton Rd., 216/281-0055
Johnny's Downtown
  1406 W. Sixth St., 216/623-0055
Piccolo Mondo
  1352 W. Sixth St., 216/241-1300

Best Japanese Food
Otani
  1625 Golden Gate Shopping Center, 6420 Mayfield
    Rd., 216/442-7098
Shuhei
  23360 Chagrin Blvd., Beachwood, 216/464-1720

Best Late-Night Food
Clifton Lunch
  11637 Clifton Blvd., 216/521-5003

Best Mexican Food
Lopez y Gonzalez
  2066 Lee Rd., 216/371-7611
Luchita's Restaurant
  3456 W. 117th St., 216/252-1169

Best Other Ethnic Food
Empress Taytu Ethiopian Restaurant (Ethiopian)
  6125 Saint Clair Ave., 216/391-9400
Phnom Penh Restaurant (Cambodian)
  13124 Lorain Ave., 216/251-0210

Best Outdoor Dining
Gamekeeper's Taverne
  87 West St., Chagrin Falls, 216/247-7744

Best Pizza
Mama Santa
  12305 Mayfield Rd., 216/231-9567
Player's Restaurant
  14527 Madison Ave., Lakewood, 216/226-5200

Best Place to Take the Kids
The Great Lakes Brewing Company
  2516 Market Ave., Beachwood, 216/771-4404

Best Regional Food
Skyline Chili
  5706 Mayfield Rd., 216/646-1011
  4752 Ridge Rd., 216/351-7632

Best Sandwiches
Grum's Sub Shoppe
  1776 Coventry Rd., Cleveland Heights,
    216/321-4781

Max's Deli and Restaurant
19337 Detroit Rd., Rocky River, 216/356-2226

Best Seafood
Pier W
12700 Lake Ave., Lakewood, 216/228-2250

Best Spanish Food
KeKA
2523 Market Ave., 216/241-5352

Best Sports Bar
Harpo's Sports Cafe
13930 Brookpark Rd., 216/267-7777
19654 W. 130th St., Strongville, 216/846-7777

Best Steaks
Hyde Park Grille
1825 Coventry Rd., Cleveland Heights,
216/321-6444
Morton's of Chicago
230 W. Huron Rd., 216/621-6200

Best Thai Food
Lemon Grass
2179 Lee Rd., 216/321-0210
Paul's Siam Cuisine
1918 Lee Rd., 216/371-9575

Best Vegetarian Food
Hunan by the Falls
508 E. Washington St., Chagrin Falls,
216/247-0808
Tommy's
1824 Coventry Rd., Cleveland Heights,
216/321-7757

Best Vietnamese Food
Phnom Penh Restaurant
13124 Lorain Ave., 216/251-0210

Best Wine Selection
Wards' Inn
34105 Chagrin Blvd., Moreland Hills,
216/595-1954

COLUMBUS, OH

Best Barbecue/Ribs
JP's Barbeque Ribs
2000 Norton Rd., 614/878-7422
1072 E. Main St., 614/258-3756

Best Beer Selection
Bernie's Bagels and Distillery
1896 N. High St., 614/291-4127

Best Bistro
Lindey's
169 E. Beck Ave., 614/228-4343
Pierre's Bistro
1788 W. Fifth Ave., 614/481-9463

Best Burgers
Max and Erma's
739 S. Third St., 614/444-0917

Best Cajun/Creole Food
Gloria Cajun Kitchen
  2170 W. Henderson Rd., 614/538-1822

Best Casual Dining
Cameron's
  2185 W. Dublin-Granville Rd., Worthington,
    614/885-3663

Best Chinese Food
China Dynasty
  1930 E. Dublin-Granville Rd., 614/523-2009
Hunan Lion
  2000 Bethel Rd., 614/459-3933
Imperial Garden
  2950 Hayden Run Plaza, 614/799-8655
Windchimes Chinese Restaurant
  5742 Frantz Rd., Dublin, 614/792-0990

Best Coffee/Coffeehouse
Cup O' Joe
  627 S. Third St., 614/221-1563
Stauf's Coffee Roasters
  1277 Grandview Ave., 614/486-4861

Best Delicatessen
Au Bon Pain
  20 S. Third St., 614/224-1922
Bermuda Onion
  50 W. Broad St., 614/228-8646
Brown Bag Deli
  898 Mohawk St., 614/443-4214
Carfagna's
  7045 E. Dublin-Granville Rd., 614/846-6340
Katzinger's Delicatessen
  475 S. Third St., 614/228-3354
Michael's Finest Market
  771 Bethel Rd., 614/457-5000
Nazareth Deli
  5663 Emporium Sq., 614/899-1177
Vincenzo's Convenient Elegance
  6393 Sawmill Rd., Dublin, 614/792-1010

Best Desserts
French Loaf
  1456 W. Fifth Ave., 614/488-6843

Best Diner
Nancy's Restaurant
  3133 N. High St., 614/265-9012

Best Eclectic Menu
Lindey's
  169 E. Beck St., 614/228-4343

Best Family Restaurant
Ohio Deli and Restaurant
  3444 S. High St., 614/497-0577

Best Fine Dining
Bexley's Monk
  2232 E. Main St., Bexley, 614/239-6665

Bistro Roti
  1693 W. Lane Ave., 614/481-7684
Handke's Cuisine
  520 S. Front St., 614/621-2500
Merlot
  5252 Norwich St., Hilliard, 614/529-1995

Best French Food
L'Antibes
  772 N. High St., 614/291-1666
The Refectory
  1092 Bethel Rd., 614/451-9774

Best German Food
Schmidt's Sausage Haus Restaurant
  1885 Henderson Rd., 614/459-7122
  6800 Schrock Hill Ct., 614/523-0900

Best Greek/Mediterranean Food
Firdous Deli and Cafe
  1538 N. High St., 614/299-1844

Best Ice Cream/Yogurt
Graeter's Ice Cream
  2282 E. Main St., 614/236-2663
  1534 W. Lane Ave., 614/488-3222

Best Indian Food
Flavors of India
  29 Spruce St., 614/621-3223
Taj Mahal
  2247 N. High St., 614/294-0208

Best Italian Food
Bravo Cucina Italiana
  3000 Hayden Rd., 614/791-1022
Butch's Italian Cafe
  4720 E. Main St., 614/864-7300
Da Vinci's Ristorante
  4740 Reed Rd., 614/451-5147
La Plaia
  5766 Columbus Sq., 614/890-2070
Moretti's Italian Cafe
  1447 Grandview Ave., 614/488-2104
Pasta Amore
  18 Dillmont Dr., 614/848-3636
Pasta Petite
  6096 Boardwalk St., 614/436-4066
Pastabilities
  Karl Plaza, 1644 E. Dublin-Granville Rd.,
    614/891-8891
Rigsby's Cuisine Volatile
  698 N. High St., 614/461-7888
Scali Ristorante and Deli
  1901 State Rte. 256, Reynoldsburg, 614/759-7764
Tony's Italian Ristorante
  16 W. Beck St., 614/224-8669
Trattoria Roma
  1270 Morse Rd., 614/888-6686

O

Best Japanese Food
Restaurant Japan
  1173 Old Henderson Rd., 614/451-5411
Sapporo Wind
  6188 Cleveland Ave., 614/895-7575

Best Mexican Food
El Vaquero Mexican Restaurant
  2195 Riverside Dr., 614/486-4547
Estrada Mexican Restaurant
  240 King Ave., 614/294-0808
La Bamba Mexican Restaurant
  1980 N. High St., 614/294-5004

Best Other Ethnic Food
Blue Nile Restaurant (Ethiopian)
  3686 E. Main St., 614/238-0591
Gold Gate (Eastern European)
  1395 S. Hamilton Rd., 614/237-4151
Kahiki (Polynesian)
  3583 E. Broad St., 614/237-5425

Best Pizza
Figlio
  1369 Grandview Ave., 614/481-0745
Rotolo's Pizza
  1749 W. Fifth Ave., 614/488-7934

Best Restaurant in Town
55 At Crosswoods
  55 Hutchinson Ave., 614/846-5555

Best Sandwiches
Ohio Deli and Restaurant
  3444 S. High St., 614/497-0577

Best Seafood
55 on The Boulevard
  55 E. Nationwide Blvd., 614/228-5555
Clarmont
  684 S. High St., 614/443-1125

Best Spanish Food
Spain Restaurant
  3777 Sullivant Ave., 614/272-6363

Best Steaks
Hyde Park Grille
  1615 Old Henderson Rd., 614/442-3310
Morton's of Chicago
  2 Nationwide Plz., 614/464-4442
The Clarmont
  684 S. High St., 614/443-1125
The Top
  2891 E. Main St., 614/231-8238

Best Thai Food
Lai Lai Restaurant
  5125 E. Main St., 614/759-6868
Thai Orchid
  7654 Sawmill Rd., Dublin, 614/792-1112

Best Vietnamese Food
Saigon Palace
   114 N. Front St., 614/464-3325
Vietnam Restaurant
   2548 Bethel Rd., 614/459-1909

DAYTON, OH

Best Barbecue/Ribs
Damon's, The Place for Ribs
   262 E. Stroop Rd., 937/294-7427

Best Chinese Food
Keeng Wha Restaurant and Lounge
   2221 Wagoner Ford Rd., 937/278-8889
Mark Pi's Ancient Wok
   1875 Needmore Rd., 937/898-1466
   5200 Salem Ave., 937/854-0705

Best Homestyle Food
Bill Knapp's
   6460 Far Hills Ave., 937/433-4455
   4465 Indian Ripple Rd., 937/429-1020

Best Italian Food
Dominic's Restaurant
   1066 S. Main St., 937/222-4801
Spaghetti Warehouse
   36 W. Fifth St., 937/461-3913

Best Mexican Food
Elsa's South
   6318 Far Hills Ave., 937/439-3897
Pepito's
   3618 Wilmington Pike, 937/293-3777
   2412 Catalpa Dr., 937/277-1476
   4904 Airway Rd., 937/252-5131

Best Pizza
Donato's Pizza
   3375 Dayton Xenia Rd., 937/427-5880

Best Romantic Dining
Peerless Mill Inn
   319 S. Second St., Miamisburg, 937/866-5968

Best Sandwiches
Max and Erma's
   8901 Kingsridge Dr., 937/433-6200
Upper Krust
   1919 N. Main St., 937/277-7200
   6149 Far Hills Ave., 937/435-9464

Best Seafood
Jay's Restaurant
   225 E. Sixth St., 937/222-2892

Best Steaks
Oakwood Club
   2414 Far Hills Ave., 937/293-6973
Paragon Club
   797 Miamisburg Centerville Rd., 937/433-1234
Pine Club
   1926 Brown St., 937/228-7463

O

Best View While Dining
Four River Place
4 River Pl., 937/224-0535
Lincoln Park Grille
580 Lincoln Park Blvd., 937/293-6293

Best Wine Selection
Jay's Restaurant
225 E. Sixth St., 937/222-2892

DELAWARE, OH

Best American Food
Bun's Restaurant
6 W. Winter St., 740/363-3731

Best Barbecue/Ribs
Damon's, The Place For Ribs
1159 Columbus Pk., 740/369-7427

Best Homestyle Food
Heartland Cafe and Grille
19 E. Winter St., 740/363-0860

Best Southwestern Food
Nacho Mama's
5277 Columbus Pike, Lewis Center, 740/548-5655

ELYRIA, OH

Best Bar
Moss' Prime Rib Restaurant
209 Broad St., 440/322-8611

Best Breakfast
Lunchbreak Cafe
353 Broad St., 440/322-3221

Best Chinese Food
Hunan King
1537 W. River Rd. N., 440/324-4095

Best Diner
Hazel's Family Restaurant
615 Cleveland St., 440/365-3513
Mid Way Oh Boy Restaurant
6620 Lake Ave., 440/324-3711

Best Other Ethnic Food
Mongo's (Tibetan)
36040 Sugar Ridge Rd., North Ridgeville,
440/327-2155

Best Pizza
East of Chicago Pizza Company
515E N. Abbe Rd., 440/365-6005

Best Salad/Salad Bar
Grassies Wayside Inn
447 Oberlin Rd., 440/322-0690

Best Steaks
Moss' Prime Rib Restaurant
209 Broad St., 440/322-8611
Mountain Jack's Restaurant
1845 Lorain Blvd., 440/324-7700

FAIRBORN, OH

Best American Food
Roush's Restaurant
305 W. Main St., 937/878-3611

Best Chinese Food
Flying Tiger Chinese Restaurant
60 S. Broad St., 937/878-2583
Kim's Oriental Restaurant
2632 Colonel Glenn Hwy., 937/427-2012
Seasons House
1210 Kauffman Ave., 937/878-7287

Best Eclectic Menu
Winds Cafe
215 Xenia Ave., Yellow Springs, 937/767-1144

Best Italian Food
Giovanni's Pizza
215 W. Main St., 937/878-1611

Best Sandwiches
Cadillac Jack's
1156 Kauffman Ave., 937/754-1061

Best Sports Bar
Cold Beer and Cheeseburgers
2638 Colonel Glenn Hwy., 937/427-2337
Tickets Pub and Eatery
7 W. Main St., 937/878-9022

O

FAIRFIELD, OH

Best Cajun/Creole Food
Jake's
622 Riegart Sq., 513/868-8492

Best Chinese Food
East West Restaurant
7245 Dixie Hwy., 513/870-0011

Best Desserts
Jake's
622 Riegart Sq., 513/868-8492

Best Family Restaurant
Boston Market
725 Nilles Rd., 513/829-1282

Best Fine Dining
Jake's
622 Riegart Sq., 513/868-8492

Best Homestyle Food
Boston Market
725 Nilles Rd., 513/829-1282

Best Pizza
Fairfield Pizzeria
680 Nilles Rd., 513/829-2200

Best Salad/Salad Bar
Jake's
622 Riegart Sq., 513/868-8492

Best Sandwiches
Boston Market
725 Nilles Rd., 513/829-1282

FINDLAY, OH

Best Bar
Rocking U Restaurant
318 W. Main Cross St., 419/423-4471

Best Burgers
Wilson's Sandwich Shop
600 S. Main St., 419/422-5051

Best Greek/Mediterranean Food
Rena's Restaurant
321 S. Main St., 419/422-0808

Best Homestyle Food
Miller's Luncheonette
203 N. Main St., 419/422-3081

Best Japanese Food
Japan West
406 S. Main St., 419/424-1007

Best Mexican Food
Oler's Bar and Grill
708 Lima Ave., 419/423-2846

GALLIPOLIS, OH

Best All-You-Can-Eat Buffet
Dale's Smorgasbord
630 Silver Bridge Plaza, 740/446-0399

Best Family Restaurant
Lollipop Candy Store
44 State St., 740/446-1199
McClure's Family Restaurant
820 Jackson Pike, 740/446-3837
Red Rooster Restaurant
218 Jackson Pike, 740/446-6635
Shake Shoppe
901 Second Ave., 740/446-2682
383 Jackson Pike, 740/446-1611

Best Sandwiches
Mogie's
39 Court St., 740/446-6647

Best Steaks
Holiday Inn
577 State Rte. 7N, 740/446-0090

HAMILTON, OH

Best Bar
Scooter's Pub
1483 Millville Ave., 513/887-9779

Best Breakfast
Frisch's Big Boy
2949 Dixie Hwy., 513/863-6159
1225 W. Main St., 513/863-6075

Best Burgers
Frisch's Big Boy
2949 Dixie Hwy., 513/863-6159
1225 W. Main St., 513/863-6075

Best Desserts
Hyde's Restaurant
130 S. Erie Hwy., 513/892-1287

Best Homestyle Food
Hyde's Restaurant
130 S. Erie Hwy., 513/892-1287
Mamaw's Home Cooking
1479 Millville Ave., 513/896-4600

Best Ice Cream/Yogurt
United Dairy Farmers
11 N. Brookwood Ave., 513/863-1272

Best Pizza
Richard's Pizza
417 Main St., 513/894-3296
2343 Dixie Hwy., 513/894-3217

Best Romantic Dining
Academy Restaurant
343 N. Third St., 513/868-7171

Best Salad/Salad Bar
Frisch's Big Boy
2949 Dixie Hwy., 513/863-6159
1225 Main St., 513/863-6075

Best Sandwiches
Deli Sandwich Shoppe
23 N. Third St., 513/844-6500
Frisch's Big Boy
2949 Dixie Hwy., 513/863-6159
1225 Main St., 513/863-6075

Best Seafood
Academy Restaurant
343 N. Third St., 513/868-7171

Best Steaks
Academy Restaurant
343 N. Third St., 513/868-7171
Shady-Nook Restaurant
879 Millville Oxford Rd., 513/863-4343
Tumbleweed Mexican Food and Mesquite
9956 Escort Dr., Mason, 513/573-9023

HILLSBORO, OH

Best All-You-Can-Eat Buffet
Wooden Spoon Restaurant
1480 N. High St., 937/393-4956

Best Burgers
Magee's Snack Shop
129 W. Main St., 937/393-2014

Best Homestyle Food
Wooden Spoon Restaurant
1480 N. High St., 937/393-4956

Best Italian Food
Stephano's Pizza
147 Catherine St., 937/393-8500

Best Steaks
Frontier Cattle Company
11145 N. Shore Dr., 937/393-6772

KENT, OH

Best Breakfast
Country Kitchen
4441 State Rte. 43, 330/678-4874

Best Casual Dining
Kentwood Restaurant and Lounge
1910 State Rte. 59, 330/673-1010

Best Chinese Food
China City
156 Cherry St., 330/673-6566

Best German Food
Henry Wahner's Restaurant
1609 E. Main St., 330/678-4055

Best Greek Food
Akropolis Family Restaurant
707 N. Mantua St., 330/678-2981

Best Ice Cream/Yogurt
Stoddard's Frozen Custards
1321 W. Main St., 330/673-2991

Best Inexpensive Meal
Chicken Manor
2108 State Rte. 59, 330/673-9355

Best Salad/Salad Bar
Cipriano's Restaurant and Lounge
6544 State Rte. 14, Ravenna, 330/296-2277

LANCASTER, OH

Best Breakfast
Snead's Restaurant
202 N. Cherry St., 740/654-1777

Best Burgers
White Cottage
525 N. High St., 740/654-9127

Best Coffee/Coffeehouse
Four Reasons
135 W. Main St., 740/654-2253

Best Desserts
Annie's Cheesecake and Tea Room
539 E. Main St., 740/654-3692

Best Homestyle Food
Roots Restaurant
1260 N. Memorial Dr., 740/653-8944

Best Pizza
Pink Cricket
929 E. Main St., 740/653-7300

Best Seafood
Mauger's Seafood Restaurant
512 E. Main St., 740/654-8237

LIMA, OH

Best All-You-Can-Eat Buffet
Old Barn Out Back
3175 W. Elm St., 419/991-3075

Best Burgers
Kewpee Hamburgers
2111 Allentown Rd., 419/227-9791
111 N. Elizabeth St., 419/228-1778
1350 Bellefontaine Ave., 419/229-1385

Best Family Restaurant
Huddle Restaurant
134 N. Metcalf St., 419/224-6851

Best Italian Food
Milano's
415 W. Market St., 419/225-4981

Best Steaks
The Beef and Bourbon
3801 Shawnee Rd., 419/999-1331
Burgundy's Restaurant
1365 N. Cable Rd., 419/224-5080

LORAIN, OH

Best Chinese Food
Hunan King Restaurant
3317 Oberlin Ave., 440/960-2162

Best French Food
Chez Francois
555 Main St., Vermilion, 216/967-0630

Best Homestyle Food
Chris' Restaurant
2812 W. Erie Ave., 440/245-5822

MANSFIELD, OH

Best American Food
Cheddar's Restaurant
979 N. Lexington Springmill Rd., 419/747-9777

Best Burgers
Big Al's Drive-In
1740 Park Ave. W., 419/529-9800
Derrenberger's Family Restaurant
1402 Lexington Ave., 419/756-1609
Mom's Hamburgers
1316 Ashland Rd., 419/589-8404

Best Chinese Food
Bethel Chinese Restaurant
205 Lexington Ave., 419/526-1877
China House
1435 Park Ave. W., 419/529-9767
Chinatown Restaurant
283 Ashland Rd., 419/524-2332

O

Zest of China
 2067 W. Fourth St., 419/529-3473

Best Diner
Mr. T's Coffee Shop
 82 Park Ave. W., 419/522-2121

Best Family Restaurant
Chris's Cafe
 1111 W. Fourth St., 419/529-6014
Daugherty Restaurant
 2413 Possum Run Rd., 419/756-3729

Best Fine Dining
Oak Park Tavern
 2519 Park Ave. E., 419/589-2637
Skyway East
 2461 Emma Ln., 419/589-9929
Sweeney's Too
 777 Lexington Ave., 419/756-2858

Best Homestyle Food
Chris's Cafe
 1111 W. Fourth St., 419/529-6014
Daugherty Restaurant
 2413 Possum Run Rd., 419/756-3729
Mansfield Family Restaurant
 948 S. Main St., 419/756-0479
Olde Keyes
 1 N. Main St., Savannah, 419/962-4610

Best Ice Cream/Yogurt
Big Al's Drive-In
 1740 Park Ave. W., 419/529-9800
Dairy Land
 800 Springmill St., 419/525-2168

Best Italian Food
Mama's Touch of Italy
 275 Park Ave. W., 419/526-5099

Best Mexican Food
Fork and Fingers
 54 Park Ave. W., 419/526-2321

Best Pizza
East of Chicago Pizza Company
 1592 Park Ave. W., 419/529-8070

MARIETTA, OH

Best Barbecue/Ribs
Damon's, The Place For Ribs
 Comfort Inn, 300 E. Pike St., 740/373-6700

Best Burgers
Cone and Shake
 219 Pike St., 740/373-1067

Best Chinese Food
Hong Kong Restaurant
 90 Acme St., 740/374-7009

Best Diner
Belrock Country Diner
 1802 Washington Blvd., Belpre, 740/423-5233

Best Health-Conscious Menu
Brighter Day Natural Foods
  10 Tiber Way, 740/374-2429

Best Sandwiches
Third Street Deli
  343 Third St., 740/374-0003

Best Seafood
Becky Thatcher Restaurant
  237 Front St., 740/373-4130
Tally-Ho
  211 Second St., 740/374-5228

Best Steaks
Becky Thatcher Restaurant
  237 Front St., 740/373-4130
Tally-Ho
  211 Second St., 740/374-5228

MARION, OH

Best All-You-Can-Eat Buffet
Gateway Smorgasboard
  1348 Mount Vernon Ave., 740/389-4712

Best Bar
Maury's on Main
  138 S. Main St., 740/382-3019

Best Chinese Food
House of Hunan
  1583 Marion Waldo Rd., 740/387-0032

Best Pizza
OK Cafe
  734 E. Center St., 740/387-6565

Best Sandwiches
Cafe George
  131 S. Main St., 740/382-5281

Best Steaks
Michael's Steak House
  1221 Delaware Ave., 740/382-6161

MASSILLON, OH

Best Chinese Food
China Kitchen
  2716 Lincoln Way E., 330/837-0188

Best Italian Food
Belleria Italian Restaurant
  2484 Lincoln Way E., 330/832-4700

Best Lunch
Meldrum's
  2144 Wales Ave. NW, 330/833-4729

Best Pizza
Kraus' Pizza
  915 Amherst Rd. NE, 330/832-2242

Best Restaurant in Town
Kurt's Inn
  4104 Lincoln Way E., 330/478-2548

O

Best Sandwiches
Irish Exchange
8009 Hills and Dales Rd. NW, 330/833-5000

MIDDLETOWN, OH

Best All-You-Can-Eat Buffet
Stefano's Italian Cafe and Catering
2200 Central Ave., 513/422-9922

Best Breakfast
Sunshine Cafe
640 N. University, 513/424-4842

Best Diner
Parrot Restaurant
100 S. Main St., 513/423-0191

Best Greek/Mediterranean Food
Grecian Delight
1300 Cincinnati Dayton Rd., 513/424-5411

Best Pizza
Capozzi's
3530 Central Ave., 513/422-3882

Best Seafood
Manchester Inn
1027 Manchester Ave., 513/422-5481

Best Steaks
Manchester Inn
1027 Manchester Ave., 513/422-5481

NEW PHILADELPHIA, OH

Best Italian Food
Uncle Primo's
435 Minnich Ave. NW, 330/364-2349

Best Other Ethnic Food
Dutch Valley (Amish)
1343 Old Route 39, Sugarcreek, 330/852-4627

Best Seafood
The Pros Table, Home of the Hanger
878 E. High Ave., 330/339-4011

Best Steaks
Leonard's Restaurant
719 S. Wooster Ave., Strasburg, 330/878-7772

NEWARK, OH

Best Burgers
Yesterday's Pub
78 Wilson St., 740/349-8009

Best Chinese Food
Golden Wok
22A N. Park Pl., 740/349-7050
Imperial Palace China Garden
1225 W. Church St., 740/344-0361

Best Dinner
Cherry Valley Lodge
2299 Cherry Valley Rd. SE, 740/788-1200

Best Fine Dining
Granville Inn
314 Broadway E., Granville, 740/587-3333

Best Homestyle Food
Sparta Restaurant
16 W. Main St., 740/345-6040

Best Italian Food
A Taste of Italy
606 W. Church St., 740/344-1121

Best Mexican Food
Casa Lupita
1671 N. 21st St., 740/366-7368

Best Other Ethnic Food
Miller's Essenplatz (Amish)
1414 N. 21st St., 740/366-7310

Best Steaks
Natoma Restaurant
10 N. Park Pl., 740/345-7260

PIQUA, OH

Best Burgers
Checkers Food and Spirits
311 N. Main St., 937/773-6641

Best Casual Dining
Dave's Place
1106 Fisk St., 937/773-3373

Best Chinese Food
China East
1239 E. Ash St., 937/778-8688

SANDUSKY, OH

Best Breakfast
Berardi's Family Kitchen
1019 W. Perkins Ave., 419/626-4592

Best Burgers
Med's 800 Club Ol' Time Saloon
1220 Sycamore Line, 419/625-3776
Plum Nilly
918 W. Perkins Ave., 419/625-8266

Best Italian Food
Cedar Villa Restaurant
1918 Cleveland Rd., 419/625-8487

Best Pizza
Cameo Pizza
702 W. Monroe St., 419/626-0187
Chet and Matt's Pizza
1013 E. Strub Rd., 419/626-6000

Best Seafood
Bay Harbor Inn
1 Causeway Dr., Cedar Point Marina, 419/625-6373

SPRINGFIELD, OH

Best Chinese Food
Hunan East
1460 Upper Valley Pike, 937/322-5432
Mark Pi's China Gate
1475 Upper Valley Pike, 937/325-1892
2149 S. Limestone St., 937/322-0055

Best Homestyle Food
Meadows Restaurant and Motel
4105 E. National Rd., 937/323-0872

Best Inexpensive Meal
Hickory Inn
652 N. Limestone St., 937/323-1702

Best Italian Food
Fazoli's Restaurant
529 E. Main St., 937/593-5503

Best Place to Take the Kids
Chuck E. Cheese Pizza
2345 Valley Loop Rd., 937/324-4155

Best Romantic Dining
Ashley's
Springfield Inn, 100 S. Fountain Ave.,
937/322-3600

Best Sandwiches
Mike and Rosy's Deli
330 W. McCreight Ave., 937/390-3511

Best Seafood
Klosterman's Derr Road Inn
4343 Derr Rd., 937/399-0822

Best Steaks
The Mill
3404 W. National Rd., 937/324-4045

STEUBENVILLE, OH

Best American Food
Jaggin' Around Restaurant and Pub
501 Washington St., 740/282-1010

Best Breakfast
Damon's Clubhouse
Holiday Inn, 1401 University Blvd.,
740/282-2745

Best Chinese Food
Hunan Chinese Restaurant
106 N. Fourth St., 740/282-8952

Best Greek/Mediterranean Food
Yorgo's Gyros Potatos
127 N. Fourth St., 740/282-9663

Best Italian Food
Naples Spaghetti House
329 North St., 740/283-3405

Best Steaks
Boots' Texas Roadhouse
4402 Sunset Blvd., 740/264-5599

Gas Lite Restaurant and Lounge
820 Canton Rd., Wintersville, 740/264-2225

STOW, OH

Best Breakfast
Cafe in Stow
4591 Darrow Rd., 330/688-0200
Charlie's Restaurant
3428 Darrow Rd., 330/688-3171

Best Desserts
Osman's Pies
4974 Darrow Rd., 330/655-2919

Best Fine Dining
Silver Pheasant
3085 Graham Rd., 330/678-2116

Best Ice Cream/Yogurt
Isaly's II
3310 Kent Rd., 330/688-4269

Best Inexpensive Meal
Swensen's Drive-in
4466 Kent Rd., 330/678-7775

Best Mexican Food
Poncho and Lefty's
3254 Kent Rd., 330/686-6781

Best Pizza
Rizzi's Pizzeria and Restaurant
4976 Darrow Rd., 330/655-2440

O

TOLEDO, OH

Best Breakfast
Original Pancake House
3310 W. Central Ave., 419/535-5927

Best Burgers
Nick and Jimmy's Bar and Grill
4956 Monroe St., 419/472-0756

Best Business Lunch
Christopher's Restaurant
5147 Main, Sylvania, 419/539-7355
Timko's Soup and Such
2500 W. Sylvania Ave., 419/475-4629

Best Casual Dining
Cooker Bar and Grill
5700 Monroe St., Sylvania, 419/882-2222
6658 Airport Hwy., Holland, 419/867-4994
J. Alexander's
4315 Talmadge Rd., 419/474-8620

Best Chinese Food
Fu Yi's
7130 Airport Hwy., Holland, 419/866-5262

Best Coffee/Coffeehouse
Sufficient Grounds
3160 Markway Rd., 419/537-1988

Best Diner
Ralphie's
3005 Navarre Ave., Oregon, 419/693-2500

Best Greek/Mediterranean Food
Theo's Taverna and Greek Restaurant
823 N. Summit St., 419/242-8312

Best Homestyle Food
Alice Harvey's Place
2521 Glendale Ave., 419/382-1011

Best Ice Cream/Yogurt
Pal's Ice Cream
3333 Airport Hwy., 419/382-0615

Best Indian Food
Tandoor Cuisine of India
2247 S. Reynolds Rd., 419/385-7467

Best Italian Food
Spaghetti Warehouse
42 S. Superior St., 419/255-5038

Best Late-Night Food
Dominic's Italian Restaurant
2121 S. Reynolds Rd., 419/381-8822

Best Mexican Food
El Matador Restaurant
3309 N. Holland Sylvania Rd., 419/841-4434
35 E. Alexis Rd., 419/476-2043
Loma Linda Restaurant
10400 Airport Hwy., Swanton, 419/865-5455

Best Middle Eastern Food
Beirut
4082 Monroe St., 419/473-0885

Best Pizza
Alexander's The Great Pizza
1808 Arlington Ave., 419/389-1200
3523 W. Alexis Rd., 419/473-2225

Best Place to Take the Kids
Major Magic's All Star Pizza Revue
5838 Monroe St., Sylvania, 419/885-1400

Best Romantic Dining
Fifi's Restaurant
1423 Bernath Pkwy., 419/866-6777
Georgio's Cafe
426 N. Superior St., 419/242-2424

Best Sandwiches
Frisco Deli
3348 Secor Rd., 419/537-1777
Grumpy's Deli
11 N. Michigan St., 419/241-6728
Salad Galley
611 Madison Ave., 419/243-3133
3301 W. Central Ave., 419/534-3322
Sufficient Grounds
3160 Markway Rd., 419/537-1988

Tony Packo's Cafe
  1902 Front St., 419/691-6054

Best Steaks
Mancy's Restaurant
  953 Phillips Ave., 419/476-4154

Best View While Dining
Aztec Grill and Bar
  One Seagate, 419/255-1116

WARREN, OH

Best Breakfast
Saratoga Restaurant
  129 E. Market St., 330/393-6646

Best Casual Dining
Mary M's Restaurant
  2940 Parkman Rd. NW, 330/898-3846

Best Chinese Food
Imperial Palace
  1212 Youngstown Warren Rd., Niles, 330/544-2388

Best Coffee/Coffeehouse
Mocha House
  467 High St. NE, 330/392-3020

Best Fine Dining
Alberini's Restaurant
  1201 Youngstown Warren Rd., Niles, 330/652-5895
Jimmy Chieffo's Restaurant and Lounge
  3860 Youngstown Rd. SE, 330/369-6507

Best Homestyle Food
Saratoga Restaurant
  129 E. Market St., 330/393-6646

Best Pizza
Sunrise Inn
  510 E. Market St., 330/392-5176

Best Sandwiches
Scrump-Deli-Icious
  176 N. Park Ave., 330/393-9311

Best Seafood
Abruzzi's Cafe 422
  4422 Youngstown Rd. SE, 330/369-2422

Best Steaks
Tall Oaks Restaurant
  Avalon Inn, 9519 E. Market St., 330/856-1900

WILLOUGHBY, OH

Best Coffee/Coffeehouse
Thinker Coffeehouse
  4148 Erie St., 440/942-5282

Best Desserts
Bakers Square Restaurant
  28601 Chardon Rd., Willoughby Hills,
    440/944-7777

O

Best Italian Food
The Italian Oven
  30170 Lake Shore Blvd., Willowick,
    440/585-0999

Best Mexican Food
Meximilian's
  9080 Mentor Ave., Mentor, 440/255-1720

Best Sunday Brunch
Big Boy Restaurant
  35441 Euclid Ave., 440/951-5040

Best Vegetarian Food
Thinker Coffeehouse
  4148 Erie St., 440/942-5282

WOOSTER, OH

Best American Food
T.J.'s Restaurant
  359 W. Liberty St., 330/264-6263

Best Breakfast
Buehler's Towne Market Cafe
  336 N. Market St., 330/264-9900
Parlor Restaurant
  203 W. Liberty St., 330/262-4871

Best Chinese Food
Sue-Min's Chinese Gourmet
  1535 Madison Ave., 330/262-5552

Best Family Restaurant
Smithville Inn
  109 E. Main St., Smithville, 330/669-2641

Best Greek/Mediterranean Food
Matsos Family Restaurant
  154 W. Liberty St., 330/264-8800

Best Homestyle Food
Hawkins Cafeteria
  2312 Akron Rd., 330/264-8908

Best Inexpensive Meal
K C's Lunch Counter
  620 W. High St., Orrville, 330/682-6921

Best Italian Food
Coccia House
  764 Pittsburg Ave., 330/262-7136

Best Lunch
Pines Golf Club and Restaurant
  1319 N. Millborne Rd., Orrville, 330/684-1010

Best Other Ethnic Food
Des Dutch Essenhaus (Amish)
  176 S. Market St., Shreve, 330/567-2212

Best Salad/Salad Bar
The Barn Restaurant
  877 E. Main St., Smithville, 330/669-2555

XENIA, OH

Best Lunch
Otis' Tavern
120 Xenia Towne Sq., 937/372-1993

YOUNGSTOWN, OH

Best Atmosphere
Rachel's Steak and Seafood
169 S. Four Mile Run Rd., 330/799-2800

Best Barbecue/Ribs
Armadillo's Restaurant
3031 Mahoning Ave., 330/792-0662

Best Breakfast
Yankee Kitchen
6635 Market St., 330/726-1300

Best Burgers
Coconut Grove
3229 South Ave., 330/788-0140

Best Business Lunch
Paonessa's
871 McKay Ct., 330/726-6001

Best Coffee/Coffeehouse
Beat Coffeehouse
215 Lincoln Ave., 330/743-4227

Best Diner
Emerald Diner
825 N. Main St., Hubbard, 330/534-1441

Best Health-Conscious Menu
Crystal's Restaurant
1931 Belmont Ave., 330/743-5381

Best Ice Cream/Yogurt
Handel's Homemade Ice Cream
3931 Handels Ct., 330/788-0356
3622 Belmont Ave., 330/759-2417
310 Churchill Hubbard Rd., 330/759-1442

Best Inexpensive Meal
Cafe Roma
17 N. Champion St., 330/746-6900

Best Late-Night Food
Splendid Restaurant and Lounge
3330 South Ave., 330/782-3062

Best Mexican Food
La Fiesta
1801 Midland Ave., 330/793-3967

Best Pizza
Belleria Pizzeria
1535 Logan Ave., 330/744-4085
The Elmton
584 Fifth Ave., Struthers, 330/755-8511
Wedgewood Pizza Shop
1622 S. Raccoon Rd., 330/799-2102

O

Best Place to Take the Kids
Antone's Restaurant
7424 Market St., Boardman, 330/758-2218

Best Romantic Dining
Rachel's Steak and Seafood
169 S. Four Mile Run Rd., 330/799-2800
The Crystal Room
Wick-Pollock Inn, 603 Wick Ave., 330/746-1200

Best Steaks
Rachel's Steak and Seafood
169 S. Four Mile Run Rd., 330/799-2800

Best View While Dining
The Moonraker
1275 Boardman Poland Rd., 330/726-8841

ZANESVILLE, OH

Best Breakfast
Tee Jaye's Country Place
1542 Maple Ave., 740/450-7555

Best Chinese Food
Mark Pi's China Gate
2502 Maple Ave., 740/453-6655

Best Italian Food
Maria Adornetto Restaurant
953 Market St., 740/453-0643

Best Mexican Food
Zak's
32 N. Third St., 740/453-2227

Best Pizza
Papa Chuck's
375 Muskingum Ave., 740/452-6303

Best Sandwiches
Adornetto's Pizzeria
2224 Maple Ave., 740/453-0789
2440 Maysville Pike, 216/454-6261

Best Steaks
Old Market House Inn
424 Market St., 740/454-2555

Oklahoma

Best Barbecue/Ribs
Little House of Barbecue
  217 W. Pecan St., 580/482-6555
Woody's Barbecue
  1100 N. Main St., 580/477-4756

Best Chinese Food
Fortune Cookie Oriental Restaurant
  119 S. Hudson St., 580/477-0775

Best Italian Food
Papa Joe's
  2200 N. Main St., 580/477-4557

Best Mexican Food
Benny's Mexican Food and Pizza
  1314 N. Main St., 580/482-8713

Best Other Ethnic Food
Polynesian Garden (Polynesian)
  1700 Falcon Rd., 580/482-2831

Best Restaurant in Town
Crystal's Restaurant
  2515 E. Broadway St., 580/477-3000
Eddie's Cafe
  1613 E. Broadway St., 580/482-1373
Val's It's About Time
  800 N. Main St., 580/482-4580

Best Steaks
Val's It's About Time
  800 N. Main St., 580/482-4580

O

Best Thai Food
Kay's Bangkok Restaurant
1000 Falcon Rd., 580/482-1469

ARDMORE, OK

Best Barbecue/Ribs
Aub's Two Frogs Grill
Hwy. 70, Lone Grove, 580/657-8645
Hick'ry House Barbecue
2200 S. Commerce St., 580/223-5855

Best Breakfast
Grandy's Restaurant
819 N. Commerce St., 580/226-2051
Kettle Restaurant
202 Holliday Dr., 580/226-8023

Best Burgers
Hamburger Inn
27 N. Washington St., 580/223-7440

Best Chinese Food
Great Wall Chinese Restaurant
2015 W. Broadway St., 580/226-4460

Best Mexican Food
Polo's
717 W. Broadway St., 580/226-7656

Best Sandwiches
Cafe Alley
107 E. Main St., 580/223-6413

Best Steaks
Benson's
110 Holliday Dr., 580/223-7848
Fireside Dining
Lake Murray Village, Hwy. 77, 580/226-4070
Sirloin Stockade
1217 N. Commerce St., 580/226-6281

BARTLESVILLE, OK

Best Barbecue/Ribs
Dink's Pit Barbecue
2929 E. Frank Phillips Blvd., 918/335-0606

Best Burgers
Murphy's Original Steak House
1625 SW Frank Phillips Blvd., 918/336-4789
Washington County Hamburger Store
412 S. Johnstone Ave., 918/336-4440

Best Chinese Food
Szechuan Chinese Restaurant
516 SE Washington Blvd., 918/335-3945

Best Coffee/Coffeehouse
Java Bean Cafe
572 SE Washington Blvd., 918/335-9276

Best Greek/Mediterranean Food
Greek Express
2350 SE Washington Blvd., 918/331-0735

Best Homestyle Food
Cotton Patch Cafe
  3813 E. Frank Phillips Blvd., 918/333-9450
Jarret Farm Country Inn
  Hwy. 75N, Collinsville, 918/371-9868
Midway Cafe
  641 SE Washington Blvd., 918/335-1000
Wing's Country Pleasin'
  1757 SW Frank Phillips Blvd., 918/336-2828

Best Italian Food
Villa Italia
  821 S. Johnstone Ave., 918/337-6660

Best Mexican Food
Alfredo's Restaurante Mexicano
  3121 E. Frank Phillips Blvd., 918/335-3585

Best Pizza
Simple Simon's Pizza
  200 NE Washington Blvd., 918/333-0238

Best Restaurant in Town
Sterling's Grille
  2905 S. Frank Phillips Blvd., 918/335-0707

Best Southwestern Food
Monterey's Tex Mex Cafe
  3815 SE Adams Rd., 918/333-5524

BROKEN ARROW, OK

O

Best Bar
C.J. Moloney's
  1849 S. Aspen Ave., 918/251-1973

Best Barbecue/Ribs
Robert's Barbecue
  12219 S. 273rd East Ave., 918/451-0322

Best Burgers
Goldie's Patio Grill
  1912 S. Elm Pl., 918/455-6128

Best Chinese Food
China Palace Restaurant
  113 N. Elm Pl., 918/258-6526

Best Coffee/Coffeehouse
Golden Bagels
  1009 N. Elm Pl., 918/258-1009

Best Desserts
Tea For Two
  804 S. Main St., 918/251-8305

Best Diner
Duffy's Restaurant
  706 S. Elm Pl., 918/251-3285

Best Family Restaurant
Delta Cafe
  3806 S. Elm Pl., 918/455-1900

Best Fine Dining
Hickory Hills Steak House
  3600 W. Jasper St., 918/451-2428

Best Ice Cream/Yogurt
Braum's Ice Cream and Dairy
804 N. Elm Pl., 918/258-2424
4640 S. Elm Pl., 918/455-6464
20200 E. 81st St., 918/251-4660

Best Inexpensive Meal
Duffy's Restaurant
706 S. Elm Pl., 918/251-3285

Best Vegetarian Food
Delta Cafe
3806 S. Elm Pl., 918/455-1900

Best View While Dining
Cafe Savannah's
7501 E. Kenosha St., 918/357-4408

DUNCAN, OK

Best Barbecue/Ribs
Hickies' Barbecue
3325 N. Hwy. 81, 580/255-1551

Best Chinese Food
Peking Garden Chinese Restaurant
1203 S. Hwy. 81, 580/255-1806

Best Mexican Food
Don Jose
3402 N. Hwy. 81, 580/252-5853
Eduardo's Mexican Restaurant
1304 N. Hwy. 81, 580/255-0781
El Palacio Mexican Restaurant
1209 W. Bois D'Arc Ave., 580/252-1314

Best Steaks
Wright's Steak and Lobster House
905 E. Bois D'Arc Ave., 580/252-4363

EDMOND, OK

Best All-You-Can-Eat Buffet
Cici's Pizza
1520 E. Second St., 405/341-1112

Best American Food
Johnnie's Charcoal Broiler
3334 S. Boulevard St., 405/348-3214
The Greystone Crab and Steakhouse
1 N. Sooner Rd., 405/340-4400

Best Business Lunch
Interurban Restaurant
1301 E. Danforth Rd., 405/348-2792

Best Chinese Food
Blue Moon
1320 S. Broadway, 405/340-3871
Edmond Mandarin Chinese
1083 S. Broadway, 405/348-6300

Best Coffee/Coffeehouse
Java Dave's
9 S. Broadway, 405/340-1693

Best Delicatessen
New York Bagel Shop
  1700 S. Broadway St., 405/359-7722

Best Diner
Around The Corner Restaurant
  11 S. Broadway, 405/341-5414

Best Fine Dining
Twelve Oaks Restaurant
  6100 N. Midwest Blvd., 405/340-1002

Best Health-Conscious Menu
Cafe 501
  501 S. Boulevard St., 405/359-1501

Best Inexpensive Meal
Braum's Ice Cream and Dairy
  3101 E. Memorial Rd., 405/478-4730
  1001 E. Danforth Rd., 405/348-7039
  1612 S. Boulevard St., 405/341-3808

Best Pizza
Godfather's Pizza
  603 S. Broadway, 405/348-7333

Best Place to Eat Alone
Hobby's Hoagies
  222 S. Santa Fe Ave., 405/348-2214

ELK CITY, OK

O

Best All-You-Can-Eat Buffet
The Gazebo
  Holiday Inn, 101 Meadowedge Dr., 580/225-6637

Best Breakfast
Flamingo Restaurant
  2000 W. Third St., 580/225-3412
Kettle Restaurant
  2700 E. Hwy. 66, 580/225-1071

Best Burgers
Billie's
  210 N. Madison Ave., 580/225-3355
Flamingo Restaurant
  2000 W. Third St., 580/225-3412

Best Coffee/Coffeehouse
Flamingo Restaurant
  2000 W. Third St., 580/225-3412

Best Ice Cream/Yogurt
Braum's Ice Cream and Dairy
  1111 W. Third St., 580/225-1011

Best Mexican Food
Lupe's Restaurant
  905 N. Main St., 580/225-7109

Best Pizza
Mazzio's Pizza
  103 Janets Way, 580/243-0000

Best Sandwiches
Cafe Elk City
  107 W. Fifth St., 580/243-0801

Best Steaks
Simon's Catch
  Southwest of City, 580/225-8400

Best Tea Room
Country Dove Gifts and Tea Room
  610 W. Third St., 580/225-7028

ENID, OK

Best American Food
Grand Avenue Cafe
  423 N. Grand St., 580/234-7544
Sneakers
  1710 W. Willow Rd., 580/237-6325
The Dutch Pantry
  Best Western Hotel, 2818 S. Van Buren St.,
    405/242-7110
Wooden Spoon
  2426 W. Owen K. Garriott Rd., 580/234-8355

Best Business Lunch
Richill's Cafeteria
  221 W. Randolph Ave., 580/237-4005

Best Chinese Food
Combo King
  4125 W. Owen K. Garriott Rd., 580/242-7733
  923 S. Van Buren St., 580/242-7788

Best Fine Dining
Sage Room Restaurant
  1927 S. Van Buren St., 580/233-1212

Best Health-Conscious Menu
Richill's Cafeteria
  221 W. Randolph Ave., 580/237-4005

Best Homestyle Food
The Dutch Pantry
  Best Western Hotel, 2818 S. Van Buren St.,
    580/242-7110

Best Ice Cream/Yogurt
Braum's Ice Cream and Dairy
  1121 W. Willow Rd., 580/242-6152
  2709 W. Owen K. Garriott Rd., 580/234-8580

Best Italian Food
Louisa's
  220 N. Independence St., 580/233-8707
Port Lugano
  813 S. Van Buren St., 580/242-4861

Best Late-Night Food
Taco Mayo
  118 N. Van Buren St., 580/233-5014

Best Pizza
Simple Simon's Pizza
  1402 E. Chestnut Ave., 580/233-8899

Best Place to Take the Kids
Godfather's Pizza
  222 Sunset Plaza, 580/233-5766

Best Steaks
Sage Room Restaurant
  1927 S. Van Buren St., 580/233-1212

LAWTON, OK

Best Breakfast
Rise and Shine Omelet Grill
  5239 NW Cache Rd., 580/353-4072
  201 SW Eleventh St., 580/355-3841
  1529 NW Cache Rd., 580/353-8150
Victoria's
  1125 E. Gore Blvd., 580/353-0200

Best Burgers
Braum's Ice Cream and Dairy
  608 NW Fort Sill Blvd., 580/353-5099
  1211 SW Lee Blvd., 580/353-0764
  4435 NW Cache Rd., 580/353-5098

Best Business Lunch
Bet's Country Ritz
  529 C Avenue, 580/355-7200

Best Coffee/Coffeehouse
Beans and Briar
  618 C Avenue, 580/357-2830
Forgotten Works Bookstore and Coffee Bar
  603 E Avenue, 580/248-1575

Best Diner
Leo and Ken's Truck Stop
  103 SE Lee Blvd., 580/357-8561

Best Fine Dining
Martin's Restaurant
  2107 NW Cache Rd., 580/355-0373

Best Homestyle Food
Calico County Restaurant
  5203 NW Cache Rd., 580/353-7976

Best Italian Food
Bianco's Italian Restaurant
  113 NW Second St., 580/353-9543
Pizano's Italian Restaurant
  1302A NW Homestead Dr., 580/357-4033

Best Mexican Food
El Zarape Restaurant
  1015 SW Park Ave., 580/353-3610
Salas Authentic Mexican Foods
  111 SW Lee Blvd., 580/357-1600

Best Sandwiches
Schlotzsky's
  3902 NW Cache Rd., 580/357-2867

Best Seafood
Fishermen's Cove
  HC 32 Hwy. 49, 580/529-2672

Best Steaks
Old Plantation
  Medicine Park, 580/529-9641

O

MCALESTER, OK

Best Barbecue/Ribs
Ball Hickory Pit Barbecue
  319 W. Shawnee Ave., 918/423-4430

Best Breakfast
Meeting Place
  104 E. Choctaw Ave., 918/426-6416

Best Burgers
Ray's Grill
  215 E. Chickasaw Ave., 918/423-1444

Best Chinese Food
Hunan Chinese Restaurant
  733 S. George Nigh Expwy., 918/426-0481

Best Desserts
Janalynn's
  324 E. Carl Albert Pkwy., 918/423-4183

Best Homestyle Food
Marilyn's Restaurant
  1211 S. George Nigh Expwy., 918/426-1629

Best Ice Cream/Yogurt
Braum's Ice Cream
  1015 E. Carl Albert Pkwy., 918/426-0167

Best Italian Food
Giacomo's Restaurant
  19 W. Comanche Ave., 918/423-2662
Isle of Capri
  150 SW Seventh St., Krebs, 918/423-3062
Pete's Place
  120 SW Eighth St., Krebs, 918/423-2042
Rosanna's
  205 E. Washington Ave., 918/423-2055

Best Mexican Food
Polo's of McAlester
  615 1/2 S. George Nigh Expwy., 918/423-7656

Best Seafood
Trolley's Restaurant
  21 E. Monroe Ave., 918/423-2446

MUSKOGEE, OK

Best American Food
Jasper's Restaurant
  1702 W. Okmulgee St., 918/682-7867

Best Barbecue/Ribs
Cowboy's Bar-B-Q
  401 N. York St., 918/682-0651
My Place Barbecue
  1311 Gibson St., 918/683-2021
  4322 W. Okmulgee St., 918/683-5202

Best Burgers
Ty's Hamburgers
  2406 Chandler Rd., 918/682-7599

Best Italian Food
Little Italy Fine Dining
2432 N. 32nd St., 918/687-5699

Best Southwestern Food
Hamlin's El Toro East
940 N. York St., 918/687-9982
Hamlin's El Toro West
3620 W. Okmulgee St., 918/687-9194

Best Steaks
Okie's Restaurant
219 S. 32nd St., 918/683-1056

NORMAN, OK

Best Bar
O'Connell's Irish Pub and Grill
120 E. Lindsey St., 405/329-8454
The Deli
309 White St., 405/329-3534

Best Barbecue/Ribs
Coaches Brewery and Restaurant
102 W. Main St., 405/360-5726
Ole Town Chicken and Barbecue
402 E. Main St., 405/447-0884

Best Bistro
La Baguette
924 W. Main St., 405/321-3424

Best Breakfast
Kendall's
100 S. Main St., Noble, 405/872-7158

Best Brewpub
Coaches Brewery and Restaurant
102 W. Main St., 405/360-5726
Interurban Restaurant and Brewpub
105 W. Main St., 405/364-7942

Best Chinese Food
Hunan Chinese Restaurant
203 Hal Muldrow Dr., 405/360-0394
Lai Lai Chinese Restaurant
3720 W. Robinson St., 405/447-1555
Little China
1118 N. Berry Rd., 405/360-2384
Orient Express
722 Asp Ave., 405/364-2100

Best Coffee/Coffeehouse
La Baguette
323 W. Boyd St., 405/321-3424

Best Delicatessen
Lovelight Restaurant
529 Buchanan Ave., 405/364-2073
New York Bagel Shop and Deli
301 W. Boyd St., 405/329-3000

Best Diner
Diner
213 E. Main St., 405/329-6642

O

Ozzie's Diner
1700 Lexington St., 405/364-9835

Best Eclectic Menu
Charleston's Restaurant
300 Ed Noble Pkwy., 405/360-0900
Mr. Bill's Restaurant
1101 Elm St., 405/364-2530

Best Fine Dining
Legend's Restaurant
1313 W. Lindsey St., 405/329-8888

Best German Food
Old Germany Wein Und Biergarten
3720 W. Robinson St., Ste. 106, 405/321-6565

Best Greek/Mediterranean Food
House of Greek
330 E. Main St., 405/364-4841

Best Homestyle Food
Kendall's
100 S. Main St., Noble, 405/872-7158

Best Ice Cream/Yogurt
Braum's Ice Cream and Dairy
1002 24th Ave. SW, 405/326-9155
1200 N. Interstate Dr., 405/364-7806
1320 E. Lindsey St., 405/360-2022
400 E. Robinson St., 405/321-3431

Best Indian Food
Misal of India
584 Buchanan Ave., 405/360-5888

Best Italian Food
Jana's Restaurant
1324 N. Interstate Dr., 405/447-7200
Othello's Italian Restaurant
434 Buchanan Ave., 405/360-2353
Victoria's
327 White St., 405/329-0377

Best Late-Night Food
Prairie Kitchen
2520 W. Main St., 405/329-2263
Kettle Restaurant
1522 W. Lindsey St., 405/321-5232

Best Lunch
Interurban Restaurant and Brewpub
105 W. Main St., 405/364-7942

Best Mexican Food
Border Crossing
606 W. Main St., 405/364-7617
Don Pablo's Mexican Kitchen
330 Ed Noble Pkwy., 405/573-9670
Los Dos Amigos
1600 S. Green Ave., Purcell, 405/527-7985
The Mont
1300 Classen Blvd., 405/329-3330

Best Outdoor Dining
The Mont
  1300 Classen Blvd., 405/329-3330

Best Pizza
Chicago's Pizza and Grill
  1337 E. Lindsey St., 405/447-2288

Best Romantic Dining
Victoria's
  327 White St., 405/329-0377

Best Steaks
Indian Hills Restaurant and Club
  6221 N. Interstate Dr., 405/364-7577

Best Tea Room
Janet's Eats and Sweets
  100 N. Main St., Blanchard, 405-485-2638

Best Thai Food
Kum Koon Thai Restaurant
  1200 24th Ave. SW, 405/321-0110

Best Vegetarian Food
Lovelight Restaurant
  529 Buchanan Ave., 405/364-2073

OKLAHOMA CITY, OK

Best American Food
Ann's Chicken Fry House
  4106 NW 39th St., 405/943-8915
Black-Eyed Pea
  1508 SW 74th St., 405/685-1000
  13702 N. Pennsylvania Ave., 405/752-9744
  6444 NW Expressway St., 405/721-2255
Charleston's Restaurant
  5907 NW Expressway St., 405/721-0060
  2000 N. Meridian Ave., 405/681-6686
Johnnie's Charcoal Broiler
  6629 NW Expressway St., 405/721-9018
  421 SW 74th St., 405/634-4681
  2652 W. Britton Rd., 405/751-2565
Johnnie's Grill
  301 S. Rock Island Ave., El Reno, 405/262-4721
  442 W. Main St., Yukon, 405/354-2030
Varsity Sports Grill
  1140 NW 63rd St., 405/842-0898
  1732 S. Meridian Ave., 405/685-7715
  115 E. Sheridan Ave., 405/235-5525

Best Bar
Bricktown Brewery Restaurant and Pub
  1 N. Oklahoma Ave., 405/232-2739
Flip's Wine Bar and Trattoria
  5801 N. Western Ave., 405/843-1527
Henry Hudson's Pub
  3509 NW 58th St., 405/946-5771
  1131 W. Memorial Rd., 405/752-1444
  7500 SE Fifteenth St., 405/732-0232
  3938 W. Reno Ave., 405/943-9080
  401 SW 74th St., 405/631-0212

O

Pearl's Oyster Bar
928 NW 63rd St., 405/848-8008
Varsity Sports Grill
1140 NW 63rd St., 405/842-0898
1732 S. Meridian Ave., 405/685-7715
115 E. Sheridan Ave., 405/235-5525
VZD's
4200 N. Western Ave., 405/524-4203

Best Barbecue/Ribs
County Line Restaurant
1226 NE 63rd St., 405/478-4955
Jack's Barbecue
4418 NW 39th St., 405/946-1865
2724 W. Britton Rd., 405/755-7510
Leo's Family Barbecue and Catering
3631 N. Kelley Ave., 405/427-3254
Oklahoma Station Barbecue
4333 NW 50th St., 405/947-7277
Piggy's Bar-B-Q
303 E. Sheridan Ave., 405/232-3912

Best Brewpub
Bricktown Brewery Restaurant and Pub
1 N. Oklahoma Ave., 405/232-2739

Best Chinese Food
Dot Wo Restaurant
3101 N. Portland Ave., 405/942-1376
Golden Palace
1224 S. Air Depot Blvd., Midwest City,
405/737-7118
Grand House Restaurant
1140 NW 24th St., 405/524-7333
Grand House Restaurant
2701 N. Classen Blvd., 405/524-7333
Hunan Chinese Restaurant
1500 SW 74th St., 405/685-5288
9211 N. Pennsylvania Pl., 405/843-6233
Lido Restaurant
2518 N. Military Ave., Ste. 101, 405/521-1902
Orient Express
7311 N. MacArthur Blvd., 405/721-0882
The Orient
101 Park Ave., 405/235-2288

Best Coffee/Coffeehouse
Java Dave's
7936 N. May Ave., 405/840-9949
10 NE Tenth St., 405/236-0272
101 N. Broadway Ave., 405/232-5728
Medina's Coffee House and Gallery
3004 Paseo, 405/524-7949
Yippee Yi-Yo Cafe
1310 NW 25th St., 405/524-5282

Best Delicatessen
Breadworks Bakery
7300 N. Western Ave., 405/842-7571
City Bites Subs
7309 S. Western Ave., 405/632-6655

4646 N. Santa Fe Ave., 405/528-6797
12058 N. May Ave., 405/752-1771
6001 N. May Ave., 405/842-3355
Earth Natural Foods and Deli
1101 NW 49th St., 405/840-0502
New York Bagel Shop
9235 N. Pennsylvania Pl., 405/848-3366
211 N. Robinson Ave., 405/235-3700
Someplace Else
2310 N. Western Ave., 405/524-0887

Best Diner
Neighbor's Country Kitchen
3401 N. Classen Blvd., 405/528-3441

Best Family Restaurant
Miller's Crossing
501 N. Mustang Rd., Yukon, 405/324-2444

Best Fine Dining
Bellini's Ristorante and Grill
6305 Waterford Blvd., Ste. 100, 405/848-1065
Nikz
5900 Mosteller Dr., 405/843-7875

Best French Food
The Metro Wine Bar and Bistro
6418 N. Western Ave., 405/840-9463

Best German Food
Ingrid's Kitchen
3701 N. Youngs Blvd., 405/946-8444
The Keller in The Kastle German Restaurant
820 N. MacArthur Blvd., 405/942-6133
Old Germany Restaurant
15920 SE 29th St., Choctaw, 405/390-8647
Royal Bavaria
3401 S. Sooner Rd., 405/799-7666

Best Greek/Mediterranean Food
The Akropolis Greek Restaurant of Del City
4734 SE 29th St., 405/670-3040

Best Health-Conscious Menu
Earth Natural Foods and Deli
1101 NW 49th St., 405/840-0502
Gopuram Taste of India
4559 NW 23rd St., 405/948-7373
Sala Thai
1614 NW 23rd St., 405/528-8424

Best Indian Food
Ajanta
11919 N. Pennsylvania Ave., 405/752-5283
Gopuram Taste of India
4559 NW 23rd St., 405/948-7373

Best Italian Food
Bellini's Ristorante and Grill
6305 Waterford Blvd., Ste. 100, 405/848-1065
Flip's Wine Bar and Trattoria
5801 N. Western Ave., 405/843-1527

O

Papa's Little Italy
10603 N. I-35 Service Rd., 405/478-4400
Portobello Ristorante
5418 N. Western Ave., 405/848-7678
Spaghetti Warehouse
101 E. Sheridan Ave., 405/235-0402
Tony's Italian Specialties
2824 N. Pennsylvania Ave., 405/524-7705

Best Japanese Food
Shogun Steak House of Japan
4475 NW 50th St., 405/949-1674
Tokyo Japanese Restaurant
7516 N. Western Ave., 405/848-6733

Best Korean Food
Sharon Garden Korean Restaurant
1400 NW 23rd St., 405/523-2121

Best Mexican Food
Chelino's Mexican Restaurant
15 E. California Ave., 405/235-3533
427 SW 36th St., 405/636-1110
4221 S. Robinson Ave., 405/636-1548
Cocina De Mino Restaurante Mexicano
6000 NW Second St., 405/495-0411
333 SE 29th St., 405/636-0335
12325 N. May Ave., 405/749-8800
3830 MacArthur Blvd., Warr Acres, 405/495-6789
Iguana Lounge
6816 N. Western Ave., 405/840-3474
La Roca Mexican Restaurant
412 S. Walker Ave., 405/235-8646
409 W. Reno Ave., 405/235-9596
Monterey Jack's Number 3
801 S. Airdepop Ave., 405/732-6399

Best Restaurant in Town
Bellini's Ristorante and Grill
6305 Waterford Blvd., Ste. 100, 405/848-1065
The Coach House
6437 Avondale Dr., Nichols Hills, 405/842-1000
Monterey Jack's Number 3
801 S. Airdepop Ave., 405/732-6399
The Ground Floor Cafe
6430 Avondale Dr., Nichols Hills, 405/842-2233

Best Sandwiches
Between the Bread
3500 N. Classen Blvd., 405/528-3136

Best Seafood
Fishkie's Seafood Restaurant
6816 N. Western Ave., 405/840-3474
Pearl's Oyster Bar
2125 SW 74th St., 405/682-1500
928 NW 63rd St., 405/848-8008
Trapper's Fish Camp
4300 W. Reno Ave., 405/943-9111

Best Sports Bar
Interurban's IU Sports Grill
  1024 SW 74th St., 405/632-1222

Best Steaks
Cattlemen's Steak House
  1309 S. Agnew Ave., 405/236-0416
Junior's
  2601 NW Expressway St., 405/848-5597

Best Sunday Brunch
Classen Grill
  5421 N. Classen Blvd., 405/842-0428
Flip's Wine Bar and Trattoria
  5801 N. Western Ave., 405/843-1527
Harrigan's Restaurant
  2125 W. Memorial Rd., 405/751-7322
  2203 SW 74th St., 405/686-1012
  6420 NW Expressway St., 405/728-1329
Jimmy's Egg Restaurant
  2801 W. I-240 Service Rd., 405/681-1191
  5829 Melton Dr., 405/728-8343
  6805 SE Fifteenth St., 405/732-6433
  2132 W. Britton Rd., 405/842-2944
The Veranda Restaurant
  Waterford Marriott Hotel, 6300 Waterford Blvd.,
    405/848-4782

Best Thai Food
Sala Thai
  1614 NW 23rd St., 405/528-8424

Best Vietnamese Food
Cao Van Restaurant
  3009 N. Classen Blvd., 405/525-3579
Pho Hoa Vietnamese Restaurant
  901 NW 23rd St., 405/557-1477

O

PONCA CITY, OK

Best American Food
Blue Moon
  1418 E. South Ave., 580/762-2425

Best Bar
Crown and Rose
  731 N. Fourteenth St., 580/762-8489

Best Barbecue/Ribs
Blue Moon
  1418 E. South Ave., 580/762-2425
Head Country Barbecue Restaurant
  1217 E. Prospect Ave., 580/767-8304

Best Family Restaurant
Cobb's Cafe
  801 S. First St., 580/762-2434
Nottingham's Grand Cafe
  423 E. Grand Ave., 580/762-2310

Best Italian Food
Ristorante Bravo
  200 N. Second St., 580/762-7280

Best Steaks
Pauline's Supper Club
  114 L.A. Cann Dr., 580/765-5460
The Rusty Barrel
  2005 N. Fourteenth St., 580/765-6689

SALLISAW, OK

Best Barbecue/Ribs
Wild Horse Mountain Barbecue
  Hwy. 59S, 918/775-9960

Best Breakfast
Dana's Restaurant
  907 Kerr Blvd., 918/775-4921

Best Chinese Food
Full Moon
  122 W. Cherokee St., 918/775-8580
Golden Wu Restaurant
  702 E. Cherokee St., 918/776-0808

Best Ice Cream/Yogurt
Braum's Ice Cream
  615 S. Kerr Blvd., 918/775-9965

Best Place to Take the Kids
Simple Simon's Pizza
  2401 E. Cherokee St., 918/775-5511

SHAWNEE, OK

Best American Food
Garfield's Restaurant and Pub
  4901 N. Kickapoo St., Ste. 1660, 405/273-3301

Best Barbecue/Ribs
Van's Pig Stand
  717 E. Highland St., 405/273-8704

Best Chinese Food
Sunrise Chinese Restaurant
  1814 N. Harrison St., 405/275-7271

Best Mexican Food
Amigo's Mexican Restaurant
  1718 N. Kickapoo St., 405/275-5552

Best Steaks
Jay's Classic Steakhouse
  37808 Old Hwy. 270, 405/275-6867

STILLWATER, OK

Best Mexican Food
Mexico Joe's
  311 E. Hall of Fame Ave., 405/372-1169

Best Restaurant in Town
Eskimo Joe's
  501 W. Elm Ave., 405/372-8896
Hideaway
  230 S. Knoblock St., 405/372-4777

Best Steaks
Sirloin Stockade
  208 N. Perkins Rd., 405/624-1681
Stillwater Bay
  612 1/2 S. Husband St., 405/743-2780

TULSA, OK

Best American Food
Blue Rose Cafe
  3421 S. Peoria Ave., 918/742-3873
East Side Cafe
  3021 E. Admiral Pl., 918/834-1725
Full Moon Cafe
  1525 E. Fifteenth St., 918/583-6666

Best Atmosphere
Royal Dragon
  7837 E. 51st St., 918/664-2245
Warren Duck Club
  6110 S. Yale Ave., 918/495-1000

Best Bar
Bistro at Brookside
  3523 S. Peoria Ave., 918/749-7737
Grapevine
  3509 S. Peoria Ave., 918/745-9155
Tucci's Cafe Italia
  1344 E. Fifteenth St., 918/582-3456

Best Barbecue/Ribs
Knotty Pine Barbecue
  3301 W. Fifth St., 918/584-0171
Mac's Barbecue
  1030 W. Rogers Blvd., Skiatook, 918/396-4165
Rib Crib
  1607 S. Harvard Ave., 918/742-6327
  5025 S. Sheridan Rd., 918/663-4295
Wilson's
  1522 E. Apache St., 918/425-9912
Wrangler's Barbecue and Roadhouse Cafe
  7915 E. 71st St., 918/252-4499

Best Breakfast
Brookside By Day
  3313 S. Peoria Ave., 918/745-9989

Best Brewpub
Tulsa Brewing Company and Restaurant
  7227 S. Memorial Dr., 918/459-2739

Best Burgers
Burger Street
  6151 E. 51st St., 918/664-1774
  2107 S. Harvard Ave., 918/747-3711
  7445 E. Admiral Pl., 918/838-7605
  4919 S. Peoria Ave., 918/744-0427
Ron's Hamburgers
  multiple locations

Best Chinese Food
Great Wall Restaurant
  7105 S. Yale Ave., 918/494-8652

Royal Dragon
  7837 E. 51st St., 918/664-2245

Best Coffee/Coffeehouse
Java Dave's Coffee
  6239 E. Fifteenth St., 918/836-7317
  3310 S. Peoria Ave., 918/744-5317
  8013D S. Sheridan Rd., 918/492-8317
  427 S. Boston Ave., 918/587-3317
  1326 E. Fifteenth St., 918/592-3317

Best Continental Food
Bistro at Brookside
  3523 S. Peoria Ave., 918/749-7737
Cardigan's in London Square
  5800 S. Lewis Ave., 918/749-9070

Best Delicatessen
Boston Deli
  6231 E. 61st St., 918/582-3353
Margaret's German Restaurant and Deli
  5107 S. Sheridan Rd., 918/622-3747
New York Bagel Shop and Deli
  1344 E. 41st St., 918/744-1100
  7125 S. Yale Ave., 918/491-6886
  1520 E. Fifteenth St., 918/587-7600

Best Desserts
Sourdough Sam's
  Fontana Center, 7877 E. 51st St., 918/663-0717
Spaghetti Warehouse
  221 E. Brady St., 918/587-4440

Best Diner
Phill's Diner
  3310 E. 32nd St., 918/742-4563
Route 66 Downtown Diner
  402 E. Second St., 918/587-6662

Best Fine Dining
Capistrano Rotisserie Cafe
  1748 Utica Sq., 918/747-2819
The Polo Grill
  2038 Utica Sq., 918/744-4280
Wild Fork
  1820 Utica Sq., 918/742-0712

Best German Food
Margaret's German Restaurant and Deli
  5107 S. Sheridan Rd., 918/622-3747
Ursula's Bavarian Inn
  4932 E. 91st St., Ste. 109, 918/496-8282

Best Health-Conscious Menu
Akin's Natural Foods Market
  7807 E. 51st St., 918/663-4137
  3321 E. 31st St., 918/742-6630
Be Le Vegetarian Restaurant
  3121 S. Mingo Rd., 918/664-0292
Big Al's Subs and Health Foods
  3303 E. Fifteenth St., 918/744-5085

Best Homestyle Food
Amish Essen Haus Restaurant
 14002 E. 21st St., 918/438-4558
Amish Kitchen
 1111 W. Seventeenth St., 918/582-1607
Betty Ann's Restaurant
 4401 S. Memorial Dr., 918/663-8269
Black-Eyed Pea
 3118 S. Garnett Rd., 918/665-7435
Nelson's Buffeteria
 514 S. Boston Ave., 918/584-9969
Ollie's Restaurant
 4070 Southwest Blvd., 918/446-0524
Ty's Restaurant
 5001 N. Peoria Ave., 918/425-3651

Best Ice Cream/Yogurt
I Can't Believe It's Yogurt
 3807A S. Peoria Ave., 918/744-5056

Best Indian Food
India Palace
 6963 S. Lewis Ave., 918/492-8040

Best Italian Food
Mondo's Italian Restaurant
 5960 S. Lewis Ave., 918/749-2233
 6746 S. Memorial Dr., 918/254-7778
Tucci's Cafe Italia
 1344 E. Fifteenth St., 918/582-3456
Zio's Italian Kitchen
 7111 S. Mingo Rd., 918/250-5999

Best Mexican Food
Cafe Ole
 3509 S. Peoria Ave., 918/745-6699
Mexicali Border Cafe
 14 W. Brady St., 918/582-3383
 7104 S. Sheridan Rd., Ste. 9, 918/481-1114
Pepper's Restaurant and Club
 1950 Utica Sq., 918/749-2163
 6175 E. 61st St., 918/494-0592

Best Middle Eastern Food
Eddy's Steakhouse
 3510 E. 31st St., 918/742-5212

Best Outdoor Dining
Full Moon Cafe
 1525 E. Fifteenth St., 918/583-6666

Best Pizza
Hideaway Pizza
 8204 S. Harvard Ave., 918/492-4777
 1503 E. Fifteenth St., 918/582-4777
Uno Chicago Bar and Grill
 8221 E. 61st St., 918/254-6611

Best Seafood
Atlantic Sea Grill
 8321A E. 61st St., 918/252-7966
Bodean Seafood Restaurant
 3323 E. 51st St., 918/743-3861

O

Landry's Seafood House
7646 E. 61st St., 918/252-1010
S and J Oyster Company
3301 S. Peoria Ave., 918/744-4440

Best Steaks
Eddy's Steakhouse
3510 E. 31st St., 918/742-5212
Silver Flame Steak and Seafood
6100 S. Sheridan Rd., 918/496-3311

Best Tea Room
Tea Cup
409 E. A St., Jenks, 918/299-8204

Best Thai Food
Thai-Siam Restaurant
6380 E. 31st St., 918/622-7667

Best Vietnamese Food
Minh Vietnamese Restaurant
10032 S. Sheridan Rd., 918/299-9061
Ri Le's
3206 S. Yale Ave., 918/747-3205
4932 E. 91st St., 918/496-2126

WOODWARD, OK

Best Barbecue/Ribs
Rib Ranch
2424 Williams Ave., 580/256-6081

Best Burgers
JB Steakhouse
225 E. Main St., 580/256-4845
West Side Restaurant
2329 Oklahoma Ave., 580/256-6992

Best Homestyle Food
Polly Anna Cafe
902 Main St., 580/256-9037

Best Ice Cream/Yogurt
Braum's Ice Cream and Dairy
2403 Williams Ave., 580/256-4630

Best Sandwiches
Chicken Roscoe's
1023 Main St., 580/254-2149

Best Steaks
JB Steakhouse
225 E. Main St., 580/256-4845

Oregon

ALBANY, OR

Best American Food
The Buzz Saw Restaurant and Lounge
 421 Water Ave. NE, 541/928-0642

Best Delicatessen
The Wine Depot and Deli
 300 Second Ave. SW, 541/967-9499

Best Italian Food
Capriccio's Ristorante
 442 First Ave. W., 541/924-9932
Pastabilities
 250 Broadalbin St. SW, 541/924-9235

Best Mexican Food
Los Dos Amigos
 1402 Pacific Blvd. SE, 541/928-5363

Best Other Ethnic Food
Novak's Hungarian Restaurant (Hungarian)
 2835 Santiam Hwy. SE, 541/967-9488

Best Seafood
Depot Cafe
 822 Lyon St. S., 541/926-7326

ASHLAND, OR

Best Casual Dining
Greenleaf Restaurant
 49 N. Main St., 541/482-2808

Best Chinese Food
Jade Dragon
 2270 Ashland St., 541/482-8220

Best Coffee/Coffeehouse
Beanery
  1602 Ashland St., 541/488-0700

Best Diner
Alex's Plaza Restaurant and Bar
  35 N. Main St., 541/482-8818

Best Dinner
Firefly Restaurant
  15 N. First St., 541/488-3212

Best Eclectic Menu
Firefly Restaurant
  15 N. First St., 541/488-3212

Best Fine Dining
Chateaulin Restaurant Francais
  50 E. Main St., 541/482-2264
Cucina Biazzi
  568 E. Main St., 541/488-3739
Firefly Restaurant
  15 N. First St., 541/488-3212
Monet Restaurant
  36 S. Second St., 541/482-1339
Primavera
  241 Hargadine St., 541/488-1994
Winchester Country Inn
  35 S. Second St., 541/488-1115

Best French Food
Chateaulin Restaurant Francais
  50 E. Main St., 541/482-2264

Best Italian Food
Il Giardino
  5 Granite St., 541/488-0816
Martino's Restaurant and Bar
  58 E. Main St., 541/488-4420

Best Lunch
Bento Express
  3 Granite St., 541/488-3582
Munchies Restaurant
  59 N. Main St., 541/488-2967

Best Outdoor Dining
Greenleaf Restaurant
  49 N. Main St., 541/482-2808
Winchester Country Inn
  35 S. Second St., 541/488-1115

Best Romantic Dining
Cucina Biazzi
  568 E. Main St., 541/488-3739
Firefly Restaurant
  15 N. First St., 541/488-3212

Best Thai Food
Jade Dragon
  2270 Ashland St., 541/482-8220
Thai Pepper
  84 N. Main St., 541/482-8058

ASTORIA, OR

Best American Food
Andrew and Steve's Cafe
1196 Marine Dr., 503/325-5762
Pier 11 Feedstore Restaurant
7711 Eleventh St., 503/325-0279

Best Breakfast
Pig and Pancake
146 W. Bond St., 503/325-3144

Best Chinese Food
House of Chan
159 W. Bond St., 503/325-7289

Best Other Ethnic Food
The Ship Inn (English)
1 Second St., 503/325-0033

BANDON, OR

Best Breakfast
Minute Cafe
145 N. Second St., 541/347-2707

Best French Food
Christophe
3235 Beach Loop Rd., 541/347-3261

Best Restaurant Meal Value
Harp's Restaurant
480 First St., 541/347-9057
Sea Star Guesthouse
370 First St., 541/347-9632

Best Seafood
Bandon Boatworks Restaurant
275 Lincoln Ave. SW, 541/347-2111
Harp's Restaurant
480 First St., 541/347-9057

Best View While Dining
Lord Bennett's Restaurant
1695 Beach Loop Dr., 541/347-3663

BEND, OR

Best Breakfast
West Side Cafe and Bakery
1005 NW Galveston Ave., 541/382-3426

Best Brewpub
Bend Brewing Company
1019 NW Brooks St., 541/383-1599
Deschutes Brewery
1044 NW Bond St., 541/382-9242

Best Burger
Bend Brewing Company
1019 NW Brooks St., 541/383-1599

Best Chinese Food
Eddie's Canton
909 NW Bond St., 541/389-5154

O

Best Coffee/Coffeehouse
Central Coffeehouse and Roastery
601 NE First St., 541/382-6349
Eastside Coffeehouse
E. Hwy. 20, 541/330-1642
Westside Coffeehouse
1075 NW Newport Ave., 541/383-0873

Best Health-Conscious Menu
Baja Norte
801 NW Wall St., 541/385-0611

Best Italian Food
Ernesto's Italian Restaurant
1203 NE Third St., 541/389-7274

Best Japanese Food
Yoko's Japanese Restaurant
1028 NW Bond St., 541/382-2999

Best Lunch
Wild Onion
163 NW Minnesota Ave., 541/389-2025

Best Mexican Food
Baja Norte
801 NW Wall St., 541/385-0611
Mexicali Rose
301 NE Franklin Ave., 541/389-0149

Best Outdoor Dining
Baja Norte
801 NW Wall St., 541/385-0611
Bend Brewing Company
1019 NW Brooks St., 541/383-1599

Best Pizza
John Dough's Pizza
35 SW Century Dr., 541/382-3645

Best Restaurant Meal Value
Baja Norte
801 NW Wall St., 541/385-0611

Best Seafood
Kayo's
61363 S. Hwy. 97, 541/389-1400
McKenzie's Restaurant
1033 NW Bond St., 541/388-3891

Best Thai Food
Toomie's Thai Cuisine
119 NW Minnesota Ave., 541/388-5590

BROOKINGS, OR

Best Casual Dining
Wharfside Seafood Restaurant
16362 Lower Harbor Rd., Harbor, 541/469-7316

Best Desserts
Hog Wild Cafe and Catering
16158 Hwy. 101S, 541/469-8869

Best Mexican Food
Los Amigos
  541 Chetco Ave., 541/469-4102

Best Sandwiches
The Tea Room
  434 Redwood St., 541/469-7240

BURNS, OR

Best Bar
Central Pastime
  211 N. Broadway Ave., 541/573-6261
Palace Cafe
  260 N. Broadway Ave., 541/573-6636

Best Breakfast
Palace Cafe
  260 N. Broadway Ave., 541/573-6636
Ye Olde Castle
  186 W. Monroe St., 541/573-6601

Best Chinese Food
Hilander Restaurant
  195 N. Broadway Ave., 541/573-2111

Best Other Ethnic Food
Steen's Mountain Cafe (Basque)
  195 N. Alder Ave., 541/573-7226

Best Pizza
Central Pastime
  211 N. Broadway Ave., 541/573-6261
Windmill Pizza Company
  673 W. Monroe St., 541/573-5421

Best Sandwiches
Wayside Delicatessen
  530 N. Broadway Ave., 541/573-7020

Best Seafood
Burns Power House Restaurant
  305 E. Monroe St., 541/573-9060
Pine Room Cafe
  543 W. Monroe St., 541/573-6631

Best Steaks
Burns Power House Restaurant
  305 E. Monroe St., 541/573-9060
Pine Room Cafe
  543 W. Monroe St., 541/573-6631

Best Thai Food
Elkhorn Club Restaurant and Lounge
  457 N. Broadway Ave., 541/573-3201

COOS BAY, OR

Best Beer Selection
Bank Brewing Company
  201 Central Ave., 541/267-0963
Blue Heron Bistro
  100 Commercial Ave., 541/267-3933

Best Burgers
Bay Burger Inn
  1175 Newmark Ave., 541/888-3688

Best Chinese Food
Kum-Yon's
  835 S. Broadway, 541/269-2662

Best Coffee/Coffeehouse
Kaffe 101
  134 S. Broadway, 541/267-4894

Best Family Restaurant
Little Richard's
  581 N. Bayshore Dr., 541/267-7711
Sea Basket
  Small Boat Basin, 541/888-5711
Timber Inn Restaurant
  1001 N. Bayshore Dr., 541/267-4622

Best Italian Food
Benetti's Italian Restaurant
  260 S. Broadway, 541/267-6066

Best Mexican Food
Playa del Sol
  525 Newport Hwy. 101, 541/469-4102
Puerto Vallarta
  230 S. Second St., 541/269-0919

Best Pizza
Papa Murphy's
  880 Ingersoll St., 541/269-9700

Best Sandwiches
Blue Heron Bistro
  100 Commercial Ave., 541/267-3933

Best Seafood
Cheryn's Seafood
  5102 Cape Arago Hwy., Charleston, 541/888-3251
Portside Restaurant
  8001 Kingfisher Rd., 541/888-5544

CORVALLIS, OR

Best Delicatessen
Old World Deli
  341 SW Second St., 541/752-8549

Best Pizza
Woodstock's Pizza Parlor
  1045 NW Kings Blvd., 541/752-5151

Best Restaurant in Town
Bombs Away Cafe
  2527 NW Monroe Ave., 541/757-7221
China Delight
  325 NW Fifteenth St., 541/753-0791
Michael's Landing
  603 NW Second St., 541/754-6141

Best Seafood
McGrath's Fish House
  350 NE Circle Blvd., 541/752-3474

The Gables Restaurant
  1121 NW Ninth St., 541/752-3364

Best Vegetarian Food
Nearly Normal's
  109 NW Fifteenth St., 541/753-0791

EUGENE, OR

Best Atmosphere
Adams Place
  30 E. Broadway, 541/344-6948
Ambrosia Restaurant and Bar
  174 E. Broadway, 541/342-4141
Piccolo's Restaurant
  999 Willamette St., 541/484-4011

Best Barbecue/Ribs
West Brothers Barbecue
  844 Olive St., 541/345-8489

Best Breakfast
French Horn Cafe and Bakery
  1591 Willamette St., 541/343-7473
Glenwood Restaurant
  2588 Willamette St., 541/687-8201
  1340 Alder St., 541/687-0355
The Original Pancake House
  782 E. Broadway, 541/343-7523

Best Brewpub
Field's Restaurant and Brewpub
  1290 Oak St., 541/341-6599
High Street Brewery and Cafe
  1243 High St., 541/345-4905
Steelhead Brewery and Cafe
  199 E. Fifth Ave., 541/686-2739
Wild Duck Brewery
  169 W. Sixth Ave., 541/485-3825

Best Chinese Food
Ocean Sky
  1601 Chambers St., 541/342-4848

Best Coffee/Coffeehouse
Full City Coffee Roasters
  842 Pearl St., 541/344-0475

Best Continental Food
Valley River Inn
  1000 Valley River Way, 541/687-0123

Best French Food
Chanterelle
  207 E. Fifth Ave., 541/484-4065

Best Ice Cream/Yogurt
Geppetto's Ice Cream
  861 Willamette St., 541/343-2621
Sweet Treats
  1605 E. Nineteenth Ave., 541/344-4418

Best Italian Food
Mazzi's Italian Food
  3377 E. Amazon Dr., 541/687-2252

O

Original Joe's Restaurant
21 W. Sixth Ave., 541/485-4820

Best Mexican Food
Tres Hermanas
99 W. Broadway, 541/342-4058

Best Pizza
Izzy's Pizza Restaurant
730 E. Broadway, 541/484-2919
210 Division Ave., 541/689-6443
Mona Lizza
830 Olive St., 541/345-1072
Pegasus Smokehouse Pizza
790 E. Fourteenth Ave., 541/344-4471

Best Sandwiches
Hawthorne's Cafe and Deli
153 E. Broadway, 541/683-0783
Rosewater's Deli and Catering
44 W. Broadway, 541/485-4342
Wild Rose Food Company
296 E. Fifth Ave., 541/484-7302

Best Seafood
Oscar's Garden Cafe
66 E. Sixth Ave., 541/342-2000

Best Steaks
Oregon Electric Station
27 E. Fifth Ave., 541/485-4444

Best Thai Food
Mekala's
296 E. Fifth Ave., 541/342-4872

FLORENCE, OR

Best Breakfast
Blue Hen Cafe
1675 Hwy. 101, 541/997-3907

Best Burgers
Blue Hen Cafe
1675 Hwy. 101, 541/997-3907

Best Casual Dining
Traveler's Cove
1362 Bay St., 541/997-6845

Best View While Dining
Surfside Restaurant and Lounge
Driftwood Shores Hotel, 88416 First Ave., 541/997-8263

GRANTS PASS, OR

Best Brewpub
The Brewery
509 G St. SW, 541/479-9850
Wild River Brewing and Pizza Company
595 NE E St., 541/471-7487

Best Coffee/Coffeehouse
Java House
412 NW Sixth St., 541/471-1922

Best French Food
Legrand's Restaurant and Bakery
  323 NE E St., 541/471-1554

Best Mexican Food
Si Casa Flores Mexican Restaurant
  1632 Williams Hwy., 541/474-7198

Best Pizza
Wild River Brewing and Pizza Company
  595 NE E St., 541/471-7487

Best Restaurant in Town
Genessee Place
  201 SW G St., 541/955-8845
Hamilton House Restaurant
  344 NE Terry Ln., 541/479-3938
Heaven and Earth Restaurant
  Wolf Creek Inn, 100 Front St., Wolf Creek,
541/866-2474
The Black Swan
  Paradise Resort, 7000 Monument Dr., 541/479-
4333
The Yankee Pot Roast
  720 NW Sixth St., 541/476-0551

Best Sandwiches
Powderhorn Cafe
  321 NE Sixth St., 541/479-9403

Best Vegetarian Food
Sunshine Natural Food Cafe
  128 SW H St., 541/474-5044

O

KLAMATH FALLS, OR

Best Coffee/Coffeehouse
Renaldo's Cafe Espresso
  2350 Dahlia St., 541/884-3846

Best French Food
Chez Nous
  3927 S. Sixth St., 541/883-8719

Best Italian Food
Fiorella's Italian Restaurant
  6139 Simmers Ave., 541/882-1878

Best Mexican Food
Maria's of Keno
  2424 Shasta Way, 541/884-0787
Sergio's Mexican Restaurant
  4650 S. Sixth St., 541/885-6885
  430 Main St., 541/883-8454

Best Steaks
Diamond Grille
  4480 S. Sixth St., 541/884-0743

Best Sunday Brunch
Shiloh's Restaurant and Lounge
  2500 Almond St., 541/885-7977

LA GRANDE, OR

Best Barbecue/Ribs
Smokehouse Restaurant
  2208 Adams Ave., 541/963-9692

Best Coffee/Coffeehouse
Highway 30 Coffee Company
  1103B Washington Ave., 541/963-6821

Best Homestyle Food
Farm House Family Restaurant
  401 Adams Ave., 541/963-9318

Best Mexican Food
Mamacita's
  110 Depot St., 541/963-6223

Best Pizza
Klondike Pizza
  2104 Island Ave., 541/963-0994
  2610 Bearco, 541/963-4949

Best Sandwiches
Cock and Bull Villa Roma
  1414 Adams Ave., 541/963-0573

Best Seafood
Ten Depot Street
  10 Depot St., 541/963-8766

Best Steaks
Wrangler Steakhouse
  1914 Adams Ave., 541/963-3131

LINCOLN CITY, OR

Best French Food
Chez Jeannette
  7150 Old Hwy. 101, Gleneden Beach, 541/764-3434

Best Seafood
Bay House
  5911 SW Hwy. 101, 541/996-3222
Shilo Inn Restaurant and Lounge
  1501 NW 40th Pl., 541/994-5255
Surfrider Resort
  3115 NW Hwy. 101, Depoe Bay, 541/764-2311
Tidal Raves
  279 N. Hwy. 101, Depoe Bay, 541/765-2995

Best Vegetarian Food
Noodle
  2185 NW Hwy. 101, 541/994-8800

Best View While Dining
The Inn at Spanish Head
  4009 SW Hwy. 101, 541/996-2161
Tidal Raves
  279 N. Hwy. 101, Depoe Bay, 541/765-2995
Whale Cove Inn
  2345 S. Hwy. 101, Depoe Bay, 541/765-2255

Best Wine Selection
The Dining Room
  Salishan Lodge, 7760 Hwy. 101N, Gleneden Beach,

541/764-2371
The Sunroom
  Salishan Lodge, 7760 Hwy. 101N, Gleneden Beach,
541/764-2371

MEDFORD, OR

Best Fine Dining
Jacksonville Inn
  175 E. California St., Jacksonville, 541/899-1900
McCulley House Inn
  240 E. California St., Jacksonville, 541/899-1942

Best Italian Food
Rudolfo's Italian Garden Cafe
  703 E. Main St., 541/773-1421

Best Mexican Food
Senoir Sam's Mexican Grill
  959 Medford Center Dr., 541/734-3299
  1234 S. Riverside Ave., 541/857-0621

Best Other Ethnic Food
Samovar Russian Restaurant (Russian)
  101 E. Main St., 541/779-4967

Best Restaurant in Town
Bel Di's
  21900 Hwy. 62, Shady Cove, 541/878-2010
Genessee Place
  203 Genessee St., 541/772-5581

Best Steaks
Hungry Woodsman
  2001 N. Pacific Hwy., 541/772-2050

Best Thai Food
Ali's Thai Kitchen
  2392 N. Pacific Hwy., 541/770-3104

NEWPORT, OR

Best Beer Selection
Bayfront Brewery and Public House
  748 SW Bay Blvd., 541/265-3188

Best Chinese Food
Kum-Yon's
  1006 SW Coast Hwy., 541/265-5330

Best Lunch
Canyon Way Bookstore and Restaurant
  1216 SW Canyon Way, 541/265-8319
Champagne Patio
  1630 N. Coast Hwy., 541/265-3044

Best Pizza
At's Pizza
  352 SW Ninth St., 541/265-6000
Izzy's Pizza Restaurant
  5251 N. Coast Hwy., 541/265-3636

Best Vegetarian Food
Whale's Tale Restaurant
  452 SW Bay Blvd., 541/265-8660

O

NORTH BEND, OR

Best Breakfast
Pancake Mill Restaurant
  23900 Tremont St., 541/756-2751

Best Burgers
Leon's
  1120 Virginia Ave., 541/756-1914

Best Chinese Food
Ming Palace
  3480 Tremont St., 541/756-2537

Best Family Restaurant
Pony Village Motor Lodge
  Virginia Ave., 541/756-3191
Virginia Street Diner
  1430 Virginia St., 541/756-3475

Best Mexican Food
Los Dos Amigos
  1611 Virginia Ave., 541/756-4799

Best Pizza
Gino's Pizza Inn
  1324 Virginia Ave., 541/756-5000

Best Restaurant Meal Value
Bay View Cafe
  The Mill Casino and Resort, 3201 Tremont St.,
541/756-8800

Best Steaks
Hilltop House
  166 N. Bay Dr., 541/756-4160

PENDLETON, OR

Best Breakfast
Kopper Kitchen Restaurant
  319 SE Nye Ave., 541/278-0678

Best Burgers
A and R Burger Island
  912 SE Emigrant Ave., 541/276-3352

Best Chinese Food
Golden Fountain
  437 S. Main St., 541/276-6130
Lee's Cafe
  502 SW Emigrant Ave., 541/276-5819

Best Fine Dining
Raphael's Restaurant and Catering
  233 SE Fourth St., 541/276-8500

Best Homestyle Food
Circle S Barbecue
  210 SE Fifth St., 541/276-9637

Best Pizza
Big John's Hometown Pizza
  225 SW Ninth St., 541/276-0550

Best Sandwiches
USA Subs
  1004 SW Court Ave., 541/278-7827

Best Steaks
Cimmiyotti's
137 S. Main St., 541/276-4314

PORTLAND, OR

Best Bistro
28 East
40 NE 28th Ave., 503/235-9060
Cafe Des Amis
1987 NW Kearney St., 503/295-6487

Best Breakfast
Bijou Cafe
132 S.W. Third Ave., 503/222-3187
Bread and Ink Cafe
3610 SE Hawthorne Blvd., 503/239-4756
Chez What Cafe
2904 NE Alberta St., 503/281-1717
Original Pancake House
8600 SW Barbur Blvd., 503/246-9007

Best Burgers
Bread and Ink Cafe
3610 SE Hawthorne Blvd., 503/239-4756
Hamburger Mary's
239 SW Broadway, 503/223-0900
Kupie Cone Drive-In
3835 SE Holgate Blvd., 503/775-3890

Best Casual Dining
Hawthorne Street Cafe
3354 SE Hawthorne Blvd., 503/232-4982

Best Chinese Food
Fong Chong and Company
301 NW Fourth Ave., 503/220-0235

Best Coffee/Coffeehouse
Papaccino's
8421 SW Terwilliger Blvd., 503/452-8859
4441 SE Woodstock Blvd., 503/771-2825

Best Desserts
Papa Haydn
5829 SE Milwaukie Ave., 503/232-9440
Papa Haydn West
701 NW 23rd Ave., 503/228-7317

Best Eclectic Menu
Three Doors Down Cafe
1429 SE 37th Ave., 503/236-6886
Zefiro Restaurant
500 NW 21st Ave., 503/226-3394

Best French Food
Couvron
1126 SW Eighteenth Ave., 503/225-1844
Heathman Restaurant and Bar
Heathman Hotel, 1001 SW Broadway, 503/241-4100
L' Auberge Restaurant
2601 NW Vaughn St., 503/223-3302

O

Best Health-Conscious Menu
Old Wives' Tales Restaurant
 1300 E. Burnside St., 503/238-0470

Best Ice Cream/Yogurt
Simply Irresistible
 1620 SE Bybee Blvd., 503/231-2960

Best Inexpensive Meal
Saigon Kitchen
 3829 SE Division St., 503/236-2312
 835 NE Broadway St., 503/281-3669

Best Italian Food
Alessandro's
 301 SW Morrison St., 503/242-2515
Assaggio
 7742 SE Thirteenth Ave., 503/232-6151
Davinci's
 12615 SE McLoughlin Blvd., 503/659-3547
Genoa Restaurant
 2832 SE Belmont St., 503/238-1464
Pazzo Ristorante
 627 SW Washington St., 503/228-1515
Rustica Italian Cafe
 1700 NE Broadway St., 503/288-0990

Best Japanese Food
Hokkaido
 6744 NE Sandy Blvd., 503/288-3731

Best Lunch
Bread and Ink Cafe
 3610 SE Hawthorne Blvd., 503/239-4756

Best Mexican Food
El Palenque Mexican Restaurant
 8324 SE Seventeenth Ave., 503/231-5140
Esparza's Tex-Mex Cafe
 2725 SE Ankeny St., 530/234-7909

Best Other Ethnic Food
Jarra's Ethiopian Restaurant (Ethiopian)
 1435 SE Hawthorne Blvd., 503/230-8990
Marrakesh Moroccan Restaurant (Moroccan)
 1201 NW 21st Ave., 503/248-9442

Best Pizza
Oasis Cafe
 3701 SE Hawthorne Blvd., 503/231-0901
Old Town Pizza
 226 NW Davis St., 503/222-9999

Best Regional Food
Atwater's Restaurant and Lounge
 111 SW Fifth Ave., Ste. 30, 503/275-3600
Higgins Restaurant
 1239 SW Broadway, 503/222-9070
Paley's Place
 1204 NW 21st Ave., 503/243-2403
Wildwood Restaurant and Bar
 1221 NW 21st Ave., 503/248-9663

Best Romantic Dining
Higgins Restaurant
1239 SW Broadway, 503/222-9070

Best Sandwiches
Woodstock Wine and Deli
4030 SE Woodstock Blvd., 503/777-2208

Best Seafood
Jake's Famous Crawfish
401 SW Twelfth Ave., 503/226-1419
Winterborne Restaurant
3520 NE 42nd Ave., 503/249-8486

Best Spanish Food
Fernando's Hideaway
824 SW First Ave., 503/248-4709

Best Sports Bar
The Kingston Saloon
2021 SW Morrison St., 503/224-2115

Best Steaks
McCormick and Schmick's
235 SW First Ave., 503/224-7522

Best Vietnamese Food
Saigon Kitchen
3829 SE Division St., 503/236-2312
835 NE Broadway St., 503/281-3669

Best View While Dining
Avalon Grill
4630 SW Macadam Ave., 503/227-4630
Old Spaghetti Factory
715 SW Bancroft Terrace, 503/222-5375
Salty's
3839 NE Marine Dr., 503/288-4444

Best Wine Selection
Woodstock Wine and Deli
4030 SE Woodstock Blvd., 503/777-2208

O

ROSEBURG, OR

Best Breakfast
Old Town Cafe
527 SE Jackson St., 541/440-4901
Sandpiper Restaurant
1450 NW Mulholland Dr., 541/673-0021

Best Brewpub
Umpqua Brewing Company
328 SE Jackson St., 541/672-0452

Best Burgers
Jersey Lilly
1430 Dee St., 541/672-9131

Best Chinese Food
China Palace
968 NE Stephens St., 541/672-8899
Kowloon Restaurant
2686 NE Diamond Lake Blvd., 541/673-0095

Best Coffee/Coffeehouse
Cafe Espresso
  368 SE Jackson St., 541/672-1859

Best Fine Dining
Brandy's Restaurant
  2566 NE Stephens St., 541/673-3721

Best German Food
Teske's Germania Restaurant
  647 SE Jackson St., 541/672-5401

Best Ice Cream/Yogurt
Gay 90's Ice Cream Parlor and Deli
  925 W. Harvard Ave., 541/672-5679

Best Mexican Food
Los Dos Amigos
  1390 NE Stephens St., 541/957-0409
  537 SE Jackson St., 541/673-1351

Best Pizza
Little Pizza Paradise
  20069 N. Umpqua Hwy., Glide, 541/496-3818
Round Table Pizza
  2040 NW Stewart Pkwy., 541/673-2047

Best Restaurant in Town
Del Rey Cafe
  5669 Murphy Stevens Rd., 541/672-1522
Kowloon Restaurant
  2686 NE Diamond Lake Blvd., 541/673-0095
Sandpiper Restaurant
  1450 NW Mulholland Dr., 541/672-8633
The Owl Restaurant
  2011 NE Stephens St., 541/672-3904

Best Sandwiches
Between the Buns Sandwich Shop
  214 SE Jackson St., 541/672-8633
  250 NE Garden Valley Blvd. - Ste. 18, 541/672-0342

Best Steaks
Beef and Brew
  2060 Stewart Pkwy., 541/673-8030

Best Thai Food
House of Siam
  2521 W. Harvard Ave., 541/673-8357

Best Vietnamese Food
Saigon Restaurant
  719 SE Jackson St., 541/440-6658

SALEM, OR

Best American Food
Eola Inn
  4250 Dallas Hwy. NW, 503/378-7521

Best Barbecue/Ribs
Jackie's Ribs
  3404 Commercial St. SE, 503/399-7464
  2155 Silverton Rd. NE, 503/371-7339

Best Breakfast
Original Pancake House
4685 Portland Rd. NE, 503/393-9124
4656 Commercial St. SE, 503/378-0431

Best Brewpub
Cascade Microbrewery
3529 Fairview Industrial Dr. SE, 503/378-0737

Best Burgers
Rock-n-Rogers
3135 Commercial St. SE, 503/315-8467
1405 Broadway St. NE, 503/364-5734
3235 Market St. NE, 503/362-5517
Tropical Cafe Beach
2653 Commercial St. SE, 503/362-1100

Best Continental Food
Inn at Orchard Heights
695 Orchard Heights Rd. NW, 503/378-1780

Best Desserts
Gerry Frank's Konditorei
310 Kearney St. SE, 503/585-7070

Best Dinner
Off Center Cafe
1741 Center St. NE, 503/363-9245

Best Health-Conscious Menu
Arbour Cafe
380 High St. NE, 503/588-2353
Heritage Tree
574 Cottage St. NE, 503/399-7075

Best Indian Food
India Palace
377 Court St. NE, 503/371-4808

Best Inexpensive Meal
Golden Crown Restaurant
365 Liberty St. NE, 503/362-9560

Best Italian Food
Alessandro's
325 High St. SE, 503/370-9951

Best Lunch
Off Center Cafe
1741 Center St. NE, 503/363-9245

Best Mexican Food
La Margarita Company Restaurant
545 Ferry St. SE, 503/362-8861

Best Outdoor Dining
Ram Border Cafe and Sports Bar
515 Twelfth St. SE, 503/363-1904

Best Pizza
Izzy's Pizza Restaurant
2205 Lancaster Dr. NE, 503/399-0915
2990 Commercial St. SE, 503/581-9831
3400 River Rd. N., 503/390-5002
Locomotion Pizza
4550 Commercial St. SE, 503/364-3004

O

Best Restaurant in Town
Morton's Bistro Northwest
   1128 Edgewater St. NW, 503/585-1113
Off Center Cafe
   1741 Center St. NE, 503/363-9245

Best Seafood
Jonathan's Oyster Bar
   445 State St., 503/362-7219
McGrath's Fish House
   831 Lancaster Dr. NE, 503/362-6729
   350 Chemeketa St. NE, 503/362-0736

Best Steaks
Holly House
   2025 Golf Course Rd. S., 503/399-0449
Night Deposit
   195 Commercial St. NE, 503/585-5588

Best Thai Food
Thai Cuisine
   4140 River Rd. N., 503/393-6216

Best Vietnamese Food
Kwan Original Cuisine
   835 Commercial St. SE, 503/362-7711

Best View While Dining
Eola Inn
   4250 Dallas Hwy. NW, 503/378-7521

THE DALLES, OR

Best Casual Dining
Tugboat Annie's
   1100 E. Marina Way, Hood River, 541/386-7999

Best Fine Dining
Ole's Supper Club
   2620 W. Second St., 541/296-6708
Stonehedge Inn
   3405 Cascade Ave., Hood River, 541/386-3940

Best Mexican Food
Casa El Mirador
   302 W. Second St., 541/298-7388

Best Sunday Brunch
O' Callahan's
   The Shilo Inn, 3223 Bret Clodfelter Way, 541/298-8225

YACHATS, OR

Best Sandwiches
Yankee Clipper Sandwich Company
   125 Ocean Dr., 541/547-4004

Best Seafood
La Serre Restaurant
   160 W. Second at Beach St., 541/547-3420

Best Steaks
The Adobe Resort and Restaurant
   1555 Hwy. 101, 541/547-3141

Best View While Dining
The Adobe Resort and Restaurant
  1555 Hwy. 101, 541/547-3141

Best Wine Selection
La Serre Restaurant
  Second at Beach St., 541/547-3420

O

Pennsylvania

Best Bar
T.K.'s Corral
  801 N. Fifteenth St., 610/437-3970

Best Breakfast
Brass Rail Restaurant
  1137 W. Hamilton St., 610/434-9383
  3015 Lehigh St., 610/797-1927

Best Chinese Food
China House
  4783 W. Tilghman St., 610/395-1855
Mandarin House South
  3025 W. Emmaus Ave., 610/791-2000

Best Family Restaurant
Your Place Restaurant
  2035 Downyflake Ln., 610/791-4819

Best Fine Dining
Ambassador Restaurant
  3750 Hamilton Blvd., 610/432-2025
Manor House Inn
  4508 Old Bethlehem Pike, Center Valley,
    610/865-8166

Best Ice Cream/Yogurt
Ice Cream World
  3512 Hamilton Blvd., 610/439-8591

Best Italian Food
Carmen's Italian Family Restaurant
  1125 Third St., Catasauqua, 610/266-2626

P

Best Mexican Food
Pancho and Sonny's
  2073 31st St. SW, 610/797-9300

Best Middle Eastern Food
Beirut Restaurant
  651 Union Blvd., 610/437-4023
Damascus Restaurant
  449 N. Second St., 610/432-2036

Best Pizza
Dino's Pizza Restaurant
  3300 Lehigh St., 610/791-5107
Vito's Italian Delights
  704 W. Emmaus Ave., 610/791-9111

Best Sandwiches
Wally's Deli
  711 N. Seventeenth St., 610/435-7177

Best Seafood
Henry's Salt of the Sea
  1926 W. Allen St., 610/434-2628
Shanty Restaurant
  617 N. Nineteenth St., 610/398-1760

Best Steaks
Spice of Life
  1259 S. Cedar Crest Blvd., 610/821-8081

Best Thai Food
Bay Leaf Restaurant
  935 E. Hamilton St., 610/433-4211

P

ALTOONA, PA

Best Breakfast
Granny's Family Restaurant
  613 Valley View Blvd., 814/942-0491

Best Casual Dining
Lena's Cafe
  2000 Eighth Ave., 814/943-9655
Phoenix
  300 Fourth Ave., 814/946-8096
Zach's
  5820 Sixth Ave., 814/943-9479

Best Chinese Food
House of Chang Peking II
  601 Logan Blvd., 814/942-3322

Best Fine Dining
U. S. Hotel
  401 S. Juniata St., Hollidaysburg, 814/695-9924

Best Homestyle Food
Granny's Family Restaurant
  613 Valley View Blvd., 814/942-0491

Best Italian Food
Allegro Restaurant
  3926 Broad Ave., 814/946-5216
Finelli's Italian Villa
  1808 Fourth Ave., 814/943-8510

Best Lunch
Gingerbread Man
206 E. Plank Rd., 814/942-2511

Best Pizza
Brother's Pizza
1600 Ninth Ave., 814/942-7444

Best Place to Take the Kids
Chuck E. Cheese Pizza
3415 Pleasant Valley Blvd., 814/942-2410

Best Romantic Dining
The Laurel Room
Ramada Inn, 1 Sheraton Dr., 814/946-1631

Best Sandwiches
Original Italian Pizza
709 Fourth Ave., 814/942-9770
Tim's American Cafe
1600 Crawford Ave., 814/949-5841

Best Steaks
Hoss's Steak and Sea House
621 Valley View Blvd., 814/946-5115

BEAVER FALLS, PA

Best Barbecue/Ribs
Bert's Wooden Indian Bar-B-Que
308 Leopard Ln, Beaver, 724/774-7992
Boots
1420 Riverside Dr., Beaver, 412/728-8002

Best Breakfast
Pappan's Family Restaurant
1635 Third St., Beaver, 412/775-5914
1198 Mulberry St., Beaver, 412/774-7711

Best Burgers
Jerry's Curb Service
Riverside Dr., Beaver,412/774-4727

Best Casual Dining
Bert's Wooden Indian Bar-B-Que
308 Leopard Ln., West Bridgewater, 724/774-7992
Christy's
Rt. 65, Ellwood City, 412/752-1155
Dockers Restaurant and Tavern
500 Market St., Beaver, 412/774-7071

Best Family Restaurant
Eat N Park
Sheffield Rd. at 21st St., Aliquippa, 724/378-4400
Pappan's Family Restaurant
2527 Darlington Rd., 412/843-5813

Best Fine Dining
Wooden Angel
100 Leopard Ln., Beaver, 412/774-7880

Best Ice Cream/Yogurt
Bruster's Old Fashion Ice Cream and Yogurt
2569 Brandt School Rd., Wexford, 412/934-0840
1525 Riverside Dr., Beaver, 412/774-4155

P

Best Italian Food
DiPietro's
  10500 Perry Hwy., Wexford, 412/934-1050

Best Late-Night Food
Eat N Park
  Twelfth St. at Seventh Ave., 412/843-3750

Best Salad/Salad Bar
Hilltop Grill
  318 New York Ave., Rochester, 724/774-8665
Rick's Place
  3551 Darlington Rd., Darlington, 724/827-2004

Best Sandwiches
Wexford Post Office Deli and Catering
  120 Wexford Bayne Rd., Wexford, 412/935-3354

BETHLEHEM, PA

Best Breakfast
Hack's
  59 E. Broad St., 610/868-9997

Best Burgers
New Street Bridge Works
  Fourth St. at New St., 610/868-1313

Best Coffee/Coffeehouse
Confetti Cafe
  462 Main St., 610/861-7484

Best Desserts
The Cafe
  221 W. Broad St., 610/866-1686
Viennese Pastries Cafe
  500 Main St., 610/866-0112

Best Family Restaurant
Jack Creek Steakhouse
  1900 Catasauqua Rd., 610/264-8888

Best Italian Food
Cafe Luigi
  2915 Schoenersville Rd., 610/694-8853
Giovanni's Italian American Restaurant
  16 W. Broad St., 610/861-9246

Best Pizza
Penn Pizza
  554 N. New St., 610/866-3532

Best Seafood
Minsi Trail Inn
  626 Stefko Blvd., 610/691-5613
New Street Bridge Works
  Fourth St. at New St., 610/868-1313

Best Steaks
Candlelight Inn
  4431 Easton Ave., 610/691-7777
Minsi Trail Inn
  626 Stefko Blvd., 610/691-5613

P

Best Sunday Brunch
Krista's Restaurant
  Holiday Inn, 512 Hwy. 22, 610/866-5800
  Freemansburg, 610/867-3711

Best Thai Food
The Cafe
  221 W. Broad St., 610/866-1686

EASTON, PA

Best Breakfast
City Diner
  1601 S. 25th St. at Freemansburg Ave.,
    610/258-5526
H.W. Crossings
  3701 Nazareth Rd., 610/258-7599

Best Casual Dining
Supreme Court
  683 Walnut St., 610/258-5812

Best Ice Cream/Yogurt
Hartman's Two Family Restaurant
  5920 Sullivan Trail, Nazareth, 610/759-5217

Best Italian Food
Apollo Pizza Restaurant
  900 Walnut St., 610/258-6955
Hilltop Italian American
  204 W. Madison St., 610/253-9903

Best Seafood
Alan's Stockyard
  1600 N. Delaware Dr., 610/253-9371

Best Steaks
Keystone Steakhouse
  1200 Northampton St., 610/253-4640

P

ERIE, PA

Best Breakfast
Pie in the Sky Cafe
  463 W. Eighth St., 814/459-8638

Best Casual Dining
Maxi's Cafe
  Bel Aire Hotel Complex, 2800 W. Eighth St.,
    814/833-1116

Best Delicatessen
Tickles Deli
  17 W. Fourth St., 814/455-5718

Best Diner
Beaners
  26 N. Park Row, 814/455-4600

Best Ice Cream/Yogurt
Kaley's Korner Ice Cream
  1537 W. 38th St., 814/864-2772

Best Inexpensive Meal
Plymouth Tavern
  1109 State St., 814/453-6454

Best Italian Food
Martucci's Tavern
  2641 Myrtle St., 814/455-6564

Best Late-Night Dining
Dominick's Restaurant
  123 E. Twelfth St., 814/459-5781

Best Middle Eastern Food
Oasis Restaurant
  3 N. Park Row, 814/452-6111

Best Outdoor Dining
Elephant Bar and Restaurant
  2826 W. Eighth St., 814/838-3613
Pufferbelly Restaurant and Bar
  414 French St., 814/454-1557

Best Pizza
Valerio's Italian Restaurant
  3205 Pittsburgh Ave., 814/833-2959

Best Romantic Dining
Stonehouse Inn
  4753 W. Lake Rd., 814/838-9296

Best Steaks
Marketplace Grill
  319 State St., 814/455-7272

Best View While Dining
Smugglers' Wharf
  3 State St., 814/459-4273
Waterfront Seafood and Steak House
  4 State St., 814/459-0606

P

GETTYSBURG, PA

Best 24-Hour Restaurant
Lincoln Diner
  32 Carlisle St., 717/334-3900

Best Fine Dining
Dobbin House Tavern
  89 Steinwehr Ave., 717/334-2100
Herr Tavern and Public House
  900 Chambersburg Rd., 717/334-4332

Best French Food
Blue Parrot Bistro
  35 Chambersburg St., 717/337-3739

Best Regional Food
The Fairfield Inn
  15 Main Trail, Fairfield, 717/642-5410

GREENSBURG, PA

Best Business Lunch
Vista Plateau Dining Room
  Four Points Sheraton Hotel, 100 Sheraton Dr.,
  412/836-6060

Best Barbecue/Ribs
Bar-B-Que and Ale
  Rte. 30E, Latrobe, 724/539-7427

Best Italian Food
Rizzo's Malabar Inn
  Keener Dr., Crabtree, 724/836-4323

Best Mexican Food
Cozumel Restaurante Mexicano
  1145 E. Pittsburgh St., Greensburg, 724/836-2653

HARRISBURG, PA

Best Bar
Rod's Road House Cafe
  1031 Eisenhower Blvd., 717/939-9915

Best Barbecue/Ribs
Red Rabbit Drive-In
  Rural Route 4, Duncannon, 717/834-4696

Best Breakfast
Arches
  4125 N. Front St., 717/233-5891

Best Burgers
Colonial Park Diner
  4301 Jonestown Rd., 717/541-9794
Harris House Tavern
  3951 Union Deposit Rd., 717/564-4270

Best Chinese Food
The Bloom
  204 Walnut St., 717/238-8355

Best Coffee/Coffeehouse
Gingerbread Man
  12 E. Park Ctr., 717/564-4078

Best Fine Dining
Circular Dining Room
  Hotel Hershey, Hotel Rd., Hershey, 717/533-2171
Colony House Restaurant
  125 W. Main St., Mechanicsburg, 717/691-3131

Best Greek/Mediterranean Food
Al Mediterraneo
  288 E. Main St., Hummelstown, 717/566-5086

Best Health-Conscious Menu
Isaac's Deli
  4408 Oakhearst Blvd., 717/541-1111

Best Indian Food
Passage to India
  525 S. Front St., 717/233-1202

Best Mexican Food
Casa Chica Restaurant
  451 Swatara St., Steelton, 717/939-4907

Best Pizza
Zephyr Express
  400 N. Second St., 717/257-1328

Best Romantic Dining
Golden Sheaf
  1 N. Second St., 717/237-6400

P

Best Sandwiches
Sandwich Man
  5640 Allentown Blvd., 717/540-1818
  111 N. Second St., 717/236-7171

Best Seafood
Kosta's
  451 N. 21st St., Camp Hill, 717/761-1118

Best Steaks
Glass Lounge
  4745 N. Front St., 717/255-9919
Maverick
  1851 Arsenal Blvd., 717/233-7688

HAVERTOWN, PA

Best Bar
Westgate Pub
  1021 W. Chester Pike, 610/446-3030

Best Chinese Food
Forbidden City
  162 W. Eagle Rd., 610/789-4488
Sampan Inn
  8 Brookline Blvd., 610/446-2188

Best French Food
Nais Cuisine
  13 W. Benedict Ave., 610/789-5983

Best Italian Food
Lamplighter Tavern
  8 Campbell Ave., 610/446-2733

Best Pizza
Primavera Pizza Kitchen
  7 E. Lancaster Ave., Ardmore, 610/642-8000

Best Restaurant in Town
Nais Cuisine
  13 W. Benedict Ave., 610/789-5983

Best Seafood
Quarry Inn
  300 W. Chester Pike, 610/789-1414

Best Thai Food
Thai Pepper Restaurant
  64 E. Lancaster Ave., Ardmore, 610/642-5951

HAZLETON, PA

Best Atmosphere
Powerhouse Eatery
  Powerhouse Rd., White Haven, 717/443-4480

Best Barbecue/Ribs
Knotty Pines
  26th St. at N. Church St., 717/455-3211

Best Breakfast
Dubatto's Family Restaurant
  615 E. Broad St., 717/454-7676
Earnie's Family Steak House
  31 N. Church St., 717/459-3070

Ferdinand's Family Restaurant
1000 W. Fifteenth St., 717/454-6397

Best Chinese Food
Five Star Chinese Restaurant
Rte. 93 at Airport Rd., Ste. C1, 717/455-3478

Best Diner
Family Diner
300 Main St., White Haven, 717/443-8797

Best Pizza
Georgio's Sub and Pizza
25 N. Laurel St., 717/459-1818
Pasquale's Pizzeria
41 E. Diamond Ave., 717/459-5085
Senape's Tavern Pitza
835 N. Vine St., 717/454-9168

Best Seafood
Library Lounge
615 E. Broad St., 717/455-3920
Ovalon Restaurant
254 N. Wyoming St., 717/454-0853
Scatton's Restaurant
1008 N. Vine St., 717/455-6630

Best Steaks
Library Lounge
615 E. Broad St., 717/455-3920
Ovalon Restaurant
254 N. Wyoming St., 717/454-0853
Scatton's Restaurant
1008 N. Vine St., 717/455-6630

P

JOHNSTOWN, PA

Best Bar
Johnnie's Restaurant and Lounge
415 Main St., 814/536-9309

Best Breakfast
Eat N Park Restaurant
1900 Minno Dr., 814/255-7711
1461 Scalp Ave., 814/266-5714

Best Chinese Food
Szechuan Chinese Restaurant
124 Main St., 814/535-8845

Best Dinner
Lombardo's
935 Scalp Ave., 814/266-4247

Best Homestyle Food
Slick's Ivy Stone Restaurant
8785 William Penn Rd., Osterburg, 814/276-3131

Best Pizza
Santo's Pizza
1749 Goucher St., 814/255-7138

Best Seafood
Surf and Turf Inn
100 Valley Pike, 814/536-9250

Best Steaks
Surf and Turf Inn
    100 Valley Pike, 814/536-9250

LANCASTER, PA

Best Atmosphere
Loft Restaurant
    201 W. Orange St., 717/299-0661

Best Breakfast
Red Rose Luncheonette
    101 E. King St., 717/392-8620
Zimmerman's Family Restaurant
    66 N. Queen St., 717/394-6977

Best Burgers
Lancaster Dispensing Company
    33 N. Market St., 717/299-4602

Best Chinese Food
China Garden Restaurant
    1254 Millersville Pike, 717/397-1327
Hong Kong Garden
    1807 Columbia Ave., 717/394-4336

Best Continental Food
Log Cabin Restaurant
    11 Lehoy Forest Dr., Leola, 717/626-1181

Best Diner
Silk City Diner
    1640 N. Reading Rd., Stevens, 717/335-3833

Best Fine Dining
Loft Restaurant
    201 W. Orange St., 717/299-0661
Donecker's
    409 N. State St., Ephrata, 717/738-9500
Stock Yard Inn
    1147 Lititz Pike, 717/394-3481
Strawberry Hill
    128 W. Strawberry St., 717/393-5544

Best Homestyle Food
Good N Plenty Restaurant
    Rte. 896, Smoketown, 717/394-7111

Best Ice Cream/Yogurt
Oregon Dairy Farm Market
    2900 Oregon Pike, Lititz, 717/656-2856

Best Indian Food
Kiran Palace
    1358 Columbia Ave., 717/295-9508

Best Italian Food
Gallo Rosso
    337 N. Queen St., 717/392-5616
Lombardo's Italian American
    216 Harrisburg Ave., 717/394-3749
Portofino Italian Ristorante
    254 E. Frederick St., 717/394-1635

Best Late-Night Food
McFly's Pub
  10 S. Prince St., 717/299-3456

Best Mexican Food
Carlos and Charlie's Bar
  915 N. Plum St., 717/293-8704
  2309 Columbia Ave., 717/399-1912

Best Pizza
House of Pizza
  23 W. Chestnut St., 717/393-1747
Sam's Pizza
  710 Columbia Ave., 717/299-7391

Best Place to Take the Kids
Garfield's Restaurant
  222 Eden Rd., 717/569-5454

Best Sandwiches
Isaac's Deli
  555 Greenfield Rd., 717/393-6067
Marion Court Room
  7 Marion Ct., 717/399-1970
Market Fare Restaurant
  50 W. Grant St., 717/299-7090
Press Room
  26-28 W. King St., 717/399-5400
Wish You Were Here
  108 W. Orange St., 717/299-5157

Best Seafood
Kegel's Seafood Restaurant
  551 W. King St., 717/397-2832
Oyster Bay Restaurant
  37 E. Orange St., 717/392-1828

Best Steaks
Loft Restaurant
  201 W. Orange St., 717/299-0661

LEBANON, PA

Best American Food
Fenwick Tavern and Restaurant
  2200 Cumberland St., 717/272-9280

Best Bar
Mookie's Tavern and Eatery
  25 Fieldstone Circle, Elizabethtown, 717/367-5544

Best Breakfast
Eat Well Diner
  1539 E. Cumberland St., 717/273-3849
Hearth Family Restaurant
  2550 Cumberland St., 717/270-1266
Kreider's Dairy Farm Restaurant
  2221 Cumberland St., 717/272-1084

Best Chinese Food
Chan's Garden
  17 W. High St., Elizabethtown, 717/361-8411

P

Best Diner
Heisey's Diner
  1740 State Rte. 72N, 717/272-0891

Best Dinner
Harper's Tavern
  Hwy. 934, Annville, 717/865-2584

Best Fine Dining
Fenwick Tavern and Restaurant
  2200 Cumberland St., 717/272-9280

Best German Food
Little Corner of Germany Cafe
  3050 Lebanon Rd., Manheim, 717/665-7641

Best Lunch
Eli's
  1010 W. Crestview Dr., 717/273-7777

Best Pizza
A and M Pizza Restaurant
  626 Quentin Rd., 717/273-9330

Best Regional Food
Elizabethtown Inn
  28 S. Market St., Elizabethtown, 717/367-7907

LEVITTOWN, PA

Best Diner
Golden Dawn
  7115 New Falls Rd., 215/945-4554

Best Restaurant in Town
Brick Hotel and Restaurant
  1 E. Washington Ave., Newtown, 215/860-8313
Isaac Newton Food and Drink
  18 S. State St., Newtown, 215/860-5100

LOCK HAVEN, PA

Best All-You-Can-Eat Buffet
Big Wrangler Family Restaurant
  Hogan Blvd., Mill Hall, 717/748-9671

Best Breakfast
Aungst Family Restaurant
  368 Hogan Blvd., Mill Hall, 717/726-6233
Blue Chimney Restaurant
  Rte. 150, Mill Hall, 717/726-6420
Clinton Hotel
  375 E. Clinton St., 717/748-2880

Best Business Lunch
Dutch Haven Restaurant
  201 E. Bald Eagle St., 717/748-7444
Fox's Market House Restaurant
  142 E. Church St., 717/748-4000

Best Family Restaurant
Black Forest Inn
  15 Black Forest Dr., 717/769-7203

Best Homestyle Food
Kathy's Kitchen
   201 Logan Ave., 717/748-7977

Best Ice Cream/Yogurt
Overdorf's Drive-In
   835 Woodward Ave., 717/748-6118
Schon's Restaurant
   241 Allegheny St., Jersey Shore, 717/398-7095

Best Italian Food
Santino's Italian Cuisine
   100 S. Main St., Jersey Shore, 717/398-4484

Best Pizza
Original Italian Pizza
   136 E. Main St., 717/748-8027

Best Sandwiches
Jeff's Place
   225 E. Main St., 717/748-2234

MONROEVILLE, PA

Best Breakfast
Eat N Park Restaurant
   805 Lysle Blvd., McKeesport, 412/664-9148
Stan's Family Restaurant
   2812 State St., McKeesport, 412/664-9792

Best Chinese Food
China Jade Restaurant
   4313 Walnut St., McKeesport, 412/751-8213

Best Dinner
Gold Rush Restaurant
   1225 Mosside Blvd., 412/372-1699

Best Italian Food
Italian Oven
   2644 Mosside Blvd., 412/373-6836

Best Mexican Food
El Campesino
   4063 William Penn Hwy., 412/373-1772

Best Sandwiches
Rudy's Submarines
   3942 William Penn Hwy., 412/372-9738
   1794 Golden Mile Hwy., 412/327-9721

Best Seafood
Monterey Bay Fish Grotto
   4099 William Penn Hwy., 412/374-8530

NEW CASTLE, PA

Best American Food
Frengel's
   1245 W. State St., 412/654-6491
Starwood Restaurant and Pub
   1115 Butler Ave., 412/658-6113

Best Homestyle Food
Hazel's Restaurant
   119 N. Mercer St., 412/654-2621

P

Best Italian Food
Medure's Restaurant
 2001 E. Washington St., 724/658-1103

Best Restaurant in Town
Olde Library Inn
 106 E. North St., 724/656-1090
Shad Hanna's East
 1046 Butler Ave., 724/654-0133
Shad Hanna's West
 1245 W. State St., 724/654-6491

Best Steaks
Olde Library Inn
 106 E. North St., 724/656-1090

NORRISTOWN, PA

Best Lunch
Bravo Bistro
 175 King of Prussia Rd., 610/293-9521

Best American Food
Mainland Inn
 17 Main St., Mainland, 215/256-8500

Best Bar
A.J.'s Pub
 22 W. Main St., 610/270-9580

Best Casual Dining
Bravo Bistro
 175 King of Prussia Rd., Wayne, 610/293-9521
Passerelle Restaurant
 175 King of Prussia Rd., Wayne, 610/293-9411
Primavera
 384 W. Lancaster Ave., Wayne, 610/254-0200

Best Chinese Food
88 Chinese Kitchen
 32 W. Main St., 610/278-6711

Best Italian Food
Giacamo's Restaurant
 368 E. Main St., 610/277-7277

Best Pizza
Perrotto's Pizzeria
 2453 W. Main St., 610/539-1936
Sala's Pizza
 12 W. Main St., 610/277-3776

Best Romantic Dining
Spring Mill Cafe
 164 Barren Hill Rd., Conshohocken, 610/828-2550

Best Sandwiches
Rich's Other Place
 924 Bethlehem Pike, Spring House, 215/628-9737
The Peanut Gallery
 1832 Markley St., 610/275-4777

Best Seafood
Barnacle Ben's Seafood Restaurant
 14 Balligomingo Rd., Conshohocken, 610/940-3900

Big Fish
140 Moorehead Ave., Conshohocken, 610/834-7224

PHILADELPHIA, PA

[See also: Camden, NJ.]

Best American Food
Central Bar and Grille
39 Morris Ave., Bryn Mawr, 610/527-1400

Best Bar
Jake and Oliver's
22 S. Third St., 215/627-4825
McGillin's Old Ale House
1310 Drury St., 215/735-5562
Roosevelt's Pub
8011 Roosevelt Blvd., 215/332-1440
Tavern on Green
2047 Green St., 215/235-6767

Best Breakfast
Down Home Diner
1100 Arch St., 215/627-1955
Emil's
1800 S. Broad St., 215/468-4498
Fairmount Bagel Institute (FBI)
2501 Olive St., 215/235-2245
267 S. Nineteenth St., 215/735-2222
Ishkabibble's
337 South St., 215/923-4337
Nifty Fifties
2491 Grant Ave., 215/676-1950
1356 E. Passyunk Ave., 215/468-1950
Pyramid Club
Mellon Bank Center, 1735 Market St.,
215/567-6510
Savoy Restaurant
232 S. Eleventh St., 215/923-2348

Best Brewpub
Dock Street Brewing Company
2 Logan Sq., 215/496-0413
Samuel Adam's Brew House
1516 Sansom St., 215/563-2326

Best Burgers
New Wave Cafe
784 S. Third St., 215/922-8484

Best Business Lunch
Thai Singha House
3939 Chestnut St., 215/382-8001
White Dog Cafe
3420 Sansom St., 215/386-9224

Best Casual Dining
Ristorante Primavera
146 South St., 215/925-7832

P

Sassafras International Cafe
  48 S. Second St., 215/925-2317

Best Chinese Food
Charlie Plaza
  234 N. Tenth St., 215/829-4383
Harmony Vegetarian Restaurant
  135 N. Ninth St., 215/627-4520
Imperial Inn
  146 N. Tenth St., 215/627-2299
Joe's Peking Duck House
  925 Race St., 215/922-3277
Lee How Fook Tea House
  219 N. Eleventh St., 215/925-7266
Sang Kee Peking Duck House
  238 N. Ninth St., 215/922-3930
  5441 Baltimore Ave., 215/472-5791
Susanna Foo Chinese Cuisine
  1512 Walnut St., 215/545-2666
Yangming
  1051 Conestoga Rd., Bryn Mawr, 610/527-3200

Best Coffee/Coffeehouse
Crimson Moon
  2005 Sansom St., 215/564-2228
La Tazza Dart Coffee House
  110 Cotton St., 215/487-6522
Millenium Coffee
  212 S. Twelfth St., 215/731-9798
Roselena's Coffee Bar
  1623 E. Passyunk Ave., 215/755-9697
Torreo Coffee and Tea
  130 S. Seventeenth St., 215/988-0061

Best Continental Food
Continental Diner
  138 Market St., 215/923-6069
Dock Street Brewing Company
  2 Logan Sq., 215/496-0413
Harry's Bar and Grill
  22 S. Eighteenth St., 215/561-5757

Best Delicatessen
Famous 4th Street Delicatessen
  700 S. Fourth St., 215/922-3274
  1136 Arch St. at Reading Terminal, 215/629-5990
Koch's
  4309 Locust St., 215/222-8662
Latimer Delicatessen
  255 S. Fifteenth St., 215/545-9244

Best Desserts
Pink Rose Pastry Shop
  630 S. Fourth St., 215/592-0565
Treetops
  Rittenhouse Hotel, 210 W. Rittenhouse Sq.,
    215/790-2533
White Dog Cafe
  3420 Sansom St., 215/386-9224

Best Diner
American Diner
  4201 Chestnut St., 215/387-1451
Mayfair Diner
  7373 Frankford Ave., 215/624-8886
Melrose Diner
  1501 Snyder Ave., 215/467-6644
Silk City Diner
  435 Spring Garden St., 215/592-8838

Best Eclectic
Circa Restaurant
  1518 Walnut St., 215/545-6800

Best Eclectic Menu
Bridget Foy's South Street Grill
  200 South St., 215/922-1813
Fountain
  Four Seasons Hotel, 1 Logan Sq., 215/963-1500
Tavern on Green
  2047 Green St., 215/235-6767

Best Family Restaurant
Spaghetti Warehouse
  1026 Spring Garden St., 215/787-0784
Tom Jones Family Restaurant
  4417 Edgmont Ave., Brookhaven, 610/874-1055

Best Fine Dining
Dilworthtown Inn
  1390 Old Wilmington Pike at Brinton Bridge Rd.,
West Chester, 610/399-1390
Lebec-Fin
  1523 Walnut St., 215/567-1000
Oxford Diner
  233 S. Third St., Oxford, 610/932-2653
Rembrandt's Bar and Restaurant
  741 N. 23rd St., 215/763-2228
Striped Bass
  1500 Walnut St., 215/732-4444
The Fountain
  Four Seasons Hotel, 1 Logan Sq., 215/963-1500

Best French Food
Caribou Cafe
  1126 Walnut St., 215/625-9535
Chanterelle's
  1312 Spruce St., 215/735-7551
Ciboulette Restaurant
  200 S. Broad St., 215/790-1210
Overtures
  609 E. Passyunk Ave., 215/627-3455

Best German Food
Old Brauhaus Restaurant
  7980 Oxford Ave., 215/728-9440

Best Greek/Mediterranean Food
Dimitri's
  795 S. Third St., 215/625-0556

P

Best Homestyle Food
Country Club Restaurant
  1717 Cottman Ave., 215/722-0500

Best Ice Cream/Yogurt
Hillary's Gourmet Ice Cream
  437 South St., 215/922-4931
  3409 Walnut St., 215/387-8837
  2006 Chestnut St., 215/561-6962
More Than Just Ice Cream
  1119 Locust St., 215/574-0586

Best Indian Food
Passage to India
  1320 Walnut St., 215/732-7300

Best Inexpensive Meal
Dock Street Brewing Company
  2 Logan Sq., 215/496-0413
East Junior
  1625 Chestnut St., Ste. 13F, 215/567-2477
Le Bus
  3402 Sansom St., 215/387-3800
Taco House
  1218 Pine St., 215/735-1880

Best Italian Food
La Famiglia Restaurant
  8 S. Front St., 215/922-2803
Marras Restaurant
  1734 E. Passyunk Ave., 215/463-9249
Mr. Martino's Trattoria
  1646 E. Passyunk Ave., 215/755-0663
Pasta Blitz by Lamberti
  212 Walnut St., 215/238-0499
Ralph's Italian Restaurant
  760 S. Ninth St., 215/627-6011
Saloon Restaurant
  750 S. Seventh St., 215/627-1811
Scampi Italian Restaurant
  2312 Garrett Rd., Drexel Hill, 610/284-3333
Upstairs at Varalli
  1345 Locust St., 215/546-4200
Villanove Restaurant
  797 E. Lancaster Ave., Villanova, 610/527-9009

Best Late-Night Food
Melrose Diner
  1501 Snyder Ave., 215/467-6644
New South Street Diner
  140 South St., 215/627-5258

Best Lunch
Little Pete's
  219 S. Seventeenth St., 215/545-5508
Magnolia Cafe
  1602 Locust St., 215/546-4180
Tony Luke's
  39 E. Oregon Ave., 215/551-5725

Best Mexican Food
Taco House
  1218 Pine St., 215/735-1880
Tequila's
  1511 Locust St., 215/546-0181
Zocala
  3600 Lancaster Ave., 215/895-0139

Best Middle Eastern Food
Alyan's Restaurant
  603 S. Fourth St., 215/922-3553

Best Other Etnic Food
Chanterelle's (French-Asian)
  1312 Spruce St., 215/735-7551

Best Outdoor Dining
Garden
  1617 Spruce St., 215/546-4455
Rock Lobster
  221 N. Delaware Ave., 215/627-7625

Best Pizza
Bertucci's
  1515 Locust St., 215/731-1400
Cafe Antonio
  107 E. Trenton Ave., Morrisville, 215/428-3999
Celebre Pizzeria
  1536 Packer Ave., 215/467-3255
Felicia's
  1148 S. Eleventh St., 215/755-9656
Imperial Pizza
  615 South Ave., Clifton Heights, 610/543-9393
Lorenzo Pizza
  900 Christian St., 215/922-2540
Pine Street Pizza
  1138 Pine St., 215/922-2526
Savas Pizzaria
  1547 Spring Garden St., 215/564-1910
Upscale Pizza Joint
  4120 Main, 215/482-9000
Zio Pizza
  122 S. Sixteenth St., 215/569-0898

Best Regional Food
Dalessandro's
  600 Wendover St., 215/482-5407
Jim's Steaks
  2311 Cottman Ave., 215/333-5467
  431 N. 62nd St., 215/747-6615
  400 South St., 215/928-1911
Pat's King of Steaks
  1237 E. Passyunk Ave., 215/468-1546
Tony Luke's
  39 E. Oregon Ave., 215/551-5725

Best Romantic Dining
Astral Plane
  1708 Lombard St., 215/546-6230
Bridgid's
  726 N. 24th St., 215/232-3232

P

City Tavern
  138 S. Second St., 215/413-1443
Frangelica
  200 S. Twelfth St., 215/731-9930
Garden
  1617 Spruce St., 215/546-4455
Mendenhall Inn
  Kennett Pike, Mendenhall, 610/388-1181
Monte Carlo Living Room
  150 South St., 215/925-2220
Mr. Martino's Trattoria
  1646 E. Passyunk Ave., 215/755-0663

Best Salad/Salad Bar
Chart House Restaurant
  555 S. Columbus Blvd., 215/625-8383
Goat Hollow
  300 W. Mount Pleasant Ave., 215/242-4710
Marathon Grill
  1617 John F. Kennedy Blvd., 215/564-4745
  121 S. Sixteenth St., 215/569-3278
Pollo Rosso
  8229 Germantown Ave., 215/248-9338

Best Sandwiches
New London Pizza
  1016 Lincoln Ave., Prospect Park, 610/461-9330
Salumeria
  1200 Filbert, 215/592-8150
Slack's Hoagie Shack
  8439 Frankford Ave., 215/338-6777
Tony Luke's
  39 E. Oregon Ave., 215/551-5725

Best Seafood
Bookbinder's Fifteenth Street House
  215 S. Fifteenth St., 215/545-1137
Brittingham's Irish Pub
  640 Germantown Pike, Lafayette Hill,
    610/828-7351
Dimitri's
  795 S. Third St., 215/625-0556
Palm Restaurant
  200 S. Broad St., 215/546-7256
Seafood Unlimited
  270 S. Twentieth St., 215/732-9012
Striped Bass
  1500 Walnut St., 215/732-4444

Best Spanish Food
Pamplona Restaurant
  225 N. Twelfth St., 215/627-9059
Tierra Columbiana
  4535 N. Fifth St., 215/324-6086

Bes Sports Bar
Philly Legends
  Holiday Inn, 900 Packer Ave., 215/755-9500

Best Steaks
Chart House Restaurant
  555 S. Columbus Blvd., 215/625-8383
Kansas City Prime
  4417 Main St., 215/482-3700
Morton's of Chicago
  Four Seasons Hotel, 1 Logan Sq., 215/557-0724
Pats King of Steaks
  1237 E. Passyunk Ave., 215/468-1546

Best Sunday Brunch
Fountain
  Four Seasons Hotel, 1 Logan Sq., 215/963-1500
Jake's Restaurant and Bar
  4365 Main St., 215/483-0444
Striped Bass
  1500 Walnut St., 215/732-4444

Best Sushi
Aoi Japanese Restaurant
  1210 Walnut St., 215/985-1838
Genji Japanese Restaurant
  4002 Spruce St., 215/387-1583
  1720 Sansom St., 215/564-1720
Hikaru
  108 S. Eighteenth St., 215/496-9950
Shiroi Hana Japanese Restaurant
  222 S. Fifteenth St., 215/735-4444

Best Thai Food
My Thai
  2200 South St., 215/985-1878
Pattaya Grill
  4006 Chestnut St., 215/387-8533
Sabai Thai
  831 E. Baltimore Ave., Lansdowne, 610/622-9878
Thai Singha House
  3939 Chestnut St., 215/382-8001

Best Vegetarian Food
Essene Cafe
  719 S. Fourth St., 215/928-3722
Harmony Vegetarian Restaurant
  135 N. Ninth St., 215/627-4520
Mary's
  400 Roxborough Ave., 215/487-2249
Rajbhog Restaurant and Sweets
  738 Adams Ave., 215/537-1937

Best Vietnamese Food
Vietnam Restaurant
  221 N. Eleventh St., 215/592-1163

Best View While Dining
Chart House Restaurant
  555 S. Columbus Blvd., 215/625-8383

Best Wine Selection
Lebec-Fin
  1523 Walnut St., 215/567-1000
Ristorante Panorama
  14 N. Front St., Penn's View Inn, 215/922-7800

P

PITTSBURGH, PA

Best American Food
Chelsea Grille
  515 Allegheny Ave., Oakmont, 412/828-0570
Chesterfield's Restaurant
  12119 Rte. 30, Irwin, 412/864-7450
Hoffstot's Cafe Monaco
  533 Allegheny Ave., Oakmont, 412/828-8555
Mr. Jones
  8300 McKnight Rd., 412/367-7777
Siena
  430 Market St., 421/338-0955
Village Inn
  500 Washington Ave., Bridgeville, 412/257-2480

Best Barbecue/Ribs
Bobby Rubino's
  10 Commerce Ct., 412/642-7427
Damon's
  855 Freeport Rd., 412/782-3750
Tessaro's
  4601 Liberty Ave., 412/682-6809
Wilson's Bar-B-Q
  700 N. Taylor Ave., 412/322-7427

Best Beer Selection
Chiodo's Tavern
  107 W. Eighth Ave., Homestead, 412/461-3113

Best Breakfast
DeLuca's Restaurant
  2015 Penn Ave., 412/566-2195
Pamela's
  3703 Forbes Ave., 412/683-4066
  5527 Walnut St., 412/683-1003
  5813 Forbes Ave., 412/422-9457
Ritter's Diner
  5221 Baum Blvd., 412/682-4852

Best Brewpub
Penn Brewery
  800 Vinial St., 412/237-9400

Best Burgers
Jergel's
  3385 Babcock Blvd., 412/364-9902
Tessaro's
  4601 Liberty Ave., 412/682-6809

Best Chinese Food
Chan's Tea House
  1009 W. View Park Dr., 412/931-0134
Jimmy Tsang's Chinese Restaurant
  5700 Centre Ave., 412/661-4226
Mark Pi's China Gate
  1500 Washington Rd., Ste. 3, 412/341-8890
Sichuan House Chinese Restaurant
  1335 Freeport Rd., 412/967-0789
  1717 Cochran Rd., 412/563-5252
  1900 Murray Ave., 412/422-2700

Best Coffee/Coffeehouse
Beehive Coffeehouse
    1327 E. Carson St., 412/488-4483

Best Continental Food
Cafe Allegro
    51 S. Twelfth St., 412/481-7788
Mallorca Restaurant
    2228 E. Carson St., 412/488-1818

Best Delicatessen
Pittsburgh Deli Company
    728 Copeland St., 412/682-3354
Rhoda's Deli Restaurant
    2201 Murray Ave., 412/521-4555

Best Desserts
Gullifty's
    1922 Murray Ave., 412/521-8222
Houlihan's
    15 Station Sq. E., 412/232-0302
    1741 Washington Rd., 412/831-9797
Mitchell's Ice Cream and Barbecue
    3123 Babcock Blvd., 412/364-9988

Best Diner
Jo Jo's Restaurant
    100 24th St., 412/261-0280
Ritter's Diner
    5221 Baum Blvd., 412/682-4852
Tom's Diner
    2937 W. Liberty Ave., 412/531-2350

Best Fine Dining
Chesterfield's Restaurant
    12119 Rte. 30, Irwin, 412/863-7450
Le Mont Restaurant
    1114 Grandview Ave., 412/431-3100
Tivoli Restaurant
    419 Rodi Rd., 412/243-9630

Best German Food
Max's Allegheny Tavern
    537 Suismon St., 412/231-1899

Best Health-Conscious Menu
Coral Garden Chinese Restaurant
    1621 S. Braddock Ave., 412/731-1101
Shadyside Balcony
    5520 Walnut St., 412/687-0110
Sweet Basil's Bar
    5882 Forbes Ave., 412/421-9958

Best Ice Cream/Yogurt
Bruster's Old Fashion Ice Cream and Yogurt
    4070 Beechwood Blvd., 412/422-9555
Dave and Andy's Homemade Ice Cream
    207 Atwood St., 412/681-9906

Best Indian Food
India Garden
    328 Atwood St., 412/682-3000

P

Star of India
  412 S. Craig St., 412/681-5700

Best Italian Food
Davio
  2100 Broadway Ave., 412/531-7422
Pasta Piatto
  736 Bellefonte St., 412/621-5547
Piccolo Piccolo Ristorante
  1 Wood St., 412/261-7234
Tigano's Inn
  6202 Leechburg Rd., Verona, 412/795-5151

Best Japanese Food
Kiku Japanese Restaurant
  Station Square, 412/765-3200

Best Mexican Food
Franklin Inn
  2313 Rochester Rd., 412/366-4140
Mad Mex
  7905 McKnight Rd., 412/366-5656

Best Middle Eastern Food
Ali Baba
  404 S. Craig St., 412/682-2829
Amel's Restaurant
  435 McNeilly Rd., 412/563-3466

Best Other Ethnic Food
Kaya (Carribean)
  2000 Smallman St., 412/261-6565
Soba Lounge (Pan-Asian)
  5847 Ellsworth Ave., 412/362-5656

Best Outdoor Dining
J. Harris' Grill
  5747 Ellsworth Ave., 412/363-0833

Best Pizza
Caruso's Pizza
  656 Washington Rd., 412/343-1722
Mineo's Pizza House
  2128 Murray Ave., 412/521-9864

Best Place to Take the Kids
Chuck E. Cheese Pizza
  249 N. Craig St., 412/655-8840

Best Restaurant in Town
Hyeholde Restaurant
  190 Hyeholde Dr., Coraopolis, 412/264-3116

Best Restaurant Meal Value
Armstrong's Restaurant
  1136 N. Thorn Run, Coraopolis, 412/262-9355

Best Romantic Dining
Rico's
  1 Rico Ln., 412/931-1989

Best Salad/Salad Bar
Blarney Stone
  30 Grant Ave., 412/781-1666

P

Best Sandwiches
Peppi's
  927 Western Ave., 412/231-9009
  12 Smithfield St., 412/281-1510
  1721 Penn Ave., 412/562-0125
Pour House
  215 E. Main St., Carnegie, 412/279-0770
Primanti Brothers
  3803 Forbes Ave., 412/621-4444
  46 Eighteenth St., 412/263-2142
  11 Cherry Way, 412/566-8051

Best Seafood
Poli's Seafood Restaurant
  2607 Murray Ave., 412/521-6400
Robert Wholey's Fish Market
  1711 Penn Ave., 412/391-3737
Wright's Seafood Inn
  1837 Washington St., Carnegie, 412/423-1255

Best Steaks
Mardi Gras Steak and Seafood
  634 Camp Horne Rd., 412/369-9916
Morton's of Chicago
  625 Liberty Ave., 412/261-7141
Ruddy Duck Restaurant and Lounge
  1 Bigelow Sq., 412/281-3825
Winchester Room
  1728 Lincoln Hwy., North Versailles, 412/823-9954

Best Sunday Brunch
Chesterfield's Restaurant
  12119 Rte. 30, Irwin, 412/863-7450
Grand Concourse Restaurant
  1 Station Sq., 412/261-1717

Best Vegetarian Food
East End Food Co-Op
  7516 Meade St., 412/242-3598
Himalayan Tibetan Restaurant
  3531 Forbes Ave., 412/687-6550
Janet's Cafe
  901 E. Carson St., 412/381-5308

Best Wine Selection
Carlton
  500 Grant St., 412/391-4099
Le Pommier
  2104 E. Carson St., 412/682-2620
Lemont Restaurant
  1114 Grandview, 412/431-3100

P

POTTSTOWN, PA

Best Chinese Food
Panda Heaven Chinese Restaurant
  11A Coventry Square Mall, 610/970-6999

Best Continental Food
Coventry Forge Inn
  3360 Coventryville Rd., 610/469-6222

Best Italian Food
Cutillo's Restaurant
  2688 E. High St., 610/327-2910

Best Lunch
Coventry Tea Room
  1161 Ridge Rd., 610/469-9134

READING, PA

Best All-You-Can-Eat Buffet
Chef Alan's Restaurant and Lounge
  525 Penn Ave., 610/375-4012

Best Atmosphere
Stokesay Castle
  Hill Rd. at Spook Lane, 610/375-4588
Widow Finney's Restaurant
  30 S. Fourth St., 610/378-1776

Best Bar
Kramer's Peanut Bar
  332 Penn St., 610/376-8500

Best Barbecue/Ribs
Wild Wings Cafe
  Reading Regional Airport Rd., 2385 Bernville Rd.,
  610/478-1747

Best Breakfast
Deluxe Restaurant
  415 Lancaster Pike W., 610/775-2577

Best Chinese Food
China Penn Restaurant
  4203A Perkiomen Ave., 610/779-9754
China Penn West
  1816 Bern St., 610/374-5656

Best Coffee/Coffeehouse
Salon Salon
  600 Penn Ave., West Reading, 610/372-3705

Best Desserts
Arner's Family Restaurant
  1714 State Hill Rd., 610/372-6101
  4643 Pottsville Pike, 610/926-9002
Chef Alan's Restaurant and Lounge
  525 Penn Ave., 610/375-4012

Best Eclectic Menu
Cafe Unicorn
  116 Lafayette St., 610/929-9992
Dan's Restaurant
  1049 Penn St., 610/373-2075

Best Fine Dining
American House Hotel
  86 Main St., Womelsdorf, 610/589-5899
Joe's Restaurant
  450 S. Seventh St., 610/373-6794
Stokesay Castle
  Hill Rd. at Spook Ln., 610/375-4588

Best French Food
Green Hills Inn
  2444 Morgantown Rd., 610/777-9611

Best German Food
Alpenhof Restaurant
  903 Morgantown Rd., 610/373-1624

Best Health-Conscious Menu
California Bar and Grill
  699 Mountain View Rd., 610/777-7224

Best Ice Cream/Yogurt
Bresler's Ice Cream and Yogurt
  3050 N. Fifth St., 610/929-3317

Best Italian Food
Bravo
  1160 Buttonwood St., 610/378-9200
Pachuilo's Italian Restaurant
  850 N. Eighth St., 610/376-2717

Best Mexican Food
El Tapatio
  801 Walnut St., 610/373-8872

Best Middle Eastern Food
Sahara Restaurant
  334 Penn St., 610/374-8500

Best Pizza
Paolo's Pizza Restaurant
  1200 Lancaster Pike W., 610/775-3500
Santino's Family Restaurant
  1 Wellington Blvd., 610/670-2052

Best Regional Food
Reeser Wegman's Restaurant
  4401 Pottsville Pike, 610/929-2538

Best Sandwiches
Butler's Pantry
  348 Penn St., 610/373-7555

Best Seafood
Crab Barn
  2613 Hampden Blvd., 610/921-8922

Best Steaks
Inn at Reading
  1040 N. Park Rd., 610/372-7811

Best Thai Food
Thai Cuisine
  502 Eisenbrown St, 610/929-6993

SCRANTON, PA

Best 24-Hour Restaurant
Waffle Shop and Family Restaurant
  917 Wyoming Ave., 717/344-2288

Best Bar
Fresno's Restaurant
  914 Scranton Carbondale Hwy., 717/383-9400

Best Chinese Food
House of China
1137 Moosic St., 717/343-8118

Best Family Restaurant
Carmella's
140 Erie St., 717/961-3070

Best Greek/Mediterranean Food
Aegean II Restaurant and Bar
134 N. Main Ave., 717/969-6080

Best Late-Night Food
Fresno's Restaurant
914 Scranton Carbondale Hwy., 717/383-9400

Best Lunch
Carmen Restaurant
Lackawanna Station, 700 Lackawanna Ave.,
717/342-8300

Best Restaurant in Town
Cooper's Seafood House
701 N. Washington Ave., 717/346-6883

STATE COLLEGE, PA

Best American Food
Corner Room
100 W. College Ave., 814/237-3051

Best Breakfast
Waffle Shop
364 E. College Ave., 814/237-9741
1229 N. Atherton St., 814/238-7460

Best Dinner
Tavern Restaurant
220 E. College Ave., 814/238-6116

Best Italian Food
Mario and Luigi's
1272 N. Atherton St., 814/234-4273
113 S. Garner St., 814/237-0374

Best Pizza
Hi-Way Pizza
1688 N. Atherton St., 814/237-0375
428 Westerly Parkway Plz., 814/237-1074
340 E. College Ave., 814/237-5718

Best Steaks
Hoss's Steak and Sea House
1450 N. Atherton St., 814/234-4009

SWARTHMORE, PA

Best Delicatessen
Anna's
303 Sutton Ave., Folsom, 610/534-9289

Best Diner
Gateway Diner
2215 MacDade Blvd., Holmes, 610/532-2825

Best Dinner
Erin's Pub
  36 W. Winona Ave., Norwood, 610/461-0991

Best Family Restaurant
Ingleneuk Tea House and Catering
  120 Park Ave., 610/543-4569

Best French Food
American Bistro
  1 S. Morton Ave., Morton, 610/543-3033

Best Italian Food
Italian Village
  902 MacDade Blvd., Folsom, 610/237-0200

Best Lunch
Occasionally Yours
  10 Park Ave., 610/328-9360

Best Sandwiches
Cheese Court
  1 Park Ave., 610/328-4140

UNIONTOWN, PA

Best All-You-Can-Eat Buffet
Sun Porch
  Rte. 40E, Hopwood, 724/439-5734

Best Diner
Herring's Dairy Store Restaurant
  Rte. 40E, Hopwood, 724/438-9823

Best Family Restaurant
Coal Baron Restaurant
  Rte. 40W, 724/439-0111

Best French Food
Chez Garand French Restaurant
  Rte. 40E, Hopwood, 724/437-9001

Best Italian Food
Luigi's Italian Restaurant
  1711 Morrell Ave., Connellsville, 724/626-0422

Best Middle Eastern Food
Sam's Restaurant
  208 Morgantown St., 724/438-7050

Best Pizza
Mom Maruca's Pizza Shop
  265 N. Gallatin Ave., 724/438-9066

Best Sandwiches
Bud Murphy's Sport's Bar and Restaurant
  718 McCormick Ave., Connellsville, 724/628-4827

WARREN, PA

Best Coffee/Coffeehouse
Roy's Texas Lunch
  214 Pennsylvania Ave. W., 814/723-5292

Best Diner
Plaza Restaurant
  328 Pennsylvania Ave. W., 814/723-5660

P

Best Italian Food
Mineral Well
  Rte. 1, Clarendon, 814/723-9840
The Stonehouse Restaurant
  Chalkhill, 412/329-8876

Best Sandwiches
V and J Pizza and Sub Shop
  601 Pennsylvania Ave. E., 814/723-3406

Best Steaks
Busy Bee Restaurant
  229 Pennsylvania Ave. W., 814/723-9868

WILKES BARRE, PA

Best Breakfast
Holiday Pancake House
  116 Wilkes Barre Township Blvd., 717/824-4927

Best Burgers
Jim Dandy's
  Mark Plaza, Kingston, 717/288-3500

Best Italian Food
Perugino's
  205 S. Main St., Ashley, 717/825-6803

Best Japanese Food
Katana
  41 S. Main St., 717/825-9080

Best Pizza
Serpico Pizza
  220 E. End Ctr., 717/824-4477

Best Sandwiches
Bakers Inn
  6 S. Main St., 717/823-8580

WILLIAMSPORT, PA

Best American Food
Johnson's Cafe
  334 Broad St., Montoursville, 717/368-8351

Best Brewpub
Bullfrog Brewery
  229 W. Fourth St., 717/326-4700

Best Chinese Food
Oriental Buffet
  1955 E. Third St., 717/322-4833

Best Diner
Donna's Food Works
  2703 Euclid Ave., 717/326-7589

Best Dinner
Tags Bar and Grill
  1254 Memorial Ave., 717/322-9288

Best Family Restaurant
Heller's Family Restaurant
  1941 Lycoming Creek Rd., 717/322-8006

Best Fine Dining
Peter Herdic House
   407 W. Fourth St., 717/322-0165

Best French Food
Phillippe's
   326 Court St., 717/326-6432

Best Health-Conscious Menu
American Chef Cafe
   313 Broad St., Montoursville, 717/368-3464

Best Homestyle Food
Thomas Lightfoot Inn
   2887 S. Reach Rd., 717/326-6396

Best Italian Food
Columbia Hotel
   525 W. Third St., 717/322-9173
Old Corner Hotel
   328 Court St., 717/326-4286

Best Lunch
Old Jail Getaway
   154 W. Third St., 717/326-5255

Best Restaurant in Town
Bridge Tavern
   222 Market St., 717/323-8839
Tag's Bar and Grill
   1254 Memorial Ave., 717/322-9288
The Villa
   2016 E. Third St., 717/323-5533

YORK, PA

Best Business Lunch
Autographs
   Yorktown Hotel, 48 E. Market St., 717/848-1111

Best Chinese Food
Peter Chang Chinese
   907 Loucks Rd., 717/845-8138
Shangrila Chinese Restaurant
   2149 White St., 717/854-3333

Best Fine Dining
Accomac Inn
   Accomac Rd., Wrightsville, 717/252-1521

Best Homestyle Food
Alexander's Family Restaurant
   840 Carlisle Rd., 717/846-1041

Best Italian Food
Alberto's Restaurant and Pizza
   2736 S. Queen St., 717/741-3854
Anthony's
   801 Loucks Rd., 717/843-0063
Bel Paese Italian Ristorante
   1201 Memory Lane Ext., 717/840-4040
Genova's Restaurant and Pizza
   2530 W. Market St., 717/792-4602

P

Best Mexican Food
El Serrano Restaurant
  3410 E. Market St., 717/757-4963

Best Pizza
Jim and Nena's Pizzaria
  501 W. Philadelphia St., 717/843-4492
  305 Parkway Blvd., 717/845-2269
  2755 W. Market St., 717/792-5015
  35 W. Market St., 717/845-0241
Marcello Pizza
  17 W. Market St., 717/854-7811

Best Restaurant in Town
Roosevelt Tavern
  400 W. Philadelphia St., 717/854-7725
Village Green Family Restaurant
  2300 E. Market St., 717/755-9839

Best Sandwiches
Isaac's Restaurant and Deli
  2960 Whiteford Rd., 717/751-0515
Jim and Nena's Pizzaria
  501 W. Philadelphia St., 717/843-4492
  305 Parkway Blvd., 717/845-2269
  2755 W. Market St., 717/792-5015
  35 W. Market St., 717/845-0241

Best Seafood
Lamotte's Restaurant
  7 E. Franklin St., New Freedom, 717/235-2295
Mr. Bill's Quarterdeck Seafood
  2600 Keyway Dr., 717/741-0872

Best Vegetarian Food
Blue Moon Cafe
  361 W. Market St., 717/854-6664

Rhode Island

Best Breakfast
Hope Diner
  742 Hope St., 401/253-1759

Best Regional Food
The Lobster Pot
  119 Hope St., 401/253-9100

Best Restaurant in Town
Redlefsen's Rotisserie and Grill
  425 Hope St., 401/254-1188
S.S. Dion Restaurant
  520 Thames St., 401/253-2884

Best Restaurant Meal Value
Tweets Balzano's Family Restaurant
  180 Mount Hope Ave., 401/253-9811

Best Breakfast
Bickford's Family Restaurant
  860 Reservoir Ave., 401/943-6004
Mike's Kitchen
  170 Randall St., 401/946-5320

Best Burgers
Chelo's Beef Hearth
  1275 Reservoir Ave., 401/942-7666

Best Coffee/Coffeehouse
Cafe Luna
  10 Midway Rd., 401/944-1438
Caffe-Bonami
  1082 Park Ave., 401/943-8400

Ocean Coffee Roasters
110 Waterman Ave., 401/331-5282

Best Ice Cream/Yogurt
Dear Hearts Ice Cream
2218 Broad St., 401/941-5167
Newport Creamery
100 Hillside Rd., 401/944-3397

Best Italian Food
Basta Italian Restaurant
2195 Broad St., 401/461-0330
Caffe Itri
1686 Cranston St., 401/942-1970
Twin Oaks Restaurant
100 Sabra St., 401/781-9693

Best Other Ethnic Food
Galaxie Restaurant (Chinese, Cambodian, Thai)
957 Reservoir Ave., 401/946-9464

Best Pizza
Calvitto's Pizza and Bakery
1391 Park Ave., 401/944-3737
Tony's Pizza and Restaurant
548 Pontiac Ave., 401/781-1334

Best Restaurant Meal Value
Marchetti's Restaurant
1463 Park Ave., 401/943-7649
Mike's Kitchen
170 Randall St., 401/946-5320
Silver Palace
623 Reservoir Ave., 401/467-0077

R

EAST PROVIDENCE, RI

Best Breakfast
Wampanoag Diner
2800 Pawtucket Ave., 401/434-9880

Best Desserts
Gregg's Restaurant
1940 Pawtucket Ave., 401/438-5700

Best Family Restaurant
Gregg's Restaurant
1940 Pawtucket Ave., 401/438-5700
Joseph's Family Restaurant
315 Waterman Ave., 401/438-5250

Best Other Ethnic Food
Estrella Do Mar (Portuguese)
736 N. Broadway, 401/434-5130
Madeira (Portuguese)
288 Warren Ave., 401/431-1322

Best Sandwiches
Waterman Avenue Deli
97 Waterman Ave., 401/434-4964

Best Seafood
Old Oyster House Restaurant
28 Water St., 401/431-1133

Best Steaks
133 Club and Restaurant
  29 Warren Ave., 401/438-1330

LINCOLN, RI

Best Breakfast
Gisele's Kitchen
  479 Great Rd., 401/722-8737

Best Delicatessen
Local Hero
  101 Higginson Ave., 401/724-0230

Best Diner
Asia Restaurant
  George Washington Hwy., 401/334-3200

Best Sunday Brunch
Breakfast Nook
  189 Front St., 401/727-2704

NARRAGANSETT, RI

Best Casual Dining
Arturo Joe's
  140 Point Judith Rd., 401/789-3230

Best Chinese Food
Chen's Restaurant
  60 Old Tower Hill Rd., Wakefield, 401/783-8516

Best Coffee/Coffeehouse
Coffee Bean
  20 Woodruff Ave., 401/782-6226

Best Continental Food
Basil's Restaurant and Lounge
  22 Kingstown Rd., 401/789-3743

Best Ice Cream/Yogurt
Heffie's Ice Cream and Restaurant
  1820 Boston Neck Rd., Saunderstown,
    401/295-1414

Best Italian Food
Casa Rossi
  90 Point Judith Rd., 401/789-6385

Best Regional Food
Aunt Carrie's Restaurant
  1240 Ocean Rd., 401/783-7930
George's of Galilee
  250 Sand Hill Cove Rd., 401/783-2306

Best Restaurant in Town
Spain Restaurant
  1144 Ocean Rd., 401/783-9770

Best Seafood
Aunt Carrie's Restaurant
  1240 Ocean Rd., 401/783-7930
Capt'n Jack's Restaurant
  706 Succotash Rd., Wakefield, 401/789-4556
Coast Guard House
  40 Ocean Rd., 401/789-0700

Best Sunday Brunch
Coast Guard House
40 Ocean Rd., 401/789-0700

NEWPORT, RI

Best American Food
Yesterday's Ale House
28 Washington Sq., 401/847-0116

Best Bar
Brick Alley Pub and Restaurant
140 Thames St., 401/849-6334
The White Horse Tavern
16 Farewell St., 401/849-3600

Best Barbecue/Ribs
Music Hall Cafe
250 Thames St., 401/848-2330

Best Breakfast
Coffee Corner
283 Broadway, 401/849-2902
Muriel's
58 Spring St., 401/849-7780

Best Chinese Food
Batik Garden Chinese Restaurant
99 E. Main Rd., 401/848-0663
Dragon Express
82 Broadway, 401/847-1686

Best Coffee/Coffeehouse
Ocean Coffee Roasters
22 Washington Sq., 401/846-6060

Best Delicatessen
Cappuccino's
92 William St., 401/846-7145
Sig's Market and Caterers
7 Carroll Ave., 401/847-9668

Best Diner
Fourth Street Diner
184 Admiral Kalbfus Rd., 401/847-2069

Best Eclectic Menu
Cheeky Monkey Cafe
14 Perry Mill Wharf, 401/845-9494
Salvation Cafe
142 Broadway, 401/847-2620

Best French Food
Courtyard La Petit Auberge
19 Charles St., 401/849-6669
Restaurant Bouchard
505 Thames St., 401/846-0123

Best Italian Food
Puerini's Italian Specialties
24 Memorial Blvd. W., 401/847-5506

Best Other Ethnic Food
Asterix and Obelix Cafe (Mediterranean-Asian)
599 Thames St., 401/841-8833

Sea Shai (Japanese/Korean)
747 Aquidneck Ave., Ste. 1B, Middletown,
401/849-5180

Best Pizza
Nikola's Pizza Newport
38 Memorial Blvd. W., 401/849-6611
Via Via
112 William St., 401/846-4074
Via Via II
372 Thames St., 401/848-0880

Best Regional Food
The Black Pearl
Bannister's Wharf, 401/846-5264

Best Restaurant Meal Value
Salas Dining Room
343 Thames St., 401/849-7895

Best Romantic Dining
Canfield House
5 Memorial Blvd., 401/847-0416
Clarke Cooke House and Candy Store
1 Bannisters Wharf, 401/849-2900
Inn at Castle Hill
590 Ocean Ave., 401/849-3800

Best Sandwiches
Newport Creamery
49 Long Wharf Mall, 401/849-8469

Best Seafood
Canfield House
5 Memorial Blvd., 401/847-0416
Christie's Restaurant
351 Thames St., 401/847-5400
The Mooring
Newport Yacht Center, Sayers Wharf, 401/846-2260

Best Steaks
Brick Alley Pub and Restaurant
140 Thames St., 401/849-6334
Chart House
22 Bowens Wharf, 401/849-7555

Best Wine Selection
The Place
28 Washington Sq., 401/847-0116

NORTH KINGSTON, RI

Best Breakfast
Breakfast Nook
6130 Post Rd., 401/884-6108

Best Delicatessen
Brown Street Cafe
85 Brown St., 401/294-1150

Best Homestyle Food
Oatley's Restaurant
1717 Ten Rod Rd., 401/295-5126

Best Restaurant Meal Value
Walt's Roast Beef
  6660 Post Rd., 401/884-9719

Best Seafood
Harborside Grill
  68 Brown St., 401/295-0444

Best Steaks
Red Rooster Tavern
  7385 Post Rd., 401/295-8804

Best Sunday Brunch
L.A. Robert's Restaurant
  6900 Post Rd., 401/885-0575

NORTH SMITHFIELD, RI

Best Breakfast
Coffee and Cream
  4 Greenville Rd., 401/762-4352
  900 Victory Hwy., 401/767-5566
Roast House
  8 Old Louisquisset Pike, 401/765-0919

Best Diner
Kennedy's Lunch
  685 Saint Paul St., 401/762-9211

PAWTUCKET, RI

Best Breakfast
Bill's Restaurant
  844 Newport Ave., 401/726-9265
Kip's Restaurant
  826 Newport Ave., 401/726-9882
Modern Diner
  364 East Ave., 401/726-8390

Best Burgers
Stanley's Restaurant
  535 Dexter St., Central Falls, 401/726-9689

Best Chinese Food
China Inn
  285 Main St., 401/723-3960
Super Dragon
  805 Broadway, 401/723-9800
Tin Tin Buffet
  223 Newport Ave., 401/725-8118

Best Coffee/Coffeehouse
Honey Dew Donuts
  1515 Newport Ave., 401/723-5580

Best Delicatessen
Barney's Bagels
  727 East Ave., 401/727-1010
Shaw's Meats
  435 Power Rd., 401/728-8120

Best Ice Cream/Yogurt
Dot's Dairy Bar
  1476 Newport Ave., 401/724-9150

R

Newport Creamery
  100 Main St., 401/724-4630
  665 Central Ave., 401/724-3170

Best Other Ethnic Food
Lisbon at Night (Portuguese)
  17 Exchange St., 401/723-2030

Best Pizza
House of Pizza
  206 Division St., 401/725-9433
Ronzio Pizzeria
  727 East Ave., 401/722-5330
Toti's Pizza Palace
  622 Central Ave., 401/728-9797

Best Vegetarian Food
Garden Grill
  727 East Ave., 401/726-2826

PROVIDENCE, RI

Best Bar
The Gatehouse
  4 Richmond Sq., 401/521-9229

Best Barbecue/Ribs
Wes' Rib House
  38 Dike St., 401/421-9090

Best Bistro
Grill 262
  262 S. Water St., 401/751-3700
Leon's on the West Side
  166 Broadway, 401/273-1055

Best Breakfast
Plaza Grille
  64 De Pasquale Ave., 401/274-8684
Seaplane Diner
  307 Allens Ave., 401/941-9547
Tony's Place
  36 Spruce St., 401/331-1452

Best Brewpub
Trinity Brewhouse
  186 Fountain St., 401/453-2337

Best Business Lunch
Capital Grille
  1 Cookson Pl., 401/521-5600

Best Casual Dining
Wyatt's Rotisserie
  165 Benefit St., 401/751-7900

Best Chinese Food
Little Chopsticks
  495 Smith St., 401/351-4290

Best Coffee/Coffeehouse
Cafe Paragon
  234 Thayer St., 401/331-6200

R

Best Continental Food
Arbor Cafe
  1 W. Exchange St., 401/598-8000
Parkside Rotisserie and Bar
  76 S. Main St., 401/331-0003

Best Delicatessen
Jim's Deli
  1702 Mendon Rd., Cumberland, 401/334-1011

Best Diner
Downcity Diner
  151 Weybosset St., 401/331-9217
Haven Brothers' Diner
  72 Spruce St., 401/861-7777

Best Eclectic Menu
Adesso
  161 Cushing St., 401/521-0770
Applause East Side Bistro
  960 Hope St., 401/274-6055
New Rivers Restaurant
  7 Steeple St., 401/751-0350
Rue De L' Espoir Restaurant
  99 Hope St., 401/751-8890

Best Family Restaurant
Gregg's Restaurant and Pub
  1303 N. Main St., 401/521-9229

Best Fine Dining
Capital Grille
  1 Cookson Pl., 401/521-5600
Christopher's On The Hill
  245 Atwells Ave., 401/274-4232

Best French Food
Cafe La France
  1 Citizens Plz., 401/861-6545
  73 Empire St., 401/454-3380

Best Health-Conscious Menu
Little Chopsticks
  495 Smith St., 401/351-4290

Best Ice Cream/Yogurt
Ice Cream Machine
  4288 Diamond Hill Rd., Cumberland, 401/333-5053
Sunshine Creamery
  305 N. Broadway, Rumford, 401/431-2828

Best Indian Food
India Cafe and Grill
  758 Hope St., 401/421-2600
Taste of India
  230 Wickenden St., 401/421-4355

Best Inexpensive Meal
Angelo's Civita Farnese
  141 Atwells Ave., 401/621-8171

Best Italian Food
Blue Grotto
  210 Atwells Ave., 401/272-9030

Cafe Gianni
  335 Newport Ave., Rumford, 401/438-2226
Camille's Roman Garden
  71 Bradford St., 401/751-4812
Caserta Pizzeria
  121 Spruce St., 401/272-3618
Jimmy's At The Italo
  256 Broadway, 401/273-5488
La Campagnola Cafe
  188 Atwells Ave., 401/861-3463
Old Canteen
  121 Atwells Ave., 401/751-5544
Raphael Bar Risto
  345 S. Water St., 401/421-4646

Best Japanese Food
Oki Japanese Steakhouse
  1270 Mineral Spring Ave., North Providence,
    401/728-7970

Best Lunch
Tony's Place
  36 Spruce St., 401/331-1452

Best Mexican Food
Cactus Grill and Bar
  370 Richmond St., 401/421-3300
Montana
  272 Thayer St., 401/273-7427
Stickyfingers
  133 Douglas Ave., 401/272-7427

Best Other Ethnic Food
Asian Paradise (Cambodian)
  165 Angell St., 401/454-0222
Hot Pockets (Lebanese)
  285 Thayer St., 401/751-3251

Best Pizza
Adesso
  161 Cushing St., 401/521-0770
Bob and Timmy's Legendary Grilled Pizza
  57 De Pasquale Ave., 401/453-2221
Caserta Pizzeria
  121 Spruce St., 401/272-3618
Sammy's House of Pizza
  1370 Mineral Spring Avenue, North Providence,
    401/353-7827
Twins Pizza
  1000 Mineral Spring Ave., North Providence,
    401/726-0549
Uncle Tony's Pizza and Pasta
  141 Newport Ave., Rumford, 401/438-4646

Best Restaurant Meal Value
Little Inn
  103 Putnam Turnpike, Johnston, 401/231-0570

Best Romantic Dining
Pot au Feu French Restaurant
  44 Custom House St., 401/273-8953

Best Sandwiches
Geoff's on Benefit
  163 Benefit St., 401/751-2248
  178 Angell St., 401/751-9214
Meeting Street Cafe
  220 Meeting St., 401/273-1066

Best Seafood
Agora
  Westin Hotel, 1 W. Exchange St., 401/598-8011
Bluepoint Oyster Bar
  99 N. Main St., 401/272-6145
Hemenway's Seafood Grill and Bar
  1 Old Stone Sq., 401/351-8570

Best Southwestern Food
Atomic Grill
  99 Chestnut St., 401/621-8888

Best Steaks
Club 44
  355 Putnam Turnpike, Smithfield, 401/231-2240

Best Sunday Brunch
Davio's
  Biltmore Hotel, 11 Dorrance St., 401/421-0700
Kountry Kitchen Restaurant
  10 Smith Ave., Greenville, 401/949-0840

Best Tea Room
Bush Berry
  466 Putnam Pike, Greenville, 401/949-5230

WARWICK, RI

Best Barbecue/Ribs
Bugaboo Creek Steak House
  30 Jefferson Blvd., 401/781-1400
Dave's Bar and Grill
  2339 Post Rd., 401/739-7444

Best Breakfast
Bickford's Family Restaurant
  24 Jefferson Blvd., 401/785-9660
  969 Bald Hill Rd., 401/828-2080

Best Casual Dining
Bobby J's Europa Pizza
  685 Airport Rd., 401/732-2727

Best Chinese Food
Islander Restaurant
  2318 W. Shore Rd., 401/738-9861
Panda Island
  300 Quaker Ln., 401/821-5553

Best Delicatessen
Ricotti's
  2792 Post Rd., 401/737-9580
Schroder's Delicatessen
  204 Willett Ave., Riverside, 401/437-1610
The Food Chalet
  874 Post Rd., 401/467-9169

Best Desserts
Chelo's of Warwick
  2225 Post Rd., 401/737-7299
Gregg's Restaurant
  1359 Post Rd., 401/467-5700

Best Ice Cream/Yogurt
Carvel Ice Cream Bakery
  1775 Post Rd., 401/738-0495
I Can't Believe It's Yogurt
  300 Quaker Ln., 401/823-3609

Best Italian Food
Portofino
  897 Post Rd., 401/461-8920

Best Pizza
Bertucci's Brick Oven Pizzeria
  1946 Post Rd., 401/732-4343
Pizza King
  1356 Greenwich Ave., 401/732-1338
Uno Pizzerio
  399 Bald Hill Rd., 401/738-5610

Best Place to Take the Kids
Bugaboo Creek Steak House
  30 Jefferson Blvd., 401/781-1400

Best Regional Food
Crow's Nest
  288 Arnolds Neck Dr., 401/732-6575
Rocky Point Chowder House
  1759 Post Rd., 401/739-4222

Best Restaurant Meal Value
Dave's Bar and Grill
  2339 Post Rd., 401/739-7444
Walt's Roast Beef
  1800 Post Rd., 401/732-0374

Best Seafood
Crow's Nest
  288 Arnolds Neck Rd., 401/732-6575
Monterey Restaurant
  1910 Post Rd., 401/738-3407

Best View While Dining
Crow's Nest
  288 Arnolds Neck Rd., 401/732-6575

WEST WARWICK, RI

Best Breakfast
A.J.'s Restaurant
  1365 Main St., 401/828-4160

Best Chinese Food
House of Wu
  52 Providence St., 401/828-7720

Best Delicatessen
Pinelli's Gourmet Deli
  701 Quaker Ln., 401/821-8828

Best Desserts
Audrey's Cafe
   315 Main St., East Greenwich, 401/884-4441

Best Dinner
Cowesett Inn
   226 Cowesett Ave., 401/828-4726

Best Inexpensive Meal
Mr. Taco
   49 Providence St., 401/828-7573

Best Italian Food
Evelyn's Villa
   272 Cowesett Ave., 401/821-0060

Best Lunch
Stephen's Backyard
   11 Curson St., 401/821-0030

Best Sandwiches
Ricotti's
   250 Cowesett Ave., 401/823-1030

WESTERLY, RI

Best Barbecue/Ribs
W.B. Cody's
   265 Post Rd., 401/322-4070

Best Chinese Food
China Pavillion
   148 Granite St., 401/596-9888

Best Delicatessen
Fortuna's Italian Deli
   140 Franklin St., 401/596-1883

Best Lunch
Brick Oven
   209 Main St., Ashaway, 401/377-2230

WOONSOCKET, RI

Best Chinese Food
Chan's Fine Oriental Dining
   267 Main St., 401/765-1900

Best Dinner
Vermette's Restaurant
   1347 Diamond Hill Rd., 401/769-0429

Best Italian Food
Bocce Club
   226 St. Louis Ave., 401/762-0155
Savini's Restaurant
   476 Rathbun St., 401/762-5114

Best Lunch
Box Seats
   350 River St., 401/762-0900

Best Pizza
Arnold Pizza
   260 Arnold St., 401/762-5662
Mezza Luna Pizzeria
   7 Park Sq., 401/769-7654

R

Best Sports Bar
Box Seats
   350 River St., 401/762-0900

South Carolina

AIKEN, SC

Best Atmosphere
Mango's Restaurant
  149 Laurens St. NW, 803/643-0620
No. 10 Downing Street
  241 Laurens St. SW, 803/642-9062
Willcox Inn
  100 Colleton Ave. SW, 803/649-1377

Best Barbecue/Ribs
Bobby's Bar-B-Q Buffet
  1897 Jefferson Davis Hwy., Warrenville,
    803/593-5900
Carolina Barbecue
  109 Main St. S., New Ellenton, 803/652-2919
Hog Heaven Barbecue
  1050 York St. NE, 803/649-6465
Whiskey Road Bar-B-Q
  4248 Whiskey Rd., 803/649-4260

Best Breakfast
Alvanoes Restaurant and Catering
  122 Laurens St. NW, 803/643-9710
New Moon Cafe
  116 Laurens St. NW, 803/643-7088
Track Kitchen
  420 Mead Ave., 803/641-9628

Best Brewpub
Aiken Brewing Company
  140 Laurens St., 803/502-0707

Best Burgers
Alvanoes Restaurant and Catering
  122 Laurens St. NW, 803/643-9710

Arris' Grill
1533 Whiskey Rd., 803/642-3930

Best Chinese Food
China Palace Restaurant
1368 Whiskey Rd., 803/642-9270

Best Delicatessen
Stoplight Deli
119 Laurens St. NW, 803/642-3354

Best Diner
Alvanoes Restaurant and Catering
122 Laurens St. NW, 803/643-9710

Best Fine Dining
Eejay's
Kalmia Mall, Ste. 180, 1680 Richland Ave.,
803/648-6328
Malia's
120 Laurens St. SW, 803/643-3086
Willcox Inn
100 Colleton Ave. SW, 803/649-1377

Best Homestyle Food
Blue Top Grill
212 Aiken Rd., Graniteville, 803/663-3971
Chick-N-Snack
102 Breezy Hill Rd., Graniteville, 803/663-9395
Ford's Lunch
406 Main St., Graniteville, 803/663-3251

Best Inexpensive Meal
Al's Family Restaurant
611 Atomic Rd., North Augusta, 803/278-3140

Best Italian Food
Olive Oil's Italian Cuisine
232 Chesterfield St. SW, 803/649-3726

Best Other Ethnic Food
Mango's Restaurant (Caribbean)
149 Laurens St. NW, 803/643-0620

Best Pizza
Acropolis Pizza Restaurant
1647 Richland Ave. E., 803/649-7601
Ferrando's Italian Pizzeria
3032 Augusta Rd., Warrenville, 803/593-6400
Nick's House of Pizza
411 Silver Bluff Rd., 803/643-8777

Best Place to Take the Kids
Stoplight Deli
119 Laurens St. NW, 803/642-3354

Best Romantic Dining
No. 10 Downing Street
241 Laurens St. SW, 803/642-9062

Best Salad/Salad Bar
West Side Bowery
151 Bee Ln., 803/648-2900

Best Sandwiches
No. 10 Downing Street
 241 Laurens St. SW, 803/642-9062
Stoplight Deli
 119 Laurens St. NW, 803/642-3354

Best Seafood
Bowery Westside
 151 Bee Ln., 803/648-2900
Up Your Alley Restaurant
 222 The Alley, 803/649-2603

Best Steaks
Up Your Alley Restaurant
 222 The Alley, 803/649-2603
Variety Restaurant
 921 York St. NE, 803/648-6987
West Side Bowery
 151 Bee Ln., 803/648-2900

Best Sunday Brunch
Riley's Whitby Bull
 218 York St. SE, 803/641-6227

ANDERSON, SC

Best Breakfast
Butterbean's
 206 Concord Rd., 864/261-3198
Mama Penn's Family Dining
 2935 N. Main St., 864/224-2402

Best Business Lunch
O'Charley's of Anderson
 3723 Clemson Blvd., 864/224-1417
Towne House Restaurant
 125 N. Main St., 864/225-9791
Tucker's Restaurant
 3501 Clemson Blvd., 864/226-5474

Best Chinese Food
Dragon Den Chinese Restaurant
 3323 Clemson Blvd., 864/224-7135
Grand China Restaurant
 4141 Clemson Blvd., 864/261-6688

Best Desserts
Friends Foods with a Flair
 110 N. Main St., 864/231-0663
The Gilded Spoon
 309 N. Main St., 864/231-7843

Best Fine Dining
1109 South Main
 1109 S. Main St., 864/225-1109

Best Italian Food
Capri's Italian
 2407 N. Main St., 864/224-5405
Fazoli's
 3432 Clemson Blvd., 864/225-7918

S

Best Mexican Food
Monterrey Mexican Restaurant
   3191 N. Main St., 864/225-1316

Best Pizza
Pizza Inn
   3420 Clemson Blvd., 864/226-6215

Best Regional Food
Liberty Hall Inn
   621 S. Mechanic St., Pendleton, 864/646-7500

Best Romantic Dining
Doni's Under the Trees
   3422 Clemson Blvd., 864/224-7107

Best Sandwiches
Grace's Coffeehouse and Restaurant
   1510 N. Murray Ave., 864/231-6739

BEAUFORT, SC

Best Barbecue/Ribs
Duke's Barbecue
   3166 Boundary St., 843/524-1128
Sergeant White's Restaurant
   1908 Boundary St., 843/522-2029

Best Breakfast
Blackstone's Deli Cafe
   915 Bay St., 843/524-4330

Best Burgers
Captain Stewbee's Cafe
   1 Landing Dr., Port Royal, 843/525-6768
Steamer
   168 Sea Island Pkwy., 843/522-0210

Best Coffee/Coffeehouse
Firehouse Books and Espresso Bar
   706 Craven St., 843/522-2665

Best Desserts
Emily's
   906 Port Republic St., 843/522-1866

Best Homestyle Food
Backstreet Cafe
   813 Port Republic St., 843/524-2100

Best Pizza
Cinelli Pizzeria
   20 Savannah Hwy., Ste. 21, 843/525-0667
Dad's Place
   2611 Boundary St., 843/522-3237
Upper Crust
   81 Sea Island Pkwy., 843/521-1999

Best Sandwiches
Bananas
   910 Bay St., 843/522-0910
Plum's
   904 1/2 Bay St., 843/525-1946

S

Best Seafood
Dockside Restaurant
  1699 Eleventh St., Port Royal, 843/524-7433
Factory Creek Landing
  67 Sea Island Pkwy., 843/525-1165

Best Sunday Brunch
Beaufort Inn and Restaurant
  809 Port Republic St., 843/521-9000

CHARLESTON, SC

Best Bar
East Bay Trading Company
  161 E. Bay St., 843/722-0722
Henry's
  54 N. Market St., 843/723-4363

Best Breakfast
Baker's Cafe
  214 King St., 843/577-2694
Bear E Patch
  801 Folly Rd., 843/762-6555
Four Corners Cafe
  38 Broad St., 843/577-0088

Best Burgers
Jack's Cafe
  41 George St., 843/723-5237

Best Chinese Food
Emperor's Garden Chinese
  874 Orleans Rd., 843/556-7212

Best Continental Food
Market East Bistro
  14 N. Market St., 843/577-5080

Best Desserts
Indigo Inn
  1 Maiden Ln., 843/577-5900
Kaminsky's Most Excellent Cafe
  78 N. Market St., 843/853-8270
Mint Julep
  68 Queen St., 843/853-6468

Best Family Restaurant
Sticky Fingers Downtown
  235 Meeting St., 843/853-7427
Sticky Fingers
  341 Johnnie Dodds Blvd., Mt. Pleasant,
    843/856-9840

Best Fine Dining
Magnolia's
  185 E. Bay St., 843/577-7771

Best Greek/Mediterranean Food
Old Towne Restaurant
  229 King St., 843/723-8170

Best Homestyle Food
Sticky Fingers Downtown
  235 Meeting St., 843/853-7427

S

Sticky Fingers
  341 Johnnie Dodds Blvd., Mt. Pleasant,
    843/856-9840

Best Inexpensive Meal
Pinckney Cafe and Espresso
  18 Pinckney St., 843/577-0961

Best Italian Food
Bocci's Italian Restaurant
  158 Church St., 843/720-2121
Vincenzo's
  232 Meeting St., 843/577-7953

Best Late-Night Food
T Bonz
  80 N. Market St., 843/577-2511
  1668 Old Towne Rd., West Ashley, 843/556-2478
  1028 Johnnie Dodds Blvd., Mt. Pleasant,
    843/971-7771

Best Mexican Food
Juanita Greenberg
  75 1/2 Wentworth St., 843/577-2877

Best Pizza
Andolini's Pizza
  82 Wentworth St., 843/722-7437

Best Place to Eat Alone
Pinckney Cafe and Espresso
  18 Pinckney St., 843/577-0961

Best Regional Food
Charleston Grill
  224 King St., 843/577-4522

Best Restaurant in Town
Anson
  12 Anson St., 843/577-0551
Captain Stacks
  205 E. Bay St., 843/853-8600

Best Romantic Dining
Blossom Cafe
  171 E. Bay St., 843/722-9200
Fulton Five
  5 Fulton St., 843/853-5555

Best Seafood
A.W. Shucks Seafood Restaurant
  70 State St., 843/723-1151
Crawdaddy's Seafood Restaurant
  1600 Peas Island Rd., James Island, 843/762-4336
Hyman's Seafood Company
  213 Meeting St., 843/723-6000

Best Steaks
Arizona Bar and Grill
  14 Chapel St., 843/577-5090

COLUMBIA, SC

Best Bar
Yesterdays Restaurant and Tavern
  2030 Devine St., 803/799-0049

Best Business Lunch
Restaurant One.Two.Three.
   7001 Saint Andrews Rd., 803/781-0118

Best Chinese Food
Eggroll Chen
   715 Crowson Rd., 803/787-6820

Best Desserts
Spinnaker's Restaurant
   Columbiana Center, 100 Columbiana Circle,
      803/781-0701

Best Ice Cream/Yogurt
Freshens Premium Yogurt
   Columbiana Center, 100 Columbiana Circle,
      Ste. 1254, 803/781-8464
Immaculate Consumption
   933 Main St., 803/799-9053

Best Italian Food
Capri's of Irmo
   7467 Saint Andrews Rd., Irmo, 803/781-0302
Garibaldi's of Columbia
   2013 Greene St., 803/771-8888

Best Mexican Food
San Jose Mexican Restaurant
   4722 Forest Dr., 803/790-0678
   559 Saint Andrews Rd., 803/772-4251

Best Romantic Dining
Garibaldi's of Columbia
   2013 Greene St., 803/771-8888

Best Sandwiches
Beulah's Bar and Grill
   902 Gervais St., 803/779-4655

S

FLORENCE, SC

Best Breakfast
Venus Pancake House
   471 W. Palmetto St., 843/669-9977

Best Italian Food
Grotto Italian Restaurant
   1749 S. Irby St., 843/667-8651

Best Mexican Food
Corona Mexican Restaurant
   2029 W. Evans St., 843/665-6508
San Jose Mexicano Restarante
   1316 S. Irby St., 843/665-0866
   2020 W. Palmetto St., 843/673-6988

Best Restaurant in Town
P.A.'s Restaurant
   South Park Shopping Center, 1534 S. Irby St.,
      843/665-0846
Percy and Willie's
   2401 David H. Mc Leod Blvd., 843/669-1620

GEORGETOWN, SC

Best American Food
Chandler's Choice
  713 Front St., 843/546-4377

Best Desserts
Kudzu Bakery
  714 Front St., 843/546-1847

Best Family Restaurant
Lafayette Restaurant
  711 Church St., 843/546-5033
Land's End Restaurant
  1 Marina Dr., 843/527-1376

Best Fine Dining
Rice Paddy Restaurant
  819 Front St., 843/546-2021

Best Ice Cream/Yogurt
JR Yogurt and Ice Cream
  1063 N. Fraser St., 843/546-1623

Best Lunch
Orange Blossom
  107 Orange St., 843/527-5060
Pink Magnolia
  719 Front St., 843/527-6506

Best Pizza
Tony's Famous Pizza
  415 N. Fraser St., 843/546-1612

Best Restaurant in Town
Land's End Restaurant
  1 Marina Dr., 843/527-1376

Best Sandwiches
River Room Restaurant
  801 Front St., 843/527-4110

Best Seafood
River Room Restaurant
  801 Front St., 843/527-4110

Best Steaks
Nanna's Steakhouse
  502 Church St., 843/527-0077

GREENVILLE, SC

Best American Food
858
  18 E. North St., 864/242-8883
Stax's Omega Diner
  72 Orchard Park Dr., 864/297-6639

Best Barbecue/Ribs
Henry's Smokehouse
  240 Wade Hampton Blvd., 864/232-7774

Best Brewpub
Blue Ridge Brewing Company
  217 N. Main St., 864/232-4677

Best Burgers
Como's Restaurant
  1611 Augusta St., 864/233-1385
Johnny Rocket's
  401 Haywood Rd., 864/627-0405
McGuffey's Restaurant
  711 Congaree Rd., 864/288-3116

Best Casual Dining
Occasionally Blues
  1 Augusta St., 864/242-6000
Stax's Grill
  850 Woods Crossing Rd., 864/288-5546

Best Chinese Food
China Palace
  2112 Wade Hampton Blvd., 864/292-3719
Dragon Den Chinese Restaurant
  420 N. Pleasantburg Dr., 864/242-1777

Best Coffee/Coffeehouse
The Coffee Underground
  1 E. Coffee St., 864/298-0494

Best Delicatessen
Two Chefs
  10 S. Main St., 864/370-9336

Best Diner
Gene's Restaurant
  527 Buncombe St., 864/235-2922

Best Fine Dining
Provencia
  Hyatt Regency, 220 N. Main St., 864/235-1234
Palms
  The Phoenix Hotel, 246 N. Pleasantburg Dr.,
  864/370-9181
Seven Oaks Restaurant
  104 Broadus Ave., 864/232-1895
Stax's Peppermill
  30 W. Orchard Park Dr., 864/288-9320
The Terrace
  100 Villa Rd., 864/242-3804

Best Homestyle Food
Bullock's Restaurant
  424 Laurens Rd., 864/233-0558
Grandma's Saloon and Deli
  723 Congaree Rd., 864/297-4145

Best Ice Cream/Yogurt
Swensen's Ice Cream
  2025 Wade Hampton Blvd., 864/268-7945

Best Italian Food
Alberto's Trattoria
  2016 Augusta St., 864/233-8868
Capri's Italian Restaurant
  1130 Woodruff Rd., 864/288-5884
  500 E. Stone Ave., 864/235-4552
Provino's Italian Restaurant
  3795 E. North St., 864/268-9432

S

Vince Perone's
  1 E. Antrim Dr., 864/233-1621

Best Japanese Food
Yagoto
  500 Congaree Rd., 864/288-8471

Best Mexican Food
Cantinflas
  120 S. Main St., 864/250-1300
Corona Mexican Restaurant
  2112 Wade Hampton Blvd., 864/292-3719
Monterrey Mexican Restaurant
  1813 Laurens Rd., 864/271-2561
  2716 Wade Hampton Blvd., 864/268-5277
  2801 Poinsett Hwy., 864/271-3625

Best Pizza
Barley's Tap Room
  25 W. Washington St., 864/232-3706

Best Place to Take the Kids
Zaxby's Restaurant
  1903 Laurens Rd., 864/370-1995

Best Sandwiches
Fatz Cafe
  225 S. Pleasantburg Dr., 864/467-9542
Schlotzsky's
  2121 Augusta St., 864/232-7229

Best Steaks
The Peddler Steak House
  2000 Poinsett Hwy., 864/235-7192

GREENWOOD, SC

Best Chinese Food
China Garden
  421 Montague Ave., 864/223-2999

Best Italian Food
Capri's Italian
  1704 Bypass 72NE, 864/223-0367

Best Lunch
Fatz Cafe
  1302 Montague Ave. St., 864/229-3711

Best Restaurant in Town
Inn on the Square
  104 Court St., 864/223-4488
Ranch House Restaurant
  1213 Bypass 72NE, 864/223-5909

HILTON HEAD ISLAND, SC

Best American Food
Scott's Fish Market Restaurant
  1 Shelter Cove Ln. at Harbourside I, 843/785-7575

Best Bar
Big Rocco's Restaurant and Lounge
  15 Park Ln., 843/785-9000
Reilley's South
  70 Greenwood Dr., 843/842-4414

Reilley's North End Pub
  Port Royal Plz., 123E Mathews Dr., 843/681-4153

Best Casual Dining
Crabby Nick's Seafood House
  2 Regency Pkwy., 843/842-2425
Remy's Restaurant and Lounge
  28 Arrow Rd., 843/842-3800

Best Continental Food
Julep's Restaurant
  14 Greenwood Dr., Ste. G, 843/842-5857

Best Diner
Hilton Head Diner
  6 Marina Side Dr., 843/686-2400

Best French Food
Gaslight Restaurant
  303 Market Pl., 843/785-5814
La Maisonette
  14 Pope Ave., 843/785-6000

Best German Food
Hofbrauhaus Restaurant
  Pope Ave., 843/785-3663

Best Italian Food
Antonio's Restaurant
  Village at Wexford, Ste. B6, 843/842-5505
Fratello's
  811 William Hilton Pkwy., 843/785-6620
Just Pasta
  1 Coligny Plz., 843/686-3900
Stellini Italian Restaurant
  15 Pope Ave., 843/785-7006

Best Mexican Food
San Miguel's Mexican Cafe
  Harbourside III at Shelter Cove, 843/842-4555

Best Pizza
Jiuseppe's Pizza and Pasta
  32B Shelter Cove Ln., 843/785-4144
  79 Lighthouse Rd., Ste. 210, 843/671-5133

Best Romantic Dining
Old Fort Pub Restaurant
  101 Marshland Rd., 843/681-6040

Best Sandwiches
Plantation Cafe
  14 Heritage Plz., 843/785-9020

Best Seafood
Abe's Native Shrimp House
  650 William Hilton Pkwy., 843/785-3675
Crazy Crab
  1 Lighthouse Rd., 843/363-2722

Best View While Dining
Old Fort Pub Restaurant
  101 Marshland Rd., 843/681-6040

S

MURRELLS INLET, SC

Best Homestyle Food
Spring House Restaurant
   3841 Hwy. 17 Business, 843/357-2785

Best Seafood
Admiral's Flagship Restaurant
   4664 Hwy. 17 Business, 843/651-3016
Dockside Restaurant
   4037 Hwy. 17 Business, 843/651-5850
Drunken Jack's Restaurant
   4031 Hwy. 17 Business, 843/651-2044
Flo's Place Restaurant and Bar
   3797 Hwy. 17 Business, 843/651-7222
Lee's Inlet Kitchen
   4460 Hwy. 17 Business, 843/651-2881
Nance's Creek Front Restaurant
   4883 Hwy. 17 Business, 843/651-2696
Oliver's Lodge
   4204 Hwy. 17 Business, 843/651-2963
Plantation Kitchen
   Hwy. 17 Business, 843/651-7919

Best Steaks
T-Bones Steak House and Saloon
   715 Pendergrass Ave., 843/651-0551

MYRTLE BEACH, SC

Best All-You-Can-Eat Buffet
Captain Benjamin's Calabash Seafood Buffet
   401 S. Kings Hwy., 843/626-9354
   2290 S. Kings Hwy., 843/448-9787
Benjamin's Calabash Seafood
   9593 N. Kings Hwy., 843/449-0821

Best Barbecue/Ribs
Prosser's Barbecue
   2394 Hwy. 501E, Conway, 843/347-2247

Best Beer Selection
Liberty Steakhouse
   Broadway at the Beach, 1321 Celebrity Circle,
      843/626-4677

Best Breakfast
Omega Pancake and Omelet House
   2800 N. Kings Hwy., 843/626-9949

Best Eclectic Menu
Latif's Bakery and Cafe
   503 61st Ave. N., 843/449-1716

Best Homestyle
K and W Cafeteria
   2001 S. Kings Hwy., 843/448-1669
   7900 N. Kings Hwy., 843/449-1442

Best Ice Cream/Yogurt
Painter's Homemade Ice Cream
   2107 Hwy. 17 Bypass S., 843/651-1255
   5706 S. Kings Hwy., 843/238-2724

S

Best Mexican Food
El Cerro Grande
 1880 Hwy. 17N, 843/238-1239

Best Restaurant in Town
Carolina Roadhouse
 4617 S. Kings Hwy., 843/497-9911
Thoroughbreds Restaurant
 9706 N. Kings Hwy., 843/497-2636

Best Sandwiches
Dagwood's
 400 Eleventh Ave. N., 843/448-0100

Best Seafood
Chesapeake House
 9918 N. Kings Hwy., 843/449-3231

NORTH MYRTLE BEACH, SC

Best American Food
Joe's Bar and Grill
 810 Conway St., 843/272-4666

Best Italian Food
Tony's Italian Restaurant
 1407 Old Hwy. 17N, 843/249-1314
Umberto's
 Barefoot Landing, 4886 Hwy. 17S, 843/272-1176
 1705 Hwy. 17N, Little River, 843/249-5552

Best Mexican Food
Rosa Linda's Cafe
 4635 Hwy. 17S, 843/272-6823

Best Seafood
Marker 350
 4 Harbour Pl., 843/249-3888
Oak Harbor Inn
 1407 Thirteenth Ave. N., 843/249-4737
Sante Fe Station
 1101 Hwy. 17N, 843/249-3463

Best Sports Bar
Oscar's Food and Spirits
 4101 Hwy. 17S, 843/272-0707

Best Steaks
Old Pro's Table
 4701 Hwy. 17S, 843/272-6060

ORANGEBURG, SC

Best Barbecue/Ribs
Earl Duke's Bar-B-Que
 1878 Charleston Rd. SW, 803/534-4493

Best Burgers
Central Park USA
 168 John C. Calhoun Dr. SE, 803/531-3444

Best Chinese Food
China Palace
 1045 Five Chop Rd. SE, 803/536-4676

S

Best Homestyle Food
Biddie Banquet
 1575 John C. Calhoun Dr. SE, 803/534-0488
Crossroads Restaurant
 1680 Neeses Hwy., 803/531-4064

Best Ice Cream/Yogurt
Dairy O
 1504 Russell St. SE, 803/536-4205

Best Sandwiches
Chestnut Grill
 1455 Chestnut St. NE, 803/531-1747
Schlotzsky's
 1208 Saint Matthews Rd. NE, 803/536-5628

Best Seafood
Fisherman's Catch
 603 Bleakley St. SE, 803/531-1033
The Shrimper
 1270 John C. Calhoun Dr. SW, 803/531-2336

PAWLEYS ISLAND, SC

Best Bar
Litchfield Beach Fish House
 Ocean Hwy. 17S, North Pawleys Island
  843/237-3949

Best Casual Dining
Island Cafe and Deli
 Ocean Hwy. 17, 843/237-9527
Island Country Store
 Ocean Hwy. 17, 843/237-8465
Frank's Outback
 10434 Ocean Hwy. 17, 843/237-1777
Shabby's
 9674 Ocean Hwy. 17S, 843/237-4205

Best Fine Dining
Community House Restaurant and Tavern
 10555 Ocean Hwy. 17S, 843/237-8353
Frank's Restaurant and Bar
 10434 Ocean Hwy. 17N, 843/237-3030

Best Italian Food
Deniro's Italian Ristorante
 105 Ocean Hwy. 17S, 843/237-1397

Best Seafood
Litchfield Beach Fish House
 Ocean Hwy. 17S, 843/237-3949
Litchfield Inn
 1 Norris Dr., 843/237-4211
Mayor's House Restaurant
 2614 Ocean Hwy. 17, 843/237-9082

ROCK HILL, SC

Best American Food
Anna J's Restaurant
 1025 Camden Ave., 803/327-9943
Thursdays Too
 147 Herlong Ave., 803/366-6117

S

The White Horse
617 Cherry Rd., 803/328-2172

Best Breakfast
The Little Cafe
1204 Mt. Gallant Rd., 803/329-1440

Best Burgers
Checkers
2615 Cherry Rd., 803/324-7538

Best Cafeteria
Jackson's Cafeteria
1735 Heckle Blvd., 803/366-6860

Best Homestyle Food
Sagebrush Steakhouse and Saloon
2445 Cherry Rd., 803/366-8331
Watkins Grill
123 Elk Ave., 803/327-4923

Best Mexican Food
El Cancun
1244 Cherry Rd., 803/366-6996

Best Other Ethnic Food
Tropical Escape Cafe (Pacific Rim)
590 N. Anderson Rd., Hwy. 21 Bypass,
803/366-3888

Best Sandwiches
For What It's Worth
122 E. Main St., 803/327-1450

Best Seafood
Tam's Tavern
1027 Oakland Ave., 803/329-2226
Tropical Escape Cafe
590 N. Anderson Rd., Hwy. 21 Bypass,
803/366-3888

S

SPARTANBURG, SC

Best Breakfast
Papa Sam's Breakfast Nook
191 E. Saint John St., 864/582-6655
Skillet Restaurant
435 E. Main St., 864/582-3206

Best Burgers
Beacon Drive In
255 Reidville Rd., 864/585-9387
Sugar and Spice Drive-In Restaurant
212 S. Pine St., 864/585-3991

Best Business Lunch
As You Like It
401 E. Kennedy St., 864/573-6633

Best Chinese Food
Great Wall
1120 Asheville Hwy., 864/583-4668
Jade Garden Chinese Restaurant
1200 E. Main St., 864/583-2532
Shanghai Restaurant
1100 Asheville Hwy., 864/574-1300

Best Coffee/Coffeehouse
The Sandwich Factory
  137 W. Main St., 864/585-8506

Best Fine Dining
Harry's on Morgan Square
  116 Magnolia St., 864/583-8121
Spice of Life
  100 Wood Row, 864/585-3737

Best German Food
Gerhard's Cafe
  1200 E. Main St., 864/591-1920

Best Homestyle Food
Wade's Restaurant
  1000 N. Pine St., 864/582-3800
Woodward's Cafe
  438 Stevens St., 864/585-5986

Best Inexpensive Meal
The Sandwich Factory
  137 W. Main St., 864/585-8506

Best Italian Food
Capri's Italian Restaurant
  299 E. Wood St., 864/583-7811
  1600 Reidville Rd., 864/576-4152
Dante Italian Restaurant
  456 Oak Grove Rd., 864/576-2107
Renato's Italian Restaurant
  221 E. Kennedy St., 864/585-7027
Stefano's Restaurant
  1560 Union St., 864/591-1941

Best Mexican Food
Corona Mexican Restaurant
  404D McCravy Dr., 864/585-9980
Monterrey Mexican Restaurant
  149 Fernwood Dr., 864/582-7700
  1450 W.O. Ezell Blvd., 864/574-7214
  1564 Asheville Hwy., 864/591-2015

Best Place to Eat Alone
Mimi's Uptown
  180 E. Main St., 864/585-8332

Best Sandwiches
Ice Creams and Coffee Beans
  551 E. Main St., 864/597-1510
  1735 Reidville Rd., Ste. 12, 864/574-2252

Best Seafood
Seven Sea's Seafood and Steaks
  1398 Boiling Springs Rd., 864/578-9768
Walnut Grove Southern Grill
  Hwy. 221 at I-26, Roebuck, 864/574-7777

Best Steaks
Le Baron Restaurant
  2600 E. Main St., 864/579-3111
Peddler Steak House
  464 E. Main St., 864/583-5874

S

Piedmont Steak House
276 Magnolia St., 864/582-4380

Best Tea Room
Grapevine Shoppe and Tea Room
113 Wall St., 864/573-1484
Piazza Tea Room
571 E. Main St., 864/582-5861

SUMTER, SC

Best Barbecue/Ribs
Ward's Barbecue
1961 McCrays Mill Rd., 803/773-2206
1087 Alice Dr., 803/775-0008
416 E. Liberty St., 803/775-2490

Best Chinese Food
Dragon Restaurant
236 S. Pike W., 803/778-1807

Best Fine Dining
Lilfred's of Camden
8425 Main St., Rembert, 803/432-7063
Mill Pond Restaurant
84 Boykin Mill Rd., Rembert, 803/424-0261

Best Italian Food
Sambino's Italian Restaurant
4742 Broad St., 803/494-9494

Best Mexican Food
Casa Linda Mexican Restaurant
1029 Broad St., 803/778-2939

Best Sandwiches
Mary Ann's Deli Restaurant
584 Bultman Dr., 803/775-4575

S

Best Steaks
Omaha Steakhouse of Sumter
1336 Broad St., 803/469-0076

South Dakota

Best Breakfast
Starlight Truck Stop and Restaurant
  702 S. Hwy. 281, 605/225-5913

Best Casual Dining
The Back Room
  Ward Hotel, 104 S. Main St., 605/225-6100

Best Chinese Food
King House Chinese Restaurant
  311 S. Main St., 605/229-2587

Best Diner
R.G.'s Restaurant
  2402 Sixth Ave. SE, 605/226-0316

Best Dinner
Helen's California Kitchen
  Melgaard Rd., 605/225-9286

Best Mexican Food
Guadalajara Mexican Restaurant
  3015 Sixth Ave. SE, 605/229-7555

Best Restaurant in Town
Flame Restaurant and Lounge
  2 S. Main St., 605/225-2082
Helen's California Kitchen
  Melgaard Rd., 605/225-9286
Refuge Oyster Bar Grill
  715 Lancelot Ln., 605/229-2681

Best Seafood
Refuge Oyster Bar Grill
  715 Lancelot Ln., 605/229-2681

S

BROOKINGS, SD

Best Breakfast
Country Kitchen of Brookings
2221 Sixth St., 605/692-6968
Dakota Inn Restaurant
1441 Sixth St., 605/692-9320

Best Burgers
Nick's Hamburger Shop
427 Main Ave., 605/692-4324

Best Coffee/Coffeehouse
Joehouse Espresso Cafe
311 Third St., 605/692-5777

Best Homestyle Food
Cook's Kitchen
304 Main Ave., 605/692-1303
Granmoo's Kitchen
417 Main Ave., 605/692-1290

Best Pizza
George's Pizza and Steak House
311 Main Ave., 605/692-6610

Best Sandwiches
Mad Jack's Brown Baggers
805 Medary Ave., 605/692-2878

Best Seafood
Casper's Cafe
420 Main Ave., 605/692-7240
Ram Pub
327 Main Ave., 605/692-2485

Best Steaks
Pheasant Restaurant
726 S. Main Ave., 605/692-4723
Steak and Buffet
1815 Sixth St., 605/692-1740

HOT SPRINGS, SD

Best American Food
Debbie's Diner
333 S. Chicago St., 605/745-6588

Best Bar
Yogi's Den
625 N. River St., 605/745-5949

Best Breakfast
Cascade Restaurant
800 Mammoth St., 605/745-3878
Maverick Restaurant and Lounge
Hwy. 18-385 at Hwy. 79, 605/745-4215

Best Burgers
Yogi's Den
625 N. River St., 605/745-5949

Best Coffee/Coffeehouse
Katz Kafe
603 N. River St., 605/745-6005

Best Family Restaurant
Cascade Restaurant
  800 Mammoth St., 605/745-3878
Dakota Rose Restaurant
  E. Hwy. 79, 605/745-6447
Maverick Restaurant and Lounge
  Hwy. 18-385 at Hwy. 79, 605/745-4215

Best Homestyle Food
Black Hills Family Restaurant
  745 Battle Mountain Ave., 605/745-3737

Best Salad/Salad Bar
Katz Kafe
  603 N. River St., 605/745-6005

Best Sandwiches
Katz Kafe
  603 N. River St., 605/745-6005

Best Steaks
Cascade Restaurant
  800 Mammoth St., 605/745-3878
Dakota Rose Restaurant
  E. Hwy. 79, 605/745-6447
Maverick Restaurant and Lounge
  Hwy. 18-385 at Hwy. 79, 605/745-4215

HURON, SD

Best All-You-Can-Eat Buffet
Barn Restaurant
  2715 Dakota Ave. S., 605/352-9238

Best Breakfast
Festivals
  100 Fourth St. SW, 605/352-3204

Best Chinese Food
Prom Oriental Kitchen
  149 Dakota Ave. S., 605/352-1844

Best Family Restaurant
Festivals
  100 Fourth St. SW, 605/352-3204

Best Inexpensive Meal
Sid's Lunch
  340 Kansas Ave. SE, 605/352-5300

Best Steaks
Prime Time Tavern
  2110 Dakota Ave. S., 605/352-9906
Shenanigan's Pub and Cafe
  1000 Eighteenth St. SW, 605/352-4617

MITCHELL, SD

Best Chinese Food
Twin Dragon
  704 E. Norway Ave., 605/996-5446

Best Dinner
Chef Louie's Steak House and Lounge
  601 E. Haven St., 605/996-7565

S

Best Inexpensive Meal
Scoreboard
  315 N. Main St., 605/996-9488

Best Steaks
The Brig Steak House
  Hwy. 37N, 605/996-7444

Best Sunday Brunch
Block and Barrel
  Holiday Inn, 1525 W. Havens St., 605/996-6501

PIERRE, SD

Best Bar
Shenanigans Sports Pub and Restaurant
  602 W. Sioux Ave., 605/224-5657

Best Family Restaurant
Country Kitchen
  221 E. Pleasant Dr., 605/224-8431
Kozy Korner Family Restaurant
  217 E. Dakota Ave., 605/224-9547

Best Health-Conscious Menu
Classy's
  1615 N. Harrison Ave., 605/224-5857

Best Homestyle Food
Town and Country Restaurant
  808 W. Sioux Ave., 605/224-7183

Best Pizza
Gator's Pizza
  1615 N. Harrison Ave., 605/224-6262
Pizza Ranch
  1610 N. Hwy. 83, Ft. Pierre, 605/223-9114

Best Sports Bar
Point After Sports Bar
  620 S. Cleveland Ave., 605/224-8326

Best Steaks
Cattleman's Club
  29608 South Dakota Hwy. 34, 605/224-9774

RAPID CITY, SD

Best Atmosphere
Pirate's Table
  3550 Sturgis Rd., 605/341-4842

Best Brewpub
Firehouse Brewing Company
  610 Main St., 605/348-1915

Best Chinese Food
Golden Phoenix
  2421 W. Main St., 605/348-4195
Imperial Chinese Restaurant
  702 E. North St., 605/394-8888

Best Desserts
Breakfast Nook
  720 N. Lacrosse St., 605/399-3975

Best Dinner
Murphy's
510 Ninth St., 605/348-7270

Best Family Restaurant
Millstone Family Restaurant
1520 N. Lacrosse St., 605/348-9022
2010 W. Main St., 605/343-5824

Best Pizza
B.J.'s Grinder King
902 Main St., 605/348-3166

Best Restaurant in Town
American Pie Bistro and Marketplace
710 Saint Joseph St., 605/343-3773
Asian Cafe
208 E. North St., 605/399-1579
Beanery Deli and Bakery
201 Main St., 605/348-6775
Carini's Italian Food
324 Saint Joseph St., 605/348-3704
Colonial House Restaurant
2501 Mount Rushmore Rd., 605/342-4640
Elk Creek Steakhouse and Lounge
I-90, Exit 46, Piedmont, 605/787-6349
Firehouse Brewing Company
610 Main St., 605/348-1915
Fireside Inn
23021 Hisega Rd., 605/342-3900
Gaslight Restaurant and Saloon
13490 Main St., 605/343-9276
Piesano's Pacchia
3618 Canyon Lake Dr., 605/341-6941
Veggies
2050 W. Main St., 605/348-5019

Best Restaurant Meal Value
Millstone Family Restaurant
2010 W. Main St., 605/343-5824
1520 N. Lacrosse St., 605/348-9022

Best Sandwiches
Sixth Street Bakery and Deli
516 Sixth St., 605/342-6660

SIOUX FALLS, SD

Best All-You-Can-Eat Buffet
Royal Fork Buffet Restaurant
4610 W. Empire Pl., 605/361-1094

Best Bar
Sioux Falls Brewing Company
431 N. Phillips Ave., 605/332-4847

Best Breakfast
Minerva's Downtown
301 S. Phillips Ave., 605/334-0386

Best Business Lunch
Minerva's Downtown
301 S. Phillips Ave., 605/334-0386

S

Best Chinese Food
Szechwan Chinese Restaurant
   415 N. Minnesota Ave., 605/332-2010
   423 S. Phillips Ave., 605/339-4116

Best Coffee/Coffeehouse
Barnes and Noble
   3800 S. Louise Ave., 605/361-9244

Best Fine Dining
Theo's Great Food
   601 W. 33rd St., 605/338-6801

Best French Food
Theo's Great Food
   601 W. 33rd St., 605/338-6801

Best Inexpensive Meal
Roll 'N Pin Restaurant
   3015 W. Russell St., 605/339-9190

Best Mexican Food
Casa Del Ray
   901 W. Russell St., 605/338-6078
   4529 E. 26th St., 605/371-3828

Best Pizza
Lucianna's
   945 S. Marion Rd., 605/334-4820

Best Salad/Salad Bar
Valentino's
   2000 W. 41st St., 605/339-9900

Best Steaks
Tea Steakhouse
   215 S. Main St., Tea, 605/368-9667

Best Tea Room
Parsonage
   3915 S. Hawthorne Ave., 605/334-8838

Best Vegetarian Food
Kristina's Cafe and Bakery
   334 S. Phillips Ave., 605/331-4860

STURGIS, SD

Best All-You-Can-Eat Buffet
Bob's Family Restaurant
   1039 Main St., 605/347-2930
Boulder Canyon Restaurant
   Hwy. 14A at Boulder Canyon Route, 605/347-3787

Best Burgers
Mom's
   2214 Junction Ave., 605/347-3709

Best Desserts
Ranch House Cafe
   S. Junction, 605/347-5503

Best Homestyle Food
Country Kitchen
   620 E. Jackson Blvd., Spearfish, 605/642-4200

Best Pizza
Gold Pan Pizza
1133 Main St., 605/347-5221

Best Restaurant in Town
Anthony's
270 Main St., Deadwood, 605/578-9777
Bay Leafe Cafe
126 W. Hudson St., Spearfish, 605/642-5462
Jake's
677 Main St., Deadwood, 605/578-3656

VERMILLION, SD

Best Burgers
Bimbo's Burger Bar
918 E. Cherry St., 605/624-4791

Best Casual Dining
Toby's Lounge
Main St., Meckling, 605/624-9905

Best Coffee/Coffeehouse
Coffee Shop Gallery
108B E. Main St., 605/624-2945

Best Desserts
Silver Dollar Saloon and Eatery
1216 E. Cherry St., 605/624-4830

Best Family Restaurant
Cowboy Family Restaurant
1122 E. Cherry St., 605/624-8879

Best Health-Conscious Menu
Emma's Kitchen
13 W. Main St., 605/624-9337

Best Homestyle Food
Whimp's Place
Main St., Burbank, 605/624-9973

Best Ice Cream/Yogurt
R-Pizza
2 W. Main St., 605/624-6757

Best Korean Food
Chae's
8 W. Main St., 605/624-2294

Best Mexican Food
Recuerdo De Mexico
112 E. Main St., 605/624-6445

WATERTOWN, SD

Best All-You-Can-Eat Buffet
Steak and Buffet
710 Tenth St. SW, 605/886-4822

Best Barbecue/Ribs
Second Street Station
15 Second St. SW, 605/886-8304

Best Breakfast
Wheel Inn
Hwy. 20N, 605/886-4649

S

Best Coffee/Coffeehouse
Java House
  1002 Fourteenth St. SE, 605/882-2000

Best Family Restaurant
Grainery
  615 Fifth Ave. SE, 605/882-3950

Best Ice Cream/Yogurt
Little Dipper
  1300 Ninth Ave. SE, 605/886-9114

Best Pizza
Godfather's Pizza
  1300 Ninth Ave. SE, 605/882-1232

Best Salad/Salad Bar
Willie Mayes Sports Cafe
  Drake Motor Inn, 621 Fifth St. SE, 605/886-8411

Best Sandwiches
Dagwood's Subs
  23 Fifth St. NE, 605/886-6568

Best Seafood
Lakeshore
  100 N. Lake Dr., 605/882-3422

S

Tennessee

BRISTOL, TN

Best Barbecue/Ribs
Pardner's
  5444 Hwy. 11E, Piney Flats, 423/538-5539
Ridgewood Restaurant
  900 Elizabethton Hwy., Bluff City, 423/538-7543

Best Burgers
Pal's
  960 Volunteer Pkwy., 423/652-2291

Best Dinner
Athens Steakhouse
  329 Eighth St., 423/652-2202

Best Ice Cream/Yogurt
Kay's Ice Cream
  9 Pennsylvania Ave., 423/968-9974

Best Inexpensive Meal
Pal's
  960 Volunteer Pkwy., 423/652-2291

Best Lunch
The Feed Room
  620 State St., 423/764-0545

Best Mexican Food
La Carreta Restaurant
  530 Volunteer Pkwy., 423/989-3361

CHATTANOOGA, TN

Best Bar
Yesterdays Restaurant
  820 Georgia Ave., 423/756-1978

Best Beer Selection
Big River Grille and Brewing Works
222 Broad St., 423/267-2739

Best Burgers
Armando's Brownie Burgers
3943 St. Elmo Ave., 423/825-1840

Best Business Lunch
Town and Country Restaurant
110 N. Market St., 423/267-8544

Best Chinese Food
New Peking Mandarin House
1801 Dayton Blvd., 423/870-9915

Best Coffee/Coffeehouse
Mudpie Coffee House and News Stand
12 Frazier Ave., 423/267-9043
Rembrandt's
204 High St., 423/267-2451

Best Desserts
Southside Grill
1400 Cowart St., 423/266-6511

Best Fine Dining
The Green Room
The Radison Read House, 827 Broad St., 423/266-4121

Best French Food
La Cabriole
1341 Burgess Rd., 423/821-0350

Best Homestyle Food
Bea's Restaurant
4500 Dodds Ave., 423/867-3618
Country Place Restaurant
5025 Dayton Blvd., 423/875-0741
7320 Shallowford Rd., 423/855-1392

Best Ice Cream/Yogurt
Mr. T's Delivery and Ice Cream
3924 Tennessee Ave., 423/821-5084

Best Italian Food
Provino's Italian Restaurant
5084 S. Terrace, 423/899-2559
Tony's Pasta Shop
212 High St., 423/757-0118

Best Late Night Food
Mudpie Coffee House and News Stand
12 Frazier Ave., 423/267-9043
Steak N Shake
2296 Gunbarrel Rd., 423/892-2993

Best Lunch
Sloppy Greeks Cafe
718B Market St., 423/752-1946

Best Mexican Food
Las Margaritas Mexican Restaurant and Cantina
1101 Hixson Pike, 423/756-3332

Best Romantic Dining
The Loft
  328 Cherokee Blvd., 423/266-3601

Best Vegetarian Food
Country Life Vegetarian Restaurant
  3748 Ringgold Rd., 423/622-2451

CLARKSVILLE, TN

Best Brewpub
Blackhorse Brewery and Pub
  132 Franklin St., 931/552-3726

Best Burgers
Buffalo Brady's Wooden Nickel
  1009 S. Riverside Dr., 931/552-1401
Johnny's Burgers and Pizza
  428 College St., 931/647-4545
Stratton's
  201 S. Main St., Ashland City, 615/792-9177

Best Chinese Food
China Star Restaurant
  804 S. Riverside Dr., 931/648-4405
Hunan Chinese Restaurant
  1947 Madison St., 931/552-7889

Best Desserts
Sweet Shoppe
  135 Franklin St., 931/551-8580

Best Homestyle Food
Mayfield's Barbecue
  247 Hwy. 149, 931/647-6237
Wilson's Catfish
  2560 Wilma Rudolph Blvd., 931/552-2342

Best Korean Food
Seoul Garden
  1913 Fort Campbell Blvd., 931/648-4536

Best Mexican Food
Cancun Mexican Restaurant
  1820 Madison St., 931/647-1493

Best Pizza
Blackhorse Brewery and Pub
  132 Franklin St., 931/552-3726
Mr. Gatti's Pizza
  1807 Madison St., 931/647-7728

Best Steaks
Hickory Stick Grill
  1979 Madison St., 931/503-8270
Logan's Roadhouse
  3072 Wilma Rudolph Blvd., 931/6458333

CLEVELAND, TN

Best Breakfast
Rebel North
  2502 N. Ocoee St., 423/472-6524

T

Best Chinese Food
China Hall
  145 Stuart Rd. NE, 423/479-6666

Best Italian Food
Gondolier Pizza
  3300 Keith St. NW, 423/472-4998

Best Lunch
Jenkins Deli
  88 Mouse Creek Rd. NW, 423/479-5315

Best Mexican Food
Monterey Mexican Restaurant
  3055 Keith St. NW, 423/339-5700

Best Steaks
Roblyn's Steak House
  1422 25th St. NW, 423/476-8808

COLUMBIA, TN

Best Barbecue/Ribs
J.J.'s Barbecue
  1122 Hampshire Pike, 931/380-1756
Nolan's Barbecue
  115 E. James Campbell Blvd., 931/381-4322

Best Burgers
Betty's Parkway Restaurant
  912 Riverside Dr., 931/388-5570
Sam Hill's Restaurant
  1144 Riverside Dr., 931/388-5555

Best Chinese Food
Chinese Panda Restaurant
  100 Berrywood Dr., 931/381-7733

Best Dinner
Legends Restaurant
  2401 Pulaski Hwy., 931/380-1888

Best Family Restaurant
Apples Grill and Bar
  Ramada Inn, 1208 Nashville Hwy., 931/388-2720

Best Greek/Mediterranean Food
Chicago's Good Eatings
  800 Hatcher Ln., 931/381-7462

Best Homestyle Food
Harlan House
  104 W. Sixth St., 931/388-6868

Best Lunch
Back Porch Barbeque
  200 W. Third St., 931/381-2225

Best Mexican Food
La Hacienda Mexican Restaurant
  119 Nashville Hwy., Ste. 117, 931/380-1565

Best Sports Bar
Sam Hill's Restaurant
  1144 Riverside Dr., 931/388-5555

Best Steaks
Sarge's Shack
  Hwy. 64 at Hwy. 65, Exit 14, 931/363-1310

COOKEVILLE, TN

Best Barbecue/Ribs
Bobby Q's
  1070 N. Washington Ave., 931/526-1024

Best Burgers
Dipsy Doodle Drive In
  1442 W. Broad St., 931/526-2986

Best Homestyle Food
City Square Cafe
  453 E. Broad St., 931/528-9120

Best Lunch
Diner on First
  120 W. First St., 931/520-0173
O'Charley's
  1401 Interstate Dr., 931/520-1898

DYERSBURG, TN

Best American Food
Catfish Corner
  1910 Upper Finley Rd., 901/285-6428

Best Bar
Chequers
  110 S. Main Ave., 901/285-0515

Best Barbecue/Ribs
Neil's Barbeque and Grill
  470A Mall Blvd., 901/287-8400

Best Breakfast
Cozy Kitchen
  100 N. Church Ave., 901/285-1054

Best Chinese Food
New China
  506 Hwy. 51 Bypass, 901/285-1573

Best Coffee/Coffeehouse
Old Hickory House
  State Hwy. 51N, 901/285-2702

Best Desserts
Plaza Restaurant
  1140 U.S. Hwy. 51N Bypass, 901/287-7893

Best Homestyle Food
Mom's Kitchen
  9595 Hwy. 78, 901/286-6689

Best Romantic Dining
Daddy Jack's Steak and Seafood
  Holiday Inn, 835 Hwy. 51N Bypass, 901/286-6744

Best Salad/Salad Bar
Grecian Steak House
  2265 St. John Ave., 901/286-6842

T

FRANKLIN, TN

Best Barbecue/Ribs
Corky's Barbeque
  100 Franklin Rd., Brentwood, 615/373-1020
Herbert's Barbecue Restaurant
  111 Royal Oaks Blvd., 615/791-0700
West Side Ribs and Bar-B-Que
  224 New Hwy. 96 W., 615/790-6787

Best Cajun/Creole Food
Copeland's of New Orleans
  1649 Westgate Circle, Brentwood, 615/661-8040

Best Casual Dining
Bunganut Pig
  1143 Columbia Ave., 615/794-4777
Uncle Bud's Catfish
  1214 Lakeview Dr., 615/790-1234

Best Dinner
Five Points Place
  438 Main St., 615/591-4787
Franklin Chop House
  1101 Murfreesboro Rd., 615/591-7666

Best Homestyle Food
Dotson's Restaurant
  99 E. Main St., 615/794-2805

Best Indian Food
The East India Club
  4926 Thoroughbred Ln., Brentwood, 615/661-9919

Best Italian Food
Antonio's Ristorante Italiano
  119 Fifth Ave. N., 615/790-1733
Bravo Ceasar
  414 Main St., 615/791-7999
Romano's Macaroni Grill
  1712 Galleria Blvd., 615/771-7002

Best Lunch
HRH Dumplin's of Franklin
  428 Main St., 615/791-4651
Meridee's Bread Basket
  110 Fourth Ave. S., 615/790-3755

Best Mexican Food
Camino Real
  548 Alexander Plz., 615/790-3104
La Hacienda Mexican Restaurant
  509 Hillsboro Rd., 615/591-9590

Best Salad/Salad Bar
J. Alexander's
  1721 Galleria Blvd., 615/771-7779

GATLINBURG, TN

[See also: Sevierville.]

Best American Food
Howard's Restaurant
  650 Parkway, 423/436-3600
The Park Grill Restaurant
  1110 Parkway, 423/436-2300

Best Breakfast
Atrium Restaurant and Lounge
  432 Parkway, 423/430-3684
Burning Bush Restaurant
  1151 Parkway, 432/436-4669
Pancake Pantry
  628 Parkway, 423/436-4724

Best Burgers
Duffy's Restaurant
  631 Parkway, 423/436-7112

Best Desserts
Cheese Cupboard and Hofbrauhaus
  634 Parkway, Ste.15, 423/436-9511

Best Dinner
Brass Lantern Restaurant
  710 Parkway, 423/436-4168
Maxwell's Beef and Seafood
  1103 Parkway, 423/436-3738
Waldo Peppers
  762 Parkway, 423/436-7003

Best Lunch
Maxwell's Beef and Seafood
  1103 Parkway, 423/436-3738

Best Pizza
Jersey Joe's
  631 Parkway, 423/436-7718

JACKSON, TN

Best All You Can Eat Buffet
Barnhill's Country Buffet
  660 Carriage House Dr., 901/664-5163

Best Casual Dining
Rafferty's Restaurant and Bar
  162 Old Hickory Blvd., 901/664-8118

Best Chinese Food
Asia Garden Chinese Restaurant
  581C Old Hickory Blvd., 901/668-9024

Best Fine Dining
Oliver's
  Old English Inn, 2267 N. Highland Ave.,
  901/668-1571

Best Homestyle Food
Catfish Cabin
  1290 S. Highland Ave., 901/422-1001

T

HRH Dumplin's of Jackson
31C Wiley Parker Rd., 901/664-4959
Old Country Store and Restaurant
88 Casey Jones Ln., 901/668-1223

Best Italian Food
Baudo's Restaurant
559 Wiley Parker Rd., 901/668-1447
Old Town Spaghetti Store
550 Carriage House Dr., 901/668-4937
Zeto's
110 S. Liberty St., 901/424-9001

Best Lunch
Davis-Kidd Cafe
Davis-Kidd Booksellers, 869 N. Parkway, 901/661-9757

Best Mexican Food
Los Portales
19B Stonebrook Pl., 901/661-9041
127 Old Hickory Blvd., 901/664-6217
1652 S. Highland Ave., 901/424-2484

Best Regional Food
Catfish Galley
2002 N. Highland Ave., 901/668-7555

Best Sunday Brunch
Brooksie's Barn
561 Oil Well Rd., 901/664-2276

JOHNSON CITY, TN

Best Barbecue/Ribs
Dixie Barbecue Company
3301 N. Roan St., 423/283-7447
Red Pig Barbecue
2201 Ferguson Rd., 423/282-6585

Best Cajun/Creole Food
Crazy Cajun Restaurant
5358 Kingsport Hwy., 423/477-2414

Best Casual Dining
Cheers Restaurant
1905 N. Roan St., 423/929-1023
Down Home
300 W. Main St., 423/929-9822
Gatsby's Cafe and Saloon
227 E. Main St., 423/928-2295

Best Chinese Food
Golden Dragon
1735 W. State St., 423/928-5068

Best Fine Dining
The Parson's Table
102 Woodrow Ave., Jonesborough, 423/753-8002

Best Lunch
Galloway's Restaurant
807 N. Roan St., 423/926-1166
Mingle's Delicatessen and Pizza
4704 Kingsport Hwy., Ste. 3, 423/282-8605

Best Pizza
Crazy Tomato Pizza Pasta
  203 Princeton Rd., 423/283-0211

Best Sandwiches
Poor Richard's Deli
  825 W. Walnut St., 423/926-8611
  106 Mountcastle Dr., 423/282-8711

Best Seafood
Peerless Restaurant
  2531 N. Roan St., 423/282-2351

KINGSPORT, TN

Best Atmosphere
Fuji House
  1804 N. Eastman Rd., Ste. 4, 423/247-1688

Best Barbecue/Ribs
Pardners Barbecue and Steak
  424 W. Stone Dr., 423/378-5555
Sharon's Barbecue and Burgers
  301 W. Center St., 423/247-5588

Best Casual Dining
Cheer's Restaurant
  2004 N. Eastman Rd., 423/245-0123

Best Chinese Food
Ming Garden Chinese Restaurant
  1205B N. Eastman Rd., 423/246-1141
Plum Tree
  4260 Fort Henry Dr., 423/239-8500

Best Family Restaurant
Happy Hostess Restaurant
  221 E. Center St., 423/246-4364

Best Italian Food
Chef Pizza
  254 W. New St., 423/245-2433
Raffaele's
  4309 Fort Henry Dr., 423/239-0026

Best Japanese Food
Fuji House
  1804 N. Eastman Rd., Ste. 4, 423/247-1688

Best Mexican Food
La Carreta Restaurant
  1336 S. John B. Dennis Hwy., 423/247-4700
  4252 Fort Henry Dr., 423/239-0014
  1001 E. Stone Dr., 423/245-7707

Best Sandwiches
Bristol Bagel and Bakery Company
  214 E. Center St., 423/378-5567

Best Steaks
Chop House
  1704 N. Eastman Rd., 423/247-1704
Prime Sirloin Steak and Seafood
  104 Indian Center Ct., 423/247-3191
Skoby's Restaurant
  1001 Konnarock Rd., 423/245-2761

KNOXVILLE, TN

Best All-You-Can-Eat-Buffet
Mandarin House
8111 Gleason Dr., 423/694-0350

Best American Food
Patrick Sullivan's Fine Foods
7545 Northshore Dr. SW, 423/694-9696
100 N. Central St., 423/522-4511
The Diner
1612 Downtown West Blvd., 423/690-2345

Best Bar
Ivory's
4705 Old Kingston Pike, 423/588-6023
Lucille's
106 N. Central St., 423/546-3742
Michael's
7049 Kingston Pike, 423/588-2455

Best Barbecue/Ribs
Buddy's Barbecue
multiple locations
Calhoun's
400 Neyland Dr., 423/673-3355
10020 Kingston Pike, 423/673-3444
Corky's Ribs and Barbecue
260 N. Peters Rd., 423/690-3137

Best Beer Selection
Amsterdam Cafe
102 S. Central St., 423/523-2437
Mill Brewery Eatery and Bakery
4429 Kingston Pike, 423/588-0080
Smoky Mountain Brewing Company
424 S. Gay St., 423/673-8400
The Sunspot Restaurant
1909 Cumberland Ave., 423/524-3380

Best Burgers
Bel Air Grill
9117 Executive Park Dr., 423/694-0606
Litton's Diner
1612 Downtown West Blvd., 423/690-2345

Best Cafeteria
Morrison's
East Town Mall, 3052 N. Mall Rd., 423/522-5952
S&S Cafeteria
4808 Kingston Pike, 423/584-5191

Best Chinese Food
China Inn
6450 Kingston Pike, 423/588-7815
Mandarin House
8111 Gleason Dr., 423/694-0350

Best Coffee/Coffeehouse
Cup-A-Joe
1911 Cumberland Ave., 423/673-3148
Java Coffee House
109 S. Central St., 423/525-1600

5115 Homberg Dr., 423/525-1600
JFG Coffee House
132 W. Jackson Ave., 423/525-0012

Best Delicatessen
Harold's Kosher Style Food Center
131 S. Gay St., 423/523-5315
New York Bagel and Deli
4622 Kingston Pike, 423/588-1364
Vic and Bill's
1501 White Ave., 423/524-9863

Best Diner
Hanna's Cafe
1901 Cumberland Ave., 423/522-9933
Line's Sweets N Eats
412 W. Clinch Ave., 423/523-2414
Litton's Diner
1612 Downtown West Blvd., 423/690-2345
Sullivan's Diner
137 S. Central St., 423/522-4511
Sutherland Deli
2011 Euclid Ave., 423/524-6272
The Diner
1612 Downtown West Blvd., 423/690-2345

Best French Food
The Orangery
5412 Kingston Pike, 423/588-2964

Best Homestyle Food
Helma's Restaurant
8606 Asheville Hwy., 423/933-2703

Best Indian Food
Kashmir Indian Restaurant
711 Seventeenth St. SW, 423/524-1982

Best Italian Food
Cappucino's
7316 Kingston Pike, 423/673-3422
Italian Market and Grill
9648 Kingston Pike, 423/690-2600
Naples Italian Restaurant
5500 Kingston Pike, 423/584-5033
Savelli Deli Restaurant
3055 Sutherland Ave., 423/521-9085

Best Lunch
Chef Bistro and Bakery
5003 Kingston Pike, 423/584-1300
Little Italian Subs and Pizza
5104A Kingston Pike, 423/584-1204
Lunch Box
6701 Baum Dr., 423/584-7682
800 S. Gay St., 423/525-7421

Best Mexican Food
Cancun
4409 Chapman Hwy., 423/577-8881
4829 N. Broadway St., 423/688-4030
Garcia's
1516 Downtown West Blvd., 423/690-9910

T

La Paz Mexican Restaurant
  8025 Kingston Pike, 423/690-5250

Best Middle Eastern Food
Dad's Cafe and Restaurant
  5032 Whitaker Dr., 615/584-2143
Falafel Hut
  601 Fifteenth St., 423/522-4963
Kashmir Indian Restaurant
  711 Seventeenth St. SW, 423/524-1982
King Tut's Grill
  4123 Martin Mill Pike, 423/573-6021

Best Pizza
Stefano's Chicago Style Pizza
  11533 Kingston Pike, 423/671-0500
  1937 Cumberland Ave., 423/522-4151
  7213 Kingston Pike, 423/588-1841
  9115 Executive Park Dr., Ste. 5C, 423/539-0033
Tomato Head
  12 Market Square Mall, 423/637-4067

Best Romantic Dining
Naples Italian Restaurant
  5500 Kingston Pike, 423/584-5033
Regas Restaurant
  318 N. Gay St., 423/637-9805
The Orangery
  5412 Kingston Pike, 423/588-2964

Best Salad/Salad Bar
Grady's Goodtimes
  6741A Kingston Pike, 423/584-4663
  318 N. Peters Rd., 423/694-4663
Silver Spoon Cafe
  7240 Kingston Pike, 423/584-1066
Tomato Head
  12 Market Square Mall, 423/637-4067

Best Sandwiches
Nixon's Deli
  220 N. Peters Rd., 423/694-3719
  1800 Cumberland Ave., 423/522-5224
  3049B N. Mall Rd., 423/525-3343
  5716 Kingston Pike, 423/558-6354
  5034 N. Broadway St., 423/281-8435
  4423 Western Ave., 423/637-6104
Sam and Andy's West
  11110 Kingston Pike, 423/675-4242

Best Seafood
Bayou Bay Seafood House
  7112 Chapman Hwy., 423/573-7936
Chesapeake's
  500 Henley St., 423/673-3433
Shrimp Shack
  8027 Kingston Pike, 423/539-1700

Best Sports Bar
Bailey's Sports Grille
  250 N. Seven Oaks Dr., 423/531-2644

T

Between The Buns
  155 West End Ave., Concord, 423/675-0900
Hooray's Sports Bar and Grill
  106 S. Central St., 423/546-6729

Best Steaks
Regas Restaurant
  318 N. Gay St., 423/637-9805
Ye Olde Steak House
  6838 Chapman Hwy., 423/577-9328

Best Sunday Brunch
Country Garden
  Hyatt Regency, 500 E. Hill Ave., 423/637-1234
Darryl's
  6604 Kingston Pike, 423/584-1879
  5616 Merchants Center Blvd., 423/688-1792
Hawkeye's Corner
  1717 White Ave., 423/524-5326
The Copper Cellar Restaurant
  7316 Kingston Pike, 423/673-3422
  3001 Industrial Pkwy. E., 423/522-3500
  1807 Cumberland Ave., 423/673-3411

Best Thai Food
China House Chinese and Thai
  11509 Kingston Pike, 423/966-7918
Stir Fry Cafe
  7240 Kingston Pike, Ste. 128, 423/588-2064

Best Vegetarian Food
The Sunspot Restaurant
  1909 Cumberland Ave., 423/524-3380
Tjaarda's Restaurant
  118 S. Central St., 423/637-8702

MARYVILLE, TN

T

Best Breakfast
411 Restaurant
  2635 Hwy. 411S, 423/982-7346

Best Chinese Food
Panda Garden
  2129 E. Broadway Ave., 423/981-4900

Best Homestyle Food
411 Restaurant
  2635 Hwy. 411S, 423/982-7346

Best Mexican Food
Los Amigos
  409 N. Cusick St., 423/983-6022

Best Sandwiches
Ham and Goody's
  227 W. Broadway Ave., 423/983-2680

MEMPHIS, TN

Best American Food
Barksdale Restaurant
  237 S. Cooper St., 901/722-2193

Ciao Baby Cucina
135 S. Main St., 423/247-1704

Best Barbecue/Ribs
Corky's Barbecue
5259 Poplar Ave., 901/685-9744
Cozy Corner
745 N. Parkway, 901/527-9158
Interstate Bar-B-Q
2265 S. Third St., 901/775-2921
Neely's
5700 Mt. Moriah Rd., 901/795-4177
670 Jefferson Ave., 901/521-9798
Rendezvous Charles Vergos
52 S. Second St., 901/523-2746

Best Beer Selection
High Point Pinch
111 Jackson Ave., 901/525-4444

Best Bistro
Lulu Grille
565 Erin Dr., 901/763-3677

Best Breakfast
Brother Juniper's College Inn
3519 Walker Ave., 901/324-0144

Best Burgers
Belmont Grill
4970 Poplar Ave., 901/767-0305
Fox Ridge Pizza
5950 Knight Arnold Rd. Ext., 901/794-8876
Huey's
1771 N. Germantown Pkwy., Cordova,
901/754-3885
1927 Madison Ave., 901/726-4372
2858 Hickory Hill Rd., 901/375-4373
Huey's Downtown
77 S. Second St., 901/527-2700

Best Business Lunch
Cafe Society
212 N. Evergreen St., 901/722-2177
Dux Restaurant
149 Union Ave., 901/529-4199
Owen Brennan's Restaurant
6150 Poplar Ave., 901/761-0990

Best Coffee/Coffeehouse
Edge
532 S. Cooper St., 901/272-3036
Java Cabana
2170 Young Ave., 901/272-7210
Otherland's Gifts
641 S. Cooper St., 901/278-4994

Best Delicatessan
Bogie's Delicatessan Midtown
2098 Lasalle Pl., 901/272-0022
Jason's Deli
Park Place Mall, 1199 Ridgeway Rd., 901/685-3333

T

Best Delicatessen
Young Avenue Deli
 2119 Young Ave., 901/278-0034

Best Desserts
Cafe Expresso
 5679 Poplar Ave., 901/763-3888
 149 Union Ave., 901/529-4160
North End
 346 N. Main St., 901/526-0319
Paulette's
 2110 Madison Ave., 901/726-5128

Best Eclectic Menu
Harry's on Teur
 2015 Madison Ave., 901/725-6054

Best Fine Dining
Automatic Slim's Tonga Lounge
 83 S. Second St., 901/525-7948
Chez Philippe
 Peabody Hotel, 149 Union Ave., 901/529-4188
Cafe Society
 212 N. Evergreen St., 901/722-2177
Erling Jensen Restaurant
 1044 S. Yates Rd., 901/763-3700
Paulette's
 2110 Madison Ave., 901/726-5128

Best Greek/Mediterranean Food
Melos Taverna
 2021 Madison Ave., 901/725-1863

Best Greek/Mediterranean Food
Fino's Italian Grocery
 1853 Madison Ave., 901/272-3466

Best Homestyle Food
Buntyn Restaurant
 3070 Southern Ave., 901/458-8776
Cupboard
 1495 Union Ave., 901/276-8015
Cupboard Too
 149 Madison Ave., 901/527-9111
Dixie Cafe
 4699 Poplar Ave., 901/683-7555
 3101 S. Mendenhall Rd., 901/794-4433
Ferguson's
 3171 Summer Ave., 901/458-2728
 2794 Coleman Rd., 901/383-1101

Best Indian Food
Delhi Palace
 6100 Macon Rd., 901/386-3600
India Palace
 1720 Poplar Ave., 901/278-1199

Best Italian Food
Frank Grisanti's
 1022 Shady Grove Rd., 901/761-9462
Ronnie Grisanti and Sons Restaurant
 2855 Poplar Ave., 901/323-0007

T

Best Japanese Food
Sekisui Midtown
  25 S. Belvedere Blvd., 901/725-0005
Sekisui of Japan
  50 Humphreys Ctr., 901/747-0001

Best Late-Night Food
Belmont Grill
  4970 Poplar Ave., 901/767-0305
C K's Coffee Shop
  multiple locations
Maxwell's
  948 S. Cooper St., 901/725-1009

Best Mexican Food
Acapulco
  3681 Jackson Ave., 901/386-1199
El Porton Mexican Restaurant
  65 S. Highland St., 901/452-7330
  5959 Winchester Rd., 901/366-1871
La Taqueria Mexican Restaurant
  3991 Jackson Ave., 901/387-1940
Los Reyes Mexican Restaurant
  3024 Covington Pike, 901/383-1873
Molly's La Casita
  2006 Madison Ave., 901/726-1873

Best Other Ethnic Food
Cafe Samovar
  83 Union Ave., 901/529-9607
In Limbo (Caribbean)
  928 S. Cooper St., 901/726-4999
Lupe and Bea's (Cuban)
  394 N. Watkins St., 901/726-9877

Best Pizza
Bosco's Pizza Kitchen and Brewery
  2250 West St., Germantown, 901/756-7310
Broadway Pizza
  2581 Broad Ave., 901/454-7930
Pete and Sam's
  3886 Park Ave., 901/458-0694

Best Restaurant Meal Value
Harry's on Teur
  2015 Madison Ave., 901/725-6054

Best Romantic Dining
Jim's Place East Restaurant
  5560 Shelby Oaks Dr., 901/388-7200
La Tourelle Restaurant
  2146 Monroe Ave., 901/726-5771

Best Seafood
Anderton's
  1901 Madison Ave., 901/726-4010
Cafe Max
  6161 Poplar Ave., 901/767-3633

Best Soul Food
Arcade Restaurant
  540 S. Main St., 901/526-5757

Miss Ellen's
601 S. Parkway E., 901/942-4888
Yellow Rose Cafe
56 N. Mid-America Mall, 901/527-5692

Best Steaks
Butcher Shop Steak House
101 S. Front St., 901/521-0856
Folk's Folly Prime Steak House
551 S. Mendenhall Rd., 901/762-8200

Best Sunday Brunch
La Tourelle
2146 Monroe Ave., 901/726-5771
Owen Brennan's Restaurant
6150 Poplar Ave., 901/761-0990
Paulette's
2110 Madison Ave., 901/726-5128
The Skyway
Peabody Hotel, 149 Union Ave., 901/529-4000

Best Sushi
Sekisui Midtown
25 S. Belvidere St., 901/725-0005

Best Vegetarian Food
La Montagne Natural Food
3550 Park Ave., 901/458-1060
Maxwell's
948 S. Cooper St., 901/725-1009
Squash Blossom
1801 Union Ave., 901/725-4823
5101 Sanderlin Ave., 901/685-2293

Best Vietnamese Food
Saigon Le
51 N. Cleveland St., 901/276-5326

Best Wine Selection
La Chardonnay Wine Bar
2105 Overton Sq., 901/725-1375

MORRISTOWN, TN

Best Atmosphere
Angelo's
3614 W. Andrew Johnson Hwy., 423/581-4882

Best Barbecue/Ribs
Buddy's Barbecue
2275 W. Andrew Johnson Hwy., 423/587-5058

Best Mexican Food
Mexico Lindo
3351 W. Andrew Johnson Hwy., 423/587-9754

Best Salad/Salad Bar
Justin's Restaurant
1825 W. Andrew Johnson Hwy., 423/581-8343

Best Steaks
Little Dutch's Restaurant
115 S. Cumberland St., 423/581-1441

MURFREESBORO, TN

Best American Food
Demo's Steak and Spaghetti House
  1115 NW Broad St., 615/895-3701
Front Porch Cafe
  114 E. College St., 615/896-6771

Best Barbecue/Ribs
Bar-B-Cutie
  905 Old Fort Pkwy., 615/890-9470

Best Beer Selection
Red Rose Coffee House and Bistro
  528 W. College St., 615/893-1405
The Boro Bar and Grill
  1211 Greenland Dr., 615/895-4800

Best Coffee/Coffeehouse
Red Rose Coffee House and Bistro
  528 W. College St., 615/893-1405

Best Lunch
City Cafe
  113 E. Main St., 615/373-5555
Clearview Restaurant
  222 S. Highland Ave., 615/896-0520

Best Mexican Food
Camino Real
  301 NW Broad St., 615/890-1412
La Siesta Mexican Restaurant
  1111 Greenland Dr., 615/890-0773
Santa Fe Cantina and Cattlemen's Club
  127 SE Broad St., 615/80-3030

Best Middle Eastern Food
Kebab Cuisine
  223 W. Main St., 615/895-4999

Best Pizza
Mazzio's Pizza
  1624 Memorial Blvd., 615/895-8646
Sir Pizza
  230 Stones River Mall Blvd., 615/896-2410

Best Steaks
Logan's Roadhouse
  740 NW Broad St., 615/895-4419

NASHVILLE, TN

Best All-You-Can-Eat-Buffet
Chinese Kitchen
  2010 Richard Jones Rd., 615/298-2929
Evergreen Restaurant
  1141 Bell Rd., Antioch, 615/731-2777
Golden Dragon Restaurant
  4115 Lebanon Rd., Hermitage, 615/889-9577
  104 Sanders Ferry Rd., Hendersonville,
    615/264-2126
  94 White Bridge Rd., 615/356-4558
Opryland Hotel
  2800 Opryland Dr., 615/889-1000

Best American Food
Sportsman's Grille
  5405 Harding Rd., 615/356-6206
  1601 21st Ave. S., 615/320-1633

Best Bar
Ace of Clubs
  114 Second Ave. S., 615/254-2237
McCabe's Pub
  4410 Murphy Rd., 615/269-9406
O'Charley's
  5500 Old Hickory Blvd., Hermitage, 615/883-6993
  1108 Murfreesboro Pike, 615/361-3651
  17 White Bridge Rd., 615/356-1344
Springwater
  115 27th Ave. N., 615/320-0345
Tin Angel
  3201 West End Ave., 615/298-3444

Best Barbecue/Ribs
Bar-B-Cutie
  5221 Nolensville Rd., 615/834-6556
  501 Donelson Pike, 615/872-0207
Calhoun's Restaurant
  2001 Gallatin Rd., Madison, 615/859-1050
  96 White Bridge Rd., 615/356-0855
Hog Heaven
  115 27th Ave. N., 615/329-1234
Mary's Old Fashion Barbecue Pit
  1106 Jefferson St., 615/256-7696
Whitt's Barbecue
  multiple locations

Best Beer Selection
The Beer Sellar
  107 Church St., 615/254-9464

Best Breakfast
Fido
  1812 21st Ave. S., 615/385-7959
Loveless Cafe
  Loveless Motel, 8400 Hwy. 100, 615/646-9700
Noshville Delicatessen
  1918 Broadway, 615/329-6674
The Pancake Pantry
  1796 21st Ave. S., 615/383-9333

Best Brewpub
Big River Grille and Brewing Works
  111 Broadway, 615/251-4677
Blackstone Restaurant and Brewery
  1918 West End Ave., 615/327-9969
Bosco's Nashville Brewing Company
  1805 21st Ave. S., 615/385-0050
Gerst Haus
  228 Woodland St., 615/256-9760
Market Street Brewery & Public House
  134 Second Ave. N., 615/259-9611

T

Best Burgers
Fat Mo's Burger
  2620 Franklin Pike, 615/298-1111
  946 Richards Rd., Antioch, 615/781-1830
  1216 Murfreesboro Pike, 615/366-3171
Rotier's Restaurant
  2413 Elliston Pl., 615/327-9892
Sportsman's Grille
  5405 Harding Rd., 615/356-6206
  1601 21st Ave. S., 615/320-1633

Best Business Lunch
Green Hills Grille
  2122 Hillsboro Dr., 615/383-6444
Houston's Restaurant
  3000 West End Ave., 615/269-3481
Jody's
  209 Tenth Ave. S., 615/259-4875
Midtown Cafe
  102 Nineteenth Ave. S., 615/320-7176
Sammy B's
  26 Music Sq. E., 615/256-6600
The Merchants Restaurant
  401 Broadway, 615/254-1892
The Nashville Country Club
  1811 Broadway, 615/321-0066
Third and Lindsley Bar and Grill
  818 Third Ave. S., 615/259-9891
Wild Boar
  2014 Broadway, 615/329-1313

Best Cajun/Creole Food
Bro's Cajun Cuisine
  5207 Nolensville Rd., 615/834-8777

Best Chinese Food
August Moon
  4004 Hillsboro Rd., 615/298-9999
  116 Wilson Pike, 615/371-1999
  7075 Hwy. 70S, 615/646-5333
Chinatown Restaurant
  3900 Hillsboro Rd., 615/269-3275
Golden Dragon Restaurant
  81 White Bridge Rd., 615/356-1110

Best Coffee/Coffeehouse
Bean Central
  2817 West End Ave., 615/321-8530
Bongo Java
  2007 Belmont Blvd., 615/385-5282
Cafe Coco
  10 Louise Ave., 615/329-0024

Best Delicatessen
Goldie's Deli
  4520 Harding Rd., 615/292-3589

Best Desserts
Cooker Bar and Grille
  1211 Murfreesboro Rd., 615/361-4747
  2609 West End Ave., 615/327-2925

4770 Lebanon Rd., 615/883-9700
317 Blue Bird Rd., Goodlettsville, 615/859-2756
McCabe's Pub
4410 Murphy Rd., 615/269-9406
Sunset Grill
2001 Belcourt Ave., 615/386-3663

Best Diner
Brown's Diner
2102 Blair Blvd., 615/269-5509

Best Eclectic Menu
Cafe 123
123 Twelfth Ave. N., 615/255-2233
Jody's
209 Tenth Ave. S., 615/259-4875
Mere Bulles
152 Second Ave. N., 615/256-1946
Tabouli
2015 Belmont Blvd., 615/386-0106
The Bound'ry Restaurant
911 Twentieth Ave. S., 615/321-3043
Twelfth & Porter
114 Twelfth Ave. N., 615/254-7236

Best Fine Dining
Arthur's
Union Station Hotel, 1001 Broadway, 615/255-1494
Capitol Grille
Westin Hermitage Hotel, 231 Sixth Ave. N.,
615/345-7116
Mario's Italian Ristorante
2005 Broadway, 615/327-3232
The Mad Platter
1239 Sixth Ave. N., 615/242-2563
Wild Boar
2014 Broadway, 615/329-1313

Best German Food
Gerst Haus
228 Woodland St., 615/256-9760

Best Greek/Mediterranean Food
Tabouli
2015 Belmont Blvd., 615/386-0106

Best Health Conscious Menu
Green Hills Grille
2122 Hillsboro Dr., 615/383-6444
The Food Company
2211 Bandywood Dr., 615/385-4311
510 Church St., 615/313-8111

Best Homestyle Food
Arnold's Country Kitchen
605 Eighth Ave. S., 615/256-4455
Belle Meade Buffet Cafeteria
4534 Harding Rd., 615/298-5571
C & J Diner
405 31st Ave. N., 615/329-1120
Elliston Place Soda Shop
2111 Elliston Pl., 615/327-1090

T

Monell's Dining and Catering
1235 Sixth Ave. N., 615/248-4747
Rotier's Restaurant
2413 Elliston Pl., 615/327-9892
Swett's Restaurant
2725 Clifton Ave., 615/329-4418
Sylvan Park Restaurant
2201 Bandywood Dr., 615/292-6449
4502 Murphy Rd., 615/292-9275
5207 Nolensville Rd., 615/781-3077
The Pie Wagon
118 Twelfth Ave. S., 615/256-5893

Best Ice Cream/Yogurt
White Mountain Creamery
416 21st Ave. S., 615/329-4016
4004 Hillsboro Rd., 615/297-0144

Best Indian Food
Shalimar Cafe Indian Cuisine
3711 Hillsboro Pike, 615/269-8577
Sitar Indian Restaurant
116 21st Ave. N., 615/321-8889

Best Inexpensive Meal
Arnold's Country Kitchen
605 Eighth Ave. S., 615/256-4455
Calypso Cafe
2424 Elliston Pl., 615/321-3878
722 Thompson Ln., 615/297-6530
21 Arcade, 615/259-9631
International Market and Restaurant
2010B Belmont Blvd., 615/297-4453
San Antonio Taco Company
416 21st Ave. S., 615/327-4322
208 Commerce St., 615/259-4413
Taste of Tokyo
1806 21st Ave. S., 615/292-8338

Best Italian Food
Amerigo
1920 West End Ave., 615/320-1740
Antonio's of Nashville
7097 Old Harding Rd., 615/646-9166
Caesar's Ristorante Italiano
88 White Bridge Rd., 615/352-3661
Finezza Trattoria
5404 Harding Rd., 615/356-9398
Mama Mia's
4671 Trousdale Dr., 615/331-7207
Nick's Italian Deli
508 Fifth Ave. S., 615/254-7210
Provino's Italian Restaurant
15542 Old Hickory Blvd., 615/831-3003

Best Japanese Food
Benkay Japanese Restaurant
40 White Bridge Rd., 615/356-6600
Goten Japanese Restaurant
110 21st Ave. S., 615/321-4537

Goten II Japanese Restaurant
  Cummins Station, 209 Tenth Ave. S., 615/251-4855
Kobe Steaks Japanese Restaurant
  210 25th Ave. N., 615/327-9081
Shintomi Japanese Restaurant
  2184 Bandywood Dr., 615/386-3022

Best Korean Food
Arirang Korean Restaurant
  1719 West End Ave., 615/327-3010

Best Lunch
Varallo's Restaurant
  817 Church St., 615/256-9109
  239 Fourth Ave. N., 615/256-1907

Best Mexican Food
Chez Jose Restaurant
  2323 Elliston Pl., 615/320-0107
La Hacienda Taqueria
  5560 Nolensville Rd., 615/833-3716
La Paz Restaurante Y Cantina
  3808 Cleghorn Ave., 615/383-5200
Las Palmas Mexican Restaurant
  15560 Old Hickory Blvd., 615/831-0432
  1905 Hayes St., 615/322-9588
  1400 Antioch Pike, Antioch, 615/831-0863
  803 Two Mile Pkwy., Goodlettsville, 615/851-7315
  110 Imperial Blvd., Hendersonville, 615/264-1919
  5511 Charlotte Pike, 615/352-0313
Monterey Mexican Restaurant
  4976 Nolensville Rd., 615/834-9522
Rio Bravo Cantina
  3015 West End Ave., 615/329-1745

Best Outdoor Dining
Blue Moon Waterfront Cafe
  525 Basswood Dr., 615/352-5892
Rio Bravo Cantina
  3015 West End Ave., 615/329-1745
San Antonio Taco Company
  208 Commerce St., 615/259-4413
  416 21st Ave. S., 615/327-4322

Best Pizza
Chanello's Pizza
  2109 Abbott Martin Rd., 615/383-4600
  3920 Apache Trail, Antioch, 615/383-4600
DaVinci's Gourmet Pizza
  1812 Hayes St., 615/329-8098
Obie's Pizza
  2217 Elliston Pl., 615/327-4772
Pizza Perfect
  4002 Granny White Pike, 615/297-0345
Pizza Perfect
  1602 21st Ave. S., 615/329-2757
Sole Mio
  94 Peabody St., 615/256-4013

Best Place to Take the Kids
Cafe Bambino
    734 Thompson Ln., 615/383-4383
Dalt's Grill
    38 White Bridge Rd., 615/352-8121

Best Regional Food
Cock of the Walk
    2624 Music Valley Dr., 615/889-1930
Tin Angel
    3201 West End Ave., 615/298-3444

Best Romantic Dining
Arthur's
    Union Station Hotel, 1001 Broadway,
        615/255-1494
Cafe 123
    123 Twelfth Ave. N., 615/255-2233
F. Scott's Restaurant
    2210 Crestmoor Rd., 615/269-5861

Best Salad/Salad Bar
Cooker Bar and Grille
    4770 Lebanon Rd., Hermitage, 615/883-9700
    317 Bluebird Dr., Goodlettsville, 615/859-2756
    2609 West End Ave., 615/327-2925
    1211 Murfreesboro Rd., 615/361-4747
Fifth Quarter
    295 E. Thompson Ln., 615/366-4268
Houston's Restaurant
    3000 West End Ave., 615/269-3481
J. Alexander's
    73 White Bridge Rd., 615/352-0981

Best Sandwiches
Bean Central
    2817 West End Ave., 615/321-8530
Jersey Mike's Subs and Salads
    2311 Elliston Pl., 615/329-4304
Major Brew
    1900 Broadway, 615/321-3363
Mosko's Muncheonette
    2204 Elliston Pl., 615/327-2658
Noshville Delicatessen
    1918 Broadway, 615/329-6674
Pizza Perfect
    4002 Granny White Pike, 615/297-0345
    1602 21st Ave. S., 615/329-2757
Provence Breads and Cafe
    1705 21st Ave. S., 615/386-0363
Star Bagel Company
    992 Davidson Dr., 615/352-2435
Sub Stop Restaurant
    1701 Broadway, 615/255-6482
Way Out West Cafe
    3415 West End Ave., Ste. 101B, 615/298-5562

Best Seafood
Blue Moon Waterfront Cafe
    525 Basswood Dr., 615/352-5892

Crab House
123 Second Ave. S., 615/242-2722
Florida Seafood Kitchen
3798 Nolensville Rd., 615/832-5081
Laurell's 2nd Avenue Oyster Bar
123 Second Ave. N., 615/244-1230
New Orleans Manor
1400 Murfreesboro Pike, 615/367-2777
South Street Restaurant
907 Twentieth Ave. S., 615/320-5555

Best Southwestern Food
Way Out West Cafe
3415 West End Ave., Ste. 101B, 615/298-5562

Best Sports Bar
Bailey's Sports Grille
786 Two Mile Pkwy., Goodlettsville, 651/851-9509
Box Seat
2221 Bandywood Dr., 615/383-8018
Jonathan's Village Cafe
1803 21st Ave. S., 615/385-9301

Best Steaks
Jimmy Kelly's
217 Louise Ave., 615/329-4349
Logan's Roadhouse
5300 Hickory Hollow Ln., Antioch, 615/731-4022
1715 Gallatin Pike N., Madison, 615/860-9220
Morton's of Chicago
625 Church St., 615/259-4558
Sperry's Restaurant
5109 Harding Rd., 615/353-0809
The Mad Platter
1239 Sixth Ave. N., 615/242-2563

Best Sunday Brunch
Granite Falls
2000 Broadway, 615/327-9250
Plaza Grill
Loew's Vanderbilt Plaza Hotel, 2100 West End
Ave., 615/320-1700
O'Charley's
5500 Old Hickory Blvd., Hermitage, 615/883-6993
1108 Murfreesboro Pike, 615/361-3651
17 White Bridge Rd., 615/356-1344

Best Sushi
Benkay Japanese Restaurant
40 White Bridge Rd., 615/356-6600
Ichiban Japanese Restaurant
109 Second Ave. N., 615/254-7185

Best Tea Room
Pineapple Room At Cheekwood
1200 Forrest Park Dr., 615/352-4859
Satsuma Tea Room
417 Union St., 615/256-0760
Towne House Tea Room
165 Eighth Ave. N., 615/254-1277

Best Thai Food
Royal Thai
204 Commerce St., 615/255-0821
Siam Cafe
316 McCall St., 615/834-3181
Thai Pattaya Restaurant
216 Thompson Ln., 615/331-5553
The Orchid Thai Cuisine
73 White Bridge Rd., 615/353-9411

Best View While Dining
The Pinnacle
Crowne Plaza, 623 Union St., 615/259-2000

OAK RIDGE, TN

Best Chinese Food
Magic Wok
202 Tyler Rd., 423/482-6628

Best Coffee/Coffeehouse
The Daily Grind
221 Jackson Sq., 423/483-9200

Best Continental Food
Bleu Hound Grill
80 E. Tennessee Ave., 423/481-6101

Best Homestyle Food
Village Restaurant
123 Central Ave., 423/483-1675

Best Pizza
Big Ed's Pizza
101 Broadway Ave., 423/482-4885

Best Sandwiches
Mustard Seed Cafe
333 Main St., 423/4829952
Time-Out Deli
138 Randolph Rd., 423/483-7349

PULASKI, TN

Best Barbecue/Ribs
Lawler's Barbecue
1520 W. College St., 931/363-3515
Legends Restaurant
1030 W. College St., 931/363-5612
Reed's Barbecue
821 Mill St., 931/363-0320

Best Breakfast
Jim's Diner
425 S. First St., 931/363-9120

Best Coffee/Coffeehouse
Bluebird Cafe
124 S. First St., 931/363-4681

Best Ice Cream/Yogurt
Reeves Drug Store
125 N. First St., 931/363-2561

SEVIERVILLE, TN

[See also: Gatlinburg.]

Best Breakfast
Apple Tree Inn
  3215 Parkway, Pigeon Forge, 423/453-4961

Best Chinese Food
Lotus Garden Chinese Restaurant
  131 Forks of the River Pkwy., 423/453-3891

Best Family Restaurant
Applewood Farm House Restaurant
  240 Apple Valley Rd., 423/428-1222
Applewood Farmhouse Grill
  250 Apple Valley Rd., 423/429-8644

Best Italian Food
Santo's Italian Restaurant
  3271 Parkway, Pigeon Forge, 423/428-5840
Tastebuds Cafe
  1198 Wears Valley Rd., Pigeon Forge, 423/428-9781

Best Sandwiches
Bel Aire Grill
  2785 Parkway, Pigeon Forge, 423/429-0101

Best Seafood
Five Oaks Beef and Seafood
  1625 Parkway, 423/453-5994

UNION CITY, TN

Best All You Can Eat Buffet
Olympia Pizza and Steak House
  1705 W. Reelfoot Ave., 901/885-3611

Best Barbecue/Ribs
Corner Bar B-Q
  1425 E. Reelfoot Ave., 901/885-9924
Dixie Barn
  1315 N. Old Troy Rd., 901/885-3663

Best Burgers
Grace's Restaurant
  3762 Ken Tenn Hwy., 901/885-1126
P.V.'s Hut
  209 E. Florida Ave., 901/885-5737

Best Chinese Food
New Jade Chinese Restaurant
  1413 S. First St., 901/885-9999

Best Desserts
Flippen's Hillbilly Barn
  3734 W. Shawtown Rd., Troy, 901/538-2933

Best Homestyle Food
Dixie Barn
  1315 N. Old Troy Rd., 901/885-3663
Dumplin's
  623 Perkins St., 901/885-9028

Searcy's Cafeteria
  306 S. First St., 901/885-0332

Best Pizza
Snappy Tomato Pizza
  509 S. First St., 901/885-7627

Texas

Best Barbecue/Ribs
Joe Allen's Pit Bar-B-Que
1185 China St., 915/672-6082

Best Breakfast
The Skillet
1750 E. I-20, 915/672-4545
3374 Turner Plz., 915/692-4280

Best Burgers
Tucson's Family Bar and Grill
3370 N. First St., 915/676-8279

Best Chinese Food
China Star
3601 S. First St., 915/677-2000

Best Coffee/Coffeehouse
McLemore-Bass
2136 Pine St., 915/673-8882

Best Family Restaurant
Furr's Cafeteria
3350 S. Clack St., 915/692-8330
Luby's Cafeteria
4310 Buffalo Gap Rd., Ste. 1184, 915/695-2000
Tucson's Family Bar and Grill
3370 N. First St., 915/676-8279

Best Homestyle Food
Betty Rose's
2402 S. Seventh St., 915/673-5809

Best Japanese Food
Shogun Japanese Steak House
3130 S. Clack St., 915/695-6660

T

Best Mexican Food
Dos Amigos
  3650 N. Sixth St., 915/672-2992

Best Outdoor Dining
Perini Ranch Steak House
  3002 State Park Rd., Hwy. 89, Buffalo Gap,
  915/572-3339

Best Pizza
Cici's Pizza
  3366 Turner Plz., 915/692-1660
Crystal's Pizza and Spaghetti
  2201 S. First St., 915/672-5616

Best Salad/Salad Bar
Greenjeans Salad Bar Plus
  4646 S. Fourteenth St., 915/692-1772

Best Seafood
Cahoots Catfish and Oyster Bar
  301 S. Eleventh St., 915/672-6540

Best Tea Room
Hickory Street Cafe
  644 Hickory St., 915/675-0465

Best View While Dining
The Petroleum Club of Abilene
  500 Chestnut St., 915/677-5218

ADDISON, TX

Best Brewpub
Rock Bottom Brewery
  4050 Belt Line Rd., 972/404-7456

Best Burgers
Humperdink's Bar and Grill
  4021 Belt Line Rd., Ste. 109, 972/934-2612
Snuffer's
  14910 Midway Rd., 972/991-8811

Best Homestyle Food
Norma's Cafe
  3330 Belt Line Rd., Farmers Branch, 972/243-8646

AMARILLO, TX

Best Barbecue/Ribs
Cattle Call
  Westgate Mall, 7701 I-40W, Ste. 398, 806/353-1227

Best Breakfast
Carrow's Restaurant
  2116 S. Georgia St., 806/359-9162

Best Burgers
Whataburger
  2424 S. Georgia St., 806/359-5472
  4111 W. 45th Ave., 806/355-9244
  3401 Coulter Dr., 806/358-8573

Best Business Lunch
Harrigan's Restaurant
  3311 Olsen Blvd., 806/358-8901

Best Casual Dining
Marty's
2740 Westhaven Village, 806/353-3523

Best Chinese Food
Peking Chinese Restaurant
2001 Paramount Blvd., 806/353-9179

Best Coffee/Coffeehouse
Roasters Coffee and Tea
2620 Wolflin Village, 806/359-7099

Best Health-Conscious Menu
Bless Your Heart
2203 Paramount Blvd., 806/351-0055

Best Homestyle Food
All the Fixin's Restaurant
3333 Coulter Dr., 806/358-7444

Best Ice Cream/Yogurt
Braum's Ice Cream and Dairy
1700 S. Western St., 806/359-7363
7401 W. 34th Ave., 806/356-9030
4629 S. Western St., 806/359-7412
801 E. Amarillo Blvd., 806/372-3626

Best Late-Night Food
Bennigan's
3401 I-40W, 806/358-7409

Best Mexican Food
Los Insurgentes
3521 W. Fifteenth Ave., 806/353-5361
Santa Fe Restaurant and Bar
3333 Coulter Dr., 806/358-8333

Best Pizza
Mr. Gatti's Pizza
429 E. 34th St., 806/355-5601

Best Regional Food
El Patio
5619 Amarillo Blvd., 806/383-8438

Best Seafood
David's Steaks and Seafood
2721 Virginia Circle, 806/355-8171

Best Steaks
Big Texan Steak Ranch
7701 I-40E, 806/372-6000

Best Tea Room
Back Porch Restaurant
3440 Bell St., 806/358-8871

Best Thai Food
Thai Star
3800 E. Amarillo Blvd., 806/383-4727

ARLINGTON, TX

[See also: Dallas, Ft. Worth, and Irving.]

Best American Food
Uno Pizzeria, Chicago Bar and Grill
1301 N. Collins St., 817/277-1080

Best Atmosphere
Piccolo Mondo Italian Restaurant
829 E. Lamar Blvd., 817/265-9174

Best Bar
J. Gilligan's Bar and Grill
407 E. South St., 817/274-8561

Best Barbecue/Ribs
Spring Creek Barbecue
3608 S. Cooper St., 817/465-0553

Best Breakfast
Country Kitchen
1409 N. Collins St., 817/261-5663
La Madeleine French Bakery
2101 N. Collins St., 817/459-1327

Best Brewpub
Humperdink's Bar and Grill
700 Six Flags Dr., 817/640-8553

Best Burgers
Al's Hamburgers
1001 NE Green Oaks Blvd., Ste. 103, 817/275-8918

Best Business Lunch
Harrigan's Restaurant
944 E. Copeland Rd., 817/277-2400
5900 I-20W, 817/483-9103

Best Cajun/Creole Food
Atchafalaya River Cafe
1520 Stadium Dr. W., 817/261-4696
Pappadeaux Seafood Kitchen
1304 E. Copeland Rd., 817/543-0544

Best Casual Dining
Mac's Bar and Grill
6077 I-20W, 817/572-0541

Best Chinese Food
Arc-En-Ciel
2208 New York Ave., 817/469-9999
China Cafe
3415 S. Cooper St., 817/468-2727

Best Coffee/Coffeehouse
La Madeleine French Bakery
2101 N. Collins St., 817/459-1327
The Coffee Haus
478 Lincoln Sq., Ste. 302, 817/274-0006

Best Desserts
Tippin's Restaurant and Pie Pantry
3321 S. Cooper St., 817/467-7437

Best Family Restaurant
Black-Eyed Pea
3808 S. Cooper St., 817/467-9555
1400 N. Collins St., 817/275-8973

Best Health-Conscious Menu
Jason's Deli
780 Road to Six Flags E., 817/860-2888

Best Ice Cream/Yogurt
Marble Slab Creamery
4261 W. Green Oaks Blvd., 817/483-9960
780 Road to Six Flags W., 817/277-3363

Best Indian Food
Tandoor The Indian Restaurant
532 Fielder North Plz., 817/261-6604

Best Italian Food
Italian Villa
6033 I-20W, 817/561-2226
Romano's Macaroni Grill
1670 I-20W, 817/784-1197

Best Late-Night Food
Cheddar's Restaurant
812 Six Flags Dr., 817/640-6073
4820 Little Rd., 817/572-2966

Best Mexican Food
Cozymel's
1300 E. Copeland Rd., 817/469-9595
Mercado Juarez Restaurant
2222 Miller Rd., 817/649-3324

Best Outdoor Dining
Don Pablo's Restaurant
3765 S. Cooper St., 817/472-5533
On The Border Cafe
2011 E. Copeland Rd., 817/261-3598
Pappadeaux Seafood Kitchen
1304 E. Copeland Rd., 817/543-0544

Best Pizza
Uno Pizzeria, Chicago Bar and Grill
1301 N. Collins St., Ste. 201, 817/277-1080

Best Place to Take the Kids
Chuck E. Cheese Pizza
2216 S. Fielder Rd., 817/861-1561
3200 Justiss Dr., 817/649-2933

Best Restaurant in Town
Cacharel Restaurant
2221 E. Lamar Blvd., Ste. 910, 817/640-9981
Pappadeaux Seafood Kitchen
1304 E. Copeland Rd., 817/543-0544
Portofino
226 Lincoln Sq., 817/861-8300

Best Restaurant Meal Value
Hibachi 93
5736 SW Green Oaks Blvd., 817/483-0553

T

Best Salad/Salad Bar
Souper Salad Restaurant
1325 I-20W, 817/557-9738

Best Sandwiches
Boo Boo's Food Shop
1130 S. Bowen Rd., 817/274-3641
Jason's Deli
780 Road to Six Flags E., 817/860-2888

Best Steaks
Arlington Steak House
1724 W. Division St., 817/275-7881

Best Vietnamese Food
Arc-En-Ciel
2208 New York Ave., 817/469-9999
Kim Hai
2420 E. Arkansas Ln., 817/275-2449

AUSTIN, TX

Best 24-Hour Restaurant
Katz's Deli
618 W. Sixth St., 512/472-2037

Best All-You-Can-Eat Buffet
Fonda San Miguel Restaurant
2330 W. North Loop Blvd., 512/459-4121
Hickory Street Bar and Grill
800 Congress Ave., 512/477-8968
The Cafe
Four Seasons Hotel, 99 San Jacinto Blvd.,
512/478-4500

Best Bar
Trudy's North Star
8800 Burnet Rd., 512/454-1474
Trudy's Texas Star
409 W. 30th St., 512/477-2935

Best Barbecue/Ribs
County Line on the Hill
6500 Bee Caves Rd., 512/327-1742
Iron Works Barbecue
100 Red River St., 512/478-4855
Ruby's Barbecue and Catering Company
512 W. 29th St., Ste. A12, 512/477-1651
Salt Lick Barbecue
1826 FM 165, Dripping Springs, 512/858-4959
Stubb's Barbecue
801 Red River St., 512/480-0203

Best Beer Selection
Dog and Duck Pub
406 W. Seventeenth St., 512/479-0598
Double Dave's Pizzaworks
9608 N. Lamar Blvd., 512/476-3283
Gingerman Pub
304 W. Fourth St., 512/473-8801
Maggie Mae's
512 Trinity St., 512/478-8541

Waterloo Ice House
  600 N. Lamar Blvd., 512/472-5400
Waterloo Ice House at 26 Doors
  1106 W. 38th St., 512/451-5245

Best Breakfast
El Zarape
  2103 E. Cesar Chavez St., 512/320-0308
Guero's Taco Bar
  1412 S. Congress Ave., 512/447-7688
Joe's Bakery and Coffee Shop
  2305 E. Seventh St., 512/472-0017
Magnolia Cafe
  2304 Lake Austin Blvd., 512/478-8645

Best Brewpub
The Bitter End Bistro and Brewery
  311 Colorado St., 512/478-2337
Draught Horse Pub and Brewery
  4112 Medical Pkwy., 512/452-6258
Waterloo Brewing Company
  401 Guadalupe St., 512/477-1836

Best Burgers
Dan's Hamburgers
  1822 S. Congress Ave., 512/444-5738
Dirty Martin's Place
  2808 Guadalupe St., 512/477-3173
Hut's Hamburgers
  801 W. Sixth St., 512/472-0693

Best Business Lunch
Kerbey Lane Cafe
  2700 S. Lamar Blvd., 512/445-4451
  12602 Research Blvd., 512/258-7757
  3704 Kerbey Ln., 512/451-1436

Best Cajun/Creole Food
Pappadeaux's Seafood Kitchen
  6319 I-35N, 512/452-9363

Best Chinese Food
Chinatown
  3407 Greystone Dr., 512/343-9307
  2712 Bee Caves Rd., 512/327-6588
Hunan Chinese Restaurant
  9306 N. Lamar Blvd., 512/837-2700
  1940 W. William Cannon Dr., 512/443-8848
Suzi's Chinese Kitchen
  1152 S. Lamar Blvd., 512/441-8400
Tien Hong
  8301 Burnet Rd., 512/458-2263

Best Coffee/Coffeehouse
Captain Quackenbush's Cafe
  2120 Guadalupe St., 512/472-4477
Chuy's Hula Hut
  3825 Lake Austin Blvd., 512/476-4852
Flipnotics
  1603 Barton Springs Rd., 512/322-9011
Mozart's Coffee Roasters
  3826 Lake Austin Blvd., 512/477-2900

T

Ruta Maya Coffee House
  218 W. Fourth St., 512/472-9637
Soma
  212 W. Fourth St., 512/474-SOMA

Best Delicatessen
Central Market
  4001 N. Lamar Blvd., 512/206-1000
Jason's Deli
  3300 Bee Caves Rd., 512/328-0200
  9722 Great Hills Trail, 512/345-9586
Katz's Deli
  618 W. Sixth St., 512/472-2037
Phoenicia Bakery and Deli
  2912 S. Lamar Blvd., 512/447-4444

Best Desserts
Dr. Chocolate
  4001 N. Lamar Blvd., 512/454-0555
Magnolia Cafe
  2304 Lake Austin Blvd., 512/478-8645
The Granite Cafe
  2905 San Gabriel St., 512/472-6483
Threadgill's Restaurant
  6416 N. Lamar Blvd., 512/451-5440

Best Diner
The Mustang Diner
  400 Lavaca St., 512/472-2363

Best French Food
Chez Nous
  510 Neches St., 512/473-2413

Best German Food
Gunther's
  11606 I-35N, 512/834-0474

Best Greek/Mediterranean Food
Phoenicia Bakery and Deli
  2912 S. Lamar Blvd., 512/447-4444
Ted's Greek Corner
  417 Congress Ave., 512/472-4494

Best Health-Conscious Menu
Boggy Creek Farm
  3414 Lyons Rd., 512/926-4650
Casa de Luz
  1701 Toomey Rd., 512/476-2535
East Side Cafe
  2113 Manor Rd., 512/476-5858
Good Eats Cafe
  1530 Barton Springs Rd., 512/476-8141
  6801 Burnet Rd., 512/451-2560
Martin Brothers Cafe
  2815 Guadalupe St., 512/478-9001

Best Ice Cream/Yogurt
Amy's Ice Cream
  1012B W. Sixth St., 512/480-0673
  10000 Research Blvd., 512/345-1006
  3500 Guadalupe St., 512/458-6895

Best Indian Food
Star of India
  2900 W. Anderson Ln., Ste. 12D, 512/452-8199
Taj Palace
  6700 Middle Fiskville Rd., 512/452-9959

Best Inexpensive Meal
Austin's Tamale House
  2218 College Ave., 512/441-3033
  2825 Guadalupe St., 512/472-0487
  5003 Airport Blvd., 512/453-9842
Dot's Place Cafeteria
  13805 Orchid Ln., 512/255-7288
Hut's Hamburgers
  801 W. Sixth St., 512/472-0693
Rosie's Tamale House
  13776 Research Blvd., 512/219-7793
  13436 Hwy. 71W, 512/263-5245
  2701 S. Congress Ave., 512/462-9484

Best Italian Food
Basil's Restaurant
  900 W. Tenth St., 512/477-4340
Madam Nadalini's Restaurant and Cafe
  3663 Bee Caves Rd., 512/328-4858
Mezzaluna
  310 Colorado St., 512/472-6770
Romeo's
  1500 Barton Springs Rd., 512/476-1090

Best Japanese Food
Kyoto II Japanese Restaurant
  4815 W. Braker Ln., 512/346-5800
Kyoto Japanese Restaurant
  315 Congress Ave., 512/482-9010

Best Lunch
Phoenicia Bakery and Deli
  2912 S. Lamar Blvd., 512/447-4444

Best Mexican Food
Fonda San Miguel Restaurant
  2330 W. Loop Blvd., 512/459-4121
Guero's Taco Bar
  1412 S. Congress Ave., 512/707-8232
Jovita's Mexican Restaurant
  1619 S. First St., 512/447-7825
Manuel's
  310 Congress Ave., 512/472-7555
San Miguel Restaurant
  2330 W. North Loop Blvd., 512/459-4121
Z Tejas Grill
  1110 W. Sixth St., 512/478-5355

Best Middle Eastern Food
Armen's Mediterranean Restaurant
  12196 N. Mo Pac Expwy., 512/835-8888

Best Other Ethnic Food
El Rinconcito Cocina Mexicana (Peruvian)
  1014 N. Lamar Blvd., 512/476-5277

Best Outdoor Dining
Magnolia Cafe South
  1920 S. Congress Ave., 512/445-0000
Shady Grove Cafe
  1624 Barton Springs Rd., 512/474-9991
The Granite Cafe
  2905 San Gabriel St., 512/472-6483

Best Pizza
Brick Oven Restaurant
  1209 Red River St., 512/477-7006
  10710 Research Blvd., 512/345-6181
  1608 W. 35th St., 512/453-4330
Conan's Pizza
  1912 Smith Rd., 512/385-5914
  603 W. 29th St., 512/478-5712
Marye's Gourmet Pizza
  3663 Bee Caves Rd., Ste. 110, 512/327-5222
Nick's Great Pizza
  11302 Ranch Rd. 2222, 512/331-4471
Pizza Nizza
  1608 Barton Springs Rd., 512/474-7470

Best Place to Take the Kids
Celebration Station
  4525 S. I-35, 512/448-3533
Chuck E. Cheese Pizza
  502 W. Ben White Blvd., 512/441-9681
  8038 Burnet Rd., 512/451-0296
Matt's El Rancho
  2613 S. Lamar Blvd., 512/462-9333
Spaghetti Warehouse
  117 W. Fourth St., 512/476-4059

Best Romantic Dining
Belgian Restaurant L'Estro Armonico
  3520 Bee Caves Rd., 512/328-0580
Castle Hill Cafe
  1101 W. Fifth St., 512/476-0728
Hudson's on the Bend
  3509 Hwy. 620N, 512/266-1369
The Granite Cafe
  2905 San Gabriel St., 512/472-6483

Best Salad/Salad Bar
The Bitter End Bistro and Brewery
  311 Colorado St., 512/478-2337
Eastside Cafe
  2113 Manor Rd., 214/476-5858
Milto's Pizza Pub
  2909 Guadalupe St., 512/476-1021
Souper Salad
  10710 Research Blvd., 512/343-0807
  2438 W. Anderson Ln., 512/451-9320
  6700 Middle Fiskville Rd., 512/453-7687
  4211 S. Lamar Blvd., 512/441-6958

Best Sandwiches
Delaware Subs
  3930 Bee Caves Rd., Ste. 1, 512/345-3816

Hyde Park Bar and Grill
4206 Duval St., 512/458-3168
Marye's Gourmet Pizza
2712 Bee Caves Rd., Ste. 110, 512/327-5222

Best Seafood
Eaves Brothers' Quality Seafood
5621 Airport Blvd., 512/454-5827
Gilligan's Seafood and Oyster Bar
407 Colorado St., 512/474-7474
Pappadeaux's Seafood Kitchen
6319 I-35N, 512/452-9363

Best Soul Food
Soul Kitchen
2931 E. Twelfth St., 512/478-0251

Best Southwestern Food
Chuy's Restaurant
1728 Barton Springs Rd., 512/474-4452
10520 N. Lamar Blvd., 512/836-3218
El Mercado
1302 S. First St., 512/447-7445
7414 Burnet Rd., 512/454-2500
El Soy y La Luna
1224 S. Congress Ave., 512/444-7770

Best Steaks
Austin Land and Cattle Company
1205 N. Lamar Blvd., 512/472-1813
Dan McKlusky's Restaurant
10000 Research Blvd., 512/346-0780
301 E. Sixth St., 512/473-8924
Hoffbrau
613 W. Sixth St., 512/472-0822
Ruth's Chris Steak House
3010 Guadalupe St., 512/477-7884
Sullivan's Steakhouse
3000 Colorado St., 512/495-6504

Best Sunday Brunch
Fonda San Miguel Restaurant
2330 W. North Loop Blvd., 512/459-4121
Red River Cafe
2912 Medical Arts St., 512/472-0385
The Cafe
Four Seasons Hotel, 99 San Jacinto Blvd.,
512/478-4500

Best Sushi
Musashino
3407 Greystone Dr., 512/795-8593
Osaka
13492 Research Blvd., Ste. 160, 512/948-8012

Best Tea Room
Mozart's Coffee Roasters
3826 Lake Austin Blvd., 512/477-2900

Best Thai Food
Kim Phung Restaurant
7601 N. Lamar Blvd., 512/451-2464

T

Satay, The Asian Cookery
  3202 W. Anderson Ln., 512/467-6731
Thai Kitchen
  3437 Bee Caves Rd., 512/327-3528
  801 E. William Cannon Dr., 512/445-4844
Thai Passion
  620 Congress Ave., Ste. 105, 512/472-1244

Best Vegetarian Food
Acorn Cafe
  2602 Guadalupe St., 512/472-2816
Mother's Cafe and Garden
  4215 Duval St., 512/451-3994
West Lynn Cafe
  1110 W. Lynn St., 512/482-0950

Best View While Dining
Oasis
  6550 Comanche Trail, 512/266-2441

Best Wine Selection
Jeffrey's Restaurant
  1204 W. Lynn St., 512/477-5584
Louie's 106
  106 E. Sixth St., 512/476-2010
Mezzaluna
  310 Colorado St., 512/472-6770

BAYTOWN, TX

Best Bar
Speakeasy
  1800 W. Main St., 281/428-8955

Best Barbecue/Ribs
Going's Barbecue Company
  1006 N. Main St., 281/422-4600

Best Breakfast
Kettle Restaurant
  4915 I-10E, 281/421-1656

Best Chinese Food
Dong Hwa Chinese Restaurant
  4529 Garth Rd., 281/591-2706
Lee Palace Restaurant
  6942 Garth Rd., 281/421-1203

Best Delicatessen
Doyle's Deli
  1504 San Jacinto Mall, 281/421-1643

Best Health-Conscious Menu
The Health Way
  407 W. Baker Rd., 281/427-9000

Best Homestyle Food
Murray's Family Restaurant
  1001 Memorial Dr., 281/422-5386

Best Inexpensive Meal
Pancho's Mexican Restaurant
  8761 Garth Rd, 281/421-2911

Best Lunch
Luna's Mexican Restaurant
4539 Garth Rd., 281/422-9090

Best Mexican Food
Tia Maria's Mexican Restaurant
1711 Garth Rd., 281/427-8666

Best Seafood
Baytown Seafood
709 W. Main St., 281/427-2478

Best Steaks
Rooster's Steak House
6 W. Texas Ave., 281/428-8222

BEAUMONT, TX

Best Barbecue/Ribs
Broussard's Links Plus Ribs
2930 S. Eleventh St., 409/842-1221

Best Burgers
Novrozsky Hamburgers
4438 Dowlen Rd., 409/899-4076
458 N. Eighth St., 409/832-3113
4230 Calder Ave., 409/898-8688

Best Cajun/Creole Food
Cajun Cookery
2308 Lutcher Dr., Orange, 409/886-0990

Best Diner
Pig Stands
1595 Calder St., 409/835-9702
3695 College St., 409/835-9394

Best Family Restaurant
Black-Eyed Pea
6455 Phelan Blvd., 409/866-2617

Best Homestyle Food
Dorothy's Front Porch
1001 Holmes Rd., 409/722-1472

Best Ice Cream/Yogurt
Marble Slab Creamery
6626 Phelan Blvd., 409/866-4740

Best Italian Food
Carlo's Restaurant and Bar
2570 Calder St., 409/833-0108
Patrizi's Restaurant
2050 I-10S, 409/842-5151

Best Late-Night Food
Bennigan's
325 I-10N, 409/833-2648

Best Mexican Food
Elena's
1865 College St., 409/832-1203

Best Pizza
Mazzio's Pizza
5025 Eastex Freeway, 409/899-1400

Best Place to Take the Kids
Pancho's Mexican Buffet
  850 S. Eleventh St., 409/835-0289

Best Regional Food
Tamale Company
  6025 Phelan Blvd., 409/769-3300

Best Romantic Dining
Carlo's Restaurant and Bar
  2570 Calder St., 409/833-0108
Sartin's
  6725 Eastex Freeway, 409/892-6771

Best Sandwiches
Jason's Deli
  414 Dowlen Rd., 409/866-9015
  112 Gateway St., 409/833-5914

Best Seafood
Don's Seafood and Steak House
  2290 I-10S, 409/842-0686
Dorothy's Front Porch
  1001 Holmes Rd., 409/722-1472
Gulf Port Restaurant
  3950 I-10S, 409/842-5995

Best Steaks
Hoffbrau Steaks
  2310 N. Eleventh St., 409/892-6911

Best Tea Room
Green Beanery Cafe
  2121 McFaddin St., 409/833-5913

Best Vegetarian Food
Luby's Cafeteria
  745 N. Eleventh St., 409/892-4181

BIG SPRING, TX

Best Breakfast
Country Fare Restaurant
  I-20W at Hwy. 87, 915/264-4444

Best Burgers
Al's and Sons Bar-B-Q
  1810 S. Gregg St., 915/267-8921

Best Coffee/Coffeehouse
Spanky's Coffee and Company
  1909A S. Gregg St., 915/264-6747

Best Mexican Food
Alberto's Crystal Cafe
  120 E. Second St., 915/267-9024
Carlos' Restaurant and Bar
  308 NW Third St., 915/267-9141
Spanish Inn Restaurant
  200 NW Third St., 915/267-9340

Best Sandwiches
Red Mesa Grill
  2401 S. Gregg St., 915/263-2205

Best Seafood
Mel's Catch of the Day Fish
   504 S. Gregg St., 915/267-6266

Best Steaks
Brandin' Iron Inn
   San Anglio Hwy., 915/267-7661
K.C. Steak and Seafood House
   N. Service Rd. at I-20W, 915/263-1651

BROWNSVILLE, TX

Best All-You-Can-Eat Buffet
Kettle Pancake House
   854 N. Expressway, 956/542-2731

Best Barbecue/Ribs
La Hacienda
   804 Paredes Line Rd., 956/550-0055

Best Burgers
Whataburger
   2021 International Blvd., 956/542-0963
   2290 N. Expressway, 956/546-2572
   2419 Boca Chica Blvd., 956/546-2361

Best Casual Dining
Palm Court Restaurant
   2235 Boca Chica Blvd., 956/542-3575

Best Chinese Food
Lotus Court Restaurant
   1774 E. Price Rd., 956/544-3331
Lotus Inn
   905 N. Expressway, 956/542-5715

Best Coffee/Coffeehouse
Toddle Inn
   1740 Central Blvd., 956/542-8838

Best Desserts
Palm Court Restaurant
   2235 Boca Chica Blvd., 956/542-3575

Best Mexican Food
Antonio's Mexican Village
   2921 Boca Chica Blvd., 956/542-6504
Jesse's Cantina and Restaurant
   2700 Padre Blvd., South Padre Island,
      956/761-4500

Best Pizza
D'Pizza Joint
   2413 Padre Blvd., South Padre Island,
      956/761-7995
Gio Villa Italian Food
   2325 Central Blvd., 956/542-9057

Best Sandwiches
Vermillion
   115 Paredes Line Rd., 956/542-9893

T

BRYAN/COLLEGE STATION, TX

Best Bar
Dixie Chicken
  307 University Dr., College Station, 409/846-2322

Best Burgers
Whataburger
  906 S. Texas Ave., Bryan, 409/822-0624

Best Chinese Food
Chinese Garden
  2901 S. Texas Ave., Bryan, 409/823-2818

Best Coffee/Coffeehouse
Sweet Eugene's
  1702 Kyle Ave. S., College Station, 409/696-5282

Best Family Restaurant
Ken Martin's Steak House
  3231 E. 29th St., Bryan, 409/776-7500

Best Mexican Food
Jose's Restaurant
  3824 Texas Ave. S., Bryan, 409/268-0036

Best Place to Be "Seen"
Bennigan's
  1505A Texas Ave. S., College Station, 409/696-9066

Best Place to Eat Alone
Chicken Oil Company
  3600 S. College Ave., Bryan, 409/463-3306

Best Restaurant in Town
Tom's Barbecue and Steak House
  3610 S. College Ave., Bryan, 409/846-4275
  2005 Texas Ave. S., College Station, 409/696-2076

Best Salad/Salad Bar
Oxford Street Restaurant and Pub
  1710 Briarcrest Dr., Bryan, 409/268-0792

CONROE, TX

Best Barbecue/Ribs
Luther's Barbeque
  27752 I-45, 281/363-2647
McKenzie's Barbecue
  1501 N. Frazier St., 409/539-4300

Best Breakfast
Village Inn
  1111 W. Dallas St., 409/756-2267

Best Burgers
Burger Boy
  217 E. Davis St., 409/756-3440

Best Chinese Food
Hunan Village Restaurant
  1402A Loop 336W, 409/539-6811
Imperial Garden
  3708E W. Davis St., 409/539-1566
  1600 I-45N, 409/539-1566

Best Continental Food
Glass Menagerie
  2301 N. Millbend Dr., The Woodlands,
    281/367-1000

Best Health-Conscious Menu
Garden Cafe
  1406A Loop 336W, 409/539-9663

Best Homestyle Food
BK Buffet
  11432 FM 2854 RD, 409/756-9985
Kuntry Katfish
  Hwy. 105W, 409/760-3386
Vernon's Kuntry Barbecue
  5000 W. Davis St., 409/539-3000

Best Ice Cream/Yogurt
I Can't Believe It's Yogurt
  1422 Loop 336W, 409/539-1109

Best Italian Food
Carrabba's Italian Grill
  25665 I-45, The Woodlands, 281/367-9423
Villa Italia
  203 Simonton St., 409/539-1915
  6035 Hwy. 105W, 409/539-5599

Best Mexican Food
El Pollino
  201 N. Frazier St., 409/756-2614
Guadalajara Mexican Grille
  27885 I-45, The Woodlands, 281/362-0774
Margarita's
  1027 N. Loop State Hwy. 336W, 409/756-8771
Ninfa's Express
  1201 Lake Woodlands Dr., Ste. 2154,
    The Woodlands, 281/362-7337
Rancho Grande Mexican
  2207 N. Frazier St., 409/441--440

Best Regional Food
Black Eyed Pea
  1330 Lake Woodlands Dr., The Woodlands,
    281/367-7143

Best Restaurant Meal Value
Rancho Grande Mexican
  2207 N. Frazier St., 409/441--440

Best Sandwiches
Garden Cafe
  1406A Loop 336W, 409/539-9663

Best Steaks
Hofbrau Steaks
  2031 Plantation Dr., 409/756-1554

CORPUS CHRISTI, TX

Best Atmosphere
Roadhouse Inn
  11223 Up River Rd., 512/241-0621

Best Barbecue/Ribs
Bar-B-Q Man
  4932 I-37, 512/888-4248
County Line Barbecue
  6102 Ocean Dr., 512/991-7427

Best Breakfast
Kettle Restaurant
  4001 S. Padre Island Dr., 512/855-4778
  6301 I-37, 512/289-5622
  5015 Ayers St., 512/852-7818

Best Burgers
EZ's Pizzas and Burgers
  5425 S. Padre Island Dr., 512/992-1292

Best Business Lunch
Water Street Oyster Bar
  309 N. Water St., 512/881-9448

Best Chinese Food
Golden Crown Chinese Restaurant
  6601 Everhart Rd., Ste. B7, 512/854-5506
  2739 S. Staples St., 512/853-8886
Mao-Tai Chinese Restaurant
  4601 S. Padre Island Dr., 512/852-8877

Best Delicatessen
Jason's Deli
  Gulfway Shopping Ctr., 1416 Airline Dr.,
  512/992-4649

Best Desserts
Ultimate Cheesecake Factory
  4210 S. Alameda St., 512/991-7892

Best Diner
Elmo's City Diner and Bar
  622 N. Water St., 512/883-1643

Best Homestyle Food
Elmo's City Diner and Bar
  622 N. Water St., 512/883-1643
Roadhouse Inn
  11223 Up River Rd., 512/241-0621

Best Italian Food
Mama Mia's
  128 N. Mesquite St., 512/883-3773

Best Mexican Food
Old Mexico Restaurant
  3329 Leopard St., 512/883-6461
Pepe's Mexican Cafe
  15 Gaslight Sq., 512/888-7373

Best Pizza
Cici's Pizza
  4102A S. Staples St., 512/814-2424

Best Place to Take the Kids
Chuck E. Cheese Pizza
  5118 S. Staples St., 512/993-8824

T

Best Romantic Dining
Lighthouse Restaurant
  444 N. Shoreline Blvd., 512/881-8210
Window on the Bay
  Howard Johnson's, 300 N. Shoreline Blvd.,
    512/887-1645

Best Seafood
Catfish Charlie's
  5830 McArdle Rd., 512/993-0363

Best Sushi
Origami
  1220 Airline Rd., 512/993-3966

Best Tea Room
Jeron's Tea Room
  5830 McArdle Rd., Ste. 4, 512/980-1939

Best Vietnamese Food
Vietnam
  4501 S. Padre Island Dr., 512/853-2682

DALLAS, TX

*[See also: Arlington, Irving, Garland, Mesquite, and
Richardson.]*

Best American Food
Dick's Last Resort
  1701 N. Market St., Ste. 110, 972/747-0001
Houston's Restaurant
  5318 Belt Line Rd., 972/960-1752

Best Barbecue/Ribs
Austin's Barbecue
  2321 W. Illinois Ave., 972/337-2242
Baker's Ribs
  4844 Greenville Ave., 972/373-0082
  2724 Commerce St., 972/748-5433
Carter's
  1621 S. Malcolm X Ave., 972/428-9461
Dickey's Barbecue
  17721 N. Dallas Pkwy., Ste. 130, 972/713-8909
  14999 Preston Rd., 972/661-2006
Hickory House Barbecue
  600 S. Industrial Blvd., 972/747-0758
Sonny Bryan's
  2202 Inwood Rd., 972/357-7120

Best Bistro
L'Ancestral
  4514 Travis St., 972/528-1081
Watel's
  2719 McKinney Ave., 972/720-0323

Best Breakfast
Barbec's
  8949 Garland Rd., 972/321-5597
Chubby's Family Restaurant
  11333 E. Northwest Hwy., 972/348-6065

T

Circle Grill
  3701 N. Buckner Blvd., 972/324-4140
Gold Rush Cafe
  1913 Skillman St., 972/823-6923
Kel's Restaurant
  5337 Forest Ln., 972/458-7221
Plaza Cafe
  Dallas Grand Hotel, 1914 Commerce St., 972/747-7000

Best Brewpub
Coppertank Brewing Company
  2600 Main St., 972/744-2739
Routh Street Brewery and Grill
  3011 Routh St., 972/922-8835
Yegua Creek Brewing Company
  2920 N. Henderson Ave., 972/824-2739

Best Burgers
Ball's Hamburgers
  4343 W. Northwest Hwy., 972/352-2525
Cheddar's
  39640 Lyndon B. Johnson Freeway, 972/780-1200
Chip's
  4501 Cole Ave., 972/526-1092
Feed Bag
  7752 Forest Ln., 972/739-3909
  3119 E. Lemmon Ave., 972/522-2630
Humperdink's Bar and Grill
  6050 Greenville Ave., 972/368-6597
Prince of Hamburgers
  5200 Lemmon Ave., 972/526-9081
Snuffer's
  3526 Greenville Ave., 972/826-6850
Theo's Diner
  111 S. Hall St., 972/747-6936

Best Cajun/Creole Food
Pappadeaux Seafood Kitchen
  3520 Oak Lawn Ave., 972/521-4700
  10428 Lombardy Ln., 972/358-3096
Razzoo's Cajun Cafe
  13949 N. Central Expwy., 972/235-3700

Best Chinese Food
Bo Bo China
  10630 Church Rd., 972/349-2600
Cafe Panda
  7979 Inwood Dr., 972/902-9500
The New Big Wong
  2121 Greenville Ave. S., 972/821-4198
China Blossom
  3107 W. Camp Wisdom Rd., 972/330-4303
Szechuan Chinese Restaurant
  4117 Lemmon Ave., 972/521-6981

Best Coffee/Coffeehouse
Cafe Brazil
  6420 N. Central Expwy., 972/691-7791
  2221 Abrams Rd., 972/826-9522

Cafe Society
  4514 Travis St., 972/528-6543

Best Desserts
Basha
  2217 Greenville Ave., 972/824-7794

Best Diner
Mecca Restaurant
  10422 Harry Hines Blvd., 972/352-0051

Best Dinner
Landmark
  Melrose Hotel, 3015 Oak Lawn Ave., 972/521-5151
Magic Time Machine
  5003 Belt Line Rd., 972/980-1903
Red Hot and Blue
  9810 N. Central Expwy., Ste. 600, 972/368-7427
Simply Fondue
  2108 Greenville Ave., 972/827-8878

Best Fine Dining
Beau Nash Restaurant
  2200 Cedar Springs, 972/871-3240
Lavendou
  19009 Preston Rd., 972/248-1911
The Mansion on Turtle Creek
  2821 Turtle Creek Blvd., 972/559-2100
Pyramid Restaurant
  1717 N. Akard St., 972/720-5249

Best German Food
Kuby's
  6601 Snider Plz., 972/363-2231

Best Homestyle Food
Celebration Restaurant and Catering
  4503 W. Lover's Ln., 972/351-5681
Gennie's Bishop Grill
  321 N. Bishop Ave., 972/946-1752
Mama's Daughter's Diner
  2014 Irving Blvd., 972/742-8646
  211 N. Record St., 972/741-6262
  2610 Royal Ln., 972/241-8646
Norma's Cafe
  1123 W. Davis St., 972/946-4711

Best Ice Cream/Yogurt
Braum's Ice Cream and Dairy
  11821 Plano Rd., 972/644-5413

Best Indian Food
Bombay Cricket Club
  2508 Maple Ave., 972/871-1333

Best Italian Food
Amore Italian Restaurant
  6931 Snider Plz., 972/739-0502
Mi Piacci
  14854 Montfort Dr., 972/934-8424
Isola Guzo
  1030 Northpark Ctr., Ste. 335, 972/691-0488

Pomodoro
   2520 Cedar Springs Rd., 972/871-1924
Ruggeri's
   2911 Routh St., 972/871-7377
Terilli's
   2815 Greenville Ave., 972/827-3993

Best Korean Food
Korea House Restaurant
   2598 Royal Ln., 972/243-0434

Best Kosher Food
Bagelstein's Restaurant and Catering
   8104 Spring Valley Rd., 972/234-3787

Best Late-Night Food
Cafe Brazil
   6420 N. Central Expwy., 972/691-7791
The Metro Diner
   3309 Gaston Ave., 972/828-2190

Best Lunch
Souper Salad Restaurant
   multiple locations
Treebeard's Restaurant
   Plaza of the Americas, 700 N. Pearl, 972/871-7477

Best Mexican Food
Don Pablos
   9039 Vantage Point Dr., 972/231-5212
   10333 Technology Blvd. E., 972/350-4086
   5345 N. Belt Line Rd., 972/385-7067
El Arroyo
   7402 Greenville Ave., 972/363-4464
El Chico Restaurant
   2031 Abrams Rd., 972/821-5785
   9005 Burton Rd., 972/381-5870
   13927 N. Central Expwy., 972/238-0011
El Fenix Restaurant
   multiple locations
Herrera's Cafe
   4001 Maple Ave., 972/528-9644
Mercado Juarez Restaurant
   1901 W. Northwest Hwy., 972/556-0796
Ojeda's Mexican Restaurant
   4617 Maple Ave., 972/528-8383
Pappasito's Cantina
   10433 Lombardy Ln., 972/350-1970
Rosita's Mexican Restaurant
   4906 Maple Ave., 972/521-4741
Tejano Mexican Restaurant
   110 W. Davis St., 972/943-8610
Uncle Julio's Restaurant
   7557 Greenville Ave., 972/987-9900
   16150 Dallas Pkwy., 972/380-0100
   4125 Lemmon Ave., 972/520-6620

Best Other Ethnic Food
Gloria's (Salvadoran)
   4140 Lemmon Ave., 972/521-7576

Best Outdoor Dining
Pappasito's Cantina
  10433 Lombardy Ln., 972/350-1970
Tejano Mexican Restaurant
  110 W. Davis St., 214/943-8610
The Green Room
  2715 Elm St., 972/748-7666

Best Pizza
Al's Pizza
  3701 W Northwest Hwy., Ste. 159, 972/350-2714
Arcodoro
  2520 Cedar Springs Rd., 972/871-1924
Campisi's Pizza To Go
  5665 E. Mockingbird Ln., 972/821-4741
  7522 Campbell Rd., Ste. 106, 972/931-2267
Olympic Pizza
  2907 W. Northwest Hwy., 972/358-4111
Pizzeria Uno Restaurant and Bar
  4002 Belt Line Rd., Ste. 100, 972/991-8181
Sal's Pizza and Restaurant
  2525 Wycliff Ave., 972/522-1828

Best Restaurant Meal Value
Norma's Cafe
  1123 W. Davis St., 972/946-4711
  3330 Belt Line Rd., 972/243-8646
St. Pete's Dancing Marlin
  2730 Commerce St., 972/698-1511

Best Romantic Dining
The French Room
  Adolphus Hotel, 1321 Commerce St., 972/742-8200
The Grape Restaurant
  2808 Greenville Ave., 972/828-1981
York Street
  6047 Lewis St., 972/826-0968

Best Salad/Salad Bar
La Madeleine French Bakery and Cafe
  Galleria Mall, 13350 Dallas Pkwy., Ste. 400,
    972/991-7788
  5290 Belt Line Rd., Ste. 112, 972/239-9051
Parigi Restaurant
  3311 Oak Lawn Ave., Ste. 102, 972/521-0295
Souper Salad Restaurant
  multiple locations
Whole Foods Market
  2218 Greenville Ave., 972/828-0052

Best Sandwiches
Pocket Sandwich Theatre
  5400 E. Mockingbird Ln., Ste. 119, 972/821-1860

Best Seafood
Daddy Jack's Lobster and Chowder House
  1916 Greenville Ave., 972/826-4910
Galveston Island Seafood
  9901 Royal Ln., 972/348-8844
Magic Time Machine
  5003 Belt Line Rd., 972/980-1903

T

Pappadeaux Seafood Kitchen
10428 Lombardy Ln., 972/358-3096
3520 Oak Lawn Ave., 972/521-4700
Pappasito's Cantina
10433 Lombardy Ln., 972/350-1970

Best Soul Food
Sweet Georgia Brown Barbecue
2840 E. Ledbetter Dr., 972/375-2020
Vern's Place
3600 Main St., 972/823-0435

Best Southwestern Food
Blue Mesa Grill
5100 Belt Line Rd., 972/934-0165
The Mansion on Turtle Creek
2821 Turtle Creek Blvd., 972/559-2100
Star Canyon
3102 Oak Lawn Ave., 972/520-7827
Y.O. Ranch Restaurant
702 Ross Ave., 972/744-3287

Best Steaks
Chamberlain's
15280 Addison Rd., Ste. 300, 972/934-8780
5330 Belt Line Rd., 972/934-2467
Del Frisco's
5251 Spring Valley Rd., 972/490-9000
Dunston's Steak House
3565 Forest Ln., 972/241-9204
8526 Harry Hines Blvd., 972/637-3513
5423 W. Lovers Ln., 972/352-8320
Hoffbrau Steaks
4180 Belt Line Rd., 972/392-1161
Ruth's Chris Steak House
17840 Dallas Pkwy., 972/250-2244
5922 Cedar Springs Rd., 972/902-8080
Trail Dust Steak House
10841 Composite Dr., 972/357-3862

Best Tea Room
Lady Primrose's Tea Room
500 Crescent Ct., 972/871-8334

Best Thai Food
Thailanna Restaurant
4315 Bryan St., 972/827-6478
Toy's Cafe
4422 Lemmon Ave., 972/528-7233

Best Vegetarian Food
Cosmic Cup
2912 Oak Lawn Ave., 972/521-6157
Kalachandji's
5430 Gurley Ave., 972/821-1048
Macro Cafe
146 Spring Creek Village, 972/385-8000
Thai Soon
2018 Greenville Ave., 972/821-7666

Best Vietnamese Food
East Wind Restaurant
2711 Elm St., 972/745-5554

Best View While Dining
Nana Grill
2201 Stemmons Freeway, 972/761-7479

DEL RIO, TX

Best Restaurant in Town
Cripple Creek Saloon
Hwy. 90W, 830/775-0153
Don Marcelino Restaurant
1110 Avenue F, 830/775-6242
Memo's
804 E. Losoya St., 830/775-8104
The Windmill
1811 Avenue F, 830/774-7003

Best Thai Food
Jitra Thai Cuisine
800 E. Gibbs St., 830/775-7553

DENISON, TX

Best Barbecue/Ribs
Carter Red
2001 S. Austin Ave., 903/465-8337

Best Chinese Food
China Inn
505 S. Armstrong Ave., 903/465-6622

Best Italian Food
Old Italian Depot
101 E. Main St., 903/463-2145

Best Mexican Food
Garcia's Mexican Cafe
119 W. Main St., 903/463-1624
2001 S. Austin Ave., 903/463-4414

Best Restaurant in Town
Old Italian Depot
101 E. Main St., 903/463-2145

Best Seafood
Grandpappy Point
Hwy. 84, 903/465-6376

DENTON, TX

Best Breakfast
Homestead
401 S. Locust St., Ste. 101, 940/566-3240
Jim's Diner
110 Fry St., 940/382-4442

Best Chinese Food
Red Pepper's Chinese Restaurant
2412 S. I-35E, 940/387-1688

Best Desserts
Cappucino Cafe
707 Sunset St., 940/565-1808

T

Best Greek/Mediterranean Food
Arcadia's
   314 W. University Dr., 940/591-8489

Best Ice Cream/Yogurt
Braum's Ice Cream and Dairy
   301 W. University Dr., 940/382-2710

Best Italian Food
Milano Restaurant
   911A Avenue C, 940/383-2021

Best Mexican Food
Mazatlan Restaurant
   1928 N. Ruddell St., 940/566-1718

Best Salad/Salad Bar
Rama's Courtyard
   222 W. Hickory St., 940/383-8491

EDINBURG, TX

Best All-You-Can-Eat Buffet
Grand View
   Echo Motor Hotel, 1903 S. Closner Blvd.,
   956/383-3823

Best Breakfast
El Taco Place
   620 S. Closner Blvd., 956/381-5452
Hec and Bec Restaurant
   317 E. University Dr., 956/383-8592

Best Burgers
Hamburger King
   524 E. University Dr., 956/383-9091

Best Homestyle Food
Kuntry Kitchen
   2207 S. Hwy. 281, 956/380-0521

Best Italian Food
The Ripe Olive
   1328 N. Closner Blvd., 956/383-0474

Best Mexican Food
La Casa Del Taco
   321 W. University Dr., 956/383-0521
Las Brasas Restaurant
   1701 W. University Dr., 956/380-6624

Best Place to Take the Kids
Peter Piper Pizza
   1009 S. Closner Blvd., 956/380-6666

Best Salad/Salad Bar
Shea-Martin Cafe and Catering
   217 S. Closner Blvd., 956/380-0401

Best Seafood
La Jaiba
   524 W. University Dr., 956/316-3474

EL PASO, TX

Best All-You-Can-Eat Buffet
K-Bob's Steakhouse
9530 Viscount Blvd., 915/598-1266
7597 N. Mesa St., 915/581-8780
10059 Dyer St., 915/751-8100

Best Barbecue/Ribs
The Brisket Bar-B-Q
11420 Rojas Dr., Ste. 5, 915/595-0114

Best Chinese Food
Uncle Bao's Restaurant
5668 N. Mesa St., 915/585-1818
9515 Gateway Blvd. W., 915/592-1101

Best Coffee/Coffeehouse
Barnes and Noble
705 Sunland Park Dr., 915/581-5353
9521 Viscount Blvd., 915/590-1932

Best Desserts
Marie Callender's
10501 Gateway Blvd. W., 915/592-6920

Best Family Restaurants
Great American Land and Cattle
7600 Alabama St., 915/751-5300
2220 N. Yarborough Dr., 915/595-1772

Best Italian Food
Dominic's
717 E. San Antonio Ave., 915/544-0011

Best Japanese Food
Samurai
7040 N. Mesa St., 915/585-8848

Best Mexican Food
Amigos
2000 Montana Ave., 915/533-0155
Kiki's Restaurant and Bar
2719 N. Piedras St., 915/565-6713

Best Pizza
Cici's Pizza
11335 Montwood Dr., 915/857-3355
7500 N. Mesa St., 915/833-4900

Best Romantic Dining
Carlos and Mickey's Restaurant
1310 Magruder St., 915/778-3323

Best Steaks
Cattlemen's Steakhouse
Indian Cliffs Ranch, I-10 at Exit 49, 5 miles N,
Fabens, 915/764-2283

Best Tea Room
La Jolla Tea Room
5411 N. Mesa St., 915/587-6020

T

FT. STOCKTON, TX

Best All-You-Can-Eat Buffet
Brazen Bean
3105 W. Dickinson Blvd., 915/336-3070

Best Barbecue/Ribs
K-Bob's Steakhouse
2800 W. Dickinson Blvd., 915/336-6233

Best Mexican Food
Burrito Inn
805 N. Alamo St., 915/336-3141
Mi Casita
405 E. Dickinson Blvd., 915/336-5368

FT. WORTH, TX

[See also: Arlington.]

Best American Food
8.0 Restaurant and Bar
111 E. Third St., 817/336-0880

Best Barbecue/Ribs
Angelo's Barbecue
2533 White Settlement Rd., 817/332-0357
Cattlemen's Restaurant
2458 N. Main St., 817/624-3945
Cousin's Pit Barbecue
6262 McCart Ave., 817/346-2511
Railhead Smokehouse
2900 Montgomery, 817/738-9808
Ricsky's Barbecue
2314 Azle Ave., 817/624-8662
300 Main St., 817/877-3306
140 E. Exchange Ave., 817/626-7777
2314 Azle Ave., 817/624-8662
9000 Hwy. 377S, 817/249-3320

Best Beer Selection
Billy Miner's Saloon
150 W. Third St., 817/877-3301
Flying Saucer
111 E. Fourth St., 817/336-7468
Pig and Whistle Pub
5731 Locke Ave., 817/731-4938

Best Breakfast
Cactus Flower Cafe
509 University Dr., 817/332-9552
Ol' South Pancake House
1507 S. University Dr., 817/336-0311
5148 E. Belknap St., Haltom City, 817/834-1291
Paris Coffee Shop
700 W. Magnolia Ave., 817/335-2041

Best Burgers
B.J. Keefer's
909 W. Magnolia Ave., 817/921-0889
Billy Miner's Saloon
150 W. Third St., 817/877-3301

Kincaid's
4901 Camp Bowie Blvd., 817/732-2881
Reata Restaurant
500 Throckmorton St., 817/336-1009

Best Cajun/Creole Food
Razzoo's Cajun Cafe
318 Main St., 817/429-7009
4700 Bryant Irvin Rd., 817/237-7237

Best Chinese Food
Abacus Chinese Restaurant
4954 Overton Ridge Blvd., 817/731-3321
BKK-Narita Restaurant
6060 Southwest Blvd., 817/738-3175
Bamboo Garden
6415 McCart Ave., 817/292-9655
Szechuan Chinese Restaurant
5712 Locke Ave., 817/738-7300
Wan Fu
6399 Camp Bowie Blvd., 817/731-2388

Best Coffee/Coffeehouse
Borders Books and Music Espresso Bar
4613 S. Hulen St., 817/370-9473
Four Star Coffee Bar
3324 W. Seventh St., 817/336-5555
La Madeleine French Bakery
6140 Camp Bowie Blvd., 817/654-0471

Best Delicatessen
Carshon's Delicatessen
3133 Cleburne Rd., 817/923-1907
Sundance Market and Deli
353 Throckmorton St., 817/335-3354

Best Desserts
Houston Street Bakery
301 Main St., 817/870-2895
Swiss Pastry Shop
3936 W. Vickery Blvd., 817/732-5661

Best Fine Dining
Bistro Louise
2900 S. Hulen St., Ste. 40, 817/922-9244
Cafe Aspen
6103 Camp Bowie Blvd., 817/738-0838
Reata Restaurant
500 Throckmorton St., 817/336-1009
Reflections Restaurant
Worthington Hotel, 200 Main St., 817/882-1660

Best German Food
Edelweiss German Restaurant
3801A Southwest Blvd., 817/738-5934

Best Homestyle Food
Black-Eyed Pea
6001 SW Loop 820, 817/370-9701
6357 Camp Bowie Blvd., Ste. 200, 817/737-6142
800 E. Loop 820, 817/496-0213
Celebration Restaurant
4600 Dexter Ave., 817/731-6272

T

Good Eats Grill
   1651 S. University Dr., 817/332-9060
Hatch's Corner
   6950 Forest Hill Dr., 817/293-8295

Best Indian Food
Maharaja
   6308 Hulen Bend Blvd., 817/263-7156

Best Italian Food
Italian Inn
   6323 Camp Bowie Blvd., Ste. B, 817/737-0123
La Piazza
   1600 S. University Dr., 817/334-0000
On Broadway Ristorante
   6306 Hulen Bend Blvd., 817/346-8841
Prego Pasta House
   301 Main St., 817/870-1908
Sardine's Ristorante Italiano
   3410 Camp Bowie Blvd., 817/332-9937
Spaghetti Warehouse
   600 E. Exchange Ave., 817/625-4171

Best Japanese Food
BKK-Narita Restaurant
   6060 Southwest Blvd., 817/738-3175

Best Mexican Food
Don Pablo's Restaurant
   7050 Ridgmar Meadow Rd., 817/731-0497
   5601 S. Hulen St., 817/346-3787
El Asadero II
   4200 South Freeway, 817/922-8113
El Asadero Mexican Restaurant
   1535 N. Main St., 817/626-3399
El Rancho Grande
   1400 N. Main St., 817/624-9206
El Sombrero Mexican Restaurant
   316 S. Saginaw Blvd., 817/232-2331
Joe T. Garcia's Mexican Bakery
   2201 N. Commerce St., 817/626-4356
   1109 Hemphill St., 817/626-5770
   2122 N. Main St., 817/626-5770
Los Vaqueros
   2629 N. Main St., 817/624-1511
Mercado Juarez Restaurant
   2222 Miller Rd., 817/649-3324
   1651 E. Northside Dr., 817/838-8285
Mercado Juarez Stonegate Hacienda
   4200 Stonegate Blvd., 817/920-9487
Mi Cocina
   400 Main St., 817/654-4466

Best Middle Eastern Food
Hedary's Lebanese Restaurant
   3308 Fairfield Ave., 817/731-6961

Best Other Ethnic Food
Blue Danube (Eastern European)
   905 Throckmorton St., 817/338-4701

Papi's Restaurant (Puerto Rican)
  5336 Birchman Ave., 817/763-8442

Best Pizza
Mama's Pizza
  1813 W. Berry St., 817/923-3541
  4801 Camp Bowie Blvd., 817/731-2451
Pizzeria Uno
  300 Houston St., 817/885-8667

Best Romantic Dining
Le Chardonnay
  2443 Forest Park Blvd., 817/926-5622
Michael's
  3413 W. Seventh St., 817/877-3413
Reflections Restaurant
  Worthington Hotel, 200 Main St., 817/882-1660
St. Emilion
  3617 W. Seventh St., 817/737-2781

Best Sandwiches
Jason's Deli
  5443 S. Hulen St., 817/370-9187
  6244 Camp Bowie Blvd., 817/738-7144

Best Seafood
Shrimpers Inc.
  215 University Dr., 817/877-3255
Water Street Seafood Company
  1540 S. University Dr., 817/877-3474
Zeke's Fish and Chips
  5920 Curzon Ave., 817/731-3321

Best Steaks
Cattlemen's Restaurant
  2458 N. Main St., 817/624-3945
Del Frisco's Double Eagle
  812 Main St., 817/877-3999
Hoffbrau Steaks
  1712 S. University Dr., 817/870-1952
The Keg Rodeo Steakhouse
  1309 Calhoun St., 817/332-1288

Best Sunday Brunch
Uncle Julio's Fine Mexican
  5301 Camp Bowie Blvd., 817/377-2777
The Bridge
  Worthington Hotel, 200 Main St., 817/882-1660

Best Vegetarian Food
King Tut
  1512 W. Magnolia Ave., 817/335-3051
Luby's Cafeteria
  3252 SE Loop 820, 817/293-0060
  4800 S. Hulen St., 817/292-5014
  251 University Dr., 817/870-9875
  1200 Bridgewood Dr., 817/457-5200

Best Vietnamese Food
BKK-Narita Restaurant
  6060 Southwest Blvd., 817/738-3175
Phuong Cafe
  4045 E. Belknap St., Haltom City, 817/831-2010

T

Tu Hai
3909 E. Belknap, Haltom City, 817/834-6473

GALVESTON, TX

Best Breakfast
El Nopalito
614 42nd St., 409/763-9815

Best Chinese Food
Happy Buddha
2827 61st St., 409/744-5774

Best Coffee/Coffeehouse
Rock and Java
213 Tremont St., 409/762-8083

Best Fine Dining
Clary's Restaurant
1002 Commodore Dr., 409/740-1103
8509 Teichman Rd., 409/740-0771

Best Greek/Mediterranean Food
Mikonos Pub and Deli
2101 Post Office St., 409/762-3985

Best Health-Conscious Menu
Yaga's Tropical Cafe
2314 Strand St., 409/762-6676

Best Homestyle Food
Schutte's Corner
8021 Post Office St., 409/763-8111

Best Ice Cream/Yogurt
Marble Slab Creamery
2705 61st St., 409/744-6215

Best Italian Food
Nash D'Amico's Pasta and Clam
2328 Strand St., 409/763-6500

Best Late-Night Food
Wentletrap, A Restaurant
2301 Strand St., 409/765-5545

Best Mexican Food
La Mixteca
1818 Mechanic St., 409/762-2235
Marco's Mexican Restaurant
2705 61st St., 409/740-2024

Best Pizza
Mario's Flying Pizza Restaurant
2202 61st St., 409/744-2975

Best Romantic Dining
Gaido's Seafood Restaurant
3800 Seawall Blvd., 409/762-9625

Best Sandwiches
Paul's Sandwich Shop
412 Twentieth St., 409/765-8319
706 Holiday Dr., 409/763-9256

Best Seafood
Clary's Restaurant
8509 Teichman Rd., 409/740-0771
1002 Commodore Dr., 409/740-1103

GARLAND, TX

[See also: Dallas and Richardson.]

Best Chinese Food
General Pao Chinese Restaurant
1311 Plaza Dr., 972/686-8691

Best Coffee/Coffeehouse
Entrees on Trays
2313 Country Hollow Ln., 972/530-6866

Best Homestyle Food
Hubbard's Cubbard
614 Main St., 972/276-4179

Best Italian Food
Giovanni's Restaurant
184 Preston Rd., Ste. 119, 972/596-8610

Best Vietnamese Food
Arc-en-Ciel
3555 W. Walnut St., 972/272-2188

GRAPEVINE, TX

Best Mexican Food
Don Pablo's Restaurant
1709 Cross Roads Dr., 817/421-2981

Best Pizza
California Pizza Kitchen
1051 W. Hwy. 114, 817/481-4255

Best Seafood
Joe's Crab Shack
201 W. Hwy. 114, 817/251-1515

GREENVILLE, TX

Best Barbecue/Ribs
Spare Rib
7818 Wesley St., 903/455-0219

Best Burgers
Lee Street Hamburger Company
2500 Lee St., 903/454-0001

Best Chinese Food
Yen Jing Chinese Restaurant
5113 Wesley St., 903/454-7413

Best Desserts
Bob Whitworth's Cafe and Patio
8119 Wesley St., 903/455-3440
Puddin' Hill Store
4007 I-30 (Exit 95), 903/455-6931

Best Ice Cream/Yogurt
Braum's Ice Cream and Dairy
4206 Wesley St., 903/454-1158

Best Mexican Food
Molina's Mexican Cuisine
4207 Wesley St., 903/455-4043

Best Sandwiches
Puddin' Hill Store
4007 I-30 (Exit 95), 903/455-6931

Best Seafood
Bob Whitworth's Cafe and Patio
8119 Wesley St., 903/455-3440

Best Steaks
Bob Whitworth's Cafe and Patio
8119 Wesley St., 903/455-3440

HENDERSON, TX

Best All-You-Can-Eat Buffet
Catfish King Restaurant
440 U.S. Hwy. 79S, 903/657-2572

Best Homestyle Food
Cotton Patch Cafe
420 U.S. Hwy. 79S, 903/657-1414

Best Mexican Food
Lupe's Mexican Restaurant
1221 U.S. Hwy. 79N, 903/657-4427

HOUSTON, TX

Best All-You-Can-Eat Buffet
Patus Thai Cuisine
2420B Rice Blvd., 713/528-6998

Best American Food
Mason Jar
7637 FM 1960 Rd. W., 281/894-7637
9005 Katy Freeway, 713/461-9005
5010 Richmond Ave., 713/626-5010
9434 Old Katy Rd., 713/464-5287
Rotisserie For Beef and Bird
2200 Wilcrest Dr., 713/977-9524

Best Bar
Baba Yega Saloon and Cafe
2607 Grant St., 713/522-0042
Cafe Noche
2409 Montrose Blvd., 713/529-2409

Best Barbecue/Ribs
Barney's Barbeque and Grill
2698 FM 1960 Rd., 281/821-1818
County Line
13580 Cutten Rd., 281/537-2454
Goode Company Barbecue
8911 Katy Freeway, 713/464-1901
5109 Kirby Dr., 713/522-2530
Luther's Barbeque
2611 FM 1960 Rd. W., 281/537-8895

Otto's Barbecue
5502 Memorial Dr., 713/864-2573
500 Dallas St., 713/659-6886
Pappas Barbecue
9815 Bissonnet St., 713/777-1661
7050 Gulf Freeway, 713/649-7236
1217 Pierce St., 713/659-1245
7007 SW Freeway, 713/772-4557
5839 Westheimer Rd., 713/780-7352

Best Beer Selection
Richmond Avenue Arms
5920 Richmond Ave., 713/784-7722
The Gingerman
5607 1/2 Morningside Dr., 713/526-2770

Best Breakfast
Buffalo Grille
3116 Bissonnet St., 713/661-3663
Cafe Artiste
1601 W. Main St., 713/528-3704
La Madeleine French Bakery
5015 Westheimer Rd., 713/993-0287
10001 Westheimer Rd., 713/266-7686
6205 Kirby Dr., 713/942-7081
Le Peep Restaurant
11199 Westheimer Rd., 713/789-7337
6128 Village Pkwy., 713/523-7337
4702 Westheimer Rd., 713/629-7337

Best Brewpub
Houston Brewery
6224 Richmond Ave., 713/953-0101
Rock Bottom Brewery
6111 Richmond Ave., 713/974-2739
Saint Arnold Brewing Company
2522 Fairway Park Dr., 713/686-9494

Best Burgers
Annie's Hamburgers
10821 S. Post Oak Rd., 713/729-9861
Beck's Prime
multiple locations
Cues Burgers and More
10423 S. Post Oak Rd., 713/726-0313
Heaven in a Blanket
8903 Cullen Blvd., 713/733-4848
Moose Cafe
1340 W. Gray St., 713/520-9696
Otto's Hamburgers
5502 Memorial Dr., 713/864-8526
Willie's Dockside Cafe
8500 Hwy. 6N, 281/859-9096

Best Cajun/Creole Food
Floyd's Cajun Shack
1200 Durham Dr., 713/862-3326
Pappadeaux Seafood Kitchen
multiple locations,
Ragin' Cajun Restaurant
4302 Richmond Ave., 713/623-6321

Best Chinese Food
Chinese Cafe
   5092 Richmond Ave., 713/621-2888
   12047 Northwest Freeway, 713/683-8288
Dong Ting
   611 Stuart St., 713/527-0005
Empress of China
   5419A FM 1960 Rd. W., 281/583-8021
Fu's Garden
   9905 S. Post Oak Rd., 713/723-2246
   4720 Richmond Ave., 713/520-7742
   5866 San Felipe St., 713/783-4419
Imperial Palace
   9160 Bellaire Blvd., 713/773-3838
   2001 Jefferson St., 713/222-2461
Joy Garden Chinese and American
   9579 Jones Rd., 281/890-2888
King Palace Chinese Restaurant
   18405 Tomball Pkwy., 281/890-7844

Best Coffee/Coffeehouse
Brasil
   2604 Dunlavy St., 713/528-1993
Empire Cafe
   1732 Westheimer Rd., 713/528-5282
Starbucks Coffee
   multiple locations

Best Delicatessen
Jason's Deli
   5860 Westheimer Rd., 713/975-7878
   2611 S. Shepherd Dr., Ste. 100, 713/520-6728
   10321A Katy Freeway, 713/467-2007
   2530 University Blvd., 713/522-2660
Victor's Delicatessen and Restaurant
   4710 FM 1960 Rd. W., 713/681-5559

Best Desserts
Empire Cafe
   1732 Westheimer Rd., 713/528-5282
Nielsen's Delicatessen
   4500 Richmond Ave., 713/963-8005
Patisserie Descours Catering
   1330D Wirt Rd., 713/681-8894

Best Diner
59 Diner
   3801 Farnham St., 713/523-2333
   8125 Katy Freeway, 713/681-5559
Simpson's Diner
   8808 Westheimer Rd., 713/789-5875

Best Dinner
Achilles Italian Cuisine
   14120 Memorial Dr., 281/558-0615
Carmelo's Italian Restaurant
   14795 Memorial Dr., 281/531-0696
Swiss Inn Restaurant
   1330B Wirt Rd., 713/688-8471

Best Family Restaurant
Family Cafe
2712 Blodgett St., 713/520-5444

Best Fine Dining
Anthony's
4007 Westheimer Rd., 713/961-0552
Brennan's Houston
3300 Smith St., 713/522-9711
Cafe Annie
1728 Post Oak Blvd., 713/840-1111
Great Caruso
10001 Westheimer Rd., 713/780-4900
Tony's Restaurant
1801 Post Oak Blvd., 713/622-6779

Best Greek/Mediterranean Food
Riviera Grill
10655 Katy Freeway, 713/974-4445

Best Health-Conscious Menu
Souper Salad Restaurant
multiple locations

Best Homestyle Food
Black-Eyed Pea
multiple locations
City Cafe
513 College Ave., South Houston, 713/944-3710
Mom's Cookin'
905 Taft St., 713/522-4500
Pappy's Grill
9041 Katy Freeway, 713/827-1811
Potato Patch
2504 FM 1960 Rd., 281/443-3530
Uncle Tom's Kitchen
12302 Jones Rd., 281/955-7907

Best Ice Cream/Yogurt
Amy's Ice Cream and Coffee
3826 Farnham St., 713/526-2697

Best Indian Food
Annapurna Fast Food
5827 Hillcroft St., 713/780-4453
Khyber Restaurant
2510 Richmond Ave., 713/942-9424
Raja Quality Restaurant
5667 Hillcroft St., 713/782-5667

Best Inexpensive Meal
Taco Cabana
multiple locations

Best Italian Food
Baci
2441 University Blvd., 713/524-1266
Carrabbas Italian Grill
5440 FM 1960 Rd. W., 713/397-8255
11339 Katy Freeway, 713/464-6595
1399 S. Voss Rd., 713/468-0868
3115 Kirby Dr., 713/522-3131

T

Ciros Cibi Italiani
  1000 Campbell Rd., Ste. 550, 713/467-9336
Josephine's Ristorante
  1209 Caroline St., 713/759-9323
Polliciniella Ristorante
  6536 FM 1960 Rd. W., 281/893-6510

Best Japanese Food
Japon
  2444 Times Blvd., 713/526-2100

Best Korean Food
Kim Son Restaurant
  8200 Wilcrest Dr., 281/498-7841
Kim Son Restaurant
  2001 Jefferson St., 713/222-2461
  7531 Westheimer Rd., 713/783-0054

Best Late-Night Food
Droubi's Bakery
  3233 Hillcroft St., 713/782-6160
  7333 Hillcroft St., 713/988-5897
House of Pies
  6314 Antoine Dr., 713/680-1641
  6142 Westheimer Rd., 713/782-1290
  3112 Kirby Dr., 713/528-3816
Spanish Flower Mexican Restaurant
  4701 N. Main St., 713/869-1706

Best Mexican Food
Bajas A Texas Grill
  9453 Jones Rd., 281/897-9200
Fajita Willie's
  14960 Northwest Freeway, 713/466-7646
  17492 Northwest Freeway, 713/466-5925
Goode Company Hamburgers and Tacqueria
  4902 Kirby Dr., 713/520-9153
Irma's
  22 N. Chenevert St., 713/222-0767
Ninfa's Mexican Restaurant
  multiple locations
Pappsitos Cantina
  multiple locations

Best Middle Eastern Food
Dimassi Middle Eastern Cafe
  5064 Richmond Ave., 713/439-7481

Best Outdoor Dining
Baba Yega Saloon and Cafe
  2607 Grant St., 713/522-0042
Backstreet Cafe
  1103 S. Shepherd Dr., 713/521-2239
Cafe Noche
  2409 Montrose Blvd., 713/529-2409
On the Border Cafe
  4608 Westheimer Rd., 713/961-4494
Patrenella's
  813 Jackson Hill St., 713/863-8223
River Cafe
  3615 Montrose Blvd., 713/529-0088

Rose's Patio Cafe
219 Main St., 713/288-0512
Yakov's Deli
3925 Richmond Ave., 713/621-3308

Best Pizza
Collina's
3933 Richmond Ave., 713/621-8844
Fuzzy's Pizza
823 Antoine Dr., 713/682-8836
Star Pizza
2111 Norfolk St., 713/523-0800
Star Pizza II
140 S. Heights Blvd., 713/869-1241

Best Place to Take the Kids
Skeeter's Mesquite Grill
5529 Weslayan St., 713/660-7090

Best Restaurant in Town
Moose Cafe
1340 W. Gray St., 713/520-9696
The Ruggles Grill
903 Westheimer Rd., 713/524-3839

Best Restaurant Meal Value
Annapurna Fast Food
5827 Hillcroft St., 713/780-4453
Cleburne Cafeteria
3606 Bissonnet St., 713/667-2386
Riviera Grill
10655 Katy Freeway, 713/974-4445

Best Romantic Dining
Bistro Vino
819 W. Alabama St., 713/526-5500
La Mora
912 Lovett Blvd., 713/522-7412
Rainbow Lodge
1 Birdsall St., 713/861-8666

Best Salad/Salad Bar
Cafe Express
210 Meyerland Plaza Malla, 713/349-9222
1422 W. Gray St., 713/522-3100
4060 Bellaire Blvd., 713/669-0069
3200 Kirby Dr., 713/522-3994
Houston's
4848 Kirby Dr., 713/529-2385
5888 Westheimer Rd., 713/975-1947

Best Sandwiches
Jason's Deli
5860 Westheimer Rd., 713/975-7878
2611 S. Shepherd Dr., Ste. 100, 713/520-6728
5403D FM 1960 Rd. W., 713/444-7515
2530 University Blvd., 713/522-2660
10321A Katy Freeway, 713/467-2007
Jax Grill
1613 Shepherd Dr., 713/861-5529
Ouisie's Table
3939 San Felipe St., 713/528-2264

T

Best Seafood
Captain Benny's Half Shell Oyster Bar
  8506 S. Main St., 713/666-5469
Denis Seafood
  12109 Westheimer Rd., 713/497-1110
Goode Company Seafood
  2621 Westpark Dr., 713/523-7154
Los Andes
  12 E. Greenway Plz., Ste. 100, 713/622-2686
Pappadeaux Seafood Kitchen
  multiple locations
Pappas Seafood House
  6894 Eastex Freeway, 713/784-4729
  11301 North Freeway, 281/999-9928
  6945 Gulf Freeway, 713/641-0318
  12010 East Freeway, 713/453-3265

Best Soul Food
Family Cafe
  2712 Blodgett St., 713/520-5444
Houston This Is It
  207 Gray St., 713/659-1608

Best Southwestern Food
Cafe Annie
  1728 Post Oak Blvd., 713/840-1111
Redwood Grill
  4611 Montrose Blvd., 713/523-4611
The Ruggles Grill
  903 Westheimer Rd., 713/524-3839

Best Steaks
Brenner's
  10911 Katy Freeway, 713/465-2901
County Line
  13580 Cutten Rd., 281/537-2454
Lynn's Steakhouse
  955 Dairy Ashford St., 281/870-0807
Ruth's Chris Steak House
  6213 Richmond Ave., 713/789-2333

Best Sunday Brunch
Ritz-Carlton
  1919 Briar Oaks Lane, 713/840-7600

Best Sushi
Miyako
  6345 Westheimer Rd., 713/781-6300
  3910 Kirby Dr., 713/520-9797

Best Thai Food
Kim Son Restaurant
  2001 Jefferson St., 713/222-2461
Morningside Thai Original
  6710 Morningside Dr., 713/661-4400
Thai Pepper Restaurant
  2049 W. Alabama St., 713/520-8225
Tubtim Siam
  6488 FM 1960 Rd. W., 281/893-8889

Best Vegetarian Food
A Moveable Feast
  2202 W. Alabama St., 713/528-3585
Hobbit Hole Cafe
  1715 S. Shepherd Dr., 713/528-3418
Wonderful Vegetarian Restaurant
  7549 Westheimer Rd., 713/977-3137
Yildizlar
  3419 Kirby Dr., 713/524-7735

Best Vietnamese Food
Mais Restaurant
  3403 Milan Rd., 713/520-7684

HUMBLE, TX

Best All-You-Can-Eat Buffet
Trigg's Cafe
  1712 First St. E., 281/540-2700

Best American Food
Black-Eyed Pea
  9710 FM 1960 Bypass Rd. W., 281/446-3399

Best Barbecue/Ribs
Luther's Barbecue
  19713 Hwy. 59N, 281/446-0441
Mo's Original Barbecue
  8331 FM 1960 Bypass Rd. W., 281/548-3777

Best Cajun/Creole Food
Mardi Gras Restaurant
  113 S. Avenue A, 281/548-3663

Best Fine Dining
Chez Nous French Restaurant
  217 S. Avenue G, 281/446-6717

Best Italian Food
Amedeo's Italian Restaurant
  22704 Loop 494, Kingwood, 281/359-4451
Hasta La Pasta
  202E FM 1960 Bypass Rd. E., 281/446-6414

Best Lunch
Humble City Cafe
  200 E. Main St., 281/319-0200
Mardi Gras Restaurant
  113 S. Avenue A, 281/548-3663
Rent-a-Chef Cafe and Catering
  813 First St. E., 281/446-3030
Two Cooks
  502 Staitti St., 281/446-1005

Best Mexican Food
Monterey's Tex-Mex Cafe
  270 First St. W., 281/446-8466
Pappasito's Cantina
  10005 FM 1960 Bypass Rd. W., 281/540-8664

T

HUNTSVILLE, TX

Best Chinese Food
Imperial Garden
1600 I-45N, 409/539-1566

Best Homestyle Food
The Texan Cafe
1120 Sam Houston Ave., 409/295-2381

Best Seafood
Junction Steak and Seafood
2641 Eleventh St., 409/291-2183

IRVING, TX

[See also: Arlington and Dallas.]

Best Atmosphere
Veranda
5433 N. MacArthur Blvd., 972/518-0939

Best Barbecue/Ribs
Spring Creek Barbecue
3514 W. Airport Freeway, 972/313-0987

Best Casual Dining
Mustang Cafe
5205 N. O'Connor Blvd., 972/869-9942

Best Chinese Food
Empress of China
2648 N. Belt Line Rd., 972/252-7677
1429 Rochelle Blvd., 972/830-6288

Best Coffee/Coffeehouse
W. W. Coffee Company
5459 N. MacArthur Blvd., 972/756-0046

Best Delicatessen
The Deli Express
5525 N. MacArthur Blvd., 972/714-0196

Best Greek/Mediterranean Food
Athens Restaurant
3866 Irving Mall, 972/255-0692

Best Homestyle Food
Black-Eyed Pea
3601 N. Belt Line Rd., 972/255-0563
Mama's Daughters' Diner
2610 W. Royal Ln., 972/241-8646
2412 W. Shady Grove Rd., 972/790-2778
The Big Feeder Restaurant
1111 W. Airport Freeway, 972/252-1162

Best Italian Food
Cafe Cipriani
220 Las Colinas Blvd. E., 972/869-0713
The Italian Oven Restaurant
7750 N. MacArthur Blvd., 972/506-7001

Best Lunch
Good Eats Cafe
3516 W. Airport Freeway, 972/313-0803
La Madeleine
3132 Skyway Circle S., 972/256-3498

Best Mexican Food
Gourmet Tamale
3516 W. Airport Freeway, 972/554-7893

Best Salad/Salad Bar
Souper Salads
3401 W. Airport Freeway, 972/255-9526

Best Seafood
Pappy's Catfish and Oyster Bar
831 N. Belt Line Rd., 972/790-7650

Best Southwestern Food
Cafe Encino
2742 N. O'Connor Rd., 972/252-1155

KILLEEN, TX

Best All-You-Can-Eat Buffet
Pancho's Mexican Buffet
1502 E. Central Texas Expwy., 254/634-4590

Best American Food
O'Phelan's Restaurant
2100 S. Young Dr., 254/699-3888

Best Barbecue/Ribs
Sam's Barbecue and Catering
1414 S. Fort Hood St., 254/526-8087

Best Breakfast
Hallmark Restaurant
4402 E. Central Texas Expwy., 254/526-6050
Henderson's Family Restaurant
525 E. Veterans Memorial Blvd., 254/554-8505

Best Chinese Food
China Star
910 E. Central Texas Expwy., 254/634-8100

Best German Food
Munchener Kind'l German Restaurant
1519 Florence Rd., 254/634-1818

Best Italian Food
The Appian Way Greek and Italian Ristorante
3301 E. Rancier Ave., 254/690-6888

Best Korean Food
Korean Kitchen
525 E. Veterans Memorial Blvd., 254/634-8172

Best Mexican Food
Casa Castillo
129 W. Veterans Memorial Blvd., 254/634-1191
Rosita's Mexican Food
615 N. Second St., 254/634-9828

Best Place to Take the Kids
Pistol Pete's Pizza
1001 E. Veterans Memorial Blvd., 254/526-5559

T

Best Romantic Dining
Remington's Restaurant
    1721 E. Central Texas Expwy., 254/634-1555

LAREDO, TX

Best Breakfast
Tacoi Palenque
    4515 San Bernardo Ave., Ste.725, 956/725-9898

Best Burgers
Santa Maria Party House
    1909 Santa Maria Ave., 956/724-6969

Best Business Lunch
La Posada Hotel Suites
    1000 Zaragoza St., 956/722-1701

Best French Food
Chez Mauricette
    500 Flores Ave., 956/726-9453

Best Indian Food
Bombay Bar and Grill
    201 W. Del Mar Blvd., 956/717-1003

Best Mexican Food
Tacoi Palenque
    4515 San Bernardo Ave., Ste.725, 956/725-9898
Unicorn Restaurant and Pegasus
    3810 San Bernardo Ave., 956/727-4663

Best Pizza
Pistol Pete's Pizza
    3615 McDonell Ave., 956/725-2508
    4600 San Dario Ave., 956/725-2508

Best Seafood
Mariscos El Pescador
    3919 San Dario Ave., 956/724-8958
Pelican's Wharf
    619 Chicago St., 956/727-5070

LEWISVILLE, TX

Best Fine Dining
Veranda
    208 E. Main St., 972/436-1853

Best Restaurant in Town
The Pantry Cafe
    1288 W. Main St., 972/221-0608

Best Steaks
The Grotto
    2300 Highland Village Rd., Ste. 500, 972/318-0515

LONGVIEW, TX

Best All-You-Can-Eat Buffet
Catfish King Restaurant
    2338 S. Mobberly Ave., 903/757-9709
    1700 Judson Rd., 903/757-2941
    4803 E. End Blvd. S., Marshall, 903/935-5277

Best American Food
Cotton Patch Cafe
  1228 McCann Rd., 903/236-4009
Rusty Nail
  414 W. Loop 281, 903/753-3899

Best Barbecue/Ribs
Bodacious Barbecue
  904 N. Sixth St., 903/753-2714

Best Burgers
Butcher Shop
  102 Lehigh St., 903/758-6066
Jucy's Hamburgers
  816 W. Marshall Ave., 903/753-8993

Best Chinese Food
Canton Restaurant
  2010 E. Marshall Ave., 903/758-0791
China Pearl
  2323 W. Loop 281, 903/297-3831
Hunan Chinese Restaurant
  420 N. High St., 903/757-9137
Hupei Chinese Restaurant
  501 N. Spur 63, 903/757-6261

Best Desserts
Oxford Street Restaurant
  421 N. Spur 63, 903/758-9130

Best Family Restaurant
Armadillo Willie's
  102 E. Tyler St., 903/236-4970

Best French Food
The Taylor House
  212 W. Bowie St., Marshall, 903/938-8549

Best Italian Food
Gucci's Pizza and Grill
  1300 E. Pinecrest Dr., Marshall, 903/938-3841
Monjuni's
  212 E. Marshall Ave., 903/236-8541

Best Mexican Food
Carlito's Restaurant
  2517 Judson Rd., 903/236-6855
Casa Ole Mexican Restaurant
  280 N. Spur 63, 903/758-3776
  410 W. Loop 281, 903/236-3491
Lupe's Mexican Restaurant
  809 Pine Tree Rd., 903/297-6916
  3022 Estes Pkwy., 903/236-0411
  1015 E. Marshall Ave., 903/757-5940
  1205 U.S. Hwy. 59S, Marshall, 903/938-9850
Posados
  110 Triple Creek Dr., 903/234-9115

Best Pizza
Pizza King
  1100 E. Marshall Ave., 903/753-0912

T

Best Restaurant in Town
The Hungry Potter
  4901 Elysian Fields Ave., Marshall, 903/935-1227

Best Romantic Dining
Summit Club
  211 E. Tyler St., Ste. 918, 903/753-0331

Best Sandwiches
Jason's Deli
  103 W. Loop 281, 903/663-5161

Best Seafood
Cace's Seafood and Steak House
  1501 E. Marshall Ave., 903/753-7691
Fisherman's Market
  116F Johnston St., 903/753-6722

Best Vegetarian Food
Jack's Natural Food
  1614 Judson Rd., 903/753-4800
  2199 Gilmer Rd., 903/759-4262

LUBBOCK, TX

Best Barbecue/Ribs
County Line
  Rural Route 3, Box 308, 806/763-6001
Stubb's Bar-B-Q
  620 Nineteenth St., 806/747-4777

Best Breakfast
Mesquite's
  2419 Broadway St., 806/763-1159

Best Brewpub
Hub City Brewery
  1807 Avenue H, 806/747-1535

Best Burgers
Pete's Drive-In
  1002 Avenue Q, 806/765-8419
  4156 34th St., 806/792-2806
  529 34th St., 806/762-8995
  11703 S. University, 806/745-4662

Best Cajun/Creole Food
Jazz, A Louisiana Kitchen
  3703C Nineteenth St., 806/799-2124

Best Desserts
Harrigan's Restaurant
  3801 50th St., 806/792-4648

Best French Food
Chez Suzette
  4423 50th St., 806/795-6796

Best German Food
Schnitzel Haus
  2407 19th St., 806/763-3223

Best Indian Food
Delhi Palace Indian Restaurant
  5401 Aberdeen Ave., 806/799-6772

T

Best Italian Food
Orlando's Italian Restaurant
  6951 Indiana Ave., 806/797-8646
  2402 Avenue Q, 806/747-5998

Best Salad/Salad Bar
Bless Your Heart Restaurant
  3701 Nineteenth St., 806/791-2211

Best Seafood
Cattle Baron Steak and Seafood
  8201 Quaker Ave., 806/798-7033
River Smith's Catering
  322 Avenue U, 806/765-8164
  1602 Main St., 806/744-3474
Shogun
  4520 50th St., 806/797-6044

Best Steaks
Depot's Restaurant and Bar
  1801 Avenue G, 806/747-1646

Best Thai Food
Choochai Thai Cuisine
  2330 Nineteenth St., 806/747-1767

Best View While Dining
County Line
  Rural Route 3, Box 308, 806/763-6001

LUFKIN, TX

Best All-You-Can-Eat Buffet
Fuller's Buffet
  1124 S. First St., 409/632-8200

Best Barbecue/Ribs
Lufkin Bar BQ
  203 S. Chestnut St., 409/639-4744

Best Burgers
Mom's Diner
  900 W. Frank Ave., 409/637-6510
Ray's Drive In Cafe
  420 N. Timberland Dr., 409/634-3262
Ray's Drive In Cafe West
  918 S. John Redditt Dr., 409/637-2525

Best Chinese Food
Chen's China Inn
  302 S. Timberland Dr., 409/634-9091

Best Desserts
Lunch Box
  1422 N. Timberland Dr., 409/639-6334

Best Diner
Mom's Diner
  900 W. Frank Ave., 409/637-6510

Best Homestyle Food
Fuller's Buffet
  1124 S. First St., 409/632-8200

T

Best Italian Food
Roma Italiano Restorante
112 S. First St., 409/637-7227

Best Lunch
Lunch Box
1422 N. Timberland Dr., 409/639-6334

Best Mexican Food
Cafe Del Rio
1901 S. First St., 409/639-4471

Best Seafood
Shrimp Boat Manny's
2802 S. First St., 409/632-0110

MCALLEN, TX

Best Bar
Pepper's Restaurant
4800 N. Tenth St., 956/631-2082

Best Barbecue/Ribs
Lone Star Bar-B-Q
315 W. Hwy. 83, 956/686-7113
Texas T Smokehouse
400 Nolana St., 956/664-1035

Best Burgers
Mesquite Tree
2009 Nolana St., 956/630-4477
Tom and Jerry's
401 N. Tenth St., 956/630-5223

Best Chinese Food
Asian Garden
2200 Nolana St., 956/686-8366
China Wok
3711 N. Tenth St., 956/631-8332
Royal China Restaurant
1020 Nolana St., 956/631-9009

Best Coffee/Coffeehouse
Kafecito's
400 W. Nolana St., 956/664-2464

Best Desserts
Irma's Sweete Shoppe
120 E. Park St., Pharr, 956/787-7131

Best Fine Dining
Oyster Bar III
600 N. Tenth St., 956/686-9924

Best Health-Conscious Menu
Yogurt Etc.
2901K N. Tenth St., 956/682-8737

Best Homestyle Food
Luby's Cafeteria
4901 N. Tenth St., 956/687-9568
1215 S. Tenth St., 956/682-3115

Best Inexpensive Meal
El Pato Mexican Food
1300 E. Tamarack Ave., 956/687-5227

1121 W. Hwy. 83, 956/687-8269
2263 Pecan Blvd., 956/682-3176
3019 N. Tenth St., 956/682-1576

Best Italian Food
Iannelli Ristorante Italiano
2316 N. Tenth St., 956/631-0666

Best Late-Night Food
Taco Cabana
1010 S. Tenth St., 956/630-2888

Best Lunch
Koko's Cafe
119 S. Broadway St., 201/630-5656

Best Mexican Food
Casa Del Taco
600 S. Tenth St., 956/682-1255
1100 W. Houston Ave., 956/631-8193
El Caballo Bayo Restaurant
705 S. Tenth St., 956/682-9555
Johnny's Mexican
1010 W. Houston Ave., 956/686-9061
La Mexicana
709 Hwy. 83 W., Pharr, 956/787-7884
La Mexicano
4019 N. Tenth St., 956/631-8191
La Terraza
Doubletree Club Hotel, 101 N. Main St.,
956/631-1101

Best Pizza
Armando's Pizza
2000 Nolana St., 956/630-2791

Best Sandwiches
Schlotzsky's
2616 N. Tenth St., 956/687-6566
The Mill
4105 N. Tenth St., 956/686-6847

Best Seafood
Oyster Bar III
600 N. Tenth St., 956/686-9924

Best Steaks
Santa Fe Steakhouse
1918 S. Tenth St., 956/630-2331

MCKINNEY, TX

Best Desserts
Pantry Restaurant
214 E. Louisiana St., 972/542-2411

Best Diner
Bill Smith Cafe
1510 W. University Dr., 972/542-5331

Best German Food
Rhinelandhaus
1330 N. McDonald St., 972/562-0124

Best Homestyle Food
Steak Kountry Restaurant
  143 S. Central Expressway, 972/542-3192
  153 Westgate Shopping Center, 972/548-9587

Best Mexican Food
Jalapenos Mexican Grill
  1502 W. University Dr., 972/542-6658
San Miguel Grill
  506 W. University Dr., 972/548-2345

Best Restaurant in Town
Pantry Restaurant
  214 E. Louisiana St., 972/542-2411

MESQUITE, TX

[See also: Dallas.]

Best American Food
Grady's American Grill
  3811 Pavillion Ct., 972/686-1919

Best Barbecue/Ribs
Colter's Bar-B-Q and Grill
  1715 N. Town East Blvd., 972/270-2091

Best Burgers
The Feed Bag
  3600 Gus Thomasson Rd., Ste. 100, 972/270-0852

Best Casual Dining
Don Pablo's
  3900 Pavillion Ct., 972/613-7832
Martinez Restaurant
  810 W. Kearney St., 972/288-7772

Best Chinese Food
Chi's Wok
  1111 N. Town East Blvd., Ste. 10, 972/279-1088
China Imperial
  120 Motley Dr., 972/270-8989
Pearl Chinese Restaurant
  4701 Gus Thomasson Rd., 972/613-8888

Best Desserts
Braum's Ice Cream and Dairy
  219 N. Galloway Ave., 972/285-6066
  4645 Gus Thomasson Rd., 972/279-2661

Best Diner
Owen's Family Restaurant
  3919 Pavillion Ct., 972/613-8690

Best Homestyle Food
Donna's Kitchen
  3600 Gus Thomasson Rd., 972/613-3651
Luby's Cafeteria
  3301 Gus Thomasson Rd., 972/279-6169

Best Indian Food
Ranjini Indian Cuisine
  1815 N. Galloway Ave., 972/329-1599

Best Italian Food
Riuniti Pizza, Pasta, and Subs
  1336 N. Galloway Ave., 972/288-4500

Best Mexican Food
El Fenix Famous Mexican Restaurant
  3904 Towne Crossing Blvd., 972/279-8900
Martinez Restaurant
  810 W. Kearney St., 972/288-7772

Best Pizza
Calzone's Pizza and Italian
  2411 N. Galloway Ave., Ste. 110, 972/686-8905
Cici's Pizza
  3330 N. Galloway Ave., 972/686-1700

Best Sandwiches
Donna's Kitchen
  3600 Gus Thomasson Rd., 972/613-3651
Grady's American Grill
  3811 Pavillion Ct., 972/686-1919

Best Southwestern Food
Tia's Tex-Mex Grill
  3817 Pavillion Ct., 972/681-0118

Best Steaks
Dunston's Steak House
  11817 Lake June Rd., 972/285-2879
Trail Dust Steak House
  21717 Lyndon B. Johnson Freeway, 972/289-5457

MIDLAND, TX

Best Chinese Food
Hunan Garden
  4410A N. Midkiff Rd., Ste. 10, 915/697-9818

Best Italian Food
Luigi's Italian Restaurant
  111 N. Big Spring St., 915/683-6363

Best Late-Night Food
Bennigan's
  4517 N. Midkiff Rd., 915/697-3237

Best Mexican Food
Abuelo's Mexican Restaurant
  4610 N. Garfield St., 915/685-3335

Best Place to Take the Kids
Luby's Cafeteria
  2510 W. Louisiana Ave., 915/682-6256

Best Romantic Dining
Venezia Restaurant
  2101 W. Wadley Ave., 915/687-0900

Best Sandwiches
Murray's Deli
  3211 W. Wadley Ave., Ste. 24, 915/697-3433

Best Steaks
Cattlemen's Restaurant
  3300 N. Big Spring St., 915/682-5668

T

NACOGDOCHES, TX

Best Barbecue/Ribs
Smokehouse
    2709 Westward Dr., 409/560-6714

Best Breakfast
Hot Biscuit
    3227 South St., 409/560-3555

Best Burgers
Butcher Boy's Meats and Deli
    603 North St., 409/560-1137

Best Chinese Food
Szechuan Chinese Restaurant
    3205 N. University Dr., 409/569-2266

Best Homestyle Food
Cotton Patch Cafe
    3117 North St., Ste. 1, 409/569-6926

Best Mexican Food
La Carreta
    3000 North St., 409/569-2800

Best Seafood
Californian
    342 N. University Dr., 409/560-1985

NEW BRAUNFELS, TX

Best American Food
Plaza Diner
    367 Main Plaza, 830/620-7070

Best German Food
Krause's Cafe
    148 S. Castell Ave., 830/625-7581

Best Mexican Food
Adobe Cafe
    124 W. Hwy. 81, 830/620-4433
Molly Joe's
    1153 Oasis St., 830/620-1234

Best Restaurant in Town
The Gristmill Restaurant
    1287 Gruene Rd., 830/625-0684

Best Seafood
Clear Springs Restaurant
    1692 Hwy. 46S, 830/629-3775

ODESSA, TX

Best Burgers
Texas Burger
    7546 W. University Blvd., 915/381-7593
    1507 John Ben Shepperd Pkwy., 915/367-9584
    5200 Andrews Hwy., 915/366-3801

Best Business Lunch
Harrigan's Restaurant
    2701 John Ben Shepperd Pkwy., 915/367-4185

Best Chinese Food
Sakura Restaurant
  4555 E. University Blvd., 915/367-6332

Best Mexican Food
Al's Mexican Food
  4651 N. Grandview Ave., 915/362-5571

Best Pizza
Mr. Gatti's Pizza
  2750 N. Grandview Ave., 915/368-4488

Best Romantic Dining
Zucchi's
  1541 John Ben Shepperd Pkwy., Ste. 18,
    915/550-7443

Best Steaks
Barn Door Restaurant
  2140 Grant Ave., 915/337-4142

Best Vegetarian Food
Calico Cafe
  2931 E. Hwy. 80, 915/334-6899

PARIS, TX

Best Barbecue/Ribs
Tommy's Barbecue
  6825 Lamar Ave., 903/785-2808

Best Chinese Food
China Star
  1810 Lamar Ave., 903/785-8872

Best Homestyle Food
McKee's 24-Hour Family Restaurant
  1355 N. Collegiate Dr., 903/785-0002

Best Ice Cream/Yogurt
Braum's Ice Cream
  2035 Bonham St., 903/784-2142
  2160 Lamar Ave., 903/784-0214

Best Mexican Food
Papacita's Mexican Restaurant
  3015 Loop 286, 903/785-7797

Best Seafood
Fish Fry
  3500 NE Loop 286, 903/785-6144

Best Steaks
Sirloin Stockade
  1167 Lamar Ave., 903/785-0319

PASADENA, TX

Best American Food
Ernie's Restaurant
  6707 Fairmont Pky., 281/487-2848

Best Atmosphere
Cowboy Ranch
  6915 Spencer Hwy., 281/479-1950

T

Best Bar
Clearlake Beach Club
  3813 NASA Road 1, Seabrook, 281/326-3066

Best Barbecue/Ribs
Buster's Bar-B-Que
  2901 Preston Ave., 281/487-5232
Feed Lot Barbecue
  1920 Richey St., 713/477-1531
Gabby's BBQ and Burgers
  4010 Spencer Hwy., 713/944-8424
No Name Bar-B-Q
  101 Pasadena Blvd., 713/472-7249

Best Beer Selection
Bradley's Restaurant and Cafe
  515 W. Bay Area Blvd., Webster, 281/332-8488

Best Burgers
Barry's Feedlot
  8200 Spencer Hwy., 281/930-8203
Joe's Texan Burger
  2406 Preston Ave., 713/472-5001

Best Casual Dining
Black-Eyed Pea
  3800 Spencer Hwy., 713/947-2776
Kettle Restaurant
  3002 Pasadena Freeway, 713/472-5270
  6926 Spencer Hwy., 713/479-0988

Best Chinese Food
Chan's Restaurant
  4111 Fairmont Pky., 281/998-0602
China River Buffet
  3807 Spencer Hwy., 713/910-8899

Best Homestyle Food
Southern Belle Diner
  3324 Shaver St., 713/943-3177

Best Inexpensive Meal
Jimmy's Taco Shack
  213 E. Main St., League City, 713/332-6706

Best Italian Food
Mitchelo's Pizza and Pasta
  1900A Strawberry Rd., 713/473-8200

Best Mexican Food
Casa Ole Mexican Restaurant
  2726 Spencer Hwy., 713/943-1455
Donkey's Mexican Food
  5010 Spencer Hwy., 281/487-1253
Fat Maria's Mexican Restaurant
  5824 Spencer Hwy., 281/487-0062
La Buena Vida Mexican Restaurant
  2328 Southmore Ave., 713/475-7160
La Noria Mexican Restaurant
  4412 Red Bluff Rd., 281/998-8488
Marco's Mexican Restaurant
  1860 E. Beltway 8, 713/472-1919
  1020 W. NASA Rd. 1, Webster, 713/338-1247

Tortillas
9602 Spencer Hwy., La Porte, 713/479-1710

Best Restaurant in Town
Pepper's Beef and Seafood
3604 Fairmont Pky., 281/998-1114

Best Romantic Dining
Monument Inn
4406 Battleground Rd., La Porte, 713/479-1521

Best Sandwiches
Schlotzsky's Deli
3830 Spencer Hwy., 713/946-2034
1221 Main St., 713/473-3930

Best Seafood
Crab House
317 Todville Rd., Seabrook, 281/474-5836

PLAINVIEW, TX

Best Barbecue/Ribs
Chuckwagon Bar-B-Q
2105 Dimmit Rd., 806/296-9907

Best Breakfast
Spudnut Shop
1806 W. Fifth St., 806/296-9198

Best Chinese Food
Far East Restaurant
910 I-27S, 806/296-6812

Best Family Restaurant
Kettle Restaurant
700 I-27N, 806/293-1423

Best Homestyle Food
Cotton Patch Cafe
3314 Olton Rd., 806/293-5522

Best Mexican Food
Leal's Mexican Restaurant
3311 Olton Rd., 806/293-5355

Best Sandwiches
Fieldhouse Sandwich Shop
3402B Olton Rd., 806/293-5092
Roaring '50s Sandwich Shop
600 Quincy St., 806/293-4264

Best Tea Room
Bridal House by Fleur-De-Lis
212 W. Ninth St., 806/296-9444

PLANO, TX

[See also: Dallas and Richardson.]

Best All-You-Can-Eat Buffet
Pancho's Mexican Buffet
3200 Alma Dr., 972/578-1722

Best American Food
Cheddar's
  2400 N. Central Expwy., 972/422-4240
Jack Astor's Bar and Grill
  2901 N. Central Expwy., 972/423-0533

Best Barbecue/Ribs
Barbeque Galore
  1801 Preston Rd., 972/735-8185
Dickey's Barbecue Pit
  1211 Fourteenth St., 972/423-9960
  1441A Coit Rd., 972/867-2901

Best Beer Selection
Bavarian Grill
  221 W. Parker Rd., 972/881-0705

Best Burgers
Chuck's Restaurant
  3308 Preston Rd., 972/596-4211

Best Chinese Food
Rice Farm Chinese Restaurant
  3100 Independence Pkwy., 972/867-6799

Best Coffee/Coffeehouse
Starbucks Coffee
  801 W. Fifteenth St., 972/422-5003
  2201 Preston Rd., 972/964-7020

Best Delicatessen
Jason's Deli
  925 N. Central Expwy., 972/578-2520

Best Desserts
Patrizio North
  1900 Preston Rd., 972/964-2200

Best Diner
Poor Richard's Cafe
  2442 K Ave., 972/423-1524

Best Dinner
Good Eats Cafe
  1101 N. Central Expwy., 972/516-3287

Best Family Restaurant
Black-Eyed Pea
  605 W. Fifteenth St., 972/423-5565
  1932 Preston Park Blvd., 972/964-1353
Chubby's Family Restaurat
  910 Parker Rd., 972/881-1348

Best Fine Dining
Plano Cafe
  1915 N. Central Expwy., 972/516-0865

Best French Food
Cafe De France
  2205 N. Central Expwy., 972/423-2323
Cafe E'Claire
  151 W. Spring Creek Pkwy., 972/517-8224
La Madeleine French Bakery
  5000 W. Park Blvd., Ste. 100, 972/407-1878

Best German Food
Bavarian Grill
  221 W. Parker Rd., 972/881-0705

Best Health-Conscious Menu
Fitness Foods
  2000 W. Parker Rd., 972/867-2620
Souper Salad
  1017 N. Central Expwy., 972/422-7022

Best Ice Cream/Yogurt
Braum's Ice Cream and Dairy
  600 E. Fifteenth St., 972/423-2801
  1401 Independence Pkwy., 972/596-1404
  2005 W. Parker Rd., 972/596-3358

Best Italian Food
Pasquale's Italian Cuisine
  1116 W. Parker Rd., 972/516-1044
Patrizio Restaurant
  1900 Preston Rd., 972/964-2200
Picasso's
  3948 Legacy Dr., 972/618-4143

Best Japanese Food
Awaji Japanese Restaurant
  4701 W. Park Blvd., 972/519-1688

Best Mexican Food
El Paso Cantina
  1320 N. Central Expwy., 972/881-8600
Tino's Mexican Restaurant
  811 N. Central Expwy., 972/424-2572
Tino's Too Mexican Restaurant
  1585 K Ave., 972/881-9226

Best Pizza
Mr. Jim's Pizzeria
  2357 Jupiter Rd., 972/422-1953
Paproni's Pizza
  1929 W. Parker Rd., 972/596-9606

Best Place to Take the Kids
Cici's Pizza
  2011 W. Spring Creek Pkwy., 972/517-8004
  3611 Fourteenth St., 972/423-0240
  2220 Coit Rd., 972/964-0061

Best Seafood
Fishmonger's Seafood Market
  1915 N. Central Expwy., 972/423-3699
Mac's Bar and Grill
  2301 N. Central Expwy., 972/881-2804

Best Sports Bar
Austin Avenue Grill and Sports Bar
  935 W. Parker Rd., 972/422-8003

Best Steaks
Hoffbrau Steaks
  3310 N. Central Expwy., 972/423-4475
Mac's Bar and Grill
  2301 N. Central Expwy., 972/881-2804

T

Best Tea Room
Homemade Delights Tearoom
1400 J Ave., 972/578-2520

Best Wine Selection
Plano Cafe
1915 N. Central Expwy., 972/516-0865

PORT ARTHUR, TX

Best Business Lunch
Port Arthur Club
441 Austin Ave., 409/982-2011

Best Chinese Food
New China Restaurant
2600 Memorial Blvd., 409/983-4937

Best Homestyle Food
French Quarter
5333 N. Twin City Hwy., 409/962-6326

Best Mexican Food
Guadalajara Restaurant
1600 Ninth Ave., 409/983-9173

Best Place to Be "Seen"
Pompano Club
330 Twin City Hwy., Port Neches, 409/727-3111

Best Place to Eat Alone
Casa Ole Mexican Restaurant
3100 Hwy. 365, 409/727-5377
4801 N. Twin City Hwy., 409/963-0185

Best Sandwiches
Jason's Deli
3100 Hwy. 365, Ste. 170, 409/727-6420

Best Sunday Brunch
Holiday Inn
2929 Jimmy Johnson Blvd., 409/724-5000

RICHARDSON, TX

[See also: Dallas, Garland, and Plano.]

Best Barbecue/Ribs
Dickey's BBQ Pit
1778 N. Plano Rd., 972/479-0424
1150 N. Plano Rd., 972/907-8494
Spring Creek Barbecue
270 N. Central Expwy., 972/669-0505

Best Breakfast
Cafe Brazil
2071 N. Central Expwy., 972/783-9011

Best Burgers
Humperdink's Restaurant
1601 N. Central Expwy., 972/690-4867

Best Cajun/Creole Food
Pappadeaux Seafood Kitchen
725 S. Central Expwy., 972/235-1181

Best Chinese Food
Monkok Chinese Restaurant
  2150 N. Collins Blvd., 972/644-0404
Tong's House
  1910 Promenade Center, 972/231-8858

Best Delicatessen
Alvin Ord's Sandwich Shop
  346 W. Campbell Rd., 972/680-2100
Jason's Deli
  385 Dal Rich Village, 972/437-9156
Mr. G's Deli
  283 W. Campbell Rd., 972/437-6747
The Greenhouse Deli
  1600 Promenade Ctr., 972/235-6376

Best Dinner
Campisi's Restaurant
  536 Centennial Blvd., 972/437-2982

Best Health-Conscious Menu
Bless Your Heart
  216 W. Campbell Rd., 972/783-0787

Best Mexican Food
Don Charros Restaurant
  108 University Village Ctr., 972/783-7671
Pappasito's Cantina
  723 S. Central Expwy., 972/480-8595

Best Other Ethnic Food
Palayok (Philoppine)
  940 E. Belt Line Rd., 972/235-6703

Best Southwestern Food
Tia's Tex-Mex Grill
  327 W. Spring Valley Rd., 972/231-6982

Best Sports Bar
Humperdink's Restaurant
  1601 N. Central Expwy., 972/690-4867

Best Vietnamese Food
Peh-Nien Tong
  1819 Promenade Center, 972/231-8858
Pho Huy
  110 S. Greenville Ave., 972/235-9729

ROSENBURG, TX

Best 24-Hour Restaurant
The Texas Grill Restaurant
  1210 Avenue H, 713/342-4775

Best Chinese Food
Hunan Garden Restaurant
  4601 Avenue H, Ste. 7, 713/342-7279

Best Mexican Food
Larry's Original Mexican
  116 E. Hwy. 60A, Richmond, 713/342-2881

Best Restaurant in Town
Hill's Cafe
  1011 FM 359, Richmond, 713/341-0030

Best Steaks
Western Steakhouse
3614 Avenue I, 713/342-9602

SAN ANGELO, TX

Best Bar
Santa Fe Junction
1524 S. Bryant Blvd., 915/658-5068

Best Burgers
Charcoal House
1205 N. Chadbourne St., 915/657-2931
1616 S. Bryant Blvd., 915/653-6666

Best Business Lunch
Michael's
Cactus Hotel, 36 E. Twohig Ave., 915/658-6373

Best Chinese Food
China Garden Restaurant
4217 S. College Hills Blvd., 915/949-2838

Best Coffee/Coffeehouse
Cactus Cafe and Espresso Bar
Cactus Hotel, 36 E. Twohig Ave., Ste. 105,
915/659-1470

Best Diner
Dixie Diner
102 N. Abe St., 915/655-6279

Best Family Restaurant
Shakey's Pizza Parlor
20 Howard St., 915/944-7611

Best Homestyle Food
Peasant Village
23 S. Park St., 915/655-4811

Best Italian Food
Spaghetti Western
2307 Loop 306, 915/944-8082
Taste of Italy
3520 Knickerbocker Rd., 915/944-3290

Best Late-Night Food
Kettle Restaurant
1811 S. Bryant Blvd., 915/655-5542

Best Mexican Food
Better Than Nothing
1911 S. Bryant Blvd., 915/655-3553
Fuentes Cafe Downtown
101 S. Chadbourne St., 915/658-2430
Henry's Diner
3015 Sherwood Way, 915/944-3245
La Casa Blanca
3020 N. Chadbourne St., 915/653-1058
Little Mexico Restaurant
4248 Sherwood Way, 915/949-5570

Best Place to Take the Kids
Shakey's Pizza Parlor
20 Howard St., 915/944-7611

Best Sandwiches
Concho Confetti
    42 E. Concho Ave., 915/655-3962

Best Seafood
Wharf
    2302 Loop 306, 915/944-3414

Best Steaks
Zentner's Daughter Steak House
    1901 Knickerbocker Rd., 915/949-2821
Zentner's Steak House
    2715 Sherwood Way, 915/942-8631

Best Tea Room
Jabberwocky's
    33 E. Concho Ave., 915/659-6903

SAN ANTONIO, TX

Best American Food
Restaurant Biga
    206 E. LocustSt., 210/255-0722

Best Barbecue/Ribs
Big Buck's A-1 Bar-B-Q
    1202 W. Commerce St., 210/212-3895
The County Line
    111 W. Crockett St., 210/229-1941
    606 W. Afton Oaks Blvd., 210/496-0011

Best Bistro
Bistro Time
    5137 Fredericksburg Rd., 210/344-6626
Boardwalk Bistro
    4011 Broadway St., 210/824-0100

Best Burgers
Chris Madrid's Nachos and Burgers
    1900 Blanco Rd., 210/735-3552

Best Cajun/Creole Food
Pappadeaux's Seafood Kitchen
    76 NE Loop 410, 210/340-7143

Best Chinese Food
Gin's Chinese Restaurant
    5337 Glen Ridge Dr., 210/684-7008
Hung Fong Restaurant
    3624 Broadway, 210/822-9211

Best Coffee/Coffeehouse
Rock and Java
    502 Embassy Oaks, Ste. 142, 210/494-5282

Best Delicatessen
Jason's Deli
    9933 I-10W, 210/690-3354

Best French Food
La Madeleine
    4820 Broadway St., 210/829-7271

Best German Food
Nadler's
    7053 San Pedro Ave., 210/340-1021

Best Greek/Mediterranean Food
Babylon
901 S. Alamo St., 210/229-9335

Best Health-Conscious Menu
Cafe Lite and Bakery
8498 Fredericksburg Rd., 210/614-2600
999 E. Basse Rd., 210/824-0027

Best Indian Food
Simi's
4535 Fredericksburg Rd., 210/737-3166

Best Italian Food
Little Italy
824 Afterglow St., 210/349-2060
Paesano's
555 E. Basse Rd., Ste. 100, 210/226-9541

Best Japanese Food
Koi Kawa Japanese Restaurant
4051 Broadway St., 210/805-8112

Best Mexican Food
El Mirador
722 S. St. Mary's St., 210/225-9444
Los Barrios
4223 Blanco Rd., 210/732-6017
Nacho Mama's
24057 Old Fredericksburg Rd., 210/698-0020

Best Pizza
EZ's
8498 N. New Braunfels Ave., 210/828-1111
5720 Bandera Rd., 210/681-2222
734 W. Bitters Rd., 210/490-6666

Best Regional Food
Cascabel Restaurant and Bar
Sheraton Fiesta Hotel, 37 NE Loop 410,
210/366-2424

Best Seafood
Sea Island Shrimp House
322 W. Rector St., 210/342-7771
10141 Wurzbach Rd., 210/558-8989

Best Steaks
Ruth's Chris Steak House
Concord Plaza, 7720 Jones Maltsberger,
210/821-5051

Best Thai Food
Dang's Thai
1146 Austin Hwy., 210/829-7345

Best Vietnamese Food
Saigon Dynasty
9226 Wurzbach Rd., 210/614-6799

SAN MARCOS, TX

Best Atmosphere
Texas Red's Steakhouse and Saloon
120 W. Grove St., 512/754-8808

Best Barbecue/Ribs
Kreuz Market
208 S. Commerce St., Lockhart, 512/398-2361

Best Breakfast
Herbert's Taco Hut
419 Riverside Dr., 512/353-9323
Wesray's
215 N. LBJ Dr., 512/353-3663

Best Burgers
Grins Restaurant
802 N. LBJ Dr., 512/392-4746

Best Chinese Food
Hong Kong Restaurant
812 S. Guadalupe St., 512/392-5665
Imperial Garden Chinese Restaurant
1104L Thorpe Ln., 512/353-3355

Best Desserts
Cottage Kitchen
400 E. Hopkins St., 512/392-4295
Palmer's Restaurant and Bar
218 Moore St., 512/353-3500

Best Homestyle Food
Cottage Kitchen
400 E. Hopkins St., 512/392-4295

Best Pizza
Schlotzsky's
909C Hwy. 80, 512/353-3354

SHERMAN, TX

Best Chinese Food
Gourmet China
4909 N. Sam Rayburn Freeway, 903/892-3882

Best Desserts
Conrad's Pies
124 S. Woods St., 903/868-1959

Best Homestyle Food
City Limits
4521 Texoma Pkwy., 903/893-9117

Best Ice Cream/Yogurt
Braum's Ice Cream & Dairy
600 N. Travis St., 903/893-2421

Best Sandwiches
Sandwich Shop
110 E. Houston St., 903/892-9305
Vitina's Deli Delights
1001 N. Travis St., 903/892-6480

Best Seafood
Tiffin Shop
221 Sunset Blvd., 903/893-4737

T

SPRING, TX

Best American Food
Happy Cooker
123A Midway St., 281/288-4882

Best Dinner
Hyde's Cafe
26608 Keith St., 281/350-8530
Wunsche Brothers' Cafe and Saloon
103 Midway St., 281/350-1902

Best Italian Food
Carrabbas Italian Grill
25665 I-45, 281/367-9423

Best Seafood
Hyden's Restaurant
25130 I-45, 281/362-7337

Best Tea Room
British Trading Post
26303 W. Hardy Rd., 281/350-5854
Gentry's Pantry
315 Gentry St., 281/353-5566
Queen Victoria Tea Room
310 Main St., 281/288-7455

TEMPLE, TX

Best Atmosphere
Market Street Cafe
300 SW H.K. Dodgen Loop, 254/778-1384

Best Barbecue/Ribs
Cyclone Corral Bar B-Q
1616 Farmers Rd., Burlington, 254/985-2317

Best Chinese Food
Emperors of China
220 SW H.K. Dodgen Loop, 254/774-7955

Best Delicatessen
Molly's Deli
20 E. Avenue A, 254/778-1384

Best Family Restaurant
Jody's Family Restaurant
1307 S. First St., 254/774-7999

Best Homestyle Food
Blue Bonnet Cafe
705 S. 25th St., 254/773-6654

Best Italian Food
Sorge's
1323 S. 57th St., 254/899-1492

Best Mexican Food
Casa Salgado
715 S. First St., 254/770-1313
La Hacienda
3030 S. 31st St., 254/791-1244
Las Casas Restaurante and Patio
2907 S. General Bruce Dr., 254/774-7476

Best Pizza
Mazzio's Pizza
 1420 SW H.K. Dodgen Loop, 254/771-3320

Best Steaks
The Great American Steak and More
 3111 S. 31st St., 254/771-1887

TEXARKANA, TX

Best Barbecue/Ribs
Bodacious BBQ
 720 Texas Blvd., Wake Village, 903/792-4787

Best Burgers
Old Tyme Burger Shoppe
 5121 Summerhill Rd., 903/832-5570
Texas Burger
 301 W. Seventh St., Wake Village, 903/794-4291
The Burger Barn
 839 Redwater Rd., Wake Village, 903/832-0359

Best Casual Dining
Catfish King Restaurant
 3301 Summerhill Rd., 903/794-0901

Best Delicatessen
Franchazi Deli-Bistro
 4055 Summerhill Square, 903/793-1695

Best Family Restaurant
Rawleigh's Family Restaurant
 3002 New Boston Rd., Wake Village, 903/838-8721

Best Homestyle Food
Bryce's Cafeteria
 2021 Mall Dr., 903/792-1611

Best Italian Food
Monjuni's
 5522 Summerhill Rd., 903/793-4550

Best Lunch
Martha's Restaurant
 I Hwy. 30W, 903/794-3131

Best Mexican Food
Poncho's Mexican Buffet
 2700 Richmond Rd., 903/831-6639

Best Pizza
Rigatoni's Pizza
 115 Central Mall, 903/832-1689

Best Seafood
Doc Alexander's
 4900 Texas Blvd., 903/792-7925
John's Seafood
 1617 New Boston Rd., Wake Village, 903/793-5787

TEXAS CITY, TX

Best Barbecue/Ribs
Grand Prize Barbeque
 2223 Palmer Hwy., 409/948-6501

T

Best Breakfast
Busy Bee Cafe
3440 Palmer Hwy., 409/945-8444

Best Chinese Food
Fortune Chinese Restaurant
3118 Palmer Hwy., 409/945-3134

Best Homestyle Food
Kelley's
4604 Gulf Freeway, LaMarque, 409/935-3131

Best Pizza
Cici's Pizza
3506 Palmer Hwy., 409/945-2021

Best Seafood
Gus' Restaurant
911 Eleventh Ave. N., 409/948-8004

TYLER, TX

Best Bar
Rick's
104 W. Erwin St., 903/531-2415

Best Breakfast
D's Royal Coffee Shop
710 E. Front St., 903/597-3653

Best Burgers
J.W. Finn's Market Cafe
2324 S. Southeast Loop 323, 903/592-2833

Best Business Lunch
Oxford Street
3300 Troup Hwy., 903/593-2655

Best Casual Dining
Armadillo Willy's
215 W. Southwest Loop 323, 903/509-0122
Jason's Deli
4740 S. Broadway Ave., 903/561-5380

Best Chinese Food
Hunan Chinese Restaurant
1610 S. Vine Ave., 903/595-6677
Hupei Chinese Restaurant
1125 E. Fifth St., 903/595-5393
Liang's Chinese Restaurant
1828 E. Southeast Loop 323, 903/593-7883

Best Desserts
Chez Bazan French Bakery
5930 Old Bullard Rd., 903/561-9644

Best Diner
Cox's Grill
706 W. Front St., 903/593-8940
Fuller's Fine Foods
601 E. Front St., 903/595-1676

Best French Food
Currents Restaurant
1121 E. Second St., 903/597-3771

Best Health-Conscious Menu
Cace's Seafood
7011 S. Broadway Ave., 903/581-0744
Honey Tree
211 Shelley Dr., 903/561-5329
Szechuan Chinese Restaurant
6421 S. Broadway Ave., 903/581-4310

Best Homestyle Food
Pauline's Country Buffet
3040 W. Gentry Pkwy., 903/592-1955

Best Inexpensive Meal
Bruno's Pizza
1400 S. Vine Ave., 903/595-1676

Best Mexican Food
Papacita's Mexican Restaurant
6704 S. Broadway Ave., 903/581-7433

Best Pizza
Bruno's Pizza
1400 S. Vine Ave., 903/595-1676

Best Romantic Dining
Mansion on the Hill
3324 Spur 124, 903/533-1628

Best Sandwiches
Schlotzsky's
4500 S. Broadway Ave., 903/561-2650
709 S. Beckham Ave., 903/592-8390

Best Steaks
Allen's Steakhouse
4111 Troup Hwy., 903/509-2535

Best Sunday Brunch
Broadway South
5701 S. Broadway Ave., 903/561-5800

Best Tea Room
Annie's Tea Room
107 S. Tyler St., Big Sandy, 903/636-4952
Tyler Square Antiques and Tea Room
117 S. Broadway Ave., 903/593-6888

VICTORIA, TX

Best Breakfast
Village Inn
2301 N. Ben Jordan St., 512/572-0770

Best Chinese Food
China Inn
3602 Houston Hwy., 512/573-0609
Dragon Palace
5223 Hallettsville Hwy., 512/573-1342
Great Wall Chinese Restaurant
2902 Houston Hwy., 512/572-3788

Best Italian Food
Olde Victoria Restaurant
207 N. Navarro St., 512/572-8840

Best Mexican Food
Del Lago Restaurant
  1002 N. Navarro St., 512/572-3846
Taqueria Victoria
  209 S. Main St., 512/572-8226
Tejas Cafe and Bar
  2902 N. Navarro St., 512/572-9433

Best Sandwiches
Fossati's
  302 S. Main St., 512/576-3354

WACO, TX

Best Burgers
Whataburger Restaurant
  100 S. Loop 340, 254/772-0642
  420 N. Valley Mills Dr., 254/772-5822
  928 S. Seventh St., 254/753-0389
  950 N. Loop 340, 254/799-0267

Best Cajun/Creole Food
Buzzard Billy's
  208 S. University Parks Dr., 254/753-2778

Best Family Restaurant
Black-Eyed Pea
  5501 Bosque Blvd., 254/772-9771

Best Mexican Food
Trujillo's Comedor Y Cantina
  2612 La Salle Ave., 254/756-1331

Best Pizza
Poppa Rollo's Pizza
  703 N. Valley Mills Dr., 254/776-6776

Best Place to Take the Kids
Mr. Gatti's Pizza
  1845 Lake Shore Dr., 254/756-6636
  1725 S. Valley Mills Dr., 254/753-7452
  1300 N. Valley Mills Dr., 254/772-6821

Best Seafood
Buzzard Billy's
  208 S. University Parks Dr., 254/753-2778

Best Southwestern Food
Diamondback's
  217 Mary St., 254/757-2871

Best Thai Food
Thai Orchid Restaurant
  1017 N. University Parks Dr., 254/752-3555

WICHITA FALLS, TX

Best Barbecue/Ribs
Stanley's
  2703 Avenue U, 940/692-8561

Best Burgers
Whataburger Restaurant
  2725 Southwest Pkwy., 940/692-0015
  1111A Holliday St., 940/723-8532
  1040 Central Freeway, 940/723-1019

3900 Sheppard Access Rd., 940/855-4411
3404 McNiel Ave., 940/696-2201

Best Chinese Food
Hunan Chinese Restaurant
3916 Kemp Blvd., 940/691-3900

Best Homestyle Food
Pioneer Restaurant
1400 Tenth St., 940/322-9461
1100 Sheppard Access Rd., 940/723-8146
812 Holliday St., 940/723-8512

Best Ice Cream/Yogurt
Braum's Ice Cream and Dairy
2304 Kemp Blvd., 940/766-0789
3808 Jacksboro Hwy., 940/322-6317
4711 Southwest Pkwy., 940/691-4251

Best Japanese Food
Japanese Steak House Samurai
2611 Plaza Pkwy., 940/696-2626

Best Pizza
Cici's Pizza
2710 Southwest Pkwy., 940/691-6060

Best Sandwiches
Bogart's Deli
2708 Southwest Pkwy., 940/692-4242

Best Steaks
Fat McBride's Steaks
4537 Maplewood Ave., 940/696-0250

T

Utah

Best Breakfast
Market Grill
  2290 W. 400N, 435/586-9325
Sullivan's Cafe
  301 S. Main St., 435/586-6761

Best Casual Dining
Adriana's
  164 S. 100W, 435/865-1234
Boomer's
  5 N. Main St., 435/865-9665

Best Chinese Food
China Garden Restaurant
  64 N. Main St., 435/586-6042
Hunan Chinese Restaurant
  501 S. Main St., 435/586-8952

Best Family Restaurant
J. B.'s Restaurant
  131 S. Main St., 435/586-6911

Best Homestyle Food
Brad's Food Hut
  546 N. Main St., 435/586-6358
Hermie's
  294 N. Main St., 435/865-0612

Best Mexican Food
Escobar's Mexican Restaurant
  155 N. Main St., 435/865-0155
La Fiesta Mexican Restaurant
  890 N. Main St., 435/586-4646

U

Best Sandwiches
Top Spot Drive Inn
650 S. Main St., 435/586-9661

Best Seafood
Milt's Stage Stop
Hwy. 14, 435/586-9344
Rusty's Ranch House
Hwy. 14, 435/586-3839

LOGAN, UT

Best Coffee/Coffeehouse
Angie's Restaurant
690 N. Main St., 435/752-9252
Straw Ibis Market Cafe
52 Federal Ave., 435/753-4777

Best Fine Dining
Grape Vine Restaurant
129 N. 100E, 435/752-1977

Best Italian Food
Gia's Restaurant and Deli
119 S. Main St., 435/752-8384

Best Pizza
Factory Pizzeria
119 S. Main St., 435/752-9384

Best Sandwiches
Factory Pizzeria
95 N. 800E, Hyrum, 435/245-3000

MURRAY, UT

Best Barbecue/Ribs
Buffalo Joe's
5927 S. State St., 801/261-3537
Joe Morley's
669 E. Center St., Midvale, 801/255-8928

Best Breakfast
Village Inn
5941 S. State St., 801/268-1292

Best Burgers
Red Robin
316 E. 6400 S., 801/266-9410
Training Table Restaurant
6957 State St., Midvale, 801/566-1911

Best Homestyle Food
Galaxy Diner
6099 S. State St., 801/262-8262
Midvale Mining Company Restaurant
390 W. 7200S, Midvale, 801/255-5511

Best Mexican Food
Restaurant Morelia
6098 S. State St., 801/265-8790

OGDEN, UT

Best Breakfast
Big Z Restaurant
1141 W. 21505, 801/621-5083
Jeremiah's Restaurant
1307 W. 1200S, 801/394-3273

Best Chinese Food
ABC Mandarin
5260 S. 1900W, Roy, 801/776-6361
Eastern Winds
3740 Washington Blvd., 801/627-2739
Mandarin Palace
505 N. Main St., Layton, 801/547-0088
Utah Noodle
3019 Washington Blvd., 801/392-6002

Best Desserts
Frontier Pies Restaurant
4137 Riverdale Rd., 801/399-4411

Best Diner
Galaxy Diner
4250 S. Harrison Blvd., 801/621-2161
Winger's
4649 S. Harrison Blvd., 801/479-1104

Best Family Restaurant
J and D's Family Restaurant
720 S. Main St., Brigham City, 435/723-3811
Maddox Ranch House
1900 Hwy. 88S, Brigham City, 435/723-8545

Best Fine Dining
Frontier Pies Restaurant
4137 Riverdale Rd., 801/399-4411
Timber Mine Restaurant
1701 Park Blvd., 435/393-2155
Ye Lion's Den Restaurant
3607 Washington Blvd., 435/399-5804

Best German Food
Bavarian Chalet German Restaurant
4387 Harrison Blvd., 801/479-7561

Best Health-Conscious Menu
Edible Art's
2070D Wall Ave., 801/621-4477

Best Ice Cream/Yogurt
Farr Better Ice Cream Shop
286 21st St., 801/272-9551

Best Inexpensive Meal
Andy's Chuck Wagon Buffet
3684 Wall Ave., 801/393-2911

Best Late-Night Food
Winger's
4649 S. Harrison Blvd., 801/479-1104

Best Lunch
Good Time Spaghetti Company
373 31st St., 801/627-4181

Rooster's 25th Street Brewing Company
253 25th St., 801/627-6171

Best Mexican Food
Chaparro's
3981 Wall Ave., 801/392-7777
El Matador
2564 Ogden Ave., 801/393-3151

Best Pizza
Ligori's Pizza and Pasta
4421 Harrison Blvd., 801/476-0476
Pizzaria
2253 N. Main St., Sunset, 801/825-4747

Best Romantic Dining
Prairie Schooner Steak House
445 Park Blvd., 801/392-2712

Best Sandwiches
Training Table Restaurant
4510 Harrison Blvd., 801/399-5050

Best Steaks
Timber Mine Restaurant
1701 Park Blvd., 801/393-2155

OREM, UT

Best Chinese Food
Great China Restaurant
380 E. Hwy. 1300S, 801/224-2238

Best Family Restaurant
Chuck-A-Rama Buffet
1408 S. State St., 801/225-9300
Prestwich Farms Restaurant
289 E. Hwy. 1300S, 801/226-7437

Best Late-Night Food
El Azteca Mexican Takeout
1230 Hwy. 46W, 801/375-9690

U

PARK CITY, UT

Best Barbecue/Ribs
Texas Red's Pit Barbecue
440 Main St., 435/649-7337

Best Burgers
Harley's Restaurant
816 E. 9400S, Sandy, 801/572-1951

Best Casual Dining
Baja Cantina
1284 Empire Ave., 435/649-2252
Spring Chicken Inn
1969 S. Hoytsville Rd., Coalville, 801/336-5334

Best Diner
Mt. Aire Cafe
1900 Park Ave., 435/649-9868

Best Eclectic Menu
Chez Betty
1637 Short Line Rd., 435/649-8181

Best Fine Dining
Riverhorse Cafe
  540 Main St., 435/649-3536
Zoom Restaurant
  660 Main St., 435/649-9108

Best Greek/Mediterranean Food
Mercato Meditterean
  312 Main St., 435/647-0030

Best Homestyle Food
Johanna's Country Kitchen
  9725 State St., Sandy, 801/566-1762

Best Italian Food
Grappa Italian Cafe
  151 Main St., 435/645-0636

Best Mexican Food
Alberto's Mexican Food
  1735 W. 7800S, West Jordan, 801/565-1730
Nacho Mama's
  1821 Sidewinder Dr., 435/645-8226

Best Pizza
Davanza's Pizza
  1776 Park Ave., Ste. 7, 435/649-7177

Best Seafood
La Caille
  9565 Wasatch Blvd., Sandy, 801/942-1751

Best Steaks
La Caille
  9565 Wasatch Blvd., Sandy, 801/942-1751

PRICE, UT

Best Burgers
JB's
  715 E. Main St., 435/637-1840

Best Greek/Mediterranean Food
Greek Streak
  84 S. Carbon Ave., 435/637-1930

Best Italian Food
Farlaino's Cafe
  87 W. Main St., 435/637-9217

Best Mexican Food
Ricardo's Restaurant
  655 E. Main St., 435/637-2020

PROVO, UT

Best Burgers
The T-Bone Restaurant
  9695 S. State St., Springville, 801/489-7920

Best Chinese Food
China Lilly
  98 W. Center St., 801/371-8888
Formosa Garden Restaurant
  265 West Ln., Ste.1230, 801/377-5654

U

Best Homestyle Food
Keith's Lunch
190S West Ln., Ste. 100, 801/375-3505

Best Italian Food
Brick Oven Restaurant
111 E. Hwy. 800N, 801/374-8800
La Dolce Vita
61 N. Hwy. 100E, 801/373-8482

Best Lunch
Gandolfo's
18 N. University Ave., 801/375-3354
Magleby's Restaurant
1675 N. Hwy. 200W, 801/374-6249

Best Mexican Food
El Azteca
746 E. Hwy. 820N, 801/373-9312
Los Hermanos
16 W. Center St., 801/375-5732

Best Steaks
Ruby River
1160 S. University Ave., 801/371-0648

SALT LAKE CITY, UT

Best All-You-Can-Eat Buffet
Chuck-A-Rama Buffet
2960 Highland Dr., 801/487-0879
744 E. 400S, 801/531-1123

Best Brewpub
Salt Lake Brewing Company
367 W. 200S, 801/363-7000

Best Burgers
Hires Big H
425 S. 700E, 801/364-4582
2900 W. 4700S, 801/965-1010

Best Continental Food
Dodo
680 S. 900E, 801/328-9348

Best Desserts
Primo Restaurant
2350 E. 7000S, 801/947-0025

Best Diner
Galaxy Diner
570 W. 500S, Bountiful, 801/298-0330
Winger's
530 W. 500S, Bountiful, 801/295-4884

Best German Food
Seigfred's Delicatessen
69 W. Broadway, 801/355-3891

Best Greek/Mediterranean Food
Greek Souvlaki No. 1 Original
1446 S. State St., 801/487-3481
404 E. 300S, 801/322-2062

Best Health-Conscious Menu
Wasatch Broiler
  4927 S. State St., 801/266-3311

Best Ice Cream/Yogurt
Red's Frozen Yogurt
  4991 S. Highland Dr., 801/278-6148
Snelgrove Ice Cream
  850 E. 2100S, 801/486-4457

Best Italian Food
Al Forno's Ristorante
  239 S. 500E, 801/359-6040

Best Japanese Food
Hashi Japanese Restaurant
  1352 S. 2100E, 801/583-5701
Rio Grande Cafe
  270 S. 455W, 801/364-3302
Shogun Restaurant
  321 S. Main St., 801/364-7142

Best Mexican Food
Alberto's Mexican Food
  2901 E. 3300S, 801/487-3850
  4931 S. State St., 801/265-3795
La Frontera
  1236 W. 400S, 801/532-3158

Best Pizza
Deloretto's Pizzeria
  2010 S. State St., 801/485-6615
Godfather's Pizza
  902 E. 2100S, 801/456-7473
Pie Pizzeria
  1320 E. 200S, 801/582-0193

Best Place to Take the Kids
Chuck E. Cheese Pizza
  4425 S. State St., 801/261-2888

Best Romantic Dining
New Yorker Club
  60 Market St., 801/363-0166
The Roof
  15 E. South Temple, 801/539-1911

Best Seafood
Market Street Broiler
  263 S. 1300E, 801/583-8808

Best Sports Bar
Port O' Call
  78 W. 400S, 801/521-0589

Best Steaks
Primo Restaurant
  2350 E. 7000S, 801/947-0025

Best Vietnamese Food
East West Connection
  1400 S. Foothill Dr., 801/581-1128

U

ST. GEORGE, UT

Best American Food
The Palms Restaurant
  Holiday Inn, 850 S. Bluff St., 435/628-4235

Best Barbecue/Ribs
Libby Lorraine's Restaurant
  567 S. Valley View Dr., 435/673-7190

Best Chinese Food
Hong Kong Dynasty
  635 E. Saint George Blvd., 435/628-3348

Best Greek/Mediterranean Food
Basila's Greek and Italian Cafe
  2 W. Saint George Blvd., 435/673-7671

Best Pizza
The Pizza Factory
  490 W. Saint George Blvd., Ste. 2, 435/634-1234
  2 W. Saint George Blvd., 435/628-1234

Best Sandwiches
Charlie's Malts and Ice Cream
  287 W. Saint George Blvd., 435/628-6304

Best Steaks
Brandin' Iron Steakhouse
  939 E. Main St., Pine Valley, 435/574-2261

VERNAL, UT

Best Breakfast
JB's Family Restaurant
  475 W. Main St., 801/789-4547
Weston Lamplighter
  120 E. Main St., 801/789-0312

Best Chinese Food
Mea Palace
  2539 N. Vernal Ave., 801/789-7703
Win On Restaurant
  578 W. Main St., 801/789-0888

Best Coffee/Coffeehouse
Spoof's Coffee and Tea Shop
  38 E. Main St., 801/789-1154

Best Homestyle Food
7-11 Ranch Restaurant
  77 E. Main St., 801/789-1170

Best Italian Food
Pizza Barn
  831 W. Main St., 801/789-2030

Best Mexican Food
Casa Rios
  2015 W. Hwy. 40, 801/789-0103
La Cabana
  56 W. Main St., 801/789-3151

Best Steaks
Bud's Steakhouse
  65 S. Vernal Ave., 801/789-9963

U

Vermont

Best Delicatessen
Belly's Deli
   100 Pleasant St., 802/442-3653

Best Desserts
Alldays and Onions
   519 Main St., 802/447-0043

Best Diner
Blue Benn Diner
   102 Hunt St., 802/442-5140

Best Dinner
Heritage House
   218 Northside Dr., 802/442-6211

Best Eclectic Menu
Main Attraction
   421 Main St., 802/442-8579

Best Pizza
Mickey's Pizza
   510 Main St., 802/447-1555

Best Restaurant in Town
Bennington Station
   150 Depot St., 802/447-1080

Best Atmosphere
TJ Buckley's
   132 Elliot St., 802/257-4922

Best Breakfast
Chelsea Royal Diner
   Rte. 9 at Marlboro Rd., 802/254-8399

V

Riverview Restaurant
9 Bridge St., 802/254-9841

Best Brewpub
Latchis Grille and Windham Brewery
6 Flat St., 802/254-4747
McNeil's Brewery
90 Elliot St., 802/254-2553

Best Burgers
Marina Restaurant
28 Springtree Rd., 802/257-7563

Best Chinese Food
Panda North Chinese Restaurant
1332 Putney Rd., 802/257-4578

Best Coffee/Coffeehouse
Cafe Beyond
29 High St., 802/258-4900
Coffee Country
1 Harmony Pl., 802/257-0032
Mocha Joe's
82 Main St., 802/257-7794

Best Family Restaurant
Picknics Rotisserie Restaurant
889 Putney Rd., 802/254-9675

Best Fine Dining
Four Columns Inn and Restaurant
230 West St., Newfane, 802/365-7713
Peter Haven's
32 Elliot St., 802/257-3333

Best Health-Conscious Menu
Common Ground
25 Elliot St., 802/257-0855

Best Indian Food
India Palace
69 Elliot St., 802/254-6143

Best Korean Food
Shin-La Restaurant
57 Main St., 802/257-5226

Best Lunch
Truffles Restaurant
E. Main St., Wilmington, 802/464-5608

Best Pizza
Frankie's Pizzeria
145 Harmony Pl., 802/254-2420
Vermont Inn Pizza
228 Canal St., 802/254-6264

Best Seafood
The Marina Restaurant
28 Springtree Rd., 802/257-7563

Best Steaks
Jolly Butcher's Tavern
Marlboro Rd., 802/254-6043

V

Best View While Dining
The Marina Restaurant
  28 Springtree Rd., 802/257-7563
Skyline Restaurant
  Rte. 9, Marlboro, 802/464-5535

BURLINGTON, VT

Best Breakfast
Sneaker's
  36 Main St., Winooski, 802/655-9081

Best Burgers
Sneaker's
  36 Main St., Winooski, 802/655-9081

Best Cajun/Creole Food
Bourbon Street Grill
  213 College St., 802/865-2800

Best Coffee/Coffeehouse
Java Blues
  197 College St., 802/860-5060
Muddy Waters
  184 Main St., 802/658-0466

Best Eclectic Menu
Daily Planet
  15 Center St., 802/862-9647

Best French Food
Cafe Shelburne Francais
  Rte. 7, Shelburne, 802/985-3939

Best Health-Conscious Menu
Five Spice Cafe
  175 Church St., 802/864-4045

Best Homestyle Food
Libby's Blue Line Diner
  1 Roosevelt Hwy., Colchester, 802/655-0343

Best Indian Food
India House Restaurant
  207 Colchester Ave., 802/862-7800

Best Italian Food
Alfredo's Restaurant
  136 Church St., 802/864-0854
Buono Appetito Italian Restaurant
  1963 Shelburne Rd., Shelburne, 802/985-2232

Best Japanese Food
Sakura Japanese Restaurant
  2 Church St., 802/863-1988

Best Pizza
Al's Pizza Towne
  28 Railroad Ave., Essex Junction, 802/878-9331

Best Sandwiches
Lillydale Bakery and Cafe
  1350 Shelburne Rd., South Burlington,
    802/658-2422
  131 Main St., 802/863-1569

V

Red Onion Restaurant
   140 1/2 Church St., 802/865-2563
   310 Pine St., 802/863-2788

Best Seafood
Dockside Restaurant
   209 Battery St., 802/864-5266
Ray's Seafood Market
   7 Pinecrest Dr., Essex Junction, 802/879-3611

Best Steaks
Sirloin Saloon
   1908 Shelburne Rd., Shelburne, 802/985-2200

Best Sunday Brunch
Sneaker's
   36 Main St., Winooski, 802/655-9081

Best Thai Food
Parima
   185 Pearl St., 802/864-7917

Best Vietnamese Food
Sai-gon Cafe
   133 Bank St., 802/863-5637

MIDDLEBURY, VT

Best American Food
Middlebury Inn
   14 Court St., 802/388-4961

Best Atmosphere
Waybury Inn
   Rte. 125, East Middlebury, 802/388-4015
Woody's Restaurant
   5 Bakery Ln., 802/388-4182

Best Bar
Amigo's Restaurant
   4 Merchants Row, 802/388-3624

Best Breakfast
Rosie's Restaurant
   Rte. 7, 802/388-7052

Best Burgers
Steve's Park Diner
   12 Merchants Row, 802/388-3297

Best Business Lunch
Middlebury Inn
   14 Court St., 802/388-4961

Best Chinese Food
Panda House
   2 Maple St., 802/388-3101

Best Coffee/Coffeehouse
Storm Cafe
   3 Mill St., 802/388-1063

Best French Food
Roland's Place
   1796 House St., New Haven, 802/453-6309

Best Italian Food
Angela's
  86 Main St., 802/388-0002
Cristall's
  3 Green St., Vergennes, 802/877-3413

Best Mexican Food
Amigo's Restaurant
  4 Merchants Row, 802/388-3624

Best Pizza
Green Peppers Restaurant
  11 Washington St., 802/388-3164

Best Place to Take the Kids
Rosie's Restaurant
  Rte. 7, 802/388-7052

Best Sandwiches
Green Peppers Restaurant
  11 Washington St., 802/388-3164

Best Seafood
Fire and Ice Restaurant
  26 Seymour St., 802/388-7166

Best Steaks
Fire and Ice Restaurant
  26 Seymour St., 802/388-7166

Best View While Dining
Mister Ups
  Bakery Ln., 802/388-6724
Woody's Restaurant
  5 Bakery Ln., 802/388-4182

MONTPELIER, VT

Best Breakfast
Burlington Bagel Bakery
  89 Main St., 802/223-0533

Best Chinese Food
China Star Chinese Restaurant
  15 Main St., 802/223-0808

Best Coffee/Coffeehouse
Crump's Coffee House
  11 Main St., 802/229-1019

Best Italian Food
Sarducci's
  3 Main St., 802/223-0229

Best Mexican Food
Julio's
  44 Main St., 802/229-9348

Best Pizza
Angeleno's Pizza
  15 Barre St., 802/229-5721

Best Restaurant in Town
Chef's Table
  118 Main St., 802/229-9202
New England Culinary Institute Restaurant
  250 Main St., 802/223-6324

V

Soup-n-Greens
321 N. Main St., Barre, 802/479-9862
The Country House Restaurant
276 N. Main St., Barre, 802/476-4282
The Hilltop Restaurant
241 Quarry Hill Rd., Barre, 802/479-2129
The Wayside Restaurant
Barre Montpelier Rd., 802/223-6611

Best Steaks
Main Street Bar and Grill
118 Main St., 802/223-3188

NEWPORT, VT

Best American Food
The Corner Restaurant
27 Main St., 802/334-1336

Best Breakfast
Brown Cow
990 E. Main St., 802/334-7887
Miss Newport Diner
985 E. Main St., 802/334-7742

Best Casual Dining
East Side Restaurant
25 Lake St., 802/334-2340

Best Desserts
Heermansmith Farm
Heermansmith Farm Rd., Coventry, 802/754-8866

Best Family Restaurant
Brown Cow
990 E. Main St., 802/334-7887

Best German Food
Forsthaus Restaurant
Rte. 14, Newport Center, 802/334-7294

Best Pizza
Village Pizza
E. Main St., 802/334-7929

Best Seafood
East Side Restaurant
25 Lake St., 802/334-2340

Best Steaks
East Side Restaurant
25 Lake St., 802/334-2340
The Corner Restaurant
27 Main St., 802/334-1336

RUTLAND, VT

Best Breakfast
Maple Sugar and Vermont Spice
Rte. 4, 802/773-7832

Best Chinese Food
Kong Chow Restaurant
48 Center St., 802/775-5244
Panda Pavilion Chinese Restaurant
Woodstock Ave., 802/775-6682

Best Coffee/Coffeehouse
Season's Circle Coffee House
  24 Wales St., 802/773-3701

Best Ice Cream/Yogurt
Seward's Family Dairy
  224 N. Main St., 802/773-2738

Best Italian Food
Casa Bianco Restaurant
  76 Grove St., 802/773-7401

Best Restaurant in Town
Royal's 121 Hearthside Restaurant
  37 N. Main St., 802/773-7148
Rutland Restaurant
  57 Merchants Row, 802/775-7447

STOWE, VT

Best Dinner
Blue Moon Cafe
  35 School St., 802/253-7006

Best Italian Food
Trattoria Delia
  152 Saint Paul St., 802/864-5253

Best Restaurant in Town
Gracie's
  Carlson Bldg., 20 S. Main St., 802/253-8741

WHITE RIVER JUNCTION, VT

Best Bistro
The Prince and The Pauper Restaurant
  24 Elm St., Woodstock, 802/457-1818

Best Breakfast
Mountain Creamery
  33 Central St., Woodstock, 802/457-1715
Polka Dot
  1 Main St., 802/295-9722

Best Brewpub
Norwich Inn
  325 Main St., Norwich, 802/649-1143

Best Diner
Wasps Snack Bar
  57 Pleasant St., Woodstock, 802/457-9805

Best Dinner
AJ's Steakhouse
  2 Bowling Ln., 802/295-3071

Best Homestyle Food
Polka Dot
  1 Main St., 802/295-9722

Best Lunch
Del Roma Restaurant
  16 Gates St., 802/295-9705
Mountain Creamery
  33 Central St., Woodstock, 802/457-1715

V

Simon Pearce Restaurant
  The Mill, Quechee, 802/295-1470
Wildflowers Restaurant
  Rte. 4, Quechee, 802/295-7051
William Tally House
  1 Sykes Ave., 802/295-3835

Best Pizza
Pizza Chef of Quechee
  610 Woodstock Rd., 802/296-6669

Best Sandwiches
Gondola Deli and Sub Shop
  2 Maple St., 802/295-9070

Best Sports Bar
Than Wheeler Coaches Corner
  15 N. Main St., 802/295-4847

Best Steaks
AJ's Steakhouse
  2 Bowling Ln., 802/295-3071

Best View While Dining
Simon Pearce Restaurant
  The Mill, Quechee, 802/295-1470

V

Virginia

[See also: Arlington, Fairfax, and Washington, DC.]

Best American Food
Gadsby's Tavern
  138 N. Royal St., 703/548-1288

Best Barbecue/Ribs
Johnny Macs
  2245 Huntington Ave., Jefferson Manor,
    703/960-1086
Rib Rack
  8113 Richmond Hwy., 703/780-7225

Best Beer Selection
Bilbo Baggins' Cafe Restaurant
  208 Queen St., 703/683-0300

Best Bistro
Cate's Bistro
  715 King St., 703/549-0533
Clyde's of Tysons Corner
  8332 Leesburg Pike, Vienna, 703/734-1900

Best Brewpub
Virgina Beverage Company
  607 King St., 703/684-5397

Best Cajun/Creole Food
Cajun Gourmet
  6500E Springfield Mall, Springfield, 703/719-0672
  5801 Duke St., 703/658-0918
Copeland's of New Orleans
  4300 King St., 703/671-7997

V

Best Casual Dining
Calvert Grill
    3106 Mount Vernon Ave., 703/836-8425
Le Gaulois Cafe Restaurant
    1106 King St., 703/739-9494

Best Chinese Food
Peking Duck Restaurant
    7531 Richmond Hwy., Community, 703/768-2774
Peking Gourmet Inn
    6029 Leesburg Pike, Baileys Crossroads,
        703/671-8088

Best Delicatessen
Mancini's Cafe and Bakery
    1508 Mount Vernon Ave., 703/838-3663
Olde Town Deli
    109 N. Washington St., 703/836-8028
Paesano Italian Deli
    1724 Duke St., 703/548-8111

Best Desserts
Amphora Restaurant
    377 Maple Ave. W., Vienna, 703/938-7877

Best Eclectic Menu
Ecco Cafe
    220 N. Lee St., 703/684-0321

Best French Food
La Bergerie Restaurant
    218 N. Lee St., 703/683-1007

Best Greek/Mediterranean Food
Taverna Cretekou
    818 King St., 703/548-8688

Best Inexpensive Meal
Hard Times Cafe
    1404 King St., 703/683-5340

Best Italian Food
Geno's Restaurant
    1300 King St., 703/549-1796
Landini Brothers
    115 King St., 703/836-8404
Paradiso Italian Restaurant
    6124 Franconia Rd., Franconia, 703/922-6222
Primi Piatti
    8045 Leesburg Pike, Vienna, 703/893-0300
Trattoria Da Franco
    305 S. Washington St., 703/548-9338

Best Mexican Food
Chirilagua City
    3606 Mount Vernon Ave., 703/549-1644
Edgardo's Restaurant
    281 S. Van Dorn St., 703/751-6700
Tio Pedro
    728 N. Henry St., 703/548-0468

Best Other Ethnic Food
Panjshir Restaurant (Afghan)
    924 W. Broad St., Falls Church, 703/536-4566

Scotland Yard (Irish)
728 King St., 703/683-1742

Best Pizza
Generous George's Pizza
6131 Backlick Rd., Springfield, 703/451-7111

Best Restaurant in Town
Bilbo Baggins' Cafe Restaurant
208 Queen St., 703/683-0300
Chart House Restaurant
1 Cameron St., 703/684-5080
Copeland's of New Orleans
4300 King St., 703/671-7997

Best Seafood
Dandy Restaurant Cruise Ship
Prince St., 703/683-6076
Fin and Hoof Bar and Grill
801 N. Saint Asaph St., 703/549-6622
Potowmack Landing Restaurant
1 Marina Dr., 703/548-0001
R T's Restaurant
3804 Mount Vernon Ave., 703/684-6010
Village Wharf Restaurant
7966 Fort Hunt Rd., 703/765-0661

Best Thai Food
Duangrat's Thai Restaurant
5878 Leesburg Pike, Baileys Crossroads,
703/820-5775

ARLINGTON, VA

*[See also: Alexandria, Fairfax, McLean, and Reston;
Washington, DC; and Bethesda, MD.]*

Best Bistro
Village Bistro
1723 Wilson Blvd., 703/522-0284

Best Brewpub
Bardo Rodeo Brewpub
2000 Wilson Blvd., 703/527-9399
Blue N Gold Brewing Company
3100 Clarendon Blvd., 703/908-4995

Best Cajun/Creole Food
Cajun Gourmet
4238 Wilson Blvd., 703/527-5286

Best Chinese Food
Hunan Number One Restaurant
3033 Wilson Blvd., 703/528-1177

Best French Food
Chez Froggy
509 23rd St. S., 703/979-7676
L'Alouette Restaurant
2045 Wilson Blvd., 703/525-1750

V

Best Greek/Mediterranean Food
Aegean Taverna
2950 Clarendon Blvd., 703/841-9494

Best Indian Food
Cafe New Delhi
1041 N. Highland St., 703/528-2511
Deli Dhaba
2424 Wilson Blvd., 703/524-0008
India Palace Restaurant
561 23rd St. S., 703/979-0777

Best Inexpensive Meal
Red, Hot, and Blue
1600 Wilson Blvd., 703/276-7427

Best Italian Food
Il Radicchio
1801 Clarendon Blvd., 703/276-2627
Tutto Bene Italian Restaurant
501 N. Randolph St., 703/522-1005

Best Korean Food
Woo Lae Oak of Seoul
1500 S. Joyce St., 703/521-3706

Best Mexican Food
Edgardo's Restaurant
922 S. Walter Reed Rd., 703/271-9400

Best Other Ethnic Food
Atilla's Restaurant (Turkish)
2705 Columbia Pike, 703/920-8255
Moby Dick House of Kabob (Persian)
2301 Jefferson Davis Hwy., 703/413-5100

Best Seafood
R T's Seafood Kitchen
2300 Clarendon Blvd., 703/841-0100

Best Sports Bar
Champion's Sports
2500 Wilson Blvd., 703/524-6000

Best Steaks
Ruth's Chris Steak House
2231 Crystal Dr., Ste. 11, 703/979-7275

Best Vietnamese Food
Nam Viet Restaurant
1127 N. Hudson Rd., 703/522-7110
Queen Bee
3181 Wilson Blvd., 703/527-3444
105 Goodson St., 540/466-8271

CHARLOTTESVILLE, VA

Best Atmosphere
Bodos Bagel Bakery Sandwich
1418 Emmet St. N., 804/977-9598
505 Preston Ave., 804/293-5224
1609 University Ave., 804/293-6021

Best Breakfast
Spudnut Shop
309 Avon St., 804/296-0590

The Tavern
1140 Emmet St. N., 804/295-0404

Best Cajun/Creole Food
Southern Culture
633 W. Main St., 804/979-1990

Best Fine Dining
Metropolitan
214 W. Water St., 804/977-1043
Silver Thatch Inn
3001 Hollymead Dr., 804/978-4686

Best Greek/Mediterranean Food
Cafe Europa
1331 W. Main St., 804/294-4040

Best Italian Food
Carmello's of Charlottesville
400 Emmet St., 804/977-5200
Casellas Italian Restaurant
1107F Emmet St. N., 804/979-7011
Northern Exposure Bar and Grill
1202 W. Main St., 804/977-6002
Oregano Joe's
1252 Emmet St. N., 804/971-9308
Rococo's
2001 Commonwealth Dr., 804/971-7371
Vivace
2244 Ivy Rd., 804/979-0994

Best Lunch
Blue Bird Cafe
625 W. Main St., 804/295-1166

Best Sandwiches
Bodo's Bagel Bakery
1609 University Ave., 804/293-6021
1418 Emmet St. N., 804/977-9598
505 Preston Ave., 804/293-5224

Best Southwestern Food
Continental Divide
511 W. Main St., 804/984-0143

CHESAPEAKE, VA

[See also: Norfolk, Portsmouth, and Virginia Beach.]

Best Bar
Hodad's Bar and Grill
136 Battlefield Blvd. N., 757/547-9619

Best Barbecue/Ribs
Billy's Bar-B-Que
1642 Sparrow Rd., 757/420-3233
Frankie's Place for Ribs
146 Battlefield Blvd., 757/546-0030
Johnson's Bar-B-Que
1903 S. Military Hwy., 757/545-6957
Ken's Barbecue
1116 Sparrow Rd., 757/420-1932

Mr. Pig's Bar-B-Q
  445 Battlefield Blvd. N., 757/547-5171

Best Beer Selection
Cheers Restaurant
  1405 Greenbrier Pkwy., 757/424-4665

Best Breakfast
Two Mom's Cafe
  1200 Battlefield Blvd. N., 757/548-0260

Best Casual Dining
Pargo's Restaurant
  1436 Greenbrier Pkwy., 757/420-1900

Best Delicatessen
Nathan's Deli
  1729 Parkview Dr., Ste. 1701, 757/523-1011

Best Dinner
Court House Cafe
  350 Battlefield Blvd. S., 757/482-7077

Best Homestyle Food
The Black-Eyed Pea
  1432 Greenbrier Pkwy., 757/523-5977

Best Inexpensive Meal
Rancho Grande
  1320 S. Military Hwy., 757/366-5128

Best Lunch
City Deli
  450 Battlefield Blvd., 757/482-5554

Best Mexican Food
Three Amigos
  200 Battlefield Blvd., 757/548-4105

Best Outdoor Dining
Cara's Restaurant
  123 N. Battlefield Blvd., 757/548-0006

Best Seafood
Locks Pointe Restaurant
  136 N. Battlefield Blvd., 757/547-9618

Best Sports Bar
Key West Restaurant
  725 Woodlake Dr., 757/523-1212

DANVILLE, VA

Best All-You-Can-Eat Buffet
Stratford Inn and Restaurant
  2500 Riverside Dr., 804/793-2500

Best Barbecue/Ribs
Short Sugar's Bar-B-Q
  2215 Riverside Dr., 804/793-4800

Best Burgers
Sir Richard's Steak House
  1513 S. Boston Rd., 804/822-6444

Best Chinese Food
Long River Restaurant
  2835 Riverside Dr., 804/799-6770

Best Coffee/Coffeehouse
Main Street Coffee Emporium
435 Main St., 804/792-4252

Best Homestyle Food
Danview Restaurant
116 Danview Dr., 804/793-3552
Mary's Diner
1203 Piney Forest Rd., 804/836-5034

Best Pizza
Joe and Mimma's Italian Pizza
3232 Riverside, Ste. 3336, 804/799-5763

Best Sandwiches
Rock Ola Cafe
140 Crown Dr., 804/793-1848
Yesterday's Cafe
443 Main St., 804/793-2629

Best Seafood
Baron's
671 Woodlawn Dr., 804/822-0120
Libby Hill Seafood Restaurant
2105 Riverside Dr., 804/791-4680
Mayflower Seafood Restaurant
2320 Riverside Dr., 804/792-8817
Stratford Inn and Restaurant
2500 Riverside Dr., 804/793-2500

FAIRFAX, VA

[See also: Alexandria, Arlington, McLean, and Reston.]

Best Breakfast
Le Peep Restaurant
3922 Old Lee Hwy., 703/273-7337
Manhattan Bagel Company
10382 Willard Way, 703/591-2525
Silver Diner
12250 Fair Lakes Pky., 703/359-5999

Best Chinese Food
China Shang Hai
9573 Braddock Rd., 703/323-8800
House of Lions
11180 Main St., 703/273-3998
Hunan Eatery
4008 University Dr., 703/352-2888
9412 Main St., 703/764-3040

Best Coffee/Coffeehouse
Kiari's Coffee Source
10380 Willard Way, 703/352-0884

Best Family Restaurant
Angie's Family Restaurant
9569 Braddock Rd., 703/978-5518
The Black-Eyed Pea
3971 Chain Bridge Rd., 703/352-0588

Best Italian Food
Cafe Italia II
10515 Main St., 703/385-6767

Best Pizza
Tony's New York Pizza
Fair Lakes Shopping Center,
13087 Fairlake Dr., 703/502-0808

Best View While Dining
House of Lions
11180 Main St., 703/273-3998

HAMPTON, VA

[See also: Newport News and Norfolk.]

Best Chinese Food
Fortune Garden
1182 Big Bethel Rd., 757/826-5277
Good Fortune Chinese Restaurant
225D Fox Hill Rd., Ste. 1, 757/851-6888
Ming Gate Restaurant
3509 Kecoughtan Rd., 757/723-9572

Best Coffee/Coffeehouse
Hung Cuong Coffee Shop
1023 N. King St., 757/727-0250

Best Delicatessen
Helen's Deli
2 Eaton St., Ste. 306, 757/728-1108

Best Family Restaurant
Darryl's Restaurant and Bar
2026 Coliseum Dr., 757/838-1862

Best Italian Food
Sal's New York Italian Restaurant
85 Lincoln St., 757/723-6154

Best Korean Food
Seoul Restaurant
1205 N. King St., 757/722-4771

Best Mexican Food
Burrito Haven
1312 E. Pembroke Ave., 757/722-7407
El Ranchito
1771 N. King St., 757/723-8818
Mi Paseo Mexican Restaurant
3326 W. Mercury Blvd., 757/825-2482

Best Outdoor Dining
Second Street Restaurant and Tavern
132 E. Queen St., 757/722-6811

Best Seafood
Captain George's
2710 W. Mercury Blvd., 757/826-1436
Fisherman's Wharf
14 Ivy Home Rd., 757/723-3113

Harpoon Larry's Oyster Bar
  2000 N. Armistead Ave., 457/827-0600
Keith's Dockside Restaurant
  38C Water St., 757/723-1781
Old Hampton Seafood Kitchen
  124 S. Armistead Ave., 757/723-4936
Sir Richard's Restaurant
  3534 Kecoughtan Rd., 757/722-0828

Best Steaks
Old Point Steak and Spaghetti
  33 E. Mellen St., 757/722-8880
The Grate Steak
  1934 Coliseum Dr., 757/827-1886

Best Sunday Brunch
Hampton Dining Room
  Chamberlin Hotel, 2 Fenwick Rd.,
    Fort Monroe, 757/723-6511

Best Vietnamese Food
Ling Nam Restaurant
  25 W. Mercury Blvd., 757/722-0997

HARRISONBURG, VA

Best Bar
Blue Foxx Cafe
  2061 S. Evelyn Bird Ave., 540/432-3699

Best Breakfast
Mr. J's Bagels and Deli
  1635 E. Market St., 540/564-0416

Best Delicatessen
Brooklyn's Delicatessen
  2035 E. Market St., 540/433-4090

Best Diner
Jess' Lunch
  22 S. Main St., 540/434-8282

Best Family Restaurant
Rowe's Family Restaurant
  486 Rowe Rd., Staunton, 540/886-1833

Best Fine Dining
Joshua Wilton House
  412 S. Main St., 540/434-4464

Best Greek/Mediterranean Food
Gus' Taverna
  95 S. Main St., 540/564-1487

Best Italian Food
L'Italia Restaurant
  815 E. Market St., 540/433-0961
Lucio's Ristorante
  1894 Fairway Dr., Basye, 540/856-8082

Best Lunch
Spanky's Delicatessen
  60 W. Water St., 540/434-7647

Best Mexican Food
El Charro Mexican Restaurant
  1570 E. Market St., 540/564-0386

Best Restaurant In Town
Hotel Strasburg
  213 S. Holliday St., Strasburg,
    540/465-9191
Inn at Little Washington
  Middle at Main, Washington, 540/675-3800

Best Barbecue/Ribs
K and L Barbecue
  1410 Maple St., 804/458-4241

Best Burgers
Burger Fair
  2510 Oaklawn Blvd., 804/458-9921

Best Cafeteria
Broadway Cafeteria
  120 E. City Point Rd., 804/458-1700

Best Chinese Food
China Inn
  2703C Oaklawn Blvd., 804/458-5748

Best Italian Food
Rosa's Pizza Restaurant
  4108 Oaklawn Blvd., 804/458-8744

Best Pizza
Luisa's Pizza
  323 Cavalier Sq., 804/458-8000

Best Seafood
Captain's Cove Seafood Restaurant
  910 N. 21st Ave., 804/452-1368

Best Breakfast
Myrt's Hot Dogs
  2810 Candlers Mountain Rd., 804/237-6124

Best Business Lunch
Shaker's Restaurant
  2095 Langhorne Rd., 804/847-0234
  3401 Candlers Mountain Rd., 804/847-7425

Best Chinese Food
China Garden
  21 Wadsworth St., 804/528-2855

Best Desserts
Billie Joe's
  4915 Fort Ave., 804/237-7825

Best Homestyle Food
Country Cookin'
  8686 Timberlake Rd., 804/239-1996

Best Italian Food
Fazoli's
  2629 Wards Rd., 804/832-1200

Best Romantic Dining
Crown Sterling Steaks
  6120 Fort Ave., 804/239-7744

Best Sandwiches
Westside Delicatessen
  7701 Timberlake Rd., 804/239-6304

Best Seafood
Harbor Inn Seafood
  3220 Old Forest Rd., 804/385-6888

Best Tea Room
Texas Inn
  422 Main St., 804/846-3823

MANASSAS, VA

Best American Food
Heritage Bar and Grill
  9110 Center St., 703/330-1004
Palm Court
  14750 Conference Center Dr., Chantilly, 703/818-3522

Best Brewpub
Hero's American Restaurant
  9412 Main St., 703/330-1534

Best Fine Dining
Hermitage Inn
  7134 Main St., Clifton, 703/266-1623

Best Italian Food
Carmello's of Charlottesville
  9108 Center St., 703/368-5522

Best Other Ethnic Food
Little Portugal Restaurant (Portuguese)
  9104 Center St., 703/368-7979

Best Regional Food
Hickory Smokehouse
  9212 Center St., 703/369-7007

Best Sandwiches
Sandwich Factory
  9420 Battle St., 703/369-6022

Best Seafood
Something Fishy
  9780 Zimbro Ave., 703/369-3474

Best Thai Food
Thai Secret Restaurant
  9114 Center St., 703/361-2500

V

MCLEAN, VA

[See also: Arlington, VA; Bethesda, MD; and Washington, DC.]

Best Barbecue/Ribs
Three Pigs of Mclean
   1394 Chain Bridge Rd., 703/356-1700

Best Chinese Food
Wok and Roll
   1371 Beverly Rd., 703/556-8811

Best Diner
Silver Diner
   8101 Fletcher St., 703/821-5666

Best Family Restaurant
Evans Farm Inn
   1696 Chain Bridge Rd., 703/356-8000

Best French Food
Cafe Tatti
   6627 Old Dominion Dr., 703/790-5164
La Mirabelle
   6645 Old Dominion Dr., 703/893-8484

Best Greek/Mediterranean Food
Greek Taverna
   6828 Old Dominion Dr., 703/556-0788

Best Indian Food
Cafe Taj
   1379 Beverly Rd., 703/827-0444

Best Italian Food
Il Borgo Restaurante
   1381A Beverly Rd., 703/893-1400
Pulcinella Italian Host
   6852 Old Dominion Dr., 703/893-7777

Best Japanese Food
Misora Japanese Restaurant
   1315 Old Chan Bridge Rd., 703/356-6200

Best Other Ethnic Food
Kazan Restaurant (Turkish)
   6813 Redmond Dr., 703/734-1960

Best Regional Food
America Restaurant
   8008 Tysons Corner Center, 703/847-6607

Best Sandwiches
Italian Deli
   6813 Elm St., 703/506-1136

Best Seafood
Legal Sea Food
   International Dr., 703/827-8900

Best Steaks
J.R.'s Stockyards Inn
   8130 Watson St., 703/893-3390

Best View While Dining
The Restaurant
Ritz-Carlton Tysons Corner,
1700 Tysons Blvd., 703/506-4300

NEWPORT NEWS, VA

[See also: Hampton, Portsmouth, and Norfolk]

Best Barbecue/Ribs
Bodine's Hickory Smoked Bar-B-Que
754 J. Clyde Morris Blvd., 757/596-7427

Best Breakfast
Belgian Waffle and Family Steak House
621 J. Clyde Morris Blvd., 757/591-8563
Warwick Restaurant
12306 Warwick Blvd., 757/595-0231

Best Chinese Food
Lotus Pond Szechuan Restaurant
12460 Warwick Blvd., 757/591-0800
Port Arthur Restaurant
11137 Warwick Blvd., 757/599-6474

Best Coffee/Coffeehouse
Coffee Beanery
12300 Jefferson Ave., 757/249-9226
Warwick Restaurant
12306 Warwick Blvd., 757/595-0231

Best Delicatessen
Danny's Deli Restaurant
10838 Warwick Blvd., 757/595-0252
Philly's Sub and Pub
736 J. Clyde Morris Blvd., 757/599-8411

Best Family Restaurant
Sam and Steve's House of Beef
10753 Jefferson Ave., 757/595-3441
Sammy and Nick's Family Restaurant
11834 Canon Blvd., 757/873-8738

Best German Food
Das Waldcafe
12529 Warwick Blvd., 757/930-1781

Best Italian Food
Carmela's Homestyle Italian Cuisine
14501 Warwick Blvd., 757/874-8421
Guiseppe's
Mulberry Inn, 16890 Warwick Blvd.,
757/887-3000

Best Japanese Food
Kappo Nara Seafood and Sushi Restaurant
550 Oyster Point Rd., 757/249-5395
Nara of Japan Steak and Seafood
10608 Warwick Blvd., 757/595-7399

V

Best Mexican Food
El Mariachi Mexican Restaurante
   660 J. Clyde Morris Blvd., 757/596-4933

Best Pizza
Anna's Italian Pizza
   9708 Warwick Blvd., 757/595-0723
Joe and Mimma's Italian Pizza Restaurant
   862 J. Clyde Morris Blvd., 757/596-6664

Best Regional Food
Cheddars
   12280 Jefferson Ave., 757/249-4000

Best Restaurant in Town
Red Maple Inn
   202 Harpersville Rd., 757/596-6333

Best Romantic Dining
Bon Appetit
   11710 Jefferson Ave., 757/873-0644

Best Sandwiches
Mike's Place
   11006 Warwick Blvd., Ste. 458, 757/599-5500

Best Seafood
Bill's Seafood House
   10900 Warwick Blvd., 757/595-4320
Crab Shack
   7601 River Rd., 757/245-2722

Best Sports Bar
R J's
   12743 Jefferson Ave., 757/874-4246
Wipeout Eddie's Rawbar and Grille
   11712 Jefferson Ave., 757/873-3339

Best Vietnamese Food
Mai Vietnamese Restaurant
   Denbigh Village Center,
      14346 Warwick Blvd., Ste. 356,
      757/874-2700

V

NORFOLK, VA

[See also: Chesapeake, Hampton, Newport News, Portsmouth, and Virginia Beach.]

Best American Food
Bistro!
   210 W. York St., 757/622-3210
Cafe 21
   742G 21st St., 757/625-4218
Crackers
   821 W. 21st. St., 757/640-0200
Dumbwaiter
   128 College Pl., 757/623-3663
Grate Steak
   235 N. Military Hwy., 757/461-5501
Magnolia Steak
   749 W. Princess Anne, 757/625-0400

Palettes Restaurant
  245 W. Olney Rd., 757/664-6291
Tandom's Madison Grill
  345 Granby St., 757/627-2222

Best Barbecue/Ribs
Harry's Famous Barbecue
  250 Granby St., 757/622-8137

Best Burgers
Elliot's Restaurant
  1421 Colley Ave., 757/625-0259
Kelly's Tavern
  1408 Colley Ave., 757/623-3216

Best Business Lunch
Freemason Abbey Restaurant
  209 W. Freemason St., 757/622-3966
Phillips Waterside
  333 Waterside Dr., 757/627-6600

Best Cajun/Creole Food
Bienville Grill
  723 W. 21st St., 757/625-5427

Best Casual Dining
Morrison's Cafeteria
  530 N. Military Hwy., 757/461-2477
Reggie's British Pub
  333 Waterside Dr., Ste. 2, 757/627-3575

Best Coffee/Coffeehouse
First Colony Coffee House
  2000 Colonial Ave., 757/622-0149
  132 E. Little Creek Rd., 757/480-1225
Prince Books and Coffee Shoppe
  109 E. Main St., 757/622-9223

Best Continental Food
Monastery Restaurant
  443 Granby St., 757/625-8193
The Norfolk Waterside Marriott Dining Room
  Norfolk Waterside Marriot,
  235 E. Main St., 757/627-4200
Seawell's Ordinary
  Hwy. 17, Ordinary, 757/642-3635

Best Delicatessen
Schlotzsky's
  700 N. Military Hwy., 757/455-2867
  246 E. Main St., 757/627-2867

Best Diner
Charlie's Breakfast and Lunch
  1800A Granby St., 757/625-0824

Best Fine Dining
Ship's Cabin Seafood Restaurant
  4110 E. Ocean View Ave., 757/362-4659

Best French Food
La Galleria Ristorante
  120 College Pl., 757/623-3939

Best Greek/Mediterranean Food
Orapax Inn
  1300 Redgate Ave., 757/627-8041

Best Homestyle Food
The Bait Shack
  333 Waterside Dr., 757/622-3654

Best Indian Food
Nawab Indian Cuisine
  888 N. Military Hwy., 757/455-8080

Best Italian Food
Fellini's
  3910 Colley Ave., 757/625-3000
Franco's Italian Ristorante
  6200A N. Miltary Hwy., 757/853-0177
Il Porto
  323 Waterside Dr., 757/627-4400

Best Lunch
Downtowner Restaurant
  209 Granby St., 757/627-9469

Best Mexican Food
El Rodeo Autentico Restaurante
  5834 E. Virginia Beach Blvd., 757/466-9077

Best Other Ethnic Food
Mo and O'Malley's Irish Pub (Irish)
  131 Granby St., 757/623-3466

Best Outdoor Dining
Phillips Waterside
  333 Waterside Dr., 757/627-6600

Best Pizza
Chanello's Pizza
  3201 E. Ocean View Ave., 757/588-2200
  4820 Hampton Blvd., 757/440-0800
  105 Greenbrier Ave., 757/440-5858
  6213 Chesapeake Blvd., 757/858-4000

Best Place to Take the Kids
Darryl's Restaurant and Bar 1930
  1020 N. Military Hwy., 757/466-1930

Best Restaurant in Town
Bobbywood
  7515 Granby St., 757/440-7515
Todd Jurich's Bistro
  210 W. York St., 757/622-3210

Best Romantic Dining
Ship's Cabin Seafood Restaurant
  4110 E. Ocean View Ave., 757/362-4659

Best Sandwiches
Famous Uncle Al's
  223 E. City Hall, 757/625-8319

Best Seafood
Fisherman's Wharf
  1571 Bayville St., 757/480-3113
Phillips Waterside
  333 Waterside Dr., 757/627-6600

Ship's Cabin Seafood Restaurant
4110 E. Ocean View Ave., 757/362-4659

Best Sports Bar
Stormy's Sports Pub
Norfolk Waterside Marriott, 235 E. Main St.,
757/627-4200

Best Steaks
The Grate Steak
235 N. Military Hwy., 757/461-5501

Best Sunday Brunch
Freemason Abbey Restaurant
209 W. Freemason St., 757/622-3966
Riverwalk Restaurant
777 Waterside Dr., 757/622-2868

Best Vegetarian Food
Green Trees
112 Bank St., 757/625-2455

PETERSBURG, VA

Best Bar
Annabelle's
2733 Park Ave., 804/732-0997

Best Barbecue/Ribs
King's Barbecue
2910 S. Crater Rd., 804/732-0975
King's Barbecue
3221 W. Washington St., 804/732-5861

Best Burgers
Aunt Sarah's Pancake House
403 E. Washington St., 804/732-5411

Best Chinese Food
Hunan Palace Restaurant
405 E. Washington St., 804/732-2331
Lee's Express
21 W. Washington St., 804/732-5337

Best Coffee/Coffeehouse
Yankee Coffee Shop
2557B S. Crater Rd., 804/861-4990

Best Fine Dining
Annabelle's
2733 Park Ave., 804/732-0997

Best Italian Food
Roma's Restaurant
2447 County Dr., 804/861-0414

Best Pizza
Roma's Restaurant
2447 County Dr., 804/861-0414

V

PORTSMOUTH, VA

[See also: Chesapeake, Newport News, and Norfolk.]

Best Barbecue/Ribs
Rodman's Bones and Buddies
  3562 Western Branch Blvd., 757/397-3900
  5917 Churchland Blvd., 757/483-2000

Best Breakfast
Waffle Town USA
  3110 High St., 757/399-6612

Best Burgers
Circle Seafood Restaurant
  3010 High St., 757/397-8196

Best Chinese Food
Dragon Town Chinese Restaurant
  4748 W. Norfolk Rd., 757/483-9189

Best Continental Food
Cafe Europa
  319 High St., 757/399-6652

Best Delicatessen
Mom's Best Deli
  340 Broad St., 757/399-1199

Best Homestyle Food
C.W. Cowling's Restaurant and Lounge
  1278 Smithfield Shopping Plaza,
    Smithfield, 757/357-0044
Jones' Restaurant
  5811 W. Norfolk Rd., 757/484-1996

Best Italian Food
Mario's Pizza and Restaurant
  611 Airline Blvd., 757/399-8970

Best Mexican Food
La Tolteca
  6031 High St. W., 757/484-8043

Best Pizza
Mario's Pizza and Restaurant
  611 Airline Blvd., 757/399-8970

Best Romantic Dining
Smithfield Station
  415 S. Church St., Smithfield,
    757/357-7700

Best Seafood
Amory's Seafood Restaurant
  5909 High St. W., 757/483-1518
Amory's Wharf
  10 Crawford Pkwy., 757/399-0991
Circle Seafood Restaurant
  3010 High St., 757/397-8196

Best Steaks
Circle Seafood Restaurant
  3010 High St., 757/397-8196

Best View While Dining
Scale O' De Whale
  3135 Shipwright St., 757/483-2772

RESTON, VA

[See also: Fairfax, VA.]

Best Barbecue/Ribs
Pepper's Texas Bar-B-Q
  1810 Michael Faraday Dr., 703/435-9696

Best Burgers
Clyde's of Reston
  11905 Market St., 703/787-6601

Best Chinese Food
China Star
  1800 Michael Faraday Ct., 703/435-8666
China Town
  1771 Library St., 703/435-4260

Best Coffee/Coffeehouse
Starbucks Coffee
  1444 Northpoint Village Ctr., 703/787-9341

Best Desserts
Jasmine Cafe
  1633A Washington Plaza N., 703/471-9114

Best Fine Dining
Market Street Bar and Grill
  1800 Presidents St., 703/709-6262
Serbian Crown Restaurant
  1141 Walker Rd., Great Falls, 703/759-4150

Best Greek/Mediterranean Food
Marie's Restaurant
  11130M S. Lakes Dr., 703/620-6555

Best Ice Cream/Yogurt
Lee's Ice Cream
  11917 Freedom Dr., 703/471-8902

Best Italian Food
Il Cigno Restaurant
  1617 Washington Plaza N., 703/471-0121
Paolo's
  11898 Market St., 703/318-8920

Best Late-Night Food
Paolo's
  11898 Market St., 703/318-8920

Best Mexican Food
Rio Grande Cafe
  1827 Library St., 703/904-0703

Best Pizza
Pizzeria Uno Restaurant and Bar
  11948 Market St., 703/742-8667

V

Best Place to Take the Kids
Roy Rogers Restaurant
  11850 Sunrise Valley Dr., 703/860-2292
  11170 S. Lakes Dr., 703/620-2249

Best Restaurant in Town
Dante Restaurant
  1148 Walker Rd., Great Falls, 703/759-3131
L'Auberge Chez Francois
  332 Springvale Rd., Great Falls, 703/759-3800

Best Seafood
Clyde's of Reston
  11905 Market St., 703/787-6601

Best Steaks
Market Street Bar and Grill
  1800 Presidents St., 703/709-6262

Best View While Dining
Marie's Restaurant
  11130M S. Lakes Dr., 703/620-6555

RICHMOND, VA

Best Bar
Castle Thunder Cafe
  1726 E. Main St., 804/648-3038
Penny Lane Pub and Restaurant
  207 N. Seventh St., 804/780-1682
Southern Culture Restaurant
  2229 W. Main St., 804/355-6939

Best Barbecue/Ribs
Bill's Barbecue
  700 E. Main St., 804/643-9857
  11230 Midlothian Turnpike, 804/379-0899
  927 Myers St., 804/355-9905
  8820 W. Broad St., 804/270-9722
  3100 N. Boulevard, 804/355-9745
  5805 W. Broad St., 804/288-9991
Extra Billy's Steak and Bar-B-Q
  5205 W. Broad St., 804/282-3949
Smokey Pig
  212 S. Washington Hwy., Ashland, 804/798-4590

Best Beer Selection
Fox and Hounds British Pub
  10455 Midlothian Turnpike, Bon Air, 804/272-8309

Best Bistro
Davis and Main
  2501 W. Main St., 804/353-6641

Best Breakfast
Aunt Sarah's Pancake House
  7927 W. Broad St., 804/747-8284
  4205 W. Broad St., 804/358-8812
  5100 S. Laburnum Ave., 804/222-2080
  8201 Midlothian Turnpike, 804/323-0639
  2126 Willis Rd., 804/271-1070

V

Best Brewpub
Cobblestone Brewery and Pub
  110 N. Eighteenth St., 804/644-2739
Richbrau Brewery
  1214 E. Cary St., 804/644-3018

Best Burgers
Solbles
  2600 W. Main St., 804/358-7843
Strawberry Street Cafe
  421 Strawberry St., 804/353-6860

Best Business Lunch
Bogart's Restaurant
  443 N. Ridge Rd., 804/285-1603
  203 N. Lombardy St., 804/353-9280

Best Casual Dining
Buddy's Place
  325 N. Robinson St., 804/355-3701
Joe's Inn
  205 N. Shields Ave., 804/355-2282
Robin Inn
  2601 Park Ave., 804/353-0298
Slip at Shockoe
  11 S. Twelfth St., 804/643-3313
Strawberry Street Cafe
  421 Strawberry St., 804/353-6860

Best Chinese Food
Full Kee Restaurant
  6400 Horsepen Rd., 804/673-2233
Peking Chinese Restaurant
  8904 W. Broad St., 804/270-9898
  5710 Grove Ave., 804/288-8371
Peking Gourmet Inn
  13132 Midlothian Pike, Midlothian, 804/794-1799

Best Coffee/Coffeehouse
Virginia Coffee and Tea Company
  1211 W. Main St., 804/355-2739

Best Delicatessen
Manhattan Deli
  9550 Midlothan Turnpike, Bon Air,
    804/330-3845
New York Delicatessen and Restaurant
  2920 W. Cary St., 804/355-6056

Best Diner
Third Street Diner
  218 E. Main St., 804/788-4750
Millie's
  2603 E. Main St., 804/643-5512

Best Dinner
Zeus Gallery Cafe
  201 N. Belmont Ave., 804/359-3219

Best Eclectic Menu
Grafiti Grille
  403B N. Ridge Rd., 804/288-0633

V

Helen's
2527 W. Main St., 804/358-4370
Rick's Cafe
1847 W. Broad St., 804/359-1224

Best Family Restaurant
Darryl's Restaurant and Bar
8240 Midlothian Turnpike, Bon Air,
804/272-1788
Melting Pot Restaurant
9704 Gayton Rd., Ridge, 804/741-3120
The Black-Eyed Pea
9498 W. Broad St., 804/762-4821

Best Fine Dining
Fox Head Inn
1840 Manakin Rd., Manakin Sabot, 804/784-5126

Best French Food
La Petite France Restaurant
2912 Maywill St., 804/353-8729

Best Greek/Mediterranean Food
Crazy Greek
1903 Staples Mill Rd., 804/355-3786
Greek Island Restaurant
10902 Hull Street Rd., Midlothian, 804/674-9199

Best Homestyle Food
Klara's Kitchun
4313 Old Hundred Rd., Chester, 804/796-3737
The Black-Eyed Pea
10201 Midlothian Turnpike, 804/560-3168

Best Ice Cream/Yogurt
Gelati Celesti Ice Cream Makers
8906A W. Broad St., 804/346-0038

Best Indian Food
Bombay Curry House
4401 W. Broad St., 804/359-0054
India House Restaurant
2313 Westwood Ave., 804/355-8378
India K'Raja Restaurant
9051 W. Broad St., 804/965-6345

Best Italian Food
Amici Ristorante
3343 W. Cary St., 804/353-4700
Azzurro Restaurant
6221 River Rd., 804/282-1509
Bella Italia
6407 Iron Bridge Rd., Ampthill, 804/743-1116
Franco's Ristorante and Cafe
9031I W. Broad St., 804/270-9124
La Grotta
1218 E. Cary St., 804/644-2466
Millie's
2603 E. Main St., 804/643-5512
Sal Federico's Italian Restaurant
1808 Staples Mill Rd., 804/358-9111

Best Japanese Food
Hana Zushi Japanese Restaurant
  1309 E. Cary St., 804/225-8801

Best Mexican Food
La Casita
  5204 Brook Rd., Bellevue, 804/262-8729
La Siesta Mexican Restaurant
  9900 Midlothian Turnpike, 804/272-7333

Best Middle Eastern Food
Casablanca
  6 E. Grace St., 804/648-2040

Best Other Ethnic Food
Havana 59 (Cuban)
  16 N. Seventeenth St., 804/649-2822

Best Outdoor Dining
Du Jour
  5806 Grove Ave., 804/285-1301

Best Pizza
Bottoms Up Pizza
  1700 Dock St., 804/644-4400
Mary Angela's Italian Subs
  3345 W. Cary St., 804/353-2333

Best Place to Take the Kids
Chuck E. Cheese Pizza
  10430 Midlothian Turnpike, 804/330-9865

Best Restaurant in Town
Franco's Ristorante and Cafe
  9031I W. Broad St., 804/270-9124
Grafiti Grille
  403 N. Ridge Rd., 804/282-0633
La Petite France Restaurant
  2912 Maywill St., 804/353-8729
Lemaire Specialty Restaurant
  Franklin St. at Adams St., 804/788-8000
Millie's
  2603 E. Main St., 804/643-5512
Season's Restaurant and Cafe
  13124 Midlothian Turnpike, Midlothian,
    804/379-0444
The Dining Room
  The Berkley Hotel, 1200 E. Cary St.,
    804/780-1300
Tobacco Company Restaurant
  1201 E. Cary St., 804/782-9555
Track Restaurant
  2915 W. Cary St., 804/359-4781
Zeus Gallery Cafe
  201 N. Belmont Ave., 804/359-3219

Best Romantic Dining
Lemaire Specialty Restaurant
  Franklin St. at Adams St., 804/788-8000

Best Salad/Salad Bar
Strawberry Street Cafe
  421 Strawberry St., 804/353-6860

V

Best Sandwiches
Mary Angela's Italian Subs
  3345 W. Cary St., 804/353-2333

Best Seafood
Blue Point Seafood Restaurant
  550 E. Grace St., 804/783-8138
Brookside Seafood Restaurant
  5221 Brook Rd., Bellevue, 804/262-5716
Crab Louie's Seafood Tavern
  1000 Sycamore Square Dr., Midlothian, 804/275-2722
Hard Shell
  1411 E. Cary St., 804/643-2333
The Frog and the Redneck
  1423 E. Cary St., 804/648-3764
Track Restaurant
  2915 W. Cary St., 804/359-4781
Westhaven Grill
  6233 Mechanicsville Turnpike,
    Mechanicsville, 804/730-7512

Best Southwestern Food
Texas Wisconsin Border Cafe
  1501 W. Main St., 804/355-2907

Best Steaks
Annabel Lee Riverboat Cruises
  3011 Dock St., 804/644-5700
Buckhead's
  8510 Patterson Ave., 804/750-2000
The North Pole
  Patterson St., Crozier, 804/784-4222
Ruth's Chris Steak House
  11500 W. Hugenot Rd., Midlothian, 804/378-0600

Best Sunday Brunch
Tobacco Company Restaurant
  1201 E. Cary St., 804/782-9555
T.J.'s in Jefferson Hotel
  Franklin St. at Adams St., 804/788-8000

Best Tea Room
Virginia Coffee and Tea Company
  1211 W. Main St., 804/355-2739

Best Thai Food
Thai Dinner
  8059 W. Broad St., 804/270-2699

Best Vietnamese Food
Mekong Vietnamese Restaurant
  6004 W. Broad St., 804/288-8929
Saigon
  903 W. Grace St., 804/355-6633
Saigon Gourmet Restaurant
  11033 Hull Street Rd., Midlothian, 804/745-0199
Vietnam Garden Restaurant
  3991 Glenside Dr., Lakeside, 804/262-6114

ROANOKE, VA

Best Bar
Awful Arthur's
  108 Campbell Ave., 540/344-2997
Charade's
  2801 Hershberger Rd. NW, 540/563-9300
Confeddy's
  24 Campbell Ave. SE, 540/343-9746

Best Coffee/Coffeehouse
Mill Mountain Coffee and Tea
  700 N. Main St., Blacksburg, 540/552-7442

Best Delicatessen
Five Boro Bagels
  2016 Electric Rd., Rte. 419, 540/989-5569
The New Yorker
  2802 Williamson Rd. NW, 540/366-0935

Best Fine Dining
Library Restaurant
  3117 Franklin Rd. SW, 540/985-0811

Best Late-Night Food
Mac and Maggie's
  4202 Electric Rd., 540/774-7427
Texas Tavern
  114 Church Ave. W, 540/342-4825

Best Restaurant in Town
Alexander's
  105 S. Jefferson St., 540/982-6983
Roanoker
  2522 Colonial Ave. SW, 540/344-7746
Stephen's
  2926 Franklin Rd. SW, 540/344-7203

Best Wine Selection
Chateau Morrisette
  Rural Route 1, Floyd, 540/593-2865
Montano's
  3733 Franklin Rd. SW, 540/344-8960

SALEM, VA

Best Beer Selection
Cheers Lounge
  1650 Braeburn Dr. E., 540/389-4600

Best Casual Dining
Mac and Bob's
  316 E. Main St., 540/389-5999
Macado's
  211 E. Main St., 540/387-2686

Best Delicatessen
Upper Crust
  1713 Riverview Dr., 540/389-7540

Best Restaurant in Town
Famous Anthony's
  1716 W. Main St., 540/389-4502

V

Best Seafood
Libby Hill Seafood Restaurant
  1941 W. Main St., 540/389-7198

SUFFOLK, VA

[See also: Portsmouth and Chesapeake.]

Best Barbecue/Ribs
Herb's Barbeque
  868 Carolina Rd., 757/539-9785

Best Breakfast
Bunny's Restaurant
  1901 Wilroy Rd., 757/538-2325

Best Burgers
Herb's Barbeque
  868 Carolina Rd., 757/539-9785

Best Chinese Food
Big Won
  827 W. Constance Rd., 757/925-1818

Best Fine Dining
Dining Room
  510 E. Pinner St., 757/539-4265

Best Homestyle Food
Bunny's Restaurant
  1901 Wilroy Rd., 757/538-2325
Dining Room
  510 E. Pinner St., 757/539-4265

Best Seafood
Main Street Restaurant and Raw Bar
  1467 N. Main St., 757/934-9235

Best Steaks
George's Steak House
  1260 Holland Rd., 757/934-1726

VIRGINIA BEACH, VA

[See also: Chesapeake and Norfolk.]

Best American Food
501 City Grill
  501 N. Birdneck Rd., 757/425-7195

Best Barbecue/Ribs
Frankie's Place for Ribs
  5200 Fairfield Shopping Ctr., 757/495-7427
  408 Laskin Rd., 757/428-7631

Best Breakfast
Village Inn
  313 Independence Blvd., 757/499-5557

Best Burgers
Raven Restaurant
  1200 Atlantic Ave., 757/425-9556

Best Casual Dining
Annabelle's
21 Pembroke Mall, Ste. 4586, 757/490-3888
Chick's Oyster Bar
2143 Vista Circle, 757/481-5757

Best Chinese Food
Chinese Gourmet
1508 Lynnhaven Pkwy., 757/471-2540
Great Wall Chinese Restaurant
1001 Providence Square Shopping Ctr., 757/467-4917
Szechuan Garden Restaurant
2720 N. Mall Dr., 757/463-1680

Best Coffee/Coffeehouse
First Colony Coffee House
1550 Laskin Rd., 757/428-2994

Best Desserts
Aldo's Ristorante
1860 Laskin Rd., 757/491-1111
Cuisine and Company
3004 Pacific Ave., 757/428-6700

Best Diner
Atlas Diner
2158 Great Neck Shopping Center,
757/496-3839

Best Fine Dining
Le Chambord
324 N. Great Neck Rd., 757/498-1234

Best French Food
La Caravelle Restaurant
1040 Laskin Rd., 757/428-2477

Best Greek/Mediterranean Food
Street Cook
1949 Lynnhaven Pky., 757/471-7810

Best Health-Conscious Menu
Heritage Health Food Store
314 Laskin Rd., 757/428-0500

Best Homestyle Food
Carolina Cookin' Family Restaurant
6567 College Park Sq., 757/523-4529

Best Indian Food
India Restaurant
5760 Northampton Blvd., 757/460-2100

Best Inexpensive Meal
La Fogata
3900 Bonney Rd., 757/463-6039

Best Italian Food
Aldo's Ristorante
1860 Laskin Rd., 757/491-1111
Il Giardino Ristorante
910 Atlantic Ave., 757/422-6464
Pasta e Pani
1069 Laskin Rd., 757/428-2299

V

Best Japanese Food
Shogun Japanese Steak House
  550 First Colonial Rd., 757/422-5150

Best Kosher Food
The Jewish Mother
  3108 Pacific Ave., 757/422-5430

Best Mexican Food
El Rodeo Mexican Restaurant
  5209 Providence Rd., 757/474-2698
La Fogata
  3900 Bonney Rd., 757/463-6039

Best Middle Eastern Food
Casablanca
  709 Deer Lake Dr., 757/495-0688

Best Outdoor Dining
Sandbridge Restaurant and Bar
  205 Sandbridge Rd., 757/426-2193

Best Place to Be "Seen"
Duck-In and Gazebo
  3324 Shore Dr., 757/481-0201

Best Place to Eat Alone
Gus' Mariner Restaurant
  57th St. at Atlantic Ave., 757/425-5699

Best Restaurant in Town
Costal Grill
  1427 N. Great Neck Rd., 757/496-3348
The Lucky Star
  1608 Pleasure House Rd., 757/363-8410

Best Romantic Dining
Tandom's
  2932 Virginia Beach Blvd., 757/340-5637

Best Sandwiches
Beach Pub
  1001 Laskin Rd., 757/422-8817
Taste Unlimited
  213 36th St., 757/425-0977
  638 Hilltop West Shopping Ctr., 757/425-1858
  4097 Shore Dr., 757/464-1566
The Jewish Mother
  3108 Pacific Ave., 757/422-5430

Best Seafood
Alexander's on the Bay
  Fentress Ave., 757/464-4999
Captain George's Seafood
  1956 Laskin Rd., 757/428-3494
  2272 Old Pungo Ferry Rd., 757/721-3463
Chick's Oyster Bar
  2143 Vista Circle, 757/481-5757
Coastal Grill
  1427 N. Great Neck Rd., 757/496-3348
Duck-In and Gazebo
  3324 Shore Dr., 757/481-0201
Harpoon Larry's Oyster Bar
  216 24th St., 757/422-6000

V

Henry's Seafood Restaurant
  3319 Shore Dr., 757/481-7300
Sandbridge Restaurant and Bar
  205 Sandbridge Rd., 757/426-2193
Steinhilber's Thalia Acres Inn
  653 Thalia Rd., 757/340-1156
The Lucky Star
  1608 Pleasure House Rd., 757/363-8410

Best Steaks
Aberdeen Barn
  5805 Northampton Blvd., 757/464-1580

Best Sunday Brunch
T.K. Tripp's Restaurant and Lounge
  101 S. Independence Blvd., 757/490-4517

Best Thai Food
Bangkok Garden Restaurant
  4000 Virginia Beach Blvd., 757/498-5009

Best Vegetarian Food
Cafe Central
  5350 Kemps River Dr., Ste. 101,
    757/420-2561
Fresh Market Deli
  550 First Colonial Rd., Ste. 309,
    757/425-5383

Best View While Dining
Sandbridge Restaurant and Bar
  205 Sandbridge Rd., 757/426-2193

WILLIAMSBURG, VA

Best American Food
Beethoven's Inn Cafe Deli
  467 Merrimac Trail, 757/229-7069
Chownings Tavern
  Duke of Gloucester St., Merrimac, 757/229-2141
Christiana Campbell's Tavern
  Waller St., 757/229-2141
King's Arms Tavern
  Duke of Gloucester St., 757/229-1000
Regency Room
  Williamsburg Inn, 136 W. Francis, 757/229-2141
Shields Tavern
  Duke of Gloucester St., 757/229-1000
Trellis Restaurant
  403 Duke of Gloucester St., 757/229-8610
Victoria's Fire
  264AB McLaws Circle, 757/220-2511

Best Barbecue/Ribs
County Grill
  1215 George Washington Memorial Hwy.,
    Yorktown, 757/591-0600
Pierce's Pitt Bar-B-Que
  447 Rochambeau Dr., 757/565-2955

Best Breakfast
Gazebo House of Pancakes
  409 Bypass Rd., 757/220-0883

V

Best Chinese Food
Dynasty Restaurant
  1621 Richmond Rd., 757/220-8888
Peking Restaurant
  122A Waller Mill Rd., 757/229-2288

Best Coffee/Coffeehouse
Prince George Espresso
  433 Prince George St., 757/220-6670

Best Delicatessen
College Deli and Pizza Restaurant
  336 Richmond Rd., 757/229-6627
Paul's Deli Restaurant
  761 Scotland St., 757/229-8976

Best Eclectic Menu
Bray Dining Room
  1010 Kingsmill Rd., 757/253-3900

Best French Food
Le Yaca
  1915 Pocahontas Trail, 757/220-3616

Best Italian Food
Ristorante Primo
  1325 Jamestown Rd., 757/229-9212

Best Japanese Food
Sakura Steak House
  601 Prince George St., 757/253-1233

Best Mexican Food
La Tolteca
  5351 Richmond Rd., 757/253-2939

Best Regional Food
Coach House Tavern
  12604 Harrison Landing, Charles City,
    757/829-6003

Best Restaurant in Town
The Kitchen at Powhatan Plantation
  3601 Ironbound Rd., 757/220-1200

Best Seafood
Backfin Resaurant
  1193 Jamestown Rd., 757/220-2249
Berret's Seafood Restaurant-Raw Bar
  199 S. Boundary St., 757/253-1847
Nick's Seafood Pavilion
  Water Street, Yorktown, 757/887-5269
The Whaling Company
  494 McLaws Circle, 757/229-0275
Trellis Restaurant
  403 Duke of Gloucester St., 757/229-8610

Best Soul Food
The Surrey House Restaurant
  11865 Rolfe Hwy., Surry, 757/294-3389

Best Steaks
The Aberdeen Barn
  1601 Richmond Rd., 757/229-6661

Best Vegetarian Food
Trellis Restaurant
  403 Duke of Gloucester St., 757/229-8610

Best Vietnamese Food
Chez Trinh Restaurant
  157 Monticello Ave., 757/253-1888

V

Washington

Best Breakfast
Sidney's
  512 W. Heron St., 360/533-6635

Best Chinese Food
Ocean Palace
  212 E. Wishkah St., 360/533-6966

Best Desserts
Bridges' Restaurant
  112 N. G St., 360/532-6563

Best Dinner
Levee Street Restaurant
  709 Levee St., Hoquiam, 360/532-1959

Best Family Restaurant
Duffy's
  1605 Simpson Ave., 360/532-3842

Best Italian Food
Parma Italian Restaurante
  116 W. Heron St., 360/532-3166

Best Mexican Food
Casa Mia
  2936 Simpson Ave., Hoquiam, 360/533-2010
Mazatlan Restaurant
  South Shore Mall, 1017 S. Boone St., 360/532-0940

Best Sandwiches
Billy's Restaurant
  322 E. Heron St., 360/533-7144

Best Steaks
707 Restaurant
  707 W. Curtis St., 360/533-2662

ANACORTES, WA

Best Bar
Brown Lantern
  412 Commercial Ave., 360/293-2544

Best Barbecue/Ribs
Charlie's Restaurant
  5407 Ferry Terminal Rd., 360/293-7377

Best Breakfast
Calico Cupboard
  901 Commercial Ave., 360/293-7315

Best Brewpub
Anacortes Brewhouse
  320 Commercial Ave., 360/293-2444

Best Chinese Food
Hong Kong Gardens
  2501 Commercial Ave., 360/293-9595

Best Delicatessen
Gere-A-Deli and Bistro
  502 Commercial Ave., 360/293-7383

Best Desserts
Dessert Show
  2302 Commercial Ave., 360/293-8042

Best Health-Conscious Menu
Calico Cupboard
  901 Commercial Ave., 360/293-7315

Best Pizza
Village Pizza
  807 Commercial Ave., 360/293-7847

Best Restaurant In Town
La Petite Restaurant
  3401 Commercial Ave., 360/293-4644

Best Restaurant Meal Value
Stork's Restaurant and Lounge
  2821 Commercial Ave., 360/293-7500

Best Seafood
Boomer's Landing Restaurant
  209 T Ave., 360/293-5108

BELLEVUE, WA

[See also: Mercer Island, Redmond, and Seattle.]

Best Barbecue/Ribs
Three Pigs Barbecue
  1044 116th Ave. NE, 425/453-0888

Best Breakfast
Coffee Garden and City Side
  Doubletree Hotel, 818 112th Ave. NE,
    425/455-1515
Yankee Diner
  13859 Bellevue Redmond Rd., 425/643-1558

Best Chinese Food
Asian Wok
  707 148th Ave. NE, 425/747-8700

Best Diner
Coco's Restaurant
  530 112th Ave. NE, 425/453-8138

Best Homestyle Food
Yankee Diner
  13859 Bellevue Redmond Rd., 425/643-1558

Best Indian Food
Raga Cuisine of India
  555 108th Ave. NE, 425/450-0336

Best Italian Food
Cucina! Cucina! Italian Cafe
  800 Bellevue Way NE, Ste. 118, 425/637-1177
Spazzo Mediterranean Grill
  10655 NE Fourth St., Ste. 9, 425/454-8255

Best Mexican Food
Azteca Mexican Restaurant
  150 112th Ave. NE, 425/453-9087

Best Middle Eastern Food
Ebru Mediterranean Deli
  15600 NE Eighth St., 425/641-4352

Best Other Ethnic Food
Pogacha Restaurant (Yugoslavian/Russian)
  119 106th Ave. NE, 425/455-5670
Restaurant Ararat (Armenian/Yugoslavian)
  10425 NE Eighth St., 425/451-3234

Best Sandwiches
Grand Central Bakery
  138 107th Ave. NE, 425/454-9661

Best Steaks
The New Jake O'Shaughnessey's
  401 Bellevue Sq., 425/455-5559

Best Sunday Brunch
Salish Lodge Restaurant
  Salish Lodge, 6501 Railroad Ave. SE, Snoqualmie,
  425/888-2556

Best Thai Food
Best Wok
  19 148th Ave. NE, 425/747-7031
King and I Restaurant
  10509 Main St., 425/462-9337
Thai Kitchen Restaurant
  14115 NE Twentieth St., 425/641-9166

BELLINGHAM, WA

Best Bar
Archer Ale House
  1212 Tenth St., 360/647-7002
Orchard Street Brewery
  709 W. Orchard Dr., Ste. 1, 360/647-1614

W

Best All-You-Can-Eat Buffet
Cathay House
 950 Lincoln St., 360/676-9100

Best Breakfast
Little Cheerful Cafe
 133 E. Holly St., 360/738-8824

Best Brewpub
Orchard Street Brewery
 709 W. Orchard Dr., Ste. 1, 360/647-1614

Best Business Lunch
Casino Bar and Grill
 1224 Cornwall Ave., 360/733-3500
Colophon Cafe
 1208 Eleventh St., 360/647-0092

Best Casual Dining
Boomer's Drive-In
 310 N. Samish Way, 360/647-2666
Pacific Cafe
 100 N. Commercial St., 360/647-0800

Best Coffee/Coffeehouse
Starbucks Coffee
 2814 Meridan St., 360/647-8128
 4285 Guide Meridian Rd., 360/650-0883
 210 36th St., 360/738-1402
 1225 E. Sunset Dr., 360/734-0702

Best Desserts
Colophon Cafe
 1208 Eleventh St., 360/647-0092
La Patisserie
 3098 Northwest Ave., 360/671-3671

Best Diner
Carol's Coffee Cup
 5415 Mount Baker Hwy., Deming, 360/592-5641

Best Family Restaurant
Red Robin
 100 Telegraph Rd., 360/734-9991

Best French Food
La Belle Rose
 1801 Roeder Ave., 360/647-0833

Best Health-Conscious Menu
Old Town Cafe
 316 W. Holly St., 360/671-4431
Pepper Sisters
 1055 N. State St., 360/671-3414

Best Homestyle Food
Mitzel's American Kitchen
 241 Telegraph Rd., 360/671-5522

Best Ice Cream/Yogurt
The Ice Creamery
 1 Bellis Fair Pkwy., 360/734-7502

Best Inexpensive Meal
The Royal Inn Restaurant
 208 E. Holly St., 360/738-3701

W

Best Italian Food
Il Fiasco Restaurant
  1309 Commercial St., 360/676-9136
Mannino's Italian Restaurant
  130 E. Champion St., 360/671-7955

Best Mexican Food
La Pinata Mexican Restaurant
  1317 Commercial St., 360/647-1101

Best Pizza
Cicchitti's East Coast
  1230 N. State St., 360/671-8447
Stanello's Restaurant
  1304 Twelfth St., 360/676-1304

Best Place to Eat Alone
Swan Cafe
  1220 N. Forest St., 360/734-0542

Best Place to Take the Kids
Red Robin
  100 Telegraph Rd., 360/734-9991

Best Restaurant in Town
Mannino's Italian Restaurant
  130 E. Champion St., 360/671-7955
Orchard Street Brewery
  709 W. Orchard Dr., Ste. 1, 360/647-1614
Pacific Cafe
  100 N. Commercial St., 360/647-0800

Best Romantic Dining
Pacific Cafe
  100 N. Commercial St., 360/647-0800

Best Salad/Salad Bar
Bob's Burgers and Brew
  1781 Main St., Ferndale, 360/384-1766

Best Sandwiches
Casino Bar and Grill
  1224 Cornwall Ave., 360/733-3500
The Bagelry
  1319 Railroad Ave., 360/676-5288

Best Seafood
Oyster Bar
  240 Chuckanut Dr., Bow, 360/766-6185
Pacific Cafe
  100 N. Commercial St., 360/647-0800

Best Sunday Brunch
Chuckanut Manor Restaurant
  302 Chuckanut Dr., Bow, 360/766-6191

Best Vegetarian Food
Pepper Sisters
  1055 N. State St., 360/671-3414

BREMERTON, WA

Best Breakfast
Big Apple Diner
  6720 Kitsap Way, 360/373-8242

Family Pancake and Dinner House
  3900 Kitsap Way, 360/479-2422
  4115 Wheaton Way, 360/479-0788

Best Burgers
Noah's Ark Restaurant
  1516 Sixth St., 360/377-8100

Best Casual Dining
Melody Lane
  536 Fourth St., 360/373-2499

Best Chinese Food
Panda Inn On The Bay
  4180 Kitsap Way, 360/377-7785

Best Italian Food
Campana's Italian Restaurant
  19815 Viking Ave. NW, Poulsbo, 360/779-2222

Best Japanese Food
Osaka Japanese Restaurant
  10408 Silverdale Way NW, Silverdale, 360/698-7266

Best Pizza
Spiro's Pizza and Pasta
  1217 Sylvan Way, 360/377-6644

Best Restaurant In Town
Boat Shed Restaurant
  101 Shore Dr., 360/377-2600

Best Seafood
Mary Mac's Restaurant
  5155 McCormick Woods Dr. SW, Port Orchard,
    360/895-0142

Best Steaks
Keg Restaurant
  2620 Wheaton Way, 360/373-8088

CENTRALIA, WA

Best Breakfast
Alva's Place
  227 SW Riverside Dr., Chehalis, 360/748-0877
Country Cousin
  1054 Harrison Ave., 360/736-2200

Best Burgers
Burgerville USA
  818 Harrison Ave., 360/736-5212

Best Chinese Food
Mandarin Chef
  705 1/2 N. Tower Ave., 360/736-9326
Shanghai Restaurant
  519 N. Tower Ave., 360/736-4539

Best Desserts
Berry Fields
  Antique Mall Cafe, 201 S. Pearl St., 360/736-1183
Sweet Inspirations
  514 N. Market Blvd., Chehalis, 360/748-7102

Best Mexican Food
Azteca Mexican Restaurant
118 N. Tower Ave., 360/736-0973
Plaza Jalisco Mexican Restaurant
1340 NW Maryland Ave., Chehalis, 360/748-4298

Best Pizza
Figaro's Italian Pizza
1704 S. Gold St., 360/736-3221

Best Sandwiches
Berry Fields
Antique Mall Cafe, 201 S. Pearl St., 360/736-1183

Best Steaks
Rib-Eye Restaurant
1336 Rush Rd., Chehalis, 360/748-0288

EDMONDS, WA

Best American Food
Maltby Cafe
8809 Maltby Rd., Snohomish, 425/483-3123

Best Casual Dining
Scott's Bar and Grill
8115 Lake Ballinger Way, 425/775-2561

Best Chinese Food
Chopsticks
10012 Edmonds Way, 425/776-1196
North China Restaurant
22814 100th Ave. W., 425/774-4310

Best Coffee/Coffeehouse
Brusseau's
117 Fifth Ave. S., 425/774-4166
Rainforest Gourmet Coffee Company
320 Fifth Ave. S., 425/771-3933

Best Lunch
Anthony's Beach Cafe
456 Admiral Way, 425/771-4400

Best Seafood
Arnie's Restaurant
300 Admiral Way, Ste. 105, 425/774-8661

EVERETT, WA

[See also: Lynnwood.]

Best Barbecue/Ribs
Down Home Bar-B-Que
1409 Hewitt Ave., 425/258-6005

Best Breakfast
Karl's Bakery and Coffee Shoppe
2814 Wetmore Ave., 425/252-1774
Sisters
2804 Grand Ave., 425/252-0480
Totem Family Dining
4410 Rucker Ave., 425/252-3277

W

Best Burgers
Buck's American Cafe
  2901 Hewitt Ave., 425/258-1351

Best Cajun/Creole Food
Alligator Soul
  2013 Hewitt Ave., 425/259-6311

Best Desserts
Pave Specialty Bakery
  2613 Colby Ave., 425/252-0250

Best Dinner
Confetti's Woodfire Grill
  1722 W. Marine View Dr., 425/258-4000

Best Indian Food
The Pride of India
  1405 Hewitt Ave., 425/252-8543

Best Inexpensive Meal
Mom's Teriyaki
  2934 Colby Ave., 425/339-5535

Best Italian Food
Anna's Italian Kitchen
  2930 Colby Ave., 425/252-8225
Bella Rosa Ristorante Italiano
  2803 Colby Ave., 425/258-8028
Gianni's Italian Restaurant
  5030 Evergreen Way, 425/252-2435

Best Lunch
Donato's
  2609 Colby Ave., 425/258-2151
Sisters
  2804 Grand Ave., 425/252-0480

Best Mexican Food
Tampico Mexican Restaurant
  2303 Broadway, 425/339-2427

Best Pizza
Giorgio's Pizza House
  9031 Evergreen Way, 425/347-1542

Best Place to Take the Kids
Alfy's Pizza
  9620 Nineteenth Ave. SE, 425/338-2577
  12720 Fourth Ave. W., 425/353-1776
  2317 Broadway, 425/258-9333
  7404 Evergreen Way, 425/355-1776

Best Restaurant Meal Value
Alligator Soul
  2013 Hewitt Ave., 425/259-6311
The Pride of India
  1405 Hewitt Ave., 425/252-8543
Sisters
  2804 Grand Ave., 425/252-0480

Best Seafood
Anthony's Homeport
  1726 W. Marine View Dr., 425/252-3333

Best Steaks
Stuart Anderson's Black Angus
  8413 Evergreen Way, 425/355-7400

Best View While Dining
Anthony's Homeport
  1726 W. Marine View Dr., 425/252-3333
Confetti's Woodfire Grill
  1722 W. Marine View Dr., 425/258-4000

FEDERAL WAY, WA

[See also: Kent and Tacoma.]

Best Breakfast
Coffee Crossing
  2500B SW 336th St., 253/838-2742

Best Business Lunch
Diamond Jim's
  1616 S. 325th St., 253/927-4045

Best Fine Dining
Salty's
  28201 Redondo Beach Dr. S., 253/946-0636

Best Italian Food
Giancarlo
  4624 SW 320th St., 253/838-1101
Verrazano's Italian-American
  28835 Pacific Hwy. S., 253/946-4122

Best Mexican Food
Azteca Mexican Restaurant
  31740 23rd Ave. S., 253/839-6693

Best Seafood
Salty's
  28201 Redondo Beach Dr. S., 253/946-0636

Best Steaks
Diamond Jim's
  1616 S. 325th St., 253/927-4045

KENNEWICK, WA

Best All-You-Can-Eat Buffet
Granny's Buffet
  6821 W. Canal, 509/735-9887

Best Burgers
Red Robin Burgers and Spirits
  1021 N. Columbia Center Blvd., 509/736-6008

Best Business Lunch
Henry's Restaurant
  3013 W. Clearwater Ave., 509/735-1996

Best Chinese Food
Chinese Garden
  1520 N. Fourth Ave., Pasco, 509/545-6324

Best Homestyle Food
Country Gentlemen
  300 N. Ely St., 509/783-0128

Lil' Pardner's Family Restaurant
1320 N. Twentieth Ave., Pasco, 509/547-6446

Best Inexpensive Meal
Shari's Restaurant
1200 N. Columbia Center Blvd., 509/735-7438

Best Mexican Food
Casa Chapala
107 E. Columbia Dr., 509/586-4224

Best Pizza
Round Table Pizza
2230 W. Court St., Pasco, 509/545-1091

Best Steaks
T.S. Cattle Company Steakhouse
6515 W. Clearwater, Ste. 400, 509/783-8251

Best Sunday Brunch
Rosso's Ristorante
2525 N. Twentieth Ave., Pasco, 509/547-0701

KENT, WA

[See also: Federal Way and Seattle.]

Best Breakfast
Black Diamond Bakery
32805 Railroad Ave., Black Diamond, 360/886-2741

Best Diner
Rose's Highway Inn
26915 Pacific Hwy. S., 253/839-7277

Best Family Restaurant
Rose's Highway Inn
26915 Pacific Hwy. S., 253/839-7277

Best Greek/Mediterranean Food
Spiro's
215 First Ave. S., 253/854-1030

Best Italian Food
Auguri Ristorante
13018 SE Kent Kangley Rd., 253/631-8262

Best Restaurant in Town
Mirabella
1819 W. Meeker St., 253/854-0967

Best Romantic Dining
The Dinner House
24306 Roberts Dr., Black Diamond, 360/886-2524

LONGVIEW, WA

Best Breakfast
Omelettes and More
3120 Washington Way, 360/425-9260
Pancake House
1425 California Way, 360/577-9966
The Pantry
919 Fifteenth Ave., 360/425-8880

Best Business Lunch
Henri's
  4545 Ocean Beach Hwy., 360/425-7970
Vintage Bistro
  1329 Commerce Ave., 360/425-8848

Best Casual Dining
Masthead Restaurant
  1210 Ocean Beach Hwy., 360/577-7972
Trophies Sports Broiler
  409 S. Pacific Ave., Kelso, 360/577-6787

Best Chinese Food
Chiu's Mongolian Grill
  970 Fourteenth Ave., 360/577-1597
Golden Palace
  1245 Fourteenth Ave., 360/423-4261

Best Desserts
Judy's Restaurant and Catering
  1036 Washington Way, 360/423-9262

Best Family Restaurant
Spaghetti Works and Deli
  1073 Fourteenth Ave., 360/577-1136

Best Homestyle Food
Country Folks Deli
  1323 Commerce Ave., 360/425-2837

Best Mexican Food
La Playa Mexican Restaurant
  1310 Ocean Beach Hwy., 360/425-1660

Best Place to Eat Alone
Commerce Cafe
  1338 Commerce Ave., 360/577-0115

Best Romantic Dining
Rutherglen Mansion
  420 Rutherglen Dr., 360/425-5816

Best Salad/Salad Bar
Bart's Restaurant
  1208 Washington Way, 360/425-2179
Emerald Room
  Monticello Hotel, 1405 Seventeenth Ave.,
    360/425-9900

Best Steaks
Elmer's Restaurant
  804 Ocean Beach Hwy., 360/577-1990

Best Vegetarian Food
Country Village Cafe
  711 Vandercook Way, 360/425-8100

W

LYNNWOOD, WA

[See also: Everett and Seattle.]

Best Burgers
California Burger Company
  3333B 184th St. SW, 425/771-1710

Best Chinese Food
Mandarin House
   6815 196th St. SW, 425/776-1204

Best Family Restaurant
Yankee Diner
   4010 196th St. SW, 425/775-5485

Best Italian Food
Eastside Mario's
   4730 196th St. SW, 425/775-2535

Best Mexican Food
Azteca Mexican Restaurant
   18920 28th Ave. W., 425/672-1771

Best Pizza
Sparta's Pizza and Spaghetti
   17630 Hwy. 99, 425/745-1880

Best Restaurant in Town
Mario's Italian Cuisine
   19226 Hwy. 99, 425/776-6525
Red Robin Burgers and Spirits
   18410 33rd Ave. W., 425/771-6492

MERCER ISLAND, WA

[See also: Bellevue and Seattle.]

Best Italian Food
Roberto's Pizza
   7619 SE 27th St., 206/232-7383

Best Mexican Food
Mi Pueblo Grill
   7811 SE 27th St., 206/232-8750

Best Restaurant in Town
Alpenland Delicatessen
   2707 78th Ave. SE, 206/232-4780

Best Thai Food
Thai on Mercer
   7691 SE 27th St., 206/236-9990

MOSES LAKE, WA

Best Breakfast
Bob's Cafe at the Inn
   1807 E. Kittelson Rd., 509/765-3211

Best Chinese Food
Lin's Restaurant
   601 S. Pioneer Way, 509/766-4257

Best Homestyle Food
Bob's Cafe at the Inn
   1807 E. Kittelson Rd., 509/765-3211

Best Japanese Food
Kiyoji's Sapporo
   440 Melva Ln., 509/765-9314

W

Best Mexican Food
Inca Mexican Restaurant
404 E. Third Ave., 509/766-2426

Best Pizza
Chico's Pizza Parlor
917 S. Dahlia Dr., 509/765-4589

OLYMPIA, WA

Best Atmosphere
Spar Restaurant
114 Fourth Ave. E., 360/357-6444

Best Bistro
Capitale Espresso Grill
609 Capitol Way S., 360/352-8007
Fifth Avenue Bistro
209 Fifth Ave. SE, 360/709-0390

Best Breakfast
San Francisco Street Bakery
1320 San Francisco St. NE, 360/753-8553

Best Brewpub
Fishbowl Brewpub and Cafe
515 Jefferson St. SE, 360/943-6480

Best Casual Dining
Budd Bay Cafe
525 Columbia St. SW, 360/357-6963

Best Coffee/Coffeehouse
Dancing Goats Expresso Company
124 Fourth Ave. E., 360/754-8187
Ruby's Coffee House
700 Fourth Ave. E., 360/352-3318

Best Desserts
Oasis Cafe
7702 Terminal St., Tumwater, 360/357-6967
Sweet Oasis Mediterranean Restaurant
507 Capitol Way S., 360/956-0470
Wagner's European Bakery
1013 Capitol Way S., 360/357-7268

Best Family Restaurant
Falls Terrace Restaurant
106 S. Deschutes Way, Tumwater, 360/943-7830

Best Fine Dining
By The Fountain
1075 Capitol Way S., 360/956-9094
Jean-Pierre's Garden Room
316 Schmidt Pl. SW, 360/754-3702
La Petite Maison
101 Division St. NW, 360/943-8812

Best Mexican Food
Saritas
909 Sleater Kinney Rd. SE, Lacey, 360/456-7269

Best Pizza
Brewery City Pizza Company
5150 Capitol Blvd. S., 360/754-6767
2705 Limited Ln. NW, 360/754-7800

W

4353 Martin Way E., 360/491-6630

Best Salad/Salad Bar
Falls Terrace Restaurant
  106 S. Deschutes Way, Tumwater, 360/943-7830

Best Seafood
Budd Bay Cafe
  525 Columbia St. SW, 360/357-6963
Gardner's Seafood and Pasta
  111 Thurston Ave. NW, 360/786-8466

Best Steaks
Falls Terrace Restaurant
  106 S. Deschutes Way, Tumwater, 360/943-7830

Best Thai Food
Saigon Rendez-Vous Restaurant
  117 Fifth Ave. SW, 360/352-1989

Best Vegetarian Food
Oasis Cafe
  7702 Terminal St. SW, Tumwater, 360/357-6967
Sweet Oasis Mediterranean Restaurant
  507 Capitol Way S., 360/956-0470
Urban Onion Restaurant
  116 Legion Way SE, 360/943-9242

Best View While Dining
Genoa's On The Bay
  1525 Washington St. NE, 360/943-7770
Oyster House
  320 Fourth Ave. W., 360/753-7000
Seven Gables Restaurant
  1205 West Bay Dr. NW, 360/352-2349

PORT TOWNSEND, WA

Best Atmosphere
Lonny's Restaurant
  2330 Washington St., 360/385-0700

Best Breakfast
Landfall Restaurant
  412 Water St., 360/385-5814
Salal Cafe
  634 Water St., 360/385-6532
Sea J's Cafe
  2501 Washington St., 360/385-6312

Best Burgers
Lighthouse Cafe
  955 Water St., 360/385-1165

Best Chinese Food
Shanghai Restaurant
  Hudson Pt., 360/385-4810
Silver Palace
  2001 Sims Way, 360/385-6175

Best Coffee/Coffeehouse
Bread and Roses
  230 Quincy St., 360/385-1044
Elevated Ice Cream Company
  627 Water St., 360/385-1156

Uptown Oasis
720 Tyler St., 360/385-2130

Best Family Restaurant
Landing Restaurant
1433C W. Sims Way, 360/385-5964
Public House Grill
1038 Water St., 360/385-9708

Best Fine Dining
Lonny's Restaurant
2330 Washington St., 360/385-0700

Best Ice Cream/Yogurt
Elevated Ice Cream Company
627 Water St., 360/385-1156

Best Mexican Food
El Sarape Mexican Restaurant
630 Water St., 360/379-9343

Best Pizza
Waterfront Pizza
951 Water St., 360/385-6629

Best Sandwiches
Bayview
1539 Water St., 360/385-1461
Water Street Deli-Restaurant
926 Water St., 360/385-2422

Best Seafood
Lanza's Ristorante and Pizzeria
1020 Lawrence St., 360/385-6221
Manresa Castle
Seventh at Sheridan, 360/385-5750
Silverwater Cafe
237 Taylor St., 360/385-6448

Best Thai Food
Khu Larb Thai Restaurant
225 Adams St., 360/385-5023

Best Vegetarian Food
Blackberries
Bldg. 210, Fort Worden State Park, 200 Battery
Way, 360/385-9950

REDMOND, WA

[See also: Bellevue.]

Best Chinese Food
Peking Restaurant
16857 Redmond Way, 425/883-9090

Best Diner
Coco's Restaurant
14804 NE 24th St., 425/746-7510

Best Family Restaurant
Billy McHale's Restaurant
15210 Redmond Way, 425/881-0316

Best French Food
Bistro Provencal
  212 Central Way, Kirkland, 425/827-3300

Best Italian Food
Frankie's Pizza and Pasta
  16630 Redmond Way, 425/883-8407

Best Japanese Food
Kikuya Restaurant
  8105 161st Ave. NE, 425/881-8771

Best Mexican Food
Circo! Circo! Mexican Restaurant
  12709 NE 124th St., Kirkland, 425/821-9405

Best Pizza
Coyote Creek Pizza Company
  228 Central Way, Kirkland, 425/822-2226

Best Restaurant in Town
The Redmond Brown Bag Cafe
  8412 164th Ave. NE, 425/861-4099

Best Thai Food
Redmond Thai Cuisine
  16421 Cleveland St., 425/869-6131

RICHLAND, WA

Best Breakfast
Sterling's Famous Steak, Seafood, and Salad Bar
  Restaurant
  890 George Washington Way, 509/943-1588

Best Burgers
Red Robin Burgers and Spirits
  924 George Washington Way, 509/943-8484

Best Business Lunch
Henry's Restaurant
  1435 George Washington Way, 509/946-8706

Best Inexpensive Meal
Shari's of Richland
  1745 George Washington Way, 509/946-0681

SEATTLE, WA

[See also: Bellevue, Lynnwood, and Mercer Island.]

Best American Food
Bick's Broadview American Grill
  10555 Greenwood Ave. N., 206/367-8481
Red Robin Burgers and Spirits
  138 Northgate Plz., 206/365-0933
  1107 Alaskan Way, 206/624-3969
  3272 Fuhrman Ave. E., 206/323-0917
  1100 Fourth Ave., 206/447-1909
  17300 Southcenter Pkwy., 206/575-8382
Yankee Diner
  5300 24th Ave. NW, 206/783-1999

Best Atmosphere
Palisade
  2601 W. Marina Pl., 206/285-1000

Best Barbecue/Ribs
Pecos Pit BBQ
  2260 First Ave. S., 206/623-0629

Best Bistro
Cafe Campagne
  1600 Post Alley, 206/728-2233

Best Breakfast
Julia's of Wallingford
  4401 Wallingford, 206/633-1175
Julia's Park Place
  5410 Ballard Ave. NW, 206/783-2033

Best Brewpub
Pike Place
  1419 First Ave., 206/622-3373
Redhook Ale Brewery
  3400 Phinney Ave. N., 206/548-8000

Best Burgers
Dick's Drive-In Restaurant
  9208 Holman Rd. NW, 206/783-5233
  115 Broadway E., 206/323-1300
  111 NE 45th St., 206/632-5125
  12325 30th Ave. NE, 206/363-7777
  4426 Second Ave. NE, 206/634-0300
Red Mill Burgers
  312 N. 67th St., 206/783-6362
Red Robin Burgers and Spirits
  138 Northgate Plz., 206/365-0933
  1107 Alaskan Way, 206/624-3969
  3272 Fuhrman Ave. E., 206/323-0917
  1100 Fourth Ave., 206/447-1909
  17300 Southcenter Pkwy., 206/575-8382
Zesto's Burger and Fish House
  6416 Fifteenth Ave. NW, 206/783-3350

Best Casual Dining
Beppo Seattle
  701 Ninth Ave. N., 206/244-2288

Best Chinese Food
Bamboo Garden
  364 Roy St., 206/282-6616
Snappy Dragon
  8917 Roosevelt Way NE, 206/528-5575

Best Coffee/Coffeehouse
Green Cat Cafe
  1514 E. Olive Way, 206/726-8756
Seattle's Best Coffee
  multiple locations
Starbucks Coffee
  multiple locations
Still Life In Fremont Coffeehouse
  709 N. 35th St., 206/547-9850
Zio Ricco European Coffee
  1415 Fourth Ave., 206/467-8616

Best Desserts
B & O Espresso
  204 Belmont Ave. E., 206/322-5028
Honey Bear Bakery
  2106 N. 55th St., 206/545-7296
Dilettante Chocolates and Cafe
  416 Broadway E., 206/329-6463

Best Dinner
Charlie's
  2727 Fairview Ave. E., 206/324-7564

Best Eclectic Menu
Gravity Bar
  424 Broadway E., 206/325-7186
Lampreia
  2400 First Ave., 206/443-3301

Best Family Restaurant
Yankee Diner
  5300 24th Ave. NW, 206/783-1999

Best Fine Dining
Canlis Restaurant
  2576 Aurora Ave. N., 206/283-3313
Palisade
  2601 W. Marina Pl., 206/285-1000

Best French Food
611 Supreme
  611 E. Pine St., 206/328-0292
Campagne Restaurant
  89 Pine St., 206/728-2800
Rover's
  2808 E. Madison St., 206/325-7442

Best Greek/Mediterranean Food
Andaluca
  407 Olive Way, 206/623-8700

Best Health-Conscious Menu
Macheezmo Mouse
  425 Queen Anne Ave. N., 206/282-9904
  701 Fifth Ave., 206/382-1730

Best Indian Food
Chautney's
  519 First Ave. N., 206/284-6799

Best Inexpensive Meal
Dick's Drive-In Restaurant
  9208 Holman Rd. NW, 206/783-5233
  115 Broadway E., 206/323-1300
  4426 Second Ave. NE, 206/634-0300
  111 NE 45th St., 206/632-5125
  12325 30th Ave. NE, 206/363-7777
Still Life In Fremont Coffeehouse
  709 N. 35th St., 206/547-9850

Best Italian Food
Angelina's Trattoria
  2311 California Ave. SW, 206/932-7311
Assaggio Ristorante
  2010 Fourth Ave., 206/441-1399

Baci
  1513 Sixth Ave., 206/292-6223
Bruno's Mexican-Italian Restaurant
  1417 Third Ave., 206/622-3180
Il Terrazzo Carmine
  411 First Ave. S., 206/467-7797
La Buca Restaurant
  102 Cherry St., 206/343-9517
Saleh Al Lago
  6804 E. Green Lake Way N., 206/524-4044
Tulio Ristorante
  1100 Fifth Ave., 206/624-5500

Best Late-Night Food
13 Coins Restaurant
  125 Boren Ave. N., 206/682-2513
Hurricane Cafe
  2230 Seventh Ave., 206/623-5750

Best Lunch
McCormick and Schmick's
  1103 First Ave., 206/623-5500
  9404 E. Marginal Way S., 206/762-4418
Rattlers Grill
  1823 Eastlake Ave. E., 206/325-7350

Best Mexican Food
Azteca Mexican Restaurants
  22003 66th Ave. W., Mountlake Terrace,
  206/672-0601
Bruno's Mexican-Italian Restaurant
  1417 Third Ave., 206/622-3180
Casa Luna
  23720 NE State Hwy. 3, 360/275-9392
El Camino
  607 N. 35th St., 206/632-7303
El Puerco Lloron
  1501 Western Ave., 206/624-0541
Guadalajara Cafe
  1715 N. 45th St., 206/632-7858
Jalisco Mexican Restaurant
  122 First Ave. N., 206/283-4242
  12336 31st Ave. NE, 206/364-3978
  1467 E. Republican St., 206/325-9005
  8517 Fourteenth Ave. S., 206/767-1943
Mama's Mexican Kitchen
  2234 Second Ave., 206/728-6262

Best Other Ethnic Food
Asia Grille (Pacific Rim)
  2820 NE University Village Mall, 206/517-5985
Boca (Latin)
  2516 Alki Ave. SW, 206/933-8000

Best Outdoor Dining
Lombardi's Cucina
  2200 NW Market St., 206/783-0055
Ray's Boathouse
  6049 Seaview Ave. NW, 206/789-3770

Best Pizza
Olympia Pizza and Spaghetti House
1500 Queen Anne Ave. N., 206/285-5550
516 Fifteenth Ave. E., 206/329-4500
Pagliacci Pizza
multiple locations

Best Place to Eat Alone
Sid's Delicatessen
250 Fourth Ave. S., 206/443-5567

Best Place to Take the Kids
The Iron Horse Restaurant
311 Third Ave. S., 206/223-9506
Yankee Diner
5300 24th Ave. NW, 206/783-1999

Best Restaurant in Town
Fuller's
Sheraton Seattle Hotel and Towers,
1400 Sixth Ave., 206/447-5544
Marco's Supper Club
2510 First Ave., 206/441-7801
Palace Kitchen
2030 Fifth Ave., 206/448-2001
Ponti Seafood Grill
3014 Third Ave. N., 206/284-3000
Wild Ginger Asian Restaurant
1400 Western Ave., 206/623-4450

Best Romantic Dining
Adriatica Restaurant
1107 Dexter Ave. N., 206/285-5000

Best Salad/Salad Bar
Still Life In Fremont Coffeehouse
709 N. 35th St., 206/547-9850

Best Sandwiches
City Foods
2522 Fifth Ave., 206/441-3663
Three Girls Bakery
1514 Pike Pl., 206/622-1045

Best Seafood
Bell Street Diner
2201 Alaskan Way, 206/448-6688
Anthony's Fish Bar
2201 Alaskan Way, 206/448-6688
Anthony's Homeport
6135 Seaview Ave. NW, 206/783-0780
421 S. 227th St., 206/824-1947
Anthony's Pier 66
2201 Alaskan Way, 206/448-6688
Arnie's Restaurant and Bar
1900 N. Northlake Way, 206/547-3242
Chandler's Crabhouse and Fresh Fish
901 Fairview Ave. N, 206/223-2722
Pescatore
5300 34th Ave. NW, 206/784-1733
Ray's Boathouse
6049 Seaview Ave. NW, 206/789-3770

W

Best Southwestern Food
Cactus Restaurant
 4220 E. Madison St., 206/324-4140

Best Sports Bar
Jersey's All-American Sports Club
 700 Virginia St., 206/343-9377

Best Steaks
Metropolitan Grill
 820 Second Ave., 206/624-3287

Best Sunday Brunch
The Garden Court
 Four Seasons Hotel, 411 University St.,
  206/621-7889

Best Sushi
Nikko
 1900 Fifth Ave., 206/322-4641
Sanmi Sushi
 2601 W. Marina Pl., 206/283-9978
Shiro's Sushi Restaurant
 2401 Second Ave., 206/443-9844

Best Thai Food
Freemont Noodle House
 3411 Fremont Ave. N., 206/547-1550
Thai Thai Restaurant
 11205 Sixteenth Ave. SW, 206/246-2246

Best Vegetarian Food
Cafe Flora
 2901 E. Madison St., 206/325-9100
Globe Cafe and Bakery
 1531 Fourteenth Ave., 206/324-8815
Gravity Bar
 424 Broadway E., 206/325-7186
Green Cat Cafe
 1514 E. Olive Way, 206/726-8756

Best Vietnamese Food
Cafe Loc
 305 Harrison St., 206/728-9292
Saigon Bistro
 1032 S. Jackson St., Ste. 202, 206/329-4939
Viet My Restaurant
 129 Prefontaine Pl. S., 206/382-9923

Best View While Dining
Palisade
 2601 W. Marina Pl., 206/285-1000
Space Needle Restaurant
 219 Fourth Ave. N., 206/443-2100

Best Wine Selection
Ponti Seafood Grill
 3014 Third Ave. N., 206/284-3000
Ray's Boathouse
 6049 Seaview Ave. NW, 206/789-3770

W

SPOKANE, WA

Best American Food
Cavanaugh's River Inn
700 N. Division St., 509/326-5577

Best Atmosphere
Patsy Clark's Mansion
2208 W. Second Ave., 509/838-8300

Best Bistro
Lindaman's Cafe North
6412 N. Monroe St., 509/325-6511

Best Breakfast
Waffles N More
5312 N. Division St., 509/484-4049
41 W. Third Ave., 509/624-3353
9425 E. Sprague Ave., 509/928-8055

Best Burgers
Benjamin's Cafe
112 N. Howard St., 509/455-6771
Red Robin Burgers and Spirits
9904 N. Newport Hwy., 509/467-3382

Best Chinese Food
Kay Lon Garden Restaurant
2819 N. Division St., 509/326-1333
Peking North
4120 N. Division St., 509/484-4321

Best Coffee/Coffeehouse
Espresso Delizioso Cafe
706 N. Monroe St., Ste. 1, 509/326-5958

Best Delicatessen
Something Else
518 W. Sprague Ave., 509/747-3946

Best Dinner
Atrium Cafe and Deli
303 W. North River Dr., 509/326-8000

Best Eclectic Menu
Fugazzi Bakery and Cafe
1 N. Post St., 509/624-1133

Best Family Restaurant
Onion
7522 N. Division St., 509/482-6100
302 W. Riverside Ave., 509/747-3852
Red Robin Burger and Spirits
9904 N. Newport Hwy., 509/467-3382

Best Fine Dining
Clinkerdagger
621 W. Mallon Ave., 509/328-5965
Scarlet Begonia's
The Mars Hotel and Casino, 312 W. Sprague Ave.,
509/747-6277
Paprika
1228 S. Grand Blvd., 509/455-7545
Patsy Clark's Mansion
2208 W. Second Ave., 509/838-8300

Best Health-Conscious Menu
Luna
  5620 S. Perry St., 509/448-2383

Best Italian Food
Cucina! Cucina! Italian Cafe
  707 W. Main Ave., 509/838-3388
Rock City Cucina Italiano
  505 W. Riverside Ave., 509/455-4400

Best Japanese Food
Mustard Seed
  9806 E. Sprague Ave., 509/924-3194
  245 W. Spokane Falls Blvd., 509/747-2689

Best Lunch
Frontier West Family Restaurant
  2121 N. Division St., 509/328-4090

Best Mexican Food
Chapala Restaurant
  2820 E. 29th Ave., 509/534-7388
  1801 N. Hamilton St., 509/484-4534

Best Outdoor Dining
C.I. Shenanigan's Restaurant
  908 N. Howard St., 509/326-3677

Best Pizza
Pete's Pizza
  2328 W. Northwest Blvd., 509/326-1900
  821 E. Sharp Ave., 509/487-9795
Pizza Factory
  123 S. Broad St., Medical Lake, 509/299-9100
Rocky Rococo
  520 W. Main Ave., 509/747-1000

Best Place to Take the Kids
Cyrus O'Leary
  516 W. Main Ave., 509/624-9000
Tomato Brothers
  6220 N. Division St., 509/484-4500

Best Sandwiches
Bruchi's
  multiple locations
Domini Sandwiches
  703 W. Sprague Ave., 509/747-2324
Sparky's Firehouse Subs
  9328 N. Division St., 509/465-3473
  926 W. Indiana Ave., 509/325-3473

Best Seafood
Clinkerdagger
  621 W. Mallon Ave., 509/328-5965
Salty's
  510 N. Lincoln St., 509/327-8888

Best Steaks
Chapter Eleven
  105 E. Mission Ave., 509/326-0466
  9304 N. Division St., 509/467-7011
  7720 E. Sprague Ave., 509/928-1787

W

Best Sunday Brunch
C.I. Shenanigan's Seafood and Chophouse
  322 N. Spokane Falls Ct., 509/326-3745

Best Thai Food
Riverview Thai Restaurant
  621 W. Mallon Ave., 509/325-8370

Best Vegetarian Food
Mizuna
  214 N. Howard St., 509/747-2004

Best View While Dining
Ankeny's Restaurant
  Cavanaugh's Ridpath Hotel, 515 W. Sprague Ave.,
  509/838-6311

Best Wine Selection
C.I. Shenanigan's Seafood and Chophouse
  322 N. Spokane Falls Ct., 509/455-6690

TACOMA, WA

[See also: Federal Way.]

Best Atmosphere
Tacoma Bar and Grill
  625 S. Commerce St., 253/572-4861

Best Bar
The Swiss
  1904 S. Jefferson Ave., 253/572-2821

Best Barbecue/Ribs
Bob's Barbecue Pit Too
  911 S. Eleventh St., 253/627-4899

Best Brewpub
Engine House Number Nine
  611 N. Pine St., 253/272-3435
Powerhouse Restaurant Brewery
  454 E. Main Ave., Puyallup, 253/845-1370

Best Burgers
Frisko Freeze
  1201 Division Ave., 253/272-4800

Best Chinese Food
East and West Cafe
  5319 Tacoma Mall Blvd., 253/475-7755

Best Fine Dining
Stanley and Seafort's Steak Chop
  115 E. 34th St., 253/473-7300

Best Greek/Mediterranean Food
It's Greek To Me
  1703 Sixth Ave., 253/272-1375

Best Homestyle Food
Southern Kitchen
  1716 Sixth Ave., 253/627-4282

W

Best Italian Food
Lorenzo's Restaurant
2811 Sixth Ave., 253/272-3331

Best Mexican Food
Moctezuma's Mexican Restaurant
4102 S. 56th St., 253/474-5593

Best Outdoor Dining
C.I. Shenanigan's Seafood and Chophouse
3017 Ruston Way, 253/752-8811

Best Pizza
Milton Tavern
7320 Pacific Hwy. E., 253/922-3340

Best Romantic Dining
Stanley and Seafort's Steak Chop
115 E. 34th St., 253/473-7300
Tacoma Bar and Grill
625 S. Commerce St., 253/572-4861

Best Salad/Salad Bar
Keg Restaurant
2212 Mildred St. W., 253/565-7300

Best Steaks
Stanley and Seafort's Steak Chop
115 E. 34th St., 253/473-7300

Best View While Dining
C.I. Shenanigan's Seafood and Chophouse
3017 N. Ruston Way, 253/752-8811
Stanley and Seafort's Steak Chop
115 E. 34th St., 253/473-7300

VANCOUVER, WA

Best Beer Selection
McMenamin's On The Columbia
1801 SE Columbia River Dr., 360/699-1521

Best Business Lunch
Chart House Restaurant
101 E. Columbia Way, 360/693-9211
Pinot Ganache
1004 Washington St., 360/695-7786

Best Chinese Food
Fa Fa Gourmet Chinese Restaurant
11712 NE Fourth Plain Rd., 360/260-7899
Silver Dragon
3605 E. Fourth Plain Blvd., 360/694-2212

Best Coffee/Coffeehouse
Java House
210 W. Evergreen Blvd., Ste. 400, 360/737-2925
Coffee Talk
907 Main St., 360/737-6765

Best Dinner
City Grill
916 SE 164th Ave., 360/253-5399

W

Best Fine Dining
Chart House Restaurant
   101 E. Columbia Way, 360/693-9211
Pinot Ganache
   1004 Washington St., 360/695-7786

Best Italian Food
Cafe Augustino's
   1109 Washington St., 360/750-1272

Best Lunch
Sheldon's Cafe
   1101 Officers Row, 360/699-1213

Best Mexican Food
Bernabes Family Cafe
   9803 NE Hwy. 99, 360/574-5993
Who Song and Larry's Mexican Restaurant
   111 E. Columbia Way, 360/695-1198

Best Outdoor Dining
Beaches Restaurant and Bar
   1919 SE Columbia River Dr., 360/699-1592

Best Restaurant In Town
Dante's
   111C E. Main St., Battle Ground, 360/687-4373
Hidden House Restaurant
   100 W. Thirteenth St., 360/696-2847
New York Richie's
   8086 E. Mill Plain Blvd., 360/696-4001

Best Sandwiches
McMenamin's On The Columbia
   1801 SE Columbia River Dr., 360/699-1521

Best Seafood
Beaches Restaurant and Bar
   1919 SE Columbia River Dr., 360/699-1592

Best Steaks
Keg Restaurant
   4250 E. Fourth Plain Blvd., 360/699-2442

Best Sunday Brunch
Who Song and Larry's Mexican Restaurant
   111 E. Columbia Way, 360/695-1198

Best Thai Food
Thai Little Home
   3214 E. Fourth Plain Blvd., 360/693-4061

Best View While Dining
Chart House Restaurant
   101 E. Columbia Way, 360/693-9211

W

WALLA WALLA, WA

Best Bar
Blue Mountain Tavern
   2025 E. Isaacs Ave., 509/525-9941

Best Burgers
Ice-Burg
   616 W. Birch St., 509/529-1793

Best Coffee/Coffeehouse
Merchants Ltd. and French Bakery
  21 E. Main St., 509/525-0900

Best Ice Cream/Yogurt
Ice-Burg
  616 W. Birch St., 509/529-1793

Best Italian Food
Pastime Cafe
  215 W. Main St., 509/525-0873

Best Mexican Food
El Sombrero Mexican Restaurant
  4 W. Oak St., 509/522-4984
La Casita
  428 Ash St., 509/525-2598

Best Pizza
Pepe's Pizza and Pasta
  1533 E. Isaacs Ave., 509/529-2550

Best Restaurant in Town
Rosita's Mexican Restaurant
  201 E. Main St., 509/525-6361
  1005 S. Ninth Ave., 509/525-5007
The Addition Restaurant and Catering
  16 S. Colville St., 509/529-7336
The Homestead Restaurant
  1528 E. Isaacs Ave., 509/522-0345

WENATCHEE, WA

Best American Food
Prospector Pies Restaurant
  731 N. Wenatchee Ave., 509/662-1118

Best Bar
McGlinn's Ale House
  111 Orondo Ave., 509/663-9073

Best Burgers
Buzz Inn
  1112 N. Wenatchee Ave., 509/663-7777

Best German Food
Gustav's
  617 U.S. Hwy. 2, Leavenworth, 509/548-4509

Best Lunch
Gingerbread House
  400 S. Chelan Ave., 509/663-2878
Jeepers! It's Bagels
  619 S. Mission St., 509/663-4594

Best Mexican Food
Plaza Jalisco Mexican Restaurant
  1650 Grant Rd., East Wenatchee, 509/886-1910

Best Restaurant in Town
Andreas Keller Restaurant
  829 Front St., Leavenworth, 509/548-6000
Cellar Cafe
  202 N. Mission St., 509/662-1722
Steven's at Mission Square
  218 N. Mission St., 509/663-6573

W

Best Sports Bar
Mickey O' Reilly's Sports Bar
  560 Valley Mall Pkwy., East Wenatchee,
    509/884-6299

Best Sunday Brunch
The Cougar Inn
  23379 Hwy. 207, Leavenworth, 509/763-3354

Best View While Dining
The Cougar Inn
  23379 Hwy. 207, Leavenworth, 509/763-3354

YAKIMA, WA

Best Bar
Bert Grant's Brewery Pub
  32 N. Front St., 509/575-2922

Best Breakfast
Cafe European Bakery
  3105 Summitview Ave., 509/248-5844
Twin Bridges Inn
  1315 N. First St., 509/452-6352

Best Burgers
Miner's Drive-In Restaurant
  2415 S. First St., 509/457-8194

Best Casual Dining
Whistlin' Jack Lodge
  20800 State Rte. 410, Naches, 509/658-2433

Best Chinese Food
China Star
  14 N. Second St., 509/248-9992
George's Wok and Grill
  1208 S. 80th Ave., 509/966-0933

Best Delicatessen
5th Avenue Deli
  415 W. Walnut St., 509/452-2332

Best Fine Dining
Gasperetti's
  1013 N. First St., 509/248-0628

Best Health-Conscious Menu
Teriyaki Grille
  901 W. Yakima Ave., Ste. 6B, 509/575-4911

Best Mexican Food
Las Margaritas Mexican Restaurant
  1460 N. Sixteenth Ave., 509/575-1553
Santiago's Gourmet Mexican
  111 E. Yakima Ave., 509/453-1644
Tequila's
  1 W. Yakima Ave., 509/457-3296

Best Place to Eat Alone
Deli De Pasta
  7 N. Front St., 509/453-0571

Best Restaurant in Town
Greystone Restaurant
  5 N. Front St., 509/248-9801

W

Best Steaks
Stuart Anderson's Black Angus Restaurant
  501 N. Front St., 509/248-4540

W

West Virginia

Best Italian Food
Pasquale Mira Restaurant
  100 Harper Park Dr., 304/255-5253

Best Mexican Food
Rio Grande Mexican Restaurante
  4006 Robert C. Byrd Dr., 304/252-7488

Best Pizza
Padrino's Pizza Restaurant
  Beaver Shopping Ctr., Rte. 19, Beaver,
    304/255-7755

Best Restaurant in Town
Char
  100 Char Dr., 304/253-1760

Best Steaks
Texas Steakhouse
  140 Harper Park Dr., 304/253-1436

W

Best American Food
Oak Supper Club
  HC 78 Box 47A, Pipestem, 304/466-4800

Best Breakfast
Manor Coffee Shop
  411 Federal St., 304/327-9311

Best Casual Dining
Gabby's
  1508 Jefferson St., 304/327-9569
Macado's Restaurant
  Bluefield Mall, Rte. 2, 304/325-8557

Best Chinese Food
Chinese Kitchen
   3022 E. Cumberland Rd., 304/327-9133

Best Family Restaurant
Bailey's Restaurant
   3175 E. Cumberland Rd., 304/325-5421

Best Homestyle Food
K & W Cafeteria
   Hwy. 460 at Rte. 52, 304/327-0251

Best Mexican Food
Taco Loco Mexican Cafe
   7172 Mercer Mall, 304/325-5189

Best Seafood
Johnston's Inn and Restaurant
   Old Oakvale Rd., Princeton, 304/425-7591

Best Steaks
Johnston's Inn and Restaurant
   Old Oakvale Rd., Princeton, 304/425-7591

CHARLESTON, WV

Best Barbecue/Ribs
Joey's Downtown
   115 Quarrier St., 304/343-4121

Best Chinese Food
Charlie Woo's
   200 Patrick St., 304/346-1111

Best Coffee/Coffeehouse
Common Grounds
   186 Summers St., 304/342-1525

Best Delicatessen
Deli-D-Lite
   6545 MacCorkle Ave. SE, 304/925-4642

Best Family Restaurant
Harding's Family Restaurant
   2772 Pennsylvania Ave., 304/344-5044

Best Greek/Mediterranean Food
Best Of Crete
   3029 Charleston Town Ctr., 304/343-3292

Best Homestyle Food
Diehl's Restaurant
   152 Main Ave., Nitro, 304/755-9353

Best Italian Food
Italian Heritage Pasta Kitchen
   705 Donnally St., 304/343-9784

Best Japanese Food
Hibachi Japanese Steak House
   741 Washington St. W., 304/342-7616

Best Lunch
Sam's Uptown Cafe
   28 Capitol St., 304/346-6222

Best Pizza
Graziano's Pizza
243 Capitol St., 304/342-8554
159 Kanawha Mall, 304/925-7794
6303 MacCorkle Ave. SE, 304/925-7292
3027 Charleston Town Ctr., 304/343-3386

Best Salad/Salad Bar
Fifth Quarter Steakhouse
201 Clendenin St., 304/345-2726

Best Sandwiches
Deli-D-Lite
6545 MacCorkle Ave. SE, 304/925-4642

Best View While Dining
Chesapeake Crab House
The Holiday Inn Charleston House Hotel
600 Kanawha Blvd. E., 304/344-4092

CLARKSBURG, WV

Best Barbecue/Ribs
Damon's
110 Emily Dr., 304/624-7427

Best Chinese Food
Peking Restaurant
Rte. 50E at Old Bridgeport Hwy., 304/623-5828

Best Coffee/Coffeehouse
Andrew and Ballard Book Cellar
215 W. Main St., 304/623-0644

Best Italian Food
Phillip's Restaurant
401 N. Fifth St., 304/624-1404
Victoria's Pasta
Greenbrier Motel, 200 Buckhannon Pike,
304/624-5518

Best Pizza
Chunki's Pizza and Subs
762 W. Pike St., 304/623-3100

Best Sandwiches
Chunki's Pizza and Subs
762 W. Pike St., 304/623-3100

Best Seafood
Jim Reid's Restaurant
1422 Buckhannon Pike, 304/623-4909

ELKINS, WV

Best Breakfast
Nanny's Kitchen
Tiger Valley Mall, Harrison St., 304/636-0940

Best Burgers
Western Steer Steakhouse
250 S. Beverly Pike, Rte. 219, 304/636-2373

Best Sandwiches
Pete's Place
413 Kerens Ave., 304/636-7383

Starr Cafe
224 Davis Ave., 304/636-7273

Best Steaks
Duke's Restaurant
Valley Point Mall, Rte. 219, 304/636-8786

FAIRMONT, WV

Best Chinese Food
China Garden
1406 Country Club Rd., 304/367-1994

Best Homestyle Food
Say Boy Restaurant
905 Country Club Rd., 304/366-7252

Best Italian Food
Muriale's Restaurant
1742 Fairmont Ave., 304/363-3190

Best Steaks
Say Boy Restaurant
905 Country Club Rd., 304/366-7252

HUNTINGTON, WV

Best Atmosphere
Calamity Cafe
1555 Third Ave., 304/525-4171

Best Cafeteria
Bailey's Cafeteria
410 Ninth St., 304/522-3663

Best Bar
Damon's
1001 Third Ave., 304/697-7427

Best Breakfast
Down Town Breakfast and Deli
625 Eighth St., 304/523-3542

Best Burgers
Heritage Station
15 Heritage Village, 304/523-6373

Best Chinese Food

China Garden
804 Sixth Ave., 304/697-5524
Happy Dragon
1238 Fourth Ave., 304/697-9061

Best Coffee/Coffeehouse
Afterward Cafe
Renaissance Book Company, 831 Fourth Ave.,
304/529-7323

Best Italian Food
Rocco's Spaghetti House
252 Main St., Ceredo, 304/453-3000

Best Late-Night Food
Dwight's
601 First St., 304/525-3591

Best Mexican Food
Chili Willi's Mexican Cantina
  841 Fourth Ave., 304/529-4857

Best Pizza
Evaroni's Pizza
  914 Oak St., Kenova, 304/453-4355

Best Place to Be "Seen"
The Drop Shop
  1318 Fourth Ave., 304/523-5282

Best Place to Eat Alone
Oliver's
  322 Tenth St., 304/522-2415

Best Place to Take the Kids
Gino's Pizza and Spaghetti House
  2501 Fifth Ave., 304/529-6086
  940 Fourth Ave., Ste. 418, 304/525-2943
  1401 Washington Ave., 304/529-3271
  1001 Third Ave., 304/529-2547
  146 Norway Ave., 304/522-9557

Best Restaurant in Town
Rebels and Redcoats Tavern
  412 Seventh Ave., 304/523-8829

Best Sandwiches
Down Town Breakfast and Deli
  625 Eighth St., 304/523-3542

MARTINSBURG, WV

Best Burgers
Hoss's Steak and Sea House
  2200 Aikens Ctr., 304/267-2224
The Peppermill
  200 W. Burke St., 304/263-3986

Best Chinese Food
Gateway Peking Restaurant
  100 W. Martin St., 304/263-6544

Best Desserts
American Deli
  315 W. Stephens St., 304/263-4656
The Peppermill
  200 W. Burke St., 304/263-3986

Best Homestyle Food
Linda and Danny's Kitchen
  1161 Winchester Ave., 304/263-7821
Warm Springs Eatery
  Berkeley Plaza Shopping Ctr., Warm Springs Ave.,
    304/264-0410

Best Ice Cream/Yogurt
Rock Hill Creamery
  313 S. Queen St., 304/264-2373

Best Italian Food
Taste of Italy Restaurant
  240 Lutz Ave., 304/264-0231

W

Best Mexican Food
Rio Grande
   127 N. Queen St., 304/267-1684

Best Pizza
Ramon's Pizza and Sub Shop
   329 Winchester Ave., 304/263-2989

Best Restaurant in Town
Bavarian Inn and Lodge
   Rte. 480, Shepherdstown, 304/876-2551

Best Sandwiches
Peppermill
   141 S. Queen St., 304/263-3986
Ramon's Pizza and Sub Shop
   329 Winchester Ave., 304/263-2989

Best Seafood
Hoss's Steak and Sea House
   2200 Aikens Ctr., 304/267-2224
Market House
   100 N. Queen St., 304/263-7615

Best Steaks
Heatherfield's Restaurant
   301 Foxcroft Ave., 304/267-8311
Peppermill
   141 S. Queen St., 304/263-3986

MORGANTOWN, WV

Best Barbecue/Ribs
BW3
   268 High St., 304/292-2999

Best Breakfast
Eat N Park Restaurant
   353 Patteson Dr., 304/598-0020

Best Brewpub
West Virginia Brewing
   1291 University Ave., 304/296-2739

Best Burgers
Boston Beanery
   383 Patteson Dr., 304/599-1870
   321 High St., 304/292-0165

Best Chinese Food
Asian Garden
   3109 University Ave., 304/599-1888
Chinese Gourmet
   2862 University Ave., 304/599-2069
Chopsticks
   1 Suburban Ct., 304/599-4848

Best Coffee/Coffeehouse
Blue Moose Cafe
   248 Walnut St., 304/292-8999

Best Family Restaurant
Boston Beanery
   383 Patteson Dr., 304/599-1870
   321 High St., 304/292-0165

W

Best Fine Dining
Glasshouse Grill
   709 Beechurst Ave., 304/296-8460

Best Greek/Mediterranean Food
Ali-Baba Downtown Restaurant
   327 High St., 304/292-4701

Best Health-Conscious Menu
Mountain People's Restaurant
   1400 University Ave., 304/291-6131

Best Homestyle Food
Ruby and Ketchy's
   Cheat Rd., 304/594-2004

Best Italian Food
Alfredo's Ristorante
   1193 Pineview Dr., 304/599-8811
Puglioni's Pasta and Pizza
   1137 Van Voorhis Rd., 304/599-7521
Tiberio's III
   Rte. 857N, Pierpoint Rd., 304/594-0832

Best Japanese Food
Yama Japanese Restaurant
   387A High St., 304/291-2456

Best Lunch
Aunt Patty's
   Morgantown Municipal Airport, 210 Hartfield Rd.,
      304/291-3663
Chestnut Street Cafe
   190 Chestnut St., 304/296-1670

Best Mexican Food
La Casa
   132 Pleasant St., 304/292-6701

Best Seafood
Back Bay
   1869 Mileground Rd., 304/296-3027

Best Steaks
Flame Steak House
   76 High St., 304/296-2976

Best Sunday Brunch
Reflections On The Lake
   Lakeview Resort and Conference Center Hotel,
      1 Lakeview Dr., 304/594-1111

Best Vegetarian Food
Maxwell's
   1 Wall St., 304/292-0982

PARKERSBURG, WV

Best 24-Hour Restaurant
Mountaineer Family Restaurant
   4006 E. Seventh St., 304/422-0101

Best American Food
Jimmy Colombo's Restaurant
   1236 Seventh St., 304/428-5472

Best Chinese Food
House of Hunan
  100 Lakeview Ctr., 304/422-1688

Best Homestyle Food
Travelers Restaurant
  328 Seventh St., 304/428-9177

Best Ice Cream/Yogurt
Broughton Ice Cream Store
  3411 Emerson Ave., 304/428-4111

Best Italian Food
Jimmy Colombo's Restaurant
  1236 Seventh St., 304/428-5472

Best Mexican Food
Don Emilio's
  2407 Ohio Ave., 304/422-8800

Best Restaurant In Town
Paradise Grille
  I-77 at Rte. 50 and Seventh St., 304/485-7147

WEIRTON, WV

Best Barbecue/Ribs
Happy's BBQ Ribs
  4075 Main St., 304/797-7427

Best Italian Food
Mario's Restaurant
  3806 Main St., 304/748-1179

Best Restaurant in Town
J. Holiday's Tavern, Steak and Seafood
  Best Western Hotel, 350 Three Springs Dr.,
    304/723-5522

Best Steaks
Dee Jay's
  1229 Penna Ave., 304/748-1150

WHEELING, WV

Best Breakfast
Blake's Family Restaurant
  800 Lafayette Ave., Moundsville, 304/845-7090

Best Brewpub
Nail City Brewing Company
  1400 Main St., 304/233-5330

Best Business Lunch
Peaches
  265 River Rd., 304/232-4199
Riverside Restaurant and Lounge
  949 Main St., 304/233-8507
TJ's Sports Garden
  808 National Rd., 304/232-9555
Undo's
  McClure Hotel, 1200 Market St., 304/232-0300

Best Chinese Food
Golden Chopsticks
  329 N. York St., 304/232-2888

Panda Restaurant
  1133 Market St., 304/232-7572
Peking Garden
  32 Twelfth St., 304/233-1044

Best Fine Dining
Ernie's Esquire
  1 W. Bethlehem Blvd., 304/242-2800
Stratford Springs
  355 Oglebay Dr., 304/233-5100

Best German Food
Keg und Kraut
  167 Sixteenth St., 304/232-5654

Best Homestyle Food
Mitchell's Restaurant
  1203 First St., Moundsville, 304/845-8440

Best Pizza
De Felice Brothers Pizza
  1000 National Rd., 304/232-8999
Greco's
  45 Washington Ave., 304/242-5400
Pizza Outlet
  1127 Market St., 304/232-1100

Best Salad/Salad Bar
Boots Texas Roadhouse
  836 National Rd., 304/233-9259
Riverside Restaurant and Lounge
  949 Main St., 304/233-8507

W

Wisconsin

Best Bar
Dos Bandidos Restaurant and Pub
  1004 S. Olde Oneida St., 920/731-3322

Best Breakfast
The Orchard
  Paper Valley Hotel and Conference Center,
    333 W. College Ave., 920/733-8000

Best Burgers
Friar Tuck's
  2120 W. College Ave., 920/730-1004

Best Chinese Food
Chef Chu's Chinese Cuisine
  719 W. College Ave., 920/749-0330

Best Eclectic Menu
Hobnobbin'
  710 W. Grove St., 920/733-5465

Best Homestyle Food
Schreiner's Diner
  2437 S. Oneida St., 920/734-9191

Best Italian Food
Victoria's
  503 W. College Ave., 920/730-9595

Best Mexican Food
Dos Bandidos Restaurant and Pub
  1004 S. Olde Oneida St., 920/731-3322

Best Restaurant in Town
Trim B's Restaurant
  201 S. Walnut St., 920/734-9204

Best Sandwiches
Pizza King
   1003 W. Northland Ave., 920/734-9996
   1717 E. Calumet St., 920/731-3234
   1326 N. Meade St., 920/731-6577

Best Seafood
Cali Restaurant
   201 N. Appleton St., 920/830-0700

Best Steaks
George's Steak House
   2208 S. Memorial Dr., 920/733-4939

Best Sunday Brunch
The Orchard
   Paper Valley Hotel and Conference Center,
      333 W. College Ave., 920/733-8000

ASHLAND, WI

Best Breakfast
Michael's
   421 Main St. E., 715/682-8838

Best Burgers
Railyard Pub
   400 Third St. W., 715/682-9199

Best Health-Conscious Menu
Black Cat Coffeehouse
   211 Chapple Ave., 715/682-3680

Best Homestyle Food
Breakwater Cafe
   1808 Lake Shore Dr. E., 715/682-8388
The Restaurant
   2300 Lake Shore Dr. W., 715/682-9808

Best Pizza
Frankie's Pizza
   1315 Lake Shore Dr. E., 715/682-9980
Hugo's Pizza
   221 Sanborn Ave., 715/682-8202
Pizza Pub
   1402 Lake Shore Dr. E., 715/682-6641

Best Steaks
The Depot
   400 Third Ave. W., 715/682-4200
Marine Supper Club
   Hwy. 2W, 715/682-3298

BELOIT, WI

Best Barbecue/Ribs
Taasbag Too
   2683 Prairie Ave., 608/365-0999

Best Breakfast
A Matter of Taste Cafe
   614 Fourth St., 608/362-0678
Little Rascals
   530 W. Grand Ave., 608/365-4949

Best Burgers
Hanson's Tavern
  615 Cranston Rd., 608/362-8559

Best Delicatessen
Dan's Restaurant
  1600A Huebbe Pkwy., 608/362-5419

Best Diner
State Street Cafe
  315 State St., 608/362-9889

Best Fine Dining
Butterfly Club
  5246 E. County Rd. X, 608/362-8577
The Gun Club
  1122 E. Colley Rd., 608/362-9900

Best Italian Food
Domenico Pizza Restaurant
  534 E. Grand Ave., 608/365-9489

Best Outdoor Dining
Butterfly Club
  5246 E. County Rd. X, 608/362-8577

Best Seafood
Manor
  2102 Freeman Pkwy., 608/365-1608

Best Steaks
Manor
  2102 Freeman Pkwy., 608/365-1608
The Gun Club Restaurant
  1122 E. Colley Rd., 608/362-9900

EAU CLAIRE, WI

Best Bar
Pioneer Tavern
  401 Water St., 715/832-4455
She-Nannigan's and Peanuts
  415 Water St., 715/832-5061

Best Burgers
Culver's Frozen Custard
  2021 Brackett Ave., 715/831-1060

Best Business Lunch
Woo's Pagoda Restaurant
  1700 S. Hastings Way, 715/832-6431

Best Coffee/Coffeehouse
Country Kitchen
  2308 E. Clairemont Ave., 715/832-3677

Best Family Restaurant
Cheese to Please and Chocolate's Too
  2159 Eastridge Center Mall, 715/834-4444

Best Ice Cream/Yogurt
Culver's Frozen Custard
  2021 Brackett Ave., 715/831-1060

Best Italian Food
Draganetti's Ristorante
  3120 Hillcrest Pkwy., Altoona, 715/834-9234

Mona Lisa's Ristorante
428 Water St., 715/839-8969

Best Late-Night Food
Country Kitchen
2308 E. Clairemont Ave., 715/832-3677

Best Restaurant in Town
Sweetwater's Restaurant
1104 W. Clairemont Ave., 715/834-5777

Best Sandwiches
Erbert and Gerbert's Subs and Clubs
405 Water St., 715/835-9995

Best Steaks
Sweetwater's Restaurant
1104 W. Clairemont Ave., 715/834-5777

Best Sunday Brunch
Burgundy's
Ramada Inn, 1202 W. Clairemont Ave.,
715/834-6328

FOND DU LAC, WI

Best Breakfast
Ransom's Restaurant
245 N. Peters Ave., 920/923-4400
Schreiner's Restaurant
168 N. Pioneer Rd., 920/922-0590

Best Chinese Food
Chinatown Kitchen
18 N. Main St., 920/923-9688

Best Homestyle Food
Oasis Family Restaurant
339 N. Main St., 920/922-3345
Rolling Meadows Family Restaurant
947 S. Rolling Meadows Dr., 920/922-9140

Best Ice Cream/Yogurt
Gilles Frozen Custard
819 S. Main St., 920/922-4900
Randall's Original Frozen
609 W. Johnson St., 920/922-8050

Best Italian Food
Tami's
109 S. Main St., 920/922-6162

Best Mexican Food
Mazatlan
237 S. Main St., 920/924-9012

Best Pizza
Joe's Fox Hut
41 N. Main St., 920/923-2300
Pizza Ville
160 W. Scott St., 920/921-1700
Sarafina's Pizza
113 N. Main St., 920/921-3600

Best Sandwiches
Friar Tuck's
  570 W. Johnson St., 920/921-4027
The Scenario
  1000 S. Main St., 920/921-9922

Best Seafood
Sunset Supper Club
  N7364 Winnebago Dr., 920/922-4540

Best Steaks
Sunset Supper Club
  N7364 Winnebago Dr., 920/922-4540
Theo's Supper Club
  24 N. Main St., 920/922-8899

Best Sunday Brunch
The Rosewood Diningroom
  Ramada Inn Plaza Hotel, 1 N. Main St.,
    920/923-3000

Best View While Dining
Carver's On The Lake
  N5529 County Rd. A, Green Lake, 920/294-6931

GERMANTOWN, WI

Best Barbecue/Ribs
Jerry's Old Town Inn
  15841 Main St., 414/251-4455

Best Casual Dining
The Barley Pop Pub
  16137 Main St., 414/255-2086

Best Steaks
Lohmann's Steak House
  W183N9609 Appleton Ave., 414/251-8430

GREEN BAY, WI

Best Bar
Gipper's Sports Bar and Grill
  1860 University Ave., 920/435-1515

Best Barbecue/Ribs
Wally's Spot Supper Club
  1979 Main St., 920/468-7924

Best Breakfast
Peytons
  Best Western Midway Hotel, 780 Packer Dr.,
    920/499-3161

Best Burgers
Settlement Inn
  3254 Bay Settlement Rd., 920/465-8415

Best Chinese Food
Lee's Pandas Wok Restaurant
  2247 University Ave., 920/468-1370
Mandarin Garden Restaurant
  2394 S. Oneida St., 920/499-4459

Best Family Restaurant
Bay Family Restaurant
  1245 E. Mason St., 920/437-9020
Metz's On B Street
  116 S. Broadway, De Pere, 920/337-4717
Peyton's Restaurant
  780 Packer Dr., 920/499-3161

Best Fine Dining
Chanterelle's
  2638 Bay Settlement Rd., 920/469-3200
The Wellington
  1060 Hansen Rd., 920/499-2000

Best German Food
Lorelei Inn
  1412 S. Webster Ave., 920/432-5921

Best Ice Cream/Yogurt
Hansen's Dairy Stores
  multiple locations

Best Italian Food
Victoria's
  2610 Bay Settlement Rd., 920/468-8070

Best Mexican Food
Los Banditos
  1258 Main St., 920/432-9462
  2335 W. Mason St., 920/494-4505

Best Pizza
Green Bay Pizza Company
  2229 University Ave., 920/465-9555
Jake's Pizza
  1149 Main St., 920/432-8012

Best Sandwiches
Erbert and Gerbert's Subs and Clubs
  227 N. Washington St., 920/435-7827

Best Seafood
Eagle's Nest Supper Club
  3261 Nicolet Dr., 920/468-0976

Best Sports Bar
Stadium View
  1963 Holmgren Way, 920/498-1989

Coaches Corner
  501 N. Adams St., 920/435-9599

Best Steaks
Kroll's East
  1658 Main St., 920/468-4422
Kroll's West Restaurant
  1990 S. Ridge Rd., 920/497-1111
Settlement Inn
  3254 Bay Settlement Rd., 920/465-8415

JANESVILLE, WI

Best American Food
Cherry's Steak and Prime
  13 N. Franklin St., 608/754-9775

Cornerstone Restaurant
2601 Morse St., 608/754-1919
Wedge Inn East
3443 E. Milwaukee St., 608/757-1626

Best Bar
Looking Glass
18 N. Main St., 608/755-9828

Best Barbecue/Ribs
Harpo's West
5201 W. State Rd. 11, 608/752-8886

Best Burgers
Geri's Hamburgers
702 Center Ave., 608/754-0838

Best Business Lunch
Looking Glass
18 N. Main St., 608/755-9828

Best Casual Dining
Duck Inn
N1416 State Rd. 89, Delevan, 608/883-6988
Jumbo's Pub
1110 Kellogg Ave., 608/752-9566
Liberty Station Fine Food
231 Front St., Milton, 608/868-2873
Roherty's
2121 Milton Ave., 608/752-2393

Best Chinese Food
Rice Bowl Restaurant
1917 Center Ave., 608/756-3533
Yummy Wok
2600 E. Milwaukee St., 608/754-5535

Best Diner
Geri's Hamburgers
702 Center Ave., 608/754-0838

Best Family Restaurant
Jessica's Restaurant and Bakery
2339 Milton Ave., 608/757-2377
Park City Family Restaurant
2002 E. Milwaukee St., 608/754-8181

Best Fine Dining
Campi's Restaurant and Lounge
4323 Milton Ave., 608/758-0321
Hoffman House
3431 Milton Ave., 608/756-2313

Best Italian Food
Frankie's on Main
54 S. Main St., 608/758-1888

Best Mexican Food
El Mariachi Southwest Cafe
307 W. Milwaukee St., 608/752-8271
La Cosina
1026 N. Washington St., 608/757-0065

Best Pizza
Lisa Pizzeria
  1650 Center Ave., 608/756-1117
Tony and Maria's
  1503 Milton Ave., 608/754-9543

Best Sandwiches
Cousin's Subs
  2528 E. U.S. Hwy. 14, 608/757-2733

Best Steaks
Cherry's Steak and Prime
  13 N. Franklin St., 608/754-9775
Prime Quarter
  1900 Old Humes Rd., 608/752-1881

KENOSHA, WI

Best Breakfast
Taste of Wisconsin
  7515 125th Ave., 414/857-9110

Best Chinese Food
China House
  4221 75th St., 414/694-0555

Best Homestyle Food
Taste of Wisconsin
  7515 125th Ave., 414/857-9110

Best Italian Food
Mangia Trattoria
  5717 Sheridan Rd., 414/652-4285
Pasta al Dente
  3715 80th St., 414/694-8844

Best Mexican Food
La Hacienda
  3823 22nd Ave., 414/658-2950

Best Pizza
Ruffolo's I
  4621 38th Ave., 414/656-0685
Ruffolo's II
  3931 45th St., 414/656-0441
Ruffolo's III
  11820 Sheridan Rd., 414/694-4003

Best Restaurant in Town
Mangia Trattoria
  5717 Sheridan Rd., 414/652-4285
Ray Radigan's Restaurant
  11712 Sheridan Rd., 414/694-0455

Best Sandwiches
Big Apple Bagel
  5902 75th St., 414/694-2330

LA CROSSE, WI

Best American Food
Mr. D's Restaurant and Bakery
  1146 State St., 608/784-6737

Best Bar
Alpine Inn
  W5717 Bliss Rd., 608/784-8470
Bikini Yacht Club Marina
  621 Park Plaza Dr., 608/784-0556
Freight House Restaurant
  107 Vine St., 608/784-6211
Howie's Hof Brau
  1128 La Crosse St., 608/784-7400
Nut Bush City Limits
  3264 W. George St., La Crosse, 608/783-0228
Recovery Room Tavern
  901 Seventh St. S., 608/782-8573

Best Barbecue/Ribs
Piggy's of La Crosse
  328 Front St. S., 608/784-4877

Best Breakfast
Fayze's
  135 Fourth St. S, 608/784-9548

Best Burgers
Fayze's
  135 Fourth St. S., 608/784-9548
Howie's Hof Brau
  1128 La Crosse St., 608/784-7400

Best Business Lunch
Picasso's Cafe
  600 Third St. N., 608/784-4485

Best Chinese Food
Dragon
  1812 Jackson St., 608/782-1334
Hunan Chinese Restaurant
  318 Fourth St. S., 608/784-7878

Best Desserts
Picasso's Cafe
  600 Third St. N., 608/784-4485

Best Greek/Mediterranean Food
Casablanca
  117 Second Ave. S., Onalaska, 608/783-7880

Best Health-Conscious Menu
Tom's Turkey Express
  223 Third St. S., 608/784-8667

Best Homestyle Food
New Villa
  2132 Ward Ave., 608/788-4400

Best Italian Food
Di Sciascio's Coon Creek Inn
  110 Central Ave., Coon Valley, 608/452-3182

Best Pizza
Big Al's Pizzeria
  115 Third St. S., 608/782-7550
Edwardo's Pizza Wagon
  1930 Rose St., 608/783-8282
Pizza Doctors
  624 King St., 608/784-0450

Pizza King
  2929 South Ave., 608/788-1926

Best Restaurant In Town
Boatworks
  200 Harborview Plz., 608/784-6680
Ed Sullivan's
  W25709 Sullivan Rd., Trempealeau, 608/534-7775
Freight House Restaurant
  107 Vine St., 608/784-6211
Traditions
  201 Main St., Onalaska, 608/783-0200

Best Salad/Salad Bar
Ed Sullivan's
  W25709 Sullivan Rd., Trempealeau, 608/534-7775
Lindy's Subs and Salads
  700 Third St. N., 608/785-7200
Picasso's Cafe
  600 Third St. N., 608/784-4485

Best Sandwiches
Lindy's Subs and Salads
  700 Third St. N., 608/785-7200
Piggy's on Front Catering
  328 Front St. S., 608/784-4877
State Street Deli
  1820 State St., 608/784-1820
Tom's Turkey Express
  223 Third St. S., 608/784-8667

Best Seafood
Freight House Restaurant
  107 Vine St., 608/784-6211
New Villa
  2132 Ward Ave., 608/788-4400

Best Steaks
Freight House Restaurant
  107 Vine St., 608/784-6211

Best Vegetarian Food
Mr. D's Restaurant and Bakery
  1146 State St., 608/784-6737

W

MADISON, WI

Best American Food
Dairyland Family Restaurant
  716 Cottage Grove Rd., 608/222-9232
Opera House
  117 Martin Luther King Jr. Blvd., 608/284-8466

Best Bar
Badger Bowl
  506 E. Badger Rd., 608/274-6662

Best Barbecue/Ribs
Big Mama and Uncle Fats'
  6824 Odana Rd., 608/829-2683

Best Beer Selection
Come Back In
  508 E. Wilson St., 608/258-8619

Best Breakfast
C's Restaurant Bakery and Coffee
  2622 Allen Blvd., Middleton, 608/836-4700
Mickie's Dairy Bar
  1511 Monroe St., 608/256-9476

Best Brewpub
Angelic Brewing Company
  322 W. Johnson St., 608/257-2707
Great Dane Pub and Brewing Company
  123 E. Doty St., 608/284-0000

Best Burgers
Culver's Frozen Custard
  2906 W. Beltline Hwy., Middleton, 608/836-5577
Dotty Dumpling's Dowry
  116 N. Fairchild St., 608/255-3175
Nau-Ti-Gal
  5360 Westport Rd., 608/246-3130
Oakcrest Tavern
  5371 Old Middleton Rd., 608/233-1243
Plaza Tavern
  319 N. Henry St., 608/255-6592
Short Stop Grill and Pub
  608 W. Verona Ave., Verona, 608/845-9669

Best Business Lunch
The Dayton Street Cafe
  The Madison Hotel and Governors Club,
    1 W. Dayton St., 608/257-6000

Best Cajun/Creole Food
Da' Cajun Way
  2611 Monroe St., 608/233-5380
Louisianne's
  7464 Hubbard Ave., Middleton, 608/831-1929

Best Chinese Food
Hong Kong Cafe
  2 S. Mills St., 608/259-1668
Imperial Garden
  4214 E. Washington Ave., 608/249-0466
Imperial Palace
  1291 N. Sherman Ave., 608/241-7708
Red Pepper Chinese Restaurant
  1518 N. Stoughton Rd., 608/249-1373

Best Coffee/Coffeehouse
Ancora Coffee House and Roasterie
  112 King St., 608/255-2900
Arthouse Cafe
  2827 Atwood Ave., 608/242-7151
Cafe Assisi
  254 W. Gilman St., 608/255-1816
Canterbury Booksellers Coffeehouse Inn
  315 W. Gorham St., 608/258-9911
Gloria Jean's Gourmet Coffee
  40 W. Towne Mall, 608/829-2739
  171 E. Towne Mall, 608/244-4776
Steep and Brew
  multiple locations

Sunporch Cafe Restaurant
  2701 University Ave., 608/231-1111
Sunprint Cafe
  704 S. Whitney Way, 608/274-7374
The Good Day Coffee Shop
  101 S. Webster St., 608/251-0157
Victor Allen's Coffee and Tea
  multiple locations

Best Continental Food
L' Etoile Restaurant
  25 N. Pinckney St., 608/251-0500

Best Delicatessen
Delitalia
  7854 Mineral Point Rd., 608/833-3354
  2850 University Ave., 608/233-4800
Ella's Deli
  425 State St., 608/257-8611
  2902 E. Washington Ave., 608/241-5291
Gino's
  540 State St., 608/257-9022
Radical Rye
  231 State St., 608/256-1200

Best Desserts
Canterbury Booksellers Coffeehouse Inn
  315 W. Gorham St., 608/258-9911
Clasen's European Bakery
  7610 Donna Dr., Middleton, 608/831-2032
Ella's Deli
  2902 E. Washington Ave., 608/241-5291
  425 State St., 608/257-8611
Michael's Frozen Custard
  3826 Atwood Ave., 608/222-4110
  2531 Monroe St., 608/231-3500
  407 W. Verona Ave., 608/845-8887
  5602 Shroeder Rd., 608/276-8100

Best Diner
Cleveland Diner
  410 E. Wilson St., 608/251-4455
The Curve
  653 S. Park St., 608/251-0311
Monty's Blue Plate
  2089 Atwood Ave., 608/244-8505

Best Dinner
Coyote Capers
  1201 Williamson St., 608/251-1313

Best Fine Dining
Blue Marlin
  101 N. Hamilton St., 608/255-2255
L'Etoile Restaurant
  25 N. Pinckney St., 608/251-0500
Otto's Restaurant and Bar
  6405 Mineral Point Rd., 608/274-4044

Best German Food
Brat Und Brau
  234 E. Towne Mall, 608/249-1011

W

Essen Haus
514 E. Wilson St., 608/255-4674

Best Greek/Mediterranean Food
Bavaria Family Restaurant
7457 Elmwood Ave., Middleton, 608/836-6614
Husnu's
547 State St., 608/256-0900
Kostas On State
117 State St., 608/255-6671

Best Ice Cream/Yogurt
Babcock Hall Dairy Store
1605 Linden Dr., 608/262-3045
Chocolate Shoppe
702 N. Midvale Blvd., 608/233-5866
2221 Daniels St., 608/221-8640
468 State St., 608/255-5454
1726 Fordem Ave., 608/241-2747
Freshens
237 E. Towne Mall, 608/244-3237
Michael's Frozen Custard
2531 Monroe St., 608/231-3500
3826 Atwood Ave., 608/222-4110
Yogurt Express
2701G University Ave., 608/233-4313
499 State St., 608/255-9876

Best Italian Food
Antonio's
1109 S. Park St., 608/251-1412
Cafe Romeo
702 N. Midvale Blvd., 608/231-9899
Portabella's
425 N. Frances St., 608/256-3186

Best Mexican Food
Pasqual's Southwestern Deli
2534 Monroe St., 608/238-4419
2098 Atwood Ave., 608/244-3142
Pedro's
3555 E. Washington Ave., 608/241-8110
Taqueria Gila Monster
106 King St., 608/255-6425

Best Middle Eastern Food
Lu Lu's Deli and Restaurant
2524 University Ave., 608/233-2172

Best Other Ethnic Food
Horn of Africa (African)
117 E. Mifflin St., 608/255-2077

Best Pizza
Buck's Pizza
525 S. Midvale Blvd., 608/238-9166
Paison's
80 University Square, 608/257-3832
Pizza Extreme
605 E. Washington Ave., 608/259-1500
Pizzeria Uno
222 W. Gorham St., 608/255-7722

W

7601 Mineral Point Rd., 608/833-7200
Rocky Roco Pan Style Pizza
    1618 W. Beltline Hwy., 608/251-0304
    4556 Monona Dr., 608/221-3818

Best Place to Take the Kids
Chuck E. Cheese Pizza
    438 Grand Canyon Dr., 608/829-2000

Best Sandwiches
Ella's Deli
    2902 E. Washington Ave., 608/241-5291
    425 State St., 608/257-8611
Radical Rye
    231 State St., 608/256-1200

Best Seafood
Blue Marlin
    101 N. Hamilton St., 608/255-2255
Captain Bill's
    2701 Century Harbor Rd., 608/831-7327
Mariner's Inn
    5339 Lighthouse Bay Dr., 608/246-3120

Best Southwestern Food
Deb and Lola's Restaurant
    227 State St., 608/255-0820

Best Spanish Food
LaPaella
    2784 S. Fish Hatchery Rd., 608/273-2666

Best Steaks
Delaney's Charcoal Steaks
    449 Grand Canyon Dr., 608/833-7337
Mariner's Inn
    5339 Lighthouse Bay Dr., 608/246-3120
Prime Quarter
    3520 E. Washington Ave., 608/244-3520
Smoky's Club
    3005 University Ave., 608/233-2120
Tornado Club Steak House
    116 S. Hamilton St., 608/256-3570

Best Sunday Brunch
Dry Bean
    5264 Verona Rd., 608/274-2326
Nau-ti-Gal
    5360 Westport Rd., 608/246-3130
White Horse Inn
    202 N. Henry St., 608/255-9933

Best Thai Food
Bahn Thai Restaurant
    944 Williamson St., 608/256-0202
    2809 University Ave., 608/233-3900

Best Vegetarian Food
Savory Thymes
    1146 Williamson St., 608/255-2292
Sunporch
    2701 University Ave., 608/231-1111

W

Sunprint Cafe
704 S. Whitney Way, 608/274-7374
Sunroom Cafe
638 State St., 608/255-1555

MANITOWAC, WI

Best Breakfast
Four Seasons Family Restaurant
3950 Calumet Ave., 920/683-1444

Best Burgers
Dugout
4117 Broadway St., 920/684-1622
Penquin Drive In Restaurant
3900 Calumet Ave., 920/684-6403

Best Chinese Food
Chinatown Kitchen
807 Buffalo St., 920/683-9330
Jade Palace
1103 S. Tenth St., 920/682-5352

Best Desserts
Inn on Maritime Bay
101 Maritime Dr., 920/682-7000
Machut's Supper Club
3911 Lincoln Ave., Two Rivers, 920/793-9432

Best Ice Cream/Yogurt
Cedar Crest Specialties
2000 S. Tenth St., 920/682-5577

Best Pizza
Luigi's Pizza Palace III
6124 U.S. Hwy. 151, 920/684-4200
Tony's Pizza
2204 Washington St., 920/682-8669

Best Sandwiches
Butch's Osman Oasis
10731 State Rd. 42, Newton, 920/726-4311

Best Seafood
Machut's Supper Club
3911 Lincoln Ave., Two Rivers, 920/793-9432

Best Steaks
Machut's Supper Club
3911 Lincoln Ave., Two Rivers, 920/793-9432
Stock's Dinner Club
8330 Center Rd., Newton, 920/726-4404

W

MARSHFIELD, WI

Best American Food
Pinewood Supper Club
1208 Half Moon Lake Dr., Mosinee, 715/693-3180
Severt's Fine Foods
421 S. Central Ave., 715/384-4431

Best Breakfast
Country Kitchen
1209 S. Central Ave., 715/387-3445

Best Burgers
Cousin's Steakhouse
  10500 State Hwy. 13, 715/389-1865

Best Casual Dining
Crabby Dave's
  501 S. Central Ave., 715/384-4868
Palomino's
  1414 W. McMillan St., 715/387-3842

Best Chinese Food
China Chef
  168 S. Central Ave., 715/384-9004

Best Dinner
Belvedere Supper Club
  329M State Hwy. 97, 715/387-4161

Best Family Restaurant
Antlers Supper Club
  1126 County Rd., Mosinee, 715/693-5050

Best Lunch
Kitchen Table
  118 E. Third St., 715/387-2601

Best Sports Bar
Palomino's
  1414 W. McMillan St., 715/387-3842

Best Steaks
Cousin's Steakhouse
  10500 State Hwy. 13, 715/389-1865

Best Sunday Brunch
Marshfield Inn
  116 W. Ives St., 715/387-6381

MENOMONEE FALLS, WI

Best Bar
Waldo Peppers
  2903 N. Grandview Blvd., Pewaukee, 414/524-9989

Best Burgers
Centennial Bar and Grille
  10352 N. Port Washington Rd., Mequon,
    414/241-4353

Best Casual Dining
Betsy's Bar and Restaurant
  N88W16495 Main St., 414/251-9852
Pop's Frozen Custard
  N87W16459 Appleton Ave., 414/251-3320
Trysting
  N71W12980 Appleton Ave., 414/255-4110

Best Chinese Food
Harvey Moy's
  N89W16754 Appleton Ave., 414/255-3307

Best Desserts
Cream and Crepe Cafe
  N70W6340 Bridge Rd., Cedarburg, 414/377-0900

W

Best Family Restaurant
JJ's Restaurant
  N96W16865 Cumberland Ct., 414/251-8330

Best French Food
Cream and Crepe Cafe
  N70W6340 Bridge Rd., Cedarburg, 414/377-0900

Best Homestyle Food
Colonial Restaurant
  N89W16829 Appleton Ave., 414/255-4544

Best Pizza
Alioto's Pizza
  N86W16396 Appleton Ave., 414/251-1800
Mancino's Grinders and Pizza
  W186N9515 Bancroft Dr., 414/250-1717

Best Sandwiches
Betsy's Bar and Restaurant
  N88W16495 Main St., 414/251-9852

Best Steaks
Club Forest
  4200 W. County Line Rd. 96N, Mequon,
    414/238-0876

Best Sunday Brunch
Boder's on the River
  11919 N. River Rd., Mequon, 414/242-0335
La Par - Silver Spring Country Club
  N56W21318 Silver Spring Dr., 414/252-4994
Seven Seas
  1807 Nagawicka Rd., Hartland, 414/367-3903

MILWAUKEE, WI

Best Barbecue/Ribs
Butler Inn
  12400 W. Hampton Ave., Butler, 414/783-5899
Pitch's Kansas City Style
  11320 W. Bluemound Rd., 414/774-7180
Saz's Grand Avenue
  275 W. Wisconsin Ave., 414/273-4404
Saz's State House
  5539 W. State St., 414/453-2410

Best Brewpub
Lakefront Brewery
  818 E. Chambers St., 414/372-8800

Best Burgers
Kopp's Frozen Custard
  5373 N. Port Washington Rd., 414/961-2006
  7631 W. Layton Ave., 414/282-4080
Solly's Coffee Shop
  4629 N. Port Washington Rd., 414/332-8808

Best Cajun/Creole Food
Crawdaddy's Cajun and Creole
  6501 W. Greenfield Ave., 414/778-2228

Best Chinese Food
East Garden Chinese Restaurant
  3600 N. Oakland Ave., 414/962-7460

W

Emperor of China
1010 E. Brady St., 414/271-8889
Toy's Chinatown Restaurant
830 N. Third St., 414/271-5166
Yen Ching Restaurant
7630 W. Good Hope Rd., 414/353-6677

Best Coffee/Coffeehouse
Brewed Awakenings
1208 E. Brady St., 414/276-2739
Coffee Trader
2625 N. Downer Ave., 414/332-9690
Fuel Cafe
818 E. Center St., 414/374-3835
Gil's Espresso Bongo Lounge
2608 N. Downer Ave., 414/964-4455

Best Delicatessen
Benji's Delicatessen and Restaurant
4156 N. Oakland Ave., 414/332-7777

Best Desserts
Baker's Square Restaurant
10200 W. National Ave., 414/546-1220
7320 W. Good Hope Rd., 414/353-0200
Sanford Restaurant
1547 N. Jackson St., 414/276-9608

Best Diner
Ed Debevic's
780 N. Jefferson St., 414/226-2200

Best Family Restaurant
Omega Family Restaurant
7822 W. Capitol Dr., 414/438-0370
3473 S. 27th St., 414/645-6595
7727 W. Greenfield Ave., 414/774-4460

Best Fine Dining
Sanford Restaurant
1547 N. Jackson St., 414/276-9608

Best French Food
Grenadier's
747 N. Broadway, 414/276-0747

Best German Food
Bavarian Wurst Haus Restaurant
8310 W. Appleton Ave., 414/464-0060
John Ernst Restaurant
600 E. Ogden Ave., 414/273-1878
Karl Ratzsch's Restaurant
320 E. Mason St., 414/276-2720
Mader's German Restaurant
1037 N. Third St., 414/271-3377

Best Greek/Mediterranean Food
Mykonos Restaurant
8501 W. Capitol Dr., 414/438-1939
Oakland Gyros
2867 N. Oakland Ave., 414/963-1393

Best Indian Food
Jee Shah Restaurant
   1854 E. Kenilworth Pl., 414/273-2625
Taste of India
   10900 W. Bluemound Rd., 414/259-9200

Best Italian Food
Bartolotta's Restaurant
   7616 W. State St., 414/771-7910
Giovanni's Restaurant
   1683 N. Van Buren St., 414/291-5600
Maniaci's Cafe Siciliano
   6904 N. Santa Monica Blvd., 414/352-5757
Mimma's Cafe
   1307 E. Brady St., 414/271-7337

Best Japanese Food
Izumi's Restaurant
   2178 N. Prospect Ave., 414/271-5278
Tokyo Japanese Restaurant
   12950 W. Bluemound Rd., Elm Grove,
      414/797-7818

Best Late-Night Food
Eagan's on Water
   1030 N. Water St., 414/271-6900
Elsa's on the Park
   833 N. Jefferson St., 414/765-0615
Ma Fisher's Family Restaurant
   2214 N. Farwell Ave., 414/271-7424
Pizza Man
   1800 E. North Ave., 414/272-1745
Red Mill
   1005 S. Elm Grove Rd., Brookfield, 414/782-8780
Saz's Grand Avenue
   275 W. Wisconsin Ave., 414/273-4404

Best Mexican Food
El Sombrero Restaurant
   809 S. Sixteenth St., 414/649-9449
Jalisco Restaurant
   2207 E. North Ave., 414/291-0645
La Fuente Restaurant
   625 S. Fifth St., 414/271-8595
Rudy's Mexican Restaurant
   631 S. Fifth St., 414/291-0296
Tres Hermano's Restaurant
   1100 W. National Ave., 414/384-8850
   1332 W. Lincoln Ave., 414/384-9050

Best Middle Eastern Food
Au Bon Appetit
   1016 E. Brady St., 414/278-1233
Shahrazad Middle Eastern
   2847 N. Oakland Ave., 414/964-5475

Best Other Ethnic Food
Cracovia Restaurant (Polish)
   1531 W. Lincoln Ave., 414/383-8688
Old Town Serbian Gourmet House (Serbian)
   522 W. Lincoln Ave., 414/672-0206

W

Three Brothers Restaurant (Serbian)
2414 S. St. Clair St., 414/481-7530

Best Outdoor Dining
Brew City Barbecue
1114 N. Water St., 414/278-7033
Cafe Knickerbocker
1030 E. Juneau Ave., 414/272-0011
Miro's Serbian Cafe
2499 N. Bartlett Ave., 414/964-9220

Best Pizza
Balistreri's Italian-American Ristorante
812 N. 68th St., 414/475-1414
Edwardo's Natural Pizza Restaurant
700 E. Kilbourn Ave., 414/277-8080
10845 W. Bluemound Rd., 414/771-7770
Lisa's Pizzeria Restaurant
2961 N. Oakland Ave., 414/332-6360
Zaffiro's Pizza and Bar
1724 N. Farwell Ave., 414/289-8776

Best Restaurant in Town
English Room
424 E. Wisconsin Ave., 414/273-8222
Grenadier's
747 N. Broadway, 414/276-0747
Pandl's in Bayside
8825 N. Lake Dr., 414/352-7300

Best Romantic Dining
Boulevard Inn
925 E. Wells St., 414/765-1166
Columns
3445 W. Edgerton Ave., 414/281-4422
English Room
424 E. Wisconsin Ave., 414/273-8222
Harold's Restaurant
4747 S. Howell Ave., 414/481-8000

Best Salad/Salad Bar
Coffee Trader
2625 N. Downer Ave., 414/332-9690

Best Seafood
Anchorage Restaurant
4700 N. Port Washington Rd., 414/962-4710
Nantucket Shores Restaurant
924 E. Juneau Ave., 414/278-8660
Red Rock Cafe
4022 N. Oakland Ave., 414/962-4545
River Lane Inn
4313 W. River Ln., 414/354-1995

Best Soul Food
Nita's Soul Food Kitchen
2510 N. Teutonia Ave., 414/374-0911

Best Sports Bar
Luke's Sport's Spectacular
1225 N. Water St., 414/223-3210
Major Goolsby's
340 W. Kilbourne Ave., 414/271-3414

Best Steaks
Clock Steak House
  720 N. Plankinton Ave., 414/272-1278
Coerper's 5 O'Clock Club
  2416 W. State St., 414/342-3553
Jake's Restaurant
  6030 W. North Ave., 414/771-0550
Third Street Pier
  1110 N. Old World Third St., 414/272-0330

Best Sunday Brunch
Cafe Rouge
  424 E. Wisconsin Ave., 414/273-8222
Pandl's In Bayside
  8825 N. Lake Dr., 414/352-7300
Pieces Of Eight Restaurant
  550 N. Harbor Dr., 920/271-0597

Best Thai Food
King and I Thai Restaurant
  823 N. Second St., 920/276-4181
  7225 N. 76th St., 920/353-6069
Siam Restaurant
  314 W. Juneau Ave., 920/272-4933

Best Vegetarian Food
Beans and Barley Market and Cafe
  1901 E. North Ave., 920/278-7878

Best Vietnamese Food
West Bank Cafe
  732 E. Burleigh St., 920/562-5555

OSHKOSH, WI

Best Bar
Tony's Place
  556 W. Seventh Ave., 414/235-4447

Best Breakfast
Annie's American Cafe
  1930 Omro Rd., 414/233-7880

Best Chinese Food
Great Wall Restaurant and Lounge
  700 N. Koeller St., 414/231-1828

Best Homestyle Food
Annie's American Cafe
  1930 Omro Rd., 414/233-7880

Best Italian Food
Vitale's Italian Cuisine
  307 W. Murdock Ave., 414/426-0886

Best Seafood
Granary Restaurant
  50 W. Sixth Ave., 414/233-3929

Best Steaks
Granary Restaurant
  50 W. Sixth Ave., 414/233-3929

W

RACINE, WI

Best Burgers
Ritzy's Restaurant
  5821 Washington Ave., 414/886-3121

Best Business Lunch
Main Street Bistro
  340 S. Main St., 414/637-4340

Best Casual Dining
Chancery Pub and Restaurant
  6430 Washington Ave., 414/886-5600

Best Chinese Food
Great Wall Chinese Restaurant
  6025 Washington Ave., 414/886-9700

Best Desserts
Main Street Bistro
  340 S. Main St., 414/637-4340

Best Family Restaurant
Chancery Pub and Restaurant
  6430 Washington Ave., 414/886-5600

Best Fine Dining
Main Street Bistro
  340 S. Main St., 414/637-4340

Best Inexpensive Meal
Athan's Family Restaurant
  2100 Douglas Ave., 414/633-8060
Infusino's Pizzeria
  3301 Washington Ave., 414/634-2727

Best Italian Food
Infusino's Pizzeria
  3301 Washington Ave., 414/634-2727
Totero's
  2343 Mead St., 414/634-9488

Best Mexican Food
Tacos El Rey
  2207 Lathrop Ave., 414/632-6340

Best Pizza
Derango's Pizza Palace
  3840 Douglas Ave., 414/639-4112
Infusino's Pizzeria
  3301 Washington Ave., 414/634-2727

Best Sandwiches
Chancery Pub and Restaurant
  6430 Washington Ave., 414/886-5600

Best Seafood
Chartroom
  209 Dodge St., 414/632-9901

Best Steaks
Corner House
  1521 Washington Ave., 414/637-1295

W

SHEBOYGAN, WI

Best Breakfast
Sy's Restaurant
1735 Calumet Dr., 920/452-7850

Best Chinese Food
Imperial Palace
2910 Kohler Memorial Dr., 920/452-2291

Best Coffee/Coffeehouse
Golden Palate Delicatessen
632 N. Eighth St., 920/457-6565

Best Desserts
Randall's Frozen Custard
3827 Superior Ave., 920/458-9699

Best Family Restaurant
Faye's Pizza
1821 Calumet Dr., 920/458-4171

Best Ice Cream/Yogurt
Randall's Frozen Custard
3827 Superior Ave., 920/458-9699

Best Italian Food
Trattoria Stefano
522 S. Eighth St., 920/452-8455

Best Pizza
Faye's Pizza
1821 Calumet Dr., 920/458-4171

Best Sandwiches
Ella's Dela Delicatessen
1113 N. Eighth St., 920/457-3034
Golden Palate Delicatessen
632 N. Eighth St., 920/457-6565

Best Steaks
Immigrant Restaurant and Winery
407 Highland Dr., Kohler, 920/457-8888

STEVENS POINT, WI

Best American Food
Arbuckle's Eatery
1320 Strongs Ave., 715/341-2444
Red Mill Country Inn
209 U.S. Hwy. 10W, 715/341-7714

Best Barbecue/Ribs
Mesquite Grill
1501 Northpoint Dr., 715/341-1340

Best Breakfast
Blueberry Muffin Restaurant
2801 Stanley St., 715/341-1993
Wooden Chair
1059 Main St., 715/341-1133

Best Cajun/Creole Food
Silver Coach
38 Park Ridge Dr., 715/341-6588

W

Best Coffee/Coffeehouse
Supreme Bean
1100A Main St., Ste. 1, 715/344-0077

Best Desserts
Blueberry Muffin Restaurant
2801 Stanley St., 715/341-1993

Best Dinner
Hot Fish Shop
1140 Clark St., 715/344-4252

Best Fine Dining
Bernard's Continental Restaurant
701 Second St. N., 715/344-3365
The Restaurant
1800 Northpoint Dr., 715/346-6010

Best Ice Cream/Yogurt
Belt's Soft Serve
2140 Division St., 715/344-0049
Sweet Treats
913 Main St., 715/341-4990

Best Italian Food
Pagliacci Taverna
1800 N. Point Dr., 715/346-6010

Best Lunch
Hilltop Pub and Grill
4901 U.S. Hwy. 10E, 715/341-3037
Sport Plate
601 N. Michigan Ave., 715/345-1600

Best Salad/Salad Bar
Wooden Chair
1059 Main St., 715/341-1133

Best Seafood
Hot Fish Shop
1140 Clark St., 715/344-4252
Pagliacci Taverna
1800 N. Point Dr., 715/346-6010

Best Steaks
Silver Coach
38 Park Ridge Dr., 715/341-6588

Best Sunday Brunch
Mesquite Grill
1501 Northpoint Dr., 715/341-1340

WAUKESHA, WI

Best Bar
Chancery Pub and Restaurant
2100 E. Moreland Blvd., 414/549-1720

Best Burgers
First Precinct Steak House
13995 W. National Ave., New Berlin, 414/785-0277
Red Rooster Inn
N14 W22032 Watertown Rd., 414/547-6668

Best Business Lunch
Chancery Pub and Restaurant
2100 E. Moreland Blvd., 414/549-1720

Best Casual Dining
Michael's Italian-American Restaurant
1400 S. Grand Ave., 414/549-0406

Best Chinese Food
Ching Hwa Chinese Restaurant
1947 E. Main St., 414/544-1983

Best Delicatessen
Strand Foods and Deli
1218 The Strand, 414/547-5835

Best Family Restaurant
Baker's Square Restaurant
1430 Moreland Blvd., 414/544-2023

Best Fine Dining
Steven Wade's Cafe
17001 W. Greenfield Ave., New Berlin,
414/784-0774

Best German Food
Gasthaus
2720 N. Grandview Blvd., 414/544-4460

Best Ice Cream/Yogurt
Charlene Kaye's Ice Cream and Sandwich Shop
280 W. Broadway, 414/521-3250

Best Italian Food
Carmille's Fattoria
105 Main St., Eagle, 414/594-5444
Michael's Italian-American Restaurant
1400 S. Grand Ave., 414/549-0406

Best Mexican Food
Jalisco Restaurant
1120 Whiterock Ave., 414/521-1986

Best Pizza
Michael's Italian-American Restaurant
1400 S. Grand Ave., 414/549-0406

Best Romantic Dining
Heaven City Restaurant
S91W27850 National Ave., Mukwonago,
414/363-5191

Best Steaks
Di Miceli's Rafters
7228 S. 27th St., Oak Creek, 414/761-2222

WAUSAU, WI

Best American Food
Annie's American Cafe
305 S. Eighteenth Ave., 715/842-0846
Billy Moy's
1819 Stewart Ave., 715/845-2237
Emma's Bakery Cafe
710 N. Second St., 715/235-1600

Best Breakfast
Tri-City Family Restaurant
  525 Grand Ave., Schofield, 715/359-9596

Best Burgers
Wausau Mine Company
  3904 Stewart Ave., 715/845-7304

Best Casual Dining
Chapter Two
  1810 Merrill Ave., 715/675-9855

Best Chinese Food
Peking Chinese and American Restaurant
  221 Scott St., 715/842-8080

Best Desserts
2510 Restaurant
  2510 Stewart Ave., 715/845-2510

Best Family Restaurant
Blue Willow Cafe
  1111 N. Fourth Ave., 715/675-4543
Larry Raymond's At Greenwood
  2002 Poplar Ln., 715/848-2900

Best Homestyle Food
George's Restaurant
  1706 1/2 Stewart Ave., 715/845-7067
Log Cabin Restaurant
  2316 Schofield Ave., Schofield, 715/359-3669

Best Ice Cream/Yogurt
Finnegan's Ice Cream Parlor
  129 N. Third Ave., 715/842-8805

Best Italian Food
Iozzo's Italian Food
  3115 Camp Phillips Rd., 715/848-2202
Mino's Cucina Italiana
  900 Golf Club Rd., 715/675-5939
Wausau Mine Company
  3904 Stewart Ave., 715/845-7304

Best Mexican Food
Chico's

  5704 State Hwy. 52, 715/842-9851
Diamond Dave's Taco Company
  B200 Wausau Ctr., 715/842-9898

Best Pizza
Sam's Pizza Palace
  111 Elm St., 715/842-3165

Best Restaurant In Town
2510 Reflections Bakery and Deli
  2510 Stewart Ave., 715/845-2510

Best Seafood
Gulliver's Landing
  2204 Rib Mountain Dr., 715/842-9098
Palms Supper Club
  5912 U.S. Hwy. 51S, Schofield, 715/359-2200

Best Steaks
Captain's Restaurant
1914 W. Stewart Ave., 715/842-2271
Michael's Supper Club
2901 Rib Mountain Dr., 715/842-9856
Palms Supper Club
5912 U.S. Hwy. 51S, Schofield, 715/359-2200

Best Sunday Brunch
Hoffman House
2901 Martin Ave., 715/842-1656

WEST BEND, WI

Best Barbecue/Ribs
Walden Supper Club
2472 Wallace Lake Rd., 414/334-4664

Best Burgers
J.D. Tasha's
147 N. Main St., 414/338-8200

Best Chinese Food
China Palace
817 S. Main St., 414/334-5952

Best Coffee/Coffeehouse
Devon Delights
102 N. Main St., 414/335-1811

Best Continental Food
Old Courthouse Inn
518 Poplar St., 414/335-6302

Best Ice Cream/Yogurt
Toucan Food and Custard
600 N. Main St., 414/338-8444

Best Pizza
Dick's Pizzaria
1750 W. Washington St., 414/334-2591

Best Steaks
Coachman House Supper Club
1006 S. Main St., 414/334-9491
White Tail Inn
5802 State Road 144S, 414/644-5553

W

WISCONSIN DELLS, WI

Best American Food
Houlihan's Restaurant and Bar
644 Wisconsin Dells Pkwy., 608/253-9109

Best Bar
Monk's Bar and Grill
220 Broadway, 608/254-2955

Best Breakfast
Mr. Pancake
1405 Wisconsin Dells Pkwy., 608/253-3663

Best Casual Dining
Cheese Factory Restaurant
521 Wisconsin Dells Pkwy., 608/253-6065

Best Dinner
Fischer's Supper Club
   441 U.S. Hwy. 12, Lake Delton, 608/253-7531
Ishnala Supper Club
   S2011 Ishnala Rd., Lake Delton, 608/253-1771

Best Family Restaurant
BJ's Restaurant
   1201 Wisconsin Dells Pkwy., 608/254-6278

Best Italian Food
Annie's Port Pizza and Pasta
   S1675 Ishnala Rd., Lake Delton, 608/254-8230

Best Mexican Food
Pedro's Mexican Restaurant
   951 Stand Rock Rd., 608/253-7233

Best Other Ethnic Food
American Club and Polish Buffet (Polish)
   400 County Road A, 608/253-4451

Best Pizza
Firestation Pizza
   420 State Road 13, 608/254-7123
Pizza Pub
   218 Broadway, 608/254-7877
   1455 Wisconsin Dells Pkwy., 608/254-7877

Best Restaurant In Town
Dell Haus
   126 Broadway, 608/253-3501
Park Restaurant
   701 Broadway, 608/254-7116
River Works At The River Inn
   1015 River Rd., 608/253-1231

Best Steaks
Field's Steak and Stein
   4079 State Road 13, 608/254-4841

W

Wyoming

Best Barbecue/Ribs
Chef's Coop
1040 N. Center St., 307/237-1132

Best Breakfast
Casper's Good Cooking
581 N. Poplar St., 307/237-3033

Best Business Lunch
Cafe Jose
1600 E. Second St., 307/235-6599

Best Chinese Food
South Sea Chinese Restaurant
2025 E. Second St., 307/237-4777

Best Dinner
Benham's
739 N. Center St., 307/234-4531

Best Family Restaurant
L.B.M. Pizza
3350 Cy Ave., 307/235-0786

Best Italian Food
Anthony's Upper Crust
241 S. Center St., 307/234-3071
Bosco's Italian Restaurant
847 E. A St., 307/265-9658

Best Lunch
Cottage Cafe
116 S. Lincoln St., 307/234-1157
Garden Creek Cafe
251 S. Center St., 307/265-9018

Best Mexican Food
Cafe Jose
  1600 E. Second St., 307/235-6599
El Jarro Restaurant
  500 W. S St., 307/577-0538

Best Sandwiches
Cheese Barrel
  544 S. Center St., 307/235-5202
Mountain View Sub Shop
  239 E. First St., 307/237-7999

Best Seafood
Goose Egg Inn
  10580 Goose Egg Rd., 307/473-8838

Best Steaks
Goose Egg Inn
  10580 Goose Egg Rd., 307/473-8838

Best Sunday Brunch
Parkway Plaza Cafe
  123 W. E St., 307/235-1777

CHEYENNE, WY

Best Burgers
C.B. & Potts Bighorn Brewery
  1650 Dell Range Blvd., 307/632-8636

Best Business Lunch
Lexie's Cafe
  216 E. Seventeenth St., 307/638-8712

Best Chinese Food
Twin Dragon
  1809 Carey Ave., 307/637-6622

Best Coffee/Coffeehouse
Java Joint
  1720 Capitol Ave., 307/638-7332

Best Fine Dining
Carriage Court
  Hitching Post Inn, 1700 W. Lincolnway,
    307/638-3301
Players Restaurant
  3307 E. Nation Way, 307/637-7339
Poor Richard's
  2233 E. Lincolnway, 307/635-5114

Best Homestyle Food
Cloud Nine Restaurant
  300 E. Eighth Ave., 307/635-1525

Best Italian Food
Avanti Restaurant
  4620 Grandview Ave., 307/634-3432

Best Mexican Food
Estevan's Cafe
  1820 Ridge Rd., 307/632-6828
Los Amigos Mexican Restaurant
  620 Central Ave., 307/638-8691

Best Salad/Salad Bar
The Western Gold Dining Room
  Little America Hotel and Resort, 2800 W.
    Lincolnway, 307/775-8400

Best Sandwiches
Little Philly
  1121 W. Lincolnway, 307/632-6824

Best Steaks
Little Bear Inn
  1700 Little Bear Rd., 307/634-3684
Senator's Steak House
  51 I-25 Service Rd., 307/634-4994

CODY, WY

Best Barbecue/Ribs
M's B Ribs
  1905 Sheridan Ave., 307/527-6373

Best Breakfast
The Irma
  Irma Hotel, 1192 Sheridan Ave., 307/587-4221

Best Burgers
Proud Cut Saloon
  1227 Sheridan Ave., 307/527-6905
Silver Dollar Bar and Grill
  1313 Sheridan Ave., 307/587-3554

Best Coffee/Coffeehouse
Cody Coffee Company
  1702 Sheridan Ave., 307/527-7879
Peter's Cafe Bakery
  1191 Sheridan Ave., 307/527-5040

Best Family Restaurant
Cattleman's Cut
  225 Yellowstone Ave., 307/527-7432
Sunset House Restaurant
  1651 Eighth St., 307/587-2257

Best Homestyle Food
Our Place
  148 Yellowstone Ave., 307/527-4420

Best Italian Food
Franca's Italian Dining
  1421 Rumsey Ave., 307/587-5354

Best Pizza
Pizza on the Run
  1453 Sheridan Ave., 307/527-7862

Best Salad/Salad Bar
Silver Dollar Bar and Grill
  1313 Sheridan Ave., 307/587-3554

Best Sandwiches
Peter's Cafe Bakery
  1191 Sheridan Ave., 307/527-5040

Best Seafood
Black Sheep Restaurant
  1901 Mountain View Dr., 307/527-5895

Best Steaks
Maxwell's
937 Sheridan Ave., 307/527-7749
Proud Cut Saloon
1227 Sheridan Ave., 307/527-6905
Wapiti Lounge and Steakhouse
3189 N. Fork Hwy., Wapiti, 307/587-6659

DOUGLAS, WY

Best All-You-Can-Eat Buffet
Madame Clementine's
1199 Mesa Dr., 307/358-5554

Best Atmosphere
Chutes Eatery and Saloon
Best Western Douglas Inn, 1450 Riverbend Dr.,
307/358-9790
Country Inn
2341 E. Richards St., 307/358-3575

Best Breakfast
Village Inn
1840 Richards St., 307/358-5600

Best Chinese Food
Four Seasons Chinese Restaurant
1120 Richards St., 307/358-5091

Best Health-Conscious Menu
Thru The Grapevine
301 Center St., 307/358-4567

Best Homestyle Food
Village Inn
1840 Richards St., 307/358-5600

Best Ice Cream/Yogurt
Covered Wagon Drive Inn
1728 Richards St., 307/358-5085

Best Mexican Food
La Costa Mexican Restaurant
1213 Teton Way, 307/358-2449
Santa Fe Cafe
1954 Richards St., 307/358-5933

Best Steaks
Country Inn
2341 E. Richards St., 307/358-3575

GILLETTE, WY

Best Bar
Bailey's Bar and Grill
301 S. Gillette Ave., 307/686-7678
Las Margaritas
2107 S. Douglas Hwy., 307/682-6545

Best Breakfast
Village Inn
806 E. Second St., 307/682-8823

Best Casual Dining
Humphrey's Bar and Grill
408 W. Juniper Ln., 307/682-0100

Best Chinese Food
Hong Kong Restaurant
1612 W. Second St., 307/682-5829

Best Coffee/Coffeehouse
Coffee Friends
320 S. Gillette Ave., 307/686-6119

Best Ice Cream/Yogurt
Polar Bear Frozen Yogurt
900 Camel Dr., Ste. GG, 307/682-3155

Best Mexican Food
Las Margaritas
2107 S. Douglas Hwy., 307/682-6545

Best Salad/Salad Bar
Bailey's Bar and Grill
301 S. Gillette Ave., 307/686-7678

Best Sports Bar
Humphrey's Bar and Grill
408 W. Juniper Ln., 307/682-0100

Best Steaks
Prime Rib Restaurant
1205 S. Douglas Hwy., 307/682-2944

JACKSON, WY

Best American Food
Granary
1800 Spirit Dance Rd., 307/733-8833

Best Atmosphere
Cadillac Grille Restaurant
55 N. Cache St., 307/733-3279

Best Barbecue/Ribs
Bubba's Barbecue Restaurant
515 W. Broadway, 307/733-2288

Best Breakfast
Jedediah's
135 E. Broadway, 307/733-5671
Nora's Fishcreek Inn
5600 W. Hwy. 22, Wilson, 307/733-8288

Best Burgers
Billy's Giant Burgers
55 N. Cache St., 307/733-3279

Best Cajun/Creole Food
Acadian House
170 N. Millward St., 307/739-1269

Best Casual Dining
Horse Creek Station
9800 Hwy. 89S, 307/733-0810

Best Chinese Food
Chinatown Restaurant
850 W. Broadway, 307/733-8856
Lame Duck
680 E. Broadway, 307/733-4311

Best Coffee/Coffeehouse
Betty Rock Cafe
  325 W. Pearl St., 307/733-0747
Shades Cafe
  75 S. King St., 307/733-2015

Best Continental Food
The Blue Lion
  160 N. Millward, 307/733-3912

Best Delicatessen
Dickie's Fat Cat Deli
  135 N. Cache St., Ste. 6, 307/733-1166

Best Eclectic Menu
Off Broadway Restaurant
  30 Kings Hwy., 307/733-9777

Best Fine Dining
Snake River Grill
  84 E. Broadway, Town Square, 307/733-0557
The Range Restaurant
  225 N. Cache St., 307/733-5481

Best Health-Conscious Menu
Sweetwater Restaurant
  85 Kings St., 307/733-3553
The Range Restaurant
  225 N. Cache Dr., 307/733-5481

Best Inexpensive Meal
Vista Grande
  Teton Village Rd., 307/733-6964

Best Italian Food
Anthony's Italian Restaurant
  50 S. Glenwood St., 307/733-3717
Nani's Genuine Pasta House
  240 N. Glenwood St., 307/733-3888

Best Mexican Food
Cafe a Mano
  45 S. Glenwood, 307/739-2500
Mama Inez
  380 W. Pearl Ave., 307/739-9166
Merry Piglets
  160 N. Cache St., 307/733-2966
Vista Grande
  Teton Village Rd., 307/733-6964

Best Other Ethnic Food
Stiegler's Restaurant and Bar (Austrian)
  The Aspens, Teton Village Rd., 307/733-1071

Best Pizza
Mountain High Pizza Pie
  120 W. Broadway St., 307/733-3646

Best Regional Food
Jenny Leigh's Dining Room
  3345 W. McCollister Dr., Teton Village,
    307/733-7102
Silver Dollar Bar and Grill
  50 N. Glenwood St., 307/733-2190

Best Restaurant in Town
Jedediah's
  135 E. Broadway, 307/733-5671
Sugarfoot Cafe
  145 N. Glenwood, 307/733-9148
The Blue Lion
  160 N. Millward, 307/733-3912

Best Sandwiches
The Bunnery
  130 N. Cache St., 307/733-5474
Pearl Street Bagels
  145 W. Pearl St., 307/739-1218

Best Steaks
Gun Barrel Steakhouse
  862 W. Broadway, 307/733-3287
Teton Steakhouse
  40 W. Pearl St., 307/733-2639

Best Sunday Brunch
Atrium Restaurant
  Snow King Resort, 400 E. Snow King Ave.,
  307/733-5200

Best View While Dining
The Mural Room
  Jackson Lake Lodge, Hwy. 89, Moran,
  307/543-2811
Rising Sage Cafe
  2820 Rungius Rd., 307/733-8649

LARAMIE, WY

Best Brewpub
The Library Restaurant and Brewing Company
  1622 Grand Ave., 307/742-0500

Best Burgers
Winger's
  3626 E. Grand Ave., 307/742-4999

Best Casual Dining
Jeffrey's Bistro
  123 E. Ivinson Ave., 307/742-7046

Best Coffee/Coffeehouse
Cowboy Coffee
  1710 E. Grand Ave., 307/745-5288

Best Pizza
Grand Avenue Pizza
  301 E. Grand Ave., 307/721-2909

Best Restaurant in Town
Cafe Jacques
  220 E. Grand Ave., 307/742-5522
Cafe Ole
  519 Boswell Dr., 307/742-8383
El Conquistador
  110 E. Ivinson Ave., 307/742-2377
Old Corral
  2750 Hwy. 130, Centennial, 307/745-5918

The Overland
  100 E. Ivinson Ave., 307/721-2800
Shari's of Laramie
  666 N. Third St., 307/721-4813

POWELL, WY

Best Breakfast
Hamilton House
  201 N. Hamilton St., 307/754-5703
Skyline Cafe
  141 E. Coulter Ave., 307/754-8052

Best Burgers
Hansel and Gretel's
  113 S. Bent St., 307/754-2191

Best Chinese Food
Chinatown
  245 N. Ferris St., 307/754-7924

Best Ice Cream/Yogurt
Linda's Sandwich & Ice Cream
  119 N. Bent St., 307/754-9553

Best Mexican Food
El Tapatio Mexican Restaurant
  112 N. Bent St., 307/754-8085

Best Steaks
Bent Street Station
  117 S. Bent St., 307/754-3384
Lamplighter Inn
  234 E. First St., 307/754-2226

RAWLINS, WY

Best American Food
Aspen House
  318 Fifth St., 307/324-4787
Country Kitchen
  1800 E. Cedar St., 307/324-7968
Golden Spike
  1617 W. Spruce St., 307/324-2284
Pantry Restaurant
  221 W. Cedar St., 307/324-7860

Best Bar
George's Bar and Grill
  309 W. Cedar St., 307/324-5474
Peppermill Bar and Grill
  1602 Inverness Blvd., 307/324-8100

Best Breakfast
Frontier Pies Restaurant
  2300 W. Spruce St., 307/328-2181

Best Chinese Food
China Panda
  1810 E. Cedar St., 307/324-2198
Ron and Mary's Golden Peacock Cafe
  1811 W. Spruce St., 307/324-8110

Best Coffee/Coffeehouse
5th Street Bistro
  112 Fifth St., 307/324-7246

Best Desserts
Frontier Pies Restaurant
  2300 W. Spruce St., 307/328-2181

Best Family Restaurant
Country Kitchen
  1800 E. Cedar St., 307/324-7968

Best Mexican Food
Rosie's Lariat
  410 E. Cedar St., 307/324-5261

ROCK SPRINGS, WY

Best American Food
Cruel Jack's
  8 Purple Sage Rd., 307/382-9018

Best Chinese Food
Hong Kong House
  1676 Sunset Dr., 307/382-5462
Sands Restaurant and Lounge
  1549 Ninth St., 307/362-5633

Best Italian Food
Park Grill and Lounge
  19 Elk St., 307/362-3701

Best Restaurant in Town
Red Feather Restaurant
  211 E. Flaming Gorge Way, Green River,
    307/875-6625
The Outlaw Inn
  1630 Elk St., 307/362-6623
White Mountain Mining Company
  240 Clearview Dr., Green River, 307/382-5265

Best Seafood
T and J's North Park Dining
  White Mountain Golf Course, 1501 Clubhouse Dr.,
    307/362-3950

Best Steaks
Ted's Supper Club
  9 Purple Sage Rd., 307/362-7323

SHERIDAN, WY

Best Burgers
Sanford's Grub and Pub
  1 E. Alger St., 307/674-1722

Best Chinese Food
Golden China Restaurant
  727 E. Brundage Ln., 307/674-7181

Best Coffee/Coffeehouse
Coffee House
  123 N. Main St., 307/674-8619

W

Best Diner
Silver Spur Cafe
 832 N. Main St., 307/672-2749

Best Italian Food
Ciao Bistro
 120 N. Main St., 307/672-2838

Best Pizza
Ole's Pizza and Spaghetti House
 1842 Sugarland Dr., Ste. 110, 307/672-3636

Best Sandwiches
Melinda's
 57 N. Main St., 307/674-9188

Best Steaks
Golden Steer
 2071 N. Main St., 307/674-9334

WHEATLAND, WY

Best American Food
Grandma's Kitchenette
 257 Whalen Canyon Rd., Guernsey, 307/836-2822

Best Breakfast
Breakfast Inn
 86 Sixteenth St., 307/322-9302

Best Mexican Food
El Gringo's
 705 Tenth St., 307/322-4402

Best Seafood
Vimbo's
 203 Sixteenth St., 307/322-3725

Best Steaks
Vimbo's
 203 Sixteenth St., 307/322-3725

Notes on Restaurants

City: _____
State: _____ Date of Visit: _____
Restaurant visited: _____
_____

Service: ❑ Satisfactory   ❑ Good
         ❑ Excellent   ❑ Unsatisfactory

Food: ❑ Satisfactory   ❑ Good
         ❑ Excellent   ❑ Unsatisfactory

Food/drink I especially enjoyed: _____
_____
_____
_____

Food/drink I did not like: _____
_____
_____
_____

Other notes: _____
_____
_____
_____
_____

City: _____
State: _____ Date of Visit: _____
Restaurant visited: _____
_____

Service: ❑ Satisfactory   ❑ Good
         ❑ Excellent   ❑ Unsatisfactory

Food: ❑ Satisfactory   ❑ Good
         ❑ Excellent   ❑ Unsatisfactory

Food/drink I especially enjoyed: _____
_____
_____

Food/drink I did not like: _____
_____
_____

Other notes: _____
_____
_____
_____

City: _____
State: _____ Date of Visit: _____
Restaurant visited: _____

Service: ❑ Satisfactory ❑ Good
          ❑ Excellent ❑ Unsatisfactory

Food: ❑ Satisfactory ❑ Good
          ❑ Excellent ❑ Unsatisfactory

Food/drink I especially enjoyed: _____
_____
_____
_____

Food/drink I did not like: _____
_____
_____
_____

Other notes: _____
_____
_____
_____

City: _____
State: _____ Date of Visit: _____
Restaurant visited: _____

Service: ❑ Satisfactory ❑ Good
          ❑ Excellent ❑ Unsatisfactory

Food: ❑ Satisfactory ❑ Good
          ❑ Excellent ❑ Unsatisfactory

Food/drink I especially enjoyed: _____
_____
_____
_____

Food/drink I did not like: _____
_____
_____
_____

Other notes: _____
_____
_____
_____

Help make Where the Locals Eat *more accurate and useful— send us your comments and suggestions.*

The editors of this directory constantly strive to improve and update the information in *Where the Locals Eat*. Your views are important to us. If you have been a guest recently at one of the restaurants listed in our directory, we want your evaluation of it— good or bad. We hope that you will take a few moments to complete this short questionnaire—or a part of it —before returning it, in confidence, to us. Thank you!

A. Have you recently visited any of the restaurants included in *Where the Locals Eat*? If so, please let us know what you thought of them.

1. _____
   (name of restaurant)

in _____
   (city and state)

What was your opinion of this restaurant?

_____
_____
_____
_____
_____

2. _____
   (name of restaurant)

in _____
   (city and state)

What was your opinion of this restaurant?

_____
_____
_____
_____
_____

3. _____
   (name of restaurant)

in _____
   (city and state)

What was your opinion of this restaurant?

_____
_____
_____
_____
_____

B. Have you recently visited any restaurants that you believe should be included in the next edition of *Where the Locals Eat*?

If so, please tell us which restaurants you want us to consider. (We are especially interested in the restaurants in your area that are your favorites.)

_____
(name of restaurant)

in _____
(city and state)

_____
(name of restaurant)

in _____
(city and state)

_____
(name of restaurant)

in _____
(city and state)

C. How can we improve *Where the Locals Eat*?
Your suggestions for improving our guide are welcome. If you have something to say about *Where the Locals Eat*—a comment, a correction, a compliment—please write your comments on the form below. Thank you for your interest.

_____
_____
_____
_____
_____
_____
_____
_____

From:

_____
(name)

_____
(street address)

_____
(city, state, ZIP)

Return this questionnaire to: Lee Wilson, Editor, *Where the Locals Eat*, Magellan Press, Inc., P.O. Box 121075, Nashville, TN 37212. Photocopies will not be accepted.

Book Orders

Additional copies of *Where the Locals Eat* may be ordered directly from the publisher. Use the order blank below (or a photocopy) to place your order.

You may also call 800/624-5359 to order with a credit card.

Please send *Where the Locals Eat* in the quantity indicated below.

Ship to:

_____
(name)

_____
(street address)

_____
(city, state, ZIP)

Number of copies ordered: _____

Amount enclosed: $_____

(Send $19.95 plus $2.00 shipping and handling *per copy ordered.* Make check payable to MAGELLAN PRESS, INC. Tennessee residents must include sales tax.)

Mail check and order blank to:

MAGELLAN PRESS, INC.
P.O. Box 121075
Nashville, TN 37212